Biological Psychology

9

James W. Kalat

North Carolina State University

Australia • Brazil • Canada • Mexico • Singapore • Spain
United Kingdom • United States

Biological Psychology
James W. Kalat

Publisher: *Vicki Knight*
Development Editor: *Kirk Bomont*
Managing Assistant Editor: *Jennifer Alexander*
Editorial Assistant: *Sheila Walsh*
Managing Technology Project Manager: *Darin Derstine*
Vice President, Director of Marketing: *Caroline Croley*
Marketing Assistant: *Natasha Coats*
Senior Marketing Communications Manager: *Kelley McAllister*
Content Project Manager: *Karol Jurado*
Creative Director: *Rob Hugel*
Senior Art Director: *Vernon Boes*
Senior Print Buyer: *Karen Hunt*
Senior Permissions Editor: *Joohee Lee*
Production Service: *Nancy Shammas, New Leaf Publishing Services*
Text Designer: *Tani Hasegawa*
Art Editor: *Lisa Torri*
Photo Researcher: *Eric Schrader*
Copy Editor: *Frank Hubert*
Illustrator: *Precision Graphics*
Cover Designer: *Denise Davidson*
Cover Image: *Runaway Technology*
Cover Printer: *Transcontinental Printing/Interglobe*
Compositor: *Thompson Type*
Printer: *Transcontinental Printing/Interglobe*

Printed in Canada
1 2 3 4 5 6 7 10 09 08 07 06

Library of Congress Control Number: 2006924488

Student Edition: ISBN 0-495-09079-4

Thomson Higher Education
10 Davis Drive
Belmont, CA 94002-3098
USA

About the Author

James W. Kalat (rhymes with ballot) is Professor of Psychology at North Carolina State University, where he teaches courses in introduction to psychology and biological psychology. Born in 1946, he received an AB degree summa cum laude from Duke University in 1968 and a PhD in psychology from the University of Pennsylvania in 1971. He is also the author of *Introduction to Psychology, Seventh Edition* (Belmont, CA: Wadsworth, 2005) and co-author with Michelle Shiota of *Emotion* (Belmont, CA: Wadsworth, 2006). In addition to textbooks, he has written journal articles on taste-aversion learning, the teaching of psychology, and other topics. A remarried widower, he has three children, two stepchildren, and two grandchildren.

To My Family

Brief Contents

Contents

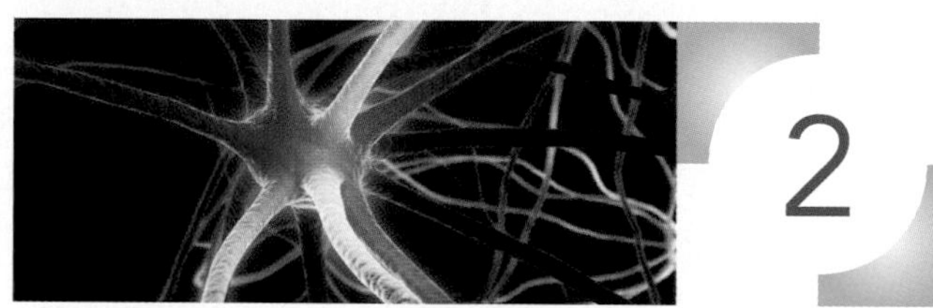

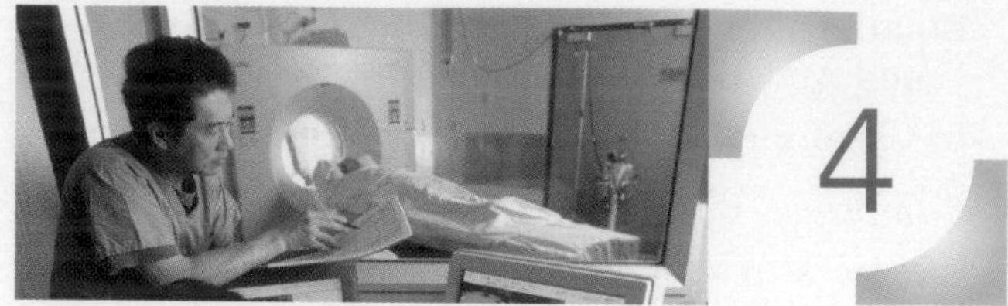

4

Anatomy of the Nervous System 81

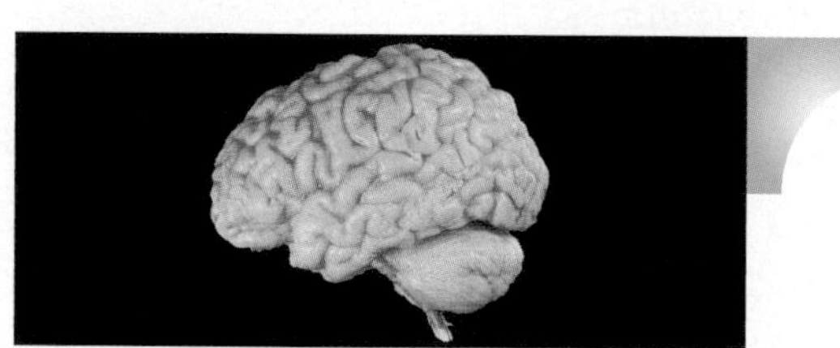

5

Development and Plasticity of the Brain 121

7

The Other Sensory Systems 195

8

9

Reproductive Behaviors 325

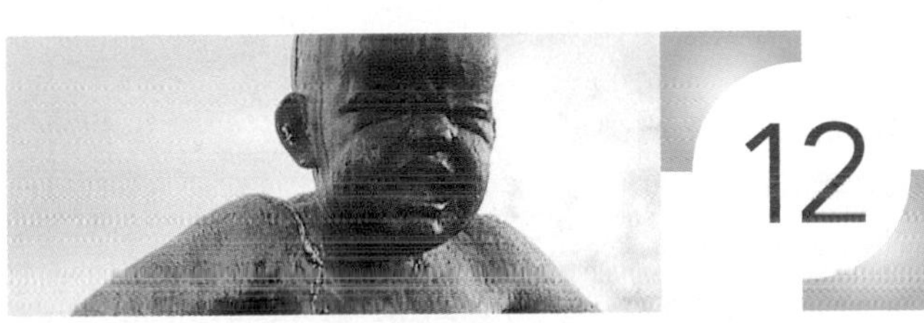

Emotional Behaviors 353

13

14

Cognitive Functions 415

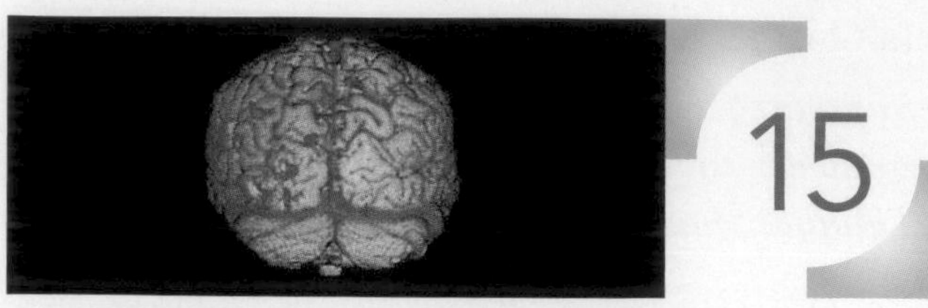

15 Psychological Disorders 451

Preface

In the first edition of this text, published in 1981, I remarked, "I almost wish I could get parts of this text . . . printed in disappearing ink, programmed to fade within ten years of publication, so that I will not be embarrassed by statements that will look primitive from some future perspective." I would say the same thing today, except that I would like for the ink to fade in much less than ten years. Biological psychology progresses rapidly, and many statements become out-of-date quickly.

The most challenging aspect of writing a text is selecting what to include and what to omit. My primary goal in writing this text through each edition has been to show the importance of neuroscience, genetics, and evolution for psychology and not just for biology. I have focused on the biological mechanisms of such topics as language, learning, sexual behavior, anxiety, aggression, attention, abnormal behavior, and the mind–body problem. I hope that by the end of the book readers will clearly see what the study of the brain has to do with "real psychology" and that they will be interested in learning more.

Each chapter is divided into modules; each module begins with its own introduction and finishes with its own summary and questions. This organization makes it easy for instructors to assign part of a chapter per day instead of a whole chapter per week. Parts of chapters can also be covered in a different order. Indeed, whole chapters can be rearranged in a different order. I know one instructor who likes to start with Chapter 14.

I assume that the reader has a basic background in psychology and biology and understands such basic terms as classical conditioning, reinforcement, vertebrate, mammal, gene, chromosome, cell, and mitochondrion. Naturally, the stronger the background is, the better. I also assume a high-school chemistry course. Those with a weak background in chemistry or a fading memory of it may consult Appendix A.

Changes in This Edition

The changes in this text are my attempt to keep pace with the rapid progress in biological psychology. This text includes more than 550 new references from 2002 through 2006 and countless major and minor changes, including new or improved illustrations, a redesigned layout, and new Try It Yourself activities, both within the text and online. Here are some highlights:

General

At relevant points throughout the text, icons and references have been added to direct the reader's attention to the Try It Yourself activities available on line and in the CD that accompanies the text.

Five new or revised Try It Yourself activities are available on the CD and on line. These demonstrations show some processes that a static display in a book cannot. When I read about a perceptual phenomenon or an experimental result, I often wonder what it would be like to experience the effect described. If I can experience it myself, I understand it better. I assume other people feel the same way.

The module on attention was moved from Chapter 7 (senses) to Chapter 14 (cognitive functions).

Most of the discussion of drugs and their mechanisms was moved from Chapter 15 (psychological disorders) to Chapter 3 (synapses).

Many of the research methods previously discussed in other chapters have been consolidated into the module on research methods in Chapter 4 (anatomy).

Chapter 1

- Added research studies examining the brain mechanisms related to consciousness.

Chapter 2

- New information indicates that in some cases axons convey information by their rhythm of firing as well as their overall frequency of firing.

Chapter 3

- Most of the material on hormones in general was moved from Chapter 11 to this chapter.
- Updated and expanded discussion of drug mechanisms.
- Added discussion of mechanisms for the postsynaptic cell to provide negative feedback to the presynaptic cell.

Chapter 4

- The module on research methods was expanded, modified, and moved to the end of the chapter.

- New explanation of binding with an improved Try-It-Yourself activity.
- New section discussing the research on the relationship between brain size and intelligence. Discussion of species differences in brain anatomy moved here from Chapter 5.

Chapter 5

- Revised order of topics in both modules.
- Experiment on reorganization of the infant ferret cortex revised and moved here from Chapter 6.
- New discussion of brain changes that result from lifelong blindness.

Chapter 6

- New examples of species differences in vision.
- Updated discussion of blindsight, face recognition, motion blindness, and visual attention.
- Added several new studies of the development of vision, including people who had vision restored in adulthood after having had little or none since early childhood.

Chapter 7

- Much expanded discussion of the auditory cortex, including parallels between the auditory and visual systems.
- Neuropsychological studies of a patient who cannot integrate vestibular sensation with other senses and therefore has "out of body" experiences.
- Neuropsychological studies of a patient who has no conscious touch sensation but nevertheless feels pleasure when touched.
- Reorganized discussion of pain.
- New research added showing that chronic pain depends on a mechanism related to learning.
- New section added on synesthesia, the tendency of certain people to experience one sense in response to stimulation of a different sense.

Chapter 8

- Added "mirror neurons" in the motor cortex that respond both to one's own movements and the sight of other people doing the same movements.
- New section on the relationship between conscious decisions and movements.

Chapter 9

- New material added on the differences between morning people and evening people.
- New research included on the role of orexin in maintaining wakefulness.
- GABA release during sleep does not decrease neuronal activity, but decreases the spread of excitation at synapses. Neuronal activity continues, although much of it is not conscious.
- Reorganized section on theories of the need for sleep.
- New examples of sleep specializations in other species: dolphins, migratory birds, European swifts (who sleep while flying).
- Added information about sleep in astronauts, submarine sailors, and people working in Antarctica.

Chapter 10

- Several new examples of seemingly odd animal behaviors that make sense in terms of temperature regulation.
- A completely rewritten section on brain mechanisms of feeding.
- Discussion of evidence suggesting that consuming high-fructose corn syrup increases the risk of obesity.

Chapter 11

- Revised discussion of hormonal effects on intellectual performance.
- New study included that shows that one gene controlling vasopressin can alter social behaviors, causing male meadow voles to establish pair bonds with females and help them rear babies—a behavior never previously seen in males of this species.
- Much revised discussion of gender identity and gender-differentiated behaviors in people with congenital adrenal hyperplasia.
- Several updates about homosexuality including: the probability of homosexuality is increased among boys with older brothers; and men with a homosexual orientation have female relatives who have a greater than average number of children—a possible explanation for maintenance of a gene promoting homosexuality.

Chapter 12

- Substantial updating and revision throughout this chapter.
- Clarification of the James-Lange theory and evidence relevant to it.
- Monkeys with low serotonin turnover become aggressive and are likely to die young, but if they survive, they are likely to achieve dominant status.
- The human amygdala responds most strongly to emotional stimuli that are sufficiently ambiguous to require processing.
- People with amygdala damage fail to identify fear in photographs because they focus their vision almost entirely on the nose and mouth.
- Genetic variance in the amygdala probably contributes to variance in predisposition to anxiety disorders.
- Stress module: Deleted the discussion of psychosomatic illness and expanded discussion of stress and the immune system.

- New evidence indicates that people with smaller than average hippocampus are predisposed to PTSD.

Chapter 13

- New studies on patient H.M.: If tested carefully, he shows slight evidence of new declarative memories since his operation, although no new episodic memories.
- Brief new discussion of individual differences in the hippocampus and their relationship to differences in memory.
- Reorganized discussion of consolidation of memory.
- Updates added on Alzheimer's disease, including some new prospects for treatment.

Chapter 14

- New section on the genetics of handedness.
- Revised module on attention.

Chapter 15

- The first module now deals with substance abuse and addiction, but not the mechanisms of drugs in general. That section is now in Chapter 3.
- Greatly revised discussion of addiction, with more explanation of the distinction between wanting and liking.
- Evidence now says depression relates more to lack of happiness than to increased sadness.
- New evidence relates depression to an interaction between a gene and a series of stressful experiences.
- New evidence on the genetics of schizophrenia.
- New evidence suggests a parasitic infection in childhood can predispose someone to schizophrenia later.
- Reorganized discussion of antipsychotic drugs and their relationship to neurotransmitters.

Supplements

The CD-ROM that accompanies this text includes animations, film clips, *Try It Yourself* activities, quizzes, and other supplements to the text. Darin Derstine took responsibility for coordinating the CD, working with Rob Stufflebeam, University of New Orleans, and me on the new online *Try It Yourself* activities. Those who adopt the book may also obtain from the publisher a copy of the Instructor's Manual, written by Cynthia Crawford, California State University at San Bernardino. The manual contains chapter outlines, class demonstrations and projects, a list of video resources, additional Websites, InfoTrac Virtual Reader, and the author's answers to the *Thought Questions.* A separate print Testbank lists multiple-choice and true–false items written and assembled by Jeffrey Stowell, Eastern Illinois University. Note the test bank includes special files of questions for a midterm and a comprehensive final exam. The test items are also available electronically on Examview. The Study Guide, written by Elaine M. Hull of Florida State University, may be purchased by students. Also available is the Multimedia Manager Instructor's Resource CD-ROM, written by Chris Hayashi, Southwestern College.

I am grateful for the excellent work of Darin Derstine, Cynthia Crawford, JeffreyStowell, Elaine Hull, and Chris Hayashi.

In addition, it is possible to use technology in a variety of ways in your course with the following new products:

JoinIn™ on TurningPoint®

Exclusive from Thomson for colleges and universities . . . turn your lecture into an interactive experience for your students, using "clickers."

WebTutor™ Advantage

Save time managing your course, posting materials, incorporating multimedia, and tracking progress with this engaging, text-specific e-learning tool. Visit **http://webtutor.thomsonlearning.com.**

ThomsonNow™

A powerful, assignable, personalized online learning companion that assesses individual study needs and builds focused Personalized Learning Plans that reinforce key concepts with interactive animations, text art, and more.

Acknowledgments

Let me tell you something about researchers in this field: As a rule, they are amazingly cooperative with textbook authors. Many of my colleagues sent me comments, ideas, articles, and photos. I thank especially the following:

Greg Allen, *University of Texas Southwestern Medical Center*
Ralph Adolphs, *University of Iowa*
Danny Benbassat, *Ohio Northern University*
Stephen L. Black, *Bishop's University*
Martin Elton, *University of Amsterdam*
Jane Flinn, *George Mason University*
Ronnie Halperin, *SUNY-Purchase*
Julio Ramirez, *Davidson College*
Sarah L. Pallas, *Georgia State University*
Alex Pouget, *University of Rochester*
Robert Provine, *University of Maryland, Baltimore County*
Roberto Refinetti, *University of South Carolina*

I have received an enormous number of letters and e-mail messages from students. Many included helpful suggestions; some managed to catch errors or inconsistencies that everyone else had overlooked. I thank especially the following:

Jacqueline Counotte, *Leiden University, Netherlands*
Terry Fidler, *University of Victoria, British Columbia*
Paul Kim, *N. C. State University*
Florian van Leeuwen, *University of Groningen, Netherlands*
Elizabeth Rose Murphy, *North Carolina State University*
Steve Williams, *Massey University, New Zealand*

I appreciate the helpful comments and suggestions provided by the following reviewers who commented on the 8th edition and provided suggestions for the 9th edition, and/or who reviewed the revised manuscript for the 9th edition:

Joseph Porter, *Virginia Commonwealth University*
Marjorie Battaglia, *George Mason University*
Anne Marie Brady, *St. Mary's College of Maryland*
Linda James, *Georgian Court University*
Mary Clare Kante, *University of Illinois at Chicago Circle*
Frank Scalzo, *Bard College*
Nancy Woolf, *University of California, Los Angeles*
Joseph Dien, *University of Kansas*
Derek Hamilton, *University of New Mexico*
Alexander Kusnecov, *Rutgers University*
Ronald Baenninger, *College of St. Benedict/ St. John's University*
Christine Wagner, *SUNY, Albany*
Amira Rezec, *Saddleback College*
Brian Kelley, *Bridgewater College*
Lisa Baker, *Western Michigan University*
Steven Brown, *Rockhurst University*
Chris Bloom, *University of Southern Indiana*
Anthony Risser, *University of Houston*
Douglas Grimsley, *University of North Carolina, Charlotte*
Yuan B. Peng, *University of Texas at Arlington*
Carlota Ocampo, *Trinity University*
Ron Salazar, *San Juan College*

In preparing this text I have been most fortunate to work with Vicki Knight, a wise, patient, and very supportive acquisitions editor/publisher. She was especially helpful in setting priorities and planning the major thrust of this text. Kirk Bomont, my developmental editor, reads manuscripts with extraordinary care, noticing discrepancies, unclear points, and ideas that need more explanation. His work helped me enormously in the preparation of this edition. Karol Jurado, Content Project Manager, did a stellar job in coordinating the production process and working closely with all of the players, including Nancy Shammas at New Leaf Publishing Services who provided the service for the book and undertook the management of all of the talented people who contributed to the production of this book—a major task for a book with such a large art and photo program. As art editor, Lisa Torri's considerable artistic abilities helped to compensate for my complete lack. And once again, Precision Graphics did an outstanding job with modifications on the art and new renderings. Joohee Lee handled all of the permissions, no small task for a book like this. Eric Schrader was the photo researcher; I hope you enjoy the new photos in this text as much as I do. Jennifer Wilkinson oversaw the development of supplements, such as the Instructor's Manual and test item file. I thank Vernon Boes, who managed the interior design and the cover, Tani Hasegawa for the outstanding changes to the interior design, Frank Hubert for the copyediting, Linda Dane for the proofreading, and Do Mi Stauber for the indexes. All of these people have been splendid colleagues.

I thank my wife, Jo Ellen, for keeping my spirits high, and my department head, David Martin, for his support and encouragement. I especially thank my son Sam for many discussions and many insightful ideas. Sam Kalat, coming from a background of biochemistry and computer science, has more original and insightful ideas about brain functioning than anyone else I know.

I welcome correspondence from both students and faculty. Write: James W. Kalat, Department of Psychology, Box 7650, North Carolina State University, Raleigh, NC 27695–7801, USA. E-mail: james_kalat@ncsu.edu

James W. Kalat

TO THE OWNER OF THIS BOOK:

I hope that you have found *Biological Psychology*, 9th Edition, useful. So that this book can be improved in a future edition, would you take the time to complete this sheet and return it? Thank you.

School and address: ______________________________

____

Department: ______________________________

Instructor's name: ______________________________

1. What I like most about this book is: ______________________________

____

____

2. What I like least about this book is: ______________________________

____

____

3. My general reaction to this book is: ______________________________

____

____

4. The name of the course in which I used this book is: ______________________________

____

5. Were all of the chapters of the book assigned for you to read? ______________________________

   If not, which ones weren't? ______________________________

6. In the space below, or on a separate sheet of paper, please write specific suggestions for improving this book and anything else you'd care to share about your experience in using this book

____

____

____

____

____

____

____

The Major Issues

1

Chapter Outline

Opposite: It is tempting to try to "get inside the mind" of people and other animals, to imagine what they are thinking or feeling. In contrast, biological psychologists try to explain behavior in terms of its physiology, development, evolution, and function.

Source: George D. Lepp/CORBIS

Main Ideas

1. Biological explanations of behavior fall into several categories, including physiology, development, evolution, and function.
2. Nearly all current philosophers and neuroscientists reject the idea that the mind exists independently of the physical brain. Still, the question remains as to how and why brain activity is connected to consciousness.
3. The expression of a given gene depends on the environment and on interactions with other genes.
4. Research with nonhuman animals can produce important information, but it sometimes inflicts distress or pain on the animals. Whether to proceed with a given experiment can be a difficult ethical issue.

> It is often said that Man is unique among animals. It is worth looking at this term "unique" before we discuss our subject proper. The word may in this context have two slightly different meanings. It may mean: Man is strikingly different—he is not identical with any animal. This is of course true. It is true also of all other animals: Each species, even each individual is unique in this sense. But the term is also often used in a more absolute sense: Man is so different, so "essentially different" (whatever that means) that the gap between him and animals cannot possibly be bridged—he is something altogether new. Used in this absolute sense the term is scientifically meaningless. Its use also reveals and may reinforce conceit, and it leads to complacency and defeatism because it assumes that it will be futile even to search for animal roots. It is prejudging the issue.
>
> *Niko Tinbergen (1973, p. 161)*

Biological psychologists study the "animal roots" of behavior, relating actions and experiences to genetics and physiology. In this chapter, we consider three major issues and themes: the relationship between mind and brain, the roles of nature and nurture, and the ethics of research. We also briefly consider prospects for further study.

Module 1.1
The Mind–Brain Relationship

Biological psychology is the study of the physiological, evolutionary, and developmental mechanisms of behavior and experience. It is approximately synonymous with the terms *biopsychology, psychobiology, physiological psychology,* and *behavioral neuroscience.* The term *biological psychology* emphasizes that the goal is to relate the biology to issues of psychology. *Neuroscience* as a field certainly includes much that is relevant to behavior, but it also includes more detail about anatomy and chemistry.

Much of biological psychology is devoted to studying brain functioning. Figure 1.1 offers a view of the human brain from the top (what anatomists call a *dorsal* view) and from the bottom (a *ventral* view). The labels point to a few important areas that will become more familiar as you proceed through this text. An inspection of brain areas reveals distinct subareas. At the microscopic level, we find two kinds of cells: the *neurons* (Figure 1.2) and the *glia.* Neurons, which convey messages to one another and to muscles and glands, vary enormously in size, shape, and functions. The glia, generally smaller than neurons, have many functions but do not convey information over great distances. The activities of neurons and glia *somehow* produce an enormous wealth of behavior and experience. This book is about researchers' attempts to elaborate on that word "somehow."

Biological psychology is the most interesting topic in the world. No doubt every professor or textbook author feels that way about his or her field. But the others are wrong. Biological psychology really *is* the most interesting topic.

When I make this statement to a group of students, I always get a laugh. But when I say it to a group of biological psychologists or neuroscientists, they nod their heads in agreement, and I do in fact mean it seriously. I do *not* mean that memorizing the names and functions of brain parts and chemicals is unusually interesting. I mean that biological psychology addresses some fascinating issues that should excite anyone who is curious about nature.

Actually, I shall back off a bit and say that biological psychology is about tied with cosmology as the most interesting topic. Cosmologists ask why the uni-

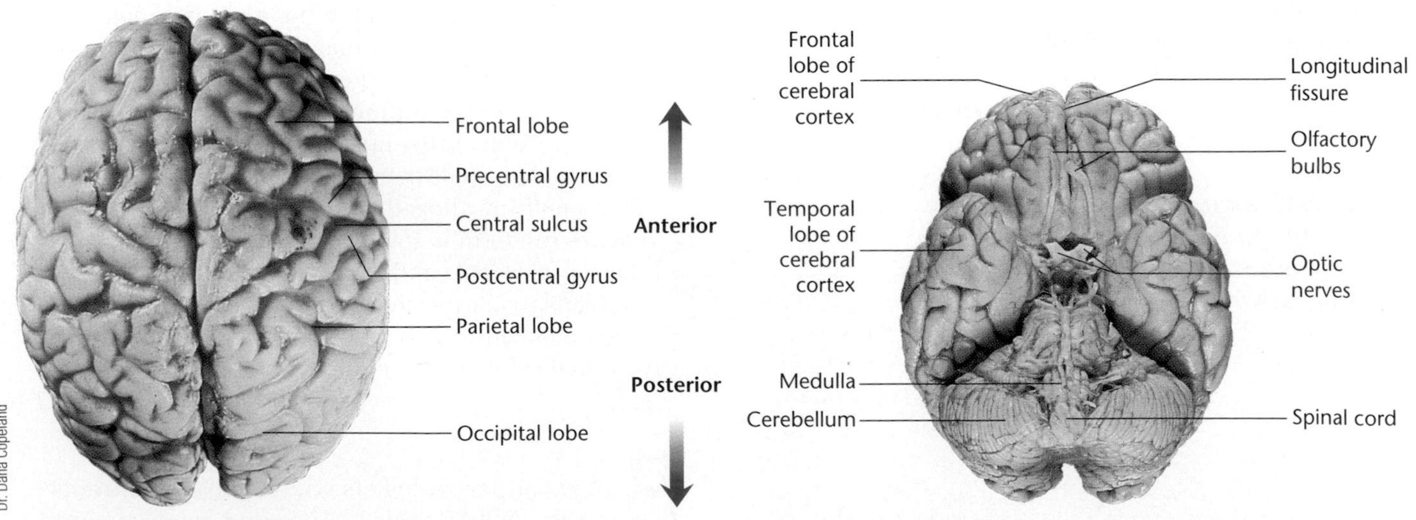

Figure 1.1 A dorsal view (from above) and a ventral view (from below) of the human brain

The brain has an enormous number of divisions and subareas; the labels point to a few of the main ones on the surface of the brain.

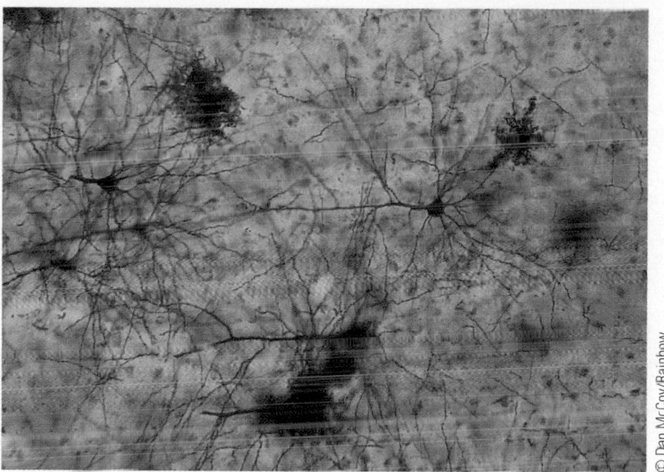
© Dan McCoy/Rainbow

Figure 1.2 Neurons, greatly magnified
The brain is composed of individual cells called neurons and glia.

© Dorr/Premium Stock/PictureQuest

Researchers continue to debate exactly what good yawning does. Yawning is a behavior that even people do without knowing its purpose.

verse exists at all: Why is there *something* instead of *nothing*? And if there is something, why is it this particular kind of something? Biological psychologists ask: Given the existence of this universe composed of matter and energy, why is there consciousness? Is it a necessary function of the brain or an accident? How does the brain produce consciousness and why?

Researchers also ask more specific questions such as: What genes, prenatal environment, or other factors predispose some people to psychological disorders? Is there any hope for recovery after brain damage? And what enables humans to learn language so easily?

Biological Explanations of Behavior

Commonsense explanations of behavior often refer to intentional goals such as, "He did this because he was trying to . . ." or "She did that because she wanted to . . . ." But frequently, we have no reason to assume any intentions. A 4-month-old bird migrating south for the first time presumably does not know why; the next spring, when she lays an egg, sits on it, and defends it from predators, again she probably doesn't know why. Even humans don't always know the reasons for their own behaviors. (Yawning and laughter are two examples. You do them but can you explain what good they accomplish?)

In contrast to commonsense explanations, biological explanations of behavior fall into four categories: physiological, ontogenetic, evolutionary, and functional (Tinbergen, 1951). A **physiological explanation** relates a behavior to the activity of the brain and other organs. It deals with the machinery of the body—for

© Steve Maslowski/Photo Researchers

Unlike all other birds, doves and pigeons can drink with their heads down. (Others fill their mouths and then raise their heads.) A physiological explanation would describe these birds' unusual pattern of nerves and throat muscles. An evolutionary explanation states that all doves and pigeons share this behavioral capacity because they inherited their genes from a common ancestor.

example, the chemical reactions that enable hormones to influence brain activity and the routes by which brain activity ultimately controls muscle contractions.

The term *ontogenetic* comes from Greek roots meaning "to be" and "origin" (or genesis). Thus, an **ontogenetic explanation** describes the development of a structure or a behavior. It traces the influences of genes, nutrition, experiences, and their interactions in molding behavior. For example, the ability to inhibit an impulse develops gradually from infancy through the teenage years, reflecting gradual maturation of the frontal parts of the brain.

An **evolutionary explanation** reconstructs the evolutionary history of a structure or behavior. For example, frightened people sometimes get "goose bumps"—erections of the hairs, especially on their arms and shoulders. Goose bumps are useless to humans because our shoulder and arm hairs are so short. In most other mammals, however, hair erection makes a frightened animal look larger and more intimidating (Figure 1.3). Thus, an evolutionary explanation of human goose bumps is that the behavior evolved in our remote ancestors and we inherited the mechanism.

A **functional explanation** describes *why* a structure or behavior evolved as it did. Within a small, isolated population, a gene can spread by accident through a process called *genetic drift.* (For example, a dominant male with many offspring spreads all his genes, including neutral and harmful ones.) However, the larger the population, the less powerful is genetic drift. Thus, a gene that becomes common in a large population presumably has provided some advantage—at least in the past, though not necessarily in today's environment. A functional explanation identifies that advantage. For example, many species have an appearance that matches their background (Figure 1.4). A functional explanation is that camouflaged appearance makes the animal inconspicuous to predators. Some species use their behavior as part of the camouflage. For example, zone-tailed hawks, which live in Mexico and parts of the southwest United States, fly among vultures and hold their wings in the same posture as vultures. Small mammals and birds run for cover when they see a hawk, but they learn to ignore vultures, which are no threat unless an animal is already dying. Because the zone-tailed hawks resemble vultures in both appearance and flight behavior, their prey disregard them, enabling the hawks to pick up easy meals (W. S. Clark, 2004).

© Gary Bell/Seapics.com

Figure 1.4 A seadragon, an Australian fish related to the seahorse, lives among kelp plants, looks like kelp, and usually drifts slowly and aimlessly, *acting* like kelp.
A functional explanation addresses why a structure or behavior has evolved and what function it serves. In this case, the function is that potential predators overlook a fish that resembles inedible plants.

© Frank Siteman/Stock Boston

Figure 1.3 A frightened cat with erect hairs
When a frightened mammal erects its hairs, it looks larger and more intimidating. (Consider, for example, the "Halloween cat.") Frightened humans sometimes also erect their body hairs, forming goose bumps. An evolutionary explanation for goose bumps is that we inherited the tendency from ancestors who had enough hair for the behavior to be useful.

Functional explanations of human behavior are often controversial because many behaviors alleged to be part of our evolutionary heritage could have been learned instead. Also, we know little about the lives of early humans. We shall examine one example of such controversies in Chapter 11.

To contrast the four types of biological explanations, consider how they all apply to one example, birdsong (Catchpole & Slater, 1995):

Physiological explanation: A particular area of a songbird brain grows under the influence of testosterone; hence, it is larger in breeding males than in females or immature birds. That brain area enables a mature male to sing.

Ontogenetic explanation: In many species, a young male bird learns its song by listening to adult males. Development of the song requires both the genes that prepare him to learn the song and the opportunity to hear the appropriate song during a sensitive period early in life.

Evolutionary explanation: In certain cases, one species' song closely resembles that of another species. For example, dunlins and Baird's sandpipers, two shorebird species, give their calls in distinct pulses, unlike other shorebirds. This similarity suggests that the two evolved from a single ancestor.

Functional explanation: In most bird species, only the male sings, and he sings only during the reproductive season and only in his territory. The functions of the song are to attract females and warn away other males. As a rule, a bird sings loudly enough to be heard only in the territory he can defend. In short, birds have evolved tendencies to sing in ways that improve their chances for mating.

We improve our understanding of behavior when we can combine as many of these approaches as possible. That is, ideally, we should understand the body mechanisms that produce the behavior, how it develops within the individual, how it evolved, and what function it serves.

STOP & CHECK

1. How does an evolutionary explanation differ from a functional explanation?

Check your answer on page 10.

The Brain and Conscious Experience

Explaining birdsong in terms of hormones, brain activity, and evolutionary selection probably does not trouble you. But how would you feel about a physical explanation of your own actions and experiences? Suppose you say, "I became frightened because I saw a man with a gun," and a neuroscientist says, "You became frightened because of increased electrochemical activity in the central amygdala of your brain." Is one explanation right and the other wrong? Or if they are both right, what is the connection between them?

Biological explanations of behavior raise the **mind–body** or **mind–brain problem:** What is the relationship between the mind and the brain? The most widespread view among nonscientists is, no doubt, **dualism,** the belief that mind and body are different kinds of substance—mental substance and physical substance—that exist independently. The French philosopher René Descartes defended dualism but recognized the vexing issue of how a mind that is not made of material could influence a physical brain. He proposed that mind and brain interact at a single point in space, which he suggested was the pineal gland, the smallest unpaired structure he could find in the brain (Figure 1.5).

Although we credit Descartes with the first explicit defense of dualism, he hardly originated the idea. Mental experience seems so different from the physical actions of the brain that most people take it for granted that mind and brain are different. However, nearly all current philosophers and neuroscientists reject dualism. The decisive objection is that dualism conflicts with a consistently documented observation in physics, known as the law of the conservation of matter and energy: So far as we can tell, the total amount of matter and energy in the universe is fixed. Matter can transform into energy or energy into matter, but neither one appears out of nothing or disappears into nothing. Because any movement of matter requires energy, a mind that is not composed of matter or energy would seem unable to make anything happen, even a muscle movement.

The alternative to dualism is **monism,** the belief that the universe consists of only one kind of substance. Various forms of monism are possible, grouped into the following categories:

- **materialism:** the view that everything that exists is material, or physical. According to one version of

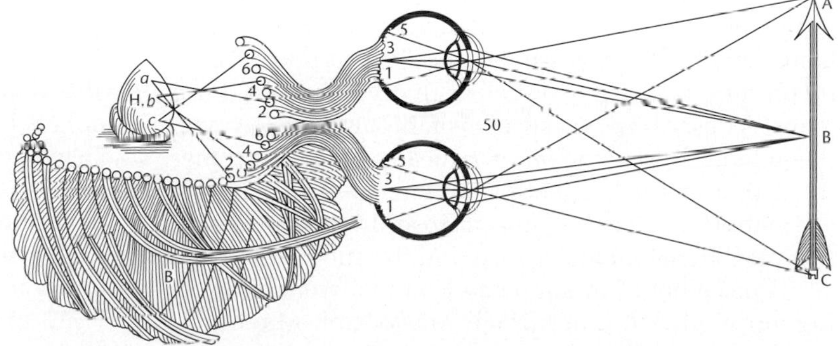

Figure 1.5 René Descartes's conception of brain and mind
Descartes understood how light from an object reached the retinas at the back of the eyes. From there, he assumed the information was all channeled back to the pineal gland, a small unpaired organ in the brain. *(Source: From Descartes' Treaties on Man)*

this view ("eliminative materialism"), mental events don't exist at all, and the common folk psychology based on minds and mental activity is fundamentally mistaken. However, most of us find it difficult to believe that our mind is a figment of our imagination! A more plausible version is that we will eventually find a way to explain all psychological experiences in purely physical terms.

- **mentalism:** the view that only the mind really exists and that the physical world could not exist unless some mind were aware of it. It is not easy to test this idea—go ahead and try!—but few philosophers or scientists take it seriously.
- **identity position:** the view that mental processes are the same thing as certain kinds of brain processes but are described in different terms. In other words, the universe has only one kind of substance, but it includes both material and mental aspects. By analogy, one could describe the *Mona Lisa* as an extraordinary painting of a woman with a subtle smile, or one could list the exact color and brightness of each point on the painting. Although the two descriptions appear very different, they refer to the same object. According to the identity position, every mental experience *is* a brain activity, even though descriptions of thoughts sound very different from descriptions of brain activities. For example, the fright you feel when someone threatens you *is the same thing as* a certain pattern of activity in your brain.

Note how the definition of the identity position is worded. It does not say that the mind is the brain. Mind is brain *activity.* In the same sense, fire is not really a "thing." Fire is what is happening to something. Similarly, mental activity is what is happening in the brain.

Can we be sure that monism is correct? No. However, we adopt it as the most reasonable working hypothesis. That is, we conduct research on the assumption of monism and see how far we can go. As you will find throughout this text, experiences and brain activities appear inseparable. Stimulation of any brain area provokes an experience, and any experience evokes brain activity. You can still use terms like *mind* or *mental activity* if you make it clear that you regard these terms as describing an aspect of brain activity. However, if you lapse into using *mind* to mean a ghostlike something that is neither matter nor energy, don't underestimate the scientific and philosophical arguments that can be marshaled against you (Dennett, 1991).

(Does a belief in monism mean that we are lowering our evaluation of minds? Maybe not. Maybe we are elevating our concept of the material world.)

Even if we accept the monist position, however, we have done little more than restate the mind–brain problem. The questions remain: *Why* is consciousness a property of brain activity? Is it important or just an accident, like the noises a machine makes? *What kind* of brain activity produces consciousness? *How* does it produce consciousness? And what is consciousness, anyway? (You may have noted the lack of a definition. A firm, clear definition of consciousness is elusive. The same is true for many other terms that we feel comfortable using. For example, you know what *time* means, but can you define it?)

The function (if any) of consciousness is far from obvious. Several psychologists have argued that many nonhuman species also have consciousness because their behavior is so complex and adaptive that we cannot explain it without assuming consciousness (e.g., Griffin, 2001). Others have argued that even if other animals are conscious, their consciousness explains nothing. Consciousness may not be a useful scientific concept (Wynne, 2004). Indeed, because we cannot observe consciousness, none of us knows for sure even that other people are conscious, much less other species. According to the position known as **solipsism** (SOL-ip-sizm, based on the Latin words *solus* and *ipse,* meaning "alone" and "self"), I alone exist, or I alone am conscious. Other people are either like robots or like the characters in a dream. (Solipsists don't form organizations because each is convinced that all other solipsists are wrong!) Although few people take solipsism seriously, it is hard to imagine evidence to refute it. The difficulty of knowing whether other people (or animals) have conscious experiences is known as the **problem of other minds.**

David Chalmers (1995) has proposed that in discussions of consciousness we distinguish between what he calls the easy problems and the hard problem. The **easy problems** pertain to many phenomena that we call *consciousness,* such as the difference between wakefulness and sleep and the mechanisms that enable us to focus our attention. These issues pose all the usual difficulties of any scientific question but no philosophical problems. In contrast, the **hard problem** concerns why and how any kind of brain activity is associated with consciousness. As Chalmers (1995) put it, "Why doesn't all this information-processing go on 'in the dark,' free of any inner feel?" (p. 203). That is, why does brain activity *feel* like anything at all? Many scientists (Crick & Koch, 2004) and philosophers (Chalmers, 2004) agree that we have no way to answer that question, at least at present. We don't even have a clear hypothesis to test. The best we can do is determine what brain activity is necessary or sufficient for consciousness. After we do so, maybe we will see a way to explain *why* that brain activity is associated with consciousness, or maybe we won't.[1]

[1]Note the phrasing "is associated with consciousness," instead of "leads to consciousness" or "causes consciousness." According to the identity position, brain activity does not cause or lead to consciousness any more than consciousness leads to brain activity. Each is the same as the other.

Why are most of us *not* solipsists? That is, why do you (I assume) believe that other people have minds? We reason by analogy: "Other people look and act much like me, so they probably have internal experiences much like mine." How far do we extend this analogy? Chimpanzees look and act somewhat like humans. Most of us, but not all, are willing to assume that chimpanzees are conscious. If chimpanzees are conscious, how about dogs? Rats? Fish? Insects? Trees? Rocks? Most people draw the line at some point in this sequence, but not all at the same point. A similar problem arises in human development: At what point between the fertilized egg and early childhood does someone become conscious? At what point in dying does someone finally lose consciousness? And how could we possibly know?

Speculating on these issues leads most people to conclude that consciousness cannot be a yes-or-no question. We can draw no sharp dividing line between those having consciousness and those lacking it. Consciousness must have evolved gradually and presumably develops gradually within an individual (Edelman, 2001).

What about computers and robots? Every year, they get more sophisticated and complicated. What if someone builds a robot that can walk, talk, carry on an intelligent conversation, laugh at jokes, and so forth? At what point, if any, would we decide that the robot is conscious?

You might respond, "Never. A robot is just a machine that is programmed to do what it does." True, but the human brain is also a machine. (A machine is anything that converts one kind of energy into another.) And we, too, are programmed—by our genes and our past experiences. (We did not create ourselves.) Perhaps no robot ever can be conscious, if consciousness is a property of carbon chemistry (Searle, 1992). Can you imagine any conceivable evidence that would persuade you that a robot is conscious? If you are curious about my answer, check page 11. But think about your own answer first.

2. What are the three major versions of monism?
3. What is meant by the "hard problem"?

Check your answers on page 10.

Research Approaches

Even if the "hard problem" is unanswerable at present, it might be possible to determine which kinds of brain activity are associated with consciousness (Crick & Koch, 2004). For the most part, researchers have assumed that even though you might be conscious of something and unable to report it in words (e.g., as infants are), if you *can* describe something you saw or heard, then you *must* have been conscious of it. Based on that operational definition of consciousness,[2] it is possible to do research on the brain activities related to consciousness. Let's consider two examples.

One clever study used this approach: Suppose we could present a visual stimulus that people consciously perceived on some occasions but not others. We could then determine which brain activities differed between the occasions with and without consciousness.

The researchers flashed a word on a screen for 29 milliseconds (ms). In some cases, it was preceded and followed by a blank screen:

In these cases, people identified the word almost 90% of the time. In other cases, however, the researchers flashed a word for the same 29 ms but preceded and followed it with a masking pattern:

Under these conditions, people almost never identify the word and usually say they didn't see any word at all. Although the physical stimulus was the same in both cases—a word flashed for 29 ms—it reached consciousness in the first case but not the second. Using a brain scan technique that we shall examine in Chapter 4, the researchers found that the conscious stimulus activated the same brain areas as the unconscious stimulus, but more strongly. Also, the conscious stimuli activated a broader range of areas, presumably because strong activation in the initial areas sent excitation to other areas (Dehaene et al., 2001).

These data imply that consciousness of a stimulus depends on the amount of brain activity. At any moment, a variety of stimuli act on your brain; in effect, they compete for control (Dehaene & Changeux, 2004). Right now, for example, you have the visual sensations from this page, as well as auditory, touch, and other sensations. You cannot be simultaneously conscious of all of them. You might, however, direct

[2] An operational definition tells how to measure something or how to determine whether it is present or absent.

your attention to one stimulus or another. For example, right now what is your conscious experience of your left foot? Until you read that question, you probably had *no* awareness of that foot, but now you do. Because you directed your attention to it, activity has increased in the brain area that receives sensation from the left foot (Lambie & Marcel, 2002). Becoming conscious of something means letting its information take over more of your brain's activity.

STOP & CHECK

4. In the experiment by Dehaene et al., how were the conscious and unconscious stimuli similar? How were they different?
5. In this experiment, how did the brain's responses differ to the conscious and unconscious stimuli?

Check your answers on page 10.

Here is a second kind of research. Look at Figure 1.6, but hold it so close to your eyes that your nose touches the page, right between the two circles. Better yet, look at the two parts through a pair of tubes, such as the tubes inside rolls of paper towels or toilet paper. You will see red and black vertical lines with your left eye and green and black horizontal lines with your right eye. (Close one eye and then the other to make sure you see completely different patterns with the two eyes.) Seeing something is closely related to seeing *where* it is, and the red vertical lines cannot be in the same place as the green horizontal lines. Because your brain cannot perceive both patterns in the same location, your perception alternates. For a while, you see the red and black lines, and then gradually the green and black invade your consciousness. Then your perception shifts back to the red and black. Sometimes you will see red lines in part of the visual field and green lines in the other. These shifts, known as **binocular rivalry**, are slow and gradual, sweeping from one side to another. The stimulus seen by each eye evokes a particular pattern of brain response, which researchers can measure with the brain scanning devices described in Chapter 4. As that first perception fades and the stimulus seen by the other eye replaces it, the first pattern of brain activity fades also, and a different pattern of activity replaces it. Each shift in perception is accompanied by a shift in the pattern of activity over a large portion of the brain (Cosmelli et al., 2004; Lee, Blake, & Heeger, 2005). (A detail of procedure: One way to mark a pattern of brain activity is to use a stimulus that oscillates. For example, someone might watch a stationary pattern with one eye and something flashing with the other. When the person perceives the flashing stimulus, brain activity has a rhythm that matches the rate of flash.)

try it yourself

By monitoring brain activity, a researcher can literally "read your mind" in this limited way—knowing which of two views you perceive at a given moment. What this result says about consciousness is that not every physical stimulus reaches consciousness. To become conscious, it has to control the activity over a significant area of the brain.

The overall point is that research on the biological basis of consciousness may be possible after all. Technological advances enable us to do research that would have been impossible in the past; future methods may facilitate still more possibilities.

Figure 1.6 Binocular rivalry
If possible, look at the two parts through tubes, such as those from the inside of rolls of toilet paper or paper towels. Otherwise, touch your nose to the paper between the two parts so that your left eye sees one pattern while your right eye sees the other. The two views will compete for your consciousness, and your perception will alternate between them.

Career Opportunities

If you want to consider a career related to biological psychology, you have a range of options. The relevant careers fall into two categories—research and therapy. Table 1.1 describes some of the major fields.

A research position ordinarily requires a PhD in psychology, biology, neuroscience, or other related field. People with a master's or bachelor's degree might work in a research laboratory but would not direct it. Many people with a PhD hold college or university positions in which they perform some combination of teaching and research. Depending on the institution and the individual, the balance can range from almost all teaching to almost all research. Other individuals have pure research positions in laboratories sponsored by the government, drug companies, or other industries.

Fields of therapy include clinical psychology, counseling psychology, school psychology, several specializations of medicine, and allied medical practice such

Table 1.1 Fields of Specialization

Specialization	Description
Research Fields	**Research positions ordinarily require a PhD. Researchers are employed by universities, hospitals, pharmaceutical firms, and research institutes.**
Neuroscientist	Studies the anatomy, biochemistry, or physiology of the nervous system. (This broad term includes any of the next five, as well as other specialties not listed.)
Behavioral neuroscientist (almost synonyms: psychobiologist, biopsychologist, or physiological psychologist).	Investigates how functioning of the brain and other organs influences behavior.
Cognitive neuroscientist	Uses brain research, such as scans of brain anatomy or activity, to analyze and explore people's knowledge, thinking, and problem solving.
Neuropsychologist	Conducts behavioral tests to determine the abilities and disabilities of people with various kinds of brain damage and changes in their condition over time. Most neuropsychologists have a mixture of psychological and medical training; they work in hospitals and clinics.
Psychophysiologist	Measures heart rate, breathing rate, brain waves, and other body processes and how they vary from one person to another or one situation to another.
Neurochemist	Investigates the chemical reactions in the brain.
Comparative psychologist (almost synonyms: ethologist, animal behaviorist)	Compares the behaviors of different species and tries to relate them to their habitats and ways of life.
Evolutionary psychologist (almost synonym: sociobiologist)	Relates behaviors, especially social behaviors, including those of humans, to the functions they have served and, therefore, the presumed selective pressures that caused them to evolve.
Practitioner Fields of Psychology	**In most cases, their work is not directly related to neuroscience. However, practitioners often need to understand it enough to communicate with a client's physician.**
Clinical psychologist	Requires PhD or PsyD. Employed by hospital, clinic, private practice, or college. Helps people with emotional problems.
Counseling psychologist	Requires PhD or PsyD. Employed by hospital, clinic, private practice, or college. Helps people make educational, vocational, and other decisions.
School psychologist	Requires master's degree or PhD. Most are employed by a school system. Identifies educational needs of schoolchildren, devises a plan to meet the needs, and then helps teachers implement it.
Medical Fields	**Practicing medicine requires an MD plus about 4 years of additional study and practice in a specialization. Physicians are employed by hospitals, clinics, medical schools and in private practice. Some conduct research in addition to seeing patients.**
Neurologist	Treats people with brain damage or diseases of the brain.
Neurosurgeon	Performs brain surgery.
Psychiatrist	Helps people with emotional distress or troublesome behaviors, sometimes using drugs or other medical procedures.
Allied Medical Field	**These fields ordinarily require a master's degree or more. Practitioners are employed by hospitals, clinics, private practice, and medical schools.**
Physical therapist	Provides exercise and other treatments to help people with muscle or nerve problems, pain, or anything else that impairs movement.
Occupational therapist	Helps people improve their ability to perform functions of daily life, for example, after a stroke.
Social worker	Helps people deal with personal and family problems. The activities of a clinical social worker overlap those of a clinical psychologist.

as physical therapy. These various fields of practice range from neurologists (who deal exclusively with brain disorders) to social workers and clinical psychologists (who need to distinguish between adjustment problems and possible signs of brain disorder).

Anyone who pursues a career in research needs to stay up to date on new developments by attending conventions, consulting with colleagues, and reading the primary research journals, such as *Journal of Neuroscience, Neurology, Behavioral Neuroscience, Brain*

Research, Nature Neuroscience, and *Archives of General Psychiatry.* However, what if you are entering a field on the outskirts of neuroscience, such as clinical psychology, school psychology, social work, or physical therapy? In that case, you probably don't want to wade through technical journal articles, but you do want to stay current on major developments, at least enough to converse intelligently with medical colleagues. I recommend the journal *Cerebrum,* published by the Dana Press, 745 Fifth Avenue, Suite 700, New York, NY 10151. Their website is **http://www.dana.org** and their e-mail address is danainfo@dana.org. *Cerebrum* provides well-written, thought-provoking articles related to neuroscience or biological psychology, accessible to nonspecialists. In many ways, it is like *Scientific American* but limited to the topic of brain and behavior.

Module 1.1
In Closing: Your Brain and Your Experience

In many ways, I have been "cheating" in this module, like giving you dessert first and saving your vegetables for later. The mind–brain issue is an exciting and challenging question, but we cannot go far with it until we back up and discuss the elements of how the nervous system works. The goals in this module have been to preview the kinds of questions researchers hope to answer and to motivate the disciplined study you will need in the next few chapters.

Biological psychologists are ambitious, hoping to explain as much as possible of psychology in terms of brain processes, genes, and the like. The guiding assumption is that the pattern of activity that occurs in your brain when you see a rabbit *is* your perception of a rabbit; the pattern that occurs when you feel fear *is* your fear. This is not to say that "your brain physiology controls you" any more than one should say that "you control your brain." Rather, your brain *is* you! The rest of this book explores how far we can go with this guiding assumption.

Summary

1. Biological psychologists try to answer four types of questions about any given behavior: How does it relate to the physiology of the brain and other organs? How does it develop within the individual? How did the capacity for the behavior evolve? And why did the capacity for this behavior evolve? (That is, what function does it serve?) (p. 3)
2. Biological explanations of behavior do not necessarily assume that the individual understands the purpose or function of the behavior. (p. 3)
3. Philosophers and scientists continue to address the mind–brain or mind–body relationship. Dualism, the popular view that the mind exists separately from the brain, is opposed by the principle that only matter and energy can affect other matter and energy. (p. 5)
4. Nearly all philosophers and scientists who have addressed the mind–brain problem favor some version of monism, the belief that the universe consists of only one kind of substance. (p. 6)
5. No one has found a way to answer the "hard question" of why brain activity is related to mental experience at all. However, new research techniques facilitate studies on what types of brain activity are necessary for consciousness. For example, a stimulus that becomes conscious activates the relevant brain areas more strongly than a similar stimulus that does not reach consciousness. (p. 6)

Answers to STOP & CHECK Questions

1. An evolutionary explanation states what evolved from what. For example, humans evolved from earlier primates and therefore have certain features that we inherited from those ancestors, even if the features are not useful to us today. A functional explanation states why something was advantageous and therefore evolutionarily selected. (p. 5)
2. The three major versions of monism are materialism (everything can be explained in physical terms), mentalism (only minds exist), and identity (the mind and the brain are the same thing). (p. 7)
3. The "hard problem" is why minds exist at all in a physical world, why there is such a thing as consciousness, and how it relates to brain activity. (p. 7)
4. The conscious and unconscious stimuli were physically the same (a word flashed on the screen for 29 ms). The difference was that a stimulus did not become conscious if it was preceded and followed by an interfering pattern. (p. 8)
5. If a stimulus became conscious, it activated the same brain areas as an unconscious stimulus, but more strongly. (p. 8)

Thought Questions[3]

1. What would you say or do to try to convince a solipsist that you are conscious?
2. Now suppose a robot just said and did the same things you did in question 1. Will you be convinced that it is conscious?

Author's Answer About Machine Consciousness (p. 7)

Here is a possibility similar to a proposal by J. R. Searle (1992): Suppose someone suffers damage to part of the visual cortex of the brain and becomes blind to part of the visual field. Now, engineers design artificial brain circuits to replace the damaged cells. Impulses from the eyes are routed to this device, which processes the information and sends electrical impulses to healthy portions of the brain that ordinarily get input from the damaged brain area. After this device is installed, the person sees the field that used to be blind, remarking, "Ah! Now I can see it again! I see shapes, colors, movement—the whole thing, just as I used to!" Evidently, the machine has enabled conscious perception of vision. Then, the person suffers still more brain damage, and engineers replace even more of the visual cortex with artificial circuits. Once again, the person assures us that everything looks the same as before. Next, engineers install a machine to replace a damaged auditory cortex, and the person reports normal hearing. One by one, additional brain areas are damaged and replaced by machines; in each case, the behavior returns to normal and the person reports having normal experiences, just as before the damage. Piece by piece, the entire brain is replaced. At that point, I would say that the machine itself is conscious.

Note that all this discussion assumes that these artificial brain circuits and transplants are possible. No one knows whether they will be. The point is merely to show what kind of evidence might persuade us that a machine is conscious.

[3]Thought Questions are intended to spark thought and discussion. The text does not directly answer any of them, although it may imply or suggest an answer in some cases. In other cases, there may be several possible answers.

Module 1.2
The Genetics of Behavior

Everything you do depends on both your genes and your environment. Without your genes or without an adequate environment, you would not exist. So far, no problem. The controversies arise when we discuss *how strongly* genes and environment affect various differences among people. For example, do differences in human intelligence depend mostly on genetic differences, mostly on environmental influences, or on both about equally? Similar issues arise for sexual orientation, alcoholism, psychological disorders, weight gain, and so forth. This module certainly does not resolve the controversies, but it should help you understand them as they arise later in this text or in other texts.

We begin with a review of elementary genetics. Readers already familiar with the concepts may skim over the first three pages.

Mendelian Genetics

Prior to the work of Gregor Mendel, a late-19th-century monk, scientists thought that inheritance was a blending process in which the properties of the sperm and the egg simply mixed, much as one might mix two colors of paint.

Mendel demonstrated that inheritance occurs through **genes,** units of heredity that maintain their structural identity from one generation to another. As a rule, genes come in pairs because they are aligned along **chromosomes** (strands of genes), which also come in pairs. (As an exception to this rule, a male has unpaired X and Y chromosomes, with different genes.) A gene is a portion of a chromosome, which is composed of the double-stranded molecule **deoxyribonucleic acid (DNA).** A strand of DNA serves as a template (model) for the synthesis of **ribonucleic acid (RNA)** molecules. RNA is a single-strand chemical; one type of RNA molecule serves as a template for the synthesis of protein molecules. Figure 1.7 summarizes the main steps in translating information from DNA through RNA into proteins, which then determine the development of the organism. Some proteins form part of the structure of the body; others serve as **enzymes,** biological catalysts that regulate chemical reactions in the body.

Anyone with an identical pair of genes on the two chromosomes is **homozygous** for that gene. An individual with an unmatched pair of genes is **heterozygous**

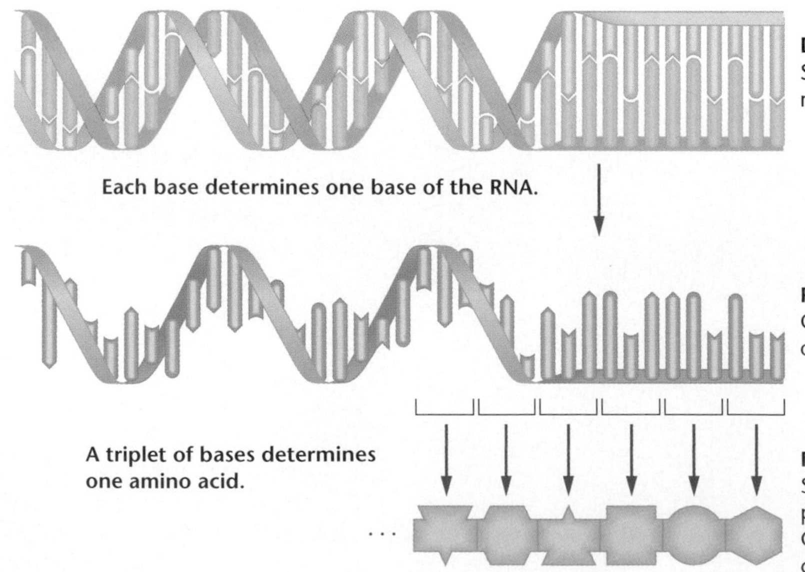

Figure 1.7
How DNA controls development of the organism
The sequence of bases along a strand of DNA determines the order of bases along a strand of RNA; RNA in turn controls the sequence of amino acids in a protein molecule.

for that gene. For example, you might have a gene for blue eyes on one chromosome and a gene for brown eyes on the other.

Certain genes are dominant or recessive. A **dominant** gene shows a strong effect in either the homozygous or heterozygous condition; a **recessive** gene shows its effects only in the homozygous condition. For example, someone with a gene for brown eyes (dominant) and one for blue eyes (recessive) has brown eyes but is a "carrier" for the blue-eye gene and can transmit it to a child. For a behavioral example, the gene for ability to taste moderate concentrations of phenylthiocarbamide (PTC) is dominant; the gene for low sensitivity is recessive. Only someone with two recessive genes has trouble tasting it (Wooding et al., 2004). Figure 1.8 illustrates the possible results of a mating between people who are both heterozygous for the PTC-tasting gene. Because each of them has one high-taste sensitivity (T) gene,[4] each can taste PTC. However, each parent transmits either a taster gene (T) or a nontaster gene (t) to a given child. Therefore, a child in this family has a 25% chance of being a homozygous (TT) taster, a 50% chance of being a heterozygous (Tt) taster, and a 25% chance of being a homozygous (tt) nontaster.

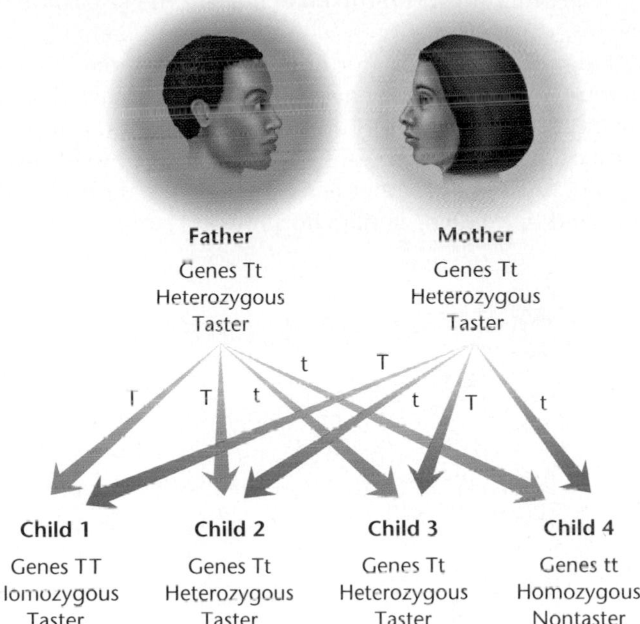

Figure 1.8 Four equally likely outcomes of a mating between parents who are heterozygous for a given gene (Tt)

A child in this family has a 25% chance of being homozygous for the dominant gene (TT), a 25% chance of being homozygous for the recessive gene (tt), and a 50% chance of being heterozygous (Tt).

Chromosomes and Crossing Over

Each chromosome participates in reproduction independently of the others, and each species has a certain number of chromosomes—for example, 23 pairs in humans, 4 pairs in fruit flies. If you have a *BbCc* genotype, and the *B* and *C* genes are on different chromosomes, your contribution of a *B* or *b* gene is independent of whether you contribute *C* or *c*. But suppose *B* and *C* are on the same chromosome. If one chromosome has the *BC* combination and the other has *bc*, then if you contribute a *B*, you probably also contribute *C*.

The exception comes about as a result of **crossing over:** A pair of chromosomes may break apart during reproduction and reconnect such that part of one chromosome attaches to the other part of the second chromosome. If one chromosome has the *BC* combination and the other chromosome has the *bc* combination, crossing over between the *B* locus (location) and the *C* locus leaves new chromosomes with the combinations *Bc* and *bC*. The closer the *B* locus is to the *C* locus, the less often crossing over occurs between them.

Sex-Linked and Sex-Limited Genes

The genes located on the sex chromosomes are known as **sex-linked genes.** All other chromosomes are autosomal chromosomes, and their genes are known as **autosomal genes.**

[4]Among geneticists, it is customary to use a capital letter to indicate the dominant gene and a lowercase letter to indicate the recessive gene.

In mammals, the two sex chromosomes are designated **X** and **Y:** A female mammal has two X chromosomes; a male has an X and a Y. (Unlike the arbitrary symbols *B* and *C* that I introduced to illustrate gene pairs, X and Y are standard symbols used by all geneticists.) During reproduction, the female necessarily contributes an X chromosome, and the male contributes either an X or a Y. If he contributes an X, the offspring is female; if he contributes a Y, the offspring is male.

The Y chromosome is small. The human Y chromosome has genes for only 27 proteins, far fewer than other chromosomes. The X chromosome, by contrast, has genes for about 1,500 proteins (Arnold, 2004). Thus, when biologists speak of sex-linked genes, they usually mean X-linked genes.

An example of a human sex-linked gene is the recessive gene for red-green color vision deficiency. Any man with this gene on his X chromosome has red-green color deficiency because he has no other X chromosome. A woman, however, is color deficient only if she has that recessive gene on both of her X chromosomes. So, for example, if 8% of human X chromosomes contain the gene for color vision deficiency, then 8% of all men will be color-deficient, but fewer than 1% of women will be (.08 × .08).

Distinct from sex-linked genes are the **sex-limited genes,** which are present in both sexes but have effects mainly or exclusively for one sex. For instance, genes control the amount of chest hair in men, breast size in women, the amount of crowing in roosters, and the rate of egg production in hens. Both sexes have those genes, but sex hormones activate them, so their effects depend on male or female hormones.

STOP & CHECK

1. Suppose you can taste PTC. If your mother can also taste it, what (if anything) can you predict about your father's ability to taste it? If your mother cannot taste it, what (if anything) can you predict about your father's ability to taste it?
2. How does a sex-linked gene differ from a sex-limited gene?

Check your answers on page 21.

Sources of Variation

If reproduction always produced offspring that were exact copies of the parents, evolution would not occur. One source of variation is **recombination,** a new combination of genes, some from one parent and some from the other, that yields characteristics not found in either parent. For example, a mother with curly blonde hair and a father with straight black hair could have a child with curly black hair or straight blonde hair.

A more powerful source of variation is a **mutation,** or change in a single gene. For instance, a gene for brown eyes might mutate into a gene for blue eyes. Mutation of a given gene is a rare, random event, independent of the needs of the organism. A mutation is analogous to having an untrained person add, remove, or distort something on the blueprints for your new house. A mutation leading to an altered protein is almost always disadvantageous. A mutation that modifies the amount or timing of protein production is closer to neutral and sometimes advantageous. Many of the differences among individuals and even among species depend on quantitative variations in the expression of genes.

Heredity and Environment

Unlike PTC sensitivity and color vision deficiency, most variations in behavior depend on the combined influence of many genes and environmental influences. You may occasionally hear someone ask about a behavior, "Which is more important, heredity or environment?" That question as stated is meaningless. Every behavior requires both heredity and environment.

However, we can rephrase it meaningfully: Do the observed *differences* among individuals depend more on differences in heredity or differences in environment? For example, if you sing better than I do, the reason could be that you have different genes, that you had better training, or both.

To determine the contributions of heredity and environment, researchers rely mainly on two kinds of evidence. First, they compare **monozygotic** ("from one egg," i.e., identical) twins and **dizygotic** ("from two eggs," i.e., fraternal) twins. A stronger resemblance between monozygotic than dizygotic twins suggests a genetic contribution. Second, researchers examine adopted children. Any tendency for adopted children to resemble their biological parents suggests a hereditary influence. If the variations in some characteristic depend largely on hereditary influences, the characteristic has high **heritability.**

Based on these kinds of evidence, researchers have found evidence for a significant heritability of almost every behavior they have tested (Bouchard & McGue, 2003). A few examples are loneliness (McGuire & Clifford, 2000), neuroticism (Lake, Eaves, Maes, Heath, & Martin, 2000), television watching (Plomin, Corley, DeFries, & Fulker, 1990), and social attitudes (S. F. Posner, Baker, Heath, & Martin, 1996). About the only behavior anyone has tested that has *not* shown a significant heritability is religious affiliation—such as Jewish, Protestant, Catholic, or Buddhist (Eaves, Martin, & Heath, 1990).

Possible Complications

Humans are difficult research animals. Investigators cannot control people's heredity or environment, and even their best methods of estimating hereditary influences are subject to error (Bouchard & McGue, 2003; Rutter, Pickles, Murray, & Eaves, 2001).

For example, it is sometimes difficult to distinguish between hereditary and prenatal influences. Consider the studies showing that biological children of parents with low IQs, criminal records, or mental illness are likely to have similar problems themselves, even if adopted by excellent parents. The parents with low IQs, criminal records, or mental illness gave the children their genes, but they also gave them their prenatal environment. In many cases, those mothers had poor diets and poor medical care during pregnancy. Many of them smoked cigarettes, drank alcohol, and used other drugs that affect a fetus's brain development. Therefore, what looks like a genetic effect could reflect influences of the prenatal environment.

Another complication: Certain environmental factors can inactivate a gene by attaching a methyl group (CH3) to it. In some cases, an early experience such as malnutrition or severe stress inactivates a gene, and then the individual passes on the inactivated gene to the next generation. Experiments have occasionally shown behavioral changes in rats based on experiences that happened to their mothers or grandmothers (Harper, 2005). Such results blur the distinction between hereditary and environmental.

Genes can also influence your behavior indirectly by changing your environment. For example, suppose your genes lead you to frequent temper tantrums. Other people—including your parents—will react harshly, giving you still further reason to feel hostile. Dickens and Flynn (2001) call this tendency a **multiplier effect:** If genetic or prenatal influences produce even a small increase in some activity, the early tendency will change the environment in a way that magnifies that tendency.

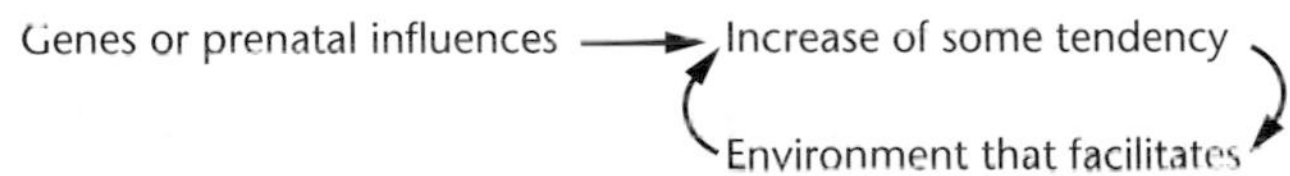

For a sports example, imagine a child born with genes promoting greater than average height, running speed, and coordination. The child shows early success at basketball, so parents and friends encourage the child to play basketball more and more. The increased practice improves skill, the skill leads to more success, and the success leads to more practice and coaching. What started as a small advantage becomes larger and larger. The same process could apply to schoolwork or any other endeavor. The outcome started with a genetic basis, but environmental reactions magnified it.

Environmental Modification

Even a trait with a strong hereditary influence can be modified by environmental interventions. For example, different genetic strains of mice behave differently in the *elevated plus maze* (Figure 1.9). Some stay almost entirely in the walled arms, like the mouse shown in the figure; others (less nervous?) venture onto the open arms. But even when different laboratories use the same genetic strains and nearly the same procedures, strains that are adventuresome in one laboratory are less active in another (Crabbe, Wahlsten, & Dudek, 1999). Evidently, the effects of the genes depend on subtle differences in procedure, such as how the investigators handle the mice or maybe even the investigators' odors. (Most behaviors do not show this much variability; the elevated plus maze appears to be an extreme example.)

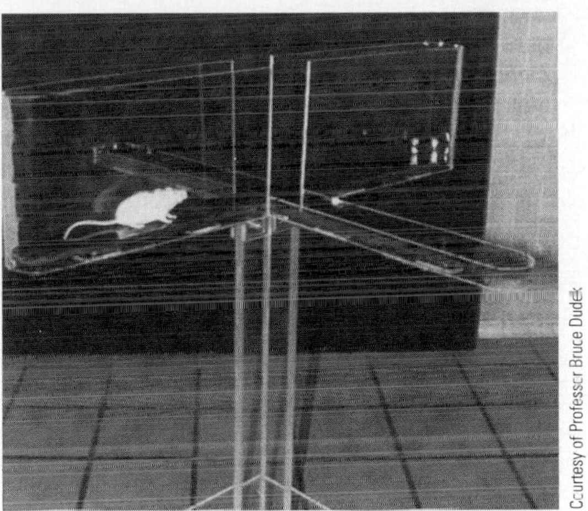

Courtesy of Professor Bruce Dudek

Figure 1.9 An elevated plus maze
Different genetic strains of mice behave differently in this apparatus, presumably displaying different levels of anxiety. But the results vary from lab to lab because of minor, unintentional variations in procedure. In short, the effects of a gene can vary depending on the environment.

For a human example, **phenylketonuria** (FEE-nil-KEET-uhn-YOOR-ee-uh), or **PKU**, is a genetic inability to metabolize the amino acid phenylalanine. If PKU is not treated, the phenylalanine accumulates to toxic levels, impairing brain development and leaving children mentally retarded, restless, and irritable. Approximately 1% of Europeans carry a recessive gene for PKU; fewer Asians and almost no Africans have the gene (T. Wang et al., 1989).

Although PKU is a hereditary condition, environmental interventions can modify it. Physicians in many countries routinely measure the level of phenylalanine or its metabolites in babies' blood or urine. If a baby has high levels, indicating PKU, physicians advise the parents to put the baby on a strict low-phenylalanine diet to minimize brain damage (Waisbren, Brown, de Sonneville, & Levy, 1994). Our ability to prevent PKU provides particularly strong evidence that *heritable* does not mean *unmodifiable*.

A couple of notes about PKU: The required diet is difficult. People have to avoid meats, eggs, dairy products, grains, and especially aspartame (NutraSweet), which is 50% phenylalanine. Instead, they eat an expensive formula containing all the other amino acids. Physicians long believed that children with PKU could quit the diet after a few years. Later experience has shown that high phenylalanine levels damage teenage and adult brains, too. A woman with PKU should be especially careful during pregnancy and when nursing. Even a genetically normal baby cannot handle the enormous amounts of phenylalanine that an affected mother might pass through the placenta.

3. Adopted children whose biological parents were alcoholics have an increased probability of becoming alcoholics themselves. One possible explanation is heredity. What is another?
4. What example illustrates the point that even if some characteristic is highly heritable, a change in the environment can alter it?

Check your answers on page 21.

How Genes Affect Behavior

A biologist who speaks of a "gene for brown eyes" does not mean that the gene directly produces brown eyes. Rather, the gene produces a protein that makes the eyes brown, assuming normal health and nutrition. If we speak of a "gene for alcoholism," we should not imagine that the gene itself causes alcoholism. Rather, it produces a protein that under certain circumstances increases the probability of alcoholism. It is important to specify these circumstances as well as we can.

Exactly how a gene increases the probability of a given behavior is a complex issue. In later chapters, we encounter a few examples of genes that control brain chemicals. However, genes also can affect behavior indirectly—for example, by changing the way other people treat you (Kendler, 2001). Suppose you have genes causing you to be unusually attractive. As a result, strangers smile at you, many people invite you to parties, and so forth. Their reactions to your appearance may change your personality, and if so, the genes produced their behavioral effects by altering your environment!

Consequently, we should not be amazed by reports that almost every human behavior has some heritability. A gene that affects almost anything in your body will indirectly affect your choice of activities and the way other people respond.

The Evolution of Behavior

Every gene is subject to evolution by natural selection. **Evolution** is a change over generations in the frequencies of various genes in a population. Note that, by this definition, evolution includes *any* change in gene frequencies, regardless of whether it is helpful or harmful to the species in the long run.

We must distinguish two questions about evolution: How *did* some species evolve, and how *do* species evolve? To ask how a species did evolve is to ask what evolved from what, basing our answers on inferences from fossils and comparisons of living species. For example, biologists find that humans are more similar to chimpanzees than to other species, and they infer a common ancestor. Similarly, humans and chimpanzees resemble monkeys in certain ways and presumably shared an ancestor with monkeys in the remoter past. Using similar reasoning, evolutionary biologists have constructed an "evolutionary tree" that shows the relationships among various species (Figure 1.10). As new evidence becomes available, biologists change their opinions of how closely any two species are related; thus, all evolutionary trees are tentative.

Nevertheless, the question of how species *do* evolve is a question of how the process works, and that process is, in its basic outlines, a logical necessity. That is, given what we know about reproduction, evolution *must* occur. The reasoning goes as follows:

- Offspring generally resemble their parents for genetic reasons.
- Mutations and recombinations of genes occasionally introduce new heritable variations, which help or harm an individual's chance of surviving and reproducing.
- Some individuals reproduce more abundantly than others.
- Certain individuals successfully reproduce more than others do, thus passing on their genes to the next generation. The percentages of various genes in the next generation reflect the kinds of individuals who reproduced in the previous generation. That is, any gene that is consistently associated with reproductive success will become more prevalent in later generations. You can witness and explore this principle with the Online Try It Yourself activity "Genetic Generations."

ONLINE try it yourself

Because plant and animal breeders have long known this principle, they choose individuals with a desired trait and make them the parents of the next generation. This process is called **artificial selection**, and over many generations, breeders have produced exceptional race horses, hundreds of kinds of dogs, chickens that lay huge numbers of eggs, and so forth. Charles Darwin's (1859) insight was that nature also selects. If certain individuals are more successful than others in finding food, escaping enemies, attracting mates, or protecting their offspring, then their genes will become more prevalent in later generations.

Common Misunderstandings About Evolution

Let us clarify the principles of evolution by addressing a few misconceptions.

- *Does the use or disuse of some structure or behavior cause an evolutionary increase or decrease in*

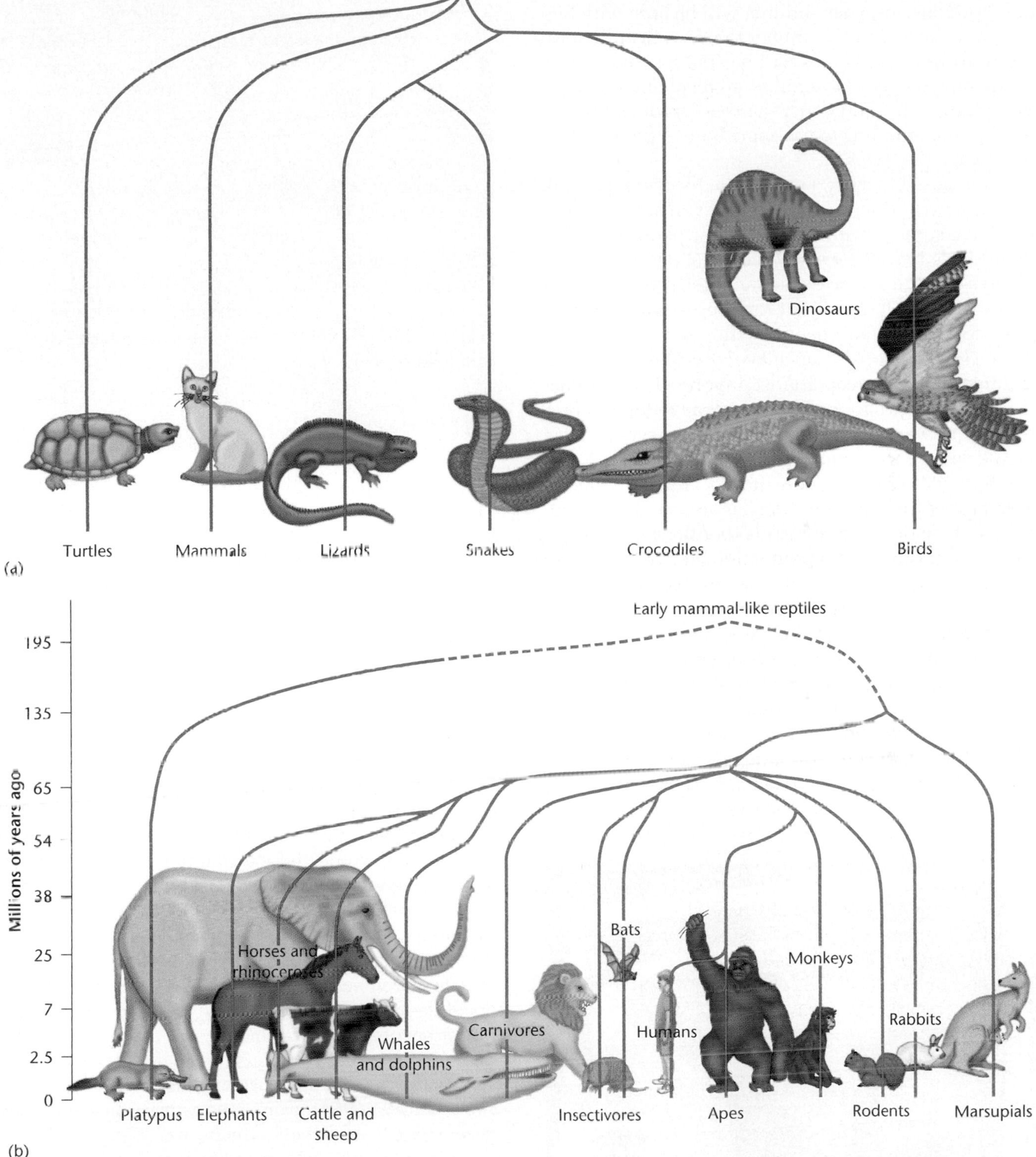

Figure 1.10 Evolutionary trees
(a) Evolutionary relationships among mammals, birds, and several kinds of reptiles.
(b) Evolutionary relationships among various species of mammals.

that feature? You may have heard people say something like, "Because we hardly ever use our little toes, they will get smaller and smaller in each succeeding generation." This idea is a carryover of the biologist Jean Lamarck's theory of evolution through the inheritance of acquired characteristics, known as **Lamarckian evolution.** According to this idea, if giraffes stretch their necks as far out as possible, their offspring will be born with longer necks. Similarly, if you exercise your arm muscles, your children will be born with bigger arm muscles, and if you fail to use your little toes, your children's little toes will be smaller than yours. However, biologists have found no mechanism for Lamarckian evolution to occur and no evidence that it does. Using or failing to use some body structure does not change the genes.

(It is possible that people's little toes might shrink in future evolution if people with even smaller little toes have some advantage over other people. But we would have to wait for a mutation that decreases little toe size—without causing some other problem—and then we would have to wait for people with this mutation to outreproduce people with other genes.)

• *Have humans stopped evolving?* Because modern medicine can keep almost anyone alive, and because welfare programs in prosperous countries provide the necessities of life for almost everyone, some people assert that humans are no longer subject to the principle of "survival of the fittest." Therefore, the argument goes, human evolution has slowed or stopped.

The flaw in this argument is that the key to evolution is not survival but reproduction. For you to spread your genes, of course you have to survive long enough to reproduce, but what counts is how many healthy children (and nieces and nephews) you have. Thus, keeping everyone alive doesn't stop human evolution. If some people have more children than others do, their genes will spread in the population.

• *Does "evolution" mean "improvement"?* It depends on what you mean by "improvement." By definition, evolution improves the average **fitness** of the population, which is operationally defined as *the number of copies of one's genes that endure in later generations.* For example, if you have more children than average, you are by definition evolutionarily fit, regardless of whether you are successful in any other sense. You also increase your fitness by supporting your brother, sister, nieces and nephews, or anyone else with the same genes you have. Any gene that spreads is by definition fit. However, genes that increase fitness at one time and place might be disadvantageous after a change in the environment. For example, the colorful tail feathers of the male peacock enable it to attract females but might become disadvantageous in the presence of a new predator that responds to bright colors. In other words, the genes of the current generation evolved because they were fit for *previous* generations; they may or may not be adaptive in the future.

© F. J. Hierschel/Okapia/Photo Researchers

Sometimes a sexual display, such as a peacock's spread of its tail feathers, leads to great reproductive success and therefore to the spread of the associated genes. In a slightly changed environment, this gene could become maladaptive. For example, if an aggressive predator with good color vision enters the range of the peacock, the bird's slow movement and colorful feathers could seal its doom.

© Alain Le Garsmeur/CORBIS

It is possible to slow the rate of evolution but not just by keeping everyone alive. China has enacted a policy that attempts to limit each family to one child. Successful enforcement of this policy would certainly limit the possibility of genetic changes between generations.

• *Does evolution act to benefit the individual or the species?* Neither: It benefits the genes! In a sense, you don't use your genes to reproduce yourself; rather, your genes use *you* to reproduce *themselves* (Dawkins, 1989). A gene spreads through a population if and only if the individuals bearing that gene reproduce more than other individuals do. For example, imagine a gene that causes you to risk your life to protect your children. That gene will spread through the population, even though it endangers you personally, provided that it enables you to leave behind more surviving children than you would have otherwise. A gene that causes you to attack other members of your species to benefit your children could also spread, even though it harms the species in general, presuming that the behavior really does benefit your children, and that others of your species do not attack you or your children in retaliation.

STOP & CHECK

5. Many people believe the human appendix is useless. Should we therefore expect that it will grow smaller from one generation to the next?

Check your answer on page 21.

Evolutionary Psychology

Evolutionary psychology, or sociobiology, deals with how behaviors have evolved, especially social behaviors. The emphasis is on *evolutionary* and *functional* explanations, as defined earlier—the presumed behaviors of our ancestors and why natural selection might have favored certain behavioral tendencies. The assumption is that any behavior that is characteristic of a species must have arisen through natural selection and must have provided some advantage. Although exceptions to this assumption are possible, it is at least a helpful guide to research. Consider a few examples:

- Some animal species have better color vision than others, and some have better peripheral vision. Presumably, the species with better vision need it for their way of life (see Chapter 7).
- We have brain mechanisms that cause us to sleep for a few hours each day and to cycle through several different stages of sleep. Presumably, we would not have such mechanisms unless sleep provided benefits (see Chapter 9).
- Mammals and birds devote more energy to maintaining body temperature than to all other activities combined. We would not have evolved such an expensive mechanism unless it gave us major advantages (see Chapter 11).
- Bears eat all the food they can find; small birds eat only enough to satisfy their immediate needs. Humans generally take a middle path. The different eating habits presumably relate to different needs by different species (see Chapter 11).

On the other hand, some characteristics of a species have a more debatable relationship to natural selection. Consider two examples:

- People grow old and die, with an average survival time of about 70 or 80 years under favorable circumstances. Do we deteriorate because we have genes that cause us to die and get out of the way so that we don't compete against our own children and grandchildren? Or are aging and death inevitable? Different people do age at different rates, largely for genetic reasons (Puca et al., 2001), so it is not ridiculous to hypothesize that our tendency to age and die is controlled by selective pressures of evolution. But the conclusion is hardly obvious either.
- More men than women enjoy the prospect of casual sex with multiple partners. Theorists have related this tendency to the fact that a man can have many children by impregnating many women, whereas a woman cannot multiply her children by having more sexual partners (Buss, 1994). So, can we conclude that men and women are prewired to have different sexual behaviors? As we shall explore in Chapter 11, the answer is debatable.

To further illustrate evolutionary psychology, let's consider the theoretically interesting example of **altruistic behavior,** an action that benefits someone other than the actor. Any gene spreads within a population if individuals with that gene reproduce more than those without it. However, a gene that encourages altruistic behavior would help *other* individuals to survive and perhaps spread their genes. How could a gene for altruism spread, if at all?

We should begin with the question of how common altruism is. It certainly occurs in humans: We contribute to charities; we try to help people in distress; a student may explain something to a classmate who is competing for a good grade in a course. Among nonhumans, we observe abundant examples of parents devoting much effort and even risking their lives to protect their young, but altruism toward nonrelatives is rare. Even apparent altruism often has a selfish motive. For example, when a crow finds food on the ground, it caws loudly, attracting other crows that will share the food. Altruism? Not really. A bird on the ground is vulnerable to attack by cats and other enemies, and when it lowers its head to eat, it cannot see the dangers. Having other crows around means more eyes to watch for dangers.

Similarly, consider meerkats (a kind of mongoose). Periodically, one or another member of any meerkat colony stands, and if it sees danger, emits an alarm call that warns the others (Figure 1.11). Its alarm call helps the others (probably including its relatives), but the one who sees the danger first and emits the alarm call is the one most likely to escape (Clutton-Brock et al., 1999).

Even in humans, we have no evidence that altruism is under genetic control. Still, for the sake of illustration, suppose some gene increases altruistic behavior.

© Nigel J. Dennis; Gallo Images/CORBIS

Figure 1.11 Sentinel behavior: altruistic or not?
As in many other prey species, meerkats sometimes show sentinel behavior in watching for danger and warning the others. However, the meerkat that emits the alarm is the one most likely to escape the danger.

Is there any way it could spread within a population? One common reply is that most altruistic behaviors cost very little. True, but being almost harmless is not good enough; a gene spreads only if the individuals with it reproduce more than those without it. Another common reply is that the altruistic behavior benefits the species. True again, but the rebuttal is the same. A gene that benefits the species but fails to help the individual dies out with that individual.

A suggestion that sounds good at first is *group selection.* According to this idea, altruistic groups survive better than less cooperative ones (D. S. Wilson & Sober, 1994). However, what will happen when a mutation favoring uncooperative behavior occurs within a cooperative group? If the uncooperative individual has a reproductive advantage within its group, its genes will spread. At best, group selection would produce an unstable outcome.

A better explanation is **reciprocal altruism,** the idea that animals help those who help them in return. Clearly, two individuals who cooperate with each other will prosper; however, reciprocal altruism requires that individuals recognize one another and learn to help only those who return the favors. Otherwise, it is easy for an uncooperative individual to accept favors, prosper greatly, and never repay the favors. In other words, reciprocal altruism requires good sensory organs and a well-developed brain. (Perhaps we now see why altruism is more common in humans than in other species.)

Another explanation is **kin selection,** selection for a gene because it benefits the individual's relatives. For example, a gene could spread if it caused you to risk your life to protect your children, who share many of your genes, including perhaps the altruism genes. Natural selection can favor altruism toward less close relatives—such as cousins, nephews, or nieces—if the benefit to them outweighs the cost to you (Dawkins, 1989; Hamilton, 1964; Trivers, 1985). In both humans and nonhumans, cooperative or altruistic behavior is more common toward relatives than toward unrelated individuals (Bowles & Posel, 2005; Krakauer, 2005).

At its best, evolutionary psychology leads to research that helps us understand a behavior. For example, someone notices that males of one species help with infant care and males of another species do not. The search for a functional explanation can direct researchers to explore the species' different habitats and ways of life until we understand why they behave differently. However, this approach is criticized, often with justification, when its practitioners assume that every behavior must be adaptive and then propose an explanation without testing it (Schlinger, 1996).

STOP & CHECK

6. What are two plausible ways for possible altruistic genes to spread in a population?

Check your answer on page 21.

Module 1.2
In Closing: Genes and Behavior

In the control of behavior, genes are neither all important nor irrelevant. Certain behaviors have a high heritability, such as the ability to taste PTC. Many other behaviors are influenced by genes but also subject to strong influence by experience. Our genes and our evolution make it possible for humans to be what we are today, but they also give us the flexibility to change our behavior as circumstances warrant.

Understanding the genetics of human behavior is particularly important, but also particularly difficult. Separating the roles of heredity and environment is always difficult, but especially so with humans, because researchers have such limited control over environmental influences. Inferring human evolution is also difficult, partly because we do not know enough about the lives of our ancient ancestors. Finally, we should remember that the way things *are* is not necessarily the same as the way they *should be*. For example, even if our genes predispose us to behave in a particular way, we can still decide to try to overcome those predispositions if they do not suit the needs of modern life.

Summary

1. Genes are chemicals that maintain their integrity from one generation to the next and influence the development of the individual. A dominant gene affects development regardless of whether a person has pairs of that gene or only a single copy per cell. A recessive gene affects development only in the absence of the dominant gene. (p. 12)
2. Some behavioral differences demonstrate simple effects of dominant and recessive genes. More often, however, behavioral variations reflect the combined influences of many genes and many environmental factors. Heritability is an estimate of the amount of variation that is due to genetic variation as opposed to environmental variation. (p. 14)
3. Researchers estimate heritability of a human condition by comparing monozygotic and dizygotic twins and by comparing adopted children to their biological and adoptive parents. (p. 14)
4. The results sometimes overestimate human heritability. First, most adoption studies do not distinguish between the effects of genes and those of prenatal environment. Second, after genes produce an early increase in some behavioral tendency, that behavior may lead to a change in the environment that magnifies the tendency. (p. 14)
5. The fact that some behavior shows high heritability for a given population does not deny the possibility that a change in the environment might significantly alter the behavioral outcome. (p. 15)
6. Genes influence behavior directly by altering brain chemicals and indirectly by affecting other aspects of the body and therefore the way other people react to us. (p. 16)
7. The process of evolution through natural selection is a logical necessity because mutations sometimes occur in genes, and individuals with certain sets of genes reproduce more successfully than others do. (p. 16)
8. Evolution spreads the genes of the individuals who have reproduced the most. Therefore, if some characteristic is widespread within a population, it is reasonable to look for ways in which that characteristic is or has been adaptive. However, we cannot take it for granted that all common behaviors are adaptive; we need to do the research to test this hypothesis. (p. 19)

Answers to STOP & CHECK Questions

1. If your mother can taste PTC, we can make no predictions about your father. You may have inherited a gene from your mother that enables you to taste PTC, and because the gene is dominant, you need only one copy of the gene to taste PTC. However, if your mother cannot taste PTC, you must have inherited your ability to taste it from your father, so he must be a taster. (p. 14)
2. A sex-linked gene is on a sex chromosome (almost always the X chromosome). A sex-limited gene is on one of the other chromosomes, but it is activated by sex hormones and therefore makes its effects evident only in one sex or the other. (p. 14)
3. If the mother drank much alcohol during pregnancy, the prenatal environment may have predisposed the child to later alcoholism. (p. 16)
4. Keeping a child with the PKU gene on a strict low-phenylalanine diet prevents the mental retardation that the gene ordinarily causes. The general point is that sometimes a highly heritable condition can be modified environmentally. (p. 16)
5. No. Failure to use or need a structure does not make it become smaller in the next generation. The appendix will shrink only if people with a gene for a smaller appendix reproduce more successfully than other people do. (p. 19)
6. Altruistic genes could spread because they facilitate care for one's kin or because they facilitate exchanges of favors with others (reciprocal altruism). (p. 20)

Thought Questions

1. What human behaviors are you sure have a heritability of 0?
2. Genetic differences probably account for part of the difference between people who age slowly and gracefully and others who grow old more rapidly and die younger. Given that the genes controlling old age have their onset long after people have stopped having children, how could evolution have any effect on such genes?

Module 1.3
The Use of Animals in Research

Certain ethical disputes resist agreement. One is abortion; another is the death penalty; still another is the use of animals in research. In each case, well-meaning people on each side of the issue insist that their position is proper and ethical. The dispute is not a matter of the good guys against the bad guys; it is between two views of what is good.

The animal welfare controversy is critical for biological psychology. As you will see throughout this book, research done on laboratory animals is responsible for a great deal of what we know about the brain and behavior. That research ranges from mere observation through painless experiments to studies that do inflict stress and pain. How shall we deal with the fact that on the one hand we want more knowledge and on the other hand we wish to minimize animal distress?

Reasons for Animal Research

Given that most biological psychologists and neuroscientists are primarily interested in the human brain and human behavior, why do they study nonhuman animals? Here are four reasons.

1. *The underlying mechanisms of behavior are similar across species and sometimes easier to study in a nonhuman species.* If you wanted to understand a complex machine, you might begin by examining a simpler machine. We also learn about brain–behavior relationships by starting with simpler cases. The brains and behavior of nonhuman vertebrates resemble those of humans in their chemistry and anatomy (Figure 1.12). Even invertebrate nerves follow the same basic principles as our own. Much research has been conducted on squid nerves, which are thicker than human nerves and therefore easier to study.
2. *We are interested in animals for their own sake.* Humans are naturally curious. We want to understand why the Druids built Stonehenge, where the moon came from, how the rings of Saturn formed, and why certain animals act the way they do. Some of this research might produce practical applications, but even if it doesn't, we would like to understand the universe just for the sake of understanding.
3. *What we learn about animals sheds light on human evolution.* What is our place in nature? How did we come to be the way we are? One way of approaching such questions is by examining other species to see how we are the same and how we are different.

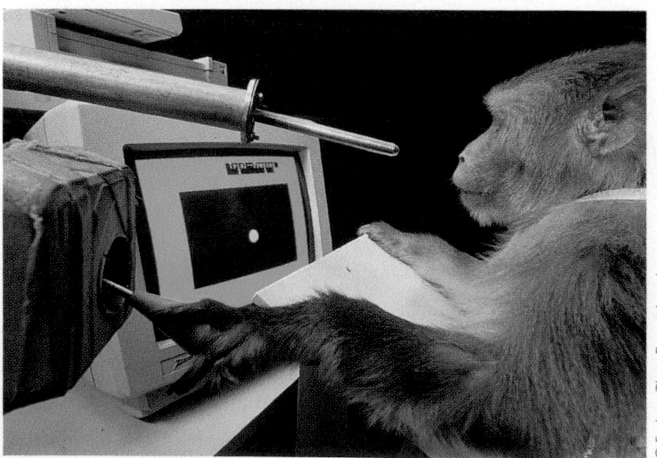

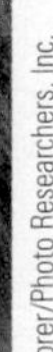

© Explorer/Photo Researchers, Inc.

© David M. Barron/Animals Animals

Animals are used in many kinds of research studies, some dealing with behavior and others with the functions of the nervous system.

4. *Certain experiments cannot use humans because of legal or ethical restrictions.* For example, investigators insert electrodes into the brain cells of rats and other animals to determine the relationship between brain activity and behavior. Such experiments answer questions that investigators cannot address in any other way. They also raise an ethical issue: If the research is unacceptable with humans, shouldn't we also object to it with nonhumans?

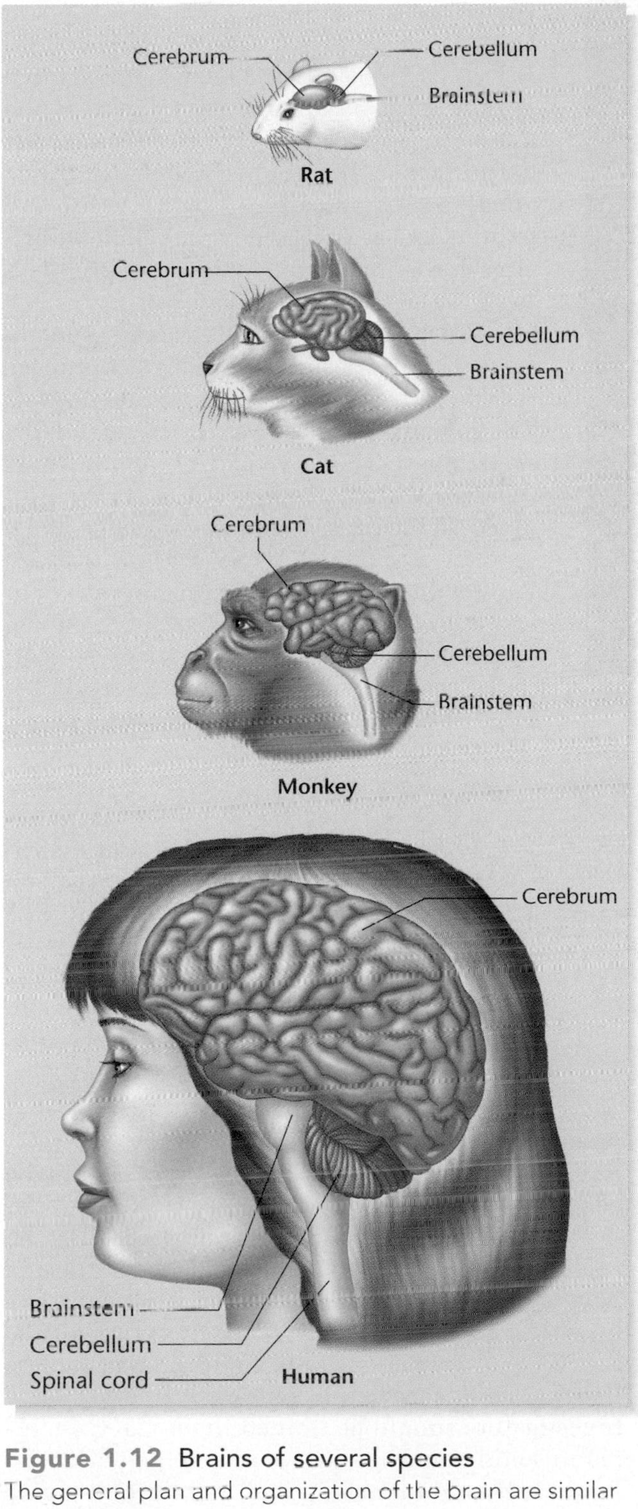

Figure 1.12 Brains of several species
The general plan and organization of the brain are similar for all mammals, even though the size varies from species to species.

The Ethical Debate

In some cases, researchers simply observe animals in nature as a function of different times of day, different seasons of the year, changes in diet, and so forth. These procedures do not even inconvenience the animals and raise no ethical problems. In other experiments, however, including many discussed in this book, animals have been subjected to brain damage, electrode implantation, injections of drugs or hormones, and so forth. Many people regard such experimentation as cruelty to animals and have reacted with tactics ranging from peaceful demonstrations to vandalizing laboratories and threatening researchers with death (Schiermeier, 1998).

The issues are difficult. On the one hand, many laboratory animals do undergo painful or debilitating procedures that are admittedly not for their own benefit. Anyone with a conscience (including scientists) is bothered by this fact. On the other hand, experimentation with animals has been critical to the medical research that led to methods for the prevention or treatment of polio, diabetes, measles, smallpox, massive burns, heart disease, and other serious conditions. Most Nobel prizes in physiology or medicine have been awarded for research conducted on nonhuman animals. The hope of finding methods to treat or prevent AIDS and various brain diseases (e.g., Alzheimer's disease) depends largely on animal research. For many questions in biological psychology, our choice is to conduct research on animals or to make much slower progress or, for certain kinds of questions, no progress at all (Figure 1.13).

Opposition to animal research ranges considerably in degree. "Minimalists" tolerate animal research under certain conditions. That is, they accept some kinds of research but wish to prohibit others depending on the probable value of the research, the amount of distress to the animal, and the type of animal. (Most people have fewer qualms about hurting an insect, say, than a dolphin.) They favor firm regulations on research.

The "abolitionists" take a more extreme position and see no room for compromise. Abolitionists maintain that all animals have the same rights as humans. They regard killing an animal as murder, regardless of whether the intention is to eat it, use its fur, or gain scientific knowledge. Keeping an animal (presumably even a pet) in a cage is, in their view, slavery. Because animals cannot give informed consent to research, abolitionists insist it is wrong to use them in any way, regardless of the circumstances. According to one op-

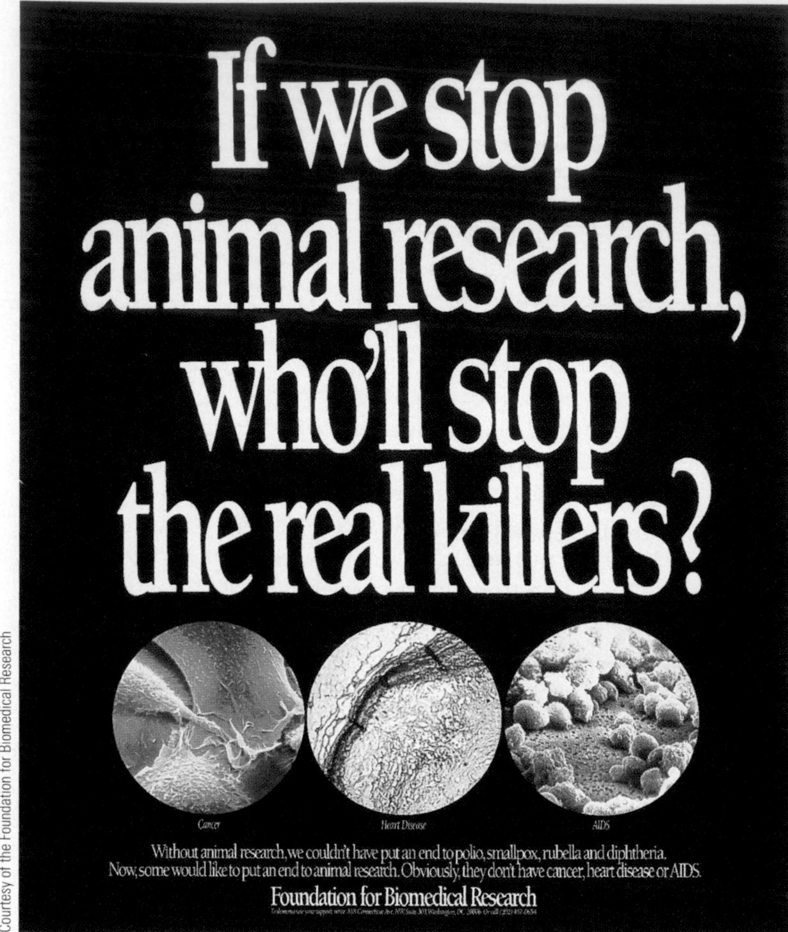

Courtesy of the Foundation for Biomedical Research

Figure 1.13 In defense of animal research
For many years, opponents of animal research have been protesting against experimentation with animals. This ad represents a reply by supporters of such research.

ponent of animal research, "We have no moral option but to bring this research to a halt. Completely. . . . We will not be satisfied until every cage is empty" (Regan, 1986, pp. 39–40). Advocates of this position sometimes claim that most animal research is painful and that it never leads to important results. However, for a true abolitionist, neither of those points really matters. Their moral imperative is that people have no right to use animals, even if the research is useful and even if it is painless.

Some abolitionists have opposed environmental protection groups as well. For example, red foxes, which humans introduced into California, so effectively rob bird nests that they have severely endangered California's least terns and clapper rails. To protect the endangered birds, the U.S. Fish and Wildlife Service began trapping and killing red foxes in the areas where endangered birds breed. Their efforts were thwarted by a ballot initiative organized by animal rights activists, who argued that killing any animal is immoral even when the motive is to protect another species from extinction (Williams, 1999). Similar objections were raised when conservationists proposed to kill the pigs (again a human-introduced species) that were destroying the habitat of native Hawaiian wildlife.

At times in the animal rights dispute, people on both sides have taken shrill "us versus them" positions. Some defenders of animal research have claimed that such research is almost always useful and seldom painful, and some opponents have argued that the research is usually painful and never useful. In fact, the truth is messier (D. Blum, 1994): Much research is both useful and painful. Those of us who value both knowledge and animal life look for compromises instead of either–or solutions.

Nearly all animal researchers sympathize with the desire to minimize painful research. That is, just about everyone draws a line somewhere and says, "I will not do this experiment. The knowledge I might gain is not worth that much distress to the animals." To be sure, different researchers draw that line at different places.

An organization of European researchers offered a series of proposals, which you can read at this website (see also van Zutphen, 2001):

http://www.esf.org/ftp/pdf/SciencePolicy/ESPB9.pdf

Here are a few highlights:

- Laboratory animals have both an instrumental value (as a means to an end) and an intrinsic value (for their own sake), which must be respected.
- While accepting the need for animal research, the European Science Foundation endorses the principles of reduction (using fewer animals), replacement (using other methods not requiring animals, when possible), and refinement (using less painful procedures).
- Research to improve animal welfare should be encouraged.
- Before any research starts, someone other than the researchers themselves should evaluate the research plan to consider likely benefits and suffering.
- Investigators should assume that a procedure that is painful to humans is also painful to animals, unless they have evidence to the contrary.
- Investigators should be trained in animal care, including ethics and alternative research methods.
- Journals should include in their publication policy a statement about the ethical use of animals.

Is this sort of compromise satisfactory? It is to researchers and minimalists, but true abolitionists have no interest in compromise. If you believe that keeping any animal in any cage is the moral equivalent of slavery, you won't endorse doing it in moderation. The disagreement between abolitionists and animal researchers is a dispute between two ethical positions: "Never knowingly harm an innocent" and "Sometimes a little harm leads to a greater good." On the one hand, permitting research has the undeniable consequence of inflicting pain or distress. On the other hand, banning the use of animals for human purposes means a great setback in medical research as well as the end of animal-to-human transplants (e.g., using pig heart valves to help people with heart diseases). For this reason, many victims of serious diseases have organized to oppose animal rights groups (Feeney, 1987).

The principles of moderation and compromise are now the legal standard. In the United States, every college or other research institution that receives federal funds is required to have an Institutional Animal Care and Use Committee, composed of veterinarians, community representatives, and scientists, that evaluates proposed experiments, decides whether they are acceptable, and specifies procedures designed to minimize pain and discomfort. Similar regulations and committees govern research on human subjects. In addition, all research laboratories must abide by national laws requiring certain standards of cleanliness and animal care. Similar laws apply in other countries, and scientific journals require a statement that researchers followed all the laws and regulations in their research. Professional organizations such as the Society for Neuroscience publish guidelines for the use of animals in research (see Appendix B). The following website describes U.S. regulations and advice on animal care: **http://oacu.od.nih.gov/index.htm**

STOP & CHECK

1. Describe reasons biological psychologists conduct much of their research on nonhuman animals.
2. How does the "minimalist" position differ from the "abolitionist" position?

Check your answers on this page.

Module 1.3
In Closing: Humans and Animals

We began this chapter with a quote from the Nobel Prize–winning biologist Niko Tinbergen. Tinbergen argued that no fundamental gulf separates humans from other animal species. Because we are similar in many ways to other species, we can learn much about ourselves from animal studies. Also because of that similarity, we identify with animals, and we wish not to hurt them. Neuroscience researchers who decide to conduct animal research do not, as a rule, take this decision lightly. They want to minimize harm to animals, but they also want to increase knowledge. They believe it is better to inflict limited distress under controlled conditions than to permit ignorance and disease to inflict much greater distress. In some cases, however, it is a difficult decision.

Summary

1. Researchers study animals because the mechanisms are sometimes easier to study in nonhumans, because they are interested in animal behavior for its own sake, because they want to understand the evolution of behavior, and because certain kinds of experiments are difficult or impossible with humans. (p. 22)
2. The ethics of using animals in research is controversial. Some research does inflict stress or pain on animals; however, many research questions can be investigated only through animal research. (p. 23)
3. Animal research today is conducted under legal and ethical controls that attempt to minimize animal distress. (p. 24)

Answers to STOP & CHECK Questions

1. Sometimes the mechanisms of behavior are easier to study in a nonhuman species. We are curious about animals for their own sake. We study animals to understand human evolution. Certain procedures are illegal or unethical with humans. (p. 25)
2. A "minimalist" wishes to limit animal research to studies with little discomfort and much potential value. An "abolitionist" wishes to eliminate all animal research, regardless of how the animals are treated or how much value the research might produce. (p. 25)

Chapter Ending

Key Terms and Activities

Terms

altruistic behavior (p. 19)
artificial selection (p. 16)
autosomal gene (p. 13)
binocular rivalry (p. 8)
biological psychology (p. 2)
chromosome (p. 12)
crossing over (p. 13)
deoxyribonucleic acid (DNA) (p. 12)
dizygotic twins (p. 14)
dominant (p. 13)
dualism (p. 5)
easy problems (p. 6)
enzyme (p. 12)
evolution (p. 16)
evolutionary explanation (p. 4)
evolutionary psychology (p. 19)
fitness (p. 18)
functional explanation (p. 4)
gene (p. 12)
hard problem (p. 6)
heritability (p. 14)
heterozygous (p. 12)
homozygous (p. 12)
identity position (p. 6)
kin selection (p. 20)
Lamarckian evolution (p. 17)
materialism (p. 5)
mentalism (p. 6)
mind–body or *mind–brain problem* (p. 5)
monism (p. 5)
monozygotic twins (p. 14)
multiplier effect (p. 15)
mutation (p. 14)
ontogenetic explanation (p. 4)
phenylketonuria (PKU) (p. 15)
physiological explanation (p. 3)
problem of other minds (p. 6)
recessive (p. 13)
reciprocal altruism (p. 20)
recombination (p. 14)
ribonucleic acid (RNA) (p. 12)
sex-limited gene (p. 14)
sex-linked gene (p. 13)
solipsism (p. 6)
X chromosome (p. 13)
Y chromosome (p. 13)

Suggestions for Further Reading

Gazzaniga, M. S. (1998). *The mind's past.* Berkeley: University of California Press. A noted neuroscientist's attempt to explain the physical origins of consciousness. This book includes a number of fascinating examples.

Koch, C. (2004). *The quest for consciousness.* Englewood, CO: Roberts. A scientist's attempt to make sense of the mind–brain relationship.

Sunstein, C. R., & Nussbaum, M. C. (Eds.). (2004). *Animal rights: Current debates and new directions.* New York: Oxford University Press. A series of essays arguing both sides of the debate about animal rights and welfare.

Websites to Explore[5]

You can go to the Biological Psychology Study Center at this address:

http://psychology.wadsworth.com/book/kalatbiopsych9e/

It would help to set a bookmark for this site because it will be helpful for each chapter. In addition to sample quiz items, a dictionary of terms, and other information, it includes links to many other websites. One way to reach any of these sites is to go to the Biological Psychology Study Cen-

[5]Websites arise and disappear without warning. The suggestions listed in this book were available at the time the book went to press; I cannot guarantee how long they will last.

ter, click the appropriate chapter, and then find the appropriate links to additional sites. You can also check for suggested articles available on InfoTrac College Edition. The sites for this chapter are:

National Society for Phenylketonuria Home Page

http://www.nspku.org

Statement on Use of Animals in Research

http://www.esf.org/ftp/pdf/SciencePolicy/ESPB9.pdf

U.S. government statement on animal care and use

http://oacu.od.nih.gov/index.htm

Here are three sites that you may find helpful at many points throughout the text:

Dana Foundation for brain information

http://www.dana.org

Biomedical terms. If you read journal articles about biological psychology, you will encounter many terms, some of which are not defined in this text or in the online Biological Psychology dictionary for this text. To look up these additional terms, try this site:

http://medical.webends.com

Founders of Neurology (biographics of major researchers)

http://www.uic.edu/depts/mcne/founders

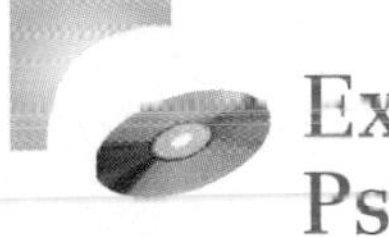

Exploring Biological Psychology CD

Binocular Rivalry (Try It Yourself)

Genetics and Evolution (Try It Yourself)

Evolutionary Studies (video)

Offspring of Parents Homozygous and Heterozygous for Brown Eyes (animation)

RNA, DNA, and Protein (animation)

Selection and Random Drift (Try It Yourself)

Critical Thinking (essay questions)

Chapter Quiz (multiple-choice questions)

ThomsonNOW™

http://www.thomsonedu.com

Go to this site for the link to ThomsonNOW, your one-stop study shop. Take a Pre-Test for this chapter, and ThomsonNOW will generate a Personalized Study Plan based on your test results. The Study Plan will identify the topics you need to review and direct you to online resources to help you master these topics. You can then take a Post-Test to help you determine the concepts you have mastered and what you still need to work on.

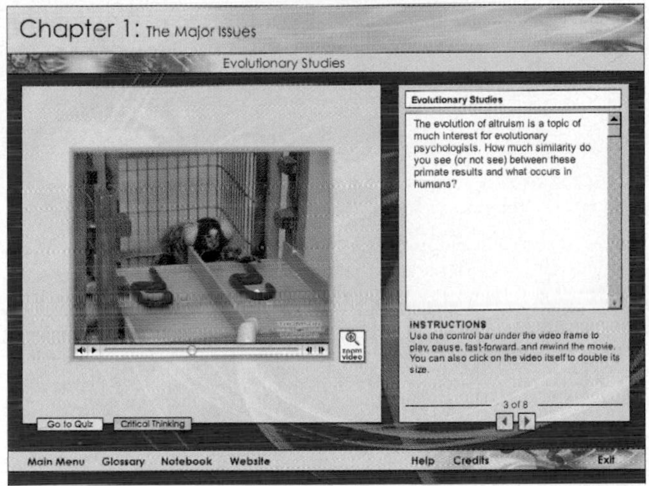

The CD includes animations and short videos, like this one.

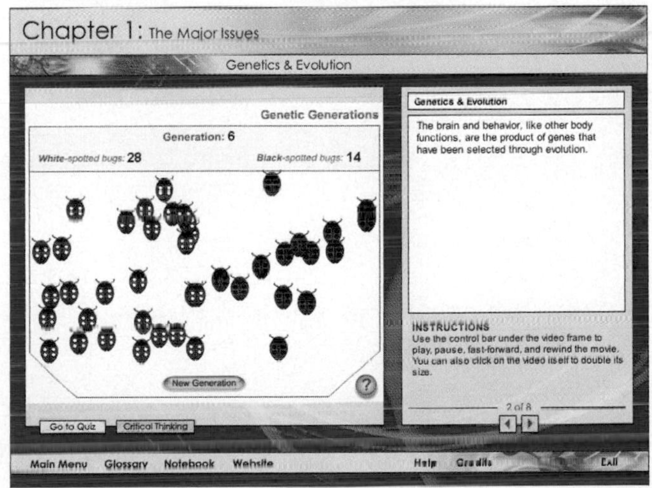

Here is one example of a Try It Yourself activity available both online and on the CD.

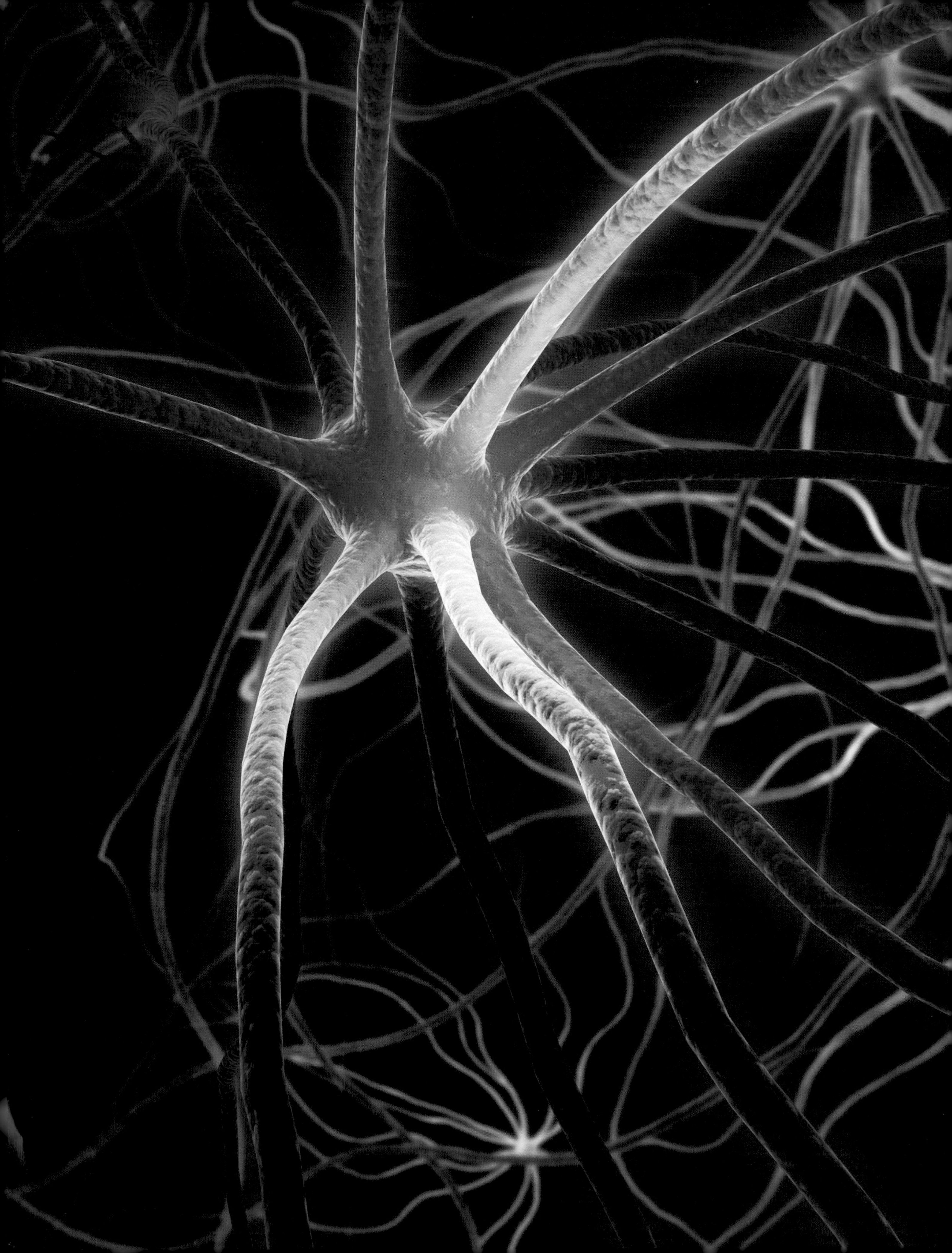

Nerve Cells and Nerve Impulses

2

Chapter Outline

Opposite: A neuron has a long, straight axon that branches at its end and many widely branching dendrites.
Source: 3D4Medical.com/Getty Images

Main Ideas

1. The nervous system is composed of two kinds of cells: neurons and glia. Only the neurons transmit impulses from one location to another.
2. The larger neurons have branches, known as axons and dendrites, which can change their branching pattern as a function of experience, age, and chemical influences.
3. Many molecules in the bloodstream that can enter other body organs cannot enter the brain.
4. The action potential, an all-or-none change in the electrical potential across the membrane of a neuron, is caused by the sudden flow of sodium ions into the neuron and is followed by a flow of potassium ions out of the neuron.
5. Local neurons are small and do not have axons or action potentials. Instead, they convey information to nearby neurons by graded potentials.

A nervous system, composed of many individual cells, is in some regards like a society of people who work together and communicate with one another or even like elements that form a chemical compound. In each case, the combination has properties that are unlike those of its individual components. We begin our study of the nervous system by examining single cells; later, we examine how cells act together.

Advice: Parts of this chapter and the next assume that you understand basic chemical concepts such as *positively charged ions*. If you need to refresh your memory, read Appendix A.

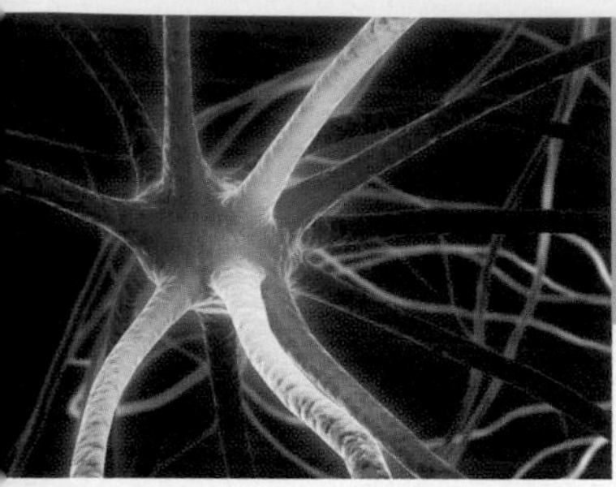

Module 2.1 The Cells of the Nervous System

Before you could build a house, you would first assemble bricks or other construction materials. Similarly, before we can address the great philosophical questions such as the mind–brain relationship or the great practical questions of abnormal behavior, we have to start with the building blocks of the nervous system—the cells.

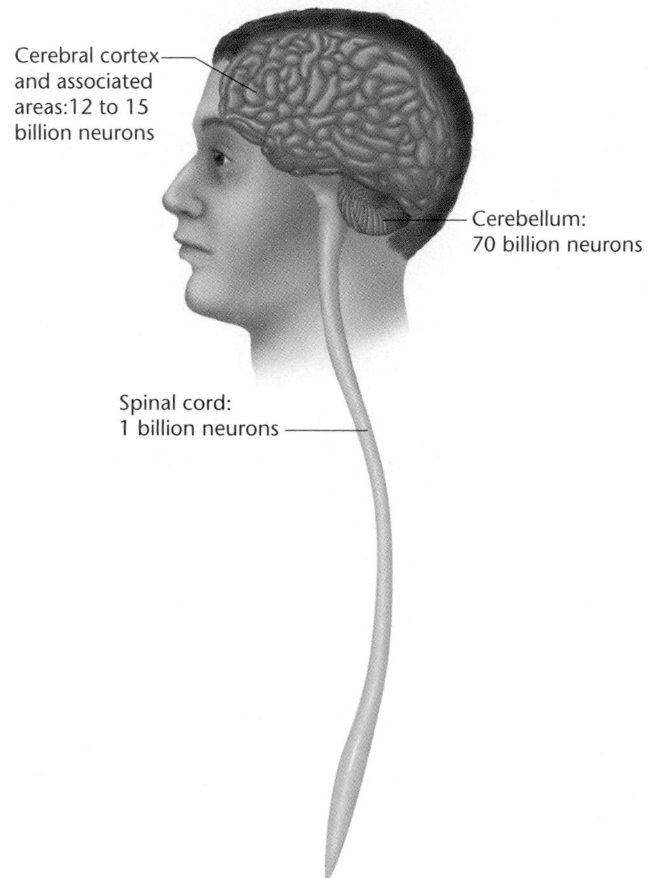

Figure 2.1 Estimated numbers of neurons in humans
Because of the small size of many neurons and the variation in cell density from one spot to another, obtaining an accurate count is difficult. *(Source: R. W. Williams & Herrup, 1988)*

Anatomy of Neurons and Glia

The nervous system consists of two kinds of cells: neurons and glia. **Neurons** receive information and transmit it to other cells. Glia provide a number of functions that are difficult to summarize, and we shall defer that discussion until later in the chapter. According to one estimate, the adult human brain contains approximately 100 billion neurons (R. W. Williams & Herrup, 1988) (Figure 2.1). An accurate count would be more difficult than it is worth, and the actual number varies from person to person.

The idea that the brain is composed of individual cells is now so well established that we take it for granted. However, the idea was in doubt as recently as the early 1900s. Until then, the best microscopic views revealed little detail about the organization of the brain. Observers noted long, thin fibers between one neuron's cell body and another, but they could not see whether each fiber merged into the next cell or stopped before it (Albright, Jessell, Kandel, & Posner, 2001). Then, in the late 1800s, Santiago Ramón y Cajal used newly developed staining techniques to show that a small gap separates the tips of one neuron's fibers from the surface of the next neuron. The brain, like the rest of the body, consists of individual cells.

EXTENSIONS AND APPLICATIONS
Santiago Ramón y Cajal, a Pioneer of Neuroscience

Two scientists are widely recognized as the main founders of neuroscience. One was Charles Sherrington, whom we shall discuss in Chapter 3; the other was the Spanish investigator Santiago Ramón y Cajal (1852–1934). (See photo and quote on the pages inside the back cover.) Cajal's early career did not progress altogether smoothly. At one point, he was imprisoned in a solitary cell, limited to one meal a day, and taken out daily for public floggings—at the age of 10—for the crime of not paying attention during his Latin class (Cajal, 1937). (And *you* thought *your* teachers were strict!)

Cajal wanted to become an artist, but his father insisted that he study medicine as a safer way to make a living. He managed to combine the two fields, becoming an outstanding anatomical researcher and illustrator. His detailed drawings of the nervous system are still considered definitive today.

Before the late 1800s, microscopy could reveal few details about the nervous system. Then the Italian investigator Camillo Golgi discovered a method of using silver salts to stain nerve cells. This method, which completely stained some cells without affecting others at all, enabled researchers to examine the structure of a single cell. Cajal used Golgi's methods but applied them to infant brains, in which the cells are smaller and therefore easier to examine on a single slide. Cajal's research demonstrated that nerve cells remain separate instead of merging into one another.

Philosophically, we can see the appeal of the idea that neurons merge. We each experience our consciousness as undivided, not as the sum of separate parts, so it seems that all the cells in the brain should be joined together physically as one unit. How the individual cells combine their influences is a complicated and still somewhat mysterious process.

The Structures of an Animal Cell

Figure 2.2 illustrates a neuron from the cerebellum of a mouse (magnified enormously, of course). A neuron has much in common with any other cell in the body, although its shape is certainly distinctive. Let us begin with the properties that all animal cells have in common.

The edge of a cell is a **membrane** (often called a *plasma membrane*), a structure that separates the inside of the cell from the outside environment. It is composed of two layers of fat molecules that are free to flow around one another, as illustrated in Figure 2.3. Most chemicals cannot cross the membrane. A few charged ions, such as sodium, potassium, calcium, and chloride, cross through specialized openings in the membrane called *protein channels*. Small uncharged chemicals, such as water, oxygen, carbon dioxide, and urea can diffuse across the membrane.

Except for mammalian red blood cells, all animal cells have a **nucleus**, the structure that contains the chromosomes. A **mitochondrion** (pl.: mitochondria) is the structure that performs metabolic activities, providing the energy that the cell requires for all its other activities. Mitochondria require fuel and oxygen to

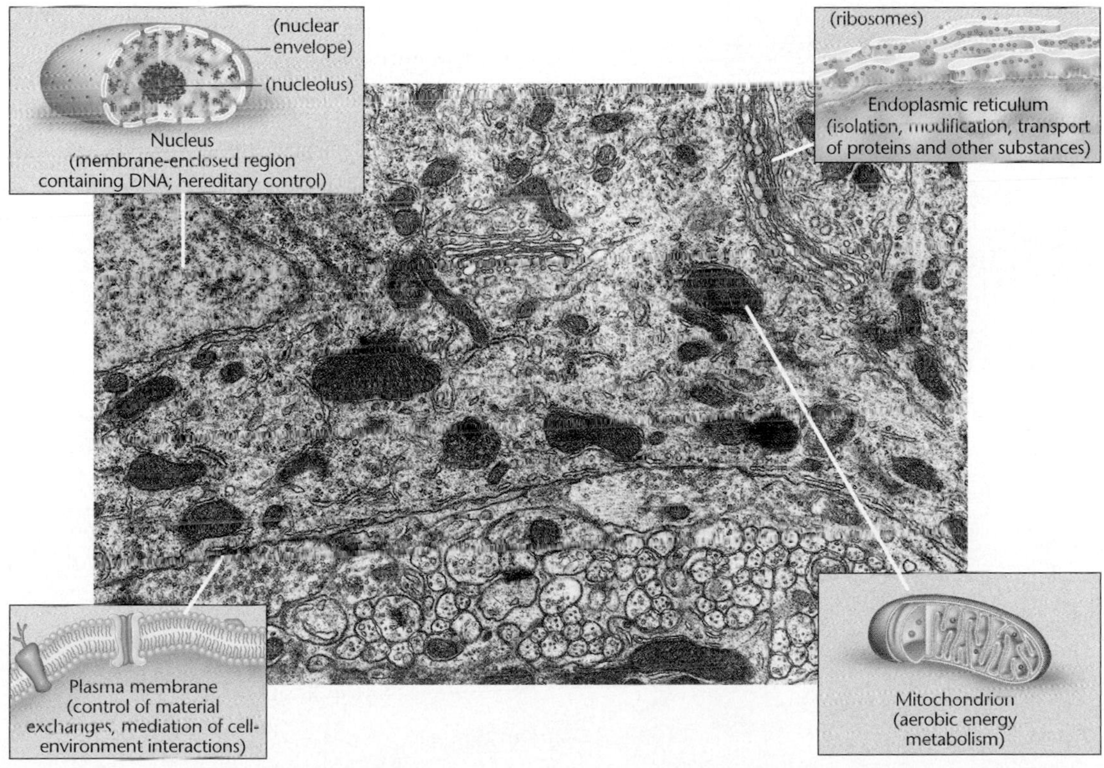

Figure 2.2 An electron micrograph of parts of a neuron from the cerebellum of a mouse
The nucleus, membrane, and other structures are characteristic of most animal cells. The plasma membrane is the border of the neuron. Magnification approximately x 20,000. *(Source: Micrograph courtesy of Dennis M. D. Landis)*

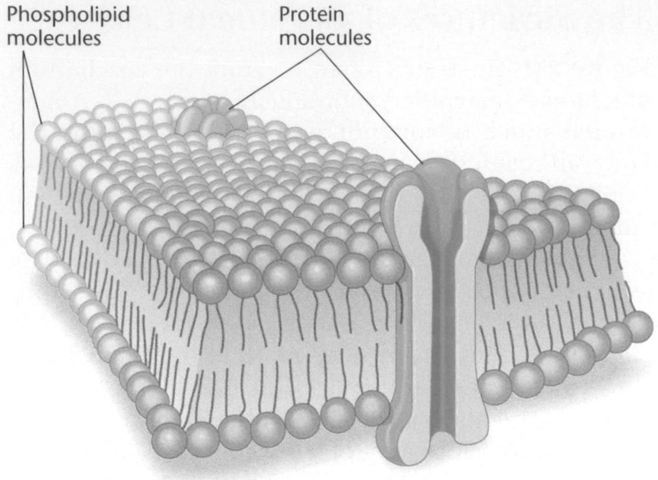

Figure 2.3 The membrane of a neuron
Embedded in the membrane are protein channels that permit certain ions to cross through the membrane at a controlled rate.

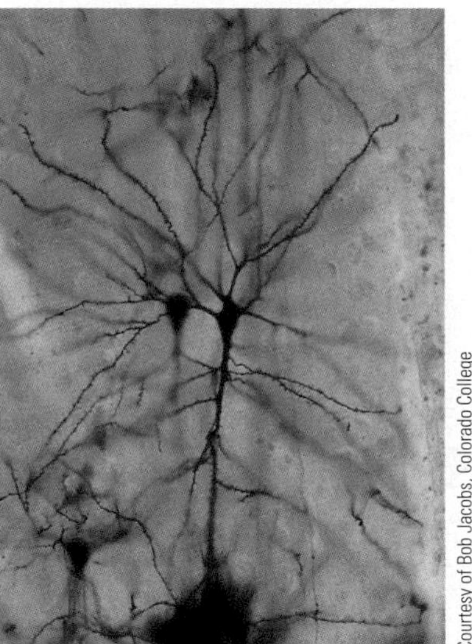

Figure 2.4 Neurons, stained to appear dark
Note the small fuzzy-looking spines on the dendrites.

function. **Ribosomes** are the sites at which the cell synthesizes new protein molecules. Proteins provide building materials for the cell and facilitate various chemical reactions. Some ribosomes float freely within the cell; others are attached to the **endoplasmic reticulum,** a network of thin tubes that transport newly synthesized proteins to other locations.

The Structure of a Neuron

A neuron (Figure 2.4) contains a nucleus, a membrane, mitochondria, ribosomes, and the other structures typical of animal cells. The distinctive feature of neurons is their shape.

The larger neurons have these major components: dendrites, a soma (cell body), an axon, and presynaptic terminals. (The tiniest neurons lack axons and some lack well-defined dendrites.) Contrast the motor neuron in Figure 2.5 and the sensory neuron in Figure 2.6. A **motor neuron** has its soma in the spinal cord. It receives excitation from other neurons through its dendrites and conducts impulses along its axon to a muscle. A **sensory neuron** is specialized at one end to be highly sensitive to a particular type of stimulation, such as touch information from the skin. Different kinds of sensory neurons have different structures; the one shown in Figure 2.6 is a neuron conducting touch information from the skin to the spinal cord. Tiny branches lead directly from the receptors into the axon, and the cell's soma is located on a little stalk off the main trunk.

Dendrites are branching fibers that get narrower near their ends. (The term *dendrite* comes from a Greek root word meaning "tree"; a dendrite is shaped like a tree.) The dendrite's surface is lined with specialized *synaptic receptors,* at which the dendrite receives information from other neurons. (Chapter 3 focuses on the synapses.) The greater the surface area of a dendrite, the more information it can receive. Some dendrites branch widely and therefore have a large surface area. Some also contain **dendritic spines,** the short outgrowths that increase the surface area available for

Figure 2.5 The components of a vertebrate motor neuron
The cell body of a motor neuron is located in the spinal cord. The various parts are not drawn to scale; in particular, a real axon is much longer in proportion to the soma.

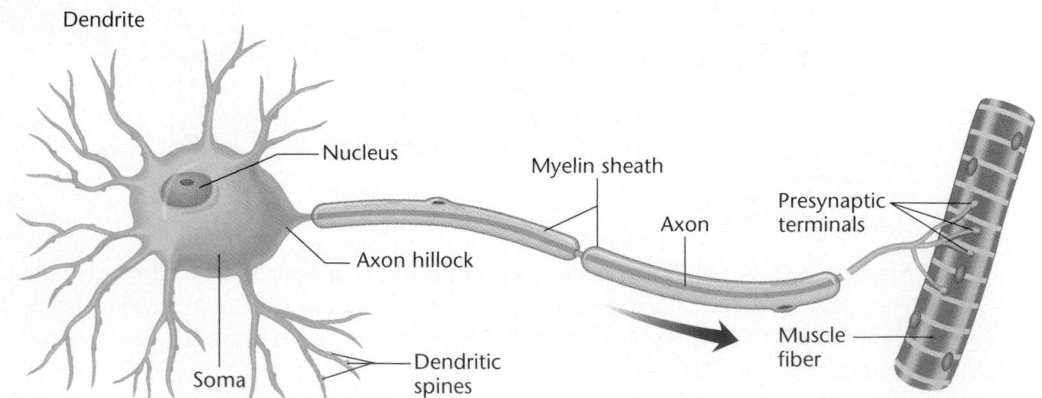

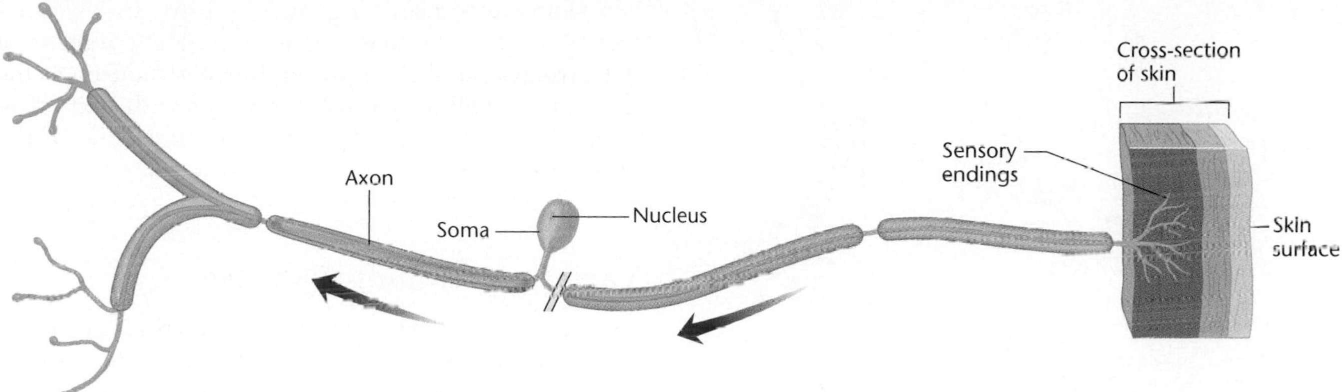

Figure 2.6 A vertebrate sensory neuron
Note that the soma is located on a stalk off the main trunk of the axon. (As in Figure 2.5, the various structures are not drawn to scale.)

synapses (Figure 2.7). The shape of dendrites varies enormously from one neuron to another and can even vary from one time to another for a given neuron. The shape of the dendrite has much to do with how the dendrite combines different kinds of input (Häusser, Spruston, & Stuart, 2000).

The **cell body,** or **soma** (Greek for "body"; pl.: somata), contains the nucleus, ribosomes, mitochondria, and other structures found in most cells. Much of the metabolic work of the neuron occurs here. Cell bodies of neurons range in diameter from 0.005 mm to 0.1 mm in mammals and up to a full millimeter in certain invertebrates. Like the dendrites, the cell body is covered with synapses on its surface in many neurons.

The **axon** is a thin fiber of constant diameter, in most cases longer than the dendrites. (The term *axon* comes from a Greek word meaning "axis.") The axon is the information sender of the neuron, conveying an impulse toward either other neurons or a gland or muscle. Many vertebrate axons are covered with an insulating material called a **myelin sheath** with interruptions known as **nodes of Ranvier.** Invertebrate axons do not have myelin sheaths. An axon has many branches, each of which swells at its tip, forming a **presynaptic terminal,** also known as an *end bulb* or *bouton* (French for "button").[1] This is the point from which the axon releases chemicals that cross through the junction between one neuron and the next.

A neuron can have any number of dendrites, but no more than one axon, which may have branches. Axons can range to a meter or more in length, as in the case of axons from your spinal cord to your feet. In most cases, branches of the axon depart from its trunk far from the cell body, near the terminals.

[1]Unfortunately, many structures in the nervous system have several names. As Candace Pert (1997, p. 64) has put it, "Scientists would rather use each other's toothbrushes than each other's terminology."

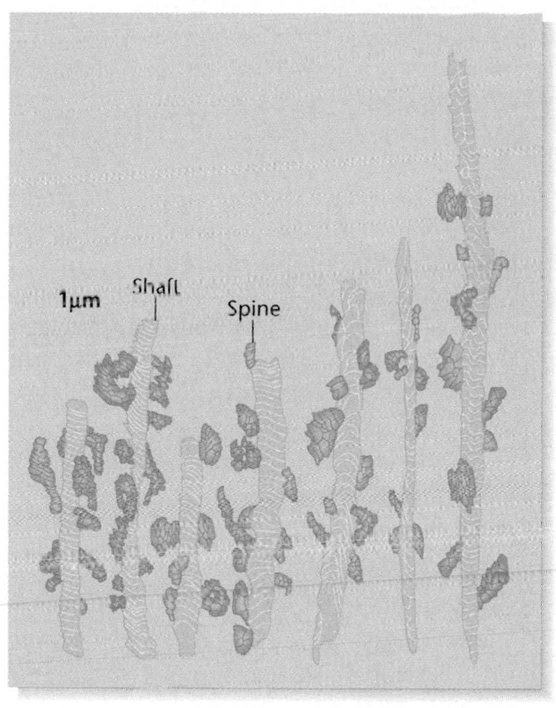

Figure 2.7 Dendritic spines
The dendrites of certain neurons are lined with spines, short outgrowths that receive specialized incoming information. That information apparently plays a key role in long-term changes in the neuron that mediate learning and memory. *(Source: From K. M. Harris and J. K. Stevens, Society for Neuroscience, "Dendritic spines of CA1 pyramidal cells in the rat hippocampus: Serial electron microscopy with reference to their biophysical characteristics."* Journal of Neuroscience, 9, 1989, *2982–2997. Copyright © 1989 Society for Neuroscience. Reprinted by permission.)*

Other terms associated with neurons are *afferent, efferent,* and *intrinsic.* An **afferent axon** brings information into a structure; an **efferent axon** carries information away from a structure. Every sensory neuron is an afferent to the rest of the nervous system; every motor neuron is an efferent from the nervous sys-

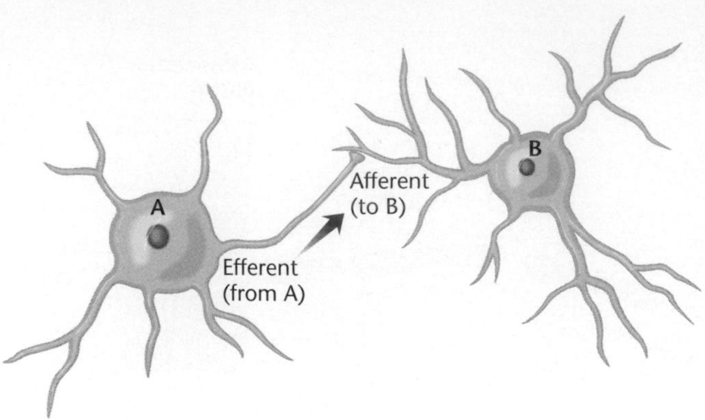

Figure 2.8 Cell structures and axons
It all depends on the point of view. An axon from A to B is an efferent axon from A and an afferent axon to B, just as a train from Washington to New York is exiting Washington and approaching New York.

tem. Within the nervous system, a given neuron is an efferent from the standpoint of one structure and an afferent from the standpoint of another. (You can remember that *efferent* starts with *e* as in *exit; afferent* starts with *a* as in *admission*.) For example, an axon that is efferent from the thalamus may be afferent to the cerebral cortex (Figure 2.8). If a cell's dendrites and axon are entirely contained within a single structure, the cell is an **interneuron** or **intrinsic neuron** of that structure. For example, an intrinsic neuron of the thalamus has all its dendrites or axons within the thalamus; it communicates only with other cells of the thalamus.

Variations Among Neurons

Neurons vary enormously in size, shape, and function. The shape of a given neuron determines its connections with other neurons and thereby determines its contribution to the nervous system. The wider the branching, the more connections with other neurons.

The function of a neuron is closely related to its shape (Figure 2.9). For example, the dendrites of the Purkinje cell of the cerebellum (Figure 2.9a) branch extremely widely within a single plane; this cell is capable of integrating an enormous amount of incoming information. The neurons in Figures 2.9c and 2.9e also have widely branching dendrites that receive and integrate information from many sources. By contrast, certain cells in the retina (Figure 2.9d) have only short branches on their dendrites and therefore pool input from only a few sources.

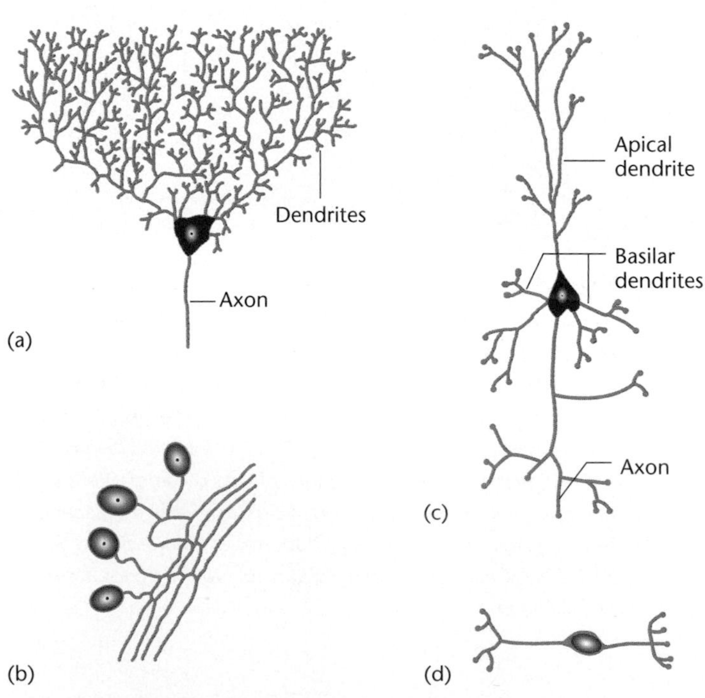

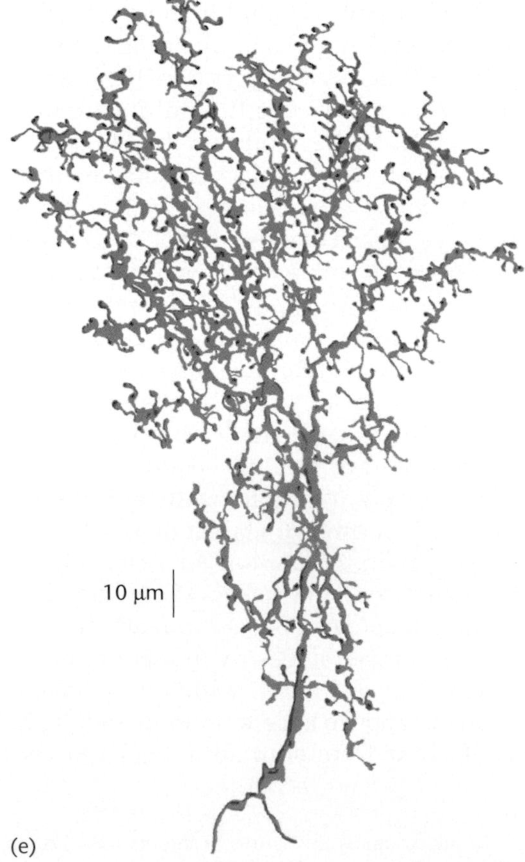

Figure 2.9 The diverse shapes of neurons
(a) Purkinje cell, a cell type found only in the cerebellum; **(b)** sensory neurons from skin to spinal cord; **(c)** pyramidal cell of the motor area of the cerebral cortex; **(d)** bipolar cell of retina of the eye; **(e)** Kenyon cell, from a honeybee. *(Source: Part e, from R. G. Coss,* Brain Research, *October 1982. Reprinted by permission of R. G. Coss.)*

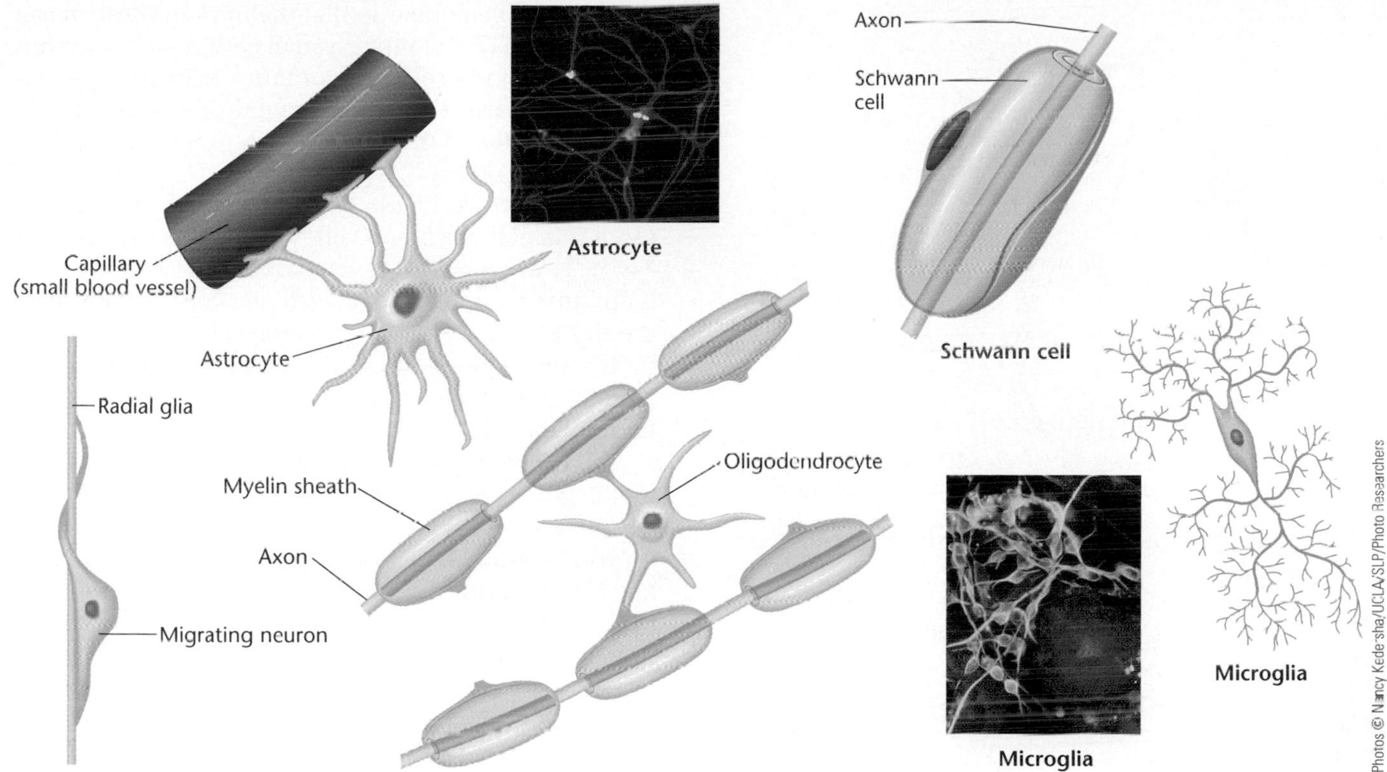

Figure 2.10 Shapes of some glia cells
Oligodendrocytes produce myelin sheaths that insulate certain vertebrate axons in the central nervous system; Schwann cells have a similar function in the periphery. The oligodendrocyte is shown here forming a segment of myelin sheath for two axons; in fact, each oligodendrocyte forms such segments for 30 to 50 axons. Astrocytes pass chemicals back and forth between neurons and blood and among neighboring neurons. Microglia proliferate in areas of brain damage and remove toxic materials. Radial glia (not shown here) guide the migration of neurons during embryological development. Glia have other functions as well.

Glia

Glia (or neuroglia), the other major cellular components of the nervous system, do not transmit information over long distances as neurons do, although they do exchange chemicals with adjacent neurons. In some cases, that exchange produces oscillations in the activity of those neurons (Nadkarni & Jung, 2003). The term *glia,* derived from a Greek word meaning "glue," reflects early investigators' idea that glia were like glue that held the neurons together (Somjen, 1988). Although that concept is obsolete, the term remains. Glia are smaller but also more numerous than neurons, so overall, they occupy about the same volume (Figure 2.10).

Glia have many functions (Haydon, 2001). One type of glia, the star-shaped **astrocytes**, wrap around the presynaptic terminals of a group of functionally related axons, as shown in Figure 2.11. By taking up chemicals released by those axons and later releasing them back to the axons, an astrocyte helps synchronize the activity of the axons, enabling them to send messages in waves (Angulo, Kozlov, Charpak, & Audinat, 2004; Antanitus, 1998). Astrocytes also remove waste material created when neurons die and help control the amount of blood flow to a given brain area (Mulligan & MacVicar, 2004).

Microglia, very small cells, also remove waste material as well as viruses, fungi, and other microorganisms. In effect, they function like part of the immune system (Davalos et al., 2005). **Oligodendrocytes** (OL-i-go-DEN-druh-sites) in the brain and spinal cord and **Schwann cells** in the periphery of the body are specialized types of glia that build the myelin sheaths that surround and insulate certain vertebrate axons. **Radial glia,** a type of astrocyte, guide the migration of neurons and the growth of their axons and dendrites during embryonic development. Schwann cells perform a related function after damage to axons in the periphery, guiding a regenerating axon to the appropriate target.

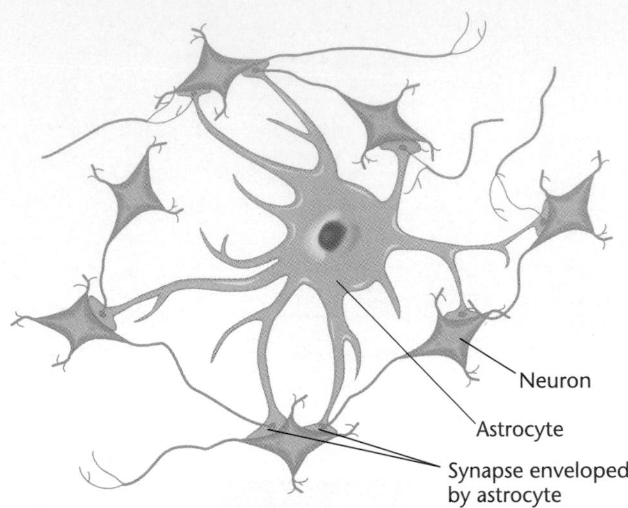

Figure 2.11 How an astrocyte synchronizes associated axons

Branches of the astrocyte (in the center) surround the presynaptic terminals of related axons. If a few of them are active at once, the astrocyte absorbs some of the chemicals they release. It then temporarily inhibits all the axons to which it is connected. When the inhibition ceases, all of the axons are primed to respond again in synchrony. *(Source: Based on Antanitus, 1998)*

STOP & CHECK

1. Identify the four major structures that compose a neuron.
2. Which kind of glia cell wraps around the synaptic terminals of axons?

Check your answers on page 38.

The Blood-Brain Barrier

Although the brain, like any other organ, needs to receive nutrients from the blood, many chemicals—ranging from toxins to medications—cannot cross from the blood to the brain (Hagenbuch, Gao, & Meier, 2002). The mechanism that keeps most chemicals out of the vertebrate brain is known as the **blood-brain barrier.** Before we examine how it works, let's consider why we need it.

Why We Need a Blood-Brain Barrier

From time to time, viruses and other harmful substances enter the body. When a virus enters a cell, mechanisms within the cell extrude a virus particle through the membrane so that the immune system can find it. When the immune system cells attack the virus, they also kill the cell that contains it. In effect, a cell exposing a virus through its membrane says, "Look, immune system, I'm infected with this virus. Kill me and save the others."

This plan works fine if the virus-infected cell is, say, a skin cell or a blood cell, which the body replaces easily. However, with few exceptions, the vertebrate brain does not replace damaged neurons. To minimize the risk of irreparable brain damage, the body literally builds a wall along the sides of the brain's blood vessels. This wall keeps out most viruses, bacteria, and harmful chemicals.

"What happens if a virus does enter the brain?" you might ask. After all, certain viruses do break through the blood-brain barrier. The brain has ways to attack viruses or slow their reproduction (Binder & Griffin, 2001) but doesn't kill them or the cells they inhabit. Consequently, a virus that enters your nervous system probably remains with you for life. For example, herpes viruses (responsible for chicken pox, shingles, and genital herpes) enter spinal cord cells. No matter how much the immune system attacks the herpes virus outside the nervous system, virus particles remain in the spinal cord and can emerge decades later to reinfect you.

A structure called the *area postrema,* which is not protected by the blood-brain barrier, monitors blood chemicals that could not enter other brain areas. This structure is responsible for triggering nausea and vomiting—important responses to toxic chemicals. It is, of course, exposed to the risk of being damaged itself.

How the Blood-Brain Barrier Works

The blood-brain barrier (Figure 2.12) depends on the arrangement of endothelial cells that form the walls of the capillaries (Bundgaard, 1986; Rapoport & Robinson, 1986). Outside the brain, such cells are separated by small gaps, but in the brain, they are joined so tightly that virtually nothing passes between them. Chemicals therefore enter the brain only by crossing the membrane itself.

Two categories of molecules cross the blood-brain barrier passively (without the expenditure of energy). First, *small uncharged molecules,* such as oxygen and carbon dioxide, cross freely. Water, a very important small molecule, crosses through special protein channels that regulate its flow (Amiry-Moghaddam & Ottersen, 2003). Second, *molecules that dissolve in the fats of the membrane* also cross passively. Examples include vitamins A and D, as well as various drugs that affect the brain, ranging from heroin and marijuana to antidepressant drugs. However, the blood-brain barrier excludes most viruses, bacteria, and toxins.

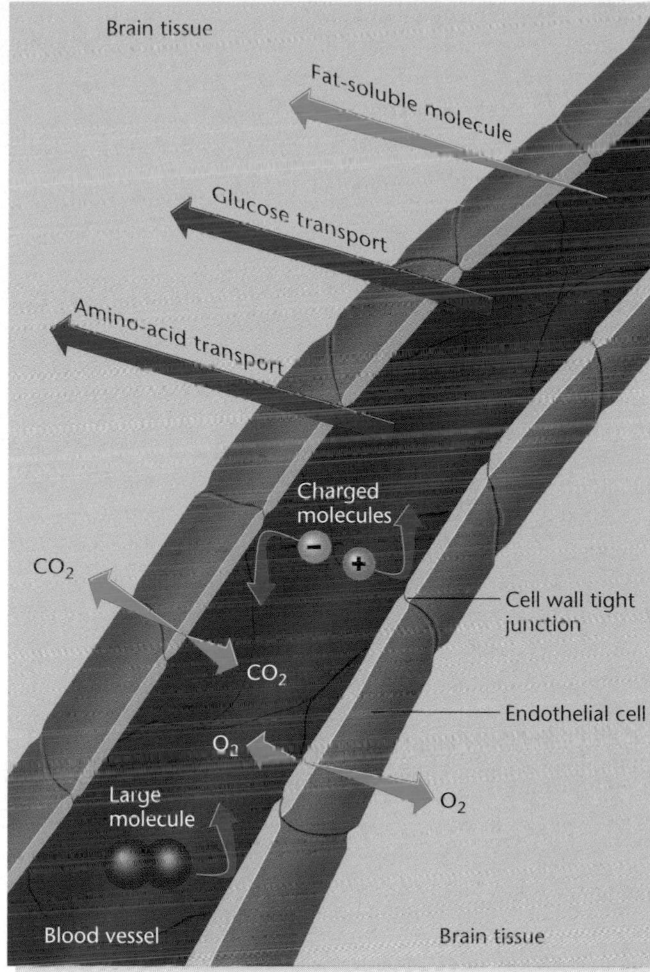

Figure 2.12 The blood-brain barrier
Most large molecules and electrically charged molecules cannot cross from the blood to the brain. A few small, uncharged molecules such as O_2 and CO_2 cross easily; so can certain fat-soluble molecules. Active transport systems pump glucose and amino acids across the membrane.

"If the blood-brain barrier is such a good defense," you might ask, "why don't we have similar walls around our other organs?" The answer is that the barrier that keeps out harmful chemicals also keeps out many useful ones, including sources of nutrition. For organs that can afford to risk a viral infection, a tight barrier would be more costly than it is worth. Getting nutrition into the brain requires an **active transport**, a protein-mediated process that expends energy to pump chemicals from the blood into the brain. Chemicals that are actively transported into the brain include glucose (the brain's main fuel), amino acids (the building blocks of proteins), and certain vitamins and hormones (Brightman, 1997). The brain also has an active transport system for moving certain chemicals from the brain to the blood (King, Su, Chang, Zuckerman, & Pasternak, 2001).

STOP & CHECK

3. What is one major advantage of having a blood-brain barrier?
4. What is a disadvantage of the blood-brain barrier?
5. Which chemicals cross the blood-brain barrier on their own?
6. Which chemicals cross the blood-brain barrier by active transport?

Check your answers on page 38.

The Nourishment of Vertebrate Neurons

Most cells use a variety of carbohydrates and fats for nutrition, but vertebrate neurons depend almost entirely on **glucose,** a simple sugar. (Cancer cells and the testis cells that make sperm also rely overwhelmingly on glucose.) The metabolic pathway that uses glucose requires oxygen; consequently, the neurons consume an enormous amount of oxygen compared with cells of other organs (Wong-Riley, 1989).

Why do neurons depend so heavily on glucose? Although neurons have the enzymes necessary to metabolize fats and several sugars, glucose is practically the only nutrient that crosses the blood-brain barrier in adults. The exceptions to this rule are *ketones* (a kind of fat), but ketones are seldom available in large amounts (Duelli & Kuschinsky, 2001), and large amounts of ketones cause medical complications.

Although neurons require glucose, a glucose shortage is rarely a problem. The liver can make glucose from many kinds of carbohydrates and amino acids, as well as from glycerol, a breakdown product from fats. An inability to *use* glucose can be a problem, however. Many chronic alcoholics have a diet deficient in vitamin B_1, **thiamine,** a chemical that is necessary for the use of glucose. Prolonged thiamine deficiency can lead to death of neurons and a condition called *Korsakoff's syndrome,* marked by severe memory impairments (Chapter 13).

Module 2.1
In Closing: Neurons

What does the study of individual neurons tell us about behavior? Perhaps the main lesson is that our experience and behavior *do not* follow from the properties of any one neuron. Just as a chemist must know about atoms to make sense of compounds, a biological psychologist or neuroscientist must know about cells to understand the nervous system. However, the nervous system is more than the sum of the individual cells, just as water is more than the sum of oxygen and hydrogen. Our behavior emerges from the communication among neurons.

Summary

1. In the late 1800s, Santiago Ramón y Cajal used newly discovered staining techniques to establish that the nervous system is composed of separate cells, now known as neurons. (p. 30)
2. Neurons receive information and convey it to other cells. The nervous system also contains *glia*. (pp. 30, 35)
3. Neurons have four major parts: a cell body, dendrites, an axon, and presynaptic terminals. Their shapes vary greatly depending on their functions and their connections with other cells. (p. 32)
4. Glia do not convey information over great distances, but they aid the functioning of neurons in many ways. (p. 35)
5. Because of the blood-brain barrier, many molecules, especially large ones, cannot enter the brain. (p. 36)
6. Adult neurons rely heavily on glucose, the only nutrient that can cross the blood-brain barrier. They need thiamine (vitamin B_1) to use glucose. (p. 37)

Answers to STOP & CHECK Questions

1. Dendrites, soma (cell body), axon, and presynaptic terminal (p. 36)
2. Astrocytes (p. 36)
3. The blood-brain barrier keeps out most viruses, bacteria, and other harmful substances. (p. 37)
4. The blood-brain barrier also keeps out most nutrients. (p. 37)
5. Small, uncharged molecules such as oxygen and carbon dioxide cross the blood-brain barrier passively. So do chemicals that dissolve in the fats of the membrane. (p. 37)
6. Glucose, amino acids, and some vitamins and hormones cross by active transport. (p. 37)

Module 2.2
The Nerve Impulse

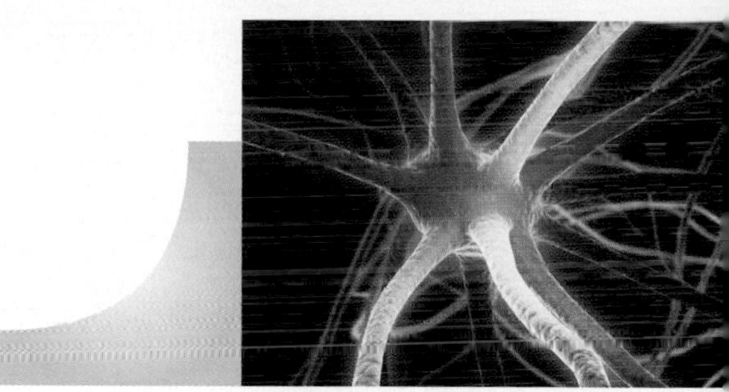

Think about the axons that convey information from your feet's touch receptors toward your spinal cord and brain. If the axons used electrical conduction, they could transfer information at a velocity approaching the speed of light. However, given that your body is made of carbon compounds and not copper wire, the strength of the impulse would decay greatly on the way to your spinal cord and brain. A touch on your shoulder would feel much stronger than a touch on your abdomen. Short people would feel their toes more strongly than tall people could.

The way your axons actually function avoids these problems. Instead of simply conducting an electrical impulse, the axon regenerates an impulse at each point. Imagine a long line of people holding hands. The first person squeezes the second person's hand, who then squeezes the third person's hand, and so forth. The impulse travels along the line without weakening because each person generates it anew.

Although the axon's method of transmitting an impulse prevents a touch on your shoulder from feeling stronger than one on your toes, it introduces a different problem: Because axons transmit information at only moderate speeds (varying from less than 1 meter/second to about 100 m/s), a touch on your shoulder will reach your brain *sooner* than will a touch on your toes. If you get someone to touch you simultaneously on your shoulder and your toe, you probably will not notice that your brain received one stimulus before the other. In fact, if someone touches you on one hand and then the other, you won't be sure which hand you felt first, unless the delay between touches exceeds 70 milliseconds (ms) (S. Yamamoto & Kitazawa, 2001). Your brain is not set up to register small differences in the time of arrival of touch messages. After all, why should it be? You almost never need to know whether a touch on one part of your body occurred slightly before or after a touch somewhere else.

try it yourself

In vision, however, your brain *does* need to know whether one stimulus began slightly before or after another one. If two adjacent spots on your retina—let's call them A and B—send impulses at almost the same time, an extremely small difference in timing indicates whether a flash of light moved from A to B or from B to A. To detect movement as accurately as possible, your visual system compensates for the fact that some parts of the retina are slightly closer to your brain than other parts are. Without some sort of compensation, simultaneous flashes arriving at two spots on your retina would reach your brain at different times, and you might perceive a flash of light moving from one spot to the other. What prevents that illusion is the fact that axons from more distant parts of your retina transmit impulses slightly faster than those closer to the brain (L. R. Stanford, 1987)!

In short, the properties of impulse conduction in an axon are well adapted to the exact needs for information transfer in the nervous system. Let's now examine the mechanics of impulse transmission.

The Resting Potential of the Neuron

The membrane of a neuron maintains an **electrical gradient,** a difference in electrical charge between the inside and outside of the cell. All parts of a neuron are covered by a membrane about 8 nanometers (nm) thick (just less than 0.00001 mm), composed of two layers (an inner layer and an outer layer) of phospholipid molecules (containing chains of fatty acids and a phosphate group). Embedded among the phospholipids are cylindrical protein molecules (see Figure 2.3, p. 32). The structure of the membrane provides it with a good combination of flexibility and firmness and retards the flow of chemicals between the inside and the outside of the cell.

In the absence of any outside disturbance, the membrane maintains an electrical **polarization,** meaning a difference in electrical charge between two locations. Specifically, the neuron inside the membrane has a slightly negative electrical potential with respect to the outside. This difference in voltage in a resting neuron is called the **resting potential.** The resting potential is mainly the result of negatively charged proteins inside the cell.

Researchers can measure the resting potential by inserting a very thin *microelectrode* into the cell body,

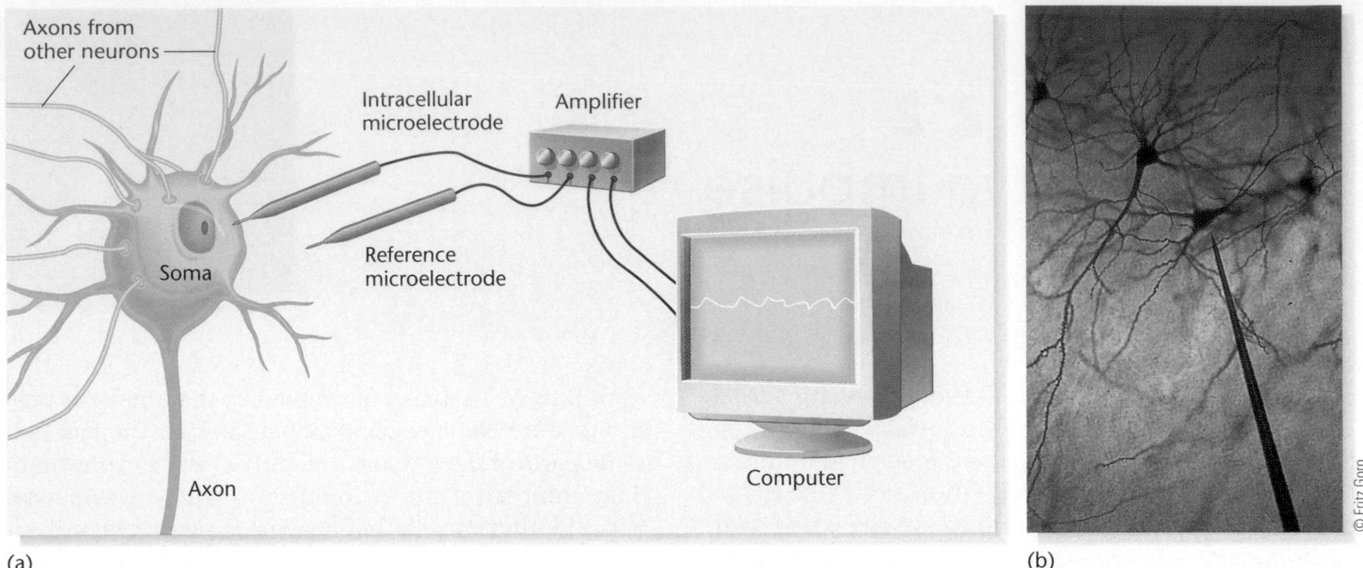

Figure 2.13 Methods for recording activity of a neuron
(a) Diagram of the apparatus and a sample recording. **(b)** A microelectrode and stained neurons magnified hundreds of times by a light microscope.

as Figure 2.13 shows. The diameter of the electrode must be as small as possible so that it can enter the cell without causing damage. By far the most common electrode is a fine glass tube filled with a concentrated salt solution and tapering to a tip diameter of 0.0005 mm or less. This electrode, inserted into the neuron, is connected to recording equipment. A reference electrode placed somewhere outside the cell completes the circuit. Connecting the electrodes to a voltmeter, we find that the neuron's interior has a negative potential relative to its exterior. The actual potential varies from one neuron to another; a typical level is –70 millivolts (mV), but it can be either higher or lower than that.

Forces Acting on Sodium and Potassium Ions

If charged ions could flow freely across the membrane, the membrane would depolarize at once. However, the membrane is **selectively permeable**—that is, some chemicals can pass through it more freely than others can. (This selectivity is *analogous* to the blood-brain barrier, but it is not the same thing.) Most large or electrically charged ions and molecules cannot cross the membrane at all. Oxygen, carbon dioxide, urea, and water cross freely through channels that are always open. A few biologically important ions, such as sodium, potassium, calcium, and chloride, cross through membrane channels (or gates) that are sometimes open and sometimes closed. When the membrane is at rest, the sodium channels are closed, preventing almost all sodium flow. These channels are shown in Figure 2.14. As we shall see in Chapter 3, certain kinds of stimulation can open the sodium channels. When the membrane is at rest, potassium channels are nearly but not entirely closed, so potassium flows slowly.

Sodium ions are more than ten times more concentrated outside the membrane than inside because

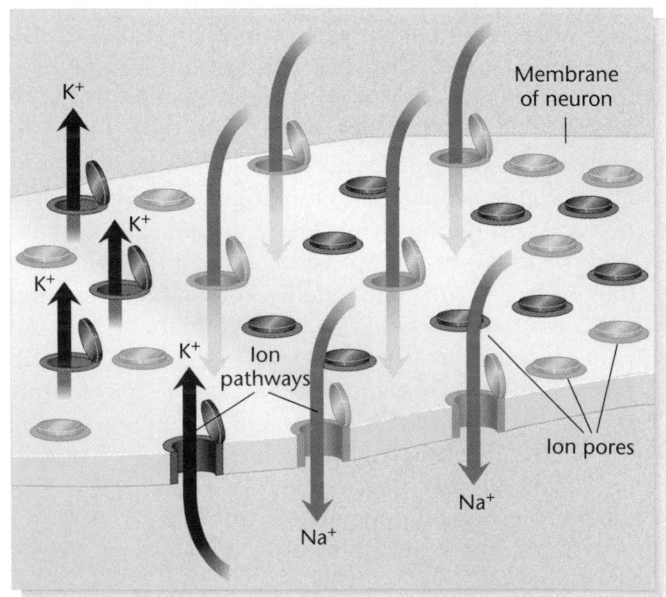

Figure 2.14 Ion channels in the membrane of a neuron
When a channel opens, it permits one kind of ion to cross the membrane. When it closes, it prevents passage of that ion.

of the **sodium-potassium pump**, a protein complex that repeatedly transports three sodium ions out of the cell while drawing two potassium ions into it. The sodium-potassium pump is an active transport requiring energy. Various poisons can stop it, as can an interruption of blood flow.

The sodium-potassium pump is effective only because of the selective permeability of the membrane, which prevents the sodium ions that were pumped out of the neuron from leaking right back in again. As it is, the sodium ions that are pumped out stay out. However, some of the potassium ions pumped into the neuron do leak out, carrying a positive charge with them. That leakage increases the electrical gradient across the membrane, as shown in Figure 2.15.

When the neuron is at rest, two forces act on sodium, both tending to push it into the cell. First, consider the electrical gradient. Sodium is positively charged and the inside of the cell is negatively charged. Opposite electrical charges attract, so the electrical gradient tends to pull sodium into the cell. Second, consider the **concentration gradient**, the difference in distribution of ions across the membrane. Sodium is more concentrated outside than inside, so just by the laws of probability, sodium is more likely to enter the cell than to leave it. (By analogy, imagine two rooms connected by a door. There are 100 cats are in room A and only 10 in room B. Cats are more likely to move from A to B than from B to A. The same principle applies to the movement of sodium.) Given that both the electrical gradient and the concentration gradient tend to move sodium ions into the cell, sodium certainly would move rapidly if it had the chance. However, the sodium channels are closed when the membrane is at rest, so almost no sodium flows except for the sodium pushed *out of* the cell by the sodium-potassium pump.

Potassium, however, is subject to competing forces. Potassium is positively charged and the inside of the cell is negatively charged, so the electrical gradient tends to pull potassium in. However, potassium is more concentrated inside the cell than outside, so the concentration gradient tends to drive it out. If the potassium gates were wide open, potassium would flow mostly out of the cell but not rapidly. That is, for potassium, the electrical gradient and concentration gradient are almost in balance. (The sodium-potassium pump keeps pulling potassium in, so the two gradients cannot get completely in balance.)

The cell has negative ions too, of course, especially chloride. However, chloride is not actively pumped in or out, and its channels are not voltage dependent, so chloride ions are not the key to the action potential.

Why a Resting Potential?

Presumably, evolution could have equipped us with neurons that were electrically neutral at rest. The resting potential must provide enough benefit to justify the energy cost of the sodium-potassium pump. The advantage is that the resting potential prepares the neuron to respond rapidly to a stimulus. As we shall see in the next section, excitation of the neuron opens channels that let sodium enter the cell explosively. Because the membrane did its work in advance by maintaining the concentration gradient for sodium, the cell is prepared to respond strongly and rapidly to a stimulus.

The resting potential of a neuron can be compared to a poised bow and arrow: An archer who pulls the

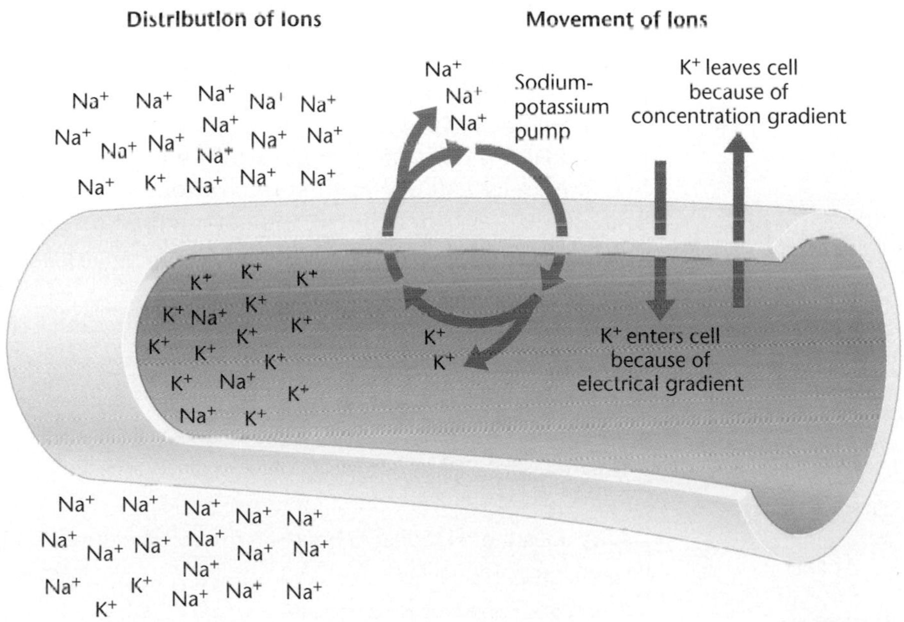

Figure 2.15 The sodium and potassium gradients for a resting membrane
Sodium ions are more concentrated outside the neuron; potassium ions are more concentrated inside. Protein and chloride ions (not shown) bear negative charges inside the cell. At rest, very few sodium ions cross the membrane except by the sodium-potassium pump. Potassium tends to flow into the cell because of an electrical gradient but tends to flow out because of the concentration gradient.

bow in advance and then waits is ready to fire as soon as the appropriate moment comes. Evolution has applied the same strategy to the neuron.

STOP & CHECK

1. When the membrane is at rest, are the sodium ions more concentrated inside the cell or outside? Where are the potassium ions more concentrated?
2. When the membrane is at rest, what tends to drive the potassium ions out of the cell? What tends to draw them into the cell?

Check your answers on page 48.

The Action Potential

The resting potential remains stable until the neuron is stimulated. Ordinarily, stimulation of the neuron takes place at synapses, which we consider in Chapter 3. In the laboratory, it is also possible to stimulate a neuron by inserting an electrode into it and applying current.

We can measure a neuron's potential with a microelectrode, as shown in Figure 2.13b. When an axon's membrane is at rest, the recordings show a steady negative potential inside the axon. If we now use an additional electrode to apply a negative charge, we can further increase the negative charge inside the neuron. The change is called **hyperpolarization,** which means increased polarization. As soon as the artificial stimulation ceases, the charge returns to its original resting level. The recording looks like this:

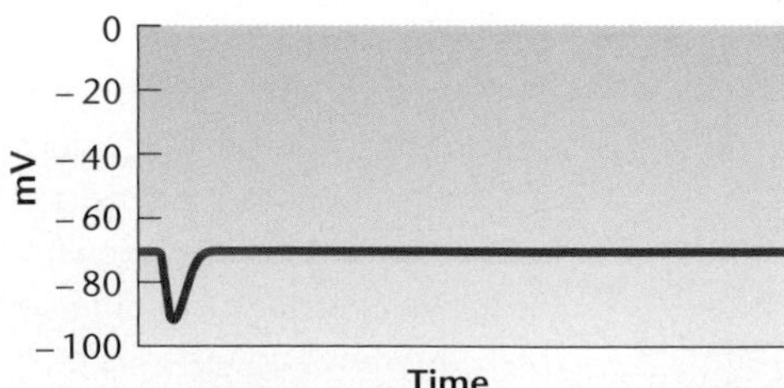

Now, let us apply a current for a slight **depolarization** of the neuron—that is, reduction of its polarization toward zero. If we apply a small depolarizing current, we get a result like this:

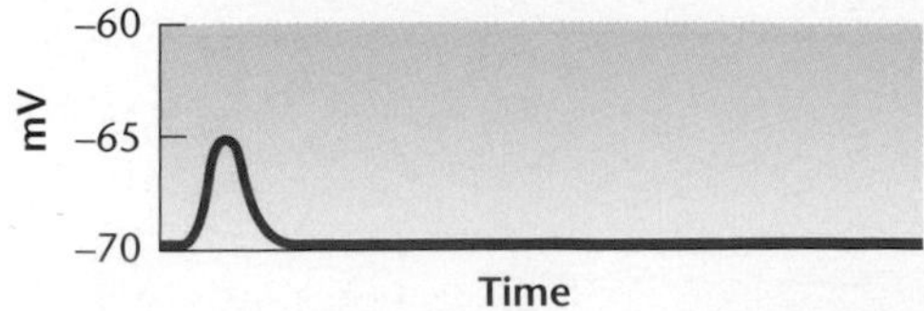

With a slightly stronger depolarizing current, the potential rises slightly higher, but again, it returns to the resting level as soon as the stimulation ceases:

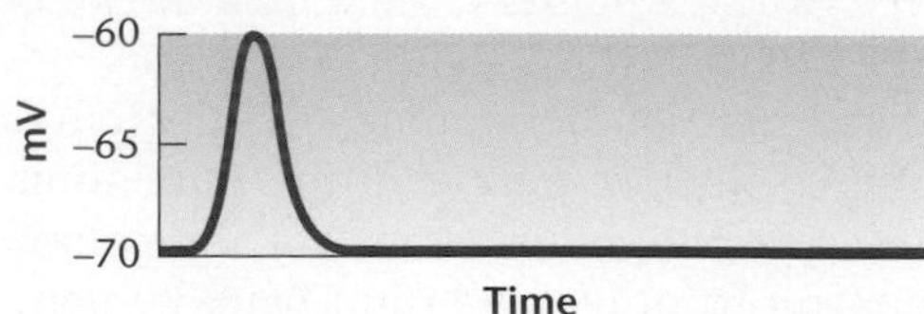

Now let us see what happens when we apply a still stronger current: Any stimulation beyond a certain level, called the **threshold of excitation,** produces a sudden, massive depolarization of the membrane. When the potential reaches the threshold, the membrane suddenly opens its sodium channels and permits a rapid, massive flow of ions across the membrane. The potential then shoots up far beyond the strength of the stimulus:

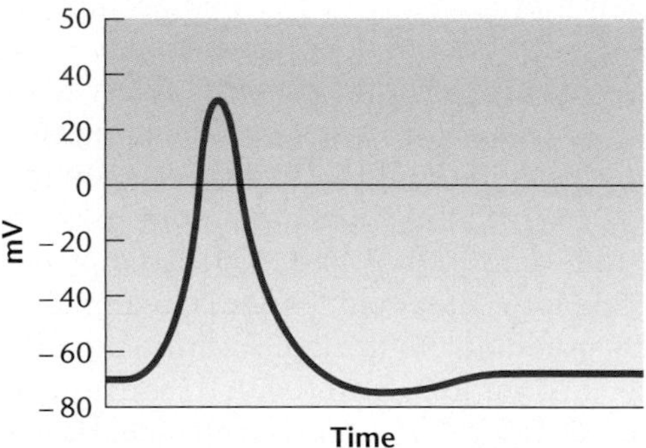

Any *subthreshold* stimulation produces a small response proportional to the amount of current. Any stimulation beyond the threshold, regardless of how far beyond, produces the same response, like the one just shown. That response, a rapid depolarization and slight reversal of the usual polarization, is referred to as an **action potential.** The peak of the action potential, shown as +30 mV in this illustration, varies from one axon to another, but it is nearly constant for a given axon.

STOP & CHECK

3. What is the difference between a hyperpolarization and a depolarization?
4. What is the relationship between the threshold and an action potential?

Check your answers on page 48.

The Molecular Basis of the Action Potential

Remember that both the electrical gradient and the concentration gradient tend to drive sodium ions into the neuron. If sodium ions could flow freely across the membrane, they would enter rapidly. Ordinarily, the membrane is almost impermeable to sodium, but during the action potential, its permeability increases sharply.

The membrane proteins that control sodium entry are **voltage-activated channels,** membrane channels whose permeability depends on the voltage difference across the membrane. At the resting potential, the channels are closed. As the membrane becomes slightly depolarized, the sodium channels begin to open and sodium flows more freely. If the depolarization is less than the threshold, sodium crosses the membrane only slightly more than usual. When the potential across the membrane reaches threshold, the sodium channels open wide. Sodium ions rush into the neuron explosively until the electrical potential across the membrane passes beyond zero to a reversed polarity, as shown in the following diagram:

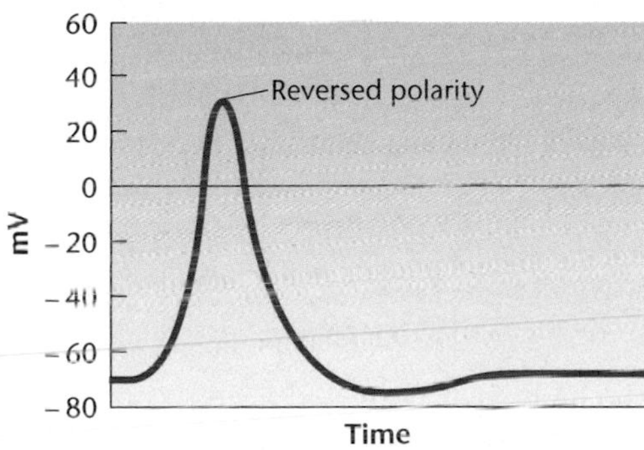

Compared to the total number of sodium ions in and around the axon, only a tiny percentage cross the membrane during an action potential. Even at the peak of the action potential, sodium ions continue to be far more concentrated outside the neuron than inside. An action potential increases the sodium concentration inside a neuron by far less than 1%. Because of the persisting concentration gradient, sodium ions should still tend to diffuse into the cell. However, at the peak of the action potential, the sodium gates quickly close and resist reopening for about the next millisecond.

After the peak of the action potential, what brings the membrane back to its original state of polarization? The answer is *not* the sodium-potassium pump, which is too slow for this purpose. After the action potential is underway, the potassium channels open. Potassium ions flow out of the axon simply because they are much more concentrated inside than outside and they are no longer held inside by a negative charge. As they flow out of the axon, they carry with them a positive charge. Because the potassium channels open wider than usual and remain open after the sodium channels close, enough potassium ions leave to drive the membrane beyond the normal resting level to a temporary hyperpolarization. Figure 2.16 summarizes the movements of ions during an action potential.

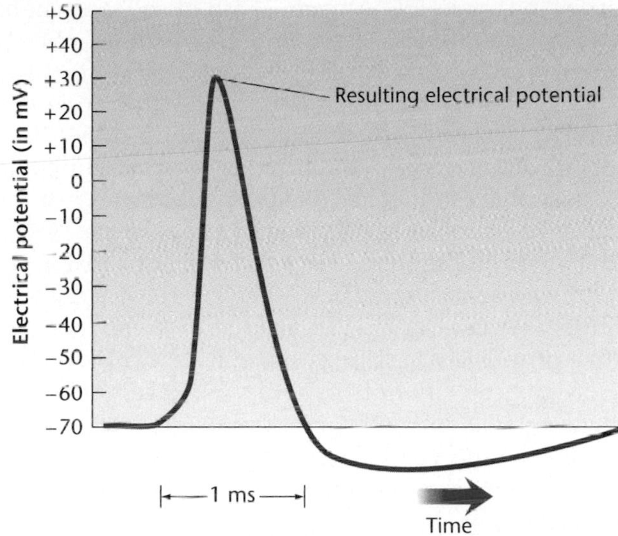

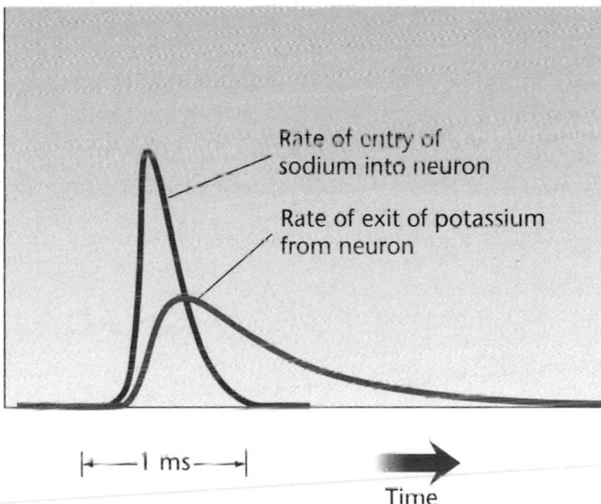

Figure 2.16 The movement of sodium and potassium ions during an action potential
Sodium ions cross during the peak of the action potential and potassium ions cross later in the opposite direction, returning the membrane to its original polarization.

At the end of this process, the membrane has returned to its resting potential and everything is back to normal, except that the inside of the neuron has slightly more sodium ions and slightly fewer potassium ions than before. Eventually, the sodium-potassium pump restores the original distribution of ions, but that process takes time. In fact, after an unusually rapid series of action potentials, the pump cannot keep up with the action, and sodium may begin to accumulate within the axon. Excessive buildup of sodium can be toxic to a cell. (Excessive stimulation occurs only under abnormal conditions, however, such as during a stroke or after the use of certain drugs. Don't worry that thinking too hard will explode your brain cells!)

For the neuron to function properly, sodium and potassium must flow across the membrane at just the right pace. Scorpion venom attacks the nervous system by keeping sodium channels open and closing potassium channels (Pappone & Cahalan, 1987; Strichartz, Rando, & Wang, 1987). As a result, the membrane goes into a prolonged depolarization and accumulates dangerously high amounts of sodium. **Local anesthetic** drugs, such as Novocain and Xylocaine, attach to the sodium channels of the membrane, preventing sodium ions from entering (Ragsdale, McPhee, Scheuer, & Catterall, 1994). In doing so, the drugs block action potentials. If anesthetics are applied to sensory nerves carrying pain messages, they prevent the messages from reaching the brain.

To explore the action potential further and try some virtual experiments on the membrane, explore this website: **http://www2.neuroscience.umn.edu/eanwebsite/metaneuron.htm**

STOP & CHECK

5. During the rise of the action potential, do sodium ions move into the cell or out of it? Why?
6. As the membrane reaches the peak of the action potential, what ionic movement brings the potential down to the original resting potential?

Check your answers on page 48.

The All-or-None Law

Action potentials occur only in axons and cell bodies. When the voltage across an axon membrane reaches a certain level of depolarization (the threshold), voltage-activated sodium channels open wide to let sodium enter rapidly, and the incoming sodium depolarizes the membrane still further. Dendrites can be depolarized, but they don't have voltage-activated sodium channels, so opening the channels a little, letting in a little sodium, doesn't cause them to open even more and let in still more sodium. Thus, dendrites don't produce action potentials.

For a given neuron, all action potentials are approximately equal in amplitude (intensity) and velocity under normal circumstances. This is the **all-or-none law:** The amplitude and velocity of an action potential are independent of the intensity of the stimulus that initiated it. By analogy, imagine flushing a toilet: You have to make a press of at least a certain strength (the threshold), but pressing even harder does not make the toilet flush any faster or more vigorously.

The all-or-none law puts some constraints on how an axon can send a message. To signal the difference between a weak stimulus and a strong stimulus, the axon can't send bigger or faster action potentials. All it can change is the timing. By analogy, suppose you agree to exchange coded messages with someone in another building who can see your window by occasionally flicking your lights on and off. The two of you might agree, for example, to indicate some kind of danger by the frequency of flashes. (The more flashes, the more danger.) You could also convey information by a rhythm.

Flash-flash . . .   long pause . . .   flash-flash

might mean something different from

Flash . . . pause . . . flash . . . pause . . . flash . . . pause . . . flash.

The nervous system uses both of these kinds of codes. Researchers have long known that a greater frequency of action potentials per second indicates "stronger" stimulus. In some cases, a different rhythm of response also carries information (Ikegaya et al., 2004; Oswald, Chacron, Doiron, Bastian, & Maler, 2004). For example, an axon might show one rhythm of responses for sweet tastes and a different rhythm for bitter tastes (Di Lorenzo, Hallock, & Kennedy, 2003).

The Refractory Period

While the electrical potential across the membrane is returning from its peak toward the resting point, it is still above the threshold. Why doesn't the cell produce another action potential during this period? Immediately after an action potential, the cell is in a **refractory period** during which it resists the production of further action potentials. In the first part of this period, the **absolute refractory period,** the membrane cannot produce an action potential, regardless of the stimulation. During the second part, the **relative refractory period,** a stronger than usual stimulus is necessary to initiate an action potential. The refractory period is based on two mechanisms: The sodium channels are closed, and potassium is flowing out of the cell at a faster than usual rate.

Most of the neurons that have been tested have an absolute refractory period of about 1 ms and a relative refractory period of another 2–4 ms. (To return to the toilet analogy, there is a short time right after you flush a toilet when you cannot make it flush again—an absolute refractory period. Then follows a period when it is possible but difficult to flush it again—a relative refractory period—before it returns to normal.)

STOP & CHECK

7. State the all-or-none law.
8. Does the all-or-none law apply to dendrites?
9. Suppose researchers find that axon A can produce up to 1,000 action potentials per second (at least briefly, with maximum stimulation), but axon B can never produce more than 200 per second (regardless of the strength of the stimulus). What could we conclude about the refractory periods of the two axons?
10. Distinguish between the absolute refractory period and the relative refractory period.

Check your answers on page 48.

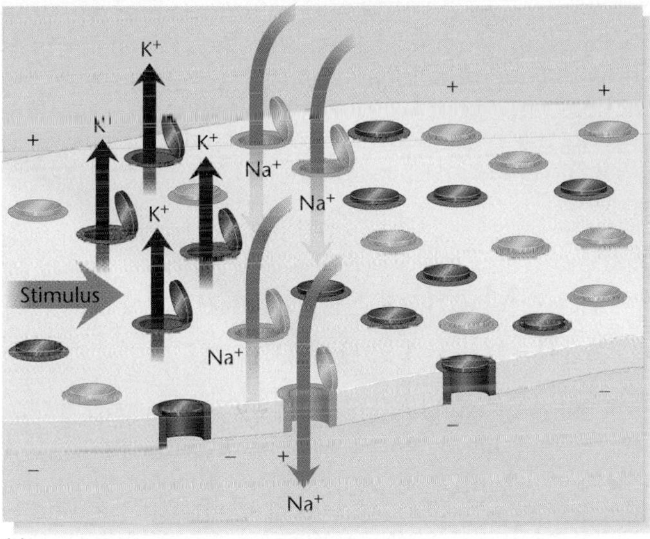

(a)

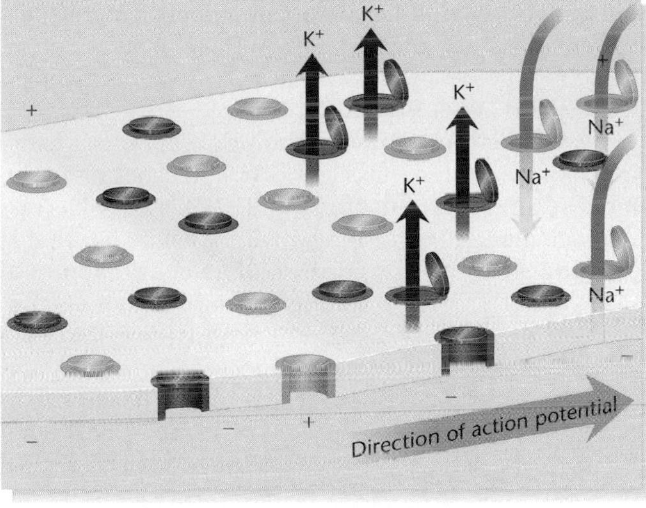

(b)

Figure 2.17
Current that enters an axon during the action potential flows down the axon, depolarizing adjacent areas of the membrane. The current flows more easily through thicker axons. Behind the area of sodium entry, potassium ions exit.

Propagation of the Action Potential

Up to this point, we have dealt with the action potential at one location on the axon. Now let us consider how it moves down the axon toward some other cell. Remember that it is important for axons to convey impulses without any loss of strength over distance.

In a motor neuron, an action potential begins on the **axon hillock**,[2] a swelling where the axon exits the soma (see Figure 2.5, p. 32). Each point along the membrane regenerates the action potential in much the same way that it was generated initially. During the action potential, sodium ions enter a point on the axon. Temporarily, that location is positively charged in comparison with neighboring areas along the axon. The positive ions flow down the axon and across the membrane, as shown in Figure 2.17. Other things being equal, the greater the diameter of the axon, the faster the ions flow (because of decreased resistance). The positive charges now inside the membrane slightly depolarize the adjacent areas of the membrane, causing the next area to reach its threshold and regenerate the action potential. In this manner, the action potential travels like a wave along the axon.

The term **propagation of the action potential** describes the transmission of an action potential down an axon. The propagation of an animal species is the production of offspring; in a sense, the action potential gives birth to a new action potential at each point along the axon. In this manner, the action potential can be just as strong at the end of the axon as it was at the beginning. The action potential is much slower than electrical conduction because it requires the diffusion of sodium ions at successive points along the axon. Electrical conduction in a copper wire with free electrons travels at a rate approaching the speed of light, 300 million meters per second (m/s). In an axon, transmission relies on the flow of charged ions through a water medium. In thin axons, action potentials travel at a velocity of less than 1 m/s. Thicker axons and those covered with an insulating shield of myelin conduct with greater velocities.

Let us reexamine Figure 2.17 for a moment. What is to prevent the electrical charge from flowing in the

[2]One exception is known to the rule that action potentials start at the axon hillock. One kind of neuron initiates its action potential at the first node of Ranvier (B. A. Clark, Monsivais, Branco, London, & Häuser, 2005). Almost any generalization about the nervous system has an exception, somewhere.

direction opposite that in which the action potential is traveling? Nothing. In fact, the electrical charge does flow in both directions. In that case, what prevents an action potential near the center of an axon from reinvading the areas that it has just passed? The answer is that the areas just passed are still in their refractory period.

The Myelin Sheath and Saltatory Conduction

The thinnest axons conduct impulses at less than 1 m/s. Increasing the diameters increases conduction velocity but only up to about 10 m/s. At that speed, an impulse from a giraffe's foot takes about half a second to reach its brain. At the slower speeds of thinner unmyelinated axons, a giraffe's brain could be seconds out of date on what was happening to its feet. In some vertebrate axons, sheaths of **myelin**, an insulating material composed of fats and proteins, increase speed up to about 100 m/s.

Consider the following analogy. Suppose it is my job to carry written messages over a distance of 3 kilometers (km) without using any mechanical device. Taking each message and running with it would be reliable but slow, like the propagation of an action potential along an unmyelinated axon. I could try tying each message to a ball and throwing it, but I cannot throw a ball even close to 3 km. The ideal compromise is to station people at moderate distances along the 3 km and throw the message-bearing ball from person to person until it reaches its destination.

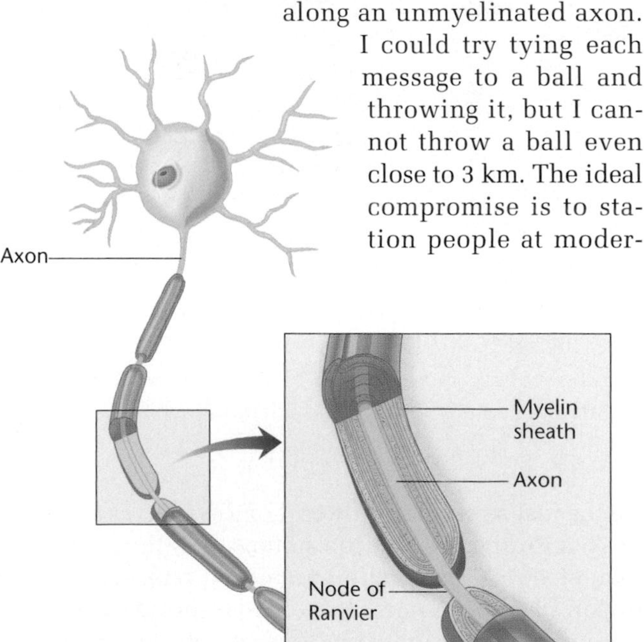

Figure 2.18 An axon surrounded by a myelin sheath and interrupted by nodes of Ranvier
The inset shows a cross-section through both the axon and the myelin sheath. Magnification approximately x 30,000. The anatomy is distorted here to show several nodes; in fact, the distance between nodes is generally about 100 times as large as the nodes themselves.

The principle behind **myelinated axons,** those covered with a myelin sheath, is the same. Myelinated axons, found only in vertebrates, are covered with a coating composed mostly of fats. The myelin sheath is interrupted at intervals of approximately 1 mm by short unmyelinated sections of axon called nodes of Ranvier (RAHN-vee-ay), as shown in Figure 2.18. Each node is only about 1 micrometer wide.

Suppose that an action potential is initiated at the axon hillock and propagated along the axon until it reaches the first myelin segment. The action potential cannot regenerate along the membrane between nodes because sodium channels are virtually absent between nodes (Catterall, 1984). After an action potential occurs at a node, sodium ions that enter the axon diffuse within the axon, repelling positive ions that were already present and thus pushing a chain of positive ions along the axon to the next node, where they regenerate the action potential (Figure 2.19). This flow of ions is considerably faster than the regeneration of an action potential at each point along the axon. The jumping of action potentials from node to node is referred to as **saltatory conduction,** from the Latin word *saltare,* meaning "to jump." (The same root shows up in the word *somersault.*) In addition to providing very rapid conduction of impulses, saltatory conduction has the benefit of conserving energy: Instead of admitting sodium ions at every point along the axon and then having to pump them out via the sodium-

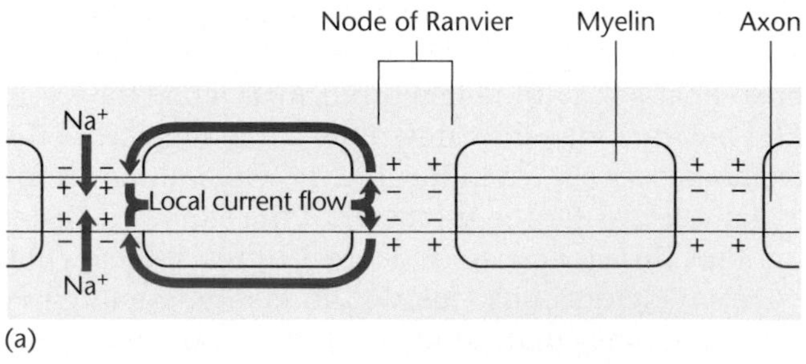

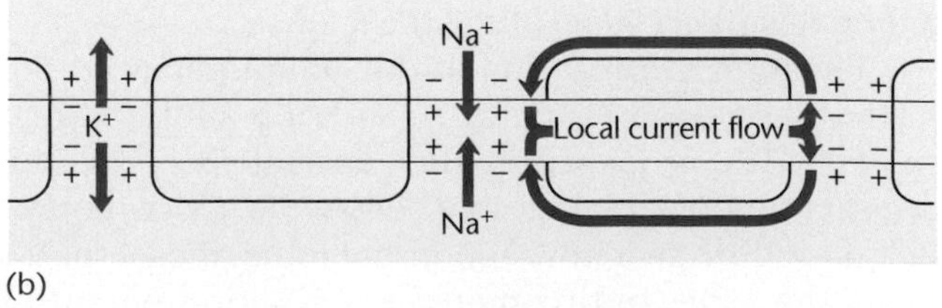

Figure 2.19 Saltatory conduction in a myelinated axon
An action potential at the node triggers flow of current to the next node, where the membrane regenerates the action potential.

potassium pump, a myelinated axon admits sodium only at its nodes.

Some diseases, including multiple sclerosis, destroy myelin sheaths, thereby slowing action potentials or stopping them altogether. An axon that has lost its myelin is not the same as one that has never had myelin. A myelinated axon loses its sodium channels between the nodes (Waxman & Ritchie, 1985). After the axon loses myelin, it still lacks sodium channels in the areas previously covered with myelin, and most action potentials die out between one node and the next. People with multiple sclerosis suffer a variety of impairments, including poor muscle coordination.

For an additional review of action potentials, visit this website: **http://faculty.washington.edu/chudler/ap.html**

STOP & CHECK

11. In a myelinated axon, how would the action potential be affected if the nodes were much closer together? How might it be affected if the nodes were much farther apart?

Check your answers on page 49.

Local Neurons

The principles we have been describing so far, especially the action potential, apply to neurons with lengthy axons. Not all neurons fall into that category.

Graded Potentials

Many neurons have only short axons, if any. They exchange information only with their closest neighbors and are therefore known as **local neurons.** A local neuron does not produce an action potential. It receives information from other neurons in its immediate vicinity and produces **graded potentials,** membrane potentials that vary in magnitude and do not follow the all-or-none law. When a local neuron is stimulated, it depolarizes or hyperpolarizes in proportion to the intensity of the stimulus. The change in membrane potential is conducted to adjacent areas of the cell, in all directions, gradually decaying as it travels. Those various areas of the cell make direct contact onto other neurons without going through an axon. In Chapter 6, we discuss in some detail a particular local neuron, the *horizontal cell,* which is essential for local interactions within the retina of the eye.

In some ways, astrocytes, although they are glia cells, operate like local neurons (Volterra & Meldolesi, 2005). They have no action potentials, but they rapidly exchange chemicals back and forth with neighboring neurons.

EXTENSIONS AND APPLICATIONS
Small Neurons and Big Misconceptions

Local neurons are somewhat difficult to study; it is almost impossible to insert an electrode into a tiny cell without damaging it. A disproportionate amount of our knowledge, therefore, has come from large neurons, and that bias in our research methods may have led to an enduring misconception.

Many years ago, long before neuroscientists could investigate local neurons, all they knew about them was that they were small. Given that nearly all knowledge about the nervous system was based on the activities of large neurons, the small neurons seemed unimportant. Many scientists assumed that they were "baby" or immature neurons. As one textbook author put it, "Many of these [neurons] are small and apparently undeveloped, as if they constituted a reserve stock not yet utilized in the individual's cerebral activity" (Woodworth, 1934, p. 194). In other words, the small cells would contribute to behavior only if they grew.

Perhaps this misunderstanding was the origin of that widespread, nonsensical belief that "we use only 10% of our brain." It is difficult to imagine any reasonable justification for this belief. Surely, no one maintained that anyone could lose 90% of the brain and still behave normally or that only 10% of neurons are active at any given moment. Whatever its source, the belief became popular, presumably because people wanted to believe it. Eventually, they were simply quoting one another long after everyone forgot what evidence they had (or didn't have) for it in the first place.

Module 2.2
In Closing: Neural Messages

We have examined what happens within a single neuron, as if each neuron acted independently. It does not, of course; all of its functions depend on communication with other neurons, as we consider in the next chapter. We may as well admit from the start, however, that neural communication is amazing. Unlike human communication, in which a speaker sometimes presents a complicated message to an enormous audience, a neuron delivers only an action potential—a mere on/off message—to only that modest number of other neurons that receive branches of its axon. At various receiving neurons, an "on" message can be converted into either excitation or inhibition (yes or no). From this limited system, all of our behavior and experience emerge.

Summary

1. The inside of a resting neuron has a negative charge with respect to the outside. Sodium ions are actively pumped out of the neuron, and potassium ions are pumped in. Potassium ions flow slowly across the membrane of the neuron, but sodium ions hardly cross it at all while the membrane is at rest. (p. 39)
2. When the charge across the membrane is reduced, sodium ions can flow more freely across the membrane. When the membrane potential reaches the threshold of the neuron, sodium ions enter explosively, suddenly reducing and reversing the charge across the membrane. This event is known as the action potential. (p. 42)
3. The magnitude of the action potential is independent of the size of the stimulus that initiated it; this statement is the all-or-none law. (p. 44)
4. Immediately after an action potential, the membrane enters a refractory period during which it is resistant to starting another action potential. (p. 44)
5. The action potential is regenerated at successive points along the axon by sodium ions flowing through the core of the axon and then across the membrane. The action potential maintains a constant magnitude as it passes along the axon. (p. 45)
6. In axons that are covered with myelin, action potentials form only in the nodes that separate myelinated segments. Transmission in myelinated axons is much faster than in unmyelinated axons. (p. 46)
7. Many small local neurons transmit messages over relatively short distances by graded potentials, which decay over time and space, instead of by action potentials. (p. 47)

Answers to STOP & CHECK Questions

1. Sodium ions are more concentrated outside the cell; potassium is more concentrated inside. (p. 42)
2. When the membrane is at rest, the concentration gradient tends to drive potassium ions out of the cell; the electrical gradient draws them into the cell. The sodium-potassium pump also draws them into the cell. (p. 42)
3. A hyperpolarization is an exaggeration of the usual negative charge within a cell (to a more negative level than usual). A depolarization is a decrease in the amount of negative charge within the cell. (p. 42)
4. A depolarization that passes the threshold produces an action potential. One that falls short of the threshold does not produce an action potential. (p. 42)
5. During the action potential, sodium ions move into the cell. The voltage-dependent sodium gates have opened, so sodium can move freely. Sodium is attracted to the inside of the cell by both an electrical and a concentration gradient. (p. 44)
6. After the peak of the action potential, potassium ions exit the cell, driving the membrane back to the resting potential. (The sodium-potassium pump is not the answer here; it is too slow.) (p. 44)
7. According to the all-or-none law, the size and shape of the action potential are independent of the intensity of the stimulus that initiated it. That is, every depolarization beyond the threshold of excitation produces an action potential of about the same amplitude and velocity for a given axon. (p. 45)
8. The all-or-none law does not apply to dendrites because they do not have action potentials. (p. 45)
9. Axon A must have a shorter absolute refractory period, about 1 ms, whereas B has a longer absolute refractory period, about 5 ms. (p. 45)
10. During the absolute refractory period, the sodium gates are locked and no amount of stimulation can produce another action potential. During the relative refractory period, a greater than usual stimulation is needed to produce an action potential. (p. 45)
11. If the nodes were closer, the action potential would travel more slowly. If they were much farther apart, the current might not be able to diffuse from one node to the next and still remain above threshold, so the action potentials might stop. (p. 47)

Thought Questions

1. Suppose that the threshold of a neuron were the same as its resting potential. What would happen? At what frequency would the cell produce action potentials?
2. In the laboratory, researchers can apply an electrical stimulus at any point along the axon, making action potentials travel in both directions from the point of stimulation. An action potential moving in the usual direction, away from the axon hillock, is said to be traveling in the *orthodromic* direction. An action potential traveling toward the axon hillock is traveling in the *antidromic* direction. If we started an orthodromic action potential at the axon hillock and an antidromic action potential at the opposite end of the axon, what would happen when they met at the center? Why? What research might make use of antidromic impulses?
3. If a drug partly blocks a membrane's potassium channels, how does it affect the action potential?

Chapter Ending

Key Terms and Activities

Terms

absolute refractory period (p. 44)
action potential (p. 42)
active transport (p. 37)
afferent axon (p. 33)
all-or-none law (p. 44)
astrocyte (p. 35)
axon (p. 33)
axon hillock (p. 45)
blood-brain barrier (p. 36)
cell body, or *soma* (p. 33)
concentration gradient (p. 41)
dendrite (p. 32)
dendritic spine (p. 32)
depolarization (p. 42)
efferent axon (p. 33)
electrical gradient (p. 39)
endoplasmic reticulum (p. 32)
glia (p. 35)
glucose (p. 37)
graded potential (p. 47)
hyperpolarization (p. 42)
interneuron (p. 34)
intrinsic neuron (p. 34)
local anesthetic (p. 44)
local neuron (p. 47)
membrane (p. 31)
microglia (p. 35)
mitochondrion (pl.: mitochondria) (p. 31)
motor neuron (p. 32)
myelin (p. 46)
myelin sheath (p. 33)
myelinated axon (p. 46)
neuron (p. 30)
node of Ranvier (p. 33)
nucleus (p. 31)
oligodendrocyte (p. 35)
polarization (p. 39)
presynaptic terminal (p. 33)
propagation of the action potential (p. 45)
radial glia (p. 35)
refractory period (p. 44)
relative refractory period (p. 44)
resting potential (p. 39)
ribosome (p. 32)
saltatory conduction (p. 46)
Schwann cell (p. 35)
selective permeability (p. 40)
sensory neuron (p. 32)
sodium-potassium pump (p. 41)
thiamine (vitamin B_1) (p. 37)
threshold of excitation (p. 42)
voltage-activated channel (p. 43)

Suggestion for Further Reading

Smith, C. U. M. (2002). *Elements of molecular neurobiology* (3rd ed.). Hoboken, NJ: Wiley. A detailed treatment of the molecular biology of neurons.

Websites to Explore

- You can go to the Biological Psychology Study Center and click this link. While there, you can also check for suggested articles available on InfoTrac College Edition. The Biological Psychology Internet address is:

http://psychology.wadsworth.com/book/kalatbiopsych9e/

MetaNeuron Program
Here you can vary temperatures, ion concentrations, membrane permeability, and so forth to see the effects on action potentials.

http://www2.neuroscience.umn.edu/eanwebsite/metaneuron.htm

Exploring Biological Psychology CD

The Parts of a Neuron (animation)
Virtual Reality Neuron (virtual reality)
Neuron Puzzle (drag & drop)
Resting Potential (animation)
Action Potential (animation)
Action Potential: Na^+ Ions (animation)
Neuron Membrane at Rest (animation)
Propagation of the Action Potential (animation)
Critical Thinking (essay questions)
Chapter Quiz (multiple-choice questions)

ThomsonNOW™

http://www.thomsonedu.com

Go to this site for the link to ThomsonNOW, your one-stop study shop, Take a Pre-Test for this chapter, and ThomsonNOW will generate a Personalized Study Plan based on your test results. The Study Plan will identify the topics you need to review and direct you to online resources to help you master these topics. You can then take a Post-Test to help you determine the concepts you have mastered and what you still need work on.

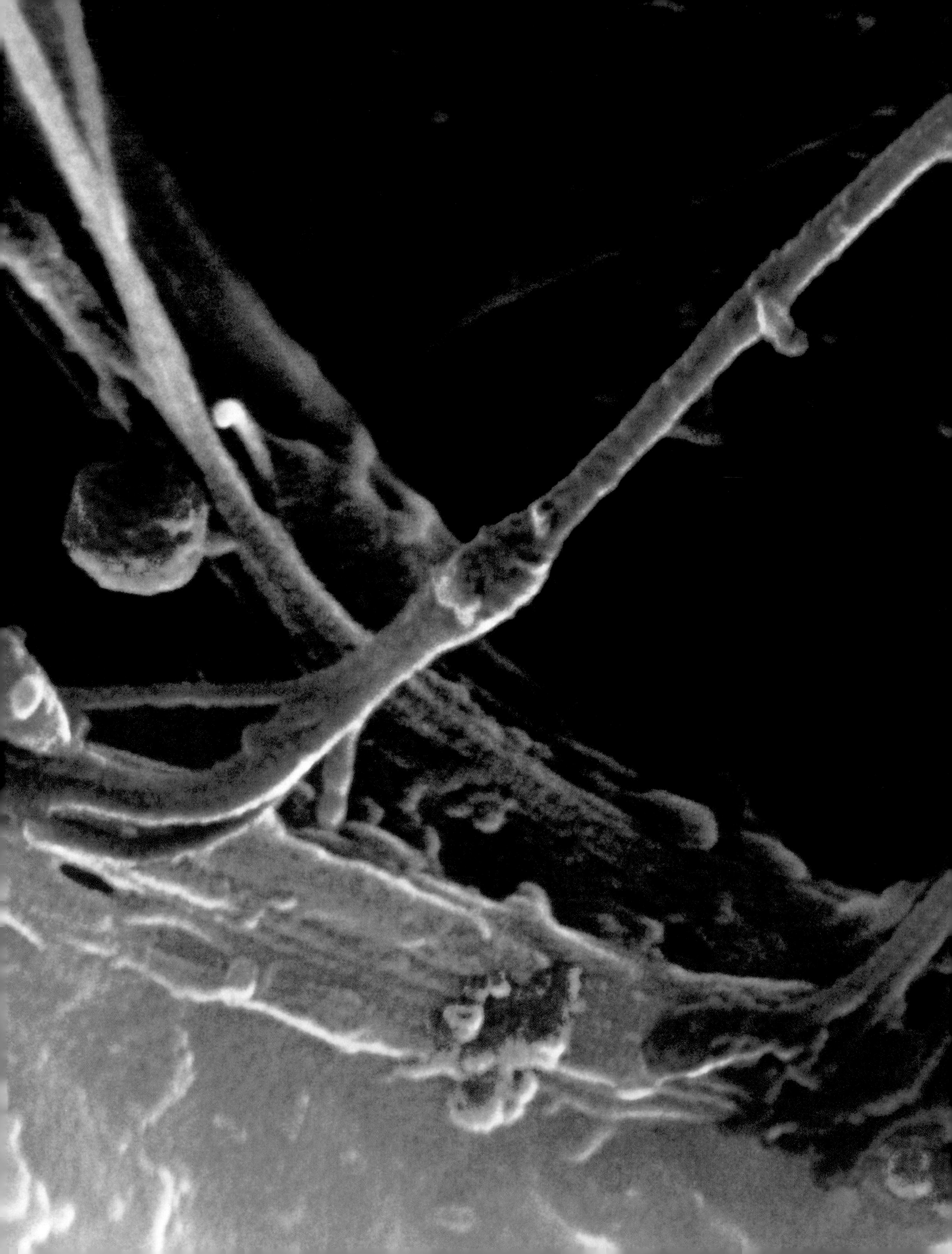

Synapses

3

Chapter Outline

Opposite: This electron micrograph, with color added artificially, shows the synapses formed by axons onto another neuron.
Source: © Eye of Science/Photo Researchers, Inc.

Main Ideas

1. At a synapse, a neuron releases a chemical known as a neurotransmitter that excites or inhibits another cell or alters its response to additional input.
2. A single release of neurotransmitter produces only a subthreshold response in the receiving cell. This response summates with other subthreshold responses to determine whether or not the cell produces an action potential.
3. Because different neurotransmitters contribute to behavior in different ways, excessive or deficient transmission at a particular type of synapse can lead to abnormal behavior.
4. Most drugs that affect behavior or experience do so by acting at synapses.
5. Nearly all abused drugs increase the release of dopamine in certain brain areas.

If you had to communicate with someone without using sound, what would you do? Chances are, your first choice would be a visual code, such as written words or sign language. Your second choice would probably be some sort of touch code or a system of electrical impulses. You might not even think of passing chemicals back and forth. Chemical communication is, however, the primary method of communication for your neurons. Considering how well the human nervous system works, chemical communication is evidently more versatile than we might have guessed. Neurons communicate by transmitting chemicals at specialized junctions called *synapses*, which are central to all information processing in the brain.

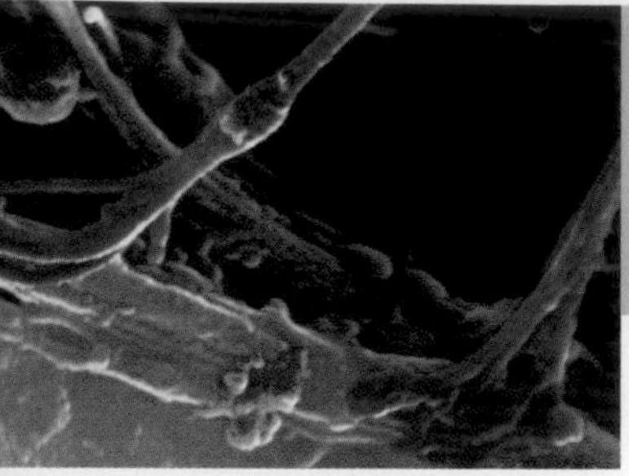

Module 3.1
The Concept of the Synapse

In the late 1800s, Ramón y Cajal anatomically demonstrated a narrow gap separating one neuron from the next. In 1906, Charles Scott Sherrington physiologically demonstrated that communication between one neuron and the next differs from communication along a single axon. (See photo and quote on the pages inside the back cover.) He inferred a specialized gap between neurons and introduced the term **synapse** to describe it. Cajal and Sherrington are regarded as the great pioneers of modern neuroscience, and their nearly simultaneous discoveries supported each other: If communication between one neuron and another was special in some way, then no doubt could remain that neurons were anatomically separate from one another. Sherrington's discovery was an amazing feat of scientific reasoning, as he used behavioral observations to infer the major properties of synapses about half a century before researchers had the technology to measure those properties directly.

The Properties of Synapses

Sherrington conducted his research on **reflexes,** automatic muscular responses to stimuli. In a leg flexion reflex, a sensory neuron excites a second neuron, which in turn excites a motor neuron, which excites a muscle, as in Figure 3.1. The circuit from sensory neuron to muscle response is called a **reflex arc.** If one neuron is separate from another, as Cajal had demonstrated, a reflex must require communication between neurons, and therefore, measurements of reflexes might reveal some of the special properties of that communication.

Figure 3.1 A reflex arc for leg flexion
The anatomy has been simplified to show the relationship among sensory neuron, intrinsic neuron, and motor neuron.

In a typical experiment, Sherrington strapped a dog into a harness above the ground and pinched one of the dog's feet. After a short delay—less than a second but long enough to measure—the dog *flexed* (raised) the pinched leg and *extended* the others. Sherrington found the same reflexive movements after he made a cut that disconnected the spinal cord from the brain; evidently, the spinal cord controlled the flexion and extension reflexes. In fact, the movements were more consistent after he separated the spinal cord from the brain. (In an intact animal, messages descending from the brain inhibit or modify the reflexes.)

Sherrington observed several properties of reflexes suggesting special processes at the junctions between neurons: (a) Reflexes are slower than conduction along an axon. (b) Several weak stimuli presented at slightly different times or slightly different locations produce a stronger reflex than a single stimulus does. (c) When one set of muscles becomes excited, a different set becomes relaxed. Let us consider each of these points and their implications.

Speed of a Reflex and Delayed Transmission at the Synapse

When Sherrington pinched a dog's foot, the dog flexed that leg after a very short but measurable delay. During that delay, an impulse had to travel up an axon from the skin receptor to the spinal cord, and then an impulse had to travel from the spinal cord back down the leg to a muscle. Sherrington measured the total distance that the impulse traveled from skin receptor to spinal cord to muscle and calculated the speed at which the impulse must have traveled to produce the response within the measured delay. He found that the speed of conduction through the reflex arc varied but was never more than about 15 meters per second (m/s). In contrast, previous research had measured action potential velocities along sensory or motor nerves at about 40 m/s. Even if the measurements were not exactly accurate, Sherrington concluded that some process was slowing conduction through the reflex, and he inferred that the delay must occur where one neuron communicates with another (Figure 3.2). This idea is critical, as it established the existence of synapses. Sherrington, in fact, introduced the term *synapse*.

Temporal Summation

Sherrington's work with reflex arcs suggested that repeated stimuli within a brief time have a cumulative effect. He referred to this phenomenon as **temporal summation.** A light pinch of the dog's foot did not evoke a reflex, but when Sherrington rapidly repeated the pinch several times, the leg flexed. Sherrington surmised that a single pinch produced a synaptic transmission too weak to reach the threshold for an action potential in the **postsynaptic neuron**, the cell that receives the message. (The neuron that delivers the synaptic transmission is the **presynaptic neuron.**) Sherrington proposed that this subthreshold excitation begins to decay shortly after it starts but can combine with a second excitation that quickly follows it. A rapid succession of pinches produces a series of weak activations at the synapse, each adding its effect to what was left of the previous ones. If enough excitations occur rapidly enough, they combine to exceed the threshold of the postsynaptic neuron.

Decades after Sherrington, John Eccles (1964) inserted microelectrodes into neurons to measure changes in the electrical potential across the membrane. He attached stimulating electrodes to axons of presynaptic neurons while recording from the postsynaptic neuron. For example, after he had briefly stimulated an axon, Eccles recorded a slight depolarization of the membrane of the postsynaptic cell (point 1 in Figure 3.3).

Note that this partial depolarization is a graded potential. Unlike action potentials, which are always depolarizations, graded potentials may be either depolarizations (excitatory) or hyperpolarizations (inhibitory). A graded depolarization is known as an **excitatory postsynaptic potential (EPSP).** Like the action potentials discussed in Chapter 2, an EPSP occurs when sodium ions enter the cell. However, in most cases, transmission at a single synapse does not open enough sodium gates to reach the threshold. Unlike an action potential, an EPSP decays over time and space; that is, its magnitude fades rapidly.

When Eccles stimulated an axon twice in close succession, he recorded two consecutive EPSPs in the postsynaptic cell. If the delay between EPSPs was short enough, temporal summation occurred; that is, the second EPSP added to what was left of the first one (point 2 in Figure 3.3). The summation of two EPSPs might or might not exceed the threshold of the postsynaptic cell depending on the size of the EPSPs, the time between them, and the threshold of the postsynaptic cell. At point 3 in Figure 3.3, three consecutive EPSPs combine to exceed the threshold and produce an action potential.

Spatial Summation

Sherrington's work with reflex arcs also suggested that synapses have the property of **spatial summation:** Several synaptic inputs originating from separate locations combine their effects on a neuron. Sherrington again began with a pinch too weak to elicit a reflex. This time, instead of pinching one point twice, he pinched two points at the same time. Although neither pinch alone elicited a response, the two together did. Sherrington concluded that pinching two points on the foot acti-

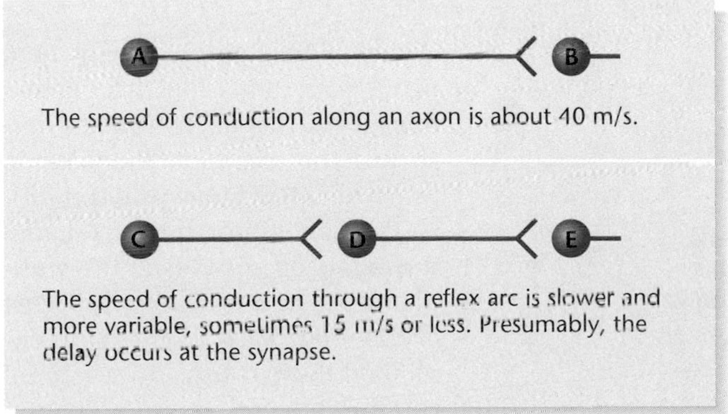

Figure 3.2 Sherrington's evidence for synaptic delay
An impulse traveling through a synapse in the spinal cord is slower than one traveling a similar distance along an uninterrupted axon.

Figure 3.3 Recordings from a postsynaptic neuron during synaptic activation

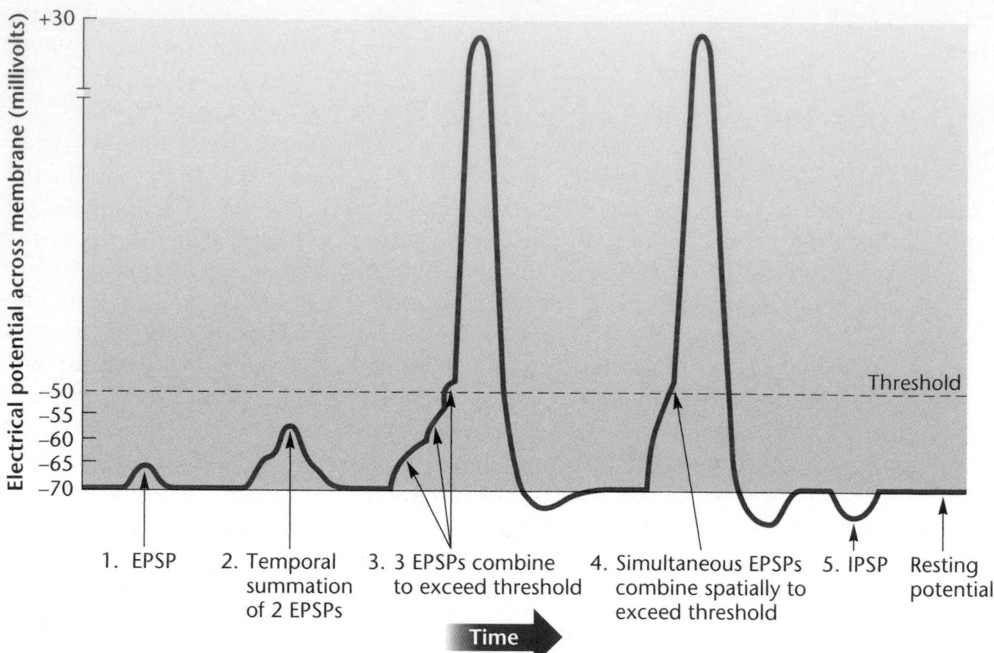

vated two sensory neurons, whose axons converged onto one neuron in the spinal cord. Excitation from either axon excited that neuron but did not reach the threshold. Two excitations exceeded the threshold and elicited an action potential (point 4 in Figure 3.3).

Again, Eccles confirmed Sherrington's inference, demonstrating that several axons were capable of producing EPSPs that summate their effects on a postsynaptic cell. Note that temporal and spatial summation both increase the depolarization of the postsynaptic cell and therefore increase the probability of an action potential (Figure 3.4).

You might guess that the synapses closer to the cell body of the postsynaptic cell might have a bigger effect than synapses on more distant parts of the dendrites because the distant inputs might decay in strength as they travel toward the cell body. Surprisingly, however, the synapses on remoter parts of the dendrites produce larger EPSPs, so their contribution to the cell's response approximately equals that of closer synapses (Magee & Cook, 2000).

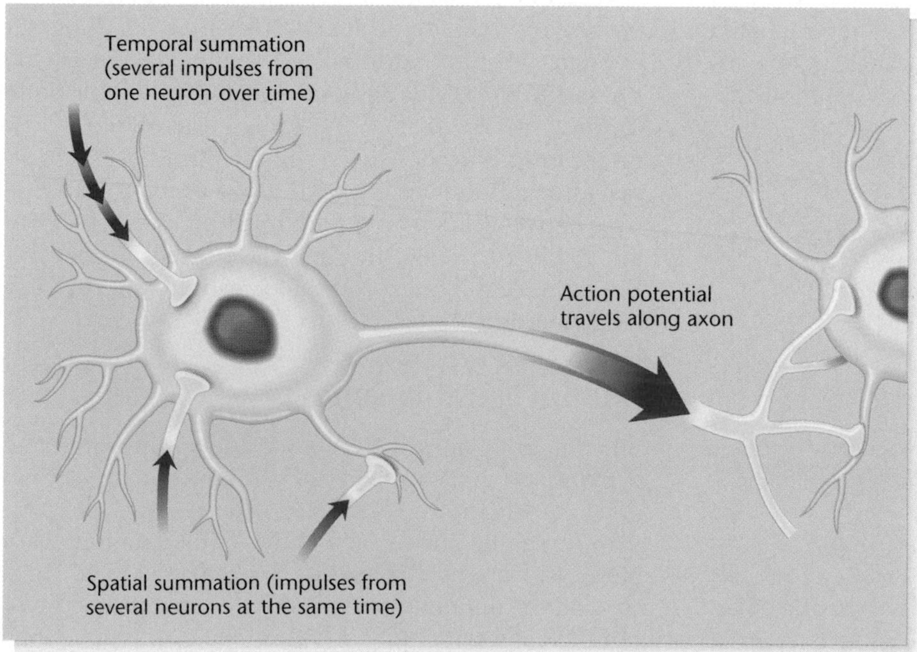

Figure 3.4 Temporal and spatial summation

Inhibitory Synapses

When Sherrington vigorously pinched a dog's foot, the flexor muscles of that leg contracted and so did the extensor muscles of the other three legs (Figure 3.5). At the same time, the dog relaxed the extensor muscles of the stimulated leg and the flexor muscles of the other legs. Sherrington explained these results by assuming certain connections in the spinal cord: A pinch on the foot sends a message along a sensory neuron to an *interneuron* (an intermediate neuron) in the spinal cord, which in turn excites the motor

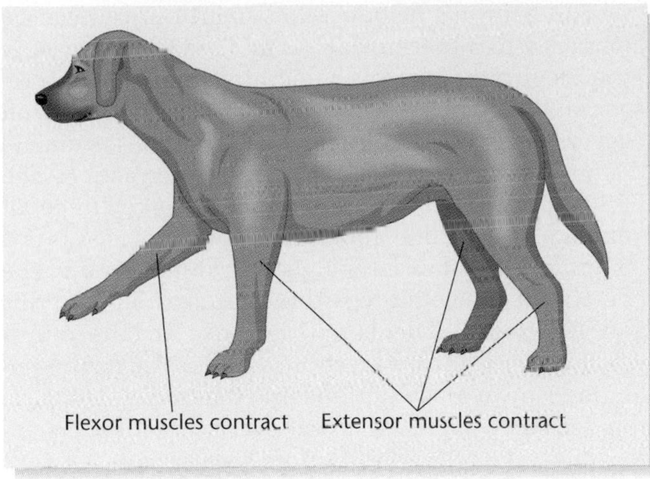

Figure 3.5 Antagonistic muscles
Flexor muscles draw an extremity toward the trunk of the body, whereas extensor muscles move an extremity away from the body.

neurons connected to the flexor muscles of that leg (Figure 3.6). Sherrington surmised that the interneuron also sends a message to block activity of motor neurons connected to the extensor muscles in the same leg, as well as the flexor muscles of the three other legs.

Eccles and later researchers physiologically demonstrated the inhibitory synapses that Sherrington had inferred. At these synapses, input from the axon hyperpolarizes the postsynaptic cell. That is, it increases the negative charge within the cell, moving it further from the threshold, and thus decreasing the probability of an action potential (point 5 in Figure 3.3). This temporary hyperpolarization of a membrane—called an **inhibitory postsynaptic potential**, or **IPSP**—resembles an EPSP in many ways. An IPSP occurs when synaptic input selectively opens the gates for potassium ions to leave the cell (carrying a positive charge with them) or for chloride ions to enter the cell (carrying a negative charge). Inhibition is more than just the absence of excitation; it is an active "brake" that suppresses excitation.

Today, we take the concept of inhibition for granted, but at Sherrington's time, the idea was controversial, as no one could imagine a mechanism to accomplish it. Establishing the idea of inhibition was critical not just for neuroscience but for psychology as well. For example, Sigmund Freud, who developed his theories in the same era as Sherrington, proposed that when a sexual "energy" was blocked from its desired outlet, it would spill over into some other activity. Today, we would simply talk about inhibiting an unwelcome activity; we see no need for the associated energy to flow somewhere else.

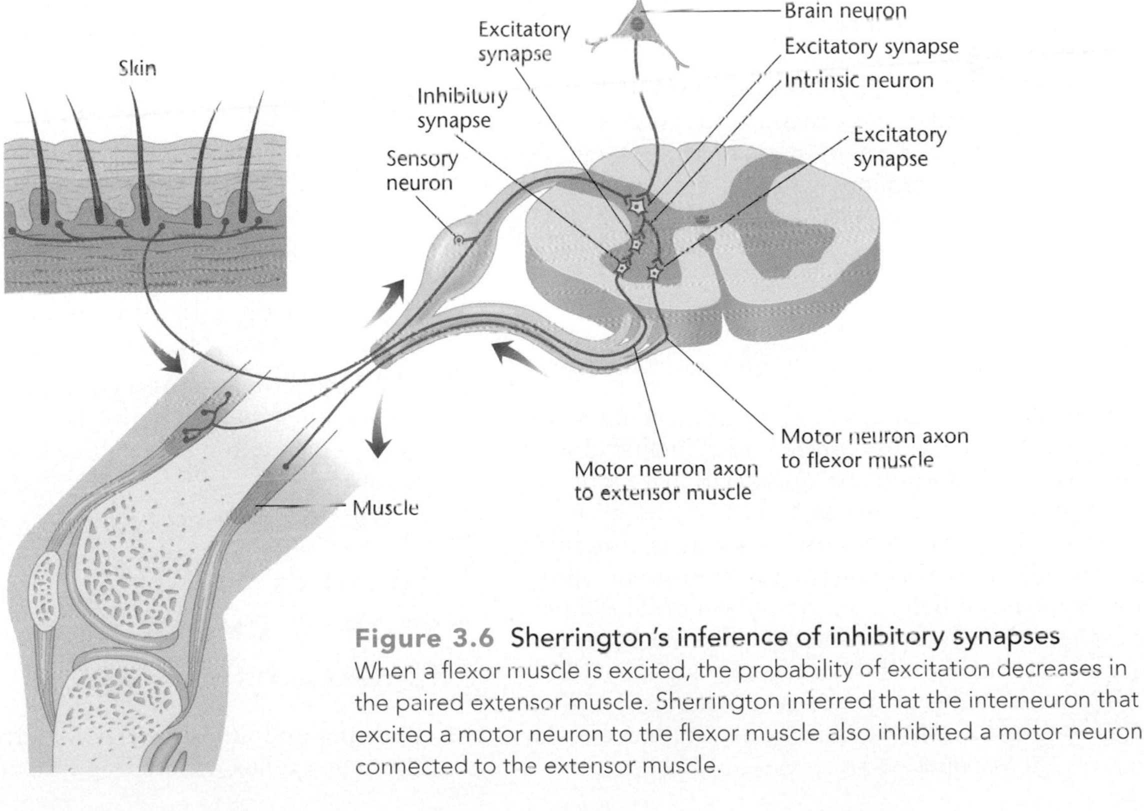

Figure 3.6 Sherrington's inference of inhibitory synapses
When a flexor muscle is excited, the probability of excitation decreases in the paired extensor muscle. Sherrington inferred that the interneuron that excited a motor neuron to the flexor muscle also inhibited a motor neuron connected to the extensor muscle.

STOP & CHECK

1. What evidence led Sherrington to conclude that transmission at a synapse is different from transmission along an axon?
2. What is the difference between temporal summation and spatial summation?
3. What was Sherrington's evidence for inhibition in the nervous system?
4. What ion gates in the membrane open during an EPSP? What gates open during an IPSP?

Check your answers on pages 56–57.

Relationship Among EPSP, IPSP, and Action Potential

A given neuron may have anywhere from a few synapses on its surface to thousands, some of them excitatory and others inhibitory. Any number and combination of synapses may be active at any time, yielding both temporal and spatial summation. The probability of an action potential depends on the ratio of EPSPs to IPSPs at a given moment.

Most neurons have a **spontaneous firing rate**, a periodic production of action potentials even without synaptic input. In such neurons, the EPSPs increase the frequency of action potentials above the spontaneous rate, whereas IPSPs decrease it below that rate. For example, if the neuron's spontaneous firing rate is 10 action potentials per second, a stream of EPSPs might increase the rate to 15 or more, whereas a preponderance of IPSPs might decrease it to 5 or fewer.

Module 3.1

In Closing: The Neuron as Decision Maker

When we learn the basics of any scientific field, we sometimes take them for granted, as if people always knew them. For example, we are taught that Earth and the other planets rotate around the sun, and we don't always pause to marvel at how Copernicus, hundreds of years ago, drew that conclusion from some observations recorded before the invention of telescopes. Sherrington's accomplishment is also amazing. Just imagine measuring reflexive leg movements and inferring the existence of synapses and their major properties long before the invention of oscilloscopes or electron microscopes.

The neuron's response to synaptic input can be compared to a thermostat, a smoke detector, or any other device that detects something and triggers a response: When input reaches a certain level, the neuron triggers an action potential. That is, synapses enable the postsynaptic neuron to integrate information. The EPSPs and IPSPs reaching a neuron at a given moment compete against one another, and the net result is a complicated, not exactly algebraic summation of the two effects. We could regard the summation of EPSPs and IPSPs as a "decision" because it determines whether or not the postsynaptic cell fires an action potential. However, do not imagine that any single neuron decides what to eat for breakfast. Complex behaviors depend on the contributions from a huge network of neurons.

Summary

1. The synapse is the point of communication between two neurons. Charles S. Sherrington's observations of reflexes enabled him to infer the properties of synapses. (p. 52)
2. Because transmission through a reflex arc is slower than transmission through an equivalent length of axon, Sherrington concluded that some process at the synapses delays transmission. (p. 53)
3. Graded potentials (EPSPs and IPSPs) summate their effects. The summation of graded potentials from stimuli at different times is temporal summation. The summation of graded potentials from different locations is spatial summation. (p. 53)
4. A single stimulation at a synapse produces a brief graded potential in the postsynaptic cell. An excitatory graded potential (depolarizing) is an EPSP. An inhibitory graded potential (hyperpolarizing) is an IPSP. (pp. 53, 55)
5. An EPSP occurs when gates open to allow sodium to enter the neuron's membrane; an IPSP occurs when gates open to allow potassium to leave or chloride to enter. (pp. 53, 55)
6. The EPSPs on a neuron compete with the IPSPs; the balance between the two increases or decreases the neuron's frequency of action potentials. (p. 56)

Answers to STOP & CHECK Questions

1. Sherrington found that the velocity of conduction through a reflex arc was significantly slower than

the velocity of an action potential along an axon. Therefore, some delay must occur at the junction between one neuron and the next. (p. 56)

2. Temporal summation is the combined effect of quickly repeated stimulation at a single synapse. Spatial summation is the combined effect of several nearly simultaneous stimulations at several synapses onto one neuron. (p. 56)
3. Sherrington found that a reflex that stimulates a flexor muscle sends a simultaneous message that inhibits nerves to the extensor muscles of the same limb. (p. 56)
4. During an EPSP, sodium gates open. During an IPSP, potassium or chloride gates open. (p. 56)

Thought Questions

1. When Sherrington measured the reaction time of a reflex (i.e., the delay between stimulus and response), he found that the response occurred faster after a strong stimulus than after a weak one. Can you explain this finding? Remember that all action potentials—whether produced by strong or weak stimuli—travel at the same speed along a given axon.
2. A pinch on an animal's right hind foot excites a sensory neuron that excites an interneuron that excites the motor neurons to the flexor muscles of that leg. The interneuron also inhibits the motor neurons connected to the extensor muscles of the leg. In addition, this interneuron sends impulses that reach the motor neuron connected to the extensor muscles of the left hind leg. Would you expect the interneuron to excite or inhibit that motor neuron? (Hint: The connections are adaptive. When an animal lifts one leg, it must put additional weight on the other legs to maintain balance.)
3. Suppose neuron X has a synapse onto neuron Y, which has a synapse onto Z. Presume that no other neurons or synapses are present. An experimenter finds that stimulating neuron X causes an action potential in neuron Z after a short delay. However, she determines that the synapse of X onto Y is inhibitory. Explain how the stimulation of X might produce excitation of Z.

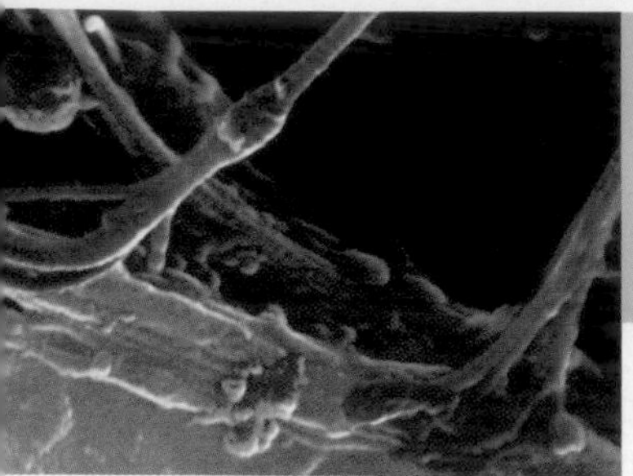

Module 3.2 Chemical Events at the Synapse

Although Charles Sherrington accurately inferred many properties of the synapse, he was wrong in one important point: Although he knew that synaptic transmission was slower than transmission along an axon, he thought it was still too fast to depend on a chemical process and therefore concluded that it must be electrical. We now know that the great majority of synapses rely on chemical processes, which are much faster and more versatile than Sherrington or anyone else of his era would have guessed.

The Discovery of Chemical Transmission at Synapses

A set of nerves called the sympathetic nervous system accelerates the heartbeat, relaxes the stomach muscles, dilates the pupils of the eyes, and regulates many other organs. T. R. Elliott, a young British scientist, reported in 1905 that applying the hormone *adrenaline* directly to the surface of the heart, the stomach, and the pupils produces the same effects as those of the sympathetic nervous system. Elliott therefore suggested that the sympathetic nerves stimulate muscles by releasing adrenaline or a similar chemical.

However, Elliott's evidence was not decisive; perhaps adrenaline merely mimicked effects that are ordinarily electrical in nature. At the time, Sherrington's prestige was so great that most scientists ignored Elliott's results and continued to assume that synapses transmitted electrical impulses. Otto Loewi, a German physiologist, liked the idea of chemical synapses but did not see how to demonstrate it more decisively. Then in 1920, he awakened one night with a sudden idea. He wrote himself a note and went back to sleep. Unfortunately, the next morning he could not read his note. The following night he awoke at 3 A.M. with the same idea, rushed to the laboratory, and performed the experiment.

Loewi repeatedly stimulated the vagus nerve, thereby decreasing the frog's heart rate. He then collected fluid from that heart, transferred it to a second frog's heart, and found that the second heart also decreased its rate of beating. (Figure 3.7 illustrates this experiment.) In a later experiment, Loewi stimulated the accelerator nerve to the first frog's heart, increasing the heart rate. When he collected fluid from that heart and transferred it to the second heart, its heart rate increased. That is, stimulating one nerve released something that inhibited heart rate, and stimulating a different nerve released something that increased heart rate. He knew he was collecting and transferring chemicals, not loose electricity. Therefore, Loewi concluded, nerves send messages by releasing chemicals.

Loewi later remarked that if he had thought of this experiment in the light of day, he probably would not have tried it (Loewi, 1960). Even if synapses did release chemicals, his daytime reasoning went, they probably did not release much. Fortunately, by the time he realized that the experiment was unlikely to work, he had already completed it, for which he later won the Nobel Prize.

Despite Loewi's work, most researchers over the next three decades continued to believe that most synapses were electrical and that chemical transmission

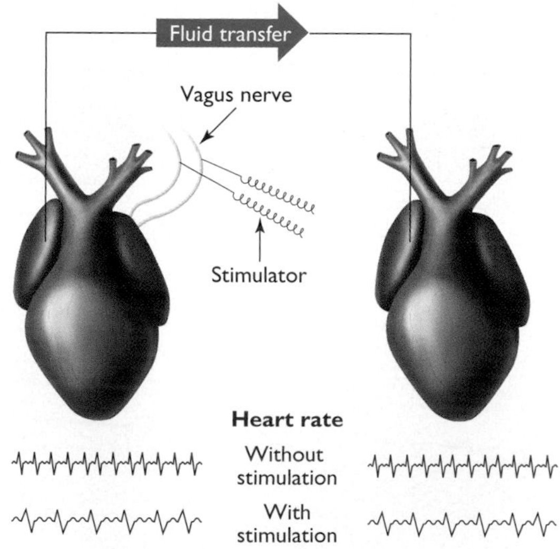

Figure 3.7 Loewi's experiment demonstrating that nerves send messages by releasing chemicals
Loewi stimulated the vagus nerve to one frog's heart, decreasing the heartbeat. When he transferred fluid from that heart to another frog's heart, he observed a decrease in its heartbeat.

was the exception. Finally, in the 1950s, researchers established that chemical transmission is the predominant type of communication throughout the nervous system. That discovery revolutionized our understanding and led to research developing new drugs for psychiatric uses (Carlsson, 2001).

The Sequence of Chemical Events at a Synapse

Understanding the chemical events at a synapse is fundamental to biological psychology. Here are the major events at a synapse:

1. The neuron synthesizes chemicals that serve as neurotransmitters. It synthesizes the smaller neurotransmitters in the axon terminals and the larger ones (peptides) in the cell body.
2. The neuron transports the peptide neurotransmitters to the axon terminals. (It doesn't have to transport smaller neurotransmitters because they are formed in the terminals.)
3. Action potentials travel down the axon. At the presynaptic terminal, an action potential enables calcium to enter the cell. Calcium releases neurotransmitters from the terminals and into the *synaptic cleft*, the space between the presynaptic and postsynaptic neurons.
4. The released molecules diffuse across the cleft, attach to receptors, and alter the activity of the postsynaptic neuron.
5. The neurotransmitter molecules separate from their receptors. Depending on the neurotransmitter, it may be converted into inactive chemicals.
6. The neurotransmitter molecules may be taken back into the presynaptic neuron for recycling or may diffuse away. In some cases, empty vesicles are returned to the cell body.
7. Although the research is not yet conclusive, it is likely that some postsynaptic cells send negative feedback messages to slow further release of neurotransmitter by the presynaptic cell.

Figure 3.8 summarizes these steps. Let's now consider each step in more detail.

Types of Neurotransmitters

At a synapse, one neuron releases chemicals that affect a second neuron. Those chemicals are known as **neurotransmitters**. Research has gradually identified more and more chemicals believed or suspected to be neurotransmitters; the current count is a hundred or more (Borodinsky et al., 2004). We shall consider many

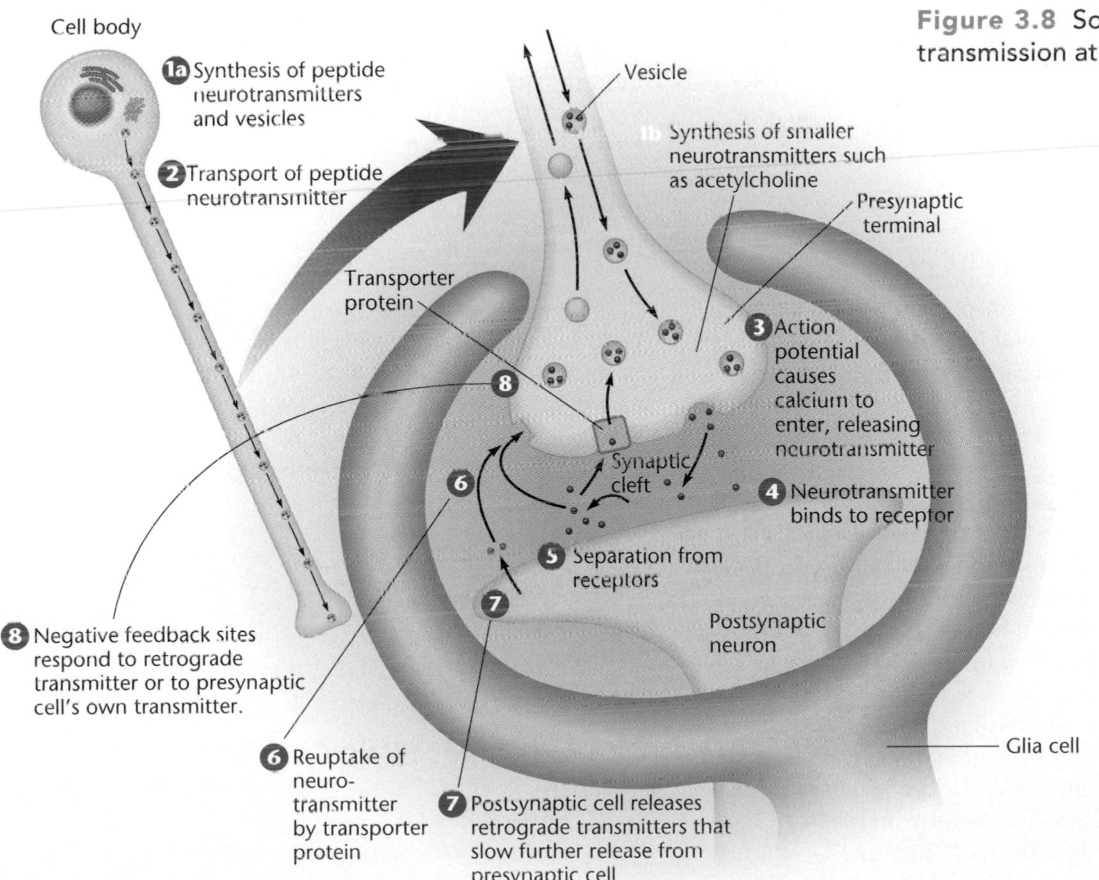

Figure 3.8 Some major events in transmission at a synapse

Table 3.1 Neurotransmitters

Neurotransmitters
Amino Acids
glutamate, GABA, glycine, aspartate, maybe others
A Modified Amino Acid
acetylcholine
Monoamines (also modified from amino acids)
indoleamines: serotonin
catecholamines: dopamine, norepinephrine, epinephrine
Peptides (chains of amino acids)
endorphins, substance P, neuropeptide Y, many others
Purines
ATP, adenosine, maybe others
Gases
NO (nitric oxide), maybe others

of them throughout this text; for now, you should familiarize yourself with some of their names (Table 3.1). Some major categories are:

amino acids acids containing an amine group (NH_2)
peptides chains of amino acids (A long chain of amino acids is called a *polypeptide;* a still longer chain is a *protein.* The distinctions among peptide, polypeptide, and protein are not firm.)
acetylcholine (a one-member "family") a chemical similar to an amino acid, except that the NH_2 group has been replaced by an $N(CH_3)_3$ group
monoamines neurotransmitters containing one amine group (NH_2), formed by a metabolic change in certain amino acids
purines a category of chemicals including adenosine and several of its derivatives
gases nitric oxide and possibly others

Note that most of the neurotransmitters are amino acids, derivatives of amino acids, or chains of amino acids. The most surprising exception is **nitric oxide** (chemical formula NO), a gas released by many small local neurons. (Do not confuse nitric oxide, NO, with nitrous oxide, N_2O, sometimes known as "laughing gas.") Nitric oxide is poisonous in large quantities and difficult to make in a laboratory. Yet many neurons contain an enzyme that enables them to make it with relatively little energy. One special function of nitric oxide relates to blood flow: When a brain area becomes highly active, blood flow to that area increases. How does the blood "know" that a brain area has become more active? The message comes from nitric oxide. Many neurons release nitric oxide when they are stimulated. In addition to influencing other neurons, the nitric oxide dilates the nearby blood vessels, thereby increasing blood flow to that area of the brain (Dawson, Gonzalez-Zulueta, Kusel, & Dawson, 1998).

Synthesis of Transmitters

Like any other cell in the body, a neuron synthesizes the chemicals it needs from substances provided by the diet. Figure 3.9 illustrates the chemical steps in the synthesis of acetylcholine, serotonin, dopamine, epinephrine, and norepinephrine. Note the relationship among epinephrine, norepinephrine, and dopamine—three closely related compounds known as **catecholamines**—because they contain a catechol group and an amine group, as shown here:

amine — NH_2, C — (other), C — (other)
catechol — HO, OH

Each pathway in Figure 3.9 begins with substances found in the diet. Acetylcholine, for example, is synthesized from choline, which is abundant in milk, eggs, and peanuts. The amino acids phenylalanine and tyrosine, present in virtually any protein, are precursors of dopamine, norepinephrine, and epinephrine.

The amino acid *tryptophan,* the precursor to serotonin, crosses the blood-brain barrier by a special transport system that it shares with other large amino acids. The amount of tryptophan in the diet controls the amount of serotonin in the brain (Fadda, 2000), so serotonin levels are higher after someone eats foods richer in tryptophan, such as soy, than after something with less tryptophan, such as maize (American corn). However, another factor limiting tryptophan entry to the brain is that it has to compete with other large amino acids, such as phenylalanine, that are more abundant than tryptophan in most proteins. One way to let more tryptophan enter the brain is to eat carbohydrates. Carbohydrates increase release of the hormone *insulin,* which takes several of the competing amino acids out of the bloodstream and into body cells, thus decreasing the competition against tryptophan (Wurtman, 1985).

1. What was Loewi's evidence that neurotransmission depends on the release of chemicals?
2. Name the three catecholamine neurotransmitters.
3. What does a highly active brain area do to increase its blood supply?

Check your answers on page 68.

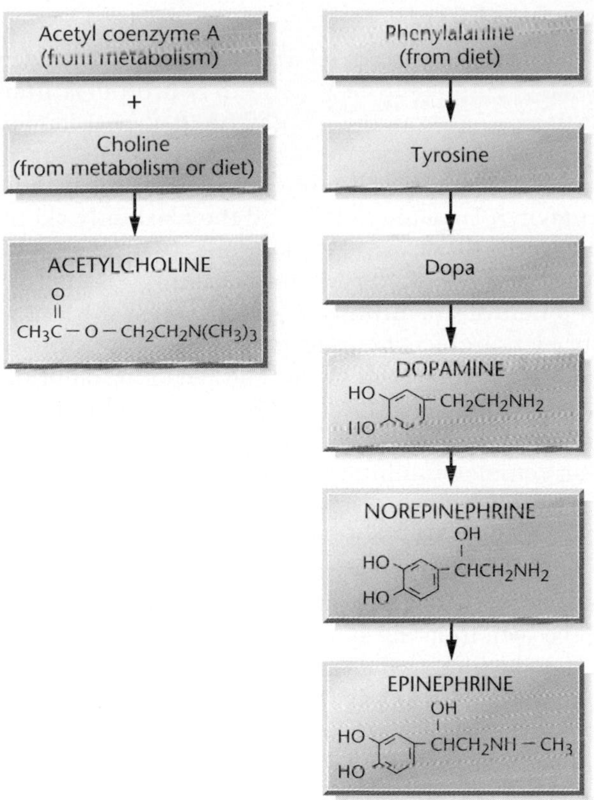

Figure 3.9 Pathways in the synthesis of acetylcholine, dopamine, norepinephrine, epinephrine, and serotonin
Arrows represent chemical reactions.

Transport of Transmitters

Many of the smaller neurotransmitters, such as acetylcholine, are synthesized in the presynaptic terminal, near their point of release. However, the larger neurotransmitters, including peptides, are synthesized in the cell body and then transported down the axon to the terminal. The speed of transport varies from only 1 millimeter (mm) per day in thin axons to more than 100 mm per day in thicker ones.

Even at the highest speeds, transport from cell body to terminal may take hours or days in a long axon. Consequently, after releasing peptides, neurons replenish their supply slowly. Furthermore, neurons reabsorb and recycle many other transmitters but not the peptides. For these reasons, a neuron can exhaust its supply of a peptide faster than that of other transmitters.

Release and Diffusion of Transmitters

The presynaptic terminal stores high concentrations of neurotransmitter molecules in **vesicles**, tiny nearly spherical packets (Figure 3.10). (Nitric oxide, the gaseous neurotransmitter mentioned earlier, is an exception to this rule. Neurons release nitric oxide as soon as they form it, instead of storing it for future use.) The presynaptic terminal also maintains much neurotransmitter outside the vesicles.

When an action potential reaches the end of an axon, the action potential itself does not release the neurotransmitter. Rather, the depolarization opens voltage-dependent calcium gates in the presynaptic terminal. Within 1 or 2 milliseconds (ms) after calcium enters the presynaptic terminal, it causes **exocytosis**—release of neurotransmitter in bursts from the presynaptic neuron into the synaptic cleft that separates this neuron from the postsynaptic neuron. The result is not always the same; an action potential often fails to release any transmitter, and even when it does, the amount varies (Craig & Boudin, 2001).

After its release from the presynaptic cell, the neurotransmitter diffuses across the synaptic cleft to the postsynaptic membrane, where it attaches to a receptor. The neurotransmitter takes no more than 0.01 ms to diffuse across the cleft, which is only 20 to 30 nano-

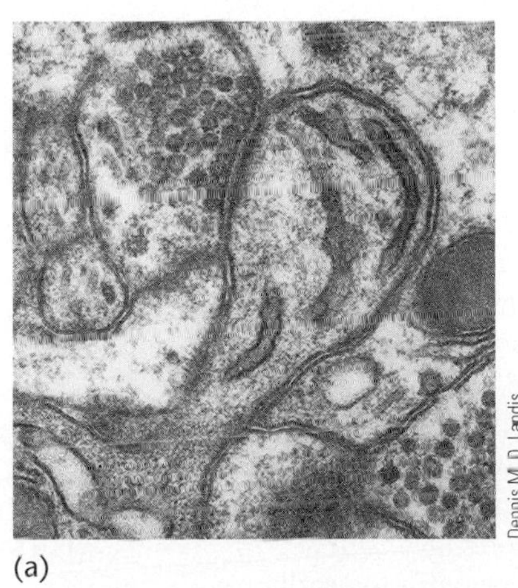
Dennis M. D. Landis
(a)

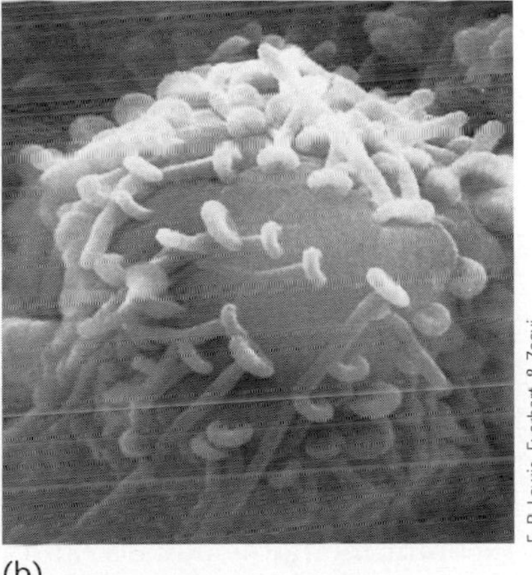
E. R. Lewis, Everhart, & Zeevi
(b)

Figure 3.10 Anatomy of a synapse
(a) An electron micrograph showing a synapse from the cerebellum of a mouse. The small round structures are vesicles. **(b)** Electron micrograph showing axon terminals onto the soma of a neuron. *(Source: From "Studying neural organization and aplysia with the scanning electron micrograph," by E. R. Lewis, et al., Science, 1969, 165:1142. Copyright 1969 by the AAAS. Reprinted with permission of AAS and E. R. Lewis.)*

meters (nm) wide. The total delay in transmission across the synapse, including the time for the presynaptic cell to release the neurotransmitter, is 2 ms or less (A. R. Martin, 1977; Takeuchi, 1977). Remember, Sherrington did not believe chemical processes could be fast enough to account for the activity at synapses. Obviously, he did not imagine such a narrow gap through which chemicals could diffuse so quickly.

Although the brain as a whole uses many neurotransmitters, no single neuron releases them all. For many years, investigators believed that each neuron released just one neurotransmitter, but later researchers found that many, perhaps most, neurons release a combination of two or more transmitters (Hökfelt, Johansson, & Goldstein, 1984). Still later researchers found that at least one kind of neuron releases different transmitters from different branches of its axon: Motor neurons in the spinal cord have one branch to the muscles, where they release acetylcholine, and another branch to other spinal cord neurons, where they release both acetylcholine and glutamate (Nishimaru, Restrepo, Ryge, Yanagawa, & Kiehn, 2005). If one kind of neuron can release different transmitters at different branches, maybe others can too. Why does a neuron release a combination of transmitters instead of just one? Presumably, the combination makes the neuron's message more complex, such as brief excitation followed by slight but prolonged inhibition (Jonas, Bischofberger, & Sandkühler, 1998).

Although a neuron releases only a limited number of neurotransmitters, it may receive and respond to many neurotransmitters at different synapses. For example, at various locations on its membrane, it might have receptors for glutamate, serotonin, acetylcholine, and so forth.

Activation of Receptors of the Postsynaptic Cell

In English, a *fern* is a kind of plant. In German, *fern* means "far away." In French, the term is meaningless. The meaning of any word depends on the listener. Similarly, the meaning of a neurotransmitter depends on its receptor. Each of the well-studied neurotransmitters interacts with several different kinds of receptors, with different functions. Therefore, a drug or a genetic mutation that affects one receptor type may affect behavior in a specific way. For example, one type of serotonin receptor mediates nausea, and the drug *ondansetron* that blocks this receptor helps cancer patients undergo treatment without nausea.

A neurotransmitter receptor is a protein embedded in the membrane. When the neurotransmitter attaches to the active site of the receptor, the receptor can directly open a channel—exerting an *ionotropic* effect—or it can produce slower but longer effects—a *metabotropic* effect.

Ionotropic Effects

Some neurotransmitters exert **ionotropic effects** on the postsynaptic neuron: When the neurotransmitter binds to a receptor on the membrane, it almost immediately opens the gates for some type of ion. Ionotropic effects begin within one to a few milliseconds (Scannevin & Huganir, 2000), and they last only about 20 ms (North, 1989; Westbrook & Jahr, 1989).

Most of the brain's excitatory ionotropic synapses use the neurotransmitter *glutamate.* Most of the inhibitory ionotropic synapses use the neurotransmitter GABA,[1] which opens chloride gates, enabling chloride ions, with their negative charge, to cross the membrane into the cell more rapidly than usual. Glycine is another common inhibitory transmitter (Moss & Smart, 2001). Acetylcholine, also a transmitter at many ionotropic synapses, has mostly excitatory effects, which have been extensively studied. Figure 3.11a shows a cross-section through an acetylcholine receptor as it might be seen from the synaptic cleft. Its outer portion (red) is embedded in the neuron's membrane; its inner portion (blue) surrounds the sodium channel. When at rest (unstimulated), the inner portion of the receptor coils together tightly enough to block sodium passage. When acetylcholine attaches, the receptor folds outward, widening the sodium channel. Figure 3.11b shows a side view of the receptor with acetylcholine attached (Miyazawa, Fujiyoshi, & Unwin, 2003). For a detailed treatment of ionotropic mechanisms, visit this website: **http://www.npaci.edu/features/98/Dec/index.html**

Metabotropic Effects and Second Messenger Systems

At other synapses, neurotransmitters exert **metabotropic effects** by initiating a sequence of metabolic reactions that are slower and longer lasting than ionotropic effects (Greengard, 2001). Metabotropic effects emerge 30 ms or more after the release of the transmitter (North, 1989) and last seconds, minutes, or even longer. Whereas most ionotropic effects depend on just glutamate and GABA, metabotropic synapses use a much larger variety of transmitters.

When the neurotransmitter attaches to a metabotropic receptor, it bends the rest of the protein, enabling a portion of the protein inside the neuron to react with other molecules, as shown in Figure 3.12 (Levitzki, 1988; O'Dowd, Lefkowitz, & Caron, 1989). The portion inside the neuron activates a **G-protein**—one that is coupled to guanosine triphosphate (GTP), an energy-storing molecule. The activated G-protein in turn increases the concentration of a second messenger, such as cyclic adenosine monophosphate (cyclic AMP), inside the cell. Just as the "first messenger" (the neurotransmitter) carries information to the postsynaptic cell,

[1]GABA (GA-buh) is an abbreviation for gamma-amino-butyric acid.

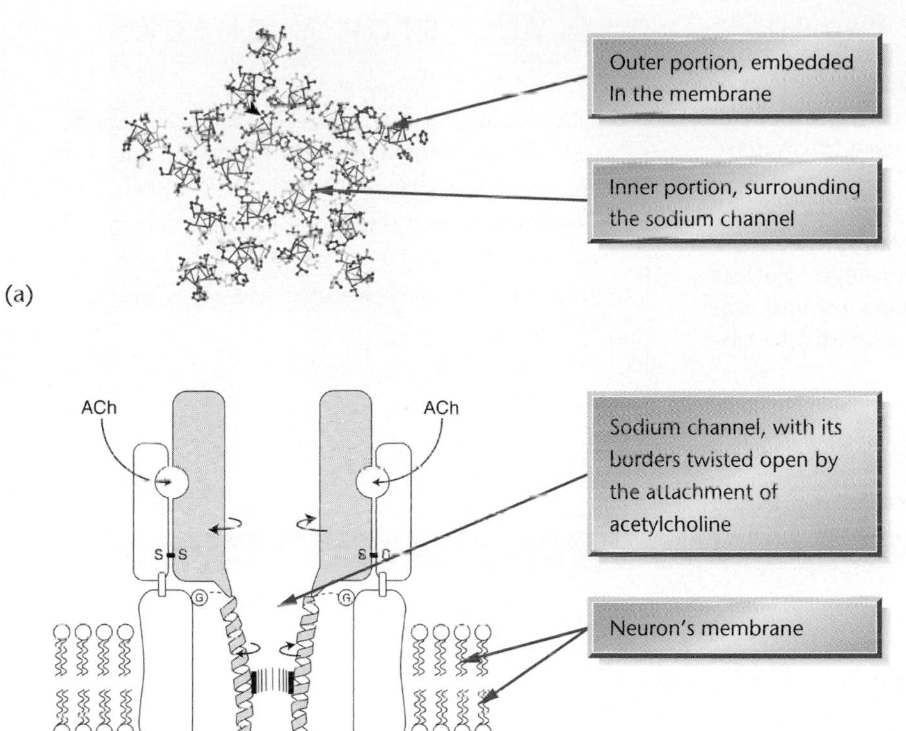

Figure 3.11 The acetylcholine receptor
(a) A cross-section, as viewed from the synaptic cleft. The membrane surrounds it. **(b)** A side view of the receptor, with the membrane to its left and right. Its inner portion surrounds the sodium channel. When the receptor is at rest, the channel is too narrow to let sodium pass through it. When acetylcholine binds to the receptor, it unfolds the protein lining the channel and lets sodium ions pass. *(Source: From A. Miyazawa et al., "Structure and gating mechanism of the acetylcholine receptor pore,"* Nature, 423, 949–955. *© 2003 Nature Publishing Group. Reprinted with permission.)*

the **second messenger** communicates to areas within the cell. The second messenger may open or close ion channels in the membrane or alter the production of proteins or activate a portion of a chromosome. Note the contrast: An ionotropic synapse has effects localized to one point on the membrane, whereas a metabotropic synapse, by way of its second messenger, influences activity in a larger area of the cell and over a longer time.

Ionotropic and metabotropic synapses contribute to different aspects of behavior. For vision and hearing, the brain needs rapid, quickly changing information, the kind that ionotropic synapses bring. In contrast, hunger, thirst, fear, and anger constitute long-term changes in the probabilities of many behaviors. Metabotropic synapses are better suited for that kind of function. Metabotropic synapses also mediate at least some of the input for taste (Huang et al., 2005) and pain (Levine, Fields, & Basbaum, 1993), which are slower and more enduring experiences than vision or hearing.

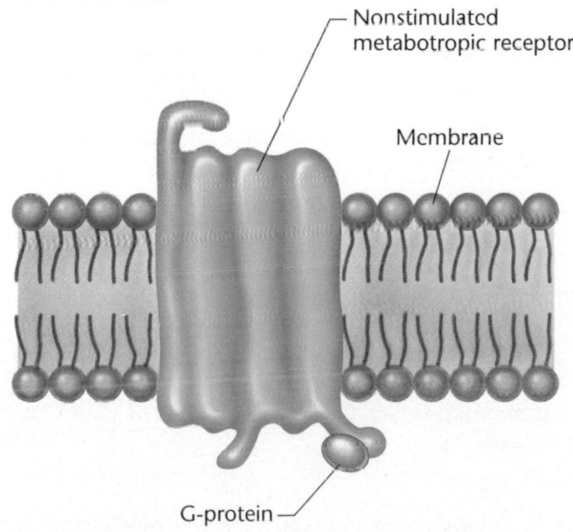

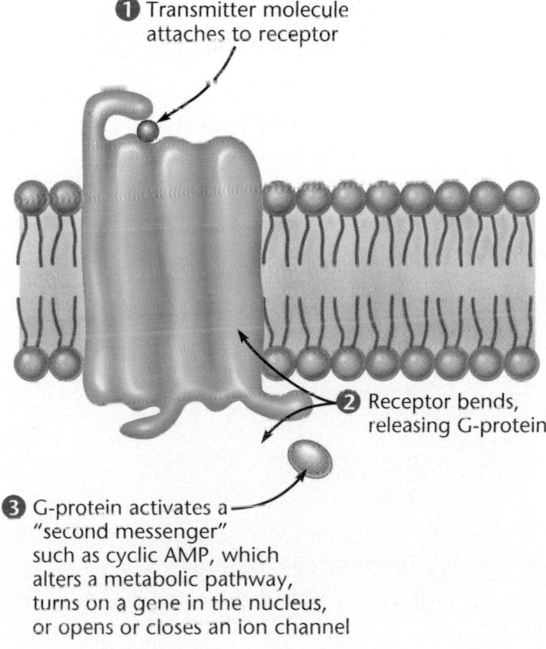

Figure 3.12 Sequence of events at a metabolic synapse, using a second messenger within the postsynaptic neuron

Researchers sometimes describe some metabotropic neurotransmitters, mainly the peptide neurotransmitters, as **neuromodulators**, with the implication that they do not directly excite or inhibit the postsynaptic cell but increase or decrease the release of other transmitters or alter the response of postsynaptic cells to various inputs. The same description applies to metabotropic synapses in general. Peptide transmitters do tend to diffuse widely enough to affect several cells, and sometimes their effects are very enduring, so the term *neuromodulator* is useful to emphasize these special characteristics.

4. When the action potential reaches the presynaptic terminal, which ion must enter the presynaptic terminal to evoke release of the neurotransmitter?
5. How do ionotropic and metabotropic synapses differ in speed and duration of effects?
6. What are second messengers, and which type of synapse relies on them?

Check your answers on page 68.

Table 3.2 Partial List of Hormone-Releasing Glands

Organ	Hormone	Hormone Functions
Hypothalamus	Various releasing hormones	Promote or inhibit release of various hormones by pituitary
Anterior pituitary	Thyroid-stimulating hormone (TSH)	Stimulates thyroid gland
	Luteinizing hormone (LH)	Increases production of progesterone (female), testosterone (male); stimulates ovulation
	Follicle-stimulating hormone (FSH)	Increases production of estrogen and maturation of ovum (female) and sperm production (male)
	ACTH	Increases secretion of steroid hormones by adrenal gland
	Prolactin	Increases milk production
	Growth hormone (GH), also known as somatotropin	Increases body growth, including the growth spurt during puberty
Posterior pituitary	Oxytocin	Controls uterine contractions, milk release, certain aspects of parental behavior, and sexual pleasure
	Vasopressin (also known as antidiuretic hormone)	Constricts blood vessels and raises blood pressure, decreases urine volume
Pineal	Melatonin	Increases sleepiness, influences sleep–wake cycle, also has role in onset of puberty
Thyroid	Thyroxine Triiodothyronine	Increase metabolic rate, growth, and maturation
Parathyroid	Parathyroid hormone	Increases blood calcium and decreases potassium
Adrenal cortex	Aldosterone	Reduces secretion of salts by the kidneys
	Cortisol, corticosterone	Stimulate liver to elevate blood sugar, increase metabolism of proteins and fats
Adrenal medulla	Epinephrine, norepinephrine	Similar to effects of sympathetic nervous system
Pancreas	Insulin	Increases entry of glucose to cells and increases storage as fats
	Glucagon	Increases conversion of stored fats to blood glucose
Ovary	Estrogens	Promote female sexual characteristics
	Progesterone	Maintains pregnancy
Testis	Androgens	Promote sperm production, growth of pubic hair, and male sexual characteristics
Liver	Somatomedins	Stimulate growth
Kidney	Renin	Converts a blood protein into angiotensin, which regulates blood pressure and contributes to hypovolemic thirst
Thymus	Thymosin (and others)	Support immune responses
Fat cells	Leptin	Decreases appetite, increases activity, necessary for onset of puberty

Hormones

A **hormone** is a chemical that is secreted, in most cases by a gland but also by other kinds of cells, and conveyed by the blood to other organs, whose activity it influences. A neurotransmitter is like a signal on a telephone line: It conveys a message directly and exclusively from the sender to the receiver. Hormones function more like a radio station: They convey a message to any receiver that happens to be tuned in to the right station. Figure 3.13 presents the major **endocrine** (hormone-producing) **glands.** Table 3.2 lists some important hormones and their principal effects.

Hormones are particularly useful for coordinating long-lasting changes in multiple parts of the body. For example, birds that are preparing to migrate secrete hormones that change their eating and digestion to store extra energy for a long journey. Among the various types of hormones are **protein hormones** and **peptide hormones,** composed of chains of amino acids. (Proteins are longer chains and peptides are shorter.) Protein and peptide hormones attach to membrane receptors where they activate a second messenger within the cell—exactly the same process as at a metabotropic synapse. In fact, many chemicals—including epinephrine, norepinephrine, insulin, and oxytocin—serve as both neurotransmitters and hormones.

Just as circulating hormones modify brain activity, hormones secreted by the brain control the secretion of many other hormones. The **pituitary gland,** attached to the hypothalamus (Figure 3.14), consists of two distinct glands, the **anterior pituitary** and the **posterior pituitary,** which release different sets of hormones (see Table 3.2). The posterior pituitary, composed of neural tissue, can be considered an extension of the hypothalamus. Neurons in the hypothalamus synthesize the hormones **oxytocin** and **vasopressin** (also known as antidiuretic hormone), which migrate down axons to the posterior pituitary, as shown in Figure 3.15. Later, the posterior pituitary releases these hormones into the blood.

The anterior pituitary, composed of glandular tissue, synthesizes six hormones, although the hypo-

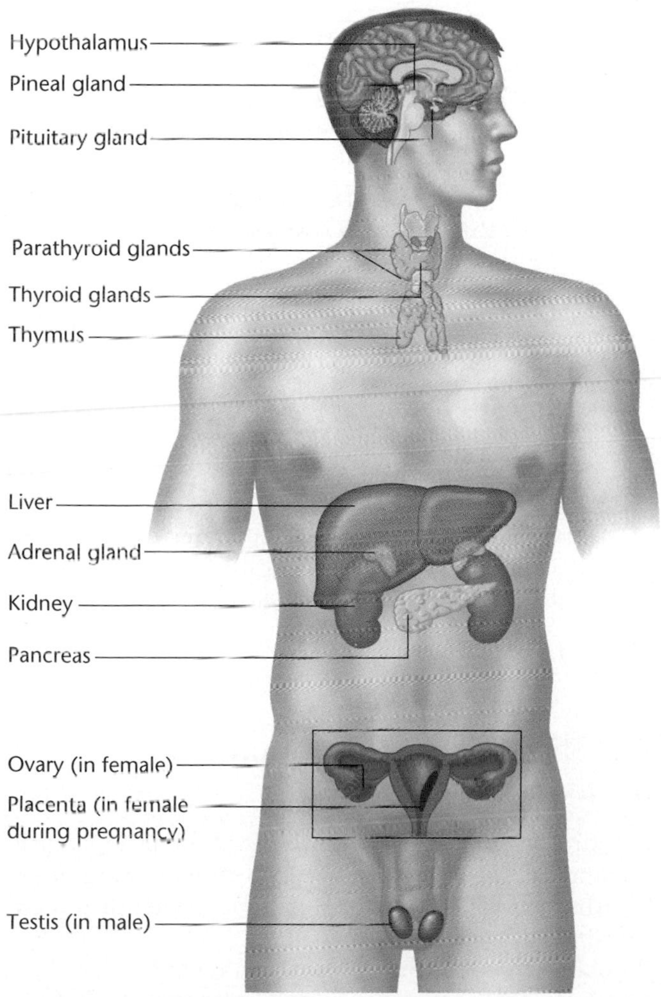

Figure 3.13 Location of some major endocrine glands
(Source: Starr & Taggart, 1989)

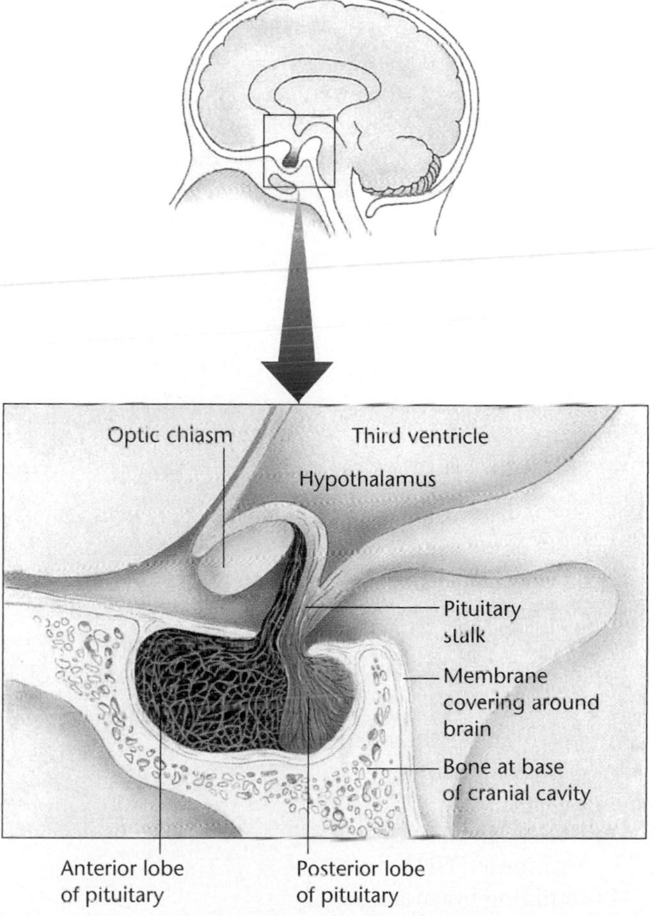

Figure 3.14 Location of the hypothalamus and pituitary gland in the human brain
(Source: Starr & Taggart, 1989)

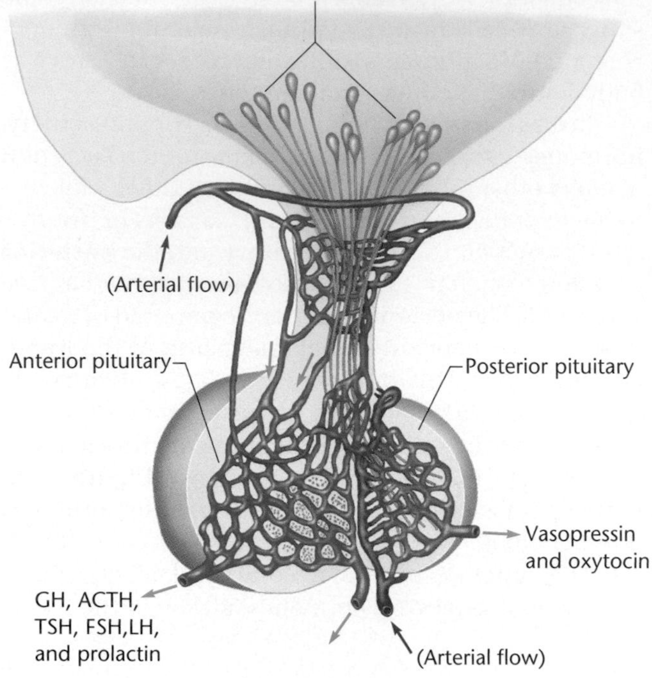

Figure 3.15 Pituitary hormones
The hypothalamus produces vasopressin and oxytocin, which travel to the posterior pituitary (really an extension of the hypothalamus). The posterior pituitary releases those hormones in response to neural signals. The hypothalamus also produces releasing hormones and inhibiting hormones, which travel to the anterior pituitary, where they control the release of six hormones synthesized there.

thalamus controls their release (see Figure 3.15). The hypothalamus secretes **releasing hormones**, which flow through the blood to the anterior pituitary. There they stimulate or inhibit the release of the following hormones:

Adrenocorticotropic hormone (ACTH)	Controls secretions of the adrenal cortex
Thyroid-stimulating hormone (TSH)	Controls secretions of the thyroid gland
Prolactin	Controls secretions of the mammary glands
Somatotropin, also known as growth hormone (GH)	Promotes growth throughout the body
Gonadotropins Follicle-stimulating hormone (FSH) Luteinizing hormone (LH)	Control secretions of the gonads

The hypothalamus maintains fairly constant circulating levels of certain hormones through a negative feedback system. For example, when the level of thyroid hormone is low, the hypothalamus releases *TSH-releasing hormone,* which stimulates the anterior pituitary to release TSH, which in turn causes the thyroid gland to secrete more thyroid hormones (Figure 3.16). For more information about hormones in general, visit this site: **http://www.endo-society.org/**

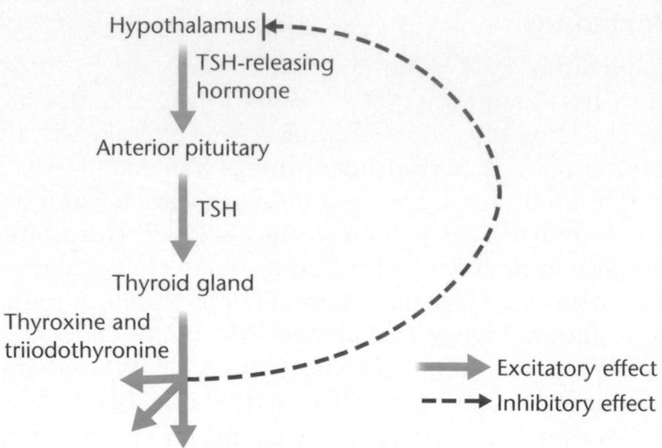

Figure 3.16 Negative feedback in the control of thyroid hormones
The hypothalamus secretes a releasing hormone that stimulates the anterior pituitary to release TSH, which stimulates the thyroid gland to release its hormones. Those hormones in turn act on the hypothalamus to decrease its secretion of the releasing hormone.

7. Which has longer lasting effects, a neurotransmitter or a hormone? Which affects more organs?
8. Which part of the pituitary—anterior or posterior—is neural tissue, similar to the hypothalamus? Which part is glandular tissue and produces hormones that control the secretions by other endocrine organs?

Check your answers on page 68.

Inactivation and Reuptake of Neurotransmitters

A neurotransmitter does not linger at the postsynaptic membrane. If it did, it might continue exciting or inhibiting the receptor. Various neurotransmitters are inactivated in different ways.

After acetylcholine activates a receptor, it is broken down by the enzyme **acetylcholinesterase** (a-SEE-til-ko-lih-NES-teh-raze) into two fragments: acetate and choline. The choline diffuses back to the presynaptic neuron, which takes it up and reconnects it with acetate already in the cell to form acetylcholine again. Although this recycling process is highly efficient, it takes time, and the presynaptic neuron does not reabsorb every molecule it releases. A sufficiently rapid series of action potentials at any synapse can deplete the neurotransmitter faster than the presynaptic cell replenishes it, thus slowing or halting transmission (Liu & Tsien, 1995).

In the absence of acetylcholinesterase, acetylcholine remains and continues stimulating its receptor. Drugs that block acetylcholinesterase can be helpful for people with diseases that impair acetylcholine transmission, such as myasthenia gravis.

Serotonin and the catecholamines (dopamine, norepinephrine, and epinephrine) do not break down into inactive fragments at the postsynaptic membrane but simply detach from the receptor. The presynaptic neuron takes up most of these neurotransmitter molecules intact and reuses them. This process, called **reuptake**, occurs through special membrane proteins called **transporters**. Many of the familiar antidepressant drugs, such as fluoxetine (Prozac), block reuptake and thereby prolong the effects of the neurotransmitter on its receptor. (Chapter 15 discusses antidepressants in more detail.)

Some of the serotonin and catecholamine molecules, either before or after reuptake, are converted into inactive chemicals that cannot stimulate the receptor. The enzymes that convert catecholamine transmitters into inactive chemicals are **COMT** (catechol-o-methyltransferase) and **MAO** (monoamine oxidase), which affects serotonin as well as catecholamines. We return to MAO in the discussion of antidepressant drugs.

The peptide neurotransmitters (or neuromodulators) are neither inactivated nor reabsorbed. They simply diffuse away.

9. What happens to acetylcholine molecules after they stimulate a postsynaptic receptor?
10. What happens to serotonin and catecholamine molecules after they stimulate a postsynaptic receptor?

Check your answers on page 68.

Negative Feedback from the Postsynaptic Cell

Suppose someone had a habit of sending you an e-mail message and then, worried that you might not have received it, sending it again and again. To prevent cluttering your inbox, you might add a system that replied to any message with an automatic reply, "Yes, I got your message; don't send it again."

A couple of mechanisms in the nervous system may serve that function. First, many presynaptic terminals have receptors sensitive to the same transmitter they release. Theoretically, these receptors may act as **autoreceptors**—receptors that detect the amount of transmitter released and inhibit further synthesis and release after it reaches a certain level. That is, they could provide negative feedback. However, the evidence on this point is mixed. For example, we should expect autoreceptors to be more strongly stimulated by repetitive release of the transmitter than by single release, but the data so far have been inconsistent on this point (Kalsner, 2001; Starke, 2001).

Second, some postsynaptic neurons respond to stimulation by releasing special chemicals that travel back to the presynaptic terminal, where they inhibit further release of transmitter. Nitric oxide is apparently one such transmitter. Two others are *anandamide* and *2-AG* (*sn*-2 arachidonylglycerol), both of which bind to the same receptors as marijuana extracts. We shall discuss them further in the next module, when we consider drugs more thoroughly. Here, the point is that neurons apparently have ways to inhibit themselves from excessive release of transmitter.

Synapses and Personality

The nervous system uses, according to current estimates, about 100 neurotransmitters in various areas. Many of the neurotransmitters have multiple kinds of receptors, each with different properties. Why such an abundance of mechanisms? Presumably, each kind of synapse has a specific function in behavior or in the development of the nervous system. If each kind of synapse has its own specific role in behavior, then anyone who has more or less than the normal amount of some neurotransmitter or receptor (for genetic or other reasons) should have some altered behavioral tendencies. That is, theoretically, variations in synapses should have something to do with variations in personality.

In the 1990s, researchers studied variations in dopamine receptors and found that people with one form of the D_2 receptor (one of five types of dopamine receptors) were more likely than others to develop severe alcoholism. Later research suggested that this gene is not specific to alcoholism but instead increases the probability of a variety of pleasure-seeking behaviors, including alcohol consumption, other recreational drug use, overeating, and habitual gambling (K. Blum, Cull, Braverman, & Comings, 1996).

Similarly, researchers studying variations in the D_4 receptor found that people with an alternative form of the receptor tend to have a "novelty-seeking" personality as measured by a standardized personality test (Benjamin et al., 1996; Ebstein et al., 1996; Elovainio, Kivimäki, Viikari, Ekelund, & Keltikangas-Järvinen, 2005; Noble et al., 1998). Novelty seeking consists of being impulsive, exploratory, and quick-tempered. Other studies have linked genes controlling various receptors to anxiety, neurotic personality, and so forth. However, most of the reported effects have been small, or based on small samples, and hard to replicate. For example, of 36 studies examining the role of one gene in anxiety, 12 found the gene significantly linked to increased anxiety, 6 found it linked to decreased anxiety, and 18 found no significant difference (Savitz & Ramesar, 2004).

Although the results so far have been far from convincing, research continues. Personality is a complicated matter, difficult to measure, and no doubt controlled by all of life's experiences as well as a great many genes. Teasing apart the contribution of any one gene will not be easy.

Module 3.2

In Closing: Neurotransmitters and Behavior

In the first module of this chapter, you read how Charles Sherrington began the study of synapses with his observations on dogs. In this module, you read about cellular and molecular processes, based on research with a wide variety of other species. For most of what we know about synapses, species differences are small or nonexistent. The microscopic structure of neuron types and ion channels is virtually the same across species. The neurotransmitters found in humans are the same as those of other species, with very few exceptions. (For example, insects apparently lack the receptors for a couple of peptide transmitters.) Evidently, evolution has been very conservative about neurotransmission. After certain chemicals proved useful for the purpose, newly evolved species have continued using those same chemicals. Therefore, the differences among species, or among individuals within a species, are quantitative. We vary in the number of various kinds of synapses, the amount of release, sensitivity of receptors, and so forth. From those quantitative variations in a few constant principles comes all the rich variation that we see in behavior.

Summary

1. The great majority of synapses operate by transmitting a neurotransmitter from the presynaptic cell to the postsynaptic cell. (p. 58)
2. Many chemicals are used as neurotransmitters. With few exceptions, each neuron releases the same combination of neurotransmitters from all branches of its axon. (p. 59)
3. At certain synapses, a neurotransmitter exerts its effects by attaching to a receptor that opens the gates to allow a particular ion, such as sodium, to cross the membrane more readily. At other synapses, a neurotransmitter may lead to slower but longer lasting changes inside the postsynaptic cell. (p. 62)
4. After a neurotransmitter (other than a peptide) has activated its receptor, many of the transmitter molecules reenter the presynaptic cell through transporter molecules in the membrane. This process, known as reuptake, enables the presynaptic cell to recycle its neurotransmitter. (p. 66)

Answers to STOP & CHECK Questions

1. When Loewi stimulated a nerve that increased or decreased a frog's heart rate, he could withdraw some fluid from the area around the heart, transfer it to another frog's heart, and thereby increase or decrease its rate also. (p. 60)
2. Epinephrine, norepinephrine, and dopamine (p. 60)
3. Many highly active neurons release nitric oxide, which dilates the blood vessels in the area and thereby increases blood flow to the area. (p. 60)
4. Calcium (p. 64)
5. Ionotropic synapses act more quickly and more briefly. (p. 64)
6. At metabotropic synapses, when the neurotransmitter attaches to its receptor, it releases a chemical (the second messenger) within the postsynaptic cell, which alters metabolism or gene expression within the postsynaptic cell. (p. 64)
7. A hormone has longer lasting effects. A hormone can affect many parts of the brain as well as other organs; a neurotransmitter affects only the neurons near its point of release. (p. 66)
8. The posterior pituitary is neural tissue, like the hypothalamus. The anterior pituitary is glandular tissue and produces hormones that control several other endocrine organs. (p. 66)
9. The enzyme acetylcholinesterase breaks acetylcholine molecules into two smaller molecules, acetate and choline, which are then reabsorbed by the presynaptic terminal. (p. 67)

10. Most serotonin and catecholamine molecules are reabsorbed by the presynaptic terminal. Some of their molecules are broken down into inactive chemicals, which then float away in the blood. (p. 67)

Thought Questions

1. Suppose that axon A enters a ganglion (a cluster of neurons) and axon B leaves on the other side. An experimenter who stimulates A can shortly thereafter record an impulse traveling down B. We want to know whether B is just an extension of axon A or whether A formed an excitatory synapse on some neuron in the ganglion, whose axon is axon B. How could an experimenter determine the answer? You should be able to think of more than one good method. Presume that the anatomy within the ganglion is so complex that you cannot simply trace the course of an axon through it.
2. Transmission of visual and auditory information relies largely on ionotropic synapses. Why is ionotropic better than metabotropic for these purposes? For what purposes might metabotropic synapses be better?

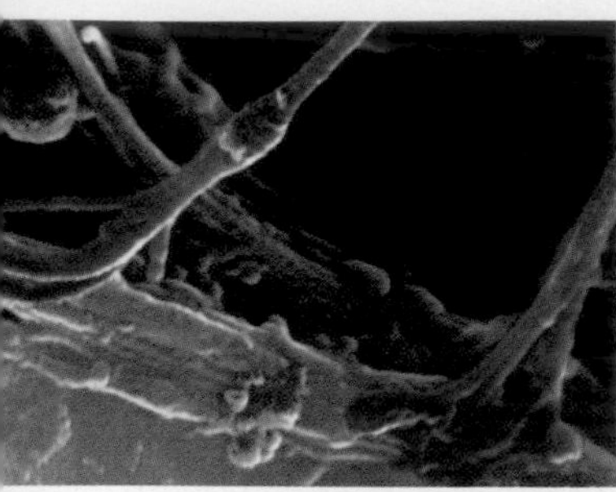

Module 3.3
Drugs and Synapses

Did you know that your brain is constantly making chemicals resembling opiates? It also makes its own marijuana-like chemicals, and it has receptors that respond to cocaine and LSD. Nearly every drug with psychological effects resembles something that the brain makes naturally and takes advantage of mechanisms that evolved to handle normal synaptic transmission. (The exceptions are Novocain and related anesthetic drugs that block sodium channels in the membrane instead of acting at synapses.) By studying the effects of drugs, we learn more about the drugs, of course, but also about synapses. This module deals mainly with abused drugs; later chapters will also discuss antidepressants, antipsychotic drugs, tranquilizers, and other psychiatric medications.

Most of the commonly abused drugs derive from plants. For example, nicotine comes from tobacco, caffeine from coffee, opiates from poppies, cocaine from coca, and tetrahydrocannabinol from marijuana. When we stop to think about it, we should be puzzled that our brains respond to plant chemicals. An explanation is more apparent if we put it the other way: Why do plants produce chemicals that affect our brains?

Part of the answer relates to the surprising fact that, with few exceptions, human neurotransmitters and

Figure 3.17 Effects of some drugs at dopamine synapses
Drugs can alter any stage of synaptic processing, from synthesis of the neurotransmitter through release and reuptake.

hormones are the same as those of other animal species (Cravchik & Goldman, 2000). So if a plant evolves some chemical to attract wasps to its flowers, to deter caterpillars from eating its leaves, or whatever, that chemical is likely to affect humans also.

Another part of the answer is that many of our neurotransmitters are also found in plants. For example, plants not only have glutamate, but they also have ionotropic glutamate receptors chemically similar to our own (Lam et al., 1998). Exactly what these receptors do in plants is uncertain; perhaps they serve for some type of communication within a plant, even though the plant has no nervous system. Evidently, a small number of chemicals are so well suited to conveying information that evolution has had no reason to replace them.

Drug Mechanisms

Drugs can either facilitate or inhibit transmission at synapses. A drug that blocks the effects of a neurotransmitter is called an **antagonist**; a drug that mimics or increases the effects is called an **agonist.** (The term *agonist* is derived from a Greek word meaning "contestant." We derive our term *agony* from the same root. An *antagonist* is an "antiagonist," or member of the opposing team.) A drug that is a *mixed agonist–antagonist* is an agonist for some behavioral effects of the neurotransmitter and an antagonist for others, or an agonist at some doses and an antagonist at others.

Drugs influence synaptic activity in many ways. As in Figure 3.17, which illustrates a dopamine synapse, a drug can increase or decrease the synthesis of the neurotransmitter, cause it to leak from its vesicles, increase its release, decrease its reuptake, block its breakdown into inactive chemicals, or directly stimulate or block the postsynaptic receptors.

Investigators say that a drug has an **affinity** for a particular type of receptor if it binds to that receptor, fitting somewhat like a lock and key. Drugs vary in their affinities from strong to weak. The **efficacy** of a drug is its tendency to activate the receptor. So, for example, a drug that binds tightly to a receptor but fails to stimulate it has a high affinity but a low efficacy.

You may have noticed that the effectiveness and side effects of tranquilizers, antidepressants, and other drugs vary from one person to another. Why? One reason is that most drugs affect several kinds of receptors. People vary in their abundance of each kind of receptor. For example, one person might have a relatively large number of dopamine type D_4 receptors and relatively few D_1 or D_2 receptors, whereas someone else has more D_1, fewer D_4, and so forth. Therefore, a drug with an affinity for dopamine receptors will affect different kinds of dopamine receptors in different people (Cravchik & Goldman, 2000).

1. Is a drug with high affinity and low efficacy an agonist or an antagonist?

Check your answers on page 77.

Common Drugs and Their Synaptic Effects

We categorize drugs based on their predominant action. For example, amphetamine and cocaine are stimulants; opiates are narcotics; LSD is a hallucinogen. Despite their differences, however, nearly all abused drugs directly or indirectly stimulate the release of dopamine, especially in the **nucleus accumbens,** a small subcortical area rich in dopamine receptors (Figure 3.18). Dopamine is in most cases an inhibitory transmitter; however, in the nucleus accumbens, sustained bursts of dopamine inhibit cells that release the inhibitory transmitter GABA. Thus, by inhibiting release of an inhibitor, dopamine has the net effect of exciting the nucleus accumbens (Hjelmstad, 2004).

Stimulant Drugs

Stimulant drugs increase excitement, alertness, and motor activity, while elevating mood. They decrease fatigue. Whereas nearly all drugs elevate dopamine activity in the nucleus accumbens in some way, stimulant drugs do so directly, especially at dopamine receptor types D_2, D_3, and D_4 (R. A. Harris, Brodie, & Dunwiddie, 1992; Wise & Bozarth, 1987).

Because dopamine is in many cases an inhibitory transmitter, drugs that increase activity at dopamine synapses decrease the activity in much of the brain. Figure 3.19 shows the results of a PET scan, which measures relative amounts of activity in various brain areas (London et al., 1990). (PET scans are a method of visualizing brain anatomy, as described in Chapter 4.) How, you might wonder, could drugs that decrease brain activity lead to behavioral arousal? One hypothesis is that high dopamine activity mostly decreases "background noise" in the brain and therefore increases the signal-to-noise ratio (Mattay et al., 1996; Willson, Wilman, Bell, Asghar, & Silverstone, 2004).

Amphetamine stimulates dopamine synapses by increasing the release of dopamine from the presynaptic terminal. The presynaptic terminal ordinarily reabsorbs released dopamine through a protein called the *dopamine transporter.* Amphetamine reverses the transporter, causing the cell to release dopamine instead of reabsorbing it (Giros, Jaber, Jones, Wightman, & Caron, 1996). Amphetamine also blocks certain receptors that inhibit dopamine release, so it enhances dopamine release in at least two ways (Paladini, Fiorillo, Morikawa, & Williams, 2001). However, amphetamine's effects are nonspecific, as it also increases the release of serotonin, norepinephrine, and other transmitters.

Cocaine blocks the reuptake of dopamine, norepinephrine, and serotonin, thus prolonging their effects. Several kinds of evidence indicate that the behavioral effects of cocaine depend mainly on increasing dopamine effects and secondarily on serotonin effects (Rocha et al., 1998; Volkow, Wang, Fischman, et al., 1997). Many of the effects of cocaine resemble those of amphetamine.

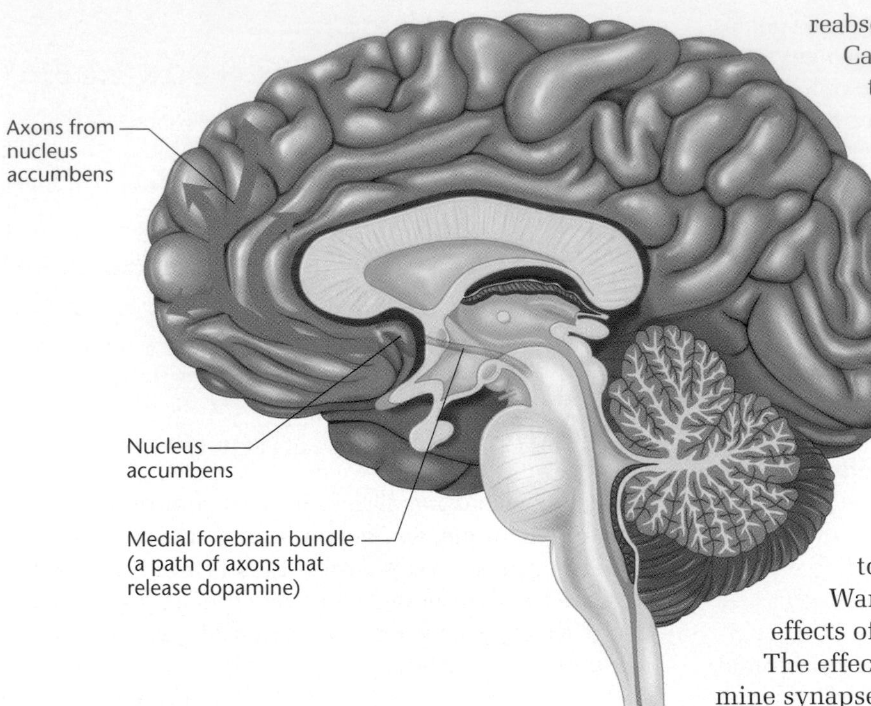

Figure 3.18 Location of the nucleus accumbens in the human brain
Nearly all abused drugs, as well as a variety of other highly reinforcing or addictive activities, increase dopamine release in the nucleus accumbens.

The effects of cocaine and amphetamine on dopamine synapses are intense but short-lived. By increasing the release of dopamine or decreasing its reuptake, the drugs increase the accumulation of dopamine in the synaptic cleft. However, the excess dopamine washes away from the synapse faster than the presynaptic cell can make more to replace it. As a result, a few hours after taking amphetamine or cocaine, a user "crashes" into a more depressed state. These withdrawal symptoms are not powerful like those of heroin, but they are easily noticeable.

Stimulant drugs are known primarily for their short-term effects, but repeated use of high doses can produce long-term problems. Cocaine users suffer lasting changes in brain metabolism and blood flow, thereby increasing their risk of stroke, epilepsy, and memory impairments (Strickland, Miller, Kowell, & Stein, 1998).

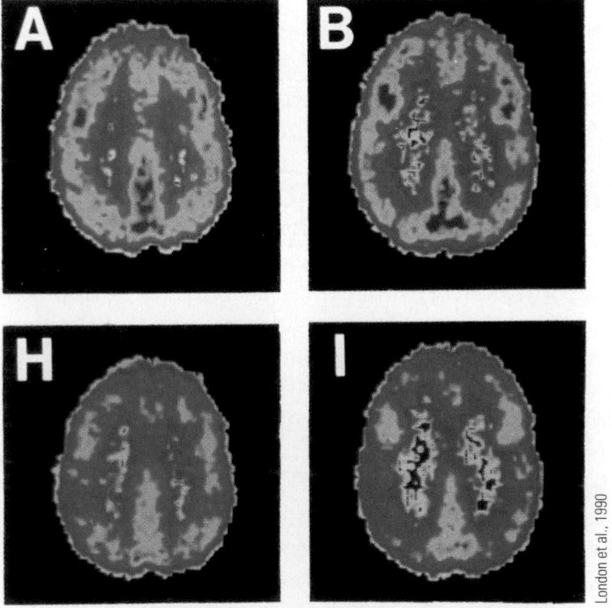

Figure 3.19 Effects of cocaine on the brain
As these positron-emission tomography (PET) scans show, cocaine lowers metabolism and overall activity in most of the brain. Red indicates highest activity, followed by yellow, green, and blue. A and B represent brain activity under normal conditions; H and I show activity after a cocaine injection.

Methylphenidate (Ritalin), another stimulant drug, is often prescribed for people with attention-deficit disorder (ADD), a condition marked by impulsiveness and poor control of attention. Methylphenidate and cocaine block the reuptake of dopamine in the same way at the same brain receptors. The differences between the drugs relate to dose and time course. Drug abusers, of course, use large doses of cocaine, whereas anyone following a physician's directions uses only small amounts of methylphenidate. Furthermore, when people take methylphenidate pills, the drug's concentration in the brain increases gradually over an hour or more and then declines slowly. In contrast, sniffed or injected cocaine produces a rapid rise and fall of effects (Volkow, Wang, & Fowler, 1997; Volkow, Wang, Fowler, et al., 1998). Therefore, methylphenidate does not produce the sudden rush of excitement, the strong withdrawal effects, the cravings, or the addiction that are common with cocaine. Larger amounts of methylphenidate produce effects resembling cocaine's.

Many people wonder whether prolonged use of methylphenidate in childhood makes people more likely to abuse drugs later. According to a review of the few studies conducted on this issue, children who take methylphenidate are *less* likely than others to abuse drugs during adolescence or early adulthood (Wilens, Faraone, Biederman, & Gunawardene, 2003). Of course, the researchers could not randomly assign children to methylphenidate and control conditions. However, experiments with rats point to the same conclusion. For example, experimenters gave young rats moderate doses of methylphenidate and then, months later, gave them cocaine and tested their preference for the room where they received cocaine versus an adjoining room where they had not received it. Compared to other rats, those with early exposure to methylphenidate showed a lower preference for the stimuli associated with cocaine and in some cases an avoidance of them (Andersen, Arvanitogiannis, Pliakas, LeBlanc, & Carlezon, 2002; Carlezon, Mague, & Andersen, 2003; Mague, Andersen, & Carlezon, 2005). Although these studies contradict the worry that early methylphenidate treatment might lead to later drug abuse, prolonged use of methylphenidate leads to other long-term disadvantages, including increased fear responses and a possibly increased risk of depression (Bolaños, Barrot, Berton, Wallace-Black, & Nestler, 2003; Carlezon et al., 2003).

The drug methylenedioxymethamphetamine (MDMA, or "ecstasy") is a stimulant at low doses, increasing the release of dopamine. At higher doses (comparable to the doses people use recreationally), it also increases serotonin release, producing hallucinogenic effects as well. In monkey studies, MDMA not only stimulates axons that release serotonin but also destroys them (McCann, Lowe, & Ricaurte, 1997).

Research on humans is difficult because researchers cannot randomly assign people to MDMA and control groups. Many studies have found that repeated MDMA users, in comparison to nonusers, have more anxiety, depression, sleep problems, memory deficits, attention problems, and impulsiveness, even a year or two after quitting (Montoya, Sorrentino, Lukas, & Price, 2002). Like laboratory animals, humans exposed to MDMA have long-term deficits in serotonin synthesis and release (Parrott, 2001). One study found that repeated MDMA users have thinner cell layers in certain brain areas, as shown in Figure 3.20 (P. M. Thompson et al., 2004). We do not know, of course, how many of the users had behavioral problems or thin cell layers in the brain prior to using MDMA. (Maybe people who already have anxiety, memory problems, and so forth are more likely than others to use MDMA.) Also, some MDMA users abuse other drugs as well. Still, the evidence suggests serious risks associated with this drug.

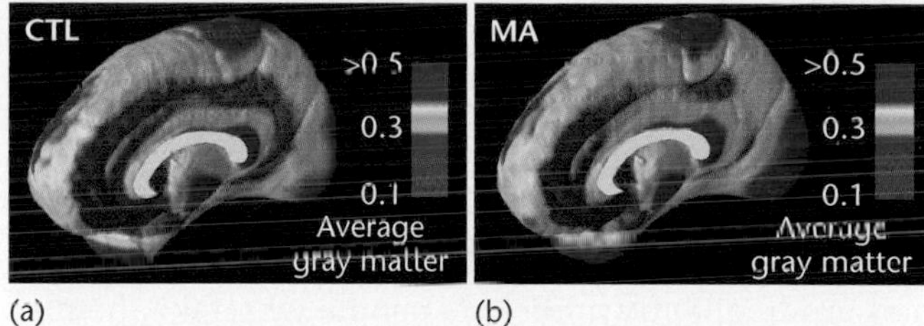

Figure 3.20 Brain thinning in MDMA users
The figure on the left is the average brain scan for 21 adults who had never been substance abusers; the figure on the right is the average of 22 adults who had used MDMA frequently for years. Red represents the thickest area of brain cells, followed by yellow, green, blue, and purple. Note the apparent thinning in certain areas for the MDMA users. *(Source: From "Structural abnormalities in the brains of human subjects who use methamphetamine," by P. M. Thompson et al.,* Journal of Neuroscience, 24. *Copyright 2004 by the Society for Neuroscience. Reprinted with permission.*

STOP & CHECK

2. How does amphetamine influence dopamine synapses?
3. How does cocaine influence dopamine synapses?
4. Why is methylphenidate generally less disruptive to behavior than cocaine is despite the drugs' similar mechanisms?
5. Does cocaine increase or decrease overall brain activity?

Check your answers on page 77.

Nicotine

Nicotine, a compound present in tobacco, has long been known to stimulate one type of acetylcholine receptor, conveniently known as the *nicotinic receptor,* which is found both in the central nervous system and at the nerve-muscle junction of skeletal muscles. Nicotinic receptors are abundant on neurons that release dopamine in the nucleus accumbens, so nicotine increases dopamine release there (Levin & Rose, 1995; Pontieri, Tanda, Orzi, & DiChiara, 1996). In fact, nicotine increases dopamine release in mostly the same cells of the nucleus accumbens that cocaine does (Pich et al., 1997).

One consequence of repeated exposure to nicotine, as demonstrated in rat studies, is that after the end of nicotine use, the nucleus accumbens cells responsible for reinforcement become less responsive than usual (Epping-Jordan, Watkins, Koob, & Markou, 1998). That is, many events, not just nicotine itself, become less reinforcing than they used to be.

Opiates

Opiate drugs are derived from (or similar to those derived from) the opium poppy. Familiar opiates include morphine, heroin, and methadone. Opiates relax people, decrease their attention to real-world problems, and decrease their sensitivity to pain. Although opiates are frequently addictive, people who take them as painkillers under medical supervision almost never abuse them. Addiction is not entirely a product of the drug; it depends on the person, the reasons for taking the drug, the dose, and the social setting.

People used morphine and other opiates for centuries without knowing how the drugs affected the brain. Then Candace Pert and Solomon Snyder found that opiates attach to specific receptors in the brain (Pert & Snyder, 1973). It was a safe guess that vertebrates had not evolved such receptors just to enable us to become drug addicts; the brain must produce its own chemical that attaches to these receptors. Soon investigators found that the brain produces peptides now known as the *endorphins*—a contraction of *endo*genous m*orphines*. This discovery was important because it indicated that opiates relieve pain by acting on receptors in the brain, not just out in the skin or organs where people felt the pain. Also, this discovery paved the way for the discovery of other peptides that regulate emotions and motivations.

Endorphin synapses may contribute directly to certain kinds of reinforcement (Nader, Bechara, Roberts, & van der Kooy, 1994), but they also act indirectly by way of dopamine. Endorphin synapses inhibit ventral tegmental neurons (in the midbrain) that release GABA, a transmitter that inhibits the firing of dopamine neurons (North, 1992). Thus, by inhibiting an inhibitor, the net effect is to increase dopamine release. Endorphins also block the locus coeruleus, a hindbrain area that responds to arousing or stressful stimuli by releasing norepinephrine, which facilitates memory storage. When endorphins or opiate drugs block this area, the result is decreased response to stress and decreased memory storage—two effects common among opiate users (Curtis, Bello, & Valentine, 2001).

STOP & CHECK

6. How does nicotine influence dopamine synapses?
7. How do opiates influence dopamine synapses?

Check your answers on page 77.

Marijuana

The leaves of the marijuana plant contain the chemical **Δ^9-tetrahydrocannabinol (Δ^9-THC)** and other **cannabinoids** (chemicals related to Δ^9-THC). Marijuana has been used medically to relieve pain or nausea, to combat glaucoma (an eye disorder), and to increase appetite. Chemically synthesized and purified THC (under the name *dronabinol*) has been approved for medical use in the United States, although marijuana itself has not—except in California, where state law and federal law are in conflict.

Common psychological effects of marijuana include an intensification of sensory experience and an illusion that time is passing very slowly. Studies have reported significant impairments of memory and cognition, especially in new users and heavy users. (Occasional moderate users develop partial tolerance.) The observed memory impairments in heavy users could mean either that marijuana impairs memory or that people with memory impairments are more likely to use marijuana. However, former users recover normal memory after 4 weeks of abstention from the drug (Pope, Gruber, Hudson, Huestis, & Yurgelun-Todd, 2001). The recovery implies that marijuana impairs memory.

Cannabinoids dissolve in the body's fats and leave slowly. One consequence is that certain behavioral effects can last hours (Howlett et al., 2004) and that traces of marijuana can be detected in the blood or urine for weeks. Another consequence is that quitting marijuana does not produce sudden withdrawal symptoms like those of opiates. Heavy marijuana smokers who abstain do report a moderate amount of irritability, restlessness, anxiety, depression, stomach pain, sleep difficulties, craving for marijuana, and loss of appetite (Budney, Hughes, Moore, & Novy, 2001).

Investigators could not explain the effects of marijuana on the brain until 1988, when researchers finally found the brain's cannabinoid receptors (Devane, Dysarz, Johnson, Melvin, & Howlett, 1988). These receptors are widespread in the animal kingdom, having been reported in every species tested so far, except for insects (McPartland, DiMarzo, de Petrocellis, Mercer, & Glass, 2001). Cannabinoid receptors are among the most abundant receptors in the mammalian brain, especially in the hippocampus, the basal ganglia, the cerebellum, and parts of the cerebral cortex (Herkenham, 1992; Herkenham, Lynn, de Costa, & Richfield, 1991). However, they are sparse in the medulla and the rest of the brainstem. That near absence is significant because the medulla includes the neurons that control breathing and heartbeat. Because marijuana has little effect on heartbeat or breathing, it poses almost no risk of a fatal overdose. Marijuana does produce other health hazards, including an increased risk of lung cancer (Zhu et al., 2000).

Just as the discovery of opiate receptors in the brain led to finding the brain's endogenous opiates, investigators searched for a brain chemical that binds to cannabinoid receptors. They found two such chemicals—

anandamide (from the Sanskrit word *ananda,* meaning "bliss") (Calignano, LaRana, Giuffrida, & Piomelli, 1998; DiMarzo et al., 1994) and the more abundant *sn*-2 arachidonylglycerol, abbreviated **2-AG** (Stella, Schweitzer, & Piomelli, 1997). The cannabinoid receptors are peculiar in being located on the *pre*synaptic neuron, not the postsynaptic one. When glutamate depolarizes the postsynaptic neuron, the postsynaptic neuron releases anandamide or 2-AG, which travels back to the presynaptic neuron, temporarily decreasing transmitter release (Kreitzer & Regehr, 2001; R. I. Wilson & Nicoll, 2002). Cannabinoids also diffuse to inhibit the release of GABA from other nearby neurons (Galante & Diana, 2004). That is, cannabinoids put the brakes on the release of both glutamate, which is excitatory, and GABA, which is inhibitory (Kreitzer & Regehr, 2001; Ohno-Shosaku, Maejima, & Kano, 2001; R. I. Wilson & Nicoll, 2001). In some cases, the result is decreased release of transmitter in a fairly wide area (Kreitzer, Carter, & Regehr, 2002).

The functions of cannabinoids are partly known, partly unknown. After a rapid burst of glutamate release, cannabinoids feed back to retard further glutamate release (the negative feedback discussed on page 67). Excessive glutamate stimulation can be harmful, even fatal, to a postsynaptic cell, so halting it is clearly helpful (Marsicano et al., 2003). The value of blocking GABA is less obvious but may be related to the formation of memories (Chevaleyre & Castillo, 2004; Gerdeman, Ronesi, & Lovinger, 2002).

Marijuana stimulates cannabinoid receptors at times when they would not ordinarily receive stimulation. In effect, they give glutamate-releasing neurons the message, "I already received your message" before the message is sent, shutting down the normal flow of information. Why are these effects pleasant or habit forming? Actually, of course, not all of the effects of marijuana are pleasant. But remember that virtually all abused drugs increase the release of dopamine in the nucleus accumbens. Cannabinoids do so indirectly. One place in which they inhibit GABA release is the ventral tegmental area of the midbrain, a major source of axons that release dopamine in the nucleus accumbens. When cannabinoids inhibit GABA there, the result is less inhibition (therefore increased activity) of the neurons that release dopamine in the nucleus accumbens (Cheer, Wassu, Heien, Phillips, & Wightman, 2004).

Researchers have tried to explain some of marijuana's other behavioral effects. Cannabinoids relieve nausea by inhibiting serotonin type 3 synapses (5-HT_3), which are known to be important for nausea (Fan, 1995). Cannabinoid receptors are abundant in areas of the hypothalamus that influence feeding, and mice lacking these receptors show decreased appetite under some circumstances (DiMarzo et al., 2001). Presumably, excess cannabinoid activity would produce extra appetite.

The report that "time passes more slowly" under marijuana's influences is harder to explain, but whatever the cause, we can demonstrate it in rats as well: Consider a rat that has learned to press a lever for food on a fixed-interval schedule, where just the first press of any 30-second period produces food. With practice, a rat learns to wait after each press before it starts pressing again. Under the influence of marijuana, rats press sooner after each reinforcer. For example, instead of waiting 20 seconds, a rat might wait only 10 or 15. Evidently, the 10 or 15 seconds *felt like* 20 seconds; time was passing more slowly (Han & Robinson, 2001).

Hallucinogenic Drugs

Drugs that distort perception are called **hallucinogenic drugs.** Many hallucinogenic drugs, such as lysergic acid diethylamide (LSD), chemically resemble serotonin (Figure 3.21) and stimulate serotonin type 2A (5-HT_{2A}) receptors at inappropriate times or for longer than usual durations. You could compare this effect to a key that almost fits a lock, so that when you get it in, it's hard to get it out. (The analogy is not perfect, but it conveys the general idea.)

HO— —$CH_2CH_2NH_2$ N H **Serotonin**

O=C—$N(C_2H_5)_2$ NCH_3 N H **LSD**

Figure 3.21 Resemblance of the neurotransmitter serotonin to LSD, a hallucinogenic drug

Note that we understand the chemistry better than the psychology. LSD exerts its effects at 5-HT_{2A} receptors, but *why* do effects at those receptors produce hallucinations? Table 3.3 summarizes the effects of some commonly abused drugs.

STOP & CHECK

8. What are the effects of cannabinoids on neurons?

9. If incoming serotonin axons were destroyed, LSD would still have its normal effects on the postsynaptic cell. However, if incoming dopamine and norepinephrine axons were destroyed, amphetamine and cocaine would have no effects. Explain the difference.

Check your answers on page 77.

Table 3.3 Summary of Some Drugs and Their Effects

Drugs	Main Behavioral Effects	Main Synaptic Effects
Amphetamine	Excitement, alertness, elevated mood, decreased fatigue	Increases release of dopamine and several other transmitters
Cocaine	Excitement, alertness, elevated mood, decreased fatigue	Blocks reuptake of dopamine and several other transmitters
Methylphenidate (Ritalin)	Increased concentration	Blocks reuptake of dopamine and others, but gradually
MDMA ("ecstasy")	Low dose: stimulant Higher dose: sensory distortions	Releases dopamine Releases serotonin, damages axons containing serotonin
Nicotine	Mostly stimulant effects	Stimulates nicotinic-type acetylcholine receptor, which (among other effects) increases dopamine release in nucleus accumbens
Opiates	Relaxation, withdrawal, decreased pain	Stimulates endorphin (e.g., heroin, morphine) receptors
Cannabinoids (marijuana)	Altered sensory experiences, decreased pain and nausea, increased appetite	Excites negative-feedback receptors on presynaptic cells; those receptors ordinarily respond to anandamide and 2AG
Hallucinogens (e.g., LSD)	Distorted sensations	Stimulates serotonin type 2A receptors (5-HT_{2A})

Module 3.3
In Closing: Drugs and Behavior

Suppose while several people are communicating by e-mail or instant messaging, we arrange for the computers to delete certain letters or words and add others in their place. The result would be garbled communication, but sometimes it might be entertaining. Abused drugs are analogous: They distort the brain's communication, blocking some messages, magnifying others, and substituting one message for another. The result can be pleasant or entertaining at times, although also troublesome.

In studying the effects of drugs, researchers have gained clues that may help combat drug abuse, as we shall consider in Chapter 15. They have also learned much about synapses. For example, the research on cocaine called attention to the importance of reuptake transporters, and the research on cannabinoids led to increased understanding of the retrograde signaling from postsynaptic cells to presynaptic cells.

However, from the standpoint of understanding the physiology of behavior, much remains to be learned. For example, research has identified dopamine activity in the nucleus accumbens as central to reinforcement and addiction, but . . . well, *why* is dopamine activity in that location reinforcing? Stimulation of 5-HT_{2A} receptors produces hallucinations, but again we ask, "Why?" In neuroscience or biological psychology, answering one question leads to new ones, and the deepest questions are usually the most difficult.

Summary

1. A drug that increases activity at a synapse is an agonist; one that decreases activity is an antagonist. Drugs act in many ways, varying in their affinity (tendency to bind to a receptor) and efficacy (tendency to activate it). (p. 71)
2. Nearly all abused drugs, as well as many other highly reinforcing experiences, increase the release of dopamine in the nucleus accumbens. (p. 71)
3. Amphetamine increases the release of dopamine. Cocaine and methylphenidate act by blocking the reuptake transporters and therefore decreasing the reuptake of dopamine and serotonin after their release. (p. 71)
4. Nicotine excites acetylcholine receptors, including the ones on axon terminals that release dopamine in the nucleus accumbens. (p. 73)
5. Opiate drugs stimulate endorphin receptors, which inhibit the release of GABA, which would otherwise inhibit the release of dopamine. Thus, the net effect of opiates is increased dopamine release. (p. 74)
6. At certain synapses in many brain areas, after glutamate excites the postsynaptic cell, the cell responds by releasing endocannabinoids, which inhibit further release of both glutamate and GABA by nearby neurons. Chemicals in marijuana mimic the effects of these endocannabinoids. (p. 74)
7. Hallucinogens act by stimulating certain kinds of serotonin receptors. (p. 75)

Answers to STOP & CHECK Questions

1. Such a drug is therefore an antagonist because, by occupying the receptor, it prevents the normal effects of the transmitter. (p. 71)
2. Amphetamine causes the dopamine transporter to release dopamine instead of reabsorbing it. (p. 73)
3. Cocaine interferes with reuptake of released dopamine. (p. 73)
4. The effects of a methylphenidate pill develop and decline in the brain much more slowly than do those of cocaine. (p. 73)
5. Cocaine decreases total activity in the brain because it stimulates activity of dopamine, which is an inhibitory transmitter in many cases. (p. 73)
6. Nicotine excites acetylcholine receptors on neurons that release dopamine and thereby increases dopamine release. (p. 74)
7. Opiates stimulate endorphin synapses, which inhibit GABA synapses on certain cells that release dopamine. By inhibiting an inhibitor, opiates increase the release of dopamine. (p. 74)
8. Cannabinoids released by the postsynaptic neuron attach to receptors on presynaptic neurons, where they inhibit further release of glutamate as well as GABA. (p. 75)
9. Amphetamine acts by releasing norepinephrine and dopamine from the presynaptic neurons. If those neurons are damaged, amphetamine is ineffective. In contrast, LSD directly stimulates the receptor on the postsynaptic membrane. (p. 75)

Thought Question

1. People who take methylphenidate (Ritalin) for control of attention-deficit disorder often report that, although the drug increases their arousal for a while, they feel a decrease in alertness and arousal a few hours later. Explain.

Chapter Ending

Key Terms and Activities

Terms

acetylcholine (p. 60)
acetylcholinesterase (p. 66)
affinity (p. 71)
2-AG (p. 75)
agonist (p. 71)
amino acids (p. 60)
amphetamine (p. 71)
anandamide (p. 75)
antagonist (p. 71)
anterior pituitary (p. 65)
autoreceptors (p. 67)
cannabinoids (p. 74)
catecholamine (p. 60)
cocaine (p. 72)
COMT (p. 67)
Δ^9-tetrahydrocannabinol (Δ^9-THC) (p. 74)
efficacy (p. 71)
endocrine glands (p. 65)
excitatory postsynaptic potential (EPSP) (p. 53)
exocytosis (p. 61)
G-protein (p. 62)
hallucinogenic drugs (p. 75)
hormone (p. 65)
inhibitory postsynaptic potential (IPSP) (p. 55)
ionotropic effect (p. 62)
MAO (p. 67)
metabotropic effect (p. 62)
methylphenidate (p. 72)
monoamines (p. 60)
neuromodulator (p. 64)
neurotransmitter (p. 59)
nicotine (p. 73)
nitric oxide (p. 60)
nucleus accumbens (p. 71)
opiate drugs (p. 74)
oxytocin (p. 65)
peptide (p. 60)
peptide hormone (p. 65)
pituitary gland (p. 65)
posterior pituitary (p. 65)
postsynaptic neuron (p. 53)
presynaptic neuron (p. 53)
protein hormone (p. 65)
purines (p. 60)
reflex (p. 52)
reflex arc (p. 52)
releasing hormone (p. 66)
reuptake (p. 67)
second messenger (p. 63)
spatial summation (p. 53)
spontaneous firing rate (p. 56)
stimulant drugs (p. 71)
synapse (p. 52)
temporal summation (p. 53)
transporter (p. 67)
vasopressin (p. 65)
vesicle (p. 61)

Suggestions for Further Reading

Cowan, W. M., Südhof, T. C., & Stevens, C. F. (2001). *Synapses.* Baltimore, MD: Johns Hopkins University Press. If you are curious about some detailed aspect of synapses, this is a good reference book to check for an answer.

McKim, W. A. (2003). *Drugs and behavior* (5th ed.). Upper Saddle River, NJ: Prentice Hall. Concise, informative text on drugs and drug abuse.

Websites to Explore

You can go to the Biological Psychology Study Center and click these links. While there, you can also check for suggested articles available on InfoTrac College Edition. The Biological Psychology Internet address is:

http://psychology.wadsworth.com/book/kalatbiopsych9e/

Exploring Biological Psychology CD

Postsynaptic Potentials (animation)
Release of Neurotransmitter (animation)
Cholinergic Synapse (animation)
Release of ACh (animation)
AChE Inactivates ACh (animation)
AChE Inhibitors
Opiate Narcotics (animation)
Critical Thinking (essay questions)
Chapter Quiz (multiple-choice questions)

ThomsonNOW™

http://www.thomsonedu.com

Go to this site for the link to ThomsonNOW, your one-stop study shop, Take a Pre-Test for this chapter, and ThomsonNOW will generate a Personalized Study Plan based on your test results. The Study Plan will identify the topics you need to review and direct you to online resources to help you master these topics. You can then take a Post-Test to help you determine the concepts you have mastered and what you still need work on.

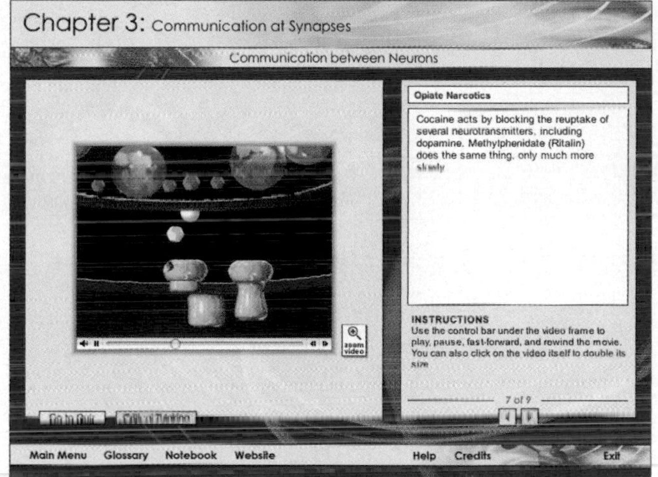

This animation shows how a drug can block reuptake of a neurotransmitter. You can find this animation in Chapter 3 on the CD.

Anatomy of the Nervous System

4

Chapter Outline

Opposite: New methods allow researchers to examine living brains. *Source: Peter Beck/CORBIS*

Main Ideas

1. Each part of the nervous system has specialized functions, and the parts work together to produce behavior. Damage to different areas results in different types of behavioral deficits.
2. The cerebral cortex, the largest structure in the mammalian brain, elaborately processes sensory information and provides for fine control of movement.
3. As research has identified the different functions of different brain areas, a difficult question has arisen: How do the areas work together to produce unified experience and behavior?
4. It is difficult to conduct research on the functions of the nervous system. Conclusions must come from multiple methods and careful behavioral measurements.

Trying to learn **neuroanatomy** (the anatomy of the nervous system) from a book is like trying to learn geography from a road map. A map can tell you that Mystic, Georgia, is about 40 km north of Enigma, Georgia. Similarly, a book can tell you that the habenula is about 4.6 mm from the interpeduncular nucleus in a rat's brain (slightly farther in a human brain). But these little gems of information will seem both mysterious and enigmatic unless you are concerned with that part of Georgia or that area of the brain.

This chapter does not provide a detailed road map of the nervous system. It is more like a world globe, describing the large, basic structures (analogous to the continents) and some distinctive features of each.

The first module introduces key neuroanatomical terms and outlines overall structures of the nervous system. In the second module, we concentrate on the structures and functions of the cerebral cortex, the largest part of the mammalian central nervous system. The third module deals with the main methods that researchers use to discover the behavioral functions of different brain areas.

Be prepared: This chapter contains a huge number of new terms. You should not expect to memorize all of them at once, and it will pay to review this chapter repeatedly.

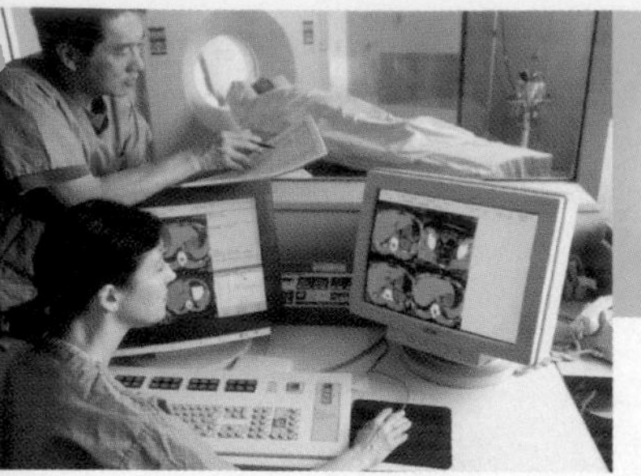

Module 4.1
Structure of the Vertebrate Nervous System

Your nervous system consists of many substructures, each of them including many neurons, each of which receives and makes many synapses. How do all those little parts work together to make one behaving unit? Does each neuron have an independent function so that, for example, one cell recognizes your grandmother, another controls your desire for pizzas, and another makes you smile at babies? Or does the brain operate as an undifferentiated whole, with each part doing the same thing as every other part?

The answer is "something in between those extremes." Individual neurons do have specialized functions, but the activity of a single cell by itself has no more meaning than the letter *h* has out of context. In some ways, neurons are like the people who compose a complex society: Each person has a specialized job, but few of us could do our jobs without the collaboration of a huge number of other people. Also, when various individuals become injured or otherwise unable to perform their jobs, other people change what they are doing to adjust. So we have neither complete specialization nor complete lack of specialization.

Terminology That Describes the Nervous System

Vertebrates have a central nervous system and a peripheral nervous system, which are of course connected (Figure 4.1). The **central nervous system (CNS)** is the brain and the spinal cord, each of which includes a great many substructures. The **peripheral nervous system (PNS)**—the nerves outside the brain and spinal

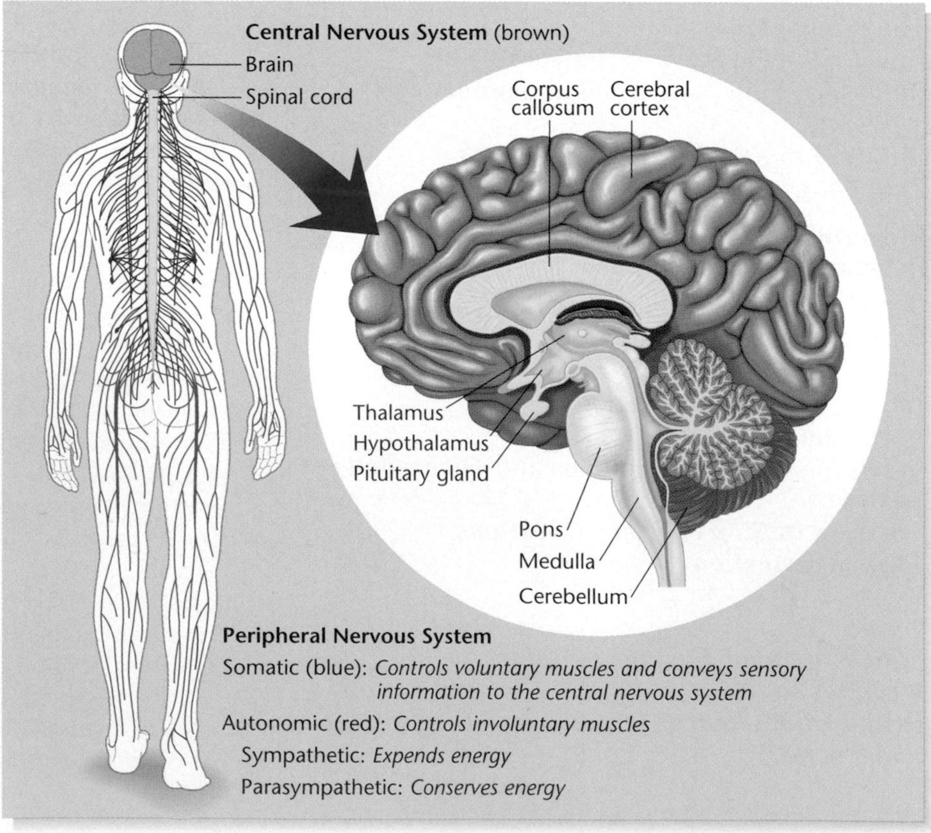

Figure 4.1 The human nervous system
Both the central nervous system and the peripheral nervous system have major subdivisions. The closeup of the brain shows the right hemisphere as seen from the midline.

Table 4.1 Anatomical Terms Referring to Directions

Term	Definition	Term	Definition
Dorsal	Toward the back, away from the ventral (stomach) side. The top of the brain is considered dorsal because it has that position in four-legged animals.	Proximal	Located close (approximate) to the point of origin or attachment
		Distal	Located more distant from the point of origin or attachment
Ventral	Toward the stomach, away from the dorsal (back) side	Ipsilateral	On the same side of the body (e.g., two parts on the left or two on the right)
Anterior	Toward the front end	Contralateral	On the opposite side of the body (one on the left and one on the right)
Posterior	Toward the rear end		
Superior	Above another part	Coronal plane (or frontal plane)	A plane that shows brain structures as seen from the front
Inferior	Below another part		
Lateral	Toward the side, away from the midline	Sagittal plane	A plane that shows brain structures as seen from the side
Medial	Toward the midline, away from the side	Horizontal plane (or transverse plane)	A plane that shows brain structures as seen from above

cord—has two divisions: The **somatic nervous system** consists of the nerves that convey messages from the sense organs to the CNS and from the CNS to the muscles. The **autonomic nervous system** controls the heart, the intestines, and other organs.

To follow a road map, you first must understand the terms *north, south, east,* and *west.* Because the nervous system is a complex three-dimensional structure, we need more terms to describe it. As Figure 4.2 and Table 4.1 indicate, **dorsal** means toward the back and **ventral** means toward the stomach. (One way to remember these terms is that a *ventri*loquist is literally a "stomach talker.") In a four-legged animal, the top of the brain (with respect to gravity) is dorsal (on the same side as the animal's back), and the bottom of the brain is ventral (on the stomach side).

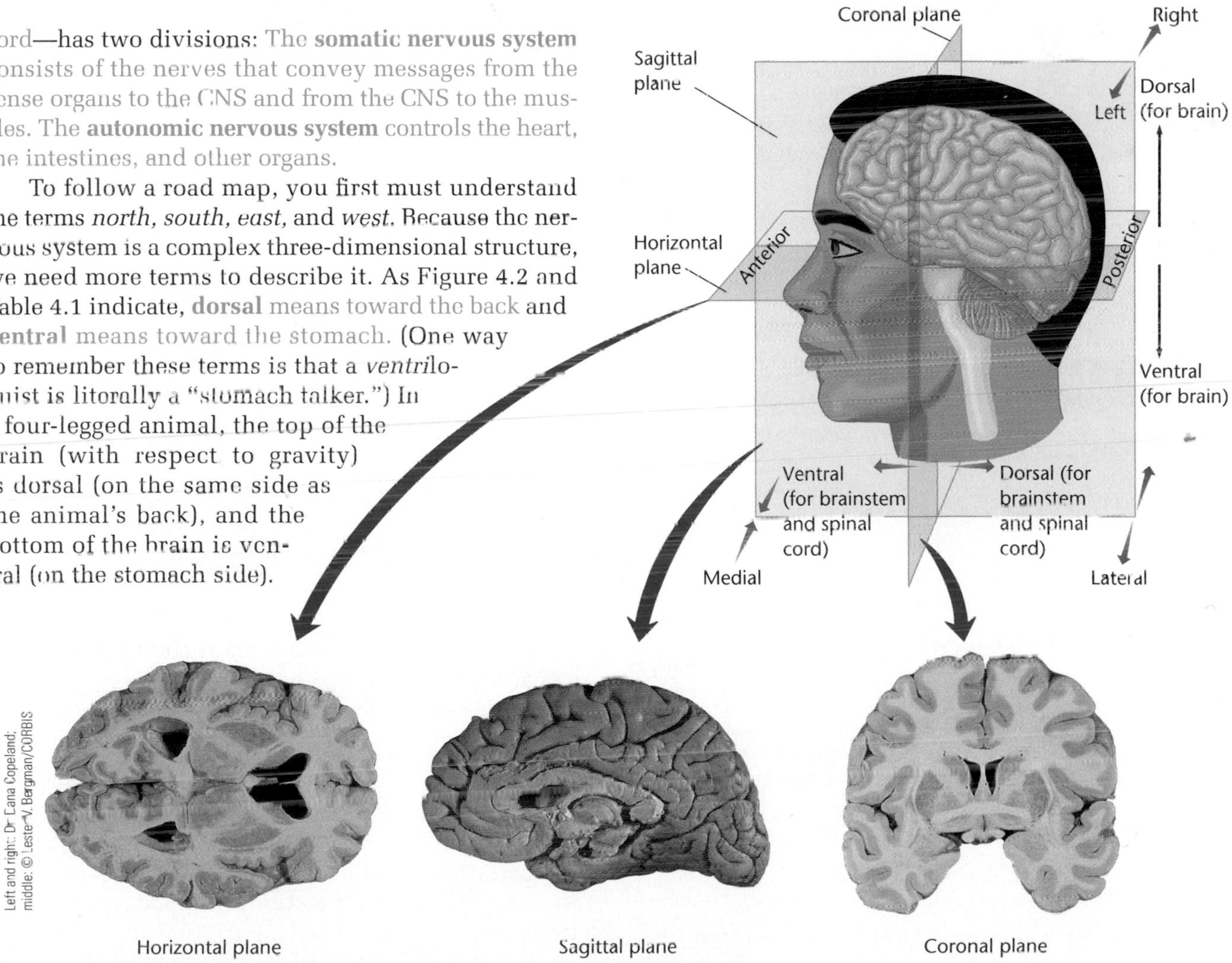

Figure 4.2 Terms for anatomical directions in the nervous system
In four-legged animals, dorsal and ventral point in the same direction for the head as they do for the rest of the body. However, humans' upright posture has tilted the head, so the dorsal and ventral directions of the head are not parallel to those of the spinal cord.

When humans evolved an upright posture, the position of our head changed relative to the spinal cord. For convenience, we still apply the terms *dorsal* and *ventral* to the same parts of the human brain as other vertebrate brains. Consequently, the dorsal–ventral axis of the human brain is at a right angle to the dorsal–ventral axis of the spinal cord. If you picture a person in a crawling position with all four limbs on the ground but nose pointing forward, the dorsal and ventral positions of the brain become parallel to those of the spinal cord.

Table 4.2 introduces additional terminology. Such technical terms may seem confusing at first, but they help investigators communicate unambiguously. Tables 4.1 and 4.2 require careful study and review. After studying the terms, check yourself with the following.

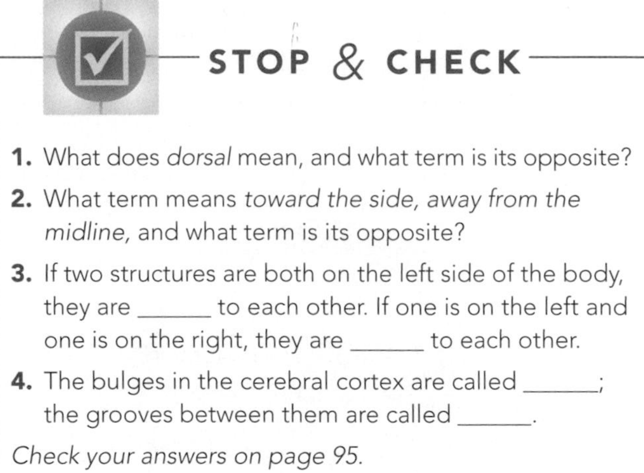

STOP & CHECK

1. What does *dorsal* mean, and what term is its opposite?
2. What term means *toward the side, away from the midline,* and what term is its opposite?
3. If two structures are both on the left side of the body, they are ______ to each other. If one is on the left and one is on the right, they are ______ to each other.
4. The bulges in the cerebral cortex are called ______; the grooves between them are called ______.

Check your answers on page 95.

Table 4.2 Terms Referring to Parts of the Nervous System

Term	Definition
Lamina	A row or layer of cell bodies separated from other cell bodies by a layer of axons and dendrites
Column	A set of cells perpendicular to the surface of the cortex, with similar properties
Tract	A set of axons within the CNS, also known as a *projection.* If axons extend from cell bodies in structure A to synapses onto B, we say that the fibers "project" from A onto B.
Nerve	A set of axons in the periphery, either from the CNS to a muscle or gland or from a sensory organ to the CNS
Nucleus	A cluster of neuron cell bodies within the CNS
Ganglion	A cluster of neuron cell bodies, usually outside the CNS (as in the sympathetic nervous system)
Gyrus (pl.: gyri)	A protuberance on the surface of the brain
Sulcus (pl.: sulci)	A fold or groove that separates one gyrus from another
Fissure	A long, deep sulcus

The Spinal Cord

The **spinal cord** is the part of the CNS found within the spinal column; the spinal cord communicates with the sense organs and muscles below the level of the head. It is a segmented structure, and each segment has on each side both a sensory nerve and a motor nerve, as shown in Figure 4.3. According to the **Bell-Magendie law,** which was one of the first discoveries about the functions of the nervous system, the entering dorsal roots (axon bundles) carry sensory information and the exiting ventral roots carry motor information. The axons to and from the skin and muscles are the peripheral nervous system. The cell bodies of the sensory neurons are located in clusters of neurons outside the spinal cord, called the **dorsal root ganglia.** (*Ganglia* is the plural of *ganglion,* a cluster of neurons. In most cases, a neuron cluster outside the central nervous system is called a ganglion, and a cluster inside the CNS is called a nucleus.) Cell bodies of the motor neurons are inside the spinal cord.

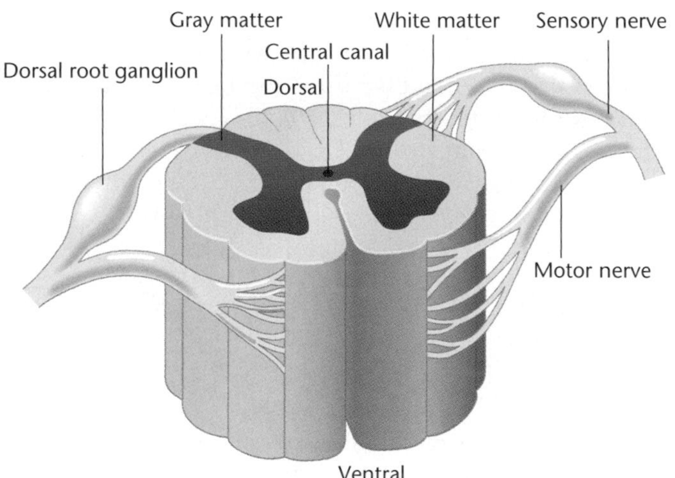

Figure 4.3 Diagram of a cross-section through the spinal cord
The dorsal root on each side conveys sensory information to the spinal cord; the ventral root conveys motor commands to the muscles.

In the cross-section through the spinal cord shown in Figures 4.4 and 4.5, the H-shaped **gray matter** in the center of the cord is densely packed with cell bodies and dendrites. Many neurons of the spinal cord send axons from the gray matter toward the brain or to other parts of the spinal cord through the **white matter,** which is composed mostly of myelinated axons.

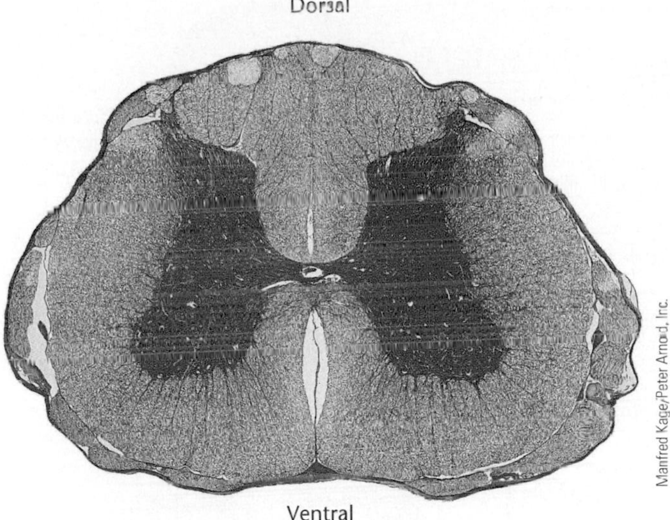

Figure 4.4 Photo of a cross-section through the spinal cord
The H-shaped structure in the center is gray matter, composed largely of cell bodies. The surrounding white matter consists of axons. The axons are organized in tracts; some carry information from the brain and higher levels of the spinal cord downward, while others carry information from lower levels upward.

Each segment of the spinal cord sends sensory information to the brain and receives motor commands from the brain. All that information passes through tracts of axons in the spinal cord. If the spinal cord is cut at a given segment, the brain loses sensation from that segment and all segments below it; the brain also loses motor control over all parts of the body served by that segment and the lower ones.

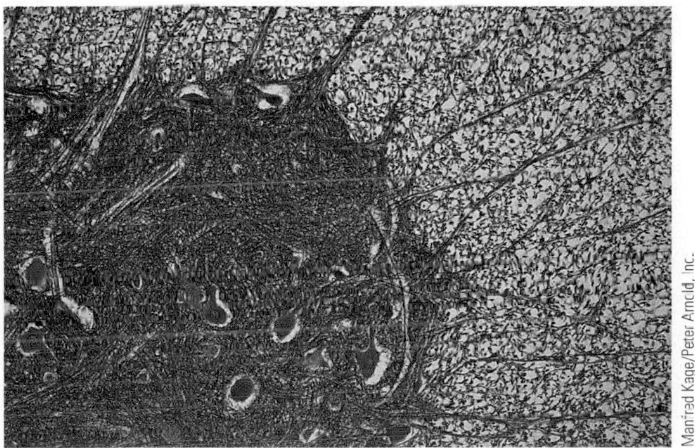

Figure 4.5 A section of gray matter of the spinal cord (lower left) and white matter surrounding it
Cell bodies and dendrites reside entirely in the gray matter. Axons travel from one area of gray matter to another in the white matter.

The Autonomic Nervous System

The autonomic nervous system consists of neurons that receive information from and send commands to the heart, intestines, and other organs. It is comprised of two parts: the sympathetic and parasympathetic nervous systems (Figure 4.6). The **sympathetic nervous system**, a network of nerves that prepare the organs for vigorous activity, consists of two paired chains of ganglia lying just to the left and right of the spinal cord in its central regions (the thoracic and lumbar areas) and connected by axons to the spinal cord. Sympathetic axons extend from the ganglia to the organs and activate them for "fight or flight"—increasing breathing and heart rate and decreasing digestive activity. Because all of the sympathetic ganglia are closely linked, they often act as a single system "in sympathy" with one another, although some parts can be more active than the others. The sweat glands, the adrenal glands, the muscles that constrict blood vessels, and the muscles that erect the hairs of the skin have only sympathetic, not parasympathetic, input.

EXTENSIONS AND APPLICATIONS
Goose Bumps

Erection of the hairs, known as "goose bumps" or "goose flesh," occurs when we are cold. What does it have to do with the fight-or-flight functions associated with the sympathetic nervous system? Part of the answer is that we also get goose bumps when we are frightened. You have heard the expression, "I was so frightened my hairs stood on end." You may also have seen a frightened cat erect its fur. Human body hairs are so short that erecting them accomplishes nothing, but a cat with erect fur looks bigger and potentially frightening. A frightened porcupine erects its quills, which are just modified hairs (Richter & Langworthy, 1933). The behavior that makes the quills so useful, their erection in response to fear, evidently evolved before the quills themselves did.

The **parasympathetic nervous system** facilitates vegetative, nonemergency responses by the organs. The term *para* means "beside" or "related to," and parasympathetic activities are related to, and generally the opposite of, sympathetic activities. For example, the sympathetic nervous system increases heart rate; the parasympathetic nervous system decreases it. The parasympathetic nervous system increases digestive activity; the sympathetic nervous system decreases it. Although the sympathetic and parasympa-

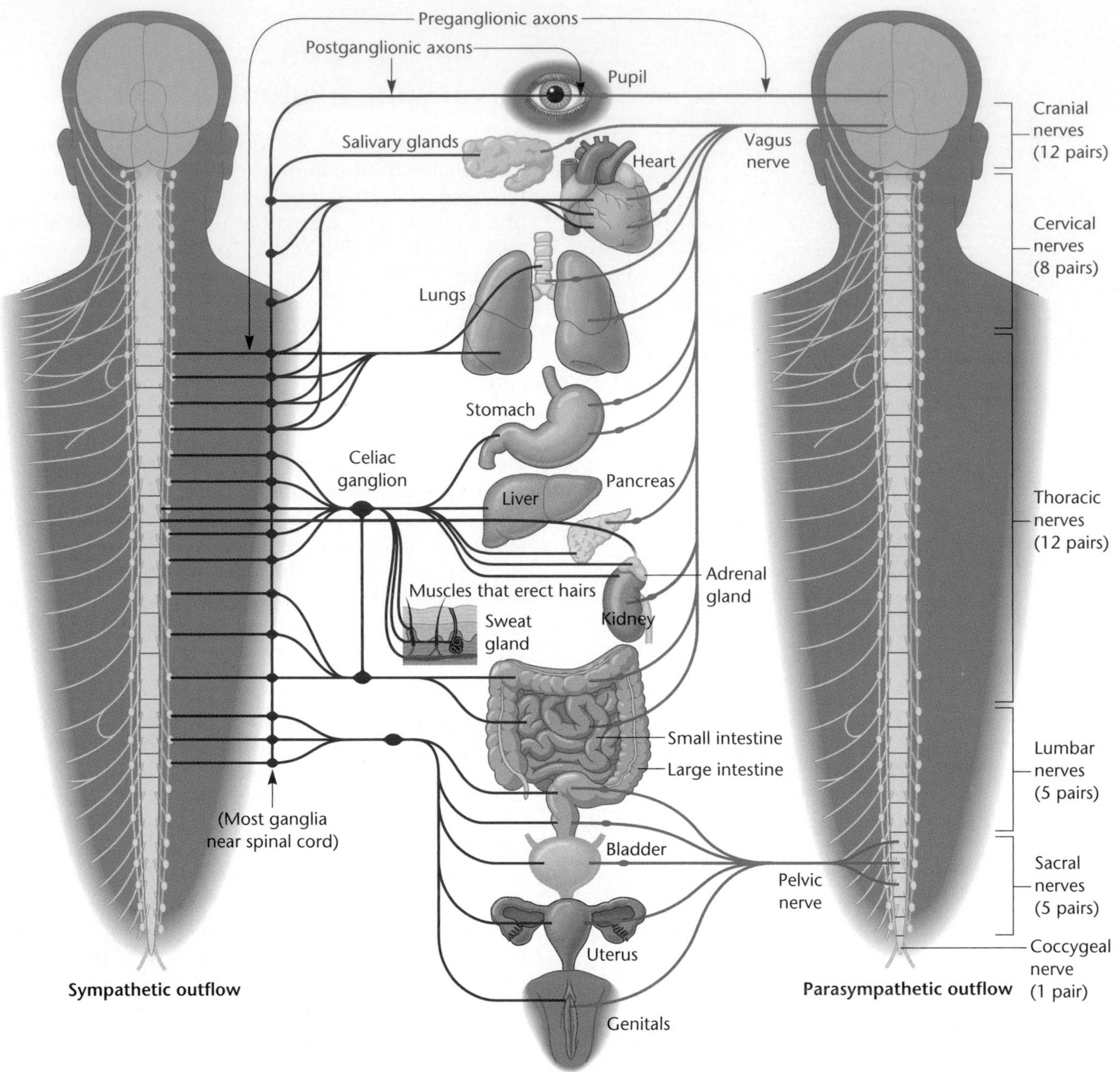

Figure 4.6 The sympathetic nervous system (red lines) and parasympathetic nervous system (blue lines)

Note that the adrenal glands and hair erector muscles receive sympathetic input only.

(Source: Adapted from Biology: The Unity and Diversity, *5th Edition, by C. Starr and R. Taggart, p. 340. Copyright © 1989 Wadsworth.)*

thetic systems act in opposition to one another, both are constantly active to varying degrees, and many stimuli arouse parts of both systems.

The parasympathetic nervous system is also known as the craniosacral system because it consists of the cranial nerves and nerves from the sacral spinal cord (see Figure 4.6). Unlike the ganglia in the sympathetic system, the parasympathetic ganglia are not arranged in a chain near the spinal cord. Rather, long *preganglionic* axons extend from the spinal cord to parasympathetic ganglia close to each internal organ; shorter *postganglionic* fibers then extend from the parasympathetic ganglia into the organs themselves. Because the parasympathetic ganglia are not linked to one another, they act somewhat more independently than the sympathetic ganglia do. Parasympathetic activity decreases heart rate, increases digestive rate, and in general, promotes energy-conserving, nonemergency functions.

The parasympathetic nervous system's postganglionic axons release the neurotransmitter acetylcholine. Most of the postganglionic synapses of the sympathetic nervous system use norepinephrine, although a few, including those that control the sweat glands, use acetylcholine. Because the two systems use different transmitters, certain drugs may excite or inhibit one system or the other. For example, over-the-counter cold remedies exert most of their effects either by blocking parasympathetic activity or by increasing sympathetic activity. This action is useful because the flow of sinus fluids is a parasympathetic response; thus, drugs that block the parasympathetic system inhibit sinus flow. The common side effects of cold remedies also stem from their sympathetic, antiparasympathetic activities: They inhibit salivation and digestion and increase heart rate. For additional detail about the autonomic nervous system, visit this website: **http://www.ndrf.org/ans.htm**

5. Sensory nerves enter which side of the spinal cord, dorsal or ventral?
6. Which functions are controlled by the sympathetic nervous system? Which are controlled by the parasympathetic nervous system?

Check your answers on page 95.

The Hindbrain

The brain itself (as distinct from the spinal cord) consists of three major divisions: the hindbrain, the midbrain, and the forebrain (Figure 4.7 and Table 4.3).

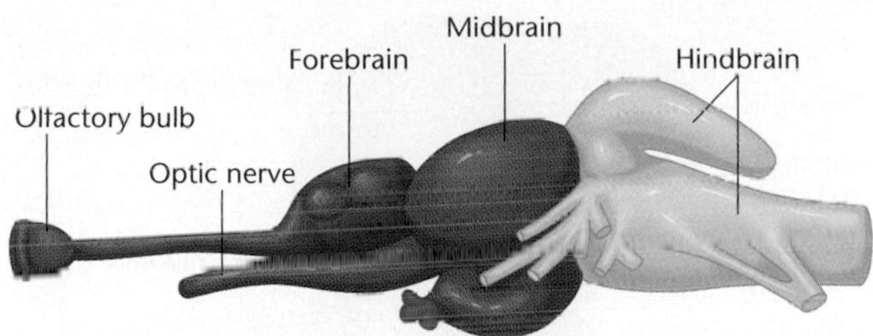

Figure 4.7 Three major divisions of the vertebrate brain
In a fish brain, as shown here, the forebrain, midbrain, and hindbrain are clearly visible as separate bulges. In adult mammals, the forebrain grows and surrounds the entire midbrain and part of the hindbrain.

Brain investigators unfortunately use a variety of terms synonymously. For example, some people prefer words with Greek roots: rhombencephalon (hindbrain), mesencephalon (midbrain), and prosencephalon (forebrain). You may encounter those terms in other reading.

The **hindbrain**, the posterior part of the brain, consists of the medulla, the pons, and the cerebellum. The medulla and pons, the midbrain, and certain central structures of the forebrain constitute the **brainstem** (Figure 4.8).

The **medulla**, or medulla oblongata, is just above the spinal cord and could be regarded as an enlarged, elaborated extension of the spinal cord, although it is located in the skull. The medulla controls a number of vital reflexes—including breathing, heart rate, vomiting, salivation, coughing, and sneezing—through the **cranial nerves**, which control sensations from the head, muscle movements in the head, and much of the parasympathetic output to the organs. Some of the cranial nerves include both sensory and motor components; others have just one or the other. Damage to the medulla is frequently fatal, and large doses of opiates are life-threatening because they suppress activity of the medulla.

Table 4.3 Major Divisions of the Vertebrate Brain

Area	Also Known as	Major Structures
Forebrain	Prosencephalon ("forward-brain")	
	Diencephalon ("between-brain")	Thalamus, hypothalamus
	Telencephalon ("end-brain")	Cerebral cortex, hippocampus, basal ganglia
Midbrain	Mesencephalon ("middle-brain")	Tectum, tegmentum, superior colliculus, inferior colliculus, substantia nigra
Hindbrain	Rhombencephalon (literally, "parallelogram-brain")	Medulla, pons, cerebellum
	Metencephalon ("afterbrain")	Pons, cerebellum
	Myelencephalon ("marrow-brain")	Medulla

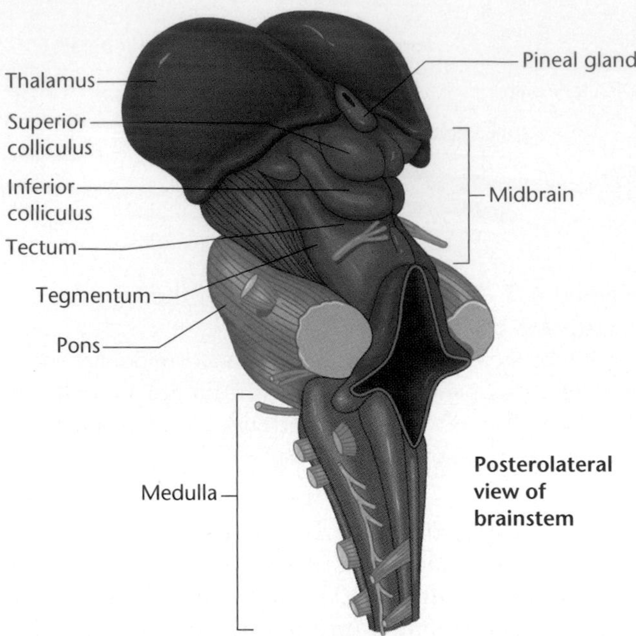

Figure 4.8 The human brainstem
This composite structure extends from the top of the spinal cord into the center of the forebrain. The pons, pineal gland, and colliculi are ordinarily surrounded by the cerebral cortex.

Just as the lower parts of the body are connected to the spinal cord via sensory and motor nerves, the receptors and muscles of the head and the internal organs are connected to the brain by 12 pairs of cranial nerves (one of each pair on the right of the brain and one on the left), as shown in Table 4.4. Each cranial nerve originates in a *nucleus* (cluster of neurons) that integrates the sensory information, regulates the motor output, or both. The cranial nerve nuclei for nerves V through XII are in the medulla and pons of the hindbrain. Those for cranial nerves I through IV are in the midbrain and forebrain (Figure 4.9).

The **pons** lies anterior and ventral to the medulla; like the medulla it contains nuclei for several cranial nerves. The term *pons* is Latin for "bridge"; the name reflects the fact that many axons in the pons cross from one side of the brain to the other. This is in fact the location where axons from each half of the brain cross to the opposite side of the spinal cord so that the left hemisphere controls the muscles of the right side of the body and the right hemisphere controls the left side.

The medulla and pons also contain the reticular formation and the raphe system. The **reticular formation** has descending and ascending portions. The descending portion is one of several brain areas that control the motor areas of the spinal cord. The ascending portion sends output to much of the cerebral cortex, selectively increasing arousal and attention in one area or another (Guillery, Feig, & Lozsádi, 1998). The **raphe system** also sends axons to much of the forebrain, modifying the brain's readiness to respond to stimuli (Mesulam, 1995).

The **cerebellum** is a large hindbrain structure with a great many deep folds. It has long been known for its contributions to the control of movement (see Chap-

Table 4.4 The Cranial Nerves

Number and Name	Major Functions
I. Olfactory	Smell
II. Optic	Vision
III. Oculomotor	Control of eye movements, pupil constriction
IV. Trochlear	Control of eye movements
V. Trigeminal	Skin sensations from most of the face; control of jaw muscles for chewing and swallowing
VI. Abducens	Control of eye movements
VII. Facial	Taste from the anterior two-thirds of the tongue; control of facial expressions, crying, salivation, and dilation of the head's blood vessels
VIII. Statoacoustic	Hearing, equilibrium
IX. Glossopharyngeal	Taste and other sensations from throat and posterior third of the tongue; control of swallowing, salivation, throat movements during speech
X. Vagus	Sensations from neck and thorax; control of throat, esophagus, and larynx; parasympathetic nerves to stomach, intestines, and other organs
XI. Accessory	Control of neck and shoulder movements
XII. Hypoglossal	Control of muscles of the tongue

Cranial nerves III, IV, and VI are coded in red to highlight their similarity: control of eye movements. Cranial nerves VII, IX, and XII are coded in green to highlight their similarity: taste and control of tongue and throat movements. Cranial nerve VII has other important functions as well. Nerve X (not highlighted) also contributes to throat movements, although it is primarily known for other functions.

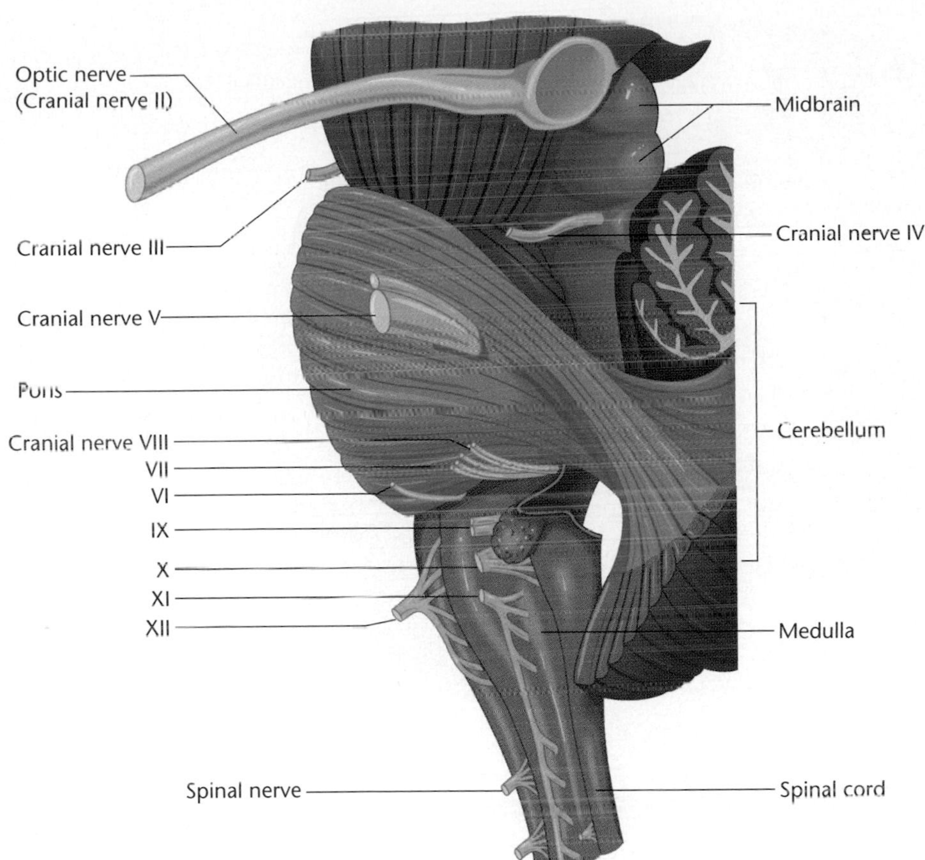

Figure 4.9 Cranial nerves II through XII
Cranial nerve I, the olfactory nerve, connects directly to the olfactory bulbs of the forebrain. *(Source: Based on Braus, 1960)*

ter 8), and many older textbooks describe the cerebellum as important for "balance and coordination." True, people with cerebellar damage are clumsy and lose their balance, but the functions of the cerebellum extend far beyond balance and coordination. People with damage to the cerebellum have trouble shifting their attention back and forth between auditory and visual stimuli (Courchesne et al., 1994). They have much difficulty with timing, including sensory timing. For example, they are poor at judging whether one rhythm is faster than another.

The Midbrain

As the name implies, the **midbrain** is in the middle of the brain, although in adult mammals it is dwarfed and surrounded by the forebrain. In birds, reptiles, amphibians, and fish, the midbrain is a larger, more prominent structure. The roof of the midbrain is called the **tectum.** (*Tectum* is the Latin word for "roof"; the same root shows up in the geological term *plate tectonics.*) The two swellings on each side of the tectum are the **superior colliculus** and the **inferior colliculus** (see Figures 4.8 and 4.10); both are part of important routes for sensory information.

Under the tectum lies the **tegmentum,** the intermediate level of the midbrain. (In Latin, *tegmentum* means a "covering," such as a rug on the floor. The tegmentum covers several other midbrain structures, although it is covered by the tectum.) The tegmentum includes the nuclei for the third and fourth cranial nerves, parts of the reticular formation, and extensions of the pathways between the forebrain and the spinal cord or hindbrain. Another midbrain structure is the **substantia nigra,** which gives rise to the dopamine-containing pathway that deteriorates in Parkinson's disease (see Chapter 8).

The Forebrain

The **forebrain** is the most anterior and most prominent part of the mammalian brain. It consists of two cerebral hemispheres, one on the left side and one on the right (Figure 4.11). Each hemisphere is organized to receive sensory information, mostly from the contralateral (opposite) side of the body, and to control muscles, mostly on the contralateral side, by way of axons to the spinal cord and the cranial nerve nuclei.

The outer portion is the cerebral cortex. (*Cerebrum* is a Latin word meaning "brain"; *cortex* is a Latin word meaning "bark" or "shell.") Under the cerebral cortex are other structures, including the thalamus, which is the main source of input to the cerebral cortex. A set of structures known as the basal ganglia plays a major

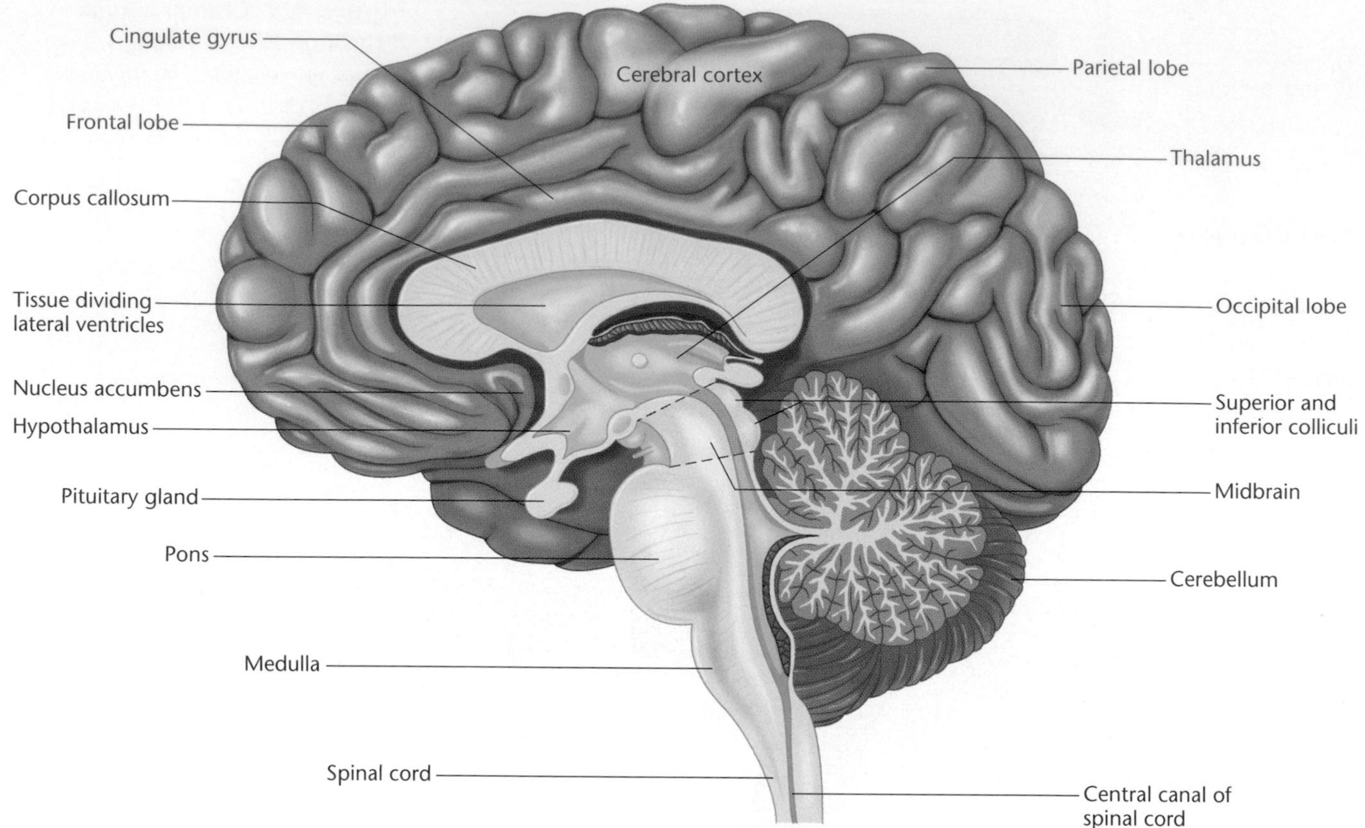

Figure 4.10 A sagittal section through the human brain
(Source: After Nieuwenhuys, Voogd, & vanHuijzen, 1988)

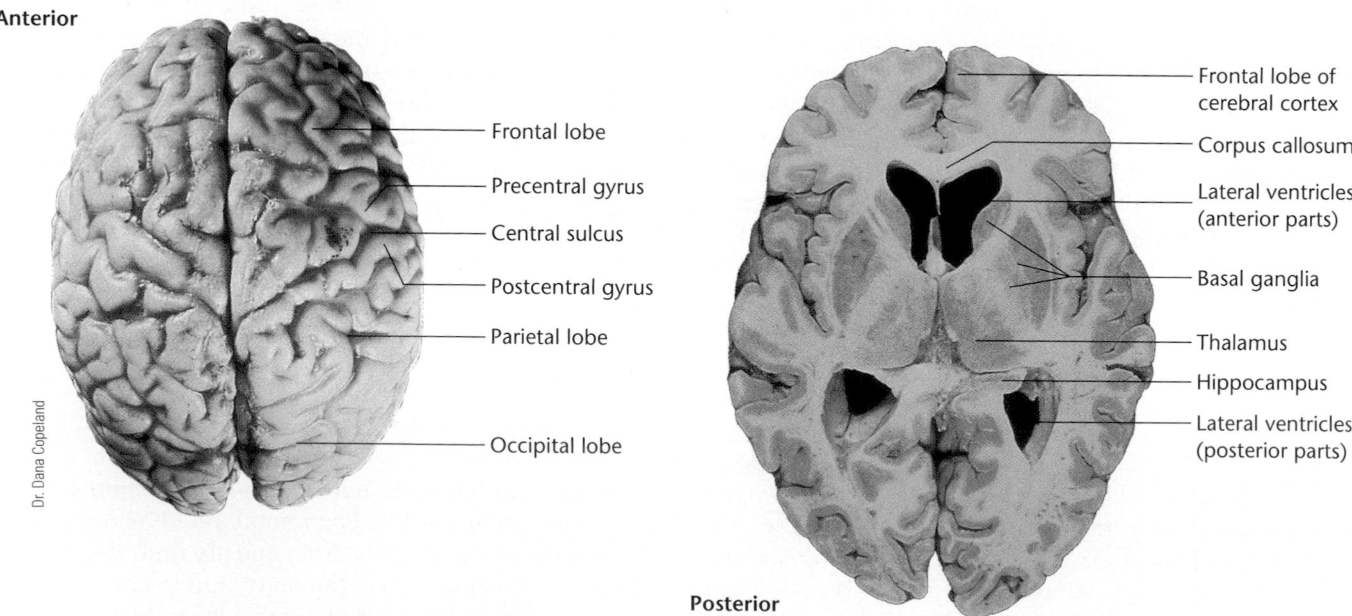

Figure 4.11 Dorsal view of the brain surface and a horizontal section through the brain

role in certain aspects of movement. A number of other interlinked structures, known as the **limbic system**, form a border (or *limbus*, the Latin word for "border") around the brainstem. These structures are particularly important for motivations and emotions, such as eating, drinking, sexual activity, anxiety, and aggression. The structures of the limbic system are the olfactory bulb, hypothalamus, hippocampus, amygdala, and cin-

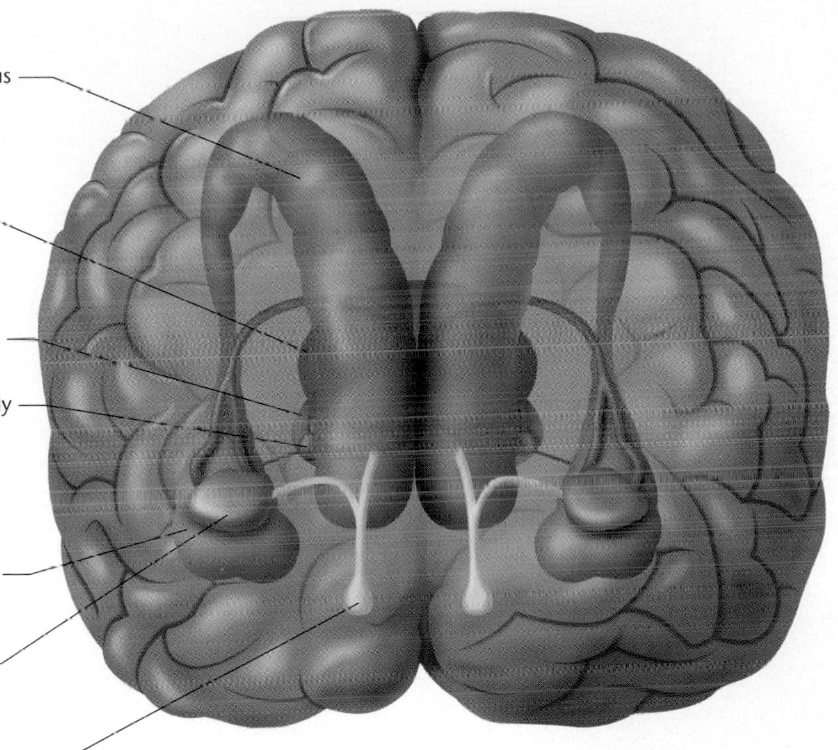

Figure 4.12 The limbic system is a set of subcortical structures that form a border (or limbus) around the brainstem

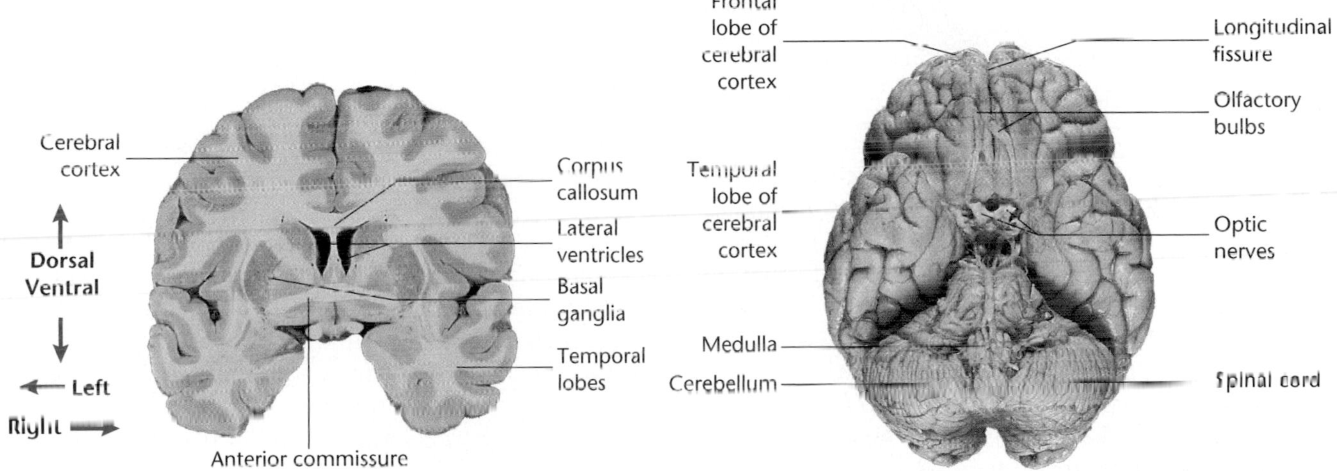

Figure 4.13 Two views of the human brain
Top: A coronal section. Note how the corpus callosum and anterior commissure provide communication between the left and right hemispheres. Bottom: The ventral surface. The optic nerves (cut here) extend to the eyes. *(Photos courtesy of Dr. Dana Copeland)*

gulate gyrus of the cerebral cortex. Figure 4.12 shows the positions of these structures in three-dimensional perspective. Figures 4.10 and 4.13 show sagittal (from the side) and coronal (from the front) sections through the human brain. Figure 4.13 also includes a view of the ventral surface of the brain.

In describing the forebrain, we begin with the subcortical areas; the next module focuses on the cerebral cortex. In later chapters, we return to each of these areas as they become relevant.

Thalamus

The thalamus and hypothalamus together form the *diencephalon,* a section distinct from the rest of the forebrain, which is known as the *telencephalon.* The **thal-**

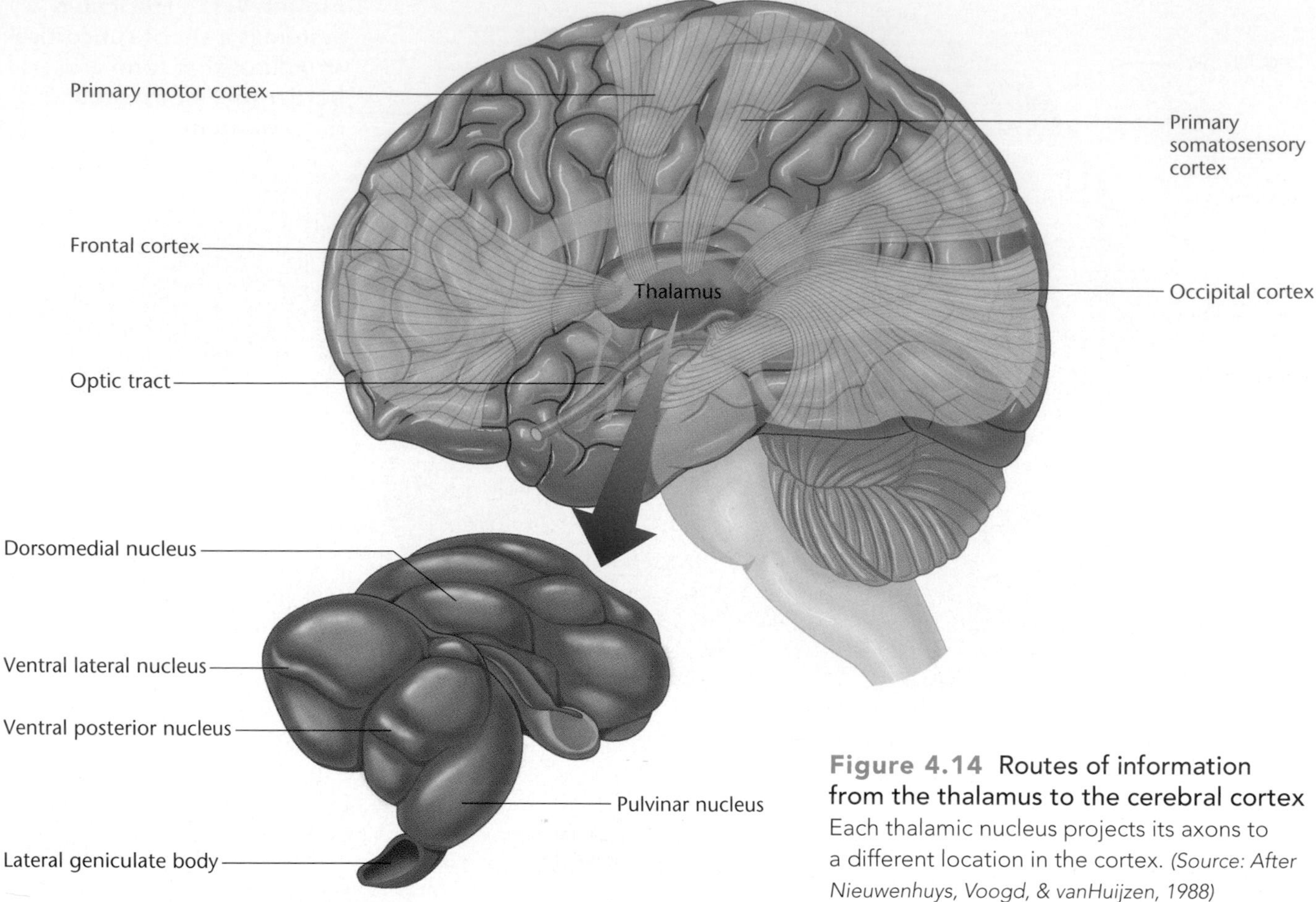

Figure 4.14 Routes of information from the thalamus to the cerebral cortex
Each thalamic nucleus projects its axons to a different location in the cortex. *(Source: After Nieuwenhuys, Voogd, & vanHuijzen, 1988)*

amus is a structure in the center of the forebrain. The term is derived from a Greek word meaning "anteroom," "inner chamber," or "bridal bed." It resembles two avocados joined side by side, one in the left hemisphere and one in the right. Most sensory information goes first to the thalamus, which then processes it and sends the output to the cerebral cortex. The one clear exception to this rule is olfactory information, which progresses from the olfactory receptors to the olfactory bulbs and from the bulbs directly to the cerebral cortex without passing through the thalamus.

Many nuclei of the thalamus receive their primary input from one of the sensory systems, such as vision, and then transmit the information to a single area of the cerebral cortex, as in Figure 4.14. The cerebral cortex then sends information back to the thalamus, prolonging and magnifying certain kinds of input at the expense of others, apparently serving to focus attention on particular stimuli (Komura et al., 2001).

Hypothalamus

The **hypothalamus** is a small area near the base of the brain just ventral to the thalamus (see Figures 4.10 and 4.12). It has widespread connections with the rest of the forebrain and the midbrain. The hypothalamus contains a number of distinct nuclei, which we examine in Chapters 10 and 11. Partly through nerves and partly through hypothalamic hormones, the hypothalamus conveys messages to the pituitary gland, altering its release of hormones. Damage to any hypothalamic nucleus leads to abnormalities in motivated behaviors, such as feeding, drinking, temperature regulation, sexual behavior, fighting, or activity level. Because of these important behavioral effects, the rather small hypothalamus attracts a great deal of research attention.

Pituitary Gland

The **pituitary gland** is an endocrine (hormone-producing) gland attached to the base of the hypothalamus by a stalk that contains neurons, blood vessels, and connective tissue (see Figure 4.10). In response to messages from the hypothalamus, the pituitary synthesizes and releases hormones into the bloodstream, which carries them to other organs.

Basal Ganglia

The **basal ganglia**, a group of subcortical structures lateral to the thalamus, include three major structures: the caudate nucleus, the putamen, and the globus pal-

Figure 4.15 The basal ganglia
The thalamus is in the center, the basal ganglia are lateral to it, and the cerebral cortex is on the outside. *(Source: After Nieuwenhuys, Voogd, & vanHuijzen, 1988)*

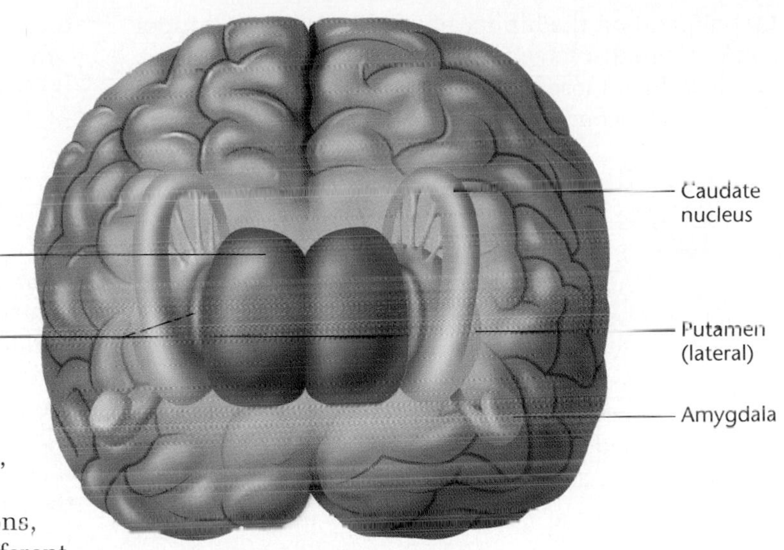

lidus (Figure 4.15). Some authorities include several other structures as well. The basal ganglia have been conserved through evolution, and the basic organization is about the same in mammals as in amphibians (Marin, Smeets, & González, 1998).

The basal ganglia have multiple subdivisions, each of which exchanges information with a different part of the cerebral cortex. The connections are most abundant with the frontal areas of the cortex, which are responsible for planning sequences of behavior and for certain aspects of memory and emotional expression (Graybiel, Aosaki, Flaherty, & Kimura, 1994). In conditions such as Parkinson's disease and Huntington's disease, in which the basal ganglia deteriorate, the most prominent symptom is impaired movement, but people also show depression, deficits of memory and reasoning, and attentional disorders.

Basal Forebrain

Several structures lie on the dorsal surface of the forebrain, including the **nucleus basalis**, which receives input from the hypothalamus and basal ganglia and sends axons that release acetylcholine to widespread areas in the cerebral cortex (Figure 4.16). We might regard the nucleus basalis as an intermediary between the emotional arousal of the hypothalamus and the information processing of the cerebral cortex. The nucleus basalis is a key part of the brain's system for arousal, wakefulness, and attention, as we consider in Chapter 9. Patients with Parkinson's disease and Alzheimer's disease have impairments of attention and intellect because of inactivity or deterioration of their nucleus basalis.

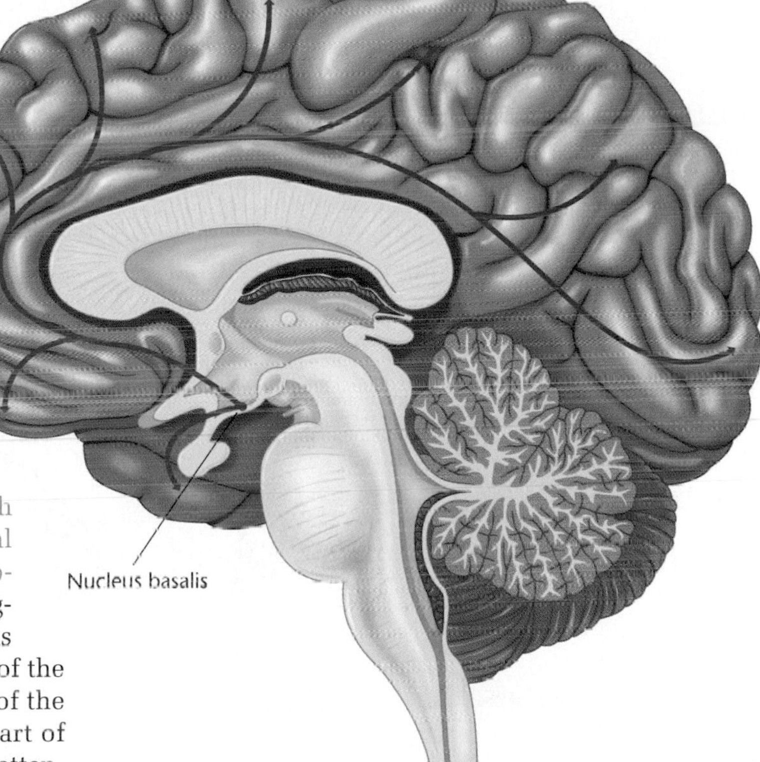

Figure 4.16 The basal forebrain
The nucleus basalis and other structures in this area send axons throughout the cortex, increasing its arousal and wakefulness through release of the neurotransmitter acetylcholine. *(Source: Adapted from "Cholinergic Systems in Mammalian Brain and Spinal Cord," by N. J. Woolf, Progress in Neurobiology, 37, pp. 475–524, 1991)*

Hippocampus

The **hippocampus** (from a Latin word meaning "sea horse," a shape suggested by the hippocampus) is a large structure between the thalamus and the cerebral cortex, mostly toward the posterior of the forebrain, as shown in Figure 4.12. We consider the hippocampus in more detail in Chapter 12; the gist of that discussion is that the hippocampus is critical for storing certain kinds of memories but not all. A debate continues about how best to describe the class of memories that depend on the hippocampus. People with hippocampal damage have trouble storing new memories, but they do not lose the memories they had from before the damage occurred.

STOP & CHECK

7. Of the following, which are in the hindbrain, which in the midbrain, and which in the forebrain: basal ganglia, cerebellum, hippocampus, hypothalamus, medulla, pituitary gland, pons, substantia nigra, superior and inferior colliculi, tectum, tegmentum, thalamus?
8. Which area is the main source of input to the cerebral cortex?

Check your answers on page 95.

The Ventricles

The nervous system begins its development as a tube surrounding a fluid canal. The canal persists into adulthood as the **central canal,** a fluid-filled channel in the center of the spinal cord, and as the **ventricles,** four fluid-filled cavities within the brain. Each hemisphere contains one of the two large lateral ventricles (Figure 4.17). Toward the posterior, they connect to the third ventricle, which connects to the fourth ventricle in the medulla.

The ventricles and the central canal of the spinal cord contain **cerebrospinal fluid (CSF),** a clear fluid similar to blood plasma. CSF is formed by groups of cells, the *choroid plexus,* inside the four ventricles. It flows from the lateral ventricles to the third and fourth ventricles. From the fourth ventricle, some CSF flows into the central canal of the spinal cord, but more goes through an opening into the narrow spaces between the brain and the thin **meninges,** membranes that surround the brain and spinal cord. (Meningitis is an inflammation of the meninges.) From one of those spaces, the subarachnoid space, CSF is gradually reabsorbed into the blood vessels of the brain.

Cerebrospinal fluid cushions the brain against mechanical shock when the head moves. It also provides buoyancy; just as a person weighs less in water than on land, cerebrospinal fluid helps support the weight of the brain. It also provides a reservoir of hormones and nutrition for the brain and spinal cord.

Sometimes the flow of CSF is obstructed, and it accumulates within the ventricles or in the subarachnoid space, thus increasing the pressure on the brain. When this occurs in infants, the skull bones may spread, causing an overgrown head. This condition, known as *hydrocephalus* (HI-dro-SEFF-ah-luss), is usually associated with mental retardation.

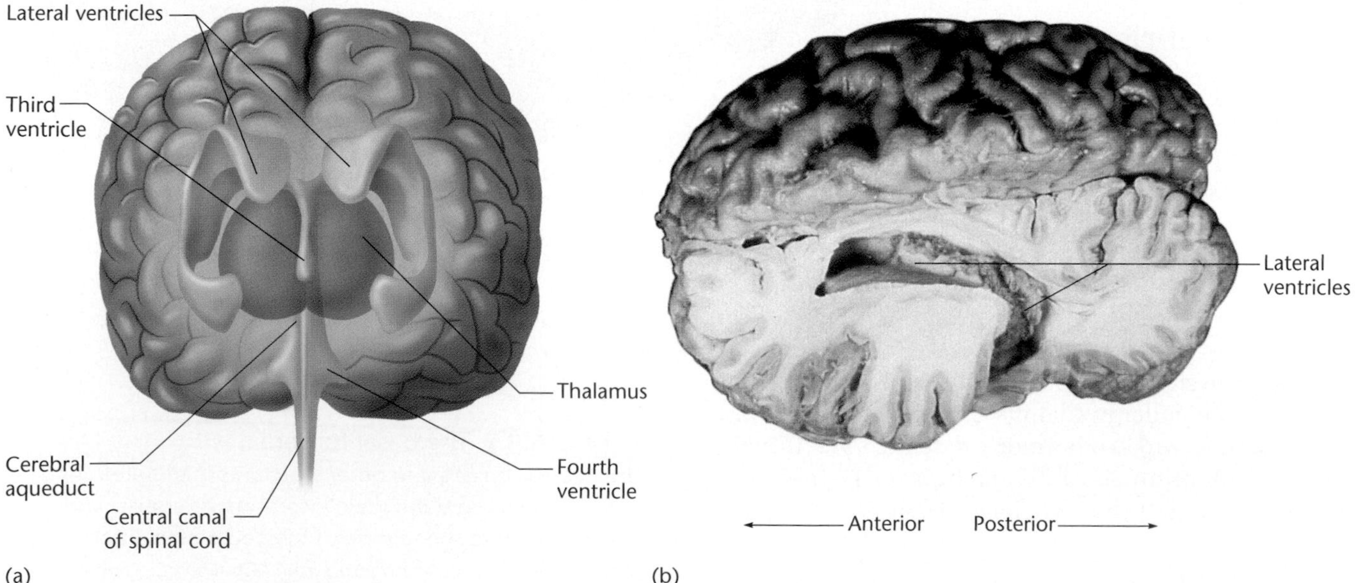

Figure 4.17 The cerebral ventricles
(a) Diagram showing positions of the four ventricles. **(b)** Photo of a human brain, viewed from above, with a horizontal cut through one hemisphere to show the position of the lateral ventricles. Note that the two parts of this figure are seen from different angles. *(Photo courtesy of Dr. Dana Copeland)*

Module 4.1

In Closing: Learning Neuroanatomy

The brain is a highly complex structure. This module has introduced a great many terms and facts; do not be discouraged if you have trouble remembering them. You didn't learn world geography all at one time either. It will help to return to this section to review the anatomy of certain structures as you encounter them again in later chapters. Gradually, the material will become more familiar.

It helps to see the brain from different angles and perspectives. Check this fantastic website, which includes detailed photos of both normal and abnormal human brains: **http://www.med.harvard.edu/AANLIB/home.html**

You might also appreciate this site, which compares the brains of different species. (Have you ever wondered what a polar bear's brain looks like? Or a dolphin's? Or a weasel's?) **http://www.brainmuseum.org/Sections/index.html**

Summary

1. The main divisions of the vertebrate nervous system are the central nervous system and the peripheral nervous system. The central nervous system consists of the spinal cord, the hindbrain, the midbrain, and the forebrain. (p. 82)
2. Each segment of the spinal cord has a sensory nerve on each side and a motor nerve on each side. Several spinal pathways convey information to the brain. (p. 84)
3. The sympathetic nervous system (one of the two divisions of the autonomic nervous system) activates the body's internal organs for vigorous activities. The parasympathetic system (the other division) promotes digestion and other nonemergency processes. (p. 85)
4. The hindbrain consists of the medulla, pons, and cerebellum. The medulla and pons control breathing, heart rate, and other vital functions through the cranial nerves. The cerebellum contributes to movement. (p. 87)
5. The subcortical areas of the forebrain include the thalamus, hypothalamus, pituitary gland, basal ganglia, and hippocampus. (p. 89)
6. The cerebral cortex receives its sensory information (except for olfaction) from the thalamus. (p. 92)

Answers to STOP & CHECK Questions

1. *Dorsal* means toward the back, away from the stomach side. Its opposite is *ventral.* (p. 84)
2. Lateral; medial (p. 84)
3. Ipsilateral; contralateral (p. 84)
4. Gyri; sulci (p. 84)
5. Dorsal (p. 87)
6. The sympathetic nervous system prepares the organs for vigorous fight-or-flight activity. The parasympathetic system increases vegetative responses such as digestion. (p. 87)
7. Hindbrain: cerebellum, medulla, and pons. Midbrain: substantia nigra, superior and inferior colliculi, tectum, and tegmentum. Forebrain: basal ganglia, hippocampus, hypothalamus, pituitary, and thalamus. (p. 94)
8. Thalamus (p. 94)

Thought Question

The drug phenylephrine is sometimes prescribed for people suffering from a sudden loss of blood pressure or other medical disorders. It acts by stimulating norepinephrine synapses, including those that constrict blood vessels. One common side effect of this drug is goose bumps. Explain why. What other side effects might be likely?

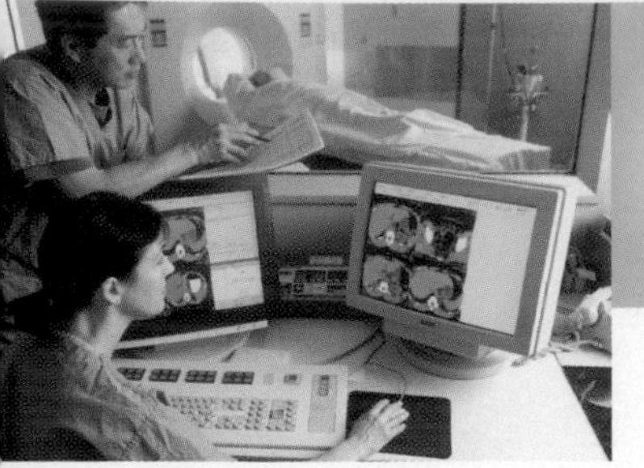

Module 4.2
The Cerebral Cortex

The most prominent part of the mammalian brain is the **cerebral cortex,** consisting of the cellular layers on the outer surface of the cerebral hemispheres. The cells of the cerebral cortex are gray matter; their axons extending inward are white matter (see Figure 4.13). Neurons in each hemisphere communicate with neurons in the corresponding part of the other hemisphere through two bundles of axons, the **corpus callosum** (see Figures 4.10, 4.11, and 4.13) and the smaller **anterior commissure** (see Figure 4.13). Several other commissures (pathways across the midline) link subcortical structures.

If we compare mammalian species, we see differences in both the size of the cerebral cortex and the degree of folding (Figure 4.18). The cerebral cortex constitutes a higher percentage of the brain in **primates**—monkeys, apes, and humans—than in other species of comparable size. Figure 4.19 shows the size of the cerebral cortex in comparison to the rest of the brain for insectivores and two suborders of primates (Barton & Harvey, 2000). Figure 4.20 compares species in another way (D. A. Clark, Mitra, & Wang, 2001). The investigators arranged the insectivores and primates from left to right in terms of what percentage of their brain was devoted to the forebrain (telencephalon), which includes the cerebral cortex. They also inserted tree shrews, a species often considered intermediate or transitional. Note that as the proportion devoted to the forebrain increases, the relative sizes of the midbrain and medulla decrease. Curiously, the cerebellum occupies a remarkably constant percentage—approximately 13% of any mammalian brain (D. A. Clark et al., 2001). That is, the cerebellum maintains an almost constant proportion to the whole brain. (Why? No one knows.)

Organization of the Cerebral Cortex

The microscopic structure of the cells of the cerebral cortex varies substantially from one cortical area to another. The differences in appearance relate to differences in function. Much research has been directed toward understanding the relationship between structure and function.

In humans and most other mammals, the cerebral cortex contains up to six distinct **laminae,** layers of cell bodies that are parallel to the surface of the cortex and separated from each other by layers of fibers (Figure 4.21). The laminae vary in thickness and prominence from one part of the cortex to another, and a given lamina may be absent from certain areas. Lamina V, which sends long axons to the spinal cord and other distant areas, is thickest in the motor cortex, which has the greatest control of the muscles. Lamina IV, which receives axons from the various sensory nuclei of the thalamus, is prominent in all the primary sensory areas

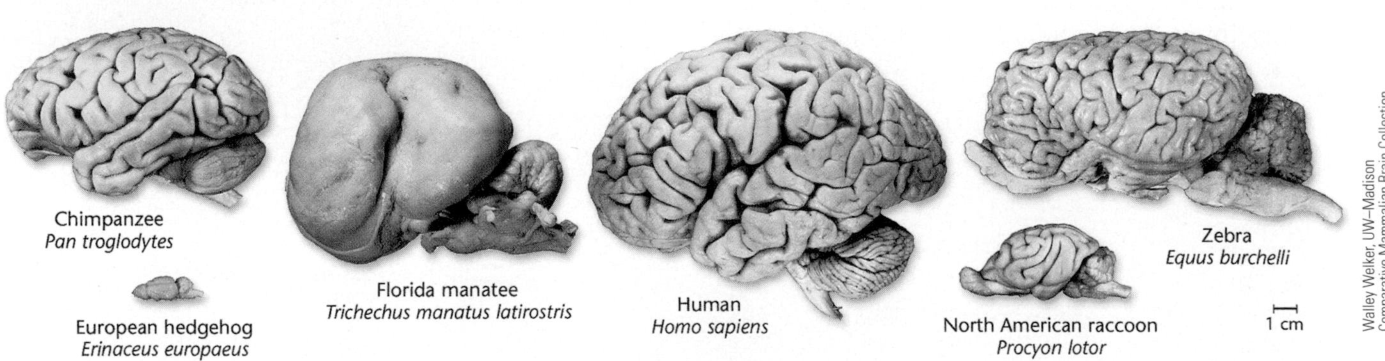

Figure 4.18 Comparison of mammalian brains
The human brain is the largest of those shown, although whales, dolphins, and elephants have still larger brains. All mammals have the same brain subareas in the same locations.

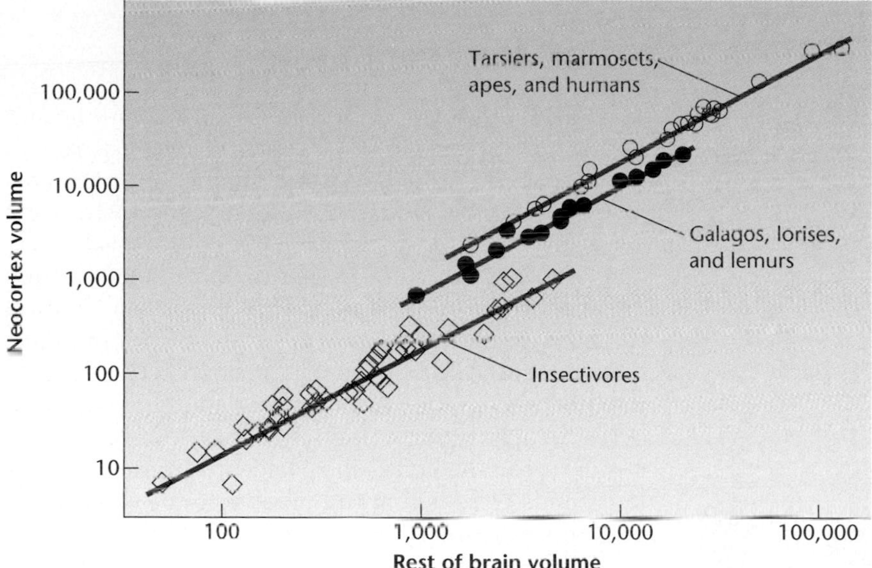

Figure 4.19 Relationship between volume of the cortex and volume of the rest of the brain
For each of the three groups, cortical volume increases quite predictably as a function of the volume of the rest of the brain. However, the lines for the two primate groups are displaced upward. *(Source: Fig. 1, p. 1055 in R. A. Barton & R. H. Harvey, "Mosaic evolution of brain structure in mammals."* Nature, 405, *pp. 1055–1058. Reprinted with permission from Nature. Copyright © 2000 Macmillan Magazine Limited.)*

(visual, auditory, and somatosensory) but absent from the motor cortex.

The cells of the cortex are also organized into **columns** of cells perpendicular to the laminae. Figure 4.22 illustrates the idea of columns, although in nature they are not so straight. The cells within a given column have similar properties to one another. For example, if one cell in a column responds to touch on the palm of the left hand, then the other cells in that column do too. If one cell responds to a horizontal pattern of light at a particular location in the retina, then the other cells in the column respond to the same pattern in nearly the same location.

We now turn to some of the specific parts of the cortex. Researchers distinguish 50 or more areas of the cerebral cortex based on differences in the thickness of

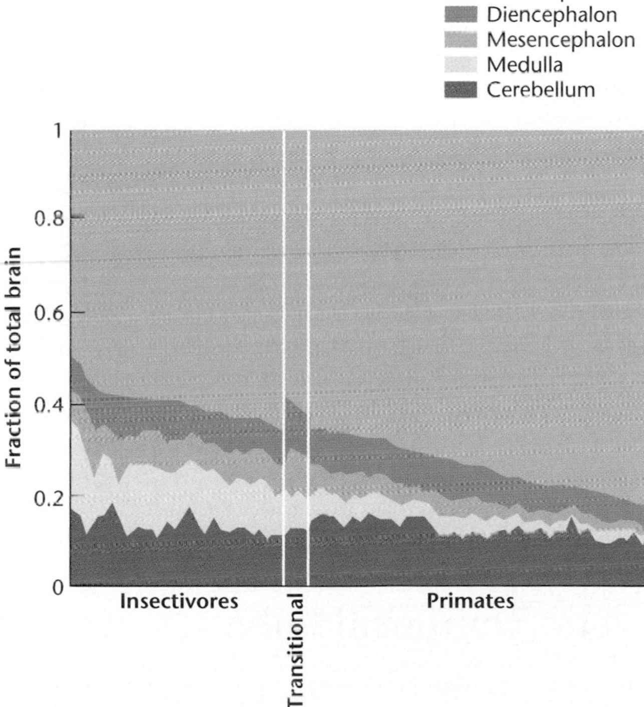

Figure 4.20 Relative sizes of five brain components in insectivores and primates
The forebrain composes a larger percentage of primate than insectivore brains. Note also the near-constant fraction devoted to the cerebellum. *(Source: Fig. 1, p. 189 in D. A. Clark, P. P. Mitra, & S. S-H. Wong, "Scalable architecture in mammalian brains."* Nature, 411, *pp. 189–193. Reprinted with permission from Nature. Copyright © 2001 Macmillan Magazine Limited.)*

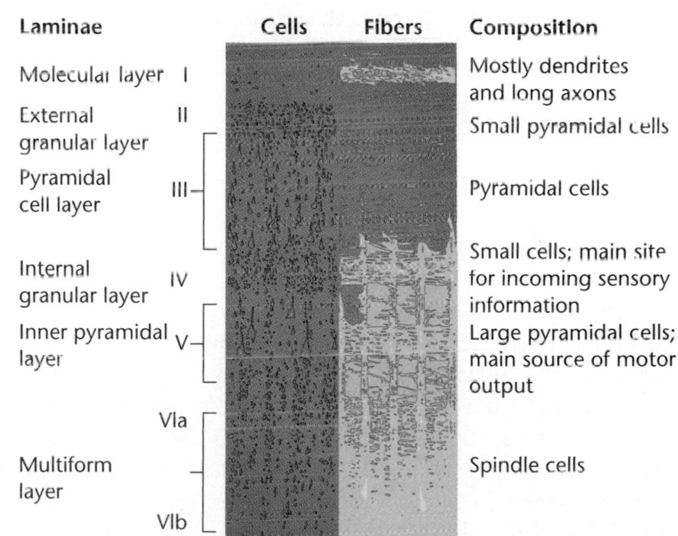

Figure 4.21 The six laminae of the human cerebral cortex
(Source: From S. W. Ranson and S. L. Clark, The Anatomy of the Nervous System, *1959, Copyright © 1959 W. B. Saunders Co. Reprinted by permission.)*

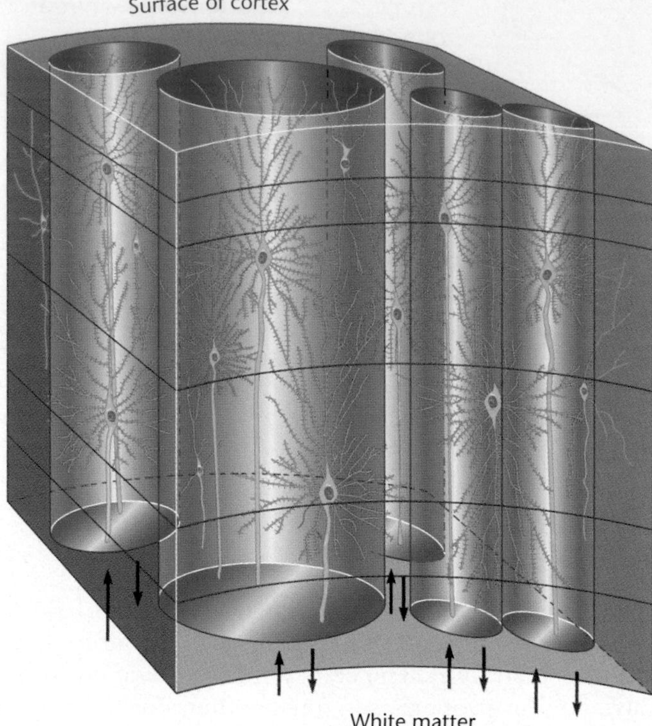

Figure 4.22 Columns in the cerebral cortex
Each column extends through several laminae. Neurons within a given column have similar properties. For example, in the somatosensory cortex, all the neurons within a given column respond to stimulation of the same area of skin.

the six laminae and on the structure of cells and fibers within each lamina. For convenience, we group these areas into four *lobes* named for the skull bones that lie over them: occipital, parietal, temporal, and frontal.

The Occipital Lobe

The **occipital lobe,** located at the posterior (caudal) end of the cortex (Figure 4.23), is the main target for axons from the thalamic nuclei that receive visual input. The posterior pole of the occipital lobe is known as the *primary visual cortex,* or *striate cortex,* because of its striped appearance in cross-section. Destruction of any part of the striate cortex causes *cortical blindness* in the related part of the visual field. For example, extensive damage to the striate cortex of the right hemisphere causes blindness in the left visual field (the left side of the world from the viewer's perspective). A person with cortical blindness has normal eyes, normal pupillary reflexes, and some eye movements but no pattern perception and not even visual imagery. People who suffer severe damage to the eyes become blind, but if they have an intact occipital cortex and previous visual experience, they can still imagine visual scenes and can still have visual dreams (Sabo & Kirtley, 1982).

The Parietal Lobe

The **parietal lobe** lies between the occipital lobe and the **central sulcus,** which is one of the deepest grooves in the surface of the cortex (see Figure 4.23). The area just posterior to the central sulcus, the **postcentral gyrus,** or the *primary somatosensory cortex,* is the primary target for touch sensations and information from muscle-stretch receptors and joint receptors. Brain surgeons sometimes use only local anesthesia (anesthetizing the scalp but leaving the brain awake). If during this process they lightly stimulate the postcentral gyrus, people report "tingling" sensations on the opposite side of the body. The postcentral gyrus includes four bands of cells that run parallel to the central sulcus. Separate areas along each band receive simultaneous information from different parts of the body, as shown in Figure 4.24a (Nicolelis et al., 1998). Two of the bands receive mostly light-touch information, one receives deep-pressure information, and one receives a combination of both (Kaas, Nelson, Sur, Lin, & Merzenich, 1979). In effect, the postcentral gyrus represents the body four times.

Information about touch and body location is important not only for its own sake but also for interpreting visual and auditory information. For example, if you see something in the upper left portion of the visual field, your brain needs to know which direction your eyes are turned, the position of your head, and the tilt of your body before it can determine the location of the object that you see and therefore the direction you should go if you want to approach or avoid it. The parietal lobe monitors all the information about eye, head, and body positions and passes it on to brain areas that control movement (Gross & Graziano, 1995). It is essential not only for processing spatial information but also numerical information (Hubbard, Piazza, Pinel, & Dehaene, 2005). That overlap makes sense when you consider all the ways in which number relates to space—from initially learning to count with our fingers, to geometry, and to all kinds of graphs.

The Temporal Lobe

The **temporal lobe** is the lateral portion of each hemisphere, near the temples (see Figure 4.23). It is the primary cortical target for auditory information. In humans, the temporal lobe—in most cases, the left temporal lobe—is essential for understanding spoken language. The temporal lobe also contributes to some of the more complex aspects of vision, including perception of movement and recognition of faces. A tumor in the temporal lobe may give rise to elaborate auditory or visual hallucinations, whereas a tumor in the oc-

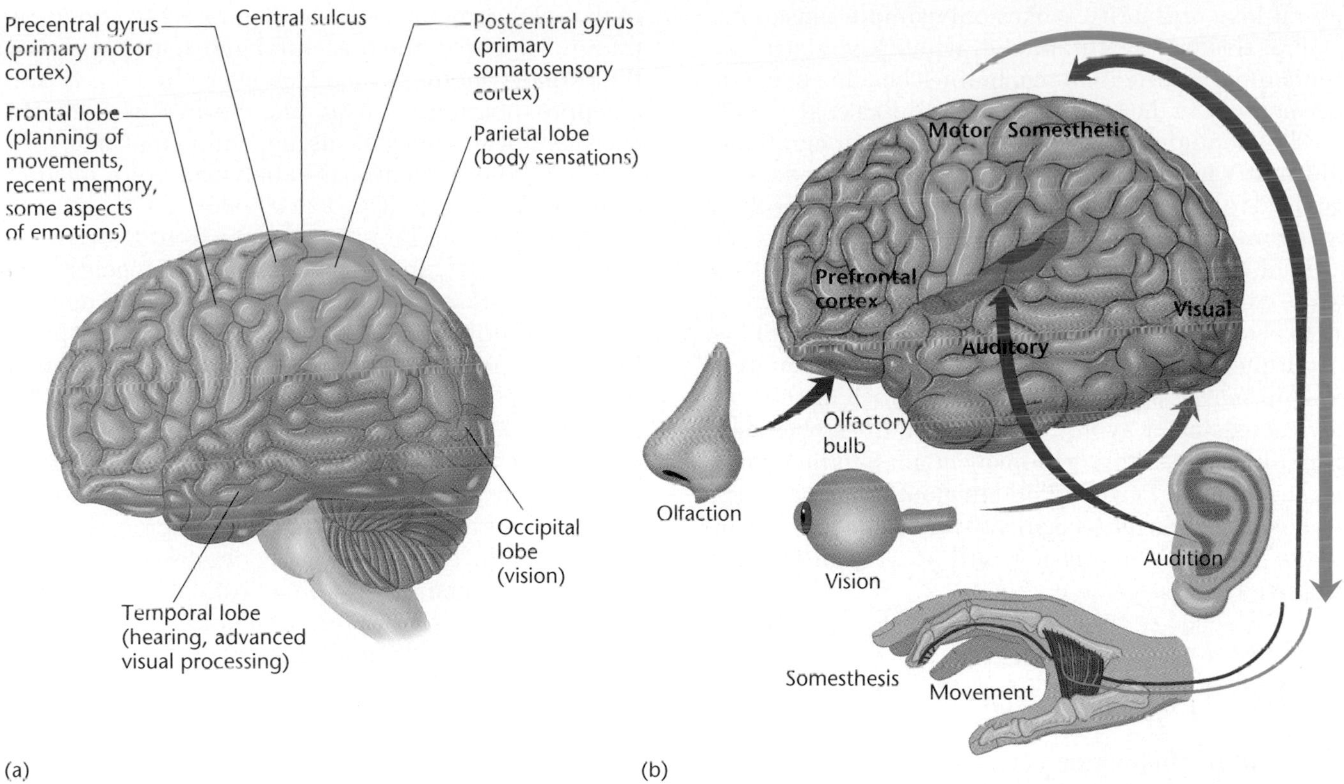

Figure 4.23 Areas of the human cerebral cortex
(a) The four lobes: occipital, parietal, temporal, and frontal. **(b)** The primary sensory cortex for vision, hearing, and body sensations; the primary motor cortex; and the olfactory bulb, a noncortical area responsible for the sense of smell. *(Source for part b: T. W. Deacon, 1990)*

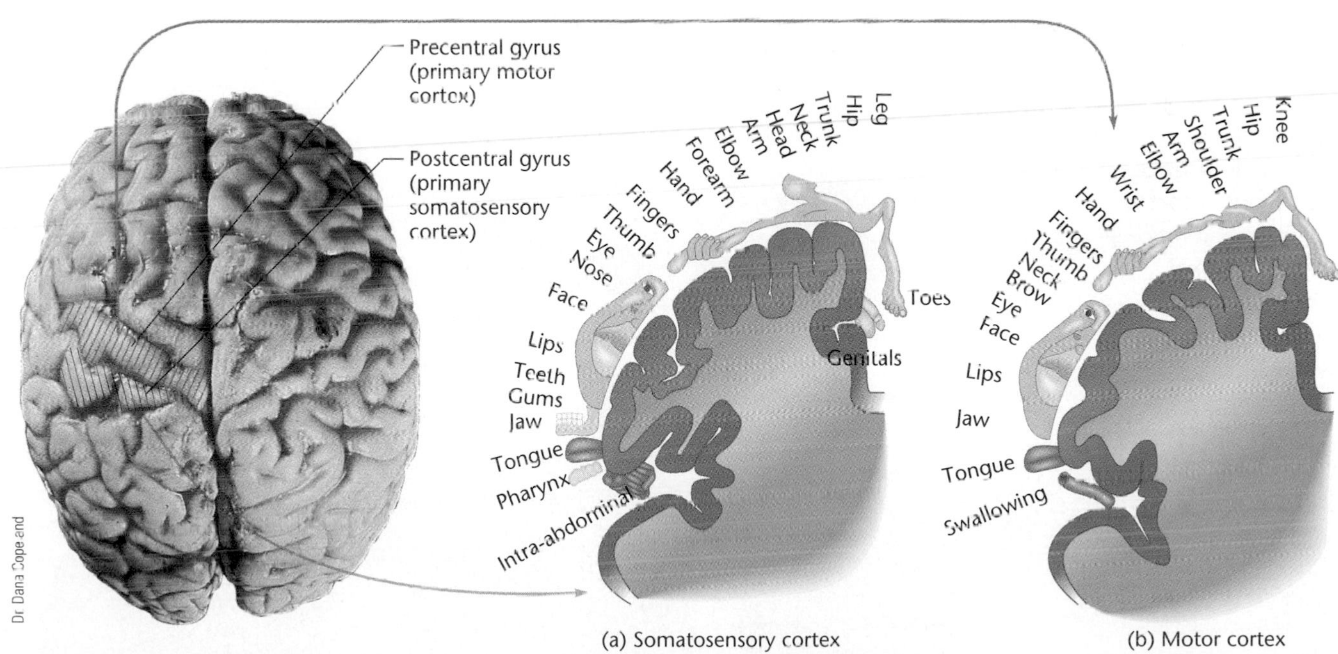

Figure 4.24 Approximate representation of sensory and motor information in the cortex
(a) Each location in the somatosensory cortex represents sensation from a different body part. **(b)** Each location in the motor cortex regulates movement of a different body part. *(Source: Adapted from* The Cerebral Cortex of Man *by W. Penfield and T. Rasmussen, Macmillan Library Reference. Reprinted by permission of The Gale Group.)*

cipital lobe ordinarily evokes only simple sensations, such as flashes of light. In fact, when psychiatric patients report hallucinations, brain scans detect extensive activity in the temporal lobes (Dierks et al., 1999).

The temporal lobes also play a part in emotional and motivational behaviors. Temporal lobe damage can lead to a set of behaviors known as the **Klüver-Bucy syndrome** (named for the investigators who first described it). Previously wild and aggressive monkeys fail to display normal fears and anxieties after temporal lobe damage (Klüver & Bucy, 1939). They put almost anything they find into their mouths and attempt to pick up snakes and lighted matches (which intact monkeys consistently avoid). Interpreting this behavior is difficult. For example, a monkey might handle a snake because it is no longer afraid (an emotional change) or because it no longer recognizes what a snake is (a cognitive change). Such issues will be a major topic in Chapter 12.

The Frontal Lobe

The **frontal lobe,** which contains the primary motor cortex and the prefrontal cortex, extends from the central sulcus to the anterior limit of the brain (see Figure 4.23). The posterior portion of the frontal lobe just anterior to the central sulcus, the **precentral gyrus,** is specialized for the control of fine movements, such as moving one finger at a time. Separate areas are responsible for different parts of the body, mostly on the contralateral (opposite) side but also with slight control of the ipsilateral (same) side. Figure 4.24b shows the traditional map of the precentral gyrus, also known as the *primary motor cortex.* However, the map is only an approximation; for example, the arm area does indeed control arm movements, but within that area, there is no one-to-one relationship between brain location and specific muscles (Graziano, Taylor, & Moore, 2002).

The most anterior portion of the frontal lobe is the **prefrontal cortex.** In general, the larger a species' cerebral cortex, the higher the percentage of it is devoted to the prefrontal cortex (Figure 4.25). For example, it forms a larger portion of the cortex in humans and all the great apes than in other species (Semendeferi, Lu, Schenker, & Damasio, 2002). It is not the primary target for any single sensory system, but it receives information from all of them, in different parts of the prefrontal cortex. The dendrites in the prefrontal cortex have up to 16 times as many dendritic spines (see Figure 2.7) as neurons in other cortical areas (Elston, 2000). As a result, the prefrontal cortex can integrate an enormous amount of information.

EXTENSIONS AND APPLICATIONS
The Rise and Fall of Prefrontal Lobotomies

The prefrontal cortex was the target of the infamous procedure known as **prefrontal lobotomy**—surgical disconnection of the prefrontal cortex from the rest of the brain. The surgery consisted of damaging the prefrontal cortex or cutting its connections to the rest of the cortex. The lobotomy trend began with a report that damaging the prefrontal cortex of laboratory pri-

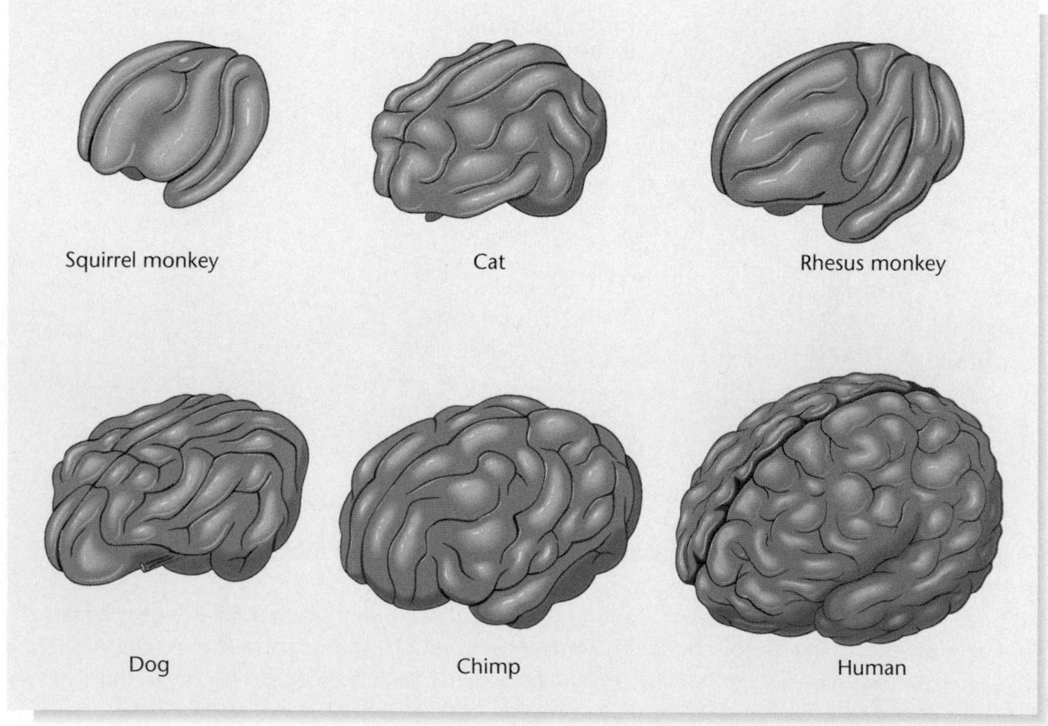

Figure 4.25
Species differences in prefrontal cortex
Note that the prefrontal cortex (blue area) constitutes a larger proportion of the human brain than of these other species. *(Source: After* The Prefrontal Cortex *by J. M. Fuster, 1989, Raven Press. Reprinted by permission.)*

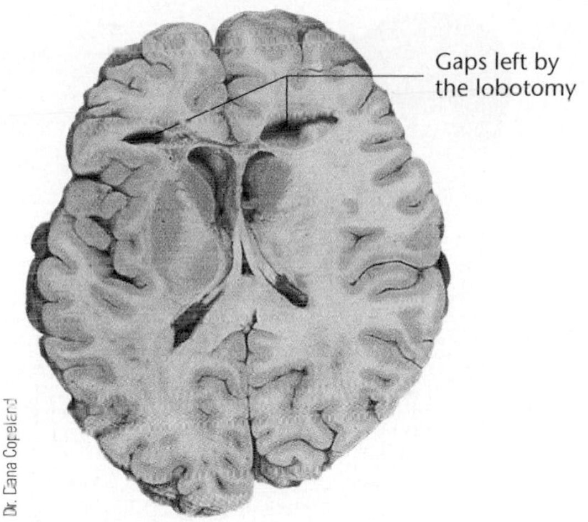

A horizontal section of the brain of a person who had a prefrontal lobotomy many years earlier. The two holes in the frontal cortex are the visible results of the operation.

mates had made them tamer without noticeably impairing their sensory or motor capacities. A few physicians reasoned (loosely) that the same operation might help people who suffered from severe, untreatable psychiatric disorders.

In the late 1940s and early 1950s, about 40,000 prefrontal lobotomies were performed in the United States (Shutts, 1982), many of them by Walter Freeman, a medical doctor untrained in surgery. His techniques were crude, even by the standards of the time, using such instruments as an electric drill and a metal pick. He performed many operations in his office or other nonhospital sites. (Freeman carried his equipment in his car, which he called his "lobotomobile.")

Freeman and others became increasingly casual in deciding who should have a lobotomy. At first, they limited the technique only in severe, apparently hopeless cases of schizophrenia. Lobotomy did calm some individuals, but the effects were usually disappointing. We now know that the frontal lobes of people with schizophrenia are relatively inactive; lobotomy was therefore damaging a structure that was already impaired. Later, Freeman lobotomized people with less serious disorders, including some whom we would consider normal by today's standards. After drug therapies became available for schizophrenia and depression, physicians quickly and almost completely abandoned lobotomies, performing only a few of them after the mid-1950s (Lesse, 1984; Tippin & Henn, 1982).

Among the common consequences of prefrontal lobotomy were apathy, a loss of the ability to plan and take initiative, memory disorders, distractibility, and a loss of emotional expressions (Stuss & Benson, 1984). People with prefrontal damage lose their social inhibitions, ignoring the rules of polite, civilized conduct. They often act impulsively because they fail to calculate adequately the probable outcomes of their behaviors.

Modern View of the Prefrontal Cortex

Lobotomies added rather little to our understanding of the prefrontal cortex. Later researchers studying people and monkeys with brain damage found that the prefrontal cortex is important for *working memory,* the ability to remember recent stimuli and events, such as where you parked the car today or what you were talking about before being interrupted (Goldman-Rakic, 1988). The prefrontal cortex is especially important for the **delayed-response task,** in which a stimulus appears briefly, and after some delay, the individual must respond to the remembered stimulus. The prefrontal cortex is much less important for remembering unchanging, permanent facts.

Neuroscientists have offered several other hypotheses about the function of the prefrontal cortex. One is that it is essential when we have to follow two or more rules at the same time in the same situation (Ramnani & Owen, 2004). Another is that it controls behaviors that depend on the context (E. Miller, 2000). For example, if the phone rings, do you answer it? It depends: In your own home, yes, but at someone else's home, probably not. If you saw a good friend from a distance, would you shout out a greeting? Again, it depends: You would in a public park but not in a library. People with prefrontal cortex damage often fail to adjust to their context, so they behave inappropriately or impulsively.

STOP & CHECK

1. If several neurons of the visual cortex all respond best when the retina is exposed to horizontal lines of light, then those neurons are probably located in the same ______.
2. Which lobe of the cerebral cortex includes the primary auditory cortex? The primary somatosensory cortex? The primary visual cortex? The primary motor cortex?
3. What are the functions of the prefrontal cortex?

Check your answers on page 104.

How Do the Parts Work Together?

We have just considered a variety of brain areas, each with its own function. How do they merge their effects to produce integrated behavior and the experience of a single self? In particular, consider the sensory areas of the cerebral cortex. The primary visual area, auditory area, and somatosensory area are in different locations, hardly even connected with one another. When you hold your radio or iPod, how does your brain know that the object you see is also what you feel and what you hear?

Consider other examples of what we need to explain:

- When you hear a ventriloquist's voice while you watch the dummy's mouth move, the dummy appears to be talking. Even infants look at someone whose mouth is moving when they hear speech; somehow they know to attribute sound to moving lips instead of stationary ones.
- If you watch a film in which the picture is slightly out of synchrony with the sound, or a foreign-language film that was badly dubbed, you know that the sound does not match the picture.
- If you see a light flash once while you simultaneously hear two beeps, you will sometimes think you saw the light flash twice, coincident with the beeps. If the tone is soft, it is also possible to experience the opposite: The tone beeps twice during one flash of light, and you think you heard only one beep. If you saw three flashes of light, you might think you heard three beeps (Andersen, Tiippana, & Sams, 2004). You can experience an example of this phenomenon with the Online Try It Yourself activity "Illustration of Binding."
- Here is another great demonstration to try (I. H. Robertson, 2005). Position yourself parallel to a large mirror, as in Figure 4.26, so that you see your right hand and its reflection in the mirror. Keep your left hand out of sight. Now repeatedly clench and unclench both hands in unison. You will feel your left hand clenching and unclenching at the same time you see the hand in the mirror doing the same thing. After 2 or 3 minutes, you may start to feel that the hand in the mirror is your own left hand. Some people even feel that they have three hands—the right hand, the real left hand, and the apparent left hand in the mirror.

The question of how the visual, auditory, and other areas of your brain produce a perception of a single object is known as the **binding problem**, or *large-scale integration* problem (Varela, Lachaus, Rodriguez, & Martinerie, 2001). In an earlier era, researchers thought that various kinds of sensory information converged onto what they called the association areas of the cortex (Figure 4.27). The guess was that those areas "associate" vision with hearing, hearing with touch, or current sensations with memories of previous experiences. However, later research found that the "association areas" perform advanced processing on a particular sensory system, such as vision or hearing, and do not combine one sense with another. Discarding the idea that various senses converge in the association areas called attention to the binding problem. If they don't converge, then how do we know that something we see is also what we hear or feel?

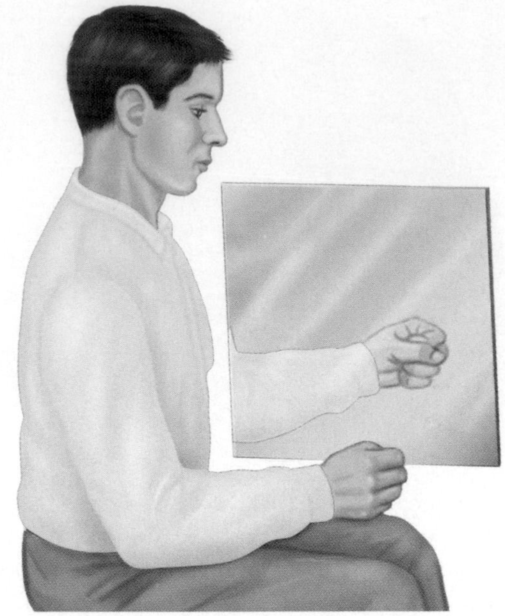

Figure 4.26 An illusion to demonstrate binding
Clench and unclench both hands while looking at your right hand and its reflection in the mirror. Keep your left hand out of sight. After a couple of minutes, you may start to experience the hand in the mirror as being your own left hand.

One hypothesis is that the binding of a perception requires precisely simultaneous activity in various brain areas (Eckhorn et al., 1988; Gray, König, Engel, & Singer, 1989). When people see a vague image and recognize it as a face, neurons in several areas of their visual cortex produce rapid activity known as **gamma waves**, ranging in frequency at various times from 30 to 80 action potentials per second (Rodriguez et al., 1999). The gamma waves are synchronized to the millisecond in various brain areas. When people look at the same image but fail to see a face, the synchronized waves do not emerge. Many but not all other studies have confirmed this relationship between recognizing or binding a visual pattern and developing synchronized activity in separate brain areas (Roelfsema, Engel, König, & Singer, 1997; Roelfsema, Lamme, & Spekreijse, 2004).

According to an alternative hypothesis (which does not contradict the first one), the key to binding a perception is to locate it in space. For example, if the location of something you see matches the location of something you hear, then you identify them as being the same thing. People with damage to the parietal cortex

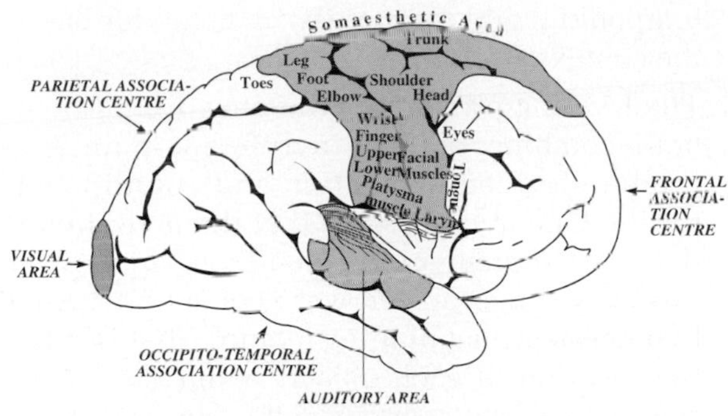

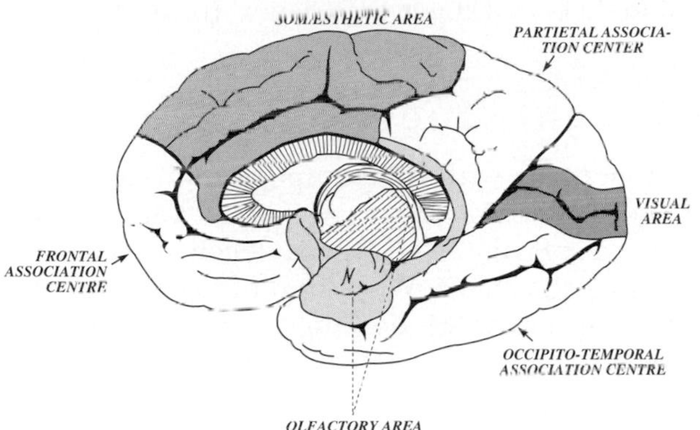

Figure 4.27 An old, somewhat misleading view of the cortex

Note the designation "association centre" in this illustration of the cortex from an old introductory psychology textbook (Hunter, 1923). Today's researchers are more likely to regard those areas as "additional sensory areas."

have trouble locating objects in space—that is, they are not sure where anything is—and they often fail to bind objects. For example, they have great trouble finding one red **X** among a group of green **X**s and red **O**s (L. C. Robertson, 2003). Also, if they see a display such as

they could report seeing a green triangle and a red square instead of a red triangle and a green square (L. Robertson, Treisman, Friedman-Hill, & Grabowecky, 1997; Treisman, 1999; R. Ward, Danziger, Owen, & Rafal, 2002; Wheeler & Treisman, 2002).

Even people with intact brains sometimes make mistakes of this kind if the displays are flashed very briefly or presented in the periphery of vision or presented during a distraction (Holcombe & Cavanagh, 2001; Lehky, 2000). You can experience this failure of binding with the Online Try It Yourself activity "Failure of Binding."

ONLINE *try it yourself*

STOP & CHECK

4. What is meant by the "binding problem" and what are two hypotheses to explain it?

Check your answer on page 104.

Module 4.2

In Closing: Functions of the Cerebral Cortex

The human cerebral cortex is so large that we easily slip into thinking of it as "the" brain, with all of the rest of the brain almost trivial. In fact, only mammals have a true cerebral cortex, and many mammals have only a small one. So subcortical areas by themselves can produce very complex behaviors, and a cerebral cortex by itself cannot do anything at all (because it would not be connected to any sense organs or muscles).

What, then, is the function of the cerebral cortex? The primary function seems to be one of elaborating sensory material. Even fish, which have no cerebral cortex, can see, hear, and so forth, but they do not recognize and remember all the complex aspects of sensory stimuli that mammals do. In a television advertisement, one company says that it doesn't make any products, but it makes lots of products better. The same could be said for the cerebral cortex.

Summary

1. Although brain size varies among mammalian species, the overall organization is similar. (p. 96)
2. The cerebral cortex has six laminae (layers) of neurons. A given lamina may be absent from certain parts of the cortex. The cortex is organized into columns of cells arranged perpendicular to the laminae. (p. 96)
3. The occipital lobe of the cortex is primarily responsible for vision. Damage to part of the occipital lobe leads to blindness in part of the visual field. (p. 98)
4. The parietal lobe processes body sensations. The postcentral gyrus contains four separate representations of the body. (p. 98)
5. The temporal lobe contributes to hearing and to complex aspects of vision. (p. 98)
6. The frontal lobe includes the precentral gyrus, which controls fine movements. It also includes the prefrontal cortex, which contributes to memories of current and recent stimuli, planning of movements, and regulation of emotional expressions. (p. 100)

7. The binding problem is the question of how we connect activities in different brain areas, such as sights and sounds. The various brain areas do not all send their information to a single central processor. (p. 102)
8. One hypothesis to answer the binding problem is that the brain binds activity in different areas when those areas produce precisely synchronous waves of activity. Still, many questions remain. (p. 102)

Answers to STOP & CHECK Questions

1. Column (p. 101)
2. Temporal lobe; parietal lobe; occipital lobe; frontal lobe (p. 101)
3. The prefrontal cortex is especially important for working memory (memory for what is currently happening) and for modifying behavior based on the context. (p. 101)
4. The binding problem is the question of how the brain combines activity in different brain areas to produce unified perception and coordinated behavior. One hypothesis is that the brain binds activity in different areas when those areas produce precisely synchronized waves of activity. Another hypothesis is that binding requires first identifying the location of each object; when the sight and sound appear to come from the same location, we bind them as a single experience. (p. 103)

Thought Question

When monkeys with Klüver-Bucy syndrome pick up lighted matches and snakes, we do not know whether they are displaying an emotional deficit or an inability to identify the object. What kind of research method might help answer this question?

Module 4.3
Research Methods

Imagine yourself trying to understand some large, complex machine. You could begin by describing the appearance and location of the machine's main parts. That task could be formidable, but it is easy compared to discovering what each part *does*.

Similarly, describing the structure of the brain is difficult enough, but the real challenge is to discover how it works. The methods for exploring brain functions are quite diverse, and throughout the text, we shall consider particular research methods as they become appropriate. However, most methods fall into a few categories. In this module, we consider those categories and the logic behind them. We also examine a few of the most common research techniques that will reappear in one chapter after another.

The main categories of methods for studying brain function are as follows:

1. *Correlate brain anatomy with behavior.* Do people with some unusual behavior also have unusual brains? If so, in what way?
2. *Record brain activity during behavior.* For example, we might record changes in brain activity during fighting, sleeping, finding food, or solving a problem.
3. *Examine the effects of brain damage.* After damage or temporary inactivation, what aspects of behavior are impaired?
4. *Examine the effects of stimulating some brain area.* Ideally, a behavior that is impaired by damage to some area should be enhanced by stimulating the same area.

Correlating Brain Anatomy with Behavior

One of the first ways ever used for studying brain function sounds easy: Find someone with unusual behavior and then look for unusual features of the brain. In the 1800s, Franz Gall observed some people with excellent verbal memories who had protruding eyes. He inferred that verbal memory depended on brain areas behind the eyes that had pushed the eyes forward. Gall then examined the skulls of people with other talents or personalities. He could not examine their brains, but he assumed that bulges and depressions on the skull corresponded to the brain areas below them. His process of relating skull anatomy to behavior is known as **phrenology**. One of his followers made the phrenological map in Figure 4.28.

One problem with phrenologists was their uncritical use of data. In some cases, they examined just one person with some behavioral quirk to define a brain area presumably responsible for it. Another problem was that skull shape has little relationship to brain anatomy. The skull is thicker in some places than others and thicker in some people than others.

Other investigators of the 1800s and 1900s rejected the idea of examining skulls but kept the idea that brain anatomy relates to behavior. One project was to remove people's brains after death and see whether the brains of eminent people looked unusual in any way. Several societies arose in which members agreed to donate their brains after death to the research cause. No conclusion resulted. The brains of the eminent varied considerably in size and external anatomy; so did the brains of everyone else. Certainly, if brain anatomy related to eminence or anything else, the relation wasn't obvious (Burrell, 2004). At the end of this module, we'll return to the issue of brain anatomy and intelligence. Modern methods enable us to approach the question more systematically than in the past, although the conclusions are still murky.

Even if we ignore the question of how overall brain size or shape relates to anything, the size of particular areas within the brain might relate to specific behaviors. For example, researchers would like to know whether people with schizophrenia or other psychiatric disorders have any brain abnormalities. Today, they can examine detailed brain anatomy in detail in living people using large enough groups for statistical analysis. We shall encounter a few examples of this kind of research throughout the text.

One method is **computerized axial tomography**, better known as a **CT** or **CAT scan** (Andreasen, 1988). A physician injects a dye into the blood (to increase contrast in the image) and then places the person's head into a CT scanner like the one shown in Figure 4.29a. X-rays are passed through the head and

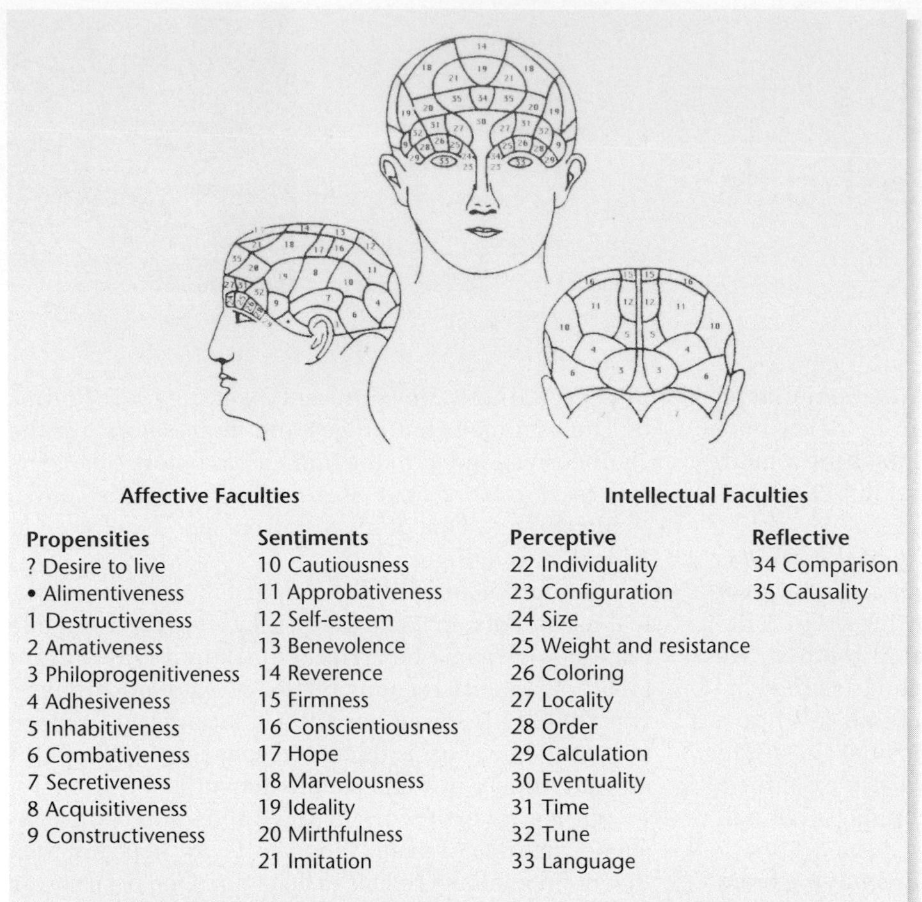

Figure 4.28 A phrenologist's map of the brain
Neuroscientists today also try to localize functions in the brain, but they use more careful methods and they study such functions as vision and hearing, not "secretiveness" and "marvelousness." *(Source: From Spurzheim, 1908)*

recorded by detectors on the opposite side. The CT scanner is rotated slowly until a measurement has been taken at each angle over 180 degrees. From the measurements, a computer constructs images of the brain. Figure 4.29b is an example.

Another method is **magnetic resonance imaging (MRI)** (Warach, 1995), which is based on the fact that any atom with an odd-numbered atomic weight, such as hydrogen, has an axis of rotation. An MRI device applies a powerful magnetic field (about 25,000 times the magnetic field of the earth) to align all the axes of rotation and then tilts them with a brief radio frequency field. When the radio frequency field is turned off, the atomic nuclei release electromagnetic energy as they relax and return to their original axis. By measuring that energy, MRI devices form an image of the brain, such as the one in Figure 4.30. MRI images anatomical details smaller than a millimeter in diameter. One drawback is that the person must lie motionless in a confining, noisy apparatus. The procedure is not suitable for children or anyone who fears enclosed places.

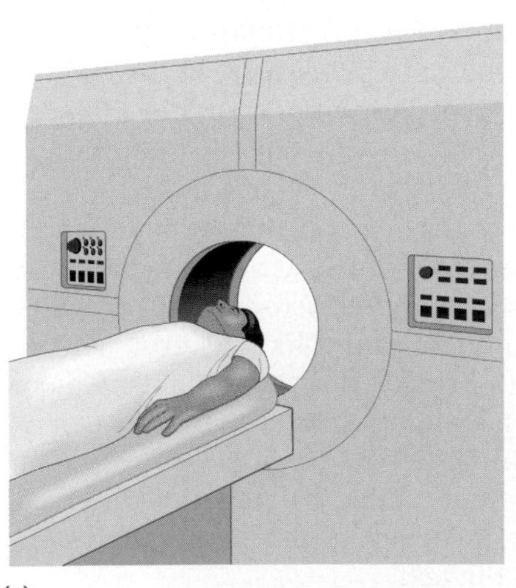

(a)

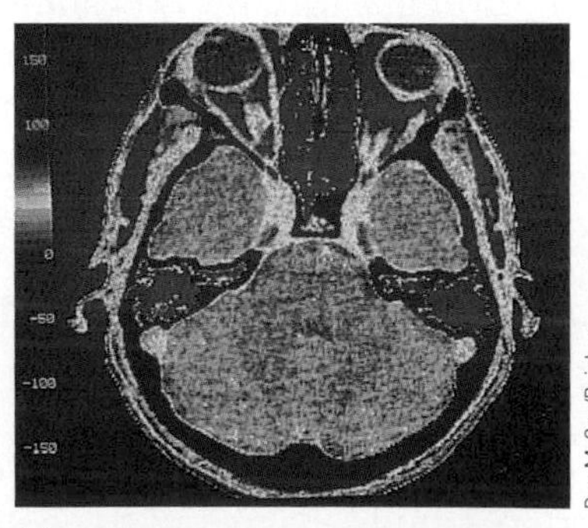

Dan McCoy/Rainbow

(b)

Figure 4.29 CT scanner
(a) A person's head is placed into the device and then a rapidly rotating source sends x-rays through the head while detectors on the opposite side make photographs. A computer then constructs an image of the brain. **(b)** A view of a normal human brain generated by computerized axial tomography (CT scanning).

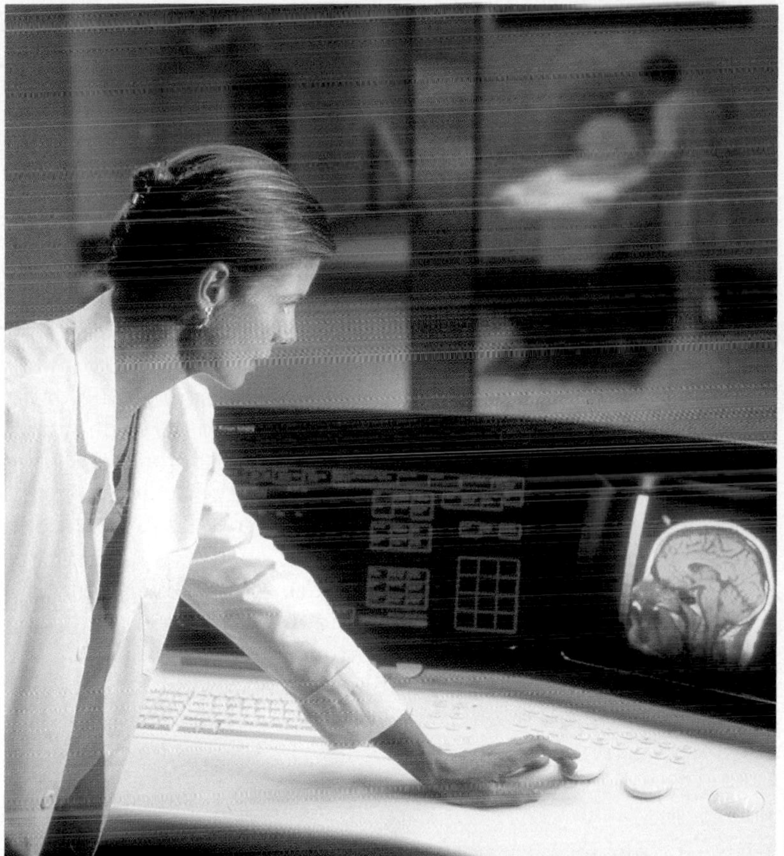

© Wil and Demi McIntyre/Photo Researchers

Figure 4.30 A view of a living brain generated by magnetic resonance imaging
Any atom with an odd-numbered atomic weight, such as hydrogen, has an inherent rotation. An outside magnetic field can align the axes of rotation. A radio frequency field can then make all these atoms move like tiny gyros. When the radio frequency field is turned off, the atomic nuclei release electromagnetic energy as they relax. By measuring that energy, we can obtain an image of a structure such as the brain without damaging it.

One limitation is something you will hear repeatedly in psychology: Correlation does not mean causation. For example, brain abnormalities could influence behavior, but it is also possible that abnormal behavior led to brain abnormalities. We need other kinds of evidence to support cause-and-effect conclusions.

STOP & CHECK

1. Researchers today sometimes relate differences in people's behavior to differences in their brain anatomy. How does their approach differ from that of the phrenologists?

Check your answer on page 116.

Recording Brain Activity

When you watch a sunset, feel frightened, or solve a mathematical problem, which brain areas change their activity? With laboratory animals, researchers insert electrodes to record brain activity (see Methods 6.1, page 173). Studies of human brains use noninvasive methods—that is, methods that don't require inserting anything.

A device called the **electroencephalograph (EEG)** records electrical activity of the brain through electrodes—ranging from just a few to more than a hundred—attached to the scalp (Figure 4.31). Electrodes glued to the scalp measure the average activity at any moment for the population of cells under the electrode. The output is then amplified and recorded. This device can record either spontaneous brain activity, or activity in response to a stimulus, in which case we call the results **evoked potentials** or **evoked responses.** For one example of a study, researchers recorded evoked potentials from young adults as they watched pictures of nudes of both sexes. Men reported high arousal by the female nudes, while women reported neutral feelings to both the males and females, but both men's and women's brains showed strong evoked potentials to the opposite-sex nudes (Costa, Braun, & Birbaumer, 2003).

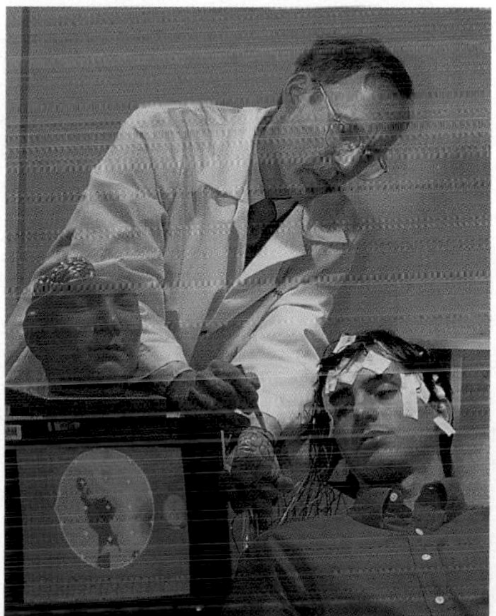

© Richard Nowitz/Photo Researchers

Figure 4.31 Electroencephalography
An electroencephalograph records the overall activity of neurons under various electrodes attached to the scalp.

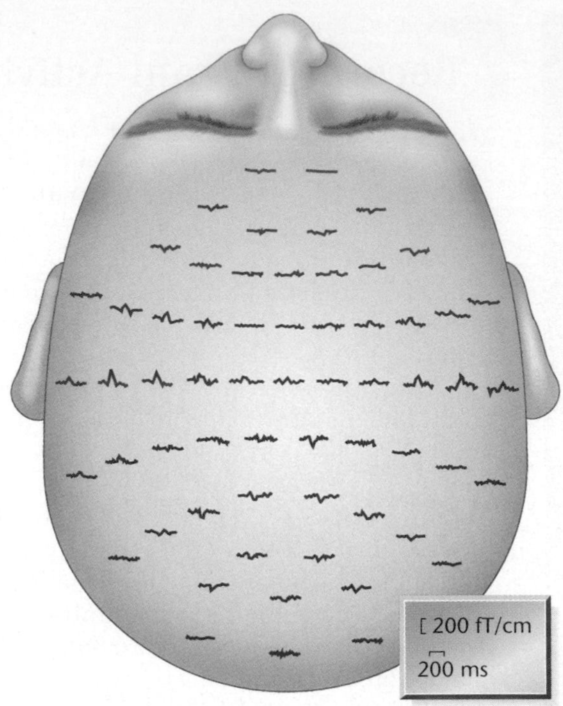

Figure 4.32 A result of magnetoencephalography, showing responses to a tone in the right ear
The nose is shown at the top. For each spot on the diagram, the display shows the changing response over a few hundred ms following the tone. (Note calibration at lower right.) The tone evoked responses in many areas, with the largest responses in the temporal cortex, especially on the left side. *(Source: Reprinted from* Neuroscience: From the Molecular to the Cognitive, *by R. Hari, 1994, p. 165, with kind permission from Elsevier Science–NL, Sara Burgerhartstraat 25, 1055 KV Amsterdam, The Netherlands.)*

That is, evoked potentials sometimes reveal information that self-reports do not.

A **magnetoencephalograph (MEG)** is similar, but instead of measuring electrical activity, it measures the faint magnetic fields generated by brain activity (Hari, 1994). Like EEG, an MEG recording identifies only the approximate location of activity to within about a centimeter. However, MEG has excellent temporal resolution, showing changes from one millisecond to another.

Figure 4.32 shows an MEG record of brain responses to a brief tone heard in the right ear. The diagram represents a human head as viewed from above, with the nose at the top (Hari, 1994). Researchers using MEG can identify the times at which various brain areas respond and thereby trace a wave of brain activity from its point of origin to all the other areas that process it (Salmelin, Hari, Lounasmaa, & Sams, 1994).

Another method, **positron-emission tomography (PET)**, provides a high-resolution image of activity in a living brain by recording the emission of radioactivity from injected chemicals. First, the person receives an injection of glucose or some other chemical containing radioactive atoms. When a radioactive atom decays, it releases a positron that immediately collides with a nearby electron, emitting two gamma rays in exactly opposite directions. The person's head is surrounded by a set of gamma ray detectors (Figure 4.33). When two detectors record gamma rays at the same time, they identify a spot halfway between those detectors as the point of origin of the gamma rays. A computer uses this information to determine how many gamma rays are coming from each spot in the brain and therefore how much of the radioactive chemical is located in each area (Phelps & Mazziotta, 1985). The areas showing the most radioactivity are the ones with the most blood flow, and therefore, presumably, the most brain activity.

Ordinarily, PET scans use radioactive chemicals with a short half-life, made in a large device called a cyclotron. Because cyclotrons are large and expensive, PET scans are available only at research hospitals. Furthermore, PET requires exposing the brain to radioactivity. For most purposes, PET scans have been re-

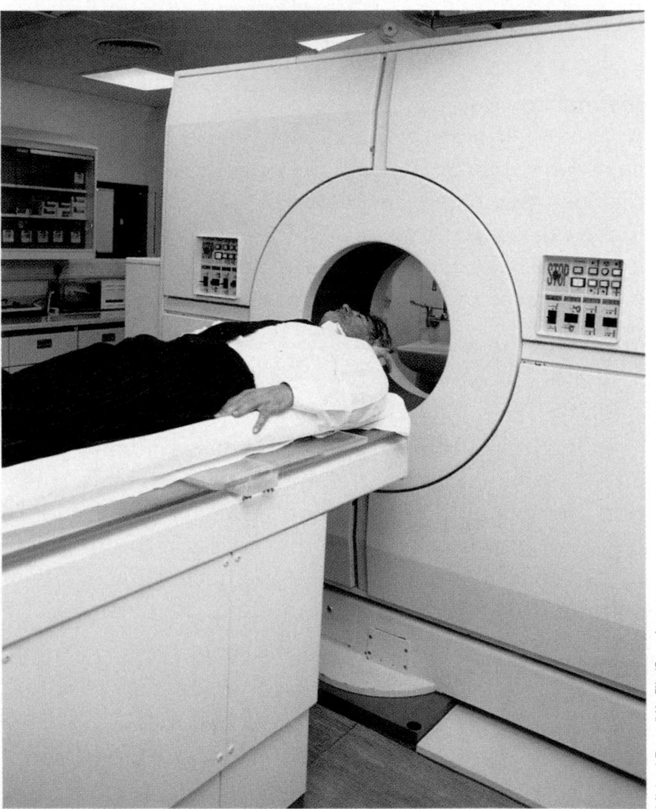

Michael Evans/Life File/Getty Images

Figure 4.33 A PET scanner
A person engages in a cognitive task while attached to this apparatus that records which areas of the brain become more active and by how much.

placed by functional magnetic resonance imaging (fMRI), which is somewhat less expensive and poses no known health risks. Standard MRI scans record the energy released by water molecules after removal of a magnetic field. Because the brain has little net flow of water, MRI doesn't show changes over time. **Functional magnetic resonance imaging (fMRI)** is a modified version of MRI based on hemoglobin (the blood protein that binds oxygen) (Detre & Floyd, 2001). Hemoglobin with oxygen reacts to a magnetic field differently from hemoglobin without oxygen. Because oxygen consumption increases in the brain areas with the greatest activity (Mukamel et al., 2005), researchers can set the fMRI scanner to detect changes in the oxygen content of the blood and thereby measure the relative levels of brain activity in various areas (Logothetis, Pauls, Augath, Trinath, & Oeltermann, 2001). An fMRI image has a spatial resolution of 1 or 2 mm (almost as good as standard MRI) and temporal resolution of about a second (Figure 4.34).

Various other methods for brain scans are also in use (Grinvald & Hildesheim, 2004). For more information about brain scan techniques and some striking pictures, check this website: **http://www.musc.edu/psychiatry/fnrd/primer_index.htm**

Unfortunately, interpreting the images is not easy. For example, a raw measure of your brain activity while you were reading would mean nothing without a comparison to something else. So researchers would record your brain activity once while you were reading, and once while you were, well, not reading, but doing what? Doing "nothing" is not an option; a healthy human brain is always doing something. As a comparison task, researchers might ask you to look at a page written in a foreign language.

Identifying the areas active during reading still does not tell us what those areas do during reading. Reading requires language, memory, visual attention, and other skills, so further research would be needed to identify which areas do what. The task might seem overwhelming, and it would be for any laboratory by itself, but researchers share their results in an online library of fMRI results (Van Horn, Grafton, Rockmore, & Gazzaniga, 2004).

One important generalization is that brain scan results vary across individuals. For example, solving a chess problem activates different areas for average players than in chess experts. For chess experts, who may have seen the same position many times before, it is not a reasoning problem but a memory problem (Amidzic, Riehle, Fehr, Wienbruch, & Elbert, 2001; Pesenti et al., 2001).

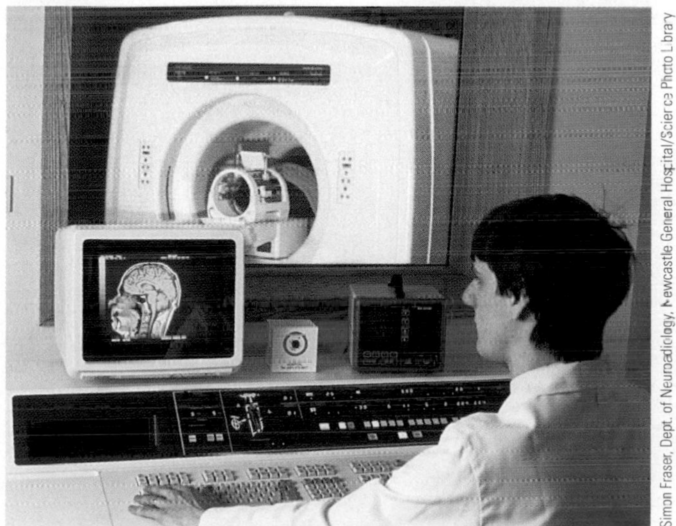

Simon Fraser, Dept. of Neuroradiology, Newcastle General Hospital/Science Photo Library

Figure 4.34 An fMRI scan of a human brain
An fMRI produces fairly detailed photos at rates up to about one per second.

Effects of Brain Damage

In 1861, the French neurologist Paul Broca found that nearly every patient who had lost the ability to speak had damage in part of the left frontal cortex, an area now known as *Broca's area*. That was the first discovery about the function of any brain area and a pioneering event in modern neurology.

Since then, researchers have made countless reports of behavioral impairments after brain damage from stroke, disease, and other causes. From a research standpoint, the problem is the lack of control. Most people with damage in any area have damage to other areas too, and no two people have exactly the same damage.

With laboratory animals, researchers can intentionally damage a selected area. A **lesion** is damage to a brain area; an **ablation** is a removal of a brain area. To damage a structure in the interior of the brain, researchers use a **stereotaxic instrument**, a device for the precise placement of electrodes in the brain (Figure 4.35). By consulting a stereotaxic atlas (map) of some species' brain, a researcher aims an electrode at the desired position with reference to landmarks on the skull (Figure 4.36). Then the researcher anesthetizes an animal, drills a small hole in the skull, inserts the electrode, and lowers it to the target.

Suppose someone makes a lesion, finds that the animal stops eating, and concludes that the area is important for eating. "Wait a minute," you might ask. "How do we know the deficit wasn't caused by anesthetizing the animal, drilling a hole in its skull, and lowering an electrode to this target?" To test this possibility, an experimenter produces a **sham lesion** in a control group, performing all the same procedures but without the electrical current. Any behavioral difference

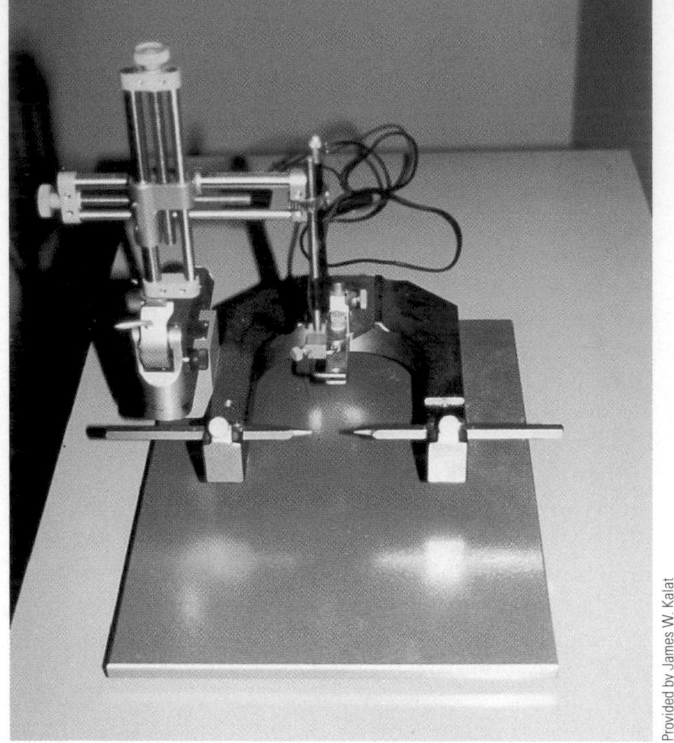

Provided by James W. Kalat

Figure 4.35 A stereotaxic instrument for locating brain areas in small animals
Using this device, researchers can insert an electrode to stimulate, record from, or damage any point in the brain.

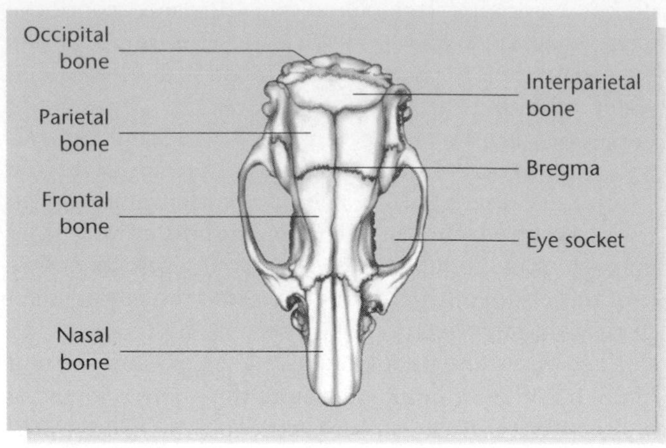

Figure 4.36 Skull bones of a rat
Bregma, the point where four bones meet on the top of the skull, is a useful landmark from which to locate areas of the brain.

between the two groups must result from the lesion and not the other procedures.

Besides lesions, several other procedures can inactivate various brain structures or systems. In the **gene-knockout approach,** researchers use biochemical methods to direct a mutation to a particular gene that is important for certain types of cells, transmitters, or receptors (Joyner & Guillemot, 1994). Certain chemicals temporarily inactivate one part of the brain or one type of synapse. **Transcranial magnetic stimulation,** the application of an intense magnetic field to a portion of the scalp, can temporarily inactivate the neurons below the magnet (Walsh & Cowey, 2000). This procedure enables researchers to study a given individual's behavior with the brain area active, then inactive, and then active again. Figure 4.37 shows the apparatus for this procedure.

With any of these approaches, a big problem is to specify the exact behavioral deficit. By analogy, suppose you cut a wire inside a television and the picture disappeared. You would know that this wire is necessary for the picture, but you would not know why. Similarly, if you damaged a brain

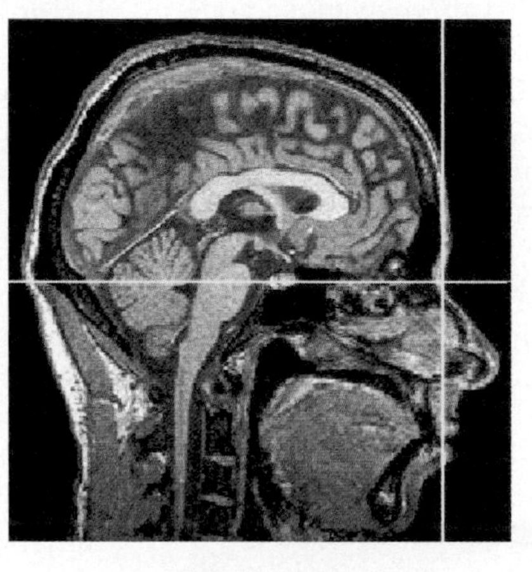

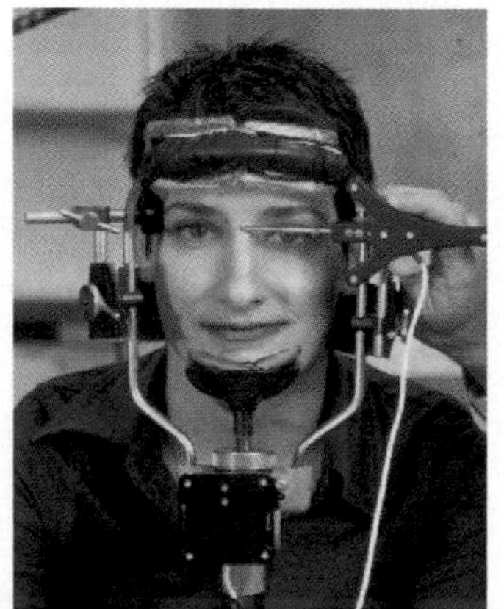

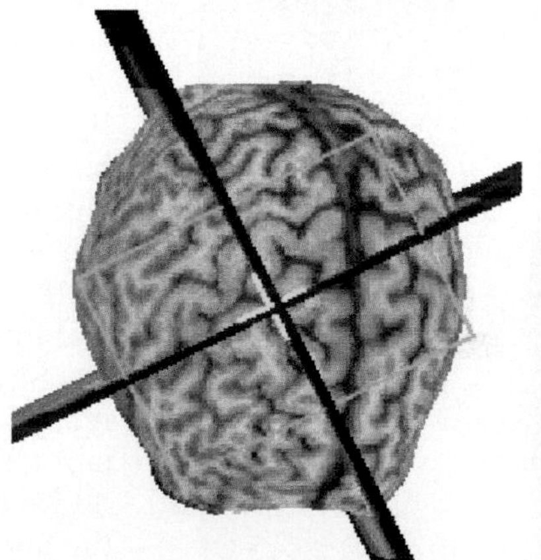

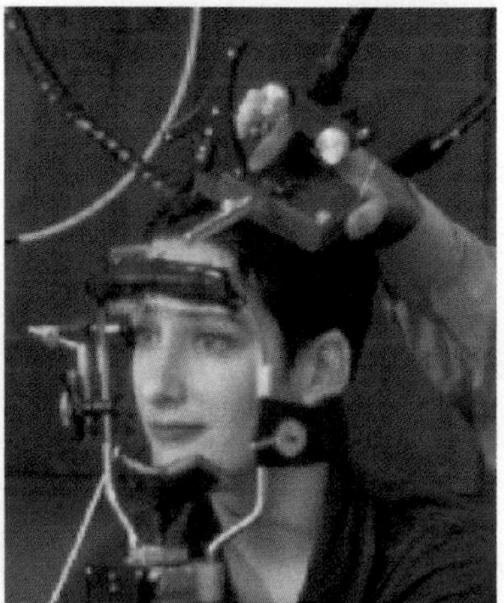

Courtesy of Tomas Paus, McGill University, Canada

Figure 4.37 Apparatus for magnetic stimulation of a human brain
The procedure is known as transcranial magnetic stimulation, or TMS.

area and the animal stopped eating, you wouldn't know how that area contributes to eating. To find out, you would need to test eating and other behaviors under many conditions.

Effects of Brain Stimulation

If brain damage impairs some behavior, stimulation should increase it. Researchers can insert electrodes to stimulate brain areas in laboratory animals. With humans, they can use a less invasive procedure (although it provides less precision). Researchers apply a magnetic field to the scalp, thereby stimulating the brain areas beneath it (Fitzgerald, Brown, & Daskalakis, 2002). Whereas intense transcranial magnetic stimulation inactivates the underlying area, a brief, milder application stimulates it. Another approach is to inject a chemical that stimulates one kind of receptor. That method, of course, stimulates those receptors throughout the brain, not just in one area.

One limitation of any stimulation study is that complex behaviors and experiences depend on many brain areas, not just one, so artificial stimulation produces artificial responses. For example, electrically or magnetically stimulating the primary visual areas of the brain produces reports of sparkling flashing points of light, not the sight of a face or other recognizable object. It is easier to discover which brain area is responsible for vision (or movement or whatever) than to discover how it produces a meaningful pattern.

Table 4.5 summarizes various methods of studying brain-behavior relationships.

STOP & CHECK

2. What is the difference between invasive and noninvasive procedures?
3. How do the effects of brief, mild magnetic stimulation differ from those of longer, more intense stimulation?
4. Why does electrical or magnetic stimulation of the brain seldom produce complex, meaningful sensations or movements?

Check your answers on page 116.

Table 4.5 Brain-Behavior Research Methods

Correlate Brain Anatomy with Behavior	
Computerized axial tomography (CAT)	Maps brain areas, but requires exposure to x-rays
Magnetic resonance imaging (MRI)	Maps brain areas in detail, using magnetic fields
Record Brain Activity During Behavior	
Record from electrodes in brain	Invasive; used with laboratory animals, seldom humans
Electroencephalograph (EEG)	Records from scalp; measures changes by ms, with but low resolution of location of the signal
Evoked potentials	Similar to EEG but in response to stimuli
Magnetoencephalograph (MEG)	Similar to EEG but measures magnetic fields
Positron emission tomography (PET)	Measures changes over both time and location but requires exposing brain to radiation
Functional magnetic resonance imaging (fMRI)	Measures changes over about 1 second, identifies location within 1–2 mm, no use of radiation
Examine Effects of Brain Damage	
Study victims of stroke etc.	Used with humans; each person has different damage
Lesion	Controlled damage in laboratory animals
Ablation	Removal of a brain area
Gene-knockout	Effects wherever that gene is active (e.g., a receptor)
Transcranial magnetic stimulation	Intense application temporarily inactivates a brain area
Examine Effects of Stimulating a Brain Area	
Stimulating electrodes	Invasive; used with laboratory animals, seldom with humans
Transcranial magnetic stimulation	Brief, mild application activates underlying brain area

Brain and Intelligence

How does intelligence relate to brain size or structure, if at all? This is a question about which you might be curious. It is also an example of how new methods facilitate more detailed research.

As mentioned at the start of this module, many researchers compared the brains of eminent (presumably intelligent) people to those of less successful people but failed to find any obvious difference in total brain size or other easily observed features. More recently, neuroscientists examined the brain of the famous scientist Albert Einstein, again hoping to find something unusual. Einstein's total brain size was just average. He did have a higher than average ratio of glia to neurons in one brain area (M. C. Diamond, Scheibel, Murphy, & Harvey, 1985). However, because researchers examined several areas and found a difference in only one, the difference could be accidental or irrelevant. Another study found expansion of part of Einstein's parietal cortex, as shown in Figure 4.38 (Witelson, Kigar, & Harvey, 1999). However, a study of a single brain produces no more than a suggestive hypothesis.

Indeed, a little reflection should convince us that brain size can't be synonymous with intelligence. If it were, then we could promote intelligence just by providing lots of good nutrition, and we wouldn't have to bother with education.

However, despite the arguments against it and the weak evidence for it, the idea has lingered: Shouldn't brain size have *something* to do with intelligence? Even if the idea isn't quite right, is it completely wrong? By analogy, muscle size isn't a good predictor of athletic ability—except for a few sports like weightlifting—but it isn't completely irrelevant either.

Comparisons Across Species

For better or worse, we humans dominate life on earth, presumably because of our brains. However, all mammalian brains have the same basic organization. The components, such as the visual cortex and the auditory cortex, are in the same relative locations, and all mammalian brains have the same cell types and same neurotransmitters.

Mammals also resemble one another in the proportions of various brain areas. Choose any two major brain areas, such as hippocampus and thalamus. Call one area A and the other B. Now choose any mammalian species. If you know the size of area A, you can fairly accurately predict the size of area B. The main exception to this rule is the olfactory bulb, which is,

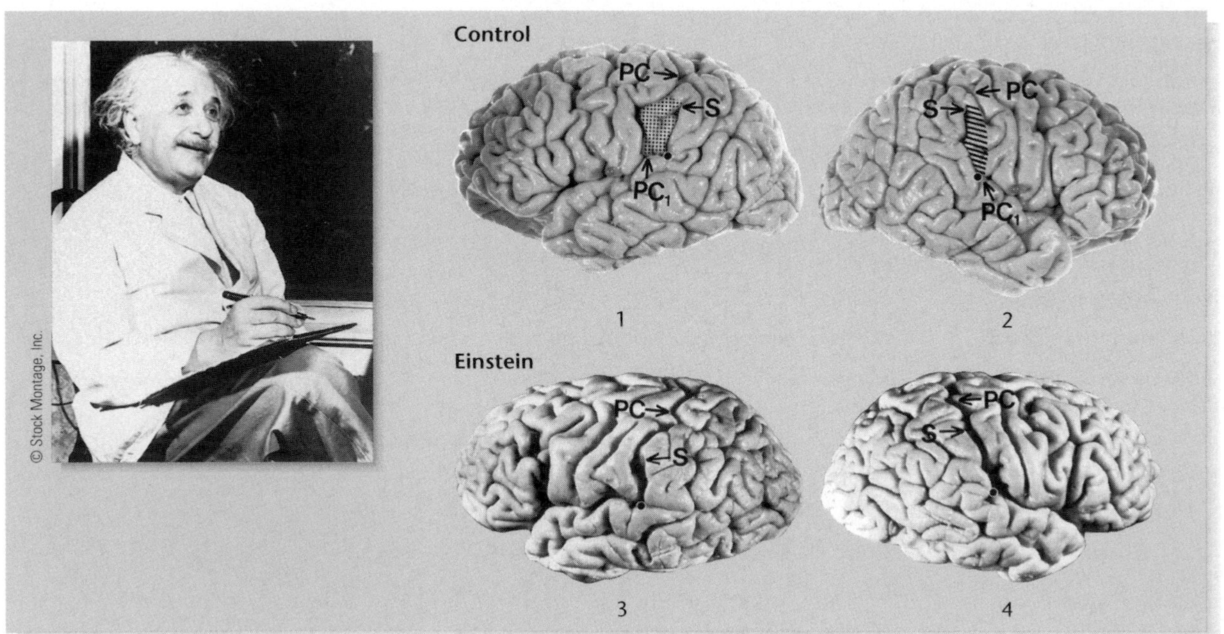

Figure 4.38 Einstein's brain

Parts 1 and 2 show the left and right hemispheres of an average brain; the stippled (left) and hatched (right) sections are a brain area called the parietal operculum. Parts 3 and 4 show Einstein's brain; the parietal operculum is absent because the inferior parietal lobe has expanded beyond its usual boundaries, occupying the area where one ordinarily finds the parietal operculum.
(Source: From "The exceptional brain of Albert Einstein," by S. F. Wittelson, D. L. Kigar, & T. Harvey (1999). Lancet, 353, *2149–2153.)*

for example, large in dogs and small in humans (Finlay & Darlington, 1995).

So, because brain organization is about the same across species, the main differences are quantitative. Do variations in overall size relate to intelligence? We humans like to think of ourselves as the most intelligent animals—after all, we're the ones defining what intelligence means! However, if we look only at size, we cannot demonstrate our intellectual superiority. Elephants' brains are four times the size of ours, and sperm whales' brains are twice as big as elephants'. Perhaps, many people suggest, the more important consideration is brain-to-body ratio. Figure 4.39 illustrates the relationship between logarithm of body mass and logarithm of brain mass for various vertebrates (Jerison, 1985). Note that the species we regard as most intelligent—for example, ahem, ourselves—have larger brains in proportion to body size than do the species we consider less impressive, such as frogs.

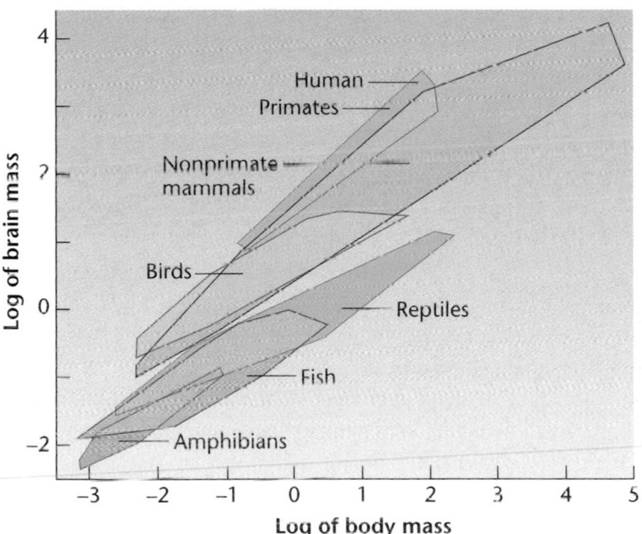

Figure 4.39 Relationship of brain mass to body mass across species

Each species is one point within one of the polygons. In general, log of body mass is a good predictor of log of brain mass. Note that primates in general and humans in particular have a large brain mass in proportion to body mass. *(Source: Adapted from Jerison, 1985)*

However, brain-to-body ratio has problems also: Chihuahuas have the highest brain-to-body ratio of all dog breeds, not because they were bred for intelligence but because they were bred for small body size (Deacon, 1997). Squirrel monkeys, which are also very thin, have a higher brain-to-body ratio than humans. (And with the increasing prevalence of human obesity, our brain-to-body ratio is declining even more!) The elephant-nose fish (Figure 4.40), which you might keep in a tropical fish aquarium, has a brain that weighs just 0.3 g, but that's 3% of the total weight of the fish, as compared

Figure 4.40 An elephant-nose fish

The brain of this odd-looking fish weighs 0.3 g (0.01 oz), which is 3% of the weight of the whole fish—a vastly higher percentage than most other fish and higher even than humans. What this fish does with so much brain, we don't know, but it may relate to the fish's unusual ability to detect electrical fields.

to humans' 2% brain-to-body ratio (Nilsson, 1999). So neither total brain mass nor brain-to-body ratio puts humans in first place.

We might look for some more complex measure that considers both total brain size and brain-to-body ratio. But before we can test various formulas, we need a clear definition of animal intelligence, which has been an elusive concept, to say the least (Macphail, 1985). Given that studies of brain and behavior in nonhumans are not helping, let's abandon the effort and turn to humans.

STOP & CHECK

5. If you know the total brain size for some species and you want to predict the size of a given structure, which structure would be hardest to predict?
6. Why are both brain size and brain-to-body ratio unsatisfactory ways of estimating animal intelligence?

Check your answers on page 116.

Comparisons Across Humans

For many years, studies of brain size and intelligence in humans found correlations barely above zero. However, a low correlation between two variables can mean either that they are truly unrelated or that at least one of them was measured poorly. In this case, the measurements of intelligence (by IQ tests) were of course imperfect, and the measurements of brain size were as bad or worse. External skull size is a poor measure of brain size because some people have thicker skulls than others. Measuring the internal volume of the skull (after death) is also imperfect because many people's brains do not fill the entire skull. Removing the brain after death and weighing it has its own problems. Brains begin to decompose immediately after death, and they begin to dry out as soon as they are removed from the skull.

Today, however, MRI scans can accurately measure brain volume in healthy, living people. Most studies, though not all (Schoenemann, Budinger, Sarich, & Wang, 2000), have found a moderate positive correlation between brain size and IQ, typically around .3 (Willerman, Schultz, Rutledge, & Bigler, 1991). Two studies on twins found greater resemblance between monozygotic than dizygotic twins for both brain size and IQ scores (Pennington et al., 2000; Posthuma et al., 2002) (Figure 4.41). Surprisingly, IQ correlated more strongly with the size of subcortical areas than with that of the cerebral cortex (Pennington et al., 2000).

Do the same genes that control brain size also influence IQ? To approach this question, investigators again examined pairs of twins. For monozygotic twins, they found that the size of one twin's brain correlated .31 with the *other* twin's IQ. For dizygotic twins, the correlation was .15. These results suggest that the genes controlling brain size also influence IQ (Pennington et al., 2000). Several genes have been identified that influence both brain structure and intellectual performance (Pezawas et al., 2004; Zhang, 2003).

Another approach is to examine the correlation between IQ scores and specific brain areas. In one study, investigators used MRI to measure the size of gray matter and white matter areas throughout the brains of 23 young adults from one university campus and 24 middle-aged or older adults from another campus. In Figure 4.42, the areas highlighted in red showed a statistically significant correlation with IQ; those highlighted in yellow showed an even stronger correlation. Note two points: First, IQ correlates with the size of many brain areas. Second, the results differed between the two samples, either because of the age difference or for other unidentified reasons (Haier, Jung, Yeo, Head, & Alkire, 2004).

As always, correlation does not mean causation. For example, brain size and IQ might correlate because good health and nutrition contribute to both brain growth and intellectual performance. In addition, how many pencils someone can hold in one hand no doubt correlates with the size of the hand. But it also correlates with the size of the foot, just because most people with large hands also have large feet. Similarly, the size of one brain area correlates with the size of others, so even if intelligence depended on only one brain area, it still might correlate with the size of other areas.

Now for the most confusing part: Although IQ correlates positively with brain size for either men or women separately, men on the average have larger brains than women but equal IQs (Willerman et al., 1991). If brain size is important, why don't men have higher IQs? One possibility is to examine brain-to-body ratio instead of just brain volume, but that may not be the whole answer. Most of the research has reported correlations between IQ and brain volume, not brain-to-body ratio. Besides, if IQ depended literally on brain-to-body ratio, it should change when people gain or lose weight, and of course, it does not.

A different hypothesis is that IQ relates more closely to the gray matter of the brain—that is, the cell bodies—rather than total mass including white matter (the axons). Women on the average have more and deeper gyri on the surface of the cortex, especially in the frontal and parietal areas (Luders et al., 2004). Consequently, the surface area of the cortex is about the

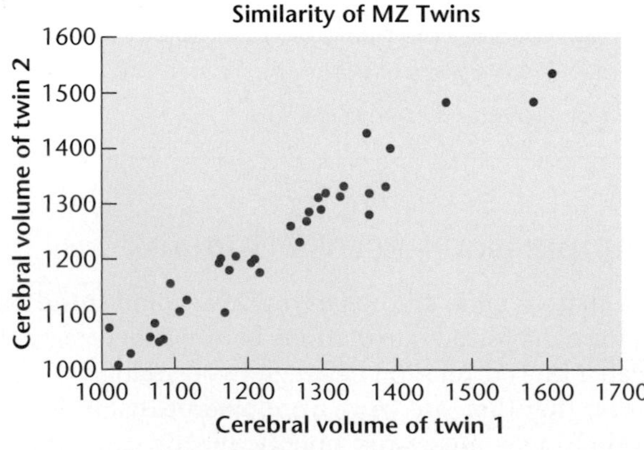

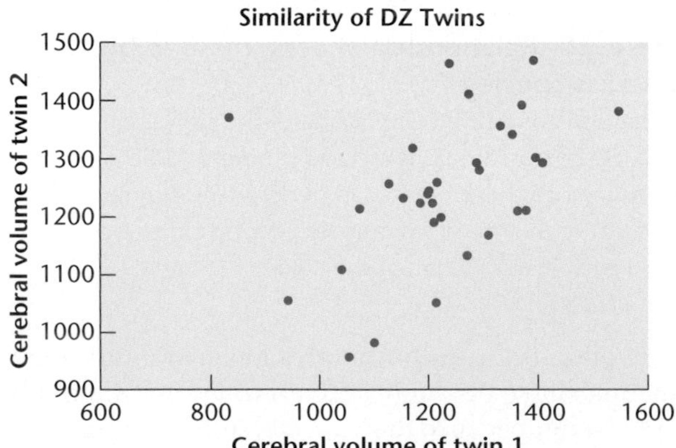

Figure 4.41 Correlations of brain size for twins

Each graph is a scatter plot, in which each dot represents one pair of twins. Brain size for one twin is shown along the *x* axis; brain size for the other twin is along the *y* axis. Note that both kinds of twins show similarities, but the correlation is stronger for the monozygotic twins. *(Source: From B. F. Pennington et al., "A twin MRI study of size variations in the human brain,"* Journal of Cognitive Neuroscience, 12, *pp. 223–232, Figures 1, 2. © 2000 by the Massachusetts Institute of Technology. Reprinted with permission.)*

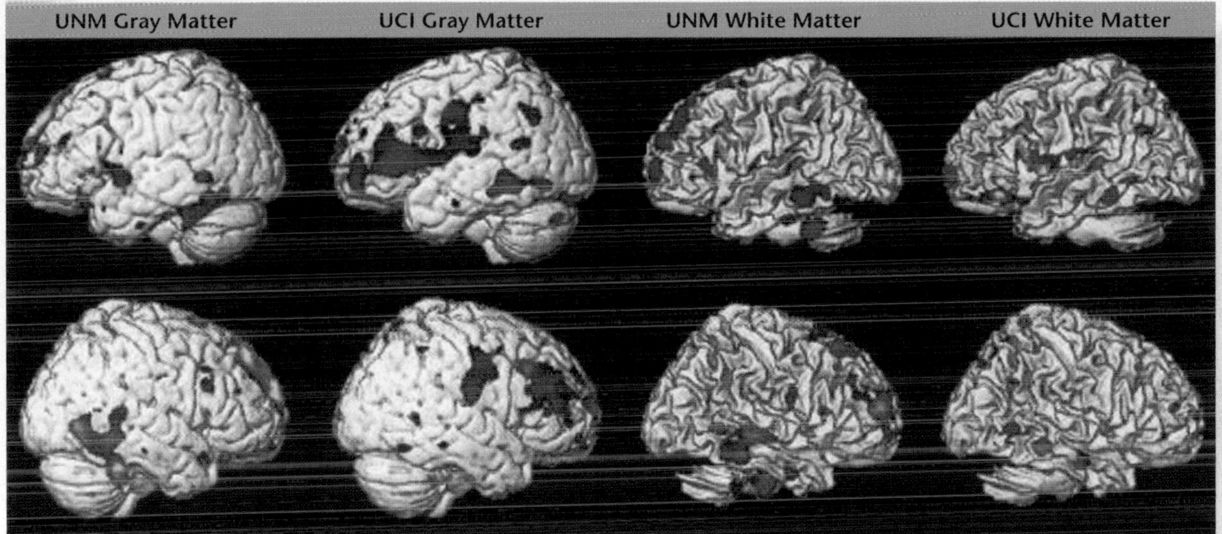

Figure 4.42 Cortical areas whose size correlated with IQ
The top row shows the left hemisphere; the bottom row shows the right. UNM and UCI columns show the results for two universities (University of New Mexico and University of California at Irvine). Areas whose size was significantly associated with IQ are shown in red; areas with the strongest relationship are shown in yellow. *(Source: Adapted from "Structural brain variation and general intelligence," by R. J. Haier, R. E. Jung, R. A. Yeo, K. Head, & M. T. Alkire,* NeuroImage, 23, *pp. 425–433, Copyright 2004 with permission from Elsevier.)*

same in men and women. Because the surface is lined with cells (gray matter), the sexes are nearly equal in gray matter, whereas men have more white matter (Allen, Damasio, Grabowski, Bruss, & Zhang, 2003). An MRI study found a .34 correlation between teenagers' IQ scores and the gray matter volumes of their brains (Frangou, Chitins, & Williams, 2004).

So a tentative conclusion is that, other things being equal, more gray matter is associated with better performance on intellectual tests. However, let's go back to species comparisons: The difference between human brains and those of chimpanzees and gorillas is more a matter of increased white matter in humans than increased gray matter (Schoenemann, Sheehan, & Glotzer, 2005). So the species difference seems to imply that white matter (i.e., connectivity within the brain) is important for intelligence. At this point, we have far better data than before about the brain and intelligence, but the overall picture is still confusing.

On the other hand, how important is this question, really? It has been a matter of curiosity for many people for a long time, but it has no great theoretical importance or practical applications. Relating total brain to total intelligence is like relating the geographical area of a country to the size of its population: Sure, the correlation is positive, but it overlooks a host of more interesting variables. Progress in both psychology and neuroscience depends on making finer-grained distinctions. How do the anatomy, chemistry, and other features of each part of the brain relate to specific aspects of behavior? In the rest of this text, we concentrate on these types of questions.

7. Why do recent studies show a stronger relationship between brain size and IQ than older studies did?
8. What evidence indicated that the genes that control human brain size also influence IQ?

Check your answers on page 116.

Module 4.3
In Closing: Research Methods and Their Limits

Descriptions of the history of science sometimes highlight a single study that "conclusively" established one theory or another. Such events are rare. Far more often, researchers gradually accumulate evidence that points in a particular direction, until eventually that view becomes dominant. Even in those rare cases when a single study appears to have been decisive, researchers often identify it as decisive only in retrospect, after several additional studies have confirmed the finding.

The reason we need so many studies is that almost any study has limitations. For example, one set of researchers found evidence linking one part of the human brain to mathematical thinking (Piazza, Izard, Pinel, Le Bihan, & Dehaene, 2004). Another study at about the same time found evidence against that conclusion (Shuman & Kanwisher, 2004). Both studies were conducted by well-respected scientists using similar methods. In a case like this, we hope additional research will identify key differences between the two studies. Do the differences depend on the age of the participants, the type of mathematical task, or the exact method of measuring brain activity? Sometimes what seem like small differences in procedure produce very different outcomes (MacAndrew, Klatzky, Fiez, McClelland, & Becker, 2002). For example, several decades ago, two laboratories studying human learning found that they got consistently different results just because one of them used chairs that resembled dentists' chairs, which reminded participants of pain or displeasure (Kimble, 1967).

Even when several studies using the same method produce similar results, the possibility remains that the method itself has a hidden flaw. Therefore, scientists prefer whenever possible to compare results from widely different methods. The more types of evidence point to a given conclusion, the greater our confidence.

Summary

1. People who differ with regard to some behavior sometimes also differ with regard to their brain anatomy. MRI is one modern method of imaging a living brain. However, correlations between behavior and anatomy should be evaluated cautiously. (p. 105)
2. Another research method is to record activity in some brain area during a given behavior. Many methods are available, including EEG, fMRI, and other noninvasive procedures. (p. 107)
3. Another way to study brain-behavior relationships is to examine the effects of brain damage. If someone loses an ability after some kind of brain damage, then that area contributes in some way, although we need more research to determine how. (p. 109)
4. If stimulation of a brain area increases some behavior, presumably that area contributes to the behavior. (p. 111)
5. Recent research using modern methods suggests a moderate positive relationship between brain size and intelligence, although many puzzles and uncertainties remain. (p. 112)
6. Each method by itself has limitations, and any conclusion must remain tentative, pending further research using additional methods and populations. (p. 115)

Answers to STOP & CHECK Questions

1. The phrenologists drew conclusions based on just one or a few people with some oddity of behavior. Today's researchers compare groups statistically. Also, today's researchers examine the brain itself, not the skull above it. (p. 107)
2. An invasive procedure is one in which the investigator inserts something, like an electrode. A noninvasive procedure inserts nothing and does not cause any known health risk. (p. 111)
3. Brief, mild magnetic stimulation on the scalp increases activity in the underlying brain areas, whereas longer, more intense stimulation blocks it. (p. 111)
4. Meaningful, complex sensations and movements require a pattern of precisely timed activity in a great many cells, not just a burst of overall activity diffusely in one area. (p. 111)
5. The olfactory bulb (p. 113)
6. If we consider ourselves to be the most intelligent species—and admittedly, that is just an assumption—we are confronted with the fact that we have neither the largest brains nor the highest brain-to-body ratio. Brain-to-body ratio depends on selection for thinness as well as selection for brain size. Furthermore, animal intelligence is undefined and poorly measured, so we cannot even determine what correlates with it. (p. 113)
7. The use of MRI greatly improves the measurement of brain size. (p. 115)
8. For pairs of monozygotic twins, the size of one twin's brain correlates significantly with the other twin's IQ (as well as his or her own). Therefore, whatever genes increase the growth of the brain also increase IQ. (p. 115)

Thought Question

Certain unusual aspects of brain structure were observed in the brain of Albert Einstein. One interpretation is that he was born with certain specialized brain features that encouraged his scientific and intellectual abilities. What is an alternative interpretation?

Chapter Ending

Key Terms and Activities

Terms

ablation (p. 109)
anterior (p. 83)
anterior commissure (p. 96)
autonomic nervous system (p. 83)
basal ganglia (p. 92)
Bell-Magendie law (p. 84)
binding problem (p. 102)
brainstem (p. 87)
central canal (p. 94)
central nervous system (CNS) (p. 82)
central sulcus (p. 98)
cerebellum (p. 88)
cerebral cortex (p. 96)
cerebrospinal fluid (CSF) (p. 94)
column (pp. 84, 97)
computerized axial tomography (CT or CAT scan) (p. 105)
contralateral (p. 83)
coronal plane (p. 83)
corpus callosum (p. 96)
cranial nerve (p. 87)
delayed-response task (p. 101)
distal (p. 83)
dorsal (p. 83)
dorsal root ganglion (p. 84)
electroencephalograph (EEG) (p. 107)
evoked potentials or *evoked responses* (p. 107)
fissure (p. 84)
forebrain (p. 89)
frontal lobe (p. 100)
functional magnetic resonance imaging (fMRI) (p. 109)
gamma waves (p. 102)
ganglion (pl.: ganglia) (p. 84)
gene-knockout approach (p. 110)
gray matter (p. 84)
gyrus (pl.: gyri) (p. 84)
hindbrain (p. 87)
hippocampus (p. 93)
horizontal plane (p. 83)
hypothalamus (p. 92)
inferior (p. 83)
inferior colliculus (p. 89)
ipsilateral (p. 83)
Klüver-Bucy syndrome (p. 100)
lamina (pl.: laminae) (pp. 84, 96)
lateral (p. 83)
lesion (p. 109)
limbic system (p. 90)
magnetic resonance imaging (MRI) (p. 106)
magnetoencephalograph (MEG) (p. 108)
medial (p. 83)
medulla (p. 87)
meninges (p. 94)
midbrain (p. 89)
nerve (p. 84)
neuroanatomy (p. 81)
nucleus (p. 84)
nucleus basalis (p. 93)
occipital lobe (p. 98)
parasympathetic nervous system (p. 85)
parietal lobe (p. 98)
peripheral nervous system (PNS) (p. 82)
phrenology (p. 105)
pituitary gland (p. 92)
pons (p. 88)
positron-emission tomography (PET) (p. 108)
postcentral gyrus (p. 98)
posterior (p. 83)
precentral gyrus (p. 100)
prefrontal cortex (p. 100)
prefrontal lobotomy (p. 100)
primates (p. 96)
proximal (p. 83)
raphe system (p. 88)
reticular formation (p. 88)
sagittal plane (p. 83)
sham lesion (p. 109)
somatic nervous system (p. 83)
spinal cord (p. 84)
stereotaxic instrument (p. 109)
substantia nigra (p. 80)
sulcus (pl.: sulci) (p. 84)
superior (p. 83)
superior colliculus (p. 89)
sympathetic nervous system (p. 85)
tectum (p. 89)
tegmentum (p. 89)
temporal lobe (p. 98)
thalamus (p. 91)
tract (p. 84)
transcranial magnetic stimulation (p. 110)
ventral (p. 83)
ventricle (p. 94)
white matter (p. 84)

Suggestions for Further Reading

Burrell, B. (2004). *Postcards from the brain museum.* New York: Broadway Books. Fascinating history of the attempts to collect brains of successful people and try to relate their brain anatomy to their success.

Klawans, H. L. (1988). *Toscanini's fumble and other tales of clinical neurology.* Chicago: Contemporary Books. Description of illustrative cases of brain damage and their behavioral consequences.

Websites to Explore

You can go to the Biological Psychology Study Center and click these links. While there, you can also check for suggested articles available on InfoTrac College Edition. The Biological Psychology Internet address is:

http://psychology.wadsworth.com/book/kalatbiopsych9e/

Autonomic Nervous System

http://www.ndrf.org/ans.htm

Brain Imaging in Psychiatry

http://www.musc.edu/psychiatry/fnrd/primer_index.htm

The Whole Brain Atlas (neuroanatomy)

http://www.med.harvard.edu/AANLIB/home.html

Exploring Biological Psychology CD

Virtual Reality Head Planes (virtual reality)
Planes Puzzle (drag & drop)
3D Virtual Brain (virtual reality)
Left Hemisphere Function (roll over with text pop-ups)
Cortex Puzzle (drag & drop)
Sagittal Section: Right Hemisphere, parts 1–3 (roll over with text pop-ups)
Brain Puzzle (drag & drop)
The Motor Cortex (animation)
The Sensory Cortex (animation)
Illustration of Binding (Try It Yourself)
Possible Failure of Binding (Try It Yourself)
Research with Brain Scans (video)
Critical Thinking (essay questions)
Chapter Quiz (multiple-choice questions

ThomsonNOW™

http://www.thomsonedu.com

Go to this site for the link to ThomsonNOW, your one-stop study shop. Take a Pre-Test for this chapter, and ThomsonNOW will generate a Personalized Study Plan based on your test results. The Study Plan will identify the topics you need to review and direct you to online resources to help you master these topics. You can then take a Post-Test to help you determine the concepts you have mastered and what you still need work on.

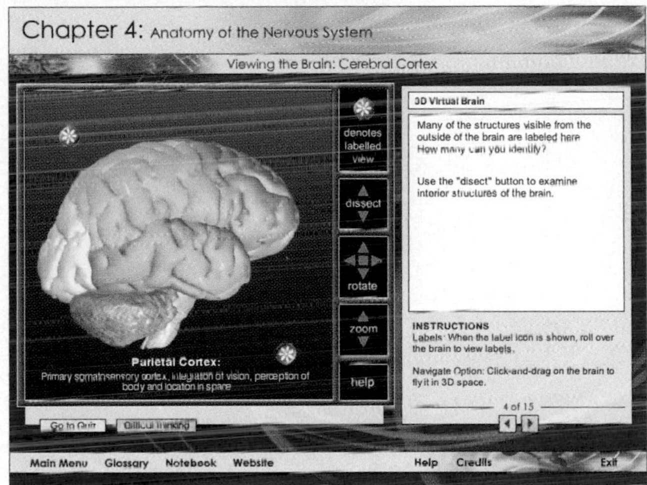

The CD includes this virtual reality brain that you can rotate to various positions and dissect with a click.

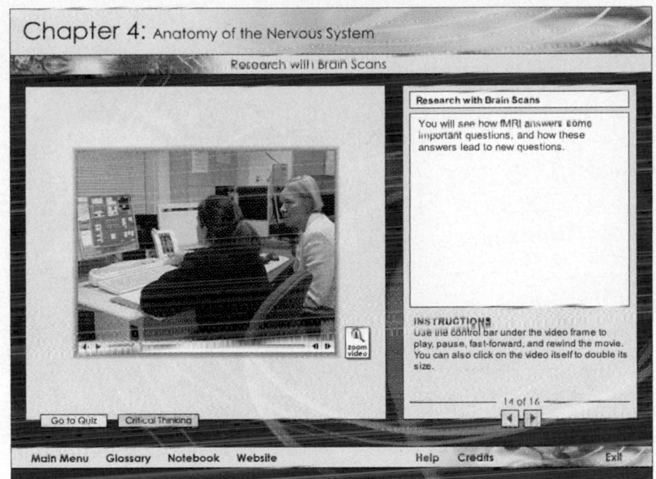

A short video illustrates the fMRI method.

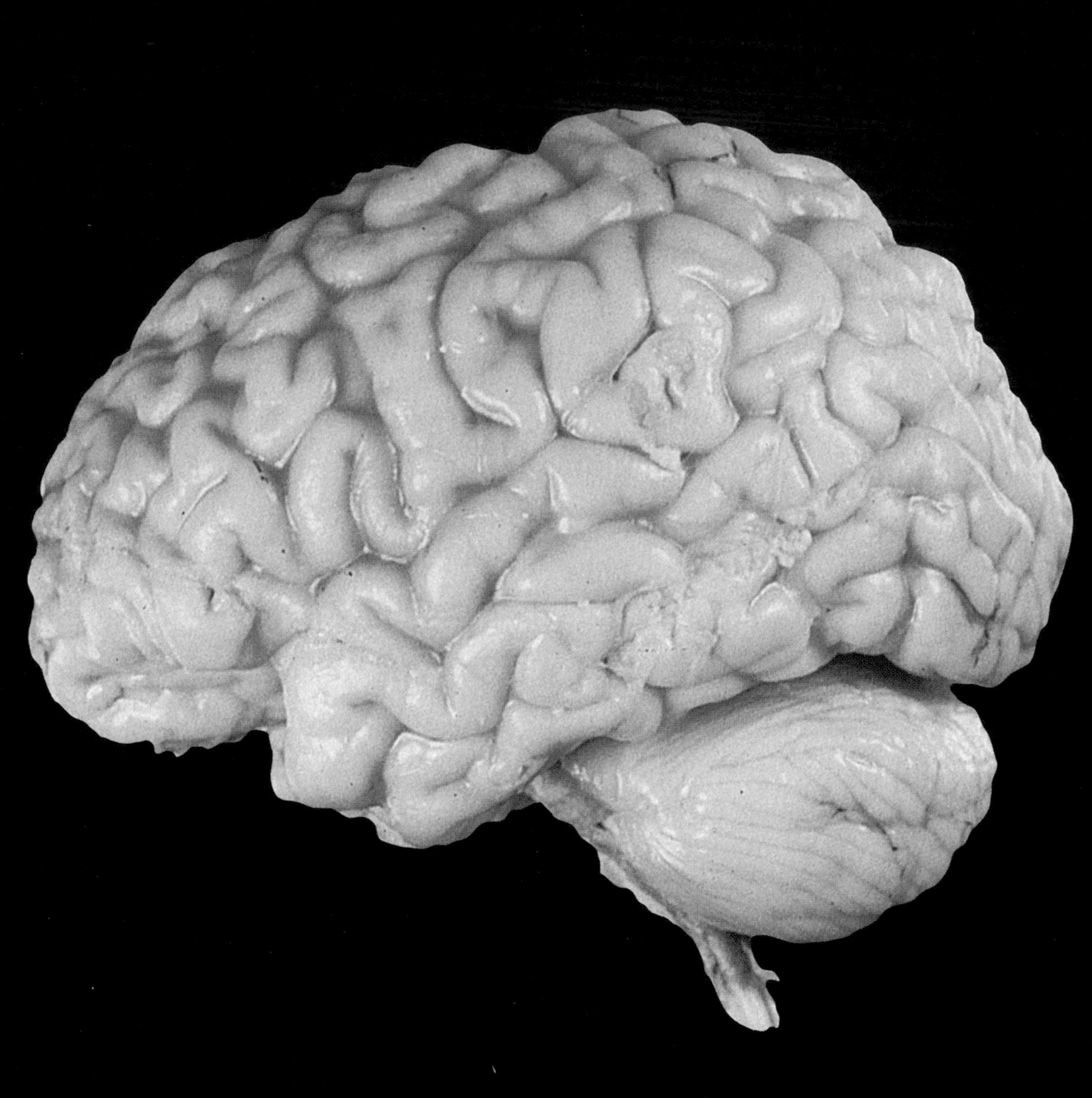

Development and Plasticity of the Brain

5

Chapter Outline

Opposite: An enormous amount of brain development has already occurred by the time a person is 1 year old.
Source: Dr. Dana Copeland

Main Ideas

1. Neurons begin by migrating to their proper locations and developing axons, which extend to approximately their correct targets by following chemical pathways.
2. The nervous system at first forms far more neurons than it needs and then eliminates those that do not establish suitable connections or receive sufficient input. It also forms excess synapses and discards the less active ones.
3. Experiences, especially early in life, can alter brain anatomy within limits.
4. Brain damage can result from a sharp blow, an interruption of blood flow, and several other types of injury.
5. Many mechanisms contribute to recovery from brain damage, including restoration of undamaged neurons to full activity, regrowth of axons, readjustment of surviving synapses, and behavioral adjustments.

"Some assembly required." Have you ever bought a package with those ominous words? Sometimes all you have to do is attach a few parts. But sometimes you face page after page of incomprehensible instructions. I remember putting together my daughter's bicycle and wondering how something that looked so simple could be so complicated.

The human nervous system requires an enormous amount of assembly, and the instructions are different from those for a bicycle. Instead of, "Put this piece here and that piece there," the instructions are, "Put these axons here and those dendrites there, and then wait to see what happens. Keep the connections that work the best and discard the others. Continue periodically making new connections and keeping only the most successful ones."

Therefore, we say that the brain's anatomy is *plastic;* it is constantly changing, within limits. The brain changes rapidly in early development and continues changing throughout life.

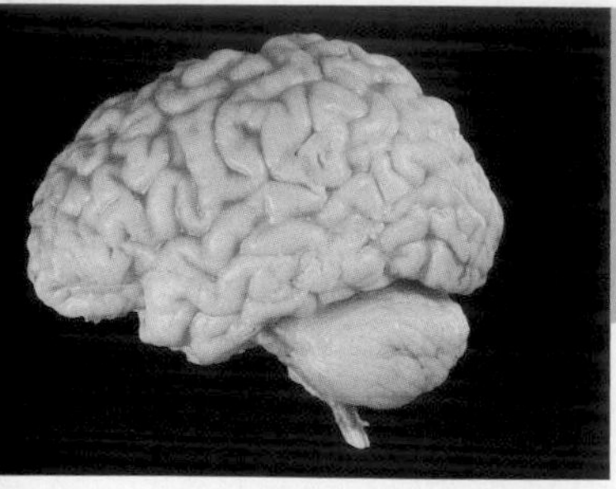

Module 5.1
Development of the Brain

Think of all the things you and other college students can do that you couldn't have done a few years ago—analyze statistics, read a foreign language, write brilliant critiques of complex issues, and so on. Have you developed these new skills because of brain growth? No, or at least not in the usual sense. Many of your dendrites have grown new branches, but we would need an electron microscope to see any of them.

Now think of all the things that 1-year-old children can do that they could not do at birth. Have *they* developed their new skills because of brain growth? To a large extent, yes. Consider, for example, Jean Piaget's object permanence task, in which an observer shows a toy to an infant and then places it behind a barrier. Generally, a child younger than 9 months old does not reach around the barrier to retrieve the toy (Figure 5.1). Why not? The biological explanation is that the prefrontal cortex is necessary for responding to a signal that appears and then disappears, and the synapses of the prefrontal cortex develop massively between 7 and 12 months (Goldman-Rakic, 1987).

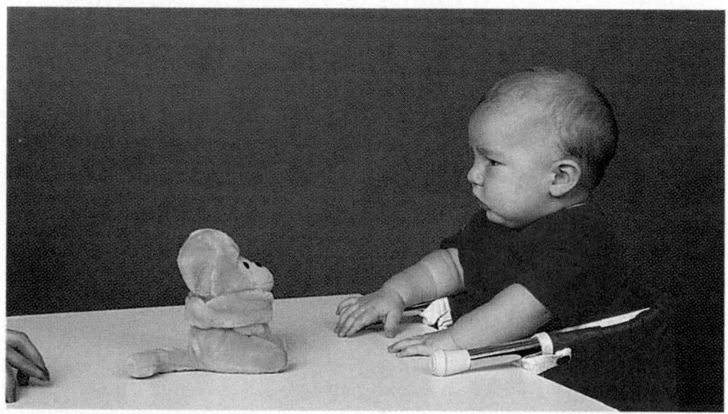

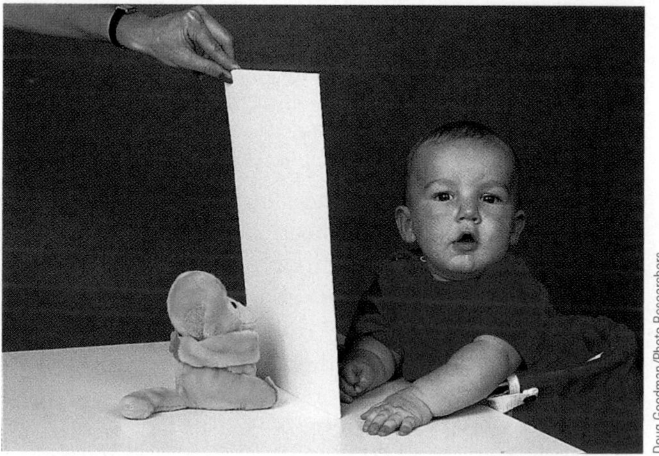

Figure 5.1 Piaget's object permanence task
An infant sees a toy and then an investigator places a barrier in front of the toy. Infants younger than about 9 months old fail to reach for the hidden toy. Tasks that require a response to a stimulus that is no longer present depend on the prefrontal cortex, a structure that is slow to mature.

An infant's behavioral development does not depend entirely on brain growth, of course; infants learn just as adults do. Furthermore, as we shall see, many processes of brain development depend on experience in complex ways that blur the distinction between learning and maturation. In this module, we consider how neurons develop, how their axons connect, and how experience modifies development.

Growth and Differentiation of the Vertebrate Brain

The human central nervous system begins to form when the embryo is about 2 weeks old. The dorsal surface thickens and then long thin lips rise, curl, and merge, forming a neural tube surrounding a fluid-filled cavity (Figure 5.2). As the tube sinks under the surface of the skin, the forward end enlarges and differentiates into the hindbrain, midbrain, and forebrain (Figure 5.3); the rest becomes the spinal cord. The fluid-filled cavity within the neural tube becomes the central canal of the spinal cord and the four ventricles of the brain; the fluid is the cerebrospinal fluid (CSF). At birth, the average human brain weighs about 350 grams. By the end of the first year, it weighs 1000 g, close to the adult weight of 1200 to 1400 g.

Growth and Development of Neurons

The development of the nervous system naturally requires the production and alteration of neurons. Neuroscientists distinguish these processes in the de-

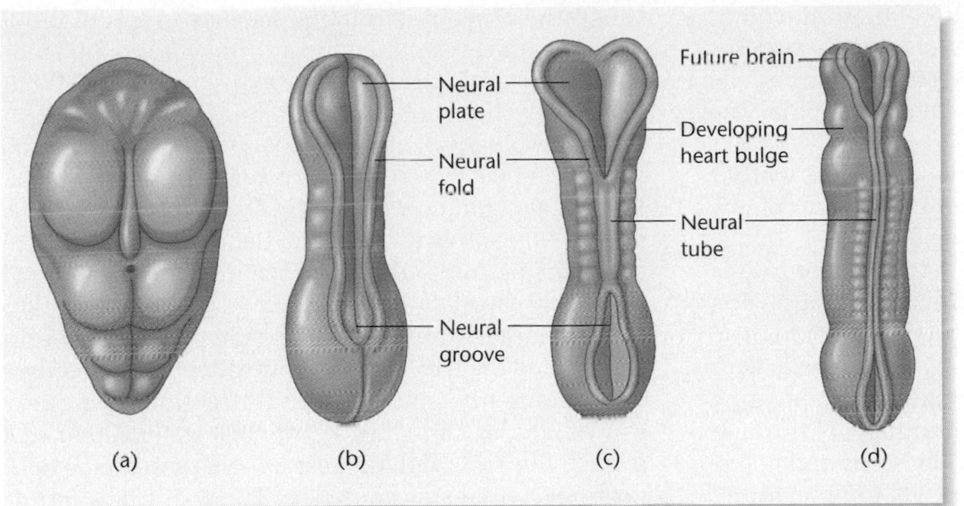

Figure 5.2 Early development of the human central nervous system
The brain and spinal cord begin as folding lips surrounding a fluid-filled canal. The stages shown occur at approximately age 2 to 3 weeks.

velopment of neurons: proliferation, migration, differentiation, myelination, and synaptogenesis.

Proliferation is the production of new cells. Early in development, the cells lining the ventricles of the brain divide. Some cells remain where they are (as *stem cells*), continuing to divide and redivide. Others become primitive neurons and glia that begin migrating to other locations. The developmental process is about the same in all vertebrates, varying in two factors: how long the cell proliferation lasts in days and the number of new neurons produced per day. For example, the main differences between human brains and chimpanzee brains are due to the fact that neurons continue proliferating longer in humans (Rakic, 1998; Vrba, 1998). Evidently, a small genetic change can produce a major difference in outcome.

After cells have differentiated as neurons or glia, they **migrate** (move) toward their eventual destinations in the brain. Different kinds of cells originate in different locations at different times, and each must migrate substantial distances, following specific chemical paths, to reach its final destination (Marín & Rubenstein, 2001). Some move radially from the inside of the brain to the outside; others move tangentially along the surface of the brain; and some move tangentially and then radially (Nadarajah & Parnavelas, 2002). Chemicals in families known as *immunoglobulins* and *chemokines* help to guide neuron migration. A deficit in these chemicals can lead to impaired migration, decreased brain size, decreased axon growth, and mental retardation (Berger-Sweeney & Hohmann, 1997; Crossin & Krushel, 2000; Tran & Miller, 2003). On the other extreme, excesses of immunoglobulins have been linked to some cases of schizophrenia (Crossin & Krushel, 2000; Poltorak et al., 1997). The brain has many kinds of immunoglobulins and chemokines, pre-

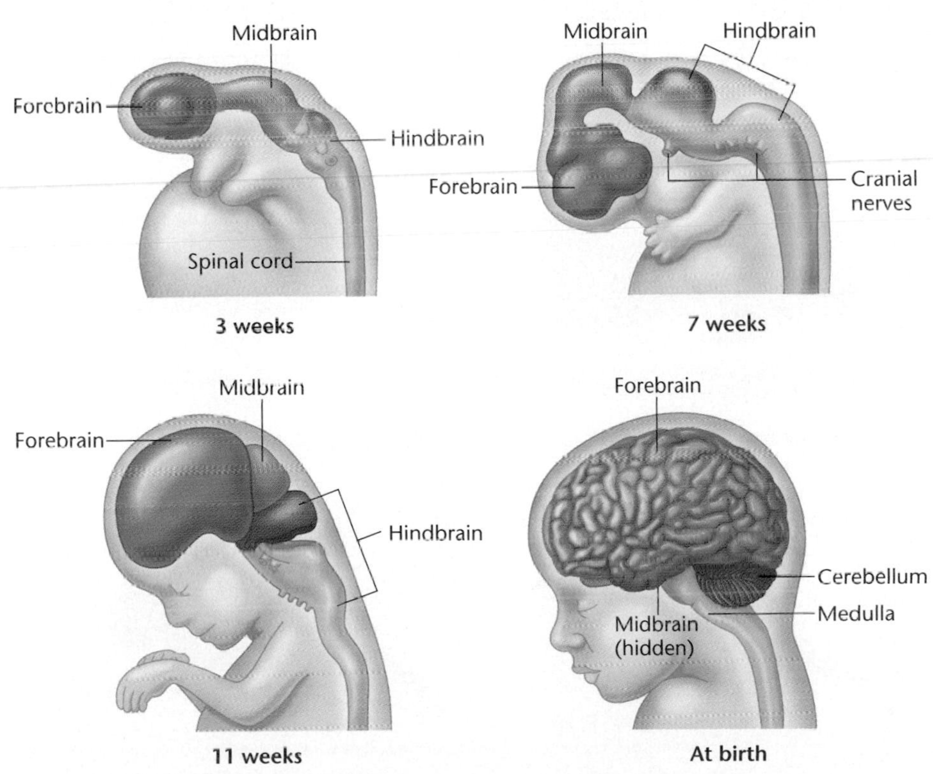

Figure 5.3 Human brain at four stages of development
Chemical processes develop the brain to an amazing degree even before the start of any experience with the world. Detailed changes in development continue to occur throughout life.

sumably reflecting the complexity of brain development. The existence of so many chemicals implies that brain development can go wrong in many ways, but it also implies that if one system fails, another one can partly compensate.

At first, a primitive neuron looks like any other cell. Gradually, the neuron **differentiates**, forming the axon and dendrites that provide its distinctive shape. The axon grows first, sometimes while the neuron is migrating. In such cases, the neuron tows its growing axon along like a tail (Gilmour, Knaut, Maischein, & Nüsslein-Volhard, 2004), allowing its tip to remain at or near its target. In other cases, the axon needs to grow toward its target, requiring it to find its way through what would seem like a jungle of other cells and fibers. After the migrating neuron reaches its final location, dendrites begin to form, slowly at first.

Neurons in different parts of the brain differ from one another in their shapes and chemical components. When and how does a neuron "decide" which kind of neuron it is going to be? Evidently, it is not a sudden all-or-none decision. In some cases, immature neurons experimentally transplanted from one part of the developing cortex to another develop the properties characteristic of their new location (S. K. McConnell, 1992). However, immature neurons transplanted at a slightly later stage develop some new properties while retaining some old ones (Cohen-Tannoudji, Babinet, & Wassef, 1994). The result resembles the speech of immigrant children: Those who enter a country when very young master the correct pronunciation, whereas slightly older children retain an accent.

In one fascinating experiment, researchers explored what would happen to the immature auditory portions of the brain if they received input from the eyes instead of the ears. Ferrets, mammals in the weasel family, are born so immature that their optic nerves (from the eyes) have not yet reached the thalamus. On one side of the brain, researchers damaged the superior colliculus and the occipital cortex, the two main targets for the optic nerves. On that side, they also damaged the inferior colliculus, a major source of auditory input. Therefore, the optic nerve, unable to attach to its usual target, attached to the auditory area of the thalamus, which lacked its usual input. The result was that the parts of the thalamus and cortex that usually receive input from the ears now received input only from the eyes. Which would you guess happened?

The result, surprising to many, was this: What would have been auditory thalamus and cortex reorganized, developing some (but not all) of the characteristic appearance of a visual cortex (Sharma, Angelucci, & Sur, 2000). But how do we know whether the animals treated that activity as vision? Remember that the researchers performed these procedures on one side of the brain. They left the other side intact. The researchers presented stimuli to the normal side of the brain and trained the ferrets to turn one direction when they heard something and the other direction when they saw a light, as shown in Figure 5.4. After the ferrets learned this task well, the researchers presented a light that the rewired side could see. The result: The ferrets turned the way they had been taught to turn when they saw something. In short, the rewired temporal cortex, receiving input from the optic nerve, produced visual responses (von Melchner, Pallas, & Sur, 2000).

A later and slower stage of neuronal development is **myelination**, the process by which glia produce the insulating fatty sheaths that accelerate transmission in many vertebrate axons. Myelin forms first in the spinal cord and then in the hindbrain, midbrain, and forebrain. Unlike the rapid proliferation and migration of

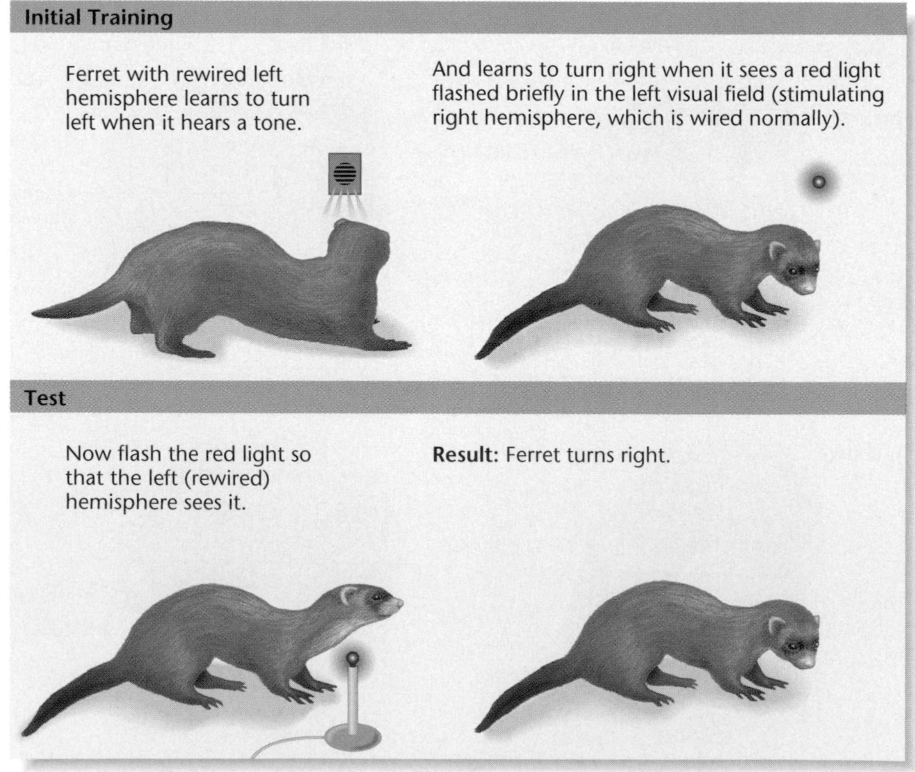

Figure 5.4 Behavior of a ferret with rewired temporal cortex
First the normal (right) hemisphere is trained to respond to a red light by turning to the right. Then the rewired (left) hemisphere is tested with a red light. The fact that the ferret turns to the right indicates that it regards the stimulus as light, not sound.

neurons, myelination continues gradually for decades (Benes, Turtle, Khan, & Farol, 1994).

The final stage, **synaptogenesis**, or the formation of synapses, continues throughout life. Neurons are constantly forming new synapses and discarding old ones. This process does, however, slow down in most older people, as does the formation of new dendritic branches (Buell & Coleman, 1981; Jacobs & Scheibel, 1993).

New Neurons Later in Life

Can the adult vertebrate brain generate any new neurons? The traditional belief, dating back to the work of Cajal in the late 1800s, was that vertebrate brains formed all their neurons during embryological development or during early infancy at the latest. Beyond that point, the brain could only lose neurons, never gain. Gradually, researchers found exceptions.

The first were the olfactory receptors, which, because they are exposed to the outside world and its toxic chemicals, usually survive only a month or two. Certain neurons in the nose remain immature throughout life. Periodically, they divide, with one cell remaining immature while the other develops to replace a dying olfactory receptor. It grows its axon back to the appropriate site in the brain (Gogos, Osborne, Nemes, Mendelsohn, & Axel, 2000; Graziadei & deHan, 1973). Later researchers also found a population of undifferentiated cells, called **stem cells**, in the interior of the brain that sometimes generate "daughter" cells that migrate to the olfactory bulb and transform into glia cells or neurons (Gage, 2000).

Still later researchers found evidence of new neuron formation in other brain areas. For example, songbirds have an area in their brain necessary for singing, and in this area, they have a steady replacement of a few kinds of neurons. Old neurons die and new ones take their place (Nottebohm, 2002). The black-capped chickadee, a small North American bird, hides seeds during the late summer and early fall and then finds them during the winter. It grows new neurons in its hippocampus (a brain area important for spatial memory) during the late summer (Smulders, Shiflett, Sporling, & deVoogd, 2000).

Stem cells can also differentiate into new neurons in the adult hippocampus of mammals (Song, Stevens, & Gage, 2002; van Praag et al., 2002). Newly formed hippocampal neurons go through a period of actively forming and altering synapses, so they are likely to be important contributors to new learning (Schmidt-Hieber, Jonas, & Bischofberger, 2004). So far, most of this research has used rodents; whether humans and other primates also form new neurons in adulthood remains controversial (Eriksson et al., 1998; Gould, Reeves, Graziano, & Gross, 1999; Rakic, 2002).

Except for olfactory neurons and the hippocampus, new neurons apparently do not form in other parts of the adult mammalian brain. Why not? Apparently, stem cells are available elsewhere; the problem is that in nearly all mature brain areas, neurons are already covered with synapses and have no availability for new neurons to establish new synapses (Rakic, 2004).

1. Which develops first, a neuron's axon or its dendrites?
2. In the ferret study, how did the experimenters determine that visual input to the auditory portions of the brain actually produced a visual sensation?
3. In which brain areas do new neurons form in adults?

Check your answers on page 136.

Pathfinding by Axons

If you asked someone to run a cable from your desk to another desk in the same room, you wouldn't have to give detailed directions. But imagine asking someone to run a cable to somewhere on the other side of the country. You would have to give detailed instructions about how to find the right city, the right building, and eventually, the right desk. The developing nervous system faces a similar challenge because it sends some of its axons over great distances. How do they find their way?

Chemical Pathfinding by Axons

A famous biologist, Paul Weiss (1924), conducted an experiment in which he grafted an extra leg to a salamander and then waited for axons to grow into it. (Unlike mammals, salamanders and other amphibians can accept transplants of extra limbs and generate new axon branches to the extra limbs. Research sometimes requires finding the right species for a given study.) After the axons reached the muscles, the extra leg moved in synchrony with the normal leg next to it.

Weiss dismissed as unbelievable the idea that each axon had developed a branch that found its way to exactly the correct muscle in the extra limb. He suggested instead that the nerves attached to muscles at random and then sent a variety of messages, each one tuned to a different muscle. In other words, it did not matter which axon was attached to which muscle. The muscles were like radios, each tuned to a different station: Each muscle received many signals but responded to only one.

Specificity of Axon Connections

Weiss was mistaken. Later evidence supported the interpretation he had rejected: The salamander's extra

Figure 5.5 Connections from eye to brain in a frog
The optic tectum is a large structure in fish, amphibians, reptiles, and birds. Its location corresponds to the midbrain of mammals, but its function is more elaborate, analogous to what the cerebral cortex does in mammals. Note: Connections from eye to brain are different in humans, as described in Chapter 14.
(Source: After Romer, 1962)

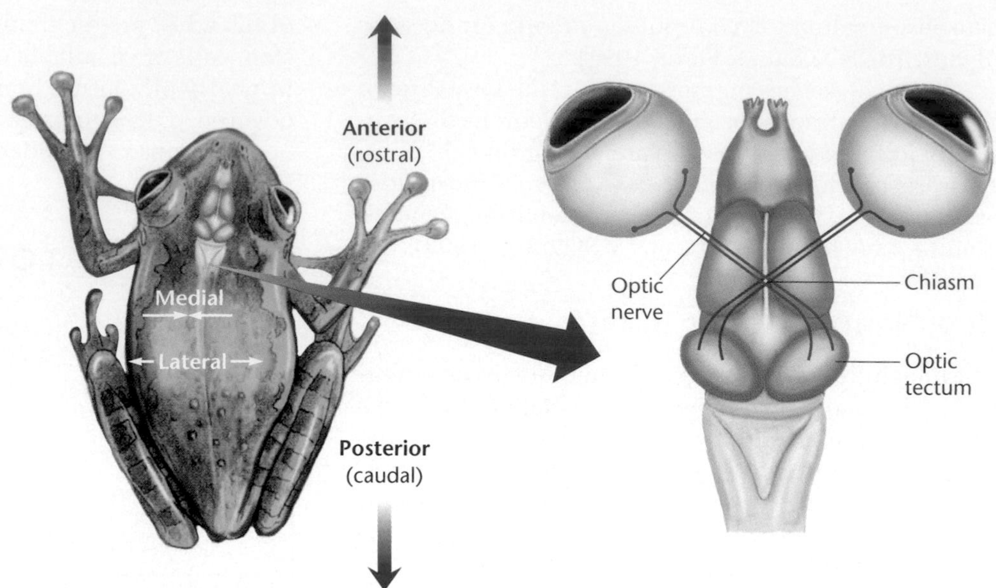

leg moved in synchrony with its neighbor because each axon had found exactly the correct muscle.

Since the time of Weiss's work, most of the research on axon growth has dealt with how sensory axons find their way to the correct targets in the brain. (The issues are the same as those for axons finding their way to muscles.) In one study, Roger Sperry, a former student of Weiss, cut the optic nerves of some newts. (See photo and quote on the pages inside the back cover.) The damaged optic nerve grew back and connected with the *tectum,* which is the main visual area of fish, amphibians, reptiles, and birds (Figure 5.5). Sperry found that when the new synapses formed, the newt regained normal vision.

Then Sperry (1943) repeated the experiment, but this time, after he cut the optic nerve, he rotated the eye by 180 degrees. When the axons grew back to the tectum, which targets would they contact? Sperry found that the axons from what had originally been the dorsal portion of the retina (which was now ventral) grew back to the area responsible for vision in the dorsal retina. Axons from what had once been the ventral retina (now dorsal) also grew back to their original targets. The newt now saw the world upside down and backward, responding to stimuli in the sky as if they were on the ground and to stimuli on the left as if they were on the right (Figure 5.6). Each axon regenerated to the area of the tectum where it had originally been, presumably by following a chemical trail.

Chemical Gradients

The next question was: How specific is the axon's aim? Must an axon from the retina find the tectal cell with exactly the right chemical marker on its surface, like a key finding the right lock? Does the body have to synthesize a separate chemical marker for each of the billions of axons in the nervous system?

No. The current estimate is that humans have only about 30,000 genes total—far too few to mark each of the brain's many billions of neurons. Nevertheless, nearly all axons grow to almost exactly their correct targets (Kozloski, Hamzei-Sichani, & Yuste, 2001). Without an extensive system of individual markers, neurons still manage to find their way. But how?

A growing axon follows a path of cell-surface molecules, attracted by some chemicals and repelled by others, in a process that steers the axon in the correct direction (Yu & Bargmann, 2001). Some axons follow a trail based on one attractive chemical until they reach an intermediate location where they become insensitive to that chemical and start following a different attractant (Shirasaki, Katsumata, & Murakami, 1998; H. Wang & Tessier-Lavigne, 1999). Eventually, axons sort themselves over the surface of their target area by following a gradient of chemicals. For example, one chemical in the amphibian tectum is a protein known as TOP_{DV} (TOP for *top*ography; DV for *d*orso*v*entral). This protein is 30 times more concentrated in the axons of the dorsal retina than of the ventral retina and 10 times more concentrated in the ventral tectum than in the dorsal tectum. As axons from the retina grow toward the tectum, the retinal axons with the greatest concentration of TOP_{DV} connect to the tectal cells with the highest concentration of that chemical; the axons with the lowest concentration connect to the tectal cells with the lowest concentration. A similar gradient of another protein aligns the axons along the anterior–posterior axis (J. R. Sanes, 1993) (Figure 5.7). (By analogy, you could think of men lining up from tallest to shortest, pairing up with women who lined up from tallest to shortest, so the tallest man dated the tallest woman and so forth.)

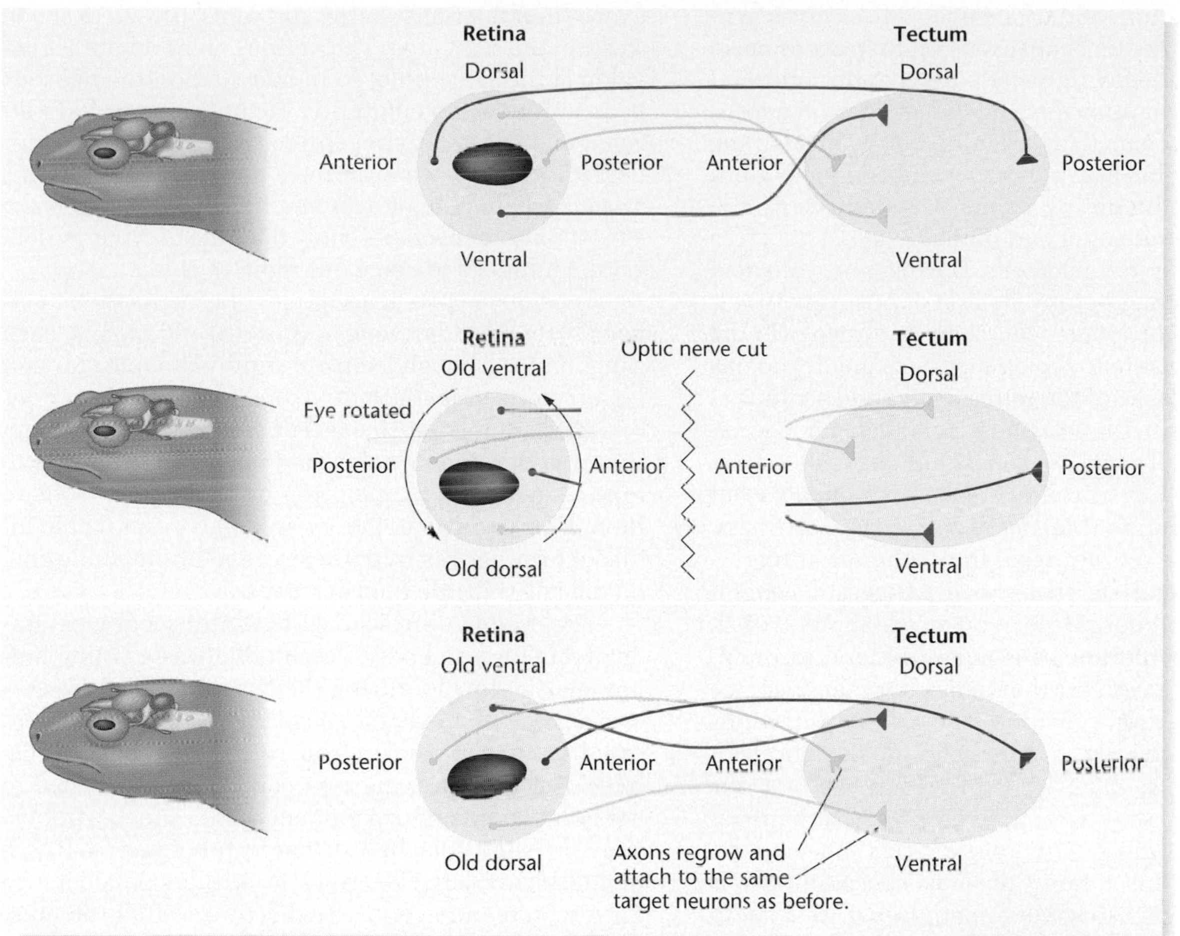

Figure 5.6 Summary of Sperry's experiment on nerve connections in newts

After he cut the optic nerve and inverted the eye, the optic nerve axons grew back to their original targets, not to the targets corresponding to the eye's current position.

4. What was Sperry's evidence that axons grow to a specific target presumably by following a chemical gradient instead of attaching at random?
5. If all cells in the tectum of an amphibian produced the same amount of TOP_{DV}, what would be the effect on the attachment of axons?

Check your answers on page 136.

Competition Among Axons as a General Principle

As you might guess from the experiments just described, when axons initially reach their targets, each one forms synapses onto several cells in approximately

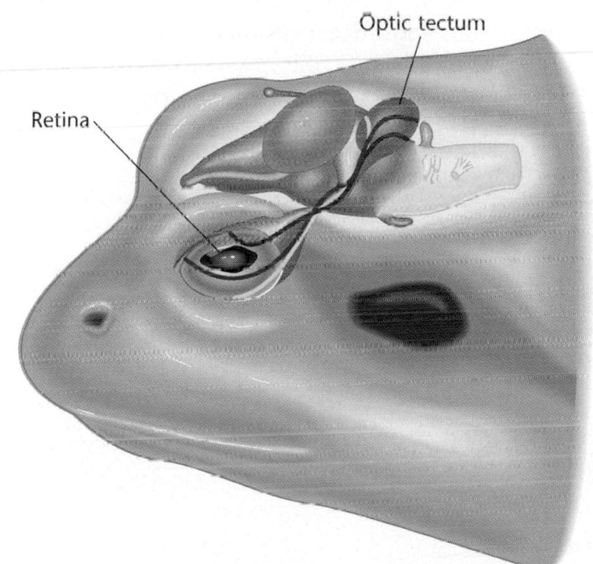

Figure 5.7 Retinal axons match up with neurons in the tectum by following two gradients

The protein TOP_{DV} is concentrated mostly in the dorsal retina and the ventral tectum. Axons rich in TOP_{DV} attach to tectal neurons that are also rich in that chemical. Similarly, a second protein directs axons from the posterior retina to the anterior portion of the tectum.

the correct location, and each target cell receives synapses from a large number of axons. At first, axons make "trial" connections with many postsynaptic cells, and then the postsynaptic cells strengthen some synapses and eliminate others (Hua & Smith, 2004). Even at the earliest stages, this fine-tuning depends on the pattern of input from incoming axons (Catalano & Shatz, 1998). For example, one part of the thalamus receives input from many retinal axons. During embryological development, long before the first exposure to light, repeated waves of spontaneous activity sweep over the retina from one side to the other. Consequently, axons from adjacent areas of the retina send almost simultaneous messages to the thalamus. Each thalamic neuron selects a group of axons that are simultaneously active; in this way, it finds a group of receptors from adjacent regions of the retina (Meister, Wong, Baylor, & Shatz, 1991). It then rejects synapses from other locations.

To some theorists, these results suggest a general principle, called **neural Darwinism** (Edelman, 1987). In Darwinian evolution, gene mutations and recombinations produce variations in individuals' appearance and actions; natural selection favors some variations and weeds out the rest. Similarly, in the development of the nervous system, we start with more neurons and synapses than we keep. Synapses form haphazardly, and then a selection process keeps some and rejects others. In this manner, the most successful axons and combinations survive; the others fail to sustain active synapses.

The principle of competition among axons is an important one, although we should use the analogy with Darwinian evolution cautiously. Mutations in the genes are random events, but neurotrophins steer new axonal branches and synapses in the right direction.

STOP & CHECK

6. If axons from the retina were prevented from showing spontaneous activity during early development, what would be the probable effect on development of the lateral geniculate?

Check your answer on page 136.

Determinants of Neuronal Survival

Getting just the right number of neurons for each area of the nervous system is more complicated than it might seem. To be of any use, each neuron must receive axons from the right source and send its own axons to a cell in the right area. The various areas do not all develop at the same time, so in many cases, the neurons in an area develop before any incoming axons have arrived and before any receptive sites are available for its own axons. If we examine a healthy adult nervous system, we find no leftover neurons that failed to make appropriate connections. How does the nervous system get the numbers to come out right?

Consider a specific example. The sympathetic nervous system sends axons to muscles and organs; each ganglion has enough axons to supply the muscles and organs in its area, with no axons left over. How does the match come out so exact? Long ago, one explanation was that the muscles sent chemical messages to tell the sympathetic ganglion how many neurons to form. Rita Levi-Montalcini was largely responsible for disconfirming this hypothesis. (See photo and quote on the pages inside the back cover.)

Levi-Montalcini's early life would seem most unfavorable for a scientific career. She was a young Italian Jewish woman during the Nazi era. World War II was destroying the Italian economy, and almost everyone discouraged women from scientific or medical careers. Furthermore, the research projects assigned to her as a young medical student were virtually impossible, as she described in her autobiography (Levi-Montalcini, 1988). Nevertheless, she developed a love for research and eventually discovered that the muscles do not determine how many axons *form;* they determine how many *survive.*

Initially, the sympathetic nervous system forms far more neurons than it needs. When one of its neurons forms a synapse onto a muscle, that muscle delivers a protein called **nerve growth factor (NGF)** that promotes the survival and growth of the axon (Levi-Montalcini, 1987). An axon that does not receive NGF degenerates, and its cell body dies. That is, each neuron starts life with a "suicide program": If its axon does not make contact with an appropriate postsynaptic cell by a certain age, the neuron kills itself through a process called **apoptosis**,[1] a programmed mechanism of cell death. (Apoptosis is distinct from *necrosis,* which is death caused by an injury or a toxic substance.) NGF cancels the program for apoptosis; it is the postsynaptic cell's way of telling the incoming axon, "I'll be your partner. Don't kill yourself."

The brain's system of overproducing neurons and then applying apoptosis enables the CNS to match the number of incoming axons to the number of receiving

[1]Apoptosis is based on the Greek root *ptosis* (meaning "dropping"), which is pronounced TOE-sis. Therefore, most scholars insist that the second *p* in *apoptosis* should be silent, a-po-TOE-sis. Others argue that *helicopter* is also derived from a root with a silent *p* *(pteron),* but we pronounce the *p* in *helicopter,* so we should also pronounce the *p* in *apoptosis.* Be prepared for either pronunciation.

cells. For example, when the sympathetic nervous system begins sending its axons toward the muscles and glands, it has no way to know the exact size of the muscles or glands. Therefore, it makes more neurons than necessary and later discards the excess.

Nerve growth factor is a **neurotrophin**, a chemical that promotes the survival and activity of neurons. (The word *trophin* derives from a Greek word for "nourishment.") In addition to NGF, the nervous system responds to *brain-derived neurotrophic factor* (BDNF) and several other neurotrophins (Airaksinen & Saarma, 2002). BDNF is the most abundant neurotrophin in the adult mammalian cerebral cortex.

For an immature neuron to avoid apoptosis and survive, it needs to receive neurotrophins not only from its target cells but also from incoming axons bringing stimulation. In one study, researchers examined mice with a genetic defect that prevented all release of neurotransmitters. The brains initially assembled normal anatomies, but neurons then started dying rapidly (Verhage et al., 2000). When neurons release neurotransmitters, they simultaneously release neurotrophins, and neurons that fail to release the neurotransmitters withhold the neurotrophins as well, so their target cells die (Poo, 2001).

All areas of the developing nervous system initially make far more neurons than will survive into adulthood. Each brain area has a period of massive cell death, becoming littered with dead and dying cells (Figure 5.8). This loss of cells does not indicate that something is wrong; it is a natural part of development (Finlay & Pallas, 1989). In fact, loss of cells in a particular brain area can indicate development and maturation. For example, late teenagers have substantial cell loss in parts of the prefrontal cortex, while showing increased neuronal activity in those areas (Sowell, Thompson, Holmes, Jernigan, & Toga, 1999) and sharp improvements in the kinds of memory that depend on those areas (D. A. Lewis, 1997). Evidently, maturation of appropriate cells is linked to simultaneous loss of less successful ones.

After maturity, the apoptotic mechanisms become dormant, except under traumatic conditions such as stroke, and neurons no longer need neurotrophins for survival (Benn & Woolf, 2004; G. S. Walsh, Orike, Kaplan, & Miller, 2004). Although adults no longer need neurotrophins for neuron survival, they do use these chemicals for other functions. Neurotrophins increase the branching of both axons and dendrites throughout life (Baquet, Gorski, & Jones, 2004; Kesslak, So, Choi, Cotman, & Gomez-Pinilla, 1998; Kolb, Côté, Ribeiro-da-Silva, & Cuello, 1997). With a deficiency of neurotrophins, cortical neurons and especially their dendrites shrink (Gorski, Zeiler, Tamowski, & Jones, 2003). Deficits in adult neurotrophins have been linked to several brain diseases (Baquet et al., 2004; Benn & Woolf, 2004) and possibly to depression, as we shall discuss in Chapter 15.

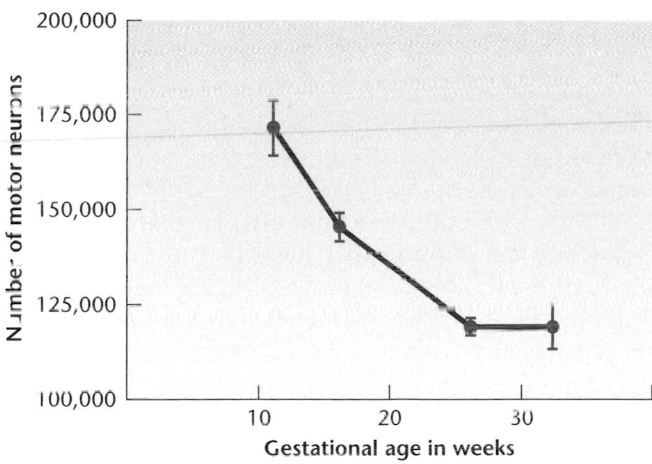

Figure 5.8 Cell loss during development of the nervous system

The graph shows the number of motor neurons in the ventral spinal cord of human fetuses. Note that the number of motor neurons is highest at 11 weeks and drops steadily until about 25 weeks, the age when motor neuron axons make synapses with muscles. Axons that fail to make synapses die. *(Source: From N. G. Forger and S. M. Breedlove, "Motoneuronal death in the human fetus."* Journal of Comparative Neurology, *264, 1987, 118–122. Copyright © 1987 Alan R. Liss, Inc. Reprinted by permission of N. G. Forger)*

7. What process enables the nervous system to have only as many axons as necessary to innervate the target neurons?
8. What class of chemicals prevents apoptosis?
9. At what age does a person have the greatest number of neurons—as an embryo, newborn, child, adolescent, or adult?

Check your answers on page 136.

The Vulnerable Developing Brain

According to Lewis Wolpert (1991, p. 12), "It is not birth, marriage, or death, but gastrulation, which is truly the important time of your life." (Gastrulation is one of the early stages of embryological development.) Wolpert's point was that if you mess up in early development, you will have problems from then on. Actually, if you mess up badly during gastrulation, your life is over.

In brain development especially, the early stages are critical. Because development is such a precarious matter, chemical distortions that the mature brain could tolerate are more disruptive in early life. The developing brain is highly vulnerable to malnutrition, toxic chemicals, and infections that would produce only brief or mild interference at later ages. For example, impaired thyroid function produces temporary lethargy in adults but mental retardation in infants. (Thyroid deficiency was common in the past because of iodine deficiencies; it is rare today because table salt is almost always fortified with iodine.) A fever is a mere annoyance to an adult, but it impairs neuron proliferation in a fetus (Laburn, 1996). Low blood glucose in an adult leads to a lack of pep, whereas before birth, it seriously impairs brain development (C. A. Nelson et al., 2000).

The infant brain is highly vulnerable to damage by alcohol. Children of mothers who drink heavily during pregnancy are born with **fetal alcohol syndrome**, a condition marked by hyperactivity, impulsiveness, difficulty maintaining attention, varying degrees of mental retardation, motor problems, heart defects, and facial abnormalities (Figure 5.9). Most dendrites are short with few branches. Rats exposed to alcohol during fetal development show some of these same deficits, including attention deficits (Hausknecht et al., 2005).

When children with fetal alcohol syndrome reach adulthood, they have a high risk of alcoholism, drug dependence, depression, and other psychiatric disorders (Famy, Streissguth, & Unis, 1998). Even in children of normal appearance, impulsive behavior and poor school performance correlate with the mother's alcohol consumption during pregnancy (Hunt, Streissguth, Kerr, & Carmichael-Olson, 1995). The mechanism of fetal alcohol syndrome probably relates to apoptosis: Remember that to prevent apoptosis, a neuron must receive neurotrophins from the incoming axons as well as from its own axon's target cell. Alcohol suppresses the release of glutamate, the brain's main excitatory transmitter, and enhances activity of GABA, the main inhibitory transmitter. Consequently, many neurons receive less excitation and neurotrophins than normal, and they undergo apoptosis (Ikonomidou et al., 2000).

Prenatal exposure to other substances can be harmful too. Children of mothers who use cocaine during pregnancy have a decrease in language skills compared to other children, a slight decrease in IQ scores, and impaired hearing (Fried, Watkinson, & Gray, 2003; Lester, LaGasse, & Seifer, 1998). Related deficits in neural plasticity have been found in rats (Kolb, Gorny, Li, Samaha, & Robinson, 2003). Children of mothers who smoked during pregnancy are at much increased risk of the following (Brennan, Grekin, & Mednick, 1999; Fergusson, Woodward, & Horwood, 1998; Finette, O'Neill, Vacek, & Albertini, 1998; Milberger, Biederman, Faraone, Chen, & Jones, 1996; Slotkin, 1998):

- Low weight at birth and many illnesses early in life
- Sudden infant death syndrome ("crib death")
- Long-term intellectual deficits
- Attention-deficit hyperactivity disorder (ADHD)
- Impairments of the immune system
- Delinquency and crime later in life (sons especially)

The overall message obviously is that pregnant women should minimize their use of drugs, even legal ones.

Finally, the immature brain is highly responsive to influences from the mother. For example, if a mother rat is exposed to stressful experiences, she becomes more fearful, she spends less than the usual amount of time licking and grooming her offspring, and her offspring become permanently more fearful in a variety of situations (Cameron et al., 2005). Analogously, the children of impoverished and abused women have, on the average, increased problems in both their academic and social life. The mechanisms in humans are not exactly the same as those in rats, but the overall principles are similar: Stress to the mother changes her behavior in ways that change her offspring's behavior.

© David H. Wells/CORBIS

Figure 5.9 Child with fetal alcohol syndrome
Note the facial pattern. Many children exposed to smaller amounts of alcohol before birth have behavioral deficits without facial signs.

STOP & CHECK

10. Anesthetic drugs increase inhibition of neurons, blocking most action potentials. Why would we predict that prolonged exposure to anesthetics would be dangerous to the brain of a fetus?

Check your answer on page 136.

Fine-Tuning by Experience

The blueprints for a house determine its overall plan, but because architects can't anticipate every detail, construction workers sometimes have to improvise. The same is true, only more so, for your nervous system. Because of the unpredictability of life, our brains have evolved the ability to remodel themselves (within limits) in response to our experience (Shatz, 1992).

Experience and Dendritic Branching

Decades ago, researchers believed that neurons never changed their shape. We now know that axons and dendrites continue to modify their structure throughout life. Dale Purves and R. D. Hadley (1985) developed a method of injecting a dye that enabled them to examine the structure of a living neuron at different times, days to weeks apart. They demonstrated that some dendritic branches extended between one viewing and another, whereas others retracted or disappeared (Figure 5.10). Later research found that when dendrites grow new spines, some spines last only days, whereas others last longer, perhaps forever (Trachtenberg et al., 2002). The gain or loss of spines means a gain or loss of synapses, and therefore potential information processing. As animals grow older, they continue altering the anatomy of their neurons but at progressively slower rates (Gan, Kwon, Feng, Sanes, & Lichtman, 2003; Grutzendler, Kasthuri, & Gan, 2002).

Experiences guide the amount and type of change in the structure of neurons. Let's start with a simple example. If you live in a complex and challenging environment, you need an elaborate nervous system. Ordinarily, a laboratory rat lives by itself in a small gray cage. Imagine by contrast ten rats living together in a larger cage with a few little pieces of junk to explore or play with. Researchers sometimes call this an enriched environment, but it is enriched only in contrast to the deprived experience of a typical rat cage. A rat in the more stimulating environment develops a thicker cortex, more dendritic branching, and improved performance on many tests of learning (Greenough, 1975; Rosenzweig & Bennett, 1996). Many of its neurons become more finely tuned. For example, for a rat living in an isolated cage, each cell in part of its somatosensory cortex responds to a group of whiskers. For a rat in the group cage, each cell becomes more discriminating and responds to a smaller number of whiskers (Polley, Kvašňák, & Frostig, 2004). At the opposite extreme, rats that have little opportunity to use their whiskers early in life (because the experimenters keep trimming them) show less than normal brain response to whisker stimulation (Rema, Armstrong-James, & Ebner, 2003).

An enriched environment enhances sprouting of axons and dendrites in a wide variety of other species also (Coss, Brandon, & Globus, 1980) (Figure 5.11). However, although an "enriched" environment promotes more neuronal development than a deprived environment, we have no evidence that a "superenriched" environment would be even better.

We might suppose that the neuronal changes in an enriched environment depend on new and interesting experiences, and no doubt, many of them do. For example, after practice of particular skills, the connections relevant to those skills proliferate, while other connections retract. Nevertheless, much of the enhancement seen in the overall "enriched environment" is due to

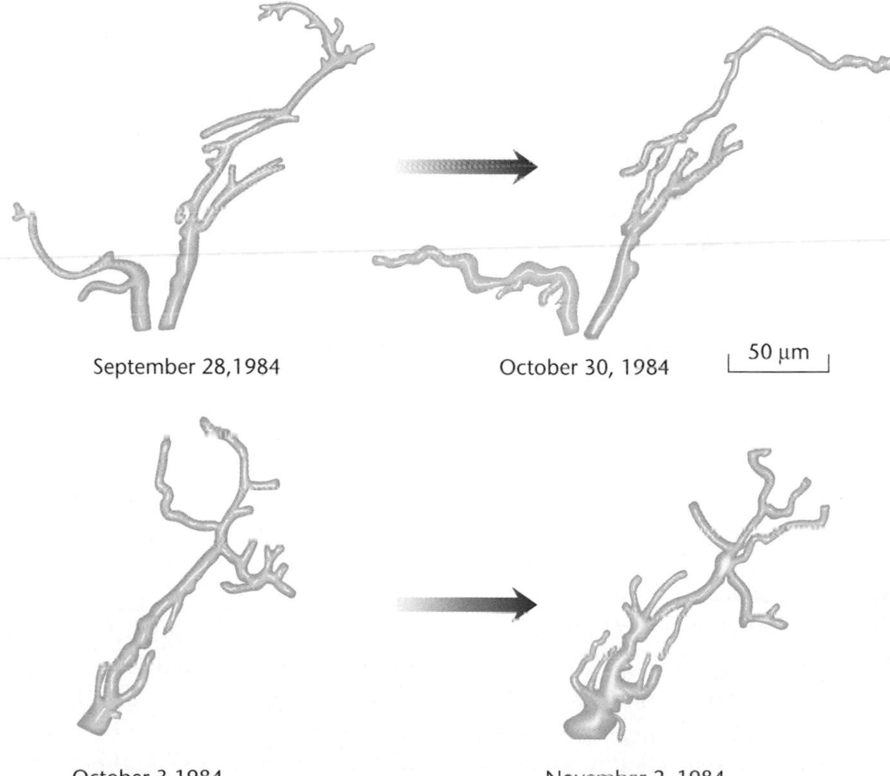

Figure 5.10 Changes over time in dendritic trees of two neurons
During a month, some branches elongated and others retracted. The shape of the neuron is in flux even during adulthood. *(Source: Reprinted from "Changes in dendritic branching of adult mammalian neurons revealed by repeated imaging in situ," by D. Purves and R. D. Hadley,* Nature, 315, pp. 404–406. *Copyright © 1985 Macmillan Magazines, Ltd. Reprinted by permission of D. Purves and Macmillan Magazines, Ltd.)*

the simple fact that rats in a group cage are more active. Using a running wheel also enhances growth of axons and dendrites, even for rats in an isolated cage (Rhodes et al., 2003; van Praag, Kempermann, & Gage, 1999). The exercise does not even have to be strenuous (Trejo, Carro, & Torres-Alemán, 2001; van Praag, Kempermann, & Gage, 2000). Measurable expansion of neurons has also been demonstrated in humans as a function of physical activity—such as daily practice of juggling balls, in one case (Draganski et al., 2004). The advice to exercise for your brain's sake is particularly important for older people. On the average, the thickness of the cerebral cortex declines in old age but much less in people who remain physically active (Colcombe et al., 2003).

People with extensive academic education also tend to have longer and more widely branched dendrites than people with less formal education (B. Jacobs, Schall, & Scheibel, 1993). It is tempting to assume that the increased learning led to brain changes, but we cannot draw cause-and-effect conclusions from correlational studies. Perhaps people who already had wider dendrites succeeded more in school and therefore stayed longer. Or of course, both explanations could be correct.

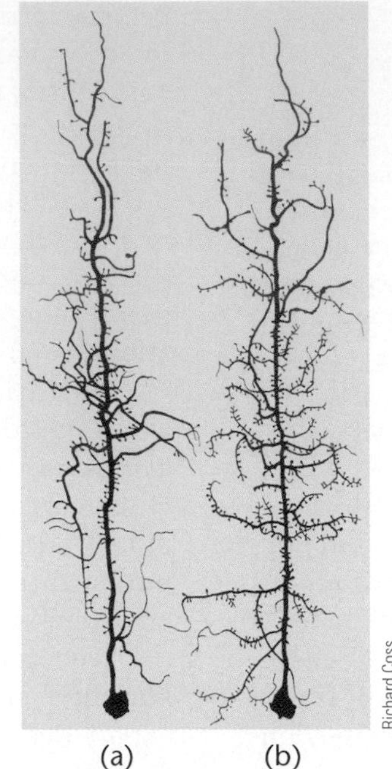

Figure 5.11 Effect of a stimulating environment on neuronal branching
(a) A jewel fish reared in isolation develops neurons with fewer branches. **(b)** A fish reared with others has more neuronal branches.

Effects of Special Experiences

The detailed structure and function of the brain can be modified by experiences. For example, neurons become more responsive and more finely tuned to stimuli that have been important or meaningful in the past (e.g., Fritz, Shamma, Elhilali, & Klein, 2003; L. I. Zhang, Bao, & Merzenich, 2001). How much plasticity might occur after experiences that are far different from the average?

Brain Adaptations in People Blind Since Infancy

One way to ask this question is to consider what happens to the brain if one sensory system is nearly or entirely absent. Recall the experiment on ferrets, in which axons of the visual system, unable to contact their normal targets, attached instead to the brain areas usually devoted to hearing and managed to convert them into more-or-less satisfactory visual areas (p. 124). Might anything similar happen in the brains of people born deaf or blind?

You will hear many people say that blind people become better than usual at touch and hearing, or that deaf people become especially acute at touch and vision. Those statements are true in a way, but we need to be more specific. Losing one sense does not affect the receptors of other sense organs. For example, being blind does not change the touch receptors in the fingers. However, losing one sense does increase attention to other senses, and after many years of altered attention, the brain shows measurable adaptations to reflect and increase that attention.

In several studies, investigators asked both sighted people and people blind since infancy to feel Braille letters, other kinds of symbols, or objects such as grooves in a board and say whether two items are same or different. On the average, blind people performed more accurately, to no one's surprise. What was more surprising was that PET and fMRI scans indicated substantial activity in the occipital cortex of the blind people while they performed these tasks (Burton et al., 2002; Sadato et al., 1996, 1998). Evidently, touch information had "invaded" this cortical area, which is ordinarily devoted to vision alone.

To double-check this conclusion, researchers asked blind and sighted people to perform the same kind of task during temporary inactivation of the occipital cortex. Remember from Chapter 4 (p. 110) that intense magnetic stimulation on the scalp can temporarily inactivate neurons beneath the magnet. Applying this procedure to the occipital cortex of blind people interferes with their ability to identify Braille symbols or to notice the difference between one tactile stimulus and another. The same procedure does not impair any aspect of touch for sighted people. In short, blind people use the occipital cortex to help identify what they feel; sighted people do not (L. G. Cohen et al., 1997). One conclusion is that touch information invades the occipital cortex of blind people. A broader conclusion is that brain areas modify their function based on the kinds of stimuli they receive.

On the average, blind people also outperform sighted people on many verbal skills. (If you can't see, you pay more attention to what you hear, including words.) One example is the task, "When you hear the name of an object (e.g., *apple*), say as quickly as possible the name of an appropriate action for that object (e.g., *eat*)." Again, performing this task activates parts of the occipital cortex in blind people but not in sighted people. Furthermore, the amount of activity in the occipital cortex (for blind people) correlates with their performance on the task (Amedi, Raz, Pianka, Malack, & Zohary, 2003). Also, inactivating the occipital cortex by intense transcranial magnetic stimulation interferes with verbal performance by blind people but not by sighted people (Amedi, Floel, Knecht, Zohary, & Cohen, 2004). So the occipital cortex of blind people serves certain verbal functions as well as touch.

As the occipital cortex increases its response to touch, sound, and verbal stimuli, does it decrease its response to visual stimuli? Applying brief transcranial magnetic stimulation (enough to stimulate, not enough to inactivate) over the occipital cortex causes sighted people to report seeing flashes of light. When the same procedure is applied to people who completely lost their sight because of eye injuries more than 10 years ago, most report seeing nothing or seeing flashes only rarely after stimulation in certain locations (Gothe et al., 2002). Note that for this experiment it is essential to test people who once had normal vision and then lost it because we can ask them whether they see anything in response to the magnetic stimulation. Someone blind since birth presumably would not understand the question.

Effects of Prolonged Practice

Cognitive psychologists have found that extensive practice of a skill, such as playing chess or working crossword puzzles, makes someone ever more adept at that skill but not necessarily at anything else (Ericsson & Charness, 1994). Presumably, developing expertise changes the brain in ways that improve the abilities required for a particular skill. In a few cases, researchers have identified some of the relevant brain changes.

One study used magnetoencephalography (MEG; see p. 108) to record responses of the auditory cortex to pure tones. The responses in professional musicians were about twice as strong as those for nonmusicians. Then an examination of their brains, using MRI, found that one area of the temporal cortex in the right hemisphere was about 30% larger in the professional musicians (Schneider et al., 2002). Of course, we do not know whether their brains were equal before they started practicing; perhaps those with certain predispositions are more likely than others to develop a passion for music.

Another study used a type of MRI scan to compare the entire brains of professional keyboard players, amateur keyboard players, and nonmusicians. Several areas showed that gray matter was thicker in the professionals than in the amateurs, and thicker in the amateurs than the nonmusicians, including the structures highlighted in Figure 5.12 (Gaser & Schlaug, 2003). The most strongly affected areas related to hand control and vision (presumably because of its importance for reading music). A related study on stringed instrument players found that a larger than normal section of the postcentral gyrus was devoted to representing the fingers of the left hand, which they use to control the strings (Elbert, Pantev, Wienbruch, Rockstroh, & Taub, 1995). The area devoted to the left fingers was largest in those who began their music practice early (and therefore also continued for more years).

These results imply that practicing a skill reorganizes the brain, within limits, to maximize performance of that skill. Part of the mechanism is that sustained attention to anything releases dopamine, and dopamine acts on the cortex to expand the response to stimuli active during the dopamine release (Bao, Chan, & Merzenich, 2001).

When Brain Reorganization Goes Too Far

Ordinarily, the expanded cortical representation of personally important information is beneficial. However, in extreme cases, the reorganization creates problems. As mentioned, when people play string instruments many hours a day for years, the representation of the left hand increases in the somatosensory cortex. Similar processes occur in people who play piano and other instruments.

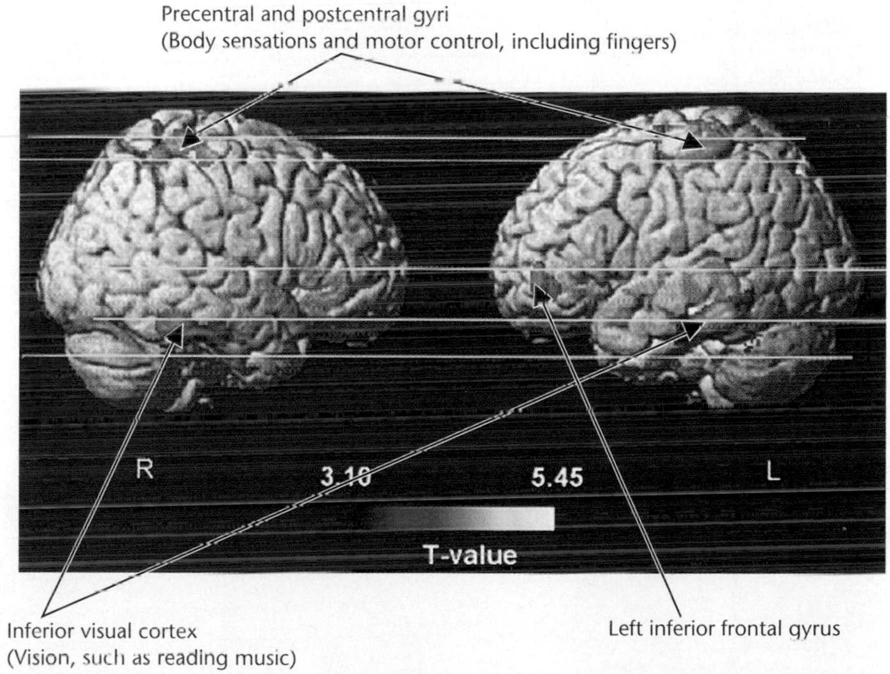

Figure 5.12 Brain correlates of extensive music practice
Areas marked in red showed thicker gray matter among professional keyboard players than in amateurs and thicker gray matter among amateurs than in nonmusicians. Areas marked in yellow showed even stronger differences in that same direction. *(Source: From "Brain structures differ between musicians and non-musicians," by C. Gaser & G. Schlaug,* Journal of Neuroscience, 23. *Copyright 2003 by the Society for Neuroscience. Reprinted with permission.)*

Imagine the normal representation of the fingers in the cortex:

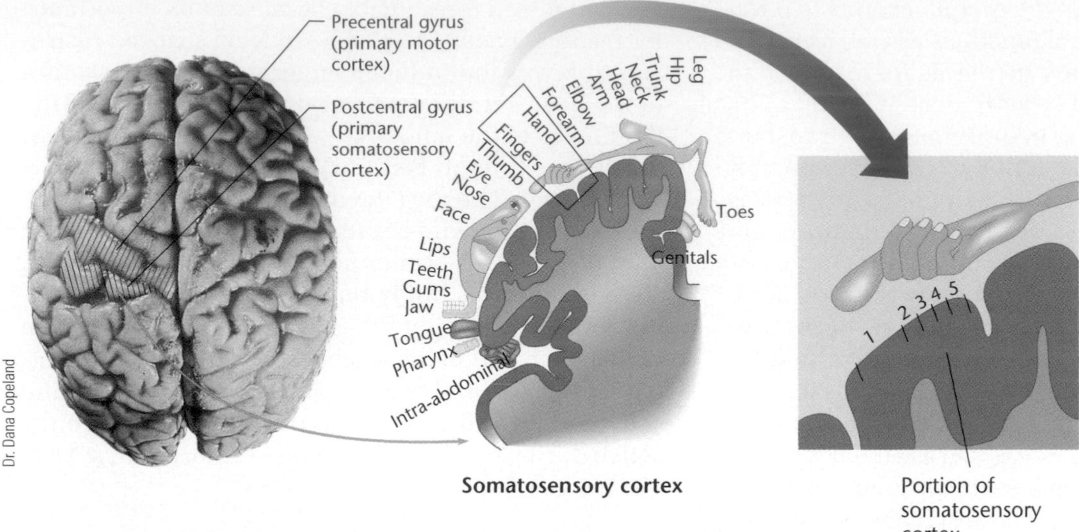

With extensive musical practice, the expanding representations of the fingers might spread out like this:

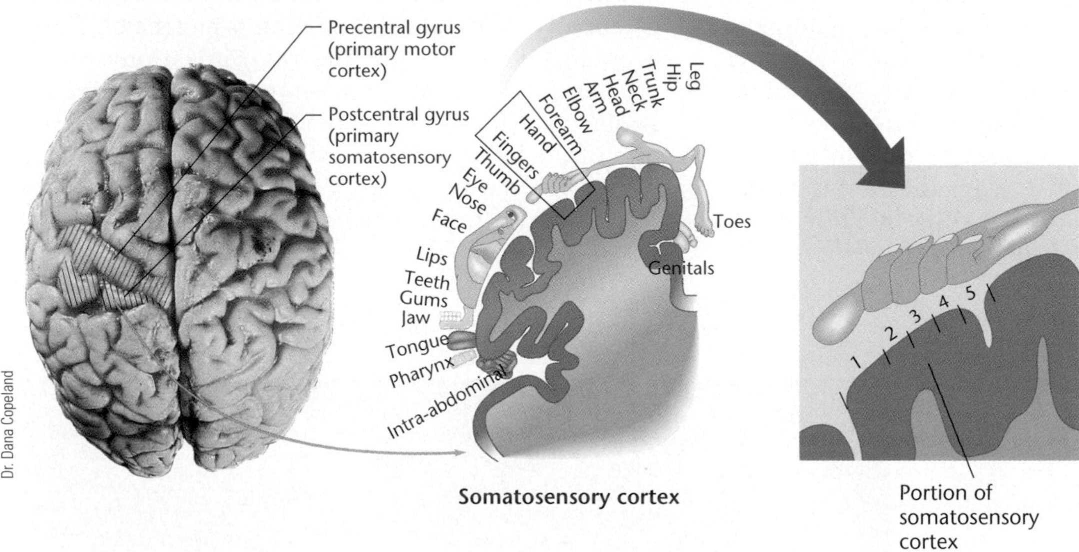

Or the representations could grow from side to side without spreading out so that representation of each finger overlaps that of its neighbor:

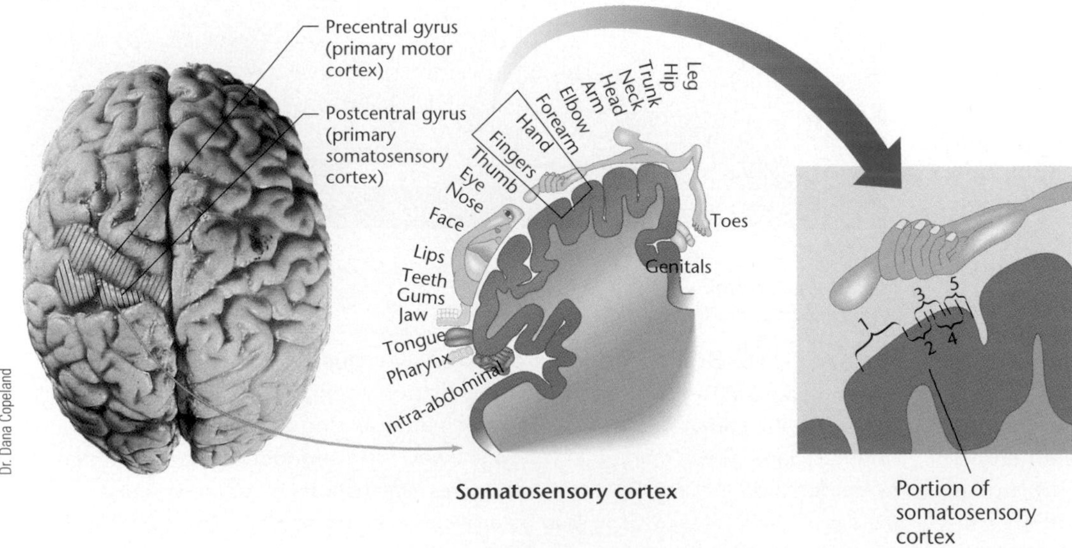

In some cases, the latter process does occur, such that stimulation on one finger excites mostly or entirely the same cortical areas as another finger. Consequently, the person has trouble distinguishing one finger from the other. Someone who can't clearly feel the difference between two fingers has trouble controlling them separately. This condition is "musician's cramp"—known more formally as **focal hand dystonia**—in which the fingers become clumsy, fatigue easily, and make involuntary movements that interfere with the task. This long-lasting condition is a potential career-ender for a serious musician. Some people who spend all day writing develop the same problem, in which case it is known as "writer's cramp." Traditionally, physicians assumed that the musician's cramp or writer's cramp was an impairment in the hands, but later research indicated that the cause is extensive reorganization of the sensory thalamus and cortex so that touch responses to one finger overlap those of another (Byl, McKenzie, & Nagarajan, 2000; Elbert et al., 1998; Lenz & Byl, 1999; Sanger, Pascual-Leone, Tarsy, & Schlaug, 2001; Sanger, Tarsy, & Pascual-Leone, 2001).

STOP & CHECK

11. An "enriched" environment promotes growth of axons and dendrites. What is known to be one important reason for this action?

12. Name two kinds of evidence indicating that touch information from the fingers "invades" the occipital cortex of people blind since birth.

13. What change in the brain is responsible for musician's cramp?

Check your answers on page 136

Module 5.1

In Closing: Brain Development

Considering the number of ways in which abnormal genes and chemicals can disrupt brain development, let alone the possible varieties of abnormal experience, it is a wonder that any of us develop normally. Evidently, the system has enough margin for error that we can function even if all of our connections do not develop quite perfectly. There are many ways for development to go wrong, but somehow the system usually manages to work.

Summary

1. In vertebrate embryos, the central nervous system begins as a tube surrounding a fluid-filled cavity. Developing neurons proliferate, migrate, differentiate, myelinate, and generate synapses. (p. 122)
2. Neuron proliferation varies among species mainly by the speed of cell division and the duration of this process in days. Therefore, differences in proliferation probably depend on very few genes. In contrast, migration depends on a large number of chemicals that guide immature neurons to their destinations. Many genes affect this process. (p. 123)
3. Even in adults, new neurons can form in the olfactory system, the hippocampus, and the song-producing brain areas of some bird species. (p. 125)
4. Growing axons manage to find their way close to the right locations by following chemicals. Then they array themselves over a target area by following chemical gradients. (p. 125)
5. After axons reach their targets based on chemical gradients, the postsynaptic cell fine-tunes the connections based on experience, accepting certain combinations of axons and rejecting others. This kind of competition among axons continues throughout life. (p. 128)
6. Initially, the nervous system develops far more neurons than will actually survive. Some axons make synaptic contacts with cells that release to them nerve growth factor or other neurotrophins. The neurons that receive neurotrophins survive; the others die in a process called apoptosis. (p. 128)
7. The developing brain is vulnerable to chemical insult. Many chemicals that produce only mild, temporary problems for adults can permanently impair early brain development. (p. 129)
8. Enriched experience leads to greater branching of axons and dendrites, partly because animals in enriched environments are more active than those in deprived environments. (p. 131)
9. Specialized experiences can alter brain development, especially early in life. For example, in people who are born blind, representation of touch, some aspects of language, and other information invades the occipital cortex, which is usually reserved for vision. (p. 132)
10. Extensive practice of a skill expands the brain's representation of sensory and motor information relevant to that skill. For example, the representation of fingers expands in people who regularly practice musical instruments. (p. 133)

Answers to STOP & CHECK Questions

1. The axon forms first, the dendrites later (p. 125)
2. They trained the ferrets to respond to stimuli on the normal side, turning one direction in response to sounds and the other direction to lights. Then they presented light to the rewired side and saw that the ferret again turned in the direction it had associated with lights. (p. 125)
3. Olfactory receptors, neurons in the hippocampus, and neurons in the song-producing areas of some bird species (p. 125)
4. Sperry found that if he cut a newt's eye and inverted it, axons grew back to their original targets, even though they were inappropriate to their new position on the eye. (p. 127)
5. Axons would attach haphazardly instead of arranging themselves according to their dorsoventral position on the retina. (p. 127)
6. The axons would attach based on a chemical gradient but could not fine-tune their adjustment based on experience. Therefore, the connections would be less precise. (p. 128)
7. The nervous system builds far more neurons than it needs and discards through apoptosis those that do not make lasting synapses. (p. 129)
8. Neurotrophins, such as nerve growth factor (p. 129)
9. The embryo has the most neurons. (p. 129)
10. Prolonged exposure to anesthetics might produce effects similar to fetal alcohol syndrome. Fetal alcohol syndrome occurs because alcohol increases inhibition and therefore increases apoptosis of developing neurons. (p. 130)
11. Animals in an "enriched" environment are more active, and their exercise enhances growth of axons and dendrites. (p. 135)
12. First, brain scans indicate increased activity in the occipital cortex while blind people perform tasks such as feeling two objects and saying whether they are the same or different. Second, temporary inactivation of the occipital cortex blocks blind people's ability to perform that task, without affecting the ability of sighted people. (p. 135)
13. Extensive practice of violin, piano, or other instruments causes expanded representation of the fingers in the somatosensory cortex. In some cases, the representation of each finger invades the area representing other fingers. If the representation of two fingers overlaps too much, the person cannot feel them separately, and the result is musician's cramp. (p. 135)

Thought Questions

1. Biologists can develop antibodies against nerve growth factor (i.e., molecules that inactivate nerve growth factor). What would happen if someone injected such antibodies into a developing nervous system?
2. Based on material in this chapter, what is one reason a woman should avoid long-lasting anesthesia during delivery of a baby?
3. Decades ago, educators advocated teaching Latin and ancient Greek because the required mental discipline would promote overall intelligence and brain development in general. Occasionally, people today advance the same argument for studying calculus or other subjects. Do these arguments seem valid, considering modern research on expertise and brain development?

Module 5.2
Plasticity After Brain Damage

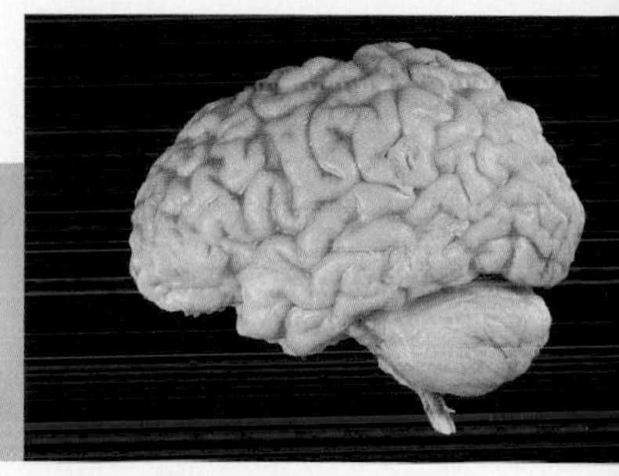

An American soldier who suffered a wound to the left hemisphere of his brain during the Korean War was at first unable to speak at all. Three months later, he could speak in short fragments. When he was asked to read the letterhead, "New York University College of Medicine," he replied, "Doctors—little doctors." Eight years later, when someone asked him again to read the letterhead, he replied, "Is there a catch? It says, 'New York University College of Medicine'" (Eidelberg & Stein, 1974).

Almost all survivors of brain damage show at least slight behavioral recovery and, in some cases, substantial recovery. Some of the mechanisms rely on the growth of new branches of axons and dendrites, quite similar to the mechanisms of brain development discussed in the first module. Understanding the process may lead to better therapies for people with brain damage and to insights into the functioning of the healthy brain.

Brain Damage and Short-Term Recovery

The possible causes of brain damage include tumors, infections, exposure to radiation or toxic substances, and degenerative conditions such as Parkinson's disease and Alzheimer's disease. In young people, the most common cause is **closed head injury,** a sharp blow to the head resulting from a fall, an automobile or other accident, an assault, or other sudden trauma that does not actually puncture the brain. The damage occurs partly because of rotational forces that drive brain tissue against the inside of the skull. Closed head injury also produces blood clots that interrupt blood flow to the brain (Kirkpatrick, Smielewski, Czosnyka, Menon, & Pickard, 1995). Many people, probably most, have suffered at least a mild closed head injury. Obviously, repeated or more severe blows increase the risk of long-term problems.

EXTENSIONS AND APPLICATIONS
How Woodpeckers Avoid Concussions

Speaking of blows to the head, have you ever wondered how woodpeckers manage to avoid giving themselves concussions or worse? If you repeatedly banged your head into a tree at 6 or 7 meters per second (about 15 miles per hour), you would almost certainly harm yourself.

Using slow-motion photography, researchers found that woodpeckers usually start with a couple of quick preliminary taps against the wood, much like a carpenter lining up a nail with a hammer. Then the birds make a hard strike in a straight line, keeping a rigid neck. The result is a near absence of rotational forces and consequent whiplash. The fact that woodpeckers are so careful to avoid rotating their heads during impact supports the claim that rotational forces are a major factor in closed head injuries (May, Fuster, Haber, & Hirschman, 1979).

The researchers suggested that football helmets, racecar helmets, and so forth would give more protection if they extended down to the shoulders to prevent rotation and whiplash. They also suggest that if you see a sudden automobile accident or something similar about to happen, you should tuck your chin to your chest and tighten your neck muscles.

Reducing the Harm from a Stroke

A common cause of brain damage in older people (more rarely in the young) is temporary loss of blood flow to a brain area during a **stroke,** also known as a **cerebrovascular accident.** The more common type of stroke is **ischemia,** the result of a blood clot or other obstruction in an artery; the less common type is **hemorrhage,** the result of a ruptured artery. Strokes vary in severity from barely noticeable to immediately fatal. Figure 5.13 shows the brains of three people: one who died immediately after a stroke, one who survived long after

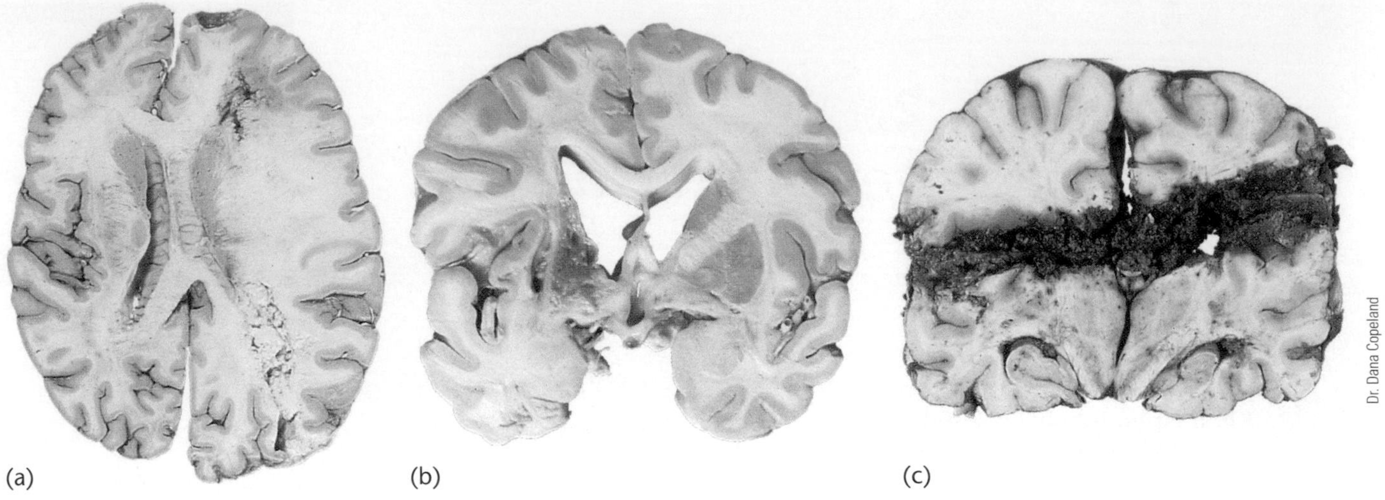

Figure 5.13 Three damaged human brains
(a) Brain of a person who died immediately after a stroke. Note the swelling on the right side. **(b)** Brain of a person who survived for a long time after a stroke. Note the cavities on the left side, where many cells were lost. **(c)** Brain of a person who suffered a gunshot wound and died immediately.

a stroke, and a bullet wound victim. For a good collection of information about stroke, visit this website: **http://www.stroke.org/**

In ischemia, neurons are deprived of blood and therefore lose much of their oxygen and glucose supplies. In hemorrhage, they are flooded with blood and therefore with excess oxygen, calcium, and other products. Both ischemia and hemorrhage lead to many of the same problems, including **edema** (the accumulation of fluid), which increases pressure on the brain and increases the probability of additional strokes (Unterberg, Stover, Kress, & Kiening, 2004). Both ischemia and hemorrhage also impair the sodium-potassium pump, leading to an accumulation of sodium inside neurons. The combination of edema and excess sodium provokes excess release of the transmitter glutamate (Rossi, Oshima, & Attwell, 2000), which overstimulates neurons: Sodium and other ions enter the neurons in excessive amounts, faster than the sodium-potassium pump can remove them. The excess positive ions block metabolism in the mitochondria and kill the neurons (Stout, Raphael, Kanterewicz, Klann, & Reynolds, 1998). As neurons die, glia cells proliferate, removing waste products and dead neurons.

If someone had a stroke and you called a hospital, what advice would you probably get? As recently as the 1980s, the staff would have been in no great hurry to see the patient because they had little to offer anyway. Today, it is possible to reduce the effects of an ischemic stroke if physicians act quickly. A drug called **tissue plasminogen activator (tPA)** breaks up blood clots (Barinaga, 1996) and has a mixture of other effects on damaged neurons (Kim, Park, Hong, & Koh, 1999). To get significant benefit, a patient should receive tPA within 3 hours after a stroke, although slight benefits are possible up to 6 hours after the stroke. Unfortunately, by the time a patient's family gets the patient to the hospital, and then waits through procedures in the emergency room, the delay is usually too long (Stahl, Furie, Gleason, & Gazelle, 2003).

Even when it is too late for tPA to save the cells in the immediate vicinity of the ischemia or hemorrhage, hope remains for cells in the **penumbra** (Latin for "almost shadow"), the region that surrounds the immediate damage (Hsu, Sik, Gallyas, Horváth, & Buzsáki, 1994; Jonas, 1995) (Figure 5.14). One idea is to prevent overstimulation by blocking glutamate synapses or preventing positive ions from entering neurons. However, most such methods have produced disappointing results (Lee, Zipfel, & Choi, 1999). A somewhat promising new drug opens potassium channels (Gribkoff et al., 2001). As calcium or other positive ions enter a neuron, potassium exits through these open channels, reducing overstimulation.

One possible reason blocking overstimulation has not worked better is that stroke-damaged neurons also can die from understimulation (Colbourne, Sutherland, & Auer, 1999; Conti, Raghupathi, Trojanowski, & McIntosh, 1998). It is possible that a stroke reactivates the mechanisms of apoptosis. According to research with laboratory animals, injections of neurotrophins and other drugs that block apoptosis can improve recovery from a stroke (Barinaga, 1996; Choi-Lundberg et al., 1997; Levivier, Przedborski, Bencsics, & Kang,

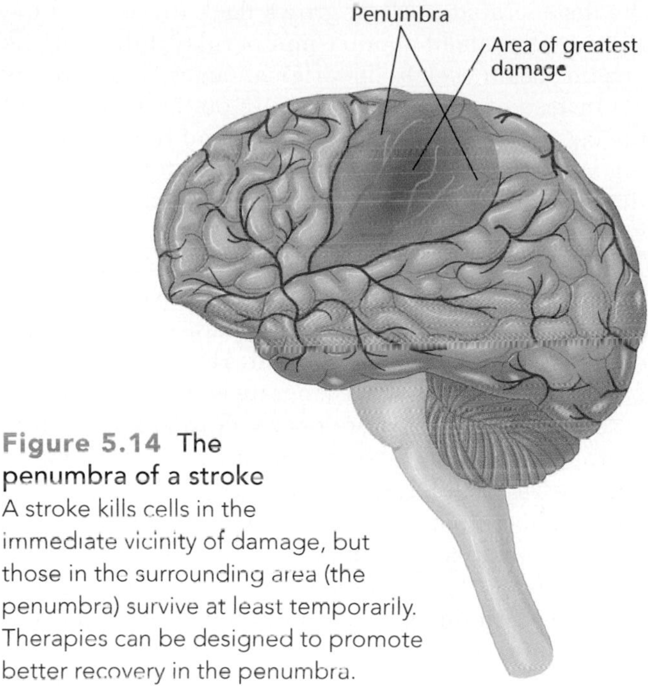

Figure 5.14 The penumbra of a stroke
A stroke kills cells in the immediate vicinity of damage, but those in the surrounding area (the penumbra) survive at least temporarily. Therapies can be designed to promote better recovery in the penumbra.

1995; Schulz, Weller, & Moskowitz, 1999). However, because these drugs do not cross the blood-brain barrier, they must be injected directly into the brain. Researchers can do so with laboratory animals, but physicians understandably hesitate to try with humans.

So far, the most effective method of preventing brain damage after strokes in laboratory animals is to cool the brain. A cooled brain has less activity, lower energy needs, and less risk of overstimulation than does a brain at normal temperature (Barone, Feuerstein, & White, 1997; Colbourne & Corbett, 1995). Humans cannot be cooled safely to the same temperature that rats can, but cooling someone to about 33–36°C (91–97°F) for the first three days after a stroke significantly improves survival and long-term behavioral functioning (Steiner, Ringleb, & Hacke, 2001). Note that this approach goes contrary to most people's first impulse, which is to keep the patient warm and comfortable.

Among other approaches that have shown promise with stroke-damaged laboratory animals, one of the more interesting is to use cannabinoids—drugs related to marijuana (Nagayama et al., 1999). Cannabinoids have been shown to reduce cell loss after stroke, closed head injury, and other kinds of brain damage, although not in all experiments (van der Stelt et al., 2002). Recall from Chapter 3 (p. 74) that cannabinoids decrease the release of glutamate. One possible explanation for how they decrease brain damage is that they probably prevent excess glutamate from overexciting neurons. They may have other mechanisms as well (van der Stelt et al., 2002). So far, researchers have not tried cannabinoids with human stroke patients.

STOP & CHECK

1. What are the two kinds of stroke and what causes each kind?
2. Why is tPA not recommended in cases of hemorrhage?
3. If one of your relatives has a stroke and a well-meaning person offers a blanket, what should you do?

Check your answers on page 147.

Later Mechanisms of Recovery

After the first few hours or at most days following brain damage, no more cells are going to die, and no new cells will replace the lost ones. Nevertheless, a variety of other changes take place in the remaining neurons.

Diaschisis

A behavioral deficit after brain damage reflects more than just the functions of the cells that were destroyed. Activity in any brain area stimulates many other areas, so damage to any area deprives other areas of their normal stimulation and thus interferes with their healthy functioning. For example, after damage to part of the left frontal cortex, activity decreases in the temporal cortex and several other areas (Price, Warburton, Moore, Frackowiak, & Friston, 2001). **Diaschisis** (di-AS-ki-sis, from a Greek term meaning "to shock throughout") refers to the decreased activity of surviving neurons after damage to other neurons.

If diaschisis contributes to behavioral deficits following brain damage, then stimulant drugs should promote recovery by decreasing the effects of diaschisis. In a series of experiments, D. M. Feeney and colleagues measured the behavioral effects of cortical damage in rats and cats. Depending on the location of the damage, the animals showed impairments in either coordinated movement or depth perception. Injecting amphetamine (which increases release of dopamine and norepinephrine) significantly enhanced both behaviors, and animals that practiced the behaviors under the influence of amphetamine showed long-lasting benefits. Injecting a drug that blocks dopamine synapses impaired behavioral recovery (Feeney & Sutton, 1988; Feeney, Sutton, Boyeson, Hovda, & Dail, 1985; Hovda & Feeney, 1989; Sutton, Hovda, & Feeney, 1989).

These results imply that people who have had a stroke should be given stimulant drugs, not immediately after the stroke, as with clot-busting drugs, but during the next days and weeks. Although amphetamine has improved recovery from brain damage in many studies with laboratory animals, it increases the risk of heart attack, and physicians rarely recommend it. In the few cases in which stroke patients have received it, the results have been disappointing (Treig, Werner, Sachse, & Hesse, 2003). However, other stimulant drugs that do not endanger the heart appear more promising (Whyte et al., 2005).

Using stimulants violates many people's impulse to calm a stroke patient with tranquilizers. Tranquilizers decrease the release of dopamine and impair recovery after brain damage (L. B. Goldstein, 1993).

STOP & CHECK

4. Following damage to someone's brain, would it be best (if possible) to direct amphetamine to the cells that were damaged or somewhere else?

Check your answer on page 147.

The Regrowth of Axons

Although a destroyed cell body cannot be replaced, damaged axons do grow back under certain circumstances. A neuron of the peripheral nervous system has its cell body in the spinal cord and an axon that extends into one of the limbs. If the axon is crushed, the degenerated portion grows back toward the periphery at a rate of about 1 mm per day, following its myelin sheath back to the original target. If the axon is cut instead of crushed, the myelin on the two sides of the cut may not line up correctly, and the regenerating axon may not have a sure path to follow. Sometimes a motor nerve attaches to the wrong muscle, as Figure 5.15 illustrates.

Within a mature mammalian brain or spinal cord, damaged axons regenerate only a millimeter or two, if at all (Schwab, 1998). Therefore, paralysis caused by spinal cord injury is permanent. However, in many kinds of fish, axons do regenerate across a cut spinal cord far enough to restore nearly normal functioning (Bernstein & Gelderd, 1970; Rovainen, 1976; Scherer, 1986; Selzer, 1978). Why do damaged CNS axons regenerate so much better in fish than in mammals? If we could answer this question, we might be able to develop new therapies for patients with spinal cord damage.

One possibility is that a cut through the adult mammalian spinal cord forms more scar tissue than it does in fish. The scar tissue not only creates a mechanical barrier to axon growth, but it also synthesizes chemicals that inhibit axon growth. We might imagine a therapy for spinal cord damage based on breaking up the scar tissue or blocking the chemicals it releases. However, despite many attempts, so far none of the methods based on breaking up scar tissue has produced much benefit (Filbin, 2003).

Another explanation for the failure of axon growth in mammals and birds is that the myelin in their central nervous system secretes proteins that inhibit axon

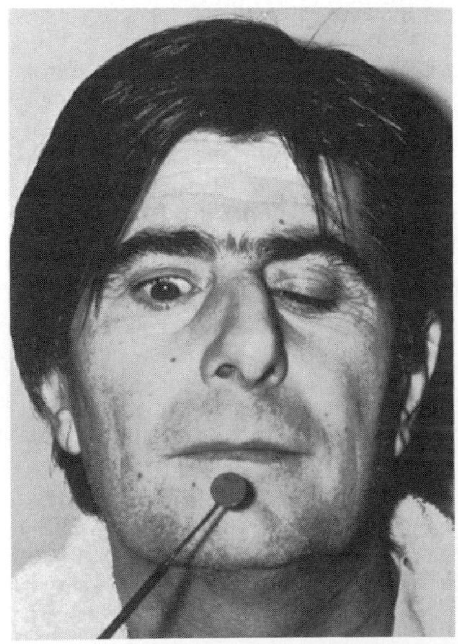

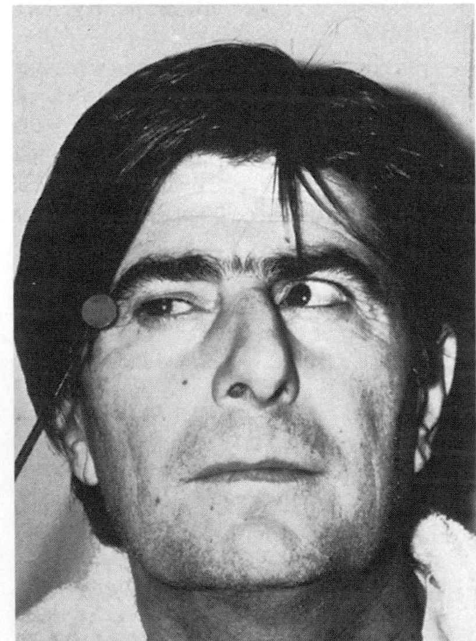

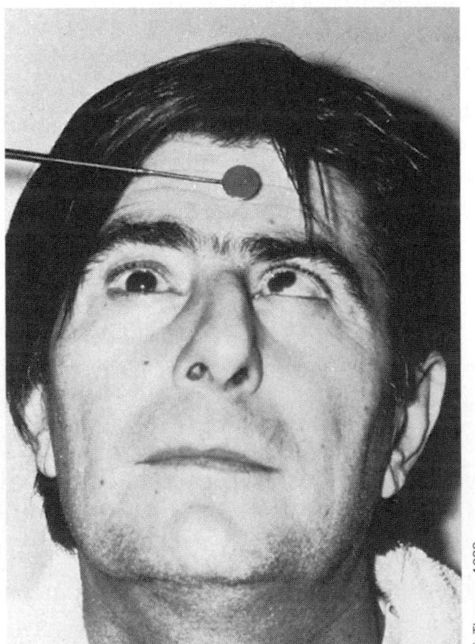

K. Thomas, 1988

Figure 5.15 What can happen if damaged axons regenerate to incorrect muscles
Damaged axons to the muscles of the patient's right eye regenerated but attached incorrectly. When he looks down, his right eyelid opens wide instead of closing like the other eyelid. His eye movements are frequently misaimed, and he has trouble moving his right eye upward or to the left.

growth (Fields, Schwab, & Silver, 1999; McClellan, 1998). However, axons also fail to regenerate in areas of the CNS that lack myelin (Raisman, 2004). So the question remains unanswered as to why axons regenerate better in fish than in mammals.

Sprouting

The brain is constantly adding new branches of axons and dendrites while withdrawing old ones (Cotman & Nieto-Sampedro, 1982). That process accelerates in response to damage. After loss of a set of axons, the cells that have lost their source of innervation react by secreting neurotrophins to induce other axons to form new branches, or **collateral sprouts,** that attach to the vacant synapses (Ramirez, 2001). Gradually over several months, the sprouts fill in most of the vacated synapses (Figure 5.16).

Most of the research has concerned the hippocampus, where two types of sprouting are known to occur. First, damage to a set of axons can induce sprouting by similar axons. For example, the hippocampus receives input from a nearby cortical area called the *entorhinal cortex,* and damage to axons from the entorhinal cortex of one hemisphere induces sprouting by axons of the other hemisphere. Those sprouts form gradually over weeks, simultaneous with improvements in memory task performance, and several kinds of evidence indicate that the sprouting is essential for the improvement (Ramirez, Bulsara, Moore, Ruch, & Abrams, 1999; Ramirez, McQuilkin, Carrigan, MacDonald, & Kelley, 1996).

Second, damage sometimes induces sprouting by unrelated axons. For example, after damage to the entorhinal cortex of both hemispheres, axons from other areas form sprouts into the vacant synapses of the hippocampus. The information they bring is certainly not the same as what was lost. In some cases, this kind of sprouting appears useful, in some cases virtually worthless, and in other cases harmful (Ramirez, 2001).

Several studies indicate that **gangliosides** (a class of glycolipids—that is, combined carbohydrate and fat molecules) promote the restoration of damaged brains. How they do so is unclear, but one possibility is that they increase sprouting or aid in the formation of appropriate synapses. The fact that gangliosides adhere to neuron membranes suggests that they contribute to the recognition of one neuron by another. Daily injections of gangliosides aid the recovery of behavior after several kinds of brain damage in laboratory animals (Cahn, Borziex, Aldinio, Toffano, & Cahn, 1989; Ramirez et al., 1987a, 1987b; Sabel, Slavin, & Stein, 1984), and in limited trials, they have shown some promise in helping people regain function after partial damage to the spinal cord (Geisler et al., 2001).

In several studies of laboratory mammals, females have recovered better than males from frontal cortex damage, especially if the damage occurred when they had high levels of the hormone *progesterone* (D. G. Stein & Fulop, 1998). Progesterone apparently exerts its benefits by increasing release of the neurotrophin BDNF, which promotes axon sprouting and the formation of new synapses (Gonzalez et al., 2004).

Denervation Supersensitivity

A postsynaptic cell that is deprived of most of its synaptic inputs develops increased sensitivity to the neurotransmitters that it still receives. For example, a normal muscle cell responds to the neurotransmitter acetylcholine only at the neuromuscular junction. If the axon is cut or if it is inactive for days, the muscle cell builds additional receptors, becoming sensitive to acetylcholine over a wider area of its surface (Johns & Thesleff, 1961; Levitt-Gilmour & Salpeter, 1986). The same process occurs in neurons. Heightened sensitivity to a neurotransmitter after the destruction of an incoming axon is known as **denervation supersensitivity** (Glick, 1974). Heightened sensitivity as a result of inactivity by an incoming axon is called **disuse supersensitivity.** The mechanisms of supersensitivity include an increased number of receptors (Kostrzewa, 1995) and increased effectiveness of receptors, perhaps by changes in second-messenger systems.

Denervation supersensitivity is a way of compensating for decreased input. In some cases, it enables people to maintain nearly

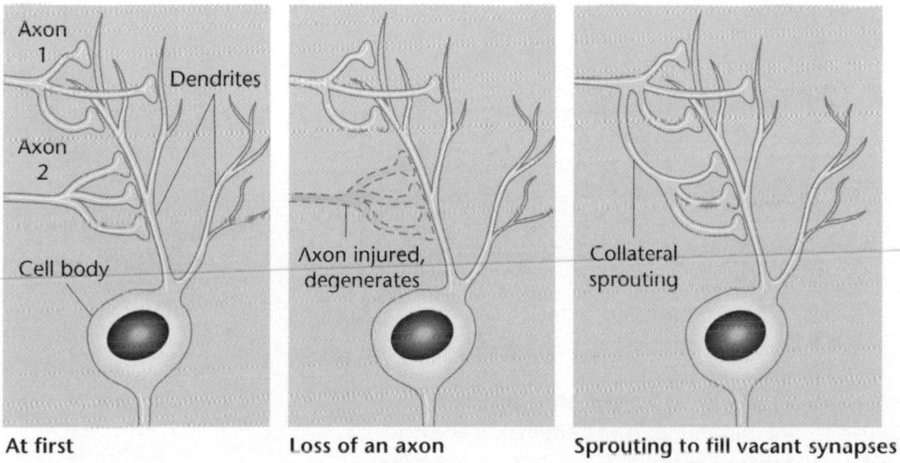

Figure 5.16 Collateral sprouting
A surviving axon grows a new branch to replace the synapses left vacant by a damaged axon.

normal behavior even after losing most of the axons in some pathway (Sabel, 1997). However, it can also have unpleasant consequences. For example, spinal cord injury often results in prolonged pain, and research with rats supports an explanation in terms of denervation supersensitivity: Because the injury damages many of the axons, postsynaptic neurons develop increased sensitivity to the remaining ones. Therefore, even normal inputs from the remaining axons produce intense responses (Hains, Everhart, Fullwood, & Hulsebosch, 2002).

5. Is collateral sprouting a change in axons or dendritic receptors?
6. Is denervation supersensitivity a change in axons or dendritic receptors?

Check your answers on page 147.

Reorganized Sensory Representations and the Phantom Limb

As described in the first module of this chapter, experiences can modify the connections within the cerebral cortex to increase the representation of personally important information. Recall that after someone has played a string instrument for many years, the somatosensory cortex has an enlarged representation of the fingers of the left hand. Such changes represent either collateral sprouting of axons or increased receptor sensitivity by the postsynaptic neurons. Similar processes occur after nervous system damage, with sometimes surprising results.

Consider how the cortex reorganizes after an amputation. Reexamine Figure 4.24 (p. 99): Each section along the somatosensory cortex receives input from a different part of the body. Within the area marked "fingers" in that figure, a closer examination reveals that each subarea responds more to one finger than to another. Figure 5.17 shows the arrangement for a monkey brain. In one study, experimenters amputated finger 3 of an owl monkey. The cortical cells that previously responded to information from that finger now had no input. Soon they became more responsive to finger 2, finger 4, or part of the palm, until the cortex developed the pattern of responsiveness shown in Figure 5.17b (Kaas, Merzenich, & Killackey, 1983; Merzenich et al., 1984).

What happens if an entire arm is amputated? For many years, neuroscientists assumed that the cortical area corresponding to that arm would remain permanently silent because axons from other cortical areas could not sprout far enough to reach the area representing the arm. Then came a surprise. Investigators recorded from the cerebral cortices of monkeys that had the sensory nerves cut from one forelimb 12 years previously. They found that the large stretch of cortex previously responsive to the limb had become responsive to the face (Pons et al., 1991). How did such connections form? After loss of sensory input from the forelimb, the axons representing the forelimb degen-

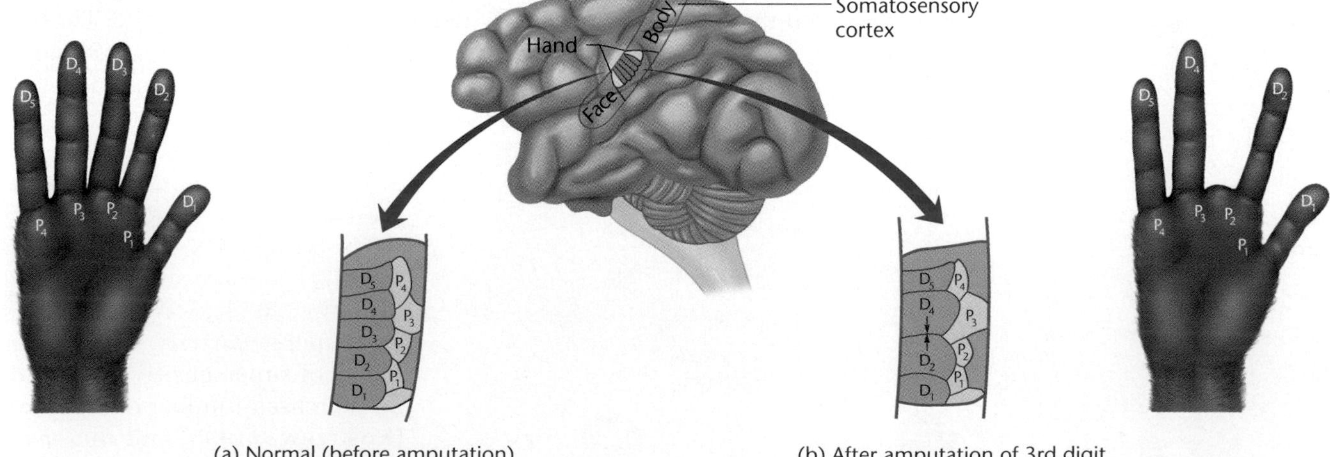

Figure 5.17 Somatosensory cortex of a monkey after a finger amputation
Note that the cortical area previously responsive to the third finger (D_3) becomes responsive to the second and fourth fingers (D_2 and D_4) and part of the palm (P_3). *(Source: Redrawn from the Annual Review of Neuroscience, Vol. 6, © 1983, by Annual Reviews, Inc. Reprinted by permission of Annual Reviews, Inc. and Jon H. Kaas.)*

METHODS 5.1
Histochemistry

Histology is the study of the structure of tissues. *Histochemistry* deals with the chemical components of tissues. One example is as follows: Investigators inject a chemical called horseradish peroxidase (HRP) into the brain of a laboratory animal. The axon terminals in that area absorb the chemical and transport it back to their cell bodies. Later, investigators treat slices of the brain with a second chemical that reacts with HRP to form granules that are visible in a microscope. By finding those granules, investigators can determine the point of origin for the axons that terminated at the spot where investigators had injected the HRP.

erated, leaving vacant synaptic sites at several levels of the CNS. Axons representing the face sprouted into those sites in the spinal cord, brainstem, and thalamus (Florence & Kaas, 1995; E. G. Jones & Pons, 1998). (Or perhaps axons from the face had already innervated those sites but were overwhelmed by the normal input. After removal of the normal input, the weaker synapses became stronger.) Also, lateral connections sprouted from the face-sensitive cortical areas into the previously hand-sensitive areas of the cortex, according to results from *histochemistry* (Florence, Taub, & Kaas, 1998) (see Methods 5.1).

Brain scan studies confirm that the same processes occur with humans. Now consider what happens when cells in a reorganized cortex become activated. Previously, those neurons responded to an arm, and now they receive information from the face. Does the response feel like stimulation on the face or on the arm?

The answer: It feels like the arm (Davis et al., 1998). Physicians have long noted that many people with amputations experience a **phantom limb**, a continuing sensation of an amputated body part. That experience can range from occasional tingling to intense pain. It is possible to have a phantom hand, foot, intestines, breast, penis, or anything else that has been amputated. Sometimes the phantom sensation fades within days or weeks, but sometimes it lasts a lifetime (Ramachandran & Hirstein, 1998).

Until the 1990s, no one knew what caused phantom pains, and most believed that the sensations were coming from the stump of the amputated limb. Some physicians even performed additional amputations, removing more and more of the limb in a futile attempt to eliminate the phantom sensations. But modern methods have demonstrated that phantom limbs develop only if the relevant portion of the somatosensory cortex reorganizes and becomes responsive to alternative inputs (Flor et al., 1995). For example, axons representing the face may come to activate the cortical area previously devoted to an amputated hand. Whenever the face is touched, the person still feels it on the face but also feels a sensation in the phantom hand. It is possible to map out which part of the face stimulates sensation in which part of the phantom hand, as shown in Figure 5.18 (Aglioti, Smania, Atzei, & Berlucchi, 1997).

The relationship between phantom sensations and brain reorganization enables us to understand some otherwise puzzling observations. Note in Figure 4.24

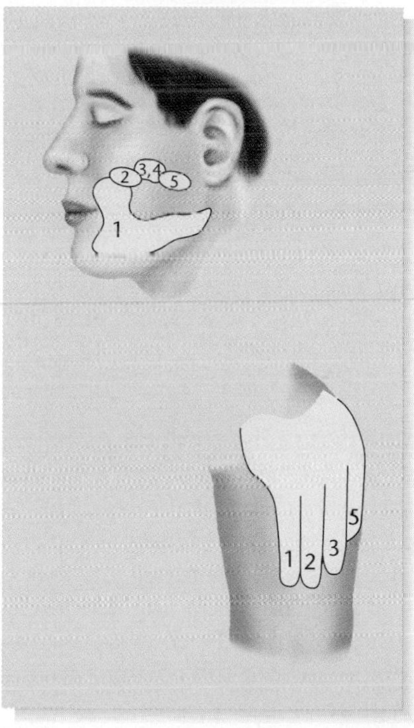

Figure 5.18 Sources of phantom sensation for one person
For this person, stimulation in the areas marked on the cheek produced phantom sensations of digits 1 (thumb), 2, 4, and 5. Stimulation on the shoulder also evoked phantom sensations of digits 1, 2, 3, and 5. *(Source: Fig. 5.29 from* Phantom in the Brain, *by V. S. Ramachandran, M.D., Ph.D. and Sandra Blakeslee. Copyright © 1998 by V. S. Ramachandran and Sandra Blakeslee. Reprinted by permission of HarperCollins Publishers and authors.)*

Amputees who feel a phantom limb are likely to lose those phantom sensations if they learn to use an artificial limb.

(p. 99) that the part of the cortex responsive to the feet is immediately next to the part responsive to the genitals. Two patients, after amputation, felt a phantom foot during sexual arousal! One in fact reported feeling orgasm not only in the genitals but also in the phantom foot—and intensely enjoying it (Ramachandran & Blakeslee, 1998). Evidently, the representation of the genitals had spread into the cortical area responsible for foot sensation.

If a phantom sensation is painful, is there any way to relieve it? In some cases, yes. Amputees who learn to use an artificial arm report that their phantom sensations gradually disappear (Lotze et al., 1999). Apparently, they start attributing sensations to the artificial arm, and in doing so, they displace abnormal connections from the face. Similarly, a study of one man found that after his hands were amputated, the area of his cortex that usually responds to the hands partly shifted to face sensitivity, but after he received hand transplants, his cortex gradually shifted back to hand sensitivity (Giraux, Sirigu, Schneider, & Dubernard, 2001).

One important message from these studies is that connections in the brain remain plastic throughout life. There are limits on the plasticity, certainly, but they are less strict than neuroscientists once supposed.

STOP & CHECK

7. Cite an example in which reorganization of the brain is helpful and one in which it is harmful.

Check your answer on page 147.

Learned Adjustments in Behavior

So far, the discussion has focused on changes in the wiring of the brain. In fact, much recovery from brain damage is based on learning, not any structural adjustments.

If you can't find your keys, perhaps you accidentally dropped them while hiking through the forest (so you will never find them), or perhaps you absentmindedly put them in an unusual place (where you will find them if you keep looking). Similarly, an individual with brain damage who seems to have lost some ability may indeed have lost it forever or may be able to find it with enough effort. Much, probably most, recovery from brain damage depends on learning to make better use of the abilities that were spared. For example, if you lost your peripheral vision, you would learn to move your head from side to side to see better (Marshall, 1985).

Sometimes a person or animal with brain damage appears unable to do something but is in fact not trying. For example, consider an animal that has incurred damage to the sensory nerves linking one forelimb to the spinal cord, as in Figure 5.19. The animal can no longer feel the limb, although the motor nerves still connect to the muscles. We say the limb is **deafferented** because it has lost its afferent (sensory) input. A monkey with a deafferented limb does not spontaneously use it for walking, picking up objects, or any other voluntary behaviors (Taub & Berman, 1968). Investigators initially assumed that the monkey *could not* use a limb that it didn't feel. In a later experiment, however, they cut the afferent nerves of both forelimbs; despite this more extensive damage, the monkey regained use of both deafferented limbs. It could walk, climb the walls of metal cages, and even pick up a raisin between its thumb and forefinger. Apparently, a monkey fails to use a deafferented forelimb only because walking on three limbs is easier than using the impaired

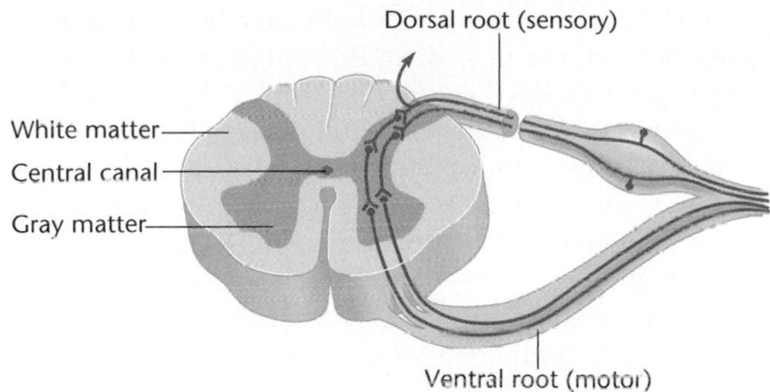

Figure 5.19 Cross-section through the spinal cord
A cut through the dorsal root (as shown) deprives the animal of touch sensations from part of the body but leaves the motor nerves intact.

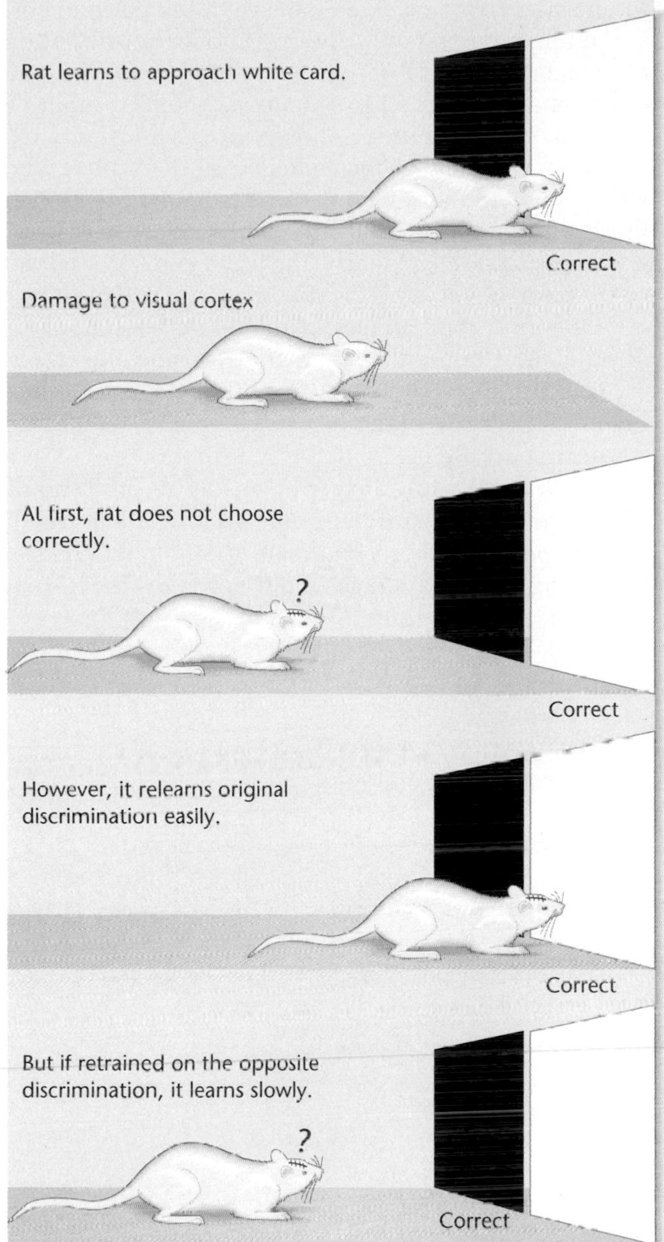

Figure 5.20 Memory impairment after cortical damage
Brain damage impairs retrieval of a memory but does not destroy it completely. *(Source: Based on T. E. LeVere & Morlock, 1973)*

limb. When it has no choice but to use its deafferented limbs, it can.

For another example, consider a rat with damage to its visual cortex. Prior to the damage, it had learned to approach a white card instead of a black card for food, but just after the damage, it approaches one card or the other randomly. Has it completely forgotten the discrimination? Evidently not because it can more easily relearn to approach the white card than learn to approach the black card (T. E. LeVere & Morlock, 1973) (Figure 5.20). Thomas LeVere (1975) proposed that a lesion to the visual cortex does not destroy the memory trace but merely impairs the rat's ability to find it. As the animal recovers, it regains access to misplaced memories.

Similarly, many people with brain damage are capable of more than they realize they can do. Often, they find ways of getting through the tasks of their day without relying on their impaired skills; for example, someone with impaired language will rely on a spouse to do the talking, or someone with impaired face recognition will learn to recognize people by their voices. Therapy for people with brain damage focuses on showing them how much they already can do and encouraging them to practice those skills. For example, someone with damage to the motor cortex of one hemisphere learns to use the pathways from the intact hemisphere more efficiently (Chollet & Weiller, 1994).

Treatment begins with careful evaluation of a patient's abilities and disabilities. Such evaluations are the specialty of neuropsychologists (see Table 1.1, p. 9), who use standardized tests and sometimes improvise new tests to try to pinpoint the problems. For example, someone who has trouble carrying out spoken instructions might be impaired in hearing, memory, language, muscle control, or alertness. Often, neuropsychologists need to test someone repeatedly under different conditions because performance fluctuates, especially when a person with brain damage becomes fatigued.

After identifying the problem, a neuropsychologist might refer a patient to a physical therapist or occupational therapist, who will help the patient practice the impaired skills. Therapists often remark that they get their best results if they start soon after a patient's stroke, and animal research confirms this impression.

In one study, rats received damage to the parietal cortex of one hemisphere, resulting in poor coordination of the contralateral forepaw. Some of the rats received experiences designed to encourage them to practice with the impaired limb. Those who began practice 5 days after the damage recovered better than those who started after 14 days, who in turn recovered better than those who started after 30 days (Biernaskie, Chernenko, & Corbett, 2004). Evidently, the brain goes through an era of plasticity during the first days after damage.

One important generalization is that behavior recovered after brain damage is effortful, and the recovery is precarious. Someone who appears to be functioning normally is working harder than usual to achieve the same end. Behavior deteriorates markedly after a couple of beers, a physically tiring day, or other kinds of stresses that would minimally affect a normal, healthy person (Fleet & Heilman, 1986). It also deteriorates more than average in old age (Corkin, Rosen, Sullivan, & Clegg, 1989).

STOP & CHECK

8. Suppose someone has suffered a spinal cord injury that interrupts all sensation from the left arm. Now he or she uses only the right arm. Of the following, which is the most promising therapy: electrically stimulate the skin of the left arm, tie the right arm behind the person's back, or blindfold the person?

Check your answer on page 147.

Module 5.2

In Closing: Brain Damage and Recovery

The mammalian body is well equipped to replace lost blood cells or skin cells but poorly prepared to deal with lost brain cells. Even the responses that do occur after brain damage, such as collateral sprouting of axons or reorganization of sensory representations, are not always helpful. It is tempting to speculate that we did not evolve many mechanisms of recovery from brain damage because, through most of our evolutionary history, an individual with brain damage was not likely to survive long enough to recover. Today, many people with brain and spinal cord damage survive for years, and we need continuing research on how to improve their lives.

For decades now, researchers have been optimistic about developing new drug therapies or surgeries for people with brain or spinal cord injury. Many kinds of treatment are in the experimental phase, although so far none has shown a good benefits-to-risk ratio. In Chapter 8, we shall focus on one of these approaches, the idea of transplanting healthy cells, preferably stem cells from an embryo, to replace dying brain cells. Greater success may be possible for replacing glia cells, such as those that produce myelin sheaths (Keirstead et al., 2005). We can and should remain optimistic about therapies of the future, but unfortunately, we don't know when that future will arrive.

Still, in the process of doing the research, we learn much about the nervous system. We can now explain some phenomena, such as the phantom limb, that previously were completely mysterious.

Summary

1. Brain damage has many causes, including blows to the head, obstruction of blood flow to the brain, or a ruptured blood vessel in the brain. Strokes kill neurons largely by overexcitation. (p. 137)
2. During the first 3 hours after an ischemic stroke, tissue plasminogen activator (tPA) can reduce cell loss by breaking up the blood clot. Theoretically, it should also be possible to minimize cell loss by preventing overexcitation of neurons, but so far none of the methods based on this idea have produced demonstrable benefits in humans. (p. 138)
3. When one brain area is damaged, other areas become less active than usual because of their loss of input. Stimulant drugs can help restore normal function of these undamaged areas. (p. 139)
4. A cut axon regrows in the peripheral nervous system of mammals and in either the central or peripheral nervous system of many fish. Researchers have tried to promote axon growth in the mammalian CNS as well, but so far without much success. (p. 140)
5. After an area of the CNS loses its usual input, other axons begin to excite it as a result of either sprouting or denervation supersensitivity. In some cases, this abnormal input produces odd sensations such as the phantom limb. (p. 141)
6. Most recovery of function after brain damage relies on learning to make better use of spared functions. Many individuals with brain damage are capable of more than they show because they avoid using skills that have become impaired or difficult. (p. 144)

Answers to STOP & CHECK Questions

1. The more common form, ischemia, is the result of an occlusion of an artery. The other form, hemorrhage, is the result of a ruptured artery. (p. 139)
2. The drug tPA breaks up blood clots, and the problem in hemorrhage is a ruptured blood vessel, not a blood clot. (p. 139)
3. Refuse the blanket. Recovery will be best if the stroke victim remains cold for the first 3 days. (p. 139)
4. It is best to direct the amphetamine to the cells that had been receiving input from the damaged cells. Presumably, the loss of input has produced diaschisis. (p. 140)
5. Axons (p. 142)
6. Dendritic receptors (p. 142)
7. The small-scale reorganization that enables increased representation of a violinist's or Braille reader's fingers is helpful. The larger-scale reorganization that occurs after amputation is harmful. (p. 144)
8. Tie the right arm behind the back to force the person to use the impaired arm instead of only the normal arm. Stimulating the skin of the left arm would accomplish nothing, as the sensory receptors have no input to the CNS. Blindfolding would be either irrelevant or harmful (by decreasing the visual feedback from left-hand movements). (p. 146)

Thought Questions

1. Ordinarily, patients with advanced Parkinson's disease (who have damage to dopamine-releasing axons) move very slowly if at all. However, during an emergency (e.g., a fire in the building), they may move rapidly and vigorously. Suggest a possible explanation.
2. Drugs that block dopamine synapses tend to impair or slow limb movements. However, after people have taken such drugs for a long time, some experience involuntary twitches or tremors in their muscles. Based on something in this chapter, propose a possible explanation.

Chapter Ending

Key Terms and Activities

Terms

apoptosis (p. 128)
closed head injury (p. 137)
collateral sprout (p. 141)
deafferent (p. 144)
denervation supersensitivity (p. 141)
diaschisis (p. 139)
differentiation (p. 124)
disuse supersensitivity (p. 141)
edema (p. 138)
fetal alcohol syndrome (p. 130)
focal hand dystonia (p. 135)
ganglioside (p. 141)
hemorrhage (p. 137)
ischemia (p. 137)
migration (p. 123)
myelination (p. 124)
nerve growth factor (NGF) (p. 128)
neural Darwinism (p. 128)
neurotrophin (p. 129)
penumbra (p. 138)
phantom limb (p. 143)
proliferation (p. 123)
stem cells (p. 125)
stroke (or cerebrovascular accident) (p. 137)
synaptogenesis (p. 125)
tissue plasminogen activator (tPA) (p. 138)

Suggestions for Further Reading

Azari, N. P., & Seitz, R. J. (2000). Brain plasticity and recovery from stroke. *American Scientist, 88,* 426–431. Good review of some of the mechanisms of recovery from brain damage.

Levi-Montalcini, R. (1988). *In praise of imperfection.* New York: Basic Books. Autobiography by the discoverer of nerve growth factor.

Ramachandran, V. S., & Blakeslee, S. (1998). *Phantoms in the brain.* New York: Morrow. One of the most thought-provoking books ever written about human brain damage, including the phantom limb phenomenon.

Websites to Explore

You can go to the Biological Psychology Study Center and click this link. While there, you can also check for suggested articles available on InfoTrac College Edition. The Biological Psychology Internet address is:

http://psychology.wadsworth.com/book/kalatbiopsych9e/

National Stroke Association Home Page

http://www.stroke.org/

Neurobehavioral Teratology Society Home Page

A society dedicated to understanding the effects of prenatal alcohol and other drugs on development of the brain and behavior

http://www.nbts.org

Exploring Biological Psychology CD

Sperry Experiment (animation)

Phantom Limb (animation)

Critical Thinking (essay questions)

Chapter Quiz (multiple-choice questions)

ThomsonNOW™

http://www.thomsonedu.com

Go to this site for the link to ThomsonNOW, your one-stop study shop, Take a Pre-Test for this chapter, and ThomsonNOW will generate a Personalized Study Plan based on your test results. The Study Plan will identify the topics you need to review and direct you to online resources to help you master these topics. You can then take a Post-Test to help you determine the concepts you have mastered and what you still need work on.

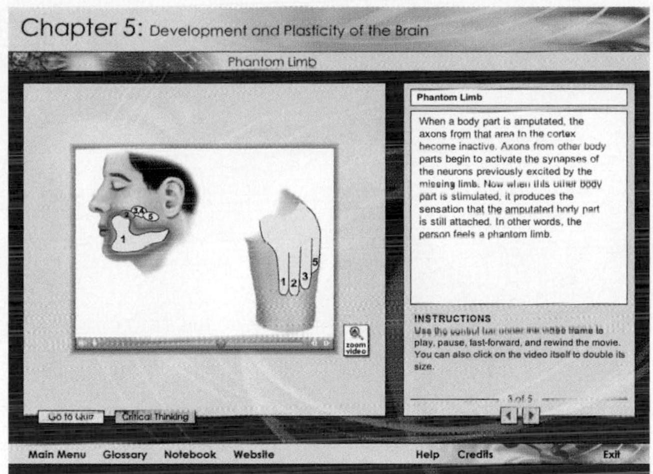

View this animation of studies of a phantom limb.

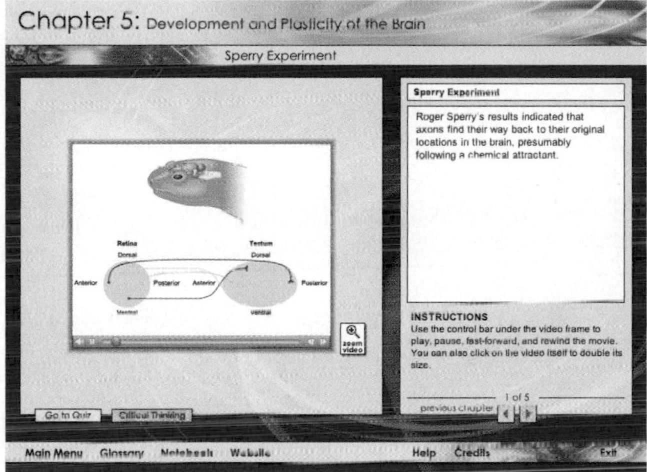

This animation explains Sperry's results showing that axons grow back to their original targets.

Vision

Chapter Outline

Opposite: Later in this chapter, you will understand why this prairie falcon has tilted its head.
Source: © *Tom McHugh/Photo Researchers*

Main Ideas

1. Each sensory neuron conveys a particular type of experience; for example, anything that stimulates the optic nerve is perceived as light.
2. Vertebrate vision depends on two kinds of receptors: cones, which contribute to color vision, and rods, which do not.
3. Every cell in the visual system has a receptive field, an area of the visual world that can excite or inhibit it.
4. After visual information reaches the brain, concurrent pathways analyze different aspects, such as shape, color, and movement.
5. Neurons of the visual system establish approximately correct connections and properties through chemical gradients that are present before birth. However, visual experience can fine-tune or alter those properties, especially early in life.

Several decades ago, a graduate student taking his final oral exam for a PhD in psychology was asked, "How far can an ant see?" He suddenly turned pale. He did not know the answer, and evidently, he was supposed to. He mentally reviewed everything he had read about the compound eye of insects. Finally, he gave up and admitted he did not know.

With an impish grin the professor told him, "Presumably, an ant can see 93 million miles—the distance to the sun." Yes, this was a trick question. However, it illustrates an important point: How far an ant can see, or how far you or I can see, depends on how far the light travels. We see because light strikes our eyes, not because we send out "sight rays." But that principle is far from intuitive. In fact, it was not known until the Arab philosopher Ibn al-Haythem (965–1040) demonstrated that light rays bounce off any object in all directions, but we see only those rays that strike the retina perpendicularly (Gross, 1999). Even today, a distressingly large number of college students believe that energy comes out of their eyes when they see (Winer, Cottrell, Gregg, Fournier, & Bica, 2002). The sensory systems, especially vision, are quite complex and do not match our commonsense notions.

Module 6.1
Visual Coding and the Retinal Receptors

Imagine that you are a piece of iron. So there you are, sitting around doing nothing, as usual, when along comes a drop of water. What will be your perception of the water?

You will have the experience of rust. From your point of view, water is above all *rustish.* Now return to your perspective as a human. You know that rustishness is not really a property of water itself but of how it reacts with iron.

The same is true of human perception. In vision, for example, when you look at a tree's leaves, you perceive them as *green.* But green is no more a property of the leaves than rustish is a property of water. Greenness is what happens when the light bouncing off the leaves reacts with the neurons in your brain. The greenness is in us—just as the rust is really in the piece of iron.

General Principles of Perception

Each receptor is specialized to absorb one kind of energy and *transduce* (convert) it into an electrochemical pattern in the brain. For example, visual receptors can absorb and sometimes respond to as little as one photon of light and transduce it into a **receptor potential**, a local depolarization or hyperpolarization of a receptor membrane. The strength of the receptor potential determines the amount of excitation or inhibition the receptor delivers to the next neuron on the way to the brain. After all the information from millions of receptors reaches the brain, how does the brain make sense of it?

From Neuronal Activity to Perception

Let us consider what is *not* an answer. The 17th-century philosopher René Descartes believed that the brain's representation of a physical stimulus had to resemble the stimulus itself. That is, when you look at something, the nerves from the eye would project a pattern of impulses arranged as a picture on your visual cortex—right-side up. The problem with this theory is that it assumes a little person in the head who can look at the picture. Even if there were a little person in the head, we would have to explain how he or she perceives the picture. (Maybe there is an even littler person inside the little person's head?) The early scientists and philosophers might have avoided this error if they had started by studying olfaction instead; we are less tempted to imagine that we create a little flower for a little person in the head to smell.

The main point is that your brain's activity *does not duplicate* the objects that you see. For example, when you see a table, the representation of the top of the table does not have to be on the top of your retina or on the top of your head. Consider an analogy to computers: When a computer stores a photograph, the top of the photograph does not have to be toward the top of the computer's memory bank.

Law of Specific Nerve Energies

An important aspect of all sensory coding is *which* neurons are active. Impulses in one neuron indicate light, whereas impulses in another neuron indicate sound. In 1838, Johannes Müller described this insight as the **law of specific nerve energies.** Müller held that whatever excites a particular nerve establishes a special kind of energy unique to that nerve. In modern terms, any activity by a particular nerve always conveys the same kind of information to the brain.

We can state the law of specific nerve energies another way: No nerve has the option of sending the message "high C note" at one time, "bright yellow" at another time, and "lemony scent" at yet another. It sends only one kind of message—action potentials. The brain somehow interprets the action potentials from the auditory nerve as sounds, those from the olfactory nerve as odors, and those from the optic nerve as light. Admittedly, the word "somehow" glosses over a deep mystery, but the idea is that some experiences are *given.* You don't have to learn how to perceive green; a certain pattern of activity in particular produces that experience automatically.

Here is a demonstration: If you rub your eyes, you may see spots or flashes of light even in a totally dark room. You have applied mechanical pressure, but that mechanical pressure excited visual receptors in your eye; anything that excites those receptors is perceived as light. (If you try this demonstration, first remove any contact lenses. Then shut your eyes and rub gently.)

1. If it were possible to flip your entire brain upside down, without breaking any of its connections to the sense organs, what would happen to your perceptions of what you see, hear, and so forth?
2. If someone electrically stimulated the receptors in your ear, how would you perceive it?

Check your answers on page 164.

The Eye and Its Connections to the Brain

Light enters the eye through an opening in the center of the iris called the **pupil** (Figure 6.1). It is focused by the lens (adjustable) and cornea (not adjustable) and projected onto the **retina**, the rear surface of the eye, which is lined with visual receptors. Light from the left side of the world strikes the right half of the retina, and vice versa. Light from above strikes the bottom half of the retina, and light from below strikes the top half. As in a camera, the image is reversed. However, the inversion of the image poses no problems for the nervous system. Remember, the visual system does not simply duplicate the image; it represents it by a code of various kinds of neuronal activity.

The Route Within the Retina

In a sense, the retina is built inside out. If you or I were designing an eye, we would probably send the receptors' messages directly back to the brain. In the vertebrate retina, however, the receptors, located on the back of the eye, send their messages not toward the brain but to **bipolar cells**, neurons located closer to the center of the eye. The bipolar cells send their messages to **ganglion cells**, located still closer to the center of the eye. The ganglion cells' axons join one another, loop around, and travel back to the brain

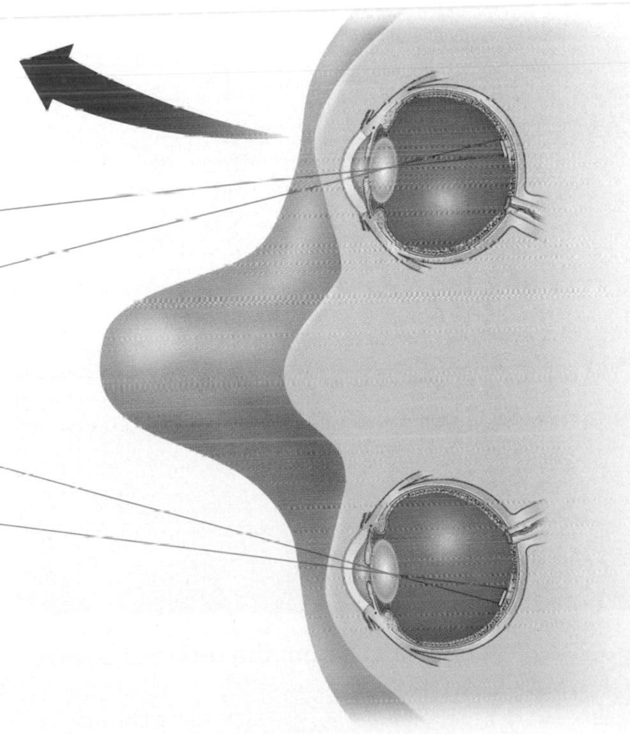

Figure 6.1 Cross-section of the vertebrate eye
Note how an object in the visual field produces an inverted image on the retina. Also note that the optic nerve exits the eyeball on the nasal side (the side closer to the nose).

Figure 6.2 Visual path within the eyeball
The receptors send their messages to bipolar and horizontal cells, which in turn send messages to the amacrine and ganglion cells. The axons of the ganglion cells loop together to exit the eye at the blind spot. They form the optic nerve, which continues to the brain.

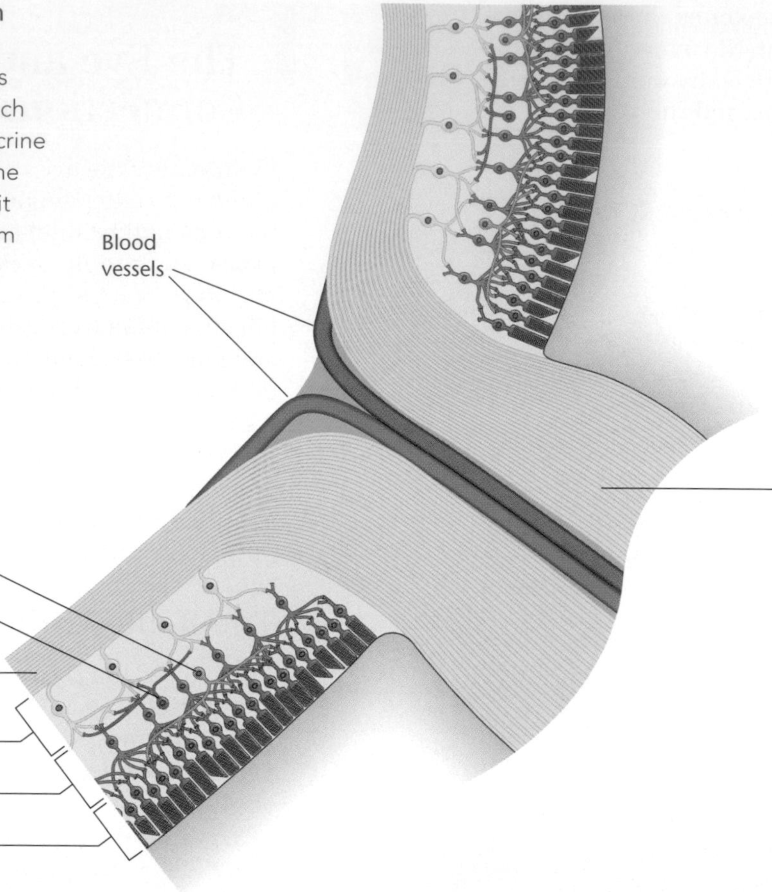

Blood vessels
Optic nerve
Horizontal cell
Amacrine cell
Axons from ganglion cells
Ganglion cells
Bipolar cells
Receptors

(Figures 6.1 and 6.2). Additional cells called *amacrine cells* get information from bipolar cells (Figure 6.3) and send it to other bipolar cells, other amacrine cells, or ganglion cells. Amacrine cells are numerous and diverse; about 50 types have been identified so far (Wässle, 2004). Different types control the ability of ganglion cells to respond to shapes, movement, or other specific aspects of visual stimuli (Fried, Münch, & Werblin, 2002; Sinclair, Jacobs, & Nirenberg, 2004).

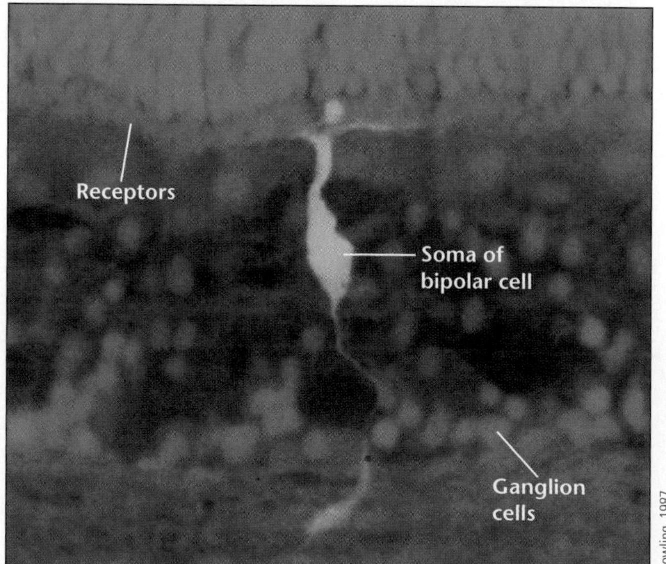

Figure 6.3 A bipolar cell from the retina of a carp, stained with Procion yellow
Bipolar cells get their name from the fact that a fibrous process is attached to each end (or pole) of the neuron.

One consequence of this anatomy is that light has to pass through the ganglion cells and bipolar cells before it reaches the receptors. However, these cells are transparent, and light passes through them without distortion. A more important consequence of the eye's anatomy is the *blind spot.* The ganglion cell axons band together to form the **optic nerve** (or optic tract), an axon bundle that exits through the back of the eye. The point at which it leaves (which is also where the major blood vessels leave) is called the **blind spot** because it has no receptors.

Every person is therefore blind in part of each eye.[1] You can demonstrate your own blind spot using Figure 6.4. Close your left eye and focus your right eye on the o at the top. Then move the page toward you and away, noticing what happens to the x. When the page is about 25 cm (10 in.) away, the x disappears because its image has struck the blind spot of your retina.

[1]This statement applies to all people, without qualification. Can you think of any other absolutes in psychology? Most statements are true "on the average," "in general," or "with certain exceptions."

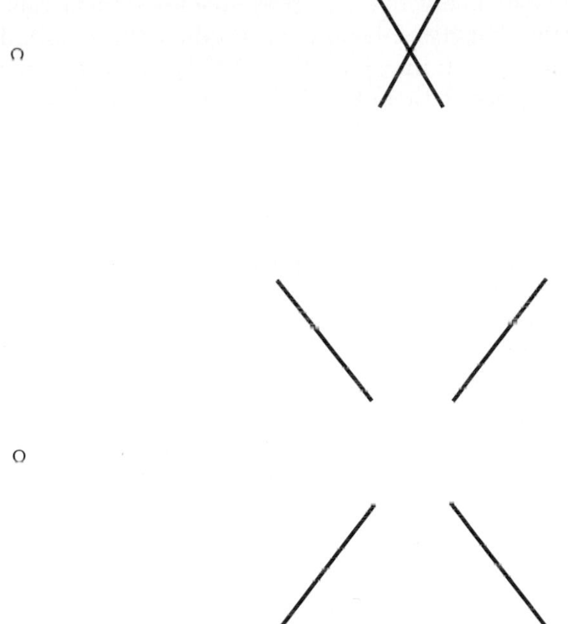

Figure 6.4 Two demonstrations of the blind spot of the retina

Close your left eye and focus your right eye on the o in the top part. Move the page toward you and away, noticing what happens to the x. At a distance of about 25 cm (10 in.), the x disappears. Now repeat this procedure with the bottom part. At that same distance, what do you see?

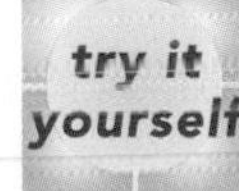

Now repeat the procedure with the lower part of the figure. When the page is again about 25 cm away from your eyes, what do you see? The *gap* disappears!

Note how your brain in effect fills in the gap. When the blind spot interrupts a straight line or other regular pattern, you tend to perceive that pattern in the blind area, as if you actually saw it. For another interesting demonstration of this phenomenon, see the Online Try It Yourself exercise "Filling in the Blind Spot."

Some people have a much larger blind spot because glaucoma has destroyed parts of the optic nerve. Generally, they do not notice it any more than you notice your smaller one. Why not? Mainly, they do not see a black spot in their blind areas, but simply no sensation at all, the same as you see in your blind spot or out the back of your head.

STOP & CHECK

3. What makes the blind spot of the retina blind?

Check your answer on page 164.

Fovea and Periphery of the Retina

When you look at any detail, such as a letter on this page, you fixate it on the central portion of your retina, especially the **fovea** (meaning "pit"), a tiny area specialized for acute, detailed vision (see Figure 6.1). Because blood vessels and ganglion cell axons are almost absent near the fovea, it has the least impeded vision available. The tight packing of receptors also aids perception of detail.

Furthermore, each receptor in the fovea connects to a single *bipolar cell,* which in turn connects to a single *ganglion cell,* which then extends its axon to the brain. The ganglion cells in the fovea of humans and other primates are called **midget ganglion cells** because each is small and responds to just a single cone. As a result, each cone in the fovea has in effect a direct line to the brain, which can register the exact location of the input.

Toward the periphery, more and more receptors converge onto bipolar and ganglion cells. As a result, the brain cannot detect the exact location or shape of a peripheral light source. However, the summation enables perception of much fainter lights in the periphery. In short, foveal vision has better *acuity* (sensitivity to detail), and peripheral vision has better sensitivity to dim light.

Peripheral vision can identify a shape by itself more easily than one surrounded by other objects (Parkes, Lund, Angelucci, Solomon, & Morgan, 2001). For example, fixate your right eye on the x in each of the following displays. With the upper display, you can probably detect the direction of the sloping lines at the right. With the lower display, you probably cannot, at least not clearly, because the surrounding elements interfere with detail perception.

```
x            ///

           #######
x          ##///##
           #######
```

You have heard the expression "eyes like a hawk." In many bird species, the eyes occupy most of the head, compared to only 5% of the head in humans. Furthermore, many bird species have two foveas per eye, one pointing ahead and one pointing to the side (Wallman & Pettigrew, 1985). The extra foveas enable perception of detail in the periphery.

Hawks and other predatory birds have a greater density of visual receptors on the top half of their retinas (looking down) than on the bottom half (looking up). That arrangement is highly adaptive because predatory birds spend most of their day soaring high in the air looking down. However, when the bird lands and needs to see above it, it must turn its head, as Figure 6.5 shows (Waldvogel, 1990).

Chase Swift

Figure 6.5 A behavioral consequence of how receptors are arranged on the retina
One owlet has turned its head almost upside down to see above itself. Birds of prey have a great density of receptors on the upper half of the retina, enabling them to see below them in great detail during flight. But they see objects above themselves poorly, unless they turn their heads. Take another look at the prairie falcon at the start of this chapter. It is not a one-eyed bird; it is a bird that has tilted its head. Do you now understand why?

Conversely, in many prey species such as rats, the greater density of receptors is on the bottom half of the retina (Lund, Lund, & Wise, 1974). As a result, they can see above them better than they can below.

Visual Receptors: Rods and Cones

The vertebrate retina contains two types of receptors: rods and cones (Figure 6.6). The **rods,** which are most abundant in the periphery of the human retina, respond to faint light but are not useful in bright daylight because bright light bleaches them. **Cones,** which are most abundant in and around the fovea, are less active in dim light, more useful in bright light, and essential for color vision. Because of the distribution of rods and cones, you have good color vision in the fovea but not in the periphery. The differences between foveal and peripheral vision are summarized in Table 6.1.

Although rods outnumber cones about 20 to 1 in the human retina, cones have a much more direct route to the brain. Remember the midget ganglion cells: In the fovea (all cones), each receptor has its own line to the brain. In the periphery (mostly rods), each receptor shares a line with tens or hundreds of others. A typical count shows about 10 cone-driven responses in the brain for every rod-driven response (Masland, 2001).

The ratio of rods to cones varies among species. A 20-to-1 ratio may sound high, but in fact, the ratio is much higher in rodents and other species that are active at night. An extreme case is that of South American oilbirds, which live in caves and emerge only at night to search for fruits. They have about 15,000 rods per cone. Furthermore, as an adaptation to detect faint lights at night, their rods are packed three deep throughout the retina (Martin, Rojas, Ramírez, & McNeil, 2004).

Both rods and cones contain **photopigments,** chemicals that release energy when struck by light. Photopigments consist of 11-*cis*-retinal (a derivative of vitamin A) bound to proteins called *opsins,* which modify the photopigments' sensitivity to different wavelengths of light. The 11-*cis*-retinal is stable in the dark; light energy converts it suddenly to another form, all-*trans*-retinal, in the process releasing energy that activates second messengers within the cell

Rod Cone

(a)

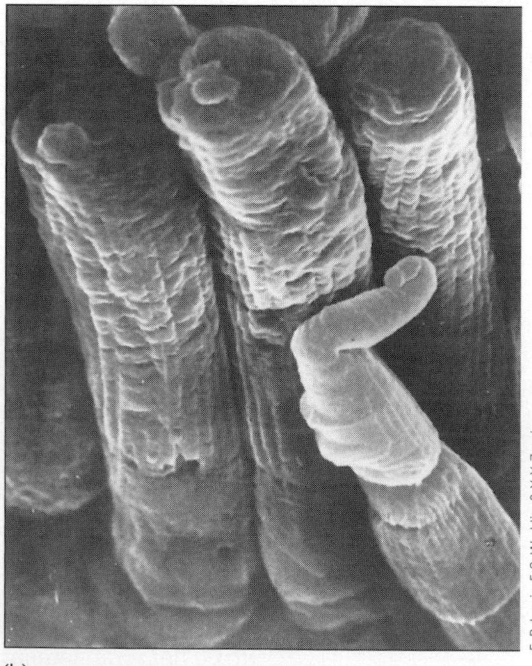

E. R. Lewis, F. S. Werblin, & Y. Y. Zeevi

(b)

Figure 6.6 Structure of rod and cone
(a) Diagram of a rod and a cone. **(b)** Photo of rods and a cone, produced with a scanning electron microscope. Magnification x 7000.

Table 6.1 Human Foveal Vision and Peripheral Vision

Characteristic	Foveal Vision	Peripheral Vision
Receptors	Cones in the fovea itself; cones and rods mix in the surrounding area	Proportion of rods increases toward the periphery; the extreme periphery has only rods
Convergence of receptors	Just a few receptors send their input to each postsynaptic cell	Increasing numbers of receptors send input to each postsynaptic cell
Brightness sensitivity	Useful for distinguishing among bright lights; responds poorly to faint lights	Responds well to faint lights; less useful for making distinctions in bright light
Sensitivity to detail	Good detail vision because few receptors funnel their input to a postsynaptic cell	Poor detail vision because so many receptors send their input to the same postsynaptic cell
Color vision	Good (many cones)	Poor (few cones)

(Q. Wang, Schoenlein, Peteanu, Mathies, & Shank, 1994). (The light is absorbed in this process; it does not continue to bounce around in the eye.) Just as neurotransmitters are virtually the same across species, so are photopigments and opsins. The opsin found in human eyes is similar to that of other vertebrates and many invertebrates (Arendt, Tessmar-Raible, Snyman, Dorresteijn, & Wittbrodt, 2004).

4. You sometimes find that you can see a faint star on a dark night better if you look slightly to the side of the star instead of straight at it. Why?
5. If you found a species with a high ratio of cones to rods in its retina, what would you predict about its way of life?

Check your answers on page 164.

Color Vision

In the human visual system, the shortest visible wavelengths, about 350 nm (1 nm = nanometer, or 10^{-9} m), are perceived as violet; progressively longer wavelengths are perceived as blue, green, yellow, orange, and red, near 700 nm (Figure 6.7). The "visible" wavelengths vary depending on a species' receptors. For example, birds' receptors enable them to see shorter wavelengths than humans can. That is, wavelengths that we describe as "ultraviolet" are simply violet to birds. (Of course, we don't know what their experience looks like.) In general, small songbirds see further into the ultraviolet range than do predatory birds such as hawks and falcons. Many songbird species have taken advantage of that tendency by evolving feathers that strongly reflect very short wavelengths, which can be seen more easily by their own species than by predators (Håstad, Victorsson, & Ödeen, 2005).

Discrimination among colors poses a special coding problem for the nervous system. A cell in the visual system, like any other neuron, can vary only its frequency of action potentials or, in a cell with graded potentials, its membrane polarization. If the cell's response indicates brightness, then it cannot simultaneously signal color. Conversely, if each response indicates a different color, the cell cannot signal brightness. The inevitable conclusion is that no single neuron can simultaneously indicate brightness and color; our perceptions must depend on a combination of responses by different neurons. Scientists of the 1800s proposed two major interpretations of color vision: the trichromatic theory and the opponent-process theory.

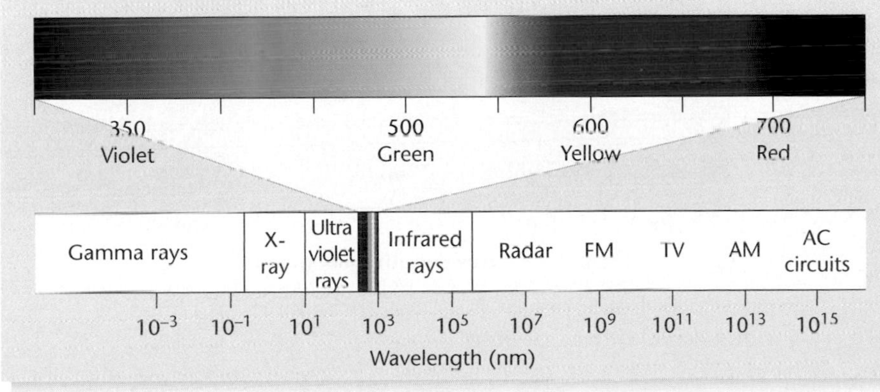

Figure 6.7 A beam of light separated into its wavelengths
Although the wavelengths vary over a continuum, we perceive them as several distinct colors.

The Trichromatic (Young-Helmholtz) Theory

People can distinguish red, green, yellow, blue, orange, pink, purple, greenish-blue, and so forth. If we don't have a separate receptor for every distinguishable color, how many types do we have?

The first person to approach this question fruitfully was an amazingly productive man named Thomas Young (1773–1829). Young was the first to decipher the Rosetta stone, although his version was incomplete. He also founded the modern wave theory of light, defined energy in its modern form, founded the calculation of annuities, introduced the coefficient of elasticity, discovered much about the anatomy of the eye, and made major contributions to many other fields (Martindale, 2001). Previous scientists thought they could explain color by understanding the physics of light. Young was among the first to recognize that color required a biological explanation. He proposed that we perceive color by comparing the responses across a few types of receptors, each of which was sensitive to a different range of wavelengths.

This theory, later modified by Hermann von Helmholtz, is now known as the **trichromatic theory** of color vision, or the **Young-Helmholtz theory.** According to this theory, we perceive color through the relative rates of response by three kinds of cones, each kind maximally sensitive to a different set of wavelengths. (*Trichromatic* means "three colors.") How did Helmholtz decide on the number three? He collected **psychophysical observations,** reports by observers concerning their perceptions of various stimuli. He found that people could match any color by mixing appropriate amounts of just three wavelengths. Therefore, he concluded that three kinds of receptors—we now call them cones—are sufficient to account for human color vision.

Figure 6.8 shows wavelength-sensitivity functions for the three cone types: *short-wavelength, medium-wavelength,* and *long-wavelength.* Note that each cone responds to a broad band of wavelengths but to some more than others.

According to the trichromatic theory, we discriminate among wavelengths by the ratio of activity across the three types of cones. For example, light at 550 nm excites the medium-wavelength and long-wavelength receptors about equally and the short-wavelength receptor almost not at all. This ratio of responses among the three cones determines a perception of yellow. More intense light increases the activity of all three cones without much change in their ratio of responses. As a result, the color appears brighter but still yellow. When all three types of cones are equally active, we see white or gray.

Note that the response of any one cone is ambiguous. For example, a low response rate by a middle-wavelength cone might indicate low-intensity 540-nm light or brighter 500-nm light or still brighter 460-nm light. A high response rate could indicate either bright light at 540 nm or bright white light, which includes 540 nm. The nervous system can determine the color and brightness of the light only by comparing the responses of the three types of cones.

Given the desirability of seeing all colors in all locations, we might suppose that the three kinds of cones would be equally abundant and evenly distributed. In fact, they are not. Long- and medium-wavelength cones are far more abundant than short-wavelength (blue) cones, and consequently, it is easier to see tiny red, yellow, or green dots than blue dots (Roorda & Williams, 1999). Try this: Look at the dots in the following display, first from close and then from greater distances. You probably will notice that the blue dots look blue when close but appear black from a greater distance. The other colors are still visible when the blue is not.

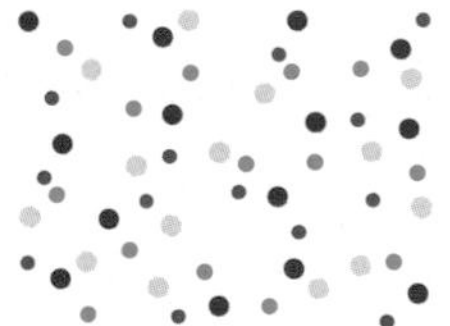

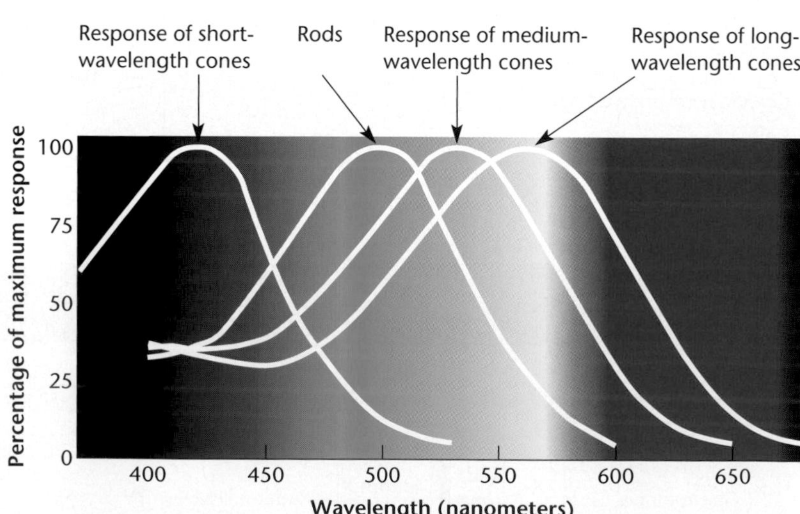

Figure 6.8 Response of rods and three kinds of cones to various wavelengths of light
Note that each kind responds somewhat to a wide range of wavelengths but best to wavelengths in a particular range. *(Source: From J. K. Bowmaker and H. J. A. Dartnell, "Visual pigments of rods and cones in a human retina," Journal of Physiology, 298, 501–511. Copyright © 1980. Reprinted by permission of the author.)*

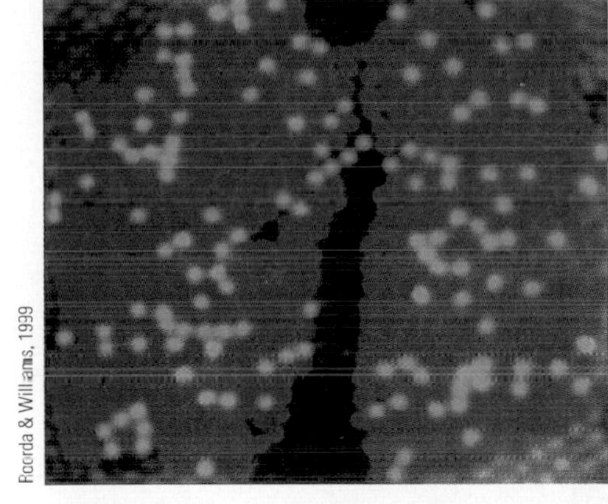

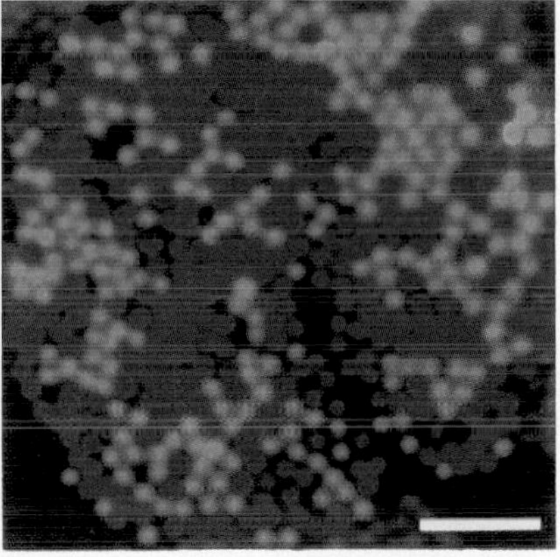

Roorda & Williams, 1999

Figure 6.9 Distribution of cones in two human retinas
Investigators artificially colored these images of cones from two people's retinas, indicating the short-wavelength cones with blue, the medium-wavelength with green, and the long-wavelength with red. Note the difference between the two people, the relative rarity of short wavelength cones, and the patchiness of the distributions.

Furthermore, the three kinds of cones are distributed randomly within the retina (Roorda, Metha, Lennie, & Williams, 2001; Roorda & Williams, 1999). Figure 6.9 shows the distribution of short-, medium-, and long-wavelength cones in two people's retinas, with colors artificially added to distinguish the three cone types. Note how few short-wavelength cones are present. Note also the patches of all medium- or all long-wavelength cones, which vary from one person to another. Some people have more than 10 times as many of one kind as the other over the whole retina. Surprisingly, these variations do not produce any easily measured difference in people's ability to discriminate one color from another (Miyahara, Pokorny, Smith, Baron, & Baron, 1998). Evidently, the brain can compensate for variations in input over a wide range.

That compensation breaks down, however, in the periphery of the retina, where cones are scare and their connections are somewhat haphazard (Diller et al., 2004; Martin, Lee, White, Solomon, & Rütiger, 2001). Try this: Get someone to mark a colored dot on the tip of your finger, or attach a colored sticker, without telling you the color. Slowly move it from behind your head into your field of vision and then gradually toward your fovea. At what point do you see the color? You will see your finger long before you can identify the color. As a rule, the smaller the dot, the farther you will have to move it into your **visual field**—that is, the part of the world that you see—before you can identify the color. The Online Try It Yourself exercise "Color Blindness in the Visual Periphery" provides a further illustration.

ONLINE try it yourself try it yourself

The Opponent-Process Theory

The trichromatic theory correctly predicted the discovery of three kinds of cones, but it is incomplete as a theory of color vision. For example, try the following demonstration: Pick any point in the top portion of Figure 6.10—such as the tip of the nose—and stare at it under a bright light, without moving your eyes, for a full minute. (The brighter the light and the longer you stare, the stronger the effect.) Then look at a plain

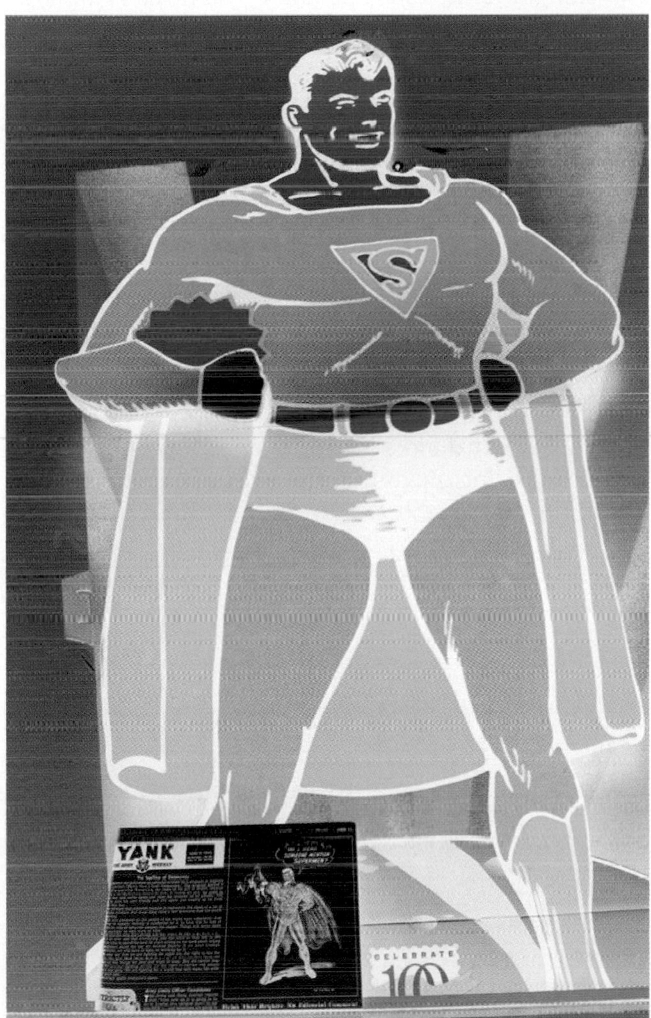

AP

Figure 6.10 Stimulus for demonstrating negative color afterimages
Stare at any point on the face under bright light for about a minute and then look at a white field. You should see a negative afterimage.

white surface, such as a wall or a blank sheet of paper. Keep your eyes steady. You will now see a **negative color afterimage**, a replacement of the red you had been staring at with green, green with red, yellow and blue with each other, and black and white with each other.

To explain this and related phenomena, Ewald Hering, a 19th-century physiologist, proposed the **opponent-process theory:** We perceive color in terms of paired opposites: red versus green, yellow versus blue, and white versus black (Hurvich & Jameson, 1957). That is, there is no such thing as reddish green, greenish red, or yellowish blue. The brain has some mechanism that perceives color on a continuum from red to green and another from yellow to blue.

Here is one possible mechanism for opponent processes: Consider the bipolar cell diagrammed in Figure 6.11. It is excited by short-wavelength (blue) light and inhibited by both long-wavelength and medium-wavelength light, and especially by a mixture of both, which we see as yellow. An increase in this bipolar cell's activity produces the experience *blue* and a decrease produces the experience *yellow.* If short-wavelength (blue) light stimulates this cell long enough, the cell becomes fatigued. If we now substitute white light, the cell is more inhibited than excited, responds less than its baseline level, and therefore produces an experience of *yellow.* Many neurons from the bipolar cells through the cerebral cortex are excited by one set of wavelengths and inhibited by another (DeValois & Jacobs, 1968; Engel, 1999).

That explanation of negative color afterimages is appealing because of its simplicity. However, it cannot be the whole story. First, try this: Stare at the x in the following diagram for at least a minute under the brightest light you can find and then look at a brightly lit white page.

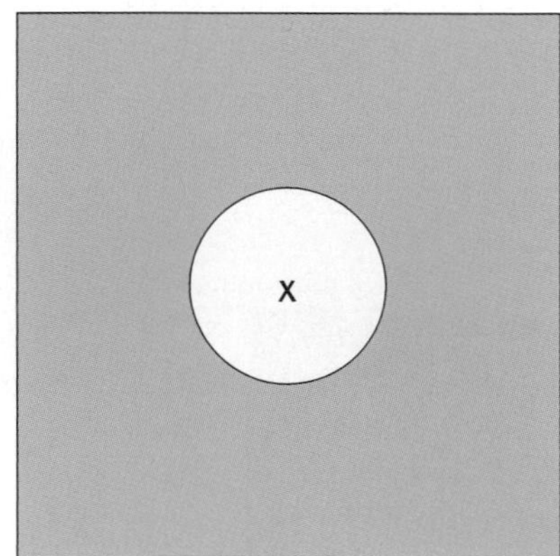

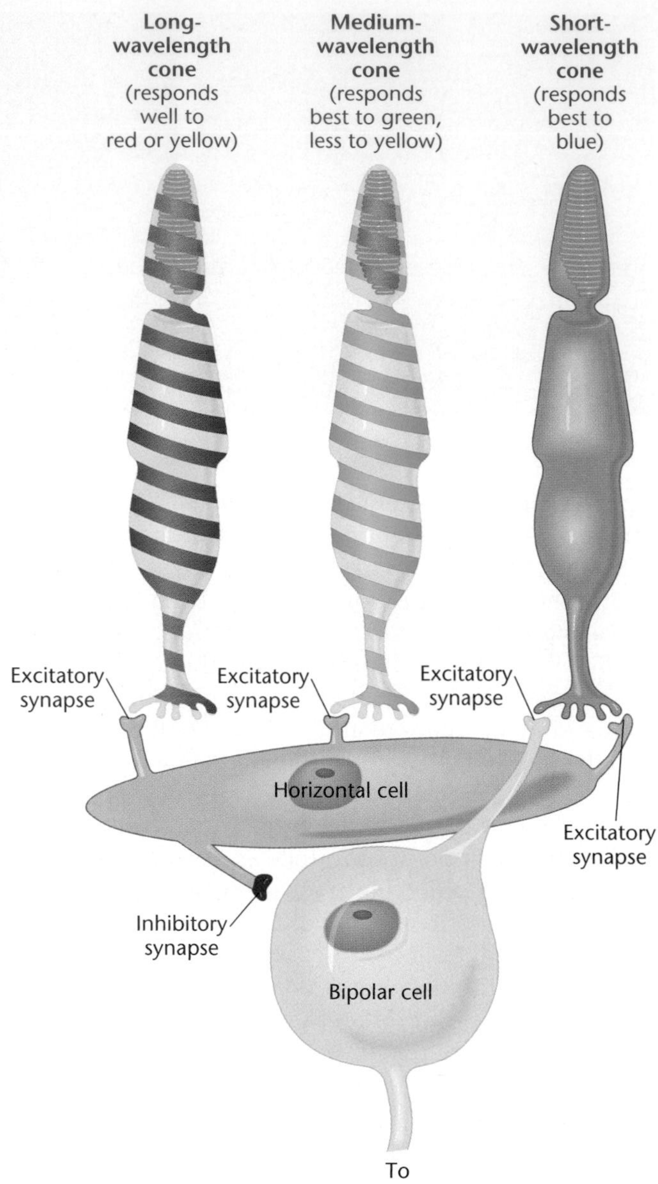

Figure 6.11 Possible wiring for one bipolar cell
Short-wavelength light (which we see as blue) excites the bipolar cell and (by way of the intermediate horizontal cell) also inhibits it. However, the excitation predominates, so blue light produces net excitation. Red, green, or yellow light inhibits this bipolar cell because they produce inhibition (through the horizontal cell) without any excitation. The strongest inhibition is from yellow light, which stimulates both the long- and medium-wavelength cones. Therefore, we can describe this bipolar cell as excited by blue and inhibited by yellow. White light produces as much inhibition as excitation and therefore no net effect.

For the afterimage of the surrounding box, you saw red, as expected from the theory. But what about the circle inside? Theoretically, you should have seen a gray or black afterimage (the opposite of white), but in fact, if you used a bright enough light, you saw a green afterimage.

Here is another demonstration: First, look at Figure 6.12. Note that although it shows four red quarter-

Figure 6.12 An afterimage hard to explain in terms of the retina
Stare at the tiny x under bright light for at least a minute and then look at a white surface. Many people report an alternation between two afterimages, one of them based on the illusion of a red square. *(Source: Reprinted with permission from "Afterimage of perceptually filled-in surface," Fig. 1A, p. 1678 (left hand) by S. Shimojo, Y. Kamitani, and S. Nishida in Science, 293, 1677–1680. Copyright 2001 American Association for the Advancement of Science.)*

circles, you have the illusion of a whole red square. (Look carefully to convince yourself that it is an illusion.) Now stare at the tiny x in Figure 6.12. Again, to get good results, stare for at least a minute under bright lights. Then look at any white surface.

People usually report that the afterimage fluctuates. Sometimes they see four green quarter circles:

And sometimes they see a whole green square (Shimojo, Kamitani, & Nishida, 2001).

Note that a whole green square is the afterimage of an illusion! The red square you "saw" wasn't really there. This demonstration suggests that afterimages depend at least partly on whatever area of the brain produces the illusion—presumably the cerebral cortex, not the retina itself.

The Retinex Theory

The trichromatic theory and the opponent-process theory have limitations, especially in explaining color constancy. **Color constancy** is the ability to recognize the color of an object despite changes in lighting (Kennard, Lawden, Morland, & Ruddock, 1995; Zeki, 1980, 1983). If you put on green-tinted glasses or replace your white light bulb with a green one, you will notice the tint, but you still identify bananas as yellow, paper as white, walls as brown (or whatever), and so forth. You do so by comparing the color of one object with the color of another, in effect subtracting a fixed amount of green from each. Color constancy requires you to compare a variety of objects.

To illustrate, examine the top part of Figure 6.13 (Purves & Lotto, 2003). Although different colors of light illuminate the two scenes, you can easily identify which of the little squares are red, yellow, blue, and so forth. Note the effects of removing context. The bottom part shows the squares that looked red in the top part. Note that they no longer look red. Without the context that indicated yellow light or blue light, those on the left look orange and those on the right look purple. (For this reason, we should avoid talking about "red light" or any other color of light. A certain wavelength of light that looks red under normal circumstances can appear to be some other color, or even white or black, depending on the background.)

Similarly, our perception of the brightness of an object requires comparing it with other objects. Examine Figure 6.14 (Purves, Shimpi, & Lotto, 1999). You see what appears to have a gray top and a white bottom. Now cover the center (the border between the top and the bottom) with your fingers. You will notice that the top of the object has exactly the same brightness as the bottom! For additional examples like this, visit this website: **http://www.purveslab.net**

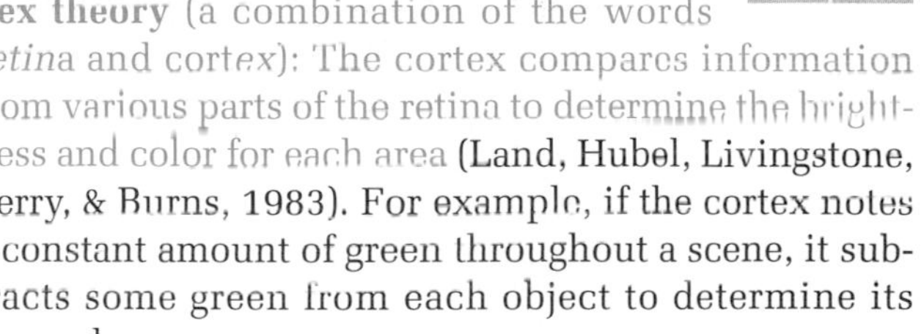

You can also try the Online Try It Yourself exercise "Brightness Contrast."

To account for color and brightness constancy, Edwin Land proposed the **retinex theory** (a combination of the words *retina* and *cortex*): The cortex compares information from various parts of the retina to determine the brightness and color for each area (Land, Hubel, Livingstone, Perry, & Burns, 1983). For example, if the cortex notes a constant amount of green throughout a scene, it subtracts some green from each object to determine its true color.

Dale Purves and colleagues have expressed a similar idea in more general terms: Whenever we see anything, we make an inference or construction. For example, when you look at the objects in Figures 6.13 and 6.14, you ask yourself, "On occasions when I have seen something that looked like this, what did it turn out to be?" You go through the same process for perceiving shapes, motion, or anything else: You calculate what objects probably produced the pattern of stimulation you just had (Lotto & Purves, 2002; Purves & Lotto, 2003). That is, visual perception requires a kind of reasoning process, not just retinal stimulation.

(a)

(b)

(c)

Figure 6.13 Effects of context on color perception

In each block, we identify certain tiles as looking red. However, after removal of the context, those that appeared red on the left now look orange; those on the right appear purple.
(Source: Why We See What We Do, *by D. Purves and R. B. Lotto, figure 6.10, p. 134. Copyright 2003 Sinauer Associates, Inc. Reprinted by permission.)*

STOP & CHECK

6. Suppose a bipolar cell received excitatory input from medium-wavelength cones and inhibitory input from all three kinds of cones. When it is highly excited, what color would one see? When it is inhibited, what color perception would result?
7. When a television set is off, its screen appears gray. When you watch a program, parts of the screen appear black, even though more light is actually showing on the screen than when the set was off and the screen appeared gray. What accounts for the black perception?
8. Figure 6.8 shows 500 nm light as blue and 550 nm light as yellow. Why should we nevertheless not call them "blue light" and "yellow light"?

Check your answers on page 164.

Figure 6.14 A powerful demonstration of brightness constancy
Do you see a gray object and a white object? With your fingers, cover the border between the two objects and then compare the brightness of the two objects. *(Source: From "An Empirical Explanation of Cornsweet Effect," by D. Purves, A. Shimpi, & R. B. Lotto, in Journal of Neuroscience, 19, 8542–8551. Copyright © 1999 by the Society for Neuroscience. Reprinted with permission.)*

Color Vision Deficiency

Encyclopedias describe many examples of discoveries in astronomy, biology, chemistry, and physics, but what are psychologists' discoveries? You might give that question some thought. One of my nominations is color blindness, better described as **color vision deficiency**, an impairment in perceiving color differences compared to other people. (Complete color blindness, the inability to perceive anything but shades of black and white, is rare.) Before color vision deficiency was discovered in the 1600s, people assumed that vision copies the objects we see (Fletcher & Voke, 1985). That is, if an object is round, we see the roundness; if it is yellow, we see the yellowness. Investigators *discovered* that it is possible to have otherwise satisfactory vision without seeing color. That is, color depends on what our brains do with incoming light; it is not a property of the light by itself.

Several types of color vision deficiency occur. For genetic reasons, some people lack one or two of the types of cones. Some have all three kinds, but one kind has abnormal properties (Nathans et al., 1989). In the most common form of color vision deficiency, people have trouble distinguishing red from green because their long- and medium-wavelength cones have the same photopigment instead of different ones. The gene causing this deficiency is on the X chromosome. About 8% of men are red-green color blind compared with less than 1% of women (Bowmaker, 1998).

EXTENSIONS AND APPLICATIONS
People with Four Cone Types

Might anyone have *more* than three kinds of cones? Apparently, some women do. People vary in the gene controlling the long-wavelength (LW) cone receptor (sensitive mainly in the red end of the spectrum). Consequently, some people's LW receptors have a peak response to a slightly longer wavelength than other people's receptors (Stockman & Sharpe, 1998). The gene controlling this receptor is on the X chromosome, so—because men have only one X chromosome—men have only one of these LW receptor types or the other. However, women have two X chromosomes. In each cell, one X chromosome is activated and the other is inhibited, apparently at random.[2] Therefore, nearly half of women have both kinds of long-wavelength genes and two kinds of red receptors (Neitz, Kraft, & Neitz, 1998). Several studies have found that such women draw slightly finer color distinctions than other people do. That is, sometimes two objects that seem the same color to other people look different to women with two kinds of LW receptors (Jameson, Highnote, & Wasserman, 2001). This effect is small, however, and emerges only with careful testing.

For more information about the retina and vision and vision in general, this site provides an excellent treatment: **http://www.webvision.med.utah.edu**

STOP & CHECK

9. As mentioned on page 158, most people can use varying amounts of three colors to match any other color that they see. Who would be an exception to this rule, and how many would they need?

Check your answer on page 164.

[2]There is a good reason one X chromosome per cell is inhibited. The genes on any chromosome produce proteins. If both X chromosomes were active in women, then either women would be getting an overdose of the X-related proteins or men would be getting an underdose. Because only one X chromosome is active per cell in women, both men and women get the same dose (Arnold, 2004).

Module 6.1

In Closing: Visual Receptors

I remember once explaining to my then-teenage son a newly discovered detail about the visual system, only to have him reply, "I didn't realize it would be so complicated. I thought the light strikes your eyes and then you see it." As you should now be starting to realize—and if not, the next module should convince you—vision requires extremely complicated processing. If you tried to build a robot with vision, you would quickly discover that shining light into its eyes accomplishes nothing unless its visual detectors are connected to devices that identify the useful information and use it to select the proper action. We have such devices in our brains, although we are still far from fully understanding them.

Summary

1. Sensory information is coded so that the brain can process it. The coded information bears no physical similarity to the stimuli it describes. (p. 152)
2. According to the law of specific nerve energies, the brain interprets any activity of a given sensory neuron as representing the sensory information to which that neuron is tuned. (p. 152)
3. Light passes through the pupil of a vertebrate eye and stimulates the receptors lining the retina at the back of the eye. (p. 153)
4. The axons from the retina loop around to form the optic nerve, which exits from the eye at a point called the blind spot. (p. 154)
5. Visual acuity is greatest in the fovea, the central area of the retina. (p. 155)
6. Because so many receptors in the periphery converge their messages to their bipolar cells, our peripheral vision is highly sensitive to faint light but poorly sensitive to detail. (p. 155)
7. The retina has two kinds of receptors: rods and cones. Rods are more sensitive to faint light; cones are more useful in bright light. Rods are more numerous in the periphery of the eye; cones are more numerous in the fovea. (p. 156)
8. Light stimulates the receptors by triggering a molecular change in 11-*cis*-retinal, releasing energy, and thereby activating second messengers within the cell. (p. 156)
9. According to the trichromatic (or Young-Helmholtz) theory of color vision, color perception begins with a given wavelength of light stimulating a distinctive ratio of responses by the three types of cones. (p. 158)
10. According to the opponent-process theory of color vision, visual system neurons beyond the receptors themselves respond with an increase in activity to indicate one color of light and a decrease to indicate the opposite color. The three pairs of opposites are red–green, yellow–blue, and white–black. (p. 159)

11. According to the retinex theory, the cortex compares the responses representing different parts of the retina to determine the brightness and color of each area. (p. 161)
12. For genetic reasons, certain people are unable to distinguish one color from another. Red-green color blindness is the most common type. (p. 163)

Answers to STOP & CHECK Questions

1. Your perceptions would not change. The way visual or auditory information is coded in the brain does not depend on the physical location within the brain. That is, seeing something as "on top" or "to the left" depends on which neurons are active but does not depend on the physical location of those neurons. (p. 153)
2. Because of the law of specific nerve energies, you would perceive it as sound, not as shock. (p. 153)
3. The blind spot has no receptors because it is occupied by exiting axons and blood vessels. (p. 155)
4. If you look slightly to the side, the light falls on an area of the retina that has rods, which are more sensitive to faint light. That portion of the retina also has more convergence of input, which magnifies sensitivity to faint light. (p. 157)
5. We should expect this species to be highly active during the day and seldom active at night. (p. 157)
6. Excitation of this cell should yield a perception of green under normal circumstances. Inhibition would produce the opposite sensation, red. (p. 162)
7. The black experience arises by contrast with the other brighter areas. The contrast occurs by comparison within the cerebral cortex, as in the retinex theory of color vision. (p. 162)
8. Color perception depends not just on the wavelength of light from a given spot but also the light from surrounding areas. As in Figure 6.13, the context can change the color perception. (p. 162)
9. Red-green color-blind people would need only two colors. People with four kinds of cones might need four. (p. 163)

Thought Question

How could you test for the presence of color vision in a bee? Examining the retina does not help; invertebrate receptors resemble neither rods nor cones. It is possible to train bees to approach one visual stimulus and not another. The difficulty is that if you trained some bees to approach, say, a yellow card and not a green card, you do not know whether they solved the problem by color or by brightness. Because brightness is different from physical intensity, you cannot assume that two colors equally bright to humans are also equally bright to bees. How might you get around the problem of brightness to test color vision in bees?

Module 6.2 The Neural Basis of Visual Perception

Long ago, people assumed that anyone who saw an object at all saw everything about it, including its shape, color, and movement. The discovery of color blindness was a huge surprise in its time, although not today. However, you may be surprised—as were late 20th-century psychologists—by the analogous phenomenon of *motion blindness:* Some people with otherwise satisfactory vision fail to see that an object is moving, or at least have great trouble determining its direction and speed. "How could anyone not see the movement?" you might ask. Your question is not very different from the question raised in the 1600s: "How could anyone see something without seeing the color?"

The fundamental fact about the visual cortex takes a little getting used to and therefore bears repeating: You have no central processor that sees every aspect of a visual stimulus at once. Different parts of the cortex process separate aspects somewhat independently of one another.

An Overview of the Mammalian Visual System

Let's begin with a general outline of the anatomy of the mammalian visual system and then examine certain stages in more detail. The structure and organization are the same across individuals and even across species, except for quantitative differences, but the quantitative differences are larger than we might have supposed. Some people have two or three times as many axons in their optic nerve as others do, and correspondingly more cells in their visual cortex (Andrews, Halpern, & Purves, 1997; Stevens, 2001; Sur & Leamey, 2001), and greater ability to detect brief, faint, or rapidly changing visual stimuli (Halpern, Andrews, & Purves, 1999).

The rods and cones of the retina make synaptic contact with **horizontal cells** and bipolar cells (see Figures 6.2 and 6.15). The horizontal cells make inhibitory contact onto bipolar cells, which in turn make synapses onto *amacrine cells* and ganglion cells. All these cells are within the eyeball. Even at this beginning stage, different cells are specialized for different visual functions, and the same is true at each succeeding stage.

The axons of the ganglion cells form the optic nerve, which leaves the retina and travels along the lower surface of the brain. The optic nerves from the two eyes meet at the optic chiasm (Figure 6.16a on page 168), where, in humans, half of the axons from each eye cross to the opposite side of the brain. As shown in Figure 6.16b, information from the nasal half of each eye crosses to the contralateral hemisphere. Information from the other half goes to the ipsilateral hemisphere. The percentage of crossover varies from one species to another depending on the location of the eyes. In species with eyes far to the sides of the head, such as rabbits and guinea pigs, nearly all the axons cross to the opposite side.

Most of the ganglion cell axons go to the **lateral geniculate nucleus,** a nucleus of the thalamus specialized for visual perception. (The term *geniculate* comes from the Latin root *genu,* meaning "knee." To *genuflect* is to bend the knee. The lateral geniculate looks a little like a knee, if you use some imagination.) A smaller number of axons go to the superior colliculus, and even fewer go to several other areas, including part of the hypothalamus that controls the waking–sleeping schedule (see Chapter 9). At any rate, most of the optic nerve goes to the lateral geniculate, which in turn sends axons to other parts of the thalamus and to the visual areas of the occipital cortex. The cortex returns many axons to the thalamus, so the thalamus and cortex constantly feed back and forth to modify each other's activity (Guillery, Feig, & van Lieshout, 2001).

STOP & CHECK

1. Where does the optic nerve start and where does it end?

Check your answer on page 183.

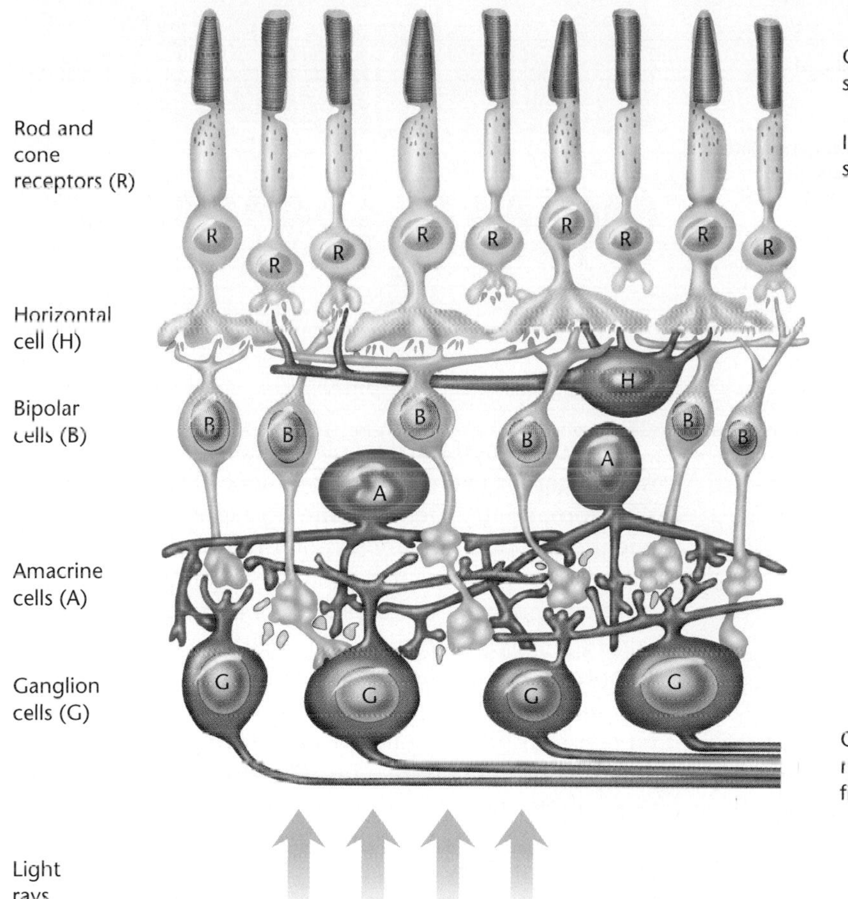

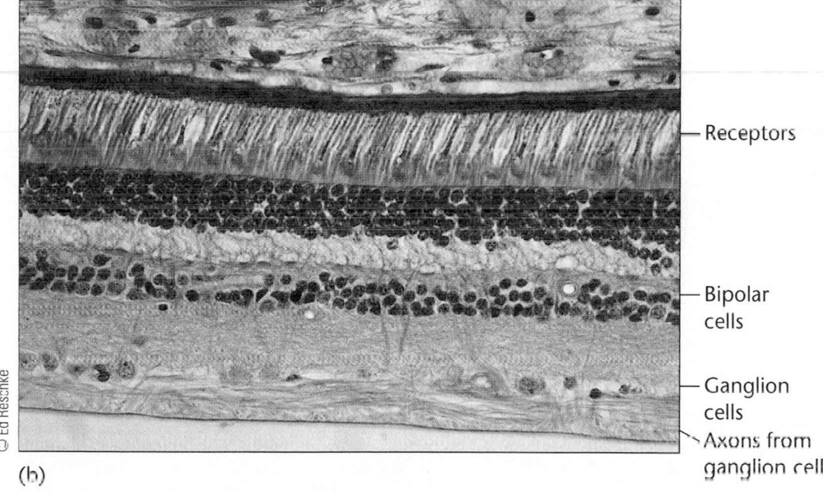

Figure 6.15 The vertebrate retina
(a) Diagram of the neurons of the retina. The top of the figure is the back of the retina. All the optic nerve fibers group together and then turn around to exit through the back of the retina, in the "blind spot" of the eye. **(b)** Photo of a cross-section through the retina. This section from the periphery of the retina has relatively few ganglion cells; a slice closer to the fovea would have a greater density. *(Source: (a) Based on "Organization of the primate retina," by J. E. Dowling and B. B. Boycott,* Proceedings of the Royal Society of London, B, *1966, 166, pp. 80–111. Used by permission of the Royal Society of London and John Dowling.)*

Processing in the Retina

The human retina contains roughly 120 million rods and 6 million cones. We cannot intelligently process that many independent messages; we need to extract the meaningful patterns, such as the edge between one object and the next. To do so, we have cells that respond to particular patterns of visual information.

The responses of any cell in the visual system depend on the excitatory and inhibitory messages it receives. To understand this idea, let's explore one example in detail. A good, well-understood example is lateral inhibition, which occurs in the first cells of the retina.

Lateral inhibition is the retina's way of sharpening contrasts to emphasize the border between one object and the next. We begin with the rods and cones. They have spontaneous levels of activity, and light striking them actually *decreases* their output. They have *inhibitory* synapses onto the bipolar cells, and therefore, light *decreases* their *inhibitory* output. Because you and I have trouble thinking in double negatives, for simplicity's sake, let's think of their output as excitation of the bipolar cells. In the fovea, each cone attaches to just one bi-

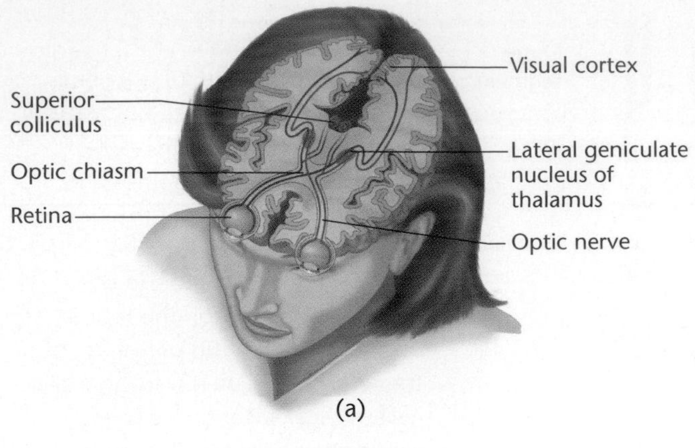

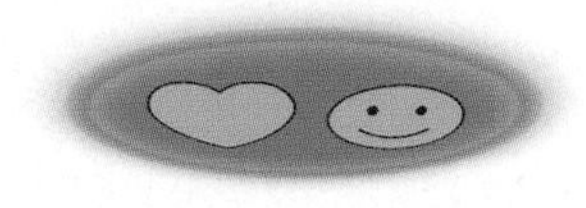

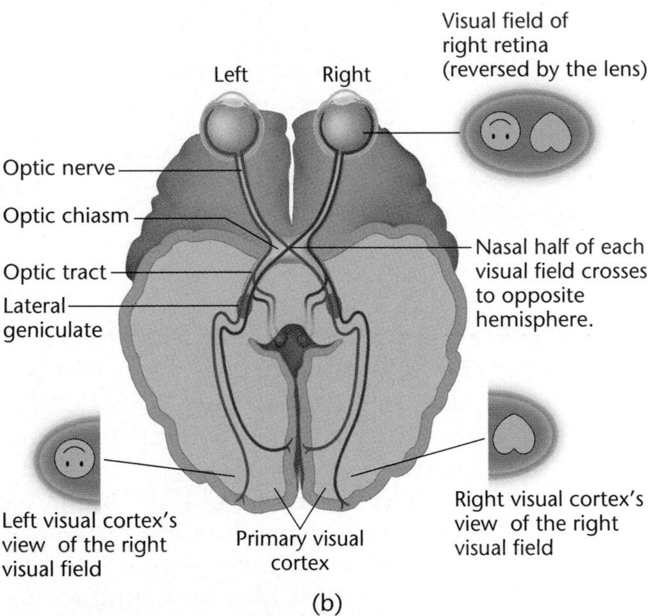

Figure 6.16 Major connections in the visual system of the brain

(a) Part of the visual input goes to the thalamus and from there to the visual cortex. Another part of the visual input goes to the superior colliculus. **(b)** Axons from the retina maintain their relationship to one another—what we call their *retinotopic organization*—throughout their journey from the retina to the lateral geniculate and then from the lateral geniculate to the cortex.

polar cell. Outside the fovea, larger numbers connect to each bipolar cell, as shown in Figure 6.2, p. 154. We'll consider the simplest case of a cone in the fovea connected to just one bipolar. In the following diagram, the green arrows represent excitation.

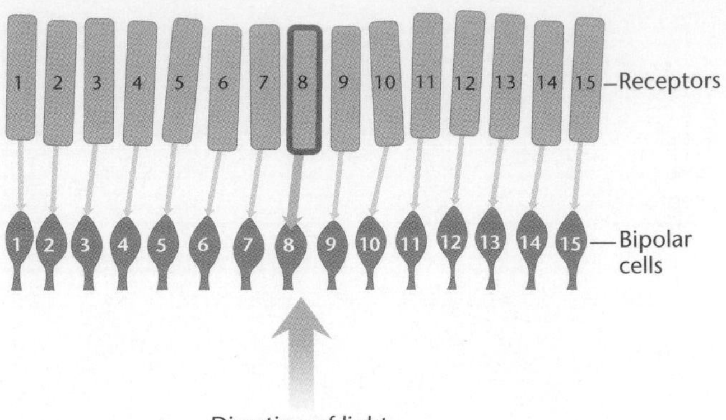

Now let's add the next element, the horizontal cells. Each receptor excites a horizontal cell, which *inhibits* the bipolar cells. Because the horizontal cell spreads widely, excitation of any receptor inhibits many bipolar cells. However, because the horizontal cell is a *local cell,* with no axon and no action potentials, its depolarization decays with distance. Mild excitation of, say, receptor 8 excites the bipolar cell to which it connects, bipolar cell 8. Receptor 8 also stimulates the horizontal cell to inhibit bipolars 7 and 9 strongly, bipolars 6 and 10 a bit less, and so on. The result is that bipolar cell 8 shows net excitation; the excitatory synapse here outweighs the effect of the horizontal cell's inhibition. However, the bipolar cells to either side (laterally) get no excitation but some inhibition by the horizontal cell. Bipolars 7 and 9 are strongly inhibited, so their activity falls well below their spontaneous level. Bipolars 6 and 10 are inhibited somewhat less, so their activity decreases a bit less. In this diagram, green arrows represent excitation from bipolar cells; red arrows represent inhibition from the horizontal cell.

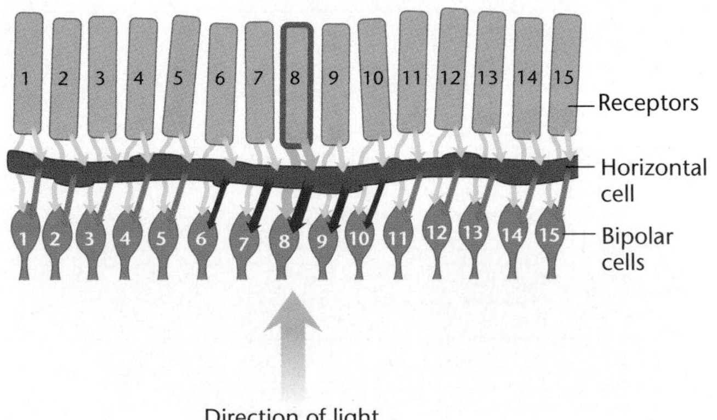

Now imagine what happens if light excites receptors 6–10. These receptors excite bipolar cells 6–10 and the horizontal cell. So bipolar cells 6–10 receive both excitation and inhibition. The excitation from the receptors is stronger than the inhibition from the horizontal cell, so bipolars 6–10 receive net excitation.

However, they do not all receive the same amount of inhibition. Remember, the response of the horizontal cell decays over distance. Bipolar cells 7, 8, and 9 are inhibited because of input on both their sides, but bipolar cells 6 and 10 are each inhibited from one side and not the other. That is, the bipolar cells on the edge of the excitation are inhibited less than those in the middle. Therefore, the overall result is that bipolar cells 6 and 10 respond *more* than bipolars 7–9.

Now think about bipolar cell 5. What excitation does it receive? None. However, it is inhibited by the horizontal cell because of the excitation of receptors 6 and 7. Therefore, bipolar 5, receiving inhibition but no excitation, responds even less than bipolars 1–4.

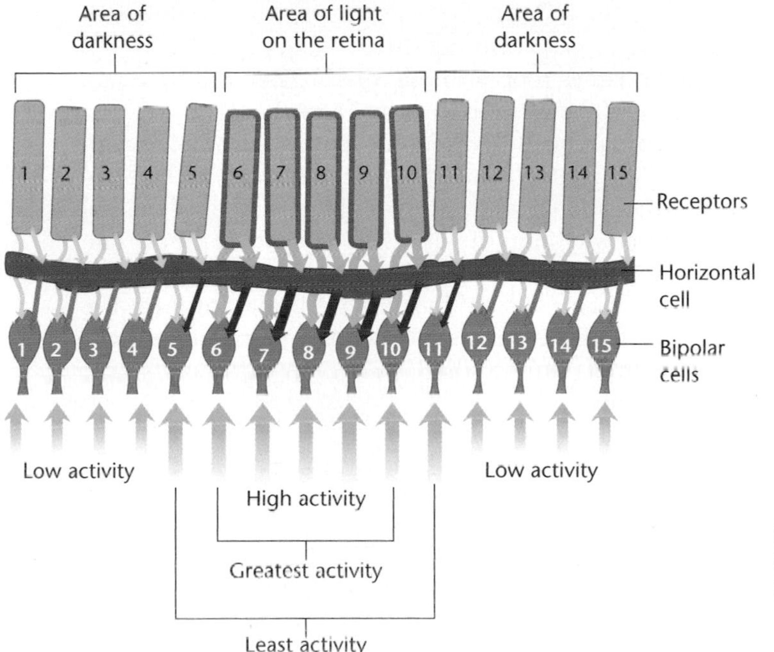

Figure 6.17 An illustration of lateral inhibition
Do you see dark diamonds at the "crossroads"?

These results illustrate **lateral inhibition,** the reduction of activity in one neuron by activity in neighboring neurons (Hartline, 1949). The main function of lateral inhibition is to heighten the contrasts. When light falls on a surface, as shown here, the bipolars just inside the border are most excited, and those outside the border are least responsive.

2. When light strikes a receptor, what effect does the receptor have on the bipolar cells (excitatory or inhibitory)? What effect does it have on horizontal cells? What effect does the horizontal cell have on bipolar cells?
3. If light strikes only one receptor, what is the net effect (excitatory or inhibitory) on the nearest bipolar cell that is directly connected to that receptor? What is the effect on bipolar cells off to the sides? What causes that effect?
4. Examine Figure 6.17. You should see grayish diamonds at the crossroads among the black squares. Explain why.

Check your answers on page 183.

Pathways to the Lateral Geniculate and Beyond

Look out your window. Perhaps you see someone walking by. Although your perception of that person seems to be an integrated whole, different parts of your brain are analyzing different aspects. One set of neurons identifies the person's shape, another set concentrates on the colors, and another sees the speed and direction of movement (Livingstone, 1988; Livingstone & Hubel, 1988; Zeki & Shipp, 1988). Your visual pathway begins its division of labor long before it reaches the cerebral cortex. Even at the level of the ganglion cells in the retina, different cells react differently to the same input.

Each cell in the visual system of the brain has what we call a **receptive field,** which is the part of the visual field that either excites it or inhibits it. For a receptor, the receptive field is simply the point in space from which light strikes the receptor. Other visual cells derive their receptive fields from the pattern of excitatory and inhibitory connections to them. For example, a ganglion cell is connected to a group of bipolar cells, which in turn are connected to receptors, so the receptive field of the ganglion cell is the combined receptive fields of those receptors, as shown in Figure 6.18. The receptive fields of the ganglion cells converge to

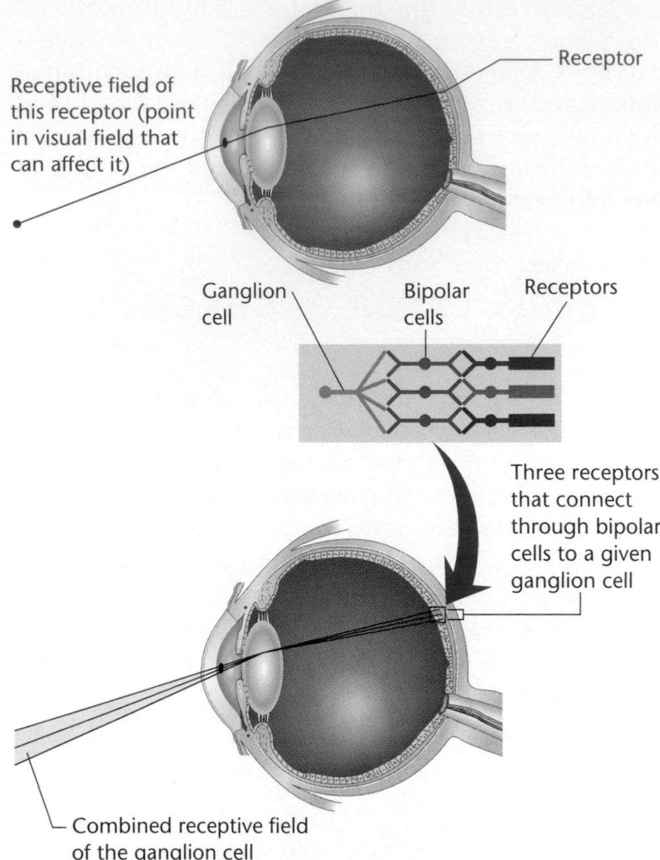

Figure 6.18 Receptive fields
The receptive field of a receptor is simply the area of the visual field from which light strikes that receptor. For any other cell in the visual system, the receptive field is determined by which receptors connect to the cell in question.

form the receptive fields of the next level of cells and so on.

To find a receptive field, an investigator can shine light in various locations while recording from a neuron. If light from a particular spot excites the neuron, then that location is part of the neuron's excitatory receptive field. If it inhibits activity, the location is in the inhibitory receptive field.

The receptive field of a ganglion cell can be described as a circular center with an antagonistic doughnut-shaped surround. That is, light in the center of the receptive field might be excitatory, with the surround inhibitory, or the opposite.

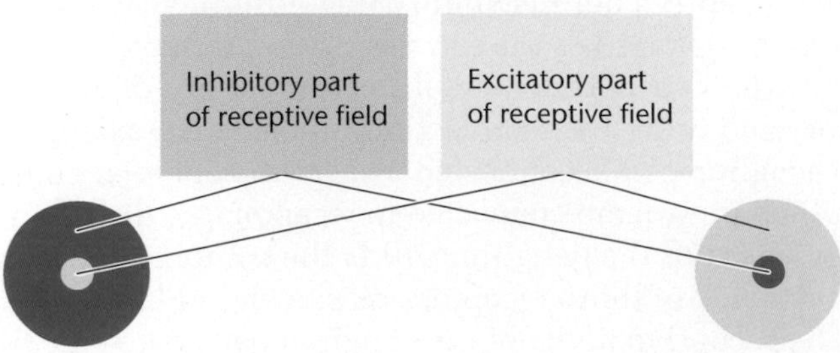

Nearly all primate ganglion cells fall into three major categories: parvocellular, magnocellular, and koniocellular (Shapley, 1995). The **parvocellular neurons**, with smaller cell bodies and small receptive fields, are located mostly in or near the fovea. (Parvocellular means "small celled," from the Latin root *parv,* meaning "small.") The **magnocellular neurons**, with larger cell bodies and receptive fields, are distributed fairly evenly throughout the retina. (Magnocellular means "large celled," from the Latin root *magn,* meaning "large." The same root appears in *magnify* and *magnificent.*) The **koniocellular neurons** have small cell bodies, similar to the parvocellular neurons, but they occur throughout the retina instead of being clustered near the fovea. (Koniocellular means "dust celled," from the Greek root meaning "dust." They got this name because of their granular appearance.)

The parvocellular neurons, with their small receptive fields, are well suited to detect visual details. They are also responsive to color, each neuron being excited by some wavelengths and inhibited by others. The high sensitivity to detail and color reflects the fact that parvocellular cells are located mostly in and near the fovea, where we have many cones. Parvocellular neurons connect only to the lateral geniculate nucleus of the thalamus.

The magnocellular neurons, in contrast, have larger receptive fields and are not color sensitive. They respond strongly to moving stimuli and to large overall patterns but not to details. Magnocellular neurons are found throughout the retina, including the periphery, where we are sensitive to movement but not to color or details. Most magnocellular neurons connect to the lateral geniculate nucleus, but a few have connections to other visual areas of the thalamus.

Koniocellular neurons have several kinds of functions, and their axons terminate in several locations (Hendry & Reid, 2000). Various types of koniocellular neurons connect to the lateral geniculate nucleus, other parts of the thalamus, and the superior colliculus. The existence of so many kinds of ganglion cells implies that the visual system analyzes information in several ways from the start. Table 6.2 summarizes the three kinds of primate ganglion cells.

The axons from the ganglion cells form the optic nerve, which exits the eye at the blind spot and proceeds to the optic chiasm, where half of axons (in humans) cross to the opposite hemisphere. Whereas the retina has more than 120 million receptors, their responses converge onto about 1 million axons in each optic nerve. Although that may sound like a loss of information, a million axons per eye still conveys an enormous amount of information—estimated to be more than one-third of all the information reaching the brain from all sources combined (Bruesch & Arey, 1942).

Most axons of the optic nerve go to the lateral geniculate nucleus of the thalamus. Cells of the lateral genic-

Table 6.2 Three Kinds of Primate Ganglion Cells

	Parvocellular Neurons	Magnocellular Neurons	Koniocellular Neurons
Cell bodies	Smaller	Larger	Small
Receptive fields	Smaller	Larger	Mostly small; variable
Retinal location	In and near fovea	Throughout the retina	Throughout the retina
Color sensitive	Yes	No	Some are
Respond to	Detailed analysis of stationary objects	Movement and broad outlines of shape	Varied and not yet fully described

ulate have receptive fields that resemble those of the ganglion cells—either an excitatory or an inhibitory central portion and a surrounding ring of the opposite effect. Again, some have large (magnocellular) receptive fields, and others have small (parvocellular) fields. However, after the information reaches the cerebral cortex, the receptive fields begin to become more specialized and complicated.

Pattern Recognition in the Cerebral Cortex

Most visual information from the lateral geniculate nucleus of the thalamus goes to the **primary visual cortex** in the occipital cortex, also known as **area V1** or the *striate cortex* because of its striped appearance. It is the area of the cortex responsible for the first stage of visual processing. Area V1 is apparently essential for most, if not all, conscious vision. If you close your eyes and imagine a visual scene, activity increases in area V1 (Kosslyn & Thompson, 2003). People who become blind because of eye damage continue having visual dreams if their visual cortex is intact. However, people with extensive damage to the visual cortex report no conscious vision, no visual imagination, and no visual images in their dreams (Hurovitz, Dunn, Domhoff, & Fiss, 1999).

Nevertheless, some people with extensive area V1 damage show a surprising phenomonon called **blindsight**, an ability to respond in some ways to visual information that they report not seeing. If a light flashes within an area where they report no vision, they can nevertheless point to it or turn their eyes toward it, while insisting that they saw nothing and are only guessing (Bridgeman & Staggs, 1982; Weiskrantz, Warrington, Sanders, & Marshall, 1974).

The explanation remains controversial. After damage to area V1, other branches of the optic nerve deliver visual information to the superior colliculus (in the midbrain) and several other areas, including parts of the cerebral cortex (see Figure 6.16a). Perhaps those areas control the blindsight responses (Cowey & Stoerig, 1995; Moore, Rodman, Repp, & Gross, 1995). However, many people with area V1 damage do not show blindsight or show it for stimuli only in certain locations (Schärli, Harman, & Hogben, 1999; Wessinger, Fendrich, & Gazzaniga, 1997). An alternative explanation is that tiny islands of healthy tissue remain within an otherwise damaged visual cortex, not large enough to provide conscious perception but nevertheless enough for blindsight (Fendrich, Wessinger, & Gazzaniga, 1992). Some patients experience blindsight after extensive (but not total) damage to the optic nerve, so the "surviving island" theory does appear valid for some cases (Wüst, Kasten, & Sabel, 2002).

Perhaps both hypotheses are correct. In some patients, a small amount of recordable activity in area V1 accompanies blindsight, supporting the "islands" explanation. In other patients, no activity in V1 is apparent, and blindsight evidently depends on other brain areas (Morland, Lê, Carroll, Hofmann, & Pambakian, 2004). In one study, experimenters temporarily suppressed a wide area of the visual cortex by transcranial magnetic stimulation (see page 110). Although people were not aware of a spot flashed on the screen during the period of suppression, the spot influenced their eye movements (Ro, Shelton, Lee, & Chang, 2004). That result also indicates that activity outside V1 can produce visually guided behavior.

Still, all these blindsight responses occur without consciousness. The conclusion remains that conscious visual perception requires strong activity in area V1.

Pathways in the Visual Cortex

The primary visual cortex sends information to the **secondary visual cortex** (area **V2**), which processes the information further and transmits it to additional areas, as shown in Figure 6.19. The connections in the visual cortex are reciprocal; for example, V1 sends information to V2 and V2 returns information to V1. Neuroscientists have distinguished 30 to 40 visual areas in the brain of a macaque monkey (Van Essen & Deyoe, 1995) and believe that the human brain has even more.

Within the cerebral cortex, a ventral pathway, with mostly parvocellular input, is sensitive to details of shape. Another ventral pathway, with mostly magnocellular input, is sensitive to movement. Still another,

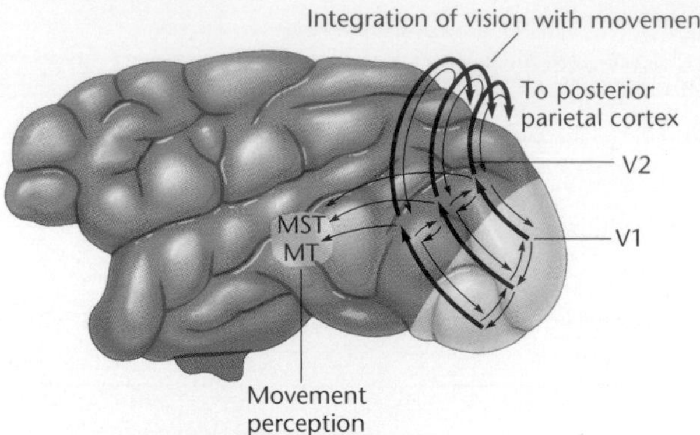

(a) Mostly magnocellular path

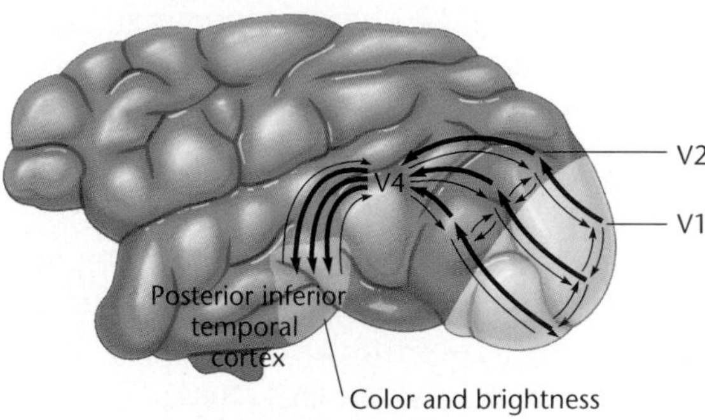

(b) Mixed magnocellular/parvocellular path

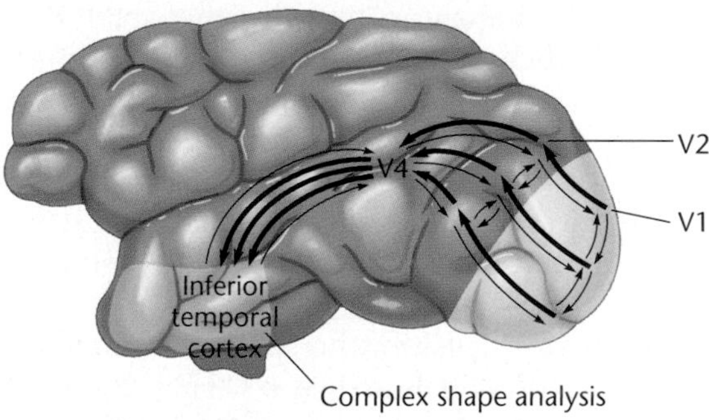

(c) Mostly parvocellular path

Figure 6.19 Three visual pathways in the monkey cerebral cortex

(a) A pathway originating mainly from magnocellular neurons. **(b)** A mixed magnocellular/parvocellular pathway. **(c)** A mainly parvocellular pathway. Neurons are only sparsely connected with neurons of other pathways. *(Sources: Based on DeYoe, Felleman, Van Essen, & McClendon, 1994; Ts'o & Roe, 1995; Van Essen & DeYoe, 1995)*

with mixed input, is sensitive mainly to brightness and color, with partial sensitivity to shape (E. N. Johnson, Hawken, & Shapley, 2001).

Note in Figure 6.19 that although the shape, movement, and color/brightness pathways are separate, they all lead to the temporal cortex. The path into the parietal cortex, with mostly magnocellular input, integrates vision with movement. Researchers refer collectively to the visual paths in the temporal cortex as the **ventral stream**, or the "what" pathway, because it is specialized for identifying and recognizing objects. The visual path in the parietal cortex is the **dorsal stream**, or the "where" or "how" pathway, because it helps the motor system find objects and determine how to move toward them, grasp them, and so forth. Don't imagine a 100% division of labor; cells in both streams have some responsiveness to shape ("what"), for example (Denys et al., 2004).

People who have damage to the ventral stream (temporal cortex) cannot fully describe the size or shape of what they see. They are also impaired in their ability to imagine shapes and faces—for example, to recall from memory whether George Washington had a beard (Kosslyn, Ganis, & Thompson, 2001). Activity in the ventral stream correlates highly with people's ability to report conscious visual perception. However, even when the ventral stream is damaged or inactive, the dorsal "where" stream can still respond strongly (Fang & He, 2005). Sometimes people with ventral stream damage reach toward objects, or walk around objects in their path, without being able to name or describe the objects. In short, they see "where" but not "what."

In contrast, people with damage to the dorsal stream (parietal cortex) can accurately describe what they see, but they cannot convert their vision into action. They cannot accurately reach out to grasp an object, even after describing its size, shape, and color (Goodale, 1996; Goodale, Milner, Jakobson, & Carey, 1991). They are also unable to imagine locations or describe them from memory—for example, to describe the rooms of a house or the arrangement of furniture in any room (Kosslyn et al., 2001).

STOP & CHECK

5. As we progress from bipolar cells to ganglion cells to later cells in the visual system, are receptive fields ordinarily larger, smaller, or the same size? Why?
6. What are the differences between the magnocellular and parvocellular systems?
7. If you were in a darkened room and researchers wanted to "read your mind" just enough to know whether you were having visual fantasies, what could they do?
8. What is an example of an "unconscious" visually guided behavior?
9. Suppose someone can describe an object in detail but stumbles and fumbles when trying to walk toward it and pick it up. Which path is probably damaged, the dorsal path or the ventral path?

Check your answers on page 183.

For additional detail about the visual cortex, check this website: **http://www.webvision.med.utah.edu/VisualCortex.html#introduction**

The Shape Pathway

In the 1950s, David Hubel and Torsten Wiesel (1959) began a research project in which they shone light patterns on the retina while recording from cells in a cat's or monkey's brain (Methods 6.1). At first, they presented just dots of light, using a slide projector and a screen, and found little response by cortical cells. The first time they got a big response was when they were moving a slide into place. They quickly realized that the cell was responding to the edge of the slide and had a bar-shaped receptive field (Hubel & Wiesel, 1998). Their research, for which they received a Nobel Prize, has often been called "the research that launched a thousand microelectrodes" because it inspired so much further research. By now, it has probably launched a million microelectrodes.

Hubel and Wiesel distinguished several types of cells in the visual cortex. The receptive fields shown in Figure 6.20 are typical of **simple cells**, which are found exclusively in the primary visual cortex. The receptive field of a simple cell has fixed excitatory and inhibitory zones. The more light shines in the excitatory zone, the more the cell responds. The more light shines in the inhibitory zone, the less the cell responds. For example, Figure 6.20c shows a vertical receptive field for a simple cell. The cell's response decreases sharply if the bar of light is moved to the left or right or tilted from the vertical because light then strikes the inhibitory regions as well (Figure 6.21). Most simple cells have bar-shaped or edge-shaped receptive fields, which may be at vertical, horizontal, or intermediate orientations. The vertical and horizontal orientations outnumber the diagonals, and that disparity probably makes sense, considering the importance of horizontal and vertical objects in our world (Coppola, Purves, McCoy, & Purves, 1998).

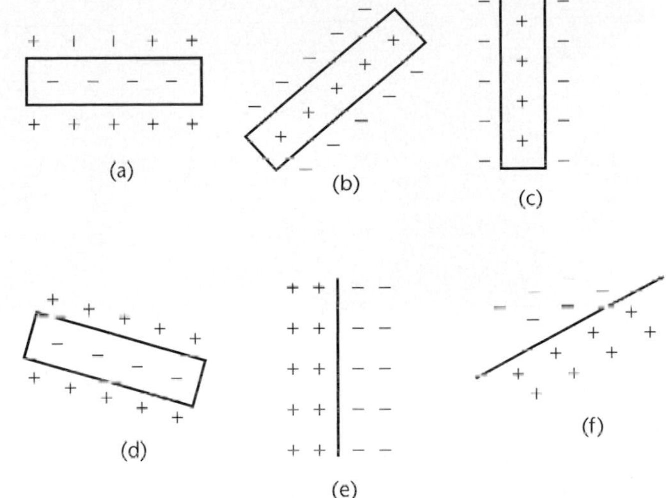

Figure 6.20 Typical receptive fields for simple visual cortex cells of cats and monkeys

Areas marked with a plus (+) are the excitatory receptive fields; areas marked with a minus (–) are the inhibitory receptive fields. *(Source: Based on Hubel & Wiesel, 1959)*

Unlike simple cells, **complex cells**, located in either area V1 or V2, have receptive fields that cannot be mapped into fixed excitatory and inhibitory zones. A complex cell responds to a pattern of light in a particular orientation (e.g., a vertical bar) anywhere within its large receptive field, regardless of the exact location of the stimulus (Figure 6.22). It responds most strongly to a stimulus moving perpendicular to its axis—for example, a vertical bar moving horizontally or a horizontal bar moving vertically. If a cell in the visual cortex responds to a bar-shaped pattern of light, the best way to classify the cell is to move the bar slightly in different directions. A cell that responds to the light in only one location is a simple cell; one that responds strongly to the light throughout a large area is a complex cell.

Researchers for decades assumed that complex cells receive input from a combination of simple cells, and eventually, it became possible to demonstrate this point. Researchers used the inhibitory transmitter GABA to block input from the lateral geniculate to the

METHODS 6.1

Microelectrode Recordings

David Hubel and Torsten Wiesel pioneered the use of microelectrode recordings to study the properties of individual neurons in the cerebral cortex. In this method, investigators begin by anesthetizing an animal and drilling a small hole in the skull. Then they insert a thin electrode—either a fine metal wire insulated except at the tip or a narrow glass tube containing a salt solution and a metal wire. They direct the electrode either next to or into a single cell and then record its activity while they present various stimuli, such as patterns of light. Researchers use the results to determine what kinds of stimuli do and do not excite the cell.

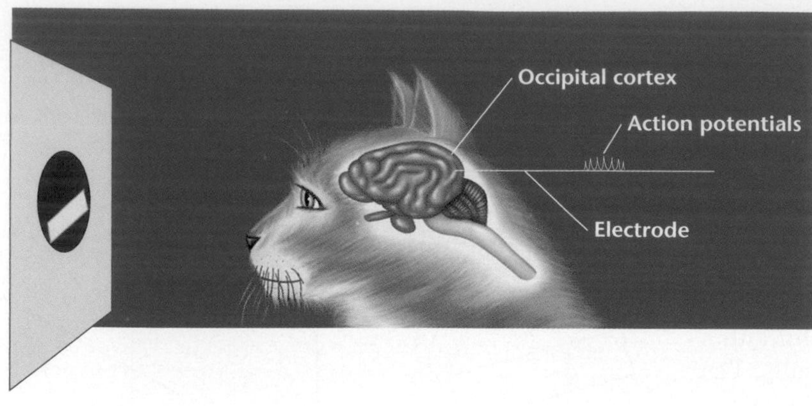

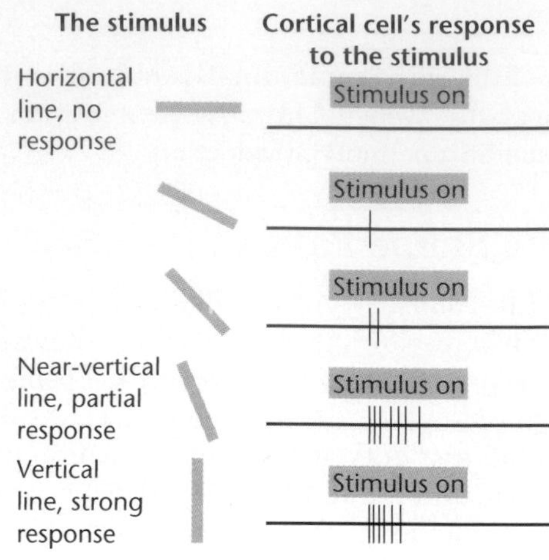

Figure 6.21 Responses of a cat's simple cell to a bar of light presented at varying angles
The short horizontal lines indicate when light is on. *(Source: Right, from D. H. Hubel and T. N. Wiesel, "Receptive fields of single neurons in the cat's striate cortex,"* Journal of Physiology, *148, 1959, 574–591. Copyright © 1959 Cambridge University Press. Reprinted by permission.)*

simple cells, and they found that as soon as the simple cells stopped responding, the complex cells stopped too (Martinez & Alonso, 2001).

Time when stimulus is present
High response
High response
High response
Low response
Low response
Time

Figure 6.22 The receptive field of a complex cell in the visual cortex
Like a simple cell, its response depends on a bar of light's angle of orientation. However, a complex cell responds the same for a bar in any position within the receptive field.

End-stopped, or **hypercomplex, cells** resemble complex cells with one additional feature: An end-stopped cell has a strong inhibitory area at one end of its bar-shaped receptive field. The cell responds to a bar-shaped pattern of light anywhere in its broad receptive field provided that the bar does not extend beyond a certain point (Figure 6.23). Table 6.3 summarizes the properties of simple, complex, and end-stopped cells.

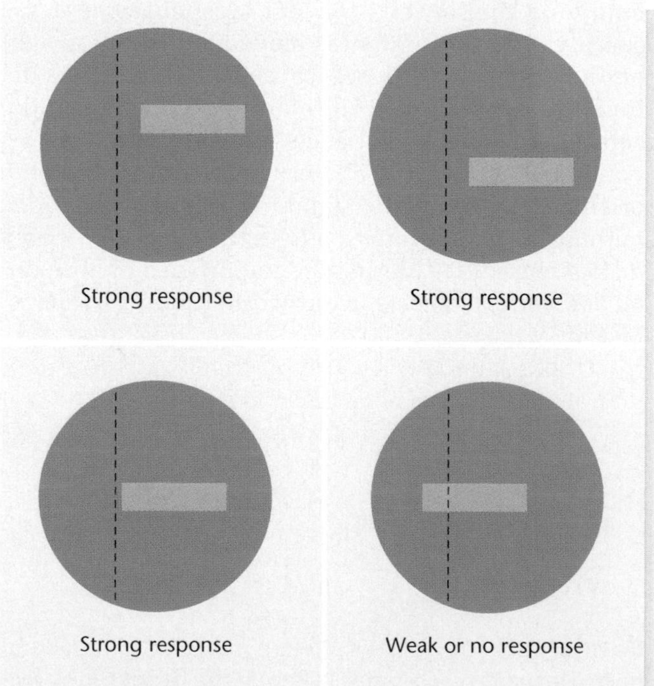

Figure 6.23 The receptive field of an end-stopped cell
The cell responds to a bar in a particular orientation (in this case, horizontal) anywhere in its receptive field provided that the bar does not extend into a strongly inhibitory area.

Table 6.3 Summary of Cells in the Primary Visual Cortex

Characteristic	Simple Cells	Complex Cells	End-Stopped Cells
Location	V1	V1 and V2	V1 and V2
Binocular input	Yes	Yes	Yes
Size of receptive field	Smallest	Medium	Largest
Receptive field	Bar- or edge-shaped, with fixed excitatory and inhibitory zones	Bar- or edge-shaped, without fixed excitatory or inhibitory zones; responds to stimulus anywhere in receptive field, especially if moving perpendicular to its axis	Same as complex cell but with strong inhibitory zone at one end

The Columnar Organization of the Visual Cortex

Cells having various properties are grouped together in the visual cortex in columns perpendicular to the surface (Hubel & Wiesel, 1977) (see Figure 4.22, p. 98). For example, cells within a given column respond either mostly to the left eye, mostly to the right eye, or to both eyes about equally. Also, cells within a given column respond best to lines of a single orientation.

Figure 6.24 shows what happens when an investigator lowers an electrode into the visual cortex and records from each cell that it reaches. Each red line represents a neuron and shows the angle of orientation of its receptive field. In electrode path A, the first series of cells are all in one column and show the same orientation preferences. However, after passing through the white matter, the end of path A invades two columns with different preferred orientations. Electrode path B, which is not perpendicular to the surface of the cortex, crosses through three columns and encounters cells with different properties. In short, the cells within a given column process similar information.

Are Visual Cortex Cells Feature Detectors?

Given that neurons in area V1 respond strongly to bar- or edge-shaped patterns, it seems natural to suppose that the activity of such a cell *is* (or at least is necessary for) the perception of a bar, line, or edge. That is, such cells might be **feature detectors**—neurons whose responses indicate the presence of a particular feature. Cells in later areas of the cortex respond to more complex shapes, and perhaps they are square detectors, circle detectors, and so forth.

Supporting the concept of feature detectors is the fact that prolonged exposure to a given visual feature decreases sensitivity to that feature, as if one has fatigued the relevant detectors. For example, if you stare at a waterfall for a minute or more and then look away, the rocks and trees next to the waterfall appear to be flowing upward. This effect, the *waterfall illusion*, suggests that you have fatigued the neurons that detect downward motion, leaving unopposed the detectors that detect the opposite motion. You can see the same effect if you watch your computer screen scroll slowly for about a minute and then examine an unmoving display.

However, just as a medium-wavelength cone responds somewhat to the whole range of wavelengths, a cortical cell that responds best to one stimulus also responds to many others. Any object stimulates a large population of cells, and any cell in the visual system responds somewhat to many stimuli (Tsunoda, Yamane, Nishizaki, & Tanifuji, 2001). The response of any cell is ambiguous unless it is compared to the responses of other cells.

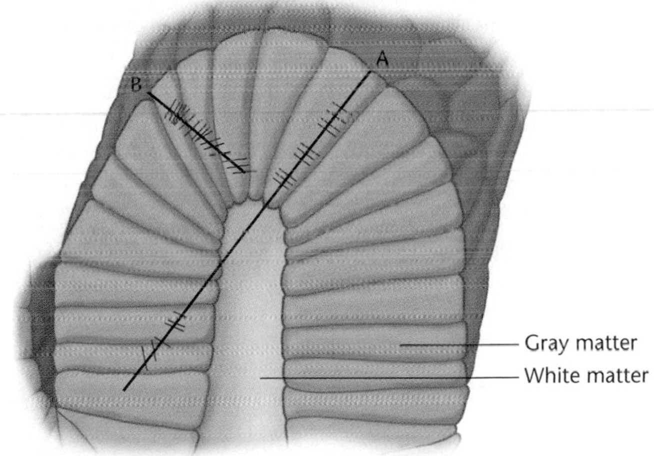

Figure 6.24 Columns of neurons in the visual cortex

When an electrode passes perpendicular to the surface of the cortex (first part of A), it encounters a sequence of neurons responsive to the same orientation of a stimulus. (The colored lines show the preferred stimulus orientation for each cell.) When an electrode passes across columns (B, or second part of A), it encounters neurons responsive to different orientations. Column borders are shown here to make the point clear; no such borders are visible in the real cortex. *(Source: From "The visual cortex of the brain," by David H. Hubel, November 1963,* Scientific American, *209, 5, p. 62. Copyright © Scientific American.)*

Furthermore, Hubel and Wiesel tested only a limited range of stimuli. Later researchers have tried other kinds of stimuli and found that a cortical cell that responds well to a single bar or line

also responds, generally even more strongly, to a sine wave grating of bars or lines:

Different cortical neurons respond best to gratings of different spatial frequencies (i.e., wide bars or narrow bars), and many are very precisely tuned; that is, they respond strongly to one frequency and hardly at all to a slightly higher or lower frequency (DeValois, Albrecht, & Thorell, 1982). Most visual researchers therefore believe that neurons in area V1 respond to spatial frequencies rather than to bars or edges. How do we translate a series of spatial frequencies into perception? From a mathematical standpoint, sine wave spatial frequencies are easy to work with. In a branch of mathematics called Fourier analysis, it can be demonstrated that a combination of sine waves can produce an unlimited variety of other more complicated patterns. For example, the graph at the top of the following display is the sum of the five sine waves below it:

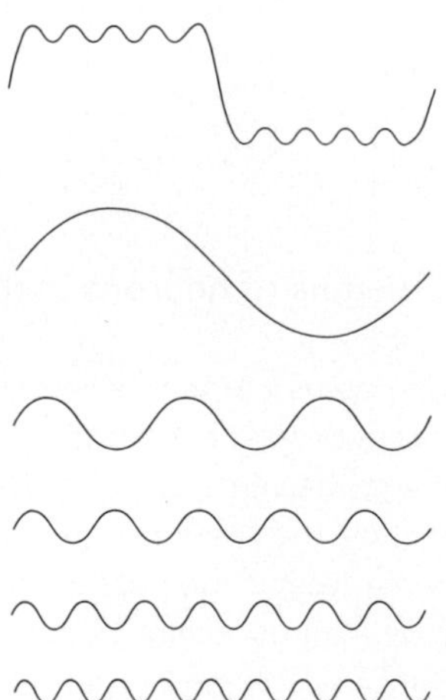

Therefore, a series of spatial frequency detectors, some sensitive to horizontal patterns and others to vertical patterns, could represent anything anyone could see. Still, we obviously do not perceive the world as an assembly of sine waves, and the emergence of object perception remains a puzzle (Hughes, Nozawa, & Kitterle, 1996). Indeed, the activities of areas V1 and V2 are probably preliminary steps that organize visual material and send it to more specialized areas that actually identify objects (Lennie, 1998).

Shape Analysis Beyond Area V1

As visual information goes from the simple cells to the complex cells and then on to later areas of visual processing, the receptive fields become larger and more specialized. For example, in area V2 (next to V1), many cells still respond best to lines, edges, and sine wave gratings, but some cells respond selectively to circles, lines that meet at a right angle, or other complex patterns (Hegdé & Van Essen, 2000). In area V4, many cells respond selectively to a particular slant of a line in three-dimensional space (Hinkle & Connor, 2002).

Response patterns are even more complex in the **inferior temporal cortex** (see Figure 6.19). Because cells in this area have huge receptive fields, always including the foveal field of vision, their responses provide almost no information about stimulus location. However, many of them respond selectively to complex shapes and are insensitive to many distinctions that are critical for other cells. For example, some cells in the inferior temporal cortex respond about equally to a black square on a white background, a white square on a black background, and a square-shaped pattern of dots moving across a stationary pattern of dots (Sáry, Vogels, & Orban, 1993). On the other hand, a cell that responds about equally to and may hardly respond at all to (Vogels, Biederman, Bar, & Lorincz, 2001). Evidently, cortical neurons can respond specifically to certain details of shape.

Most inferior temporal neurons that respond strongly to a particular shape respond almost equally to its mirror image (Rollenhagen & Olson, 2000). For example, a cell might respond equally to and to . Cells also respond equally after a reversal of contrast, where white becomes black and black becomes white. However, they do not respond the same after a figure–ground reversal. Examine Figure 6.25. Researchers measured responses in monkeys' inferior temporal cortex to a number of stimuli and then to three kinds of transformations. The response of a neuron to each original stimulus correlated highly with its response to the contrast reversal and mirror image but correlated poorly with its response to the figure–ground reversal (Baylis & Driver, 2001). That is, cells in this area detect an object, no matter how it is displayed, and not the amount of light or darkness in any location on the retina.

The ability of inferior temporal neurons to ignore changes in size and direction probably contributes to

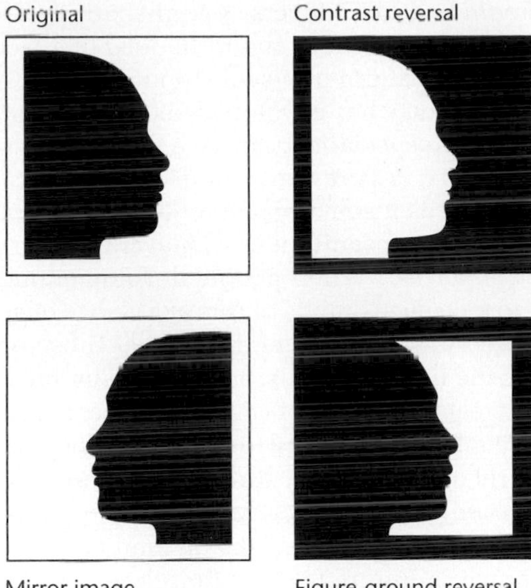

Figure 6.25 Three transformations of an original drawing
In the inferior temporal cortex, cells that respond strongly to the original respond about the same to the contrast reversal and mirror image but not to the figure–ground reversal. Note that the figure–ground reversal resembles the original very strongly in terms of the pattern of light and darkness; however, it is not perceived as the same object. *(Source: Based on Baylis & Driver, 2001)*

our capacity for **shape constancy**—the ability to recognize an object's shape even as it changes location or direction. However, although shape constancy helps us recognize an object from different angles, it interferes in reading, where we need to treat mirror-image letters as different. (Consider the difficulty some children have in learning the difference between b and d or p and q.)

Disorders of Object Recognition

Damage to the shape pathway of the cortex should lead to specialized deficits in the ability to recognize objects. Neurologists have reported such cases for decades, although they frequently met with skepticism. Now that we understand *how* such specialized defects might arise, we find them easier to accept.

An inability to recognize objects despite otherwise satisfactory vision is called **visual agnosia** (meaning "visual lack of knowledge"). It usually results from damage somewhere in the temporal cortex. A person with brain damage might be able to point to visual objects and slowly describe them but fail to recognize what they are or mean. For example, one patient, when shown a key, said, "I don't know what that is; perhaps a file or a tool of some sort." When shown a stethoscope, he said that it was "a long cord with a round thing at the end." When he could not identify a pipe, the examiner told him what it was. He then replied, "Yes, I can see it now," and pointed out the stem and bowl of the pipe. Then the examiner asked, "Suppose I told you that the last object was not really a pipe?" The patient replied, "I would take your word for it. Perhaps it's not really a pipe" (Rubens & Benson, 1971).

Many other types of agnosia occur. One closed head injury patient could recognize faces of all kinds, including cartoons and face pictures made from objects (Figure 6.26). However, he could not recognize any of

Figure 6.26 Faces made from other objects
One man, after a closed head injury, could recognize these as faces and could point out the eyes, nose, and so forth, but could not identify any of the component objects. He was not even aware that the faces were composed of objects.

the individual objects that composed the face (Moscovitch, Winocur, & Behrmann, 1997).

The opposite disorder—inability to recognize faces—is known as **prosopagnosia** (PROSS-oh-pag-NOH-see-ah). People with prosopagnosia can recognize other objects, including letters and words, and they can recognize familiar people from their voices or other cues, so their problem is neither vision in general nor memory in general but just face recognition (Farah, Wilson, Drain, & Tanaka, 1998). Furthermore, if they feel clay models of faces, they are worse than other people at determining whether two clay models are the same or different (Kilgour, de Gelder, & Lederman, 2004). Again, the conclusion is that the problem is not with vision but something special about faces.

When people with prosopagnosia look at a face, they can describe whether the person is old or young, male or female, but they cannot identify the person. (You would perform about the same if you viewed faces quickly, upside-down.) One patient was shown 34 photographs of famous people and was offered a choice of two identifications for each. By chance alone he should have identified 17 correctly; in fact, he got 18. He remarked that he seldom enjoyed watching movies or television programs because he had trouble keeping track of the characters. Curiously, his favorite movie was *Batman,* in which the main characters wore masks much of the time (Laeng & Caviness, 2001).

Prosopagnosia occurs after damage to the *fusiform gyrus* of the inferior temporal cortex, especially after such damage in the right hemisphere (Figure 6.27). According to fMRI scans, recognizing a face depends on increased activity in the fusiform gyrus and part of the prefrontal cortex (McCarthy, Puce, Gore, & Allison, 1997; Ó Scalaidhe, Wilson, & Goldman-Rakic, 1997). The fusiform gyrus also increases activity when people look at the faces of dogs (Blonder et al., 2004) or a blurry area on a picture at the top of a body where a face *should* be (Cox, Meyers, & Sinha, 2004). That is, it responds to something about the *idea* of a face, not to a particular pattern of visual stimulation.

Fusiform gyrus

Dr. Dana Copeland

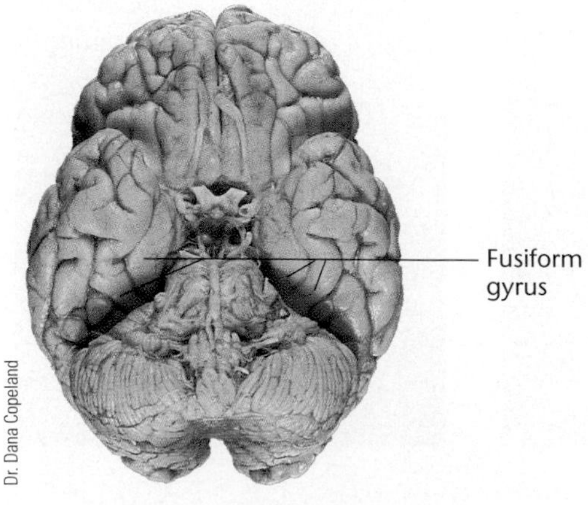

Figure 6.27 The fusiform gyrus
Many cells here are especially active during recognition of faces.

A controversy has developed about how narrowly these areas are specialized for face recognition. Is the fusiform gyrus, or part of it, a built-in face perception "module"? Or is it something a bit broader, pertaining to expert visual recognition in whatever field we might achieve expertise? When people develop enough expertise to recognize brands of cars at a glance or species of birds or types of flowers, looking at those objects activates the fusiform gyrus, and the greater the expertise, the greater the level of activation (Tarr & Gauthier, 2000). People with damage to the fusiform gyrus have trouble recognizing cars, bird species, and so forth (Farah, 1990). Furthermore, when people with intact brains are shown "greebles," the unfamiliar-looking objects shown in Figure 6.28, at first they have trouble recognizing them individually, and the fusiform gyrus responds to them only weakly. As people gain familiarity and learn to recognize them, the fusiform gyrus becomes more active and reacts to them more like faces (Gauthier, Tarr, Anderson, Skudlarski, & Gore, 1999; Rossion, Gauthier, Goffaux, Tarr, & Crommelinck, 2002). These results imply that the fusiform gyrus pertains to visual expertise of any kind. However, even in people with extreme levels of expertise, the fusiform gyrus cells that respond most vigorously to faces do not respond equally well to anything else (Grill-Spector,

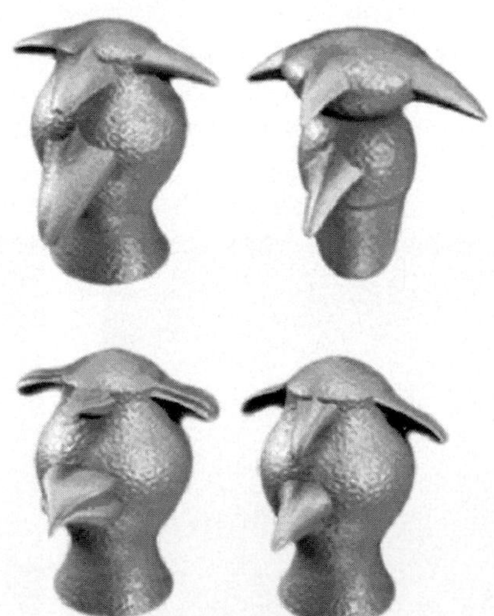

Figure 6.28 "Greebles"
When people are asked to recognize individual greebles or to sort them into "families" of related individuals, at first they have low accuracy. As they practice and improve, the fusiform gyrus becomes more responsive to greebles. *(Source: Figure 1a, p. 569, from Gauthier, I., Tarr, M. J., Anderson, A. W., Skudlarski, P. L., & Gore, J. C., (1999). "Activation of the middle fusiform 'face area' increases with experience in recognizing novel objects,"* Nature Neuroscience, *2, 568–573.)*

Knouf, & Kanwisher, 2004; Kanwisher, 2000). Also, the fusiform gyrus continues responding strongly to faces, regardless of whether the viewer is paying attention to the face as a whole or just one part, such as the mouth (Yovel & Kanwisher, 2004). So face recognition may indeed be special, not quite like any other kind of expert pattern recognition.

10. How could a researcher determine whether a given neuron in the visual cortex was simple or complex?
11. What is prosopagnosia and what does its existence tell us about separate shape recognition systems in the visual cortex?

Check your answers on page 183.

The Color, Motion, and Depth Pathways

Color perception depends on both the parvocellular and koniocellular paths, whereas brightness depends mostly on the magnocellular path. Particular clusters of neurons in cortical areas V1 and V2 respond selectively to color (Xiao, Wang, & Felleman, 2003); they then send their output through particular parts of area V4 to the posterior inferior temporal cortex, as shown in Figure 6.19b.

Several investigators have found that either area V4 or a nearby area is particularly important for color constancy (Hadjikhani, Liu, Dale, Cavanagh, & Tootell, 1998; Zeki, McKeefry, Bartels, & Frackowiak, 1998). Recall from the discussion of the retinex theory that color constancy is the ability to recognize the color of an object even if the lighting changes. Monkeys with damage to area V4 can learn to pick up a yellow object to get food but cannot find it if the overhead lighting is changed from white to blue (Wild, Butler, Carden, & Kulikowski, 1985). That is, they retain color vision but lose color constancy. In humans also, after damage to an area that straddles the temporal and parietal cortices, perhaps corresponding to monkey area V4, people recognize and remember colors but lose their color constancy (Rüttiger et al., 1999).

In addition to a role in color vision, area V4 has cells that contribute to visual attention (Leopold & Logothetis, 1996). Animals with damage to V4 have trouble shifting their attention from the larger, brighter stimulus to any less prominent stimulus.

Many of the cells of the magnocellular pathway are specialized for **stereoscopic depth perception**, the ability to detect depth by differences in what the two eyes see. To illustrate, hold a finger in front of your eyes and look at it, first with just the left eye and then just the right eye. Try again, holding your finger at different distances. Note that the two eyes see your finger differently and that the closer your finger is to your face, the greater the difference between the two views. Certain cells in the magnocellular pathway detect the discrepancy between the two views, presumably mediating stereoscopic depth perception. When you look at something with just one eye, the same cells are almost unresponsive.

Structures Important for Motion Perception

Moving objects grab our attention, for good reasons. A moving object might be alive, and if so it might be dangerous, it might be good to eat, or it might be a potential mate. If nonliving things such as rocks are moving, they may be a sign of an earthquake or landslide. Almost any moving object calls for a decision of whether to chase it, ignore it, or run away from it. Several brain areas are specialized to detect motion.

Imagine yourself sitting in a small boat on a river. The waves are all flowing one direction, and in the distance, you see rapids. Meanwhile, a duck is swimming slowly against the current, the clouds are moving yet another direction, and your perspective alters as the boat rocks back and forth. In short, you simultaneously see several kinds of motion. Viewing a moving pattern activates many brain areas spread among all four lobes of the cerebral cortex (Sunaert, Van Hecke, Marchal, & Orban, 1999; Vanduffel et al., 2001). Two temporal lobe areas that are consistently and strongly activated by any kind of visual motion are area **MT** (for middle-temporal cortex), also known as area **V5**, and an adjacent region, area **MST** (medial superior temporal cortex) (see Figure 6.19). Areas MT and MST receive their direct input from a branch of the magnocellular path, although they also receive some parvocellular input (Yabuta, Sawatari, & Callaway, 2001). The magnocellular path detects overall patterns, including movement over large areas of the visual field. The parvocellular path includes cells that detect the disparity between the views of the left and right eyes, an important cue to distance (Kasai & Morotomi, 2001).

Most cells in area MT respond selectively to a stimulus moving in a particular direction, almost independently of its size, shape, brightness, or color of the object (Perrone & Thiele, 2001). They also respond somewhat to a still photograph that implies movement, such as a photo of people running or cars racing (Kourtzi & Kanwisher, 2000). To other kinds of stationary stimuli they show little response.

Many cells in area MT respond best to moving borders within their receptive fields. Cells in the dor-

Figure 6.29 Stimuli that excite the dorsal part of area MST
Cells here respond if a whole scene expands, contracts, or rotates. That is, such cells respond if the observer moves forward or backward or tilts his or her head.

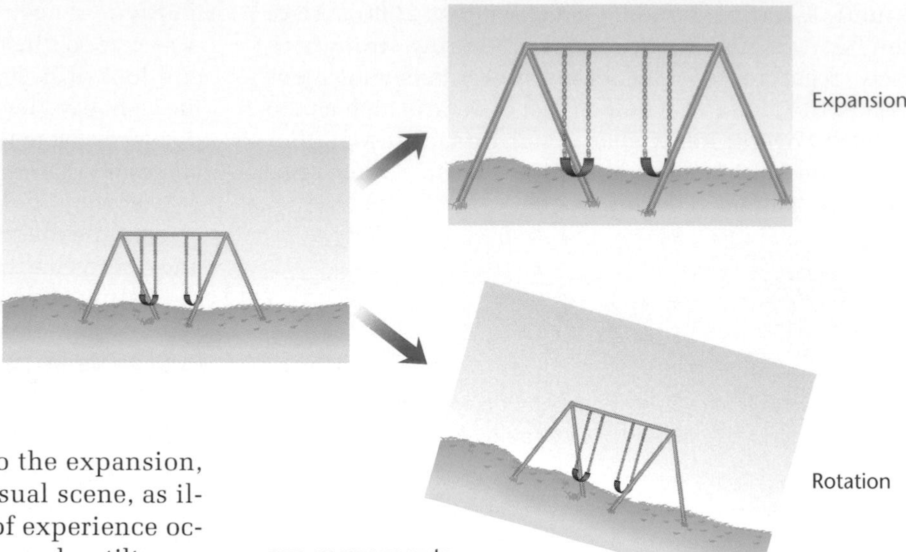

sal part of area MST respond best to the expansion, contraction, or rotation of a large visual scene, as illustrated in Figure 6.29. That kind of experience occurs when you move forward or backward or tilt your head. These two kinds of cells—the ones that record movement of single objects and the ones that record movement of the entire background—converge their messages onto neurons in the ventral part of area MST, where cells respond whenever an object moves in a certain direction *relative to its background* (K. Tanaka, Sugita, Moriya, & Saito, 1993) (Figure 6.30).

A cell with such properties is enormously useful in determining the motion of objects. When you move your head or eyes from left to right, all the objects in your visual field move across your retina as if the world itself had moved right to left. (Go ahead and try it.) Yet when you do so, the world looks stationary because the objects are stationary with respect to one another. Many neurons in area MST are silent during eye movements (Thiele, Henning, Kubischik, & Hoffmann, 2002). However, MST neurons respond briskly if an object really is moving during the eye movement—that is, if it is moving relative to the background. In short, MST neurons enable you to distinguish between the result of eye movements and the result of object movements.

Several other brain areas have specialized roles for particular types of motion perception. For example, the brain is particularly adept at detecting biological motion—the kinds of motion produced by people and animals. If you attach glow-in-the-dark dots to someone's elbows, knees, hips, shoulders, and a few other points, then when that person moves in an otherwise dark room, you perceive a moving person, even though you are actually seeing only a few spots of light. Perceiving biological motion activates an area near, but not identical with, area MT (Grossman & Blake, 2001; Grossman et al., 2000). Other areas become active when people pay close attention to the speed or direction of movement (Cornette et al., 1998; Sunaert, Van Hecke, Marchal, & Orban, 2000).

Figure 6.30 Stimuli that excite the ventral part of area MST
Cells here respond when an object moves relative to its background. They therefore react either when the object moves or when the object is steady and the background moves.

EXTENSIONS AND APPLICATIONS
Suppressed Vision During Eye Movements

The temporal cortex has cells that distinguish between moving objects and visual changes due to head movements. An additional mechanism prevents confusion or blurring during eye movements. Before the explanation, try this demonstration: Look at yourself in a mirror and focus on your left eye. Then shift your focus to your right eye. *(Please do this now.)* Did you see your eyes move? No, you did not. *(I said to try this. I bet you didn't. None of this is going to make any sense unless you try the demonstration!)*

try it yourself

Why didn't you see your eyes move? Your first impulse is to say that the movement was too small or too fast. Wrong. Try looking at someone else's eyes while he or she focuses first on your left eye and then on your right. You *do* see the other person's eyes move. So an eye movement is neither too small nor too fast for you to see.

One reason you do not see your own eyes move is that your brain decreases the activity in its visual cortex during quick eye movements, known as **saccades**. In effect, the brain areas that monitor saccades tell the visual cortex, "We're about to move the eye muscles, so take a rest for the next split second, or you will see nothing but a blur anyway." Consequently, neural activity and blood flow in the visual cortex decrease shortly before and during eye movements (Burr, Morrone, & Ross, 1994; Paus, Marrett, Worsley, & Evans, 1995). Even direct electrical stimulation of the retina produces less effect than usual during a saccade (Thilo, Santoro, Walsh, & Blakemore, 2004).

However, neural activity does not cease altogether, and so, for example, you would detect a sudden flash of light during your saccade (García-Pérez & Peli, 2001). Nevertheless, processing by the visual cortex is slowed during a saccade (Irwin & Brockmole, 2004). For example, if two stimuli flash on the screen during a saccade, 100 ms apart, the delay seems shorter than if the same stimuli flashed while no saccade was occurring (Morrone, Ross, & Burr, 2005). This finding fits with many other reports that people underestimate the duration of less-attended stimuli.

Motion Blindness

Some people with brain damage become **motion blind**, able to see objects but unable to determine whether they are moving or, if so, in which direction or how fast. People with motion blindness have trouble with the same tasks as monkeys with damage in area MT (Marcar, Zihl, & Cowey, 1997) and probably have damage in that same area (Greenlee, Lang, Mergner, & Seeger, 1995).

One patient with motion blindness reported that she felt uncomfortable with people walking around because "people were suddenly here or there but I have not seen them moving." She could not cross a street without help: "When I'm looking at the car first, it seems far away. But then, when I want to cross the road, suddenly the car is very near." Even such a routine task as pouring coffee became difficult; the flowing liquid appeared to be frozen and unmoving, so she did not stop pouring until the cup overfilled (Zihl, von Cramon, & Mai, 1983).

The opposite of motion blindness also occurs: Some people are blind *except* for the ability to detect which direction something is moving. You might wonder how someone could see something moving without seeing the object itself. A possible explanation is that area MT gets some visual input directly from the lateral geniculate nucleus of the thalamus. Therefore, even after extensive damage to area V1 (enough to produce blindness), area MT still has enough input to permit motion detection (Sincich, Park, Wohlgemuth, & Horton, 2004).

STOP & CHECK

12. Why is it useful to suppress activity in the visual cortex during saccadic eye movements?

13. What symptoms occur after damage limited to area MT? What may occur if MT is intact but area V1 is damaged?

Check your answers on page 183.

Visual Attention

Of all the stimuli striking your retina at any moment, you attend to only a few. A stimulus can grab your attention by its size, brightness, or movement, but you can also voluntarily direct your attention to one stimulus or another in what is called a "top-down" process—that is, one governed by other cortical areas, principally the frontal and parietal cortex. To illustrate, keep your eyes fixated on the central *x* in the following display. Then attend to the *G* at the right, and step by step shift your attention clockwise around the circle. Notice how you can indeed see different parts of the circle without moving your eyes.

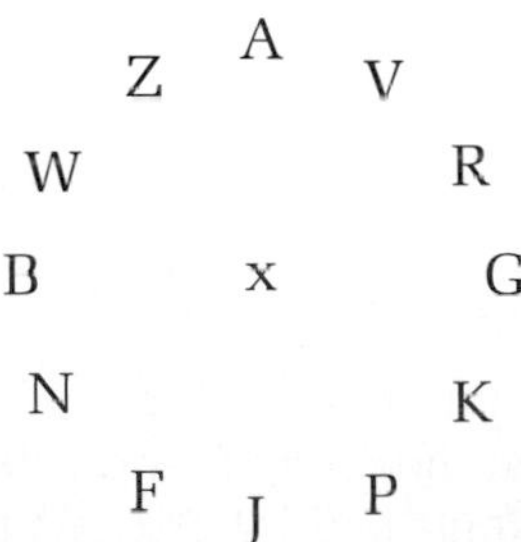

The difference between attended and unattended stimuli pertains to the amount and duration of activity in a cortical area. For example, suppose the letter Q flashes for a split second on a screen you are watching. That stimulus automatically produces a response in your area V1, but only a brief one if you are attending to something else on the screen. However, if you pay attention to the Q (perhaps because someone told you to count the times a letter flashes on the screen), then the brief response in V1 excites V2 and other areas, which feed back onto the V1 cells to enhance and prolong their responses (Kanwisher & Wojciulik, 2000; Supér, Spekreijse, & Lamme, 2001). Activity in V1 then feeds back to enhance activity in the corresponding portions of the lateral geniculate (O'Connor, Fukui, Pinsk, & Kastner, 2002). While you are increasing your brain's response to the attended stimulus, the responses to other stimuli decrease (Wegener, Freiwald, & Kreiter, 2004).

Similarly, suppose you are looking at a screen that shows a plaid grating, like this:

When you are instructed to attend to the lines in one direction or the other, activity increases in the V1 neurons that respond to lines in that orientation. As your attention shifts from one orientation to the other, so does activity in the two sets of neurons. In fact, someone who is monitoring your visual cortex with fMRI could tell you which set of lines you were attending to (Kamitani & Tong, 2005).

Also, if you are told to pay attention to color or motion, activity increases in the areas of your visual cortex responsible for color or motion perception (Chawla, Rees, & Friston, 1999). In fact, activity increases in those areas even before the stimulus (Driver & Frith, 2000). Somehow the instructions prime those areas, so that they can magnify their responses to any appropriate stimulus. They in turn feed back to area V1, enhancing that area's response to the stimulus. Again, it appears that the feedback increase in V1 responses is necessary for attention or conscious awareness of a stimulus (Pascual-Leone & Walsh, 2001).

Module 6.2

In Closing: From Single Cells to Vision

In this module, you have read about single cells that respond to shape, movement, and other aspects of vision. Does any single cell identify what you see?

Several decades ago, the early computers used to crash frequently. Some of the pioneers of computer science were puzzled. A single neuron in the brain, they realized, was surely no more reliable than a single computer chip. Individual neurons must make mistakes all the time, but your brain as a whole continues functioning well. It might make some stupid decisions, but it doesn't "crash." Why not? The computer scientists surmised, correctly, that your brain has a great deal of redundancy so that the system as a whole works well even when individual units fail. The visual system offers many examples of this point. In the retina, each ganglion cell shares information with its neighbors, such that adjoining ganglion cells respond similarly (Puchalla, Schneidman, Harris, & Berry, 2005). In area MT (or V5), no one neuron consistently detects a moving dot within its receptive field, but a population of cells almost always detects the movement within a tenth of a second (Osborne, Bialek, & Lisberger, 2004). In short, each individual neuron contributes to vision, but no neuron is ever indispensable for any perception. Vision arises from the simultaneous activity of many cells in many brain areas.

Summary

1. The optic nerves of the two eyes join at the optic chiasm, where half of the axons from each eye cross to the opposite side of the brain. Most of the axons then travel to the lateral geniculate nucleus of the thalamus, which communicates with the visual cortex. (p. 166)
2. Lateral inhibition is a mechanism by which stimulation in any area of the retina suppresses the responses in neighboring areas, thereby enhancing the contrast at light–dark borders. (p. 167)
3. Lateral inhibition in the vertebrate retina occurs because receptors stimulate bipolar cells and also stimulate the much wider horizontal cells, which inhibit both the stimulated bipolar cells and those to the sides. (p. 168)
4. Each neuron in the visual system has a receptive field, an area of the visual field to which it is connected. Light in the receptive field excites or inhibits the neuron depending on the light's location, wavelength, movement, and so forth. (p. 169)
5. The mammalian vertebrate visual system has a partial division of labor. In general, the parvocellular system is specialized for perception of color and fine details; the magnocellular system is specialized for perception of depth, movement, and overall patterns. (p. 170)
6. Area V1 is apparently essential to conscious visual perception. Without it, people report no vision, even in dreams. However, some kinds of response to light (blindsight) can occur after damage to V1, despite the lack of conscious perception. (p. 171)

7. The ventral stream in the cortex is important for shape perception ("what"), and the dorsal stream is specialized for localizing visual perceptions and integrating them with action ("where"). (p. 172)
8. Within the primary visual cortex, neuroscientists distinguish simple cells, which have fixed excitatory and inhibitory fields, and complex cells, which respond to a light pattern of a particular shape regardless of its exact location. (p. 173)
9. Neurons sensitive to shapes or other visual aspects may or may not act as feature detectors. In particular, cells of area V1 are highly responsive to spatial frequencies, even though we are not subjectively aware of spatial frequencies in our visual perception. (p. 175)
10. Specialized kinds of visual loss can follow brain damage. For example, after damage to the fusiform gyrus of the temporal cortex, people have trouble recognizing faces. (p. 176)
11. The visual cortex is specialized to detect visual motion and to distinguish it from apparent changes due to head movement. The visual cortex becomes less responsive during quick eye movements. (p. 179)
12. When two or more objects are present in the visual field, attention to one of them is related to increased cortical response to that object and decreased response to other objects. (p. 181)

Answers to STOP & CHECK Questions

1. It starts with the ganglion cells in the eye. Most of its axons go to the lateral geniculate nucleus of the thalamus; some go to the hypothalamus, superior colliculus, and elsewhere. (p. 166)
2. The receptor excites both the bipolar cells and the horizontal cell. The horizontal cell inhibits the same bipolar cell that was excited plus additional bipolar cells in the surround. (p. 169)
3. It produces more excitation than inhibition for the nearest bipolar cell. For surrounding bipolar cells, it produces only inhibition. The reason is that the receptor excites a horizontal cell, which inhibits all bipolar cells in the area. (p. 169)
4. In the parts of your retina that look at the long white arms, each neuron is maximally inhibited by input on two of its sides (either above and below or left and right). In the crossroads, each neuron is maximally inhibited by input on all four sides. Therefore, the response in the crossroads is decreased compared to that in the arms. (p. 169)
5. They become larger because each cell's receptive field is made by inputs converging at an earlier level. (p. 172)
6. Neurons of the parvocellular system have small cell bodies with small receptive fields, are located mostly in and near the fovea, and are specialized for detailed and color vision. Neurons of the magnocellular system have large cell bodies with large receptive fields, are located in all parts of the retina, and are specialized for perception of large patterns and movement. (p. 172)
7. Researchers could use fMRI, EEG, or other recording methods to see whether activity was high in your primary visual cortex. (p. 172)
8. In blindsight, someone can point toward an object or move the eyes toward the object, despite insisting that he or she sees nothing. (p. 172)
9. The inability to guide movement based on vision implies damage to the dorsal path. (p. 172)
10. First identify a stimulus, such as a horizontal line, that stimulates the cell. Then shine the stimulus at several points in the cell's receptive field. If the cell responds only in one location, it is a simple cell. If it responds in several locations, it is a complex cell. (p. 179)
11. Prosopagnosia is the inability to recognize faces. Its existence implies that the cortical mechanism for identifying faces is different from the mechanism for identifying other complex stimuli. (p. 179)
12. Vision during quick eye movements is sure to be blurry. Besides, suppressing vision during saccades may help us distinguish between changes due to eye movements and those due to movements of object. (p. 181)
13. Damage in area MT can produce motion blindness. If area MT is intact but area V1 is damaged, the person may be able to report motion direction, despite no conscious identification of the moving object. (p. 181)

Thought Question

After a receptor cell is stimulated, the bipolar cell receiving input from it shows an immediate strong response. A fraction of a second later, the bipolar's response decreases, even though the stimulation from the receptor cell remains constant. How can you account for that decrease? (Hint: What does the horizontal cell do?)

Module 6.3 Development of Vision

Suppose you had lived all your life in the dark. Then today, for the first time, you came out into the light and looked around. Would you understand anything?

Unless you were born blind, you did have this experience—on the day you were born. At first, presumably you had no idea what you were looking at. Within months, however, you were beginning to recognize faces and crawl toward your favorite toys. How did you learn to make sense of what you saw?

Infant Vision

When cartoonists show an infant character, they draw the eyes large in proportion to the head. Infant eyes approach full size sooner than the rest of the head does. Even a newborn has some functional vision, although much remains to develop.

Attention to Faces and Face Recognition

Human newborns come into the world predisposed to pay more attention to some stimuli than others. Even in the first 2 days, they spend more time looking at faces than at other stationary displays (Figure 6.31). That tendency is interesting, as it supports the idea of a built-in "face recognition module," presumably centered in the fusiform gyrus (see p. 178). However, the infant's concept of "face" is not clearly developed. Experimenters recorded infants' times of gazing at one face or the other, as shown in Figure 6.32. Newborns showed a strong preference for a right-side-up face over an upside-down face, regardless of whether the face was realistic (left pair) or badly distorted (central pair). When confronted with two right-side-up faces (right pair), they showed no significant preference between a realistic one and a distorted one (Cassia, Turati, & Simion, 2004). Evidently, a newborn's concept of "face" is not well developed, except that it requires most of its content (e.g., eyes) to be on top.

Of course, a person gradually becomes more and more adept at recognizing faces. Some day you may go to a high school reunion and quickly recognize people you haven't seen in decades, in spite of the fact that they have grown older, gained or lost weight (mostly gained), changed their hair style or gone bald, and so forth. Artificial intelligence specialists have been trying to build machines that would be equally good at recognizing faces but have found the task to be stunningly difficult.

Face recognition improves with practice early in life. For example, most adults are poor at recognizing monkey faces, but infants who get frequent practice at it between ages 6 and 9 months develop much better ability to recognize monkey faces (Pascalis et al., 2005).

Visual Attention and Motor Control

The ability to control visual attention develops gradually. A highly attractive display, such as twirling dots on a computer screen, can capture an infant's gaze and hold it, sometimes until the infant starts to cry (M. H. Johnson, Posner, & Rothbart, 1991). From about 4 to 6 months, infants can look away from the display briefly but then they shift back to it (Clohessy, Posner, Rothbart, & Veccra, 1991). Not until about age 6 months can an infant shift visual attention from one object to another.

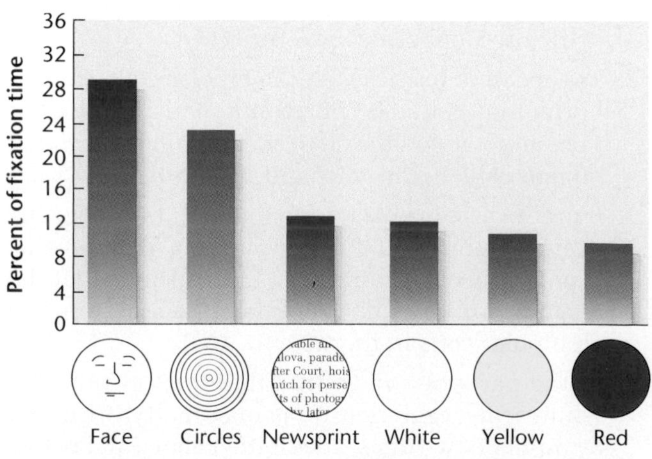

Figure 6.31 Amount of time infants spend looking at various patterns
Even in the first 2 days after birth, infants look more at faces than at most other stimuli. *(Source: Based on Fantz, 1963)*

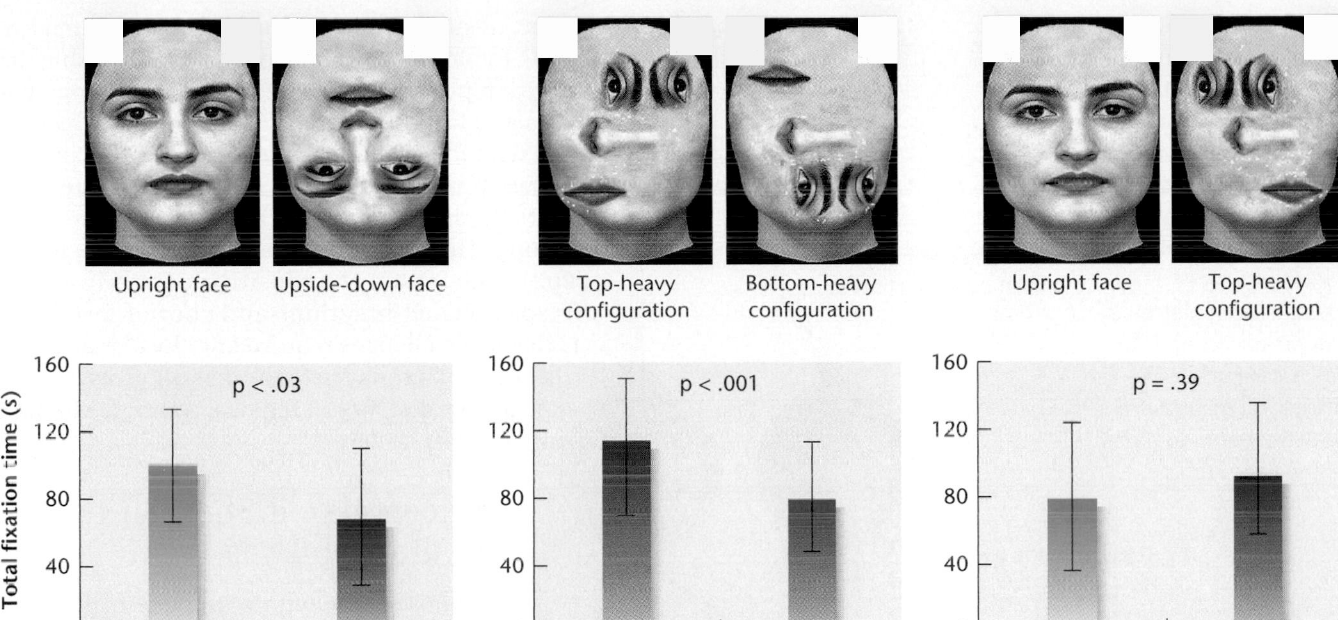

Figure 6.32 How infants divided their attention between two faces

A right-side-up face drew more attention than an upside-down one, regardless of whether the faces were realistic (left pair) or distorted (central pair). They divided their attention about equally between two right-side-up faces (right pair), even though one was realistic and the other was distorted. *(Source: From "Can a nonspecific bias toward top-heavy patterns explain newborns' face preference?" by V. M. Cassia, C. Turati, & F. Simion, 2004.* Psychological Science, *15, 379–383.)*

Here is a fascinating demonstration that combines visual attention with motor control: Hold one hand to the left of a child's head and the other hand to the right. Tell the child that when you wiggle a finger of one hand, he or she should look at the *other* hand. Before about age 5 or 6 years, most children find it almost impossible to ignore the wiggling finger and to look at the other one. Ability to perform this task smoothly develops gradually all the way to age 18, requiring areas of the prefrontal cortex that mature slowly. Even some adults—especially those with neurological or psychiatric disorders—have trouble on this task (Munoz & Everling, 2004).

To examine visual development in more detail, investigators turn to studies of animals. The research in this area has greatly expanded our understanding of brain development and has helped alleviate certain human abnormalities.

Early Experience and Visual Development

Developing axons of the visual system approach their targets by following chemical gradients, as discussed in Chapter 5. In a newborn mammal, the lateral geniculate and visual cortex already resemble an adult's (Gödecke & Bonhoeffer, 1996; Horton & Hocking, 1996), and many of the normal properties develop even for animals with retinal damage (Rakic & Lidow, 1995; Shatz, 1996) or those reared in complete darkness (Lein & Shatz, 2001; White, Coppola, & Fitzpatrick, 2001). However, without normal visual experience, those properties deteriorate. The visual system can mature to a certain point without experience, but it needs visual experience to maintain and fine-tune its connections.

Early Lack of Stimulation of One Eye

What would happen if a young animal could see with one eye but not the other? For cats and primates—which have both eyes pointed in the same direction—most neurons in the visual cortex receive **binocular input** (stimulation from both eyes). As soon as a kitten opens its eyes at about age 9 days, each neuron responds to approximately corresponding areas in the two retinas—that is, areas that focus on about the same point in space (Figure 6.33).

If an experimenter sutures one eyelid shut for a kitten's first 4 to 6 weeks of life, synapses in the visual cortex gradually become unresponsive to input from the deprived eye (Rittenhouse, Shouval, Paradiso, & Bear, 1999). Consequently, even after the deprived eye is opened, the kitten does not respond to it (Wiesel, 1982; Wiesel & Hubel, 1963).

Figure 6.33 The anatomical basis for binocular vision in cats and primates
Light from a point in the visual field strikes points in each retina. Those two retinal areas send their axons to separate layers of the lateral geniculate, which in turn send axons to a single cell in the visual cortex. That cell is connected (via the lateral geniculate) to corresponding areas of the two retinas.

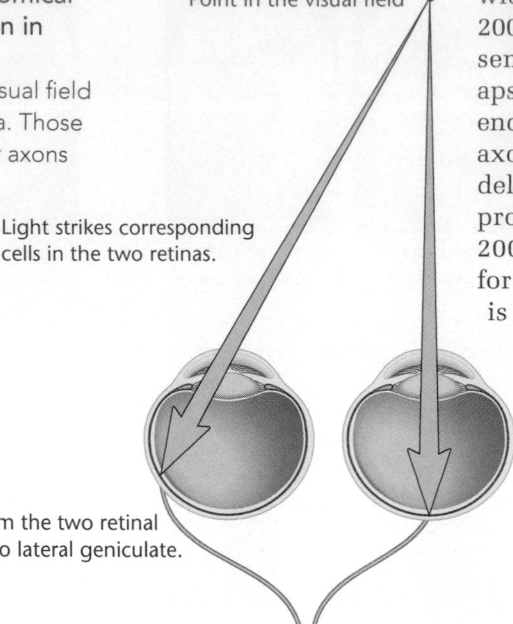

Early Lack of Stimulation of Both Eyes

If *both* eyes are kept shut for the first few weeks, we might expect the kitten to become blind in both eyes, but it does not. Evidently, when one eye remains shut during early development, the active synapses from the open eye displace the inactive synapses from the closed eye. If neither eye is active, no axon displaces any other. For at least 3 weeks, the kitten's cortex remains normally responsive to both eyes. If the eyes remain shut still longer, the cortical responses become sluggish and lose their crisp, sharp receptive fields (Crair, Gillespie, & Stryker, 1998). That is, they respond to visual stimuli, but not much more strongly to one orientation than to another.

Because the effects of abnormal experiences on cortical development depend on age, researchers identify a **sensitive period** or **critical period**, when experiences have a particularly strong and long-lasting influence. The length of the sensitive period varies from one species to another and from one aspect of vision to another (Crair & Malenka, 1995; T. L. Lewis & Maurer, 2005). It lasts longer during complete visual deprivation—for example, if a kitten is kept in total darkness—than in the presence of limited experience (Kirkwood, Lee, & Bear, 1995). The critical period begins when GABA, the brain's main inhibitory transmitter, becomes widely available in the cortex (Fagiolini & Hensch, 2000). Evidently, the changes that occur during the sensitive period require excitation of some synapses and inhibition of others. The critical period ends with the onset of some chemicals that inhibit axonal sprouting. Rearing an animal in the dark delays the spread of these chemicals and therefore prolongs the sensitive period (Pizzorusso et al., 2002). One reason the sensitive period is longer for some visual functions and shorter for others is that some changes require only local rearrangements of axons instead of axon growth over greater distances (Tagawa, Kanold, Majdan, & Shatz, 2005).

Uncorrelated Stimulation in the Two Eyes

Almost every neuron in the human visual cortex responds to approximately corresponding areas of both eyes. (The exception: A few cortical neurons respond to only what the left eye sees at the extreme left or what the right eye sees at the extreme right.) By comparing the slightly different inputs from the two eyes, you achieve stereoscopic depth perception, a powerful method of perceiving distance.

Stereoscopic depth perception requires the brain to detect **retinal disparity,** the discrepancy between what the left eye sees and what the right eye sees. But how do cortical neurons adjust their connections to detect retinal disparity? Genetic instructions could not provide enough information; different individuals have slightly different head sizes, and the genes cannot predict how far apart the two eyes will be. The fine-tuning of binocular vision must depend on experience.

And indeed, it does. Suppose an experimenter sets up a procedure in which a kitten can see with the left eye one day, the right eye the next day, and so forth. The kitten therefore receives the same amount of stimulation in both eyes, but it never sees with both eyes at the same time. After several weeks, almost every neuron in the visual cortex responds to one eye or the other but not both. The kitten therefore cannot detect retinal disparities and has no stereoscopic depth perception.

Similarly, suppose a kitten has weak or damaged eye muscles, and its eyes cannot focus in the same direction at the same time. Both eyes are active simultaneously, but no cortical neuron consistently gets a message from both eyes at the same time. Again, the result is that each neuron in the visual cortex becomes fully responsive to one eye, ignoring the other (Blake & Hirsch, 1975; Hubel & Wiesel, 1965).

A similar phenomenon occurs in humans. Certain children are born with **strabismus** (or **strabismic amblyopia**), a condition in which the eyes do not point in the same direction. Such children do not develop stereoscopic depth perception; they perceive depth no better with two eyes than they do with one.

The apparent mechanism is that each cortical cell increases its responsiveness to groups of axons with synchronized activity (Singer, 1986). For example, if a portion of the left retina frequently focuses on the same object as some portion of the right eye, then axons from those two retinal areas frequently carry synchronous messages, and a cortical cell strengthens its synapses with both axons. However, if the two eyes carry unrelated inputs, the cortical cell strengthens its synapses with axons from only one eye (usually the contralateral one).

Restoration of Response After Early Deprivation of Vision

After the cortical neurons have become insensitive to the inactive eye, can experience restore their sensitivity? Yes, if the restorative experience comes soon enough. If a kitten is deprived of vision in one eye for a few days during the sensitive period (losing sensitivity to light in that eye) and then receives normal experience with both eyes, it rapidly regains sensitivity to the deprived eye. However, in the long run, it recovers better if it goes through a few days with the opposite eye deprived of vision (Mitchell, Gingras, & Kind, 2001). Evidently, the deprived eye regains more cortical functioning if it doesn't have to overcome a competitor.

This animal research relates to the human condition called **lazy eye**, a result of strabismus or amblyopia, in which a child fails to attend to the vision in one eye. The animal results imply that the best way to facilitate normal vision in the ignored eye is to prevent the child from using the active eye. A physician puts a patch over the active eye, and the child gradually increases his or her attention to vision in the previously ignored eye. Eventually, the child is permitted to use both eyes together. The patch is most effective if it begins early, although humans do not appear to have a sharply defined critical period. That is, the division between "early enough" and "too late" is gradual, not sudden (T. L. Lewis & Maurer, 2005).

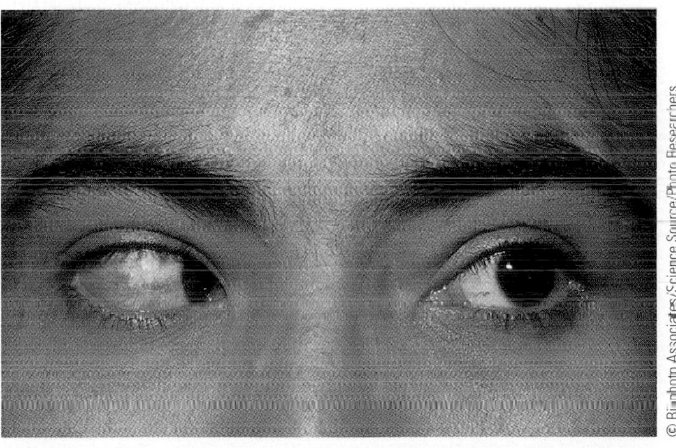
© Biophoto Associates/Science Source/Photo Researchers

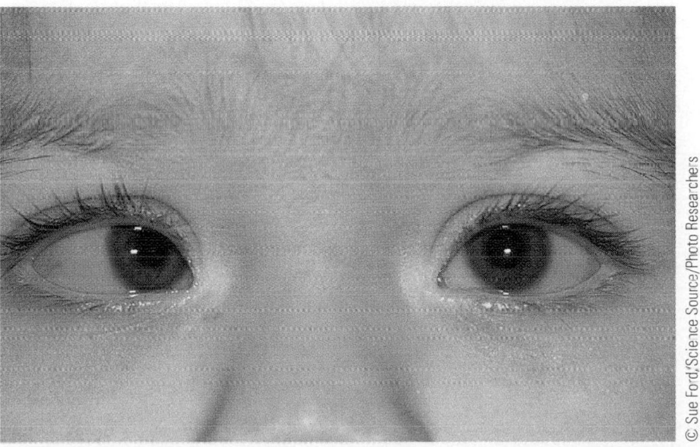
© Sue Ford/Science Source/Photo Researchers

Two examples of "lazy eye."

STOP & CHECK

1. How is vision affected by closing one eye early in life? What are the effects of closing both eyes?
2. What is "lazy eye" and how can it be treated?
3. What early experience is necessary to maintain binocular input to the neurons of the visual cortex?

Check your answers on page 191.

Early Exposure to a Limited Array of Patterns

If a kitten spends its entire early sensitive period wearing goggles with horizontal lines painted on them (Figure 6.34), nearly all its visual cortex cells become responsive only to horizontal lines (Stryker & Sherk, 1975; Stryker, Sherk, Leventhal, & Hirsch, 1978). Even after months of later normal experience, the cat does not respond to vertical lines (D. E. Mitchell, 1980).

What happens if human infants are exposed mainly to vertical or horizontal lines instead of both equally? You might wonder how such a bizarre thing could happen. No parents would let an experimenter subject their child to such a procedure, and it never happens accidentally in nature. Right?

Wrong. In fact, it probably happened to you! About 70% of all infants have **astigmatism**, a blurring of vision for lines in one direction (e.g., horizontal, vertical, or one of the diagonals). Astigmatism is caused by an asymmetric curvature of the eyes (Howland & Sayles, 1984). The prevalence of astigmatism declines to about 10% in 4-year-old children as a result of normal growth.

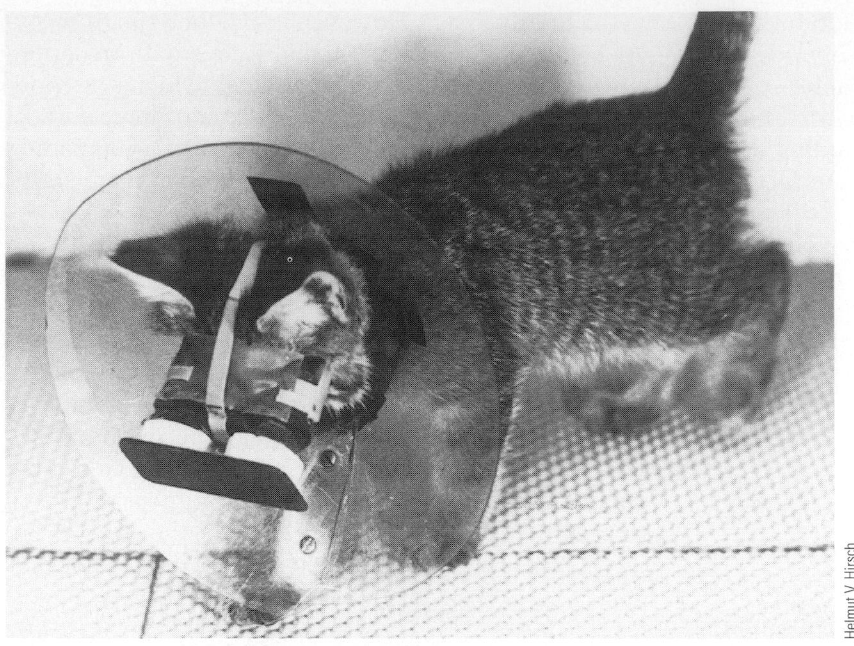

Figure 6.34 Procedure for restricting a kitten's visual experience during early development

For a few hours a day, the kitten wears goggles that show just one stimulus, such as horizontal stripes or diagonal stripes. For the rest of the day, the kitten stays with its mother in a dark room without the mask.

If your eyes had strong astigmatism during the sensitive period for the development of your visual cortex, you saw lines more clearly in one direction than in another direction. If your astigmatism was not corrected early, then the cells of your visual cortex probably became more responsive to the kind of lines you saw more clearly, and you will continue throughout life to see lines in other directions as slightly faint or blurry, even if your eyes are now perfectly spherical (Freedman & Thibos, 1975). However, if you began wearing corrective lenses before age 3 to 4 years, you thereby improved your adult vision (Friedburg & Klöppel, 1996). The moral of the story: Children should be tested for astigmatism early and given corrective lenses as soon as possible.

You can informally test yourself for astigmatism with Figure 6.35. Do the lines in some directions look faint or fuzzy? If so, rotate the page. You will notice that the appearance of the lines depends on their position. If you wear corrective lenses, try this demonstration with and without them. If you see a difference in the lines only without your lenses, then the lenses have corrected your astigmatism.

Figure 6.35 An informal test for astigmatism

Do the lines in one direction look darker or sharper than the other lines do? If so, notice what happens when you rotate either the page or your head. The lines really are identical; certain lines appear darker or sharper because of the shape of your eye. If you wear corrective lenses, try this demonstration both with and without your lenses.

Adults' cortical neurons can also change in response to altered visual experience, but the effects are smaller. If an adult mammal is trained to respond to a particular stimulus, some of its visual neurons become more responsive to that stimulus and less responsive to other stimuli (Drăgoi, Rivadulla, & Sur, 2001; Schoups, Vogels, Qian, & Orban, 2001). In short, the cortex develops specializations for dealing with the patterns it encounters most often.

What happens if kittens grow up without seeing anything move? You can imagine the difficulty of arranging such a world; the kitten's head would move, even if nothing else did. Max Cynader and Garry Chernenko (1976) used an ingenious procedure: They raised kittens in an environment illuminated only by a strobe light that flashed eight times a second for 10 microseconds each. In effect, the kittens saw a series of still photographs. After 4 to 6 months, each neuron in the visual cortex responded normally to shapes but not to moving stimuli. The kittens had become motion blind.

People with Vision Restored After Early Deprivation

What about humans? If someone were born completely blind and got to see years later, would the new vision make any sense? No cases quite like that have occurred, but several cases approximate it. Some humans become visually impaired because of *cataracts*—cloudy areas on the lenses. Although cataracts can be removed surgically, the delay before removal varies, and therefore, some people have a longer or shorter history of limited vision.

In one study, investigators examined 14 people who had been born with cataracts in both eyes but had them repaired at ages 2–6 months. Although they all eventually developed nearly normal vision, they had lingering problems in subtle regards. For example, for the faces shown in Figure 6.36, they had no trouble detecting the difference between the two lower faces, which have different eyes and mouth, but had trouble detecting any difference between the two upper faces, which differ in the spacing between the eyes or between the eyes and the mouth (Le Grand, Mondloch, Maurer, & Brent, 2001).

We might imagine that an early cataract on just one eye would not pose a problem, but it does if it is on the left eye. Remember from p. 178 that prosopagnosia is linked most strongly to damage to the fusiform gyrus in the right hemisphere. Apparently, the right hemisphere needs early experience to develop its particular expertise at face recognition.

(a)

(b)

Le Grand, et al., 2001

Figure 6.36 Faces that differ only in the eyes and mouth
The two upper faces **(a)** have the same eyes and mouth but in slightly different locations. The lower faces **(b)** have different eyes and mouth. People who had cataracts for the first few months of life detect the difference between the faces in **(b)** but have trouble detecting the difference in **(a).** Evidently, the early visual deprivation left deficits that could not be fully remedied by later experience.

In an adult, a cataract on just one eye would not affect one hemisphere much more than the other because each hemisphere receives input from both eyes:

However, during early infancy, the crossed pathways from the two eyes develop faster than the uncrossed pathways:

Consequently, each hemisphere gets its input almost entirely from the contralateral eye. Furthermore, the corpus callosum is immature in infancy, so information reaching one hemisphere does not cross to the other. In short, an infant with a left eye cataract has limited visual input to the right hemisphere. Researchers examined people who had left eye cataracts during the first few months of infancy. When they were tested at ages 8–29 years, they continued to show mild impairments in face recognition. For example, when confronted with a pair of photos like those in Figure 6.36a, they had difficulty determining whether two photos were "the same" or "different" (Le Grand, Mondloch, Maurer, & Brent, 2003). In short, good face recognition depends on practice and experience by the right hemisphere early in life.

The impairment is more extreme if the cataracts remain until later in life. Patient PD developed cataracts at approximately age 1½ years. His physician treated him with eye drops to dilate the pupils wide enough to "see around" the cataracts, with limited success. After removal of his cataracts at age 43, his ability to perceive detail improved quickly but never reached normal levels. Evidently, all those years without detailed pattern vision had made his cortical cells less able to respond sharply to patterns (Fine, Smallman, Doyle, & MacLeod, 2002). He remarked that the edges between one object and another were exaggerated. For example, where a white object met a dark one, the border of the white object looked extremely bright and the edge of the dark one looked extremely dark—suggesting lateral inhibition well beyond what most people experience. He was amazed by the strong emotional expressions on people's faces. He had been able to see faces before but not in so much detail. He was also struck by the brightness of colors. "In fact, it made me kind of angry that people were walking around in this colorful world that I had never had access to" (Fine et al., 2002, p. 208).

A more extreme case is patient MM. When he was 3½, hot corrosive chemicals splashed on his face, destroying one eye and obliterating the cornea of the other. For the next 40 years, he could see only light and dark through the surviving eye, with no patterns. He had no visual memories or visual imagery. At age 43, he received a corneal transplant. Immediately, he could identify simple shapes such as a square, detect whether a bar was tilted or upright, state the direction of a moving object, and identify which of two objects is "in front." These aspects of vision were evidently well established by age 3½ and capable of emerging again without practice (Fine et al., 2003). However, his perception of detail was poor and did not improve. Because his retina was normal, the failure to develop detail perception implied a limitation in his visual cortex. Over the next 2 years, he improved in his ability to understand what he was seeing but only to a limited extent. Prior to the operation, he had competed as a blind skier. (Blind contestants memorize the hills.) Immediately after the operation, he found all the sights frightening as he skied, so he deliberately closed his eyes while skiing! After 2 years, he found vision somewhat helpful on the easy slopes, but he still closed his eyes on the difficult slopes, where vision was still more frightening than helpful. He summarized his progress, "The difference between today and over two years ago is that I can guess better what I am seeing. What is the same is that I am still guessing" (Fine et al., 2003, p. 916).

What can we conclude? In humans as in cats and other species, the visual cortex is more plastic in infancy than in adulthood. A few aspects of vision, such as motion perception, are well established early and continue to function after decades without further experience. However, detail perception suffers and cannot recover much. The kinds of visual expertise that most of us take for granted depend on years of practice.

STOP & CHECK

4. Why does a cataract on one eye produce greater visual impairments in infants than in adults?

Check your answer on page 191.

Module 6.3
In Closing: The Nature and Nurture of Vision

The nature–nurture issue arises in one disguise or another in almost every area of psychology. In vision, consider what happens when you look out your window. How do you know that what you see are trees, people, and buildings? In fact, how do you know they are objects? How do you know which objects are close and which are distant? Were you born knowing how to interpret what you see or did you have to learn to understand it? The main message of this module is that vision requires a complex mixture of nature and nurture. We are indeed born with a certain amount of understanding, but we need experience to maintain, improve, and refine it. As usual, the influences of heredity and environment are not fully separable.

Summary

1. Even newborn infants gaze longer at faces than other stationary objects. However, they are as responsive to distorted as to realistic faces, provided

the eyes are on top. Patterned visual experience early in life, especially by the right hemisphere, is necessary to develop good face recognition. (p. 184)

2. For the first few months, infants have trouble shifting their gaze away from a captivating stimulus. For years, children have trouble shifting their attention away from a moving object toward an unmoving one. (p. 184)
3. The cells in the visual cortex of infant kittens have nearly normal properties. However, experience is necessary to maintain and fine-tune vision. For example, if a kitten has sight in one eye and not in the other during the early sensitive period, its cortical neurons become responsive only to the open eye. (p. 185)
4. Cortical neurons become unresponsive to axons from the inactive eye mainly because of competition from the active eye. If both eyes are closed, cortical cells remain somewhat responsive to axons from both eyes, although that response becomes sluggish and unselective as the weeks of deprivation continue. (p. 186)
5. To develop good stereoscopic depth perception, kittens must have experience seeing the same object with corresponding portions of the two eyes early in life. Otherwise, each neuron in the visual cortex becomes responsive to input from just one eye. (p. 186)
6. Abnormal visual experience has a stronger effect during an early sensitive period than later in life. The sensitive period begins when sufficient GABA levels become available in the visual cortex. It ends with the onset of chemicals that slow axonal growth. (p. 186)
7. If cortical cells have become unresponsive to an eye because it was inactive during the early sensitive period, normal visual experience later does not restore normal responsiveness. However, prolonged closure of the previously active eye can increase the response to the previously inactive eye. (p. 187)
8. If a kitten sees only horizontal or vertical lines during its sensitive period, most of the neurons in its visual cortex become responsive to such lines only. For the same reason, a young child who has a strong astigmatism may have permanently decreased responsiveness to one kind of line or another. (p. 187)
9. Those who do not see motion early in life lose their ability to see it. (p. 188)
10. Some people have cataracts or other impediments to vision during infancy or childhood and then, after surgery, regain vision in adulthood. Visual impairment for the first few months leaves subtle visual deficits that evidently last throughout life. Someone who had vision, lost it in childhood, and then regained it decades later shows retention of some aspects of vision (e.g., motion perception) but loss of detail and many other aspects of vision. (p. 188)

Answers to STOP & CHECK Questions

1. If one eye is closed during early development, the cortex becomes unresponsive to it. If both eyes are closed, cortical cells remain somewhat responsive to both eyes for several weeks and then gradually become sluggish and unselective in their responses. (p. 187)
2. "Lazy eye" is inattentiveness to one eye, in most cases an eye that does not move in conjunction with the active eye. It can be treated by closing or patching over the active eye, forcing the child to use the ignored eye. (p. 187)
3. To maintain binocular responsiveness, cortical cells must receive simultaneous activity from both eyes fixating on the same object at the same time. (p. 187)
4. First, infants' brains are more plastic; an adult's brain is already fairly set and resists change in the event of distorted or deficient input. Furthermore, in the infant brain, each hemisphere gets nearly all its visual input from its contralateral eye. The crossed paths from the eyes to the hemispheres are more mature than the uncrossed paths, and the corpus callosum is immature. (p. 190)

Thought Questions

1. A rabbit's eyes are on the sides of its head instead of in front. Would you expect rabbits to have many cells with binocular receptive fields—that is, cells that respond to both eyes? Why or why not?
2. Would you expect the cortical cells of a rabbit to be just as sensitive to the effects of experience as are the cells of cats and primates? Why or why not?

Chapter Ending

Key Terms and Activities

Terms

astigmatism (p. 187)
binocular input (p. 185)
bipolar cell (p. 153)
blind spot (p. 154)
blindsight (p. 171)
color constancy (p. 161)
color vision deficiency (p. 163)
complex cell (p. 173)
cone (p. 156)
dorsal stream (p. 172)
end-stopped cell (p. 174)
feature detector (p. 175)
fovea (p. 155)
ganglion cell (p. 153)
horizontal cell (p. 166)
hypercomplex cell (p. 174)
inferior temporal cortex (p. 176)
koniocellular neuron (p. 170)
lateral geniculate nucleus (p. 166)
lateral inhibition (p. 169)
law of specific nerve energies (p. 152)
lazy eye (p. 187)
magnocellular neuron (p. 170)
midget ganglion cell (p. 155)
motion blindness (p. 181)
MST (p. 179)
MT (or area V5) (p. 179)
negative color afterimage (p. 160)
opponent-process theory (p. 160)
optic nerve (p. 154)
parvocellular neuron (p. 170)
photopigment (p. 156)
primary visual cortex (or area V1) (p. 171)
prosopagnosia (p. 178)
psychophysical observations (p. 158)
pupil (p. 153)
receptive field (p. 169)
receptor potential (p. 152)
retina (p. 153)
retinal disparity (p. 186)
retinex theory (p. 161)
rod (p. 156)
saccade (p. 181)
secondary visual cortex (or area V2) (p. 171)
sensitive period (or critical period) (p. 186)
shape constancy (p. 177)
simple cell (p. 173)
stereoscopic depth perception (p. 179)
strabismus (or *strabismic amblyopia)* (p. 186)
trichromatic theory (or Young-Helmholtz theory) (p. 158)
ventral stream (p. 172)
visual agnosia (p. 177)
visual field (p. 159)

Suggestions for Further Reading

Chalupa, L. M., & Werner, J. S. (Eds.). (2004). *The visual neurosciences.* Cambridge, MA: MIT Press. A collection of 114 chapters detailing research on nearly all aspects of vision.

Purves, D., & Lotto, R. B. (2003). *Why we see what we do: An empirical theory of vision.* Sunderland, MA: Sinauer Associates. Discussion of how our perception of color, size, and other visual qualities depends on our previous experience with objects and not just on the light striking the retina.

Websites to Explore

You can go to the Biological Psychology Study Center and click these links. While there, you can also check for suggested articles available on InfoTrac College Edition. The Biological Psychology Internet address is:

http://psychology.wadsworth.com/book/kalatbiopsych9e/

Colorblind Home Page

http://colorvisiontesting.com/

The Primary Visual Cortex, by Matthew Schmolesky

http://webvision.med.utah.edu/VisualCortex.html#introduction

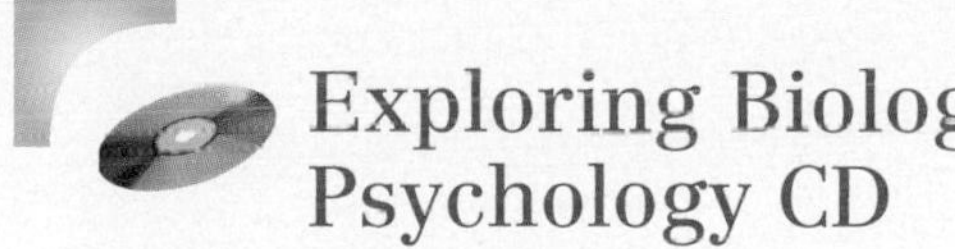

Exploring Biological Psychology CD

The Retina (animation)
Virtual Reality Eye (virtual reality)
Blind Spot (Try It Yourself)
Color Blindness in Visual Periphery (Try It Yourself)
Brightness Contrast (Try It Yourself)
Motion Aftereffect (Try It Yourself)
Visuo-Motor Control (Try It Yourself)
Critical Thinking (essay questions)
Chapter Quiz (multiple-choice questions)

ThomsonNOW™

http://www.thomsonedu.com

Go to this site for the link to ThomsonNOW, your one-stop study shop. Take a Pre-Test for this chapter, and ThomsonNOW will generate a Personalized Study Plan based on your test results. The Study Plan will identify the topics you need to review and direct you to online resources to help you master these topics. You can then take a Post Test to help you determine the concepts you have mastered and what you still need work on.

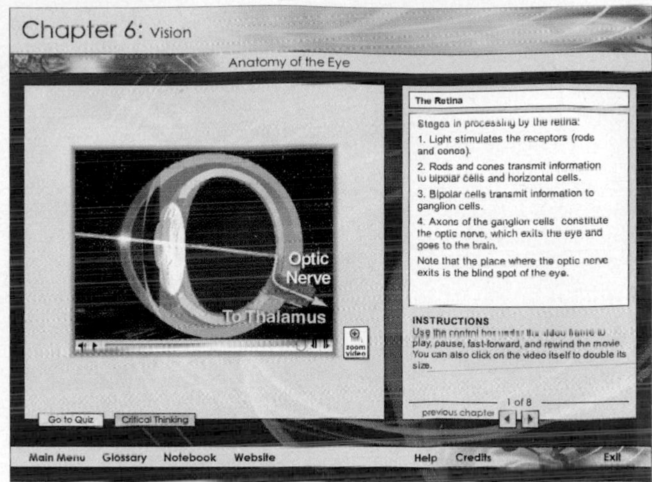

An animation of the eye shows its parts and illustrates how light excites receptors.

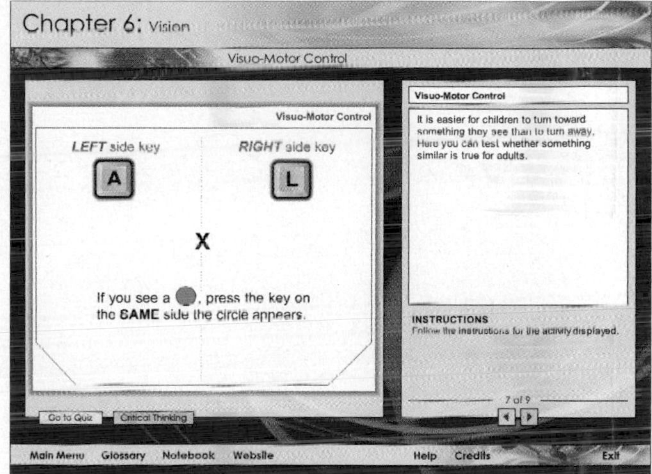

Children have trouble directing a response to the direction opposite of a stimulus. Is the same true to any extent in adulthood?

The Other Sensory Systems

7

Chapter Outline

Opposite: The sensory world of bats—which find insects by echolocation—must be very different from that of humans.
Source: Frans Lanting/Corbis

Main Ideas

1. Our senses have evolved not to give us complete information about the world but to give us information we can use.

2. Different sensory systems code information in different ways. As a rule, the activity in a single sensory axon is ambiguous by itself; its meaning depends on its relationship to a pattern across a population of axons.

According to a Native American saying, "A pine needle fell. The eagle saw it. The deer heard it. The bear smelled it" (Herrero, 1985). Different species are sensitive to different kinds of information. Bats locate insect prey by echoes from sonar waves that they emit at 20000 to 100000 hertz (Hz, cycles per second), well above the range of adult human hearing (Griffin, Webster, & Michael, 1960). Ganglion cells in a frog's eye detect small, dark, moving objects such as insects (Lettvin, Maturana, McCulloch, & Pitts, 1959). The ears of the green tree frog, *Hyla cinerea,* are highly sensitive to sounds at two frequencies—900 and 3000 Hz—prominent in the adult male's mating call (Moss & Simmons, 1986). Mosquitoes have a specialized receptor that detects the odor of human sweat—and therefore enables them to find us and bite us (Hallem, Fox, Zwiebel, & Carlson, 2004). Many biting insects also smell carbon dioxide (which is odorless to us); carbon dioxide also helps them find mammals (Grant & Kline, 2003).

Humans' visual and auditory abilities respond to a wider range of stimuli, perhaps because so many stimuli are biologically relevant to us. However, humans too have important sensory specializations. For example, our sense of taste alerts us to the bitterness of poisons (Richter, 1950; Schiffman & Erickson, 1971) but does not respond to substances such as cellulose that are neither helpful nor harmful to us. Our olfactory systems are unresponsive to gases that it would be useless for us to detect (e.g., carbon dioxide) and are highly responsive to such biologically useful stimuli as the smell of rotting meat. Thus, this chapter concerns not how our sensory systems enable us to perceive reality but how they process biologically useful information.

Module 7.1
Audition

If a tree falls in a forest where no one can hear it, does it make a sound? The answer depends on what we mean by "sound." If we define it simply as a vibration, then of course, a falling tree makes a sound. However, we usually define sound as a psychological phenomenon, a vibration that some organism hears. By that definition, a vibration is not a sound unless someone hears it.

The human auditory system enables us to hear not only falling trees but also the birds singing in the branches and the wind blowing through the leaves. Some people who are blind learn to click their heels as they walk and use the echoes to locate obstructions. Our auditory systems are amazingly well adapted for detecting and interpreting useful information.

Sound and the Ear

Sound waves are periodic compressions of air, water, or other media. When a tree falls, both the tree and the ground vibrate, setting up sound waves in the air that strike the ears. If something hit the ground on the moon, where there is no air, people would not hear it—unless they put an ear to the ground.

Physical and Psychological Dimensions of Sound

Sound waves vary in amplitude and frequency. The **amplitude** of a sound wave is its intensity. A very intense compression of air, such as that produced by a bolt of lightning, produces sound waves of great amplitude. **Loudness,** the perception of intensity, is related to amplitude but not the same as it. When a sound doubles its amplitude, its loudness increases but does not double. Many factors influence loudness; for example, a rapidly talking person sounds louder than slow music of the same physical amplitude. So if you complain that television advertisements are louder than the program, one reason is that the people in the advertisements talk faster.

The **frequency** of a sound is the number of compressions per second, measured in hertz (Hz, cycles per second). **Pitch** is a perception closely related to frequency. As a rule, the higher the frequency of a sound, the higher its pitch. Figure 7.1 illustrates the amplitude and frequency of sounds. The height of each wave corresponds to amplitude, and the number of waves per second corresponds to frequency.

Most adult humans can hear air vibrations ranging from about 15 Hz to somewhat less than 20000 Hz. Children can hear higher frequencies than adults because the ability to perceive high frequencies decreases with age and with exposure to loud noises (B. A. Schneider, Trehub, Morrongiello, & Thorpe, 1986).

Structures of the Ear

Rube Goldberg (1883–1970) drew cartoons about complicated, far-fetched inventions. For example, a person's tread on the front doorstep would pull a string that raised a cat's tail, awakening the cat, which would then chase a bird that had been resting on a balance, which would swing up to strike a doorbell. The func-

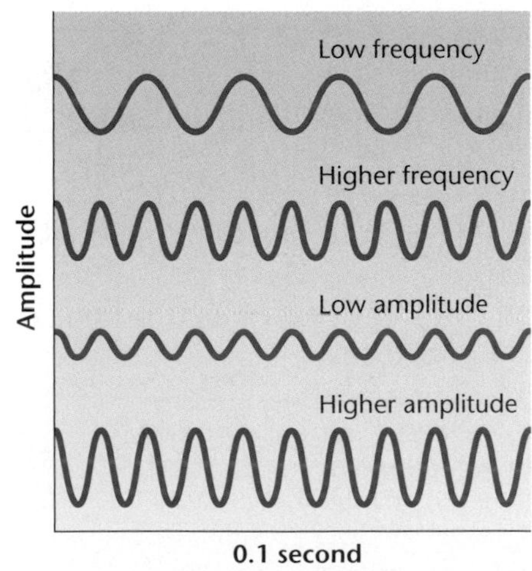

Figure 7.1 Four sound waves
The time between the peaks determines the frequency of the sound, which we experience as pitch. Here the top line represents five sound waves in 0.1 second, or 50 Hz—a very low-frequency sound that we experience as a very low pitch. The other three lines represent 100 Hz. The vertical extent of each line represents its amplitude or intensity, which we experience as loudness.

tioning of the ear may remind you of a Rube Goldberg device because sound waves are transduced into action potentials through a many-step, roundabout process. Unlike Goldberg's inventions, however, the ear actually works.

Anatomists distinguish among the outer ear, the middle ear, and the inner ear (Figure 7.2). The outer ear includes the **pinna**, the familiar structure of flesh and cartilage attached to each side of the head. By altering the reflections of sound waves, the pinna helps us locate the source of a sound. We have to learn to use that information because each person's pinna is shaped differently from anyone else's (Van Wanrooij & Van Opstal, 2005). Rabbits' large movable pinnas enable them to localize sound sources even more precisely.

After sound waves pass through the auditory canal (see Figure 7.2), they strike the **tympanic membrane**, or eardrum, in the middle ear. The tympanic membrane vibrates at the same frequency as the sound waves that strike it. The tympanic membrane is attached to three tiny bones that transmit the vibrations to the **oval window**, a membrane of the inner ear. These bones are sometimes known by their English names (hammer, anvil, and stirrup) and sometimes by their Latin names (malleus, incus, and stapes). The tympanic membrane is about 20 times larger than the footplate of the stirrup, which is connected to the oval window. As in a hydraulic pump, the vibrations of the tympanic membrane are transformed into more forceful vibrations of the smaller stirrup. The net effect of the system is to

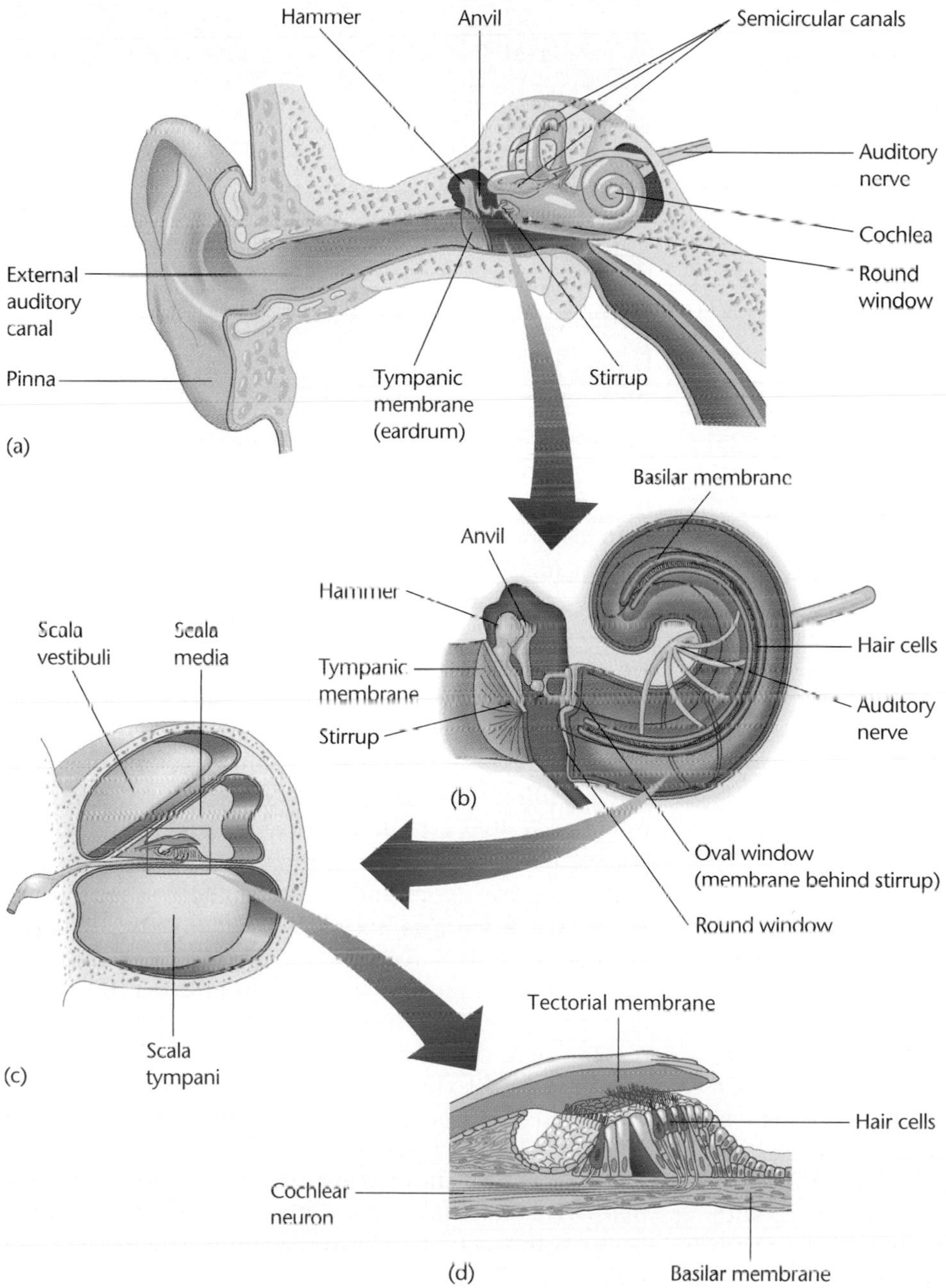

Figure 7.2 Structures of the ear
When sound waves strike the tympanic membrane in **(a)**, they cause it to vibrate three tiny bones—the hammer, anvil, and stirrup—that convert the sound waves into stronger vibrations in the fluid-filled cochlea **(b).** Those vibrations displace the hair cells along the basilar membrane in the cochlea. **(c)** A cross-section through the cochlea. **(d)** A closeup of the hair cells.

convert the sound waves into waves of greater pressure on the small oval window. This transformation is important because more force is required to move the viscous fluid behind the oval window than to move the eardrum, which has air on both sides of it.

In the inner ear is a snail-shaped structure called the **cochlea** (KOCK-lee-uh, Latin for "snail"). A cross-section through the cochlea, as in Figure 7.2c, shows three long fluid-filled tunnels: the scala vestibuli, scala media, and scala tympani. The stirrup makes the oval window vibrate at the entrance to the scala vestibuli, thereby setting in motion all the fluid in the cochlea. The auditory receptors, known as **hair cells,** lie between the basilar membrane of the cochlea on one side and the tectorial membrane on the other (Figure 7.2d). Vibrations in the fluid of the cochlea displace the hair cells. A hair cell responds within microseconds to displacements as small as 10^{-10} meter (0.1 nanometer, about the diameter of one atom), thereby opening ion channels in its membrane (Fettiplace, 1990; Hudspeth, 1985). Figure 7.3 shows electron micrographs of the hair cells of three species. The hair cells synaptically excite the cells of the auditory nerve, which is part of the eighth cranial nerve.

Figure 7.3 Hair cells from the auditory systems of three species
(a, b) Hair cells from a frog sacculus, an organ that detects ground-borne vibrations. **(c)** Hair cells from the cochlea of a cat. **(d)** Hair cells from the cochlea of a fence lizard. Kc = kinocilium, one of the components of a hair bundle.

Pitch Perception

Our ability to understand speech or enjoy music depends on our ability to differentiate among sounds of different frequencies. How do we do it?

Frequency Theory and Place Theory

According to the **frequency theory,** the basilar membrane vibrates in synchrony with a sound, causing auditory nerve axons to produce action potentials at the same frequency. For example, a sound at 50 Hz would cause 50 action potentials per second in the auditory nerve. The downfall of this theory in its simplest form is that the refractory period of a neuron is about $\frac{1}{1,000}$ second, so the maximum firing rate of a neuron is about 1 Hz, far short of the highest frequencies we hear.

According to the **place theory,** the basilar membrane resembles the strings of a piano in that each area along the membrane is tuned to a specific frequency and vibrates in its presence. (If you loudly sound one note with a tuning fork near a piano, you vibrate the piano string tuned to that note.) According to this theory, each frequency activates the hair cells at only one place along the basilar membrane, and the nervous system distinguishes among frequencies based on which neurons are activated. The downfall of this theory is that the various parts of the basilar membrane are bound together too tightly for any part to resonate like a piano string.

The current theory combines modified versions of both frequency and place theories. For low-frequency sounds (up to about 100 Hz—more than an octave below middle C in music, which is 264 Hz), the basilar membrane does vibrate in synchrony with the sound waves, in accordance with the frequency theory, and auditory nerve axons generate one action potential per wave. Weak sounds activate few neurons, whereas stronger sounds activate more. Thus, at low frequencies, the frequency of impulses identifies the pitch, and the number of firing cells identifies the loudness.

Because of the refractory period of the axon, as sounds exceed 100 Hz, it is harder and harder for a neuron to continue firing in synchrony with the sound waves. At higher frequencies, it fires on every second, third, fourth, or later wave. Its action potentials are phase-locked to the peaks of the sound waves (i.e., they occur at the same phase in the sound wave), as illustrated here:

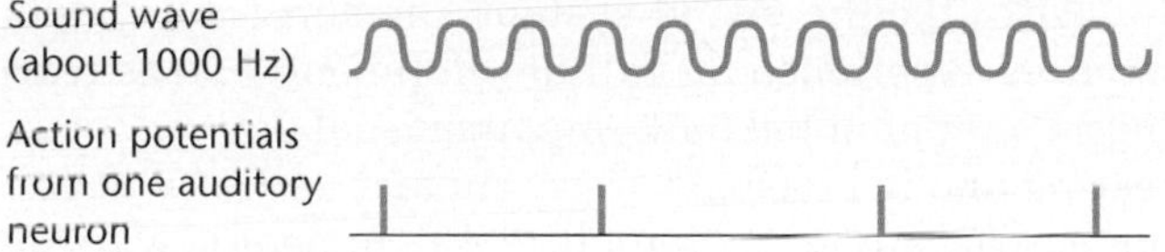

Other auditory neurons also produce action potentials that are phase locked with peaks of the sound wave, but they can be out of phase with one another:

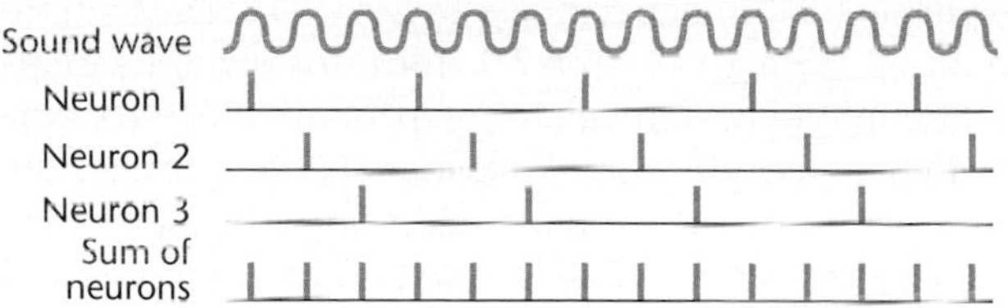

If we consider the auditory nerve as a whole, we find that with a tone of a few hundred Hz, each wave excites at least a few auditory neurons. According to the **volley principle** of pitch discrimination, the auditory nerve as a whole can have volleys of impulses up to about 4000 per second, even though no individual axon approaches that frequency by itself (Rose, Brugge, Anderson, & Hind, 1967). Beyond about 4000 Hz, even staggered volleys of impulses can't keep pace with the sound waves. Neuroscientists assume that these volleys contribute to pitch perception, although no one understands how the brain uses the information.

Most human hearing takes place below 4000 Hz, the approximate limit of the volley principle. For comparison, the highest key on a piano is 4224 Hz. Frequencies much above that level are not important in music or human speech, although they are important in the lives of rats, mice, bats, and other small animals. When we hear these very high frequencies, we use a mechanism similar to the place theory. The basilar membrane varies from stiff at its base, where the stirrup meets the cochlea, to floppy at the other end of the cochlea, the apex (von Békésy, 1956) (Figure 7.4). The hair cells along the basilar membrane have different properties based on their location, and they act as tuned resonators that vibrate only for sound waves of a particular frequency. The highest frequency sounds vibrate hair cells near the base, and lower frequency sounds vibrate hair cells farther along the membrane (Warren, 1999). Actually, the mechanisms of hearing at frequencies well over 1000 Hz are not entirely understood, as these ultra-high frequencies alter several of the properties of neurons and their membranes (Fridberger et al., 2004).

Some people are "tone deaf." The fancy term for this condition is *amusia*. Anyone who was completely insensitive to frequency differences could not understand speech because every sound we make depends on fast and slight changes in pitch. However, a substantial number of people—by one estimate, about 4%—are seriously impaired at detecting small changes in frequency, such as between C and C#. As you can imagine, they don't enjoy music (Hyde & Peretz, 2004). The explanation for this phenomenon is not known.

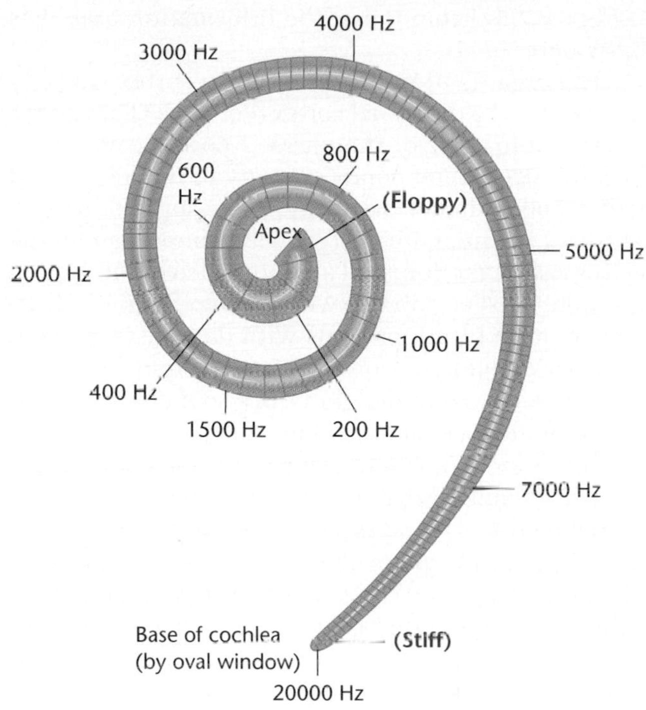

Figure 7.4 The basilar membrane of the human cochlea
High-frequency sounds excite hair cells near the base. Low-frequency sounds excite cells near the apex.

1. Through what mechanism do we perceive low-frequency sounds (up to about 100 Hz)?
2. How do we perceive middle-frequency sounds (100 to 4000 Hz)?
3. How do we perceive high-frequency sounds (above 4000 Hz)?

Check your answers on page 204.

The Auditory Cortex

Information from the auditory system passes through several subcortical structures, with a crossover in the midbrain that enables each hemisphere of the forebrain to get most of its input from the opposite ear (Glendenning, Baker, Hutson, & Masterton, 1992). The information ultimately reaches the **primary auditory cortex (area A1)** in the superior temporal cortex, as shown in Figure 7.5. From there, the information branches out widely.

The organization of the auditory cortex strongly parallels that of the visual cortex (Poremba et al., 2003). For example, part of the parietal cortex (the dorsal "where" stream) responds strongly to the location of both visual and auditory stimuli. The superior temporal cortex includes area MT, which is important for detecting visual motion, and areas that detect the motion of sounds. Just as patients with damage in area MT become motion blind, patients with damage in parts of the superior temporal cortex become motion deaf. They can hear sounds, but the source of a sound never seems to be moving (Ducommun et al., 2004).

Just as area V1 is active during visual imagery, area A1 is important for auditory imagery. In one study, people listened to several familiar and unfamiliar songs. At various points, parts of each song were replaced by 3 to 5 second gaps. When people were listening to familiar songs, they reported that they heard "in their heads" the notes or words that belonged in the gaps. That experience was accompanied by activity in area A1. During similar gaps in the unfamiliar songs, they did not hear anything "in their heads," and area A1 showed no activation (Kraemer, Macrae, Green, & Kelley, 2005).

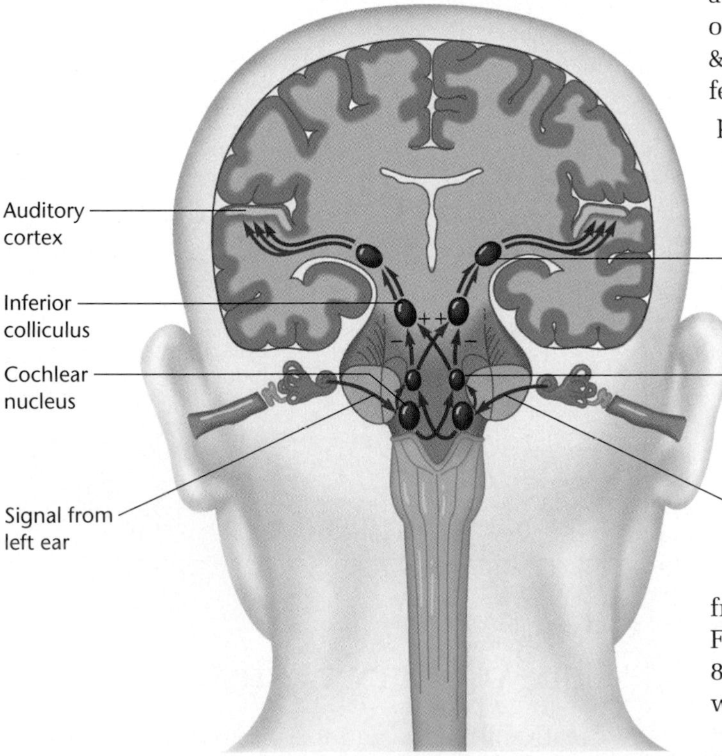

Figure 7.5 Route of auditory impulses from the receptors in the ear to the auditory cortex

The cochlear nucleus receives input from the ipsilateral ear only (the one on the same side of the head). All later stages have input originating from both ears.

Also like the visual system, the auditory system requires experience for full development. Just as rearing an animal in the dark impairs visual development, rearing one in constant noise impairs auditory development (Chang & Merzenich, 2003). In people who are deaf from birth, the axons leading from the auditory cortex develop less than in other people (Emmorey, Allen, Bruss, Schenker, & Damasio, 2003).

However, the visual and auditory systems differ in this respect: Whereas damage to area V1 leaves someone blind, damage to area A1 does not produce deafness. People with damage to the primary auditory cortex can hear simple sounds reasonably well, unless the damage extends into subcortical brain areas (Tanaka, Kamo, Yoshida, & Yamadori, 1991). Their main deficit is in the ability to recognize combinations or sequences of sounds, like music or speech. Evidently, the cortex is not necessary for all hearing, only for advanced processing of it.

When researchers record from cells in the primary auditory cortex while playing pure tones, they find that each cell has a preferred tone, as shown in Figure 7.6. Note the gradient from one area of the cortex responsive to lower tones up to areas responsive to higher and higher tones. The auditory cortex provides a kind of map of the sounds—researchers call it a *tonotopic* map.

In alert, waking animals, each cell in area A1 gives a prolonged response to its preferred sound and little or no response to other sounds (X. Wang, Lu, Snider, & Liang, 2005). However, although each cell has a preferred frequency, many cells respond better to a complex sound than to a pure tone. That is, a cell might respond when its preferred tone is the dominant one but several other tones are present also (Barbour & Wang, 2003; Griffiths, Uppenkamp, Johnsrude, Josephs, & Patterson, 2001; Wessinger et al., 2001). Most cortical cells also respond best to the kinds of sounds that capture our attention. For example, other things being equal, they respond more to an unusual sound than to one that has been repeated many times (Ulanovsky, Las, & Nelken, 2003). They also respond more strongly to a tone with its harmonics than to a single, pure frequency (Penagos, Melcher, & Oxenham, 2004). For example, for a tone of 400 Hz, the harmonics are 800 Hz, 1200 Hz, and so forth. We experience a tone with harmonics as "richer" than one without them.

Surrounding the primary auditory cortex are several additional auditory areas, in which most cells respond more to changes in sounds than to any single prolonged sound (Seifritz et al., 2002). Just as the visual system starts with cells that respond to simple lines and progresses to cells that detect faces and other complex stimuli, the same is true for the auditory system.

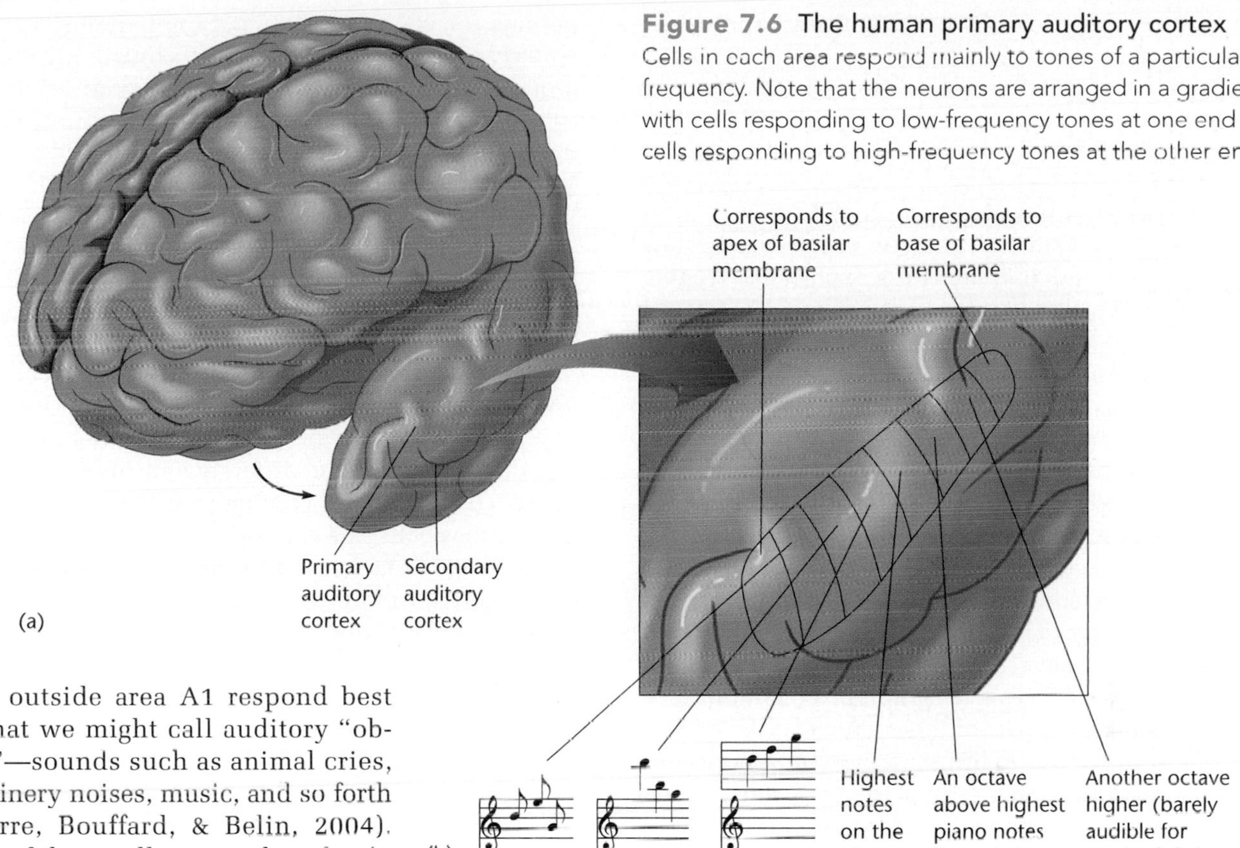

Figure 7.6 The human primary auditory cortex
Cells in each area respond mainly to tones of a particular frequency. Note that the neurons are arranged in a gradient, with cells responding to low-frequency tones at one end and cells responding to high-frequency tones at the other end.

Cells outside area A1 respond best to what we might call auditory "objects"—sounds such as animal cries, machinery noises, music, and so forth (Zatorre, Bouffard, & Belin, 2004). Many of these cells respond so slowly that they probably are not part of the initial perception of the sound itself; rather, they interpret what the sound means (Gutschalk, Patterson, Scherg, Uppenkamp, & Rupp, 2004).

STOP & CHECK

4. What is one way in which the auditory cortex is like the visual cortex?
5. What is one way in which the auditory and visual cortices differ?
6. What kinds of sounds most strongly activate the primary auditory cortex?

Check your answers on page 204.

Hearing Loss

Complete deafness is rare. About 99% of hearing-impaired people have at least some response to loud noises. We distinguish two categories of hearing impairment: conductive deafness and nerve deafness.

Conductive deafness, or **middle-ear deafness**, occurs if the bones of the middle ear fail to transmit sound waves properly to the cochlea. Such deafness can be caused by diseases, infections, or tumorous bone growth near the middle ear. Conductive deafness is sometimes temporary. If it persists, it can be corrected either by surgery or by hearing aids that amplify the stimulus. Because people with conductive deafness have a normal cochlea and auditory nerve, they hear their own voices, which can be conducted through the bones of the skull directly to the cochlea, bypassing the middle ear. Because they hear themselves clearly, they may blame others for talking too softly.

Nerve deafness, or **inner-ear deafness**, results from damage to the cochlea, the hair cells, or the auditory nerve. It can occur in any degree and may be confined to one part of the cochlea, in which case someone hears certain frequencies and not others. Hearing aids cannot compensate for extensive nerve damage, but they help people who have lost receptors in part of the cochlea. Nerve deafness can be inherited (A. Wang et al., 1998), or it can develop from a variety of prenatal problems or early childhood disorders (Cremers & van Rijn, 1991; Robillard & Gersdorff, 1986), including:

- Exposure of the mother to rubella (German measles), syphilis, or other diseases or toxins during pregnancy
- Inadequate oxygen to the brain during birth
- Deficient activity of the thyroid gland
- Certain diseases, including multiple sclerosis and meningitis

- Childhood reactions to certain drugs, including aspirin
- Repeated exposure to loud noises

Many people with nerve deafness experience **tinnitus** (tin-EYE-tus)—frequent or constant ringing in the ears. Tinnitus has also been demonstrated after nerve deafness in hamsters, and you might wonder how anyone could know that hamsters experience ringing in their ears. (They can't tell us.) Experimenters trained water-deprived hamsters to turn toward a sound to obtain water. Then they produced partial nerve deafness in one ear by exposing that ear to a very loud sound. Afterward, the hamster turned toward that ear even when no external sound was present, indicating that they heard something in that ear (Heffner & Koay, 2005).

In some cases, tinnitus is due to a phenomenon like phantom limb, discussed in Chapter 5. Recall the example in which someone has an arm amputated, and then the axons reporting facial sensations invade the brain areas previously sensitive to the arm so that stimulation of the face produces a sensation of a phantom arm. Similarly, damage to part of the cochlea is like an amputation: If the brain no longer gets its normal input, axons representing other parts of the body may invade a brain area previously responsive to sounds, especially the high-frequency sounds. Several patients have reported ringing in their ears whenever they move their jaws (Lockwood et al., 1998). Presumably, axons representing the lower face invaded their auditory cortex. Some people report a decrease in tinnitus after they start wearing hearing aids.

For practical information about coping with hearing loss, visit this website: **http://www.marky.com/hearing/**

STOP & CHECK

7. Which type of hearing loss would be more common among members of rock bands and why? For which type of hearing loss is a hearing aid generally more successful?

Check your answers on page 204.

Sound Localization

You are walking alone when suddenly you hear a loud noise. You want to know what produced it (friend or foe), but equally, you want to know where it came from (so you can approach or escape). Determining the direction and distance of a sound requires comparing the responses of the two ears—which are in effect just two points in space. And yet this system is accurate enough for you to turn almost immediately toward a sound, and for owls in the air to locate mice on the ground in the middle of the night (Konishi, 1995). You can identify a sound's direction even if it occurs just briefly and while you are turning your head (Vliegen, Van Grootel, & Van Opstal, 2004).

One cue for sound location is the difference in intensity between the ears. For high-frequency sounds, with a wavelength shorter than the width of the head, the head creates a *sound shadow* (Figure 7.7), making the sound louder for the closer ear. In adult humans, this mechanism produces accurate sound localization for frequencies above 2000 to 3000 Hz and less accurate localizations for progressively lower frequencies. Another method is the difference in *time of arrival* at the two ears. A sound coming from directly in front of you reaches both ears at once. A sound coming directly from the side reaches the closer ear about 600 microseconds (μs) before the other. Sounds coming from intermediate locations reach the two ears at delays between 0 and 600 μs. Time of arrival is most useful for localizing sounds with a sudden onset. Most birds' alarm calls increase gradually in loudness, making them difficult for a predator to localize.

A third cue is the *phase difference* between the ears. Every sound wave has phases with two consecutive peaks 360 degrees apart. Figure 7.8 shows sound waves that are in phase and 45 degrees, 90 degrees, or

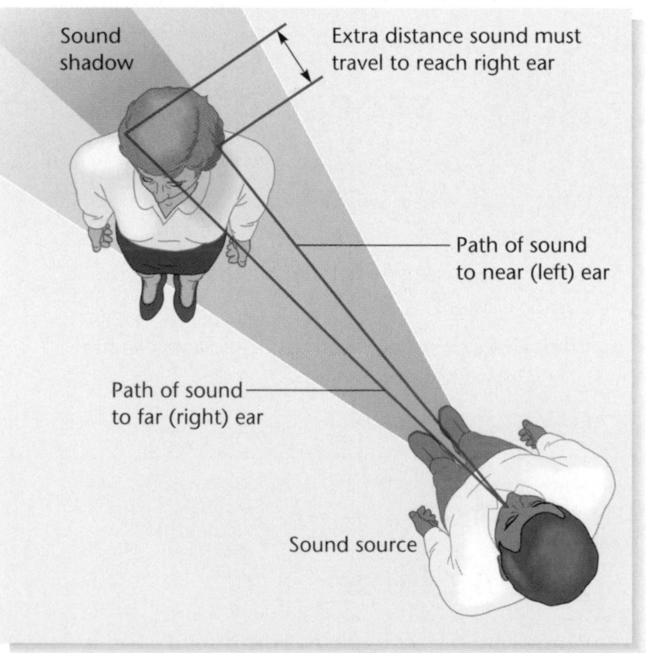

Figure 7.7 Differential loudness and arrival times as cues for sound localization
Sounds reaching the closer ear arrive sooner as well as louder because the head produces a "sound shadow."
(Source: After Lindsay & Norman, 1972)

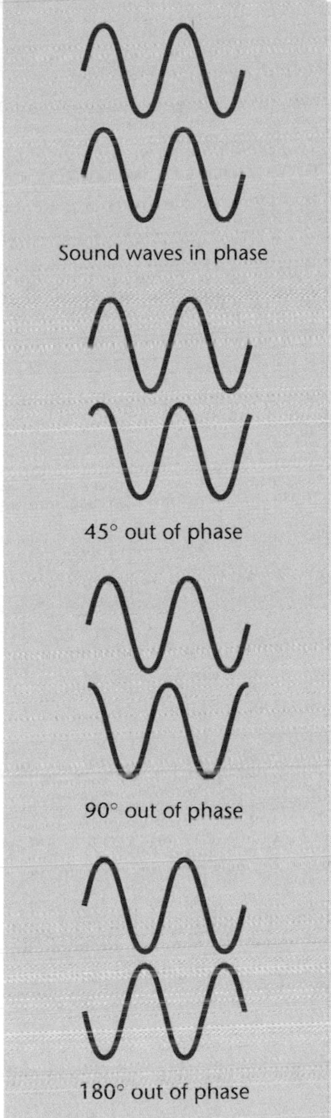

Figure 7.8 Sound waves can be in phase or out of phase

Sound waves that reach the two ears in phase are localized as coming from directly in front of (or behind) the hearer. The more out of phase the waves, the farther the sound source is from the body's midline.

180 degrees out of phase. If a sound originates to the side of the head, the sound wave strikes the two ears out of phase, as shown in Figure 7.9. How much out of phase depends on the frequency of the sound, the size of the head, and the direction of the sound. Phase differences provide information that is useful for localizing sounds with frequencies up to about 1500 Hz in humans.

In short, humans localize low frequencies by phase differences and high frequencies by loudness differences. We can localize a sound of any frequency by its time of onset if it occurs suddenly enough.

Figure 7.9 Phase differences between the ears as a cue for sound localization

A sound coming from anywhere other than straight ahead or straight behind reaches the two ears at different phases of the sound wave. The difference in phase is a signal to the sound's direction. With high-frequency sounds, the phases can become ambiguous.

What would happen if someone became deaf in one ear? At first, as you would expect, all sounds seem to come from directly to the side of the intact ear. (Obviously, that ear hears a sound louder and sooner than the other ear because the other ear doesn't hear it at all.) Eventually, however, people learn to interpret loudness cues, but only with familiar sounds in a familiar location. They infer that louder sounds come from the side of the intact ear and softer sounds come from the opposite side. Their accuracy does not match that of people with two ears, but it becomes accurate enough to be useful under some conditions (Van Wanrooij & Van Opstal, 2004).

STOP & CHECK

8. Which method of sound localization is more effective for an animal with a small head? Which is more effective for an animal with a large head? Why?

Check your answers on page 204.

Module 7.1

In Closing: Functions of Hearing

We spend much of our day listening to language, and we sometimes forget that the original, primary function of hearing has to do with simpler but extremely important issues: What do I hear? Where is it? Is it coming closer? Is it a potential mate, a potential enemy, potential food, or something irrelevant? The organization of the auditory system is well suited to resolving these questions.

Summary

1. We detect the pitch of low-frequency sounds by the frequency of action potentials in the auditory system. At intermediate frequencies, we detect volleys of responses across many receptors. We detect the pitch of the highest frequency sounds by the area of greatest response along the basilar membrane. (p. 198)
2. The auditory cortex resembles the visual cortex in many ways. Both have a "where" system in the parietal cortex and a "what" system in the temporal cortex. Both have specialized areas for detecting motion, and therefore, it is possible for a person with brain damage to be motion blind or motion deaf. The primary visual cortex is essential for visual imagery, and the primary auditory cortex is essential for auditory imagery. (p. 200)
3. Each cell in the primary auditory cortex responds best to a particular frequency of tones, although many respond better to complex tones than to a single frequency. (p. 200)
4. Cells in the auditory cortex respond most strongly to the same kinds of sounds to which we pay the most attention, such as unusual sounds and those rich in harmonics. (p. 200)
5. Areas bordering the primary auditory cortex analyze the meaning of sounds. (p. 201)
6. Deafness may result from damage to the nerve cells or to the bones that conduct sounds to the nerve cells. (p. 201)
7. We localize high-frequency sounds according to differences in loudness between the ears. We localize low-frequency sounds on the basis of differences in phase. (p. 202)

Answers to STOP & CHECK Questions

1. At low frequencies, the basilar membrane vibrates in synchrony with the sound waves, and each responding axon in the auditory nerve sends one action potential per sound wave. (p. 199)
2. At intermediate frequencies, no single axon fires an action potential for each sound wave, but different axons fire for different waves, and so a volley (group) of axons fires for each wave. (p. 199)
3. At high frequencies, the sound causes maximum vibration for the hair cells at one location along the basilar membrane. (p. 199)
4. Any of the following: (a) The parietal cortex analyzes the "where" of both visual and auditory stimuli. (b) Areas in the superior temporal cortex analyze movement of both visual and auditory stimuli. Damage there can cause motion blindness or motion deafness. (c) The primary visual cortex is essential for visual imagery, and the primary auditory cortex is essential for auditory imagery. (d) Both the visual and auditory cortex need normal experience early in life to develop normal sensitivities. (p. 201)
5. Damage to the primary visual cortex leaves someone blind, but damage to the primary auditory cortex merely impairs perception of complex sounds without making the person deaf. (p. 201)
6. Each cell in the primary auditory cortex has a preferred frequency. In addition, cells of the auditory cortex respond most strongly to the kinds of sounds most likely to capture our attention, such as unusual sounds and sounds rich in harmonics. (p. 201)
7. Nerve deafness is common among rock band members because their frequent exposure to loud noises causes damage to the cells of the ear. Hearing aids are generally successful for conductive deafness; they are not always helpful in cases of nerve deafness. (p. 202)
8. An animal with a small head localizes sounds mainly by differences in loudness because the ears are not far enough apart for differences in onset time to be very large. An animal with a large head localizes sounds mainly by differences in onset time because its ears are far apart and well suited to noting differences in phase or onset time. (p. 203)

Thought Questions

1. Why do you suppose that the human auditory system evolved sensitivity to sounds in the range of 20 to 20000 Hz instead of some other range of frequencies?
2. The text explains how we might distinguish loudness for low-frequency sounds. How might we distinguish loudness for a high-frequency tone?

Module 7.2
The Mechanical Senses

The next time you turn on your radio or stereo set, place your hand on its surface. You can feel the same vibrations that you hear. If you practiced enough, could you learn to "hear" the vibrations with your fingers? No, they would remain just vibrations. If an earless species had enough time, might its vibration detectors evolve into sound detectors? Yes! In fact, our ears evolved in just that way.

The *mechanical senses* respond to pressure, bending, or other distortions of a receptor. They include touch, pain, and other body sensations, as well as vestibular sensation, a system that detects the position and movement of the head. Audition is a mechanical sense also because the hair cells are modified touch receptors; we considered it separately because of its complexity and great importance to humans.

Vestibular Sensation

Try to read this page while you jiggle your head up and down, back and forth. You will find that you can read it fairly easily. Now hold your head steady and jiggle the book up and down, back and forth. Suddenly, you can hardly read it at all. Why?

When you move your head, the vestibular organ adjacent to the cochlea monitors each movement and directs compensatory movements of your eyes. When your head moves left, your eyes move right; when your head moves right, your eyes move left. Effortlessly, you keep your eyes focused on what you want to see (Brandt, 1991). When you move the page, however, the vestibular organ cannot keep your eyes on target. Sensations from the vestibular organ detect the direction of tilt and the amount of acceleration of the head. We are seldom aware of our vestibular sensations except under unusual conditions such as riding a roller coaster; they are nevertheless critical for guiding eye movements and maintaining balance. Astronauts, of course, become acutely aware of the *lack* of vestibular sensation while they are in orbit.

The vestibular organ, shown in Figure 7.10, consists of the *saccule* and *utricle* and three semicircular canals. Like the hearing receptors, the vestibular receptors are modified touch receptors. Calcium carbonate particles called *otoliths* lie next to the hair cells. When the head tilts in different directions, the otoliths push against different sets of hair cells and excite them (Hess, 2001).

The three **semicircular canals,** oriented in three different planes, are filled with a jellylike substance and lined with hair cells. An acceleration of the head at any angle causes the jellylike substance in one of these canals to push against the hair cells. Action potentials initiated by cells of the vestibular system travel through part of the eighth cranial nerve to the brainstem and cerebellum. (The eighth cranial nerve contains both an auditory component and a vestibular component.)

For the vestibular organ, so far as we can tell, the ideal size is nearly constant, regardless of the size of the animal. Whales are 10 million times as massive as mice, but their vestibular organ is only 5 times as large (Squires, 2004).

To be useful, of course, vestibular sensation has to be integrated with other kinds of sensation. People with damage to the *angular gyrus*—an area at the border between the parietal cortex and the temporal cortex—have trouble integrating or binding one kind of sensation with another, including vestibular sensations. One patient was given several bouts of electrical stimulation to the angular gyrus as part of an exploratory procedure prior to brain surgery. The electrical stimulation presumably disrupted the normal activity. The patient reported an "out of the body experience" each time, as if viewing the body from somewhere else (Blanke, Ortigue, Landis, & Seeck, 2002). The researchers suggested that out of the body experiences represent a failure to bind vestibular sensation with vision and touch.

STOP & CHECK

1. People with damage to the vestibular system have trouble reading street signs while walking. Why?

Check your answer on page 214.

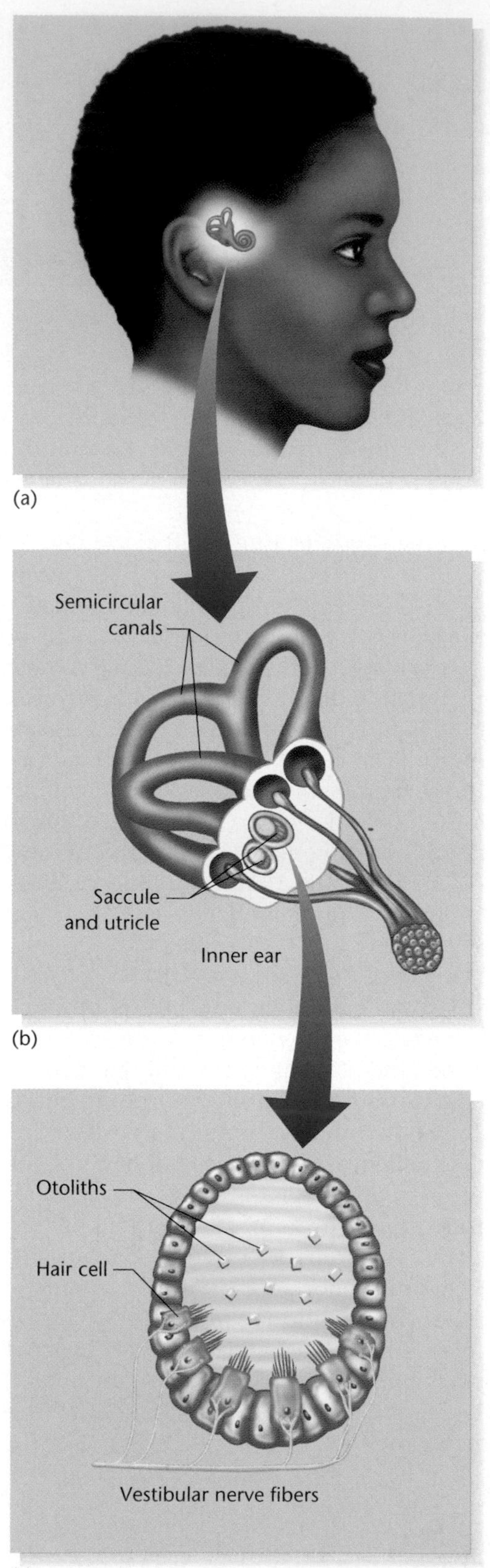

Figure 7.10 Structures for vestibular sensation
(a) Location of the vestibular organs. **(b)** Structures of the vestibular organs. **(c)** Cross-section through a utricle. Calcium carbonate particles, called otoliths, press against different hair cells depending on the direction of tilt and rate of acceleration of the head.

Somatosensation

The **somatosensory system,** the sensation of the body and its movements, is not one sense but many, including discriminative touch (which identifies the shape of an object), deep pressure, cold, warmth, pain, itch, tickle, and the position and movement of joints.

Somatosensory Receptors

The skin has many kinds of somatosensory receptors, including those listed in Figure 7.11. Table 7.1 lists the probable functions of these and other receptors (Iggo & Andres, 1982; Paré, Smith, & Rice, 2002). However, each receptor probably contributes to several kinds of somatosensory experience. Many respond to more than one kind of stimulus, such as touch and temperature. Others (not in the table) respond to deep stimulation, joint movement, or muscle movement.

A touch receptor may be a simple bare neuron ending (e.g., many pain receptors), an elaborated neuron ending (Ruffini endings and Meissner's corpuscles), or a bare ending surrounded by nonneural cells that modify its function (Pacinian corpuscles). Stimulation of a touch receptor opens sodium channels in the axon, thereby starting an action potential (Price et al., 2000).

One example of a receptor is the **Pacinian corpuscle,** which detects sudden displacements or high-frequency vibrations on the skin (Figure 7.12). Inside its onionlike outer structure is the neuron membrane. When mechanical pressure bends the membrane, its resistance to sodium flow decreases, and sodium ions enter, depolarizing the membrane (Loewenstein, 1960). Only a sudden or vibrating stimulus can bend the membrane; the onionlike outer structure provides mechanical support that resists gradual or constant pressure on the skin.

Certain chemicals can also stimulate the receptors for heat and cold. The heat receptor responds to capsaicin, the chemical that makes jalapeños and similar peppers taste hot. The coolness receptor responds to menthol and less strongly to mint (McKemy, Neuhausser, & Julius, 2002). So advertisements mentioning "the cool taste of menthol" are literally correct.

EXTENSIONS AND APPLICATIONS
Tickle

The sensation of tickle is interesting but poorly understood. Why does it exist at all? Why do you laugh if someone rapidly fingers your armpit, neck, or the soles of your feet? Chimpanzees respond to similar sensations with bursts of panting that resemble laughter. And yet tickling is unlike humor. Most people do not enjoy

Table 7.1 Somatosensory Receptors and Their Possible Functions

Receptor	Location	Responds to
Free nerve ending (unmyelinated or thinly myelinated axons)	Near base of hairs and elsewhere in skin	Pain, warmth, cold
Hair-follicle receptors	Hair-covered skin	Movement of hairs
Meissner's corpuscles	Hairless areas	Sudden displacement of skin; low-frequency vibration (flutter)
Pacinian corpuscles	Both hairy and hairless skin	Sudden displacement of skin; high-frequency vibration
Merkel's disks	Both hairy and hairless skin	Tangential forces across skin
Ruffini endings	Both hairy and hairless skin	Stretch of skin
Krause end bulbs	Mostly or entirely in hairless areas, perhaps including genitals	Uncertain

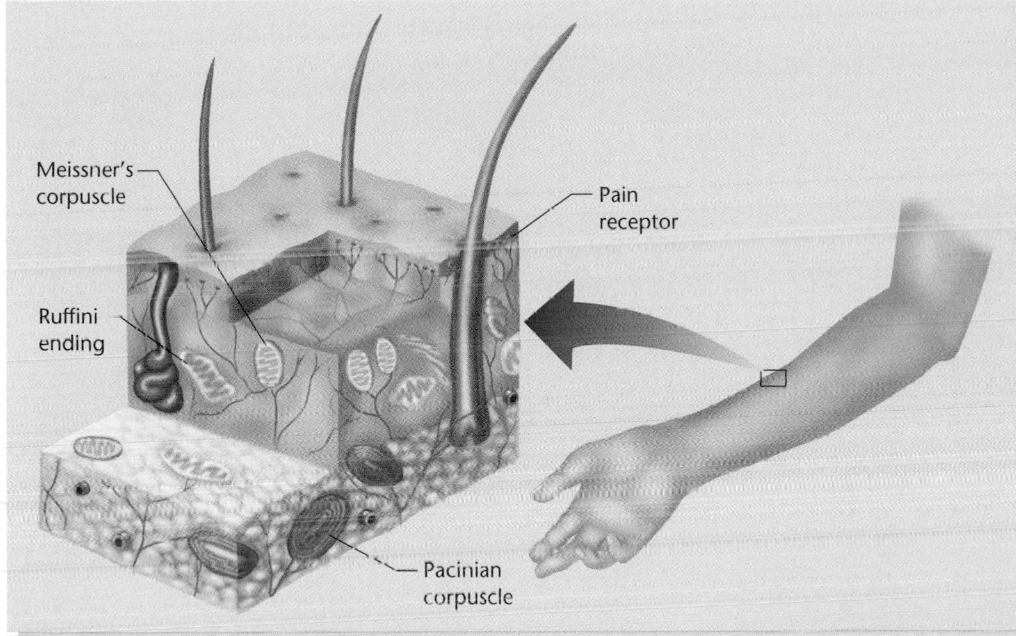

Figure 7.11 Some sensory receptors found in the skin, the human body's largest organ
Different receptor types respond to different stimuli, as described in Table 7.1.

being tickled for long—if at all—and certainly not by a stranger. If one joke makes you laugh, you are more likely than usual to laugh at the next joke. But being tickled doesn't change your likelihood of laughing at a joke (C. R. Harris, 1999).

Why can't you tickle yourself? It is for the same reason that you can't surprise yourself. When you touch yourself, your brain compares the resulting stimulation to the "expected" stimulation and generates a weak somatosensory response. When someone else touches you, the response is stronger (Blakemore, Wolpert, & Frith, 1998). Evidently, while you are trying to tickle yourself, the brain gets messages about the movements, which subtract from the touch sensations. (Actually, some people can tickle themselves—a little—if they tickle the right side of the body with the left hand or the left side with the right hand. Try it.)

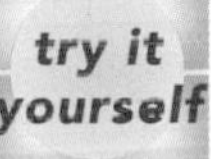

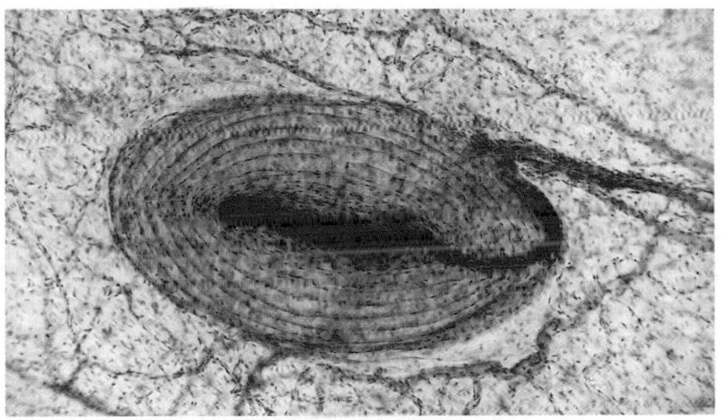

Figure 7.12 A Pacinian corpuscle
Pacinian corpuscles are a type of receptor that responds best to sudden displacement of the skin or to high-frequency vibrations. They respond only briefly to steady pressure on the skin. The onionlike outer structure provides a mechanical support to the neuron inside it so that a sudden stimulus can bend it but a sustained stimulus cannot.

Input to the Spinal Cord and the Brain

Information from touch receptors in the head enters the central nervous system (CNS) through the cranial nerves. Information from receptors below the head enters the spinal cord and passes toward the brain through the 31 spinal nerves (Figure 7.13), including 8 cervical nerves, 12 thoracic nerves, 5 lumbar nerves, 5 sacral nerves, and 1 coccygeal nerve. Each spinal nerve has a sensory component and a motor component.

Each spinal nerve *innervates,* or connects to, a limited area of the body. The skin area connected to a single sensory spinal nerve is called a **dermatome** (Figure 7.14). For example, the third thoracic nerve (T3) innervates a strip of skin just above the nipples as well as the underarm area. But the borders between dermatomes are not so distinct as Figure 7.14 implies; there is actually an overlap of one-third to one-half between adjacent pairs.

The sensory information that enters the spinal cord travels in well-defined pathways toward the brain. For example, the touch pathway in the spinal cord is separate from the pain pathway, and the pain pathway itself has different populations of axons conveying sharp pain, slow burning pain, and painfully cold sensations (Craig, Krout, & Andrew, 2001). One patient had an illness that destroyed all the myelinated somatosensory axons from below his nose but spared all his unmyelinated axons. He still felt temperature, pain, and itch, which depend on the unmyelinated axons. However, he had no sense of

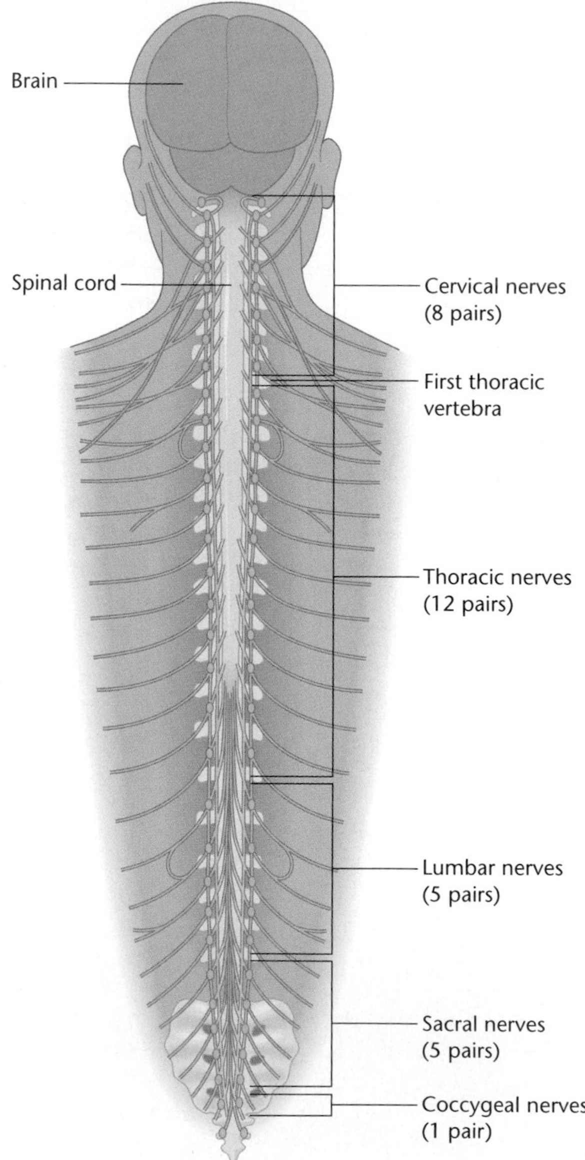

Figure 7.13 The human central nervous system (CNS)

Spinal nerves from each segment of the spinal cord exit through the correspondingly numbered opening between vertebrae. *(Source: From C. Starr and R. Taggart,* Biology: The Unity and Diversity of Life, *5th edition, 1989, 338. Copyright © 1989 Wadsworth Publishing Co. Reprinted by permission.)*

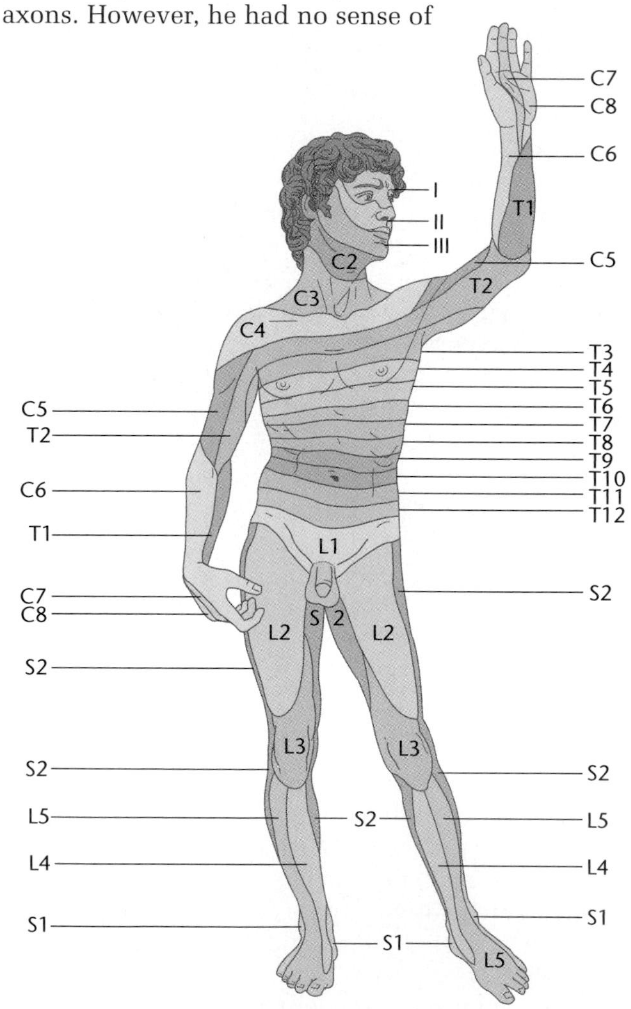

Figure 7.14 Dermatomes innervated by the 31 sensory spinal nerves

Areas I, II, and III of the face are not innervated by the spinal nerves but instead by three branches of the fifth cranial nerve. Although this figure shows distinct borders, the dermatomes actually overlap one another by about one-third to one-half of their width.

touch below the nose. Curiously, if someone lightly stroked his skin, all he experienced was a vague sense of pleasure. Recordings from his brain indicated no arousal of his primary somatosensory cortex but increased activity in the insular cortex, an area responsive to taste and to several kinds of emotional experience (Olausson et al., 2002). That is, evidently, the pleasurable, sensual aspects of touch depend on unmyelinated axons and do not require feeling the touch.

The various areas of the somatosensory thalamus send their impulses to different areas of the primary somatosensory cortex, located in the parietal lobe. Two parallel strips in the somatosensory cortex respond mostly to touch on the skin; two other parallel strips respond mostly to deep pressure and movement of the joints and muscles (Kaas, 1983). In short, various aspects of body sensation remain at least partly separate all the way to the cortex. Along each strip of somatosensory cortex, different subareas respond to different areas of the body; that is, the somatosensory cortex acts as a map of body location, as shown in Figure 4.24, p. 99.

Just as conscious vision and hearing depend on the primary visual and auditory cortex, the primary somatosensory cortex is essential for conscious touch experiences. When weak, brief stimuli are applied to the fingers, people are consciously aware of only those that produce a certain minimum level of arousal in the primary somatosensory cortex (Palva, Linkenkaer-Hansen, Näätäen, & Palva, 2005). If someone touches you quickly on two nearby points on the hand, you will probably have an illusory experience of a single touch midway between those two points. When that happens, the activity in the primary somatosensory cortex corresponds to that midway point (Chen, Friedman, & Roe, 2003). In other words, the activity corresponds to what you experience, not what has actually stimulated your receptors.

After damage to the somatosensory cortex, people generally experience an impairment of body perceptions. One patient with Alzheimer's disease, who had damage in the somatosensory cortex as well as elsewhere, had much trouble putting her clothes on correctly, and she could not point correctly in response to such directions as "show me your elbow" or "point to my knee," although she pointed correctly to various objects in the room. When told to touch her elbow, her most frequent response was to feel her wrist and arm and suggest that the elbow was probably around there, somewhere. She acted as if she had only a blurry map of her own body parts (Sirigu, Grafman, Bressler, & Sunderland, 1991).

The primary somatosensory cortex sends output to additional cortical areas that are less clearly related to any map of the body. Activity in the primary somatosensory cortex increases during attention to touch stimuli (Krupa, Weist, Shuler, Laubach, & Nicolelis, 2004), but activity in the additional somatosensory areas depends even more strongly on attention. For example, they are only mildly activated when someone merely touches something and more strongly activated when someone touches something and tries to determine what it is (Young et al., 2004).

2. In what way is somatosensation several senses instead of one?

3. What evidence suggests that the somatosensory cortex is essential for conscious perception of touch?

Check your answers on page 214.

Pain

Pain, the experience evoked by a harmful stimulus, directs our attention toward a danger and holds our attention. The prefrontal cortex, which responds briefly to almost any stimulus, responds to a painful stimulus as long as it lasts (Downar, Mikulis, & Davis, 2003).

Have you ever wondered why morphine decreases pain after surgery but not during the surgery itself? Or why some people seem to tolerate pain so much better than others? Or why even the slightest touch on sunburned skin is so painful? Research on pain addresses these and other questions.

Pain Stimuli and the Pain Pathways

Pain sensation begins with the least specialized of all receptors, a bare nerve ending (see Figure 7.11). Some pain receptors also respond to acids and heat above 43°C (110°F). **Capsaicin**, a chemical found in hot peppers such as jalapeños, also stimulates those receptors. Capsaicin can produce burning or stinging sensations on many parts of your body, as you may have experienced if you ever touched the insides of hot peppers and then rubbed your eyes. Animals react to capsaicin by sweating or salivating, as if they were indeed hot (Caterina et al., 2000).

The axons carrying pain information have little or no myelin and therefore conduct impulses relatively slowly, in the range of 2 to 20 meters per second (m/s). The thicker and faster axons convey sharp pain; the thinnest ones convey duller pain, such as postsurgical pain. The axons enter the spinal cord, where they release two neurotransmitters. Mild pain releases the neurotransmitter glutamate, whereas stronger pain releases both glutamate and **substance P** (Cao et al., 1998). Mice that lack receptors for substance P react normally to mild pain, but they react to a severe injury as if it were a mild injury (DeFelipe et al., 1998). That is, without substance P, they do not detect the increased intensity.

The pain-sensitive cells in the spinal cord relay the information to several sites in the brain. One pathway extends to the ventral posterior nucleus of the thalamus and from there to the somatosensory cortex in the parietal lobe (which also responds to touch and other body sensations). The somatosensory cortex detects the nature of the pain and its location on the body. It responds both to painful stimuli and to signals that warn of impending pain (Babiloni et al., 2005).

Painful stimuli also activate a pathway through the reticular formation of the medulla and then to several of the central nuclei of the thalamus, the amygdala, hippocampus, prefrontal cortex, and cingulate cortex (Figure 7.15). These areas react not to the sensation itself but to the unpleasant emotional quality associated with it (Hunt & Mantyh, 2001). If you watch someone—especially someone you care about—experiencing pain, you experience a "sympathetic pain" that shows up as activity in your cingulate cortex but not in your somatosensory cortex (Singer et al., 2004).

STOP & CHECK

4. How do jalapeños produce a hot sensation?

5. What would happen to a pain sensation if glutamate receptors in the spinal cord were blocked? What if substance P receptors were blocked?

Check your answers on page 214.

Ways of Relieving Pain

Pain alerts us to danger, but once we are aware of it, further pain messages accomplish little. Our brains put the brakes on prolonged pain by **opioid mechanisms**—systems that respond to opiate drugs and similar chemicals. Candace Pert and Solomon Snyder (1973) discovered that opiates exert their effects by binding to certain receptors found mostly in the spinal cord and the **periaqueductal gray area** of the midbrain. Later researchers found that opiate receptors act by blocking the release of substance P (Kondo et al., 2005; Reichling, Kwiat, & Basbaum, 1988) (Figures 7.16 and 7.17).

The discovery of opiate receptors was exciting because it was the first evidence that opiates act on the nervous system rather than the injured tissue. Furthermore, it implied that the nervous system must have its own opiate-type chemicals. Two of them are *met-enkephalin* and *leu-enkephalin*. The term *enkephalin* (en-KEFF-ah-lin) reflects the fact that these chemicals were first found in the brain, or encephalon. The enkephalins are chains of amino acids; met-enkephalin ends with the amino acid methionine and leu-enkephalin ends with leucine. Although the enkephalins are chemically unlike morphine, they and several other transmitters, including *β-endorphin*, bind to the same receptors as morphine. Collectively, the transmitters that attach to the same receptors as morphine are known as **endorphins**—a contraction of *endo*genous mor*phines*.

Both pleasant and unpleasant stimuli can release endorphins and thereby inhibit pain. Inescapable pain

Figure 7.15 Representation of pain in the human brain
A pathway to the thalamus, and from there to the somatosensory cortex, conveys the sensory aspects of pain. A separate pathway to the hypothalamus, amygdala, and other structures produces the emotional aspects. *(Source: Hunt & Mantyh, 2001)*

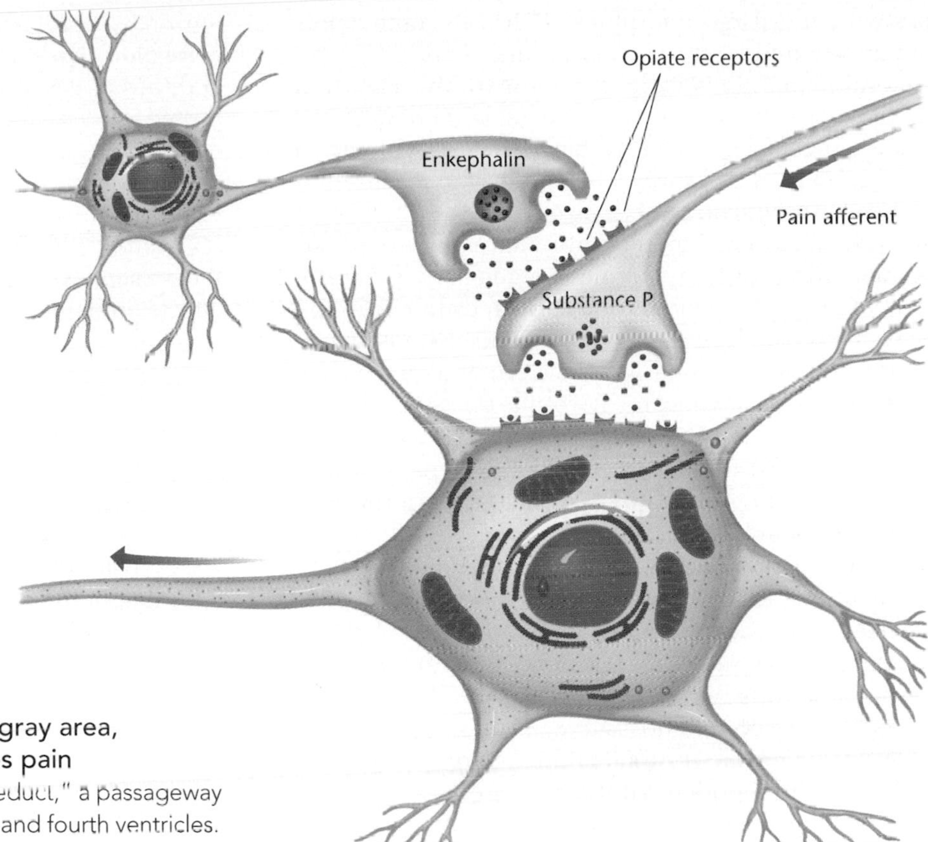

Figure 7.16 Synapses responsible for pain and its inhibition
The pain afferent neuron releases substance P as its neurotransmitter. Another neuron releases enkephalin at presynaptic synapses; the enkephalin inhibits the release of substance P and therefore alleviates pain.

Figure 7.17 The periaqueductal gray area, where electrical stimulation relieves pain
Periaqueductal means "around the aqueduct," a passageway of cerebrospinal fluid between the third and fourth ventricles.

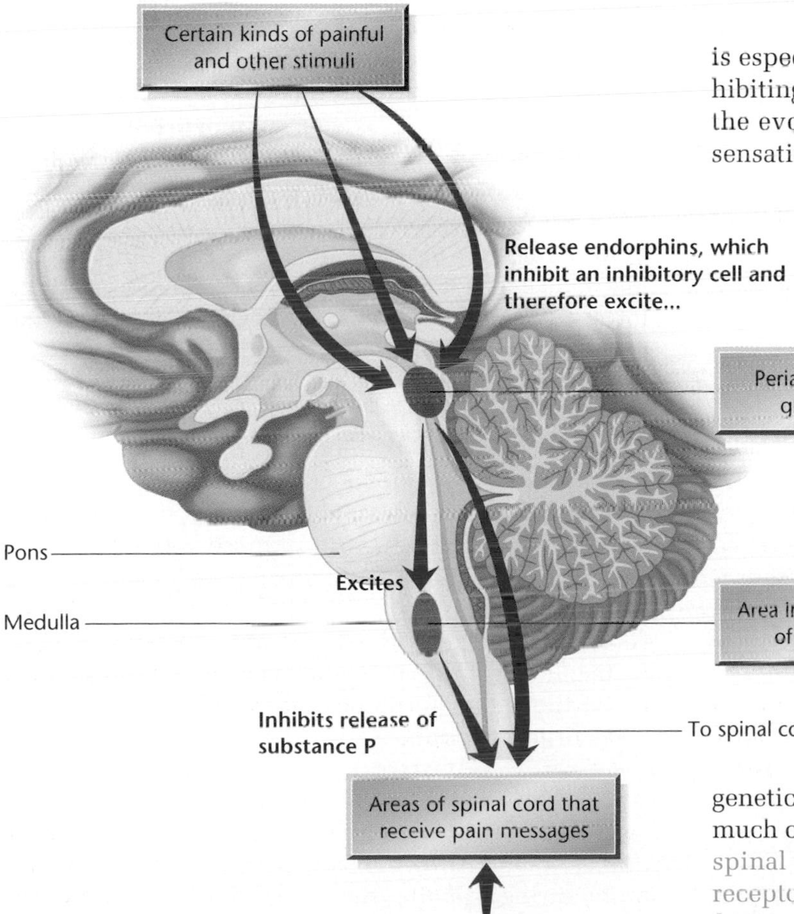

Certain kinds of painful and other stimuli
Release endorphins, which inhibit an inhibitory cell and therefore excite...
Periaqueductal gray area
Pons
Excites
Medulla
Area in rostral part of medulla
Inhibits release of substance P
To spinal cord
Areas of spinal cord that receive pain messages
Axons carrying pain messages

is especially potent at stimulating endorphins and inhibiting further pain (Sutton et al., 1997). Presumably, the evolutionary function is that continued intense sensation of pain accomplishes nothing when escape is impossible. Endorphins are also released during sex and when you listen to thrilling music that sends a chill down your spine (A. Goldstein, 1980). Those experiences tend to decrease pain. You decrease your endorphin release if you brood about sad memories (Zubieta et al., 2003).

The discovery of endorphins provides physiological details for the gate theory, proposed decades earlier by Ronald Melzack and P. D. Wall (1965). The gate theory was an attempt to explain why some people withstand pain better than others and why the same injury hurts worse at some times than others. People differ partly because of genetics (Wei et al., 2001), but experiences account for much of the variation too. According to the **gate theory**, spinal cord neurons that receive messages from pain receptors also receive input from touch receptors and from axons descending from the brain. These other inputs can close the "gates" for the pain messages—at least partly by releasing endorphins. Although some details of Melzack and Wall's gate theory turned out wrong, the general principle is valid: Nonpain stimuli can modify the intensity of pain. You have no doubt noticed this principle yourself. When you have an injury, you can decrease the pain by gently rubbing the skin around it or by concentrating on something else.

Morphine does not block the sharp pain of the surgeon's knife; for that, you need a general anesthetic. Instead, morphine blocks the slower, duller pain that lingers after surgery. Larger diameter axons, unaffected by morphine, carry sharp pain. Thinner axons convey dull postsurgical pain, and morphine does inhibit them (Taddese, Nah, & McCleskey, 1995). Marijuana and related chemicals also block certain kinds of pain by stimulating anandamide and 2-AG receptors in the midbrain (Hohmann et al., 2005).

Another approach to relieving pain uses capsaicin. As mentioned, capsaicin produces a burning or painful sensation. It does so by releasing substance P. However, it releases substance P faster than neurons can resynthesize it, leaving the cells less able to send pain messages. Also, high doses of capsaicin damage pain receptors. Capsaicin rubbed onto a sore shoulder, an arthritic joint, or other painful area produces a temporary burning sensation followed by a longer period of decreased pain. However, do not try eating hot peppers to reduce pain in, say, your legs. The capsaicin you eat passes through the digestive system without entering the blood. Therefore, eating it will not relieve your pain—unless it is your tongue that hurts (Karrer & Bartoshuk, 1991).

People also sometimes experience pain relief from placebos. A **placebo** is a drug or other procedure with no pharmacological effects. In many experiments, the experimental group receives the potentially active treatment, and the control group receives a placebo. Theoretically, placebos should not have much effect, and in most kinds of medical research, they don't, but they sometimes do relieve pain (Hróbjartsson & Gøtzsche, 2001). Evidently, the pain decreases just because people expect it to decrease. People are not just *saying* the pain decreased; brain scans indicate that placebos decrease the brain's response to painful stimuli. However, a placebo's effects are mainly on emotion, not sensation. That is, a placebo decreases the response in the cingulate cortex but not the somatosensory cortex (Petrovic, Kalso, Petersson, & Ingvar, 2002; Wager et al., 2004). Similarly, when a hypnotized person is told to feel no pain, activity decreases in the cingulate cortex but not in the somatosensory cortex (Rainville, Duncan, Price, Carrier, & Bushnell, 1997). The hypnotized person still feels the painful stimulus but does not react emotionally.

Do placebos and hypnotic suggestion decrease pain just by increasing relaxation? No. In one study, people were given injections of capsaicin (which produces a burning sensation) into both hands and both feet. They were also given a placebo cream on one hand or foot and told that it was a powerful painkiller. People reported decreased pain in the area that got the placebo but normal pain on the other three extremities (Benedetti, Arduino, & Amanzio, 1999). If placebos were simply producing relaxation, the relaxation should have affected all four extremities, not just the area where the placebo was applied. The mechanism of placebos' effects on pain is not yet understood.

Sensitization of Pain

In addition to mechanisms for decreasing pain, the body has mechanisms that increase pain. For example, even a light touch on sunburned skin is painful. Damaged or inflamed tissue, such as sunburned skin, releases histamine, nerve growth factor, and other chemicals that help repair the damage but also magnify the responses in nearby pain receptors (Devor, 1996; Tominaga et al., 1998), including those responsive to heat (Chuang et al., 2001). Nonsteroidal anti-inflammatory drugs, such as ibuprofen, relieve pain by reducing the release of chemicals from damaged tissues (Hunt & Mantyh, 2001). In animal experiments, the neurotrophin GDNF has shown even greater potential to block the heightened pain sensitivity after tissue damage (Boucher et al., 2000).

Sometimes people suffer chronic pain long after an injury has healed. Why this pain develops in some people and not others remains unknown, but the mechanism is partly understood. As we shall see in Chapter 13, a barrage of intense stimulation of a neuron can "potentiate" its synaptic receptors so that it responds more vigorously to the same input in the future. That mechanism is central to learning and memory, but unfortunately, pain activates the mechanism as well. An intense barrage of painful stimuli potentiates the cells responsive to pain so that they respond more vigorously to minor stimulation in the future (Ikeda, Heinke, Ruscheweyh, & Sandkühler, 2003). In effect, the brain learns how to feel pain, and it gets better at it.

Therefore, to prevent chronic pain, it is important to limit pain from the start. Suppose you are about to undergo major surgery. Which approach is best?

A. Start taking morphine before the surgery.
B. Begin morphine soon after awakening from surgery.
C. Postpone the morphine as long as possible and take as little as possible.

Perhaps surprisingly, the research supports answer A: Start the morphine before the surgery (Keefe & France, 1999). Allowing pain messages to bombard the brain during and after the surgery increases the sensitivity of the pain nerves and their receptors (Malmberg, Chen, Tonagawa, & Basbaum, 1997). People who begin taking morphine before surgery need less of it afterward.

For more information about pain, including links to research reports, check either of these websites:

http://www.painnet.com/

http://www.ampainsoc.org/

STOP & CHECK

6. How do opiates relieve pain? Why do they relieve dull pain but not sharp pain?
7. How do the pain-relieving effects of placebos differ from those of morphine?
8. How do ibuprofen and other nonsteroidal anti-inflammatory drugs decrease pain?
9. Why is it preferable to start taking morphine before an operation instead of waiting until later?

Check your answers on page 214.

Itch

Have you ever wondered, "What is itch, anyway? Is it a kind of pain? A kind of touch? Or something else altogether?" For many years, no one knew, and we still have not identified the receptors responsible for itch. However, we do know that when your skin rubs against certain plants, when an insect crawls along your skin, or when you have mild tissue damage, your skin releases histamines, and histamines produce an itching sensation.

Researchers have identified a spinal cord pathway of itch sensation (Andrew & Craig, 2001). Histamines in the skin excite axons of this pathway, and other kinds of skin stimuli do not. Even when a stimulus releases histamines, however, this pathway is slow to respond, and when it does respond, the axons transmit impulses at the unusually slow velocity of only about half a meter per second. At that rate, an action potential from your foot needs 3 or 4 seconds to reach your head. For a giraffe or elephant, the delay is even longer. You might try very rubbing some rough leaves against your ankle. Note how soon you feel the touch sensation and how much more slowly you notice the itchiness.

try it yourself

Itch is useful because it directs you to scratch the itchy area and presumably remove whatever is irritating your skin. Vigorous scratching produces mild pain, and pain inhibits itch. Opiates, which decrease pain, increase itch (Andrew & Craig, 2001). This inhibitory relationship between pain and itch is the strongest evidence that itch is not a type of pain.

This research helps explain an experience that you may have had. When a dentist gives you Novocain before drilling a tooth, part of your face becomes numb. An hour or more later, as the Novocain's effects start to wear off, you may feel an intense itchy sensation in the numb portion of your face. But when you try to scratch the itch, you feel nothing because the touch and pain sensations are still numb. (Evidently, the effects of Novocain wear off faster for itch than for touch and pain axons.) The fact that you can feel itch at this time is evidence that it is not just a form of touch or pain. It is interesting that scratching the partly numb skin does not relieve the itch. Evidently, your scratching has to produce some pain to decrease the itch.

STOP & CHECK

10. Would antihistamine drugs increase or decrease itch sensations? What about opiates?

Check your answers on page 214.

Module 7.2

In Closing: The Mechanical Senses

We humans generally pay so much attention to vision and hearing that we take our mechanical senses for granted. However, a mere moment's reflection should reveal how critical they are for survival. At every moment, your vestibular sense tells you whether you are standing or falling; your sense of pain can tell you that you have injured yourself. If you moved to a television-like universe with only vision and hearing, you might get by if you had already learned what all the sights and sounds mean. But it is hard to imagine how you could have learned their meaning without much previous experience of touch and pain.

Summary

1. The vestibular system detects the position and acceleration of the head and adjusts body posture and eye movements accordingly. (p. 205)
2. The somatosensory system depends on a variety of receptors that are sensitive to different kinds of stimulation of the skin and internal tissues. The brain maintains several parallel somatosensory representations of the body. (p. 206)
3. Activity in the primary somatosensory cortex corresponds to what someone is experiencing, even

if it is illusory and not the same as the actual stimulation. (p. 209)

4. Injurious stimuli excite pain receptors, which are bare nerve endings. Some pain receptors also respond to acids, heat, and capsaicin—the chemical that makes hot peppers taste hot. (p. 209)
5. Axons conveying pain stimulation to the spinal cord and brainstem release glutamate in response to moderate pain and a combination of glutamate and substance P for stronger pain. (p. 209)
6. Painful information takes two routes to the brain. A route leading to the somatosensory cortex conveys the sensory information, including location in the body. A route to the cingulate cortex and several other structures conveys the unpleasant emotional aspect. (p. 210)
7. Opiate drugs attach to the brain's endorphin receptors. Endorphins decrease pain by blocking release of substance P and other transmitters from pain neurons. Both pleasant and unpleasant experiences can release endorphins. (p. 210)
8. A harmful stimulus may give rise to a greater or lesser degree of pain depending on other current and recent stimuli. According to the gate theory of pain, other stimuli can close certain gates and block the transmission of pain. (p. 211)
9. Chronic pain bombards pain synapses with repetitive input, and increases their responsiveness to later stimuli, through a process like learning. (p. 212)
10. Morphine is most effective as a painkiller if it is used promptly. Allowing the nervous system to be bombarded with prolonged pain messages increases the overall sensitivity to pain. (p. 212)
11. Skin irritation releases histamine, which excites a spinal pathway responsible for itch. The axons of that pathway transmit impulses very slowly. They can be inhibited by pain messages. (p. 213)

Answers to STOP & CHECK Questions

1. The vestibular system enables the brain to shift eye movements to compensate for changes in head position. Without feedback about head position, a person would not be able to correct the eye movements, and the experience would be like watching a jiggling book page. (p. 205)
2. We have several types of receptors, sensitive to touch, heat, and so forth, and different parts of the somatosensory cortex respond to different kinds of skin stimulation. (p. 209)
3. People are consciously aware of only those touch stimuli that produce sufficient arousal in the primary somatosensory cortex. (p. 209)
4. Jalapeños and other hot peppers contain capsaicin, which stimulates neurons that are sensitive to pain, acids, and heat. (p. 210)
5. Blocking glutamate receptors would eliminate weak to moderate pain. (However, doing so would not be a good strategy for killing pain. Glutamate is the most abundant transmitter, and blocking it would disrupt practically everything the brain does.) Blocking substance P receptors makes intense pain feel mild. (p. 210)
6. Opiates relieve pain by stimulating the same receptors as endorphins, thereby blocking the release of substance P. Endorphins block messages from the thinnest pain fibers, conveying dull pain, and not from thicker fibers, carrying sharp pain. (p. 213)
7. Placebos reduce the emotional reaction to pain but have less effect than morphine on the sensation itself. (p. 213)
8. Anti-inflammatory drugs block the release of chemicals from damaged tissues, which would otherwise magnify the effects of pain receptors. (p. 213)
9. The morphine will not decrease the sharp pain of the surgery itself. However, it will decrease the subsequent barrage of pain stimuli that can sensitize pain neurons. (p. 213)
10. Antihistamines decrease itch; opiates increase it. (p. 213)

Thought Questions

1. Why is the vestibular sense generally useless under conditions of weightlessness?
2. How could you determine whether hypnosis decreases pain by increasing the release of endorphins?

Module 7.3
The Chemical Senses

Suppose you had the godlike power to create a new species of animal, but you could equip it with only one sensory system. Which sense would you give it?

Your first impulse might be to choose vision or hearing because of their importance to humans. But an animal with only one sensory system is not going to be much like humans, is it? To have any chance of survival, it will probably have to be small and slow, maybe even one-celled. What sense will be most useful to such an animal?

Most theorists believe that the first sensory system of the earliest animals was a chemical sensitivity (G. H. Parker, 1922). A chemical sense enables a small animal to find food, avoid certain kinds of danger, and even locate mates.

Now imagine that you have to choose one of your senses to lose. Which one will it be? Most of us would not choose to lose vision, hearing, or touch. Losing pain sensitivity can be dangerous. You might choose to sacrifice your smell or taste.

Curious, isn't it? If an animal is going to survive with only one sense, it almost has to be a chemical sense, and yet to humans, with many other well-developed senses, the chemical senses seem dispensable. Perhaps we underestimate their importance.

General Issues About Chemical Coding

Suppose you run a bakery and need to send frequent messages to your supplier down the street. Suppose further that you can communicate only by ringing three large bells on the roof of your bakery. You would have to work out a code.

One possibility would be to label the three bells: The high-pitched bell means "I need flour." The medium-pitched bell means "I need sugar." And the low-pitched bell means "I need eggs." The more you need something, the faster you ring the bell. We shall call this system the *labeled-line* code because each bell has a single unchanging label. Of course, it is limited to flour, sugar, and eggs.

Another possibility would be to set up a code that depends on a relationship among the three bells. Ringing the high and medium bells equally means that you need flour. The medium and low bells together call for sugar; the high and low bells together call for eggs. Ringing all three together means you need vanilla extract. Ringing mostly the high bell while ringing the other two bells slightly means you need hazelnuts. And so forth. We call this the *across-fiber pattern* code because the meaning depends on the pattern across bells. This code is versatile and can be highly useful, unless we make it too complicated.

A sensory system could theoretically use either type of coding. In a system relying on the **labeled-line principle**, each receptor would respond to a limited range of stimuli and send a direct line to the brain. In a system relying on the **across-fiber pattern principle**, each receptor responds to a wider range of stimuli and contributes to the perception of each of them. In other words, a given response by a given sensory axon means little unless the brain knows what the other axons are doing at the same time (Erickson, 1982).

Vertebrate sensory systems probably do not have any pure labeled-line codes. In color perception, we encountered a good example of an across-fiber pattern code. For example, a medium-wavelength cone might produce the same level of response to a moderately bright green light, a brighter blue light, or a white light, so the response of that cone is ambiguous unless the brain compares it to other cones. In auditory pitch perception, the responses of the hair cell receptors are narrowly tuned, but even in this case, the meaning of a particular receptor's response depends on the context: A given receptor may respond best to a certain high-frequency tone, but it also responds in phase with a number of low-frequency tones (as do all the other receptors). Each receptor also responds to white noise (static) and to various mixtures of tones. Auditory perception depends on a comparison of responses across all the receptors. Similarly, each taste and smell stimulus excites several kinds of neurons, and the meaning of a particular response by a particular neuron depends on the context of responses by other neurons.

1. Of the following, which use a labeled-line code and which use an across-fiber pattern code?
   A. A fire alarm
   B. A light switch
   C. The shift key plus another key on a keyboard

Check your answers on page 227.

Taste

Taste refers to the stimulation of the **taste buds,** the receptors on the tongue. When we talk about the taste of food, we generally mean flavor, which is a combination of taste and smell. Whereas other senses remain separate throughout the cortex, taste and smell axons converge onto some of the same cells in an area called the endopiriform cortex (Fu, Sugai, Yoshimura, & Onoda, 2004). That convergence presumably enables taste and smell to combine their influences on food selection.

Taste Receptors

The receptors for taste are not true neurons but modified skin cells. Like neurons, taste receptors have excitable membranes and release neurotransmitters to excite neighboring neurons, which in turn transmit information to the brain. Like skin cells, however, taste receptors are gradually sloughed off and replaced, each one lasting about 10 to 14 days (Kinnamon, 1987).

Mammalian taste receptors are in taste buds, located in **papillae,** structures on the surface of the tongue (Figure 7.18). A given papilla may contain from zero to ten or more taste buds (Arvidson & Friberg, 1980), and each taste bud contains about 50 receptor cells.

In adult humans, taste buds are located mainly along the outside edge of the tongue, with few or none in the center. You can demonstrate this principle as follows: Soak a small cotton swab in sugar water, saltwater, or vinegar. Then touch it lightly on the center of your tongue, not too far toward the back. If you get the position right, you will experience little or no taste. Then try it again on the edge of your tongue and notice how much stronger the taste is.

try it yourself

Now change the procedure a bit. Wash your mouth out with water and prepare a cotton swab as before. Touch the soaked portion to one edge of your tongue and then slowly stroke it to the center of your tongue. Now it will seem as if you are moving the taste to the center of your tongue. In fact, you are getting only a touch sensation from the center of your tongue; you attribute the taste you had on the side of your tongue to every other spot you stroke (Bartoshuk, 1991).

How Many Kinds of Taste Receptors?

Traditionally, people in Western society have described sweet, sour, salty, and bitter as the "primary" tastes. However, some tastes defy categorization in terms of these four labels (Schiffman & Erickson, 1980; Schiffman, McElroy, & Erickson, 1980). How could we determine how many kinds of taste we have?

EXTENSIONS AND APPLICATIONS
Chemicals That Alter the Taste Buds

One way to identify taste receptor types is to find procedures that alter one receptor but not others. For example, chewing a miracle berry (native to West Africa) gives little taste itself but temporarily changes sweet receptors. Miracle berries contain a protein, miraculin, that modifies sweet receptors in such a way that they can be stimulated by acids (Bartoshuk, Gentile, Moskowitz, & Meiselman, 1974). If you ever get a chance to chew a miracle berry (and I do recommend it), for the next half hour anything acidic will taste sweet in addition to its usual sour taste.

A colleague and I once spent an evening experimenting with miracle berries. We drank straight lemon juice, sauerkraut juice, even vinegar. All tasted extremely sweet, but we awoke the next day with mouths full of ulcers.

Miraculin was, for a time, commercially available in the United States as a diet aid. The idea was that dieters could coat their tongue with a miraculin pill and then enjoy unsweetened lemonade and so forth, which would taste sweet but provide almost no calories.

Have you ever drunk orange juice just after brushing your teeth? Did you wonder why something so wonderful suddenly tasted so bad? Most toothpastes contain sodium lauryl sulfate, a chemical that intensifies bitter tastes and weakens sweet ones, apparently by coating the sweet receptors and preventing anything from reaching them (DeSimone, Heck, & Bartoshuk, 1980; Schiffman, 1983).

Another taste-modifying substance is an extract from the plant *Gymnema sylvestre* (R. A. Frank, Mize, Kennedy, de los Santos, & Green, 1992). Some health-food and herbal-remedy stores sell dried leaves of *Gymnema sylvestre,* from which you can brew a tea. (*Gymnema sylvestre* pills won't work for this demonstration.) Soak your tongue in the tea for about 30 seconds and then try tasting various substances. Salty, sour, and bitter substances taste the same as usual, but sugar becomes utterly tasteless, as if you had sand on

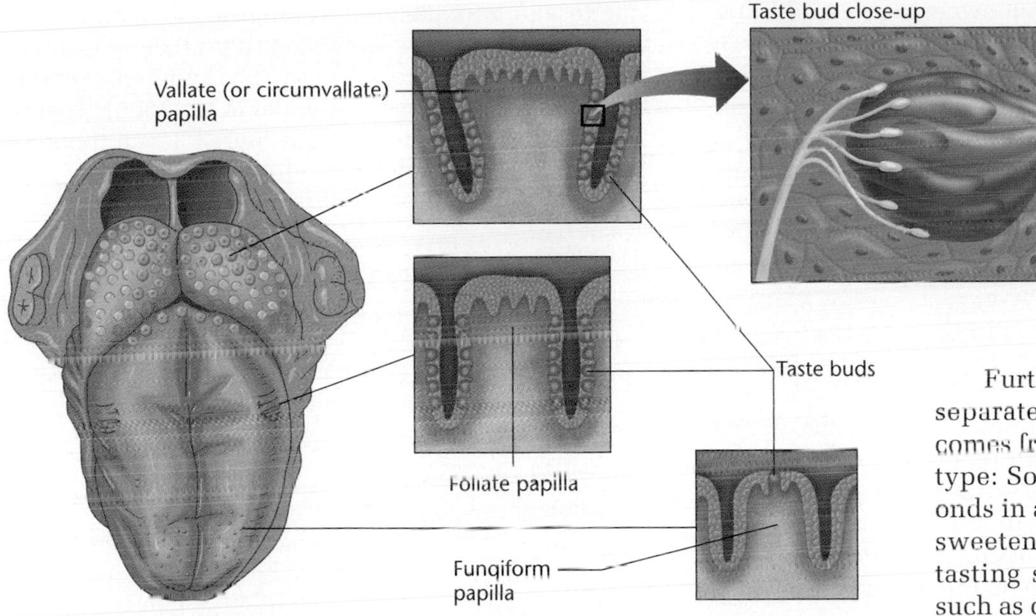

(a)

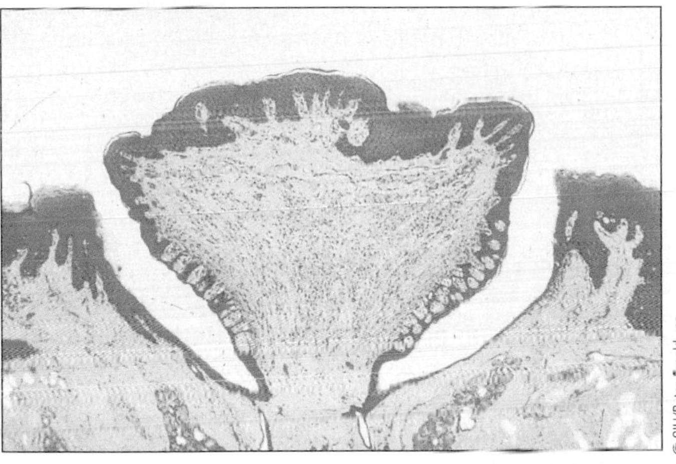

(b)

Figure 7.18 The organs of taste
(a) The tip, back, and sides of the tongue are covered with taste buds. Taste buds are located in papillae. **(b)** Photo showing cross-section of a taste bud. Each taste bud contains about 50 receptor cells.

your tongue. Candies lose their sweetness and now taste sour, bitter, or salty. (Those tastes were already present, but you barely noticed them because the sweetness dominated.) Curiously, the artificial sweetener aspartame (NutraSweet®) loses only some, not all, of its sweetness, implying that it stimulates an additional receptor besides the sugar receptor (Schroeder & Flannery-Schroeder, 2005). Note: Anyone with diabetes should refrain from this demonstration because *Gymnema sylvestre* also alters sugar absorption in the intestines. **try it yourself**

Further behavioral evidence for separate types of taste receptors comes from studies of the following type: Soak your tongue for 15 seconds in a sour solution, such as unsweetened lemon juice. Then try tasting some other sour solution, such as dilute vinegar. You will find that the second solution tastes less sour than usual. Depending on the concentrations of the lemon juice and vinegar, the second solution may not taste sour at all. This phenomenon, called **adaptation**, reflects the fatigue of receptors sensitive to sour tastes. Now try tasting something salty, sweet, or bitter. These substances taste about the same as usual. In short, you experience little **cross-adaptation**—reduced response to one taste after exposure to another (McBurney & Bartoshuk, 1973). Evidently, the sour receptors are different from the other taste receptors. Similarly, you can show that salt receptors are different from the others and so forth. **try it yourself**

Although we have long known that people have at least four kinds of taste receptors, several kinds of evidence suggested a fifth as well, that of glutamate, as found in monosodium glutamate (MSG). Researchers in fact located a glutamate taste receptor, which closely resembles the brain's receptors for glutamate as a neurotransmitter (Chaudhari, Landin, & Roper, 2000). The taste of glutamate resembles that of unsalted chicken broth. The English language did not have a word for this taste, but Japanese did, so English-speaking researchers have adopted the Japanese word, *umami*. Researchers have also reported a fat receptor in the taste buds of mice and rats, so perhaps we shall add the taste of fat as a sixth kind of taste (Laugerette et al., 2005).

In addition to the fact that different chemicals excite different receptors, they also produce different rhythms of action potentials. For example, the following two records have the same total number of action potentials in the same amount of time but different temporal patterns:

Time

Researchers noticed that sweet, salty, and bitter chemicals produced different patterns of activity in the taste-sensitive area of the medulla. They recorded the pattern while rats were drinking quinine (a bitter substance) and later used an electrode to generate the same patterns while rats were drinking water. The rats then avoided the water, as if it tasted bad (Di Lorenzo, Hallock, & Kennedy, 2003). Evidently, the "code" to represent a taste includes the rhythm of activity and not just which cells are most active.

Mechanisms of Taste Receptors

The saltiness receptor is particularly simple. Recall that a neuron produces an action potential when sodium ions cross its membrane. A saltiness receptor, which detects the presence of sodium, simply permits sodium ions on the tongue to cross its membrane. The higher the concentration of sodium on the tongue, the greater the receptor's response. Chemicals such as amiloride, which prevents sodium from crossing the membrane, reduce the intensity of salty tastes (DeSimone, Heck, Mierson, & DeSimone, 1984; Schiffman, Lockhead, & Maes, 1983).

Sourness receptors operate on a different principle. When an acid binds to the receptor, it closes potassium channels, preventing potassium from leaving the cell. The result is an increased accumulation of positive charges within the neuron and therefore a depolarization of the membrane (Shirley & Persaud, 1990).

Sweetness, bitterness, and umami receptors have much in common chemically (He et al., 2004). After a molecule binds to one of these receptors, it activates a G-protein that releases a second messenger within the cell, as in the metabotropic synapses discussed in Chapter 3 (Lindemann, 1996).

Bitter sensations have long been a puzzle. It is easy to describe the chemicals that produce a sour taste (acids), a salty taste (Na^+ ions), or umami (glutamate). Sweets are more difficult, as they include naturally occurring sugars plus artificial chemicals such as saccharin and aspartame. But bitter substances include a long list of chemicals that apparently have nothing in common, except that they are to varying degrees toxic. What receptor could identify such a large and diverse set of chemicals? The answer is that we have not one bitter receptor but a whole family of 40 or more (Adler et al., 2000; Matsunami, Montmayeur, & Buck, 2000). Most taste cells sensitive to bitterness contain just a small number of the possible bitter receptors, not all 40 (Caicedo & Roper, 2001).

One consequence of having so many bitter receptors is that we can detect a great variety of dangerous chemicals. The other is that because each type of bitter receptor is present in small numbers, we can't detect very low concentrations of bitter substances, the way we can with sour or salty substances, for example.

Researchers genetically engineered some mice with salty or sweet receptors on the cells that ordinarily have bitter receptors. Those mice avoided anything that tasted salty or sweet (Mueller et al., 2005). That is, the cells still send the message "bitter," even though a different kind of chemical is stimulating them.

STOP & CHECK

2. Suppose you find a new, unusual-tasting food. How could you determine whether we have a special receptor for that food or whether we taste it with a combination of the other known taste receptors?
3. Although the tongue has receptors for bitter tastes, researchers have not found neurons in the brain itself that respond more strongly to bitter than to other tastes. Explain, then, how it is possible for the brain to detect bitter tastes.
4. If someone injected into your tongue some chemical that blocks the release of second messengers, how would it affect your taste experiences?

Check your answers on page 227.

Taste Coding in the Brain

Although you may assume that the five kinds of receptors imply five labeled lines to the brain, research suggests a more complicated system (Hettinger & Frank, 1992). The receptors converge their input onto the next cells in the taste system, each of which responds best to a particular taste, but somewhat to other tastes also. The brain can determine what the tongue is tasting only by comparing the responses of several kinds of taste neurons. In other words, taste depends on a pattern of responses across fibers (R. P. Erickson, DiLorenzo, & Woodbury, 1994).

Information from the receptors in the anterior two-thirds of the tongue is carried to the brain along the chorda tympani, a branch of the seventh cranial nerve (the facial nerve). Taste information from the posterior tongue and the throat is carried along branches of the ninth and tenth cranial nerves. What do you suppose would happen if someone anesthetized your chorda tympani? You would no longer taste anything in the anterior part of your tongue, but you probably would not notice because you would still taste with the posterior part. However, the probability is about 40% that you would experience taste "phantoms," analogous to the phantom limb experience discussed in Chapter 5 (Yanagisawa, Bartoshuk, Catalanotto, Karrer, & Kveton, 1998). That is, you might experience tastes even when nothing was on your tongue. Evidently, the inputs from the anterior and posterior parts of your tongue interact in complex ways. Silencing the anterior part releases the posterior part from inhibition and causes it to report tastes more actively than before.

The taste nerves project to the **nucleus of the tractus solitarius (NTS)**, a structure in the medulla (Travers, Pfaffmann, & Norgren, 1986). From the NTS, information branches out, reaching the pons, the lateral hypothalamus, the amygdala, the ventral-posterior thalamus, and two areas of the cerebral cortex (Pritchard, Hamilton, Morse, & Norgren, 1986; Yamamoto, 1984). One of these, the somatosensory cortex, responds to the touch aspects of tongue stimulation. The other area, known as the insula, is the primary taste cortex. Curiously, each hemisphere of the cortex receives input mostly from the ipsilateral side of the tongue (Aglioti, Tassinari, Corballis, & Berlucchi, 2000; Pritchard, Macaluso, & Eslinger, 1999). In contrast, each hemisphere receives mostly contralateral input for vision, hearing, and touch. A few of the major connections are illustrated in Figure 7.19.

Individual Differences in Taste

You may have had a biology instructor who asked you to taste phenylthiocarbamide (PTC) and then take samples home for your relatives to try. Some people experience it as bitter, and others hardly taste it at all; most of the variance among people is controlled by a dominant gene and therefore provides an interesting example for a genetics lab (Kim et al., 2003). (Did your instructor happen to mention that PTC is mildly toxic?)

For decades, this difference was widely studied as an interesting, easily measurable genetic difference among people, and we have extensive data about the percentage of nontasters in different populations (Guo & Reed, 2001). Figure 7.20 shows some representative results. Although we might expect the prevalence of nontasters to influence cuisine, the figure shows no obvious relationship. For example, nontasters are common in India, where the food is spicy, and in Britain, where it is relatively bland.

In the 1990s, researchers discovered that people who are insensitive to PTC are also less sensitive than most people to other tastes as well, including other bitter substances, sours, salts, and so forth. Furthermore, people at the opposite extreme, known as **supertasters**, have the highest sensitivity to all tastes, as well as to mouth sensations in general (Drewnowski, Henderson, Shore, & Barratt-Fornell, 1998). Supertasters tend to avoid strong-tasting or spicy foods. However, culture and familiarity exert larger effects on people's food preferences. Consequently, even after you think about how much you do or do not like strongly flavored foods, you cannot confidently identify yourself as a supertaster, taster, or nontaster.

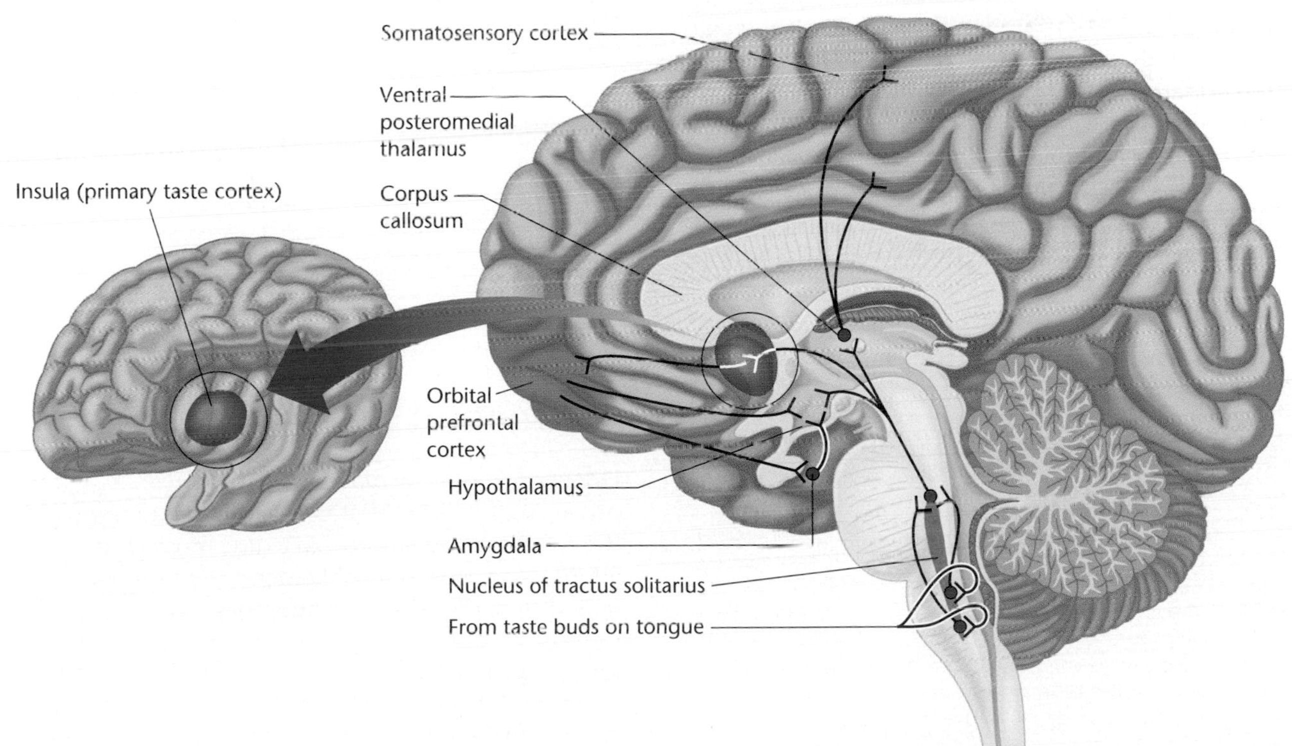

Figure 7.19 Major routes of impulses related to the sense of taste in the human brain
The thalamus and cerebral cortex receive impulses from both the left and the right sides of the tongue. *(Source: Based on Rolls, 1995)*

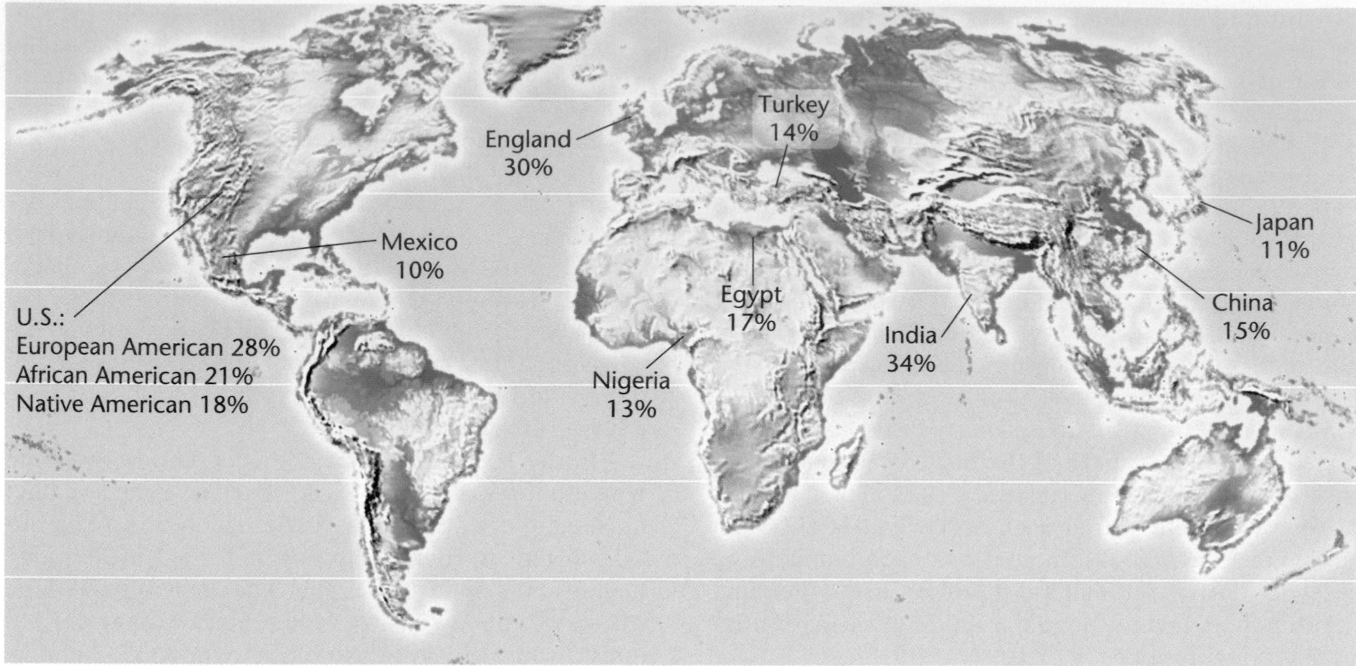

Figure 7.20 Percentage of nontasters in several human populations
Most of the percentages are based on large samples, including more than 31,000 in Japan and 35,000 in India. *(Source: Based on Guo & Reed, 2001)*

The variations in taste sensitivity relate to the number of *fungiform papillae* near the tip of the tongue. Supertasters have the most; nontasters have the fewest. That anatomical difference depends mostly on genetics but also on hormones and other influences. Women's taste sensitivity rises and falls with their monthly hormone cycles and reaches its maximum during early pregnancy, when estradiol levels are very high (Prutkin et al., 2000). That tendency is probably adaptive: During pregnancy, a woman needs to be more careful than usual to avoid harmful foods.

Table 7.2 Are You a Supertaster, Taster, or Nontaster?

Equipment: ¼-inch hole punch, small piece of wax paper, cotton swab, blue food coloring, flashlight, and magnifying glass.

Punch a ¼-inch hole with a standard hole punch in a piece of wax paper. Dip the cotton swab in blue food coloring. Place the wax paper on the tip of your tongue, just right of the center. Rub the cotton swab over the hole in the wax paper to dye a small part of your tongue. With the flashlight and magnifying glass, have someone count the number of pink, unstained circles in the blue area. They are your fungiform papillae. Compare your results to the following averages:

Supertasters:	25 papillae
Tasters:	17 papillae
Nontasters:	10 papillae

If you would like to classify yourself as a taster, nontaster, or supertaster, follow the instructions in Table 7.2.

5. What are several reasons why some people like spicier foods than others do?

Check your answer on page 227.

Olfaction

Olfaction, the sense of smell, is the detection and recognition of chemicals that contact the membranes inside the nose. During an ordinary day, most of us pay little attention to scents, and the deodorant industry is dedicated to decreasing our olfactory experience. Nevertheless, we enjoy many smells, especially in foods. We rely on olfaction for discriminating good from bad wine or edible from rotting meat. Many odors, such as that of a campfire or fresh popcorn, tend to evoke highly emotional memories (Herz, 2004).

Decades ago, researchers described olfaction as relatively slow to respond, but later studies found that mice can respond to an odor within 200 ms of its presentation, comparable to reaction times for other senses (Abraham et al., 2004). However, olfaction is subject to more rapid adaptation than sight or hearing (Kurahashi, Lowe, & Gold, 1994). To demonstrate adaptation, take a bottle of an odorous chemical, such as lemon extract, and determine how far away you can hold the bottle and still smell it. Then hold it up to your nose and inhale deeply and repeatedly for a minute. Now test again: From how far away can you smell it?

try it yourself

Behavioral Methods of Identifying Olfactory Receptors

The neurons responsible for smell are the **olfactory cells**, which line the olfactory epithelium in the rear of the nasal air passages (Figure 7.21). In mammals, each olfactory cell has cilia (threadlike dendrites) that extend from the cell body into the mucous surface of the nasal passage. Olfactory receptors are located on the cilia.

How many kinds of olfactory receptors do we have? Researchers answered the analogous question for color vision more than a century ago, using only behavioral observations. They found that, by mixing various amounts of three colors of light—say, red, green, and blue—they could match any other color that people can see. Researchers therefore concluded that we have three, and probably only three, kinds of color receptors (which we now call cones).

We could imagine doing the same experiment for olfaction. Take a few odors—say, almond, lilac, and skunk spray—and test whether people can mix various

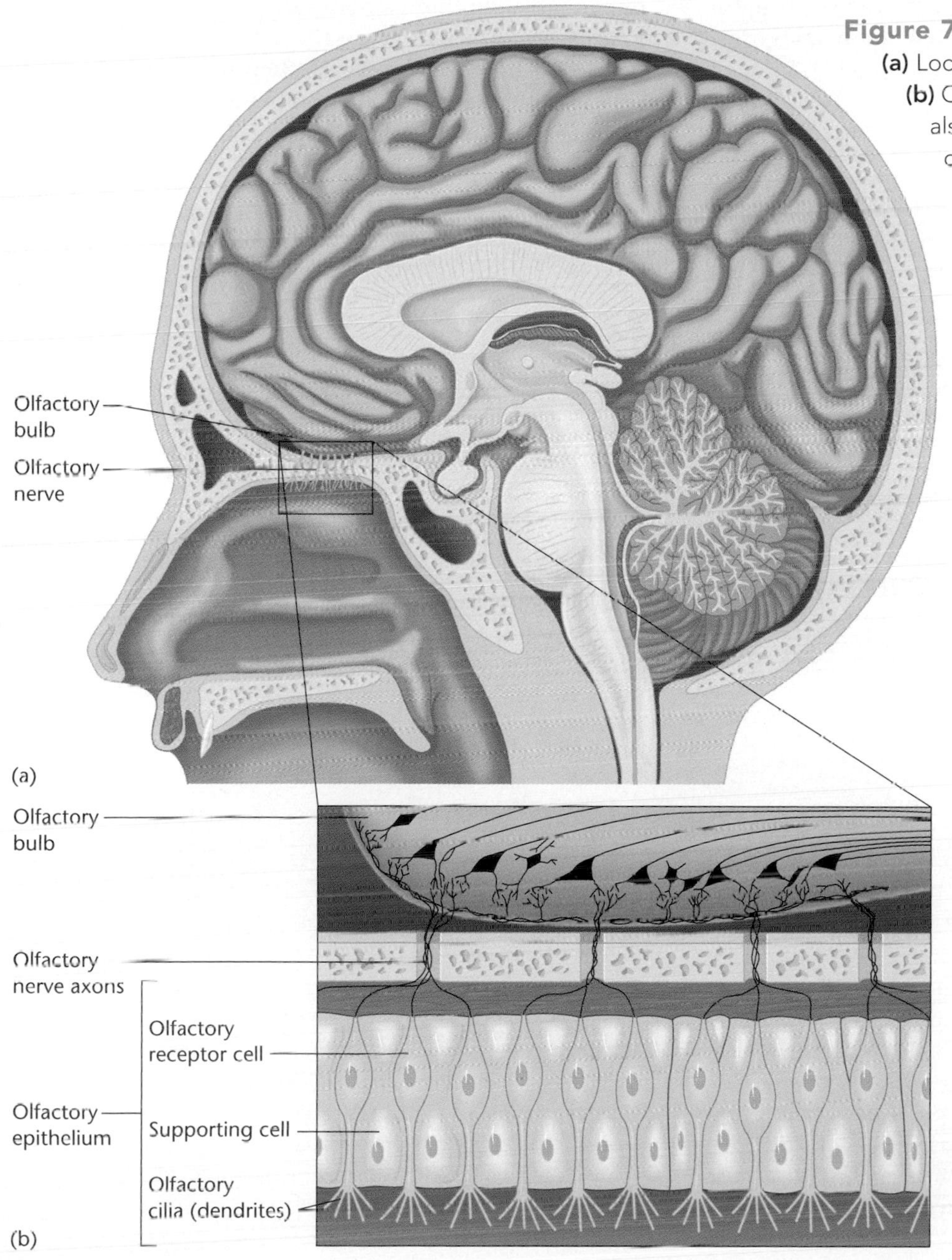

Figure 7.21 Olfactory receptors
(a) Location of receptors in nasal cavity. **(b)** Closeup of olfactory cells. Note also the vomeronasal organ, to be discussed later.

proportions of those odors to match all other odors. If three odors are not enough, add more until eventually we can mix them to match every other possible odor. Because we do not know what the "primary odors" are (if indeed there are such things), we might have to do a great deal of trial-and-error testing to find the best set of odors to use. So far as we know, however, either no one ever tried this study, or everyone who did gave up in discouragement.

A second approach is to study people who have trouble smelling one type of chemical. A general lack of olfaction is known as **anosmia;** the inability to smell a single chemical is a **specific anosmia.** For example, about 2% to 3% of all people are insensitive to the smell of isobutyric acid, the smelly component of sweat (Amoore, 1977). (Few complain about this disability.) Because people can lose the ability to smell just this one chemical, we may assume that there is a receptor specific to isobutyric acid. We might then search for additional specific anosmias on the theory that each specific anosmia represents the loss of a different type of receptor.

One investigator identified at least five other specific anosmias—musky, fishy, urinous, spermous, and malty—and less convincing evidence suggested 26 other possible specific anosmias (Amoore, 1977). But the more specific anosmias one finds, the less sure one can be of having found them all.

Biochemical Identification of Receptor Types

Ultimately, the best way to determine the number of olfactory receptor types is to isolate the receptor molecules themselves. Linda Buck and Richard Axel (1991) identified a family of proteins in olfactory receptors, as shown in Figure 7.22. Like metabotropic neurotransmitter receptors, each of these proteins traverses the cell membrane seven times and responds to a chemical outside the cell (here an odorant molecule instead of a neurotransmitter) by triggering changes in a G-protein inside the cell; the G-protein then provokes chemical activities that lead to an action potential. The best estimate is that humans have several hundred olfactory

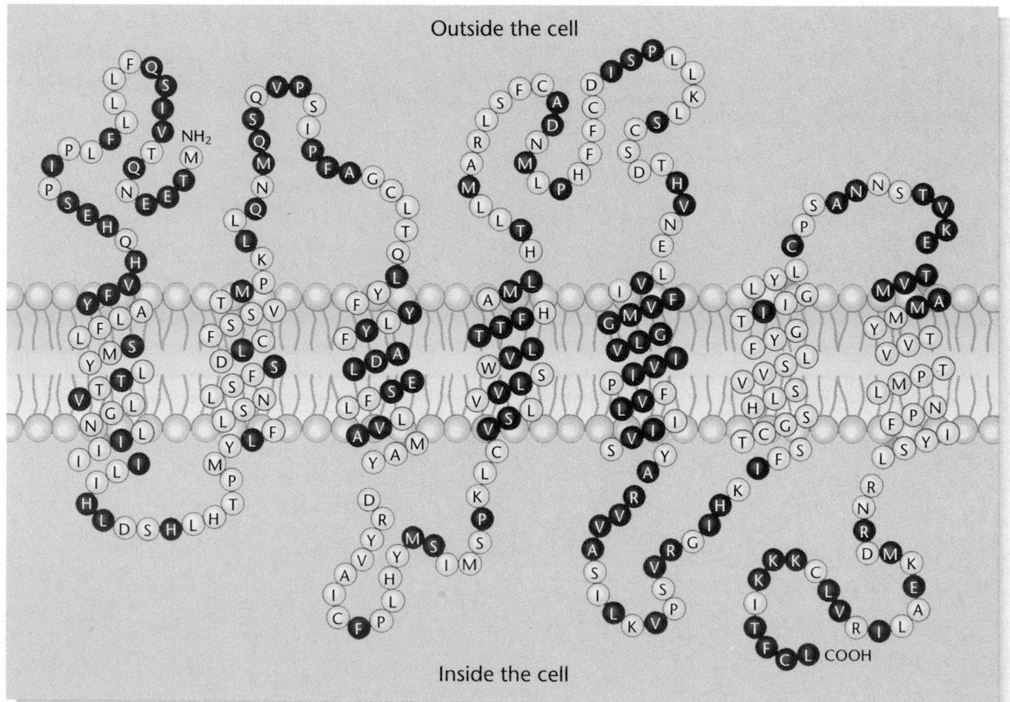

Figure 7.22 One of the olfactory receptor proteins
This protein resembles those of neurotransmitter receptors. Each protein traverses the membrane seven times; each responds to a chemical outside the cell and triggers activity of a G-protein inside the cell. The protein shown is one of a family; different olfactory receptors contain different proteins, each with a slightly different structure. Each of the little circles in this diagram represents one amino acid of the protein. The white circles represent amino acids that are the same in most of the olfactory receptor proteins; the purple circles represent amino acids that vary from one protein to another. *(Source: Based on Buck & Axel, 1991)*

receptor proteins, whereas rats and mice have about a thousand types (Zhang & Firestein, 2002). Correspondingly, rats can distinguish among odors that seem the same to humans (Rubin & Kaatz, 2001).

Although each chemical excites several types of receptors, the most strongly excited receptor inhibits the activity of other ones in a process analogous to lateral inhibition (Oka, Omura, Kataoka, & Touhara, 2004). The net result is that a given chemical produces a major response in one or two kinds of receptors and weaker responses in a few others.

6. If someone sees no need to shower after becoming sweaty, what is one (admittedly unlikely) explanation?

7. How do olfactory receptors resemble metabotropic neurotransmitter receptors?

Check your answers on page 227.

Implications for Coding

We have only three kinds of cones and probably five kinds of taste receptors, so it was a surprise to find hundreds of kinds of olfactory receptors. That diversity makes possible narrow specialization of functions. To illustrate: Because we have only three kinds of cones with which to see a great variety of colors, each cone must contribute to almost every color perception. In olfaction, we can afford to have receptors that respond to few stimuli. The response of one olfactory receptor might mean, "I smell a fatty acid with a straight chain of about three to five carbon atoms." The response of another receptor might mean, "I smell either a fatty acid or an aldehyde with a straight chain of about five to seven carbon atoms" (Araneda, Kini, & Firestein, 2000; Imamura, Mataga, & Mori, 1992; Mori, Mataga, & Imamura, 1992). The combined activity of those two receptors would identify the chemical precisely.

The question may have occurred to you, "Why did evolution go to the bother of designing so many olfactory receptor types? After all, color vision gets by with just three types of cones." The main reason is that light energy can be arranged along a single dimension, wavelength. Olfaction processes an enormous variety of airborne chemicals that are not arranged along a single continuum. To detect them all, we need a great variety of receptors. A secondary reason has to do with localization. In olfaction, space is no problem; we arrange our olfactory receptors over the entire surface of the nasal passages. In vision, however, the brain needs to determine precisely where on the retina a stimulus originates. Hundreds of different kinds of wavelength receptors could not be compacted into each spot on the retina.

Messages to the Brain

When an olfactory receptor is stimulated, its axon carries an impulse to the olfactory bulb (see Figure 4.13, p. 91). Each odorous chemical excites only a limited part of the olfactory bulb. Evidently, olfaction is coded in terms of which area of the olfactory bulb is excited. Chemicals that smell similar excite neighboring areas, and chemicals that smell different excite more separated areas (Uchida, Takahashi, Tanifuji, & Mori, 2000). The olfactory bulb sends axons to the olfactory area of the cerebral cortex, where, again, neurons responding to a particular kind of smell cluster together. The mapping is consistent across individuals; that is, the cortical area responding to a given odor is the same from one individual to another (Zou, Horowitz, Montmayeur, Snapper, & Buck, 2001). From the cortex, information connects to other areas that control feeding and reproduction, two kinds of behavior that are very sensitive to odors.

Olfactory receptors are vulnerable to damage because they are exposed to everything in the air. Unlike your receptors for vision and hearing, which remain with you for a lifetime, an olfactory receptor has an average survival time of just over a month. At that point, a stem cell matures into a new olfactory cell in the same location as the first and expressing the same receptor protein (Nef, 1998). Its axon then has to find its way to the correct target in the olfactory bulb. Each olfactory neuron axon contains copies of its olfactory receptor protein, which it uses like an identification card to find its correct partner (Barnea et al., 2004; Strotmann, Levai, Fleischer, Schwarzenbacher, & Breer, 2004). However, if the entire olfactory surface is damaged at once by a blast of toxic fumes, so that the system has to replace all the receptors at the same time, many of them fail to make the correct connections, and olfactory experience does not recover fully to normal (Iwema, Fang, Kurtz, Youngentob, & Schwob, 2004).

Individual Differences

In olfaction, as with almost anything else, people differ. One strong correlate of that difference is gender. On the average, women detect odors more readily than men, and the brain responses to odors are stronger in women than in men. Those differences occur at all ages and in all cultures that have been tested (Doty, Applebaum, Zusho, & Settle, 1985; Yousem et al., 1999). Women also seem to pay more attention to smells. Surveys have found that women are much more likely than men to care about the smell of a potential romantic partner (Herz & Inzlicht, 2002).

In addition, if people repeatedly attend to some faint odor, young adult women gradually become more and more sensitive to it, until that they can detect it in concentrations one ten-thousandth of what they could at the start (Dalton, Doolittle, & Breslin, 2002). Men, girls before puberty, and women after menopause do not show that effect, so it apparently depends on female hormones. We can only speculate on why we evolved a connection between female hormones and odor sensitization.

We don't yet know much about genetic differences in olfactory sensitivity, but consider this one surprising study: Through the wonders of bioengineering, researchers can examine the effects of deleting any particular gene. One gene controls a channel through which most potassium passes in the membranes of certain neurons of the olfactory bulb. Potassium, you will recall from Chapter 2, leaves a neuron after an action potential, thereby restoring the resting potential. With no particular hypothesis in mind, researchers tested what would happen if they deleted that potassium channel in mice.

Ordinarily, deleting any gene leads to deficits, and deleting an important gene can leave an animal incapable of survival. So imagine the researchers' amazement when they found that the mice lacking this potassium channel had a much greater than normal sense of smell. In fact, you could say they had developed mice with a superpower: These mice could detect faint smells, less than one-thousandth the minimum that other mice could detect. Their olfactory bulb had an unusual anatomy, with more numerous but smaller clusters of neurons (Fadool et al., 2004). Exactly how the deletion of a gene led to this superpower remains uncertain, and presumably, the mice are deficient in some other way (or evolution would have deleted this gene long ago). Still, it is a noteworthy example of how a single gene can make a huge difference.

For more information about olfaction, check this website: **http://www.leffingwell.com/olfaction.htm**

STOP & CHECK

8. If two olfactory receptors are located near each other in the nose, in what way are they likely to be similar?
9. What is the mean life span of an olfactory receptor?
10. What good does it do for an olfactory axon to have copies of the cell's olfactory receptor protein?

Check your answers on page 227.

Vomeronasal Sensation and Pheromones

An additional sense is important for most mammals, although less so for humans. The **vomeronasal organ (VNO)** is a set of receptors located near, but separate from, the olfactory receptors. The VNO has relatively few types of receptors—12 families of them in mice (Rodriguez, Del Punta, Rothman, Ishii, & Mombaerts, 2002).

Unlike the olfactory system, which can identify an enormous number of chemicals, the VNO's receptors are specialized to respond only to **pheromones**, which are chemicals released by an animal that affect the behavior of other members of the same species, especially sexually. For example, if you have ever had a female dog that wasn't neutered, whenever she was in her fertile (estrus) period, even though you kept her indoors, your yard attracted every male dog in the neighborhood that was free to roam.

Each VNO receptor responds to just one pheromone, such as the smell of a male or a female mouse. It responds to the preferred chemical in concentrations as low as one part in a hundred billion, but it hardly responds at all to other chemicals (Leinders-Zufall et al., 2000). Furthermore, the receptor shows no adaptation to a repeated stimulus. Olfaction, by contrast, shows massive adaptation. Have you ever been in a room that seems smelly at first but not a few minutes later? Your olfactory receptors respond to a new odor but not to a continuing one. VNO receptors, however, continue responding just as strongly even after prolonged stimulation (Holy, Dulac, & Meister, 2000).

What do you suppose would happen if a male mouse's vomeronasal receptors were inactive because of a genetic abnormality or surgical removal of the organ? Results of various studies have differed. In one study, the males lost practically all sexual behaviors (Del Punta et al., 2002). In another, they attempted indiscriminately to mate with both males and females (Stowers, Holy, Meister, Dulac, & Koentges, 2002). In still another, they mated normally, although they could not find a female by her odor (Pankevich, Baum, & Cherry, 2004).

Although the VNO is reasonably prominent in most mammals and easy to find in a human fetus, in adult humans it is tiny (Monti-Bloch, Jennings-White, Dolberg, & Berliner, 1994) and has no receptors (Keverne, 1999). It seems to be vestigial—that is, a leftover from our evolutionary past.

Humans nevertheless do respond to pheromones. Researchers have found at least one pheromone receptor in humans. Its structure resembles that of other mammals' pheromone receptors, but for us, it is located in the olfactory mucosa along with normal olfactory receptors, not in the VNO (Rodriguez, Greer, Mok, & Mombaerts, 2000).

The behavioral effects of pheromones apparently occur unconsciously. That is, people respond behaviorally to certain chemicals in human skin even though they describe them as "odorless." Exposure to these chemicals—especially chemicals from the opposite sex—alters our skin temperature, sweating, and other autonomic responses (Monti-Bloch, Jennings-White, & Berliner, 1998) and increases activity in the hypothalamus, an area important for sexual behavior (Savic, Berglund, Gulyas, & Roland, 2001).

Several studies indicate a role for pheromones in human sexual behaviors. The best-documented effect relates to the timing of women's menstrual cycles. Women who spend much time together find that their menstrual cycles become more synchronized (McClintock, 1971; Weller, Weller, Koresh-Kamin, & Ben-Shoshan, 1999; Weller, Weller, & Roizman, 1999), unless one of them is taking birth-control pills. To test whether pheromones are responsible for the synchronization, researchers in two studies exposed young volunteer women to the underarm secretions of a donor woman. In both studies, most of the women exposed to the secretions became synchronized to the donor's menstrual cycle (Preti, Cutler, Garcia, Huggins, & Lawley, 1986; Russell, Switz, & Thompson, 1980).

Another study dealt with the phenomenon that a woman who is in an intimate relationship with a man tends to have more regular menstrual periods than other women do. According to one hypothesis, the man's pheromones promote this regularity. In the study, young women who were not sexually active were exposed daily to a man's underarm secretions. (Getting women to volunteer for this study wasn't easy.) Gradually, over 14 weeks, most of these women's menstrual periods became more regular than before, with a mean of 29–30 days each (Cutler et al., 1986). In short, human body secretions apparently do act as pheromones, although the effects are more subtle than in nonhuman mammals.

STOP & CHECK

11. What is one major difference between olfactory receptors and those of the vomeronasal organ?

Check your answer on page 227.

Synesthesia

Finally, let's briefly consider something that is not one sense or another but rather a combination of them: **Synesthesia** is the experience of one sense in response to stimulation of a different sense. In the words of one person with synesthesia, "To me, the taste of beef is dark blue. The smell of almonds is pale orange. And when tenor saxophones play, the music looks like a floating, suspended coiling snake-ball of lit-up purple neon tubes" (Day, 2005, p. 11). No two people have quite the same synesthetic experience. It is estimated that about 1 person in 500 is synesthetic (Day, 2005), but that estimate probably overlooks people with a milder form of the condition, as well as many who hide their condition because other people consider it a sign of mental illness. (It is, in fact, neither particularly helpful nor harmful.)

Various studies attest to the reality of synesthesia. For example, try to find the 2 among the 5s in each of the following displays:

555555555555   **555555555555**   **555555555555**
555555555555   **555555555555**   **552555555555**
555555525555   **555555555555**   **555555555555**
555555555555   **555555555525**   **555555555555**

One person with synesthesia was able to find the 2 consistently faster than other people, explaining that he just scanned each display looking for a patch of orange! However, he was slower than other people to find an 8 among 6s because both 8 and 6 look bluish to him (Blake, Palmeri, Marois, & Kim, 2005). Another person had trouble finding an A among 4s because both look red, but could easily find an A among 0s because 0 looks black (Laeng, Svartdal, & Oelmann, 2004). Oddly, however, someone who sees the letter P as yellow had no trouble finding it when it was printed (in black ink) on a yellow page. In some way, he sees the letter both in its real color (black) *and* its synesthetic color (Blake et al., 2005).

In another study, people were asked to identify as quickly as possible the shape formed by the less common character in a display like this:

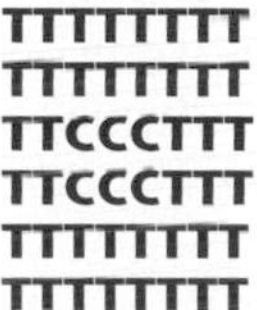

Here, the correct answer is "rectangle," the shape formed by the Cs. People who perceive C and T as different colors find the rectangle faster than the average for people without synesthesia. However, they do not find it as fast as some other person would find the rectangle of Cs in this display, where the Cs really are in color:

In short, people with synesthesia see letters as if in color but not as bright as real colors (Hubbard, Arman, Ramachandran, & Boynton, 2005).

Researchers used fMRI to map brain responses in a group of 12 women who all reported seeing colors when they heard people speak. In each case, listening to speech elicited activity in both the auditory cortex and the area of the visual cortex most responsive to color (Nunn et al., 2002). Results like these suggest that for people with synesthesia, some of the axons from one cortical area have branches into another cortical area. Although that seems a plausible hypothesis, surely it can't be the whole explanation. Obviously, no one is born with a connection between P and yellow or between 4 and red; we have to learn to recognize numbers and letters. Exactly how synesthesia develops remains for further research.

STOP & CHECK

12. If someone reports seeing a particular letter in color, in what way is it different from a real color?

Check your answer on page 227.

Module 7.3

In Closing: Different Senses as Different Ways of Knowing the World

Ask the average person to describe the current environment, and you will probably get a description of what he or she sees and maybe hears. If nonhumans could talk, most species would start by describing what they smell. A human, a dog, and a snail may be in the same place, but the environments they perceive are very different.

We sometimes underestimate the importance of taste and smell. The rare people who lose their sense of taste say they no longer enjoy eating and in fact find it difficult to swallow (Cowart, 2005). A loss of smell can be a problem too. Taste and smell can't compete with vision and hearing for telling us about what is happening in the distance, but they are essential for telling us about what is right next to us or about to enter our bodies.

Summary

1. Sensory information can be coded in terms of either a labeled-line system or an across-fiber pattern system. (p. 215)
2. Taste receptors are modified skin cells inside taste buds in papillae on the tongue. (p. 216)
3. According to current evidence, we have five kinds of taste receptors, sensitive to sweet, sour, salty, bitter, and umami (glutamate) tastes. (p. 217)
4. Taste is coded by the relative activity of different kinds of cells but also by the rhythm of responses within a given cell. (p. 217)
5. Salty receptors respond simply to sodium ions crossing the membrane. Sour receptors respond to a stimulus by blocking potassium channels. Sweet, bitter, and umami receptors act by a second messenger within the cell, similar to the way a metabotropic neurotransmitter receptor operates. (p. 218)
6. Mammals have about 40 kinds of bitter receptors, enabling them to detect a great variety of harmful substances that are chemically unrelated to one another. However, a consequence of so many bitter receptors is that we are not highly sensitive to low concentrations of any one bitter chemical. (p. 218)
7. Taste information from the anterior two-thirds of the tongue is carried by a different nerve from the posterior tongue and throat. The two nerves interact in complex ways, such that suppressing activity in the anterior tongue increases responses from the posterior tongue. (p. 218)
8. Some people, known as supertasters, have more fungiform papillae than other people do and are more sensitive to a great variety of tastes. They tend to avoid strong-tasting foods. (p. 219)
9. Olfactory receptors are proteins, each of them highly responsive to a few related chemicals and unresponsive to others. Vertebrates have hundreds of olfactory receptors, each contributing to the detection of a few related odors. (p. 222)
10. Olfactory neurons responsive to a particular odor all send their axons to the same part of the olfactory bulb and from there to the same clusters of cells in the olfactory cortex. (p. 223)
11. Olfactory neurons survive only a month or so. When the brain generates new cells to replace them, the new ones become sensitive to the same

chemicals as the ones they replace, and they send their axons to the same targets. (p. 223)

12. In most mammals, each vomeronasal organ (VNO) receptor is sensitive to only one chemical, a pheromone. A pheromone is a social signal, usually for mating purposes. Unlike olfactory receptors, VNO receptors show little or no adaptation to a prolonged stimulus. (p. 224)
13. Humans also respond somewhat to pheromones, although our receptors are in the olfactory mucosa, not the VNO. (p. 224)
14. A small percentage of people experience synesthesia, a sensation in one modality after stimulation in another one. For example, someone might see something while listening to music. The explanation is not known. (p. 225)

Answers to STOP & CHECK Questions

1. The shift key plus another is an example of an across-fiber pattern code. (The meaning of one key depends on what else is pressed.) A fire alarm and a light switch are labeled lines; they convey only one message. (p. 216)
2. You could test for cross-adaptation. If the new taste cross-adapts with others, then it uses the same receptors. If it does not cross-adapt, it may have a receptor of its own. Another possibility would be to find some procedure that blocks this taste without blocking other tastes. (p. 218)
3. Two possibilities: First, bitter tastes produce a distinctive temporal pattern of responses in cells sensitive to taste. Second, even if no one cell responds strongly to bitter tastes, the pattern of responses across many cells may be distinctive. Analogously, in vision, no cone responds primarily to purple, but we nevertheless recognize purple by its pattern of activity across a population of cones. (p. 218)
4. The chemical would block your experiences of sweet, bitter, and umami but should not prevent you from tasting salty and sour. (p. 218)
5. Both genes and hormones influence the strength of tastes, and people who taste foods most strongly tend to avoid spicy foods. In addition, and more important, people prefer familiar foods and foods accepted by their culture. (p. 220)
6. The person may have a specific anosmia and therefore may regard sweat as odorless. (p. 223)
7. Like metabotropic neurotransmitter receptors, an olfactory receptor acts through a G-protein that triggers further events within the cell. (p. 223)
8. Olfactory receptors located near each other are probably sensitive to structurally similar chemicals. (p. 224)
9. Most olfactory receptors survive a little more than a month before dying and being replaced. (p. 224)
10. The receptor molecule acts as a kind of identification to help the axon find its correct target cell in the brain. (p. 224)
11. Olfactory receptors adapt quickly to a continuous odor, whereas receptors of the vomeronasal organ continue to respond. Also, vomeronasal sensations are apparently capable of influencing behavior even without being consciously perceived. (p. 225)
12. Someone who perceives a letter as yellow (when it is actually in black ink) can nevertheless see it on a yellow page. (p. 226)

Thought Questions

1. In the English language, the letter *t* has no meaning out of context. Its meaning depends on its relationship to other letters. Indeed, even a word, such as *to*, has little meaning except in its connection to other words. So is language a labeled-line system or an across-fiber pattern system?
2. Suppose a chemist synthesizes a new chemical that turns out to have an odor. Presumably, we do not have a specialized receptor for that chemical. Explain how our receptors detect it.

Chapter Ending

Key Terms and Activities

Terms

across-fiber pattern principle (p. 215)
adaptation (p. 217)
amplitude (p. 196)
anosmia (p. 222)
capsaicin (p. 209)
cochlea (p. 198)
conductive deafness (middle-ear deafness) (p. 201)
cross-adaptation (p. 217)
dermatome (p. 208)
endorphin (p. 210)
frequency (p. 196)
frequency theory (p. 198)
gate theory (p. 211)
hair cell (p. 198)
labeled-line principle (p. 215)
loudness (p. 196)
nerve deafness (inner-ear deafness) (p. 201)
nucleus of the tractus solitarius (NTS) (p. 219)
olfaction (p. 220)
olfactory cell (p. 221)
opioid mechanisms (p. 210)
oval window (p. 197)
Pacinian corpuscle (p. 206)
papilla (pl.: papillae) (p. 216)
periaqueductal gray area (p. 210)
pheromone (p. 224)
pinna (p. 197)
pitch (p. 196)
place theory (p. 198)
placebo (p. 212)
primary auditory cortex (area A1) (p. 199)
semicircular canal (p. 205)
somatosensory system (p. 206)
specific anosmia (p. 222)
substance P (p. 209)
supertasters (p. 219)
synesthesia (p. 225)
taste bud (p. 216)
tinnitus (p. 202)
tympanic membrane (p. 197)
volley principle (p. 199)
vomeronasal organ (VNO) (p. 224)

Suggestions for Further Reading

Beauchamp, G. K., & Bartoshuk, L. (1997). *Tasting and smelling.* San Diego, CA: Academic Press. Excellent book covering receptors, psychophysics, and disorders of taste and smell.

Pert, C. B. (1997). *Molecules of emotion.* New York: Simon & Schuster. Autobiographical statement by the woman who, as a graduate student, first demonstrated the opiate receptors.

Robertson, L. C., & Sagiv, N. (2005). *Synesthesia: Perspectives from cognitive neuroscience.* Oxford, England: Oxford University Press. A review of research on this fascinating phenomenon.

Websites to Explore

You can go to the Biological Psychology Study Center and click these links. While there, you can also check for suggested articles available on InfoTrac College Edition. The Biological Psychology Internet address is:

psychology.wadsworth.com/book/kalatbiopsych9e/

Mark Rejhon's Frequently Asked Questions About Hearing Impairment
http://www.marky.com/hearing/

Pain Net, with many links
http://www.painnet.com/

American Pain Society
http://www.ampainsoc.org/

Nontaster, Taster, or Supertaster?
http://www.neosoft.com/~bmiller/taste.htm

Sense of Smell Institute
http://www.senseofsmell.org

Exploring Biological Psychology CD

Hearing (learning module)
Hearing Puzzle (puzzle)
Somesthetic Experiment (drag & drop)
Chapter Quiz (multiple-choice questions)
Critical Thinking (essay questions)

ThomsonNOW™

http://www.thomsonedu.com

Go to this site for the link to ThomsonNOW, your one-stop study shop, Take a Pre-Test for this chapter, and ThomsonNOW will generate a Personalized Study Plan based on your test results. The Study Plan will identify the topics you need to review and direct you to online resources to help you master these topics. You can then take a Post-Test to help you determine the concepts you have mastered and what you still need work on.

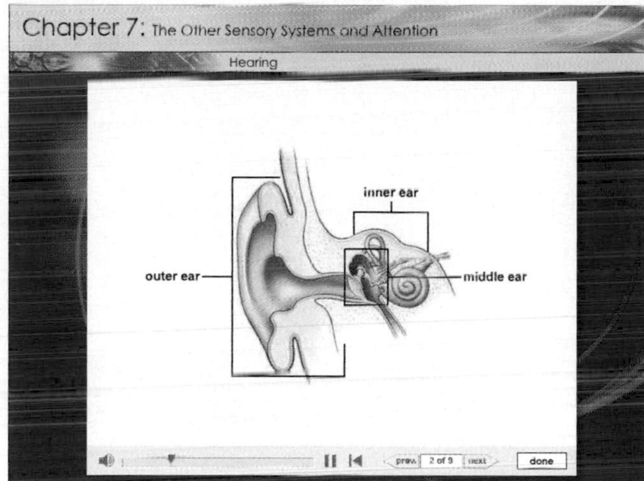

This item reviews the structure of the ear.

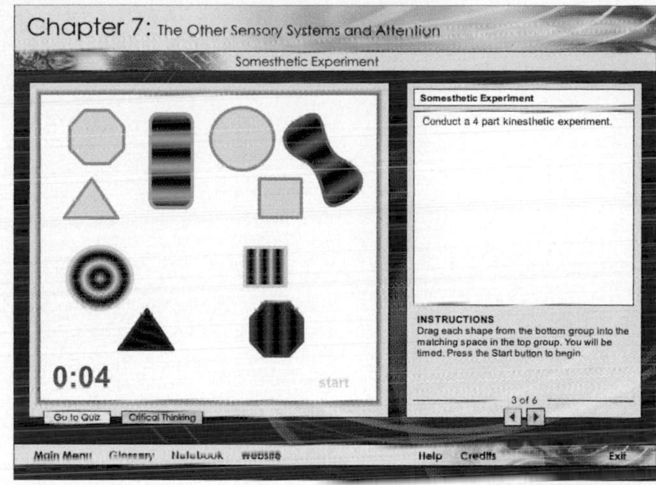

Test what happens when your hand movements produce the opposite of their visual effects.

Movement

Chapter Outline

Opposite: Ultimately, what brain activity accomplishes is the control of movement—a far more complex process than it might seem.
Source: Jim Rider/Zeis Images

Main Ideas

1. Movement depends on overall plans, not just connections between a stimulus and a muscle contraction.
2. Movements vary in sensitivity to feedback, skill, and variability in the face of obstacles.
3. Damage to different brain locations produces different kinds of movement impairment.
4. Brain damage that impairs movement also impairs cognitive processes. That is, control of movement is inseparably linked with cognition.

Before we get started, please try this: Get out a pencil and a sheet of paper, and put the pencil in your nonpreferred hand. For example, if you are right-handed, put it in your left hand. Now, with that hand, draw a face in profile—that is, facing one direction or the other, but not straight ahead. *Please do this now before reading further.*

try it yourself

If you tried the demonstration, you probably notice that your drawing is much more childlike than usual. It is as if some part of your brain stored the way you used to draw as a young child. Now, if you are right-handed and therefore drew the face with your left hand, why did you draw it facing to the right? At least I assume you did because more than two-thirds of right-handers drawing with their left hand draw the profile facing right. Young children, age 5 or so, when drawing with the right hand, almost always draw people and animals facing left, but when using the left hand, they almost always draw them facing right. But *why*? The short answer is we don't know. We have much to learn about the control of movement and how it relates to perception, motivation, and other functions.

Module 8.1
The Control of Movement

Why do we have brains at all? Plants survive just fine without them. So do sponges, which are animals, even if they don't act like them. But plants don't move, and neither do sponges. A sea squirt (a marine invertebrate) swims and has a brain during its infant stage, but when it transforms into an adult, it attaches to a surface, becomes a stationary filter-feeder, and digests its own brain, as if to say, "Now that I've stopped traveling, I won't need this brain thing anymore." Ultimately, the purpose of a brain is to control behaviors, and all behaviors are movements.

"But wait," you might reply. "We need brains for other things too, don't we? Like seeing, hearing, finding food, talking, understanding speech . . ."

Well, what would be the value of seeing and hearing if you couldn't do anything? Finding food requires movement, and so does talking. Understanding isn't movement, but again, it wouldn't do you much good unless you could do something with it. A great brain without muscles would be like a computer without a monitor, printer, or other output. No matter how powerful the internal processing, it would be useless.

Nevertheless, most psychology texts ignore movement, and journals have few articles about it (Rosenbaum, 2005). For example, one of the high points of artificial intelligence so far was the computer that won a chess tournament against the world's greatest player. During that tournament, the computer didn't actually *do* anything; a human took the computer's instructions and moved the chess pieces. It is as if we consider "intelligence" to mean great thoughts and actions to be something uninteresting tacked on at the end. Nevertheless, the rapid movements of a skilled typist, musician, or athlete require complex coordination and planning. Understanding movement is a significant challenge for psychologists as well as biologists.

Gary Bell/Getty Images

Adult sea squirts attach to the surface, never move again, and digest their own brains.

Muscles and Their Movements

All animal movement depends on muscle contractions. Vertebrate muscles fall into three categories (Figure 8.1): **smooth muscles**, which control the digestive system and other organs; **skeletal**, or **striated, muscles**, which control movement of the body in relation to the environment; and **cardiac muscles** (the heart muscles), which have properties intermediate between those of smooth and skeletal muscles.

Each muscle is composed of many individual fibers, as Figure 8.2 illustrates. A given axon may innervate more than one muscle fiber. For example, the eye muscles have a ratio of about one axon per three muscle fibers, and the biceps muscles of the arm have a ratio of one axon to more than a hundred fibers (Evarts, 1979). This difference allows the eye to move more precisely than the biceps.

A **neuromuscular junction** is a synapse where a motor neuron axon meets a muscle fiber. In skeletal muscles, every axon releases acetylcholine at the neuromuscular junction, and the acetylcholine always excites the muscle to contract. Each muscle can make just one movement—contraction—in just one direction. In the absence of excitation, it relaxes, but it never moves actively in the opposite direction. Moving a leg or arm in two directions requires opposing sets of muscles, called **antagonistic muscles.** An arm, for example, has a **flexor** muscle that flexes or raises it and an **extensor** muscle that extends or straightens it (Figure 8.3).

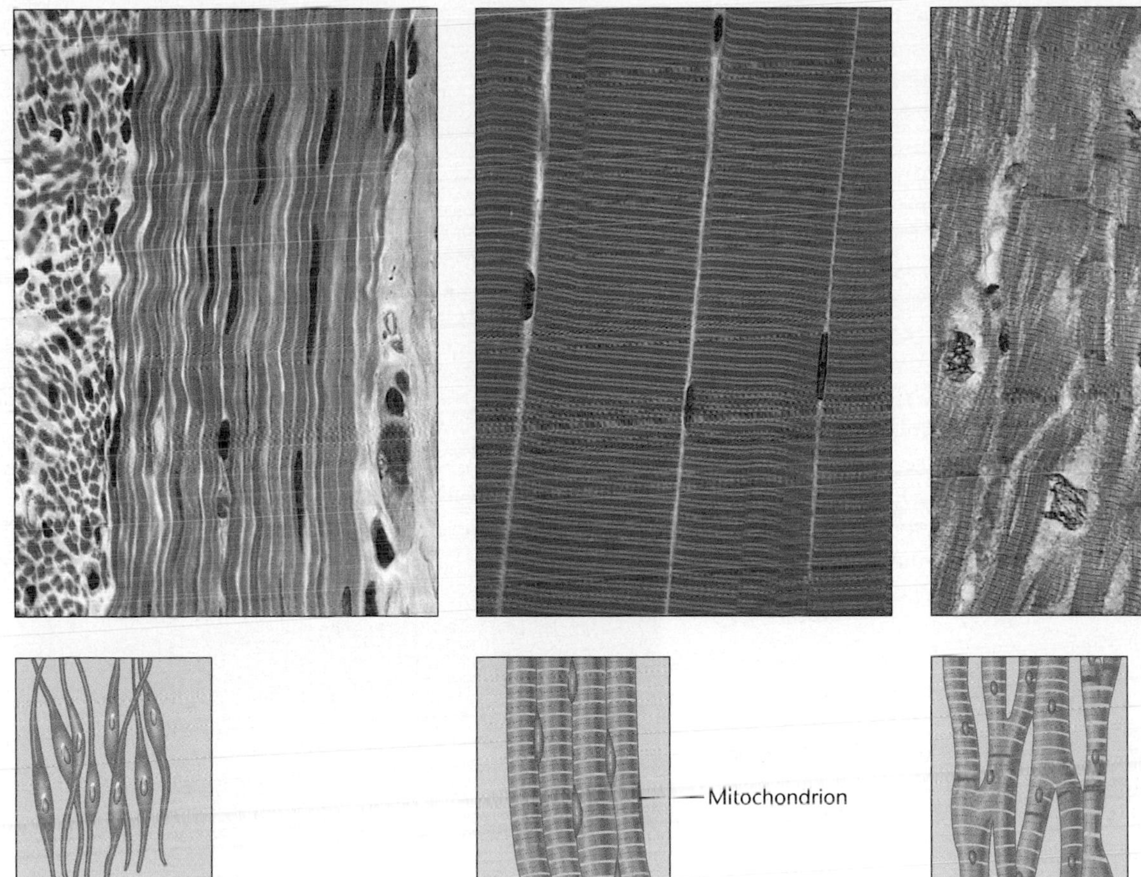

Figure 8.1 The three main types of vertebrate muscles
(a) Smooth muscle, found in the intestines and other organs, consists of long, thin cells. **(b)** Skeletal, or striated, muscle consists of long cylindrical fibers with stripes. **(c)** Cardiac muscle, found in the heart, consists of fibers that fuse together at various points. Because of these fusions, cardiac muscles contract together, not independently. *(Source: Illustrations after Starr & Taggart, 1989)*

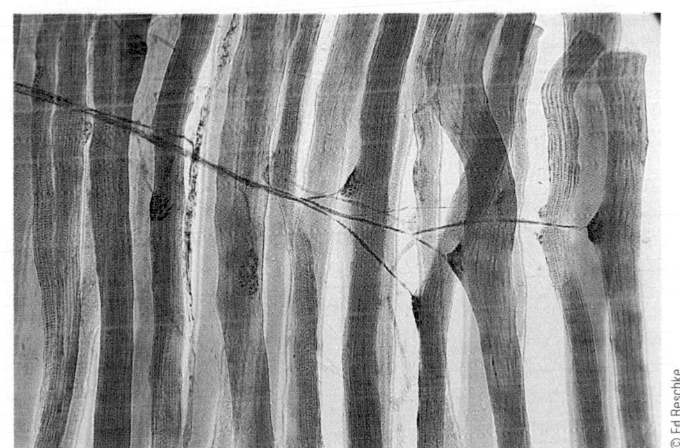

Figure 8.2
An axon branching to innervate separate muscle fibers within a muscle
Movements can be much more precise where each axon innervates only a few fibers, as with eye muscles, than where it innervates many fibers, as with biceps muscles.

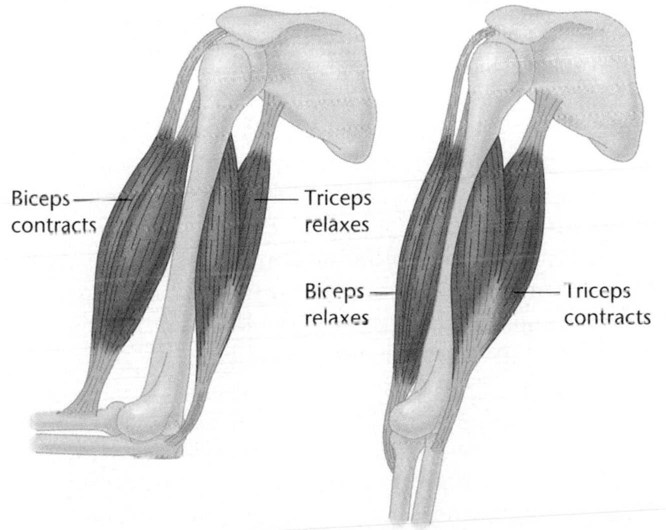

Figure 8.3 A pair of antagonistic muscles
The biceps of the arm is a flexor; the triceps is an extensor. *(Source: Starr & Taggart, 1989)*

Walking, clapping hands, and other coordinated sequences require a regular alternation between contraction of one set of muscles and contraction of another.

Any deficit of acetylcholine or its receptors in the muscles can greatly impair movement. **Myasthenia gravis** (MY-us-THEE-nee-uh GRAHV-iss) is an *autoimmune disease,* in that the immune system forms antibodies that attack the individual's own body. In myasthenia gravis, the immune system attacks the acetylcholine receptors at neuromuscular junctions (Shah & Lisak, 1993), causing progressive weakness and rapid fatigue of the skeletal muscles. Whenever anyone excites a given muscle fiber a few times in succession, later action potentials on the same motor neuron release less acetylcholine than before. For a healthy person, a slight decline in acetylcholine poses no problem. However, because people with myasthenia gravis have lost many of their receptors, even a slight decline in acetylcholine input produces clear deficits (Drachman, 1978).

Fast and Slow Muscles

Imagine that you are a small fish. Your only defense against bigger fish, diving birds, and other predators is your ability to swim away (Figure 8.4). A fish has the same temperature as the water around it, and muscle contractions, being chemical processes, slow down in the cold. So when the water gets cold, presumably you will move slowly, right? Strangely, you will not. You will have to use more muscles than before, but you will swim at about the same speed (Rome, Loughna, & Goldspink, 1984).

A fish has three kinds of muscles: red, pink, and white. Red muscles produce the slowest movements, but they are not vulnerable to fatigue. White muscles produce the fastest movements, but they fatigue rapidly. Pink muscles are intermediate in both speed and susceptibility to fatigue. At high temperatures, a fish relies mostly on its red and pink muscles. At colder temperatures, the fish relies more and more on its white muscles. By recruiting enough white muscles, the fish can swim rapidly even in cold water, at the expense of fatiguing faster.

All right, you can stop imagining that you are a fish. Human and other mammalian muscles have various kinds of muscle fibers mixed together, not in separate bundles as in fish. Our muscle types range from **fast-twitch fibers** that produce fast contractions but fatigue rapidly to **slow-twitch fibers** that produce less vigorous contractions without fatiguing (Hennig & Lømo, 1985). We rely on our slow-twitch and intermediate fibers for nonstrenuous activities. For example, you could talk for hours without fatiguing your lip muscles. You could probably walk for hours too. But if you run up a steep hill at full speed, you will have to switch to fast-twitch fibers, which will fatigue rapidly.

Tui De Roy/Minden Pictures

Figure 8.4 Temperature regulation and movement
Fish are "cold blooded," but many of their predators (e.g., this pelican) are not. At cold temperatures, a fish must maintain its normal swimming speed, even though every muscle in its body contracts more slowly than usual. To do so, a fish calls upon white muscles that it otherwise uses only for brief bursts of speed.

Slow-twitch fibers do not fatigue because they are **aerobic**—they use air (specifically oxygen) during their movements. You can think of them as "pay as you go." Vigorous use of fast-twitch fibers results in fatigue because the process is **anaerobic**—using reactions that do not require oxygen at the time, although oxygen is eventually necessary for recovery. Using them builds up an "oxygen debt." Prolonged exercise can start with aerobic activity and shift to anaerobic. For example, imagine yourself bicycling at a moderately challenging pace for hours. Your aerobic muscle activity uses glucose, and as the glucose supplies begin to dwindle, they activate a gene that *inhibits* further glucose use. The probable function is to save the dwindling glucose supplies for the brain to use (Booth & Neufer, 2005). The muscles then shift to anaerobic use of fatty acids as fuel. You will continue bicycling for a while, but the muscles will gradually fatigue.

People have varying percentages of fast-twitch and slow-twitch fibers. For example, the Swedish ultramarathon runner Bertil Järlaker built up so many slow-twitch fibers in his legs that he once ran 3,520 km (2,188 mi) in 50 days (an average of 1.7 marathons per day) with only minimal signs of pain or fatigue (Sjöström, Friden, & Ekblom, 1987). Conversely, competitive sprinters have a higher percentage of fast-twitch fibers. Individual differences depend on both genetics and training. In one study, investigators studied male sprinters before and after a 3-month period of intensive training. After the training, they found more fast-twitch leg muscle fibers and fewer slow-twitch fibers (Andersen, Klitgaard, & Saltin, 1994). Part of the change relates to alterations of the myosin molecules within muscles (Canepari et al., 2005).

STOP & CHECK

1. Why can the eye muscles move with greater precision than the biceps muscles?
2. In what way are fish movements impaired in cold water?
3. Duck breast muscles are red ("dark meat") whereas chicken breast muscles are white. Which species probably can fly for a longer time before fatiguing?
4. Why is an ultramarathoner like Bertil Järlaker probably mediocre or poor at short-distance races?

Check your answers on page 239.

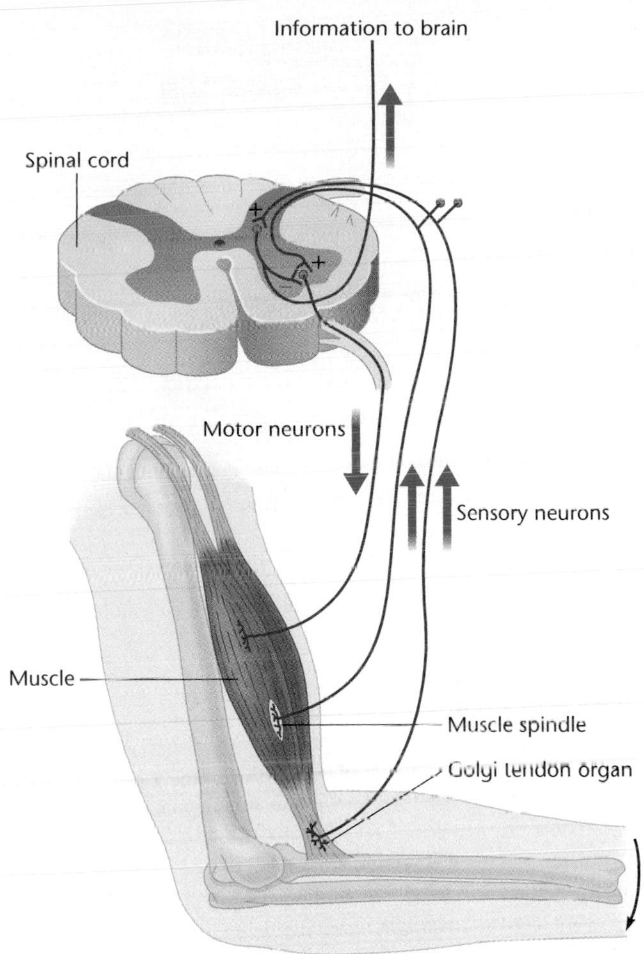

Figure 8.5 Two kinds of proprioceptors regulate the contraction of a muscle
When a muscle is stretched, the nerves from the muscle spindles transmit an increased frequency of impulses, resulting in a contraction of the surrounding muscle. Contraction of the muscle stimulates the Golgi tendon organ, which acts as a brake or shock absorber to prevent a contraction that is too quick or extreme.

Muscle Control by Proprioceptors

You are walking along on a bumpy road. What happens if the messages from your spinal cord to your leg muscles are not exactly correct? You might set your foot down a little too hard or not quite hard enough. Nevertheless, you adjust your posture almost immediately and maintain your balance without even thinking about it. How do you do that?

A baby is lying on its back. You playfully tug its foot and then let go. At once, the leg bounces back to its original position. How and why?

In both cases, the mechanism is under the control of proprioceptors (Figure 8.5). A **proprioceptor** is a receptor that detects the position or movement of a part of the body—in these cases, a muscle. Muscle proprioceptors detect the stretch and tension of a muscle and send messages that enable the spinal cord to adjust its signals. When a muscle is stretched, the spinal cord sends a reflexive signal to contract it. This **stretch reflex** is *caused* by a stretch; it does not *produce* one.

One kind of proprioceptor is the **muscle spindle**, a receptor parallel to the muscle that responds to a stretch (Merton, 1972; Miles & Evarts, 1979). Whenever the muscle spindle is stretched, its sensory nerve sends a message to a motor neuron in the spinal cord, which in turn sends a message back to the muscles surrounding the spindle, causing a contraction. Note that this reflex provides for negative feedback: When a muscle and its spindle are stretched, the spindle sends a message that results in a muscle contraction that opposes the stretch.

When you set your foot down on a bump on the road, your knee bends a bit, stretching the extensor muscles of that leg. The sensory nerves of the spindles send action potentials to the motor neuron in the spinal cord, and the motor neuron sends action potentials to the extensor muscle. Contracting the extensor muscle straightens the leg, adjusting for the bump on the road.

A physician who asks you to cross your legs and then taps just below the knee (Figure 8.6) is testing your stretch reflexes. The tap stretches the extensor muscles and their spindles, resulting in a message that jerks

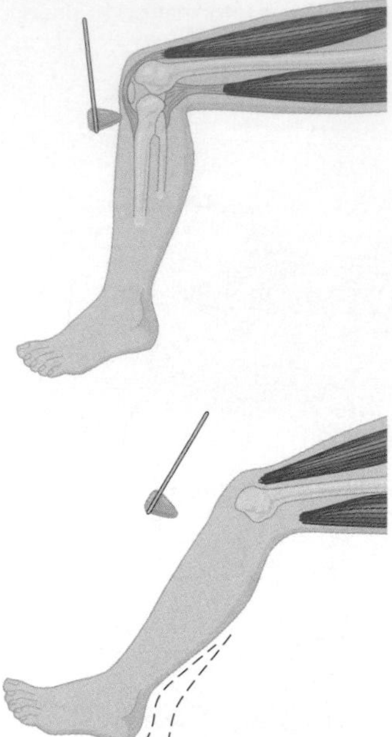

Figure 8.6 The knee-jerk reflex
Here is one example of a stretch reflex.

the lower leg upward. The same reflex contributes to walking; raising the upper leg reflexively moves the lower leg forward in readiness for the next step.

The **Golgi tendon organ**, another proprioceptor, responds to increases in muscle tension. Located in the tendons at opposite ends of a muscle, it acts as a brake against an excessively vigorous contraction. Some muscles are so strong that they could damage themselves if too many fibers contracted at once. Golgi tendon organs detect the tension that results during a muscle contraction. Their impulses travel to the spinal cord, where they inhibit the motor neurons through messages from interneurons. In short, a vigorous muscle contraction inhibits further contraction by activating the Golgi tendon organs.

The proprioceptors not only control important reflexes but also provide the brain with information. Here is an illusion that you can demonstrate yourself: Find a small, dense object and a larger, less dense object that weighs the same as the small one. For example, you might try a lemon and a hollowed-out orange, with the peel pasted back together so it appears to be intact. Drop one of the objects onto someone's hand while he or she is watching. (The watching is essential.) Then remove it and drop the other object onto the same hand. Most people report that the small one felt heavier. The reason is that with the larger object, people set themselves up with the expectation of a heavier weight. The actual weight displaces their proprioceptors less than expected and therefore yields the perception of a lighter object.

5. If you hold your arm straight out and someone pulls it down slightly, it quickly bounces back. What proprioceptor is responsible?
6. What is the function of Golgi tendon organs?

Check your answers on page 239.

Units of Movement

The stretch reflex is a simple example of movement. More complex kinds include speaking, walking, threading a needle, and throwing a basketball through a hoop while off balance and evading two defenders. In many ways, these movements are different from one another, and they depend on different kinds of control by the nervous system.

Voluntary and Involuntary Movements

Reflexes are consistent automatic responses to stimuli. We generally think of reflexes as *involuntary* because they are insensitive to reinforcements, punishments, and motivations. The stretch reflex is one example; another is the constriction of the pupil in response to bright light.

EXTENSIONS AND APPLICATIONS
Infant Reflexes

Humans have few reflexes, although infants have several not seen in adults. For example, if you place an object firmly in an infant's hand, the infant will reflexively grasp it tightly (the **grasp reflex**). If you stroke the sole of the foot, the infant will reflexively extend the big toe and fan the others (the **Babinski reflex**). If you touch an infant's cheek, the head will turn toward the stimulated cheek, and the infant will begin to suck (the **rooting reflex**). The rooting reflex is not a pure reflex, as its intensity depends on the infant's arousal and hunger levels.

Although such reflexes fade away with time, the connections remain intact, not lost but suppressed by axons from the maturing brain. If the cerebral cortex is damaged, the infant reflexes are released from inhibition. In fact, neurologists and other physicians frequently test adults for infant reflexes. A physician who strokes the sole of your foot during a physical exam is probably looking for evidence of brain damage. This is hardly the most dependable test, but it is easy. If a stroke on the sole of your foot makes you fan your toes like a baby, your cerebral cortex may be impaired.

Infant reflexes sometimes return temporarily if alcohol, carbon dioxide, or other chemicals decrease the activity in the cerebral cortex. (You might try testing for infant reflexes in a friend who has consumed too much alcohol.)

try it yourself

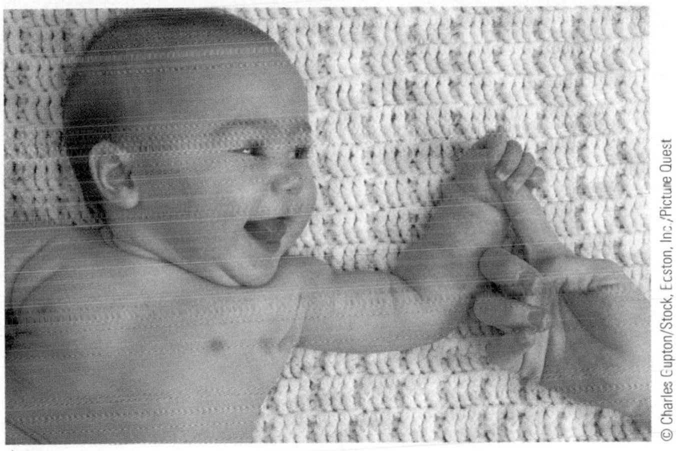

(a)

© Charles Gupton/Stock, Boston, Inc./Picture Quest

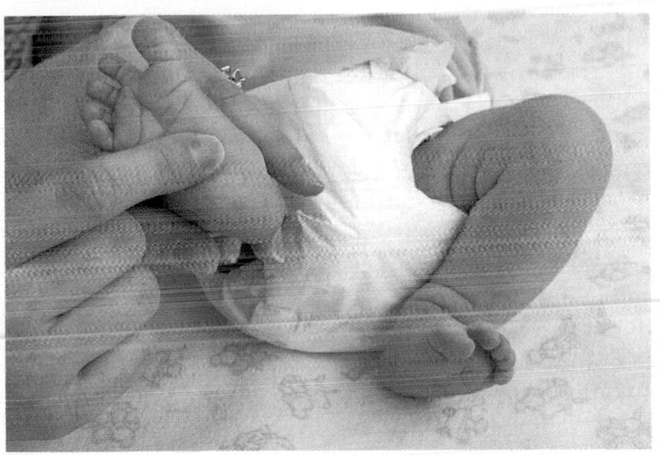

(b)

© Laura Dwight/PhotoEdit

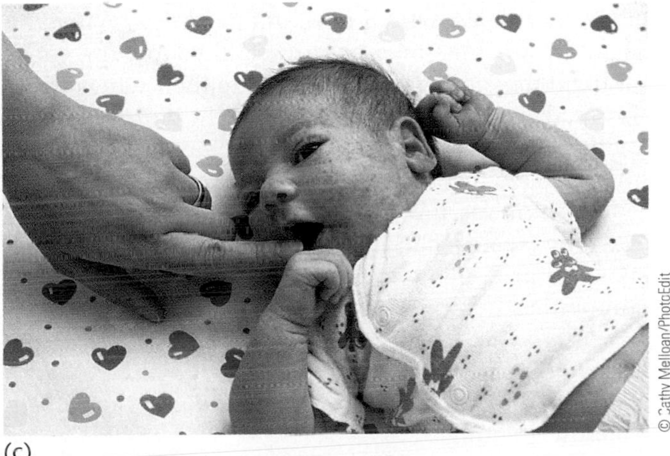

(c)

© Cathy Melloan/PhotoEdit

Three reflexes in infants but ordinarily not in adults: **(a)** grasp reflex, **(b)** Babinski reflex, and **(c)** rooting reflex.

Jo Ellen Kalat

The grasp reflex enables an infant to cling to the mother while she travels.

Infants and children also tend more strongly than adults to have certain *allied reflexes*. If dust blows in your face, you will reflexively close your eyes and mouth and probably sneeze. These reflexes are *allied* in the sense that each of them tends to elicit the others. If you suddenly see a bright light—as when you emerge from a dark theater on a sunny afternoon—you will reflexively close your eyes, and you may also close your mouth and perhaps sneeze. Some adults react this way; a higher percentage of children do (Whitman & Packer, 1993).

Few behaviors can be classified as purely voluntary or involuntary, reflexive or nonreflexive. Take swallowing, for example. You can voluntarily swallow or inhibit swallowing, but only within certain limits. Try to swallow ten times in a row voluntarily (without drinking). The first swallow or two are easy, but soon you will find additional swallows difficult and unpleasant. Now try to inhibit swallowing for as long as you can, without spitting. Chances are you will not last long.

try it yourself

You might think of a behavior like walking as being purely voluntary, but even that example includes involuntary components. When you walk, you automatically compensate for the bumps and irregularities in the road. You probably also swing your arms automatically as an involuntary consequence of walking.

Or try this: While sitting, raise your right foot and make clockwise circles. Keep your foot moving while you draw the number 6 in the air with your right hand. Or just move your right hand in counterclockwise circles. You will probably reverse the direction of your foot movement. It is difficult to make "voluntary" clockwise and counterclockwise movements on the same side of the body at the same time. (Curiously, it is less difficult to move your left hand one direction while moving the right foot in the opposite direction.) In short, the distinction between voluntary and involuntary is blurry.

Movements with Different Sensitivity to Feedback

The military distinguishes between ballistic missiles and guided missiles. A ballistic missile is simply launched, like a thrown ball, with no way to make a correction if the aim is off. A guided missile, however, detects the target location and adjusts its trajectory one way or the other to correct for error in the original aim.

Similarly, some movements are ballistic, and others are corrected by feedback. A **ballistic movement** is executed as a whole: Once initiated, it cannot be altered or corrected while it is in progress. A reflex, such as the stretch reflex or the contraction of the pupils in response to light, is a ballistic movement.

Completely ballistic movements are rare; most behaviors are subject to feedback correction. For example, when you thread a needle, you make a slight movement, check your aim, and then make a readjustment. Similarly, a singer who holds a single note hears any wavering of the pitch and corrects it.

Sequences of Behaviors

Many of our behaviors consist of rapid sequences, as in speaking, writing, dancing, or playing a musical instrument. In certain cases, we can attribute these sequences to **central pattern generators,** neural mechanisms in the spinal cord or elsewhere that generate rhythmic patterns of motor output. Examples include the spinal cord mechanisms that generate wing flapping in birds, fin movements in fish, and the "wet dog shake." Although a stimulus may activate a central pattern generator, it does not control the frequency of the alternating movements. For example, cats scratch themselves at a rate of three to four strokes per second. This rhythm is generated by cells in the lumbar segments of the spinal cord (Deliagina, Orlovsky, & Pavlova, 1983). The spinal cord neurons generate this same rhythm even if they are isolated from the brain and even if the muscles are paralyzed.

We refer to a fixed sequence of movements as a **motor program.** A motor program can be either learned or built into the nervous system. For an example of a built-in program, a mouse periodically grooms itself by sitting up, licking its paws, wiping them over its face, closing its eyes as the paws pass over them, licking the paws again, and so forth (Fentress, 1973). Once begun, the sequence is fixed from beginning to end. Many people develop learned but predictable motor sequences. An expert gymnast will produce a familiar pattern of movements as a smooth, coordinated whole; the same can be said for skilled typists, piano players, and so forth. The pattern is automatic in the sense that thinking or talking about it interferes with the action.

Nearly all birds reflexively spread their wings when dropped. However, emus—which lost the ability to fly through evolutionary time—do not spread their wings.

By comparing species, we begin to understand how a motor program can be gained or lost through evolution. For example, if you hold a chicken above the ground and drop it, its wings will extend and flap. Even chickens with featherless wings make the same movements, though they fail to break their fall (Provine, 1979, 1981). Chickens, of course, still have the genetic programming to fly. On the other hand, ostriches, emus, and rheas, which have not used their wings for flight for millions of generations, have lost the genes for flight movements and do not flap their wings when dropped (Provine, 1984). (You might pause to think about the researcher who found a way to drop these huge birds to test the hypothesis.)

Do humans have any built-in motor programs? Yawning is one example (Provine, 1986). A yawn consists of a prolonged open-mouth inhalation, often accompanied by stretching, and a shorter exhalation. Yawns are very consistent in duration, with a mean of just under 6 seconds. Certain facial expressions are also programmed, such as smiles, frowns, and the raised-eyebrow greeting.

Module 8.1
In Closing: Categories of Movement

Charles Sherrington described a motor neuron in the spinal cord as "the final common path." He meant that regardless of what sensory and motivational processes occupy the brain, the final result was always either a muscle contraction or the delay of a muscle contraction. However, a motor neuron and its associated muscle participate in a great many different kinds of movements, and we need many brain areas to control them.

Summary

1. Vertebrates have smooth, skeletal, and cardiac muscles. (p. 232)
2. Skeletal muscles range from slow muscles that do not fatigue to fast muscles that fatigue quickly. We rely on the slow muscles most of the time, but we recruit the fast muscles for brief periods of strenuous activity. (p. 234)
3. Proprioceptors are receptors sensitive to the position and movement of a part of the body. Two kinds of proprioceptors, muscle spindles and Golgi tendon organs, help regulate muscle movements. (p. 235)
4. Some movements, especially reflexes, proceed as a unit, with little if any guidance from sensory feedback. Other movements, such as threading a needle, are constantly guided and redirected by sensory feedback. (p. 237)

Answers to STOP & CHECK Questions

1. Each axon to the biceps muscles innervates about a hundred fibers; therefore, it is not possible to change the movement by just a few fibers more or less. In contrast, an axon to the eye muscles innervates only about three fibers. (p. 235)
2. Although a fish can move rapidly in cold water, it fatigues easily. (p. 235)
3. Ducks can fly enormous distances without evident fatigue, as they often do during migration. The white muscle of a chicken breast has the great power that is necessary to get a heavy body off the ground, but it fatigues rapidly. Chickens seldom fly far. (p. 235)
4. An ultramarathoner builds up large numbers of slow-twitch fibers at the expense of fast-twitch fibers. Therefore, endurance is great but maximum speed is not. (p. 235)
5. The muscle spindle (p. 236)
6. The Golgi tendon organ responds to muscle tension and thereby prevents excessively strong muscle contractions. (p. 236)

Thought Question

Would you expect jaguars, cheetahs, and other great cats to have mostly slow-twitch, nonfatiguing muscles in their legs or mostly fast-twitch, quickly fatiguing muscles? What kinds of animals might have mostly the opposite kind of muscles?

Module 8.2 Brain Mechanisms of Movement

Why do we care how the brain controls movement? One practical goal is to help people with spinal cord damage or limb amputations. Their brains plan movements, but the messages cannot reach the muscles. Suppose we could listen in on their brain messages and decode their meaning. Then biomedical engineers might route those messages to muscle stimulators or robotic limbs. Researchers mapped the relationships between rats' brain activity and their movements and then connected wires from the brains to robotic limbs. The rats learned to control the robotic movements with brain activity (Chapin, Moxon, Markowitz, & Nicolelis, 1999). In later studies, monkeys learned to move a joystick to control a cursor on a computer monitor, receiving reinforcement when the cursor reached its target. Researchers recorded the monkeys' brain activity during these actions, and then attached electrodes from the brain to a computer, so that whenever the monkey *intended* a cursor movement, it happened (Lebedev et al., 2005; Serruya, Hatsopoulos, Paninski, Fellows, & Donoghue, 2002). We can imagine that the monkeys were impressed with their apparent psychic powers!

People who suffer severe spinal cord damage continue to produce normal activity in the motor cortex when they want to move (Shoham, Halgren, Maynard, & Normann, 2001), so researchers are encouraged about the possibility of connecting their brains to robotic limbs as well (Nicolelis, 2001). To achieve precise movements, presumably physicians would need to insert electrodes directly into the motor areas of the brain. However, people can achieve a moderate degree of control using evoked potential recordings from the surface of the scalp (Millán, Renkens, Mouriño, & Gerstner, 2004; Wolpaw & McFarland, 2004). Improved understanding of the brain mechanisms of movement may improve these technologies.

Controlling movement is a more complicated matter than we might have guessed. Figure 8.7 outlines the major motor areas of the mammalian central nervous system. Don't get too bogged down in details at this point; we shall attend to each area in due course.

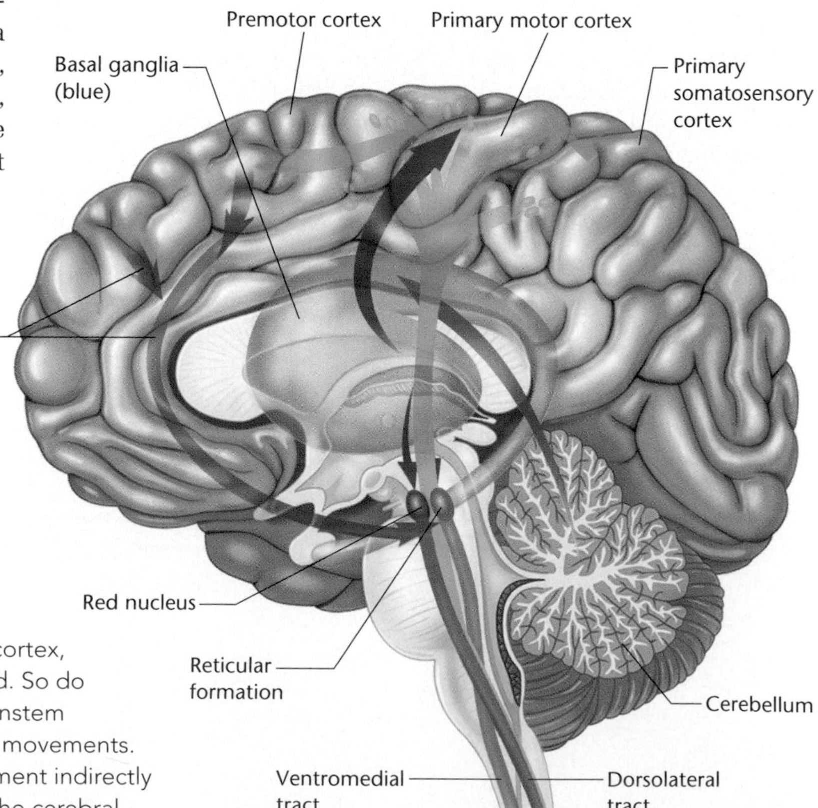

Figure 8.7 The major motor areas of the mammalian central nervous system
The cerebral cortex, especially the primary motor cortex, sends axons directly to the medulla and spinal cord. So do the red nucleus, reticular formation, and other brainstem areas. The medulla and spinal cord control muscle movements. The basal ganglia and cerebellum influence movement indirectly through their communication back and forth with the cerebral cortex and brainstem.

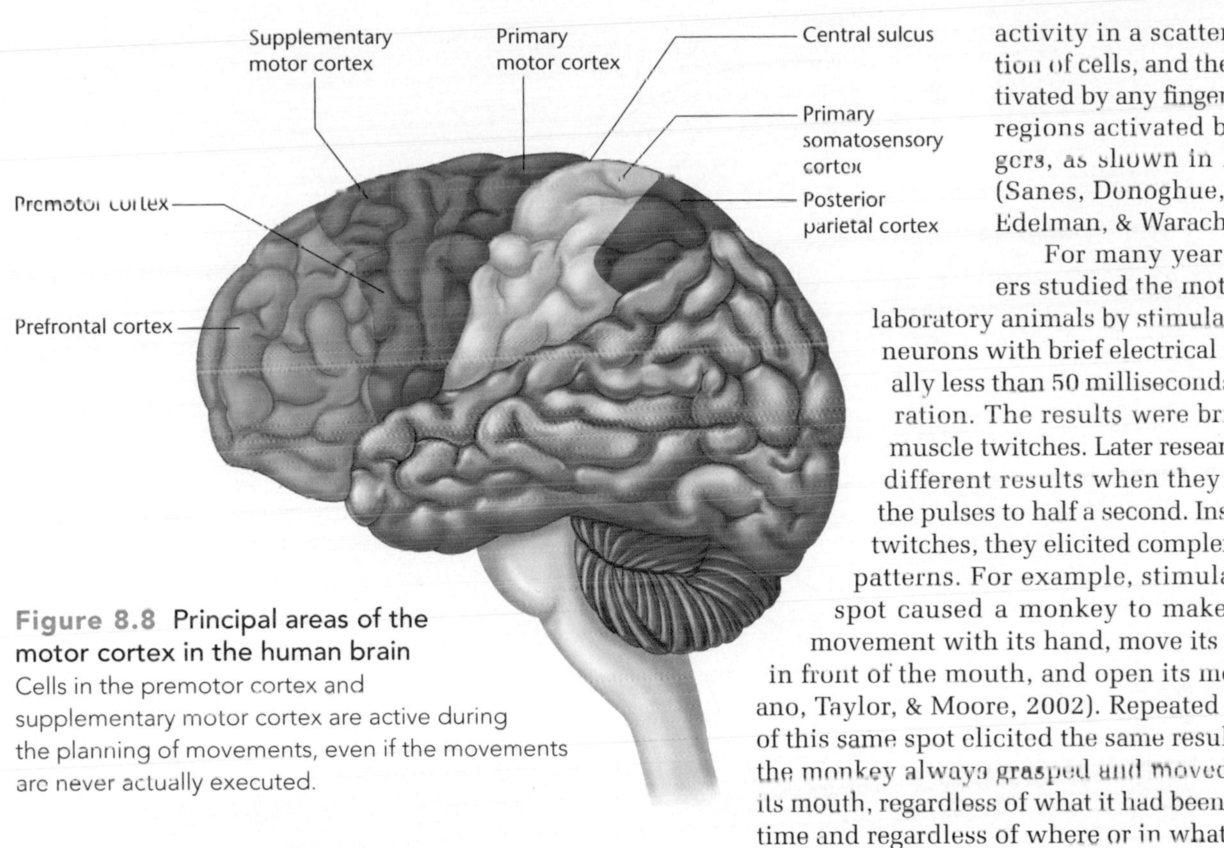

Figure 8.8 Principal areas of the motor cortex in the human brain
Cells in the premotor cortex and supplementary motor cortex are active during the planning of movements, even if the movements are never actually executed.

activity in a scattered population of cells, and the regions activated by any finger overlap the regions activated by other fingers, as shown in Figure 8.10 (Sanes, Donoghue, Thangaraj, Edelman, & Warach, 1995).

For many years, researchers studied the motor cortex in laboratory animals by stimulating various neurons with brief electrical pulses, usually less than 50 milliseconds (ms) in duration. The results were brief, isolated muscle twitches. Later researchers found different results when they lengthened the pulses to half a second. Instead of brief twitches, they elicited complex movement patterns. For example, stimulation of one spot caused a monkey to make a grasping movement with its hand, move its hand to just in front of the mouth, and open its mouth (Graziano, Taylor, & Moore, 2002). Repeated stimulation of this same spot elicited the same result each time; the monkey always grasped and moved its hand to its mouth, regardless of what it had been doing at the time and regardless of where or in what position its

The Cerebral Cortex

Since the pioneering work of Gustav Fritsch and Eduard Hitzig (1870), neuroscientists have known that direct electrical stimulation of the **primary motor cortex**—the precentral gyrus of the frontal cortex, just anterior to the central sulcus (Figure 8.8)—elicits movements. The motor cortex has no direct connections to the muscles; its axons extend to the brainstem and spinal cord, which generate the activity patterns that control the muscles (Shik & Orlovsky, 1976). The cerebral cortex is particularly important for complex actions such as talking, writing, or hand gestures. It is less important for coughing, sneezing, gagging, laughing, or crying (Rinn, 1984). Perhaps the lack of cerebral control explains why it is hard to perform such actions voluntarily. Laughing or coughing voluntarily is not the same as laughing or coughing spontaneously, and most people cannot cry or sneeze voluntarily.

Figure 8.9 (which repeats part of Figure 4.24, p. 99) indicates which area of the motor cortex controls which area of the body. For example, the brain area shown next to the hand is active during hand movements. In each case, the brain area controls a structure on the opposite side of the body. However, don't read this figure as implying that each spot in the motor cortex controls a single muscle. For example, movement of any finger or the wrist is associated with

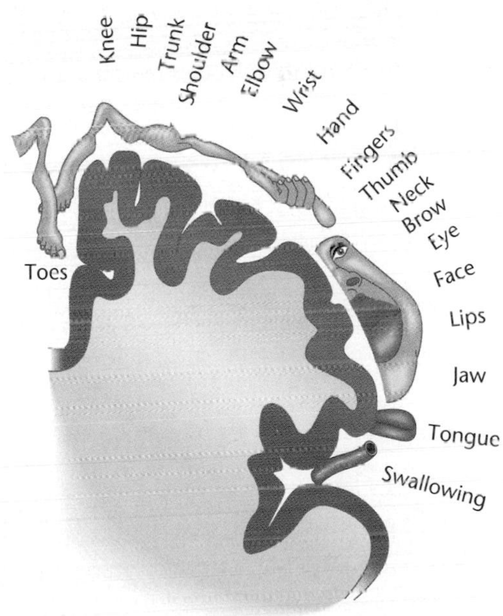

Figure 8.9 Coronal section through the primary motor cortex
Stimulation at any point in the primary motor cortex is most likely to evoke movements in the body area shown. However, actual results are usually messier than this figure implies: For example, individual cells controlling one finger may be intermingled with cells controlling another finger. *(Source: Adapted from Penfield & Rasmussen, 1950)*

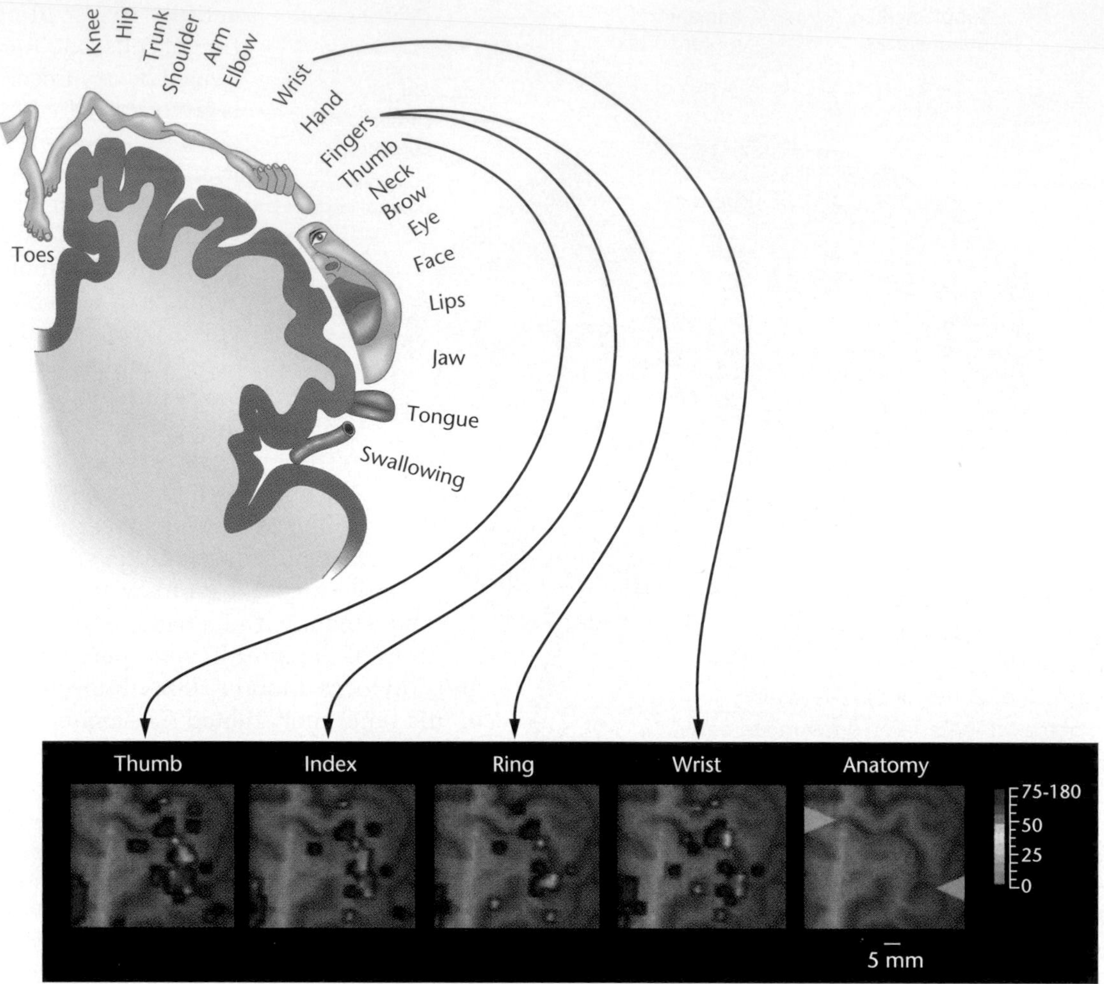

Figure 8.10 Motor cortex during movement of a finger or the wrist
In this functional MRI scan, red indicates the greatest activity, followed by yellow, green, and blue. Note that each movement activated a scattered population of cells and that the areas activated by any one part of the hand overlapped the areas activated by any other. The scan at the right (anatomy) shows a section of the central sulcus (between the two yellow arrows). The primary motor cortex is just anterior to the central sulcus. *(Source: From "Shared neural substrates controlling hand movements in human motor cortex," by J. Sanes, J. Donoghue, V. Thangaraj, R. Edelman, & S. Warach,* Science, *1995 268:1774–1778. Copyright 1995 by AAA. Reprinted by permission of AAAS and J. Sanes.)*

hand had been. That is, the stimulation produced a certain *outcome,* not a fixed set of muscle movements. Depending on the position of the arm, the stimulation might activate biceps muscles, triceps, or whatever. Although the motor cortex *can* direct contractions of a specific muscle, more often it orders an outcome and leaves it to the spinal cord and other areas to find the combination of contractions to produce that outcome (S. H. Scott, 2004).

Just as the visual cortex becomes active when we imagine seeing something, the motor cortex becomes active when we imagine movements. For example, expert pianists say that when they listen to familiar, well-practiced music, they imagine the finger movements and often start tapping the appropriate fingers as if they were playing the music. Brain recordings have confirmed that the finger area of the motor cortex is active when pianists listen to familiar music, even if they keep their fingers motionless (Haueisen & Knösche, 2001).

Neurons in part of the inferior parietal cortex of monkeys are active during a movement *and* while a monkey watches another monkey do the same movement (Cisek & Kalaska, 2004; Fogassi et al., 2005). Brain-scan studies have demonstrated similar neurons in humans. These neurons, called **mirror neurons,** presumably enable the observer to understand and identify with the movements another individual is making. They respond when a monkey watches another monkey or a human watches another human. They do not respond when a monkey watches a human do something or when a human watches a robot (Tai, Scherfler, Brooks, Sawamoto, & Castiello, 2004). Evidently, there-

Table 8.1 Some Disorders of the Spinal Column

Disorder	Description	Cause
Paralysis	Lack of voluntary movement in part of the body.	Damage to spinal cord, motor neurons, or their axons.
Paraplegia	Loss of sensation and voluntary muscle control in both legs. Reflexes remain. Although no messages pass between the brain and the genitals, the genitals still respond reflexively to touch. Paraplegics have no genital sensations, but they can still experience orgasm (Money, 1967).	Cut through the spinal cord above the segments attached to the legs.
Quadriplegia	Loss of sensation and muscle control in all four extremities.	Cut through the spinal cord above the segments controlling the arms.
Hemiplegia	Loss of sensation and muscle control in the arm and leg on one side.	Cut halfway through the spinal cord or (more commonly) damage to one hemisphere of the cerebral cortex.
Tabes dorsalis	Impaired sensation in the legs and pelvic region, impaired leg reflexes and walking, loss of bladder and bowel control.	Late stage of syphilis. Dorsal roots of the spinal cord deteriorate.
Poliomyelitis	Paralysis.	Virus that damages cell bodies of motor neurons.
Amyotrophic lateral sclerosis	Gradual weakness and paralysis, starting with the arms and later spreading to the legs. Both motor neurons and axons from the brain to the motor neurons are destroyed.	Unknown.

fore, their response reflects identification of the viewer with the actor: "The actor is like me, doing something I might do." Many psychologists believe that the existence of such neurons is important for the complex social behaviors typical of humans and other primates.

Connections from the Brain to the Spinal Cord

All the messages from the brain must eventually reach the medulla and spinal cord, which control the muscles. Diseases of the spinal cord can impair the control of movement in various ways (Table 8.1). The various axons from the brain organize into two paths, the dorsolateral tract and the ventromedial tract. Nearly all movements rely on a combination of both the dorsolateral and ventromedial tracts, but many movements rely on one tract more than the other.

The **dorsolateral tract** of the spinal cord is a set of axons from the primary motor cortex, surrounding areas, and the **red nucleus**, a midbrain area with output mainly to the arm muscles (Figure 8.11). Axons of the dorsolateral tract extend directly from the motor cortex to their target neurons in the spinal cord. In bulges of the medulla called *pyramids*, the dorsolateral tract crosses from one side of the brain to the contralateral (opposite) side of the spinal cord. (For that reason, the dorsolateral tract is also called the pyramidal tract.) It controls movements in peripheral areas, such as the hands, fingers, and toes.

Why does each hemisphere control the contralateral side instead of its own side? We do not know, but all vertebrates have this pattern. In newborn humans, the immature primary motor cortex has partial control of both ipsilateral and contralateral muscles. As the contralateral control improves over the first year and a half of life, it displaces the ipsilateral control, which gradually becomes weaker. In some children with cerebral palsy, the contralateral path fails to mature, and the ipsilateral path remains relatively strong. In fact, sometimes part of the clumsiness of children with cerebral palsy comes from competition between the ipsilateral and contralateral paths (Eyre, Taylor, Villagra, Smith, & Miller, 2001).

In contrast to the dorsolateral tract, the **ventromedial tract** includes axons from the primary motor cortex, surrounding areas, and also from many other parts of the cortex. In addition, it includes axons that originate from the midbrain tectum, the reticular formation, and the **vestibular nucleus**, a brain area that receives input from the vestibular system (see Figure 8.11). Axons of the ventromedial tract go to *both* sides of the spinal cord, not just the contralateral side. The ventromedial tract controls mainly the muscles of the neck, shoulders, and trunk and therefore such movements such as walking, turning, bending, standing up, and sitting down (Kuypers, 1989). Note that these movements are necessarily bilateral; you can move your fingers on just one side, but any movement of your neck or trunk must include both sides.

Suppose someone has suffered a stroke that damaged the primary motor cortex of the left hemisphere. The result is a loss of the dorsolateral tract from that hemisphere and a loss of movement control on the right

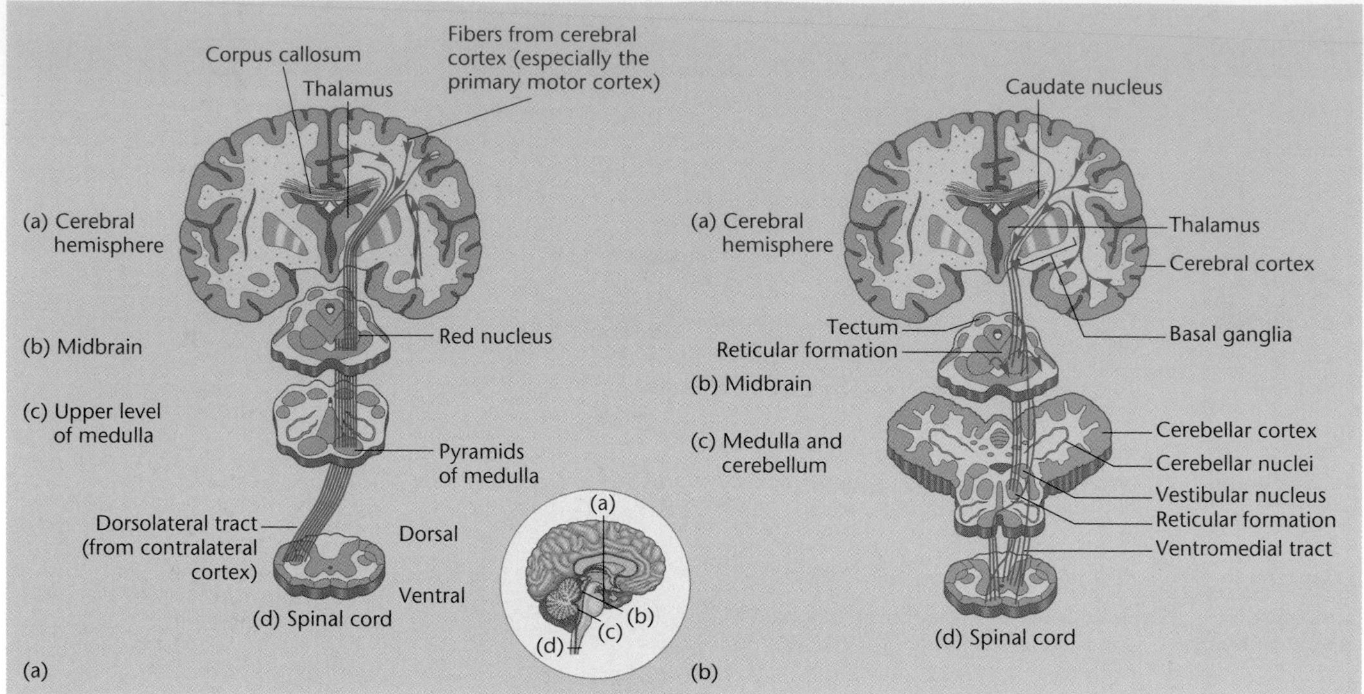

Figure 8.11 The dorsolateral and ventromedial tracts
The dorsolateral tract **(a)** crosses from one side of the brain to the opposite side of the spinal cord and controls precise and discrete movements of the extremities, such as hands, fingers, and feet. The ventromedial tract **(b)** produces bilateral control of trunk muscles for postural adjustments and bilateral movements such as standing, bending, turning, and walking.

side of the body. Eventually, depending on the exact location and amount of damage, the person may regain some muscle control from spared axons in the dorsolateral tract. If not, the possibility remains of using the ventromedial tract to approximate the intended movement. For example, someone who has no direct control of the hand muscles might move the shoulders, trunk, and hips in a way that repositions the hand in a crude way. Also, because of connections between the left and right halves of the spinal cord, normal movements of one arm or leg can induce associated movements on the other side, at least to a limited degree (Edgley, Jankowska, & Hammar, 2004).

STOP & CHECK

1. What evidence indicates that cortical activity represents the "idea" of the movement and not just the muscle contractions?
2. What kinds of movements does the dorsolateral tract control? The ventromedial tract?

Check your answers on page 252.

Areas Near the Primary Motor Cortex

A number of areas near the primary motor cortex also contribute to movement in diverse ways (see Figure 8.8). In the **posterior parietal cortex,** some neurons respond primarily to visual or somatosensory stimuli, others respond mostly to current or future movements, and still others respond to a complicated mixture of the stimulus and the upcoming response (Shadlen & Newsome, 1996). You might think of the posterior parietal cortex as keeping track of the position of the body relative to the world (Snyder, Grieve, Brotchie, & Andersen, 1998). Contrast the effects of posterior parietal damage with those of occipital or temporal damage. People with posterior parietal damage can accurately describe what they see, but they have trouble converting their perception into action. Although they can walk toward something they hear, they cannot walk toward something they see, nor can they reach out to grasp something—even after describing its size, shape, and angle. They seem to know what it is but not where it is. In contrast, people with damage to parts of the occipital or temporal cortex have trouble describing what they see, but they can reach out and pick up objects, and when walking, they step over or go around the objects in their way (Goodale, 1996; Goodale, Milner,

Jakobson, & Carey, 1991). In short, seeing *what* is different from seeing *where,* and seeing *where* is critical for movement.

The primary somatosensory cortex is the main receiving area for touch and other body information, as mentioned in Chapter 7. It sends a substantial number of axons directly to the spinal cord and also provides the primary motor cortex with sensory information. Neurons in this area are especially active when the hand grasps something, responding both to the shape of the object and the type of movement, such as grasping, lifting, or lowering (Gardner, Ro, Debowy, & Ghosh, 1999).

Cells in the prefrontal cortex, premotor cortex, and supplementary motor cortex (see Figure 8.8) actively prepare for a movement, sending messages to the primary motor cortex that actually instigates the movement. These three areas contribute in distinct ways. The **prefrontal cortex** responds to lights, noises, and other sensory signals that lead to a movement. It also calculates probable outcomes of various actions and plans movements according to those outcomes (Tucker, Luu, & Pribram, 1995). If you had damage to this area, you might shower with your clothes on, salt the tea instead of the food, and pour water on the tube of toothpaste instead of the toothbrush (M. F. Schwartz, 1995). Interestingly, this area is inactive during dreams, and the actions we dream about doing are usually as illogical and poorly planned as those of people with prefrontal cortex damage (Braun et al., 1998; Maquet et al., 1996).

The **premotor cortex** is active during preparations for a movement and somewhat active during movement itself. It receives information about the target in space, to which the body is directing its movement, as well as information about the current position and posture of the body itself (Hoshi & Tanji, 2000). Both kinds of information are, of course, necessary to move a body part toward some target. The premotor cortex sends output to both the primary motor cortex and the spinal cord, organizing the direction of the movements in space. For example, you would have to use different muscles to move your arm upward depending on whether your hand was palm-up or palm-down at the time, but the same premotor cortex cells would be active in either case (Kakei, Hoffman, & Strick, 2001).

The **supplementary motor cortex** is important for planning and organizing a rapid sequence of movements, such as pushing, pulling, and then turning a stick, in a particular order (Tanji & Shima, 1994). In one study, researchers compared fMRI results when people simply made movements and when they concentrated on their feelings of intention prior to the movements. Concentrating on intentions increased activity of the supplementary motor cortex (Lau, Rogers, Haggard, & Passingham, 2004). In another study, researchers electrically stimulated the supplementary motor cortex while people had their brains exposed in preparation for surgery. Light stimulation elicited reports of an "urge" to move some body part or an expectation that such a movement was about to start. Longer or stronger stimulation produced the movements themselves (Fried et al., 1991).

STOP & CHECK

3. How does the posterior parietal cortex contribute to movement? The prefrontal cortex? The premotor cortex? The supplementary motor cortex?

Check your answers on page 252.

Conscious Decisions and Movements

Where does conscious decision come into all of this? Each of us has the feeling, "I consciously decide to do something, and then I do it." That sequence seems so obvious that we might not even question it, but research on the issue has found results that most people consider surprising.

Imagine yourself in the following study (Libet, Gleason, Wright, & Pearl, 1983). You are instructed to flex your wrist whenever you choose. That is, you don't choose which movement to make, but you can choose the time freely. You should not decide in advance when to move, but let the urge occur as spontaneously as possible. The researchers are interested in three measurements. First, they attach electrodes to your scalp to record evoked electrical activity over your motor cortex (p. 107). Second, they attach a sensor to your hand to record when it starts to move. The third measurement is your self-report: You watch a clocklike device, as shown in Figure 8.12, in which a spot of light moves around the circle every 2.56 seconds. You are to watch that clock. Do not decide in advance that you will move when the spot on the clock gets to a certain point; however, when you do decide to move, note exactly where the spot of light is at that moment, and remember it so you can report it later.

The procedure starts. You think, "Not yet . . . not yet . . . not yet . . . NOW!" You note where the spot was at that critical instant and report, "I made my decision when the light was at the 25 position." The researchers compare your report to their records of your brain activity and your wrist movement. On the average, people report that their decision to move occurred about 200 ms before the actual movement. (Note: It's the *decision* that occurred then. People make the *report* a few seconds later.) For example, if you reported that

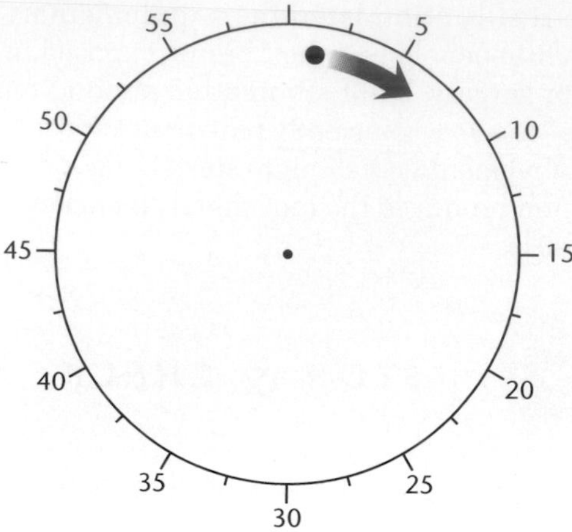

Figure 8.12 Procedure for a study of conscious decision and movement

As the light went rapidly around the circle, the participant was to make a spontaneous decision to move the wrist and remember where the light was at the time of that decision. *(Source: From "Time of conscious intention to act in relation to onset of cerebral activities (readiness potential): The unconscious initiation of a freely voluntary act," by B. Libet et al., in* Brain, *106, 623–624 (12). Reprinted by permission of Oxford University Press.)*

your decision to move occurred at position 25, your decision preceded the movement by 200 ms, so the movement itself began at position 30. (Remember, the light moves around the circle in 2.56 seconds.) However, your motor cortex produces a particular kind of activity called a **readiness potential** before any voluntary movement, and on the average, the readiness potential begins at least 500 ms before the movement. In this example, it would start when the light was at position 18, as illustrated in Figure 8.13.

The results varied among individuals, but most were similar. The key point is that the brain activity responsible for the movement apparently began *before* the person's conscious decision! The results seem to indicate that your conscious decision does not cause your action; rather, you become conscious of the decision after the process leading to action has already been underway for about 300 milliseconds.

As you can imagine, this experiment has been highly controversial. The result itself has been replicated in several laboratories, so the facts are solid (e.g., Lau et al., 2004; Trevena & Miller, 2002). One challenge to the interpretation was that perhaps people cannot accurately report the time they become conscious of something. However, when people are asked to report the time of a sensory stimulus, or the time that they made a movement (instead of the decision to move), their estimates are usually within 30–50 ms of the correct time (Lau et al., 2004; Libet et al., 1983). That is, they cannot exactly report the time when something happened, but they are close enough.

Both scientists and philosophers have raised other objections, and we should not expect the question to be settled soon. Nevertheless, the study at least raises the serious possibility that what we identify as a "conscious" decision is more the perception of an ongoing process than the cause of it. If so, we return to the issues raised in Chapter 1: What is the role of consciousness? Does it serve a useful function, or is it just an accident of the way we are built?

These results do not deny that you make a *voluntary* decision. The implication, however, is that your

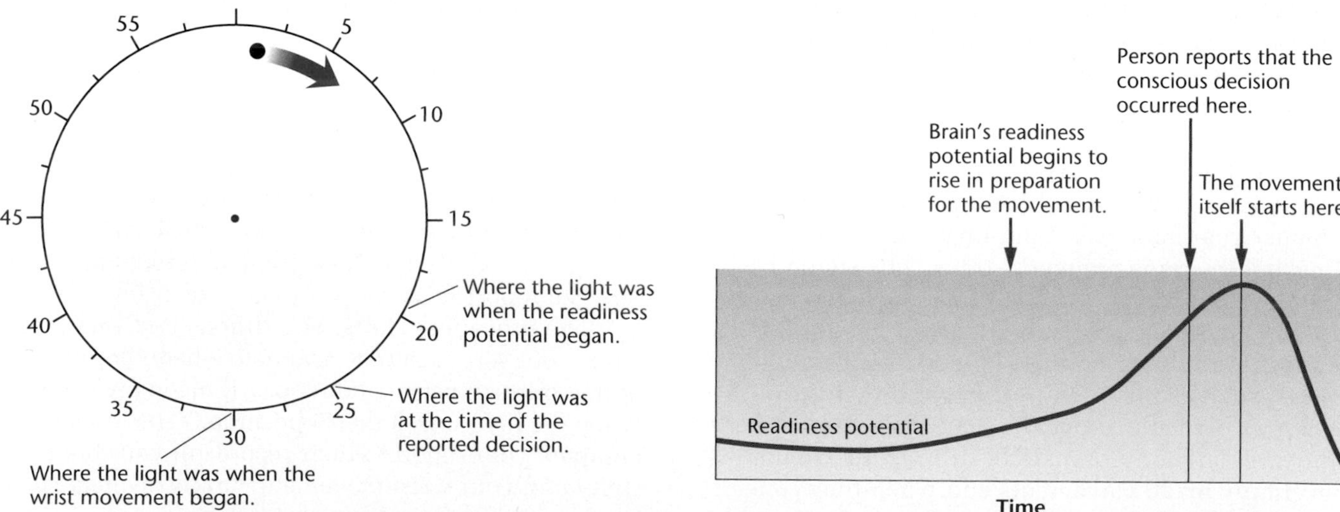

Figure 8.13 Results from study of conscious decision and movement

On the average, the brain's readiness potential began almost 300 ms before the reported decision, which occurred 200 ms before the movement.

voluntary decision is, at first, unconscious. Just as a sensory stimulus has to reach a certain strength before it becomes conscious, your decision to do something has to reach a certain strength before it becomes conscious. Of course, if you think of "voluntary" as synonymous with "conscious," then you have a contradiction.

Studies of patients with brain damage shed further light on the issue. Researchers used the same spot-going-around-the-clock procedure with patients who had damage to the parietal cortex. These patients were just as accurate as other people in reporting when a tone occurred. However, when they tried to report when they formed an intention to make a hand movement, the time they reported was virtually the same as the time of the movement itself. That is, they seemed unaware of any intention before they began the movement. Evidently, the parietal cortex monitors the preparation for a movement, including whatever it is that people ordinarily experience as their feeling of "intention" (Sirigu et al., 2004). Without the parietal cortex, they experienced no such feeling.

Another kind of patient shows a different peculiarity of consciousness. Patients with damage to the primary motor cortex of the right hemisphere are unable to make voluntary movements with their left arm or leg, but some of them deny that they have a problem. That is, they insist that they can and do make voluntary movements on the left side. Neurologists call this condition **anosognosia** (uh-NO-sog-NO-see-uh), meaning ignorance of the presence of disease. Most people with an intact motor cortex but damaged white matter leading to the spinal cord are aware of their paralysis. Anosognosia occurs in people with damage to the right hemisphere motor cortex itself and parts of the surrounding areas. Evidently, the motor cortex monitors feedback from the muscles to determine whether the movements that it ordered have occurred. In the absence of the motor cortex, the premotor cortex generates an "intention" or representation of the intended movement, but it fails to receive any feedback about whether the intended movement was executed (Berti et al., 2005).

STOP & CHECK

4. Explain the evidence that someone's conscious decision to move does not cause the movement.
5. After damage to the parietal cortex, what happens to people's reports of their intentions to move?
6. What is anosognosia, and what brain abnormality is associated with it?

Check your answers on page 252.

The Cerebellum

The term *cerebellum* is Latin for "little brain." Decades ago, the function of the cerebellum was described as simply "balance and coordination." Well, yes, people with cerebellar damage do lose balance and coordination, but that description greatly understates the importance of this structure. The cerebellum contains more neurons than the rest of the brain combined (R. W. Williams & Herrup, 1988) and an enormous number of synapses. So the cerebellum has far more capacity for processing information than its small size might suggest.

The most obvious effect of cerebellar damage is trouble with rapid movements that require accurate aim and timing. For example, people with cerebellar damage have trouble tapping a rhythm, clapping hands, pointing at a moving object, speaking, writing, typing, or playing a musical instrument. They are impaired at almost all athletic activities except a few like weightlifting that do not require aim or timing. Even long after the damage, when they seem to have recovered, they remain slow on sequences of movements and even on *imagining* sequences of movements (González, Rodríguez, Ramirez, & Sabate, 2005). They are normal, however, at a *continuous* motor activity, even if it has a kind of rhythm (Spencer, Zelaznik, Diedrichsen, & Ivry, 2003). For example, they can draw continuous circles, like the ones below. Although the drawing has a rhythm, it does not require rhythmically starting or stopping an action.

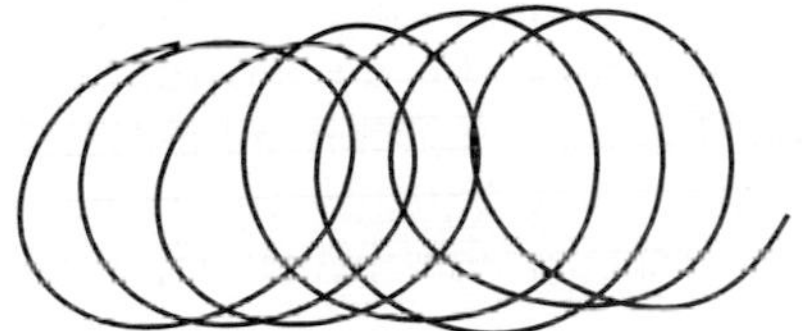
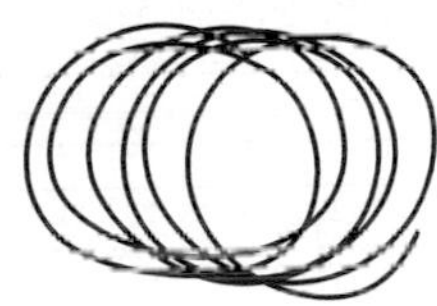

Here is one quick way to test someone's cerebellum: Ask the person to focus on one spot and then to move the eyes quickly to another spot. Saccades (sa-KAHDS), ballistic eye movements from one fixation point to another, depend on impulses from the cerebellum and the frontal cortex to the cranial nerves. A healthy person's eyes move from one fixation point to another by a single movement or by one large movement and a small correction at the end. Someone with cerebellar damage, however, has difficulty programming the angle and distance of eye movements (Dichgans, 1984). The eyes make many short movements until, by trial and error, they eventually find the intended spot.

Another test of cerebellar damage is the *finger-to-nose test.* The person is instructed to hold one arm straight out and then, at command, to touch his or her nose as quickly as possible. A normal person does so in three steps. First, the finger moves ballistically to a point just in front of the nose. This *move* function depends on the cerebellar cortex (the surface of the cerebellum), which sends messages to the deep nuclei (clusters of cell bodies) in the interior of the cerebellum (Figure 8.14). Second, the finger remains steady at that spot for a fraction of a second. This *hold* function depends on the nuclei alone (Kornhuber, 1974). Finally, the finger moves to the nose by a slower movement that does not depend on the cerebellum.

try it yourself

After damage to the cerebellar cortex, a person has trouble with the initial rapid movement. Either the finger stops too soon or it goes too far, striking the face. If certain cerebellar nuclei have been damaged, the person may have difficulty with the hold segment: The finger reaches a point just in front of the nose and then wavers.

The symptoms of cerebellar damage resemble those of alcohol intoxication: clumsiness, slurred speech, and inaccurate eye movements. A police officer testing someone for drunkenness may use the finger-to-nose test or similar tests because the cerebellum is one of the first brain areas that alcohol affects.

Evidence of a Broad Role

The cerebellum is not only a motor structure. In one study, functional MRI measured cerebellar activity while people performed several tasks with a single set of objects (Gao et al., 1996). When they simply lifted objects, the cerebellum showed little activity. When they felt things with both hands to decide whether they were the same or different, the cerebellum was much more active. The cerebellum showed activity even when someone held a hand steady and the experimenter rubbed an object across it. That is, the cerebellum responded to sensory stimuli even in the absence of movement.

What, then, is the role of the cerebellum? Masao Ito (1984) proposed that one key role is to establish new motor programs that enable one to execute a sequence of actions as a whole. Inspired by this idea, many researchers reported evidence that cerebellar damage impairs motor learning. Richard Ivry and his colleagues have emphasized the importance of the cerebellum for behaviors that depend on precise timing of short intervals (from about a millisecond to 1.5 seconds). Any sequence of rapid movements obviously requires timing. Many perceptual and cognitive tasks also require timing—for example, judging which of two visual stimuli is moving faster or listening to two pairs of tones and judging whether the delay was longer between the first pair or the second pair.

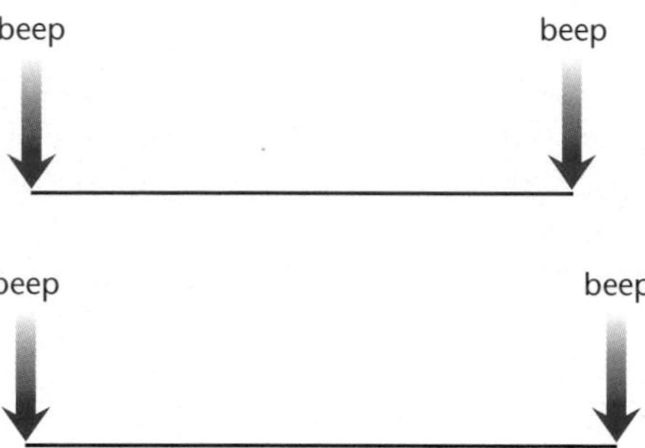

People who are accurate at one kind of timed movement, such as tapping a rhythm with a finger, tend also to be good at other timed movements, such as tapping a rhythm with a foot, and at judging which visual stimulus moved faster and which intertone delay was longer. People with cerebellar damage are impaired at all of these tasks but unimpaired at controlling the force of a movement or at judging which tone is louder (Ivry & Diener, 1991; Keele & Ivry, 1990). Evidently, the cerebellum is important mainly for tasks that require timing.

The cerebellum also appears critical for certain aspects of attention. For example, in one experiment, people were told to keep their eyes fixated on a central

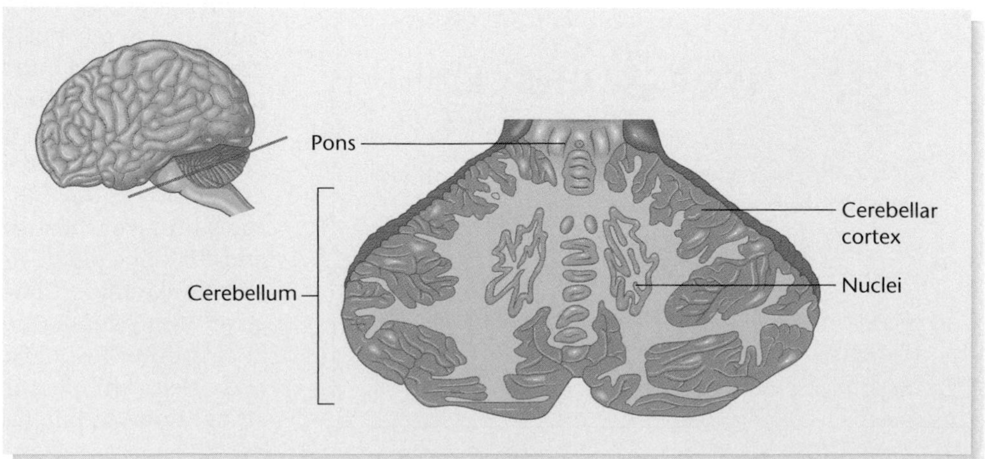

Figure 8.14 Location of the cerebellar nuclei relative to the cerebellar cortex
In the inset at the upper left, the line indicates the plane shown in detail at the lower right.

point. At various times, they would see the letter E on either the left or right half of the screen, and they were to indicate the direction in which it was oriented (E, Ǝ, ш, or ᗰ) without moving their eyes. Sometimes they saw a signal telling where the letter would be on the screen. For most people, that signal improved their performance even if it appeared just 100 ms before the letter. For people with cerebellar damage, the signal had to appear nearly a second before the letter to be helpful. Evidently, people with cerebellar damage need longer to shift their attention (Townsend et al., 1999).

So the cerebellum appears to be linked to timing, certain aspects of attention, and probably other abilities as well. Are these separate functions that just happen to be located in the same place? Or can we reduce them all to a single theme? (For example, maybe shifting attention requires timing or aim.) These unanswered questions require a careful analysis of behavior, not just a study of the nervous system.

Cellular Organization

The cerebellum receives input from the spinal cord, from each of the sensory systems by way of the cranial nerve nuclei, and from the cerebral cortex. That information eventually reaches the **cerebellar cortex**, the surface of the cerebellum (see Figure 8.14).

Figure 8.15 shows the types and arrangements of neurons in the cerebellar cortex. The figure is complex, but concentrate on these main points:

- The neurons are arranged in a precise geometrical pattern, with multiple repetitions of the same units.

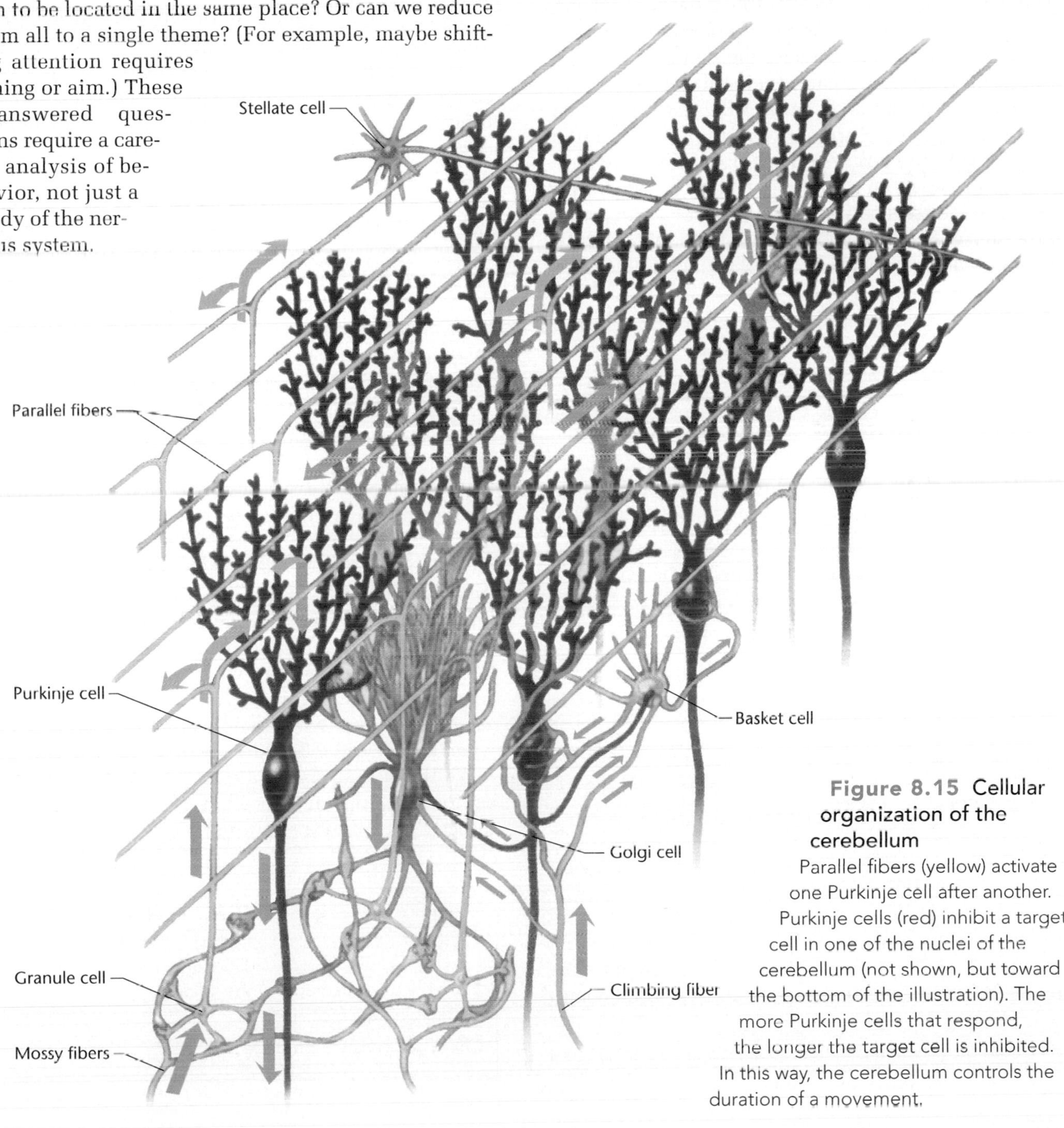

Figure 8.15 Cellular organization of the cerebellum
Parallel fibers (yellow) activate one Purkinje cell after another. Purkinje cells (red) inhibit a target cell in one of the nuclei of the cerebellum (not shown, but toward the bottom of the illustration). The more Purkinje cells that respond, the longer the target cell is inhibited. In this way, the cerebellum controls the duration of a movement.

- The **Purkinje cells** are flat cells in sequential planes.
- The **parallel fibers** are axons parallel to one another and perpendicular to the planes of the Purkinje cells.
- Action potentials in varying numbers of parallel fibers excite one Purkinje cell after another. Each Purkinje cell then transmits an inhibitory message to cells in the **nuclei of the cerebellum** (clusters of cell bodies in the interior of the cerebellum) and the vestibular nuclei in the brainstem, which in turn send information to the midbrain and the thalamus.
- Depending on which and how many parallel fibers are active, they might stimulate only the first few Purkinje cells or a long series of them. Because the parallel fibers' messages reach different Purkinje cells one after another, the greater the number of excited Purkinje cells, the greater their collective *duration* of response. That is, if the parallel fibers stimulate only the first few Purkinje cells, the result is a brief message to the target cells; if they stimulate more Purkinje cells, the message lasts longer. The output of Purkinje cells controls the timing of a movement, including both its onset and offset (Thier, Dicke, Haas, & Barash, 2000).

7. What kind of perceptual task would be most impaired by damage to the cerebellum?
8. How are the parallel fibers arranged relative to one another and to the Purkinje cells?
9. If a larger number of parallel fibers are active, what is the effect on the collective output of the Purkinje cells?
10. Do Purkinje cells control the strength or duration of a movement?

Check your answers on page 253.

The Basal Ganglia

The term **basal ganglia** applies collectively to a group of large subcortical structures in the forebrain (Figure 8.16).[1] Various authorities differ in which structures they include as part of the basal ganglia, but everyone includes at least the **caudate nucleus,** the **putamen** (pyuh-TAY-men), and the **globus pallidus.** Input comes to the caudate nucleus and putamen, mostly from the cerebral cortex. Output from the caudate nucleus and putamen goes to the globus pallidus and from there mainly to the thalamus, which relays it to the cerebral cortex, especially its motor areas and the prefrontal cortex (Hoover & Strick, 1993).

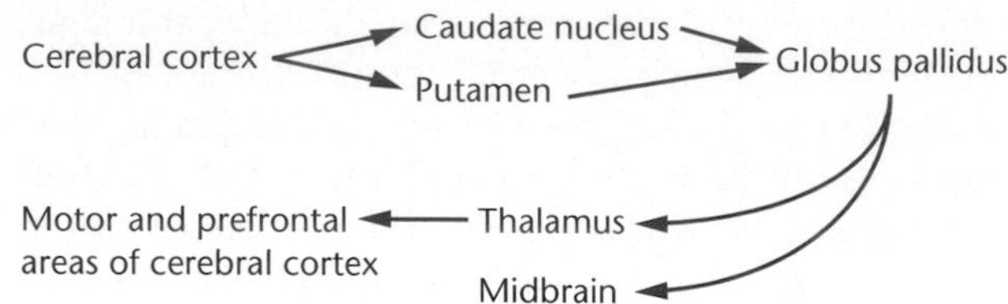

Most of the output from the globus pallidus to the thalamus releases GABA, an inhibitory transmitter, and neurons in the globus pallidus show much spontaneous activity. Thus, the globus pallidus is constantly inhibiting the thalamus. Input from the caudate nucleus and putamen tells the globus pallidus which movements to *stop inhibiting.* With extensive damage to the globus pallidus, as in people with Huntington's disease (which we shall consider later), the result is a lack of inhibition of all movements and therefore many involuntary, jerky movements.

In effect, the basal ganglia select which movement to make by ceasing to inhibit it. This circuit is particularly important for self-initiated behaviors. For example, a monkey in one study was trained to move one hand to the left or right to receive food. On trials when it heard a signal indicating exactly when to move, the basal ganglia showed little activity. However, on other trials, the monkey saw a light indicating that it should start its movement in not less than 1.5 seconds and finish in not more than 3 seconds. Therefore, the monkey had to judge the interval and choose its own starting time. Under those conditions, the basal ganglia were highly active (Turner & Anderson, 2005).

In another study, people used a computer mouse to draw lines on a screen while researchers used PET scans to examine brain activity. Activity in the basal ganglia increased when people drew a new line but not when they traced a line already on the screen (Jueptner & Weiller, 1998). Again, the basal ganglia seem critical for initiating an action but not when the action is directly guided by a stimulus.

11. How does damage to the basal ganglia lead to involuntary movements?

Check your answer on page 253.

[1]Ganglia is the plural of ganglion, so the term *basal ganglia* is a plural noun.

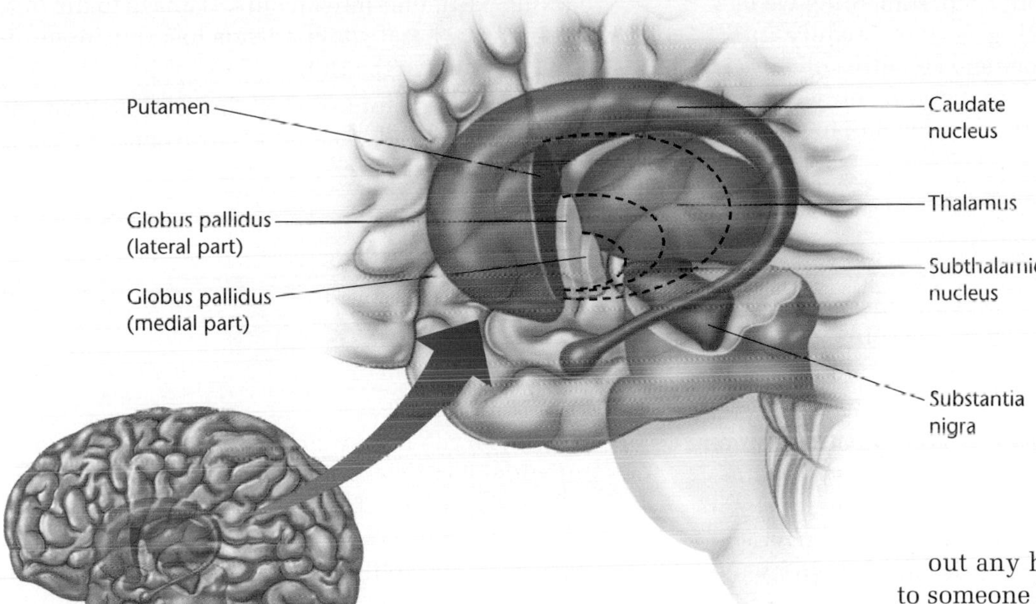

Figure 8.16 Location of the basal ganglia The basal ganglia surround the thalamus and are surrounded by the cerebral cortex.

Brain Areas and Motor Learning

Of all the brain areas responsible for control of movement, which are important for learning new skills? The apparent answer is, all of them.

Neurons in the motor cortex adjust their responses as a person or animal learns a motor skill. At first, movements are slow and inconsistent. As movements become faster, relevant neurons in the motor cortex increase their firing rates (D. Cohen & Nicolelis, 2004). After prolonged training, the movement patterns become more consistent from trial to trial, and so do the patterns of activity in the motor cortex. In engineering terms, the motor cortex increases its signal-to-noise ratio (Kargo & Nitz, 2004).

The basal ganglia are critical for learning motor skills, for organizing sequences of movement into a whole, and in general, for the kinds of learning that we can't easily express in words (Graybiel, 1998; Seger & Cincotta, 2005). For example, when you are first learning to drive a car, you have to think about everything you do. After much experience, you can signal for a left turn, change gears, turn the wheel, and change speed all at once in a single smooth movement. If you try to explain exactly what you do, you will probably find it difficult. Similarly, if you know how to tie a man's tie, try explaining it to someone who doesn't know—without any hand gestures. Or explain to someone how to draw a spiral without using the word *spiral* and again without any hand gestures. People with basal ganglia damage are impaired at learning motor skills like these and at converting new movements into smooth, "automatic" responses (Poldrack et al., 2005; Willingham, Koroshetz, & Peterson, 1996).

try it yourself

STOP & CHECK

12. What kind of learning depends most heavily on the basal ganglia?

Check your answer on page 253.

Module 8.2

In Closing: Movement Control and Cognition

It is tempting to describe behavior in three steps—first we perceive, then we think, and finally we act. As you have seen, the brain does not handle the process in such discrete steps. For example, the posterior parietal cortex monitors the position of the body relative to visual space and therefore helps guide movement. Thus, its functions are sensory, cognitive, and motor. The cerebellum has traditionally been considered a major part of the motor system, but it is now known to be equally important in timing sensory processes. People with basal ganglia damage are slow to start or select a movement. They are also often described as cognitively slow; that is, they hesitate to make any kind of choice. In short, organizing a movement is not something we tack on at the end of our thinking; it is intimately intertwined with all of our sensory and cognitive processes. The study of movement is not just the study of muscles; it is the study of how we decide what to do.

Summary

1. The primary motor cortex is the main source of brain input to the spinal cord. The spinal cord contains central pattern generators that actually control the muscles. (p. 241)
2. The primary motor cortex produces patterns representing the intended outcome, not just the muscle contractions. Neurons in part of the parietal cortex respond to both a self-produced movement and an observation of a similar movement by another individual. (p. 242)
3. The dorsolateral tract, which controls movements in the periphery of the body, has axons that cross from one side of the brain to the opposite side of the spinal cord. (p. 243)
4. The ventromedial tract controls bilateral movements near the midline of the body. (p. 243)
5. Areas near the primary motor cortex—including the prefrontal, premotor, and supplementary motor cortices—are active in detecting stimuli for movement and preparing for a movement. (p. 245)
6. When people identify the instant when they formed a conscious intention to move, their time precedes the actual movement by about 200 ms but follows the start of motor cortex activity by about 300 ms. These results suggest that what we call a conscious decision is our perception of a process already underway, not really the cause of it. (p. 245)
7. People with damage to part of the parietal cortex fail to perceive any intention prior to the start of their own movements. (p. 247)
8. Some people with damage to the primary motor cortex of the right hemisphere are paralyzed on the left side but insist that they can still move. Evidently, they fail to receive the feedback that indicates lack of movement. (p. 247)
9. The cerebellum has multiple roles in behavior, including sensory functions related to perception of the timing or rhythm of stimuli. Its role in the control of movement is especially important for timing, aiming, and correcting errors. (p. 247)
10. The cells of the cerebellum are arranged in a very regular pattern that enables them to produce outputs of well-controlled duration. (p. 249)
11. The basal ganglia are a group of large subcortical structures that are important for selecting and inhibiting particular movements. Damage to the output from the basal ganglia leads to jerky, involuntary movements. (p. 250)
12. The learning of a motor skill depends on changes occurring in both the cerebral cortex and the basal ganglia. (p. 251)

Answers to STOP & CHECK Questions

1. Activity in the motor cortex leads to a particular outcome, such as movement of the hand to the mouth, regardless of what muscle contractions are necessary given the hand's current location. Also, neurons in part of the parietal cortex respond similarly to self-produced movement and to observation of a similar movement by another individual. (p. 244)
2. The dorsolateral tract controls detailed movements in the periphery on the contralateral side of the body. (For example, the dorsolateral tract from the left hemisphere controls the right side of the body.) The ventromedial tract controls the trunk muscles bilaterally. (p. 244)
3. The posterior parietal cortex is important for perceiving the location of objects and the position of the body relative to the environment, including those objects. The prefrontal cortex responds to sensory stimuli that call for some movement. The premotor cortex is active in preparing a movement immediately before it occurs. The supplementary motor cortex is especially active in preparing for a rapid sequence of movements. (p. 245)
4. Researchers recorded a readiness potential in the motor cortex, beginning about 500 ms before the start of the movement. When people reported the time that they felt the intention to move, the reported intention occurred about 200 ms before the movement and therefore 300 ms after the start of motor cortex activity that led to the movement. (p. 247)
5. After damage to the parietal cortex, people do not monitor the processes leading up to a movement. When they try to report the time of an intention to move, they report the same time when the movement actually began. That is, they are not aware of any intention before the movement itself. (p. 247)
6. Anosognosia occurs when someone is paralyzed on the left side but denies having such a problem. It is associated with damage to the motor cortex of the right hemisphere and parts of the surrounding areas. (p. 247)

7. Damage to the cerebellum strongly impairs perceptual tasks that depend on timing. (p. 250)
8. The parallel fibers are parallel to one another and perpendicular to the planes of the Purkinje cells. (p. 250)
9. As a larger number of parallel fibers become active, the Purkinje cells increase their duration of response. (p. 250)
10. Duration (p. 250)
11. Output from the basal ganglia to the thalamus consists mainly of the inhibitory transmitter GABA. Ordinarily, the basal ganglia produce steady output, inhibiting all movements or all except the ones selected at the time. After damage to the basal ganglia, the thalamus, and therefore the cortex, receive less inhibition. Thus, they produce unwanted actions. (p. 250)
12. The basal ganglia are essential for learning habits that are difficult to describe in words. (p. 251)

Thought Question

Human infants are at first limited to gross movements of the trunk, arms, and legs. The ability to move one finger at a time matures gradually over at least the first year. What hypothesis would you suggest about which brain areas controlling movement mature early and which areas mature later?

Module 8.3 Disorders of Movement

Even if your nervous system and muscles are completely healthy, you may sometimes find it difficult to move in the way you would like. For example, if you have just finished a bout of unusually strenuous exercise, your muscles may be so fatigued that you can hardly move them voluntarily, even though they keep twitching. Or if your legs "fall asleep" while you are sitting in an awkward position, you may stumble and even fall when you try to walk.

Certain neurological disorders produce exaggerated and lasting movement impairments. We consider two examples: Parkinson's disease and Huntington's disease.

Parkinson's Disease

The symptoms of **Parkinson's disease** (also known as *Parkinson disease*) are rigidity, muscle tremors, slow movements, and difficulty initiating physical and mental activity (M. T. V. Johnson et al., 1996; Manfredi, Stocchi, & Vacca, 1995; Pillon et al., 1996). It strikes about 1 or 2 people per thousand over the age of 40, with increasing incidence at later ages. Although the motor problems are the most obvious, the disorder goes beyond movement. Parkinsonian patients are also slow on cognitive tasks, such as imagining events or actions, even when they don't have to make any movements (Sawamoto, Honda, Hanakawa, Fukuyama, & Shibasaki, 2002). Most patients also become depressed at an early stage, and many show deficits of memory and reasoning. These mental symptoms are probably part of the disease itself, not just a reaction to the muscle failures (Ouchi et al., 1999).

People with Parkinson's disease are not paralyzed or weak; they are impaired at initiating spontaneous movements in the absence of stimuli to guide their actions. Rats with Parkinsonian-type brain damage have few spontaneous movements, but they respond well to strong stimuli (Horvitz & Eyny, 2000). Parkinsonian patients sometimes walk surprisingly well when following a parade, when walking up a flight of stairs, or when walking across lines drawn at one-step intervals (Teitelbaum, Pellis, & Pellis, 1991).

The immediate cause of Parkinson's disease is the gradual progressive death of neurons, especially in the substantia nigra, which sends dopamine-releasing axons to the caudate nucleus and putamen. People with Parkinson's disease lose these axons and therefore all the effects that their dopamine would have produced. One of the effects of dopamine is inhibition of the caudate nucleus and putamen, and a decrease in that inhibition means that the caudate nucleus and putamen increase their stimulation of the globus pallidus. The result is *increased inhibition* of the thalamus and cerebral cortex, as shown in Figure 8.17 (Wichmann, Vitek, & DeLong, 1995). In summary, a loss of dopamine activity leads to less stimulation of the motor cortex and slower onset of movements (Parr-Brownlie & Hyland, 2005).

Researchers estimate that the average person over age 45 loses substantia nigra neurons at a rate of almost 1% per year. Most people have enough to spare, but some either start with fewer or lose them faster. If the number of surviving substantia nigra neurons declines below 20%–30% of normal, Parkinsonian symptoms begin (Knoll, 1993). Symptoms become more severe as the cell loss continues.

Possible Causes

In the late 1990s, the news media excitedly reported that researchers had located a gene that causes Parkinson's disease. That report was misleading. The research had found certain families in which people sharing a particular gene all developed Parkinson's disease with onset before age 50 (Shimura et al., 2001). Since then, several other genes have been found that lead to early-onset Parkinson's disease (Bonifati et al., 2003; Singleton et al., 2003; Valente et al., 2004). However, none of these genes have any link to later-onset Parkinson's disease, which is far more common.

One study examined Parkinson's patients who had twins. As shown in Figure 8.18, if you have a monozygotic (MZ) twin who develops early-onset Parkinson's disease, you are almost certain to get it too. In other words, early-onset Parkinson's disease has a strong genetic basis. However, if your twin develops Parkinson's

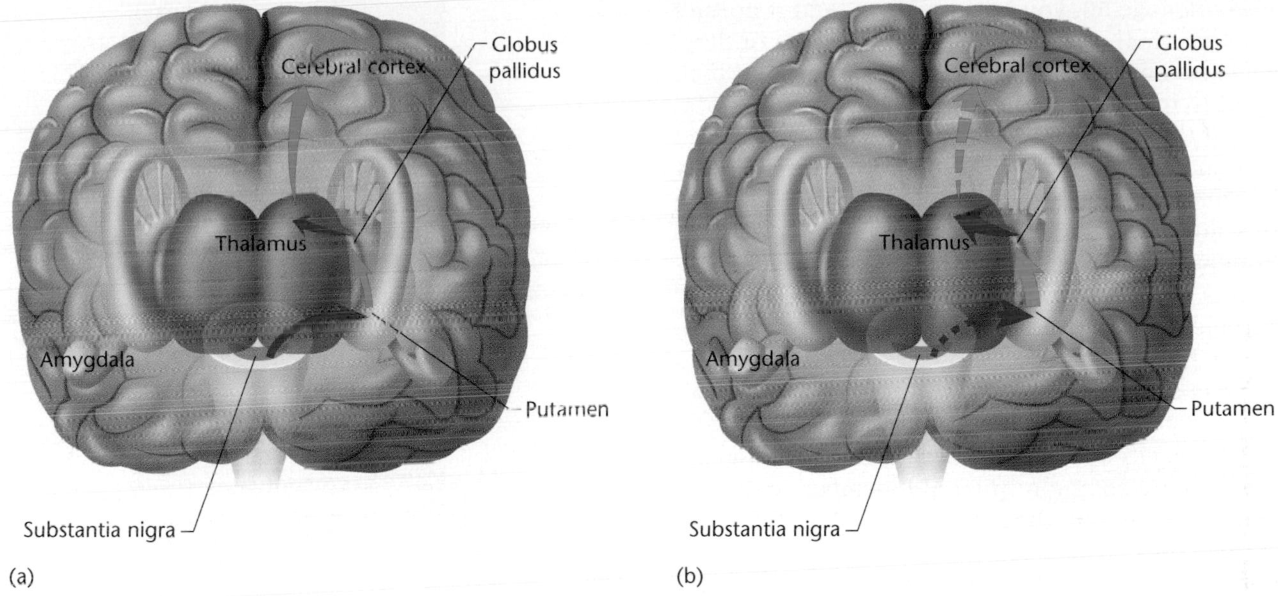

Figure 8.17 Connections from the substantia nigra: (a) normal and (b) in Parkinson's disease

Excitatory paths are shown in green; inhibitory are in red. The substantia nigra's axons inhibit the putamen. Axon loss increases excitatory communication to the globus pallidus. The result is increased inhibition from the globus pallidus to the thalamus and decreased excitation from the thalamus to the cerebral cortex. People with Parkinson's disease show decreased initiation of movement, slow and inaccurate movement, and psychological depression. *(Source: Based on Wichmann, Vitek, & DeLong, 1995)*

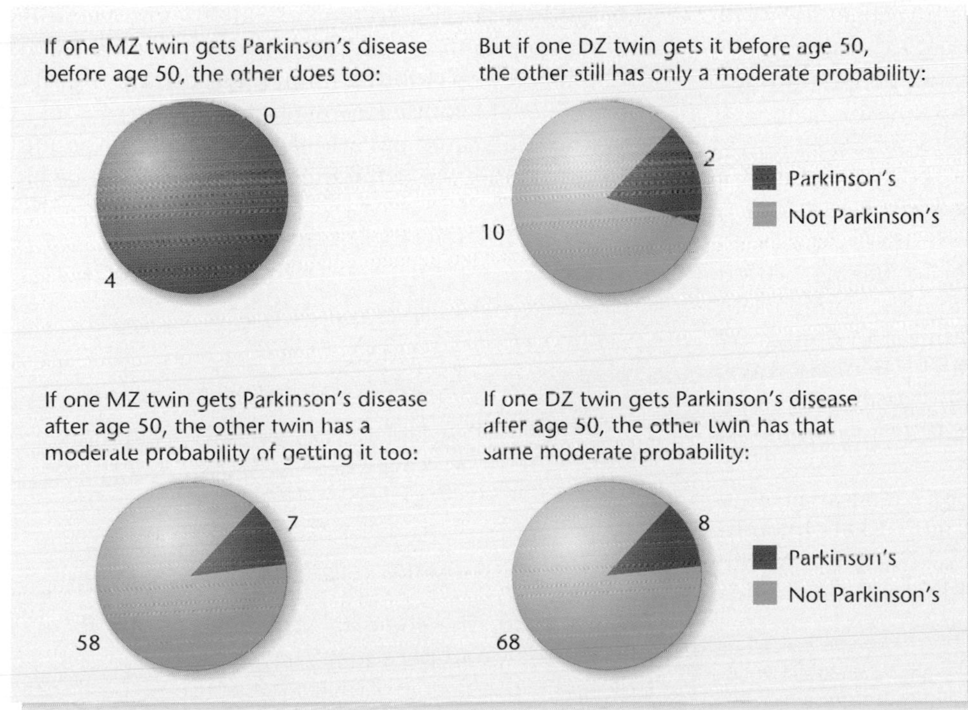

Figure 8.18 Probability of developing Parkinson's disease if you have a twin who developed the disease before or after age 50

Having a monozygotic (MZ) twin develop Parkinson's disease before age 50 means that you are very likely to get it too. A dizygotic (DZ) twin who gets it before age 50 does not pose the same risk. Therefore, early-onset Parkinson's disease shows a strong genetic component. However, if your twin develops Parkinson's disease later (as is more common), your risk is the same regardless of whether you are a monozygotic or dizygotic twin. Therefore, late-onset Parkinson's disease has little or no heritability. *(Source: Based on data of Tanner et al., 1999)* disease *after* age 50, your risk is lower, and it doesn't depend on whether your twin is monozygotic or dizygotic (Tanner et al., 1999). Equal concordance for both kinds of twins implies low heritability. That is, it implies that the family resemblance depends on shared environment rather than genes. However, this study had a small sample size. Furthermore, a study using brain scans found that many of the monozygotic twins without symptoms of Parkinson's disease did have indications of minor brain damage that could lead to symptoms later in life (Piccini, Burn, Ceravolo, Maraganore, & Brooks, 1999).

A later study examined the chromosomes of people in 174 families that included more than one person with Parkinson's disease. Researchers looked for genes that were more common in family members with Parkinson's disease than those withoutit. They found no gene that was consistently linked to the disease, but five genes were more common among people with Parkinson's (E. Martin et al., 2001; W. K. Scott et al., 2001). However, none of these genes had a powerful impact. For example, one gene was found in 82% of the people with Parkinson's disease and in 79% of those without it. Clearly, the great majority of people with this gene do not get Parkinson's disease. In short, genetic factors are only a small contributor to late-onset Parkinson's disease.

What environmental influences might be relevant? Sometimes Parkinson's disease results from exposure to toxins. The first solid evidence was discovered by accident (Ballard, Tetrud, & Langston, 1985). In northern California in 1982, several people aged 22 to 42 developed symptoms of Parkinson's disease after using a drug similar to heroin. Before the investigators could alert the community to the danger of this heroin substitute, many other users had developed symptoms ranging from mild to fatal (Tetrud, Langston, Garbe, & Ruttenber, 1989).

The substance responsible for the symptoms was **MPTP**, a chemical that the body converts to **MPP^+**, which accumulates in, and then destroys, neurons that release dopamine[2] (Nicklas, Saporito, Basma, Geller, & Heikkila, 1992). Postsynaptic neurons compensate for the loss by increasing their number of dopamine receptors (Chiueh, 1988) (Figure 8.19). In many ways, the extra receptors help, but they also produce a jumpy overresponsiveness that creates additional problems (W. C. Miller & DeLong, 1988).

No one supposes that Parkinson's disease is often the result of using illegal drugs. A more likely hypothesis is that people are sometimes exposed to MPTP or similar chemicals in herbicides and pesticides (Figure 8.20), many of which can damage cells of the substantia nigra (Betarbet et al., 2000). For example, rats exposed to the pesticide *rotenone* develop a condition closely resembling human Parkinson's disease (Betarbet et al., 2000). However, if exposure to a toxin were the main cause of Parkinson's disease, we should expect to find great differences in the prevalence be-

[2]The full names of these chemicals are 1-methyl-4 phenyl-1,2,3,6-tetrahydropyridine and 1-methyl-4-phenylpyridinium ion. (Let's hear it for abbreviations!)

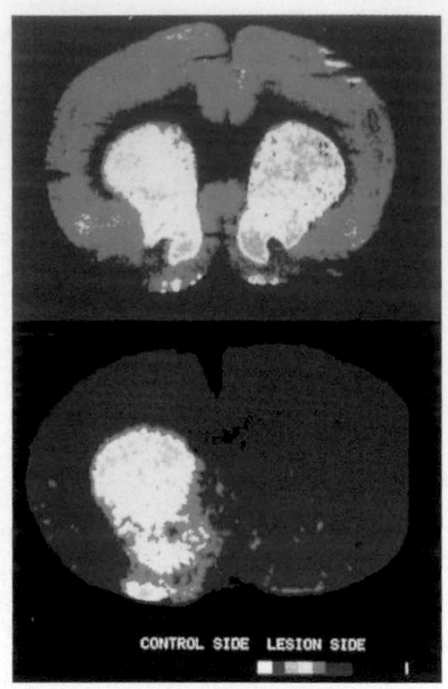

Figure 8.19 Results of injecting MPP^+ into one hemisphere of the rat brain
The autoradiography above shows D_2 dopamine receptors; the one below shows axon terminals that contain dopamine. Red indicates the highest level of activity, followed by yellow, green, and blue. Note that the MPP^+ greatly depleted the number of dopamine axons and that the number of D_2 receptors increased in response to this lack of input. However, the net result is a great decrease in dopamine activity. *(Source: From "Dopamine in the extrapyramidal motor function: A study based upon the MPTP-induced primate model of Parkinsonism," by C. C. Chiueh, 1988,* Annals of the New York Academy of Sciences, *515, p. 223. Reprinted by permission.)*

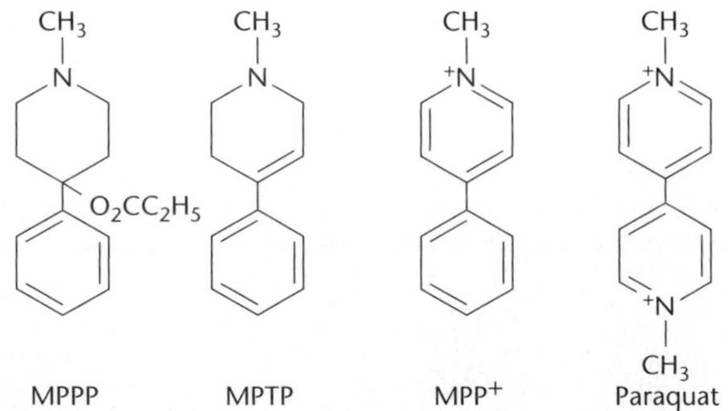

Figure 8.20 The chemical structures of MPPP, MPTP, MPP^+, and paraquat
Exposure to paraquat and similar herbicides and pesticides may increase the risk of Parkinson's disease.

tween one geographical area and another. The more or less random distribution of the disease suggests that toxins are just one cause among others yet to be discovered (C. A. D. Smith et al., 1992).

What else might influence the risk of Parkinson's disease? Researchers have compared the lifestyles of people who did and didn't develop the disease. One factor that stands out consistently is cigarette smoking and coffee drinking: People who smoke cigarettes or drink coffee have less chance of developing Parkinson's disease (Hernán, Takkouche, Caamaño-Isorna, & Gestal-Otero, 2002). (Read that sentence again.) One study took questionnaire results from pairs of young adult twins and compared the results to medical records decades later. Cigarette smoking was about 70% as common in people who developed Parkinson's disease as in their twins who did not (Wirdefeldt, Gatz, Pawitan, & Pedersen, 2004). A study of U.S. adults compared coffee drinking in middle-aged adults to their medical histories later in life; drinking coffee decreased the risk of Parkinson's disease, especially for men (Ascherio et al., 2004). Needless to say, smoking cigarettes increases the risk of lung cancer and other diseases more than it decreases the risk of Parkinson's disease. Coffee has somewhat less benefit for decreasing Parkinson's disease, but it's safer than smoking. In contrast to the effects of tobacco, marijuana increases the risk of Parkinson's disease (Glass, 2001). Researchers do not yet know how any of these drugs alters the risk of Parkinson's disease.

In short, Parkinson's disease probably results from a mixture of causes. Perhaps what they have in common is damage to the mitochondria. When a neuron's mitochondria begin to fail—because of genes, toxins, infections, or whatever—a chemical called α-synuclein clots into clusters that damage neurons containing dopamine (Dawson & Dawson, 2003). Dopamine-containing neurons are evidently more vulnerable than most other neurons to damage from almost any metabolic problem (Zeevalk, Manzino, Hoppe, & Sonsalla, 1997).

STOP & CHECK

1. Do monozygotic twins resemble each other more than dizygotic twins do for early-onset Parkinson's disease? For late-onset? What conclusion do these results imply?
2. How does MPTP exposure influence the likelihood of Parkinson's disease? What are the effects of cigarette smoking?

Check your answers on page 261.

L-Dopa Treatment

If Parkinson's disease results from a dopamine deficiency, then the goal of therapy should be to restore the missing dopamine. However, a dopamine pill would be ineffective because dopamine does not cross the blood-brain barrier. **L-dopa,** a precursor to dopamine, does cross the barrier. Taken as a daily pill, L-dopa reaches the brain, where neurons convert it to dopamine. L-dopa continues to be the main treatment for Parkinson's disease.

However, L-dopa is disappointing in several ways. First, it is ineffective for some patients, especially those in the late stages of the disease. Second, it does not prevent the continued loss of neurons. In fact, there is some evidence that too much dopamine *kills* dopamine-containing cells (Weingarten & Zhou, 2001). For that reason, L-dopa could do harm as well as good. Third, L-dopa enters not only the brain cells that need extra dopamine but also others, producing unpleasant side effects such as nausea, restlessness, sleep problems, low blood pressure, repetitive movements, hallucinations, and delusions. Generally, the more severe the patient's symptoms, the more severe the side effects.

Therapies Other Than L-Dopa

Given the limitations of L-dopa, researchers have sought alternatives and supplements. The following possibilities show promise (Dunnett & Björklund, 1999; Siderowf & Stern, 2003):

- Antioxidant drugs to decrease further damage
- Drugs that directly stimulate dopamine receptors
- Neurotrophins to promote survival and growth of the remaining neurons
- Drugs that decrease apoptosis (programmed cell death) of the remaining neurons
- High-frequency electrical stimulation of the globus pallidus or the subthalamic nucleus (This procedure is especially effective for blocking tremor.)

A potentially exciting strategy is still in the experimental stage but has been "in the experimental stage" for more than a quarter of a century already. In a pioneering study, M. J. Perlow and colleagues (1979) injected the chemical 6-OHDA into rats to make lesions in the substantia nigra of one hemisphere, producing Parkinson's-type symptoms in the opposite side of the body. After the movement abnormalities stabilized, the experimenters removed the substantia nigra from rat fetuses and transplanted them into the damaged brains. The grafts survived in 29 of the 30 recipients, making synapses in varying numbers. Four weeks later, most recipients had recovered much of their normal movement. Control animals that suffered the same brain damage without receiving grafts showed little or no behavioral recovery.

If such surgery works for rats, might it also for humans? The procedure itself is feasible. Perhaps because the blood-brain barrier protects the brain from foreign substances, the immune system is less active in the brain than elsewhere (Nicholas & Arnason, 1992), and physicians can give drugs to further suppress rejection of the transplanted tissue. However, only immature cells transplanted from a fetus can make connections, and simply making connections is not enough. In laboratory research, the recipient animal still has to relearn the behaviors dependent on those cells (Brasted, Watts, Robbins, & Dunnett, 1999). In effect, the animal has to practice using the transplanted cells.

Ordinarily, scientists test any experimental procedure extensively with laboratory animals before trying it on humans, but with Parkinson's disease, the temptation was too great. People in the late stages have little to lose and are willing to try almost anything. The obvious problem is where to get the donor tissue. Several early studies used tissue from the patient's own adrenal gland. Although that tissue is not composed of neurons, it produces and releases dopamine. Unfortunately, the adrenal gland transplants seldom produced much benefit (Backlund et al., 1985).

Another possibility is to transplant brain tissue from aborted fetuses. Fetal neurons transplanted into the brains of Parkinson's patients sometimes survive for years and do make synapses with the patient's own cells. However, the operation is difficult and expensive, requiring brain tissue from four to eight aborted fetuses. According to two studies, most patients show little or no benefit a year after surgery (Freed et al., 2001; Olanow et al., 2003). Patients with only mild symptoms showed a significant benefit, but that benefit consisted only of failing to deteriorate over the year, not actually improving (Olanow et al., 2003). At best, this procedure needs more research.

One problem is that many transplanted cells do not survive or do not form effective synapses, especially in the oldest recipients. Aging brains produce less volume of neurotrophins than younger brains do. Researchers have found improved success of brain transplants in aging rats if the transplant includes not only fetal neurons but also a source of neurotrophins (Collier, Sortwell, & Daley, 1999).

One way to decrease the need for aborted fetuses is to grow cells in tissue culture, genetically alter them so that they produce large quantities of L-dopa, and then transplant them into the brain (Ljungberg, Stern, & Wilkin, 1999; Studer, Tabar, & McKay, 1998). That idea is particularly attractive if the cells grown in tissue culture are **stem cells,** immature cells that are capable of differentiating into a wide variety of other cell types depending on where they are in the body. It may be possible to nurture a population of stem cells that are capable of becoming dopamine-releasing neurons and then deposit them into damaged brain areas (Kim et al., 2002). However, so far this method has also produced only modest benefits (Lindvall, Kokaia, & Martinez-Serrano, 2004).

The research on brain transplants has suggested yet another possibility for treatment. In several experiments, the transplanted tissue failed to survive, but the recipient showed behavioral recovery anyway. Evidently, the transplanted tissue releases neurotrophins that stimulate axon and dendrite growth in the recipient's own brain (Bohn, Cupit, Marciano, & Gash, 1987; Dunnett, Ryan, Levin, Reynolds, & Bunch, 1987; Ensor, Morley, Redfern, & Miles, 1993). Further research has demonstrated that brain injections of neurotrophins can significantly benefit brain-damaged rats and monkeys, presumably by enhancing the growth of axons and dendrites (Eslamboli et al., 2005; Gash et al., 1996; Kolb, Côte, Ribeiro-da-Silva, & Cuello, 1997). Because neurotrophins do not cross the blood-brain barrier, researchers are developing novel ways to get them into the brain (Kordower et al., 2000).

For the latest information about Parkinson's disease, visit the website of the World Parkinson Disease Association: **http://www.wpda.org/**

3. What is the likely explanation for how L-dopa relieves the symptoms of Parkinson's disease?

4. In what ways is L-dopa treatment disappointing?

5. What are some other possible treatments?

Check your answers on pages 261–262.

Huntington's Disease

Huntington's disease (also known as *Huntington disease* or *Huntington's chorea*) is a severe neurological disorder that strikes about 1 person in 10,000 in the United States (A. B. Young, 1995). Motor symptoms usually begin with arm jerks and then facial twitches; later, tremors spread to other parts of the body and develop into writhing (M. A. Smith, Brandt, & Shadmehr, 2000). (*Chorea* comes from the same root as *choreography;* the writhings of chorea sometimes resemble dancing.) Gradually, the twitches, tremors, and writhing interfere more and more with the person's walking, speech, and other voluntary movements. The ability to learn and improve new movements is especially limited (Willingham et al., 1996). The disorder is associated with gradual, extensive brain damage, especially

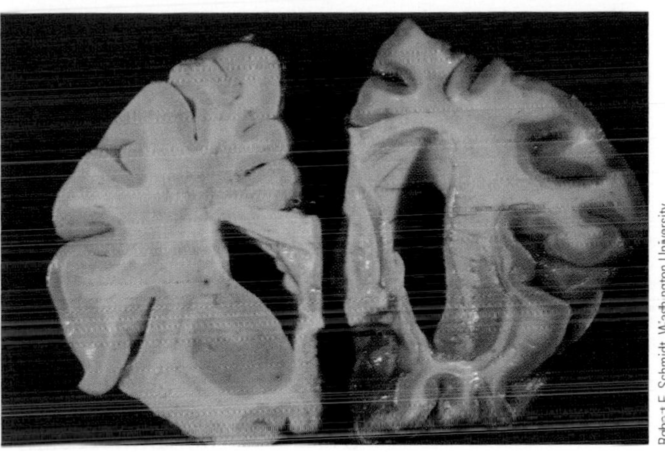

Figure 8.21 Brain of a normal person (left) and a person with Huntington's disease (right)
The angle of cut through the normal brain makes the lateral ventricle look larger in this photo than it actually is. Even so, note how much larger it is in the patient with Huntington's disease. The ventricles expand because of the loss of neurons.

in the caudate nucleus, putamen, and globus pallidus but also in the cerebral cortex (Tabrizi et al., 1999) (Figure 8.21).

People with Huntington's disease also suffer psychological disorders, including depression, memory impairment, anxiety, hallucinations and delusions, poor judgment, alcoholism, drug abuse, and sexual disorders ranging from complete unresponsiveness to indiscriminate promiscuity (Shoulson, 1990). The psychological disorders sometimes develop before the motor disorders, and occasionally, someone in the early stages of Huntington's disease is misdiagnosed as having schizophrenia.

Huntington's disease most often appears between the ages of 30 and 50, although onset can occur at any time from early childhood to old age. Once the symptoms emerge, both the psychological and the motor symptoms grow progressively worse and culminate in death. The earlier the onset, the more rapid the deterioration. At this point, no treatment is effective at either controlling the symptoms or slowing the course of the disease. However, mouse research suggests that a stimulating environment can delay the onset of symptoms (van Dellen, Blakemore, Deacon, York, & Hannan, 2000).

Heredity and Presymptomatic Testing

Huntington's disease is controlled by an autosomal dominant gene (i.e., one not on the X or Y chromosome). As a rule, a mutant gene that causes the loss of a function is recessive. The fact that the Huntington's gene is dominant implies that it produces the gain of some undesirable function.

Imagine that as a young adult you learn that your mother or father has Huntington's disease. In addition to your grief about your parent, you know that you have a 50% chance of getting the disease yourself. Your uncertainty may make it difficult to decide whether to have children and perhaps even what career to choose. (For example, you might decide against a career that requires many years of education.) Would you want to know in advance whether or not you were going to get the disease?

Investigators worked for many years to discover an accurate **presymptomatic test** to identify who would develop the disease later. In the 1980s, researchers established that the gene for Huntington's disease is on chromosome number 4, and in 1993, they identified the gene itself (Huntington's Disease Collaborative Research Group, 1993). Now an examination of your chromosomes can reveal with almost perfect accuracy whether or not you will get Huntington's disease. Not everyone who is at high risk for the disease wants to take the test, but many do.

The critical area of the gene includes a sequence of bases C-A-G (cytosine, adenine, guanine), which is repeated 11 to 24 times in most people. That repetition produces a string of 11 to 24 glutamines in the resulting protein. People with up to 35 C-A-G repetitions are considered safe from Huntington's disease. Those with 36 to 38 might get it, but probably not until old age, if at all. People with 39 or more repetitions are likely to get the disease, unless they die of other causes earlier. The more C-A-G repetitions someone has, the earlier the probable onset of the disease, as shown in Figure 8.22 (Brinkman, Mezei, Theilmann, Almqvist, & Hayden, 1997). In people with more than 50 repeats, the symptoms are likely to begin even younger, although too few such cases have been found to present reliable statistics. In short, a chromosomal examination can predict not only whether a person will get Huntington's disease but also approximately when.

Figure 8.23 shows comparable data for Huntington's disease and seven other neurological disorders. Each of them is related to an unusually long sequence of C-A-G repeats in some gene. Note that in each case, the greater the number of C-A-G repeats, the earlier the probable onset of the disease (Gusella & MacDonald, 2000). Those with a smaller number will be older when they get the disease, if they get it at all. You will recall a similar fact about Parkinson's disease: Several genes have been linked to early-onset Parkinson's disease, but the late-onset condition is less predictable and appears to depend on environmental factors more than genes. As we shall see in later chapters, genetic factors are clearly important for early-onset Alzheimer's disease, alcoholism, depression, and schizophrenia. For people with later onset, the role of genetics is weaker

disease, L-dopa produces fewer benefits and more severe side effects. (p. 258)

5. Other possible treatments include antioxidants, drugs that directly stimulate dopamine receptors, neurotrophins, drugs that decrease apoptosis, high-frequency electrical stimulation of the globus pallidus, and transplants of neurons from a fetus. (p. 258)
6. A presymptomatic test is given to people who do not yet show symptoms of a condition to predict who will eventually develop it. (p. 261)
7. Physicians can examine human chromosome 4. In one identified gene, they can count the number of consecutive repeats of the combination C-A-G. If the number is fewer than 36, the person will not develop Huntington's disease. For repeats of 36 or more, the larger the number, the more certain the person is to develop the disease and the earlier the probable age of onset. (p. 261)

Thought Questions

1. Haloperidol is a drug that blocks dopamine synapses. What effect would it be likely to have in someone suffering from Parkinson's disease?
2. Neurologists assert that if people lived long enough, sooner or later everyone would develop Parkinson's disease. Why?

Chapter Ending

Key Terms and Activities

Terms

aerobic (p. 234)
anaerobic (p. 234)
anosognosia (p. 247)
antagonistic muscles (p. 232)
Babinski reflex (p. 236)
ballistic movement (p. 238)
basal ganglia (caudate nucleus, putamen, globus pallidus) (p. 250)
cardiac muscle (p. 232)
central pattern generator (p. 238)
cerebellar cortex (p. 249)
dorsolateral tract (p. 243)
extensor (p. 232)
fast-twitch fiber (p. 234)
flexor (p. 232)
Golgi tendon organ (p. 236)
grasp reflex (p. 236)
huntingtin (p. 260)
Huntington's disease (p. 258)
L-dopa (p. 257)
mirror neurons (p. 242)
motor program (p. 238)
MPTP, MPP^+ (p. 256)
muscle spindle (p. 235)
myasthenia gravis (p. 234)
neuromuscular junction (p. 232)
nuclei of the cerebellum (p. 250)
parallel fibers (p. 250)
Parkinson's disease (p. 254)
posterior parietal cortex (p. 244)
prefrontal cortex (p. 245)
premotor cortex (p. 245)
presymptomatic test (p. 259)
primary motor cortex (p. 241)
proprioceptor (p. 235)
Purkinje cell (p. 250)
readiness potential (p. 246)
red nucleus (p. 243)
reflex (p. 236)
rooting reflex (p. 236)
skeletal muscle (or striated muscle) (p. 232)
slow-twitch fiber (p. 234)
smooth muscle (p. 232)
stem cell (p. 258)
stretch reflex (p. 235)
supplementary motor cortex (p. 245)
ventromedial tract (p. 243)
vestibular nucleus (p. 243)

Suggestions for Further Reading

Cole, J. (1995). *Pride and a daily marathon.* Cambridge, MA: MIT Press. Biography of a man who lost his sense of touch and proprioception from the neck down and eventually learned to control his movements strictly by vision.

Klawans, H. L. (1996). *Why Michael couldn't hit.* New York: W. H. Freeman. A collection of fascinating sports examples related to the brain and its disorders.

Lashley, K. S. (1951). The problem of serial order in behavior. In L. A. Jeffress (Ed.), *Cerebral mechanisms in behavior* (pp. 112–136). New York: Wiley. One of the true classic articles in psychology; a thought-provoking appraisal of what a theory of movement should explain.

Websites to Explore

- You can go to the Biological Psychology Study Center and click these links. While there, you can also check for suggested articles available on InfoTrac College Edition. The Biological Psychology Internet address is:

http://psychology.wadsworth.com/book/kalatbiopsych9e/

Myasthenia Gravis Links

http://pages.prodigy.net/stanley.way/myasthenia/

Huntington's Disease Society of America

http://www.hdsa.org

World Parkinson Disease Association

http://www.wpda.org/

Exploring Biological Psychology CD

The Withdrawal Reflex (animation)

The Crossed Extensor Reflex (animation)

Major Motor Areas (animation)

Critical Thinking (essay questions)

Chapter Quiz (multiple-choice questions)

ThomsonNOW™

http://www.thomsonedu.com

Go to this site for the link to ThomsonNOW, your one-stop study shop, Take a Pre-Test for this chapter, and ThomsonNOW will generate a Personalized Study Plan based on your test results. The Study Plan will identify the topics you need to review and direct you to online resources to help you master these topics. You can then take a Post-Test to help you determine the concepts you have mastered and what you still need work on.

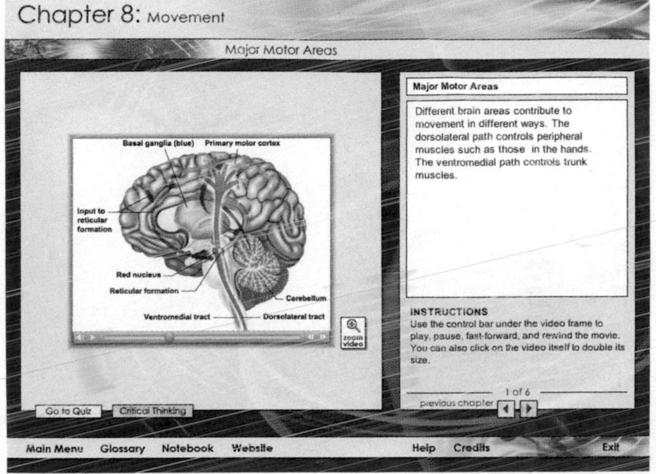

View an animation of the dorsolateral and ventromedial tracts.

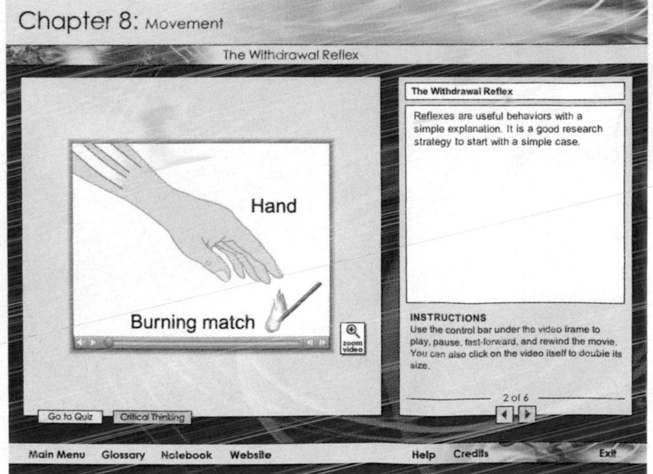

This animation illustrates one example of a reflex.

Wakefulness and Sleep

9

Chapter Outline

Main Ideas

1. Wakefulness and sleep alternate on a cycle of approximately 24 hours. The brain itself generates this cycle.
2. Sleep progresses through various stages, which differ in brain activity, heart rate, and other aspects. A special type of sleep, known as paradoxical or REM sleep, is light in some ways and deep in others.
3. Areas in the brainstem and forebrain control arousal and sleep. Localized brain damage can produce prolonged sleep or wakefulness.
4. People have many reasons for failing to sleep well enough to feel rested the following day.
5. We need sleep and REM sleep, although much about their functions remains uncertain.

Every multicellular animal that we know about has daily rhythms of wakefulness and sleep, and if we are deprived of sleep, we suffer. But if life evolved on another planet with different conditions, could animals evolve life without a need for sleep? Imagine a planet that doesn't rotate on its axis. Some animals evolve adaptations to live in the light area, others in the dark area, and still others in the twilight zone separating light from dark. There would be no need for any animal to alternate active periods with inactive periods on any fixed schedule and perhaps no need at all for prolonged inactive periods. If you were the astronaut who discovered these nonsleeping animals, you might be surprised.

Now imagine that astronauts from that planet set out on their first voyage to Earth. Imagine *their* surprise to discover animals like us with long inactive periods resembling death. To someone who hadn't seen sleep before, it would seem strange and mysterious indeed. For the purposes of this chapter, let us adopt their perspective and ask why animals as active as we are spend one-third of our lives doing so little.

Opposite: Rock hyraxes at a national park in Kenya.
Source: © Norbert Wu

Module 9.1 Rhythms of Waking and Sleeping

You are, I suspect, not particularly surprised to learn that your body spontaneously generates its own rhythm of wakefulness and sleep. Psychologists of an earlier era, however, considered that idea revolutionary. When behaviorism dominated experimental psychology from about the 1920s through the 1950s, many psychologists believed that any behavior could be traced to an external stimulation. For example, alternation between wakefulness and sleep must depend on something in the outside world, such as the cycle of sunrise and sunset or temperature fluctuations. The research of Curt Richter (1922) and others implied that the body generates its own cycles of activity and inactivity. Gradually, the evidence became stronger that animals generate approximately 24-hour cycles of wakefulness and sleep even in an environment that was as constant as anyone could make it. The idea of self-generated wakefulness and sleep was an important step toward viewing animals as active producers of behaviors.

Endogenous Cycles

An animal that produced its behavior entirely in response to current stimuli would be at a serious disadvantage; in many cases, an animal has to prepare for changes in sunlight and temperature before they occur. For example, migratory birds start flying toward their winter homes before their summer territory becomes too cold for survival. A bird that waited for the first frost would be in serious trouble. Similarly, squirrels begin storing nuts and putting on extra layers of fat in preparation for winter long before food becomes scarce.

Animals' readiness for a change in seasons comes partly from internal mechanisms. For example, several cues tell a migratory bird when to fly south for the winter, but after it reaches the tropics, no external cues tell it when to fly north in the spring. (In the tropics, the temperature doesn't change much from season to season, and neither does the length of day or night.) Nevertheless, it flies north at the right time. Even if it is kept in a cage with no cues to the season, it becomes restless in the spring, and if it is released, it flies north (Gwinner, 1986). Evidently, the bird's body generates a rhythm, an internal calendar, that prepares it for seasonal changes. We refer to that rhythm as an **endogenous circannual rhythm.** (*Endogenous* means "generated from within." *Circannual* comes from the Latin words *circum,* for "about," and *annum,* for "year.")

Similarly, all studied animals produce **endogenous circadian rhythms,** rhythms that last about a day.[1] (*Circadian* comes from *circum,* for "about," and *dies,* for "day.") Our most familiar endogenous circadian rhythm controls wakefulness and sleepiness. If you go without sleep all night—as most college students do, sooner or later—you feel sleepier and sleepier as the night goes on, until early morning. But as morning arrives, you actually begin to feel less sleepy. Evidently, your urge to sleep depends largely on the time of day, not just how recently you have slept (Babkoff, Caspy, Mikulincer, & Sing, 1991).

Figure 9.1 represents the activity of a flying squirrel kept in total darkness for 25 days. Each horizontal line represents one 24-hour day. A thickening in the line represents a period of activity by the animal. Even in this unchanging environment, the animal generates a regular rhythm of activity and sleep. The self-generated cycle may be slightly shorter than 24 hours, as in Figure 9.1, or slightly longer depending on whether the environment is constantly light or constantly dark and on whether the species is normally active in the light or in the dark (Carpenter & Grossberg, 1984). The cycle may also vary from one individual to another, partly for genetic reasons. Nevertheless, the rhythm is highly consistent for a given individual in a given environment, even if the environment provides no clues to time.

Mammals, including humans, have circadian rhythms in their waking and sleeping, frequency of eating and drinking, body temperature, secretion of hormones, volume of urination, sensitivity to drugs, and other variables. For example, although we ordinarily think of human body temperature as 37°C, normal tem-

[1]It would be interesting to know about a few species that have not been studied, such as fish that live deep in the sea, where light never reaches. Do they also have 24-hour cycles of activity and sleep?

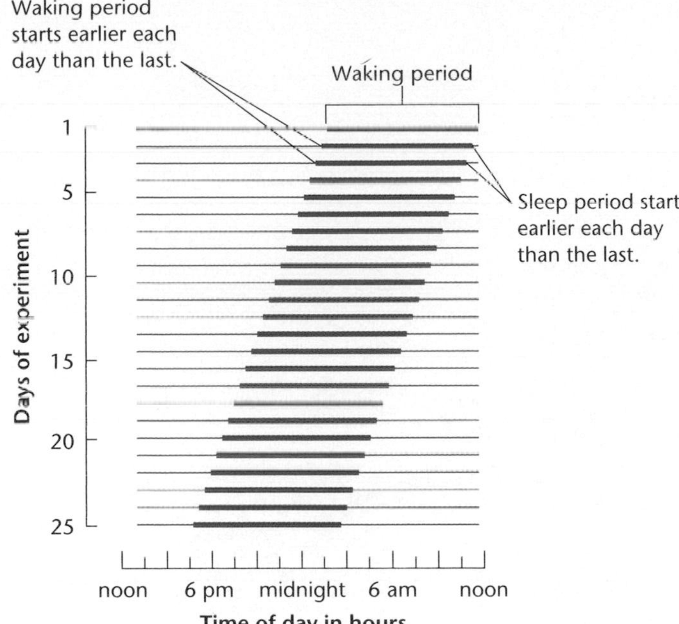

Figure 9.1 Activity record of a flying squirrel kept in constant darkness

The thickened segments indicate periods of activity as measured by a running wheel. Note that the free-running activity cycle lasts slightly less than 24 hours. *(Source: Modified from "Phase Control of Activity in a Rodent," by P. J. DeCoursey,* Cold Spring Harbor Symposia on Quantitative Biology, *1960, 25:49–55. Reprinted by permission of Cold Spring Harbor and P. J. DeCoursey)*

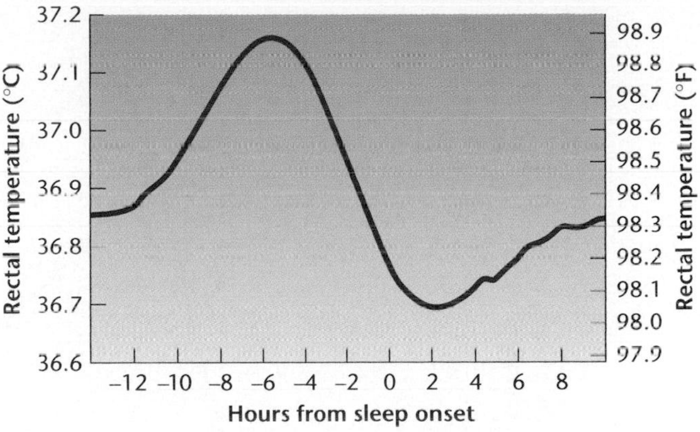

Figure 9.2 Mean rectal temperatures for nine adults

Body temperature reaches its low for the day about 2 hours after sleep onset; it reaches its peak about 6 hours before sleep onset. *(Source: From "Sleep-onset insomniacs have delayed temperature rhythms," by M. Morris, L. Lack, and D. Dawson,* Sleep, *1990, 13, 1–14. Reprinted by permission)*

perature fluctuates over the course of a day from a low near 36.7°C during the night to about 37.2°C in late afternoon (Figure 9.2).

However, circadian rhythms differ from one person to another. Some people ("morning people," or "larks") awaken early, quickly become productive, and gradually lose alertness as the day progresses. Others ("evening people," or "owls") are slower to warm up, both literally and figuratively. They reach their peak in the late afternoon or evening, and they can tolerate staying up all night better than morning people can (Taillard, Philip, Coste, Sagaspe, & Bioulac, 2003). A study of military pilots found that those who function well after sleep deprivation—mostly "evening people"—have greater levels of brain activation (as indicated by fMRI) even when they are not sleep-deprived (Caldwell et al., 2005).

Not everyone falls neatly into one extreme or the other, of course. A convenient way to compare people is to ask, "On days when you have no obligations, such as holidays and vacations, what time is the middle of your sleep?" For example, if you slept from 1 A.M. until 9 A.M. on those days, your middle time would be 5 A.M. As Figure 9.3 shows, one of the main determinants of circadian rhythm type is age. When you were a young child, you were almost certainly a "morning" type, you went to bed early and woke up early. As you entered adolescence, you started staying up later and waking up later, at least on weekends and vacations, when you had the opportunity. Most teenagers qualify either as "evening" types or as intermediates. The percentage of "evening" types increases until about age 20 and then starts a steady decrease (Roenneberg et al., 2004).

Do people older than 20 learn to go to bed earlier because they have jobs that require them to get up early? Two facts point to a biological explanation rather than an explanation in terms of learning. First, in Figure 9.3, note how the shift continues gradually over decades. If people were simply making a learned adjustment to their jobs, we might expect a sudden shift followed by later stability. Second, a similar trend occurs in rats: Older rats reach their best performance shortly after awakening, whereas younger rats tend to improve performance as the day progresses (Winocur & Hasher, 1999, 2004).

STOP & CHECK

1. If we wanted to choose people for a job that requires sometimes working without sleep, how could we quickly determine which ones were probably best able to tolerate sleep deprivation?

Check your answer on page 274.

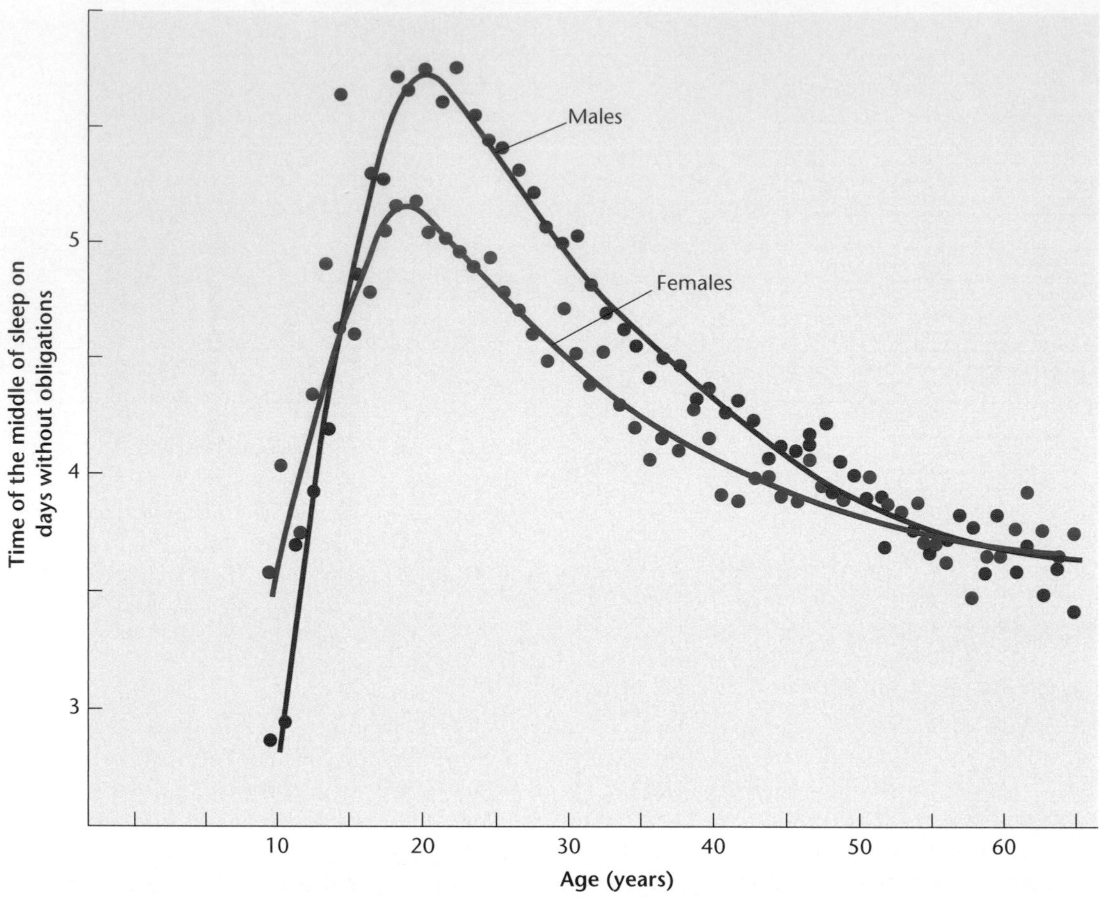

Figure 9.3 Age differences in circadian rhythms
People of various ages identified the time of the middle of their sleep, such as 3 A.M. or 5 A.M., on days when they had no obligations. People around age 20 were the most likely to go to bed late and wake up late. *(Source: Reprinted from T. Roenneberg et al., "A marker for the end of adolescence,"* Current Biology, *14, R1038–R1039, Figure 1, copyright 2004, with permission from Elsevier.)*

Duration of the Human Circadian Rhythm

It might seem simple to determine the duration of the human circadian rhythm: Put people in an environment with no cues to time and observe their waking–sleeping schedule. However, the results depend on the amount of light (Campbell, 2000). Under constant bright lights, people have trouble sleeping, they complain about the experiment, and their rhythms run faster than 24 hours. In constant darkness, they have trouble waking up, again they complain about the experiment, and their rhythms run slower. In several studies, people were allowed to turn on bright lights whenever they chose to be awake and turn them off when they wanted to sleep. Under these conditions, most people followed a cycle closer to 25 than to 24 hours a day. The problem, which experimenters did not realize at first, was that bright light late in the day lengthens the circadian rhythm.

A different way to run the experiment is to provide light and darkness on a cycle that people cannot follow. Researchers had already known that most people can adjust to a 23- or 25-hour day but not to a 22- or 28-hour day (Folkard, Hume, Minors, Waterhouse, & Watson, 1985; Kleitman, 1963). Later researchers kept healthy adults in rooms with an artificial 28-hour day. None of them could, in fact, synchronize to that schedule; they all therefore produced their own self-generated rhythms of alertness and body temperature. Those rhythms varied among individuals, with a mean of 24.2 hours (Czeisler et al., 1999).

Yet another approach is to examine people living under unusual conditions. Naval personnel on U.S. nuclear powered submarines are cut off from sunlight for months at a time, living under faint artificial light. In many cases, they have been asked to live on a schedule of 6 hours of work alternating with 12 hours of rest. Even though they sleep (or *try* to sleep) on this 18-hour schedule, their bodies generate rhythms of alertness and body chemistry that average about 24.3 to 24.4 hours (Kelly et al., 1999). In short, humans' circadian clock generates a rhythm slightly longer than 24 hours when it has nothing to reset it.

Mechanisms of the Biological Clock

What kind of biological clock within our body generates our circadian rhythm? Curt Richter (1967) introduced the concept that the brain generates its own rhythms—that is, a biological clock—and he reported that the biological clock is insensitive to most forms of interference. Blind or deaf animals generate nearly normal circadian rhythms, although they slowly drift out of phase with the external world. The circadian rhythm is surprisingly steady despite food or water deprivation, x-rays, tranquilizers, alcohol, anesthesia, lack of oxygen, most kinds of brain damage, or the removal of hormonal organs. Even an hour or so of induced hibernation often fails to reset the biological clock (Gibbs, 1983; Richter, 1975). Evidently, the biological clock is a hardy, robust mechanism.

The Suprachiasmatic Nucleus (SCN)

The surest way to disrupt the biological clock is to damage an area of the hypothalamus called the **suprachiasmatic** (soo-pruh-kie-as-MAT-ik) **nucleus,** abbreviated **SCN.** It gets its name from its location just above the optic chiasm (Figure 9.4). The SCN provides the main control of the circadian rhythms for sleep and temperature (Refinetti & Menaker, 1992). After damage to the SCN, the body's rhythms are less consistent and no longer synchronized to environmental patterns of light and dark.

The SCN generates circadian rhythms itself in a genetically controlled, unlearned manner. If SCN neurons are disconnected from the rest of the brain or removed from the body and maintained in tissue culture, they continue to produce a circadian rhythm of action potentials (Earnest, Liang, Ratcliff, & Cassone, 1999; Inouye & Kawamura, 1979). Even a single iso-

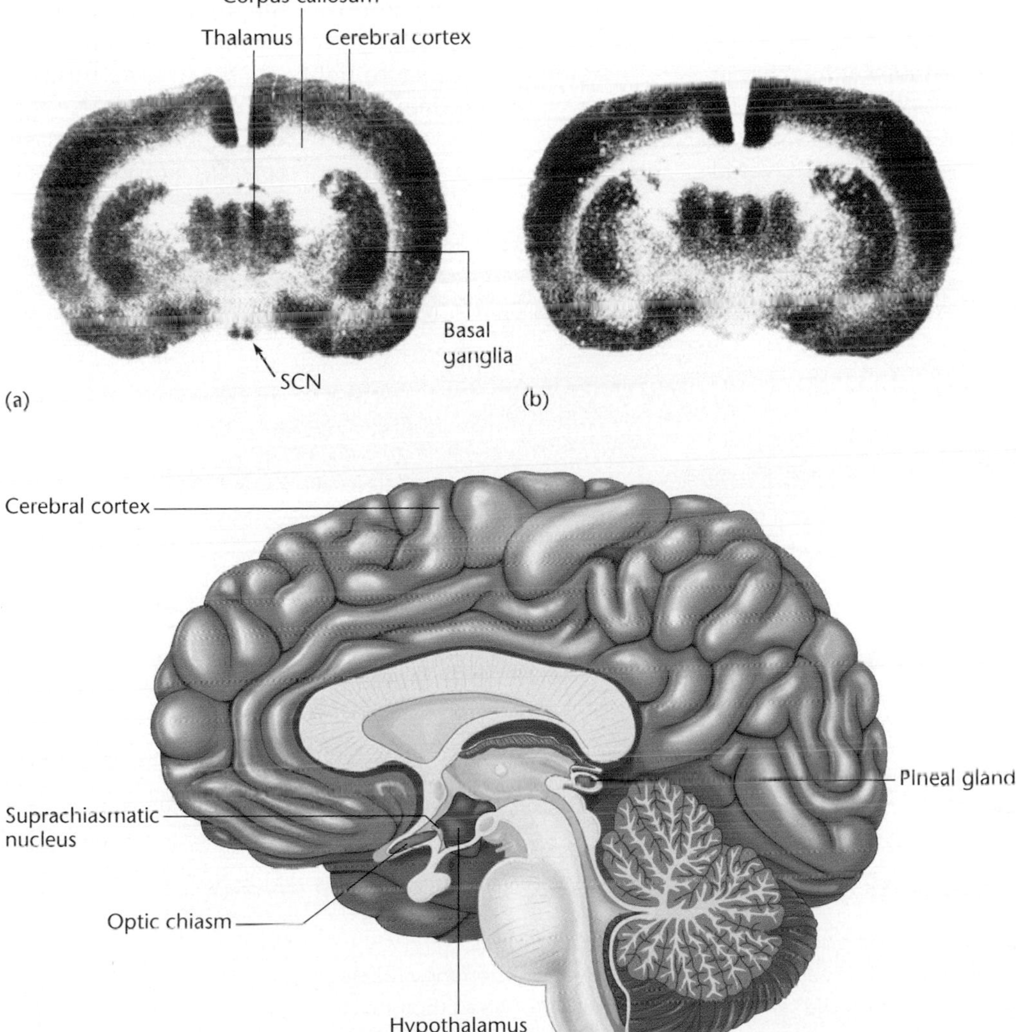

Figure 9.4 The suprachiasmatic nucleus (SCN) of rats and humans
The SCN is located at the base of the brain, just above the optic chiasm, which has torn off in these coronal sections through the plane of the anterior hypothalamus. Each rat was injected with radioactive 2-deoxyglucose, which is absorbed by the most active neurons. A high level of absorption of this chemical produces a dark appearance on the slide. Note that the level of activity in SCN neurons is much higher in section **(a),** in which the rat was injected during the day, than it is in section **(b),** in which the rat received the injection at night. **(c)** A sagittal section through a human brain showing the location of the SCN and the pineal gland. *(Source: (a) and (b) W. J. Schwartz & Gainer, 1977)*

lated SCN cell can maintain a moderately steady circadian rhythm, but cells communicate with one another to sharpen the accuracy of the rhythm, partly by neurotransmitters and partly by electrical synapses (Long, Jutras, Connors, & Burwell, 2005; Yamaguchi et al., 2003).

One group of experimenters discovered hamsters with a mutant gene that makes the SCN produce a 20-hour instead of 24-hour rhythm (Ralph & Menaker, 1988). The researchers surgically removed the SCN from adult hamsters and then transplanted SCN tissue from hamster fetuses into the adults. When they transplanted SCN tissue from fetuses with a 20-hour rhythm, the recipients produced a 20-hour rhythm. When they transplanted tissue from fetuses with a 24-hour rhythm, the recipients produced a 24-hour rhythm (Ralph, Foster, Davis, & Menaker, 1990). That is, the rhythm followed the pace of the donors, not the recipients, so again, the results show that the rhythms come from the SCN itself.

The Biochemistry of the Circadian Rhythm

Research on the mechanism of circadian rhythms began with insects, where the genetic basis is easier to explore, because they reproduce in weeks instead of months or years. Studies on the fruit fly *Drosophila* discovered genes that generate a circadian rhythm (Liu et al., 1992; Sehgal, Ousley, Yang, Chen, & Schotland, 1999). Two genes, known as *period* (abbreviated *per*) and *timeless* (*tim*), produce the proteins Per and Tim. Those proteins start in small amounts early in the morning and increase during the day. By evening, they reach a high level that makes the fly sleepy; that high level also feeds back to the genes to shut them down. During the night, while the genes no longer produce Per or Tim, their concentration declines until the next morning, when the cycle begins anew. When the Per and Tim levels are high, they interact with a protein called Clock to induce sleepiness. When they are low, the result is wakefulness. Furthermore, a pulse of light during the night inactivates the Tim protein, so extra light during the evening decreases sleepiness and resets the biological clock. Figure 9.5 summarizes this feedback mechanism.

Why do we care about flies? The answer is that after researchers understood the mechanism in flies, they found virtually the same genes and proteins in mammals (Reick, Garcia, Dudley, & McKnight, 2001; Zheng et al., 1999). The mechanisms are similar but not identical across species. For example, light directly alters the Tim protein in flies (Shearman et al., 2000), but in mammals, a pulse of light acts by altering input to the SCN, which then alters its release of Tim (Crosio, Cermakian, Allis, & Sassone-Corsi, 2000). In any case, the Per and Tim proteins increase the activity of cer-

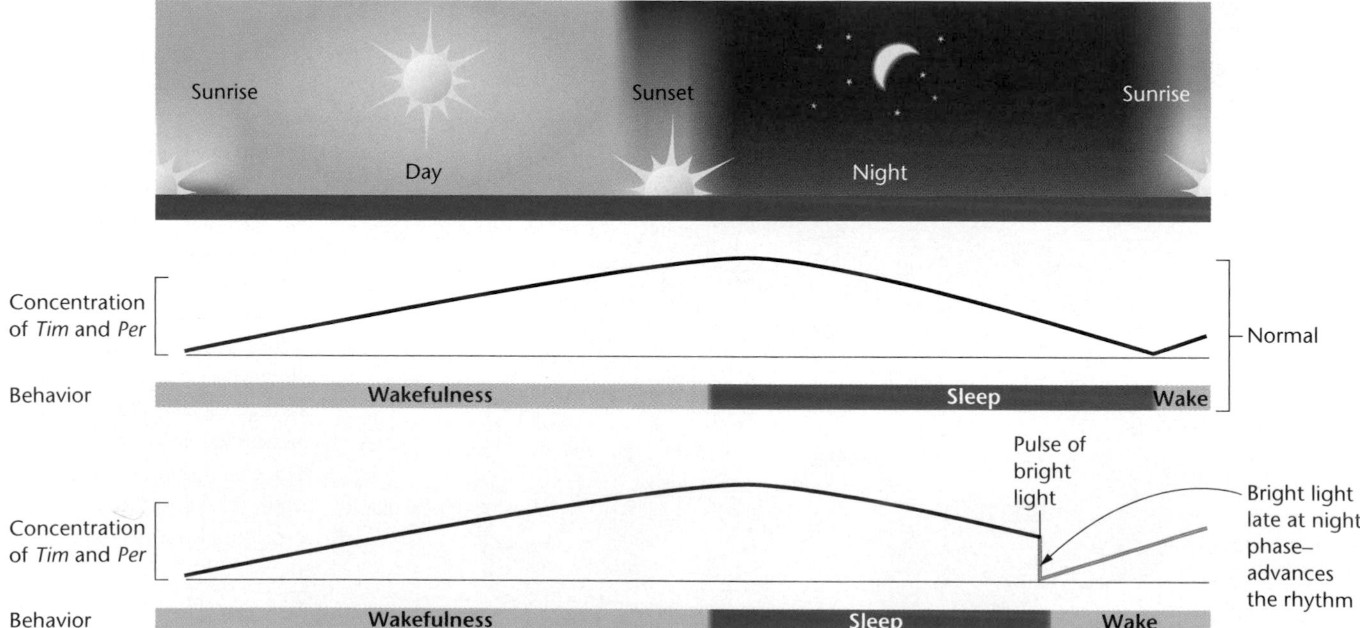

Figure 9.5 Feedback between proteins and genes to control sleepiness
In fruit flies (*Drosophila*), the Tim and Per proteins accumulate during the day. When they reach a high level, they induce sleepiness and shut off the genes that produce them. When their levels decline sufficiently, wakefulness returns and so does the gene activity. A pulse of light during the night breaks down the Tim protein, thus increasing wakefulness and resetting the circadian rhythm.

tain kinds of neurons in the SCN (Kuhlman, Silver, LeSauter, Bult-Ito, & McMahon, 2003).

Understanding these mechanisms helps make sense of some unusual sleep disorders. Mice with damage to their *clock* gene sleep less than normal (Naylor et al., 2000), and presumably, some cases of decreased sleep in humans might have the same cause. Also, some people with a mutation in their *per* gene have odd circadian rhythms: Their biological clock runs faster than 24 hours (C. R. Jones et al., 1999), and so they consistently get sleepy early in the evening and awaken early in the morning (Toh et al., 2001; Xu et al., 2005). Most people who are on vacation with no obligations say, "Oh, good! I can stay up late and then sleep late tomorrow morning!" People with the altered *per* gene say, "Oh, good! I can go to bed even earlier than usual and wake up really early tomorrow!" As with other sleep disorders, most people with this gene suffer from depression (Xu et al., 2005). As we shall see again in Chapter 15, sleep difficulties and depression are closely linked.

Melatonin

The SCN regulates waking and sleeping by controlling activity levels in other brain areas, including the **pineal gland** (PIN-ee-al; see Figure 9.4), an endocrine gland located just posterior to the thalamus (Aston-Jones, Chen, Zhu, & Oshinsky, 2001; von Gall et al., 2002). The pineal gland releases **melatonin**, a hormone that increases sleepiness. The human pineal gland secretes melatonin mostly at night, making us sleepy at that time. When people shift to a new time zone and start following a new schedule, they continue to feel sleepy at their old times until the melatonin rhythm shifts (Dijk & Cajochen, 1997). People who have pineal gland tumors sometimes stay awake for days at a time (Haimov & Lavie, 1996).

Melatonin secretion usually starts to increase about 2 or 3 hours before bedtime. Taking a melatonin pill in the evening has little effect on sleepiness because the pineal gland produces melatonin at that time anyway. However, people who take melatonin at other times become sleepy within 2 hours (Haimov & Lavie, 1996). Therefore, some people take melatonin pills when they travel to a new time zone or start a new work schedule and need to sleep at an unaccustomed time.

Melatonin also feeds back to reset the biological clock through its effects on receptors in the SCN (Gillette & McArthur, 1996). A moderate dose of melatonin (0.5 mg) in the afternoon phase-advances the clock; that is, it makes the person get sleepy earlier in the evening and wake up earlier the next morning. A single dose of melatonin in the morning has little effect (Wirz-Justice, Werth, Renz, Müller, & Kräuchi, 2002), although repeated morning doses can phase-delay the clock, causing the person to get sleepy later than usual at night and awaken later the next morning.

Taking melatonin has become something of a fad. Melatonin is an antioxidant, so it has some health benefits (Reiter, 2000). Low pill doses (up to 0.3 mg/day) produce blood levels similar to those that occur naturally and therefore seem unlikely to do any harm. Larger doses seldom produce obvious side effects. However, for rats with movement problems, melatonin aggravates the problem still further (Willis & Armstrong, 1999). Long-term use also impairs animals' reproductive fertility and, if taken during pregnancy, harms the development of the fetus (Arendt, 1997; Weaver, 1997). The long-term effects on humans are not known, but the cautious advice is, as with any medication, don't take it unless you need it.

STOP & CHECK

2. What evidence indicates that humans have an internal biological clock?
3. What evidence indicates that the SCN produces the circadian rhythm itself?
4. How do the proteins Tim and Per relate to sleepiness in *Drosophila*?

Check your answers on page 274.

Setting and Resetting the Biological Clock

Our circadian rhythms have a period close to 24 hours, but they are hardly perfect. We have to readjust our internal workings daily to stay in phase with the outside world. On weekends, when most of us are freer to set our own schedules, we expose ourselves to lights, noises, and activity at night and then awaken late the next morning. By Monday morning, when the electric clock indicates 7 A.M., the biological clock within us says about 5 A.M., and we stagger off to work or school without much pep (Moore-Ede, Czeisler, & Richardson, 1983).

Although circadian rhythms persist in the absence of light, light is critical for periodically resetting them. Consider this analogy: I used to have a windup wristwatch that lost about 2 minutes per day, which would accumulate to an hour per month if I didn't reset it. It had a **free-running rhythm** of 24 hours and 2 minutes—that is, a rhythm that occurs when no stimuli reset or alter it. The circadian rhythm is similar to that wristwatch. The stimulus that resets the circadian rhythm is referred to by the German term **zeitgeber** (TSITE-gay-ber), meaning "time-giver." Light is the dominant zeitgeber for land animals (Rusak & Zucker, 1979). (The tides are important for many marine animals.) Light is not our only zeitgeber; others include exercise (Eastman, Hoese, Youngstedt, & Liu, 1995), noises, meals, and the temperature of the environment (Refinetti, 2000). Even keeping an animal awake for a few hours in the middle of the night, by gentle handling, can shift the circadian rhythm (Antle & Mistlberger, 2000). However, these additional zeitgebers merely supplement or alter the effects of light; on their own, their effects are weak under most circumstances. For example, according to a study of people working in Antarctica, during the Antarctic winter, with no sunlight, each person generated his or her own free-running rhythm. Even though they were living together and trying to maintain a 24-hour rhythm, their bodies generated rhythms ranging from 24½ hours to more than 25 hours (Kennaway & Van Dorp, 1991). People living in the Scandinavian countries report high rates of insomnia and other sleep problems in the winter, when they see little or no sunlight (Ohayon & Partinen, 2002).

What about blind people, who are forced to set their circadian rhythms by zeitgebers other than light? The results vary. Some do set their circadian rhythms by noise, temperature, activity, and other signals. However, others who are not sufficiently sensitive to these secondary zeitgebers produce free-running circadian rhythms that run a little longer than 24 hours. When those cycles are in phase with the person's activity schedule, all is well, but when they drift out of phase, the result is insomnia at night and sleepiness during the day (Sack & Lewy, 2001).

In one study of hamsters living under constant light, the SCN of the left hemisphere got out of phase with the one in the right hemisphere in some cases. Evidently, without an external zeitgeber, the two SCNs generated independent rhythms without synchronizing each other. As a result, these hamsters had two wakeful periods and two sleep periods every 24 hours (de la Iglesia, Meyer, Carpino, & Schwartz, 2000).

Jet Lag

A disruption of circadian rhythms due to crossing time zones is known as **jet lag**. Travelers complain of sleepiness during the day, sleeplessness at night, depression, and impaired concentration. All these problems stem from the mismatch between internal circadian clock and external time (Haimov & Arendt, 1999). Most of us find it easier to adjust to crossing time zones going west than east. Going west, we stay awake later at night and then awaken late the next morning, already partly adjusted to the new schedule. That is, we *phase-delay* our circadian rhythms. Going east, we have to go to sleep earlier and awaken earlier; we *phase-advance* (Figure 9.6). Most people find it difficult to go to sleep before their body's usual time.

Adjusting to jet lag is more stressful for some people than for others. Stress elevates blood levels of the adrenal hormone *cortisol,* and many studies have shown that prolonged elevations of cortisol can lead to a loss of neurons in the hippocampus, a brain area important for memory. One study examined female flight attendants who had spent the previous 5 years making flights across seven or more time zones—such as Chicago to Italy—with mostly short breaks (fewer than 6 days) between trips. On the average, they showed smaller than average volumes of the hippocampus and surrounding structures, and they showed some memory impairments (Cho, 2001). These results suggest a danger from repeated adjustments of the circadian rhythm, although the problem here could be just air travel itself. (A good control group would have been flight attendants who flew long north–south routes.)

Shift Work

People who sleep irregularly—such as pilots and truck drivers, medical interns, and shift workers in factories—find that their duration of sleep depends on what time they go to sleep. When they have to sleep in the morning or early afternoon, they sleep only briefly, even though they have been awake for 16 hours or more (Frese & Harwich, 1984; Winfree, 1983).

Figure 9.6 Jet lag
Eastern time is later than western time. People who travel six time zones east fall asleep on the plane and then must awaken when it is morning at their destination but still night back home.

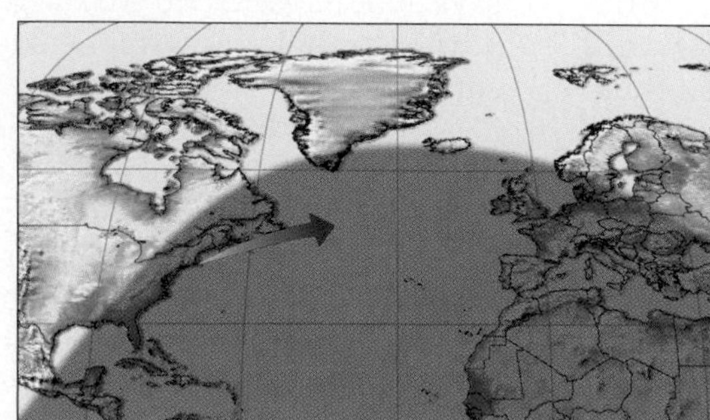
(a) Leave New York at 7 PM

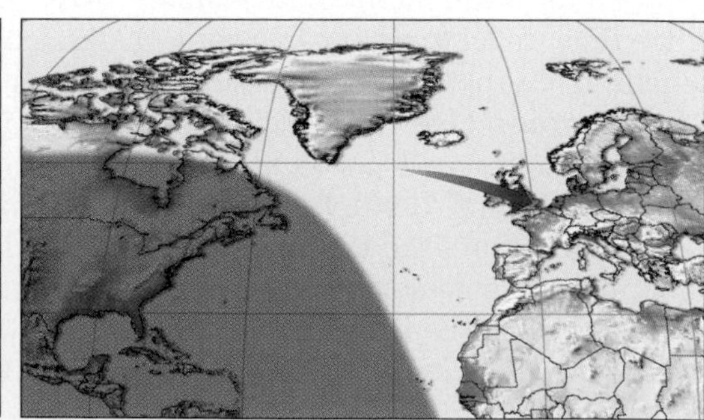
(b) Arrive in London at 7 AM, which is 2 AM in New York

People who work on a night shift, such as midnight to 8 A.M., sleep during the day. At least they try to. Even after months or years on such a schedule, many workers adjust incompletely. They continue to feel groggy on the job, they do not sleep soundly during the day, and their body temperature continues to peak when they are trying to sleep in the day instead of while they are working at night. In general, night-shift workers have more accidents than day-shift workers.

Working at night does not reliably change the circadian rhythm because most buildings use artificial lighting in the range of 150–180 lux, which is only moderately effective in resetting the rhythm (Boivin, Duffy, Kronauer, & Czeisler, 1996). People adjust best to night work if they sleep in a very dark room during the day and work under very bright lights at night, comparable to the noonday sun (Czeisler et al., 1990).

How Light Resets the SCN

The SCN is located just above the optic chiasm. (Figure 9.4 shows the positions in the human brain; the relationship is similar in other mammals.) A small branch of the optic nerve, known as the *retinohypothalamic path,* extends directly from the retina to the SCN. Axons of that path alter the SCN's settings.

Most of the input to that path, however, does not come from normal retinal receptors. Mice with genetic defects that destroy nearly all their rods and cones nevertheless reset their biological clocks in synchrony with the light (Freedman et al., 1999; Lucas, Freedman, Muñoz, Garcia-Fernández, & Foster, 1999). Also, consider blind mole rats (Figure 9.7). Their eyes are covered with folds of skin and fur; they have neither eye muscles nor a lens with which to focus an image. They have fewer than 900 optic nerve axons, as compared with 100,000 in hamsters. Even a bright flash of light evokes no startle response and no measurable change in brain activity. Nevertheless, light resets their circadian rhythms (de Jong, Hendriks, Sanyal, & Nevo, 1990).

Figure 9.7 A blind mole rat
Although blind mole rats are indeed blind in all other regards, they reset their circadian rhythms in response to light.

The surprising explanation is that the retinohypothalamic path to the SCN comes from a special population of retinal ganglion cells that have their own photopigment, called *melanopsin,* unlike the ones found in rods and cones (Hannibal, Hindersson, Knudsen, Georg, & Fahrenkrug, 2001; Lucas, Douglas, & Foster, 2001). These special ganglion cells respond directly to light and do not require any input from rods or cones (Berson, Dunn, & Takao, 2002). They are located mainly near the nose, not evenly throughout the retina (Visser, Beersma, & Daan, 1999). (That is, they see toward the periphery.) They respond to light slowly and turn off slowly when the light ceases (Berson et al., 2002). Therefore, they respond to the overall average amount of light, not to instantaneous changes in light. The average intensity over a period of minutes or hours is, of course, exactly the information the SCN needs to gauge the time of day. Because they do not contribute to vision, they do not need to respond to momentary changes in light.

Apparently, however, these neurons are not the only input to the SCN. Mice lacking the gene for melanopsin do adjust their cycles to periods of light and dark, although not as well as normal mice (Panda et al., 2002; Ruby et al., 2002). Evidently, the SCN can respond to either normal retinal input or input from the ganglion cells containing melanopsin, and either can substitute for the other.

STOP & CHECK

5. What stimulus is the most effective zeitgeber for humans?

6. How does light reset the biological clock?

Check your answers on page 274.

Module 9.1
In Closing: Sleep–Wake Cycles

Unlike an electric appliance that stays on until someone turns it off, the brain periodically turns itself on and off. Sleepiness is definitely not a voluntary or optional act. People who try to work when they are sleepy are prone to errors and injuries. Someone who sleeps well may not be altogether healthy or happy, but one who consistently fails to get enough sleep is almost certainly headed for troubles.

Summary

1. Animals, including humans, have internally generated rhythms of activity lasting about 24 hours. (p. 266)
2. The suprachiasmatic nucleus (SCN), a part of the hypothalamus, generates the body's circadian rhythms for sleep and temperature. (p. 269)
3. The genes controlling the circadian rhythm are almost the same in mammals as in insects. Across species, certain proteins increase in abundance during the day and then decrease during the night. (p. 270)
4. The SCN controls the body's rhythm partly by directing the release of melatonin by the pineal gland. The hormone melatonin increases sleepiness; if given at certain times of the day, it can also reset the circadian rhythm. (p. 271)
5. Although the biological clock can continue to operate in constant light or constant darkness, the onset of light resets the clock. The biological clock can reset to match an external rhythm of light and darkness slightly different from 24 hours, but if the discrepancy exceeds about 2 hours, the biological clock generates its own rhythm instead of resetting. (p. 271)
6. It is easier for people to follow a cycle longer than 24 hours (as when traveling west) than to follow a cycle shorter than 24 hours (as when traveling east). (p. 272)
7. If people wish to work at night and sleep during the day, the best way to shift the circadian rhythm is to have bright lights at night and darkness during the day. (p. 273)
8. Light resets the biological clock partly by a branch of the optic nerve that extends to the SCN. Those axons originate from a special population of ganglion cells that respond directly to light, rather than relaying information from rods and cones synapsing onto them. (p. 273)

Answers to STOP & CHECK Questions

1. Use fMRI to measure brain activation. Those with strongest responses tend to tolerate sleeplessness better than others. (p. 267)
2. People who have lived in an environment with a light–dark schedule much different from 24 hours fail to follow that schedule and instead become wakeful and sleepy on about a 24-hour basis. (p. 271)
3. SCN cells produce a circadian rhythm of activity even if they are kept in cell culture isolated from the rest of the body. (p. 271)
4. The proteins Tim and Per accumulate during the wakeful period. When they reach a high enough level, they trigger sleepiness and turn off the genes that produced them. Therefore, their levels decline until they reach a low enough level for wakefulness to begin anew. (p. 271)
5. Light is the most effective zeitgeber for humans and other land animals. (p. 273)
6. A branch of the optic nerve, the retinohypothalamic path, conveys information about light to the SCN. The axons comprising that path originate from special ganglion cells that respond to light by themselves, without needing input from rods or cones. (p. 273)

Thought Questions

1. Is it possible for the onset of light to reset the circadian rhythms of a person who is blind? Explain.
2. Why would evolution have enabled blind mole rats to synchronize their SCN activity to light, even though they cannot see well enough to make any use of the light?
3. If you travel across several time zones to the east and want to use melatonin to help reset your circadian rhythm, at what time of day should you take it? What if you travel west?

Module 9.2
Stages of Sleep and Brain Mechanisms

Suppose I buy a new radio. After I play it for 4 hours, it suddenly stops. I wonder whether the batteries are dead or whether the radio needs repair. Later, I discover that this radio always stops after playing for 4 hours but operates again a few hours later even without repairs or a battery change. I begin to suspect that the manufacturer designed it this way on purpose, perhaps to prevent me from listening to the radio all day. Now I want to find the device that turns it off whenever I play it for 4 hours. Notice that I am asking a new question. When I thought that the radio stopped because it needed repairs or new batteries, I did not ask which device turned it off.

Similarly, if we think of sleep as something like the "off" state of a machine, we do not ask which part of the brain produces it. But if we think of sleep as a specialized state evolved to serve particular functions, we look for the mechanisms that regulate it.

The Stages of Sleep

Nearly all scientific advances come from new or improved measurements. Researchers did not even suspect that sleep has different stages until they accidentally measured them. The electroencephalograph (EEG), as described on page 107, records an average of the electrical potentials of the cells and fibers in the brain areas nearest each electrode on the scalp (Figure 9.8). That is, if half of the cells in some area increase their electrical potentials while the other half decrease, the EEG recording is flat. The EEG record rises or falls when cells fire in synchrony—doing the same thing at the same time. You might compare it to a record of the noise in a crowded football stadium: It shows only slight fluctuations until some event gets everyone yelling at once. The EEG provides an objective way for brain researchers to compare brain activity at different times of night.

Figure 9.9 shows data from a **polysomnograph**, a combination of EEG and eye-movement records, for a male college student during various stages of sleep. Figure 9.9a presents a period of relaxed wakefulness for comparison. Note the steady series of **alpha waves** at a frequency of 8 to 12 per second. Alpha waves are characteristic of relaxation, not of all wakefulness.

In Figure 9.9b, sleep has just begun. During this period, called stage 1 sleep, the EEG is dominated by irregular, jagged, low-voltage waves. Overall brain activity is still fairly high but starting to decline. As Figure 9.9c shows, the most prominent characteristics of stage 2 are sleep spindles and K-complexes. A **sleep spindle** consists of 12- to 14-Hz waves during a burst that lasts at least half a second. Sleep spindles result from oscillating interactions between cells in the thalamus and the cortex. A **K-complex** is a sharp high-amplitude wave. Sudden stimuli can evoke K-complexes during other stages of sleep (Bastien & Campbell, 1992), but they are most common in stage 2.

In the succeeding stages of sleep, heart rate, breathing rate, and brain activity decrease, and slow, large-amplitude waves become more common (see Figures 9.9d and e). By stage 4, more than half the record

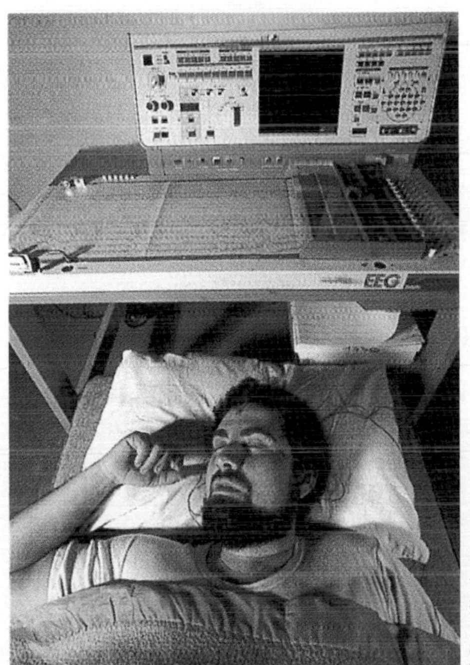

Figure 9.8 Sleeping person with electrodes in place on the scalp for recording brain activity
The printout above his head shows the readings from each electrode.

includes large waves of at least a half-second duration. Stages 3 and 4 together constitute **slow-wave sleep (SWS)**.

Slow waves indicate that neuronal activity is highly synchronized. In stage 1 and in wakefulness, the cortex receives a great deal of input, much of it at high frequencies. Nearly all the neurons are active, but different populations of neurons are active at different times. Thus, the EEG is full of short, rapid, choppy waves. By stage 4, however, sensory input to the cerebral cortex is greatly reduced, and the few remaining sources of input can synchronize many cells. As an analogy, imagine that the barrage of stimuli arriving at the brain is like thousands of rocks dropped into a pond over the course of a minute: The resulting waves largely cancel one another out. The surface of the pond is choppy, with few large waves. By contrast, the result of just one rock dropping is fewer but larger waves, such as those in stage 4 sleep.

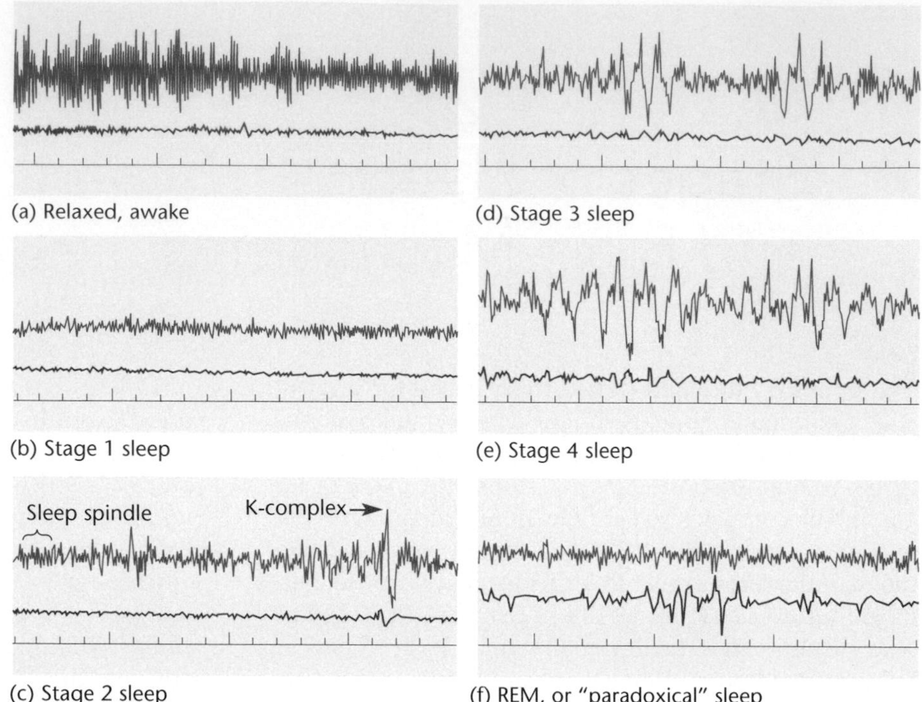

Figure 9.9 Polysomnograph records from a male college student
A polysomnograph includes records of EEG, eye movements, and sometimes other data, such as muscle tension or head movements. For each of these records, the top line is the EEG from one electrode on the scalp; the middle line is a record of eye movements; and the bottom line is a time marker, indicating 1-second units. Note the abundance of slow waves in stages 3 and 4. *(Source: Records provided by T. E. LeVere)*

STOP & CHECK

1. What do long, slow waves on an EEG indicate?

Check your answer on page 285.

Paradoxical or REM Sleep

Many discoveries occur when researchers stumble upon something by accident and then notice that it might be important. In the 1950s, the French scientist Michel Jouvet was trying to test the learning abilities of cats after removal of the cerebral cortex. Because decorticate mammals are generally inactive, Jouvet recorded slight movements of the muscles and EEGs from the hindbrain. During periods of apparent sleep, the cats' brain activity was relatively high, but their neck muscles were completely relaxed. Jouvet (1960) then recorded the same phenomenon in normal, intact cats and named it **paradoxical sleep** because it is deep sleep in some ways and light in others. (The term *paradoxical* means "apparently self-contradictory.")

Meanwhile in the United States, Nathaniel Kleitman and Eugene Aserinsky were observing eye movements of sleeping people as a means of measuring depth of sleep, assuming that eye movements would stop during sleep. At first, they recorded only a few minutes of eye movements per hour because the recording paper was expensive and they did not expect to see anything interesting in the middle of the night anyway. When they occasionally found periods of eye movements in people who had been asleep for hours, the investigators assumed that something was wrong with their machines. Only after repeated careful measurements did they conclude that periods of rapid eye movements do exist during sleep (Dement, 1990). They called these periods **rapid eye movement (REM) sleep** (Aserinsky & Kleitman, 1955; Dement & Kleitman, 1957a) and soon realized that REM sleep was synonymous with what Jouvet called *paradoxical sleep*. Researchers use the term *REM sleep* when referring to humans; most prefer the term *paradoxical sleep* for nonhumans because many species lack eye movements.

During paradoxical or REM sleep, the EEG shows irregular, low-voltage fast waves that indicate increased neuronal activity; in this regard, REM sleep is light. However, the postural muscles of the body, such as those that support the head, are more relaxed during

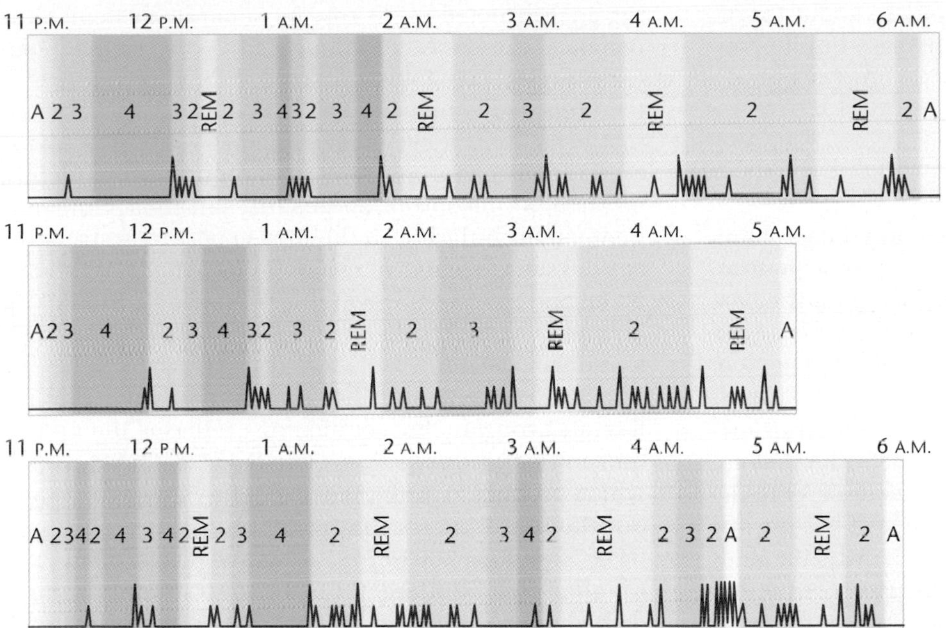

Figure 9.10 Sequence of sleep stages on three representative nights
Columns indicate awake (A) and sleep stages 2, 3, 4, and REM. Deflections in the line at the bottom of each chart indicate shifts in body position. Note that stage 4 sleep occurs mostly in the early part of the night's sleep, whereas REM sleep becomes more prevalent toward the end. *(Source: Based on Dement & Kleitman, 1957a)*

REM than in other stages; in this regard, REM is deep sleep. REM is also associated with erections in males and vaginal moistening in females. Heart rate, blood pressure, and breathing rate are more variable in REM than in stages 2 through 4. In short, REM sleep combines deep sleep, light sleep, and features that are difficult to classify as deep or light. Consequently, it is best to avoid the terms *deep* and *light* sleep.

In addition to its steady characteristics, REM sleep has intermittent characteristics such as facial twitches and eye movements, as shown in Figure 9.9(f). The EEG record is similar to that for stage 1 sleep, but notice the difference in eye movements. The stages other than REM are known as **non-REM (NREM) sleep.**

Anyone who falls asleep first enters stage 1 and then slowly progresses through stages 2, 3, and 4 in order, although loud noises or other intrusions can interrupt this sequence. After about an hour of sleep, the person begins to cycle back from stage 4 through stages 3, 2, and then REM. The sequence repeats, with each complete cycle lasting about 90 minutes. Early in the night, stages 3 and 4 predominate. Toward morning, the duration of stage 4 grows shorter and the duration of REM grows longer. Figure 9.10 shows typical sequences. The tendency to increase REM depends on time, not on how long you have been asleep. That is, if you go to sleep later than usual, you still begin to increase your REM at about the same time that you would have ordinarily (Czeisler, Weitzman, Moore-Ede, Zimmerman, & Knauer, 1980). Most depressed people enter REM quickly after falling asleep, even at their normal time, suggesting that their circadian rhythm is out of synchrony with real time.

Initially after the discovery of REM, researchers believed it was almost synonymous with dreaming. William Dement and Nathaniel Kleitman (1957b) found that people who were awakened during REM sleep reported dreams 80% to 90% of the time. Later researchers, however, found that people also sometimes reported dreams when they were awakened from NREM sleep. REM dreams are more likely than NREM dreams to include striking visual imagery and complicated plots, but not always. Some people with brain damage continue to have REM sleep but do not report any dreams (Bischof & Bassetti, 2004), and other people continue to report dreams despite no evidence of REM sleep (Solms, 1997). In short, REM and dreams usually overlap, but they are not the same thing.

STOP & CHECK

2. How can an investigator determine whether a sleeper is in REM sleep?
3. During which part of a night's sleep is REM most common?

Check your answers on page 285.

Brain Mechanisms of Wakefulness and Arousal

Recall from Chapter 1 the distinction between the "easy" and "hard" problems of consciousness. The "easy" problems include such matters as, "Which brain areas increase overall alertness, and by what kinds of transmitters do they do so?" As you are about to see, that question may be philosophically easy but it is scientifically complex.

Brain Structures of Arousal and Attention

After a cut through the midbrain separates the forebrain and part of the midbrain from all the lower structures, an animal enters a prolonged state of sleep for the next few days. Even after weeks of recovery, the wakeful periods are brief. We might suppose a simple explanation: The cut isolated the brain from the sensory stimuli that come up from the medulla and spinal cord. However, if a researcher cuts each individual tract that enters the medulla and spinal cord, thus depriving the brain of the sensory input, the animal still has normal periods of wakefulness and sleep. Evidently, the midbrain does more than just relay sensory information; it has its own mechanisms to promote wakefulness.

A cut through the midbrain decreases arousal by damaging the **reticular formation,** a structure that extends from the medulla into the forebrain. Of all the neurons in the reticular formation, some neurons have axons ascending into the brain and some have axons descending into the spinal cord. Those with axons descending into the spinal cord form part of the ventromedial tract of motor control, as discussed in Chapter 8. In 1949, Giuseppe Moruzzi and H. W. Magoun proposed that those with ascending axons are well suited to regulate arousal. The term *reticular* (based on the Latin word *rete,* meaning "net") describes the widespread connections among neurons in this system. One part of the reticular formation that contributes to cortical arousal is known as the **pontomesencephalon** (Woolf, 1996). (The term derives from *pons* and *mesencephalon,* or "midbrain.") These neurons receive input from many sensory systems and generate spontaneous activity of their own. Their axons extend into the forebrain, as shown in Figure 9.11, releasing acetylcholine and glutamate, which produce excitatory effects in the hypothalamus, thalamus, and basal forebrain. Consequently, the pontomesencephalon maintains arousal during wakefulness and increases it in response to new or challenging tasks (Kinomura, Larsson, Gulyás, & Roland, 1996). Stimulation of the pontomesencephalon awakens a sleeping individual or increases alertness in one already awake, shifting the EEG from long, slow waves to short, high-frequency waves (Munk, Roelfsema, König, Engel, & Singer, 1996). However, subsystems within the pontomesencephalon control different sensory modalities, so a stimulus sometimes arouses one part of the brain more than others (Guillery, Feig, & Lozsádi, 1998).

Arousal is not a unitary process, and neither is attention (Robbins & Everitt, 1995). Waking up, directing attention to a stimulus, storing a memory, and increasing goal-directed effort rely on separate systems. For instance, the **locus coeruleus** (LOW-kus ser-ROO-lee-us; literally, "dark blue place"), a small structure in the pons, is inactive at most times but emits bursts of impulses in response to meaningful events. The axons of the locus coeruleus release norepinephrine widely throughout the cortex, so this tiny area has a huge influence. Stimulation to the locus coeruleus strengthens the storage of recent memories (Clayton & Williams, 2000) and increases wakefulness (Berridge, Stellick, & Schmeichel, 2005). The locus coeruleus is usually silent during sleep.

The hypothalamus has several pathways that influence arousal. One set of axons releases the neurotransmitter *histamine* (Lin, Hou, Sakai, & Jouvet, 1996), which produces widespread excitatory effects throughout the brain, increasing wakefulness and alertness (Haas & Panula, 2003). Antihistamine drugs, often used for allergies, counteract this transmitter and produce drowsiness. Antihistamines that do not cross the blood-brain barrier avoid that side effect.

Another pathway from the hypothalamus, mainly from the lateral nucleus of the hypothalamus, releases a peptide neurotransmitter called either **orexin** or **hypocretin.** For simplicity, this text will stick to one term, orexin, but you might find the term hypocretin in other reading. The axons releasing orexin extend widely throughout the forebrain and brainstem, where they stimulate acetylcholine-releasing cells, thereby increasing wakefulness and arousal (Kiyashchenko et al., 2002). Orexin is not necessary for waking up, but it is for *staying* awake. That is, most adult humans stay awake for roughly 16–17 hours at a time, even when nothing much is happening. Staying awake depends on orexin, especially toward the end of the day (Lee, Hassani, & Jones, 2005). A study of squirrel monkeys, which have waking and sleeping schedules similar to those of humans, found low orexin levels early in the morning. As the day continued, orexin levels rose, and if the monkeys were kept awake beyond their usual sleep time, orexin levels stayed high. As soon as the monkeys went to sleep, the orexin levels began to drop (Zeitzer et al., 2003).

Other pathways from the lateral hypothalamus regulate cells in the **basal forebrain** (an area just anterior and dorsal to the hypothalamus). Basal forebrain cells provide axons that extend throughout the thalamus and cerebral cortex (see Figure 9.11). Some of these axons release acetylcholine, which is excitatory and tends to increase arousal (Mesulam, 1995; Szymusiak, 1995). People with Alzheimer's disease (Chapter 13) lose many of these acetylcholine-releasing cells. Damage to these cells does not increase sleep, but it does impair alertness and attention (Berntson, Shafi, & Sarter, 2002).

Other axons from the basal forebrain release GABA, the brain's main inhibitory transmitter. GABA is essen-

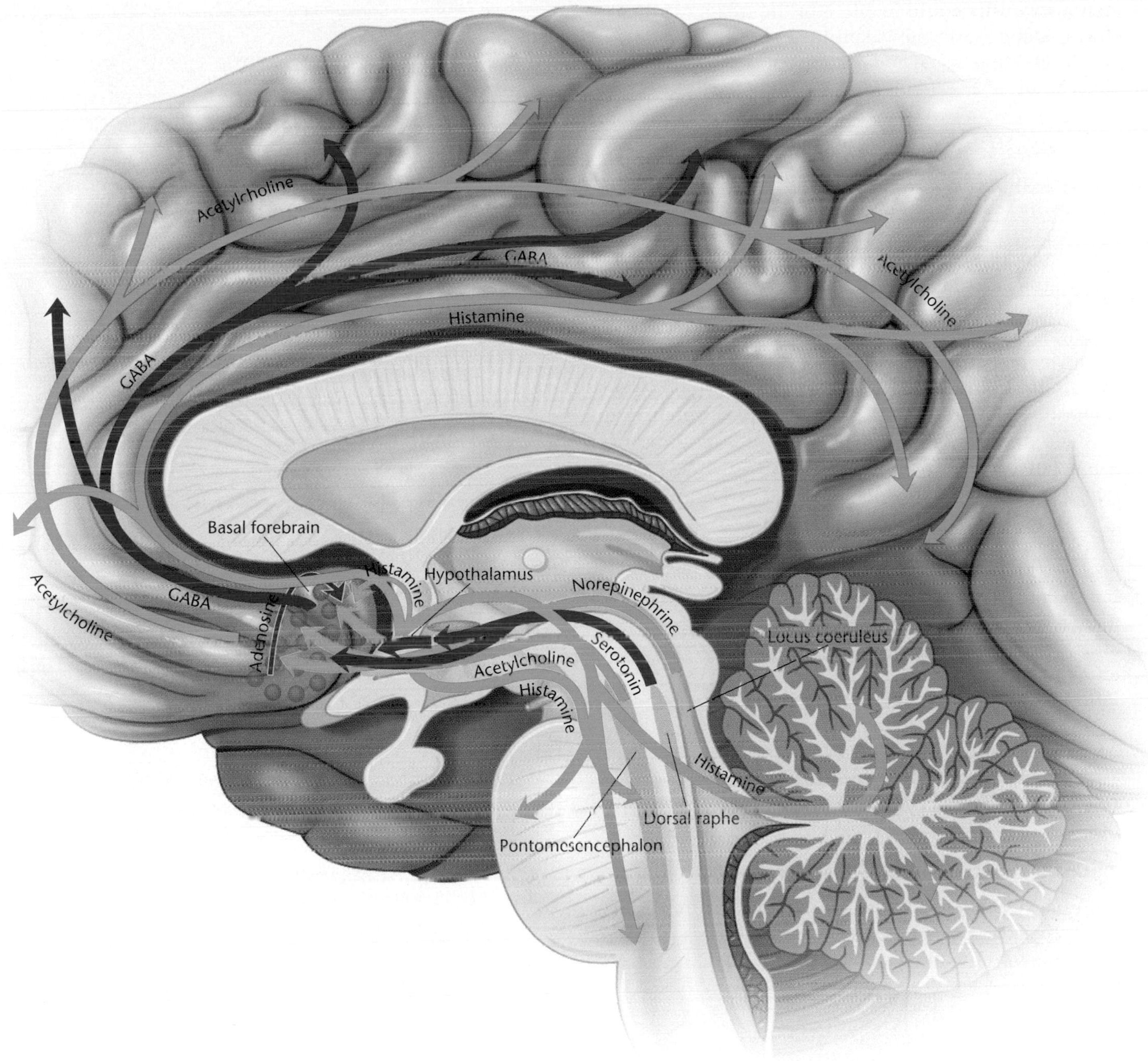

Figure 9.11 Brain mechanisms of sleeping and waking
Green arrows indicate excitatory connections; red arrows indicate inhibitory connections. Neurotransmitters are indicated where they are known. Although adenosine is shown as a small arrow, it is a metabolic product that builds up in the area, not something released by axons.
(Source: Based on Lin, Hou, Sakai, & Jouvet, 1996; Robbins & Everitt, 1995; and Szymusiak, 1995)

tial for sleep; that is, without the inhibition provided by GABA, sleep would not occur (Gottesmann, 2004). The functions of GABA help explain what we experience during sleep: During sleep, body temperature and metabolic rate decrease slightly, and so does the activity of neurons, but by less than we might expect. Spontaneously active neurons continue to fire at almost their usual rate, and neurons in the brain's sensory areas continue to respond to sounds and other stimuli. Nevertheless, we are unconscious. An explanation is that GABA inhibits synaptic activity. A neuron may be active, either spontaneously or in response to a stimulus, but its axons do not spread the stimulation to other areas because of inhibition by GABA. Researchers demonstrated that a stimulus could excite a brain area as strongly during sleep as during wakefulness, but the excitation was briefer than usual and did not spread to other areas (Massimini et al., 2005).

Getting to Sleep

Sleep requires decreased arousal, largely by means of **adenosine** (ah-DENN-o-seen). During metabolic activity, adenosine monophosphate (AMP) breaks down into adenosine; thus, when the brain is awake and active, adenosine accumulates. In most of the brain, adenosine has little effect, but adenosine inhibits the basal forebrain cells responsible for arousal (Figure 9.12), acting by metabotropic synapses that produce an effect lasting hours (Basheer, Rainnie, Porkka-Heiskanen, Ramesh, & McCarley, 2001). When people are deprived of sleep, the accumulating adenosine produces prolonged sleepiness—a phenomenon known as "sleep debt."

Caffeine, a drug found in coffee, tea, and many soft drinks, increases arousal by blocking adenosine receptors (Rainnie, Grunze, McCarley, & Greene, 1994). It also constricts the blood vessels in the brain, thereby decreasing its blood supply. (Abstention from caffeine after repeated use can increase blood flow to the brain enough to cause a headache.) The message: Just as you might use caffeine to try to keep yourself awake, you might try decreasing your caffeine intake if you have trouble sleeping.

Prostaglandins are additional chemicals that promote sleep, among other functions. Like adenosine, prostaglandins build up during the day until they provoke sleep, and they decline during sleep (Ram et al., 1997; Scamell et al., 1998). In response to infection, the immune system produces more prostaglandins, resulting in the sleepiness that accompanies illness.

Table 9.1 summarizes the effects of some key brain areas on arousal and sleep.

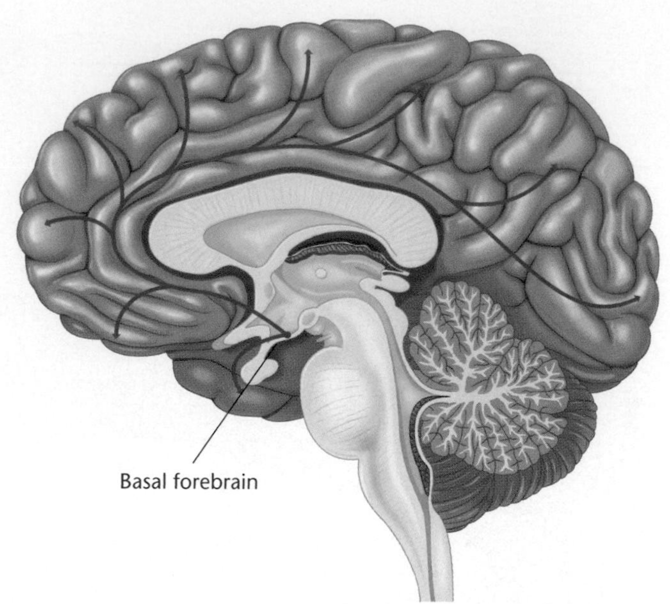

Figure 9.12 Basal forebrain
The basal forebrain is the source of many excitatory axons (releasing acetylcholine) and inhibitory axons (releasing GABA) that regulate arousal of the cerebral cortex.

STOP & CHECK

4. What would happen to the sleep–wake schedule of someone who took a drug that blocked GABA?
5. Why do most antihistamines make people drowsy?
6. What would happen to the sleep–wake schedule of someone who lacked orexin?
7. How does caffeine increase arousal?

Check your answers on page 285.

Table 9.1 Brain Structures for Arousal and Sleep

Structure	Neurotransmitter(s) It Releases	Effects on Behavior
Pontomesencephalon	Acetylcholine, glutamate	Increases cortical arousal
Locus coeruleus	Norepinephrine	Increases information storage during wakefulness; suppresses REM sleep
Basal forebrain		
Excitatory cells	Acetylcholine	Excites thalamus and cortex; increases learning, attention; shifts sleep from NREM to REM
Inhibitory cells	GABA	Inhibits thalamus and cortex
Hypothalamus (parts)	Histamine	Increases arousal
	Orexin	Maintains wakefulness
Dorsal raphe and pons	Serotonin	Interrupts REM sleep

Brain Function in REM Sleep

Researchers who were interested in the brain mechanisms of REM decided to use a PET scan to determine which areas increased or decreased their activity during REM. Although that research might sound simple, PET requires injecting a radioactive chemical. Imagine trying to give sleepers an injection without awakening them. Further, a PET scan yields a clear image only if the head remains motionless during data collection. If the person tosses or turns even slightly, the image is worthless.

To overcome these difficulties, researchers in two studies persuaded some young people to sleep with their heads firmly attached to masks that did not permit any movement. They also inserted a cannula (plastic tube) into each person's arm so that they could inject radioactive chemicals at various times during the night. So imagine yourself in that setup. You have a cannula in your arm and your head is locked into position. Now try to sleep.

Because the researchers foresaw the difficulty of sleeping under these conditions (!), they had their participants stay awake the entire previous night. Someone who is tired enough can sleep even under trying circumstances. (Maybe.)

Now that you appreciate the heroic nature of the procedures, here are the results. During REM sleep, activity increased in the pons and the limbic system (which is important for emotional responses). Activity decreased in the primary visual cortex, the motor cortex, and the dorsolateral prefrontal cortex but increased in parts of the parietal and temporal cortex (Braun et al., 1998; Maquet et al., 1996). In the next module, we consider what these results imply about dreaming, but for now note that activity in the pons triggers the onset of REM sleep.

REM sleep is associated with a distinctive pattern of high-amplitude electrical potentials known as **PGO waves**, for pons-geniculate-occipital (Figure 9.13). Waves of neural activity are detected first in the pons, shortly afterward in the lateral geniculate nucleus of the thalamus, and then in the occipital cortex (D. C. Brooks & Bizzi, 1963; Laurent, Cespuglio, & Jouvet, 1974). Each animal maintains a nearly constant amount of PGO waves per day. During a prolonged period of REM deprivation, PGO waves begin to emerge during sleep stages 2 to 4—when they do not normally occur—and even during wakefulness, often in association with strange behaviors, as if the animal were hallucinating. At the end of the deprivation period, when an animal is permitted to sleep without interruption, the REM periods have an unusually high density of PGO waves.

Besides originating the PGO waves, cells in the pons contribute to REM sleep by sending messages to the spinal cord, inhibiting the motor neurons that control the body's large muscles. After damage to the floor of the pons, a cat still has REM sleep periods, but its muscles are not relaxed. During REM, it walks (though awkwardly), behaves as if it were chasing an imagined prey, jumps as if startled, and so forth (Morrison, Sanford, Ball, Mann, & Ross, 1995) (Figure 9.14). Is the cat acting out dreams? We do not know; the cat cannot tell us. Evidently, one function of the messages from the pons to the spinal cord is to prevent action during REM sleep.

REM sleep apparently depends on a relationship between the neurotransmitters serotonin and acetylcholine. Injections of the drug *carbachol*, which stimulates acetylcholine synapses, quickly move a sleeper into REM sleep (Baghdoyan, Spotts, & Snyder, 1993).

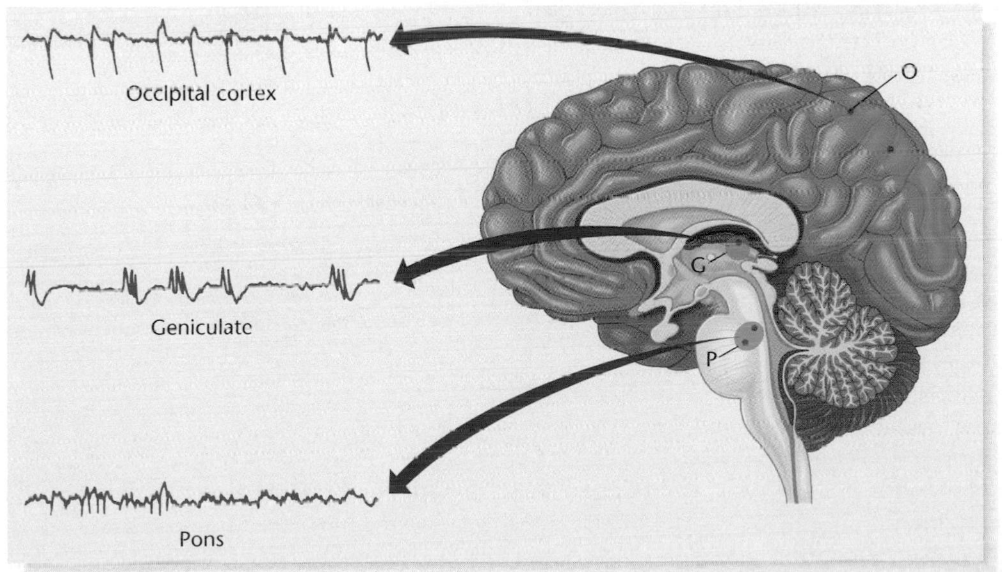

Figure 9.13 PGO waves
PGO waves start in the pons (P) and then show up in the lateral geniculate (G) and the occipital cortex (O). Each PGO wave is synchronized with an eye movement in REM sleep.

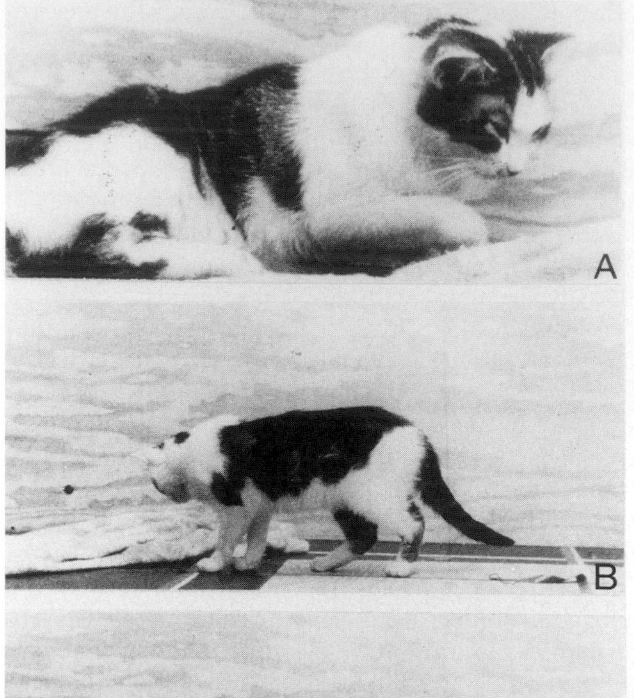

Figure 9.14 A cat with a lesion in the pons, wobbling about during REM sleep
Cells of an intact pons send inhibitory messages to the spinal cord neurons that control the large muscles.

Note that acetylcholine is important for both wakefulness and REM sleep, two states that activate most of the brain. Serotonin, however, interrupts or shortens REM sleep (Boutrel, Franc, Hen, Hamon, & Adrien, 1999). So does norepinephrine from the locus coeruleus; bursts of activity in the locus coeruleus block REM sleep (Singh & Mallick, 1996).

Sleep Disorders

How much sleep is enough? Different people need different amounts. The best gauge of **insomnia**—inadequate sleep—is whether someone feels rested the following day. If you consistently feel tired, you are not sleeping enough. Inadequate sleep is a major cause of accidents by workers and poor performance by college students. Driving while sleep deprived is comparable to driving under the influence of alcohol (Falleti, Maruff, Collie, Darby, & McStephen, 2003).

Causes of insomnia include noise, uncomfortable temperatures, stress, pain, diet, and medications. Insomnia can also be the result of epilepsy, Parkinson's disease, brain tumors, depression, anxiety, or other neurological or psychiatric conditions. Some children suffer insomnia because they are milk-intolerant, and their parents, not realizing the intolerance, give them milk to drink right before bedtime (Horne, 1992). One man suffered insomnia for months until he realized that he dreaded going to sleep because he hated waking up to go jogging. After he switched his jogging time to late afternoon, he slept without difficulty. In short, try to identify the reasons for your sleep problems before you try to solve them.

Many cases of insomnia relate to shifts in circadian rhythms (MacFarlane, Cleghorn, & Brown, 1985a, 1985b). Ordinarily, people fall asleep while their temperature is declining and awaken while it is rising, as in Figure 9.15(a). Someone whose rhythm is *phase delayed,* as in Figure 9.15(b), has trouble falling asleep at the usual time, as if the hypothalamus thinks it isn't late enough (Morris et al., 1990). Someone whose rhythm is *phase advanced,* as in Figure 9.15(c), falls asleep easily but awakens early.

Another cause of insomnia is, paradoxically, the use of tranquilizers as sleeping pills. Although tranquilizers may help a person fall asleep, taking them

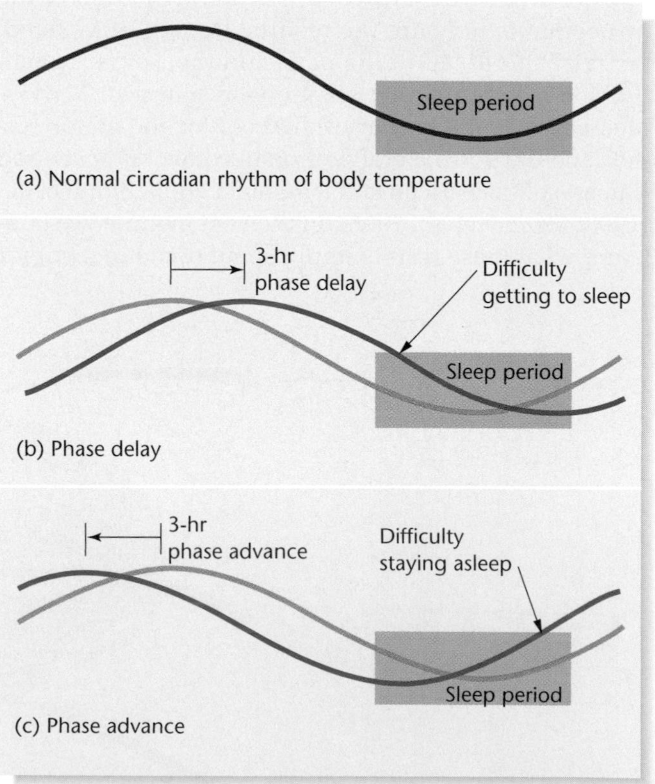

Figure 9.15 Insomnia and circadian rhythms
A delay in the circadian rhythm of body temperature is associated with onset insomnia; an advance, with termination insomnia.

repeatedly may cause dependence. Without the pills, the person goes into a withdrawal state that includes prolonged wakefulness (Kales, Scharf, & Kales, 1978). Similar problems arise when people use alcohol to get to sleep.

Sleep Apnea

One special cause of insomnia is **sleep apnea,** the inability to breathe while sleeping. Most people beyond age 45 have occasional periods during their sleep when they go at least 9 seconds without breathing, usually during the REM stage (Culebras, 1996). However, people with sleep apnea go without breathing for longer periods, sometimes a minute or more, and then awaken, gasping for breath. Some do not remember all their nighttime awakenings, although they certainly notice the consequences—sleepiness during the day, impaired attention, depression, and sometimes heart problems. People with sleep apnea have multiple areas in their brains where they appear to have lost neurons, and consequently, they show deficiencies of learning, reasoning, attention, and impulse control (Beebe & Gozal, 2002; Macey et al., 2002). These correlational data do not tell us whether the brain abnormalities led to sleep apnea or sleep apnea led to the brain abnormalities. However, research with rats suggests the latter: Rats that are subjected to frequent periods of low oxygen (as if they hadn't been breathing) lose neurons throughout the cerebral cortex and hippocampus and show impairments of learning and memory (Gozal, Daniel, & Dohanich, 2001).

Sleep apnea results from several causes, including genetics, hormones, and old-age deterioration of the brain mechanisms that regulate breathing. Another cause is obesity, especially in middle-age men. Many obese men have narrower than normal airways and have to compensate by breathing more frequently or more vigorously than others do. During sleep, they cannot keep up that rate of breathing. Furthermore, their airways become even narrower than usual when they adopt a sleeping posture (Mezzanotte, Tangel, & White, 1992).

People with sleep apnea are advised to lose weight and avoid alcohol and tranquilizers (which impair the breathing muscles). Medical options include surgery to remove tissue that obstructs the trachea (the breathing passage) or a mask that covers the nose and delivers air under enough pressure to keep the breathing passages open (Figure 9.16).

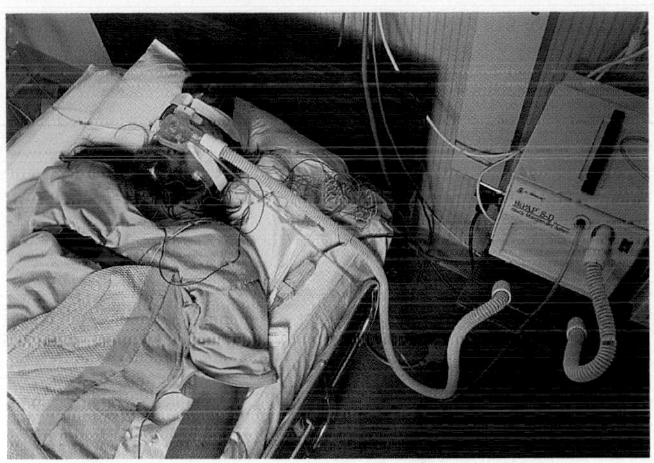

Figure 9.16 A Continuous Positive Airway Pressure (CPAP) mask
The mask fits snugly over the nose and delivers air at a fixed pressure, strong enough to keep the breathing passages open.

Narcolepsy

Narcolepsy, a condition characterized by frequent periods of sleepiness during the day (Aldrich, 1998), strikes about 1 person in 1,000. It sometimes runs in families, although no gene for narcolepsy has been identified, and many people with narcolepsy have no close relatives with the disease. Narcolepsy has four main symptoms, although not every patient has all four:

1. Gradual or sudden attacks of sleepiness during the day.
2. Occasional **cataplexy**—an attack of muscle weakness while the person remains awake. Cataplexy is often triggered by strong emotions, such as anger or great excitement. (One man suddenly collapsed during his own wedding ceremony.)
3. Sleep paralysis—an inability to move while falling asleep or waking up. Other people may experience sleep paralysis occasionally, but people with narcolepsy experience it more frequently.
4. *Hypnagogic hallucinations*—dreamlike experiences that the person has trouble distinguishing from reality, often occurring at the onset of sleep.

Each of these symptoms can be interpreted as an intrusion of a REM-like state into wakefulness. REM sleep is associated with muscle weakness (cataplexy), paralysis, and dreams (Mahowald & Schenck, 1992).

The cause relates to the neurotransmitter orexin. People with narcolepsy lack the hypothalamic cells that produce and release orexin (Thanickal et al., 2000). Why they lack those cells is not known, although one hypothesis is that they have an autoimmune disease that attacks these cells. Recall that orexin is important for maintaining wakefulness (p. 278). Consequently, people lacking orexin cannot stay awake throughout the day; they have many brief sleepy periods. Dogs that lack the gene for orexin receptors have symptoms much like human narcolepsy, with frequent alternations between wakefulness and sleep (Lin et al., 1999). The same is true for mice that lack orexin (Hara, 2001).

Over the course of a day, they have about a normal amount of wakefulness and sleep, but they do not stay awake for long at any one time (Mochizuki et al., 2004).

As discussed in Chapter 8, people with Huntington's disease have widespread damage in the basal ganglia. In addition, most lose neurons in the hypothalamus, including the neurons that make orexin. As a result, they have problems staying awake during the day; they also have periods of arousal and activity while in bed at night (Morton et al., 2005).

Theoretically, we might imagine combating narcolepsy with drugs that restore orexin. Perhaps eventually, such drugs will become available. Currently, the most common treatment is stimulant drugs, such as methylphenidate (Ritalin), which increase wakefulness by enhancing dopamine or norepinephrine activity.

Periodic Limb Movement Disorder

Another factor occasionally linked to insomnia is **periodic limb movement disorder,** a repeated involuntary movement of the legs and sometimes arms (Edinger et al., 1992). Many people, perhaps most, experience an occasional involuntary kick, especially when starting to fall asleep. Leg movements are not a problem unless they become persistent. In some people, mostly middle-aged and older, the legs kick once every 20 to 30 seconds for a period of minutes or even hours, mostly during NREM sleep. Frequent or especially vigorous leg movements may awaken the person. In some cases, tranquilizers help suppress the movements (Schenck & Mahowald, 1996).

REM Behavior Disorder

For most people, the major postural muscles are relaxed and inactive during REM sleep. However, people with **REM behavior disorder** move around vigorously during their REM periods, apparently acting out their dreams. They frequently dream about defending themselves against attack, and they may punch, kick, and leap about. Most of them injure themselves or other people and damage property (Olson, Boeve, & Silber, 2000).

REM behavior disorder occurs mostly in older people, especially older men with brain diseases such as Parkinson's disease (Olson et al., 2000). Presumably, the damage includes the cells in the pons that send messages to inhibit the spinal neurons that control large muscle movements.

Night Terrors, Sleep Talking, and Sleepwalking

Night terrors are experiences of intense anxiety from which a person awakens screaming in terror. A night terror should be distinguished from a nightmare, which is simply an unpleasant dream. Night terrors occur during NREM sleep and are far more common in children than in adults.

Sleep talking is common and harmless. Many people, probably most, talk in their sleep occasionally. Unless someone hears you talking in your sleep and later tells you about it, you could talk in your sleep for years and never know about it. Sleep talking occurs during both REM and non-REM sleep (Arkin, Toth, Baker, & Hastey, 1970).

Sleepwalking runs in families, occurs mostly in children ages 2 to 5, and is most common during stage 3 or stage 4 sleep early in the night. (It does not occur during REM sleep because the large muscles are completely relaxed.) The causes are not known. Sleepwalking is generally harmless both to the sleepwalker and to others. No doubt you have heard people say, "You should never waken a sleepwalker." In fact, it would not be harmful or dangerous, although the person would awaken confused (Moorcroft, 1993).

In an individual case, it is sometimes difficult to know whether someone is sleepwalking. One man pleaded "not guilty" to a charge of murder because he had been sleepwalking at the time and did not know what he was doing. The jury agreed with him, partly because he had a family history of sleepwalking. However, especially for a one-time event, it is difficult to know whether he was sleepwalking, subject to REM behavior disorder, or perhaps even awake at the time (Broughton et al., 1994).

For more information about a variety of sleep disorders, check this website: **http://www.thesleepsite.com/**

STOP & CHECK

8. What kinds of people are most likely to develop sleep apnea?

9. What is the relationship between orexin and narcolepsy?

Check your answers on page 285.

Module 9.2

In Closing: Stages of Sleep

In many cases, scientific progress depends on drawing useful distinctions. Chemists divide the world into different elements, biologists divide life into different species, and physicians distinguish one disease from another. Similarly, psychologists try to recognize the most natural or useful distinctions among types of behavior or experience. The discovery of different stages of sleep was a major landmark in psychology because researchers found a previously unrecognized distinction that is both biologically and psychologically important. It also demonstrated that external measurements—in this case, EEG recordings—can be used to identify internal experiences. We now take it largely for granted that an electrical or magnetic recording from the brain can tell us something about a person's experience, but it is worth pausing to note what a surprising discovery that was in its time.

Summary

1. Over the course of about 90 minutes, a sleeper goes through stages 1, 2, 3, and 4 and then returns through stages 3 and 2 to a stage called REM. REM is characterized by rapid eye movements, more brain activity than other sleep stages, complete relaxation of the trunk muscles, irregular breathing and heart rate, penile erection or vaginal lubrication, and an increased probability of vivid dreams. (p. 275)
2. The brain has multiple systems for arousal. The pontomesencephalon, dorsal raphe, and parts of the hypothalamus control various cell clusters in the basal forebrain that send axons releasing acetylcholine throughout much of the forebrain. Other cells in the basal forebrain have axons that release GABA, which is essential for sleep. (p. 278)
3. The locus coeruleus is active in response to meaningful events. It facilitates attention and new learning; it also blocks the onset of REM sleep. (p. 282)
4. Sleep is facilitated by decreased stimulation, adenosine and prostaglandins that inhibit the arousal systems of the brain, and increased activity by certain clusters of basal forebrain cells that release GABA throughout much of the forebrain. (p. 280)
5. REM sleep is associated with increased activity in a number of brain areas, including the pons, limbic system, and parts of the parietal and temporal cortex. Activity decreases in the prefrontal cortex, the motor cortex, and the primary visual cortex. (p. 281)
6. REM sleep begins with PGO waves, which are waves of brain activity transmitted from the pons to the lateral geniculate to the occipital lobe. (p. 281)
7. Insomnia sometimes results from a shift in phase of the circadian rhythm of temperature in relation to the circadian rhythm of sleep and wakefulness. It can also result from difficulty in breathing while asleep, overuse of tranquilizers, and numerous other causes. (p. 282)
8. People with sleep apnea have long periods without breathing while they sleep. Many have indications of neuronal loss, probably as a result of decreased oxygen while they sleep. (p. 283)
9. People with narcolepsy have attacks of sleepiness during the day. Narcolepsy is associated with deficiency of the peptide neurotransmitter orexin. (p. 283)

Answers to STOP & CHECK Questions

1. Long, slow waves indicate a low level of activity, with much synchrony of response among neurons. (p. 276)
2. Examine EEG pattern and eye movements. (p. 277)
3. REM becomes more common toward the end of the night's sleep. (p. 277)
4. Someone who took a drug that blocks GABA would remain awake. (Conversely, tranquilizers put people to sleep by facilitating GABA.) (p. 280)
5. Paths from the hypothalamus use histamine as their neurotransmitter to increase arousal. Antihistamines that cross the blood-brain barrier block those synapses. (p. 280)
6. Someone without orexin would alternate between brief periods of waking and sleeping. (p. 280)
7. Caffeine inhibits adenosine, which builds up during wakefulness and inhibits the arousal-inducing cells of the basal forebrain. (p. 280)
8. Sleep apnea is most common among people with a genetic predisposition, old people, and overweight middle-aged men. (p. 284)
9. Orexin is important for staying awake. Therefore, people or animals lacking either orexin or the receptors for orexin develop narcolepsy, characterized by bouts of sleepiness during the day. (p. 284)

Thought Question

When cats are deprived of REM sleep and then permitted uninterrupted sleep, the longer the period of deprivation—up to about 25 days—the greater the rebound of REM when they can sleep uninterrupted. However, REM deprivation for more than 25 days produces no additional rebound. Speculate on a possible explanation. (Hint: Consider what happens to PGO waves during REM deprivation.)

Module 9.3
Why Sleep? Why REM? Why Dreams?

Why do you sleep? "That's easy," you reply. "I sleep because I get tired." Well, yes, but you are not tired in the sense of muscle fatigue. You need almost as much sleep after a day of sitting around the house as after a day of intense physical or mental activity (Horne & Minard, 1985; Shapiro, Bortz, Mitchell, Bartel, & Jooste, 1981). Furthermore, you could rest your muscles just as well while awake as while asleep. (In fact, if your muscles ache after strenuous exercise, you probably find it difficult to sleep.)

You feel tired at the end of the day because inhibitory processes in your brain force you to become less aroused and less alert. That is, we evolved mechanisms to cause us to sleep—to "turn us off," one might say. Why?

Functions of Sleep

Sleep serves many functions. During sleep, we rest our muscles, decrease metabolism, rebuild proteins in the brain (Kong et al., 2002), reorganize synapses, and strengthen memories (Sejnowski & Destexhe, 2000). People who are deprived of sleep have trouble concentrating and become more vulnerable to illness. Clearly, we need to sleep for many reasons. Can we identify one primary reason?

Sleep and Energy Conservation

Even if we could agree on the most important function of sleep for humans today, it might not be the function for which sleep originally evolved. By analogy, consider computers: Important functions today include writing papers, sending e-mail, searching the Internet, playing video games, storing and displaying photographs, playing music, and finding a date. Someone who didn't know the history might not guess that computers were built originally for mathematical calculations.

Similarly, sleep could have, and probably did, start with a simple function to which evolution added others later. All species sleep, not just vertebrates with big brains and complex memories. Even bacteria have circadian rhythms (Mihalcescu, Hsing, & Leibler, 2004). What benefit of sleep could apply to all species, including the smallest and simplest?

A likely hypothesis is that originally sleep was simply a way of conserving energy (Kleitman, 1963; Webb, 1974). Virtually every species, even one-celled animals, is more efficient at some times of day than at others. (Some are more efficient in the day, when they can see. Those that rely on olfaction rather than vision are more efficient at night, when their predators cannot see them.) Sleep conserves energy during the inefficient times, when activity would do more harm than good. Even NASA's Rover, built to explore Mars, had a mechanism to make it "sleep" at night to conserve its batteries. During sleep, a mammal's body temperature decreases by 1 or 2°C, enough to save a significant amount of energy. Muscle activity decreases, saving still more energy. Animals increase their sleep duration during food shortages, when energy conservation is especially important (Berger & Phillips, 1995).

Sleep is therefore in some ways analogous to hibernation. Hibernation is a true need; a ground squirrel that is prevented from hibernating can become as disturbed as a person who is prevented from sleeping. However, the function of hibernation is simply to conserve energy while food is scarce.

EXTENSIONS AND APPLICATIONS
Hibernation

Hibernating animals decrease their body temperature to that of the environment (but they don't let it go low enough for their blood to freeze). A few curious facts about hibernation:

1. Hibernation occurs in certain small mammals such as ground squirrels and bats. Whether or not bears hibernate is a matter of definition. Bears sleep most of the winter, but they do not lower their body temperatures as much as smaller animals do.
2. Hamsters sometimes hibernate. If you keep your pet hamster in a cool, dimly lit place during the winter, and it appears to have died, make sure that it is not just hibernating before you bury it!
3. Hibernating animals come out of hibernation for a few hours every few days, raising their body temper-

ature to about normal. However, they spend most of this nonhibernating time asleep (Barnes, 1996).

4. Hibernation retards the aging process. Hamsters that spend longer times hibernating have proportionately longer life expectancies than other hamsters do (Lyman, O'Brien, Greene, & Papafrangos, 1981). Hibernation is also a period of relative invulnerability to infection and trauma. Procedures that would ordinarily damage the brain, such as inserting a needle into it, produce little if any harm during hibernation (Zhou et al., 2001).

Animal species vary in their sleep habits in accordance with how many hours per day they devote to finding food, how safe they are from predators while they sleep, and other aspects of their way of life (Allison & Cicchetti, 1976; Campbell & Tobler, 1984). For example, cats and bats eat nutrition-rich meals and face little threat of attack while they sleep; they sleep many hours per day. Herbivores (plant eaters) graze many hours per day and need to be alert for predators even while they sleep; their sleep is briefer and easily interrupted (Figure 9.17).

Several other species show interesting specializations in their sleep. For example, consider dolphins and other aquatic mammals. At night, they need to be alert enough to occasionally surface for a breath of air. Dolphins and several other species have evolved the ability to sleep on one side of the brain at a time. That is, the two hemispheres take turns sleeping while the other is awake enough to control swimming and breathing (Rattenborg, Amlaner, & Lima, 2000). (Evidently, sleep serves functions for dolphins other than energy conservation because a sleeping dolphin is still expending a fair amount of energy.)

Migratory birds face a different kind of problem. During a week or two in fall and spring, many species forage for food during the day and do their migratory flying at night. That schedule leaves little or no time for sleep. The birds apparently decrease their *need* for sleep during migration. If a white crowned sparrow is kept in a cage, during the migration season it flutters around restlessly, even at night, sleeping only one-third its usual amount. Despite this lack of sleep, the bird remains alert and performs normally on learning tasks. If the same species is deprived of a few hours' sleep during other seasons of the year, its performance suffers (Rattenborg et al., 2004). Exactly how a bird decreases its sleep need is unknown, although drugs that excite glutamate receptors can decrease sleep need in primates (Porrino, Daunais, Rogers, Hampson, & Deadwyler, 2005). Perhaps something similar happens for migratory birds. The fact that it is possible to decrease the need for sleep argues that sleep is not necessary for repair and restoration, or at least that sleep usually lasts longer than required for repair and restoration.

Swifts are small, dark birds that chase insects. The world has many species of swifts. Here is a trivia question for you: When a baby European swift first takes off from its nest, how long would you guess its first flight lasts, until it comes to land again?

The answer: Up to 2 years. It doesn't come down until it is old enough to mate and build a nest. In the meantime, it spends both days and nights in the air, except during huge storms. A swift at night heads into the wind, sticks out its wings, and moves them slowly.

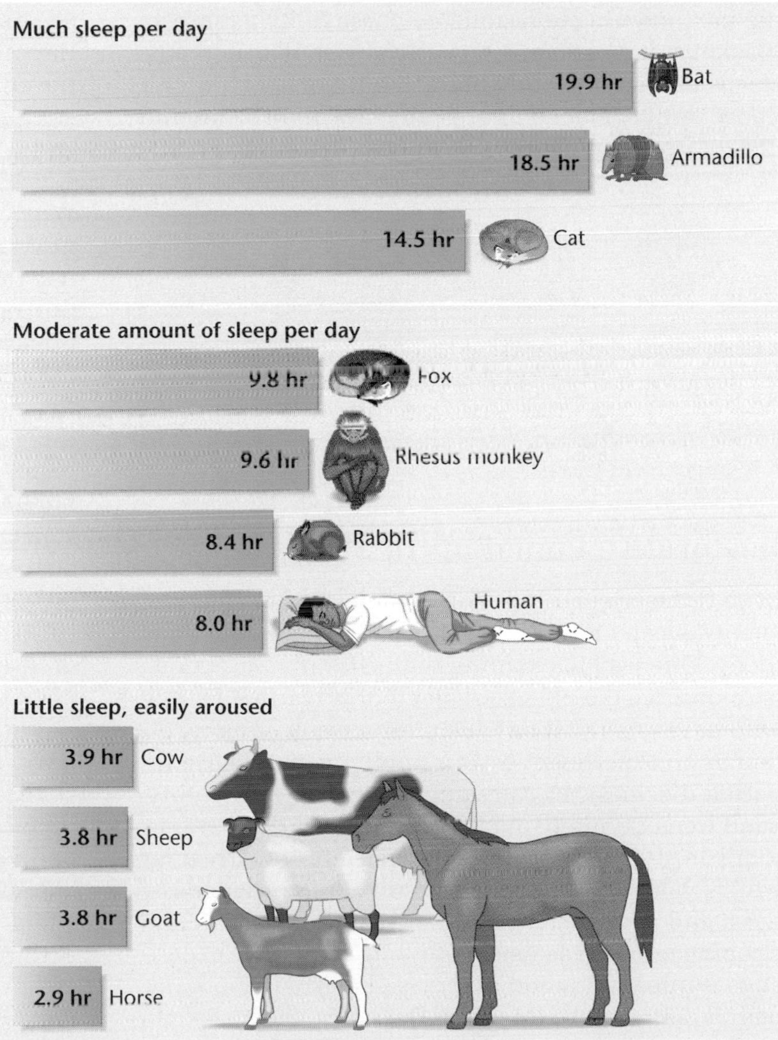

Figure 9.17 Hours of sleep per day for various animal species
Generally, predators and others that are safe when they sleep tend to sleep a great deal; animals in danger of being attacked while they sleep spend less time asleep.

Alan Williams/Alamy

A European swift.

It picks an altitude where the air is not too cold, accepts the risk of being blown far from home, and awakens the next morning to resume its chase of flying insects (Bäckman & Alerstam, 2001). Perhaps it, like dolphins, sleeps on one side of its brain at a time, but we won't know until someone figures out how to measure the EEG of a bird in flight.

STOP & CHECK

1. Some fish live in caves or the deep ocean with no light. What might one predict about their sleep?

Check your answer on page 292.

Restorative Functions of Sleep

Even if the original function of sleep was to conserve energy, sleep undeniably serves additional functions today. One way to examine the restorative functions is to observe the effects of sleep deprivation. People who have gone without sleep for a week or more, either as an experiment or as a publicity stunt, have reported dizziness, impaired concentration, irritability, hand tremors, and hallucinations (Dement, 1972; L. C. Johnson, 1969). Astronauts in space follow irregular work schedules, sleep in spacesuits under weightlessness, and for a variety of other reasons have trouble sleeping as much as usual. On long trips, they experience unpleasant mood, decreased alertness, and impaired performance (Mallis & DeRoshia, 2005). People working during the winter in Antarctica sleep poorly and feel depressed (Palinkas, 2003). Even one night of sleeplessness temporarily increases activity of the immune system (Matsumoto et al., 2001). That is, you react to sleep deprivation as if you were ill.

However, individuals vary in their need for sleep. Two men were reported to average only 3 hours of sleep per night and to awaken feeling refreshed (H. S. Jones & Oswald, 1968). A 70-year-old woman was reported to average only 1 hour of sleep per night; many nights she felt no need to sleep at all (Meddis, Pearson, & Langford, 1973).

Prolonged sleep deprivation in laboratory animals, usually rats, has produced more severe consequences. A major difference is that the animals were forced to stay awake, whereas the human volunteers knew they could quit if necessary. (Stressors take a greater toll when they are unpredictable and uncontrollable.) During a few days of sleep deprivation, rats show increased body temperature, metabolic rate, and appetite, indicating that the body is working harder than usual. With still longer sleep deprivation, the immune system begins to fail, the animal loses its resistance to infection, and brain activity decreases (Everson, 1995; Rechtschaffen & Bergmann, 1995). However, it is difficult to separate the effects of sleep deprivation from those of the various kinds of prods that were necessary to keep the animals awake.

Sleep and Memory

When people learn something and then get tested the next day, their performance is often better the second day than the first, but only if they get adequate sleep during the night (Stickgold, James, & Hobson, 2000; Stickgold, Whidbee, Schirmer, Patel, & Hobson, 2000). (The obvious message to students: When you are studying, get enough sleep.) When people practice something repeatedly, sometimes their performance deteriorates during the day, but it recovers if they get a short nap (Mednick et al., 2002). These results imply that sleep enhances memory. Sleep also helps people reanalyze their memories: In one study, people who had just practiced a complex task were more likely to perceive a hidden rule (an "aha" experience) after a period of sleep than after a similar period of wakefulness (Wagner, Gais, Haider, Verleger, & Born, 2004).

In several studies, researchers recorded brain activity as people learned a motor skill—similar to the skills you might learn in a video game—and then monitored brain activity during sleep. Later, they recorded brain activity while these people slept and found increased activity in the same areas that had been activated while these participants had been learning the skill. Furthermore, the amount of activity in those areas during sleep correlated highly with the improvement in skill seen the next day (Huber, Ghilardi, Massimini, & Tononi, 2004; Maquet et al., 2000; Peigneux et al., 2004). Similar results have been reported for birds learning to sing (Derégnaucourt, Mitra, Fehér, Pytte, & Tchernichovski, 2005). All these results point to sleep as a time when memories are strengthened.

Functions of REM Sleep

An average person spends about one-third of his or her life asleep and about one-fifth of sleep in REM, totaling about 600 hours of REM per year. Presumably, REM serves some biological function. But what is it? To approach this question, we can consider who gets more REM sleep than others and what happens after REM deprivation. Then we consider a couple of hypotheses.

Individual and Species Differences

REM sleep is widespread in mammals and birds, indicating that the capacity for it is part of our ancient evolutionary heritage. Some species, however, have more than others; as a rule, the species with the most total sleep also have the highest percentage of REM sleep (J. M. Siegel, 1995). Cats spend up to 16 hours a day sleeping, much or most of it in REM sleep. Rabbits, guinea pigs, and sheep sleep less and spend little time in REM.

Figure 9.18 illustrates the relationship between age and REM sleep for humans; the trend is the same for other mammalian species. Infants get more REM and more total sleep than adults do, confirming the pattern that more total sleep predicts a higher percentage of REM sleep. Among adult humans, those who get the most sleep per night (9 or more hours) have the highest percentage of REM sleep, and those who get the least sleep (5 or fewer hours) have the lowest percentage of REM.

Effects of REM Sleep Deprivation

What would happen if someone had almost no opportunity for REM sleep? William Dement (1960) observed the behavior of eight men who agreed to be deprived of REM sleep for four to seven consecutive nights. During that period, they slept only in a laboratory. Whenever the EEG and eye movements indicated that someone was entering REM sleep, an experimenter promptly awakened him and kept him awake for several minutes. He could then return to sleep until he started REM sleep again.

Over the course of the four to seven nights, the experimenters found that they had to awaken the subjects more and more frequently, beginning with 12 times the first night and reaching 26 on the final night. That is, people deprived of REM increased their attempts at REM sleep. On the first night after the deprivation period, most of them spent about 50% more time than usual in the REM stage. Similarly, cats and rats react to a period of REM deprivation by increasing their REM sleep when they get the opportunity (Dement, Ferguson, Cohen, & Barchas, 1969; Endo, Schwierin, Borbély, & Tobler, 1997).

Hypotheses

The results presented so far suggest that we need REM sleep but not *why*. One hypothesis is that REM is important for memory storage or that it helps the brain discard useless connections that formed accidentally during the day (Crick & Mitchison, 1983). Discarding useless connections would help the correct connections stand out by comparison.

As already discussed, sleep in general is a time for strengthening memories. The results have been less consistent on whether REM in particular aids memory formation beyond what sleep in general does (J. M. Siegel, 2001). REM and non-REM sleep may be important for consolidating different types of memories. Depriving people of sleep early in the night (mostly non-REM sleep) impairs verbal learning, such as memorizing a list of words, whereas depriving people of

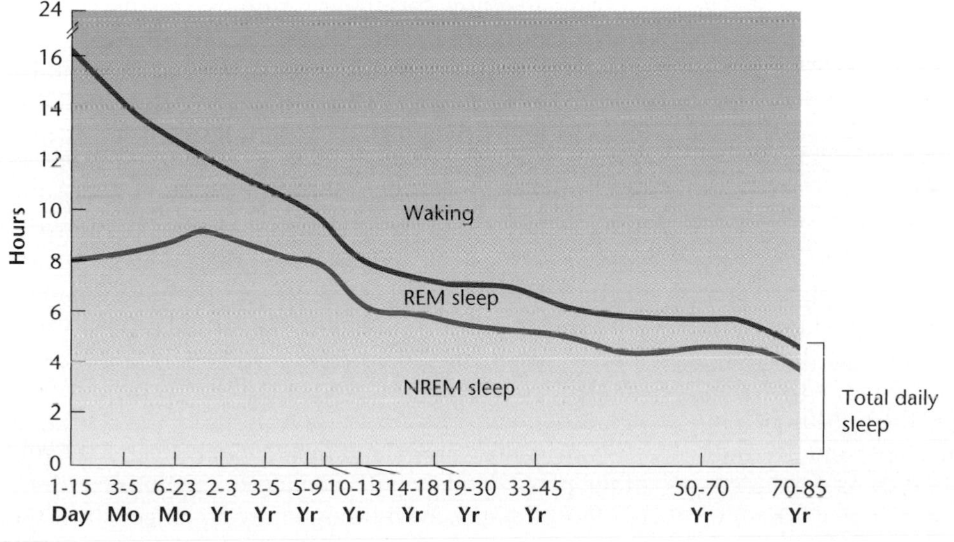

Figure 9.18 Time spent by people of different ages in waking, REM sleep, and NREM sleep

REM sleep occupies about 8 hours a day in newborns but less than 2 hours in most adults. The sleep of infants is not quite like that of adults, however, and the criteria for identifying REM sleep are not the same. *(Source: From "Ontogenetic development of human sleep-dream cycle," by H. P. Roffwarg, J. N. Muzio, and W. C. Dement, Science, 152, 1966, 604–609. Copyright 1966 AAAS. Reprinted by permission.)*

sleep during the second half of the night (more REM) impairs consolidation of learned motor skills (Gais, Plihal, Wagner, & Born, 2000; Plihal & Born, 1997). On the other hand, many people take MAO inhibitors, antidepressant drugs that severely decrease REM sleep. They nevertheless report no memory problems, and research on laboratory animals indicates that the drugs sometimes even enhance memory (Parent, Habib, & Baker, 1999).

Another hypothesis sounds odd because we have for so long imagined a glamorous role for REM sleep: David Maurice (1998) proposed that the primary role of REM is just to shake the eyeballs back and forth enough to get sufficient oxygen to the corneas of the eyes. The corneas, unlike the rest of the body, ordinarily get much of their oxygen supply directly from the surrounding air, not from the blood. During sleep, because they are shielded from the air, they deteriorate slightly (Hoffmann & Curio, 2003). They do get some oxygen from the fluid behind them (see Figure 6.1, p. 153), but when the eyes are motionless, that fluid becomes stagnant. Moving the eyes increases the oxygen supply to the corneas. According to this view, REM is a way of arousing a sleeper just enough to shake the eyes back and forth, and the other manifestations of REM—including dreams—are just by-products. It's an interesting idea, worth further research. However, as mentioned, many people take MAO inhibitors, which greatly restrict REM sleep; they are not known to suffer damage to the cornea. In short, the evidence does not convincingly support any current hypothesis about the function of REM.

2. What kinds of individuals get more REM sleep than others? (Think in terms of age, species, and long versus short sleepers.)

Check your answer on page 292.

Biological Perspectives on Dreaming

What causes dreams? For decades, psychologists were heavily influenced by Sigmund Freud's theory of dreams, which was based on the assumption that they reflect hidden and often unconscious wishes, which the brain distorted in an effort to "censor" them. Although it is true that dreams reflect the dreamer's personality and recent experiences, Freud's theory of dreams depended on certain ideas about the nervous system that are now discarded (McCarley & Hobson, 1977). He believed, for example, that brain cells were inactive except when nerves from the periphery brought them energy.

Dream research faces a special problem: All we know about dreams comes from people's self-reports, and researchers have no way to check the accuracy of those reports. In fact, we all know that we forget most dreams quickly, and even when we do remember them, we lose much of the detail. Thus, any discussion of dream content is inherently filled with difficulty.

The Activation-Synthesis Hypothesis

Whereas Freud thought the brain actively distorted messages to make a dream, an alternative view holds that a dream represents the brain's effort to make sense of information that is already distorted. According to the **activation-synthesis hypothesis,** dreams begin with periodic bursts of spontaneous activity in the pons—the PGO waves previously described—which partly *activate* many but not all parts of the cortex. The cortex combines this haphazard input with whatever other activity was already occurring and does its best to *synthesize* a story that makes sense of all this information (Hobson & McCarley, 1977; Hobson, Pace-Schott, & Stickgold, 2000; McCarley & Hoffman, 1981). Because activity is suppressed in the primary visual cortex (area V1) and primary somatosensory cortex, normal sensory information cannot compete with the self-generated stimulation, and hallucinations result (Rees, Kreiman, & Koch, 2002). The input from the pons usually activates the amygdala, a portion of the temporal lobe highly important for emotional processing, and therefore, most dreams have strong emotional content. Because much of the prefrontal cortex is inactive during PGO waves, memory is weak. We not only forget most dreams after we awaken, but we even lose track of what has been happening within a dream, so sudden scene changes are common.

Consider how this theory handles a couple of common dreams. Most people have had occasional dreams of falling or flying. Well, while you are asleep you lie flat, unlike your posture for the rest of the day. Your brain in its partly aroused condition feels the vestibular sensation of your position and interprets it as flying or falling. Have you ever dreamt that you were trying to move but couldn't? Most people have. An interpretation based on the activation-synthesis theory is that during REM sleep (which accompanies most dreams), your major postural muscles are virtually paralyzed. That is, when you are dreaming, you really *can't* move, you feel your lack of movement, and thus, you dream of failing to move.

One controversy about this theory concerns the role of the pons. Patients with damage to the pons continue to report dreams, even though they no longer show the eye movements and other typical features of REM (Solms, 1997). Therefore, some researchers argue that the pons cannot be essential for dreaming. The reply to this criticism is that none of those patients have very extensive damage to the pons. People who do have extensive damage there are either paralyzed, unconscious, or dead (Hobson et al., 2000). So when people have partial damage to the pons and still have dreams, it is possible that the surviving areas of the pons are essential for the dreams.

Another criticism is that the theory's predictions are vague. If we dream about falling because of the vestibular sensations from lying down, why don't we *always* dream of falling? If we dream we can't move because our muscles are paralyzed during REM sleep, why don't we *always* dream of being paralyzed? This criticism is reasonable, although one could counter that no other theory is any better at predicting anyone's dreams.

An interesting paradox is that the brain produces dreams, but we do not perceive them as self-produced. When you awaken from a dream, there is a brief period when you still fail to fully perceive your own actions as self-produced. A consequence is that just after awakening from a dream, some people can tickle themselves and actually feel it as a tickling sensation, at least slightly (Blagrove, Thayer, & Blakemore, 2004). See whether you can remember to try this yourself some time.

The Clinico-Anatomical Hypothesis

An alternative view of the biology of dreams has been labeled the **clinico-anatomical hypothesis** because it was derived from clinical studies of dreaming by patients with various kinds of brain damage (Solms, 1997, 2000). In several important regards, this theory resembles the activation-synthesis theory: In both theories, dreams begin with arousing stimuli that are generated within the brain, combined with recent memories and any information the brain is receiving from the senses (which are largely suppressed during sleep). The key difference is that the clinico-anatomical hypothesis puts less emphasis on the pons, PGO waves, or even REM sleep. It regards dreams as just thinking, except that the thinking takes place under unusual conditions.

One of those conditions is that the brain is getting little information from the sense organs, so it is free to generate images without constraints or interference. Also, the primary motor cortex is suppressed, as are the motor neurons of the spinal cord, so arousal cannot lead to action. Activity is suppressed in the prefrontal cortex, which is important for working memory (memory of very recent events) and for processes loosely described as "use of knowledge." Consequently, the dream is free to wander without the criticisms of "wait a minute; that's not possible!"

Meanwhile, activity is relatively high in the inferior (lower) part of the parietal cortex, an area important for visuospatial perception. Patients with damage here have problems binding body sensations with vision. They also report no dreams. Fairly high activity is also found in the areas of visual cortex outside V1. Those areas are presumably important for the visual imagery that accompanies most dreams. Finally, activity is high in the hypothalamus, amygdala, and other areas important for emotions and motivations. People usually report some emotion in their dreams (Fosse, Stickgold, & Hobson, 2001).

So the idea is that either internal or external stimulation activates parts of the parietal, occipital, and temporal cortex. No sensory input from V1 overrides the stimulation and no criticism from the prefrontal cortex censors it, so it develops into hallucinatory perceptions. This idea, like the activation-synthesis hypothesis, is hard to test because it does not make specific predictions about who will have what dream and when.

For more information about the content of dreams, visit this website: **http://www.dreamresearch.net**

3. An adult who sustains extensive damage limited to the primary visual cortex (V1) becomes blind. Would you expect such a person to report visual dreams? Why or why not?

Check your answer on page 292.

Module 9.3
In Closing: Our Limited Self-Understanding

Without minimizing how much we do understand about sleep, it is noteworthy how many basic questions remain. What is the function of REM sleep? Does dreaming have a function, or is it just an accident? Our lack of knowledge about activities that occupy so much of our time underscores a point about the biology of behavior: We evolved tendencies to behave in certain ways that lead to survival and reproduction. The behavior can serve its function even when we do not fully understand what that function is.

Summary

1. Sleep is a mechanism we evolved to force us to save energy. It also serves a variety of other functions, including restoration of the brain and consolidation of memories. (p. 286)

2. REM sleep occupies the greatest percentage of sleep in individuals and species that sleep the most total hours. (p. 289)
3. After a period of REM deprivation, people compensate by spending more time than usual in REM sleep. (p. 289)
4. According to the activation-synthesis hypothesis, dreams are the brain's attempts to make sense of the information reaching it, based mostly on haphazard input originating in the pons. (p. 290)
5. According to the clinico-anatomical hypothesis, dreams originate partly with external stimuli but mostly from the brain's own motivations, memories, and arousal. The stimulation often produces peculiar results because it does not have to compete with normal visual input and does not get censored by the prefrontal cortex. (p. 291)

Answers to STOP & CHECK Questions

1. These fish might not need to sleep because they are equally efficient at all times of day and have no need to conserve energy at one time more than another. The fish might sleep, however, as a relic left over from ancestors that lived in the light—just as humans still erect our arm hairs in response to cold, a response that was useful for our hairier ancestors but not for us. Still, if they sleep, they could sleep on any irregular schedule; there should be no reason for a 24-hour cycle. (p. 288)
2. Much REM sleep is more typical of the young than the old, of those who get much sleep than those who get little, and of species that sleep much of the day and are unlikely to be attacked during their sleep. (p. 290)
3. After adult damage to the primary visual cortex, people become blind but some still report visual dreams (Rees et al., 2002). The explanation is that the primary visual cortex is nearly inactive during dreaming anyway, so further suppression is not a problem. However, damage to other parts of the visual cortex, outside V1, do abolish visual imagery in dreams. Also, people who suffered V1 damage in early childhood have no visual imagery in dreams because they never experienced vision to form visual memories. (p. 291)

Thought Question

Why would it be harder to deprive someone of just NREM sleep than just REM sleep?

Chapter Ending

Key Terms and Activities

Terms

activation-synthesis hypothesis (p. 290)
adenosine (p. 280)
alpha wave (p. 275)
basal forebrain (p. 278)
caffeine (p. 280)
cataplexy (p. 283)
clinico-anatomical hypothesis (p. 291)
endogenous circadian rhythm (p. 266)
endogenous circannual rhythm (p. 266)
free-running rhythm (p. 271)
insomnia (p. 282)
jet lag (p. 272)
K-complex (p. 275)
locus coeruleus (p. 278)
melatonin (p. 271)
narcolepsy (p. 283)
night terror (p. 284)
non-REM (NREM) sleep (p. 277)
orexin (or *hypocretin*) (p. 278)
paradoxical sleep (p. 276)
periodic limb movement disorder (p. 284)
PGO wave (p. 281)
pineal gland (p. 271)
polysomnograph (p. 275)
pontomesencephalon (p. 278)
prostaglandin (p. 280)
rapid eye movement (REM) sleep (p. 276)

REM behavior disorder (p. 284)
reticular formation (p. 278)
sleep apnea (p. 283)
sleep spindle (p. 275)
slow-wave sleep (SWS) (p. 276)
suprachiasmatic nucleus (SCN) (p. 269)
zeitgeber (p. 272)

Suggestions for Further Reading

Dement, W. C. (1992). *The sleepwatchers.* Stanford, CA: Stanford Alumni Association. Fascinating, entertaining account of sleep research by one of its leading pioneers.

Foster, R. G., & Kreitzman, L. (2004). *Rhythms of life.* New Haven, CT: Yale University Press. Nontechnical discussion of research on circadian rhythms.

Moorcroft, W. H. (2003) *Understanding sleep and dreaming.* New York: Kluwer. Excellent review of research on many aspects of sleep and dreams.

Refinetti, R. (2005). *Circadian physiology* (2nd ed.). Boca Raton, FL: CRC Press. Marvelous summary of research on circadian rhythms and the relevance to human behavior.

Websites to Explore

You can go to the Biological Psychology Study Center and click these links. While there, you can also check for suggested articles available on InfoTrac College Edition. The Biological Psychology Internet address is:

http://psychology.wadsworth.com/book/kalatbiopsych9e/

The Sleep Site, specializing in sleep disorders

http://www.thesleepsite.com/

The Quantitative Study of Dreams, by Adam Schneider and G. William Domhoff

http://www.dreamresearch.net

Exploring Biological Psychology CD

Sleep Rhythms (learning module)
Sleep Cycle (video)
Critical Thinking (essay questions)
Chapter Quiz (multiple-choice questions)

ThomsonNOW™

http://www.thomsonedu.com

Go to this site for the link to ThomsonNOW, your one-stop study shop. Take a Pre-Test for this chapter, and ThomsonNOW will generate a Personalized Study Plan based on your test results. The Study Plan will identify the topics you need to review and direct you to online resources to help you master these topics. You can then take a Post-Test to help you determine the concepts you have mastered and what you still need work on.

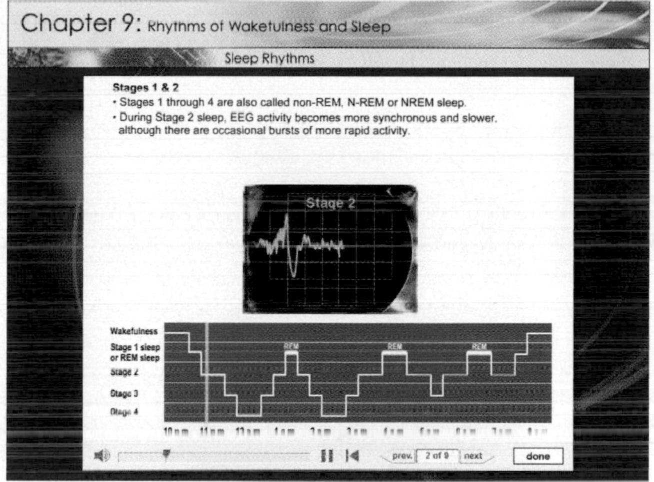

Here is a step by step view of the stages of sleep.

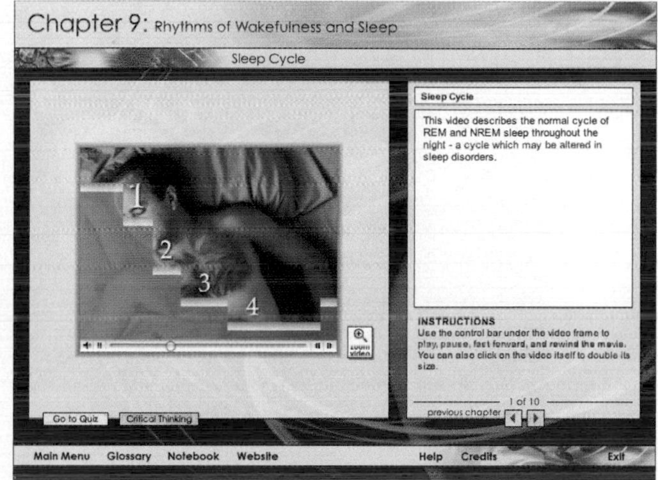

Explore the progression through the stages of sleep.

BOIL
WATER
BEFORE
DRINKING

Internal Regulation

Chapter Outline

Opposite: All life on Earth requires water, and animals drink it wherever they can find it.
Source: Courtesy of Gail R. Hill/Bimbimbie Ornithological Services

Main Ideas

1. Many physiological and behavioral processes maintain a near constancy of certain body variables, and they anticipate as well as react to needs.
2. Mammals and birds maintain constant body temperature as a way of staying ready for rapid muscle activity at any temperature of the environment. They use both behavioral and physiological processes to maintain temperature.
3. Thirst mechanisms respond to the osmotic pressure and total volume of the blood.
4. Hunger and satiety are regulated by many factors, including taste, stomach distention, the availability of glucose to the cells, and chemicals released by the fat cells. Many brain peptides help regulate feeding and satiety.

What is life? Life can be defined in different ways depending on whether our interest is medical, legal, philosophical, or poetic. Biologically, what is necessary for life is *a coordinated set of chemical reactions.* Not all chemical reactions are alive, but all life has precisely regulated chemical reactions.

Every chemical reaction in the body takes place in a water solution at a rate that depends on the identity and concentration of molecules in the water, the temperature of the solution, and the presence of contaminants. Much of our behavior is organized to keep the right chemicals in the right proportions and at the right temperature.

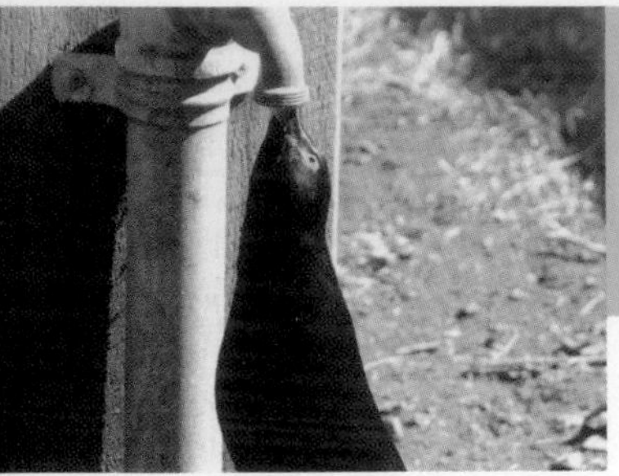

Module 10.1
Temperature Regulation

Here's an observation that puzzled biologists for years: When a small male garter snake emerges from hibernation in early spring, it emits female pheromones for the first day or two. The pheromones attract larger males that swarm all over him, trying to copulate. Presumably, the tendency to release female pheromones must have evolved and must offer the small male some advantage. But what? Biologists speculated about ways in which this pseudomating experience might help the small male attract real females. The truth is simpler: A male that has just emerged from hibernation is so cold that it has trouble slithering out of its burrow. The larger males emerged from hibernation earlier and already had a chance to warm themselves in a sunny place. When the larger males swarm all over the smaller male, they warm him and increase his activity level (Shine, Phillips, Waye, LeMaster, & Mason, 2001).

Here are some other examples of otherwise puzzling behaviors that make sense in terms of temperature regulation:

- Have you ever noticed gulls, ducks, or other large birds standing on one leg (Figure 10.1)? Why do they do that, when balancing on two legs would seem easier? The answer is they stand this way when their legs are getting cold. Tucking a leg under the body keeps it warm (Ehrlich, Dobkin, & Wheye, 1988).
- Vultures sometimes defecate onto their own legs. Are they just being careless slobs? No, they defecate onto their legs on hot days so that the evaporating excretions will cool their legs (Ehrlich et al., 1988).
- Decades ago, psychologists found that infant rats had apparent deficiencies in several aspects of learning, as well as in regulation of eating and drinking. Later results showed that the real problem was temperature control. Researchers generally work at "normal room temperature," about 20°–23°C (68–73°F), which is comfortable for adult humans but dangerously cold for an isolated baby rat (Figure 10.2). In a warmer room, even infant rats show abilities that we once assumed required more brain maturity (Satinoff, 1991).

f1 online/Alamy

Figure 10.1 Why do birds sometimes stand on one foot?
Like many other puzzling behaviors, this one makes sense in terms of temperature regulation. The bird keeps one leg warm by holding it next to the body.

© A. Cosmos Blank/NAS/Photo Researchers

Figure 10.2 The special difficulties of temperature regulation for a newborn rodent
A newborn rat has no hair, thin skin, and little body fat. If left exposed to the cold, it becomes inactive.

- According to some studies, female rats learn best during their fertile period (estrus). According to other studies using the same apparatus, they learn best a day or two before their fertile period (proestrus). The difference depends on temperature. Rats in estrus do better in a cooler environment, presumably because they are generating so much heat on their own. Rats in proestrus do better in a warmer environment (Rubinow, Arseneau, Beverly, & Juraska, 2004).

The point is that temperature affects behavior in many ways that we don't always notice. Temperature regulation is more important and more interesting than many psychologists realize.

Homeostasis and Allostasis

Physiologist Walter B. Cannon (1929) introduced the term **homeostasis** (HO-mee-oh-STAY-sis) to refer to temperature regulation and other biological processes that keep certain body variables within a fixed range. The process is analogous to the thermostat in a house with heating and cooling systems. Someone sets the minimum and maximum temperatures on the thermostat. When the temperature in the house drops below the minimum, the thermostat triggers the furnace to provide heat. When the temperature rises above the maximum, the thermostat turns on the air conditioner.

Similarly, homeostatic processes in animals trigger physiological and behavioral activities that keep certain variables within a set range. In many cases, the range is so narrow that we refer to it as a **set point,** a single value that the body works to maintain. For example, if calcium is deficient in your diet and its concentration in the blood begins to fall below the set point of 0.16 g/L (grams per liter), storage deposits in your bones release additional calcium into the blood. If the calcium level in the blood rises above 0.16 g/L, part of the excess is stored in the bones and part is excreted. Analogous mechanisms maintain constant blood levels of water, oxygen, glucose, sodium chloride, protein, fat, and acidity (Cannon, 1929). Processes that reduce discrepancies from the set point are known as **negative feedback.** Most motivated behavior can be described as negative feedback: Something happens to cause a disturbance, and behavior continues in varying ways until it relieves the disturbance.

However, the body's set points change from time to time (Mrosovsky, 1990). For example, many animals increase their body fat in fall and decrease it in spring. Your body maintains a higher temperature in the afternoon than in the middle of the night, even if the room temperature is the same throughout the day. In a frightening situation, you begin to sweat even before you begin the activity that would call for sweating. To describe these dynamic changes in set points, researchers use the term **allostasis** (from the Greek roots meaning "variable" and "standing"), which means the adaptive way in which the body changes its set points in response to changes in its life or changes in the environment (McEwen, 2000).

Controlling Body Temperature

If you were to list your strongest motivations in life, you might not think to include temperature regulation, but it is a very high priority biologically. An average young adult expends about 2,600 kilocalories (kcal) per day. Where do you suppose all that energy goes? It is not to muscle movements or mental activity. You use about two-thirds of your energy for **basal metabolism,** the energy you use to maintain a constant body temperature while at rest (Burton, 1994).

Amphibians, reptiles, and most fish are **poikilothermic** (POY-kih-lo-THER-mik)—that is, their body temperature matches the temperature of their environment. They lack physiological mechanisms of temperature regulation such as shivering and sweating. Nevertheless, they avoid wide swings in body temperature by choosing their location within the environment. A desert lizard burrows into the ground in the middle of the day, when the surface is too hot, and again in the middle of the night, when the surface is too cold. On the surface, it moves from sun to shade as necessary to keep its temperature fairly steady.

Mammals and birds are **homeothermic:**[1] They use physiological mechanisms to maintain an almost constant body temperature over a wide range of environmental temperatures. Homeothermy requires energy and therefore fuel, especially for small animals. An animal *generates* heat in proportion to its total mass; it *radiates* heat in proportion to its surface area. A small mammal or bird, such as a mouse or a hummingbird, has a high surface-to-volume ratio and therefore radiates heat rapidly. Such animals need a great deal of fuel each day to maintain their body temperature.

Homeothermic animals can use physiological mechanisms to control body temperature. To cool ourselves when the air is warmer than body temperature, we have only one mechanism, which is sweating. Species that don't sweat will instead pant or lick themselves. Sweating, panting, or licking exposes water, which cools the body as it evaporates. This mechanism is limited, however: If the air is humid as well as hot, the moisture will not evaporate. Furthermore, if you

[1]Two exceptions: When a small mammal goes into hibernation, it becomes temporarily poikilothermic as a way of conserving energy. Also, one species of mole rat that lives in underground burrows is poikilothermic (Park et al., 2003).

lose more water by sweating than you gain by drinking, your body runs into other kinds of problems.

In contrast, several physiological mechanisms increase body heat in a cold environment. One is shivering. Any muscle contractions, such as those of shivering, generate heat. Second, decreased blood flow to the skin prevents the blood from cooling before it reaches the brain, heart, muscles, and so forth. A third mechanism works well for other mammalian species, though not for humans: They fluff out their fur to increase insulation. (We humans have an evolutionary relic of that mechanism. We too fluff out our "fur" by erecting the tiny hairs on our skin—"goose bumps." Back when our ancestors had a fuller coat of fur, that mechanism did some good.)

However, we also use behavioral mechanisms, just as poikilothermic animals do. In fact, we prefer to rely on behavioral mechanisms when we can. The more we regulate our temperature behaviorally, the less we need to rely on energetically costly physiological efforts (Refinetti & Carlisle, 1986). Finding a cool place on a hot day is much better than sweating (Figure 10.3).

AP

Figure 10.3 One way to cope with the heat
Overheated animals, like overheated people, look for the coolest spot they can find.

Finding a warm place on a cold day is much better (and smarter) than standing around shivering. Here are a few other behavioral mechanisms of temperature regulation:

- Put on more clothing or take it off. This human strategy accomplishes what other mammals accomplish by fluffing out or sleeking their fur.
- Become more active to get warmer or less active to avoid overheating.
- To get warm, huddle or cuddle with others. You might be shy about hugging strangers to keep warm, but many other species are not (Figure 10.4). For example, spectacled eiders (in the duck family) spend their winters in the Arctic Ocean, which is mostly covered with ice. With more than 150,000 eiders crowded together, they not only keep one another warm but also maintain a 20-mile hole in the ice so they can dive for fish throughout the winter (Weidensaul, 1999).

Figure 10.4 Behavioral regulation of body temperature
A 1-month-old emperor penguin chick is poorly insulated against antarctic temperatures that often drop below –30°C (–22° F). However, when many chicks huddle together tightly, they act like one large well-insulated organism. The cold ones on the outside push their way inward, and the warm ones on the inside passively drift outward. The process is so effective that a cluster of penguin chicks has to move frequently to prevent melting a hole in the ice.

EXTENSIONS AND APPLICATIONS
Surviving in Extreme Cold

If the atmospheric temperature drops below 0°C (32°F), you and I can maintain our normal body temperature by shivering, shifting blood flow away from the skin, and so forth. However, a poikilothermic animal, which by definition takes the temperature of its environment, is vulnerable. If its body temperature drops below the freezing point of water, ice crystals will form. Because

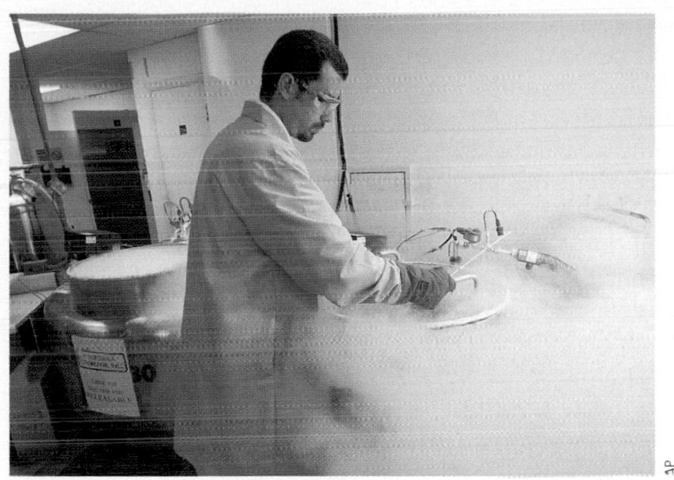

AP

Companies will freeze a dead body with the prospect that future technologies can restore the person to life.

water expands when it freezes, ice crystals would tear apart blood vessels and cell membranes, killing the animal.

Ordinarily, amphibians and reptiles avoid that risk by burrowing underground or finding other sheltered locations. However, some frogs, fish, and insects survive through winters in northern Canada where even the underground temperature approaches −40°C (which is also −40°F). How do they do it? Some insects and fish stock their blood with glycerol and other antifreeze chemicals at the start of the winter (Liou, Tocilj, Davies, & Jia, 2000). Wood frogs actually do freeze, but they have several mechanisms to reduce the damage. They start by withdrawing most fluid from their organs and blood vessels and storing it in extracellular spaces. Therefore, ice crystals have room to expand when they do form, without tearing the blood vessels and cells. Also, they have chemicals that cause ice crystals to form gradually, not in chunks. Finally, they have such extraordinary blood-clotting capacity that they can quickly repair any blood vessels that do rupture (Storey & Storey, 1999).

As you may have heard, some people have had their bodies frozen after death, in hopes that scientists will discover a cure for their disease *and* a way to bring a frozen body back to life. What do you think? If you had enough money, would you choose this route to possible life after death?

My advice is don't bother. The wood frogs that survive after freezing begin by dehydrating their organs and blood vessels. Unless a person underwent similar dehydration—before dying!—ice crystals are sure to tear up blood vessels and cell membranes throughout the body. Repairing all those membranes sounds pretty close to impossible.

The Advantages of Constant High Body Temperature

As mentioned, we spend about two-thirds of our total energy maintaining body temperature (basal metabolism). A poikilothermic animal, such as a frog, has a lower level of basal metabolism and consequently needs far less fuel. If we didn't maintain a constant, high body temperature, we could eat much less and therefore spend less effort finding food. So why is body temperature so important? Why did we evolve mechanisms to maintain constant body temperature at such a high cost?

For the answer, think back to Chapter 8: Remember what happens to a fish's activity level when water temperature changes. As the water gets colder, a fish has to recruit more and more fast-twitch muscle fibers to remain active at the risk of rapid fatigue. Birds and mammals, in contrast, keep their muscles warm at all times, regardless of air temperature, and therefore stay constantly ready for vigorous activity. In other words, we eat a great deal to support our high metabolism so that even when the weather is cold, we can still run as fast and far as possible.

Why did mammals evolve a body temperature of 37°C (98°F) instead of some other value? From the standpoint of muscle activity, we gain an advantage by being as warm as possible. A warmer animal has warmer muscles and therefore runs faster and with less fatigue than a cooler animal. However, we have tradeoffs. To get even hotter than 37° would require still more energy. Furthermore, beyond about 40° or 41°C, proteins begin to break their bonds and lose their useful properties. Birds' body temperatures are in fact about 41°C (105°F).

It is possible to evolve proteins that are stable at higher temperatures; indeed, odd microscopic animals called thermophiles survive in water close to its boiling point (Hoffman, 2001). However, to do so, they need many extra bonds to stabilize their proteins. The enzymatic properties of proteins depend on the proteins' flexible structure, so making them rigid enough to withstand high temperatures decreases their versatility and usefulness (Somero, 1996).

Reproductive cells require a somewhat cooler environment than the rest of the body (Rommel, Pabst, & McLellan, 1998). Birds lay eggs and sit on them, instead of developing them internally, because the birds' internal temperature is too hot for an embryo. Similarly, in most male mammals, the scrotum hangs outside the body because sperm production requires a cooler temperature than the rest of the body. (A man who wears his undershorts too tight keeps his testes too close to the body, overheats them, and therefore produces fewer healthy sperm cells.) Pregnant women are advised to avoid hot baths and anything else that might overheat a developing fetus.

STOP & CHECK

1. How does the idea of allostasis differ from homeostasis?
2. What is the primary advantage of maintaining a constant body temperature?
3. Why did we evolve a temperature of 37°C (98°F) instead of some other temperature?

Check your answers on pages 301–302.

Brain Mechanisms

All the physiological changes that defend body temperature—such as shivering, sweating, and changes in blood flow to the skin—depend predominantly on certain areas in and near the hypothalamus, at the base of the brain (Figure 10.5). The most critical areas for temperature control are the anterior hypothalamus and the preoptic area, which is just anterior to the anterior hypothalamus. (It is called *preoptic* because it is near the optic chiasm, where the optic nerves cross.) Because of the close relationship between the preoptic area and the anterior hypothalamus, they are often treated as a single area, the **preoptic area/anterior hypothalamus**, or **POA/AH.**

The POA/AH monitors body temperature partly by monitoring its own temperature (D. O. Nelson & Prosser, 1981). When an experimenter heats the POA/AH, an animal pants or sweats, even in a cool environment. If the same area is cooled, the animal shivers, even in a warm room. These responses are not simply reflexive. An animal will also react to a heated or cooled POA/AH by pressing a lever or doing other work for cold air or hot air reinforcements (Satinoff, 1964).

Besides monitoring their own temperature, cells of the POA/AH also receive input from temperature-sensitive receptors in the skin and spinal cord. The animal shivers most vigorously when both the POA/AH and the other receptors are cold; it sweats or pants most vigorously when both are hot. Damage to the POA/AH impairs a mammal's ability to regulate temperature (Satinoff, Valentino, & Teitelbaum, 1976). After that kind of damage, mammals are reduced to using just behavioral mechanisms such as seeking a warmer or colder location (Satinoff & Rutstein, 1970; Van Zoeren & Stricker, 1977).

Fever

Bacterial and viral infections generally cause fever, an increase in body temperature. The fever is not part of the illness; it is part of the body's defense against the illness. When bacteria, viruses, fungi, or other intruders invade the body, it mobilizes *leukocytes* (white blood cells) to attack them.

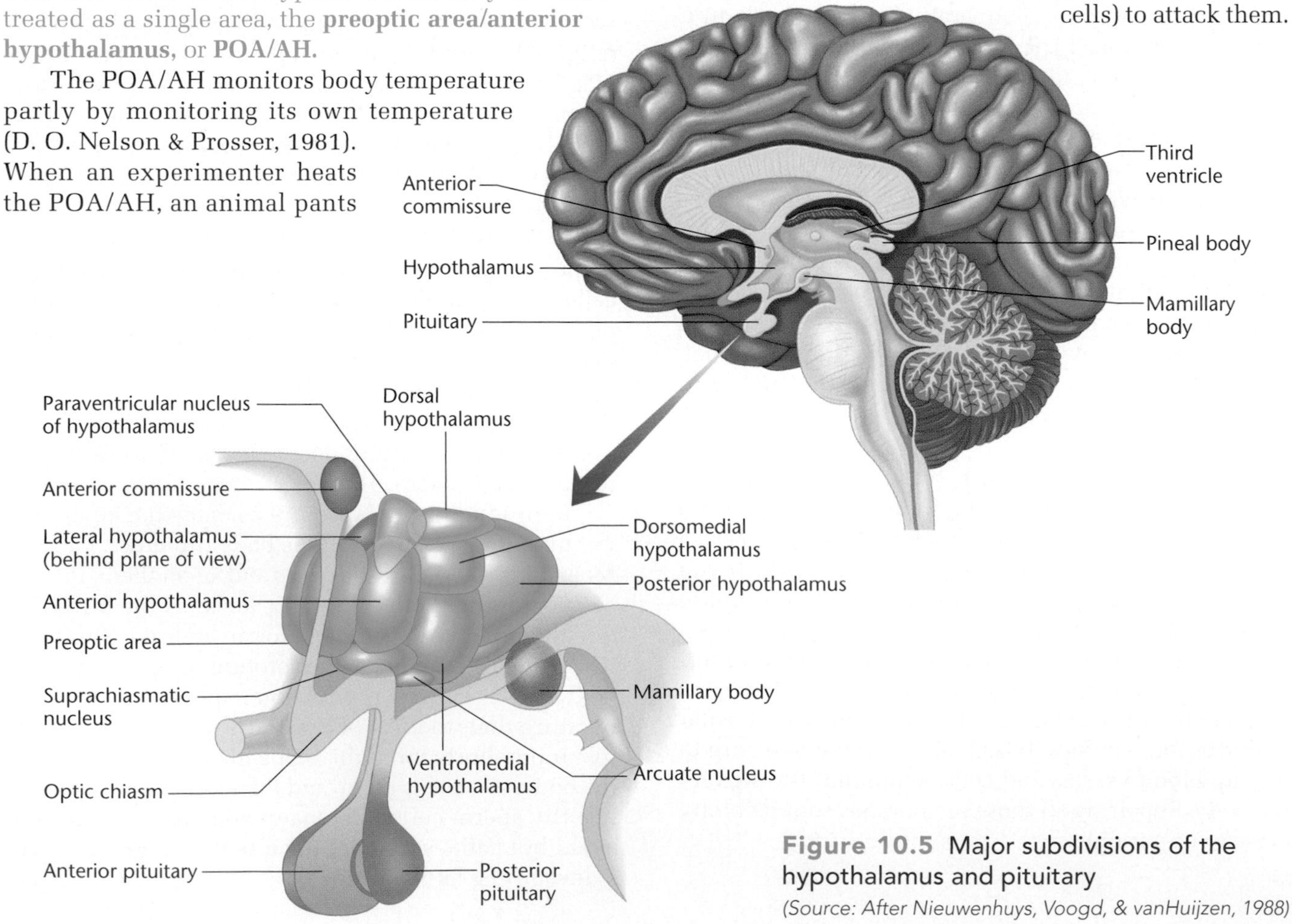

Figure 10.5 Major subdivisions of the hypothalamus and pituitary
(Source: After Nieuwenhuys, Voogd, & vanHuijzen, 1988)

The leukocytes release small proteins called **cytokines** that attack the intruders and also communicate with the brain. Some cytokines probably cross the blood-brain barrier; however, the main route of communication is that cytokines stimulate the vagus nerve, which sends signals to the hypothalamus to initiate a fever (Ek et al., 2001; Leon, 2002).

A fever represents an increased set point for body temperature. Just as you shiver or sweat when your body temperature goes below or above its usual 37°C, when you have a fever of, say, 39°C, you shiver or sweat whenever your temperature deviates from that level. Moving to a cooler room does not lower your fever; it just makes your body work harder to keep its temperature at the feverish level.

Newborn rabbits, whose hypothalamus is immature, do not shiver in response to infections. If they are given a choice of environments, however, they select a spot warm enough to raise their body temperature (Satinoff, McEwen, & Williams, 1976). That is, they develop a fever by behavioral means. Fish and reptiles with an infection also choose a warm enough environment, if they can find one, to produce a feverish body temperature (Kluger, 1991). Again, the point is that fever is something the animal does to fight an infection.

Does fever do an animal any good? Certain types of bacteria grow less vigorously at high temperatures than at normal mammalian body temperatures. Other things being equal, developing a moderate fever increases an individual's chance of surviving a bacterial infection (Kluger, 1991). However, a fever above about 39°C (103°F) in humans does more harm than good, and a fever above 41°C (109°F) can be life-threatening (Rommel et al., 1998).

4. What evidence do we have that the POA/AH controls body temperature?
5. How can an animal regulate body temperature after damage to the POA/AH?
6. What evidence indicates that fever is an adaptation to fight illness?

Check your answers on page 302.

Module 10.1
In Closing: Combining Physiological and Behavioral Mechanisms

One of the key themes of this module has been the redundancy of mechanisms. Your body has various physiological mechanisms to maintain constant body temperature, including shivering, sweating, and changes in blood flow. You also rely on behavioral mechanisms, such as finding a cooler or warmer place, adding or removing clothing, and so forth. Redundancy reduces your risk: If one mechanism fails, another mechanism comes to your rescue. It is not, however, a true redundancy in the sense of two mechanisms doing exactly the same thing. Each of your mechanisms of temperature regulation solves a different aspect of the problem in a different way. We shall see this theme again in the discussions of thirst and hunger.

Summary

1. It is easy to overlook the importance of temperature regulation. Many seemingly odd animal behaviors make sense as ways to heat or cool the body. (p. 296)
2. Homeostasis is a tendency to maintain a body variable near a set point. Temperature, hunger, and thirst are almost homeostatic, but the set point changes in varying circumstances. (p. 297)
3. A high body temperature enables a mammal or bird to move rapidly and without fatigue even in a cold environment. (p. 299)
4. From the standpoint of muscle activity, the higher the body temperature, the better. However, as temperatures exceed 41°C, protein stability decreases, and more energy is needed to maintain body temperature. Mammalian body temperature of 37°C is apparently a compromise between these competing considerations. (p. 299)
5. The preoptic area and anterior hypothalamus (POA/AH) are critical for temperature control. Cells there monitor both their own temperature and that of the skin and spinal cord. (p. 300)
6. Even homeothermic animals rely partly on behavioral mechanisms for temperature regulation, especially in infancy and after damage to the POA/AH. (p. 300)
7. A moderate fever helps an animal combat an infection. (p. 300)

Answers to STOP & CHECK Questions

1. Homeostasis is a set of processes that keep certain body variables within a fixed range. Allostasis is an adjustment of that range, increasing it or decreasing it as circumstances change. (p. 300)

2. The primary advantage of a constant (high) body temperature is that it keeps the animal ready for rapid, prolonged muscle activity even if the air is cold. (p. 300)
3. Animals gain an advantage in being as warm as possible and therefore as fast as possible. However, proteins lose stability at temperatures much above 37°C (98°F). (p. 300)
4. Direct cooling or heating of the POA/AH leads to shivering or sweating. Also, damage there impairs physiological control of temperature. (p. 301)
5. It can regulate temperature through behavior, such as by finding a warmer or cooler place. (p. 301)
6. The body will shiver or sweat to maintain its elevated temperature. Also, fish, reptiles, and immature mammals use behavioral means to raise their temperature to a feverish level. Furthermore, a moderate fever inhibits bacterial growth and increases the probability of surviving a bacterial infection. (p. 301)

Thought Question

Speculate on why birds have higher body temperatures than mammals.

Module 10.2
Thirst

Water constitutes about 70% of the mammalian body. Because the concentration of chemicals in water determines the rate of all chemical reactions in the body, the water must be regulated within narrow limits. The body also needs enough fluid in the circulatory system to maintain normal blood pressure. People sometimes survive for weeks without food, but not without water.

Mechanisms of Water Regulation

Different species have different strategies for maintaining the water they need. Beavers and other species that live in rivers or lakes drink plenty of water, eat moist foods, and excrete copious amounts of dilute urine. In contrast, gerbils and other desert animals may go through their entire lives without drinking. They gain enough water from their food, and they have many adaptations to avoid losing water, including the fact that they excrete very dry feces and very concentrated urine. Unable to sweat, they avoid the heat of the day by burrowing deep under the ground. Their highly convoluted nasal passages minimize water loss when they exhale.

We humans vary our strategy depending on circumstances. If you cannot find enough to drink, or if the water tastes bad, you will conserve water by excreting more concentrated urine, decreasing your sweat, and other autonomic responses. Your posterior pituitary (see Figure 10.5) releases a hormone called **vasopressin**, which raises blood pressure by constricting the blood vessels. (The term *vasopressin* comes from *vas*cular *press*ure.) The increased pressure helps compensate for the decreased volume. Vasopressin is also known as **antidiuretic hormone (ADH)** because it enables the kidneys to reabsorb water from urine and therefore make the urine more concentrated. (*Diuresis* means "urination.") You cannot succeed as well as gerbils, however. Gerbils can drink ocean water, and we certainly cannot.

In most cases, our strategy is closer to that of beavers: We drink more than we need and excrete the excess. (However, if you drink extensively without eating, as many alcoholics do, you may excrete enough body salts to harm yourself.) Most of our drinking is with meals or in social situations, and people in prosperous countries seldom experience intense thirst.

STOP & CHECK

1. If you lacked vasopressin, would you drink like a beaver or like a gerbil? Why?

Check your answers on page 306.

Osmotic Thirst

Not all thirst is the same. Eating salty foods causes *osmotic* thirst, and losing fluid, such as by bleeding or sweating, induces *hypovolemic* thirst. The two kinds of thirst motivate different kinds of behavior.

The combined concentration of all *solutes* (molecules in solution) in mammalian body fluids remains at a nearly constant level of 0.15 M (molar). (A concentration of 1.0 M has a number of grams of solute equal to the molecular weight of that solute dissolved in 1 liter of solution.) This fixed concentration of solutes can be regarded as a set point, similar to the set point for temperature. Any deviation activates mechanisms that restore the concentration of solutes to the set point.

The solutes inside and outside a cell produce an **osmotic pressure**, the tendency of water to flow across a semipermeable membrane from the area of low solute concentration to the area of higher concentration. A semipermeable membrane is one through which water can pass but solutes cannot. The membrane surrounding a cell is almost a semipermeable membrane because water flows across it freely and various solutes flow either slowly or not at all between the *intracellular fluid* inside the cell and the *extracellular fluid* outside it. Osmotic pressure occurs when solutes are more concentrated on one side of the membrane than on the other.

If you eat something salty, sodium ions spread through the blood and the extracellular fluid but do

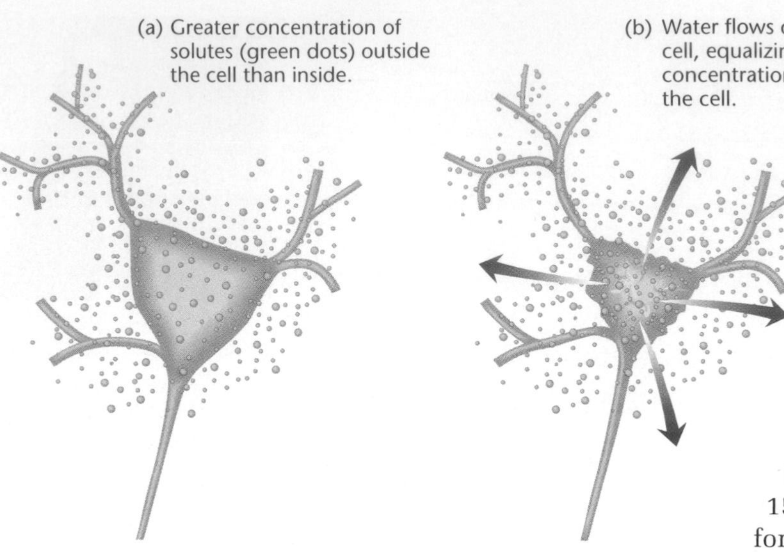

Figure 10.6 The consequence of a difference in osmotic pressure
(a) A solute such as NaCl is more concentrated outside the cell than inside. **(b)** Water flows by osmosis out of the cell until the concentrations are equal. Neurons in certain brain areas detect their own dehydration and trigger thirst.

not cross the membranes into cells. The result is a higher concentration of solutes outside the cells than inside, and the resulting osmotic pressure draws water from the cells into the extracellular fluid. Certain neurons detect their own loss of water and then trigger **osmotic thirst,** which helps restore the normal state (Figure 10.6). The kidneys also excrete more concentrated urine to rid the body of excess sodium and maintain as much water as possible.

How does the brain detect osmotic pressure? It gets part of the information from receptors around the third ventricle (Figure 10.7). Of all brain areas, those around the third ventricle have the leakiest blood-brain barrier (Simon, 2000). A weak blood-brain barrier would be harmful for most neurons, but it is helpful for those monitoring the contents of the blood. The areas important for detecting osmotic pressure and the salt content of the blood include the **OVLT** (organum vasculosum laminae terminalis) and the **subfornical organ (SFO)** (Hiyama, Watanabe, Okado, & Noda, 2004). The brain also gets information from receptors in the periphery, including the stomach, that detect high levels of sodium (Kraly, Kim, Dunham, & Tribuzio, 1995), enabling the brain to anticipate an osmotic need before the rest of the body actually experiences it.

Receptors in the OVLT, the subfornical organ, the stomach, and elsewhere relay their information to several parts of the hypothalamus, including the **supraoptic nucleus** and the **paraventricular nucleus (PVN),** which control the rate at which the posterior pituitary releases vasopressin. Receptors also relay information to the **lateral preoptic area** and surrounding parts of the hypothalamus, which control drinking (Saad, Luiz, Camargo, Renzi, & Manani, 1996).

When osmotic pressure triggers thirst, how do you know when to stop drinking? You do *not* wait until water has restored normal osmotic pressure for the receptors in the brain. The water you drink has to be absorbed through the digestive system and then pumped through the blood to the brain. That process takes 15 minutes or so, and if you continued drinking for that long, you would consume far too much water. The body monitors swallowing and detects the water contents of the stomach and intestines. Those messages inhibit thirst long before the ingested water could reach the brain (Huang, Sved, & Stricker, 2000).

Hypovolemic Thirst and Sodium-Specific Hunger

Suppose you lose a significant amount of body fluid by bleeding, diarrhea, or sweating. Although osmotic

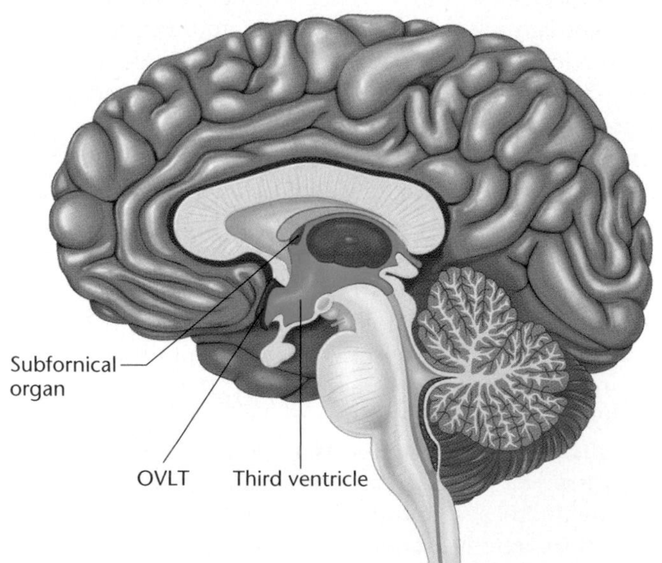

Figure 10.7 The brain's receptors for osmotic pressure and blood volume
These neurons are in areas surrounding the third ventricle of the brain, where no blood-brain barrier prevents blood-borne chemicals from entering the brain. *(Source: Based in part on DeArmond, Fusco, & Dewey, 1974; Weindl, 1973)*

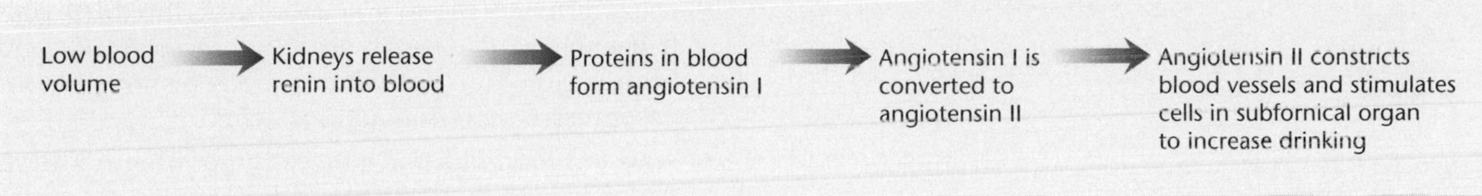

Figure 10.8 Hormonal response to hypovolemia

pressure has not changed anywhere in your body, you need fluid. Your heart has trouble pumping blood up to the head, and nutrients do not flow as easily as usual into the cells. Your body will react with hormones that constrict blood vessels. Vasopressin is one such hormone; another is *angiotensin II.* When blood volume drops, the kidneys release the enzyme *renin,* which splits a portion off angiotensinogen, a large protein in the blood, to form angiotensin I, which other enzymes convert to **angiotensin II.** Like vasopressin, angiotensin II constricts the blood vessels, compensating for the drop in blood pressure (Figure 10.8).

Angiotensin II also helps trigger thirst in conjunction with receptors that detect blood pressure in the large veins. However, this thirst is different from osmotic thirst because you need to restore your body fluids, including the salts, and not just water. This kind of thirst is known as **hypovolemic** (HI-po-vo-LEE-mik) **thirst,** meaning thirst based on low volume. When angiotensin II reaches the brain, it stimulates neurons in areas adjoining the third ventricle (Fitts, Starbuck, & Ruhf, 2000; Mangiapane & Simpson, 1980; Tanaka et al., 2001). Those neurons send axons to the hypothalamus, where they release angiotensin II as their neurotransmitter (Tanaka, Hori, & Nomura, 2001). That is, the neurons surrounding the third ventricle both respond to angiotensin II and release it. This example suggests that the connection between a neurotransmitter and its function is not at all arbitrary; the brain uses a chemical that was already performing a related function elsewhere in the body.

An animal with osmotic thirst has an increased preference for pure water, but one with hypovolemic thirst can't drink much pure water without diluting its body fluids and changing their osmotic pressure. The animal therefore increases its preference for slightly salty water (Stricker, 1969). If the animal is offered both pure water and salt, it alternates between them to yield an appropriate mixture. If sufficient salt is not readily available, it shows a strong craving for salty tastes. This preference, known as **sodium-specific hunger,** develops automatically as soon as the need exists, even in infant animals (Leshem, 1999; Richter, 1936). In contrast, specific hungers for other vitamins and minerals have to be learned by trial and error (Rozin & Kalat, 1971). You may have noticed this phenomenon yourself. A woman around the time of menstruation, or anyone who has sweated heavily, finds that salty snacks taste especially good.

Sodium-specific hunger depends partly on hormones (Schulkin, 1991). When the body's sodium reserves are low, the adrenal glands produce the hormone **aldosterone** (al-DOSS-ter-one), which causes the kidneys, salivary glands, and sweat glands to retain salt (Verrey & Beron, 1996). Aldosterone and angiotensin II together change the properties of the neurons in the nucleus of the tractus solitarius, part of the taste system (see Figure 7.19), such that they begin reacting to salt in nearly the same way they would to sugar (McCaughey & Scott, 2000).

Table 10.1 summarizes the differences between osmotic thirst and hypovolemic thirst.

Table 10.1 Comparison of Osmotic and Hypovolemic Thirst

Type of Thirst	Stimulus	Best Relieved by Drinking	Receptor Location	Hormone Influences
Osmotic	High solute concentration outside cells causes loss of water from cells	Water	OVLT, a brain area adjoining the third ventricle	Accompanied by vasopressin secretion to conserve water
Hypovolemic	Low blood volume	Water containing solutes	1. Receptors, measuring blood pressure in the veins 2. Subfornical organ, a brain area adjoining the third ventricle	Increased by angiotensin II

STOP & CHECK

2. Would adding salt to the body's extracellular fluids increase or decrease osmotic thirst?
3. Who would drink more pure water—someone with osmotic thirst or someone with hypovolemic thirst?

Check your answers on this page.

Module 10.2
In Closing: The Psychology and Biology of Thirst

You may have thought that temperature regulation happens automatically and that water regulation depends on your behavior. You can see now that the distinction is not entirely correct. You control your body temperature partly by automatic means, such as sweating or shivering, but also partly by behavioral means, such as choosing a warm or a cool place. You control your body water partly by the behavior of drinking but also by hormones that alter kidney activity. If your kidneys cannot regulate your water and sodium adequately, your brain gets signals to change your drinking or sodium intake. In short, keeping your body's chemical reactions going depends on both skeletal and autonomic controls.

Summary

1. Different mammalian species have evolved different ways of maintaining body water, ranging from frequent drinking (beavers) to extreme conservation of fluids (gerbils). Humans alter their strategy depending on the availability of acceptable fluids. (p. 303)
2. An increase in the osmotic pressure of the blood draws water out of cells, causing osmotic thirst. Neurons in the OVLT, an area adjoining the third ventricle, detect changes in osmotic pressure and send information to hypothalamic areas responsible for vasopressin secretion and for drinking. (p. 303)
3. Loss of blood volume causes hypovolemic thirst. Animals with hypovolemic thirst drink more water containing solutes than pure water. (p. 304)
4. Hypovolemic thirst is triggered by the hormone angiotensin II, which increases when blood pressure falls. (p. 305)
5. Loss of sodium salts from the body triggers sodium-specific cravings. (p. 305)

Answers to STOP & CHECK Questions

1. If you lacked vasopressin, you would have to drink more like a beaver. You would excrete much fluid, so you would need to drink an equal amount to replace it. (p. 303)
2. Adding salt to the extracellular fluids would increase osmotic thirst because it would draw water from the cells into the extracellular spaces. (p. 306)
3. The person with osmotic thirst would have a stronger preference for pure water. The one with hypovolemic thirst would drink more if the solution contained some salts. (p. 306)

Thought Questions

1. An injection of concentrated sodium chloride triggers osmotic thirst, but an injection of equally concentrated glucose does not. Why not?
2. If all the water you drank leaked out through a tube connected to the stomach, how would your drinking change?
3. Many women crave salt during menstruation or pregnancy. Why?

Module 10.3
Hunger

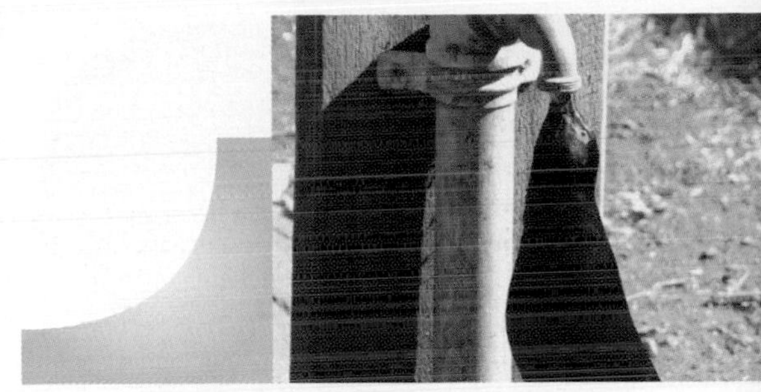

Different species use different strategies of eating. A snake or crocodile might have a huge meal (Figure 10.9) and then eat nothing more for months. Bears eat as much as they can whenever they can. It is a sensible strategy because bears' main foods—fruits and nuts—are available in large quantities for only short times. Bears' occasional feasts tide them over through times of starvation. You might think of it as survival of the fattest. (Sorry about that one.)

Small birds, at the other extreme, eat only what they need at the moment and store almost no fat at all. Such restraint is risky, as a bird can starve quickly if it can't find food. The advantage is that its low weight helps it fly away from predators (Figure 10.10). Even small birds switch strategies, however, and eat larger meals when food is hard to find or if predators are scarce (Gosler, Greenwood, & Perrins, 1995).

Humans eat more than we need at the moment, unlike small birds, but we do not stuff ourselves like bears—not as a rule, anyway. Choosing which food to eat and how much is an important decision. We have a wide array of learned and unlearned mechanisms to help in the process.

© Gunter Ziesler/Bruce Coleman

Figure 10.9 A python swallowing a gazelle
The gazelle weighs about 50% more than the snake. Many reptiles eat huge but infrequent meals, and their total intake over a year is far less than that of a mammal. We mammals need far more fuel because we use so much more energy, mainly for maintaining basal metabolism.

David M. Cottridge

Figure 10.10 A great tit, a small European bird
Ordinarily, when food is abundant, tits eat just what they need each day and maintain very low fat reserves. When food is harder to find, they eat all they can and live off fat reserves between meals. During one era when their predators were scarce, tits started putting on more fat regardless of the food supplies.

How the Digestive System Influences Food Selection

To start, let's quickly examine the digestive system, as diagramed in Figure 10.11. Its function is to break food down into smaller molecules that the cells can use. Digestion begins in the mouth, where enzymes in the saliva break down carbohydrates. Swallowed food travels down the esophagus to the stomach, where it mixes with hydrochloric acid and enzymes that digest proteins. The stomach stores food for a time, and then a round sphincter muscle opens at the end of the stomach to release food to the small intestine.

The small intestine has enzymes that digest proteins, fats, and carbohydrates. It is also the site for

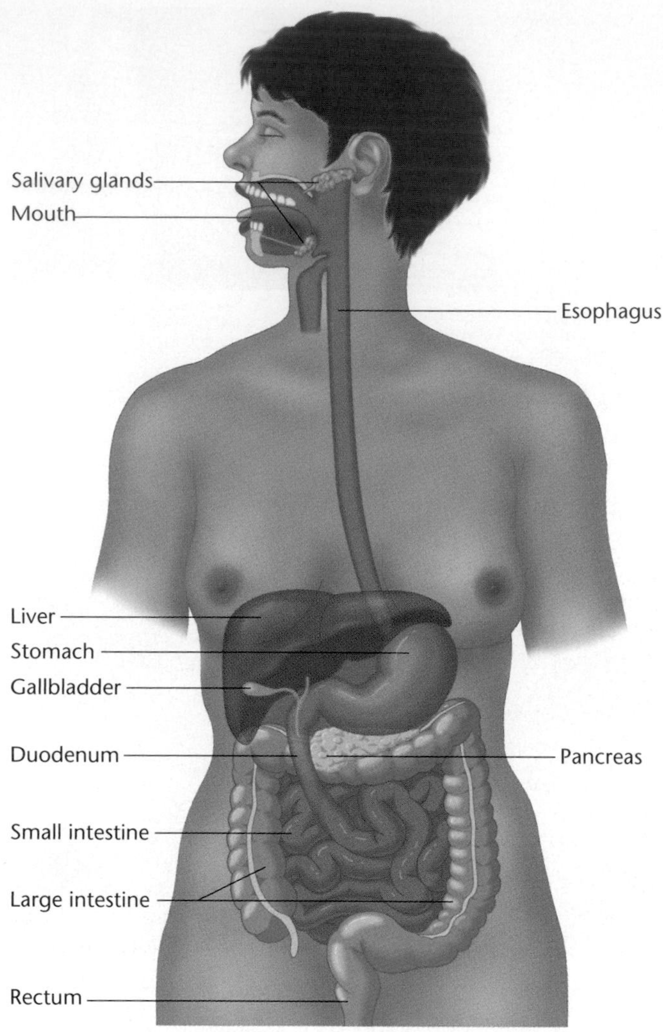

Figure 10.11 The human digestive system

absorbing digested materials into the bloodstream. The blood then carries those chemicals to body cells that either use them or store them for later use. The large intestine absorbs water and minerals and lubricates the remaining materials to pass as feces.

Enzymes and Consumption of Dairy Products

Newborn mammals survive at first on mother's milk. As they grow older, they stop nursing for several reasons: The milk dries up, the mother pushes them away, and they begin to try other foods. Also, most mammals at about the age of weaning lose the intestinal enzyme **lactase,** which is necessary for metabolizing **lactose,** the sugar in milk. From then on, milk consumption causes stomach cramps and gas (Rozin & Pelchat, 1988). Adult mammals can drink a little milk, as you may have noticed with a pet dog, but generally not much. The declining level of lactase may be an evolved mechanism to encourage weaning at the appropriate time.

Humans are a partial exception to this rule. Many adults have enough lactase levels to consume milk and other dairy products throughout life. Worldwide, however, most adults cannot comfortably tolerate large amounts of milk products. Most human beings, after all, are Asians, and nearly all the people in China and surrounding countries lack the gene that enables adults to metabolize lactose (Flatz, 1987). They can eat cheese and yogurt, which are easier to digest than milk, and small quantities of other dairy products, but they develop cramps or gas pains if they consume too much. Consequently, they generally avoid dairy products. Figure 10.12 shows the worldwide distribution of lactose tolerance.

Other Influences on Food Selection

For a **carnivore** (meat eater), selecting a satisfactory diet is relatively simple. A lion won't get vitamin deficient unless it eats vitamin-deficient zebras. However, **herbivores** (plant eaters) and **omnivores** (those that eat both meat and plants) must distinguish between edible and inedible substances and find enough vitamins and minerals. One way to do so is to learn from the experiences of others. For example, juvenile rats tend to imitate the food selections of their elders (Galef, 1992). Similarly, children acquire their culture's food preferences, especially the spices, even if they do not like every food their parents enjoy (Rozin, 1990).

But how did their parents, or grandparents, or whoever, learn what to eat? If you parachuted onto an uninhabited island covered with unfamiliar plants, you would use many strategies to select edible foods (Rozin & Vollmecke, 1986). First, you would select sweet foods, avoid bitter ones, and eat salty or sour foods in moderation. Most sweets are nutritious, and bitter substances are harmful (T. R. Scott & Verhagen, 2000). Second, you would prefer anything that tasted familiar. After all, familiar foods are safe, and new foods may not be. What did you think of coffee the first time you tried it? Hot peppers? Most people like any flavor better after it becomes familiar.

Third, you would learn the consequences of eating each food you try. If you try something new and then become ill, even hours later, your brain blames the illness on the food, and it won't taste good to you the next time (Rozin & Kalat, 1971; Rozin & Zellner, 1985). This phenomenon is known as **conditioned taste aversion.** It is a robust phenomenon that occurs reliably after just a single pairing of food with illness, even if the illness came hours after the food. In fact, you will come to dislike a food that is followed by intestinal discomfort even if you know that the nausea came from a thrill ride at the amusement park.

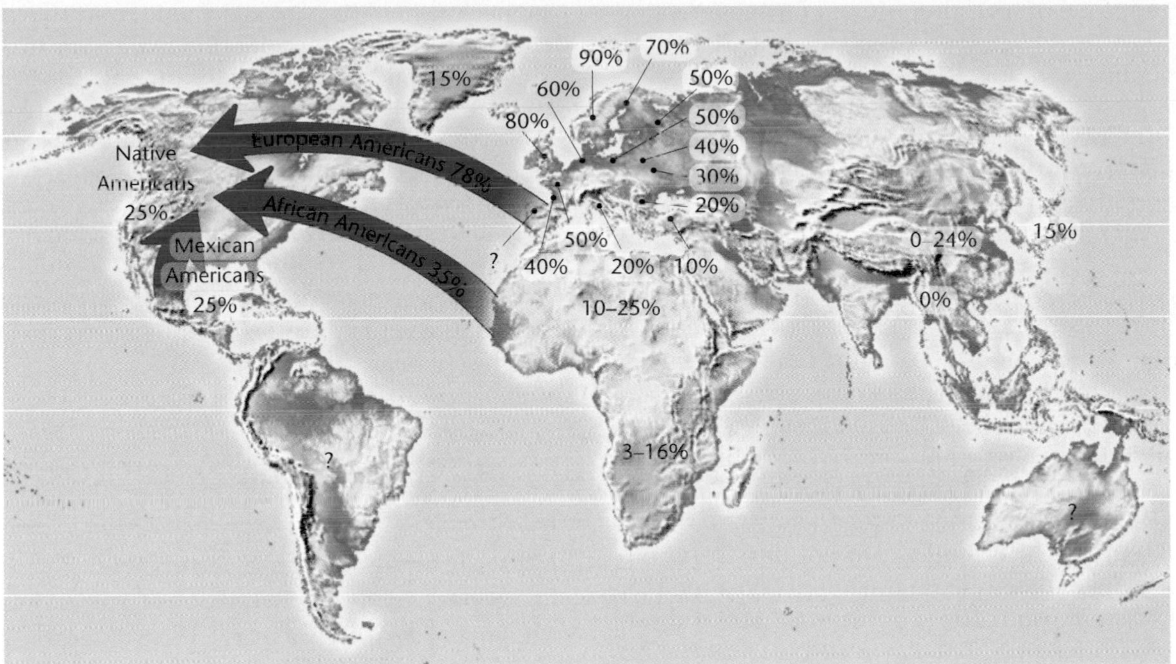

Figure 10.12 Percentage of adults who are lactose tolerant
People in areas with high lactose tolerance (e.g., Scandinavia) are likely to enjoy milk and other dairy products throughout their lives. Adults in areas with low tolerance (including much of Southeast Asia) do not ordinarily drink milk. *(Source: Based on Flatz, 1987; Rozin & Pelchat, 1988)*

STOP & CHECK

1. Why do most Southeast Asian cooks not use milk and other dairy products?

Check your answer on page 321.

Short- and Long-Term Regulation of Feeding

Eating is far too important to be entrusted to just one mechanism. Your brain gets messages from your mouth, stomach, intestines, fat cells, and elsewhere to regulate your eating.

Oral Factors

You're a busy person, right? If you could get all the nutrition you needed by swallowing a pill, would you do it? Most of us would not. Never mind how much time we would save; we *like* to eat. In fact, many people like to taste and chew even when they are not hungry. Figure 10.13 shows a piece of 6,500-year-old chewing gum made from birch-bark tar. The tooth marks indicate that a child or teenager chewed it. Anthropologists don't know how the ancient people removed the sap to make the gum, and they aren't sure why anyone would chew something that tasted as bad as this gum probably did (Battersby, 1997). Clearly, the urge to chew is strong.

Figure 10.13 Chewing gum from about 4500 B.C.
The gum, made from birch-bark tar, has small tooth marks indicating that it was chewed by a child or adolescent.

If necessary, could you become satiated without tasting your food? In one experiment, college students consumed lunch five days a week by swallowing one end of a rubber tube and then pushing a button to pump a liquid diet into the stomach (Jordan, 1969; Spiegel, 1973). (They were paid for participating.) After a few days of practice, each person established a consistent pattern of pumping in a constant volume of the liquid each day and maintaining a constant body weight. Most found the untasted meals unsatisfying, however, and reported a desire to taste or chew something (Jordan, 1969).

The opposite of ingesting without tasting is tasting without ingesting. In **sham-feeding** experiments, everything an animal swallows leaks out of a tube connected to the esophagus or stomach. Sham-feeding animals eat and swallow almost continually without becoming satiated (G. P. Smith, 1998). In short, taste and other mouth sensations contribute to satiety, but they are not enough by themselves.

The Stomach and Intestines

Ordinarily, we end a meal before the food reaches the blood, much less the muscles and other cells. The main signal to end a meal is distention of the stomach. In one experiment, researchers attached an inflatable cuff at the connection between the stomach and the small intestine (Deutsch, Young, & Kalogeris, 1978). When they inflated the cuff, food could not pass from the stomach to the duodenum. They carefully ensured that the cuff was not traumatic to the animal and did not interfere with feeding. The key result was that, with the cuff inflated, an animal ate a normal-size meal and then stopped, even though the food stayed in the stomach. Evidently, stomach distension produces satiety.

The stomach conveys satiety messages to the brain via the vagus nerve and the splanchnic nerves. The **vagus nerve** (cranial nerve X) conveys information about the stretching of the stomach walls, providing a major basis for satiety. The **splanchnic** (SPLANK-nik) **nerves** convey information about the nutrient contents of the stomach (Deutsch & Ahn, 1986).

However, the stomach is not the *only* part of the digestive system important for satiety. Later researchers repeated the experiment with the inflatable cuff and replicated the result that a rat stopped eating when the stomach filled, confirming that stomach distension is *sufficient* for satiety. However, when the cuff was open, much food passed to the duodenum before the end of the meal, so the stomach never reached full distension. The **duodenum** (DYOU-oh-DEE-num or dyuh-ODD-ehn-uhm) is the part of the small intestine adjoining the stomach; it is the first digestive site that absorbs a significant amount of nutrients. When the rats in this experiment stopped a meal, the duodenum was partly distended and the stomach was far from full (Seeley, Kaplan, & Grill, 1995). Evidently, an eater can become satiated when food distends either the stomach or the duodenum. Indeed, people after surgical removal of the stomach still report being full, so stomach distension can't be necessary.

Food in the duodenum releases several peptides that in various ways decrease meal size (Woods & Seeley, 2000). One of these is the hormone **cholecystokinin** (ko-leh-SIS-teh-KI-nehn) **(CCK)**, which acts to limit meal size (Gibbs, Young, & Smith, 1973). One mechanism is that CCK closes the sphincter muscle between the stomach and the duodenum, causing the stomach to hold its contents and fill more quickly than usual (McHugh & Moran, 1985; G. P. Smith & Gibbs, 1998). Second, CCK stimulates the vagus nerve, which sends a message to the hypothalamus, causing cells there to release as their neurotransmitter a shorter version of the CCK molecule itself (G. J. Schwartz, 2000). The process is something like sending a fax: The CCK in the intestines can't cross the blood-brain barrier, but it stimulates cells to release something almost like it. As in the case of angiotensin and thirst, the body uses the same chemical in the periphery and in the brain for closely related functions.

STOP & CHECK

2. What is the evidence that taste is not sufficient for satiety?

3. What is the evidence that stomach distension is sufficient for satiety?

4. What is the evidence that stomach distension, though sufficient, is not necessary for satiety?

5. What are two mechanisms by which CCK increases satiety?

Check your answers on page 321.

Glucose, Insulin, and Glucagon

Much digested food enters the bloodstream as glucose, an important source of energy throughout the body and nearly the only fuel used by the brain. When the blood's glucose level is high, liver cells convert some of the excess into glycogen, and fat cells convert some of it to fat. When the blood's glucose level starts to fall, the liver converts some of its glycogen back into glucose. So blood glucose levels stay fairly steady for most people most of the time.

However, the glucose in the blood is not equally available to the cells at all times. Two pancreatic hormones, insulin and glucagons, regulate the flow of glucose. **Insulin** enables glucose to enter the cells, with the exception of brain cells, where glucose can enter without insulin. Consequently, times of high insulin are times when cells receive glucose easily. Insulin levels rise as someone is getting ready for a meal; the insulin lets some of the blood glucose enter the cells in preparation for the rush of additional glucose about to enter the blood. Insulin increases even more during and after a meal. As you might guess, high levels of insulin generally decrease appetite.

As time passes after a meal, the blood glucose level falls. Insulin levels drop, glucose enters the cells more slowly, and hunger increases (Pardal & López-Barneo, 2002) (Figure 10.14). **Glucagon** stimulates the liver to

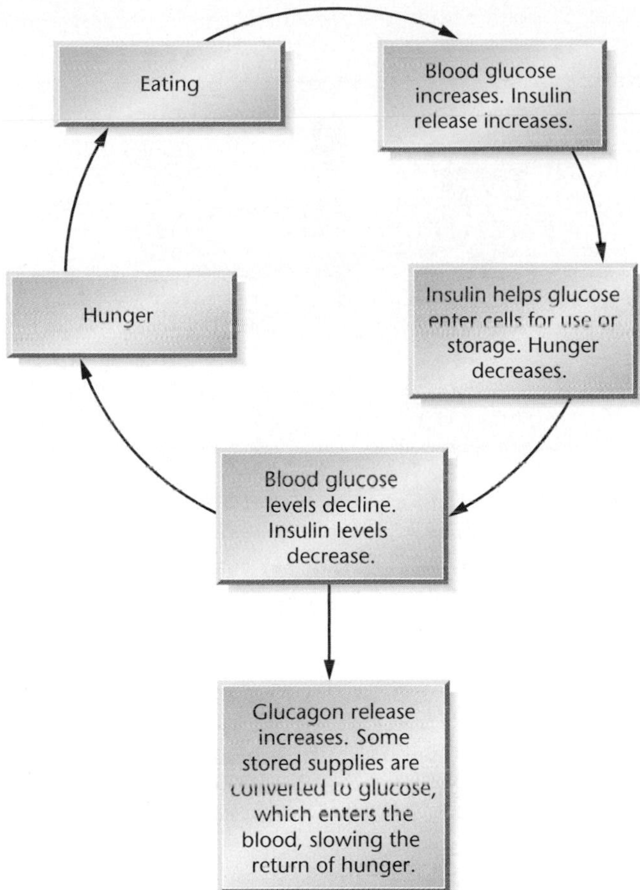

Figure 10.14 Insulin and glucagon feedback system
When glucose levels rise, the pancreas releases the hormone insulin, which causes cells to store the excess glucose as fats and glycogen. The entry of glucose into cells suppresses hunger and decreases eating, thereby lowering the glucose level.

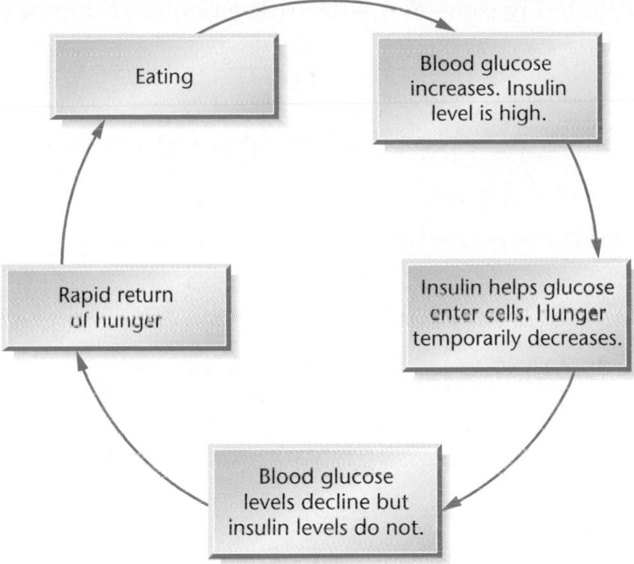

Figure 10.15 Effects of steadily high insulin levels on feeding
Constantly high insulin causes blood glucose to be stored as fats and glycogen. Because it becomes difficult to mobilize the stored nutrients, hunger returns soon after each meal.

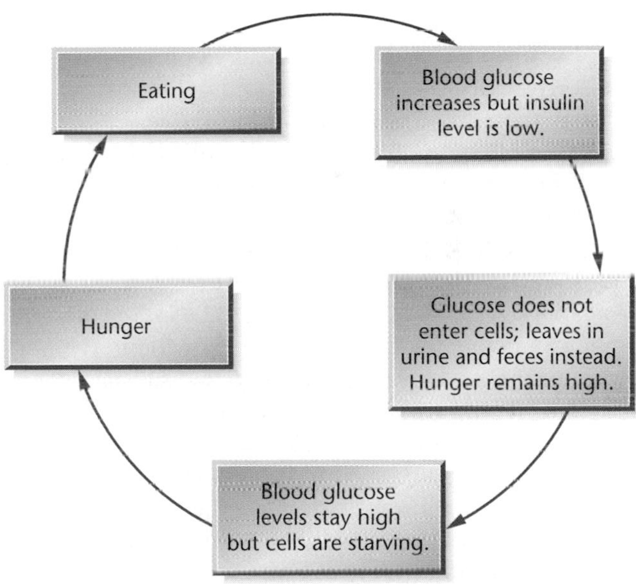

Figure 10.16 People with untreated diabetes eat much but lose weight
Because of their low insulin levels, the glucose in their blood cannot enter the cells, either to be stored or to be used. Consequently, they excrete glucose in their urine while their cells are starving.

convert some of its stored glycogen to glucose to replenish low supplies in the blood.

If the insulin level stays constantly high, the body continues rapidly moving blood glucose into the cells, including the liver cells and fat cells, long after a meal. Consequently, blood glucose drops and hunger increases in spite of the high insulin level. For example, in late autumn, animals that are preparing for hibernation have constantly high insulin levels. They rapidly deposit much of each meal as fat and glycogen, grow hungry again, and continue gaining weight (Figure 10.15). At that time, weight gain is a valuable preparation for a season when the animal will have to survive off its fat reserves.

If the insulin level remains constantly low, as in people with diabetes, blood glucose levels may be three or more times the normal level, but little of it enters the cells (Figure 10.16). People and animals with diabetes eat more food than normal because their cells are starving (Lindberg, Coburn, & Stricker, 1984), but they excrete most of their glucose unused, and they lose weight. (Note that either prolonged high or prolonged low insulin levels can increase eating, although for different reasons and with different effects on body weight.)

6. Why do people with very low insulin levels eat so much? Why do people with constantly high levels eat so much?
7. What would happen to someone's appetite if insulin levels and glucagon levels were both high?

Check your answers on page 321.

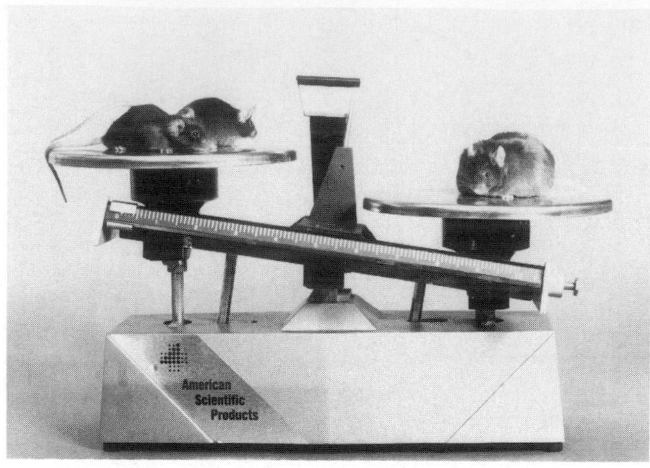

Zhang et al., 1994

Figure 10.17 The effects of the obese gene on body weight in mice
A gene that has been located on a mouse chromosome leads to increased eating, decreased metabolic rate, and increased weight gain.

Leptin

The mechanisms we have considered so far produce short-term regulation: If less glucose than usual is entering your cells, you are motivated to start eating. If your stomach or intestines are full, you stop eating. However, we can't expect those mechanisms to be completely accurate. Suppose the mechanisms that monitor your stomach, intestines, or glucose make an error of even 1%. If you ate 1% too much or 1% too little every day, the consequences would accumulate. Eventually, you would be much too heavy or much too light. The body needs to compensate for day-to-day mistakes by some type of long-term regulation.

It does so by monitoring fat supplies. Researchers had long suspected some kind of fat monitoring, but they discovered the actual mechanism more or less by accident. Researchers identified a genetic strain of mice that consistently become obese, as shown in Figure 10.17 (Zhang et al., 1994). After they identified the gene responsible for the condition, they found the peptide it makes, a previously unrecognized substance now known as **leptin**, from the Greek word *leptos,* meaning "slender" (Halaas et al., 1995). In genetically normal mice, as well as humans and other species, the body's fat cells produce leptin: The more fat cells, the more leptin. Mice with the *obese* gene fail to produce leptin.

Leptin signals the brain about the body's fat reserves—a long-term indicator of whether to increase or decrease eating. A meal can also increase the release of leptin, so the amount of circulating leptin indicates something about short-term nutrition as well. When leptin levels are high, animals act as if they have plenty of nutrition. They eat less (Campfield, Smith, Guisez, Devos, & Burn, 1995), become more active (Elias, Lee, et al., 1998), and increase the activity of their immune systems (Lord et al., 1998). (If you have enough fat supplies, you can afford to devote energy to your immune system. If you have no fat, you are starving and you have to conserve energy wherever you can.) In adolescence, a certain level of leptin triggers the onset of puberty. Again, if your fat supply is low, you don't have enough energy to provide for a baby. On the average, thinner people enter puberty later.

Because a mouse with the *obese* gene does not make leptin, its brain reacts as if the body has no fat stores and is therefore starving. The mouse eats as much as possible, conserves its energy by not moving much, and fails to enter puberty. Injections of leptin reverse these symptoms: The mouse then eats less, loses weight, becomes more active, and enters puberty (Pellymounter et al., 1995).

As you might imagine, news of this research inspired pharmaceutical companies to hope they could make a fortune by selling leptin. Leptin, after all, is something the body ordinarily makes, so it should not have unpleasant side effects. Unfortunately, researchers soon discovered that almost all overweight people already have high levels of leptin (Considine et al., 1996). (Remember—the more fat, the more leptin.) Evidently, low levels of leptin increase hunger, but high levels do not necessarily decrease it, at least not for everyone. A very few people become obese because of a genetic inability to produce leptin (Farooqi et al., 2001). Leptin helps them decrease their appetite and lose weight (D. Williamson et al., 2005). However, for the vast majority of obese people who already have high leptin levels, giving them still more is seldom an effective treatment. Presumably, they are less sensitive to leptin than other people are (Münzberg & Myers, 2005). Furthermore, excess leptin levels increase the risk of diabetes and other medical problems (B. Cohen, Novick, & Rubinstein, 1996; Naggert et al., 1995). If we are going to improve medical treatments for obesity, we need to understand more of the brain mechanisms.

Brain Mechanisms

How does your brain decide when you should eat and how much? As we have seen, your appetite at any moment depends on the taste of the food, the contents of your stomach and intestines, the availability of glucose to the cells, and your body's fat supplies. It also depends on your health, body temperature, and various other factors. Somehow the brain has to put all this information together and determine whether the "votes" for hunger outweigh those for satiety. The key areas for making this decision include several nuclei of the hypothalamus (see Figure 10.5). These brain areas have changed very little during mammalian evolution, and the mechanisms are apparently the same across species.

As shown in Figure 10.18, many kinds of information impinge onto two kinds of cells in the arcuate nucleus, which send axons to several kinds of neurons in the hypothalamus. This figure is tentative and incomplete, as feeding depends on many transmitters and mechanisms. Even in this simplified form, the figure may be intimidating. Nevertheless, it highlights some of the key mechanisms. Let's go through them step by step.

The Arcuate Nucleus and Paraventricular Hypothalamus

The **arcuate nucleus** of the hypothalamus has one set of neurons sensitive to hunger signals and a second set sensitive to satiety signals. In Figure 10.18, excitatory paths are noted in green and the inhibitory ones are in red. The hunger-sensitive cells receive input from the taste pathway; you have surely noticed that good-tasting food stimulates your hunger. Another input to the hunger-sensitive cells comes from axons releasing the neurotransmitter *ghrelin* ("GRELL-in"). This odd-looking word takes its name from the fact that it binds to the same receptors as growth-hormone releasing hormone (GHRH). The stomach releases **ghrelin** during a period of food deprivation, where it triggers stomach contractions. Although ghrelin does not cross the blood-brain barrier, certain brain neurons release it as a transmitter at the same times the stomach releases it as a hormone (Cowley et al., 2003). Again, we see how evolution uses a chemical in both the periphery and the brain for closely related functions (Hoebel, 1988).

Input to the satiety-sensitive cells of the arcuate nucleus includes signals of both short-term and long-term satiety. Distention of the intestines triggers neurons to release the neurotransmitter CCK, a short-term signal (Fan et al., 2004). Blood glucose (a short-term signal) increases secretion of the hormone insulin. Some neurons also release a smaller peptide related to insulin as a transmitter (Brüning et al., 2000). Body fat (a long-term signal) releases leptin, a signal of body fat reserves (Münzberg & Myers, 2005). Insulin and leptin combine their effects onto the satiety-sensitive cells.

Much of the output from the arcuate nucleus goes to the paraventricular nucleus of the hypothalamus. The paraventricular nucleus (PVN) inhibits the lateral hypothalamus, an area important for eating. So the paraventricular nucleus is important for satiety. Rats with damage in the paraventricular nucleus eat larger than normal meals, as if they were insensitive to the usual signals for ending a meal (Leibowitz, Hammer, & Chang, 1981).

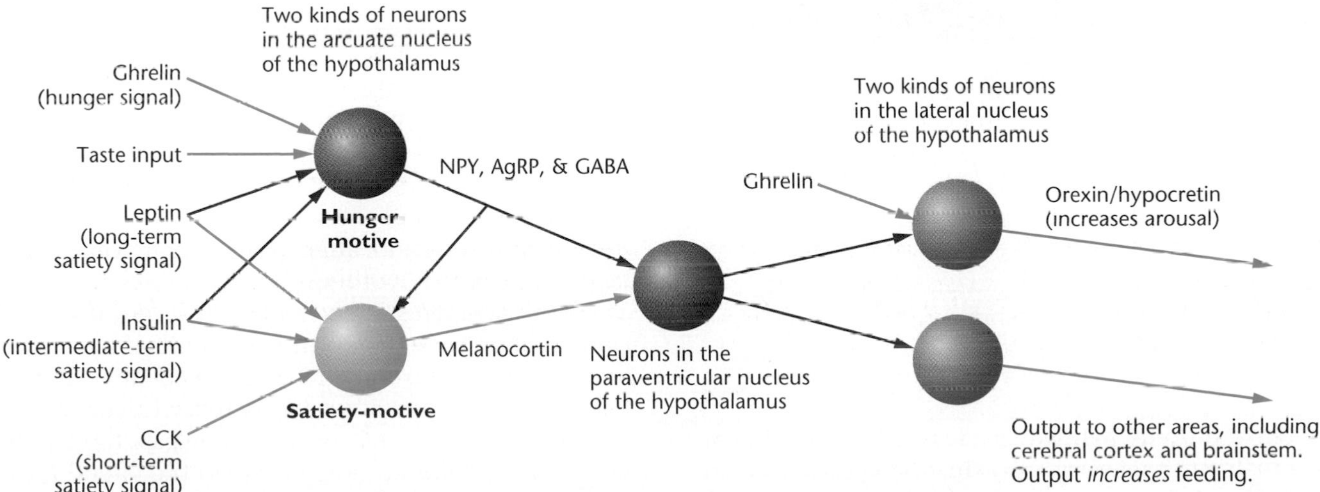

Figure 10.18 Some areas and transmitters of feeding
Hunger signals increase feeding by inhibiting the paraventricular nucleus, which inhibits the lateral hypothalamus. *(Source: Based on reviews by Horvath, 2005, and Minokoshi et al., 2004)*

Axons from the satiety-sensitive cells of the arcuate nucleus deliver an excitatory message to the paraventricular nucleus, releasing the transmitter α-melanocyte stimulating hormone (αMSH), which is a type of chemical called a **melanocortin** (Ellacott & Cone, 2004). People who have deficiencies in their melanocortin receptors fail to respond to satiety signals and consequently overeat.

Input from the hunger-sensitive neurons of the arcuate nucleus is inhibitory to both the paraventricular nucleus and the satiety-sensitive cells of the arcuate nucleus itself. The inhibitory transmitters here are a combination of GABA (the brain's main inhibitory transmitter) and two others that are used mainly in the feeding circuit: **neuropeptide Y (NPY)** (Stephens et al., 1995) and **agouti-related peptide (AgRP)** (Kas et al., 2004). Activity of these transmitters blocks the satiety actions of the paraventricular nucleus, in some cases provoking extreme overeating, as tastelessly illustrated in Figure 10.19 (Billington & Levine, 1992; Leibowitz & Alexander, 1991; Morley, Levine, Grace, & Kneip, 1985).

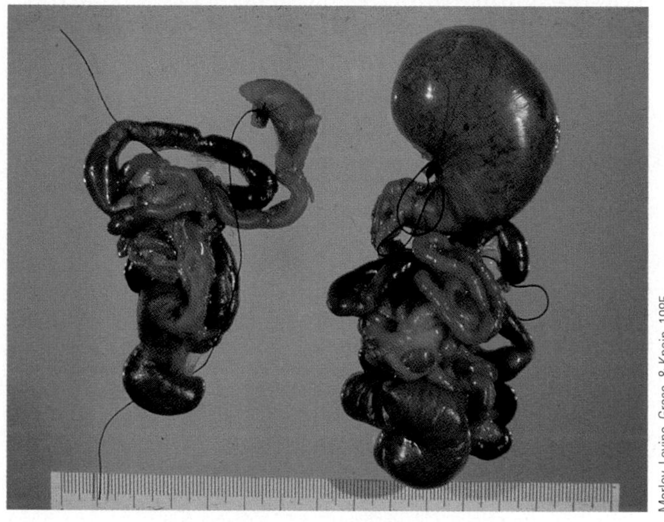

Morley, Levine, Grace, & Kneip, 1985

Figure 10.19 The effects of inhibiting the paraventricular nucleus of the hypothalamus
On the left is the digestive system of a normal rat. On the right is the digestive system of a rat that has had its paraventricular hypothalamus inhibited by injections of peptide YY, a neurotransmitter closely related to neuropeptide Y. The rat continued eating even though its stomach and intestines distended almost to the point of bursting. (All right, I admit this is a little bit disgusting.)

An additional pathway leads to cells in the lateral hypothalamus that release orexin, also known as hypocretin (Fu, Acuna-Goycolea, & van den Pol, 2004). We encountered these neurons in Chapter 9 because a deficiency of orexin leads to narcolepsy. Orexin stimulates activity and the onset of meals. However, its role in feeding is limited, as these cells increase their release of orexin only after prolonged periods of food deprivation (Williams, Cai, Elliott, & Harrold, 2004). That is, orexin motivates a near-starving animal to search for food, but it has little influence on most meals.

In addition to the chemicals in Figure 10.18, several others contribute to the control of appetite. One consequence of control by so many chemicals is that the control of feeding can go wrong in many ways. However, when an error occurs in one way, the brain has many other mechanisms to compensate for it. A closely related point is that researchers could develop drugs to control appetite by working on many routes—leptin, insulin, NPY, and so forth—but changing any one circuit might be ineffective because of compensations by the others. At present, one of the most promising hopes for drug researchers is the melanocortin receptors. As shown in Figure 10.18, many kinds of input converge onto the cells of the arcuate nucleus, but the input to the paraventricular nucleus is more limited. Insulin, diet drugs, and other procedures that affect eating produce their effects largely by altering input to the melanocortin receptors (Benoit et al., 2002; Heisler et al., 2002).

STOP & CHECK

8. Why are leptin injections probably less helpful for overweight people than for obese mice?
9. What would be the effect on eating of a drug that blocks NPY receptors? One that blocks CCK receptors?

Check your answers on page 321.

The Lateral Hypothalamus

Output from the paraventricular nucleus acts on the **lateral hypothalamus,** which includes so many neuron clusters and passing axons that that it has been compared to a crowded train station (Leibowitz & Hoebel, 1998) (Figure 10.20). The lateral hypothalamus controls insulin secretion, alters taste responsiveness, and facilitates feeding in other ways. An animal with damage in this area refuses food and water, averting its head as if the food were distasteful. The animal may starve to death unless it is force-fed, but if kept alive, it gradually recovers much of its ability to eat (Figure 10.21).

Many axons containing dopamine pass through the lateral hypothalamus, so damage to the lateral hypothalamus interrupts these fibers. To separate the roles of hypothalamic cells from those of passing fibers, experimenters used chemicals that damage only the cell bodies, or induced lesions in very young rats, before the dopamine axons reached the lateral hypothalamus. The result was a major loss of feeding without loss of arousal and activity (Almli, Fisher, & Hill, 1979; Grossman, Dacey, Halaris, Collier, & Routtenberg, 1978; Stricker, Swerdloff, & Zigmond, 1978).

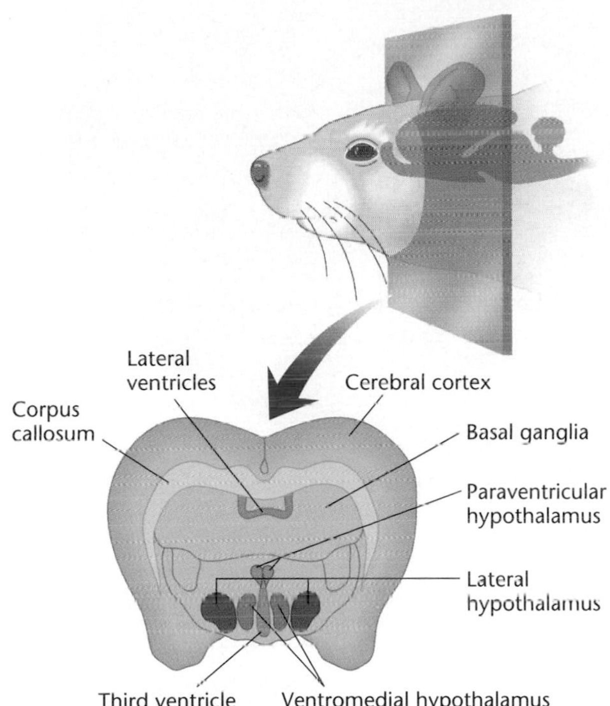

Figure 10.20 The lateral hypothalamus, ventromedial hypothalamus, and paraventricular hypothalamus
The side view above indicates the plane of the coronal section of the brain below. *(Source: After Hart, 1976)*

The question remains: *How* does the lateral hypothalamus contribute to feeding? It contributes in several ways (Leibowitz & Hoebel, 1998) (Figure 10.22):

- Axons from the lateral hypothalamus to the NTS (nucleus of the tractus solitarius), part of the taste pathway (see p. 219), alter the taste sensation and the salivation response to the tastes. In short, when the lateral hypothalamus detects hunger, it sends messages to make the food taste better.
- Axons from the lateral hypothalamus extend into several parts of the cerebral cortex, facilitating ingestion and swallowing and causing cortical cells to increase their response to the taste, smell, or sight of food (Critchley & Rolls, 1996).
- The lateral hypothalamus increases the pituitary gland's secretion of hormones that increase insulin secretion.
- The lateral hypothalamus sends axons to the spinal cord, controlling autonomic responses such as digestive secretions (van den Pol, 1999). An animal with damage to the lateral hypothalamus has trouble digesting its foods.

Medial Areas of the Hypothalamus

Neuroscientists have known since the 1940s that a large lesion centered on the **ventromedial hypothalamus (VMH)** leads to overeating and weight gain (see Figure 10.20). Some people with a tumor in that area have gained more than 10 kg (22 lb) per month (Al-Rashid, 1971; Killeffer & Stern, 1970; Reeves & Plum, 1969). Rats with similar damage sometimes double or triple their weight (Figure 10.23). Eventually, body weight

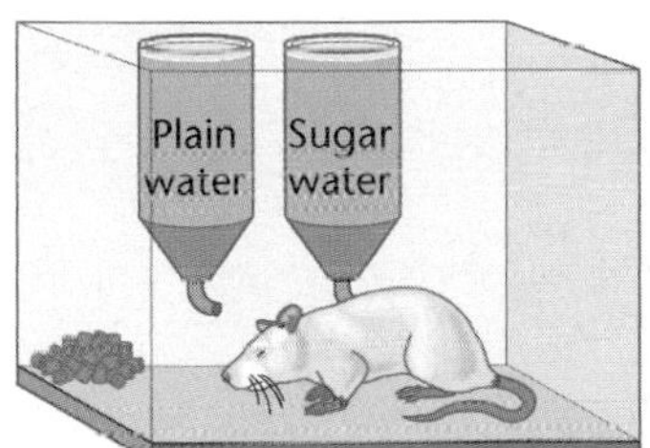

Stage 1. *Aphagia and adipsia.* Rat refuses all food and drink; must be force-fed to keep it alive.

Stage 2. *Anorexia.* Rat eats a small amount of palatable foods and drinks sweetened water. It still does not eat enough to stay alive.

Stage 3. *Adipsia.* The rat eats enough to stay alive, though at a lower-than-normal body weight. It still refuses plain water.

Stage 4. *Near-recovery.* The rat eats enough to stay alive, though at a lower-than-normal body weight. It drinks plain water, but only at mealtimes to wash down its food. Under slightly stressful conditions, such as in a cold room, the rat will return to an earlier stage of refusing food and water.

Figure 10.21 Recovery of feeding after damage to the lateral hypothalamus
At first, the rat refuses all food and drink. If kept alive for several weeks or months by force-feeding, it gradually recovers its ability to eat and drink enough to stay alive. However, even at the final stage of recovery, its behavior is not the same as that of normal rats. *(Source: Based on Teitelbaum & Epstein, 1962)*

Figure 10.22 Pathways from the lateral hypothalamus
Axons from the lateral hypothalamus modify activity in several other brain areas, changing the response to taste, facilitating ingestion and swallowing, and increasing food-seeking behaviors. Also (not shown), the lateral hypothalamus controls stomach secretions.

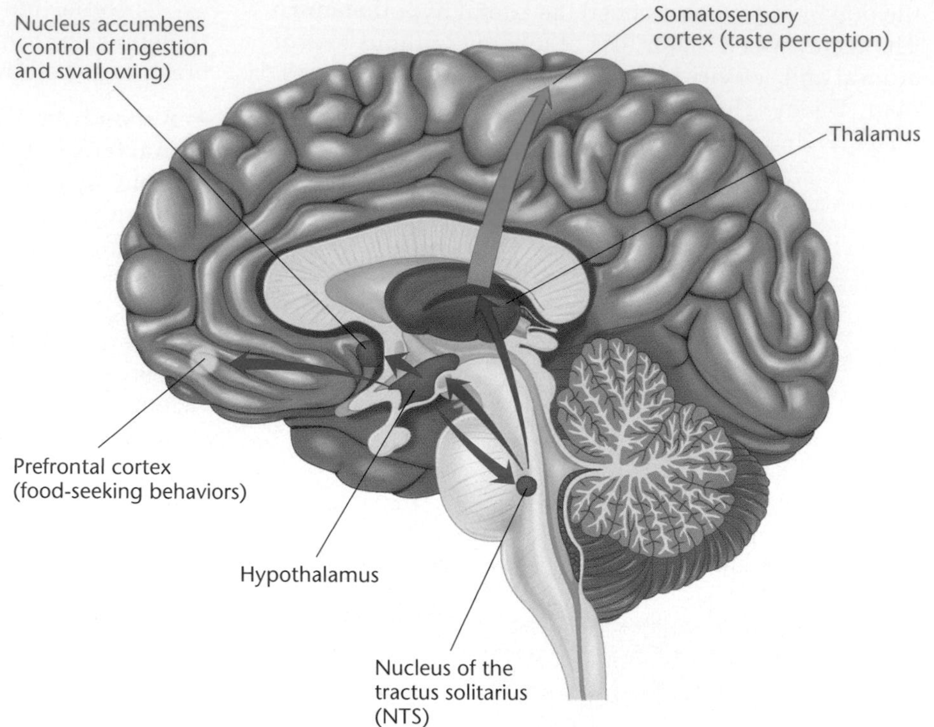

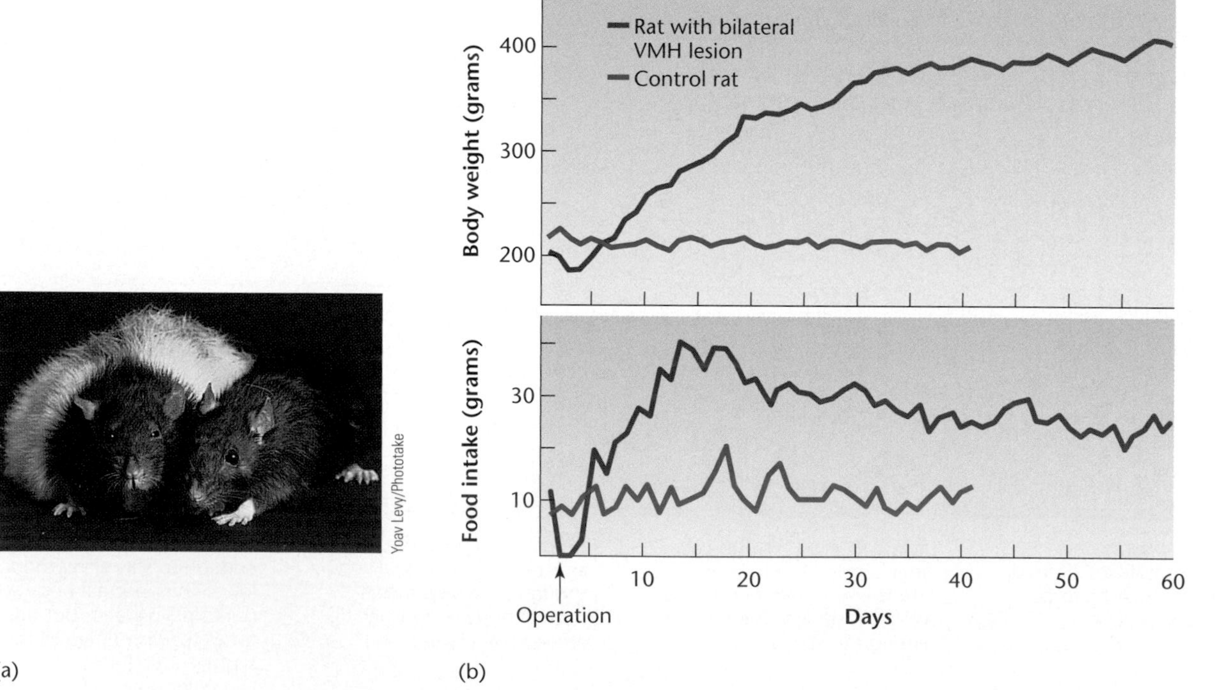

Figure 10.23 The effects of damage to the ventromedial hypothalamus
(a) On the right is a normal rat. On the left is a rat after damage to the ventromedial hypothalamus. The brain-damaged rat may weigh up to three times as much as a normal rat. **(b)** Changes in weight and eating in a rat after damage to the ventromedial hypothalamus. Within a few days after the operation, the rat begins eating much more than normal. As it gains weight, its eating decreases, although it remains above normal.
(Source: (b) Reprinted by permission of the University of Nebraska Press from "Disturbances in feeding and drinking behavior after hypothalamic lesions," by T. Teitelbaum, pp. 39–69, in M. R. Jones, Ed., 1961, Nebraska Symposium on Motivation. *Copyright © 1961 by the University of Nebraska Press. Copyright © renewed 1988 by the University of Nebraska Press.)*

levels off at a stable but high set point, and total food intake declines to nearly normal levels.

Although these symptoms have been known as the *ventromedial hypothalamic syndrome,* damage limited to the ventromedial hypothalamus does not consistently increase eating or body weight. To produce a large effect, the lesion must extend outside the ventromedial nucleus to invade nearby axons, especially the ventral noradrenergic bundle (Figure 10.24) (Ahlskog & Hoebel, 1973; Ahlskog, Randall, & Hoebel, 1975; Gold, 1973).

Rats with damage in and around the ventromedial hypothalamus show an increased appetite compared to undamaged rats of the same weight (Peters, Sensenig, & Reich, 1973). After they gain much weight, they become finicky eaters. If their diet is bitter or otherwise untasty, they eat less than normal. However, with a sweetened diet, they eat far more than normal (Ferguson & Keesey, 1975; Teitelbaum, 1955). Recall that rats with damage to the paraventricular nucleus eat large meals. In contrast, those with damage in the ventromedial area eat normal-sized but unusually frequent meals (Hoebel & Hernandez, 1993). One reason is that they have increased stomach motility and secretions, and their stomachs empty faster than normal. The faster the stomach empties, the sooner the animal is ready for its next meal. Another reason for their frequent meals is that the damage increases insulin production (King, Smith, & Frohman, 1984), so much of each meal is stored as fat. If animals with this kind of damage are prevented from overeating, they gain weight anyway! According to Mark Friedman and Edward Stricker (1976), the problem is not that the rat gets fat from overeating; rather, the rat overeats because it is storing so much fat. The high insulin levels keep moving blood glucose into storage, even when the blood glucose level is low.

Table 10.2 summarizes the effects of lesions in several areas of the hypothalamus.

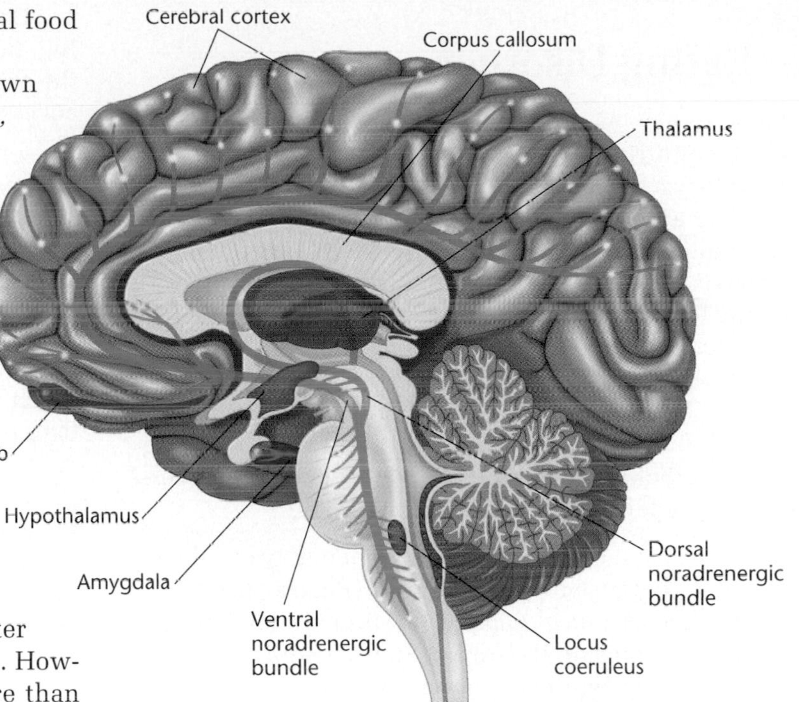

Figure 10.24 Major norepinephrine pathways in the human brain
Damage to the ventral noradrenergic bundle leads to overeating and weight gain. *(Source: Based on Valzelli, 1980)*

STOP & CHECK

10. In what ways does the lateral hypothalamus facilitate feeding?
11. In what way does eating increase after damage in and around the ventromedial hypothalamus? After damage to the paraventricular nucleus?

Check your answers on pages 321–322.

Table 10.2 Effects of Lesions in Certain Hypothalamic Areas

Hypothalamic Area	Effect of Lesion
Preoptic area	Deficit in physiological mechanisms of temperature regulation
Lateral preoptic area	Deficit in osmotic thirst due partly to damage to cells and partly to interruption of passing axons
Lateral hypothalamus	Undereating, weight loss, low insulin level (because of damage to cell bodies); underarousal, underresponsiveness (because of damage to passing axons)
Ventromedial hypothalamus	Increased meal frequency, weight gain, high insulin level
Paraventricular nucleus	Increased meal size, especially increased carbohydrate intake during the first meal of the active period of the day

Eating Disorders

Obesity has become a serious problem in more and more countries, as people become wealthy enough to afford large quantities of tasty foods. Simultaneously, smaller but still significant numbers of people suffer from anorexia, in which they refuse to eat enough to survive, and bulimia, in which they alternate between eating too much and eating too little. Evidently, our homeostatic or allostatic mechanisms are not fully doing their job.

We shall consider possible biological contributors to eating disorders, but let's start by acknowledging some of the important social and cultural influences. Here are a few examples (de Castro, 2000):

- People eat more in groups than when they eat alone, largely because meals last longer (Figure 10.25).
- The size of a meal depends on time of day and the local customs. In the United States, people eat more in the evening than at noon; in France, people eat more at noon than at night.
- Americans eat more if they think a food is "low-fat," even if in fact it isn't.
- If people drink an alcoholic beverage with a meal, they eat the same amount as usual, failing to compensate for the calories in the beverage.

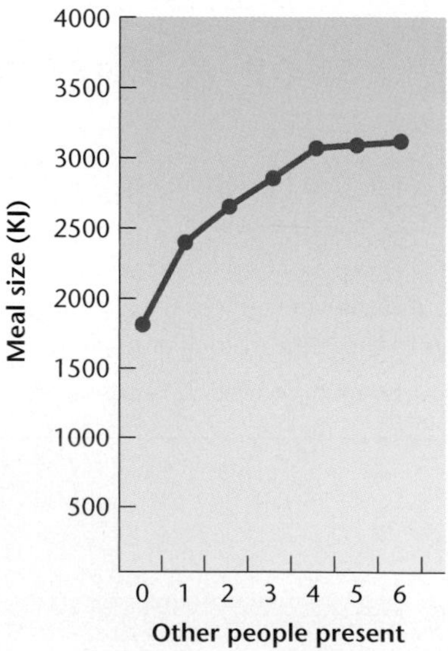

Figure 10.25 Eating in social settings
On the average, the more other people are present during a meal, the more food one is likely to eat. Meal size is expressed in kilojoules. One kilojoule = approximately 1/4 calorie. *(Source: Reprinted from* Nutrition, 16, *J. M. de Castro, "Eating behavior: Lessons from the real world of humans," pp. 800–813, copyright 2000, with permission from Elsevier Science)*

Despite the obviously huge effects of culture on eating, not everyone within the same culture develops the same eating pattern or weight. Some of the differences among people relate to their biology.

Genetics and Body Weight

You have probably noticed that most thin parents have thin children, and most heavy parents have heavy children. The resemblance relates to both the family's food choices and their genetics. A Danish study found that the weights of 540 adopted children correlated much more strongly with that of their biological relatives than with that of their adoptive relatives (Stunkard et al., 1986). Another study found that mildly obese people spent more time sitting, and less time moving about, both while they were obese and after they had lost weight (J. A. Levine et al., 2005). Evidently, their sedentary habits were a lifelong trait, presumably genetic in origin, rather than a reaction to being overweight.

In some cases, obesity can be traced to the effects of a single gene. The most common of these is a mutated gene for the receptor to melanocortin, one of the neuropeptides responsible for hunger (p. 313). People with a mutation in that gene overeat and become obese from childhood onward (Mergen, Mergen, Ozata, Oner, & Oner, 2001). However, only about 5% of obese people have that genetic problem.

Prader-Willi syndrome is a genetic condition marked by mental retardation, short stature, and obesity. People with this syndrome have blood levels of ghrelin four to five times higher than average (Cummings et al., 2002). Ghrelin, you will recall (p. 313), is a peptide related to food deprivation. Eating causes a decrease in ghrelin, and most obese people have low ghrelin levels. The fact that people with Prader-Willi syndrome overeat and still produce high ghrelin levels suggests that their problem relates to an inability to turn off ghrelin release.

A few other genes have been linked to obesity, but they are even less common (Farooqi & O'Rahilly, 2004). In more numerous cases, we have evidence for a genetic influence, though without the identification of a particular gene. For example, monozygotic twins resemble each other more than dizygotic twins do with regard to how much stomach distension is needed to end a meal, whether they prefer to eat big breakfasts or big dinners, how much they overeat when the food tastes great, and how much they overeat when in a big friendly group (de Castro, 2002; de Castro & Plunkett, 2002). Such differences probably reflect the influence of many genes, each with a small or indirect influence.

In some cases, the effect of a gene depends on the environment. Consider the Native American Pimas of Arizona and Mexico. Most are seriously overweight, apparently because of several genes (Norman et al., 1998). However, few of them were obese in the early 1900s. At that time, they ate mostly the plants of the Sonoran desert, which ripen only in brief seasons. The Pimas apparently evolved an eating strategy like bears: Eat all you can when food is available because it will have to carry you through a period of scarcity. They also evolved a tendency to conserve energy by limiting their activity. Now, with a more typical U.S. diet that is equally available at all times, the strategy of overeating and inactivity is maladaptive. In short, their weight depends on the combination of genes and environment; neither one by itself would have this effect.

Obesity has become common throughout the United States and increasingly in other countries as well, and the problem has increased sharply since the early 1970s. What might have caused this trend? Hypotheses include an inactive lifestyle, increased eating at fast-food restaurants, and increased portion sizes at restaurants (especially all-you-can-eat buffets). Another hypothesis is that the obesity relates to a change in soft drinks. Before about 1970, they were sweetened with sucrose or glucose, which are two kinds of sugar. Around 1970, manufacturers started using high-fructose corn syrup, which is today the principal sweetener for soft drinks and many other products. Fructose, also a sugar, tastes sweeter than sucrose or glucose, so using it makes drinks sweeter without adding calories. However, when fructose is present in large amounts, the body stores it as fat instead of using it for immediate needs. Also, the metabolism of fructose does not increase insulin or leptin release nearly as much as sucrose and glucose do (Teff et al., 2004). Therefore, it does not trigger satiety. For this combination of reasons, people consuming high-fructose corn syrup tend to overeat and gain weight (Bray, Nielsen, & Popkin, 2004).

Weight-Loss Techniques

Losing weight permanently is like quitting smoking, quitting alcohol, or breaking any other strong habit: It is difficult, more people try than succeed, but it can be done.

A survey found that weight-loss specialists agreed on little, except that almost any weight-loss plan should include increased exercise (M. B. Schwartz & Brownell, 1995). Exercise by itself won't trim much weight. For example, walking 4.5 km (a little less than 3 mi) expends about the energy equivalent of a handful of potato chips (Burton, 1994). However, exercise in combination with decreased eating can be effective. Furthermore, exercise lowers blood pressure, lowers cholesterol levels, and improves health, which is the ultimate goal, anyway (Campfield, Smith, & Burn, 1998).

Weight loss requires the habit of stopping a meal even when one is still enjoying it. One difficulty is that many high-calorie foods taste *very* good, especially foods with a combination of fats and carbohydrates, such as cake icing. Low-carbohydrate diets (e.g., the Atkins diet) and low-fat diets are both somewhat successful for helping people lose weight, possibly because both steer people away from fat-carbohydrate combinations (Volkow & Wise, 2005).

Some people benefit from appetite-suppressant drugs. For years, the most effective combination was "fen-phen": *Fenfluramine* increases the release of serotonin and blocks its reuptake. *Phentermine* blocks reuptake of norepinephrine and dopamine and therefore prolongs their activity. The fen-phen combination produces brain effects similar to those of a completed meal (Rada & Hoebel, 2000). Unfortunately, fenfluramine often produces medical complications, so it has been withdrawn from use. A replacement drug, *sibutramine* (Meridia), which blocks reuptake of serotonin and norepinephrine, decreases meal size and binge eating (Appolinario et al., 2003). Another drug, *orlistat* (Xenical), prevents the intestines from absorbing fats. However, a user may suffer intestinal discomfort from the large globs of undigested fats, and the bowel movements are also thick with fat. Both sibutramine and olistat produce about a 5% loss of body weight in most users. Pharmaceutical companies continue to do research for new weight-loss drugs, including some that bind to receptors for melanocortin, NPY, leptin, and other hormones and transmitters (Jandacek & Woods, 2004).

Anorexia Nervosa

Inadequate eating is less common than obesity but also dangerous. People with **anorexia nervosa** are unwilling to eat as much as they need; they therefore become extremely thin and in some cases die. About 0.3% of women in their teens or early 20s have anorexia nervosa. The prevalence is about one-tenth as high in young men, and the prevalence drops for both men and women as they grow older (Hoek & van Hoeken, 2003). A genetic predisposition is likely (Grice et al., 2002), although the relationship between the gene and the behavior is not clearly established.

People with anorexia are often interested in food; many enjoy cooking and the taste and smell of food. Their problem is not a lack of appetite but a fear of becoming fat or of losing self-control. Most people with anorexia are hardworking perfectionists who are amazingly active, unlike other people on the verge of starvation.

The causes of anorexia nervosa are poorly understood. People with this condition have many biochemical abnormalities in both their blood and brain, but those are probably the result of weight loss and not the cause, as they return to normal levels after the person regains weight (Ferguson & Pigott, 2000). One fascinating speculation compares anorexia to elk and other large mammals when they migrate long distances in search of a better feeding ground. During the migration, they are highly active, and they refuse all food, even when they find a small patch of grass. Conceivably, anorexia may occur when a combination of exercise and dieting triggers the same kind of mechanism in the human brain (Guisinger, 2003). Obviously, this hypothesis raises at least as many questions as it answers, but it might be a useful guide to further research.

For further information about anorexia, visit this website: **http://www.mentalhealth.com/dis/p20-et01.html**

Bulimia Nervosa

Bulimia nervosa is a condition in which people (again, mostly women) alternate between extreme dieting and binges of overeating. Some (not all) force themselves to vomit after huge meals. Repeated overeating and vomiting can endanger one's health. On the average, people with bulimia have decreased release of CCK, increased release of ghrelin, and alterations of several other hormones and transmitters associated with feeding (Jimerson & Wolfe, 2004). However, as with anorexia, these trends may be results of eating disorders rather than the causes of them.

One analysis of bulimia compares it to drug addiction (Hoebel, Rada, Mark, & Pothos, 1999). Eating tasty foods activates the same brain areas as addictive drugs. Drug addicts who cannot get drugs sometimes overeat as a substitute, and food-deprived people or animals become more likely than others to use drugs. A cycle of food deprivation followed by overeating strongly stimulates the brain's reinforcement areas in much the same way that drug deprivation followed by drug use does. Researchers examined rats that were food deprived for 12 hours a day, including the first 4 hours of their wakeful period, and then offered a solution of 25% glucose—a very sweet, syrupy liquid. Over several weeks on this regimen, the rats drank more and more each day and especially increased how much they drank in the first hour. The eating released dopamine and opiatelike compounds in the brain, similar to the effects of highly addicting drugs (Colantuoni et al., 2001, 2002). It also increased the levels of dopamine type 3 receptors in the brain—again, a trend resembling that of rats that received morphine (Spangler et al., 2004). If they were then deprived of this liquid, they showed withdrawal symptoms, including head shaking and teeth chattering, which could be relieved by an injection of morphine. In other words, they had developed a sugar dependence or addiction. Similarly, it is possible that bulimic cycles of dieting and binge eating may constitute a kind of addiction (Hoebel, Rada, Mark, & Pothos, 1999). Note the difficulty of quitting this kind of addiction. Someone addicted to heroin or alcohol can try to quit altogether (a difficult task). Someone addicted to bulimia cannot quit eating. The goal is to learn to eat in moderation. Imagine, by analogy, the extreme difficulty for an alcoholic or heroin addict to try to use those substances in moderation.

STOP & CHECK

12. Why is it plausible that consuming beverages with high-fructose corn syrup might lead to obesity?
13. Researchers have found many abnormalities of brain chemistry in people with anorexia nervosa or bulimia nervosa. Why do they *not* believe these abnormalities cause anorexia or bulimia?
14. What evidence from rats suggests that bulimia resembles an addiction?

Check your answers on page 322.

Module 10.3
In Closing: The Multiple Controls of Hunger

Eating is controlled by many brain areas, which monitor blood glucose, stomach distention, duodenal contents, body weight, fat cells, and more. Because the system is so complex, it can produce errors in many ways. However, the complexity of the system also provides a kind of security: If one part of the system makes a mistake, another part can counteract it. We notice people who choose a poor diet or eat the wrong amount. Perhaps we should be even more impressed by how many people eat more or less appropriately. The regulation of eating succeeds not in spite of its complexity but because of it.

Summary

1. The ability to digest a food is one major determinant of preference for that food. For example, people who cannot digest lactose generally do not like to eat dairy products. (p. 308)
2. Other major determinants of food selection include innate preferences for certain tastes, a preference for familiar foods, and learned consequences of foods. (p. 308)
3. People and animals eat partly for the sake of taste. However, a sham-feeding animal, which tastes its foods but does not absorb them, eats far more than normal. (p. 309)

4. Factors controlling hunger include distension of the stomach and intestines, secretion of CCK by the duodenum, and the availability of glucose and other nutrients to the cells. (p. 310)
5. The hormone insulin increases the entry of glucose to the cells, including cells that store nutrients for future use. Glucagon mobilizes stored fuel and converts it to glucose in the blood. Thus, the combined influence of insulin and glucagon determines how much glucose is available at any time. (p. 310)
6. Fat cells produce a protein called leptin, which provides the brain with a signal about weight loss or gain and therefore corrects day-to-day errors in the amount of feeding. Deficiency of leptin production leads to obesity and inactivity. However, leptin deficiency is an extremely rare condition among humans. (p. 312)
7. The arcuate nucleus of the hypothalamus receives signals of both hunger and satiety. Good-tasting foods and the transmitter ghrelin stimulate neurons that promote hunger. Leptin, insulin, and CCK stimulate neurons that promote satiety. (p. 313)
8. Axons from the two kinds of neurons in the arcuate nucleus send competing messages to the paraventricular nucleus, releasing transmitters that are specific to the feeding system—NPY, agouti-related peptide, and α MSH. The paraventricular nucleus inhibits the lateral nucleus of the hypothalamus, which ordinarily stimulates eating. (p. 313)
9. The lateral nucleus of the hypothalamus facilitates feeding by axons that enhance taste responses elsewhere in the brain and increase the release of insulin and digestive juices. (p. 314)
10. The ventromedial nucleus of the hypothalamus, and especially the axons passing by it, influence eating by regulating stomach emptying time and insulin secretion. Animals with damage in this area eat more frequently than normal because they store much of each meal as fat and then fail to mobilize their stored fats for current use. (p. 315)
11. Obesity is partly under genetic control, although no single gene accounts for more than 5% of all cases of obesity. The effects of genes depend on what foods are available. People tend to overeat when extremely palatable foods are available, especially those containing both fats and carbohydrates. (p. 318)
12. Anorexia nervosa is a condition in which people refuse to eat or fear to eat. Its causes are not yet understood. (p. 319)
13. Bulimia nervosa is characterized by alternation between undereating and overeating. It has been compared to addictive behaviors, especially to the effects of abstaining from a drug and then returning to it. (p. 320)

Answers to STOP & CHECK Questions

1. Most Southeast Asian adults lack the digestive enzyme lactase, which is needed to metabolize the sugar in milk. (p. 309)
2. When animals sham-feed (and the food leaks out of their digestive system), they chew and taste their food but do not become satiated. (p. 310)
3. If a cuff is attached to the junction between the stomach and duodenum so that food cannot leave the stomach, an animal becomes satiated when the stomach is full. (p. 310)
4. Ordinarily, an animal stops a meal without filling the stomach. It stops eating when some food is in the stomach and some has already passed to the duodenum, distending it. (p. 310)
5. When the duodenum is distended, it releases CCK, which closes the sphincter muscle between the stomach and duodenum. CCK therefore increases the rate at which the stomach distends. Also, neural signals from the intestines cause certain cells in the hypothalamus to release CCK as a neurotransmitter, and at its receptors, it triggers decreased feeding. (p. 310)
6. Those with very low levels, as in diabetes, cannot get glucose to enter their cells, and therefore, they are constantly hungry. They pass much of their nutrition in the urine and feces. Those with constantly high levels deposit much of their glucose into fat and glycogen, so within a short time after a meal, the supply of glucose drops. (p. 312)
7. When glucagon levels rise, stored glycogen is converted to glucose, which enters the blood. If insulin levels are high also, the glucose entering the blood is free to enter all the cells. So the result would be decreased appetite. (p. 312)
8. Unlike obese mice, nearly all overweight people produce leptin in proportion to body fat; however, they are apparently insensitive to it. Also, very large amounts of leptin can induce diabetes. (p. 314)
9. A drug that blocks NPY receptors would decrease feeding. A drug that blocks CCK receptors would increase feeding. (p. 314)
10. Activity of the lateral hypothalamus improves taste, enhances cortical responses to food, and increases secretions of insulin and digestive juices. (p. 317)

11. Animals with damage to the ventromedial hypothalamus eat more frequent meals. Animals with damage to the paraventricular nucleus of the hypothalamus eat larger meals. (p. 317)
12. When the body has much fructose, it stores it as fat instead of using it for its immediate needs. Also, fructose is less effective than other sugars at stimulating the release of insulin and leptin, which promote satiety. (p. 320)
13. When people recover from anorexia or bulimia, the brain chemistry returns to normal levels. (p. 320)
14. Rats that alternated between food deprivation and a very sweet diet gradually ate more and more of it, and they reacted to deprivation of the sweet diet with head-shaking and teeth-chattering, like the symptoms of morphine withdrawal. (p. 320)

Thought Question

For most people, insulin levels tend to be higher during the day than at night. Use this fact to explain why people grow hungry a few hours after a daytime meal but not so quickly at night.

Chapter Ending

Key Terms and Activities

Terms

agouti-related peptide (AgRP) (p. 314)
aldosterone (p. 305)
allostasis (p. 297)
angiotensin II (p. 305)
anorexia nervosa (p. 319)
arcuate nucleus (p. 313)
basal metabolism (p. 297)
bulimia nervosa (p. 320)
carnivore (p. 308)
cholecystokinin (CCK) (p. 310)
conditioned taste aversion (p. 308)
cytokines (p. 301)
duodenum (p. 310)
ghrelin (p. 313)
glucagon (p. 310)
herbivore (p. 308)
homeostasis (p. 297)
homeothermic (p. 297)
hypovolemic thirst (p. 305)
insulin (p. 310)
lactase (p. 308)
lactose (p. 308)
lateral hypothalamus (p. 314)
lateral preoptic area (p. 304)
leptin (p. 312)
melanocortin (p. 314)
negative feedback (p. 297)
neuropeptide Y (NPY) (p. 314)
omnivore (p. 308)
osmotic pressure (p. 303)
osmotic thirst (p. 304)
OVLT (p. 304)
paraventricular nucleus (PVN) (pp. 304, 313)
poikilothermic (p. 297)
preoptic area/anterior hypothalamus (POA/AH) (p. 300)
set point (p. 297)
sham-feeding (p. 310)
sodium-specific hunger (p. 305)
splanchnic nerve (p. 310)
subfornical organ (SFO) (p. 304)
supraoptic nucleus (p. 304)
vagus nerve (p. 310)
vasopressin (also known as antidiuretic hormone, ADH) (p. 303)
ventromedial hypothalamus (VMH) (p. 315)

Suggestions for Further Reading

Gisolfi, C. V., & Mora, F. (2000). *The hot brain: Survival, temperature, and the human body.* Cambridge, MA: MIT Press. Discusses research on temperature regulation.

Stricker, E., & Woods, S. (Eds.). (2004). *Neurobiology of food and fluid intake* (2nd ed.). New York: Kluwer. Collection of scholarly reviews of the literature.

Widmaier, E. P. (1998). *Why geese don't get obese (and we do).* New York: W. H. Freeman. Lighthearted and often entertaining discussion of the physiology of eating, thirst, and temperature regulation.

Websites to Explore

You can go to the Biological Psychology Study Center and click these links. While there, you can also check for suggested articles available on InfoTrac College Edition. The Biological Psychology Internet address is:

http://psychology.wadsworth.com/book/kalatbiopsych9e/

Internet Mental Health: Anorexia Nervosa

http://www.mentalhealth.com/dis/p20-et01.html

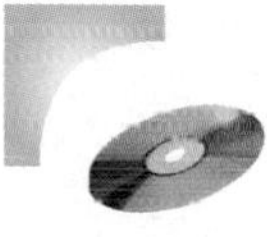

Exploring Biological Psychology CD

Pathways from the Lateral Hypothalamus (animation)
Hypothalamic Control of Feeding (animation)
Anorexia Patient: Susan (video)
Chapter Quiz (multiple-choice questions)
Critical Thinking (essay questions)

ThomsonNOW™

http://www.thomsonedu.com

Go to this site for the link to ThomsonNOW, your one-stop study shop, Take a Pre-Test for this chapter, and ThomsonNOW will generate a Personalized Study Plan based on your test results. The Study Plan will identify the topics you need to review and direct you to online resources to help you master these topics. You can then take a Post-Test to help you determine the concepts you have mastered and what you still need work on.

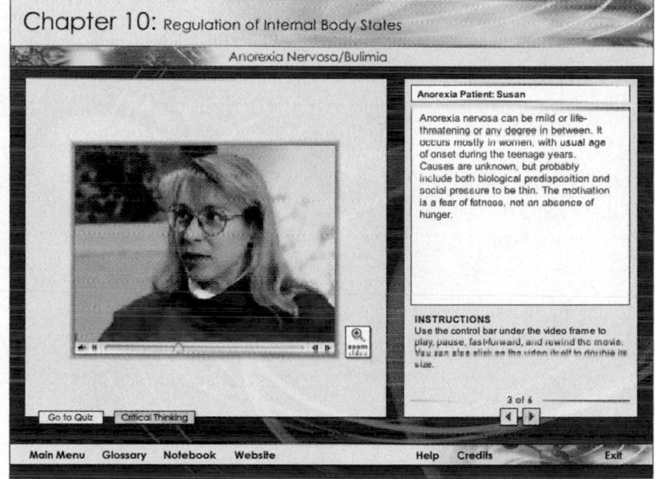

A video interview presents a patient with anorexia nervosa.

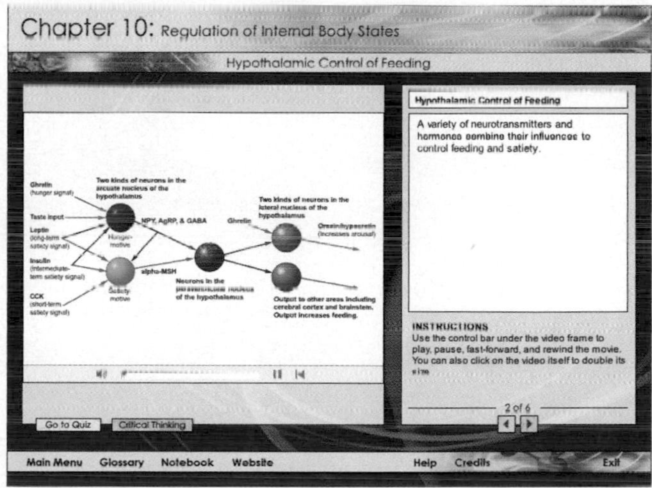

This animation goes through the neurotransmitters of feeding step-by-step.

Reproductive Behaviors

Chapter Outline

Opposite: Humans may be the only species that plans parenthood, but all species have a strong biological drive that can lead to parenthood.
Source: Art Wolfe.

Main Ideas

1. Sex hormones exert organizing and activating effects on the genitals and the brain. Organizing effects occur during an early sensitive period and last indefinitely. Activating effects are transient and may occur at any time.
2. In mammals, organizing effects of hormones influence the external genitals, the hypothalamus, the cerebral cortex, and certain aspects of thinking, including spatial reasoning.
3. Parental behavior depends on both hormones and experience.
4. Much about men's and women's sexual behavior, including mate choice, could be the product of evolutionary selection. However, current data do not enable us to determine how much is built-in and how much is determined by our experiences.
5. Hormones contribute to the development of sexual identity and orientation, although the mechanisms are not yet clear.

What good is sex? Well, yes, I know: We enjoy it. But why did we evolve to reproduce sexually instead of individually? In some species, including one kind of lizard, the female makes an egg with two copies of each chromosome instead of one. She then doesn't have to wait for a male; her egg simply starts dividing and differentiating. In many ways, it would be more efficient if you could reproduce without sex. You wouldn't have to find a mate, and you could make babies that are entirely like yourself, instead of just 50%. We wouldn't go to all the bother of courtship and mating if it didn't provide an advantage.

Biologists are not entirely settled on the advantages of sexual reproduction, and you are welcome to generate your own ideas. Currently, the dominant hypothesis is that sexual reproduction increases variation and thereby enables quick evolutionary adaptations to any change in the environment (Colgreave, 2002; Goddard, Godfray, & Burt, 2005).

In this chapter, we shall consider questions about sexual reproduction that we often ignore or take for granted. We also consider some of the ways in which being male or female influences our behavior.

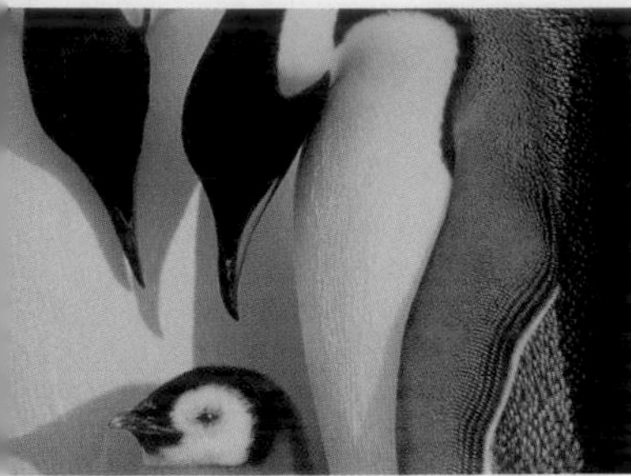

Module 11.1
Sex and Hormones

If you want to tell someone something personal, you say it face to face. If you have a message for everyone—such as the opening of a new store—you place an ad in the newspaper or make an announcement on the radio. The nervous system does its one-to-one communications at synapses. For more widespread messages, it mobilizes hormones.

One class of hormones, the **steroid hormones** contain four carbon rings, as Figure 11.1 shows. Steroids are derived from cholesterol; we are often warned about the risks of excessive cholesterol, but a moderate amount is necessary for generating these important hormones. Steroids exert their effects in three ways (Nadal, Díaz, & Valverde, 2001). First, they bind to membrane receptors, like neurotransmitters. Second, they enter cells and activate certain kinds of proteins in the cytoplasm. Third, they bind to chromosomes where they activate or inactivate specific genes (Figure 11.2).

Backbone of all steroid molecules

CH_2OH, C=O, HO, OH, Cortisol

OH, O, Testosterone (an androgen)

OH, HO, Estradiol (an estrogen)

CH_3, C=O, O, Progesterone

Figure 11.1 Steroid hormones
Note the similarity between the sex hormones testosterone and estradiol.

The "sex hormones"—the estrogens, progesterone, and the androgens—are a special category of steroids, released mostly by the gonads (testes and ovaries) and to a lesser extent by the adrenal glands. We generally refer to the **androgens,** a group that includes testosterone and several others, as "male hormones" because men have higher levels. The **estrogens,** which include **estradiol** and others, are "female hormones" because their level is higher in women. (Androgens and estrogens are categories of chemicals; neither androgen nor estrogen is a specific chemical itself.) However, both sexes have both types of hormones. **Progesterone,** another predominantly female hormone, prepares the uterus for the implantation of a fertilized ovum and promotes the maintenance of pregnancy. Sex hormones affect the brain, the genitals, and other organs.

On the average, male and female bodies differ in many ways, including some differences in the brain. Traditionally, biologists have assumed that all such differences relate to **sex-limited genes,** which are genes that androgens or estrogens activate. Sex-limited genes control most of the differences you see between male and female animals, such as the antlers of male deer. In humans, estrogen activates the genes responsible for breast development in women, and androgen activates the genes responsible for the growth of facial hair in men. Within the brain, sex hormones increase or decrease the rate of apoptosis (cell death) in various regions, causing certain areas to be slightly larger in males and others slightly larger in females (Forger et al., 2004; Morris, Jordan, & Breedlove, 2004). However, other mechanisms may be responsible for a few of the sex differences in the brain. At least three genes on the Y chro-

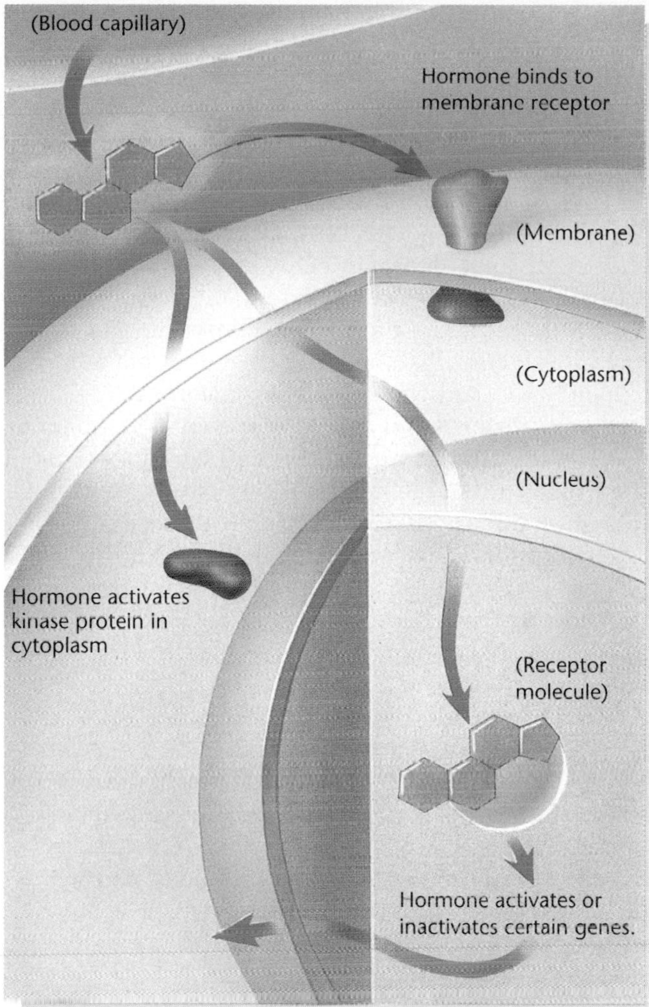

Figure 11.2 Three routes of action for steroid hormones
Steroid hormones such as estrogens and androgens bind to membrane receptors, activate proteins in the cytoplasm, and activate or inactivate specific genes. *(Source: Revised from Starr & Taggart, 1989)*

mosome (found only in men) are active in specific brain areas, and at least one gene on the X chromosome is active only in the female brain. Presumably, these genes have some behavioral consequence, although at present no one knows what the genes do (Arnold, 2004; Carruth, Reisert, & Arnold, 2002; Vawter et al., 2004).

1. How do sex hormones affect neurons?

Check your answer on page 337.

Organizing Effects of Sex Hormones

If we injected estrogens into adult males and androgens into adult females, could we make males act like females and females act like males? Researchers of the 1950s and 1960s, working with a variety of mammals and birds, were surprised to find that the answer was usually *no.* But the same hormones injected early in life have much stronger effects.

We distinguish between the organizing and activating effects of sex hormones. The **organizing effects** of sex hormones occur mostly at a sensitive stage of development—shortly before and after birth in rats and well as before birth in humans—and determine whether the brain and body will develop female or male characteristics. **Activating effects** can occur at any time in life, when a hormone temporarily activates a particular response. Activating effects on an organ may last longer than the hormone remains in an organ, but they do not last indefinitely. The distinction between the two kinds of effects is not absolute; hormones early in life exert temporary effects even while they are organizing body development, and during puberty, hormones can induce long-lasting structural changes as well as activating effects (Arnold & Breedlove, 1985; C. L. Williams, 1986).

Sex Differences in the Gonads

Sexual differentiation begins with the chromosomes. In addition to the autosomal (nonsex) chromosomes, a female mammal has two X chromosomes; a male has an X and a Y. During an early stage of prenatal development in mammals, both male and female have a set of Müllerian ducts and a set of Wolffian ducts, as well as primitive gonads (testes or ovaries). The male's Y chromosome includes the **SRY** (sex-determining region on the Y chromosome) **gene,** which causes the primitive gonads to develop into **testes,** the sperm-producing organs. The developing testes produce the hormone **testosterone** (an androgen), which increases the growth of the testes, causing them to produce more testosterone and so forth. Testosterone also causes the primitive **Wolffian ducts,** which are precursors to other male reproductive structures, to develop into *seminal vesicles* (saclike structures that store semen) and the *vas deferens* (a duct from the testis into the penis). A peptide hormone, *Müllerian inhibiting hormone (MIH),* causes degeneration of the **Müllerian ducts,** precursors to the female's oviducts, uterus, and upper vagina (Graves, 1994). The result of all the testosterone-induced changes is the development of a penis and scrotum. Because typical females are not exposed to high testosterone levels, their gonads develop into **ovaries**, the egg-producing organs. The Wolffian ducts degenerate, and the primitive Müllerian ducts develop and mature. Figure 11.3 shows how the primitive unisex structures develop into male or female external genitals.

Sexual differentiation depends mainly on the level of testosterone during a **sensitive period**, an early period when hormones have long-lasting effects. The human sensitive period for genital formation is about the third and fourth months of pregnancy (Money & Ehrhardt, 1972). In rats, testosterone begins masculinizing the external genitals during the last several days of pregnancy and first few days after birth and then continues at a declining rate for the next month (Bloch & Mills, 1995; Bloch, Mills, & Gale, 1995; Davis, Shryne, & Gorski, 1995; Rhees, Shryne, & Gorski, 1990).

A female rat that is injected with testosterone shortly before or after birth is partly masculinized, just as if her own body had produced the testosterone (I. L. Ward & Ward, 1985). Her clitoris grows larger than normal. At maturity, her pituitary and ovaries produce steady levels of hormones instead of the cycles that are characteristic of females. Anatomically, certain parts of her hypothalamus appear more male than female. Her behavior is also masculinized. She approaches sexually receptive females (Woodson & Balleine, 2002). She mounts them and makes copulatory thrusting movements rather than arching her back and allowing males to mount her. In short, early testosterone promotes the male pattern and inhibits the female pattern (Gorski, 1985; J. D. Wilson, George, & Griffin, 1981).

The anatomy and behavior of a genetic male can develop in the female-typical pattern if he lacks androgen receptors, if he is castrated (deprived of his testes), or if he is exposed to substances that block testosterone effects. Drugs that tend to feminize or demasculinize development include alcohol, marijuana, haloperidol (an antipsychotic drug), and cocaine (Ahmed, Shryne, Gorski, Branch, & Taylor, 1991; Dalterio & Bartke, 1979; Hull et al., 1984; Raum, McGivern, Peterson, Shryne, & Gorski, 1990). To a slight extent, even aspirin interferes with the male pattern of development (Amateau & McCarthy, 2004). Although estradiol does not feminize a male to the same degree that testosterone masculinizes a female, estradiol and several related compounds do produce mild abnormalities and malformations of the prostate gland—the gland that stores sperm and releases it during intercourse. Some of those estradiol-like compounds are now prevalent in the linings of plastic bottles and cans, so almost everyone is exposed to them (Timms, Howdeshell, Barton, Richter, & vom Saal, 2005). In short, male development is a fragile and vulnerable process.

The overall mechanism of early sexual differentiation has been described by saying that nature's "default setting" is to make every mammal a female. Add early testosterone and the individual becomes a male; without testosterone, it develops as a female, regardless of the amount of estradiol or other estrogens. That generalization, however, is an overstatement. A genetic female that lacks estradiol during the early sensitive period develops approximately normal female external anatomy but does not develop normal sexual behav-

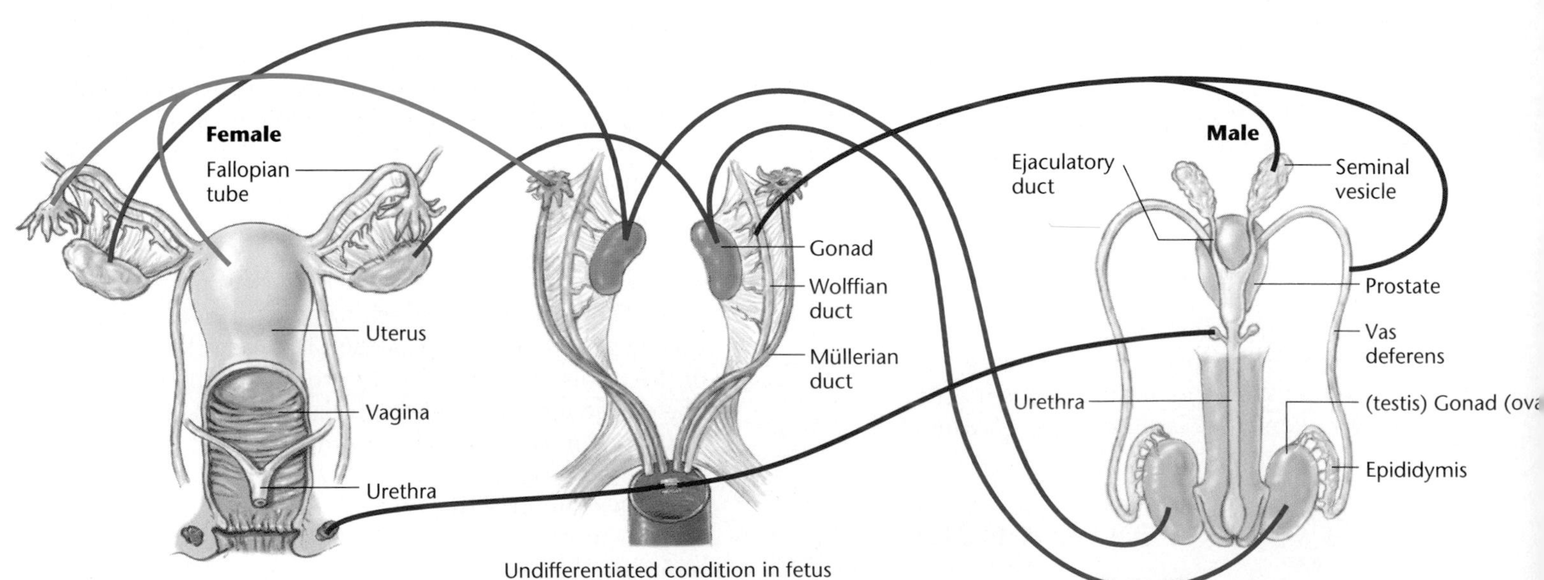

Figure 11.3 Differentiation of human genitals
The male's SRY gene causes the gonad to become a testis, and the testis produces testosterone, which masculinizes development. In the absence of testosterone, development follows the female pattern. *(Source: Based on Netter, 1983)*

ior. Even if she is given estradiol injections as an adult, she shows little sexual response toward either male or female partners (Bakker, Honda, Harada, & Balthazart, 2002). So estradiol contributes to female development, including some aspects of brain differentiation.

Sex Differences in the Hypothalamus

In addition to controlling differences in the external genitals, sex hormones early in life bind to receptors in specific areas of the hypothalamus, amygdala, and other brain areas (Shah et al., 2004). The hormones thereby induce both anatomical and physiological differences between the sexes. For example, one area in the anterior hypothalamus, known as the **sexually dimorphic nucleus,** is larger in the male than in the female and contributes to control of male sexual behavior. Parts of the female hypothalamus can generate a cyclic pattern of hormone release, as in the human menstrual cycle. The male hypothalamus cannot, and neither can the hypothalamus of a female who was exposed to extra testosterone early in life. Typical female rats have a characteristic way of holding food and dodging from other rats that might try to take it away. A female rat that was either deprived of estrogens or exposed to extra testosterone in infancy pivots around the midpoint of her trunk, like males, instead of around her pelvis, like other females (Field, Whishaw, Forgie, & Pellis, 2004).

In rodents—the mechanism in humans is less certain—testosterone exerts much of its organizing effect on the hypothalamus through a surprising route. After it enters a neuron in early development, it is converted to estradiol! Testosterone and estradiol are chemically very similar, as you can see in Figure 11.1 (p. 326). In organic chemistry, a ring of six carbon atoms containing three double bonds is an *aromatic* compound. An enzyme found in the brain can *aromatize* testosterone into estradiol. Other androgens that cannot be aromatized into estrogens are less effective in masculinizing the hypothalamus. Drugs that prevent testosterone from being aromatized to estradiol block some of the organizing effects of testosterone on sexual development and thereby permanently impair male sexual behavior and fertility (Gerardin & Pereira, 2002; Rochira et al., 2001).

Why, then, is the female rodent not masculinized by her own estradiol? During the early sensitive period, immature mammals of many species have in their bloodstream a protein called **alpha-fetoprotein,** which is not present in adults (Gorski, 1980; MacLusky & Naftolin, 1981). Alpha-fetoprotein binds with estrogen and blocks it from leaving the bloodstream and entering the cells that are developing in this early period. Because testosterone does not bind to alpha-fetoprotein, it freely enters the cells, where enzymes convert it into estradiol. That is, testosterone is a way of getting estradiol into the cells when estradiol itself cannot leave the blood.

This explanation of testosterone's effects makes sense of an otherwise puzzling fact: Injecting a large amount of estradiol actually masculinizes a female rodent's development. The reason is that normal amounts are bound to alpha-fetoprotein, but a larger amount exceeds the capacity of alpha-fetoprotein and therefore enters the cells and masculinizes them.

Sex Differences in the Cerebral Cortex and Cognition

Early hormones also influence the cerebral cortex, controlling the relative rates of apoptosis in different areas. For example, some areas are proportionately larger in men, and others are proportionately larger in women (J. M. Goldstein et al., 2001; Nopoulos, Flaum, O'Leary, & Andreasen, 2000). Men tend to have more white matter than women (Allen, Damasio, Grabowski, Bruss, & Zhang, 2003). Women on the average have a greater density of neurons in part of the temporal lobe that is important for language (Witelson, Glezer, & Kigar, 1995). The language-related areas are larger in the left than right hemisphere for both sexes, but that difference is usually larger in men than women (Good et al., 2001). The various brain differences are not tightly linked with one another. Because different brain areas mature at different times and rates, it is possible to have a "male-typical" brain in some ways and a "female-typical" brain in others (Woodson & Gorski, 2000).

Do sex hormones influence intellectual performance? On the average, males and females differ in many small but consistent regards. Girls generally receive higher grades than boys at most school subjects, especially reading (Halpern, 2004). On the average, boys do better than girls at mental rotation tasks and line orientation tasks like the ones in Figure 11.4. However, performance on these tasks does not consistently correlate with people's current levels of male or female sex hormones (Halari et al., 2005). Therefore, if performance relates to hormones, it probably depends more on organizational than activating effects.

We might assume that the male–female differences in performance are specific to our culture, but in fact, they are not even limited to our species. For example, on a variety of mazes and other spatial orientation tasks, males usually do better than females in species ranging from monkeys to mice (C. M. Jones, Braithwaite, & Healy, 2003). However, much of the difference relates to the strategies with which individuals approach spatial problems. If you ask people for directions to some location, more men than women answer in terms of coordinates, such as, "Go two blocks north and then three blocks east." More women than men respond in terms of landmarks: "Go until you reach the elemen-

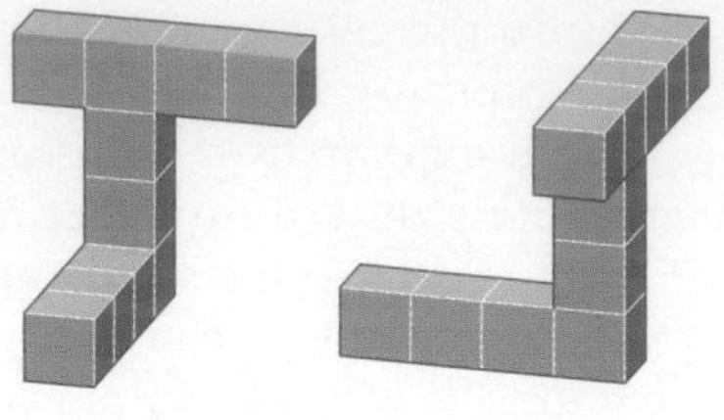

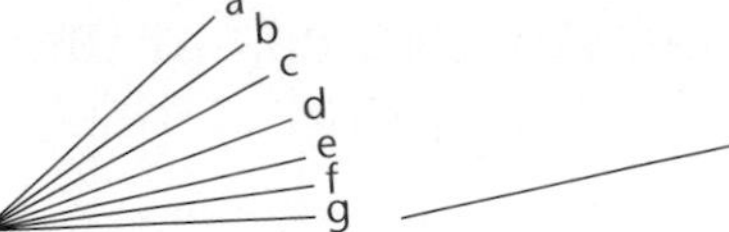

Figure 11.4 A spatial rotation task
People are presented with a series of pairs such as this one and asked whether the first figure could be rotated to match the second one. Here the answer is *no*. For the line-angle question, the correct answer is *e*. On the average, men perform better on this task than women, and women perform better while they are menstruating (and their sex hormone levels are low) than at other times. However, women perform verbal fluency and manual dexterity tasks better at other times than they do while menstruating.

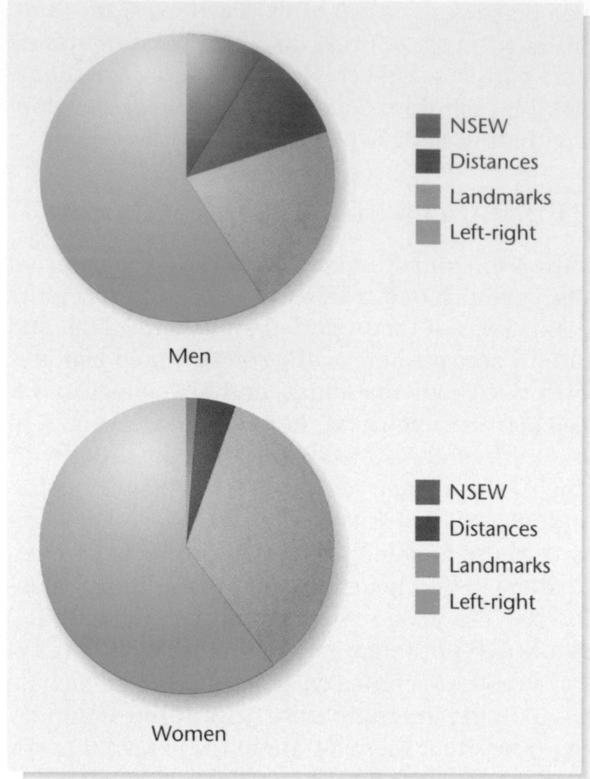

Figure 11.5 Relative use of different kinds of directions
Women used more landmark terms than men; men were more likely than women to use terms relating to north-south-east-west or to distances. *(Based on data of Rahman, Andersson, & Govier, 2005)*

tary school, then go down the hill toward the coffee shop . . ." (Saucier et al., 2002), possibly because women remember the landmarks better (Levy, Astur, & Frick, 2005). Figure 11.5 shows the results of one study recording the kinds of information people provided when giving directions. As you can see, both men and women gave left–right directions, but women described more landmarks. Men were much more likely than women to use the directions north, south, east, and west (Rahman, Andersson, & Govier, 2005).

Most of the spatial tasks that researchers use are easier to solve in terms of directions than in terms of landmarks. In one study, men and women were asked to "swim" through a computer-generated virtual tank of water to find a hidden platform to stand on. In the standard form of the task, with no landmarks as guides, men learned faster. However, if people could see consistent landmarks in various locations, women did just as well as men (Sandstrom, Kaufman, & Huettel, 1998). In short, men don't always do better than women on spatial tasks; the results depend on whether a directional strategy or a landmark strategy can apply.

Why did we evolve such that men and women use different spatial strategies? The most commonly held hypothesis is that males of many species travel over wider geographical areas than females do, often in search of mating opportunities. That hypothesis fits with the fact that in some species, males perform best on spatial tasks during the breeding season (C. M. Jones et al., 2003). Similarly, we could ask why women tend to do better on language tasks. We can make up plausible hypotheses, but they are hard to test. Overall, little can be said with confidence about the evolution of male–female differences.

STOP & CHECK

2. What would be the appearance of a mammal's external genitals if it were exposed to high levels of both androgens and estrogens during early development? What if it were exposed to low levels of both?
3. From the standpoint of protecting a fetus's sexual development, what are some drugs that a pregnant woman should avoid?
4. How would the external genitals appear on a genetic female rat that lacked alpha-fetoprotein?
5. Why do men outperform women on some spatial tasks but not others?

Check your answers on page 337.

Activating Effects of Sex Hormones

At any time in life, not just during an early sensitive period, current levels of testosterone or estradiol exert activating effects, temporarily modifying behavior. Behaviors can also influence hormonal secretions. For example, when doves court each other, each stage of their behavior initiates hormonal changes that alter the birds' readiness for the next sequence of behaviors (C. Erickson & Lehrman, 1964; Lehrman, 1964; Martinez-Vargas & Erickson, 1973).

In no case do hormones *cause* sexual behavior. They alter the activity in various brain areas to change the way the brain responds to various stimuli. They also change sensitivity in the penis, vagina, and cervix (Etgen, Chu, Fiber, Karkanias, & Morales, 1999).

Rodents

After removal of the testes from a male rodent or the ovaries from a female, sexual behavior declines as the sex hormones decline. It may not disappear altogether, partly because the adrenal glands also produce steroid hormones. Testosterone injections to a castrated male restore sexual behavior, as do injections of testosterone's two major metabolites, dihydrotestosterone and estradiol (M. J. Baum & Vreeburg, 1973). A combination of estradiol and progesterone is the most effective combination for females (Matuszewich, Lorrain, & Hull, 2000).

Sex hormones activate sexual behavior partly by enhancing sensations. Estrogens increase the sensitivity of the *pudendal nerve,* which transmits tactile stimulation from the pubic area to the brain (Komisaruk, Adler, & Hutchison, 1972). Sex hormones also bind to receptors that increase responses of certain areas of the hypothalamus, including the ventromedial nucleus, the medial preoptic area (MPOA), and the anterior hypothalamus. Part of the anterior hypothalamic area, known as the *sexually dimorphic nucleus (SDN),* is distinctly larger in males than in females. The exact importance of the SDN is still unclear. Stimulating this area increases male sexual behavior in many species (Bloch, Butler, & Kohlert, 1996), but lesions produce only mild deficits in sexual behavior (De Jonge et al., 1989).

Testosterone and estradiol prime the MPOA and several other brain areas to release dopamine. MPOA neurons release dopamine strongly during sexual activity, and the more dopamine they release, the more likely the male is to copulate (Putnam, Du, Sato, & Hull, 2001). Castrated male rats produce normal amounts of dopamine in the MPOA, but they do not release it in the presence of a receptive female, and they do not attempt to copulate (Hull, Du, Lorrain, & Matuszewich, 1997).

In moderate concentrations, dopamine stimulates mostly type D_1 and D_5 receptors, which facilitate erection of the penis in the male (Hull et al., 1992) and sexually receptive postures in the female (Apostolakis et al., 1996). In higher concentrations, dopamine stimulates type D_2 receptors, which lead to orgasm (Giuliani & Ferrari, 1996; Hull et al., 1992). The sudden burst of dopamine in several brain areas at the time of orgasm resembles the "rush" that addictive drugs produce (Holstege et al., 2003). Whereas dopamine stimulates sexual activity, the neurotransmitter serotonin inhibits it, in part by blocking dopamine release (Hull et al., 1999). Many popular antidepressant drugs increase serotonin activity, and one of their side effects is to decrease sexual arousal and orgasm.

Researchers found what appeared to be a major difference between male and female rats in their sexual motivation: If a pair of rats have had sexual relations in a particular cage, the opportunity to return to that cage is strongly reinforcing for males but not for females. Then they tried varying the procedure. The male rat was confined to that cage, but the female was free to enter or leave at any time. She could therefore control the timing of when their sexual activity started, stopped, and started again. Under these conditions, females developed a clear preference for that cage (Paredes & Vazquez, 1999). Evidently, female rats find sex very reinforcing if they can control the timing. (The rumor is that the same trend may be true for other species as well.)

STOP & CHECK

6. By what mechanism do testosterone and estradiol affect the hypothalamic areas responsible for sexual behavior?

Check your answer on page 337.

Humans

Although humans are less dependent on current sex hormone levels than other species are, hormonal changes can increase or decrease people's sexual arousal. They also affect several brain systems with functions not immediately related to sex. For example, testosterone decreases pain and anxiety, and estrogens probably do too (Edinger & Frye, 2004). Estrogen stimulates growth of dendritic spines in the hippocampus (Behl, 2002; McEwen, 2001) and increased production of dopamine type D_2 receptors and serotonin type 5-HT$_{2A}$ receptors in the nucleus accumbens, the prefrontal cortex, the olfactory cortex, and several other cortical areas (Fink, Sumner, Rosie, Grace, & Quinn, 1996).

Men

Among males, sexual excitement is generally highest when testosterone levels are highest, about ages 15 to 25. The hormone oxytocin also contributes to sexual pleasure. The body releases enormous amounts of oxytocin during orgasm, more than tripling the usual concentration in the blood. Several studies support a relationship between oxytocin and sexual pleasure (M. R. Murphy, Checkley, Seckl, & Lightman, 1990).

Decreases in testosterone levels generally decrease male sexual activity. For example, castration (removal of the testes) generally decreases a man's sexual interest and activity (Carter, 1992). However, low testosterone is not the usual basis for **impotence**, the inability to have an erection. The most common cause is impaired blood circulation, especially in older men. Other common causes include neurological problems, reactions to drugs, and psychological tension (Andersson, 2001). Erection depends partly on the fact that testosterone increases the release of nitric oxide (NO). Nitric oxide facilitates the hypothalamic neurons important for sexual behavior (Lagoda, Muschamp, Vigdorchik, & Hull, 2004) and increases blood flow to the penis. The drug sildenafil (Viagra) increases male sexual ability by prolonging the effects of nitric oxide (Rowland & Burnett, 2000). A drug that stimulates melanocortin receptors increases sexual arousal and motivation for both males and females; it is still in the experimental stage for use with humans (Pfaus, Shadiack, Van Soest, Tse, & Molinoff, 2004).

Testosterone reduction has sometimes been tried as a means of controlling sex offenders, including exhibitionists, rapists, child molesters, and those who commit incest. Sex offenders are a diverse group. Most have about average testosterone levels (Lang, Flor-Henry, & Frenzel, 1990), but one study found elevated levels among child molesters (Rösler & Witztum, 1998). (They reported masturbating about four or five times a day, on average.) Even for sex offenders with high testosterone levels, the hormones do not explain their behaviors. (Many other men with high levels do not engage in offensive behaviors.) Nevertheless, reducing the testosterone levels of sex offenders does reduce their sexual activities, as it would for other men.

Some sex offenders have been treated with *cyproterone,* a drug that blocks the binding of testosterone to receptors within cells. Others have been treated with *medroxyprogesterone,* which inhibits gonadotropin, the pituitary hormone that stimulates testosterone production. Within 4 to 8 weeks of treatment with either of these drugs, most sex offenders experience a decrease in sexual fantasies and offensive sexual behaviors. However, these drugs are not always effective, and they produce unpleasant side effects, including depression, breast growth, weight gain, and blood clots.

Therefore, researchers have sought a more satisfactory testosterone-blocking procedure. A promising possibility is *triptorelin,* a long-lasting drug that blocks gonadotropin and therefore decreases testosterone production. In one study, monthly injections of triptorelin decreased sex offenders' testosterone levels to less than 5% of their previous level. The drug also abolished deviant sexual fantasies and abnormal sexual behavior (Rösler & Witztum, 1998).

Women

A woman's hypothalamus and pituitary interact with the ovaries to produce the **menstrual cycle,** a periodic variation in hormones and fertility over the course of about 28 days (Figure 11.6). After the end of a menstrual period, the anterior pituitary releases **follicle-stimulating hormone (FSH),** which promotes the growth of a follicle in the ovary. The follicle nurtures the *ovum* (egg cell) and produces several types of estrogen, in-

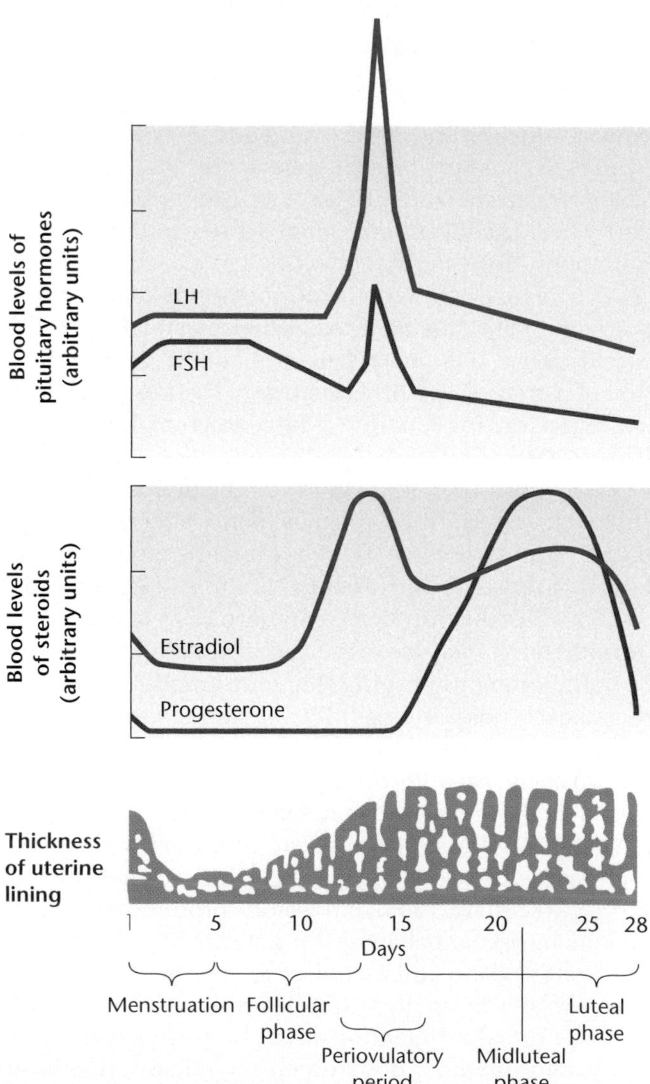

Figure 11.6 Blood levels of four hormones during the human menstrual cycle
Note that estrogen and progesterone are both at high levels during the midluteal phase but drop sharply at menstruation.

cluding estradiol. Toward the middle of the menstrual cycle, the follicle builds up more and more receptors to FSH, so even though the actual concentration of FSH in the blood is decreasing, its effects on the follicle increase. As a result, the follicle produces increasing amounts of estradiol. The increased release of estradiol causes an increased release of FSH as well as a sudden surge in the release of **luteinizing hormone (LH)** from the anterior pituitary (see the top graph in Figure 11.6). FSH and LH combine to cause the follicle to release an ovum.

The remnant of the follicle (now called the *corpus luteum*) releases the hormone progesterone, which prepares the uterus for the implantation of a fertilized ovum. Progesterone also inhibits the further release of LH. Toward the end of the menstrual cycle, the levels of LH, FSH, estradiol, and progesterone all decline. If the ovum is not fertilized, the lining of the uterus is cast off (menstruation), and the cycle begins again. If the ovum is fertilized, the levels of estradiol and progesterone increase gradually throughout pregnancy. One consequence of high estradiol and progesterone levels is fluctuating activity at the serotonin 3 ($5HT_3$) receptor, which is responsible for nausea (Rupprecht et al., 2001). Pregnant women often experience nausea because of the heightened activity of that receptor. Figure 11.7 summarizes the interactions between the pituitary and the ovary.

Birth-control pills prevent pregnancy by interfering with the usual feedback cycle between the ovaries and the pituitary. The most widely used birth-control pill, the *combination pill,* containing both estrogen and progesterone, prevents the surge of FSH and LH that would otherwise release an ovum. The estrogen-progesterone combination also thickens the mucus of the cervix, making it harder for a sperm to reach the egg, and prevents an ovum, if released, from implanting in the uterus. Thus, the pill prevents pregnancy in many ways. Note, however, that it does not protect against sexually transmitted diseases such as AIDS or syphilis. "Safe sex" must go beyond just prevention of pregnancy.

Changes in hormones over the menstrual cycle also alter women's sexual interest. The midway point, the **periovulatory period,** when ovulation occurs, is the time of maximum fertility and increased estrogen levels. According to two studies, women not taking birth-control pills initiate more sexual activity (either with a partner or by masturbation) during the periovulatory period than at other times during the month (Adams,

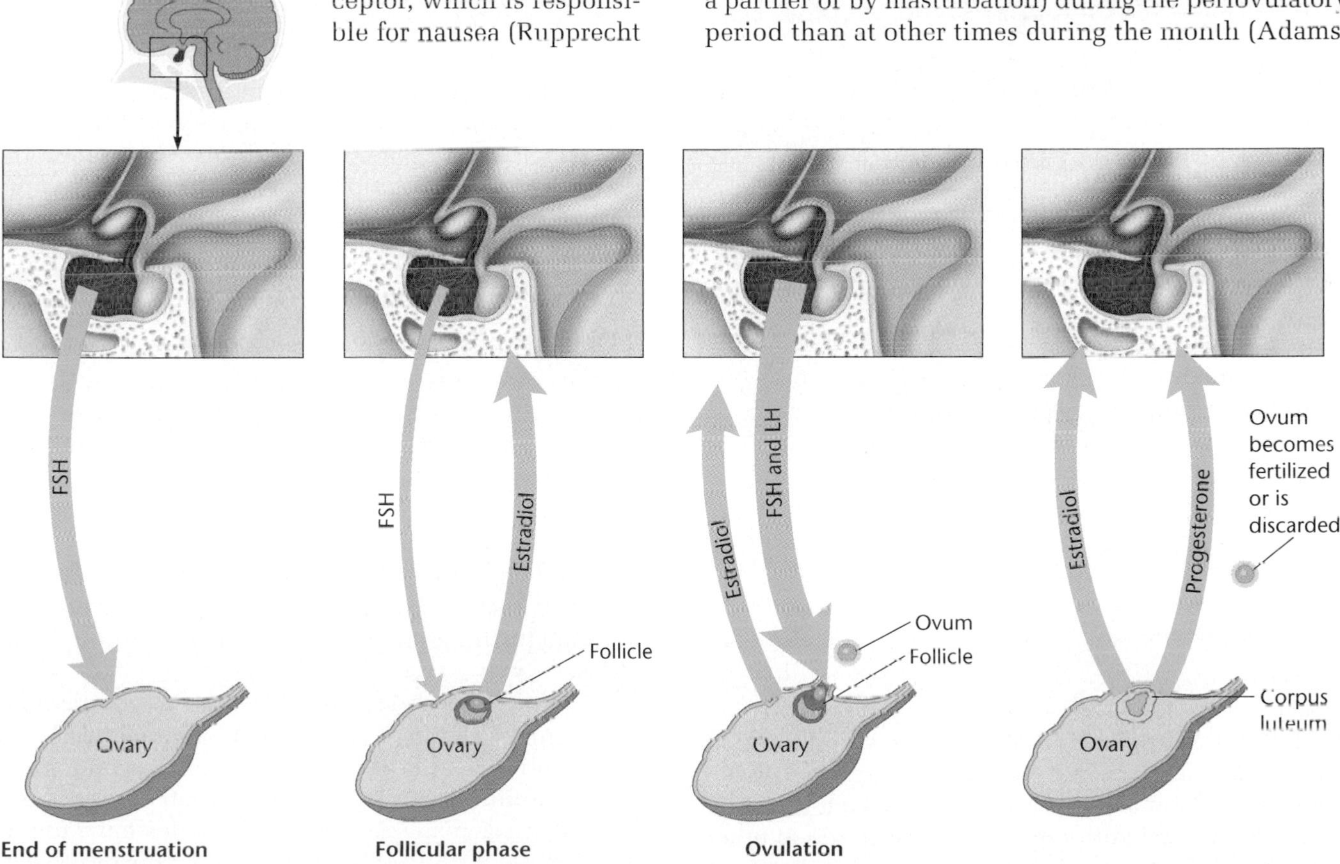

Figure 11.7 Interactions between the pituitary and the ovary
FSH from the pituitary stimulates a follicle of the ovary to develop and produce estradiol, triggering a release of a burst of FSH and LH from the pituitary. Those hormones cause the follicle to release its ovum and become a corpus luteum. The corpus luteum releases progesterone while the ovary releases estradiol.

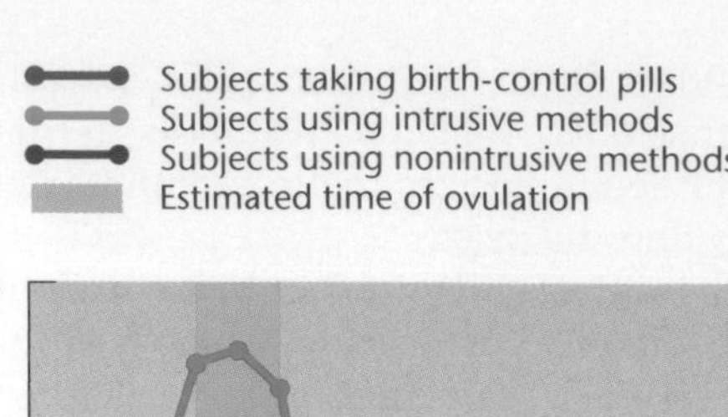

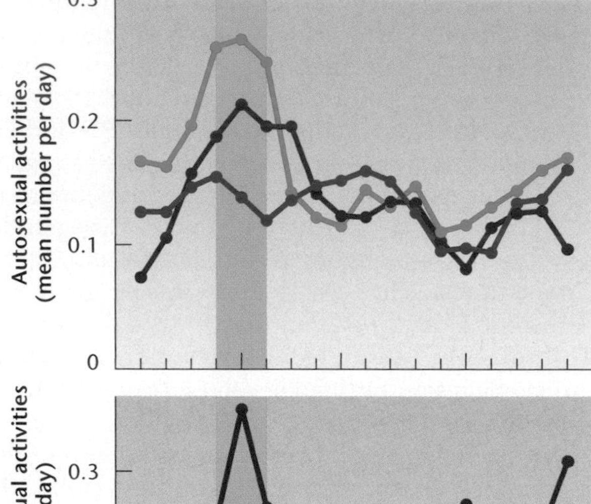

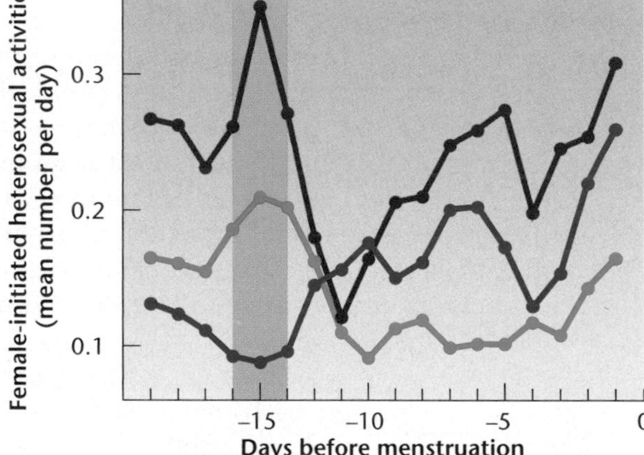

Figure 11.8 Female-initiated sexual activities during the monthly cycle

The top graph shows autosexual activities (masturbation and sexual fantasies); the bottom graph shows female-initiated activities with a male partner. "Intrusive" birth-control methods are diaphragm, foam, and condom; "nonintrusive" methods are IUD and vasectomy. Note that women other than pill users increase self-initiated sex activities when their estrogen levels peak. *(Source: From "Rise in female-initiated sexual activity at ovulation and its suppression by oral contraceptives," by D. B. Adams, A. R. Gold, and A. D. Burt, 1978,* New England Journal of Medicine, 299, *pp. 1145–1150. Reprinted by permission of The New England Journal of Medicine.)*

Gold, & Burt, 1978; Udry & Morris, 1968) (Figure 11.8). According to another study, women rate an erotic video as more pleasant and arousing if they watch it during the periovulatory period than if they watch it at other times (Slob, Bax, Hop, Rowland, & van der Werff ten Bosch, 1996). These effects are small, though.

Sex hormones also influence women's attention to sex-related stimuli. Women in one study were asked to look at facial photos on a screen and classify each as male or female as quickly as possible. They made the classifications more quickly when they were in their periovulatory period than at other times of the cycle (Macrae, Alnwick, Milne, & Schloerscheidt, 2002). In another study, women were presented with a computer that enabled them to modify pictures of men's faces to make each one look more feminine or more masculine. When they were asked specifically to show the face of the man they would prefer for a "short-term sexual relationship," women who were in their periovulatory period preferred more masculine-looking faces than did women in other phases of the menstrual cycle (Penton-Voak et al., 1999). When women were asked to view videotapes of two men and choose one for a short-term relationship, women in the periovulatory period were more likely to choose a man who seemed athletic, competitive, and assertive and who did *not* describe himself as having a "nice personality" (Gangestad, Simpson, Cousins, Garver-Apgar, & Christensen, 2004). In short, the hormones associated with fertility move women's mate preferences toward men who look and act more masculine.

EXTENSIONS AND APPLICATIONS
Premenstrual Syndrome

Some women experience anxiety, irritability, and depression during the days just before menstruation, an experience known as **premenstrual syndrome (PMS)** or *premenstrual dysphoric disorder.* The terms *syndrome* and *disorder* imply a medical problem requiring medical treatment and are therefore inappropriate in most cases. Nevertheless, the terms are widely used.

Because PMS occurs at a time of major hormonal changes, it seems reasonable to explore the possible relationship between hormones and PMS. Just before menstruation, estradiol and progesterone levels decrease, while levels of cortisol (an adrenal hormone) increase. However, women with PMS have about the same fluctuations in these hormones as women without PMS (Schmidt, Nieman, Danaceau, Adams, & Rubinow, 1998). If anything, women with PMS may have *weaker* fluctuations: Throughout the menstrual cycle, they have steadier levels of estradiol, progesterone, and norepinephrine than do other women (I. Blum et al., 2004).

Much research interest focuses on the metabolism of progesterone. Progesterone is metabolized into several other chemicals, including *allopregnanolone,* which modifies GABA synapses, which control anxiety and stress responses. Several studies have found that women with PMS have normal levels of progesterone but lower than normal levels of allopregnanolone, particularly during the premenstrual period (Follesa et al., 2000; Monteleone et al., 2000; Rapkin et al., 1997).

STOP & CHECK

7. What evidence indicates that testosterone is important for men's sex drive?
8. At what time in a woman's menstrual cycle are her levels of estrogen and progesterone highest? When are they lowest?
9. What is the relationship between sex hormones and premenstrual syndrome?

Check your answers on page 337.

Parental Behavior

In birds and mammals—with the possible exception of humans—hormonal changes prepare the mother for parental behavior. Late in pregnancy (or egg incubation for birds), the female secretes large amounts of estradiol, prolactin, and oxytocin (Pedersen, Caldwell, Walker, Ayers, & Mason, 1994). Prolactin is necessary for milk production and also for aspects of maternal behavior such as retrieving any wandering young back to the nest (Lucas, Ormandy, Binart, Bridges, & Kelly, 1998). In those species in which fathers contribute to parental care, prolactin is important for their behavior too (Schradin & Anzenberger, 1999). Oxytocin is a fascinating hormone, with effects ranging from maternal behavior to sexual arousal, social attachment (Kosfeld, Heinrichs, Zak, Fischbacher, & Fehr, 2005), and the enhancement of learning (Tomizawa et al., 2003).

In addition to secreting these hormones, the female also changes her pattern of hormone receptors. For example, late in pregnancy, her brain increases its sensitivity to estradiol in the areas responsible for maternal behavior but not in those responsible for sexual behavior (Rosenblatt, Olufowobi, & Siegel, 1998). The hormonal changes increase the mothers' attention to their young after delivery. Hormones act by increasing activity in the medial preoptic area and anterior hypothalamus (Featherstone, Fleming, & Ivy, 2000), areas that are necessary for rats' maternal behavior (J. R. Brown, Ye, Bronson, Dikkes, & Greenberg, 1996) (Figure 11.9). (We have already encountered the preoptic area/anterior hypothalamus, or POA/AH, because of its importance for temperature regulation, thirst, and sexual behavior. It's a busy little area.)

Another key hormone is vasopressin, synthesized by the hypothalamus and secreted by the posterior pituitary gland. Male prairie voles, which secrete large amounts of vasopressin, establish long-term pair bonds with females and help rear their young. A male meadow vole, with much lower vasopressin levels, mates with a female and then virtually ignores her (Figure 11.10). If a male meadow vole is put in a cage where he can choose to sit next to the female with whom he just mated or with a new female, he neither prefers nor avoids the one he mated with, as if he didn't even recognize her. In fact, most of the time, he sits by himself, near neither female. However, male meadow voles' behavior changed after researchers found a way to increase activity of the genes responsible for vasopressin in one part of the voles' brain. Suddenly, they showed a strong preference for a recent mate and, if placed into the same cage, even helped her take care of her babies (Lim et al., 2004). Whether the female was surprised, we don't know. This result is a remarkably strong example of altering social behavior by manipulating the activity of a single gene. (Whether vasopressin has similar effects in humans, we do not know.)

Although rodent maternal behavior depends on hormones for the first few days, it becomes less de-

J. R. Brown, H. Ye, R. T. Bronson, P. Dikkes, & M. E. Greenberg, 1996

Figure 11.9 Brain development and maternal behavior in mice
The mouse on the left shows normal maternal behavior. The one on the right has a genetic mutation that, among other effects, impairs the development of the preoptic area and anterior hypothalamus.

Figure 11.10 Effects of vasopressin on social and mating behaviors

(a) Prairie voles form long-term pair bonds. Staining of their brain shows much expression of the hormone vasopressin. **(b)** A closely related species, meadow voles, mate but then separate and show no social attachments. Their brains have much lower vasopressin levels. *(Reprinted with permission from "Enhanced partner preference in a promiscuous species by manipulating the expression of a single gene." by M. M. Lim, Z. Wang, D. E. Olazabal, X. Ren, E. F. Terwilliger, & L. J. Young,* Nature, *429, 754–757. Copyright 2004 Nature Publishing Group.)*

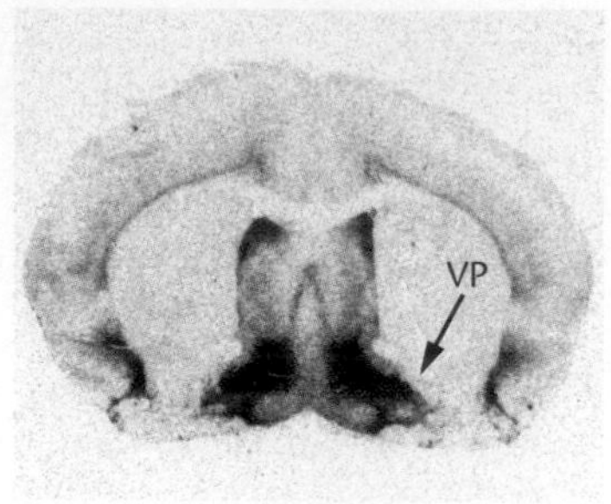

(a)

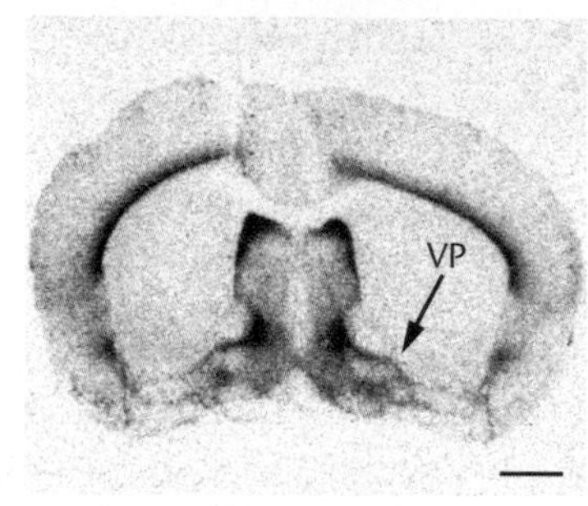

(b)

pendent at a later stage. If a female that has never been pregnant is left with some baby rats, she ignores them at first but gradually becomes more attentive. (Because the babies cannot survive without parental care, the experimenter must periodically replace them with new, healthy babies.) After about 6 days, the adoptive mother builds a nest, assembles the babies in the nest, licks them, and does everything else that a normal mother would, except nurse them. This experience-dependent behavior does not require hormonal changes and occurs even in rats that have had their ovaries removed (Mayer & Rosenblatt, 1979; Rosenblatt, 1967). That is, humans are not the only species in which a mother can adopt young without first going through pregnancy.

An important influence from being with babies is that the mother becomes accustomed to their odors. Infant rats release some chemicals that stimulate the mother's vomeronasal organ, which responds to pheromones (see Chapter 7). We might imagine that evolution would have equipped infants with pheromones that elicit maternal behavior, but actually, their pheromones interfere with maternal behavior by stimulating aggressive behaviors (Sheehan, Cirrito, Numan, & Numan, 2000). For a mother that has just gone through pregnancy, this interference does not matter; her hormones have primed her medial preoptic area so strongly that it overrides competing impulses. A female without hormonal priming, however, rejects the young until she has become familiar with their smell (Del Cerro et al., 1995).

Why do mammals need two mechanisms for maternal behavior—one hormone-dependent and one not? In the early phase, hormones compensate for the mother's lack of familiarity with the young. In the later phase, experience maintains the maternal behavior even though the hormones start to decline (Rosenblatt, 1970).

Are hormones important for human parental behavior? Hormonal changes are necessary for a woman to nurse a baby, but otherwise, hormonal changes are not necessary to prepare anyone for infant care. After all, both men and never-pregnant women can adopt children and be excellent parents. It is possible that hormonal changes facilitate or increase some aspects of human parental behavior, but research data are not available on this point.

STOP & CHECK

10. What factors are responsible for maternal behavior shortly after rats give birth? What factors become more important in later days?

Check your answers on page 337.

Module 11.1
In Closing: Reproductive Behaviors and Motivations

A mother rat licks her babies all over shortly after their birth, and that stimulation is essential for their survival. Why does she do it? Presumably, she does not understand that licking will help them. She licks because they are covered with a salty fluid that tastes good to her. If she has access to other salty fluids, she stops licking her young (Gubernick & Alberts, 1983). Analogously, sexual behavior in general serves the function of passing on our genes, but we don't crave sexual excitement just to pass on our genes. In fact, people often use contraceptives to avoid reproducing. We evolved a tendency to enjoy the sex act. The same principle holds for hunger, thirst, and other motivations: We evolved tendencies to enjoy acts that have, in general, increased our ancestors' probability of surviving and reproducing.

Summary

1. Male and female behaviors differ because of sex hormones that activate particular genes. Also, certain genes on the Y chromosome are active in the brain, and at least one gene on the X chromosome is active only in female brains. (p. 326)
2. Organizing effects of a hormone, exerted during an early sensitive period, produce relatively permanent alterations in anatomy and physiology. (p. 327)
3. In the absence of sex hormones, an infant mammal develops female-looking external genitals. The addition of testosterone shifts development toward the male pattern. Extra estradiol, within normal limits, does not determine whether the individual looks male or female. However, estradiol and other estrogens modify various aspects of development of the brain and the internal sexual organs. (p. 328)
4. During early development in rodents, testosterone is converted within certain brain cells to estradiol, which actually masculinizes their development. Estradiol in the blood does not masculinize development because it is bound to proteins in the blood. The mechanisms of sexual differentiation of the human brain are less well understood. (p. 329)
5. Organizing effects of sex hormones apparently also influence patterns of spatial reasoning. Males are more likely than females to orient by directions such as north and south, whereas females are more likely to rely on landmarks. (p. 329)
6. In adulthood, sex hormones can activate sex behaviors, partly by facilitating activity in the medial preoptic area and anterior hypothalamus. The hormones prime cells to release dopamine in response to sexual arousal. Dopamine release during orgasm resembles the effects of addictive drugs. (p. 331)
7. A woman's menstrual cycle depends on a feedback cycle that increases and then decreases the release of several hormones. In many species, females are sexually responsive only when they are fertile. Women can respond sexually at any time in their cycle, although they may have a slight increase in sexual interest around the time of ovulation, when estrogen levels are highest. (p. 332)
8. Hormones released around the time of giving birth facilitate maternal behavior in females of many mammalian species. Nevertheless, prolonged exposure to young is also sufficient to induce parental behavior. Hormonal facilitation is not necessary for human parental behavior. (p. 335)

Answers to STOP & CHECK Questions 

1. Sex hormones are steroids. They bind to receptors on the membrane, activate certain proteins in the cell's cytoplasm, and activate or inactivate particular genes. (p. 327)
2. A mammal exposed to high levels of both male and female hormones will appear male. One exposed to low levels of both will appear female. Genital development depends mostly on the presence or absence of androgens. (p. 330)
3. Pregnant women should avoid alcohol, marijuana, haloperidol, and cocaine because these drugs interfere with male sexual development. Even aspirin and the chemicals lining bottles and cans produce mild abnormalities. Obviously, the results depend on both quantities and timing of these chemicals. (p. 330)
4. A female that lacked alpha-fetoprotein would be masculinized by her own estrogens. (p. 330)
5. Men are more likely than women to solve a spatial task in terms of directions such as north and south; women are more likely to rely on landmarks. Men have an advantage on tasks with no reliable landmarks but lose that advantage when landmarks are available. (p. 330)
6. Testosterone and estradiol prime hypothalamic cells to be ready to release dopamine. (p. 331)
7. Drugs such as triptorelin that block testosterone decrease sexual drive and behavior. Also, men's sex drive is generally strongest during the ages when their testosterone levels are highest. (p. 335)
8. Estrogen and progesterone are highest at the periovulatory and midluteal phases; they are lowest during and just after menstruation. (p. 335)
9. Premenstrual syndrome is an abnormal reaction to the normal changes that occur in sex hormones. If anything, women with PMS may have weaker hormonal fluctuations than other women do. One hypothesis relates PMS to low levels of one metabolite of progesterone. (p. 335)
10. The early stage of rats' maternal behavior depends on a surge in the release of the hormones prolactin and oxytocin. A few days later, her experience with

the young decreases the vomeronasal responses that would tend to make her reject them. Experience with the young maintains maternal behavior after the hormone levels begin to drop. (p. 336)

Thought Questions

1. The pill RU-486 produces abortions by blocking the effects of progesterone. Explain how this process works.
2. The presence or absence of testosterone determines whether a mammal will differentiate as a male or a female. In birds, the story is the opposite: The presence or absence of estrogen is critical (Adkins & Adler, 1972). What problems would sex determination by estrogen create if that were the mechanism for mammals? Why do those problems not arise in birds? (Hint: Think about the difference between live birth and hatching from an egg.)
3. Antipsychotic drugs, such as haloperidol and chlorpromazine, block activity at dopamine synapses. What side effects might they have on sexual behavior?

Module 11.2
Variations in Sexual Behavior

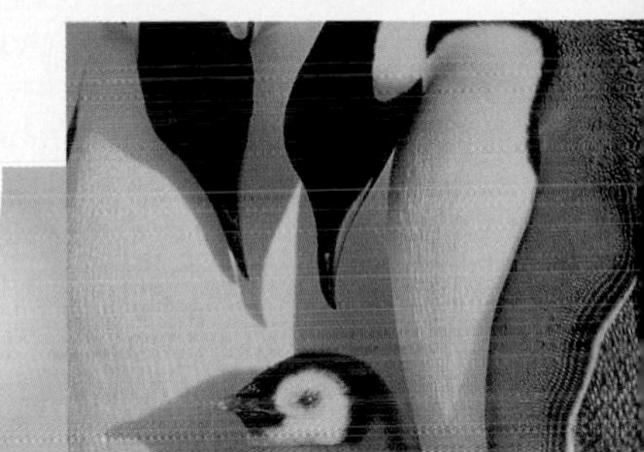

People vary considerably in their frequency of sexual activity, preferred types of sexual activity, and sexual orientation. Because sexual activity occurs mostly in private, most of us are not aware of how much diversity exists. In this module, we shall explore some of that diversity, but first we consider a few differences between men and women in general. Several researchers have been trying to go beyond just describing those differences to perhaps explaining them in terms of evolution, and the proposed explanations are both interesting and controversial.

Evolutionary Interpretations of Mating Behavior

Let's start with a few common observations: First, men are more likely than women are to seek multiple sex partners, especially for short-term encounters. Second, women are more likely than men to be concerned about a potential mate's earning ability, whereas men are more likely to be concerned about a mate's youth. Third, men usually show greater jealousy than women do at any indication of sexual infidelity.

Although these generalizations vary among individuals, they are reasonably consistent across cultures and similar to tendencies seen in many other species. Granted, a great deal about human mating behavior differs from that of other species, so we should not carelessly generalize from one species to another. Still, several theorists have argued that the different behaviors of men and women reflect the influence of past evolutionary pressures (Buss, 2000). We may or may not accept these arguments, but we should examine them carefully.

Interest in Multiple Mates

Why are men more likely to be interested in brief sexual relationships with many partners? From the evolutionary standpoint of spreading one's genes, men can succeed by either of two strategies (Gangestad & Simpson, 2000): Be loyal to one woman and devote your energies to helping her and her babies, or mate with many women and hope that some of them can raise your babies without your help. No one needs to be conscious of these strategies, of course. In contrast, a woman can have no more than one pregnancy per 9 months, regardless of her number of sex partners. So evolution may have predisposed men, or at least some men, to be more interested in multiple mates than women are.

One objection is that a woman does sometimes gain from having multiple sex partners (Hrdy, 2000). If her husband is infertile, mating with another man could be her only way of reproducing. Also, another sexual partner may provide her with valuable gifts and may be kind to her children. She also has the possibility of "trading up," abandoning her first mate for a better one. So the prospect of multiple mates may be more appealing to men, but it can have some advantages for women too.

Another objection is that researchers have no direct evidence that genes influence whether people prefer one mate or many. We shall return to this issue later.

What Men and Women Seek in a Mate

Men and women both prefer a healthy, intelligent, honest, physically attractive mate. Women have some additional interests that are not prominent for men. For example, most women prefer mates who are likely to be good providers. As you might guess, that tendency is strongest in societies where women have no income of their own. However, in all known societies, women are more interested in men's wealth and success than men care about women's wealth and success (Buss, 2000). According to evolutionary theorists, the reason is clear: While a woman is pregnant or taking care of a small child, she needs help getting food and other requirements. Evolution would have favored any gene that caused women to seek good providers. Related to this tendency, most women tend to be cautious during courtship. Even if a man seems to be very interested in her, a woman waits for a while before concluding that he has a strong commitment to her (Buss, 2001). She would not want a man who acts interested for a while and then leaves when she needs him.

Men tend to have a stronger preference for a young partner. An evolutionary explanation is that younger women are more likely than older women to be fertile, so a man can spread his genes best by mating with a young woman. Men remain fertile into old age, so a woman has less need to insist on youth. A contrary interpretation is that women also prefer young partners when possible, but in many societies, only older men have enough financial resources to get married.

Differences in Jealousy

Why might men be more jealous about wives' sexual infidelities than women should be about husbands' infidelities? If a man is to pass on his genes—the key point in evolution—he needs to be sure that the children he supports are his own. An unfaithful wife threatens that certainty. A woman's children are necessarily her own, so she has no similar worry.

One way to test this interpretation is to compare cultures. Attitudes about sexual fidelity differ from one culture to another, ranging from acceptance of extramarital sex to complete prohibition. However, although some cultures consider it more acceptable for men to have extramarital sex, no known culture considers it more tolerable for women. Should we be more impressed that jealousy is always at least as strong for men as for women, and usually more, or should we be more impressed that jealousy varies among cultures? Here reasonable people can draw different conclusions.

Which would upset you more: if your partner had a brief sexual affair with someone else, or if he or she became emotionally close to someone else? According to several studies, men say they would be more upset by the sexual infidelity, whereas women would be more upset by the emotional infidelity (Shakelford, Buss, & Bennett, 2002). However, those studies dealt with hypothetical situations. Most men and women who have actually dealt with an unfaithful partner say they were more upset by their partner's becoming emotionally close to someone else than by the sexual affair (C. H. Harris, 2002).

Evolved or Learned?

If a behavior has clear advantages for survival or reproduction, and is similar across cultures, can we conclude that it developed by evolution? Not necessarily. Of course, the brain evolved, just like any other organ, and of course, our behavioral tendencies are a product of evolution. But the key question is whether evolution has micromanaged our behavior down to such details as whether to look for a mate with high earning potential.

Cross-cultural similarity is not strong evidence for an evolved tendency. For example, people throughout the world agree that 2 + 2 = 4, but we don't assume that they have a gene for that belief. Likewise, it is possible that women throughout the world discover that they gain benefits from marrying a man who can provide well.

To establish that we evolved a tendency to act in some way, the most decisive evidence would be the demonstration of particular genes with demonstrable effects. For example, if most men have genes influencing them to prefer attractive young women, then presumably we should be able to find some men with a mutation in that gene, causing them to prefer *unattractive* women! Okay, this particular example may not be the best, but the point is this: We need to be cautious about inferring what is a product of our evolution versus what we learn in our own lifetime.

Conclusions

Discussing these issues is difficult. Ideally, we would like to consider the evidence and logical arguments entirely on their scientific merits. However, when someone describes how evolutionary selection may have led men to be interested in multiple sex partners or to be more jealous than women are, it sometimes sounds like a justification for men to act that way.

No gene forces men or women to behave in any particular way. We shall see in Chapter 15 that genes predispose some people to be more likely than others to become alcoholics, but that fact doesn't mean that some people are sure to be alcoholics or other people sure not to be.

Even leaving aside the social implications as far as we can, no firm scientific conclusion emerges. We need more data, especially about the effects of particular genes, before we can draw a conclusion.

STOP & CHECK

1. What evolutionary advantage is suggested for why women are more interested in men's wealth and success than men are interested in the same things about women?

Check your answer on page 350.

Gender Identity and Gender-Differentiated Behaviors

The coral goby is a species of fish in which the male and female tend their eggs and young together. If one of them dies, the survivor looks for a new partner. But it does not look far. This is a very stay-at-home kind of fish. If it cannot easily find a partner of the opposite sex, but does find an unmated member of its own sex—oh, well—it simply changes sex and mates with the neighbor. Male-to-female and female-to-male switches are equally common (Nakashima, Kuwamura, & Yogo, 1995).

People cannot switch sexes and remain fertile, but we do have intermediates and variations in sexual development. Sexual development is a sensitive issue, so let us specify from the start: "Different" does not mean "wrong." People naturally differ in their sexual development just as they do in their height, weight, emotions, and memory.

Gender identity is how we identify sexually and what we call ourselves. The biological differences between males and females are often referred to as *sex differences;* the differences that result from people's thinking about themselves as male or female are *gender differences.* To maintain this useful distinction, we should resist the trend to speak of the "gender" of dogs, fruit flies, and so forth. Gender identity is a human characteristic.

Most people accept the gender identity that matches their external appearance, which is ordinarily also the way they were reared. However, some are dissatisfied with their assigned gender, and many would describe themselves as being more masculine in some ways and more feminine in others. Psychologists have long assumed that gender depends mainly or entirely on the way people rear their children. However, several kinds of evidence suggest that biological factors, especially prenatal hormones, may be important also.

Courtesy of Intersex Society of North America

This group of adult intersexed people have gathered to provide mutual support and to protest against the early surgical treatments they received. They requested that their names be used to emphasize their openness about their condition and to emphasize that intersexuality should not be considered shameful. They are from left to right: Martha Coventry, Max Beck, David Vandertie, Kristi Bruce, and Angela Moreno.

Intersexes

Some people are not exactly male or female but are something intermediate (Haqq & Donahoe, 1998). For example, some XY males with a mutation in the SRY gene have poorly developed genitals. Some people are born with an XX chromosome pattern but an SRY gene that translocated from the father's Y chromosome onto another chromosome. Despite their XX chromosomes, they have either an ovary and a testis, or two testes, or a mixture of testis and ovary tissue on each side.

Others develop an intermediate appearance because of an atypical hormone pattern. Recall that testosterone masculinizes the genitals and the hypothalamus during early development. A genetic male who has low levels of testosterone or a mutation of the testosterone receptors may develop a female or intermediate appearance (Misrahi et al., 1997). A genetic female who is exposed to more testosterone than the average female can be partly masculinized.

The most common cause of this condition is **congenital adrenal hyperplasia (CAH),** meaning overdevelopment of the adrenal glands from birth. Ordinarily, the adrenal gland has a negative feedback relationship with the pituitary gland. The pituitary secretes adrenocorticotropic hormone (ACTH), which stimulates the adrenal gland. The adrenal gland secretes several hormones, including cortisol, which feeds back to decrease the release of ACTH. Some people have a genetic limitation in their ability to produce cortisol. Because the pituitary fails to receive much cortisol as a feedback signal, it continues secreting more ACTH, causing the adrenal gland to secrete larger amounts of its other hormones, including testosterone. In a genetic male, the extra testosterone has little effect, although the malfunctioning adrenal gland may cause problems with salt retention. However, genetic females with this condition develop various degrees of masculinization of their external genitals. (Internal organs such as the ovaries are less affected.) Figure 11.11 provides an example. Note a structure that appears intermediate between clitoris and penis and swellings that appear intermediate between labia and scrotum. After birth, these children are given medical treatments to bring their adrenal hormones within normal levels; some are also given surgery to alter their external genital appearance, as we shall discuss later.

Individuals whose genitals do not match the usual development for their genetic sex are referred to as **hermaphrodites** (from Hermes and Aphrodite in Greek mythology). The *true hermaphrodite,* a rarity, has some normal testicular tissue and some normal ovarian tissue—for example, a testis on one side of the body and an ovary on the other. Individuals whose sexual development is intermediate or ambiguous, such as the one in Figure 11.11, are usually called **intersexes** or

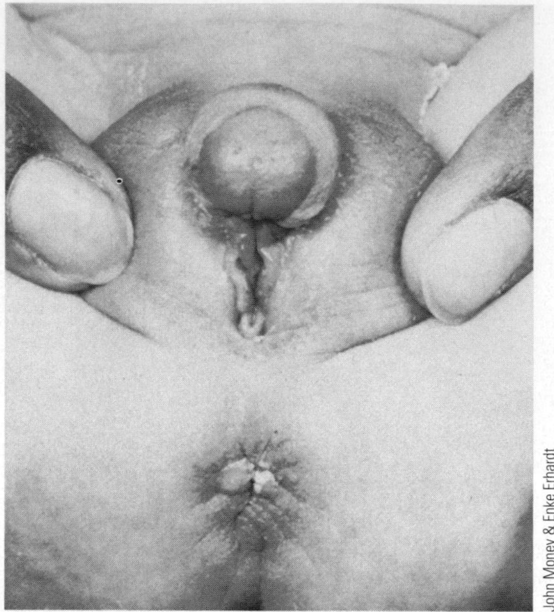

Figure 11.11 External genitals of a genetic female, age 3 months
Masculinized by excess androgens from the adrenal gland before birth, the infant shows the effects of the adrenogenital syndrome.

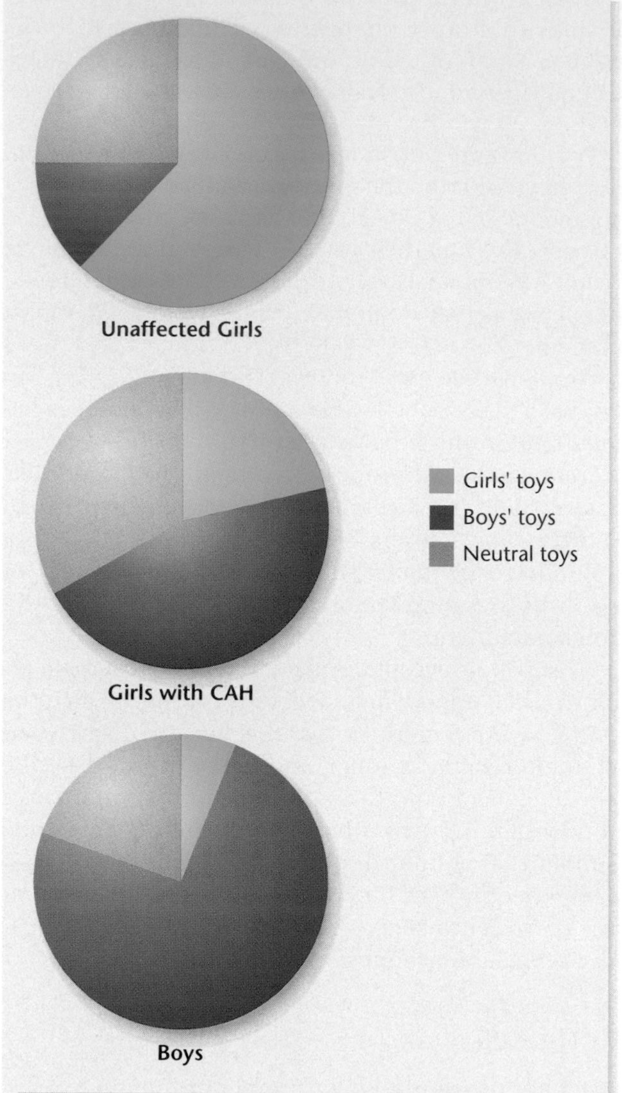

Figure 11.12 Toy preferences by CAH girls, unaffected girls, and unaffected boys
CAH girls were intermediate between unaffected girls and boys. These data show results when the children played alone. Results changed slightly when the mother or father was present, but in each case, the CAH girls were intermediate between the other groups. *(Source: Based on data of Pasterski et al., 2005)*

pseudohermaphrodites. Most dislike the term *pseudohermaphrodite,* which sounds insulting, so we shall use the term *intersex.*

How common are intersexes? An estimated 1 child in 100 in the United States is born with some degree of genital ambiguity, and 1 in 2,000 has enough ambiguity to make its male or female status uncertain (Blackless et al., 2000). However, the accuracy of these estimates is doubtful, as hospitals and families keep the information private. Maintaining confidentiality is of course important, but an unfortunate consequence of secrecy is that intersexed people have trouble finding others like themselves. For more information, consult the following website: **http://www.isna.org/**

Interests and Preferences of CAH Girls

Genetic females with CAH or similar conditions are in most cases reared as girls. However, their brains were exposed to higher than normal testosterone levels during prenatal and early postnatal life compared to other girls. Is their behavior masculinized? In several studies, girls with CAH were observed in a room full of toys—including some that are girl-typical (dolls, plates and dishes, cosmetics kits), some that are boy-typical (toy car, tool set, gun), and some that are neutral (puzzles, crayons, board games). Figure 11.12 shows the results from one such study (Pasterski et al., 2005). Note how girls with CAH were intermediate between the preferences of boys and girls without CAH. All three groups were also tested with either the mother or father present; the results changed slightly, but in each case, the girls with CAH were intermediate between the other two groups.

Other studies have reported similar results and have found that the girls exposed to the largest amount of testosterone in early development showed the largest preference for boys' toys (Berenbaum, Duck, & Bryk, 2000; Nordenström, Servin, Bohlin, Larsson, & Wedell, 2002). You might wonder whether the parents, knowing that these girls had been partly masculinized in appearance, might have encouraged "tomboyish" activities. The observations suggest quite the opposite: The parents gave extra encouragement to the girls with CAH any time they played with "girl-typical" toys (Pasterski et al., 2005). A study of some CAH girls in adolescence found that, on the average, their interests were intermediate between those of typical male and female adolescents. For example, they read more sports magazines and fewer teen and glamour magazines than the average for other teenage girls (Berenbaum, 1999). Another study found an influence of prenatal hormones on the toy preferences even for girls without CAH. The researchers took blood samples from pregnant women, measuring their testosterone levels (some of which would enter the fetus). When the daughters reached age 3½, researchers observed their toy play. Those who had been exposed to higher testosterone levels in prenatal life showed slightly elevated preferences for boys' toys (Hines et al., 2002).

A study of young women with a history of CAH found that they had fewer than average sexual experiences with men. Few had homosexual experiences, either, although some reported a mixture of heterosexual and homosexual fantasies. Many reported *no* sexual fantasies—an unusual finding, compared to other young adult women (Zucker et al., 1996).

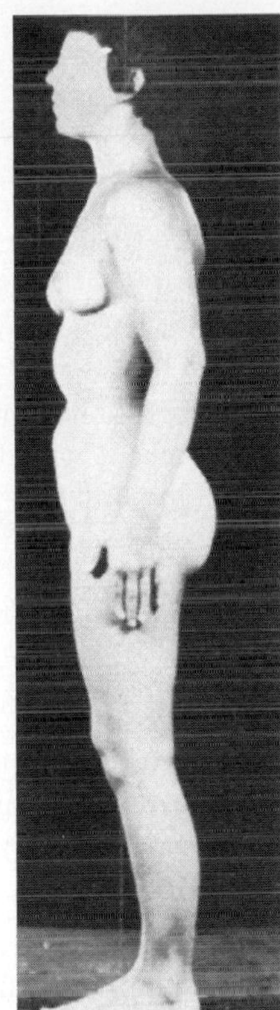

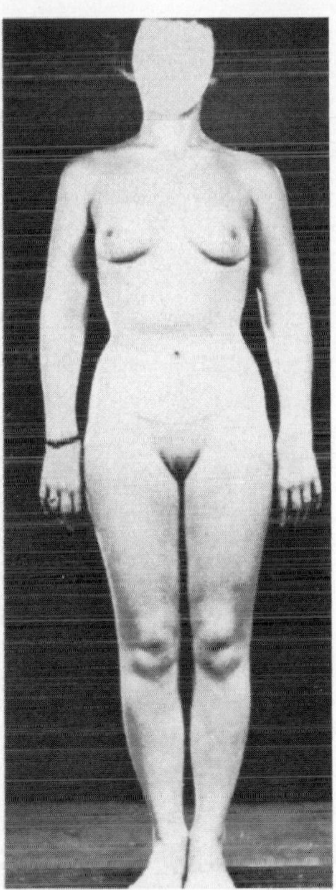

Federman, 1967

Figure 11.13 A woman with an XY chromosome pattern but insensitivity to androgens

Two undescended testes produce testosterone and other androgens, to which the body is insensitive. The testes and adrenal glands also produce estrogens that are responsible for the pubertal changes.

Testicular Feminization

Certain individuals with an XY chromosome pattern have the genital appearance of a female. This condition is known as **androgen insensitivity**, or **testicular feminization**. Although such individuals produce normal amounts of androgens (including testosterone), they lack the androgen receptor that enables it to activate genes in a cell's nucleus. Consequently, the cells are insensitive to androgens, and development proceeds as if the level of testosterone and related hormones was very low. This condition occurs in various degrees, resulting in anatomy that ranges from a smaller than average penis to genitals like those of a normal female. In some cases, no one has any reason to suspect the person is anything other than a normal female, until puberty. Then, in spite of breast development and broadening of the hips, menstruation does not begin because the body has internal testes instead of ovaries and a uterus. (The vagina is short and leads to nothing.) Also, pubic hair is sparse or absent because it depends on androgens in females as well as males (Figure 11.13).

Issues of Gender Assignment and Rearing

Many girls with CAH and related conditions are born looking only slightly masculinized, but some look as much male as female. Some genetic males are born with a very small penis for various reasons not limited to androgen insensitivity. How should they be reared? Beginning in the 1950s, medical doctors began recommending that all intersex people be reared as girls, using surgery if necessary to make their genitals look more feminine (Dreger, 1998). The reason was that it is easier to reduce an enlarged clitoris to normal size than expand it to penis size. If necessary, surgeons can build an artificial vagina or lengthen a short one. After the surgery, the child looks female. Physicians and psychologists assumed that any child who was consistently reared as a girl would fully accept that identity.

And she lives happily ever after, right? Not necessarily. Many intersexes have complained about their treatment. A surgically created or lengthened vagina may be satisfactory to a male partner, but it provides no sensation to the woman and requires almost daily attention to prevent it from scarring over. Many intersexes wish they had their original "abnormal" penis/clitoris instead of the mutilated, insensitive structure left to them by a surgeon. A few—3 of 53 people in one study—ask to be reassigned from female to male (Zucker et al., 1996). Moreover, intersexes resent being deceived. Historian Alice Dreger (1998) describes the case of one intersex:

> As a young person, [she] was told she had "twisted ovaries" that had to be removed; in fact, her testes were removed. At the age of twenty, "alone and scared in the stacks of a [medical] library," she discovered the truth of her condition. Then "the pieces finally fit together. But what fell apart was my relationship with both my family and physicians. It was not learning about chromosome or testes that caused enduring trauma, it was discovering that I had been told lies. I avoided all medical care for the next 18 years. . . . [The] greatest source of anxiety is not our gonads or karyotype. It is shame and fear resulting from an environment in which our condition is so unacceptable that caretakers lie." (p. 192)

So how *should* such a child be reared? On that question, specialists do not agree. A growing number, however, follow these recommendations (Diamond & Sigmundson, 1997):

- Be completely honest with the intersexed person and the family, and do nothing without their informed consent. (Some doctors in the past conducted surgery on infants without even explaining what they were doing or why.)
- Identify the child as male or female based mainly on the predominant external appearance. That is, there should be no bias toward calling every intersex a female.
- Rear the child as consistently as possible, but be prepared that the person might later be sexually oriented toward males, females, both, or neither.
- Do *not* perform surgery to reduce the ambiguous penis/clitoris to the size of a normal clitoris. Such surgery impairs the person's erotic sensation and is at best premature, as no one knows how the child's sexual orientation will develop. If the intersexed person makes an informed request for such surgery in adulthood, then it is appropriate, but otherwise it should be avoided.

STOP & CHECK

2. What is a common cause for a genetic female (XX) to develop a partly masculinized anatomy?
3. If a genetic female is exposed to extra testosterone during prenatal development, what behavioral effect is likely?
4. What would cause a genetic male (XY) to develop a partly feminized anatomy?

Check your answers on page 350.

Discrepancies of Sexual Appearance

The evidence from intersexes does not indisputably resolve the roles of rearing and hormones in determining gender identity. From a scientific viewpoint, the most decisive way to settle the issue would be to raise a normal male baby as a female or to raise a normal female baby as a male. If the process succeeded in producing an adult who was fully satisfied in the assigned role, we would know that upbringing determines gender identity. Although no one would perform such an experiment intentionally, we can learn from accidental events. In some cases, someone was exposed to a more-or-less normal pattern of male hormones before and shortly after birth but then reared as a girl.

One kind of case was reported first in the Dominican Republic, and then in many other places throughout the world, usually in communities with much inbreeding. In each case, certain genetic males fail to produce *5α-reductase 2,* an enzyme that converts testosterone to *dihydrotestosterone.* Dihydrotestosterone is an androgen that is more effective than testosterone for masculinizing the external genitals. At birth, some of these individuals look almost like a typical female, while others have a swollen clitoris and somewhat "lumpy" labia. Nearly all are considered girls and reared as such. However, their brains had been exposed to male levels of testosterone during early development. At puberty, the testosterone levels increase sharply, the body makes increased amounts of a different enzyme that converts testosterone to dihydrotestosterone, and the result is the growth of a penis and scrotum.

Women: Imagine that at about age 12 years, your external genitals suddenly changed from female to male. Would you say, "Yep, okay, I guess I'm a boy now"? Most (but not all) of these people reacted exactly that way. The girl-turned-boy developed a male gender identity and directed his sexual interest toward females (Cohen-Kettenis, 2005; Imperato-McGinley, Guerrero, Gautier, & Peterson, 1974). Remember, these were not typical girls; their brains had been exposed to male levels of testosterone from prenatal life onward.

In other cases, genetic males have been born without a penis, or with almost no penis, because of severe malformations of the entire pelvic region. A few others lost their penis in early infancy because of a dog bite or various other accidents. In some of these cases, the families decided to rear the child as female on the theory that it is best to have an assigned gender that matches the appearance of the external genitals. By adolescence or adulthood, many (though not all) of these people asked to be reassigned as males, and some of those who continued to live as females said they felt conflicts and discontent with being female. Of those who were originally assigned and reared as males, none expressed any desire to switch to female (Meyer-Bahlburg, 2005). Unfortunately, we do not know how many of these individuals are fully satisfied with either the female or male identity, as most of the reports provide only limited information or cover the individual's life only through childhood or early adolescence. Still, it seems clear that the results vary from one person to another.

A well-known and particularly upsetting case is that of one infant boy whose penis foreskin would not retract enough for easy urination. His parents took him to a physician to circumcise the foreskin, but the physician, using an electrical procedure, set the current too high and accidentally burned off the entire penis. On the advice of respected and well-meaning authorities, the parents elected to rear the child as a female, with the appropriate corrective surgery. What makes this a particularly interesting case is that the child had a twin brother (whom the parents did not let the physician try to circumcise). If both twins developed satisfactory gender identities, one as a girl and the other as a boy, the results would imply that rearing was decisive in gender identity.

Initial reports claimed that the child reared as a girl had a female gender identity, though she also had strong tomboyish tendencies (Money & Schwartz, 1978). However, by about age 10, she had figured out that something was wrong and that "she" was really a boy. She had preferred boys' activities and played only with boys' toys. She even tried urinating in a standing position, despite always making a mess. By age 14, she insisted that she wanted to live as a boy. At that time, her (now his) father tearfully explained the earlier events. The child changed names and became known as a boy; at age 25, he married a somewhat older woman and adopted her children. Clearly, a biological predisposition had won out over the family's attempts to rear the child as a girl (Colapinto, 1997; Diamond & Sigmundson, 1997). Some years later, the story ended tragically with this man's suicide.

We should not draw universal conclusions from a single case. However, the point is that it was a mistake to impose surgery and hormonal treatments to try to force this child to become female. When the prenatal hormone pattern of the brain is in conflict with a child's appearance, no one can be sure how that child will develop psychologically. Hormones don't have complete control, but rearing patterns don't, either.

STOP & CHECK

5. What does the enzyme 5α-reductase 2 do?

Check your answer on page 350.

Possible Biological Bases of Sexual Orientation

Most people are sexually attracted to members of the opposite sex. Others are attracted to members of their own sex. What accounts for this difference? Most people say they *discovered* their sexual orientation; they did not *decide* it any more than they decided whether to be right-handed or left-handed. Most of our discussion will focus on male homosexuality, which is more common than female homosexuality and more heavily investigated.

Genetics

Some animals in captivity show a homosexual orientation, although no one knows how frequently such orientations occur in the wild. Some cases of nonhuman homosexuality can be traced to genetics (Pinckard, Stellflug, Resko, Roselli, & Stormshak, 2000). For example, male *Drosophila* with the *fruitless* gene court only other males.

Several studies of the genetics of human sexual orientation have advertised in gay or lesbian publications for homosexual men or women who have twins. Then they contacted the twins, not telling them how they got their names, and asked them to fill out a questionnaire. The questionnaire included diverse items to conceal the fact that the real interest was sexual orientation. Figure 11.14 shows the results for two such studies. Note that the probability of homosexuality is highest in monozygotic (identical) twins of the originally identified homosexual person, lower in dizygotic twins, and still lower in adopted brothers or sisters (Bailey & Pillard, 1991; Bailey, Pillard, Neale, & Agyei, 1993).

One concern is that the people who answer ads in gay publications may not be typical. To deal with this concern, another study examined the data from 794 pairs of twins who had responded to a national (U.S.A.) survey not related to sex. Of those 794 pairs, only 43 included at least one homosexual person, so the sample size was small. When one twin (either male or female) had a homosexual orientation, the other did also in 31% of monozygotic pairs and 8% of dizygotic pairs (Kendler, Thornton, Gilman, & Kessler, 2000). These results support the conclusion of a genetic tendency, although they also confirm that genetic factors are not the only influence. If they were, monozygotic twins would be 100% concordant. Note also that this study suggests a weaker genetic contribution than the previous studies did.

Several studies reported a higher incidence of homosexuality among the maternal than paternal relatives of homosexual men (Camperio-Ciani, Corna, &

Figure 11.14
Sexual orientations in adult relatives of a homosexual man or woman
Note that the probability of a homosexual orientation is highest among monozygotic twins of a homosexual individual, lower among dizygotic twins, and still lower among adopted brothers or sisters. These data suggest a genetic contribution toward the development of sexual orientation. *(Source: Based on the data of Bailey & Pillard, 1991; Bailey, Pillard, Neale, & Agyei, 1993)*

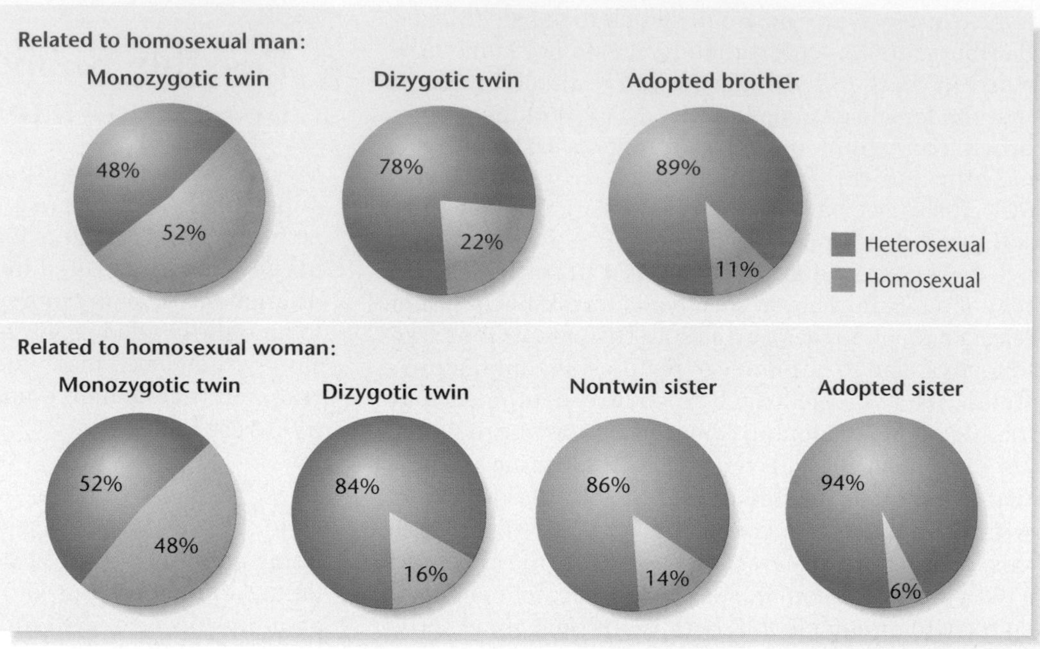

Capiluppi, 2004; Hamer, Hu, Magnuson, Hu, & Pattatucci, 1993). For example, uncles and cousins on the mother's side were more likely to be homosexual than uncles and cousins on the father's side. These results suggest a gene on the X chromosome, which a man necessarily receives from his mother. However, other studies have not replicated these results, and the current status is inconclusive (Bailey et al., 1999; Rice, Anderson, Risch, & Ebers, 1999).

If certain genes promote a homosexual orientation, why hasn't evolution selected strongly against those genes, which decrease the probability of reproduction? One hypothesis is that homosexual people help their brothers or sisters rear children and thereby perpetuate genes that the whole family shares (LeVay, 1993). However, survey data indicate that homosexual men are no more likely than heterosexuals to help their nephews or nieces (Bobrow & Bailey, 2001). Indeed, many are quite estranged from their relatives. A second hypothesis is that certain genes sometimes lead to homosexuality (perhaps in men homozygous for the gene) but in other men produce advantages, such as increased tendency to form friendships and alliances (Rahman & Wilson, 2003). So far, this hypothesis has not been tested.

According to another hypothesis, genes that produce homosexuality in males are in some way advantageous to their female relatives, increasing their probability of reproducing and therefore spreading the genes. The results of one study support this hypothesis. Homosexual men's mothers, and aunts on the mother's side, had more children on the average than other women did (Camperio-Ciani et al., 2004). Obviously, we need more research to decide among these and other hypotheses, if indeed genes have much to do with sexual orientation.

Hormones

Sexual orientation is clearly *not* related to adult hormone levels. Most homosexual men have testosterone and estrogen levels similar to those for heterosexual men; most lesbian women have hormone levels similar to those for heterosexual women. A more plausible hypothesis is that sexual orientation depends on testosterone levels during a sensitive period of brain development (Ellis & Ames, 1987). In studies of animals ranging from rats to pigs to zebra finches, males that were exposed to much-decreased levels of testosterone early in life have as adults shown sexual interest in other males (Adkins-Regan, 1988). Females exposed to extra testosterone during that period show an increased probability of attempting to mount sexual partners in the way that males typically do (Figure 11.15). However, in many of these studies, the animals not only acted somewhat like the opposite sex but also looked like them.

Homosexual and heterosexual humans look like each other in most ways but differ in subtle regards. On the average, the bones of the arms, legs, and hands are longer in heterosexual men than in homosexual men and longer in homosexual women than in heterosexual women. That is, in this regard, homosexual men are partly "feminized" and homosexual women are partly "masculinized" (Martin & Nguyen, 2004). The length of those bones begins to differ between boys and girls early in life—before puberty—so the differences probably relate to prenatal hormones.

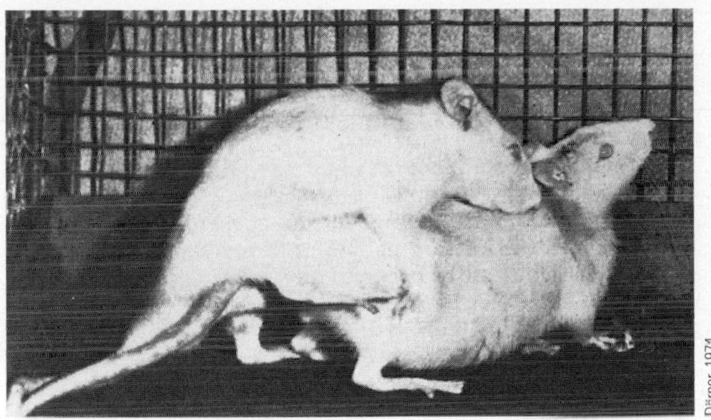
Dörner, 1974

Figure 11.15 A female rat mounting a male
The female was injected with androgens during an early sensitive period; the male was castrated at birth and injected with androgens at adulthood.

Researchers have examined brain structures that tend to be larger in heterosexual men than heterosexual women. The results are complex. In some ways, homosexual men are shifted partly in the female-typical direction but not in other ways. Similarly, on the average, homosexual women's brains are slightly shifted in the male direction in some ways but not others (Rahman & Wilson, 2003).

Consider another task: Experimenters repeatedly present a loud noise and measure the startle response. On some trials, they present a weaker noise just before the loud noise; the first noise decreases the startle response to the louder one. The decrease is called "prepulse inhibition." Prepulse inhibition is ordinarily stronger in men than in women. In this regard, homosexual men do not differ significantly from heterosexual men, but homosexual women are slightly shifted in the male direction compared to heterosexual women (Rahman, Kumari, & Wilson, 2003).

Overall, what do these results indicate? Homosexual women appear to have been masculinized, on the average, in some ways and not others. Homosexual men appear to be shifted in the female direction in some ways and not others. These results cannot make sense in terms of an *overall* increase or decrease in prenatal exposure to testosterone. They might, however, indicate altered amounts of testosterone at particular stages of development. They might also indicate that certain brain areas have altered sensitivities to testosterone (Rahman & Wilson, 2003). Bear in mind that each of the results varies from one individual to another, and there are no doubt many factors influencing sexual orientation.

Prenatal Events

The probability of a homosexual orientation is higher among men with older brothers than among oldest sons. The greater the number of older brothers, the greater the probability. The number of younger brothers makes no difference, nor does the number or age of sisters (Bogaert, 2003b; Purcell, Blanchard, & Zucker, 2000). Nothing about older or younger brothers or sisters relates significantly to homosexuality among women. These results suggest that a mother's immune system sometimes reacts against a protein in a son and then attacks subsequent sons enough to alter their development. That hypothesis fits with the observation that later-born homosexual men tend to be shorter than average (Bogaert, 2003a). However, this hypothesis seems to predict that if one son is homosexual, all later sons will be also, and that prediction is incorrect. If this hypothesis is on the right track, it will need to be refined.

Laboratory research has shown that prenatal stress can alter sexual development. In several experiments, rats in the final week of pregnancy had the stressful experience of confinement in tight Plexiglas tubes for more than 2 hours each day under bright lights. In some cases, they were given alcohol as well. These rats' daughters looked and acted approximately normal. The sons, however, had normal male anatomy but, at adulthood, often responded to the presence of another male by arching their backs in the typical rat female posture for sex (I. L. Ward, Ward, Winn, & Bielawski, 1994). Most males that were subjected to either prenatal stress or alcohol developed male sexual behavior in addition to these female sexual behaviors, but those who were subjected to both stress and alcohol had decreased male sexual behaviors (I. L. Ward, Bennett, Ward, Hendricks, & French, 1999).

Prenatal stress and alcohol may alter brain development through several routes. Stress releases endorphins, which can antagonize the effects of testosterone on the hypothalamus (O. B. Ward, Monaghan, & Ward, 1986). Stress also elevates levels of the adrenal hormone corticosterone, which decreases testosterone release (O. Ward, Ward, Denning, French, & Hendricks, 2002; M. Williams, Davis, McCrea, Long, & Hennessy, 1999). The long-term effects of either prenatal stress or alcohol include several changes in the structure of the nervous system, making the affected males' anatomy closer to that of females (Nosenko & Reznikov, 2001; I. Ward, Romeo, Denning, & Ward, 1999).

Although the relevance of these results to humans is debatable, they prompted investigators to examine possible effects of prenatal stress on humans. One approach is to ask the mothers of homosexual men whether they experienced any unusual stress during pregnancy. Three surveys compared mothers of homosexual sons to mothers of heterosexual sons. In two of the three, the mothers of homosexual sons recalled more than average stressful experiences during their pregnancies (Bailey, Willerman, & Parks, 1991; Ellis, Ames, Peckham, & Burke, 1988; Ellis & Cole-Harding, 2001). However, these studies relied on women's memories of pregnancies more than 20 years earlier. A better but more difficult procedure would be to measure stress during pregnancy and examine the sexual orientation of the sons many years later.

Brain Anatomy

On the average, men's brains differ from women's in several ways, including the sizes of several parts of the hypothalamus (Swaab, Chung, Kruijver, Hofman, & Ishunina, 2001). Do the brains of homosexual men differ from those of heterosexual men?

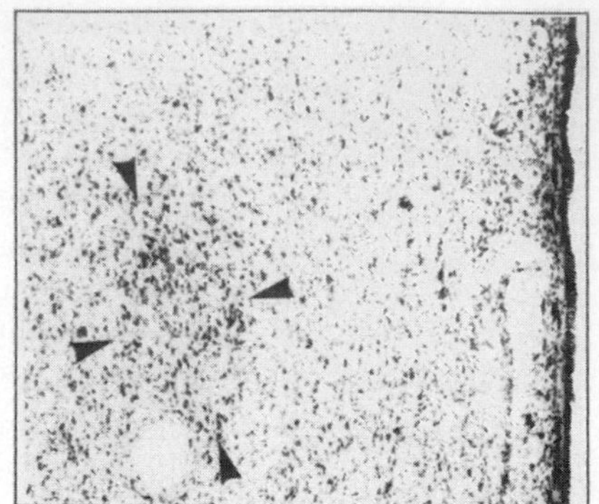
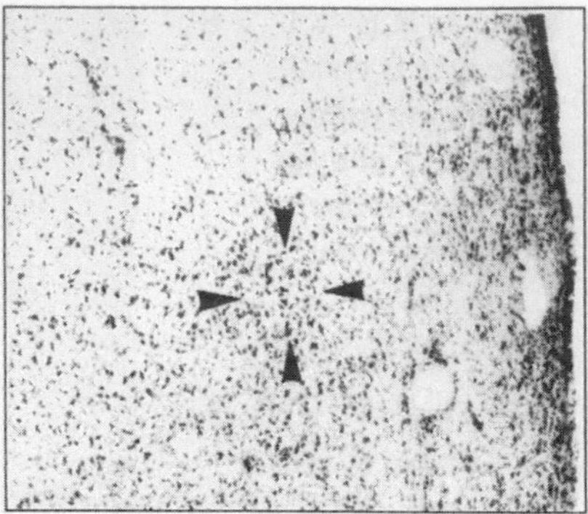

Figure 11.16 Typical sizes of interstitial nucleus 3 of the anterior hypothalamus
On the average, the volume of this structure was more than twice as large in a sample of heterosexual men (left) than it was in a sample of homosexual men (right), for whom it was about the same size as that in women. Animal studies have implicated this structure as important for male sexual activities. *(Source: Reprinted with permission from "A difference in hypothalamic structure between heterosexual and homosexual men," by S. LeVay, Science, 253, pp. 1034–1037. Copyright © 1991 American Association for the Advancement of Science.)*

Results vary from one brain area to another. The anterior commissure (see p. 91) is, on the average, larger in heterosexual women than in heterosexual men; in homosexual men, it is at least as large as in women, perhaps even slightly larger (Gorski & Allen, 1992). The implications of this difference are unclear, as the anterior commissure has no known relationship to sexual behavior. The suprachiasmatic nucleus (SCN) is also larger in homosexual men than in heterosexual men (Swaab & Hofman, 1990). Recall from Chapter 9 that the SCN controls circadian rhythms. How might a difference in the SCN relate to sexual orientation? The answer is not clear, but male rats that are deprived of testosterone during early development also show abnormalities in the SCN, and their preference for male or female sexual partners varies with time of day. They make sexual advances toward both male and female partners early in their active period of the day but mostly toward females as the day goes on (Swaab, Slob, Houtsmuller, Brand, & Zhou, 1995). Does human sexual orientation fluctuate depending on time of day? No research has been reported.

The most suggestive studies concern the third interstitial nucleus of the anterior hypothalamus (INAH-3), which is generally more than twice as large in heterosexual men as in women. This area corresponds to part of the sexually dimorphic nucleus, which is larger in male than female rats. Simon LeVay (1991) examined INAH-3 in 41 people who had died between the ages of 26 and 59. Of these, 16 were heterosexual men, 6 were heterosexual women, and 19 were homosexual men. All of the homosexual men, 6 of the 16 heterosexual men, and 1 of the 6 women had died of AIDS. LeVay found that the mean volume of INAH-3 was 0.12 mm^3 in heterosexual men, 0.056 mm^3 in heterosexual women, and 0.051 mm^3 in homosexual men. Figure 11.16 shows typical cross-sections for a heterosexual man and a homosexual man. Figure 11.17 shows the distribution of volumes for the three groups. Note that the difference between heterosexual men and the other two groups is fairly large and that the cause of death (AIDS versus other) has no clear relationship to the results. LeVay (1993) later examined the hypothalamus of a homosexual man who died of lung cancer; he had a small INAH-3, like the homosexual men who died of AIDS.

A later study partly replicated these general trends. Researchers found that the INAH-3 nucleus was slightly larger in heterosexual than homosexual men, although in this study the homosexual men's INAH-3 nucleus was larger than that of heterosexual women (Byne et al., 2001). Among heterosexual men or women, the INAH-3 nucleus was larger in those who were HIV negative than those who were HIV positive, but even if we look only at HIV+ men, we still find a difference in the hypothalamus between heterosexual and homosexual men. Figure 11.18 displays the means for the five groups. On microscopic examination of the INAH-3, researchers found that heterosexual men had larger neurons than homosexual men but about the same number. (Neither this study nor LeVay's earlier study included homosexual females.)

Interpreting these studies is another matter, however. One possibility is that brain differences predisposed some men to become homosexual and others to become heterosexual. Another possibility is that different kinds of sexual activity produce changes in the size of the adult hypothalamic neurons. Some brain areas do grow or shrink in adults as a result of hormonal or behavioral influences (Cooke, Tabibnia, & Breedlove, 1999). A further limitation is that we do not know the role of INAH-3 in human sexual behavior.

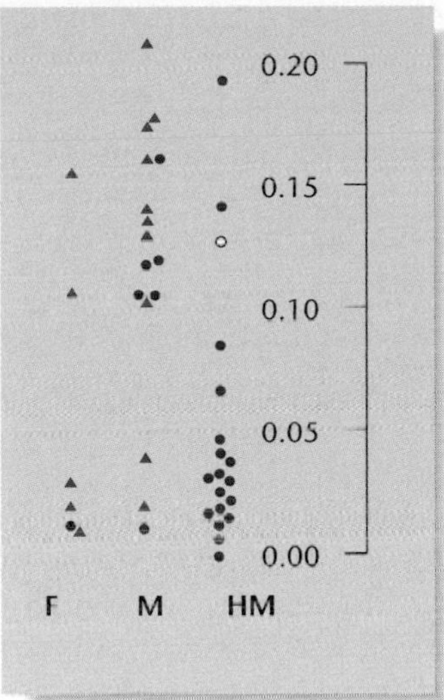

Figure 11.17 Volumes of the interstitial nucleus 3 of the anterior hypothalamus (INAH-3)
Samples are females (F), heterosexual males (M), and homosexual males (HM). Each filled circle represents a person who died of AIDS; each triangle represents a person who died from other causes. The one open circle represents a bisexual man who died of AIDS. *(Source: Reprinted with permission from "A difference in hypothalamic structure between heterosexual and homosexual men," by S. LeVay, Science, 253, pp. 1034–1037. Copyright © 1991 American Association for the Advancement of Science.)*

STOP & CHECK

6. What kind of experience in early development can cause a male rat to develop sexual responsiveness to other males and not to females? How does that experience probably produce its effects?
7. What is the relationship between birth order and homosexuality?
8. What evidence argues against the hypothesis that homosexual men have been feminized in general or that homosexual women have been masculinized in general?

Check your answers on page 350.

Module 11.2
In Closing: We Are Not All the Same

When Alfred Kinsey conducted the first massive surveys of human sexual behavior, he found that people varied enormously in their frequency of sexual acts, but each person considered his or her own frequency "normal." Many believed that sexual activity much more frequent than their own was excessive and abnormal and might even lead to insanity (Kinsey, Pomeroy, & Martin, 1948; Kinsey, Pomeroy, Martin, & Gebhard, 1953).

How far have we come since then? People today are more aware of sexual diversity than they were in Kinsey's time and generally more accepting. Still, intolerance remains common. Biological research will not tell us how to treat one another, but it can help us understand how we come to be so different.

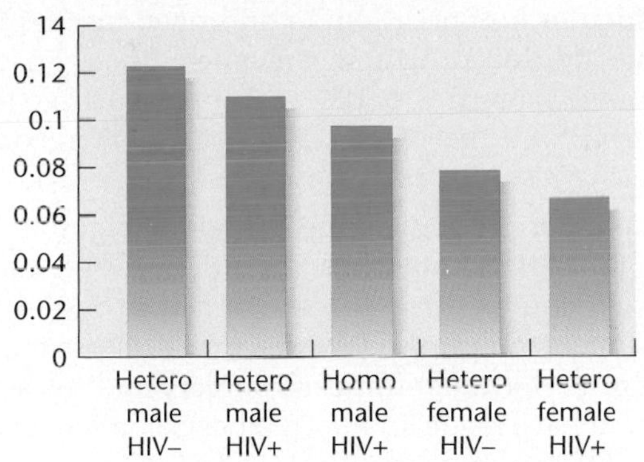

Figure 11.18 Another comparison of INAH-3
In this study, the mean volume for homosexual men was larger than that of women but smaller than that of men. *(Source: Based on data of Byne et al., 2001)*

Summary

1. Many of the mating habits of people make sense in terms of increasing the probability of passing on our genes. If we saw the same behaviors in nonhumans, we probably assume a genetic, evolved basis. However, in humans, we cannot assume a genetic basis because people may have learned these behaviors and preferences. (p. 339)
2. People can develop ambiguous genitals or genitals that don't match their chromosomal sex for several reasons. One is congenital adrenal hyperplasia, in which a genetic defect in cortisol production leads to overstimulation of the adrenal gland and therefore extra testosterone production. When that condition occurs in a female fetus, she becomes partly masculinized. (p. 341)
3. On the average, girls with a history of congenital adrenal hyperplasia show more interest in boy-typical toys than other girls do, and during adolescence and young adulthood, they continue to show partly masculinized interests. These trends apparently relate to the influence of prenatal hormones. (p. 342)

4. Testicular feminization, or androgen insensitivity, is a condition in which someone with an XY chromosome pattern is partly or fully insensitive to androgens and therefore develops a female external appearance. (p. 343)
5. People born with intermediate or ambiguous genitals are called intersexes. Traditionally, physicians have recommended surgery to make these people look more feminine. However, many intersexed people protest against imposed surgery and insist they should have made an informed decision themselves. (p. 343)
6. Some children have a gene that decreases their early production of dihydrotestosterone. Such a child looks female at birth and is considered a girl but develops a penis at adolescence. Most of these people then accept a male gender identity. (p. 344)
7. One genetic male was exposed to normal male hormones until infancy, when his penis was accidentally removed and then his testes intentionally removed. In spite of being reared as a girl, he had typically male interests and eventually insisted on a male gender identity. (p. 345)
8. Plausible biological explanations for homosexual orientation include genetics, prenatal hormones, and (in males) reactions to the mother's immune system. Hormone levels in adulthood are within the normal range. (p. 345)
9. On the average, homosexual people differ from heterosexual people in several anatomical and physiological regards. However, the data do not fit a hypothesis of anyone's being masculinized or feminized *in general*. Different aspects of anatomy and behavior are affected in different ways. (p. 346)

Answers to STOP & CHECK Questions

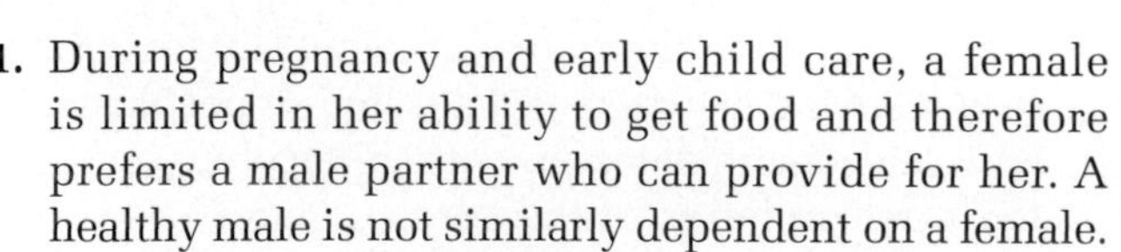

1. During pregnancy and early child care, a female is limited in her ability to get food and therefore prefers a male partner who can provide for her. A healthy male is not similarly dependent on a female. (p. 340)
2. If a genetic female is genetically deficient in her ability to produce cortisol, the pituitary does not receive negative feedback signals and therefore continues stimulating the adrenal gland. The adrenal gland then produces large amounts of other hormones, including testosterone, which masculinizes development. (p. 344)
3. A girl who is exposed to extra testosterone during prenatal development is more likely than most other girls to prefer boy-typical toys. (p. 344)
4. A genetic male with a gene that prevents testosterone from binding to its receptors will develop an appearance that partly or completely resembles females. (p. 344)
5. The enzyme 5α-reductase 2 catalyzes the conversion of testosterone to dihydrotestosterone, which is more effective in masculinizing the genitals. (p. 345)
6. Stressful experiences given to a rat late in her pregnancy can cause her male offspring to show a later preference for male partners. Evidently, the stress increases the release of endorphins in the hypothalamus, and very high endorphin levels can block the effects of testosterone. (p. 349)
7. The probability of homosexuality is somewhat elevated among boys who have older brothers. (p. 349)
8. On the average, homosexual men are shifted in the feminine direction in some ways and not others; homosexual women are shifted in the male direction in some ways and not others. (p. 349)

Thought Questions

1. In all human cultures, men prefer to mate with attractive young women, and women prefer men who are wealthy and successful (as well as attractive, if possible). It was remarked on page 340 that the similarity across cultures is not sufficient evidence to demonstrate that these preferences depend on genetics. What would be better evidence?
2. On the average, intersexes have IQ scores in the 110 to 125 range, well above the mean for the population (Dalton, 1968; Ehrhardt & Money, 1967; Lewis, Money, & Epstein, 1968). One possible interpretation is that a hormonal pattern intermediate between male and female promotes great intellectual development. Another possibility is that intersexuality may be more common in intelligent families than in less intelligent ones or that the more intelligent families are more likely to bring their intersex children to an investigator's attention. What kind of study would be best for deciding among these hypotheses? (For one answer, see Money & Lewis, 1966.)
3. Recall LeVay's study of brain anatomy in heterosexual and homosexual men (p. 348). Certain critics have suggested that one or more of the men classified as "heterosexual" might actually have been homosexual or bisexual. If so, would that fact strengthen or weaken the overall conclusions?

Chapter Ending

Key Terms and Activities

Terms

activating effect (p. 327)
alpha-fetoprotein (p. 329)
androgen (p. 326)
androgen insensitivity (or testicular feminization) (p. 343)
congenital adrenal hyperplasia (CAH) (p. 341)
estradiol (p. 326)
estrogen (p. 326)
follicle-stimulating hormone (FSH) (p. 332)
gender identity (p. 341)
hermaphrodite (p. 341)
impotence (p. 332)
intersex (or pseudohermaphrodite) (p. 341)
luteinizing hormone (LH) (p. 333)
menstrual cycle (p. 332)
Müllerian duct (p. 327)
organizing effect (p. 327)
ovary (p. 328)
periovulatory period (p. 333)
premenstrual syndrome (PMS) (p. 334)
progesterone (p. 326)
sensitive period (p. 328)
sex-limited genes (p. 326)
sexually dimorphic nucleus (p. 329)
SRY gene (p. 327)
steroid hormones (p. 326)
testis (p. 327)
testosterone (p. 327)
Wolffian duct (p. 327)

Suggestions for Further Reading

Colapinto, J. (2000). *As nature made him: The boy who was raised as a girl.* New York: HarperCollins. Describes the boy whose penis was accidentally removed, as presented on page 345.

Diamond, J. (1997). *Why is sex fun?* New York: Basic Books. Human sexual behavior differs from that of other species in many ways and therefore raises many evolutionary issues, which this book addresses. For example, why do humans have sex at times when the woman cannot become pregnant? Why do women have menopause? Why don't men breast-feed their babies? And what good are men, anyway? If you haven't thought about such questions before, you should read this book.

Dreger, A. D. (1998). *Hermaphrodites and the medical invention of sex.* Cambridge, MA: Harvard University Press. A fascinating history of how the medical profession has treated and mistreated hermaphrodites.

Websites to Explore

- You can go to the Biological Psychology Study Center and click these links. While there, you can also check for suggested articles available on InfoTrac College Edition. The Biological Psychology Internet address is:

http://psychology.wadsworth.com/book/kalatbiopsych9e/

The Endocrine Society

http://www.endo-society.org/

Intersex Society of North America

http://www.isna.org/

Exploring Biological Psychology CD

Menstruation Cycle (animation)
Erectile Dysfunction (video)
Chapter Quiz (multiple-choice questions)
Critical Thinking (essay questions)

ThomsonNOW™

http://www.thomsonedu.com

Go to this site for the link to ThomsonNOW, your one-stop study shop. Take a Pre-Test for this chapter, and ThomsonNOW will generate a Personalized Study Plan based on your test results. The Study Plan will identify the topics you need to review and direct you to online resources to help you master these topics. You can then take a Post-Test to help you determine the concepts you have mastered and what you still need work on.

Emotional Behaviors

12

Chapter Outline

Opposite: Even a static photo or statue can convey strong emotion, as in this statue, *The Angry Boy.* With movement, we can express even more.
Source: Gunnar Strom

Main Ideas

1. Emotions include cognitions, actions, and feelings. Several kinds of evidence support the theory that emotional feelings result from actions of the muscles or organs.
2. Many brain areas contribute to emotions. It is not clear that different emotions are localized differently in the brain.
3. Aggressive and fearful behaviors represent the combined outcome of many biological and environmental influences.
4. The amygdala responds quickly to emotional stimuli. Damage to the amygdala interferes with attention to information that is relevant to emotions.
5. Stressful events arouse the sympathetic nervous system and later the adrenal cortex. Prolonged or severe stress produces some of the same bodily responses that illness does.

> [W]e know the meaning [of consciousness] so long as no one asks us to define it.
>
> William James (1892/1961, p. 19)

> Unfortunately, one of the most significant things ever said about emotion may be that everyone knows what it is until they are asked to define it.
>
> Joseph LeDoux (1996, p. 23)

Suppose researchers have discovered a new species—let's call it species X—and psychologists begin testing its abilities. They let X touch a blue triangle that is extremely hot. X makes a loud sound and backs away. Then someone picks up the blue triangle (with padded gloves) and starts moving with it rapidly toward X. As soon as X sees this happening, it makes the same sound, turns, and starts moving rapidly away. Shall we conclude that it feels the emotion of fear?

If you said yes, now let me add: I said this was a new species, and so it is, but it's a new species of robot, not animal. Do you still think X feels emotions?

If such behavior isn't adequate evidence for emotion in a robot, is it adequate evidence for an animal? Biological researchers therefore concentrate mostly on emotional *behaviors,* which are observable, even if the emotions behind them are not.

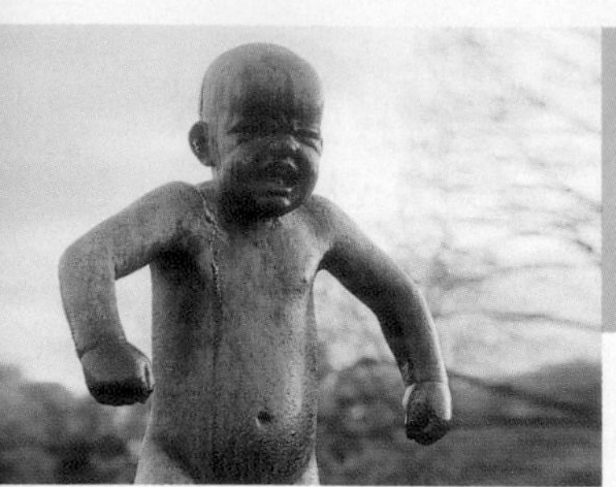

Module 12.1
What Is Emotion?

When you feel a strong emotion, you are inclined to do something vigorously. If you are afraid, you want to run away; if you are angry, you want to attack. If you are extremely joyful, your response is less predictable but usually vigorous. The last time your favorite team won a big game, did you jump, scream, hug nearby people?

Consider for a moment an apparent exception: You're lying in bed when you hear an intruder break into the house. You might lie there frozen with fear, feeling a strong emotion but doing nothing. True, you are not moving, but your heart is racing. You might continue lying there, hoping the intruder will leave without noticing you, but you are ready to run away or attack or do whatever else becomes necessary. Certainly, whatever has aroused your emotions has also captured your attention.

In short, it is hard to imagine an emotion without some readiness for action. The most general theories of emotion deal with the relationship between emotion and action.

Emotions, Autonomic Response, and the James-Lange Theory

An emotional state, such as fear, includes three aspects—a cognition ("dangerous situation"), readiness for action (escape), and a feeling. Readiness for action depends on the autonomic nervous system, which has two branches—the sympathetic and the parasympathetic. Figure 12.1 provides a reminder of the anatomy of the autonomic nervous system. The sympathetic nervous system prepares the body for brief, intense, vigorous "fight-or-flight" responses. The parasympathetic nervous system increases digestion and other processes that save energy and prepare for later events. However, each situation calls for its own special mixture of sympathetic and parasympathetic arousal (Wolf, 1995). For a simple example, running away from danger and swimming away from it require different patterns of blood flow. Nausea is associated with sympathetic stimulation of the stomach (decreasing its contractions and secretions) and with parasympathetic stimulation of the intestines and salivary glands.

Exactly how does the autonomic nervous system relate to emotions? Common sense holds that first we feel an emotion, and the emotion changes our heart rate and other responses. In contrast, according to the **James-Lange theory** (James, 1884), the autonomic arousal and skeletal actions come first; what we experience as an emotion is the label we give to our responses: I am afraid *because* I run away; I am angry *because* I attack.

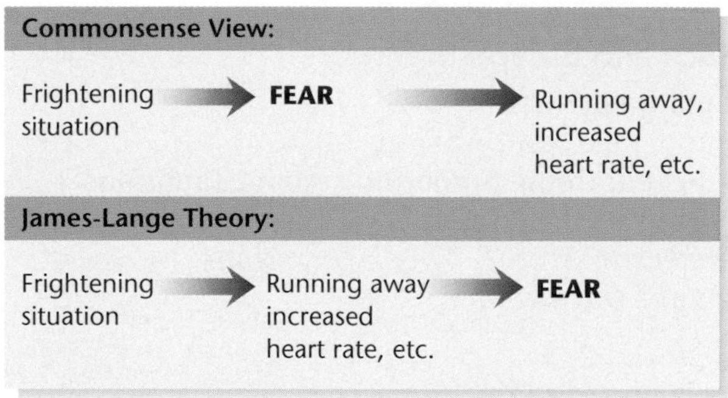

You might object, "How would I know that I should run away before I was scared?" In a later paper, William James (1894) clarified his position. An emotion has three components—cognitions, actions, and feelings. The cognitive aspect comes first. You appraise something as good or bad, frightening or irritating. That process is often amazingly quick; certain cells in the prefrontal cortex respond differently to "pleasant" or "unpleasant" photos within as little as an eighth of a second (Kawasaki et al., 2001). Your appraisal of the situation leads to actions, such as running away, attacking, or just sitting motionless with your heart racing. When William James had said that arousal and actions lead to emotions, what he meant was the *feeling* aspect of an emotion. That is,

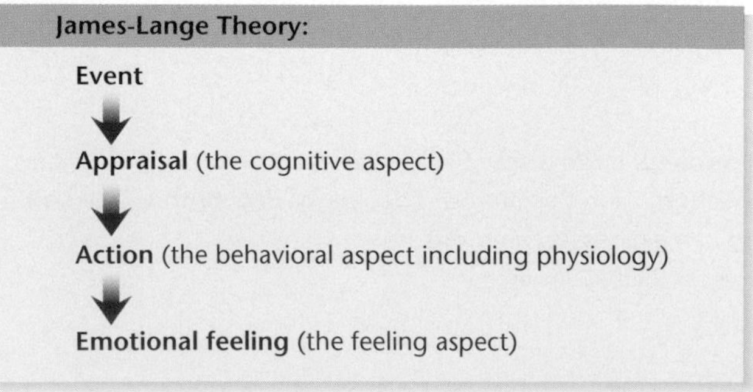

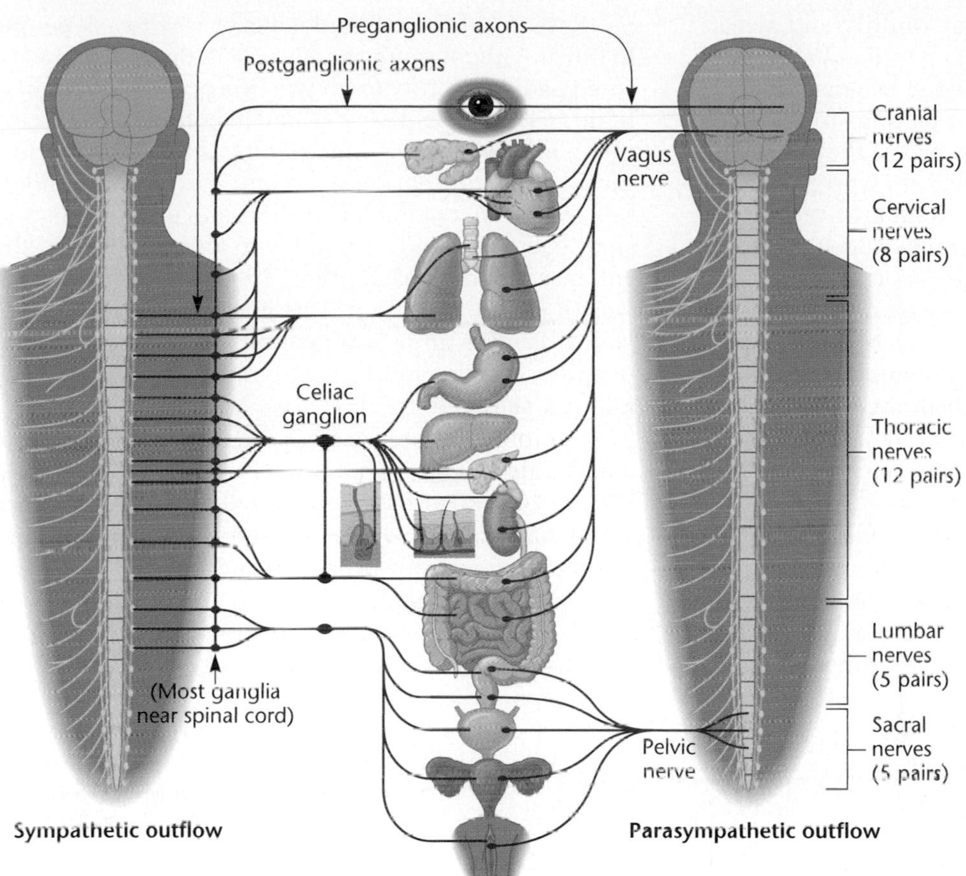

Figure 12.1 The sympathetic and parasympathetic nervous systems
Review Chapter 4 for more information.

The James-Lange theory leads to two predictions: People with weak autonomic or skeletal responses should feel less emotion, and causing or increasing someone's responses should enhance an emotion. Let's consider the evidence.

Is Physiological Arousal *Necessary* for Emotions?

People with damage to the spinal cord are paralyzed from the level of the damage downward. People who are unable to move their arms and legs certainly cannot attack or run away. Most such people report that they feel emotions about the same as before their injury (Cobos, Sánchez, Pérez, & Vila, 2004). This finding indicates that emotions do not depend on feedback from muscle movements. However, paralysis does not affect the autonomic nervous system, so it remains possible that emotional feelings depend on feedback from autonomic responses.

In people with an uncommon condition called **pure autonomic failure**, output from the autonomic nervous system to the body fails, either completely or almost completely. Heart beat and other activities continue to occur, but the nervous system no longer regulates them. One effect occurs when people stand up. When you suddenly stand up, gravity and inertia would pull the blood from your head toward the ground, except that your autonomic nervous system increases your heart rate and constricts the veins in your head. In someone with pure autonomic failure, those reflexes do not occur. To avoid fainting, people have to learn to stand up slowly. Also, people with this condition have no changes in heart rate, blood pressure, or sweating during any kind of psychological stress or physical challenge. According to the James-Lange theory, we would expect them to report no emotions. In fact, they report the same emotions as anyone else and have little difficulty identifying what emotion a character in a story would probably experience (Heims, Critchley, Dolan, Mathias, & Cipolotti, 2004). However, they report that they feel their emotions much less intensely than before the onset of the disease (Critchley, Mathias, & Dolan, 2001). Presumably, when they report emotions, they are reporting the cognitive aspect: "Yes, I'm angry; this is a situation that calls for anger." But they do not *feel* much anger. Their decreased emotional feeling is consistent with predictions from the James-Lange theory.

Is Physiological Arousal *Sufficient* for Emotions?

According to the James-Lange theory, emotional feelings result from our body's actions. If your heart started racing, and you started breathing rapidly and sweating, would you suddenly feel an emotion? Well, it depends. If all those changes occurred because you ran a mile, you would attribute your feelings to the exercise instead of any emotion. However, if they occurred spontaneously, you might indeed interpret your increased sympathetic nervous system arousal as fear. The rapid breathing in particular makes people worry that they are suffocating, and they experience a **panic attack,** marked by extreme sympathetic nervous system arousal (Klein, 1993). If someone has repeated panic attacks and starts to worry about them, the result is a clinical condition called panic disorder.

What about other emotions? For example, if you find yourself smiling, would you become happier? This is not an easy hypothesis to test. How could we get people to smile without first making them happy? Yes, of course, we could tell them to smile. However, if experimenters tell people to smile and then ask whether they are happy, people guess what the experiment is about and say what they think the experimenter wants to hear. Clever researchers did, however, find a way to get people to smile while concealing the purpose of the study, and it is a method you could easily try yourself: Hold a pen in your mouth, either with your teeth or with your lips, as shown in Figure 12.2. Now examine a page of comic strips in your newspaper. Mark each one + for very funny, ± for somewhat funny, or – for not funny. Most people rate cartoons funnier when holding a pen with their teeth—which forces a smile—than when holding it with their lips—which prevents a smile (Strack, Martin, & Stepper, 1988). That is, the sensation of smiling increases happiness, although only slightly. (Telling a depressed person to cheer up and smile does not help.)

try it yourself

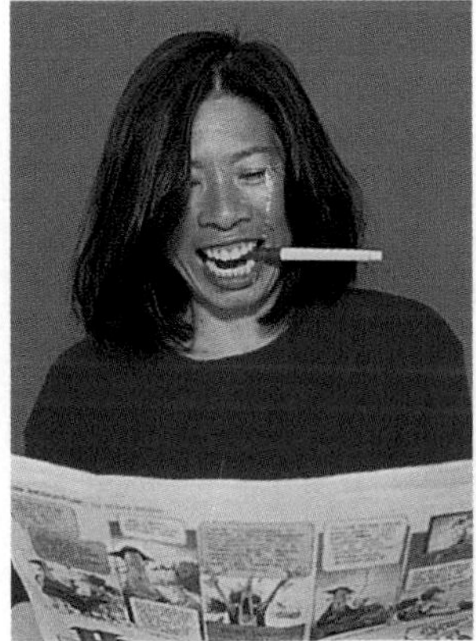

Kathleen Olson

Figure 12.2 Effect of facial expression on emotion
People who hold a pen in their teeth, and who are therefore forced to smile, are more likely to report amusement or humor than are people who hold a pen in their lips, who are therefore not smiling.

Researchers also found a clever way to ask people to frown without saying so. They said the research measured people's ability to do two things at the same time, in this case, a cognitive task and a motor task. The cognitive task was to examine photographs and rate how pleasant or unpleasant each one was. For the motor task, researchers attached golf tees to each of the person's eyebrows and said to try to keep the tips of the golf tees touching each other. The only way to do that was to frown. People in this group rated the photographs as more unpleasant compared to the average for people who were not induced to frown (Larsen, Kasimatis, & Frey, 1992).

In other studies, participants were asked to adopt a particular breathing pattern (Philippot, Chapelle, & Blairy, 2002) or posture (Flack, Laird, & Cavallaro, 1999). For example, to induce sadness, they were told to sigh frequently, or to sit with a dropped head and a limp body, lowering the eyebrows and pushing up the lower lip. Participants reported mild emotional feelings, usually appropriate to the instructions, although some reported anger when they were supposed to report fear or disgust when they were supposed to feel anger. We should not be surprised, as the physiological response of any emotion overlaps with those of others (Lang, 1994).

Overall, these results suggest that our perceptions of the body's actions do contribute to our emotional feelings, as the James-Lange theory proposed. They do not imply that feedback from the body is sufficient to identify one emotion from another—such as fear from anger. Labeling one emotion or another requires the cognitive aspect, and the James-Lange theory does not deny that it does.

STOP & CHECK

1. According to the James-Lange theory, what kind of person should feel no emotions?
2. How did researchers get people to smile or frown without using those words?

Check your answers on page 360.

Brain Areas Associated with Emotion

Do different emotions activate different brain areas, or do they activate the same brain areas in different ways? Moreover, which brain areas react most strongly to emotions?

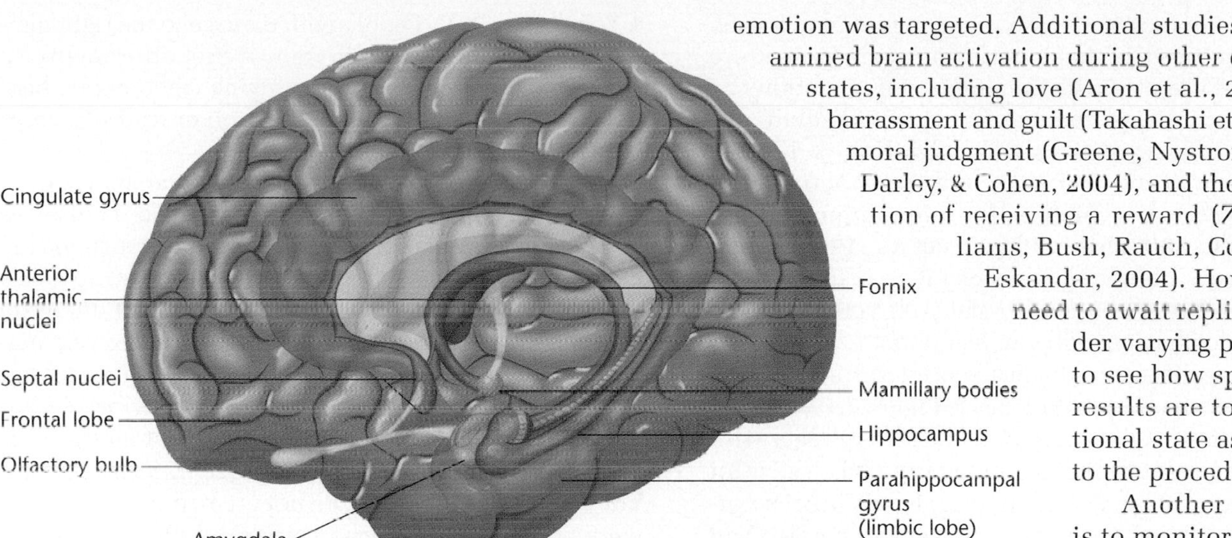

Figure 12.3 The limbic system
The limbic system is a group of structures in the interior of the brain. Here you see them as if you could look through a transparent exterior of the brain. *(Source: Based on MacLean, 1949)*

Attempts to Localize Specific Emotions

Traditionally, the **limbic system**—the forebrain areas surrounding the thalamus—has been regarded as critical for emotion (Figure 12.3). We shall especially encounter one part of it, the amygdala, later in this chapter. Much of the cerebral cortex also reacts to emotional situations. In many studies, participants have looked at photographs, listened to stories, or recalled personal experiences associated with a particular emotion. The researchers used PET or fMRI techniques to identify the cortical areas more active during that emotion than during a neutral period. Figure 12.4 shows the results of many studies. Each dot represents one research study that found significant activation of a particular cortical area associated with an emotion, and the color of the dot labels the emotion (Phan, Wager, Taylor, & Liberzon, 2002). The frontal and temporal cortices have many dots, and other kinds of research also point to these areas as important for emotions (Kringelbach, 2005). Otherwise, the main point that stands out is variability. We note some tendency for sadness dots, fear dots, or happiness dots to cluster together, but for the most part, the results look scattered. The results apparently depended heavily on details of procedure and not just on which emotion was targeted. Additional studies have examined brain activation during other emotional states, including love (Aron et al., 2005), embarrassment and guilt (Takahashi et al., 2004), moral judgment (Greene, Nystrom, Engell, Darley, & Cohen, 2004), and the anticipation of receiving a reward (Z. M. Williams, Bush, Rauch, Cosgrove, & Eskandar, 2004). However, we need to await replication under varying procedures to see how specific the results are to the emotional state as opposed to the procedure.

Another approach is to monitor electrical activity in various brain areas, using EEG or similar technology, as people examine pictures or other emotional stimuli. Different emotions activate different brain areas in the first half-second after stimulus presentation (Esslen, Pascual-Marqui, Hell, Kochi, & Lehmann, 2004). Still another approach is to use transcranial magnetic stimulation (Chapter 4) to temporarily inactivate an area; one study found that inactivation of the medial frontal cortex impaired the ability to recognize angry expressions (Harmer, Thilo, Roth-

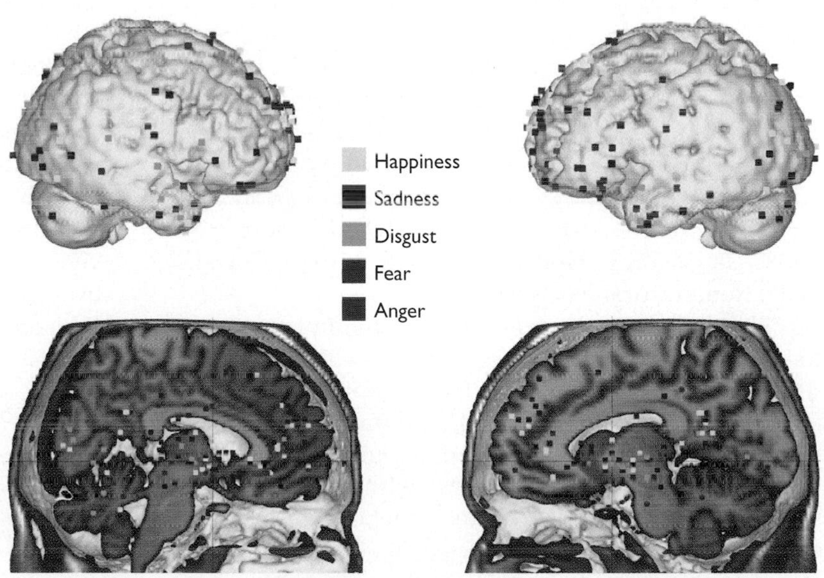

Figure 12.4 Brain areas associated with particular emotions
Each dot represents one study that found increased activity in a given brain area associated with the emotion designated by the color of the dot. *(Source: Reprinted from NeuroImage, 16, Phan, K. L., Wagner, T., Taylor, S. F., & Liberzon, I., "Functional neuroanatomy of emotion: A meta analysis of emotion activation studies in PET and fMRI," page 331–348, Copyright 2002, with permission from Elsevier.)*

well, & Goodwin, 2001). However, the problem in each of these methods is that small changes in procedure produce different results from one study to another.

Of all emotions, the one for which the evidence most strongly suggests brain localization is disgust. The *insular cortex,* or *insula,* is strongly activated if you see a disgusting picture (Murphy, Nimmo-Smith, & Lawrence, 2003; M. L. Phillips et al., 1997) or the facial expression of someone else who is feeling disgusted (Wicker et al., 2003). That is, if you see someone who looks disgusted, you feel it too.

Locating disgust in the insula is interesting because that is the primary taste cortex (see Figure 7.19, p. 219). *Disgust* is literally *dis-gust* or bad taste. To react with disgust is to react as if something tasted bad; we want to spit it out. One man with damage to his insular cortex not only failed to experience disgust but also had trouble recognizing other people's disgust expressions and did not recognize that a retching sound meant nausea or disgust (Calder, Keane, Manes, Antoun, & Young, 2000). However, the insula reacts to frightening pictures as well as disgusting ones, so it may not be specific to disgust (Schienle et al., 2002).

Contributions of the Left and Right Hemispheres

Another hypothesis relates the two hemispheres of the brain to different categories of emotion. Activity of the left hemisphere, especially its frontal and temporal lobes, relates to what Jeffrey Gray (1970) called the **Behavioral Activation System (BAS),** marked by low to moderate autonomic arousal, and a tendency to approach, which could characterize either happiness or anger. Increased activity of the frontal and temporal lobes of the right hemisphere is associated with the **Behavioral Inhibition System (BIS),** which increases attention and arousal, inhibits action, and stimulates emotions such as fear and disgust (Davidson & Fox, 1982; Davidson & Henriques, 2000; Murphy et al., 2003; Reuter-Lorenz & Davidson, 1981).

The difference between the hemispheres relates to personality: On the average, people with greater activity in the frontal cortex of the left hemisphere tend to be happier, more outgoing, and more fun-loving; people with greater right-hemisphere activity tend to be socially withdrawn, less satisfied with life, and prone to unpleasant emotions (Knyazev, Slobodskaya, & Wilson, 2002; Schmidt, 1999; Urry et al., 2004). We shall return to this point in Module 15.2.

The right hemisphere appears to be more responsive to emotional stimuli than the left. For example, listening to either laughter or crying activates the right amygdala more than the left (Sander & Scheich, 2001). When people look at faces, drawing their attention to the emotional expression increases the activity in the right temporal cortex (Narumoto, Okada, Sadato, Fukui, & Yonekura, 2001). People with damage to the right temporal cortex have trouble identifying other people's emotional expressions or even saying whether two people are expressing the same emotion or different ones (Rosen et al., 2002).

In one fascinating study, people watched videotapes of 10 people. All of those 10 described themselves honestly during one speech and completely dishonestly during another. The task of the observers was to guess which of the two interviews was the honest one. The task is more difficult than it might sound; the vast majority of people are no more correct than chance (about 5 of 10). The *only* group tested that performed better than chance was a group of people with left-hemisphere brain damage (Etcoff, Ekman, Magee, & Frank, 2000). They got only 60% correct—not great, but at least they were better than chance. Evidently, the right hemisphere is better not only at expressing emotions but also at detecting other people's emotions, and with the left hemisphere out of the way, the right hemisphere was free to do what it does best.

In yet another study, 11 patients went through a procedure in which one hemisphere at a time was anesthetized by drug injection into one of the carotid arteries, which provide blood to the head. (This procedure, called the Wada procedure, is used before certain kinds of brain surgery, as described in Methods 14.1, p. 421.) All 11 patients had left-hemisphere language, so they could not be interviewed with the left hemisphere inactivated. When they were tested with the right hemisphere inactivated, something fascinating happened: They could still describe any of the sad, frightening, or irritating events they had experienced in life, but they remembered only the facts, not the emotion. For example, one patient remembered a car wreck, another remembered visiting his mother while she was dying, and another remembered a time his wife threatened to kill him. But they denied they had felt any significant fear, sadness, or anger. When they described the same events with both hemispheres active, they remembered strong emotions indeed. So evidently, when the right hemisphere is inactive, people do not experience strong emotions and do not even remember feeling them (Ross, Homan, & Buck, 1994).

STOP & CHECK

3. Which kind of emotion, and which kind of sensation, depend most heavily on the insula?
4. What are the contributions of the right hemisphere to emotional behaviors and interpreting other people's emotions?

Check your answers on page 360.

The Functions of Emotions

If we evolved the capacity to experience and express emotions, emotions must have been adaptive to our ancestors, and presumably to us as well. What good do emotions do?

For certain emotions, the answer is clear. Fear alerts us to escape from danger. Anger directs us to attack an intruder. Disgust tells us to avoid something that might cause illness. The adaptive value of happiness, sadness, embarrassment, and other emotions is less obvious, although researchers have suggested some plausible possibilities.

In addition, emotions can provide a fairly useful guide when we need to make a quick decision. Although it is often best to suppress your emotional responses and consider a decision rationally, sometimes your "gut feeling" is a useful guide. In one study, college students viewed a series of slides of snakes and spiders, each presented for just 10 ms, followed by a masking stimulus—a random array of unrecognizable patterns. Under these conditions, people cannot identify what they saw, and if they have to guess whether it was a snake or a spider, they guess randomly. For each participant, one kind of stimulus—either the snakes or the spiders—was always followed by a mild shock 5.6 seconds later. Most people did show stimulus-specific conditioned responses. That is, those shocked after spider pictures showed a bigger heart rate increase after spider pictures, and people shocked after snake pictures showed increased heart rate after snake pictures, even though neither group could consciously identify any of the pictures. On certain trials, participants were asked to report any perceived changes in their heart rate, which were compared to external measurements of their actual heart rate. On other trials, after the stimulus, they guessed whether a shock was forthcoming. In general, those who were most accurate at reporting their heart rate increases were the most accurate at predicting whether they were about to get a shock (Katkin, Wiens, & Öhman, 2001). In short, people who are good at detecting their autonomic responses may have valid "gut feelings" about dangers that they cannot identify consciously.

People with a severe loss of emotions often make poor decisions. Antonio Damasio (1994) examined a man with prefrontal cortex damage who expressed almost no emotions. Nothing angered him; he was never very sad, even about his own brain damage. Nothing gave him much pleasure, not even music. Far from being purely rational, he frequently made bad decisions that cost him his job, his marriage, and his savings. When tested in the laboratory, he successfully predicted the probable outcomes of various decisions. For example, when asked what would happen if he cashed a check and the bank teller handed him too much money, he knew the probable consequences of returning it or walking away with it. But he admitted, "I still wouldn't know what to do" (A. R. Damasio, 1994, p. 49). He knew that one action would win him approval and another would get him in trouble, but he apparently did not anticipate that approval would feel good and trouble would feel bad. In a sense, any choice requires some consideration of values and emotions—how we think one outcome or another will make us feel. In Damasio's words, "Inevitably, emotions are inseparable from the idea of good and evil" (A. Damasio, 1999, p. 55).

Investigators also studied two young adults who had suffered prefrontal cortex damage in infancy (S. W. Anderson, Bechara, Damasio, Tranel, & Damasio, 1999). Apparently, they never learned moral behavior. From childhood onward, they frequently stole, lied, physically and verbally abused others, and failed to show any guilt. Neither had any friends or could keep a job.

Here is an experiment to explore further the role of emotions in making decisions. In the Iowa Gambling Task, people can draw one card at a time from four piles. They always win $100 in play money from decks A and B, $50 from C and D. However, some of the cards also have penalties:

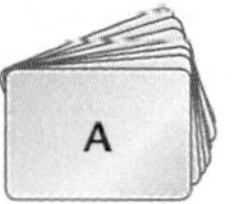

Gain $100; one-half of all cards also have penalties averaging $250

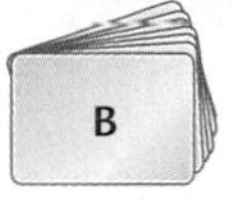

Gain $100; one-tenth of all cards also have penalties of $1250

Gain $50; one-half of all cards also have penalties averaging $50

Gain $50; one-tenth of all cards also have penalties of $250

When you see all the payoffs laid out, you can easily determine that the best strategy is to pick cards from decks C and D. In the experiment, however, people have to discover the payoffs by trial and error. Ordinarily, as people sample from all four decks, they gradually start showing signs of nervous tension whenever they draw a card from A or B, and they start shifting their preference toward C and D. People with damage to either the prefrontal cortex or the amygdala (part of the temporal lobe) show difficulties processing emotional information, and those with prefrontal damage have weak emotional expressions. In this experiment, they do not show any nervous tension associated with decks A and B, and they continue drawing from those decks (Bechara, Damasio, Damasio, & Lee, 1999). In short, failure to anticipate the unpleasantness of likely outcomes leads to bad decisions.

To be fair, it is also true that emotions sometimes interfere with good decisions. If you were driving and suddenly started skidding on a patch of ice, what would you do? A patient with damage to his prefrontal cortex who happened to face this situation calmly followed the advice he had always heard: Take your foot off the accelerator and steer in the direction of the skid (Shiv, Loewenstein, Bechara, Damasio, & Damasio, 2005). Most people in this situation panic, hit the brakes, steer away from the skid, and quickly make a bad situation worse.

STOP & CHECK

5. On what basis might someone argue that good decision-making requires an intermediate amount of emotion—not too much or too little?

Check your answer on this page.

Module 12.1

In Closing: Emotions and the Nervous System

Although we regard emotions as nebulous internal states, they are fundamentally biological. As William James observed well over a century ago, emotions are "embodied"—an emotional feeling requires some action of the body and perception of that action.

Biological research can shed light on many of the central questions about the psychology of emotions. For example, one issue is whether people have a few "basic" emotions or continuous dimensions along which emotions vary. If researchers find that different emotions depend on different brain areas, or that brain damage can alter one without altering others, the results would be strong evidence for basic emotions. If, however, all emotions overlap in the brain and no procedure impairs one kind of emotion without also impairing others, we would become more skeptical of the "basic emotions" approach. In short, understanding emotions and understanding their biology go hand in hand.

Summary

1. According to the James-Lange theory, the feeling aspect of an emotion results from feedback from actions of the muscles and organs. (p. 354)
2. Consistent with this theory, people who have impaired autonomic responses have weaker emotional feelings, although they continue to identify the cognitive aspects of emotion. (p. 355)
3. Feedback from facial movements, breathing, and posture can induce or strengthen an emotional feeling. (p. 356)
4. Emotional experiences arouse many brain areas, as measured by fMRI scans or EEG recordings. So far, the research does not convincingly assign different emotions to different brain areas, with the possible exception of disgust. (p. 357)
5. Activation of the frontal and temporal areas of the left hemisphere is associated with approach and the Behavioral Activation System. The corresponding areas of the right hemisphere are associated with withdrawal, decreased activity, and the Behavioral Inhibition System. (p. 358)
6. People with severely impaired emotions have trouble imagining which outcome they would prefer because they cannot imagine their emotional responses to those outcomes. Therefore, they often make poor decisions. (p. 359)
7. On the other hand, sometimes emotions also lead people to panic and act inappropriately. Although emotions can be helpful guides, we need to constrain them at times. (p. 359)

Answers to STOP & CHECK Questions

1. Someone who had no muscle movements and no perceivable changes in any organ should feel no emotions. However, such a person might still recognize the cognitive aspects of emotion. ("This is a sad situation.") (p. 356)
2. They got people to smile by telling them to hold a pen between their teeth. They got people to frown by attaching golf tees to their eyebrows and then telling them to keep the two tees touching each other. (p. 356)
3. The insula is important for disgust and taste. (p. 358)
4. Activation of the right hemisphere is associated with withdrawal from events and social contact. The right hemisphere is also more specialized than the left for interpreting other people's expressions of emotions. (p. 358)
5. People with severe impairments of emotion make poor and impulsive decisions, apparently unable to imagine how one outcome might make them feel better than another. However, a suddenly intense emotional feeling sometimes leads to ignoring sound advice, such as when a driver skidding on the ice suddenly hits the brakes. (p. 360)

Thought Question

According to the James-Lange theory, we should expect people with pure autonomic failure to experience weaker than average emotions. What kind of people might experience stronger than average emotions?

Module 12.2
Attack and Escape Behaviors

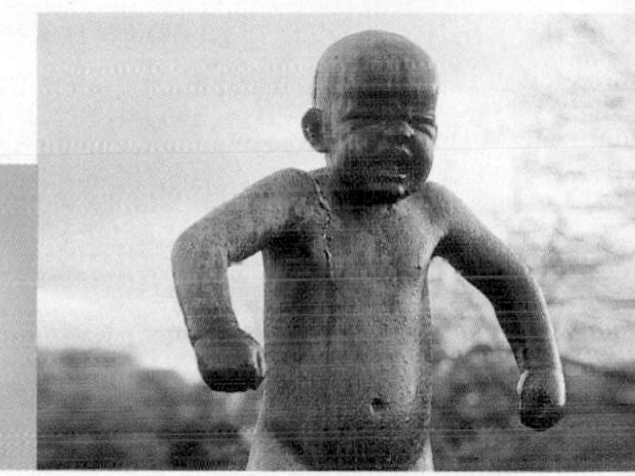

Have you ever watched a cat play with a rat or mouse before killing it? It might kick, bat, toss, pick up, shake, and carry the rodent. Is the cat sadistically tormenting its prey? No. Most of what we call its "play" behaviors are a compromise between attack and escape: When the rodent is facing away, the cat approaches; if the rodent turns around to face the cat, and especially if it bares its teeth, the cat bats it or kicks it defensively (Pellis et al., 1988). A cat usually goes for a quick kill if the rodent is small and inactive or if the cat has been given drugs that lower its anxiety. The same cat withdraws altogether if confronted with a large, menacing rodent. "Play" occurs in intermediate situations (Adamec, Stark-Adamec, & Livingston, 1980; Biben, 1979; Pellis et al., 1988).

Most of the vigorous emotional behaviors we observe in animals fall into the categories of attack and escape, and it is no coincidence that we describe the sympathetic nervous system as the fight-or-flight system. These behaviors and their corresponding emotions—anger and fear—attract much interest from both neuroscience researchers and clinical psychologists.

Attack Behaviors

Attack behavior may be wildly passionate or calm and detached. For example, a soldier in battle may feel no anger toward the enemy, and people sometimes make "cold-blooded" attacks for financial gain. We can hardly expect to find a single explanation for all aggressive behaviors.

Pains, threats, and other unpleasant events trigger most attacks, but attack behavior depends on the individual as well as the situation. For example, consider hamsters. If one intrudes into another's territory, the home hamster sniffs the intruder and eventually attacks, but usually not at once. Suppose the intruder leaves, and a little later, another hamster intrudes. The home hamster attacks faster and more vigorously than before. The first attack increases the probability of a second attack against any intruder for the next 30 minutes or more (Potegal, 1994). In other words, the first attack primes the hamster for another attack. You might say it's in a fighting mood. During that period, activity increases in the corticomedial area of the amygdala, a structure in the temporal lobe (Potegal, Ferris, Hebert, Meyerhoff, & Skaredoff, 1996) (Figure 12.5). It is pos-

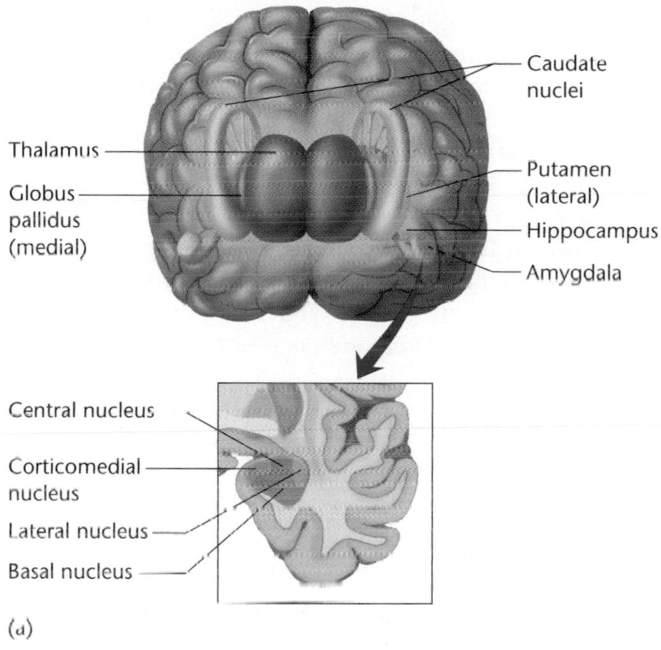

(a)

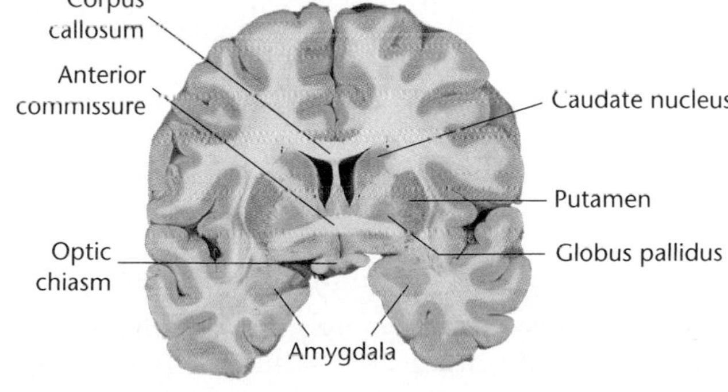

(b)

Figure 12.5 Location of amygdala in the human brain
The amygdala, located in the interior of the temporal lobe, receives input from many cortical and subcortical areas. Part (a) shows a blowup of separate nuclei of the amygdala. *[Source: (a) After Hanaway, Woolsey, Gado, & Roberts, 1998; Nieuwenhuys, Voogd, & vanHuijzen, 1988; (b) Photo courtesy of Dr. Dana Copeland]*

sible to bypass the experience and prime an attack by directly stimulating the corticomedial amygdala (Potegal, Hebert, DeCoster, & Meyerhoff, 1996).

Human behaviors are similar in this regard: After experiencing an insult or other provocation, people are more aggressive than usual for the next few minutes and not just against the person who first provoked them (Potegal, 1994). After someone has irritated you, you might yell at either that person or someone else. You have probably been told, "If you become angry, count to 10 before you act." Counting to a few thousand would work better, but the idea is correct.

Heredity and Environment in Violence

Why do some people turn to violence more readily than others do? Monozygotic twins resemble each other more closely than dizygotic twins do with regard to violent and criminal behaviors, and adopted children resemble their biological parents more closely than their adoptive parents (Mason & Frick, 1994). These results imply a genetic contribution. To explore this relationship further, researchers in one study distinguished between juvenile crimes and adult crimes. They found that dizygotic twins resembled each other in delinquent behavior just as much as monozygotic twins did during childhood and adolescence. However, monozygotic twins resembled each other much more than dizygotic twins did in *adult* crimes, suggesting that environmental similarities were more important early in life but that genetic factors became more important later (Lyons et al., 1995). How might a genetic influence become more important in adulthood than in childhood? The researchers suggested that adults have more control over their own environment. Those who are disposed to criminal behavior choose friends and activities that heighten that tendency and therefore magnify the influence of the genetic predisposition.

An important prenatal factor is the mother's smoking habits during pregnancy. Two studies found that the more a woman smoked during pregnancy, the more likely her son was to be arrested for criminal activities in adolescence and early adulthood (Brennan, Grekin, & Mednick, 1999; Fergusson, Woodward, & Horwood, 1998). The effect was particularly strong if the woman smoked *and* had complications during delivery (Figure 12.6). Of course, these results are correlational, and we do not know whether the women who smoked differed from other women in other ways that might also be important. For example, women who smoke during pregnancy may rear their children differently from other women in ways that contribute to antisocial behaviors.

In what ways could we imagine genes acting to increase the probability of violent crime? For one possibility, genes influence body size and therefore the probability of winning a fight. One study found that boys who were taller than average at age 3 years tended to be relatively fearless and aggressive at that age, and still to be relatively aggressive at age 11, even if they were no longer especially tall (Raine, Reynolds, Venables, Mednick, & Farrington, 1998). Perhaps fearlessness and aggressiveness had become habitual.

Environmental factors combine with genetic factors. One study of adopted children found the highest probability of aggressive behaviors and conduct disorders among those who had biological parents with criminal records *and* adoptive parents with marital discord, depression, substance abuse, or legal problems. A biological predisposition alone or a troubled adoptive family by itself produced only moderate effects (Cadoret, Yates, Troughton, Woodworth, & Stewart, 1995).

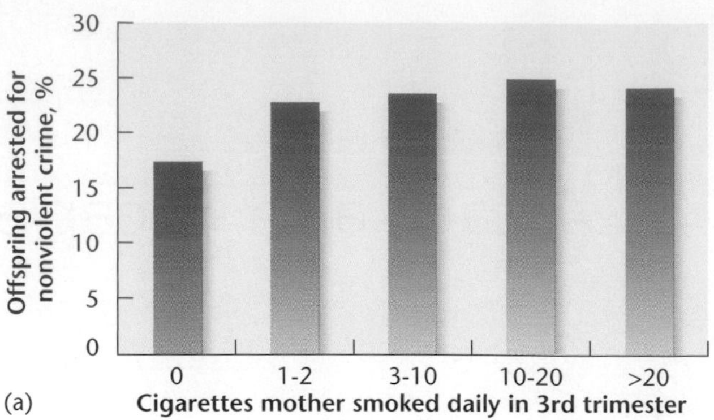

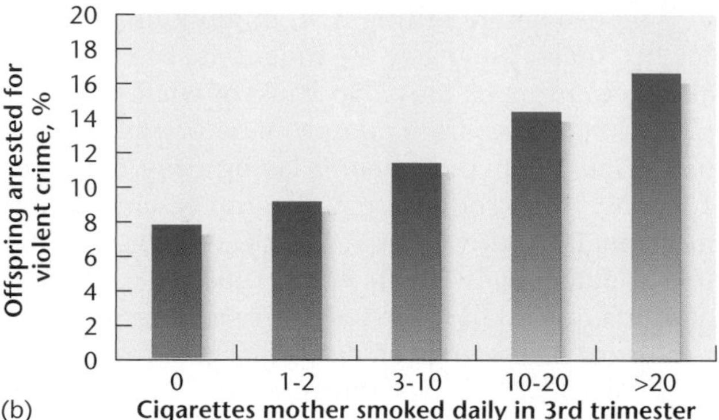

Figure 12.6 Effects of maternal smoking on later criminal behavior by her sons

The greater the number of cigarettes the mother smoked during the third trimester of pregnancy, the greater the percentage of her sons eventually arrested for violent crimes (bottom). Cigarette use did not correlate with nonviolent crimes (top). *(Source: From "Maternal smoking during pregnancy and adult male criminal outcomes," by P. A. Brennan, E. R. Grekin, and S. A. Mednick,* Archives of General Psychiatry, *56, pp. 215–219. Copyright © 1999 American Medical Association. Reprinted by permission.)*

STOP & CHECK

1. With regard to criminal behavior, adopted children resemble their biological relatives more closely than their adoptive relatives. One explanation for this observation is a genetic influence. What is the other?
2. What evidence suggests that criminal behavior depends on a combination of biological predisposition and family environment?

Check your answers on page 374.

Hormones

Most fighting throughout the animal kingdom is by males competing for mates or females defending their young. Male aggressive behavior depends heavily on testosterone, which is highest for adult males in the reproductive season.

Similarly, throughout the world, men fight more often than women, get arrested for violent crimes more often, shout insults at each other more often, and so forth. Moreover, the highest incidence of violence, as measured by crime statistics, is in men 15 to 25 years old, who have the highest testosterone levels. The studies that report high rates of violence by women tend to be those that include relatively minor acts (Archer, 2000).

Do the men with the highest testosterone levels also have the highest rates of violent behavior? Yes, somewhat, although the differences are small (Bernhardt, 1997; Brooks & Reddon, 1996). Figure 12.7 shows a typical set of results. Note that high testosterone levels were more common among men imprisoned for rape or murder than among those imprisoned for nonviolent crimes. Note also that the differences are not huge. They are also hard to interpret because environmental stressors could affect hormone levels and violent behavior independently.

Testosterone does not compel violent behavior, but it alters the way people react to various stimuli. In one study, young women who received injections of testosterone showed a greater than usual increase in heart rate when they looked at photographs of angry faces (van Honk et al., 2001). Testosterone may induce people to attend longer and respond more vigorously to situations related to aggression and conflict.

Brain Abnormalities and Violence

Several brain areas contribute to attack behaviors, and electrical stimulation of the brain can evoke aggressive behaviors. Depending on the exact location of the activation, an animal might attack another animal or just make a series of undirected growls and facial movements (A. Siegel & Pott, 1988) (Figure 12.8).

Intermittent explosive disorder, a condition marked by occasional outbursts of violent behavior with little or no provocation, is sometimes linked to temporal lobe epilepsy. An epileptic attack occurs when a population of neurons produces a sustained period of synchronous activity. When the epileptic focus is in the temporal lobe, the symptoms include hallucinations, lip smacking, other repetitive acts, and for some people, occasional emotional outbursts.

Here is a description of one patient with temporal lobe epilepsy and intermittent explosive disorder (Mark & Ervin, 1970):

> Thomas was a 34-year-old engineer, who, at the age of 20, had suffered a ruptured peptic ulcer. The resulting internal bleeding deprived his brain of blood and produced brain damage. Although his intelligence and creativity were unimpaired, there were some serious changes in his behavior, including outbursts of violent rage, sometimes against strangers and sometimes against people he knew. Sometimes his episodes began when he

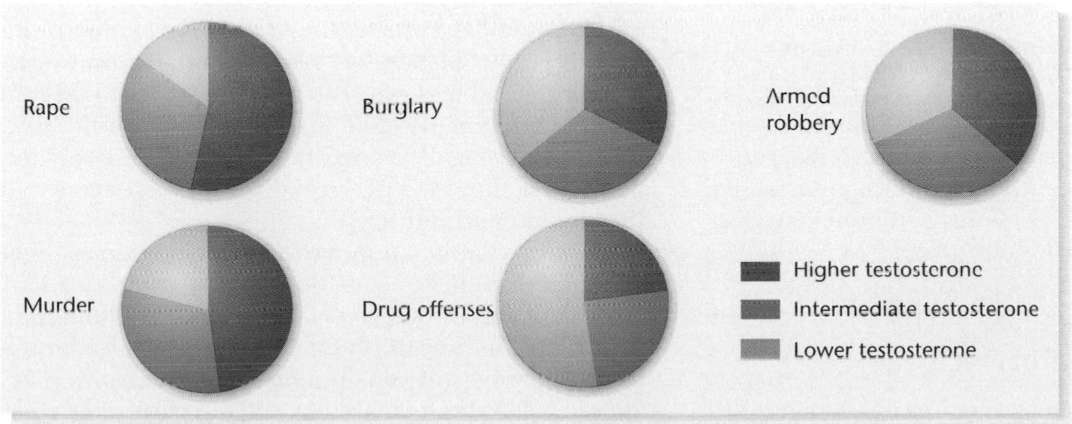

Figure 12.7 Testosterone levels for men convicted of various crimes
Men convicted of rape and murder have higher testosterone levels, on the average, than men convicted of burglary or drug offenses. *(Source: Based on Dabbs, Carr, Frady, & Riad, 1995)*

Figure 12.8 Effects of stimulation in the medial hypothalamus
Stimulation in some brain areas can lead to a full attack; in this case the result was undirected growling and facial expressions, a mere fragment of a normal attack.

was talking to his wife. He would then interpret something she said as an insult, throw her against the wall and attack her brutally for 5 to 6 minutes. After one of these attacks, he would go to sleep for a half hour and wake up feeling refreshed.

Eventually, he was taken to a hospital, where epileptic activity was found in the temporal lobes of his cerebral cortex. For the next 7 months, he was given a combination of anti-anxiety drugs, antiepileptic drugs, and other medications. None of these treatments reduced his violent behavior. Psychiatrists had previously treated him for 7 years without apparent effect. Eventually, he agreed to a surgical operation to destroy a small part of the amygdala on both sides of the brain. Afterwards, he had no more episodes of rage, although he continued to have periods of confusion and disordered thinking.

Temporal lobe epilepsy is uncommon, and most people with this kind of epilepsy do not show aggressive behaviors. Consequently, this brain abnormality accounts for only a small percentage of human aggressive acts.

Serotonin Synapses and Aggressive Behavior

Several lines of evidence link aggressive behavior to low serotonin release. Nearly all the evidence relies on correlations, not experiments, and we should be cautious about inferring cause and effect.

Nonhuman Animals

Much of the earliest evidence came from studies on mice. Luigi Valzelli (1973) found that isolating male mice for 4 weeks increased their aggressive behavior and decreased their serotonin turnover. **Turnover** is the amount of release and resynthesis of a neurotransmitter by presynaptic neurons. That is, a brain with low serotonin turnover releases relatively small amounts of serotonin and therefore does not need to resynthesize much of it. Serotonin turnover can be low even if the brain's total serotonin content is normal. Researchers infer turnover from the concentration of **5-hydroxyindoleacetic acid (5-HIAA)**, a serotonin metabolite, in the blood, cerebrospinal fluid (CSF), or urine. High levels of 5-HIAA imply much serotonin release and turnover.

Comparing different genetic strains of mice, Valzelli and his colleagues found the lowest serotonin turnover in strains that fought the most (Valzelli & Bernasconi, 1979). Social isolation does not decrease serotonin turnover in female mice in any genetic strain, and it does not make the females aggressive.

In a fascinating study, investigators measured 5-HIAA levels in 2-year-old male monkeys living in a natural environment and then observed their behavior closely. The monkeys in the lowest quartile for 5-HIAA, and therefore the lowest serotonin turnover, were the most aggressive, had the greatest probability of attacking larger monkeys, and incurred the most injuries. Most of them died by age 6, whereas all monkeys with high serotonin turnover survived (Higley et al., 1996). Female monkeys with low 5-HIAA levels are also likely to get injured and die young (Westergaaard, Cleveland, Trenkle, Lussier, & Higley, 2003).

If most monkeys with low turnover die young, why hasn't natural selection eliminated the genes for low serotonin turnover? One possibility is that evolution selects for an intermediate amount of aggression and anxiety (Trefilov, Berard, Krawczak, & Schmidtke, 2000). The most fearless animals get into fights and die young, but those with excessively high fears have other problems. A study of laboratory rats found that those showing the greatest fear—measured by hesitance to explore a new environment—died of natural causes earlier than other rats (Cavigelli & McClintock, 2003). A likely hypothesis is that they overreact to stressful events and thereby impair their health.

Another explanation sees aggressiveness as a high-risk, high-payoff strategy: Most monkeys with 5-HIAA die young, but the survivors often achieve a dominant status within their troop. In contrast, those with high 5-HIAA survive but remain submissive (Fairbanks et al., 2004). A dominant male has the opportunity to impregnate females beginning at an earlier age than other males (Gerald, Higley, Westergaard, Suomi, & Higley, 2002). A dominant female gets more than the average share of food for herself and her offspring. Thus, from an evolutionary standpoint, risking death to achieve a dominant status might make sense.

Humans

Many studies have found low serotonin turnover in people with a history of violent behavior, including people convicted of arson and other violent crimes (Virkkunen, Nuutila, Goodwin, & Linnoila, 1987) and people who attempt suicide by violent means (G. L. Brown et al., 1982; Edman, Åsberg, Levander, & Schalling, 1986; Mann, Arango, & Underwood, 1990; Pandey et al., 1995; Spreux-Varoquaux et al., 2001). Serotonin turnover varies by 5% to 10% from one time of year to another; a study in Belgium found higher suicide rates in spring, when serotonin turnover was lowest, and lower rates in fall and winter, when serotonin turnover was highest (Maes et al., 1995).

A study of children and adolescents with a history of aggressive behavior found that those with the lowest serotonin turnover were most likely to get into trouble for additional aggressive behavior during the following 2 years (Kruesi et al., 1992). Follow-up studies on people released from prison found that those with lower serotonin turnover had a greater probability of further convictions for violent crimes (Virkkunen, DeJong, Bartko, Goodwin, & Linnoila, 1989; Virkkunen, Eggert, Rawlings, & Linnoila, 1996). A study of people who had survived suicide attempts found that low serotonin turnover levels predicted additional suicide attempts within the next 5 years (Roy, DeJong, & Linnoila, 1989) (Figure 12.9). However, although each of these relationships is statistically reliable, blood tests do not enable anyone to identify dangerous people with confidence and then take preventive measures.

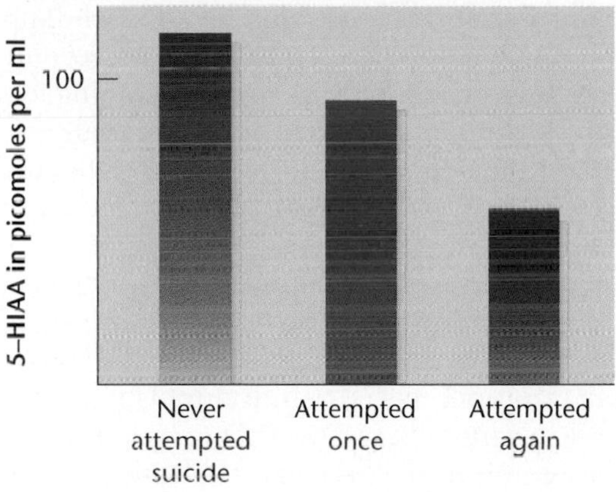

Figure 12.9 Levels of 5-HIAA in the CSF of depressed people

Measurements for the two suicide-attempting groups were taken after the first attempt. Low levels of 5-HIAA indicate low serotonin turnover. *(Source: Based on results of Roy, DeJong, & Linnoila, 1989)*

It is possible to alter serotonin synthesis by changes in diet. Neurons synthesize serotonin from tryptophan, an amino acid found in proteins, though seldom in large amounts. Tryptophan crosses the blood-brain barrier by an active transport channel that it shares with phenylalanine and other large amino acids. Thus, a diet high in other amino acids impairs the brain's ability to synthesize serotonin. One study found that many young men on such a diet showed an increase in aggressive behavior a few hours after eating (Moeller et al., 1996). Under the circumstances, it would seem prudent for anyone with aggressive or suicidal tendencies to reduce consumption of aspartame (NutraSweet), which is 50% phenylalanine, and maize (American corn), which is high in phenylalanine and low in tryptophan (Lytle, Messing, Fisher, & Phebus, 1975).

Might some of the variation in serotonin activity, and therefore violence, relate to genetics? People vary in the gene that controls *tryptophan hydroxylase,* the enzyme that converts tryptophan into serotonin. People with less active forms of this enzyme are more likely than other people to report frequent anger and aggression (Hennig, Reuter, Netter, Burk, & Landt, 2005; Rujescu et al., 2002) and more likely than others to make violent suicide attempts (Abbar et al., 2001). Another relevant gene controls the serotonin transporter—the protein in the membrane of the presynaptic neuron, which reabsorbs serotonin after its release and use. The "short" form of this gene, linked to decreased activity of the transporter, theoretically should increase serotonin transmission by prolonging the presence of serotonin in the synapse after its release. Behaviorally, this gene is linked to increased anxiety, which usually depresses aggressive behavior (Gross & Hen, 2004; Hariri et al., 2002).

Still another gene controls production of the enzyme *monoamine oxidase (MAO),* which breaks down serotonin into inactive chemicals. People who produce less of this enzyme, and who were also mistreated as children, are prone to violence and antisocial behaviors (Caspi et al., 2002). This result is interesting in its emphasis on the combination of both genetics and social environment. People with either the genetic or environmental influence, but not both, were only mildly prone to violence. Theoretically, however, the result is puzzling because decreased MAO should increase serotonin levels and therefore presumably decrease aggression.

Another problem: We shall get to depression in Chapter 15, but you might already know from other readings that depression is linked to low serotonin activity. Nevertheless, most depressed people are not violent. If some treatment suddenly lowered your serotonin level, would you at once become violent, depressed, or what? When researchers use drugs or diet to suppress serotonin levels, some people feel depressed, others become more aggressive or impulsive, and those with previous drug problems report a craving for drugs (Kaplan, Muldoon, Manuck, & Mann, 1997; Van der Does, 2001; S. N. Young & Leyton, 2002). In short, the role of serotonin is complicated, and you should not think of it as the "anti-aggression" transmitter.

An even more severe complication comes from reports that the brain releases serotonin during aggressive behavior (van der Vegt et al., 2003). If aggression releases serotonin, why are individuals with low serotonin release more aggressive? One hypothesis is that if one's serotonin release is usually low, the serotonin receptors become highly sensitive, and then when serotonin is released under conditions of possible aggression, they overreact. Another proposal is that although serotonin is released during aggressive behavior, it does not cause the aggressive behavior. One study found that serotonin was released during all social encounters among rats, regardless of whether the rats fought (Haller, Tóth, & Halász, 2005). Again, the conclusion is that serotonin's role is complicated and not well understood.

STOP & CHECK

3. How can one measure the amount of serotonin turnover in the brain?
4. What change in diet can alter the production of serotonin?
5. Given that monkeys with low serotonin turnover pick many fights and in most cases die young, what keeps natural selection from eliminating the genes for low serotonin turnover?

Check your answers on page 374.

Joe McBride/Getty Images

People's choices of activities depend in part on how easily they develop anxiety.

Escape, Fear, and Anxiety

We distinguish two closely related emotions: fear and anxiety. Fear is associated with a strong tendency to escape from some immediate threat. Anxiety is a general sense that something dangerous might occur, but you are not sure what, where, or when. With anxiety, you do not try to escape; you might even approach something to learn more about the possible danger (McNaughton & Corr, 2004). Often, however, people use these terms in overlapping ways.

Fear, Anxiety, and the Amygdala

Do we have any built-in, unlearned fears? Yes, at least one: Even newborns are frightened by loud noises. The response to an unexpected loud noise, known as the **startle reflex**, is extremely fast: Auditory information goes first to the cochlear nucleus in the medulla and from there directly to an area in the pons that commands the tensing of the muscles, especially the neck muscles. Tensing the neck muscles is important because the neck is so vulnerable to injury. (Recall from Chapter 5 how woodpeckers protect their necks while pecking a tree.) Information reaches the pons within 3 to 8 ms after a loud noise, and the full startle reflex occurs within two-tenths of a second (Yeomans & Frankland, 1996).

Although you don't learn your fear of loud noises, your current mood or past experiences can modify your reaction. Your startle reflex is more vigorous if you are already tense. People with posttraumatic stress disorder, who are certainly known for their intense anxiety, show a much stronger than normal startle reflex (Grillon, Morgan, Davis, & Southwick, 1998).

Studies of Rodents

Psychologists measure the enhancement of a startle reflex as a gauge of fear or anxiety. In research with nonhumans, psychologists typically first measure the normal response to a loud noise. Then they repeatedly pair a stimulus, such as a light, with shock. Finally, they present the light just before the loud noise and determine how much the light increases the startle response. A control group is tested with a light stimulus that has not been paired with shock. Results of such studies consistently show that after animals have learned to associate a stimulus with shock, that stimulus becomes a fear signal; presenting the stimulus just before a loud noise enhances the animal's response to the noise. Conversely, a stimulus previously associated with pleasant stimuli becomes a safety signal that decreases the startle reflex (Schmid, Koch, & Schnitzler, 1995).

Investigators have determined which brain areas are most important for enhancing the startle reflex. One key area is the amygdala (see Figures 12.5 and 12.10). Many cells in the amygdala, especially in the basolateral and central nuclei, get input from pain fibers as well as vision or hearing, so the circuitry is well suited to establishing conditioned fears (Uwano, Nishijo, Ono, & Tamura, 1995).

Output from the amygdala to the hypothalamus controls autonomic fear responses, such as increased blood pressure. The amygdala also has axons to areas of the prefrontal cortex that control approach and avoidance responses (Garcia, Vouimba, Baudry, & Thompson, 1999; Lacroix, Spinelli, Heidbreder, & Feldon, 2000). Additional axons extend to various areas in the midbrain that relay information to the nucleus in the pons that controls the startle reflex (Zhao & Davis, 2004). By this relay, the amygdala can enhance the startle reflex (LeDoux, Iwata, Cicchetti, & Reis, 1988). Figure 12.10 shows the connections.

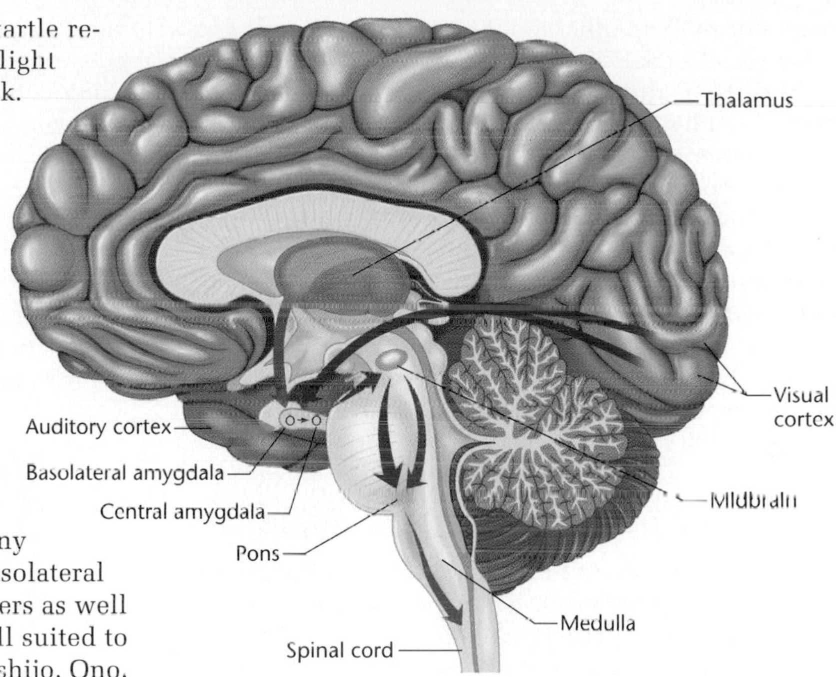

Figure 12.10 Amygdala and connections relevant to learned fears
Cells in the lateral and basolateral parts of the amygdala receive visual and auditory information and then send messages to the central amygdala, which then sends its output to the central gray area of the midbrain, which relays the information to a nucleus in the pons responsible for the startle reflex. Damage at any point along the route from amygdala to pons interferes with learned fears, although only damage to the pons would block the startle reflex itself.

Although a rat with damage to the amygdala still shows a normal startle reflex, a fear signal before the loud noise does not enhance the reflex. In one study, rats were repeatedly exposed to a light followed by shock and then tested for their responses to a loud noise. Intact rats showed a moderate startle reflex to the loud noise and an enhanced response if the light preceded the noise. In contrast, rats with damage in the path from the amygdala to the hindbrain showed a startle reflex but no enhancement by the light (Hitchcock & Davis, 1991). Damage to the amygdala interferes with both the learning of fear responses and retention of fear responses learned previously (Blair et al., 2005; Gale et al., 2004).

Do these results indicate that amygdala damage destroys fear? No, an alternative explanation is that the rats have trouble interpreting or understanding stimuli with emotional consequences. The same issue arises with humans, as we shall see.

An odd parasite has evolved a way to exploit the consequences of amygdala damage (Berdoy, Webster, & Macdonald, 2000). *Toxoplasma gondii* is a protozoan parasite that infects many mammals but reproduces only in cats. Cats excrete the parasite's eggs in their feces, thereby releasing them into the ground. Rats that burrow in the ground can become infected with the parasite. When the parasite enters a rat, it migrates to the brain where it apparently damages the amygdala. The rat then fearlessly approaches a cat, guaranteeing that the cat will eat the rat and that the parasite will find its way back into a cat!

Studies of Monkeys

The effect of amygdala damage in monkeys was described in classic studies early in the 1900s and is known as the *Klüver-Bucy syndrome*, from the names of the primary investigators. Monkeys showing this syndrome are tame and placid. They attempt to pick up lighted matches and other objects that they ordinarily avoid. They display less than the normal fear of snakes or of larger, more dominant monkeys (Kalin, Shelton, Davidson, & Kelley, 2001).

Amygdala damage, with the concomitant decrease of fear, alters monkeys' social behaviors. In one study, male monkeys with amygdala lesions sank to the bottom of the dominance hierarchy because they did not react normally to other monkeys' threat gestures and other social signals (Rosvold, Mirsky, & Pribram, 1954). That is, they approached other monkeys when they should not have.

In other studies, monkeys with amygdala lesions became more likely to approach snakes and unfamiliar people (Kalin, Shelton, & Davidson, 2004), as well as other monkeys (Emery et al., 2001). That is, in the process of becoming fearless, they also became "friendlier." People sometimes show a similar effect after taking anti-anxiety drugs. We all have a conflict about approaching other people: We desire the interaction, but we are afraid of rejection. After a decrease of fear, the approach motive becomes dominant.

Activation of the Human Amygdala

Many studies have used fMRI scans to measure brain activity while people looked at photos of faces. Looking at emotional expressions activates the amygdala, but the responses are not specific to fear. Rather, the amygdala apparently responds to expressions that require some emotional processing or that call for some emotional response. For example, in one study, participants looked at a first picture, which showed something threatening such as a gun or a snake. If their task was to look at two additional pictures and pick the one that matched the first, they showed enhanced activity in the amygdala. However, if their task was simply to classify objects as natural (like a snake) or artificial (like a gun), they showed enhanced activity in the prefrontal cortex but not much in the amygdala (Hariri, Mattay, Tessitore, Fera, & Weinberger, 2003). Presumably, the task of classifying objects as natural or artificial induced people to think about the objects in a way that interfered with emotional processing.

Ordinarily, people experience strong emotions when they see other people expressing emotions, especially anger and fear, and the amygdala responds strongly as well. Your experienced emotion depends on where the other person appears to be gazing. An angry face directed at you is threatening, whereas a fearful face directed toward you is usually puzzling. ("Why would someone look at me with fear? I'm not scary.") In contrast, an angry face directed to the side is less upsetting. ("That person is angry with someone else.") A fearful face directed to the side is more upsetting. ("Something over there is dangerous! I need to find out what, and why!") Consequently, you ordinarily recognize an angry expression faster if it is directed toward you and a fearful expression faster if it is directed to the side (Adams & Kleck, 2005).

The response of the amygdala to angry and fearful expressions also depends on gaze direction but not in the simple way we might guess. For angry expressions, one study found greater amygdala response to faces directed toward the viewer (Sato, Yoshikawa, Kochiyama, & Matsumura, 2004), and another study found greater response to faces directed to the side (Adams, Gordon, Baird, Ambady, & Kleck, 2003). The one study that compared gaze directions for fearful expressions found greater amygdala response for faces directed toward the viewer (Adams et al., 2003) (Figure 12.11). That is, a fearful face directed toward the viewer is *less* emotionally arousing, but it stimulates the amygdala more strongly. The researchers suggested that the amygdala responds strongly when the emotional interpretation is not obvious—when emotional processing is somewhat difficult.

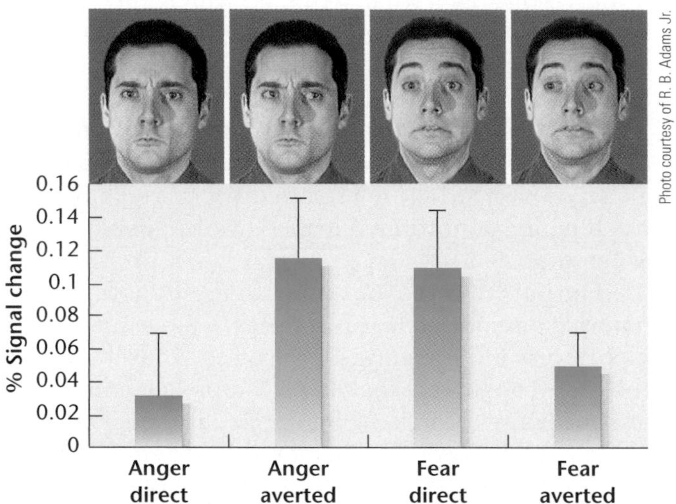

Figure 12.11 Amygdala response and direction of gaze

The amygdala responds more strongly to an angry face directed toward the viewer and to a frightened face directed toward something else. *(Source: Reprinted with permission from "Effects of gaze on amygdala sensitivity and fear faces," by R. B. Adams et al., Science, 300, 1536, Figure 1. Copyright © 2003 AAAS.)*

In most studies, looking at happy faces activates the amygdala only weakly in comparison to a neutral face. However, exceptions occur. Highly extraverted people show an enhanced response of the left amygdala to happy expressions (Canli, Sivers, Whitfield, Gotlib, & Gabrieli, 2002). People feeling strong anxiety actually show a stronger amygdala response to neutral faces than to happy faces (Somerville, Kim, Johnstone, Alexander, & Whalen, 2004). One interpretation is that they react to neutral faces as potentially unpleasant.

The amygdala responds even to emotional stimuli that people cannot identify consciously. For example, if an angry or frightened face is flashed on a screen briefly, while the person is attending to something else, the person may not recognize what appeared or even that anything appeared. The amygdala nevertheless responds and stimulates sweating and other autonomic responses (Kubota et al., 2000; Vuilleumier, Armony,

Driver, & Dolan, 2001). (Recall the earlier discussion about "gut feelings." Sometimes our body reacts emotionally when we do not consciously understand why.) Flashing similar pictures does not affect the autonomic responses of people with damage to the amygdala (Gläscher & Adolphs, 2003).

In one study, people wore a red filter over one eye and a green filter over the other eye while examining photos like the ones in Figure 12.12. The result is binocular rivalry, as discussed in Chapter 1, but because the pictures were flashed on the screen for only half a second, people almost always reported seeing only the red or the green image but not the other. On trials when they reported seeing a house and not a face, the amygdala responded anyway if the face expressed emotion (M. A. Williams, Morris, McGlone, Abbott, & Mattingley, 2004).

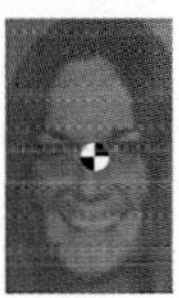

Figure 12.12 Stimuli to test unconscious arousal of the amygdala

People wore filters so that one eye saw the green picture and the other eye saw the red picture. Here the green pictures are houses and the red ones are faces with emotional expressions; in other cases, green and red were reversed. *(Source: Reprinted with permission from "Amygdala responses to fearful and happy facial expressions under conditions of binocular suppression," by M. A. Williams et al.,* Journal of Neuroscience, 24, *2898–2904. Copyright 2004 by the Society for Neuroscience.)*

Further evidence that the amygdala can react to emotional information even without conscious identification comes from studies of cortical blindness. One patient lost all conscious vision after strokes damaged his visual cortex in both hemispheres. Although he could not detect the presence of light, colors, or other visual information, when a face was displayed on a screen, he could guess whether it was happy or sad, or happy or fearful, with about 60% accuracy. Looking at emotional expressions activated his right amygdala and no cortical areas (Pegna, Khateb, Lazeyrus, & Seghier, 2004).

Damage to the Human Amygdala

People with the rare genetic disorder *Urbach-Wiethe disease* suffer skin lesions; many of them also accumulate calcium in the amygdala until it wastes away. Other people incur damage to the amygdala because of strokes or brain surgery. People with amygdala damage do not lose their emotions; they report that they continue to feel fear, anger, happiness, and other emotions more or less normally as a result of life events (A. K. Anderson & Phelps, 2002). However, they are impaired at processing emotional information when the signals are subtle or complicated (Baxter & Murray, 2002; Whalen, 1998).

For example, amygdala damage interferes with the social judgments that we constantly make about other people. When we look at other people's faces, some of them strike us, rightly or wrongly, as "untrustworthy," and looking at a face we regard as untrustworthy strongly activates the amygdala (Winston, Strange, O'Doherty, & Dolan, 2002). People with damage to the amygdala regard all faces as about equally trustworthy, and they approach people for help indiscriminately, instead of trying to find people who look and act friendly (Adolphs, Tranel, & Damasio, 1998).

People with amygdala damage also fail to focus their attention on emotional stimuli the way other people do. For example, when most people with an intact brain look at a picture of something highly emotional, such as one person attacking another, they remember the emotional part and forget most of the details in the background (Adolphs, Denburg, & Tranel, 2001). When they hear a highly emotional story, such as one about children who died in a plane crash, they remember the emotional gist and forget the details. When they see a series of words flashed briefly on the screen under distracting conditions, they notice more of the emotionally charged words like *kill* than unemotional words like *pear*. In all these regards, people with amygdala damage are different. They remember many of the irrelevant details of a story as much as the emotional gist (Adolphs, Tranel, & Buchanan, 2005), and they notice a flashed word like *pear* about as much as one like *kill* (A. K. Anderson & Phelps, 2001).

Such people also often fail to recognize the emotions that people in photographs express, especially when they express fear or disgust (Boucsein, Weniger, Mursch, Steinhoff, & Irle 2001). They also have some trouble recognizing anger, surprise, arrogance, guilt, admiration, and flirtation (Adolphs, Baron-Cohen, & Tranel, 2002; Adolphs, Tranel, Damasio, & Damasio, 1994). When one woman was asked to rate the apparent intensity of emotional expressions, she rated the intensity in the frightened, angry, or surprised faces much lower than any other observer did. Finally, when she was asked to draw faces showing certain emotions (Figure 12.13), she made good drawings of most expressions but had trouble drawing a fearful expression, saying that she did not know what such a face would look like. When the researcher insisted that she try, she drew someone crawling away with hair on end, as cartoonists often indicate fear (Adolphs, Tranel, Damasio, & Damasio, 1995).

But exactly why do people with amygdala damage fail to identify fearful expressions in photographs?

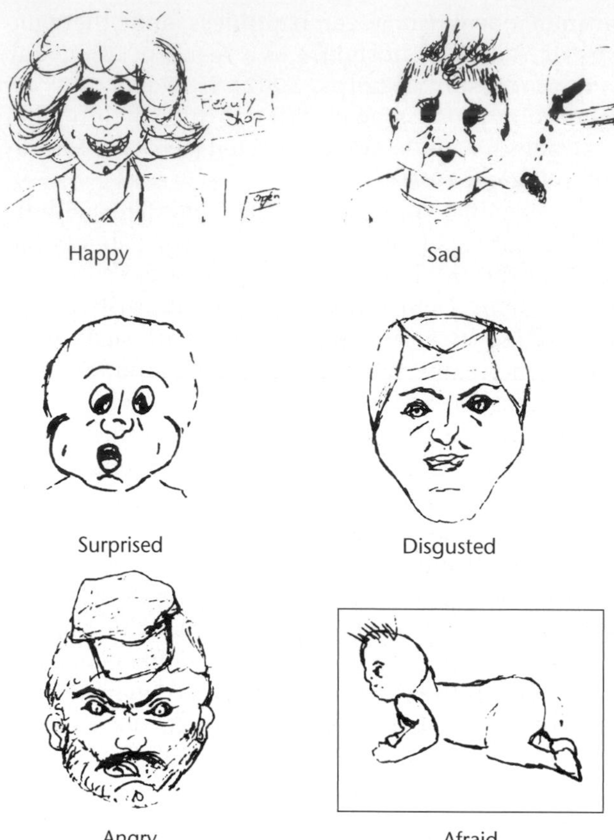

Figure 12.13 Drawings by a woman with a damaged amygdala
Note that her drawings of emotional expressions are fairly realistic and convincing except for fear. She at first declined to draw a fearful expression because, she said, she could not imagine it. When urged to try, she used the fact that frightened people try to escape, and she remembered that frightened people are often depicted with their hair on end, at least in cartoons. *(Source: From "Fear and the human amygdala," by R. Adolphs, D. Tranel, H. Damasio, and A. Damasio,* Journal of Neuroscience, 15, *pp. 5879–5891. Copyright © 1995 Oxford University Press. Reprinted by permission.)*

They are not incapable of recognizing fear; they recognize it well enough in everyday life and in movies, so the problem seems mainly limited to drawings and photographs (Adolphs, Tranel & Damasio, 2003). Ralph Adolphs and his colleagues observed that a woman with amygdala damage focused her view almost entirely on the nose and mouth of each photograph. When they instructed her to look at the eyes, she easily recognized the fearful expression (Adolphs et al., 2005). Focusing on the nose and mouth impairs fear recognition much more than that of other emotions. People express happiness mainly with the mouth, but fear almost entirely with the eyes (Morris, deBonis, & Dolan, 2002; Vuilleumier, 2005). Examine Figure 12.14, which shows only the whites of the eyes of people who were expressing two emotions. Most people react to the face

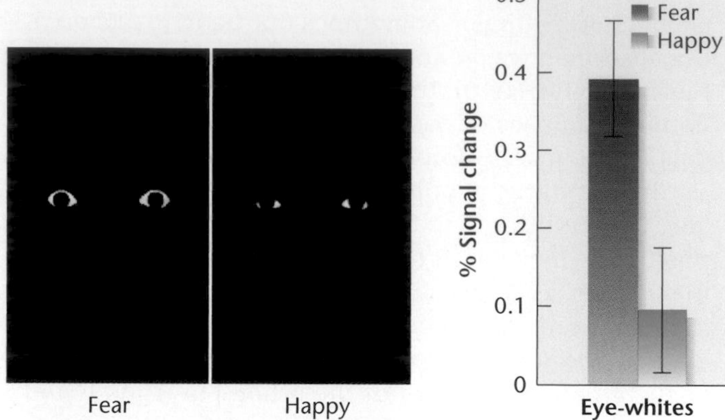

Figure 12.14 Eye whites for two facial expressions
The eye whites alone enable most people to guess that the person on the left was feeling afraid. Eye whites do not enable us to identify happiness (right). The amygdala responds more strongly to the fearful eye whites than to happy eye whites. *(Source: Reprinted with permission from "Human amygdala responsivity to masked fearful eye whites," by P. J. Whalen et al.,* Science, 306, *2061. Copyright 2004 AAAS.)*

on the left as showing fear (Whalen et al., 2004). From the eyes alone, we cannot recognize the expression on the right—happiness.

Might differences in the amygdala relate to differences in personality and anxiety disorders? Most people's tendency toward anxiety generally remains fairly consistent over years and decades. Most infants with an "inhibited" temperament develop into shy, fearful children and then into adults who show an enhanced amygdala response to the sight of any unfamiliar face (Schwartz, Wright, Shin, Kagan, & Rauch, 2003). Arousal of the amygdala, and therefore the tendency to experience strong negative emotions, relates strongly to a gene that interferes with serotonin reuptake in the amygdala (Hariri et al., 2002). It probably relates to several other genes as well (Flint, 2004). In short, genetic variations in amygdala arousal probably underlie some of the variation in anxiety and its disorders.

STOP & CHECK

6. What brain mechanism enables the startle reflex to be so fast?

7. How could a researcher use the startle reflex to determine whether some stimulus causes a person fear?

8. Why do people with amygdala damage have trouble recognizing expressions of fear?

Check your answers on pages 374–375.

METHODS 12.1
Microdialysis

In microdialysis, an investigator implants into the brain a double fluid-filled tube with a thin membrane tip across which chemicals can diffuse. The experimenter slowly delivers some fluid through one tube, while an equal amount of fluid exits through the other tube and brings with it some of the brain chemicals that have diffused across the membrane. In this manner, researchers discover which neurotransmitters are released during particular behaviors (e.g., Stanley, Schwartz, Hernandez, Leibowitz, & Hoebel, 1989).

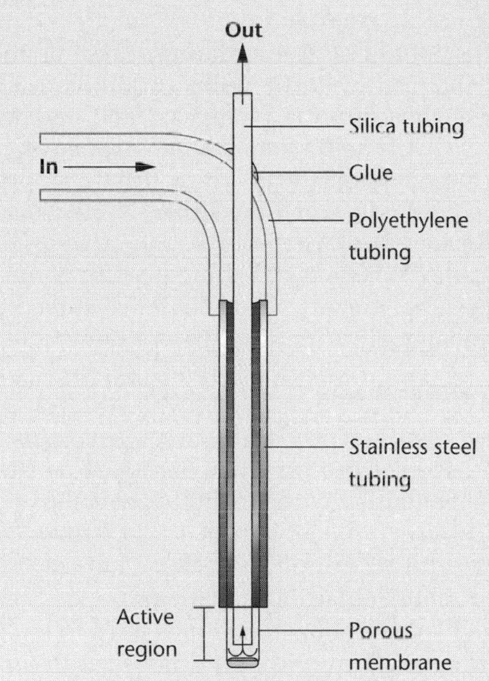

Source: Reprinted with permission from Dr. Juan Dominguez

Anxiety-Reducing Drugs

A little anxiety can be a useful thing by alerting us to danger. However, some people have exaggerated fears and excessive reactions to frightening events, partly for genetic reasons (Garpenstrand, Annas, Ekblom, Oreland, & Fredrikson, 2001; Gratacòs et al., 2001; Kendler, Myers, Prescott, & Neale, 2001). As you might guess, people with excessive fears have a hyperactive amygdala. One study found that children with panic disorder or generalized anxiety disorder had exaggerated amygdala responses to photos showing fearful faces (K. M. Thomas et al., 2001).

Drugs intended to control anxiety alter activity at amygdala synapses. One of the amygdala's main excitatory neuromodulators is CCK (cholecystokinin), which increases anxiety, and the main inhibitory transmitter is GABA, which inhibits anxiety.

Here is a good experiment showing the role of CCK: Male "intruder" rats were placed in a protected area within a resident male rat's cage for 30 minutes at a time, at which point the protective barrier was removed (Figure 12.15). For some of the intruders, the resident male was removed at the same time as the barrier. For the others, the protection was removed but not the resident. Those intruders were always attacked and defeated. (The "home field advantage" is enormous for rats. A resident male almost always defeats an intruder.) After four repetitions of this experience, the researchers implanted a cannula into the intruder male's brain and used microdialysis (Methods 12.1) to measure brain chemistry. The result was that an intruder male that had been defeated four times by the resident male showed clear signs of anxiety when again placed into that male's cage (motionlessness, defensive postures, and squeals); his prefrontal cortex showed an enormous increase in release of CCK. However, if he was given a drug that blocked his CCK type B receptors, he showed no anxiety, even when placed in the dangerous cage (C. Becker et al., 2001). The brain also has CCK type A receptors, less abundant, with different

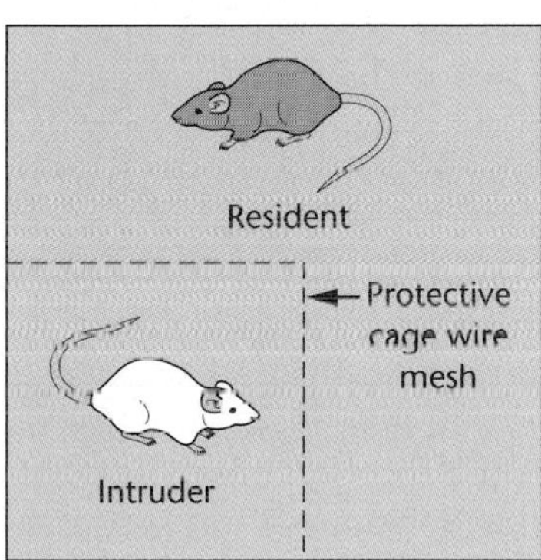

Figure 12.15 Procedure for giving male rats anxiety
Male rats were placed in a cage, protected from the resident male. Later, the protection was removed. For some, the resident male was removed at the same time, so the intruder was safe. For others, the protection was removed but the resident male was left to attack the intruder. Those who were attacked (and inevitably defeated) developed great anxiety when again placed in the same location.

and probably even opposite effects on behavior (Yamamoto et al., 2000).

Injections of CCK-stimulating drugs into the amygdala enhance the startle reflex (Frankland, Josselyn, Bradwejn, Vaccarino, & Yeomans, 1997), and drugs that block GABA type B receptors can induce an outright panic (Strzelczuk & Romaniuk, 1996). In principle, drugs could reduce anxiety either by blocking CCK or by increasing GABA activity. So far, no drugs based on blocking CCK have reached the market, although animal research suggests that they have some potential (Wiedemann, Jahn, Yassouridis, & Kellner, 2001).

Benzodiazepines

Decades ago, **barbiturates** were widely used anti-anxiety drugs. However, large doses can be fatal, especially if combined with alcohol. Today, the most commonly used anti-anxiety drugs are the **benzodiazepines** (BEN-zo-die-AZ-uh-peens), such as diazepam (trade name Valium), chlordiazepoxide (Librium), and alprazolam (Xanax). Benzodiazepines bind to the **$GABA_A$ receptor complex,** which includes a site that binds GABA as well as sites that that modify the sensitivity of the GABA site (Figure 12.16). (The brain also has other kinds of GABA receptors, such as $GABA_B$, with different behavioral effects.)

At the center of the $GABA_A$ receptor complex is a chloride channel. When open, it permits chloride ions (Cl^-) to cross the membrane into the neuron, hyperpolarizing the cell. (That is, the synapse is inhibitory.) Surrounding the chloride channel are four units, each containing one or more sites sensitive to GABA. Benzodiazepines bind to additional sites on three of those four units (labeled α in Figure 12.16). When a benzodiazepine molecule attaches, it neither opens nor closes the chloride channel but bends the receptor so that the GABA binds more tightly (Macdonald, Weddle, & Gross, 1986). Benzodiazepines thus facilitate the effects of GABA. Alcohol binds at a different site but also facilitates GABA binding (Nie et al., 2004).

Benzodiazepines exert their anti-anxiety effects in the amygdala, hypothalamus, midbrain, and several other areas. A minute amount of benzodiazepines injected directly to a rat's amygdala decreases learned shock-avoidance behaviors (Pesold & Treit, 1995), relaxes the muscles, and increases social approaches to other rats (Sanders & Shekhar, 1995). Benzodiazepines also decrease the responses in a rat's brain to the smell of a cat. Ordinarily, that smell triggers an apparently built-in fear (McGregor, Hargreaves, Apfelbach, & Hunt, 2004).

Given that benzodiazepines decrease anxiety, we should expect a strong effect on the startle reflex. Research results vary on whether the drugs decrease the startle reflex itself. However, the results are more consistent that benzodiazepines suppress influences that would otherwise increase the startle reflex. For example, ordinarily the startle reflex is enhanced in the presence of a signal previously paired with shock. Benzodiazepines decrease that effect (Gifkins, Greba, & Kokkinidis, 2002).

Benzodiazepines produce a variety of additional effects. When the drug reaches the thalamus and cerebral cortex, it induces sleepiness, blocks epileptic convulsions, and impairs memory (Rudolph et al., 1999). The mixture of effects is a problem. Some people take benzodiazepines to decrease anxiety; others take them as sleeping pills or antiepileptic treatments, but few people need all three effects, and no one wants the memory impairment. Researchers hope to develop drugs that are more specifically targeted to specific types of GABA receptors, thereby producing more limited behavioral effects (Korpi & Sinkkonen, 2006).

Other naturally occurring chemicals bind to the same sites as benzodiazepines. One such chemical is the protein **diazepam-binding inhibitor (DBI),** which

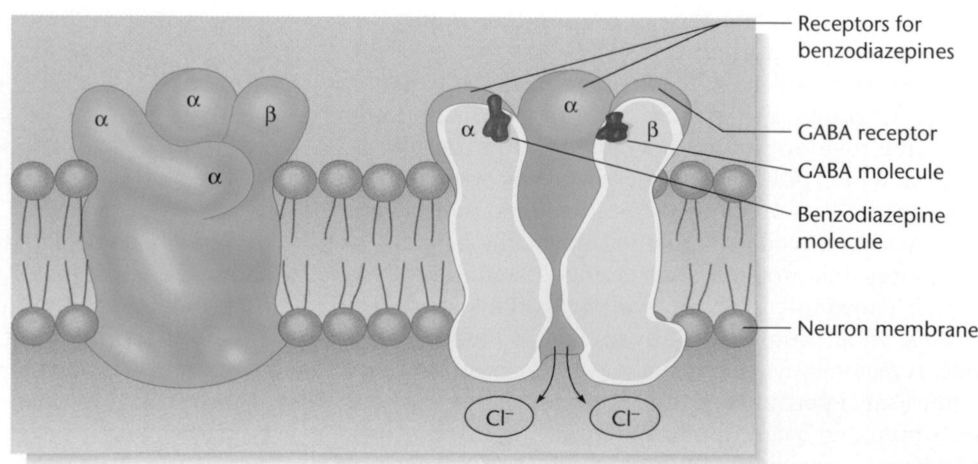

Figure 12.16 The $GABA_A$ receptor complex
Of its four receptor sites sensitive to GABA, the three a sites are also sensitive to benzodiazepines. *(Source: Based on Guidotti, Ferrero, Fujimoto, Santi, & Costa, 1986)*

blocks the behavioral effects of diazepam and other benzodiazepines (Guidotti et al., 1983). This and several related proteins are also known as **endozepines,** a contraction of "*endo*genous benzodia*zepine*," although their effects are actually the opposite to those of benzodiazepines. So really, an endozepine is an endogenous *anti*benzodiazepine. Keeping a mouse in social isolation elevates the release of endozepines in several brain areas, and presumably, that increase relates to the mouse's fearfulness and aggression when it is again placed with other mice (Dong, Matsumoto, Tohda, Kaneko, & Watanabe, 1999).

Endozepines are still not well understood, but they are an odd kind of neuromodulator. They are released mainly by glia cells, not by neurons (Patte et al., 1999). Why do our brains secrete endozepines and thereby increase our level of fears and anxieties? Presumably the "right" level of fear varies from time to time, and these chemicals help regulate that level.

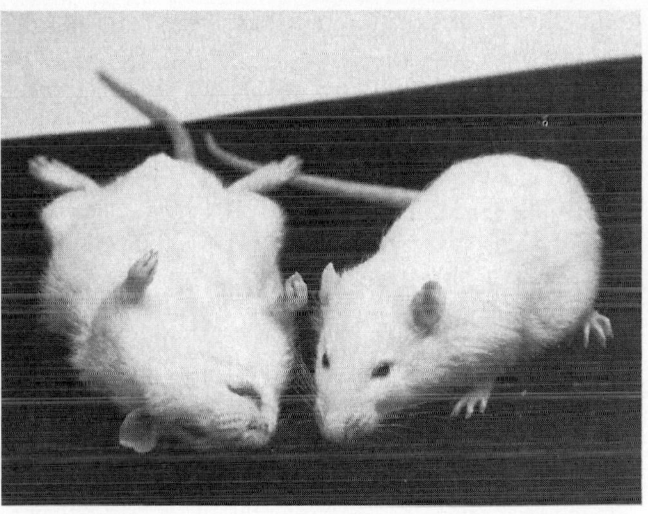

Figure 12.17 Two rats that were given the same amount of alcohol

The one on the right was later given the experimental drug Ro15-4513. Within 2 minutes, its performance on motor tasks improved significantly.

Jules Asfe

EXTENSIONS AND APPLICATIONS
Alcohol as an Anxiety Reducer

Ethyl alcohol, the beverage alcohol, has behavioral effects similar to those of benzodiazepines. It decreases anxiety and behavioral inhibitions. Moreover, a combination of alcohol and benzodiazepines depresses body activities and brain functioning more severely than either drug alone would. (A combination of both can be fatal.) Furthermore, alcohol, benzodiazepines, and barbiturates all exhibit the phenomenon of **cross-tolerance:** An individual who has used one of the drugs enough to develop a tolerance to it will show a partial tolerance to other depressant drugs as well.

Alcohol promotes the flow of chloride ions through the $GABA_A$ receptor complex, just as benzodiazepines do (Suzdak et al., 1986), probably by facilitating the binding of GABA to its receptors. Alcohol influences the brain in other ways as well, but the effects on GABA are responsible for alcohol's anti-anxiety and intoxicating effects. Drugs that block the effects of alcohol on the $GABA_A$ receptor complex also block most of alcohol's behavioral effects. One experimental drug, known as Ro15-4513, is particularly effective in this regard (Suzdak et al., 1986). Besides affecting the $GABA_A$ receptor complex, Ro15-4513 blocks the effects of alcohol on motor coordination, its depressant action on the brain, and its ability to reduce anxiety (H. C. Becker, 1988; Hoffman, Tabakoff, Szabo, Suzdak, & Paul, 1987; Ticku & Kulkarni, 1988) (Figure 12.17).

Could Ro15-4513 be useful as a "sobering-up" pill or as a treatment to help people who want to stop drinking alcohol? Hoffman-LaRoche, the company that discovered it, eventually concluded that the drug would be too risky. People who relied on the pill might think they were sober and try to drive home when they were still somewhat impaired. Furthermore, giving such a pill to alcoholics could easily backfire. Alcoholics generally drink to get drunk; a pill that decreased their feeling of intoxication would probably lead them to drink even more. Ro15-4513 reverses the behavioral effects of moderate alcohol doses, but a large dose can still be a health hazard or even fatal (Poling, Schlinger, & Blakely, 1988). For these reasons, Ro15-4513 is used only in experimental laboratories.

STOP & CHECK

9. What would be the effect of benzodiazepines on someone who had no GABA?

Check your answer on page 375

Module 12.2
In Closing: Doing Something About Emotions

Today, we understand the physiology of violence and fearfulness far better than we used to, but clearly, we have a long way to go. If we do make major advances, what then? Imagine we could take a blood sample—measuring 5-HIAA or whatever—plus an fMRI scan and a few other measurements, and then with reasonable accuracy predict which people will commit violent crime. Shall we then use that information to decide who stays in prison and who gets out on parole? Shall we go a step further and use brain tests to prevent crimes before they even occur?

And what about anxiety? Today, we have anti-anxiety drugs that work moderately well. Suppose research advances to the point that we could modulate people's anxiety precisely without undesirable side effects. Would it be a good idea to use these new methods to assure that everyone had the "right" anxiety level—not too much, not too little? Future research will give us new options and opportunities; deciding what to do with them is another matter.

Summary

1. Either a provoking experience, such as fighting, or the direct stimulation of the corticomedial area of the amygdala can temporarily heighten the readiness to attack. (p. 361)
2. Genetic or prenatal influences can alter the tendency toward violent behavior in conjunction with family environment and other experiences. (p. 361)
3. Testosterone can increase the readiness to attack. However, differences in testosterone levels across individuals account for very little of the difference in aggressive behavior. (p. 363)
4. Low serotonin turnover is associated with an increased likelihood of impulsive behavior, sometimes including violence. Monkeys with low serotonin turnover get into many fights and in most cases die young. However, those who survive have a high probability of achieving a dominant status. (p. 364)
5. The exact role of serotonin is still uncertain, and we should not think of it as the "anti-aggression" transmitter. (p. 365)
6. Researchers measure enhancement of the startle reflex as an indication of anxiety or learned fears. The amygdala is critical for increasing or decreasing the startle reflex on the basis of learned information. (p. 366)
7. Animals with damage to the amygdala often act fearless, apparently because they are slow to process emotional information. (p. 367)
8. According to studies using fMRI, the human amygdala responds strongly to emotional stimuli and facial expressions, especially when the meaning is less than obvious and requires some processing. (p. 368)
9. The amygdala responds to emotional stimuli even when they are presented under conditions that prevent people from recognizing them consciously. (p. 368)
10. People with damage to the amygdala fail to focus their attention on stimuli with important emotional content. Although they usually do not recognize facial expressions of fear, they do recognize fear if they are instructed to look at the eyes instead of the mouth. (p. 369)
11. People vary genetically in how strongly their amygdalas respond to frightening information. That variation probably contributes to differences in vulnerability to anxiety and its disorders. (p. 370)
12. Anti-anxiety drugs decrease fear by facilitating the binding of the neurotransmitter GABA to the $GABA_A$ receptors, especially in the amygdala. (p. 371)

Answers to STOP & CHECK Questions

1. The other likely explanation is that families that include members with a criminal record probably do not provide the best prenatal environment; the mothers may smoke or drink during pregnancy or otherwise endanger their fetuses' brain development. (p. 363)
2. Aggressive behaviors and conduct disorders are most common among those whose biological parents had criminal records and whose adoptive parents had marital discord, depression, substance abuse, or legal problems. (p. 363)
3. One can measure the concentration of 5-HIAA, a serotonin metabolite, in the cerebrospinal fluid or other body fluids. The more 5-HIAA, the more serotonin has been released and presumably resynthesized. (p. 366)
4. To raise production of serotonin, increase consumption of tryptophan or decrease consumption of proteins high in phenylalanine and other large amino acids that compete with tryptophan for entry to the brain. (p. 366)
5. Although most monkeys with low serotonin turnover die young, many of the survivors achieve a dominant status that enables them to get more of the food and enables males to reproduce more frequently. (p. 366)
6. Loud noises activate a path from the cochlea to cells in the pons that directly trigger a tensing of neck muscles. (p. 370)

7. Present the stimulus before giving a loud noise. If the stimulus increases the startle reflex beyond its usual level, then the stimulus produced fear. (p. 370)
8. They focus their vision on the nose and mouth. Expressions of fear depend almost entirely on the eyes. (p. 370)
9. Benzodiazepines facilitate the effects of GABA, so a person without GABA would have no response at all to benzodiazepines. (p. 373)

Thought Questions

1. Much of the play behavior of a cat can be analyzed into attack and escape components. Is the same true for children's play?
2. People with amygdala damage approach other people indiscriminately instead of trying to choose people who look friendly and trustworthy. What might be a possible explanation?

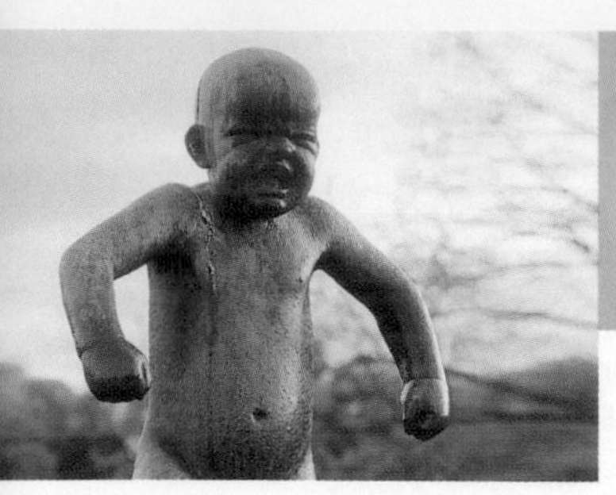

Module 12.3
Stress and Health

In the early days of scientific medicine, physicians made little allowance for the relation of personality or emotions to health and disease. If someone became ill, the cause had to be structural, like a virus or bacterium. Today, **behavioral medicine** emphasizes the effects on health of diet, smoking, exercise, stressful experiences, and other behaviors. We accept the idea that emotions and other experiences influence people's illnesses and patterns of recovery. This view does not imply mind–body dualism; stress and emotions are brain activities, after all.

Concepts of Stress

The term *stress,* like the term *emotion,* is hard to define and hard to quantify. Many people use some variant of Hans Selye's (1979) definition that **stress** is the nonspecific response of the body to any demand made upon it. When Selye was in medical school, he noticed that patients with a wide variety of illnesses had much in common: They develop a fever, they lose their appetite, they become inactive, they are sleepy most of the day, and their immune systems become more active. Later, when doing laboratory research, he found that rats exposed to heat, cold, pain, confinement, or the sight of a cat responded to these dissimilar stimuli in similar ways, including increased heart rate, breathing rate, and adrenal secretions. Selye therefore inferred that any threat to the body, in addition to its specific effects, activated a generalized response to stress, which he called the **general adaptation syndrome.** The initial stage, which he called *alarm,* is characterized by increased activity of the sympathetic nervous system, readying the body for brief emergency activity. During the second stage, *resistance,* the sympathetic response declines, but the adrenal cortex secretes **cortisol** and other hormones that enable the body to maintain prolonged alertness, fight infections, and heal wounds. After intense, prolonged stress, the body enters the third stage, *exhaustion.* During this stage, the individual is tired, inactive, and vulnerable because the nervous system and immune systems no longer have the energy to sustain their heightened responses (Sapolsky, 1998).

Stress-related illnesses and psychiatric problems are widespread in industrial societies of today, possibly because of changes in the type of stresses that we face. As Robert Sapolsky (1998) has argued, our ancestors of long ago faced many life-or-death challenges, but today's crises are more prolonged, such as advancing in one's career, paying a mortgage, or caring for a relative with a chronic health problem. If a long-term, almost inescapable issue activates the general adaptation syndrome, the result can be harmful to our well-being.

Selye's concept of stress included any change in one's life, such that either getting fired from your job or getting promoted would be considered stressful, as would either improvements or impairments of any other aspect of your life. Bruce McEwen (2000, p. 173) proposed an improved definition of stress: "events that are interpreted as threatening to an individual and which elicit physiological and behavioral responses." Although this definition differs from Selye's, the idea remains that many kinds of events can be stressful, and the body reacts to all kinds of stress in similar ways.

For access to many websites dealing with stress, visit this site: **http://www.stressless.com/AboutSL/StressLinks.cfm**

Stress and the Hypothalamus-Pituitary-Adrenal Cortex Axis

Stress activates two body systems. One is the autonomic nervous system, which prepares the body for brief emergency responses—"fight or flight." The other is the **HPA axis**—the hypothalamus, pituitary gland, and adrenal cortex. Activation of the hypothalamus induces the anterior pituitary gland to secrete adrenocorticotropic hormone (**ACTH**), which in turn stimulates the human adrenal cortex to secrete cortisol, which enhances metabolic activity and elevates blood levels of sugar and other nutrients (Figure 12.18). (In rats, it releases corticosterone instead.) Compared to the autonomic nervous system, the HPA axis reacts more slowly, but it becomes the dominant response to prolonged stressors, such as living with an abusive parent or spouse.

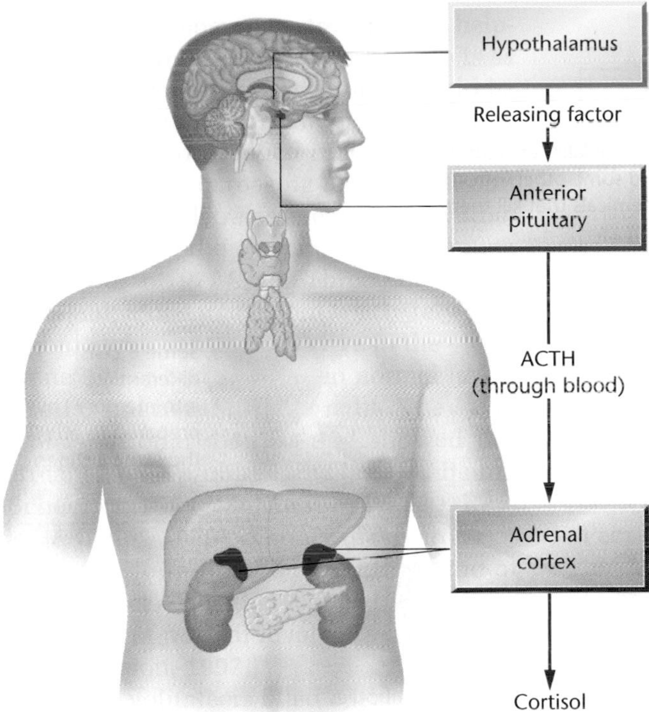

Figure 12.18 The hypothalamus-pituitary-adrenal cortex axis
Prolonged stress leads to the secretion of the adrenal hormone cortisol, which elevates blood sugar and increases metabolism. These changes help the body sustain prolonged activity but at the expense of decreased immune system activity.

Many researchers refer to cortisol as a "stress hormone" and use measurements of cortisol level as an indication of someone's recent stress level. One problem in that regard is that cortisol levels rise and fall during the day, so measurements taken from different people at different times of day are not comparable (Bremner et al., 2003).

Cortisol helps the body mobilize its energies to fight a difficult situation, but the effects depend on amount. For example, moderate levels of cortisol improve attention and memory formation (Abercrombie, Kalin, Thurow, Rosenkranz, & Davidson, 2003), and either higher or lower levels impair them (Kuhlmann, Piel, & Wolf, 2005; Mizoguchi, Ishige, Takeda, Aburada, & Tabira, 2004). Temporary increases in cortisol enhance activity of the immune system, helping it fight illnesses (Benschop et al., 1995), but prolonged increases impair immune activity. To see why, we start with an overview of the immune system.

The Immune System

The **immune system** consists of cells that protect the body against such intruders as viruses and bacteria. The immune system is like a police force: If it is too weak, the "criminals" (viruses and bacteria) run wild and create damage; if it becomes too strong or unselective, it attacks "law-abiding citizens" (the body's own cells). When the immune system attacks normal cells, we call the result an *autoimmune disease.* Myasthenia gravis, mentioned in Chapter 8, is one example of an autoimmune disease; rheumatoid arthritis is another.

Leukocytes

The most important elements of the immune system are the **leukocytes**, commonly known as white blood cells (Kiecolt-Glaser & Glaser, 1993; O'Leary, 1990).

We distinguish several types of leukocytes, including B cells, T cells, and natural killer cells (Figure 12.19):

- **B cells**, which mature mostly in the bone marrow, secrete **antibodies**, which are Y-shaped proteins that attach specifically to particular kinds of antigen, just as a key fits a lock. Every cell has surface proteins called **antigens** (antibody-generator molecules), and your own body's antigens are as unique as your fingerprints. The B cells recognize the "self" antigens, but when they find an unfamiliar antigen, they attack the cell. This kind of attack defends the body against viruses and bacteria; it also causes rejection of organ transplants, unless physicians take special steps to minimize the attack. After the body has made antibodies against a particular intruder, it "remembers" the intruder and quickly builds more of the same kind of antibody if it encounters that intruder again.
- **T cells** mature in the thymus gland. Several kinds of T cells attack intruders directly (without secreting antibodies), and some help other T cells or B cells to multiply.
- **Natural killer cells**, another kind of leukocytes, attack tumor cells and cells that are infected with viruses. Whereas each B or T cell attacks a particular kind of foreign antigen, natural killer cells nonspecifically attack all intruders.

In response to an infection, leukocytes and other cells produce small proteins called **cytokines** (e.g., interleukin-1, or IL-1), which combat infections and also communicate with the brain to elicit appropriate behaviors (Maier & Watkins, 1998). Cytokines are the immune system's way of telling the brain that the body is ill. Although cytokines do not cross the blood-brain barrier, they stimulate receptors on the vagus nerve (see Figure 4.9, p. 89), which relays a message to hypothalamic and hippocampal cells that release cytokines themselves. You might think of it as sending a fax, where the original material doesn't travel but tells the recipient to make a copy. The release of cytokines in the brain produces symptoms of illness, such as fever, sleepiness, lack of energy, lack of appetite, and loss of sex drive. In other words, cytokines are responsible for what Selye called the general adaptation syndrome.

fore more vulnerable to the damaging effects of stress and more prone than other people to PTSD.

To determine whether certain people are predisposed to PTSD, investigators examined men who developed PTSD during a war. First, they confirmed earlier reports that most PTSD victims had a smaller than average hippocampus. Then they found cases in which the PTSD victim had an identical twin who had not been in battle and who did not have PTSD. The results showed that the twin without PTSD *also* had a smaller than average hippocampus (Gilbertson et al., 2002). Presumably both twins had a smaller than average hippocampus from the start, which increased the susceptibility to PTSD.

STOP & CHECK

5. Name one way in which PTSD differs from a normal stress reaction.

6. What evidence indicates that a smaller than average hippocampus makes people more vulnerable to PTSD?

Check your answers on this page.

Module 12.3

In Closing: Emotions and Body Reactions

Research on stress and health provides an interesting kind of closure. Decades ago, Hans Selye argued that any stressful event leads to the general adaptation syndrome, marked by fever and other signs of illness. We now see why: The body reacts to prolonged stress by activating the adrenal cortex and the immune system, and the resulting increase in cytokines produces the same reactions that an infection would. Research has also improved our understanding of the predispositions behind posttraumatic stress disorder and makes it possible to foresee a new era of advances in psychosomatic medicine. Emotional states, which once seemed too ephemeral for scientific study, are now part of mainstream biology.

Summary

1. Hans Selye introduced the idea of the general adaptation syndrome, which is the way the body responds to all kinds of illness and stress. (p. 376)
2. Brief stress activates the sympathetic nervous system. More prolonged stress activates the hypothalamus-pituitary-adrenal cortex axis. The adrenal cortex releases cortisol, which increases the availability of fuels. Although the increased fuels are helpful, a prolonged increase begins to drain the body of the resources it needs for other purposes. (p. 376)
3. Stress activates the immune system, helping to fight viruses and bacteria. The immune system releases cytokines, which stimulate the hypothalamus to initiate activities to combat illness. Consequently, stress can lead to fever, sleepiness, and other symptoms that resemble those of illness. (p. 377)
4. The high cortisol levels associated with prolonged stress can damage cells in the hippocampus, thereby impairing memory. (p. 379)
5. After a severely trying event, some people but not others develop posttraumatic stress disorder (PTSD). Evidently, people with a smaller than average hippocampus and lower than average cortisol levels are predisposed to PTSD. (p. 379)

Answers to STOP & CHECK Questions

1. Cells of the immune system release cytokines. Cytokines activate the vagus nerve, which stimulates cells in the hypothalamus to release cytokines. (p. 378)
2. Cytokines stimulate neurons to produce fever, decreased hunger, decreased appetite, decreased sex drive, and other reactions to illness. (p. 378)
3. False. Fear, anger, or any other stressor impairs health if continued for a long time, but brief experiences arouse the sympathetic nervous system and enhance the activity of the immune system. (p. 379)
4. Stress increases the release of cortisol, which enhances metabolic activity throughout the body. When neurons in the hippocampus have high metabolic activity, they become more vulnerable to damage by toxins or overstimulation. (p. 379)
5. Ordinarily, stress elevates cortisol levels. People with PTSD have lower than normal cortisol levels. (p. 380)
6. On the average, PTDS victims have a smaller than average hippocampus. For those who have an identical twin, the twin also has a smaller than average hippocampus, even if he or she does not have PTSD. (p. 380)

Thought Question

If someone were unable to produce cytokines, what would be the consequences?

Chapter Ending

Key Terms and Activities

Terms

ACTH (p. 376)
antibody (p. 377)
antigen (p. 377)
B cell (p. 377)
barbiturate (p. 372)
Behavioral Activation System (BAS) (p. 358)
Behavioral Inhibition System (BIS) (p. 358)
behavioral medicine (p. 376)
benzodiazepine (p. 372)
cortisol (p. 376)
cross-tolerance (p. 373)
cytokines (p. 377)
diazepam-binding inhibitor (DBI) or endozepine (p. 372)
$GABA_A$ receptor complex (p. 372)
general adaptation syndrome (p. 376)
HPA axis (p. 376)
5-hydroxyindoleacetic acid (5-HIAA) (p. 364)
immune system (p. 377)
intermittent explosive disorder (p. 363)
James-Lange theory (p. 354)
leukocyte (p. 377)
limbic system (p. 357)
natural killer cell (p. 377)
panic attack (p. 356)
posttraumatic stress disorder (PTSD) (p. 379)
psychoneuroimmunology (p. 378)
pure autonomic failure (p. 355)
startle reflex (p. 366)
stress (p. 376)
T cell (p. 377)
turnover (p. 364)

Suggestions for Further Reading

Damasio, A. (1999). *The feeling of what happens.* New York: Harcourt Brace. A neurologist's account of the connection between emotion and consciousness, full of interesting examples.

McEwen, B. S., with Lasley, E. N. (2002). *The end of stress as we know it.* Washington, DC: Joseph Henry Press. Readable review by one of the leading researchers.

Websites to Explore

- You can go to the Biological Psychology Study Center and click these links. While there, you can also check for suggested articles available on InfoTrac College Edition. The Biological Psychology Internet address is:

http://psychology.wadsworth.com/book/kalatbiopsych9e/

Stress-Related Links

http://www.stressless.com/AboutSL/StressLinks.cfm

Exploring Biological Psychology CD

Facial analysis (video)
Amygdala and Fear Conditioning (animation)
GABA Receptors (animation)
CNS Depressants (animation)
Health and Stress (video)
Cells of the Immune System (animation)
Chapter Quiz (multiple-choice questions)
Critical Thinking (essay questions)

ThomsonNOW

http://www.thomsonedu.com

Go to this site for the link to ThomsonNOW, your one-stop study shop, Take a Pre-Test for this chapter, and ThomsonNOW will generate a Personalized Study Plan based on your test results. The Study Plan will identify the topics you need to review and direct you to online resources to help you master these topics. You can then take a Post-Test to help you determine the concepts you have mastered and what you still need work on.

The Biology of Learning and Memory

13

Chapter Outline

Opposite: Learning produces amazingly complex behaviors. Research progress requires distinctions among various types of learning and memory.
Source: Tim Davis/CORBIS

Main Ideas

1. To understand the physiology of learning, we must answer two questions: What changes occur in a single cell during learning, and how do changed cells work together to produce adaptive behavior?
2. Psychologists distinguish among several types of memory, each of which can be impaired by a different kind of brain damage.
3. During learning, a variety of changes occur that facilitate or decrease the activity at particular synapses. These changes may be the physiological basis of learning and memory.

Suppose you type something on your computer and then store it. A year later, you come back, click the correct file name, and retrieve what you wrote. How did the computer remember what to do?

That question is really two questions. One is: How does the computer store a representation of the keys that you typed? To explain how that happened, we need to understand the physics of the storage devices inside your computer. The second question is: How does the computer convert all those stored messages into the array on your computer screen? To answer that question, we need to understand the computer's wiring diagram.

Similarly, when we try to explain how you remember some experience, we are really answering two questions. One is: How did a pattern of sensory information create lasting changes in certain neurons? The second question is: After neurons change their properties, how does the nervous system as a whole produce the behavioral change that we call a memory? That question concerns the wiring diagram. Learning requires changes in individual cells, but what happens in a single cell does not explain learned behaviors.

We shall begin this chapter by considering how the various areas of the nervous system interact to produce learning and memory. In the second module, we turn to the more detailed physiology of how experience changes the properties of the individual cells and synapses.

Module 13.1
Learning, Memory, Amnesia, and Brain Functioning

Suppose you lost your ability to form long-lasting memories. You can remember what you just did and what someone just said to you, but nothing that happened earlier. It's as if you just awakened from a long sleep. So you write on a sheet of paper, "Just now, for the first time, I have suddenly become conscious!" A little later, you forget this experience too. So far as you can tell, you have just now emerged into consciousness after a long sleeplike period. You look at this sheet of paper on which you wrote about becoming conscious, but you don't remember writing it. How odd! You must have written it when in fact you were not conscious! Irritated, you cross off that statement and write anew, "*NOW* I am for the first time conscious!" And a minute later, you cross that one off and write it again. And again. Eventually, someone finds this sheet of paper on which you have repeatedly written and crossed out statements about suddenly being conscious for the first time.

Sound far-fetched? It really happened to a patient known as C who developed severe memory impairments after encephalitis damaged his temporal cortex (B. A. Wilson, Baddeley, & Kapur, 1995). Life without memory means no sense of existing across time. Your memory is almost synonymous with your sense of "self."

Localized Representations of Memory

What happens in the brain during learning and memory? One early, influential idea was that a connection grew between two brain areas. The Russian physiologist Ivan Pavlov pioneered the investigation of what we now call **classical conditioning** (Figure 13.1a), in which pairing two stimuli changes the response to one of them (Pavlov, 1927). Ordinarily, the experimenter starts by presenting a **conditioned stimulus (CS)**, which initially elicits no response of note, and then presents the **unconditioned stimulus (UCS)**, which automatically elicits the **unconditioned response (UCR)**. After some pairings of the CS and the UCS (perhaps just one or two pairings, perhaps many), the individual begins making a new, learned response to the CS, called a **conditioned response (CR)**. In his original experiments, Pavlov presented a dog with a sound (CS) followed by meat (UCS), which stimulated the dog to salivate (UCR). After many such pairings, the sound alone (CS) stimulated the dog to salivate (CR). In that case and many others, the CR resembles the UCR, but in some cases, it does not. For example, if a rat experiences a CS paired with shock, the shock elicits screaming and jumping, but the CS elicits a freezing response.

In **operant conditioning**, an individual's response is followed by a reinforcer or punishment (Figure 13.1b). A **reinforcer** is any event that increases the future probability of the response; a **punishment** is an event that suppresses the frequency of the response. For example, when a rat enters one arm of a maze and finds Froot Loops cereal (a potent reinforcer for a rat), its probability of entering that arm again increases. If it receives a shock instead, the probability decreases. The primary difference between the two kinds of conditioning is that in operant conditioning the individual's response determines the outcome (reinforcer or punishment), whereas in classical conditioning the CS and UCS will be presented at certain times independent of the individual's behavior. (The behavior is useful, however, in anticipating the effects of the UCS.)

Some cases of learning are difficult to label as classical or operant. For example, after a male songbird hears the song of his own species during his first few months, he imitates it the following year. The song that he heard was not paired with any other stimulus, as in classical conditioning. He learned the song without reinforcers or punishments, so we can't call it operant conditioning either. That is, animals have specialized methods of learning other than classical and operant conditioning (Rozin & Kalat, 1971; Rozin & Schull, 1988).

Lashley's Search for the Engram

Pavlov believed that classical conditioning reflected a strengthened connection between a CS center and a UCS center in the brain. That strengthened connection lets any excitation of the CS center flow to the UCS center, evoking the unconditioned response (Figure 13.2). Karl Lashley set out to test this hypothesis. (See photo

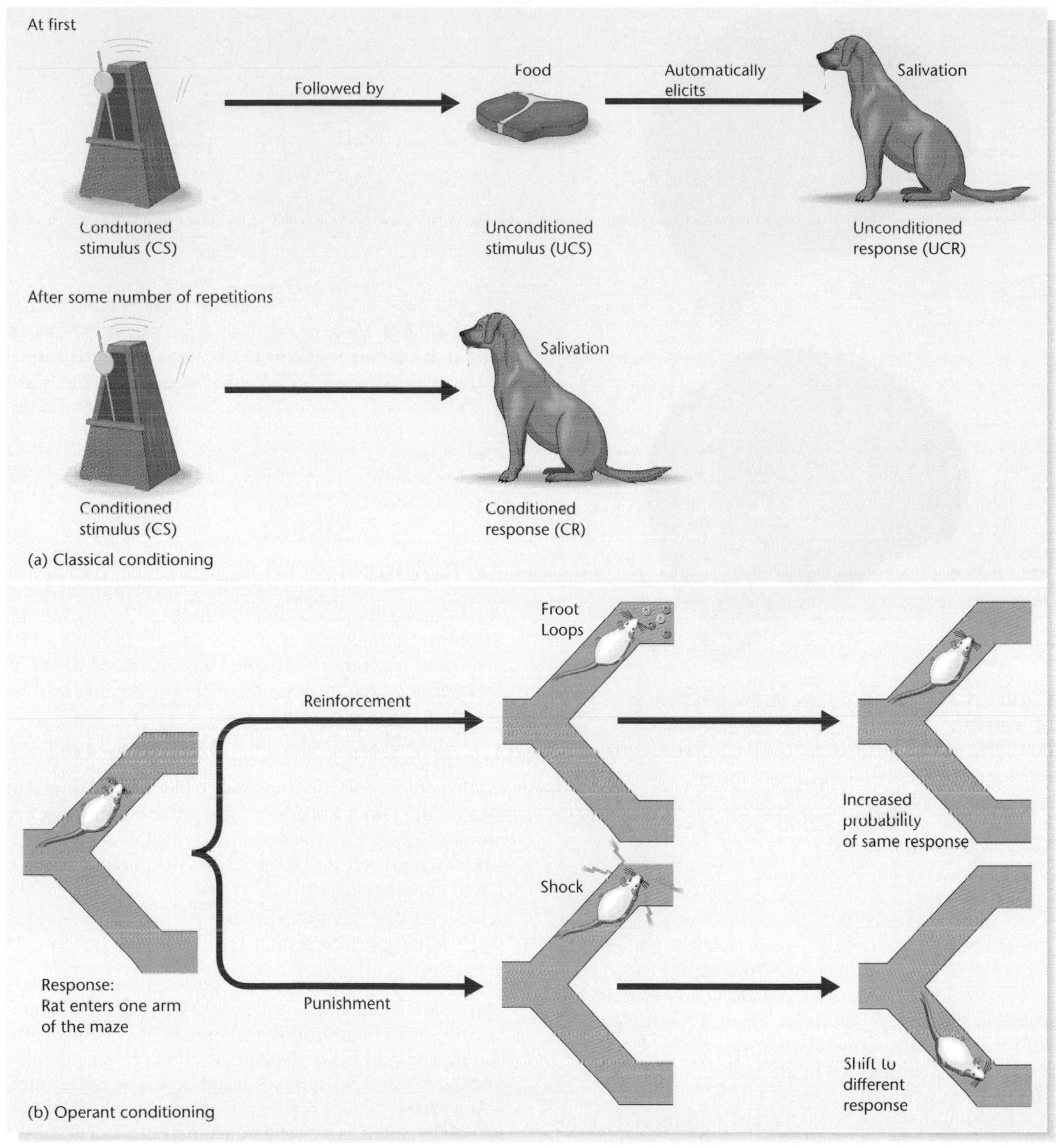

Figure 13.1 Procedures for classical conditioning and operant conditioning
(a) In classical conditioning, two stimuli (CS and UCS) are presented at certain times regardless of what the learner does. **(b)** In operant conditioning, the learner's behavior controls the presentation of reinforcer or punishment.

and quote on pages inside the back cover.) Lashley was searching for the **engram**—the physical representation of what has been learned. (A connection between two brain areas would be a possible example of an engram.)

Lashley reasoned that if learning depends on new or strengthened connections between two brain areas, a knife cut somewhere in the brain should interrupt that connection and abolish the learned response. He

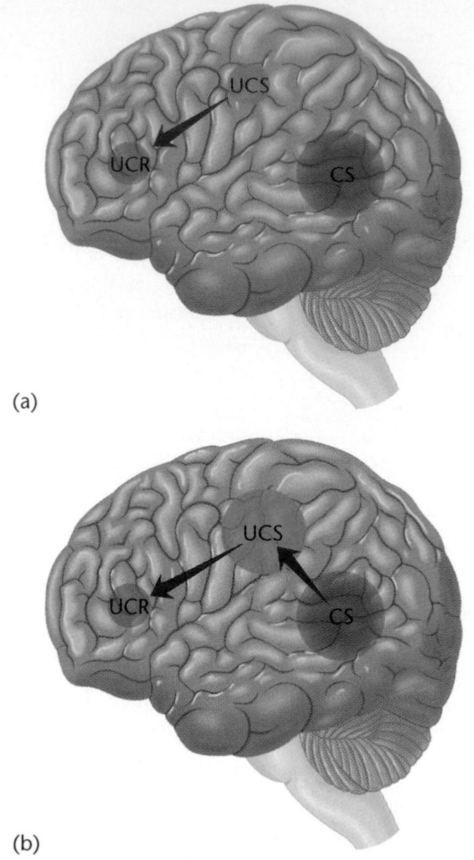

Figure 13.2 Pavlov's view of the physiology of learning

(a) Initially, the UCS excites the UCS center, which then excites the UCR center. The CS excites the CS center, which elicits no response of interest. **(b)** After training, excitation in the CS center flows to the UCS center, thus eliciting the same response as the UCS.

trained rats on a variety of mazes and a brightness discrimination task and then made one or more deep cuts in varying locations in their cerebral cortices (Lashley, 1929, 1950) (Figure 13.3). However, no knife cut significantly impaired the rats' performances. Evidently, the types of learning that he studied did not depend on connections across the cortex.

Lashley also tested whether any portion of the cerebral cortex is more important than others for learning. He trained rats on mazes before or after he removed large portions of the cortex. The lesions impaired performance, but the amount of retardation depended more on the amount of brain damage than on its location. Learning and memory apparently did not rely on a single cortical area. Lashley therefore proposed two principles about the nervous system:

- **equipotentiality**—all parts of the cortex contribute equally to complex behaviors such as learning; any part of the cortex can substitute for any other.

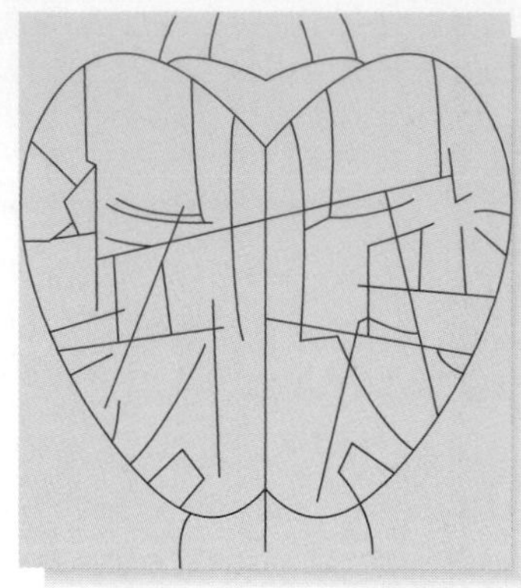

Figure 13.3 View of rat brain from above, showing cuts that Lashley made in the brains of various rats

He found that no cut or combination of cuts interfered with a rat's memory of a maze. *(Source: Adapted from Lashley, 1950)*

- **mass action**—the cortex works as a whole, and the more cortex the better..

Note, however, another interpretation of Lashley's results: Maze learning and visual discrimination learning are more complex tasks than they might appear. A rat finding its way to food attends to visual and tactile stimuli, the location of its body, the position of its head, and any other available cues. Learning depends on many cortical areas, but different areas could be contributing in different ways.

Eventually, researchers discovered that Lashley's conclusions reflected two unnecessary assumptions: (a) that the cerebral cortex is the best or only place to search for an engram and (b) that all kinds of memory are physiologically the same. As we shall see, investigators who discarded these assumptions reached different conclusions.

The Modern Search for the Engram

Richard F. Thompson and his colleagues used a simpler task than Lashley's and sought the engram of memory not in the cerebral cortex but in the cerebellum. Thompson and his colleagues studied classical conditioning of eyelid responses in rabbits. They presented first a tone (CS) and then a puff of air (UCS) to the cornea of the rabbit's eye. At first, a rabbit blinked at the air puff but not at the tone; after repeated pairings, classical conditioning occurred and the rabbit blinked at the tone also. Investigators recorded the activity in various brain cells to determine which ones changed their responses during learning.

Thompson and other investigators consistently found changes in cells of one nucleus of the cerebellum, the **lateral interpositus nucleus (LIP)**. At the start of training, those cells showed little response to the tone, but as learning proceeded, their responses increased (Thompson, 1986). However, the fact that a brain area changed its response does not necessarily mean that the learning took place in that area. Imagine a sequence of brain areas:

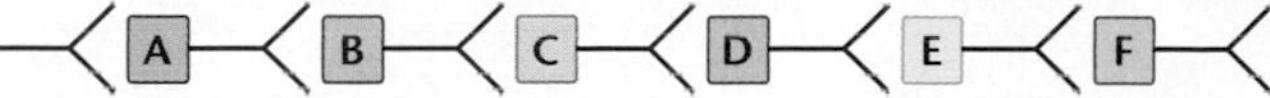

If learning occurs in any one of them (say, area D), we could record changes in D and in every area after it. Also we could disrupt the learned response by damaging any of the areas from A through F. (D has to get input from A, B, and C and has to send output to E and F.) How, then, can anyone determine where learning occurs?

Thompson and his colleagues reasoned that if learning occurred in D, then areas E and F need to be active to pass the information along to the muscles, but they wouldn't have to be active while learning itself took place. (Everything up to D would have to be active, of course, just to get the information to D.) To investigate the role of the LIP, investigators temporarily suppressed activity in that nucleus at the start of training, either by cooling it or by injecting a drug into it. They presented the CS and UCS as usual and found no evidence of learning—that is, no responses while the LIP was suppressed. Then they waited for the effects of the cooling or the drugs to wear off and continued training. At that point, the rabbits began to learn, but they learned *at the same speed as animals that had received no previous training.* Evidently, while the LIP was suppressed, the training had no effect.

But did learning actually occur *in* the LIP, or does this area just relay the information to a later area where learning occurs? In the next experiments, investigators suppressed activity in the red nucleus, a midbrain motor area that receives input from the cerebellum: When the red nucleus was suppressed, the rabbits again showed no responses during training. However, as soon as the red nucleus had recovered from the cooling or drugs, the rabbits showed strong learned responses to the tone (R. E. Clark & Lavond, 1993; Krupa, Thompson, & Thompson, 1993). In other words, suppressing the red nucleus temporarily prevented the response but did not prevent learning. The researchers concluded, therefore, that the learning occurred in the LIP. (The LIP was the last structure in the sequence that had to be awake for learning to occur.) Figure 13.4 summarizes these experiments. Later experiments demonstrated that the LIP has to be intact not only during learning but also during any later test. That is, the structure is necessary both for learning and for retention (Christian & Thompson, 2005).

The mechanisms for this type of conditioning are probably the same in humans. According to PET scans on young adults, when pairing a stimulus with an airpuff produces a conditioned eye blink, activity increases in the cerebellum, red nucleus, and several other areas (Logan & Grafton, 1995). People who have damage in the cerebellum have weaker conditioned eye blinks, and the blinks are less accurately timed relative to the onset of the airpuff (Gerwig et al., 2005).

STOP & CHECK

1. Thompson found a localizable engram, whereas Lashley did not. What key differences in procedures or assumptions were probably responsible for their different results?
2. What evidence indicates that the red nucleus is necessary for performance of a conditioned response but not for learning the response?

Check your answers on page 402.

Types of Memory

Although eyelid conditioning and several other kinds of learning depend on the cerebellum, many other kinds do not. You will recall from Chapter 6 that different parts of the brain contribute to different aspects of visual perception. The same principle holds for memory, and much research progress comes from distinguishing various types of memory.

Short-Term and Long-Term Memory

Donald Hebb (1949) reasoned that no one mechanism could account for all the phenomena of learning. (See photo and quote on pages inside the back cover.) We can form memories almost instantaneously, and some last a lifetime. Hebb considered it unlikely that any chemical process could occur fast enough to account for immediate memory yet remain stable enough to provide permanent memory. He therefore distinguished between **short-term memory** of events that have just occurred, and **long-term memory** of events from previous times. Several types of evidence support such a distinction:

- Short-term memory and long-term memory differ in their capacity. For illustration, read each of these letter sequences and then look away and try to repeat them:

DZLAUV
CYXGMBF
OBGSFKIE
RJNWSCFPT

Most healthy adults can repeat about seven unrelated items in short-term memory—sometimes slightly more or fewer depending on circumstances. In contrast, long-term memory has a vast, difficult-to-estimate capacity. When you learn something new,

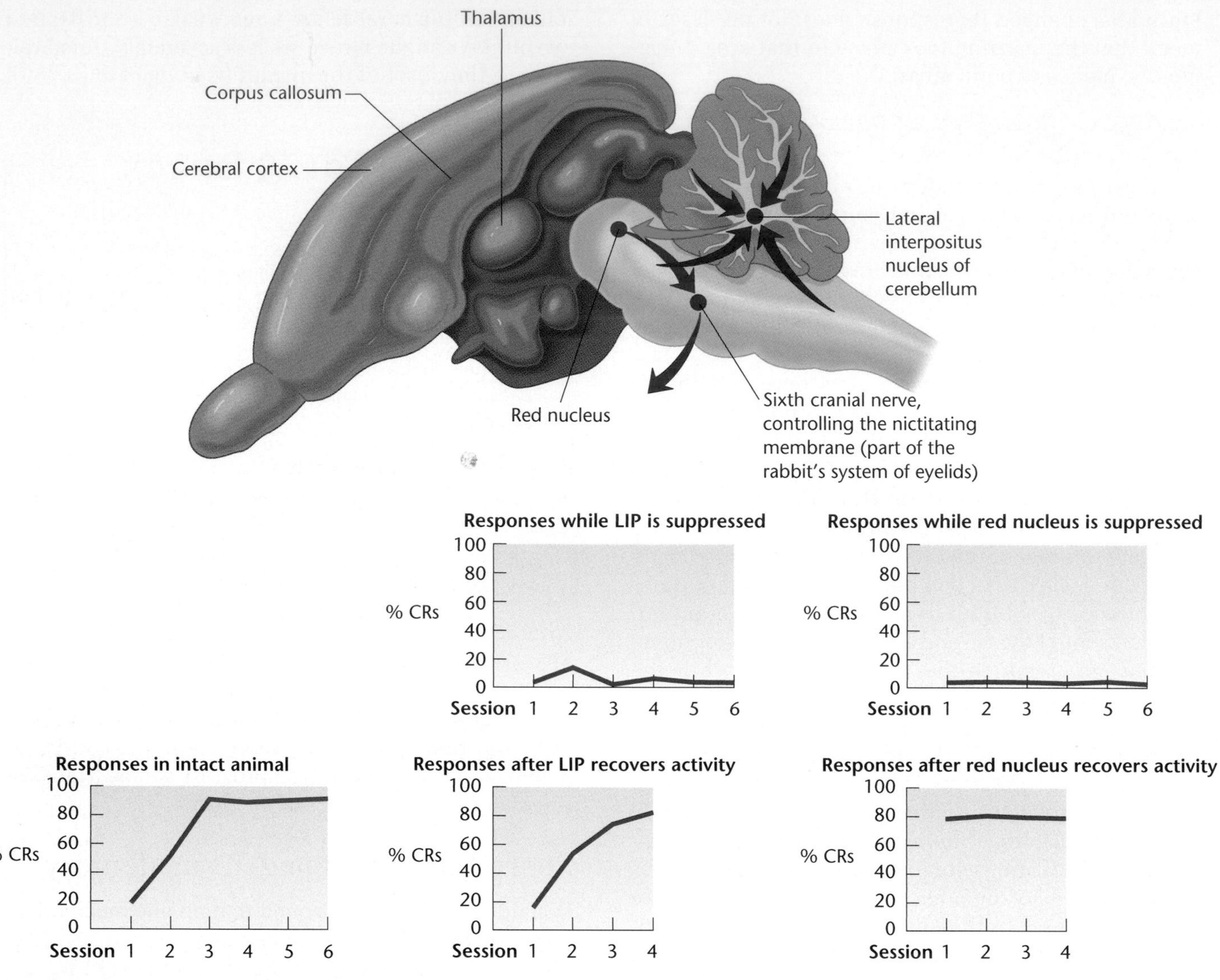

Figure 13.4 Localization of an engram
Temporary inactivation of the lateral interpositus nucleus of a rabbit blocked all indications of learning. After the inactivation wore off, the rabbits learned as slowly as rabbits with no previous training. Temporary inactivation of the red nucleus blocked the response during the period of inactivation, but the learned response appeared as soon as the red nucleus recovered. *(Source: Based on the experiments of Clark & Lavond, 1993; Krupa, Thompson, & Thompson, 1993)*

you don't have to forget something old to make room for it.

- Short-term memories fade quickly unless you rehearse them. For example, if you read the letter sequence DZLAUV and then something distracts you so that you cannot rehearse those letters, your chance of repeating them correctly is fairly good 5 seconds later, less after 10 seconds, and poor at 20 seconds or beyond (Peterson & Peterson, 1959). In contrast, you can recall many long-term memories that you haven't thought about in years. Note, however, that the research demonstrating rapid loss of short-term memory has dealt almost entirely with meaningless material. How long would you remember the number sequence 64-57-2-15 without constant rehearsal? Probably not long. How long would you remember, "The score is 64 to 57 with 2 minutes and 15 seconds left to play"? Providing a meaningful context makes the material easier to remember, even though it is still a temporary memory.
- With short-term memory, once you have forgotten something, it is lost. For example, if you read CYXGMBF and then forget it, you probably won't gain from the hint "starts with CY." With long-term memory, however, you might think you have forgotten something and yet find that some hint helps you reconstruct it. For example, try naming all your high school teachers. After you have named all you can, you will be able to name still more if someone shows you photos and tells you the teachers' initials.

Working Memory

Later studies weakened the distinction between short-term and long-term memory. For example, you probably remember what you ate for dinner last night, who was the last person you talked to, approximately how much money is in your wallet or purse, where you parked your car today, and how well your favorite sports team did in its last game. None of those are classical short-term memories: They happened more than a few seconds ago, and you can recall them without constantly rehearsing them. They are not exactly long-term memories either, as you will forget most of them within hours, days, or weeks.

As an alternative to the concept of short-term memory, A. D. Baddeley and G. J. Hitch (1974, 1994) introduced the term **working memory** to emphasize that temporary storage is not just a station on the way to long-term memory; it is the way we store information while we are working with it or attending to it. Here is a task you can use to test working memory. Read the following sequence of words to someone else, or have someone read them to you. After each word, say *the previous word.* That is, when you hear the first word, say nothing. When you hear the second word, say the first word. And so forth. Here are the words (you could use any words, of course):

try it yourself

peach, apple, blueberry, melon, orange, mango, raspberry, banana, lemon, papaya, fig, plum, tangerine, grape

Now do it again, but this time say *what was two words back.* That is, say nothing after the first two words; after the third say the first word and so forth. You begin to see that working memory means "working *with* memory" and that it requires well-controlled attention.

Baddeley and Hitch distinguished three components of working memory:

- a **phonological loop,** which stores auditory information, including words;
- a **visuospatial sketchpad,** which stores visual information; and
- the **central executive,** which directs attention toward one stimulus or another and determines which items will be stored in working memory.

They distinguished the phonological loop from the visuospatial sketchpad because verbal memory seems to be in many ways independent of visual memory. If you try to memorize a long list of words or a long list of pictures, you will find that one gets confused with another. But if you memorize a mixture of words and pictures, the words and pictures do not interfere with each other (Hale, Myerson, Rhee, Weiss, & Abrams, 1996). Presumably, we also have working memory for touch, smell, and taste, but researchers have done less with those sense.

A common test of working memory is the **delayed response task,** which requires responding to a stimulus that one heard or saw a short while earlier. For example, imagine that a light shines above one of several doors. The light goes off, you have to wait a few seconds, and then you have to go to the door where you saw the light. The delay can be increased or decreased to test your limits. Many studies have found that when humans or other mammals perform a delayed response task, cells in the prefrontal cortex, especially the dorsolateral prefrontal cortex, maintain high activity during the delay, presumably meaning that they are storing the memory (Kikuchi-Yorioka & Sawaguchi, 2000; Leung, Gore, & Goldman-Rakic, 2002). The stronger the activation of this area, the better the individual's performance (Klingberg, Forssberg, & Westerberg, 2002; Sakai, Rowe, & Passingham, 2002).

Many older people have impairments of working memory, probably because of changes in the prefrontal cortex. Studies on aged monkeys find decreases in the number of neurons and the amount of input in certain parts of the prefrontal cortex (D. E. Smith, Rapp, McKay, Roberts, & Tuszynski, 2004). Older humans who show declining memory show declining activity in the prefrontal cortex, whereas those with intact memory show *greater* activity than young adults (A. C. Rosen et al., 2002; Rossi et al., 2004). Presumably, the increased activity means that the prefrontal cortex is working harder in these older adults to compensate for impairments elsewhere in the brain. Furthermore, stimulant drugs that enhance activity in the prefrontal cortex produce a long-lasting improvement in the memory of aged monkeys (Castner & Goldman-Rakic, 2004). Such treatments may have potential for treating people with failing memory.

STOP & CHECK

3. What is one brain location and mechanism for working memory?

Check your answer on page 403.

The Hippocampus and Amnesia

Amnesia is memory loss, sometimes to an extreme degree. One patient ate lunch, and 20 minutes later ate a second lunch, apparently having forgotten the first meal. Another 20 minutes later, he started on a third lunch and ate most of it. A few minutes later, he said he would like to "go for a walk and get a good meal" (Rozin, Dow, Moscovitch, & Rajaram, 1998). However, even in severe cases like this one, no one loses all kinds of memory equally. This patient still remembered how to eat with a knife and fork, for example, even though he could not remember what he had eaten or when. Studies on amnesia help clarify the distinctions among different kinds of memory and enable us to understand the mechanisms of memory more clearly.

Amnesia After Hippocampal Damage

In 1953, a man known as H. M. suffered about 10 minor epileptic seizures per day and a major seizure about once a week, despite trying every available antiepileptic drug. Eventually, he and his neurosurgeon considered desperate measures. Because of evidence suggesting that epilepsy sometimes originates in the hippocampus, the neurosurgeon removed it from both hemispheres, as well as much of the amygdala and other nearby structures in the temporal cortex. Researchers knew almost nothing about the hippocampus at the time, and no one knew what to expect after the surgery. We now know that various parts of the hippocampus are active during both the formation of memories and later recall (Eldridge, Engel, Zeineh, Bookheimer, & Knowlton, 2005). Although the operation reduced H. M.'s epilepsy to no more than two major seizures per year, he almost certainly would have preferred to remain epileptic (Milner, 1959; Penfield & Milner, 1958; Scoville & Milner, 1957). Figure 13.5 shows the normal anatomy of the hippocampus and the damage in H. M. For more about the hippocampus, explore this website: **http://braininfo.rprc.washington.edu/menumain.html**

After the surgery, H. M.'s intellect and language abilities remained intact; his IQ score even increased slightly, presumably because of the decrease in epileptic interference. His personality remained the same except for emotional placidity, probably related to the amygdala damage (Eichenbaum, 2002). For example, he rarely complained (even about pain) or requested anything (even food). His main problem was massive **anterograde amnesia** (loss of memories for events that happened after brain damage). He also suffered a moderate **retrograde amnesia** (loss of memory for events that occurred shortly before brain damage). That is, he had some trouble recalling events that happened within 1 to 3 years before the operation.

Despite his huge deficits in forming long-term memories, his ability for short-term or working memory remained intact. In one test, Brenda Milner (1959) asked H. M. to remember the number 584. After a 15-minute delay without distractions, he recalled it correctly, explaining, "It's easy. You just remember 8. You see, 5, 8, and 4 add to 17. You remember 8, subtract it from 17, and it leaves 9. Divide 9 in half and you get 5 and 4, and there you are, 584. Easy." A moment later, after his attention had shifted to another subject, he had forgotten both the number and the complicated line of thought he had associated with it.

In contrast, the surgery severely impaired his ability to form long-term memories. He shows no ability to form **episodic memories,** memories of single events. He cannot describe a single experience that he has had since 1953. He can read a magazine repeatedly without losing interest. Sometimes he tells someone about a childhood incident and then, a minute or two later, tells the same person the same story again (Eichenbaum, 2002). In 1980, he moved to a nursing home. Four years later, he could not say where he lived or who cared for him. Although he watched the news on television every night, he recalls only a few fragments of events since 1953. Over the years, many new words have entered the English language, such as *jacuzzi* and *granola.* H. M. cannot define them and treats them as nonsense (Corkin, 2002). For several years after the operation, whenever he was asked his age and the date, he answered "27" and "1953." After a few years, he started guessing wildly, generally underestimating his age by 10 years or more and missing the date by as many as 43 years (Corkin, 1984).

You might wonder whether he is surprised at his own appearance in a mirror or photo. Yes and no. When asked his age or whether his hair has turned gray, he replies that he does not know. When shown a photo of himself with his mother, taken long after his surgery, he recognizes his mother but not himself. However, when he sees himself in the mirror, he shows no surprise (Corkin, 2002). He has, of course, seen himself daily in the mirror over all these years. He also has the context of knowing that the person in the mirror must be himself, whereas the person in the photo could be anyone.

Although he has apparently formed no episodic memories, he has formed a few weak semantic (factual) memories for information he encountered repeatedly (Corkin, 2002). For example, after he moved with his parents to a new house, he eventually learned the floor plan of the house, although he needed many years to do so. Although he does not recognize the faces of people who became famous after 1953, he has learned the names of people who were in the news repeatedly (O'Kane, Kensinger, & Corkin, 2004). When he was given first names and asked to fill in appropriate last names, his replies included some who became famous after 1953, such as these:

	H. M.'s Answer
Elvis	Presley
Martin Luther	King
Billy	Graham
Fidel	Castro
Lyndon	Johnson

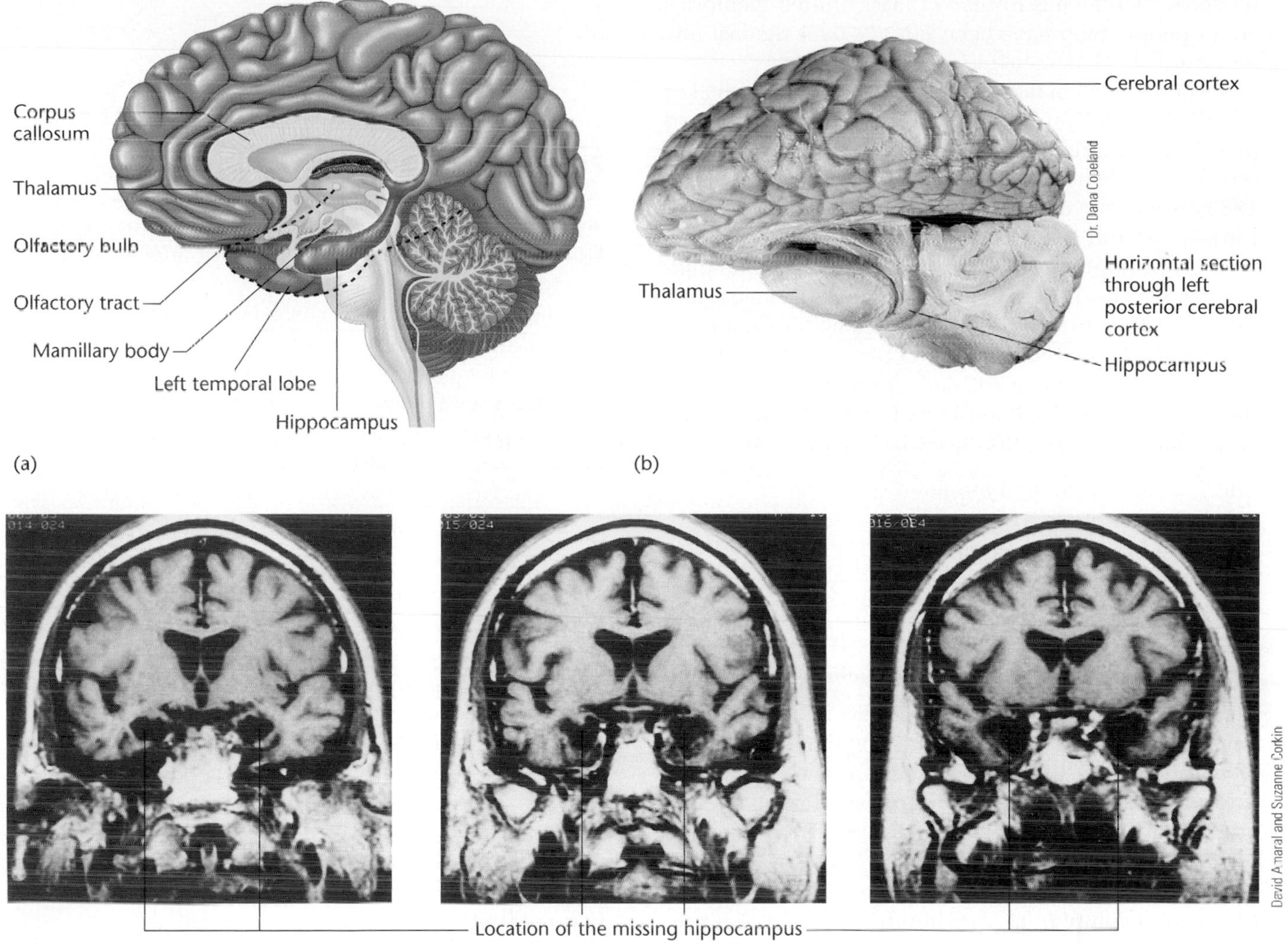

Figure 13.5 The hippocampus
(a) Location of the hippocampus in the human brain. The hippocampus is in the interior of the temporal lobe, so the left hippocampus is closer to the viewer than the rest of this plane; the right hippocampus is behind the plane. The dashed line marks the location of the temporal lobe, which is not visible in the midline. **(b)** Photo of a human brain from above. The right hemisphere is intact. The top part of the left hemisphere has been cut away to show how the hippocampus loops over (dorsal to) the thalamus, posterior to it, and then below (ventral to) it **(c)** MRI scan of the brain of H. M., showing absence of the hippocampus. Note the large size of this lesion. The three views show coronal planes at successive locations, anterior to posterior.

He provided even more names when he was given additional information:

	H. M.'s Answer
Famous artist, born in Spain . . .Pablo	Picasso

When he was given the names of people who became famous after 1953, he was able to provide relevant information about some of them, such as:

	H. M.'s Answer
John Glenn	First rocketeer, the first to be in a rocket, he went to the moon.
Mikhail Gorbachev	Famous for making speeches, head of the Russian parliament

Compared to other people, H. M.'s replies were brief and not always accurate. (Glenn was not the first in space, and he never went to the moon; Gorbachev was Soviet president, not the head of parliament.) Still, it is clear that he has formed at least limited memories about people who have been famous over the last few decades.

Another way of testing his semantic memory makes use of H. M.'s lifelong hobby of working crossword puzzles. Researchers tested him on several kinds of crosswords. When all the items were familiar before 1953—such as "invented the light bulb" (answer: Edison)—H. M. did about as well as other people, although he did not improve from day to day on the same puzzle, despite checking his answers against the key. When the items were from after 1953—such as "current president of the United States"—he could not answer them. The more interesting result came from puzzles in which the answer was a term familiar before 1953, but the clue depended on information from later. Examples are:

Country that developed atomic bomb after the U.S.	Answer: Russia
Childhood disease successfully treated by Salk vaccine.	Answer: polio
Former U.S. president who died in 1972.	Answer: Truman

On these items, he answered only 20% correctly on the first day but, after seeing the key, improved from day to day until getting 45% correct on the fifth day. The researchers suggested that H. M. can learn some new information if he can link it to information he already knew (Skotko et al., 2004). However, these answers were guessable without necessarily learning anything. Which country that can be spelled with six letters was likely to develop an atomic bomb? Russia. What previously incurable disease has five letters? Polio. Two former presidents were alive in 1953—Hoover and Truman. Which one was more likely to survive until 1972? In 1953, Hoover was already 79 years old, whereas Truman was 69. Granted, H. M.'s answers improved from day to day, but that improvement might reflect something other than learning new facts.

Although H. M. has enormous trouble learning new facts and keeping track of current events, he acquires new skills without apparent difficulty. That is, he has impaired **declarative memory,** the ability to state a memory in words, but intact **procedural memory,** the development of motor skills and responses. For example, he has learned to read words written backwards, as they would be seen in a mirror, although he is surprised at this skill, as he does not remember having tried it before. Similarly, he has learned to draw something to match what he sees in a mirror (Corkin, 2002). For another example, consider the drawing in Figure 13.6(a). Most people are not sure what it represents. If you don't know, check part 13.6(b) on the next page, then 13.6(c) on the next page, and so forth. After seeing the complete version, Figure 13.6(e), you will "see" the object even in the simplest version, 13.6(a), and you will continue to recognize this object even an hour or more later. The Gollin Partial Picture Test includes a whole series of different objects like this. H. M. does not improve as much as normal on the Gollin Partial Picture Test, but he does improve. That is, after seeing the later versions, he has a better chance of recognizing the simplified originals, even after a delay, although he says he does not remember doing this task before (Warrington & Weiskrantz, 1968).

try it yourself

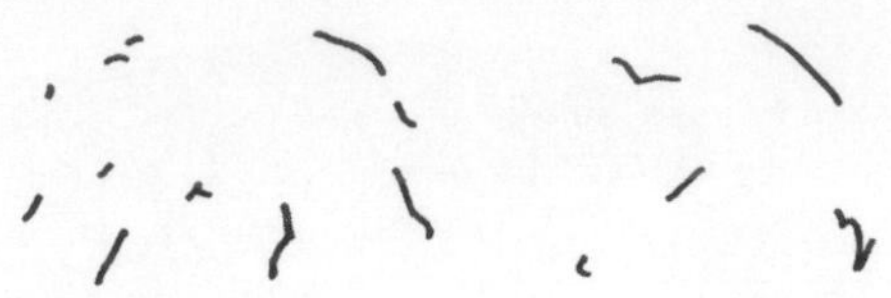

Figure 13.6(a) The Gollin Partial Picture Test
What is this object? If you are not sure—as most people are not—examine Figure 13.6(b). If you are still not sure, flip additional pages to Figure 13.6(c), (d), and (e). After seeing the full picture, most people can recognize it in the original picture as shown here, even an hour or more later. Patient H. M. also improves on this task, even though he doesn't remember having done it before. *(Source: Reproduced with permission of author and publisher from Gollins, E. S. "Developmental studies of visual recognition of incomplete objects."* Perceptual and Motor Skills, *1960, 11, 289–298. © Southern Universities Press 1960. This source also applies to parts b–e.)*

The distinction between declarative and procedural memory is not a firm one, and sometimes it is possible to use either type of memory for the same task. For example, imagine that you have to learn to choose ✂ instead of ⌘, ✈ instead of ✳, and so forth through a series of eight pairs. Most normal adults learn all the pairs quickly and can describe the correct and incorrect patterns. People with damage to the temporal lobes, including the hippocampus, learn very slowly. After learning, they cannot describe what they have learned and report that they do not recognize the task. From all indication, they are learning motor habits or procedures, rather than declarative memories, the way other people do (Bayley, Frascino, & Squire, 2005).

H. M. also shows better *implicit* than *explicit* memory. **Explicit memory** is deliberate recall of information that one recognizes as a memory. It is tested by such questions as: "Who were the main characters in the last novel you read?" **Implicit memory** is the influence of recent experience on behavior, without necessarily realizing that one is using memory. For example, you might be talking to someone about sports while other people nearby are carrying on a conversation about the latest movies. If asked, you could not say what the others were talking about, but suddenly, you comment for no apparent reason, "I wonder what's on at the movies?" To experience implicit memory, try the Online Try It Yourself exercise "Implicit Memories."

To understand what is meant by poor explicit and good implicit memory, consider several examples. In one experiment, people viewed a sequence of flashing circles and then were asked to guess whether that sequence should be called red, yellow, or green. For each sequence, one of those answers was usually considered correct but not always. After sufficient practice, normal people can describe which sequence is usually associated with which color name. Patients with amnesia do not verbalize this memory, but they guess the correct answer more often than by chance (Ptak, Gutbrod, Perrig, & Schnider, 2001). Their correct answers can be considered a kind of implicit memory.

Here is another example: Have you ever played the video game Tetris? In the game, geometrical forms such as ▭ and ┼ fall from the top, and the player must move and rotate them to fill available spaces at the bottom of the screen. Normal people improve their skill over a few hours and can describe the game and its strategy. After playing the same number of hours, patients with amnesia cannot describe the game and say they don't remember playing it. Nevertheless, they improve—a little. Moreover, when they are about to fall asleep, they report seeing images of little piles of blocks falling and rotating (Stickgold, Malia, Maguire, Roddenberry, & O'Connor, 2000). They are puzzled and wonder what these images mean.

Still another example of implicit memory: As an experiment, three hospital workers agreed to act in special ways toward a patient with amnesia. One was as pleasant as possible; the second was neutral; the third was stern, refused all requests, and made the patient perform boring tasks. After 5 days, the patient was asked to look at photos of the three workers and try to identify them or say anything he knew about them. He said he did not recognize any of them. Then he was asked which one he would approach as a possible friend or which one he would ask for help. He was asked this question repeatedly—it was possible to ask repeatedly because he never remembered being asked before—and he usually chose the photo of the "friendly" person and never chose the "unfriendly" person in spite of the fact that the "unfriendly" person was a beautiful woman, smiling in the photograph (Tranel & Damasio, 1993). He could not say why he preferred one to the others.

In summary, H. M. and similar patients with amnesia have:

- Normal short-term or working memory
- Severe anterograde amnesia for declarative memory—that is, difficulty forming new declarative memories
- Intact procedural memory
- Better implicit than explicit memory

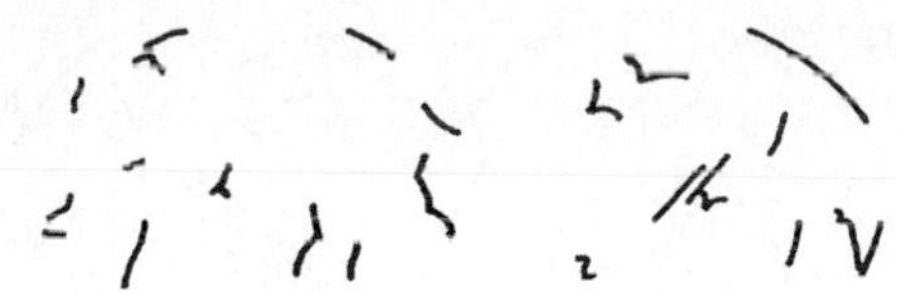

Figure 13.6(b) The Gollin Partial Picture Test
See instruction on page 392.

Individual Differences in Hippocampus and Memory

Given the importance of the hippocampus for memory, we might wonder whether people with a bigger hippocampus have a better memory. As discussed in Chapter 4, research on the relationship between intelligence and total brain size has found confusing and often conflicting results. The same is true for research on hippocampal size. Studies of children, adolescents, and young adults have found better memory performance, on the average, for those with a *smaller* hippocampus (Van Petta, 2004). One hypothesis is that apoptosis improves the hippocampus by weeding out ineffective neurons; people with a larger hippocampus underwent less of this weeding process. That idea is only a hypothesis, however. Studies of older adults have found inconsistent results. As people grow older, the hippocampus gradually shrinks; one study found impaired memory among people whose hippocampus shrank faster than average (Rodrigue & Raz, 2004). Another study of older adults found a strong correlation between verbal memory and the combined size of the hippocampus and entorhinal cortex, an area closely linked to the hippocampus (A. C. Rosen et al., 2003). However, other studies have found little relationship between hippocampal size and memory in old age, or even a reversal: better memory among those with a smaller hippocampus (Van Petta, 2004).

The results look stronger for hippocampal activity rather than size. People vary with regard to a gene that controls BDNF, a neurotrophin. The more common form of the gene codes for the amino acid valine at one location on the BDNF protein, whereas the less common form codes for methionine. People with a gene for methionine show worse than average performance on memory tasks and less than average activity in the hippocampus during the tasks (Hariri, Mattay, Tessitore, Fera, & Weinberger, 2003).

Theories of the Function of the Hippocampus

Exactly how does the hippocampus contribute to memory? The research on H. M. is important, but H. M.'s brain damage includes parts of several other structures, not just the hippocampus. Because of what happened to H. M., surgeons have not done the same operation

Figure 13.6(c) The Gollin Partial Picture Test
See instruction on page 392.

on anyone else. Sometimes strokes or other disorders damage the hippocampus, but seldom on both sides of the brain and never without also damaging other nearby structures. Researchers therefore supplement the human studies by examining laboratory animals.

The Hippocampus and Declarative Memory

One hypothesis is that the hippocampus is critical for declarative memory, especially episodic memory (Squire, 1992). How could we test this hypothesis with nonhumans, who cannot "declare" anything? What could they do that would be the equivalent of describing an episode?

Here is one attempt to examine episodic memory: A rat digs food out of five piles of sand, each with a different odor. Then it gets a choice between two of the odors and is rewarded if it goes toward the one it smelled first. Intact rats learn to respond correctly, apparently demonstrating memory of not only what they smelled but also when they smelled it. Memory of a specific event qualifies as episodic, at least by a broad definition. Rats with hippocampal damage do poorly on this task (Fortin, Agster, & Eichenbaum, 2002; Kesner, Gilbert, & Barua, 2002).

In the **delayed matching-to-sample task,** an animal sees an object (the sample) and then, after a delay, gets a choice between two objects, from which it must choose the one that matches the sample. In the **delayed nonmatching-to-sample task,** the procedure is the same except that the animal must choose the object that is different from the sample (Figure 13.7). In both cases, the animal must remember which object was present on this occasion, thereby showing what we might call a declarative memory, perhaps an episodic memory. Hippocampal damage strongly impairs performance in many cases (Zola et al., 2000). Unfortunately for theorists, performance varies enormously with changes in procedure. For example, if the delayed matching- (or nonmatching-) to-sample task uses constantly changing varieties of objects, then hippocampal damage greatly impairs performance. However, if researchers use the same two objects over and over again, then hippocampal damage has little effect, even though both versions of the task would appear to tap declarative memory (Aggleton, Blindt, & Rawlins, 1989). This study and others suggest that the hippocampus and the entorhinal cortex, which provides input to the hippocampus, are more important for processing novel stimuli than familiar stimuli (McGaughy, Koene, Eichenbaum, & Hasselmo, 2005).

The Hippocampus and Spatial Memory

A second hypothesis is that the hippocampus is especially important for spatial memories. Electrical recordings indicate that many neurons in a rat's hippocampus are tuned to particular spatial locations, responding best when an animal is in a particular place (O'Keefe & Burgess, 1996) or looking in a particular direction (Dudchenko & Taube, 1997; Rolls, 1996a). In a large enough environment, a given cell responds strongly in several locations (Hafting, Fyhn, Molden, Moser, & Moser, 2005). Ordinarily, a given cell responds in the same way whenever the rat is in a particular environment. If we move the rat to a new environment or change the current environment—for example, widening the cage—the various cells establish new patterns of response to different locations. That is, they "re-map" their new environment (Leutgeb et al., 2005; Moita, Rosis, Zhou, LeDoux, & Blair, 2004). Younger rats readjust their hippocampal maps faster than older rats and more quickly learn to find their way to important places within the environment (Rosenzweig, Redish, McNaughton, & Barnes, 2003). When people perform spatial tasks, such as imagining the best route between one friend's house and another, fMRI results show enhanced activity in the hippocampus (Kumaran & Maguire, 2005). All these results suggest that the hippocampus might be particularly important for spatial memory.

In one study, researchers conducted PET scans on the brains of London taxi drivers as they answered questions such as, "What's the shortest legal route from the Carlton Tower Hotel to the Sherlock Holmes Museum?" (London taxi drivers are well trained and answer with impressive accuracy.) Answering these route questions

Monkey lifts sample object to get food.

Food is under the new object.

Figure 13.7 Procedure for delayed nonmatching-to-sample task

Figure 13.6(d) The Gollin Partial Picture Test
See instruction on page 392.

activated their hippocampus much more than did answering nonspatial questions. MRI scans also revealed that the taxi drivers have a larger than average posterior hippocampus and that the longer they had been taxi drivers, the larger their posterior hippocampus (Maguire et al., 2000). This surprising result suggests actual growth of the adult human hippocampus in response to spatial learning experiences.

People with hippocampal damage show impairments on tests of spatial memory. For example, one task is to find your way from one place to another. A second task is to observe objects in a room and then sketch their positions on a map of the room (Bohbot, Allen, & Nadel, 2000).

Consider a couple of nonhuman examples of spatial memory. A **radial maze** has eight or more arms, some of which have a bit of food or other reinforcer at the end (Figure 13.8). A rat placed in the center can find food by exploring each arm once and only once. In a variation of the task, a rat might have to learn that the arms with a rough floor never have food or that the arms pointing toward the window never have food. So a rat can make a mistake either by entering a never-correct arm or by entering a correct arm twice.

Rats with damage to the hippocampus seldom enter the never-correct arms, but they often enter a correct arm twice.

Figure 13.8 A radial maze
A rat that reenters one arm before trying other arms has made an error of spatial working memory.

That is, they forget which arms they have already tried (Jarrard, Okaichi, Steward, & Goldschmidt, 1984; Olton & Papas, 1979; Olton, Walker, & Gage, 1978). Rats show similar impairments after damage to the areas of thalamus and cortex that send information to the hippocampus (Mair, Burk, & Porter, 2003).

Hippocampal damage also impairs performance on another test of spatial memory, the **Morris water maze task,** in which a rat must swim through murky water to find a rest platform that is just under the surface (Figure 13.9). (Rats swim as little as they can. Humans are about the only land mammals that swim recreationally.) A rat with hippocampal damage does find

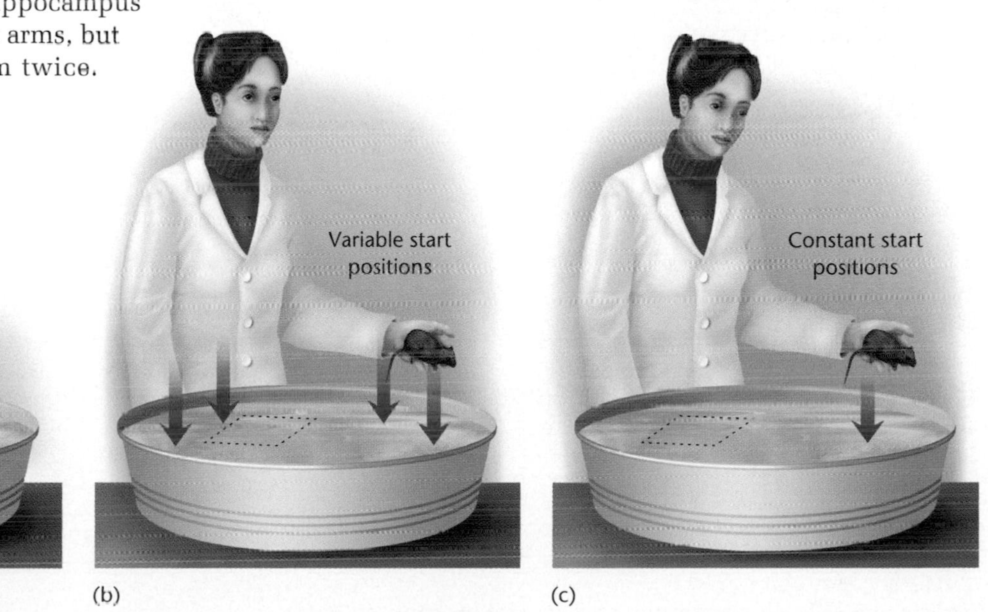

Figure 13.9 The Morris water maze task
A rat is placed in murky water. A platform that would provide support is submerged so the rat cannot see it. Rats with hippocampal damage have trouble remembering the location of the platform.

Figure 13.6(e) The Gollin Partial Picture Test
See instruction on page 392.

the platform. If it always starts from the same place and the rest platform is always in the same place, it gradually learns the route. However, if it has to start from a different location, or if the rest platform occasionally moves from one location to another, the rat has much trouble finding the platform (Eichenbaum, 2000; Liu & Bilkey, 2001).

Interesting evidence for the role of the hippocampus in spatial memory comes from comparisons of closely related species that differ in their spatial memory. Clark's nutcracker, a member of the jay family, lives year-round at high altitudes in western North America. During the summer and fall, it buries seeds in thousands of locations. Unlike squirrels, which bury nuts but often cannot find them, nutcrackers return to their hiding places in the winter and find enough to survive when no other food is available. Pinyon jays, which live at slightly lower elevations, bury less food and depend on it less to survive the winter. Scrub jays and Mexican jays, living at still lower altitudes, depend even less on stored food. Researchers have found that of these four species, the Clark's nutcrackers have the largest hippocampus and perform best on radial mazes and other laboratory tests of spatial memory. Pinyon jays are second best in both respects. On nonspatial tasks, such as color memory, size of hippocampus does not correlate with success (Basil, Kamil, Balda, & Fite, 1996; Olson, Kamil, Balda, & Nims, 1995) (Figure 13.10). In short, the species comparisons support a link between the hippocampus and spatial memory.

	Habitat	Size of Hippocampus Relative to Rest of Brain	Spatial Memory	Color Memory
Clark's nutcracker 	Lives high in mountains; stores food in summer and relies on finding it to survive the winter.	Largest	Best	Slightly worse
Pinyon jay 	Lives at fairly high altitude; depends on stored food to survive the winter.	Second largest	Second best	Slightly better
Scrub jay 	Stores some food but less dependent on it.	Smaller	Less good	Slightly worse
Mexican jay 	Stores some food but less dependent on it.	Smaller	Less good	Slightly better

Figure 13.10 Hippocampus and spatial memory in jays
Of four western North American birds in the jay family, the species that rely most heavily on stored food to get through the winter have the largest hippocampus and perform best on laboratory tests of spatial memory. They have no consistent advantage on nonspatial memory.
(Source: Based on results of Basil, Kamil, Balda, & Fite, 1996; Olson, Kamil, Balda, & Nims, 1995)

However, even while an animal is performing a single task, some parts of the hippocampus code spatial information and others code nonspatial aspects of the task (Hampson, Simeral, & Deadwyler, 1999). Thus, the hippocampus is important for spatial tasks but not exclusively for spatial tasks.

The Hippocampus, Configural Learning, and Binding

The third prominent hypothesis has been modified over the years. An early version held that the hippocampus is necessary for **configural learning**, in which the meaning of a stimulus depends on what other stimuli are paired with it. For example, an animal might have to learn that stimulus A signals food, B also signals food, but a combination of A and B signals no food. Or people might have to learn to choose a square rather than a triangle, a triangle rather than a circle, and a circle rather than a square:

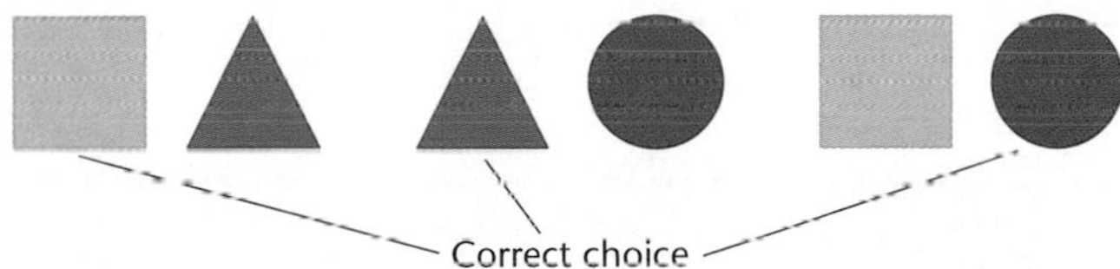

In many cases, hippocampal damage impairs configural learning (Rickard & Grafman, 1998). However, hippocampal damage also impairs memory on nonconfigural tasks when they are sufficiently difficult (Reed & Squire, 1999). Also, hippocampally damaged animals do eventually (though slowly) learn difficult configural tasks. Consequently, psychologists have abandoned the idea that the hippocampus is *necessary* for configural learning.

A modified version is that the hippocampus is specialized to quickly record combinations of stimuli that occur together at a single time, whereas the cerebral cortex detects combinations that occur repeatedly (O'Reilly & Rudy, 2001). By that view, the hippocampus is not really necessary for configural learning; the cerebral cortex can handle such learning if given enough opportunity. However, hippocampal damage impairs memory of single events, such as episodic memories.

Here is an elaboration of this theory: At any moment, you experience many sights, sounds, and so forth. Later, you get a reminder, which causes you to reconstruct as much of that experience as you can. Memory therefore requires connecting or binding various pieces of the experience. The role of the hippocampus may be not so much to establish the memory itself but to bind the pieces together, or lay out a map of where the pieces are stored so that later they can be reunited. The rich interconnections between the hippocampus and the rest of the forebrain make it well suited to this function (Rolls, 1996b). This theory has the potential to encompass the importance of the hippocampus in declarative memory and complex spatial memory, as well as single-event configural memory.

STOP & CHECK

4. What is the difference between anterograde and retrograde amnesia?
5. Which types of memory are least impaired in H. M.?
6. Under what circumstances can H. M. name someone who became famous since 1953?
7. What are three views of the contribution of the hippocampus to memory formation?

Check your answers on page 403.

The Hippocampus and Consolidation

One way of describing H. M.'s memory problem is that he forms short-term but not long-term memories. That idea relates to a proposal by Donald Hebb (1949) that short-term memories are gradually **consolidated** (strengthened) into long-term memories. If the hippocampus is necessary for consolidation, H. M. would be unable to consolidate his memories. Rats with damage to the hippocampus, or the input from other structures to the hippocampus, can learn proper responses in the Morris water maze task, but they forget rapidly, suggesting that they cannot consolidate long-term memories (Remondes & Schuman, 2004). Damage to the rat hippocampus and surrounding areas impairs recent learning more than older learning, implying that as memory becomes consolidated, it is less dependent on the hippocampus (Frankland & Bontempi, 2005). Injection of various drugs after learning can strengthen or weaken later memories. Although the drugs act at many locations and not just the hippocampus, they are most effective shortly after learning and then gradually decline in effect, again implying that memories gradually consolidate (LaLumiere, Buen, & McGaugh, 2003; Santini, Ge, Ren, Pena de Ortiz, & Quirk, 2004).

Still, researchers are not sure exactly what consolidation is or how it develops. Hebb guessed that consolidation depended mainly on time. In his view, a short-term memory might depend on a *reverberating circuit* of neuronal activity in the brain, with a self-exciting loop of neurons (Figure 13.11). If the reverberating circuit remained active long enough, the brain might synthesize proteins, grow new connections, or make some other long-lasting structural changes. To test this idea, researchers gave animals training experiences and then at various delays gave them a powerful shock to the head, producing a convulsion that should disrupt any reverberating circuit. The idea was to wipe out short-term memories before they had time to be-

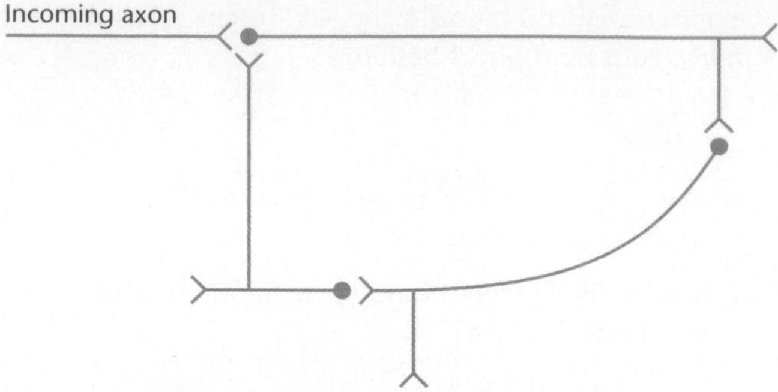

Figure 13.11 A hypothetical reverberating circuit
According to Hebb, neurons might reexcite one another, maintaining a trace of some stimulation long enough to form a more permanent storage.

come long-term memories. Electroconvulsive shock to the head did indeed impair many memories. Similarly, people who suddenly lose consciousness from a blow to the head usually forget the events right before the loss of consciousness. However, further research led to more complex results. For example, sometimes electroconvulsive shock impairs a memory that was already well established. Also, sometimes an apparently obliterated memory returns later, after some reminder (Riccio, Millin, & Gisquet-Verrier, 2003). The shock apparently attaches an impediment to retrieving the memory as opposed to wiping it out.

Furthermore, consolidating a long-term memory clearly depends on more than the passage of time. Think about your high school experiences. You probably spent hours memorizing names and dates for a history test, and now you can hardly remember them at all. Yet you clearly remember the first time a special person smiled at you, the time you said something foolish in class and people laughed at you, the time you won a major honor, the frightening moment when you heard that a friend was hurt in a car accident. Emotionally stirring memories consolidate quickly.

How does the emotional response enhance consolidation? Remember from Chapter 12 that stressful or emotionally exciting experiences increase the secretion of epinephrine (adrenaline) and cortisol. Small to moderate amounts of cortisol activate the amygdala and hippocampus, where they enhance the storage and consolidation of recent experiences (Cahill & McGaugh, 1998). Even unexciting kinds of learning activate the amygdala (Fried et al., 2001), but increased excitement activates it more, improving long-term retention. The amygdala in turn stimulates the hippocampus and cerebral cortex, which are both important for memory storage. However, prolonged stress, which releases even more cortisol, impairs memory (deQuervain, Roozendaal, & McGaugh, 1998; Newcomer et al., 1999).

Nevertheless, even if time is not the only or main influence in consolidation, memories do sometimes grow stronger over time. In one study, eight people aged 60 to 70 years examined photos of people who were famous at various times in the past. According to fMRI scans, several brain areas responded most strongly to recently famous people and least to those famous long ago, even though the participants easily recognized all of the faces (Haist, Gore, & Mao, 2001). In two other studies, fMRI showed stronger responses while people recalled recent events from their own lives than when they recalled autobiographical events from longer ago, despite equal accuracy (Maguire & Frith, 2003; Niki & Luo, 2002). One interpretation is that the brain works harder to identify the recent items, whereas the older ones are stored more firmly. However, the interpretation is uncertain: Did early memories consolidate over the decades, or did they form more strongly in the first place? People generally remember music, movies, politicians, and almost anything else from their adolescence and young adulthood better than they remember similar items from later in life; events from ages 10 to 30 are sometimes called the "autobiographical memory bump" (Berntsen & Rubin, 2002).

STOP & CHECK

8. How do epinephrine and cortisol enhance memory storage?

Check your answer on page 403.

Other Types of Brain Damage and Amnesia

Different kinds of brain damage produce different types of amnesia. Here we examine two more disorders: Korsakoff's syndrome and Alzheimer's disease.

Korsakoff's Syndrome and Other Prefrontal Damage

Korsakoff's syndrome, also known as *Wernicke-Korsakoff syndrome,* is brain damage caused by prolonged thiamine deficiency. Severe thiamine deficiency occurs mostly in chronic alcoholics who go for weeks at a time on a diet of nothing but alcoholic beverages, which contain carbohydrates but no vitamins. The brain needs thiamine (vitamin B_1) to metabolize glucose, its primary fuel. Prolonged thiamine deficiency leads to a loss or shrinkage of neurons throughout the brain, especially in the mamillary bodies (part of the hypothalamus) and in the dorsomedial thalamus, a nucleus that sends axons to the prefrontal cortex (Squire,

Amaral, & Press, 1990; Victor, Adams, & Collins, 1971). Therefore, the symptoms of Korsakoff's syndrome are similar to those of people with damage to the prefrontal cortex, including apathy, confusion, and both retrograde and anterograde amnesia. Hospitals in large cities report about 1 person with Korsakoff's syndrome per 1,000 admissions. Treatment with thiamine sometimes helps, but the longer someone has been thiamine deficient, the poorer the outlook.

To illustrate one aspect of memory in Korsakoff's syndrome, try this demonstration. Here are the first three letters of some words. For each, fill in letters to make any complete word:

met	pro	con
per	thi	def

(Please try the demonstration before reading further.)

Each of these three-letter combinations can start many English words; *pro-*, *con-*, and *per-* start well over 50 each. Did you happen to fill in any of the following—*metabolize, prolonged, confusion, person, thiamine, deficient/deficiency*? Those six words were in the paragraph just before the demonstration. After you had read those words, you were *primed* to think of them. **Priming,** one type of implicit memory, is the phenomenon that seeing or hearing words temporarily increases one's probability of using them. Patients with Korsakoff's syndrome sometimes read a list of words and then show strong priming effects on a fill-in-the-rest-of-the-word task, even though they don't remember even seeing a list of words, much less remember what the words were (Schacter, 1985). That is, like H. M., people with Korsakoff's syndrome show better implicit than explicit memory.

Korsakoff's patients and other patients with frontal lobe damage have difficulties in reasoning about their memories, such as deciding the order of events (Moscovitch, 1992). Suppose I ask, "Which happened to you most recently—graduation from high school, getting your first driver's license, or reading Chapter 2 of *Biological Psychology*?" You reason it out: "I started driving during my junior year of high school so that came before graduation. *Biological Psychology* is one of my college texts, so I started reading it after high school." Someone with frontal lobe damage has trouble with even this simple kind of reasoning.

A distinctive symptom of Korsakoff's syndrome is **confabulation,** in which the patient takes a guess to fill in the gaps in his or her memory. They do not confabulate on all questions, but only on those for which they would expect to know the answer. For example, to a nonsense question like "Who is Princess Lolita?" they reply, "I don't know." They confabulate mainly on questions about themselves, their family, and other familiar topics (Schnider, 2003). Usually, the confabulated answer was true in the past but not now, such as, "I went dancing last night," or "I need to go home and take care of my children." Most of the confabulated answers are more pleasant than the currently true answers (Fotopoulou, Solms, & Turnbull, 2004). That tendency may reflect the patient's attempt to maintain pleasant emotions or merely the fact that for a patient in a hospital, life in the past was, on the whole, more pleasant than the present.

Some patients remember their confabulations and repeat them consistently. One patient always said that he had been in the hospital "since yesterday" (Burgess & McNeil, 1999). Much of the problem seems to be that patients have trouble inhibiting an answer they have previously made. In one study, patients were shown a series of photos and then shown some additional photos and asked which ones matched photos in that series. They did reasonably well up to this point. Then they were shown a second series of photos and again were asked which of several new photos matched the ones in the series they just saw. They generally said "yes" to photos that had been on the first list even though they were not on the second (Schnider & Ptak, 1999). They could not suppress an answer that was correct previously.

The tendency to confabulate produces a fascinating influence on the strategies for studying. Suppose you had to learn a long list of three-word sentences such as: "Medicine cured hiccups" and "Tourist desired snapshot." Would you simply reread the list many times? Or would you alternate between reading the list and testing yourself?

Medicine cured ____________________.
Tourist desired ____________________.

Almost everyone learns better the second way. Completing the sentences forces you to be more active and calls your attention to the items you have not yet learned. Korsakoff's patients, however, learn much better the first way, by reading the list over and over. The reason is, when they test themselves, they confabulate. (*"Medicine cured headache. Tourist desired passport."*) Then they remember their confabulation instead of the correct answer (Hamann & Squire, 1995).

Alzheimer's Disease

Another cause of memory loss is **Alzheimer's** (AHLTZ-hime-ers) **disease.** For example, Daniel Schacter (1983) reported playing golf with an Alzheimer's patient who remembered the rules and jargon of the game correctly but could not remember how many strokes he took on any hole. On five occasions, he teed off, waited for the other player to tee off, and then teed off again, having forgotten his previous shot. As with H. M. and Korsakoff's patients, Alzheimer's patients have better procedural than declarative memory. They learn new hand skills but then surprise themselves with their good performance because they don't remember doing it before (Gabrieli, Corkin, Mickel, & Growdon, 1993). Alzheimer's patients have deficits in both explicit and implicit memory, probably because of impaired attention (Randolph, Tierney, & Chase, 1995), but more severe problems with explicit memory.

Alzheimer's disease gradually progresses to more serious memory loss, confusion, depression, restlessness, hallucinations, delusions, sleeplessness, and loss of appetite. It occasionally strikes people younger than age 40, but becomes more common with age, affecting almost 5% of people between ages 65 and 74 and almost 50% of people over 85 (D. A. Evans et al., 1989).

The first major clue to the cause of Alzheimer's was the fact that people with *Down syndrome* (a type of mental retardation) almost invariably get Alzheimer's disease if they survive into middle age (Lott, 1982). People with Down syndrome have three copies of chromosome 21 rather than the usual two. That fact led investigators to examine chromosome 21, where they found a gene linked to many cases of early-onset Alzheimer's disease (Goate et al., 1991; Murrell, Farlow, Ghetti, & Benson, 1991). Later researchers found genes on other chromosomes that are associated with larger percentages of early-onset Alzheimer's disease (Levy-Lahad et al., 1995; Schellenberg et al., 1992; Sherrington et al., 1995).

However, more than 99% of cases have a late onset, after age 60 to 65. Researchers identified genes that increase the risk of late-onset Alzheimer's disease (Bertram et al., 2000; Corder et al., 1993; Ertekin-Taner et al., 2000; Myers et al., 2000; Pericak-Vance et al., 1991; Strittmatter & Roses, 1995), but these genes account for only a small percentage of cases. About half of all patients have no known relatives with the disease (St George-Hyslop, 2000).

Further evidence that genes do not explain late-onset Alzheimer's disease comes from cross-cultural studies. The Yoruba people of Nigeria have a much lower incidence of Alzheimer's than do Americans, despite having similar frequencies of the genes linked to Alzheimer's disease. A likely hypothesis is that the Yorubas' low-calorie, low-fat, low-sodium diet decreases their vulnerability (Hendrie, 2001).

Although genes do not completely control Alzheimer's disease, understanding their mode of action sheds light on the underlying causes. The emerging pattern is that Alzheimer's disease is caused by brain proteins that fold abnormally, clump together, and interfere with neuronal activity. The same general idea holds for Parkinson's disease and several other brain diseases, although each is associated with a different protein (Taylor, Hardy, & Fischbeck, 2002).

The genes controlling early-onset Alzheimer's disease lead to the accumulation of a protein called amyloid. Brain cells contain *amyloid precursor protein*, which is *cleaved* (broken) to form a smaller protein. In most people, it is cleaved into a protein of 40 amino acids, called amyloid beta protein 40 ($A\beta_{40}$), which presumably serves some useful function. However, in people with Alzheimer's disease, amyloid precursor protein is cleaved mostly to a longer protein with 42 amino acids, **amyloid beta protein 42 ($A\beta_{42}$)**, which accumulates, clumps with other $A\beta_{42}$ molecules, and damages the membranes of axons and dendrites (Lorenzo et al., 2000). For simplicity, researchers usually refer to amyloid beta protein 42 as simply amyloid-β or β-amyloid. Much evidence favors the importance of amyloid-β in the onset of Alzheimer's. Most Alzheimer's patients accumulate amyloid plaques before the onset of behavioral symptoms (Selkoe, 2000). Amyloid deposits produce widespread atrophy (wasting away) of the cerebral cortex, hippocampus, and other areas, as Figures 13.12 and 13.13 show.

In addition to amyloid-β, Alzheimer's patients also accumulate an abnormal form of the **tau** protein that is part of the intracellular support structure of neurons (Davies, 2000). *Amyloid* produces **plaques**, structures formed from degenerating axons and dendrites. Plaques accumulate in the spaces between neurons. *Tau*

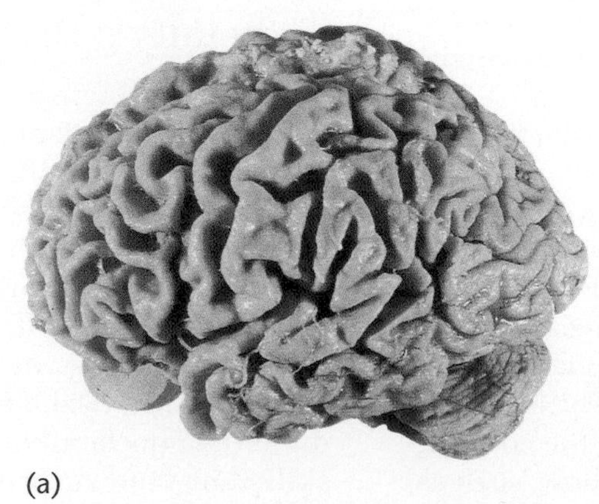
(a)

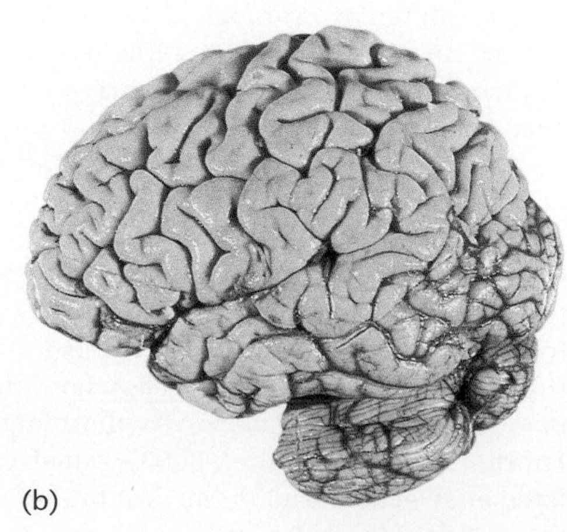
(b)

Figure 13.12 Brain atrophy in Alzheimer's disease
The cerebral cortex of a patient with Alzheimer's **(a)** has gyri that are clearly shrunken in comparison with those of a normal person **(b)**.

Dr. Robert D. Terry, Department of Neurosciences, School of Medicine, University of California at San Diego.

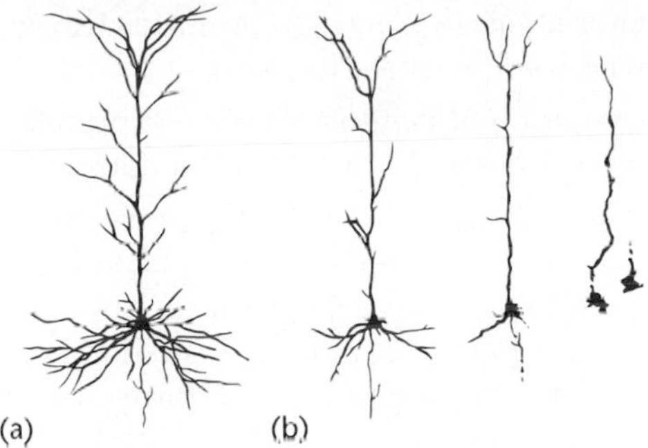

Figure 13.13 Neuronal degeneration in Alzheimer's disease

(a) A cell in the prefrontal cortex of a normal human; **(b)** cells from the same area of cortex in Alzheimer's disease patients at various stages of deterioration. Note the shrinkage of the dendritic tree. *(Source: After "Dendritic changes," by A. B. Scheibel, p. 70. In B. Reisberg, Ed.,* Alzheimer's Disease, *1983. Free Press)*

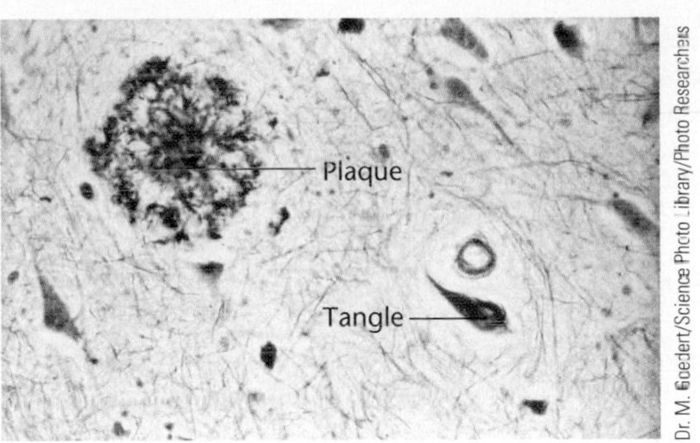

Figure 13.14 Cerebral cortex of an Alzheimer's patient

Amyloid plaque is composed of the protein $A\beta_{42}$. *(Source: From Taylor, Hardy, & Fischbeck, 2002)*

produces **tangles,** structures formed from degenerating structures within neuronal cell bodies (Figure 13.14).

Researchers have debated the relative roles of amyloid-β and tau in the onset of Alzheimer's disease. Although the research continues, most of the evidence favors amyloid-β as the primary cause. Injections of amyloid-β disrupt learning and memory in rats, whereas tau by itself does not produce significant symptoms (Cleary et al., 2005; Hardy & Selkoe, 2002). Nevertheless, tau is part of the problem, as treatments that suppress tau decrease the memory impairments of mice with a condition resembling Alzheimer's disease (SantaCruz et al., 2005).

Although the biochemical details are incomplete, the net outcome is clear: The buildup of abnormal chemicals damages many brain areas, prominently including the basal forebrain, whose cells arouse the rest of the cortex (as discussed in Chapter 9). Many of the behavioral problems follow from the impaired arousal and attention. Amyloid-β also interferes with the NMDA type of glutamate receptor, which—as we shall see in the next module—is critical for the biochemistry of learning (E. M. Snyder et al., 2005).

What can we do to prevent or treat Alzheimer's disease? A common treatment is to use drugs that stimulate acetylcholine receptors or prolong acetylcholine release (McDonald, Willard, Wenk, & Crawley, 1998). An area of major damage is the basal forebrain, which arouses brain activity via axons containing acetylcholine. Enhanced acetylcholine activity increases some aspects of memory even in healthy people (Furey, Pietrini, & Haxby, 2000).

Another drug, still in the experimental stage, stimulates cannabinoid receptors (the same ones that marijuana stimulates). As discussed in Chapter 3, such a drug limits overstimulation by glutamate. Researchers have demonstrated benefits of this drug for rats with a condition resembling Alzheimer's disease (Ramírez, Blázquez, Gómez del Pulgar, Guzmán, & de Ceballos, 2005).

Another approach is to block amyloid-β production with antioxidants, such as those found in dark fruits and vegetables (Joseph et al., 1998). A particularly promising possibility is *curcumin,* a component of yellow food dye and of turmeric, a spice in Indian curries. Research with aged mice found that curcumin reduced amyloid levels and plaques (Yang et al., 2005).

Finally, research with mice suggests the possibility of immunizing against Alzheimer's. One genetic strain of mice overproduces amyloid-β and develops symptoms resembling Alzheimer's disease. Researchers injected small amounts of amyloid-β into young mice, causing their immune system to produce antibodies that protected against the brain deterioration and learning deficits that the mice would have developed otherwise (Janus et al., 2000; Morgan et al., 2000; Schenk et al., 1999). Later researchers found they could also induce people with Alzheimer's disease to produce antibodies against amyloid-β; those with the strongest immune response stopped deteriorating in memory and cognition (Hock et al., 2003). Unfortunately, the treatment produced life-threatening side effects in a few patients, so the research stopped.

For links to more information about Alzheimer's disease, check this website: **http://www.alzforum.org/default.asp**

What Patients with Amnesia Teach Us

The study of patients with amnesia reveals that people do not lose all aspects of memory equally. A patient with great difficulty establishing new memories may be able to remember events from long ago, and someone with greatly impaired factual memory may be able to learn new skills reasonably well. Evidently, people have several somewhat independent kinds of memory that depend on different brain areas.

STOP & CHECK

9. On what kind of question is someone with Korsakoff's syndrome most likely to confabulate?
10. What is amyloid-β and how does it relate to Alzheimer's disease?

Check your answers on page 403.

Module 13.1
In Closing: Different Types of Memory

"Overall intelligence," as measured by an IQ test, is a convenient fiction. It is convenient because, under most circumstances, people who are good at one kind of intellectual task are also good at other kinds, so an overall test score makes useful predictions. However, it is a fiction because different kinds of abilities rely on different brain processes, and it is possible to damage one without another. Even memory is composed of separate abilities, and it is possible to lose one type or aspect of memory without impairing others. The study of amnesia shows how the brain operates as a series of partly independent mechanisms serving specific purposes.

Summary

1. Ivan Pavlov suggested that learning depends on the growth of a connection between two brain areas. Karl Lashley showed that learning does *not* depend on new connections across the cerebral cortex. (p. 384)
2. Later researchers found that some instances of classical conditioning take place in small areas of the cerebellum. More complex learning undoubtedly requires more widespread changes. (p. 386)
3. Psychologists distinguish between short-term memory and long-term memory. Short-term memory holds only a small amount of information and retains it only briefly unless it is constantly rehearsed. Long-term memory retains vast amounts of material indefinitely, but recalling this information sometimes requires great effort. (p. 387)
4. Working memory, a modern alternative to the concept of short-term memory, stores information that one is currently using. The prefrontal cortex and other areas store working memories through repetitive cellular activity. (p. 389)
5. Deterioration of memory in old age probably relates to impairments of the prefrontal cortex. (p. 389)
6. People with damage to the hippocampus, such as the patient H. M., have great trouble forming new long-term declarative memories, although they can still recall events from before the damage and can still form new procedural memories. (p. 390)
7. The hippocampus is important for some kinds of learning and memory but not all. According to various hypotheses, the hippocampus is critical for declarative memory, spatial memory, or binding configurations of events that happen together on a single occasion. (p. 393)
8. The hippocampus is important for consolidation of some kinds of memories. Consolidation depends more on arousal than on the mere passage of time. Arousing events increase the release of epinephrine and cortisol, which directly or indirectly stimulate the amygdala. The amygdala enhances activity in the hippocampus and cerebral cortex. (p. 397)
9. Much about consolidation remains poorly understood. For example, electroconvulsive shock, which is intended to impair consolidation, sometimes impairs old memories that should have been consolidated long ago. (p. 398)
10. Patients with Korsakoff's syndrome or other types of prefrontal damage have impairments of memory, including difficulty drawing inferences from memories. They often fill in their memory gaps with confabulations, which they then remember as if they were true. (p. 398)
11. Alzheimer's disease is a progressive disease, most common in old age, that is characterized by a severe impairment of memory and attention. It is caused partly by the deposition of amyloid-β protein in the brain. (p. 399)

Answers to STOP & CHECK Questions

1. Thompson studied a different, probably simpler type of learning. Also, he looked in the cerebellum instead of the cerebral cortex. (p. 387)
2. If the red nucleus is inactivated during training, the animal makes no conditioned responses during the training, so the red nucleus is necessary for the response. However, as soon as the red nucleus recovers, the animal can show conditioned responses at once, without any further training, so

learning occurred while the red nucleus was inactivated. (p. 387)

3. The dorsolateral prefrontal cortex maintains activity while one stores a working memory, presumably holding a representation of the sensory stimulus. (p. 389)
4. Retrograde amnesia is forgetting events before brain damage; anterograde amnesia is failing to store memories of events after brain damage. (p. 397)
5. H. M. is least impaired on short-term memory, procedural memory, implicit memory, and memory of events that occurred more than 1–3 years before his surgery. (p. 397)
6. If H. M. is given the first name, and preferably also some information about the person, sometimes he can provide the last name. (p. 397)
7. Various theorists emphasize the importance of the hippocampus for declarative memory, spatial memory, and single-occurrence configural memory. (p. 397)
8. Epinephrine and cortisol both enhance emotional memories by stimulating the amygdala. (p. 398)
9. Patients with Korsakoff's syndrome confabulate on questions where they would expect to know the answer, such as questions about themselves. Their confabulations are usually statements that were true at one time. (p. 402)
10. The protein amyloid-β accumulates in the brains of patients with Alzheimer's disease and is probably the cause of the disease. (p. 402)

Thought Questions

1. Lashley sought to find the engram, the physiological representation of learning. In general terms, how would you recognize an engram if you saw one? That is, what would someone have to demonstrate before you could conclude that a particular change in the nervous system was really an engram?
2. Benzodiazepine tranquilizers impair memory. Use what you have learned in this chapter and the previous one to propose an explanation.

Module 13.2
Storing Information in the Nervous System

Anything you see, hear, or do leaves traces in your nervous system. Which of these many traces are important for memory?

If you walk through a field, are the footprints that you leave "memories"? How about the mud that you pick up on your shoes? If the police wanted to know who walked across that field, a forensics expert could check your shoes to answer the question. And yet we would not call these physical traces memories in the usual sense.

Similarly, when a pattern of activity passes through the brain, it leaves a path of physical changes, but not every change is a memory. The task of finding how the brain stores memories is a little like searching for the proverbial needle in a haystack, and researchers have explored many avenues that seemed promising for a while but now seem fruitless.

EXTENSIONS AND APPLICATIONS
Blind Alleys and Abandoned Mines

Textbooks, this one included, concentrate mostly on successful research that led to our current understanding of a field. You may get the impression that science progresses smoothly, with each investigator contributing to the body of knowledge. However, if you look at old journals or textbooks, you will find discussions of many "promising" or "exciting" findings that we disregard today. Scientific research does not progress straight from ignorance to enlightenment; it explores one direction after another, a little like a rat in a complex maze, abandoning the dead ends and pursuing arms that lead further.

The problem with the maze analogy is that an investigator seldom runs into a wall that clearly identifies the end of a route. Perhaps a better analogy is a prospector digging in one location after another, never entirely certain whether to abandon an unprofitable spot or to keep digging just a little longer. Many once-exciting lines of research in the physiology of learning are now of little more than historical interest. Here are three examples.

1. Wilder Penfield sometimes performed brain surgery for severe epilepsy on conscious patients who had only scalp anesthesia. When he applied a brief, weak electrical stimulus to part of the brain, the patient could describe the experience that the stimulation evoked. Stimulation of the temporal cortex sometimes evoked vivid descriptions such as:

   I feel as though I were in the bathroom at school.
   I see myself at the corner of Jacob and Washington in South Bend, Indiana.
   I remember myself at the railroad station in Vanceburg, Kentucky; it is winter and the wind is blowing outside, and I am waiting for a train.

   Penfield (1955; Penfield & Perot, 1963) suggested that each neuron stores a particular memory, almost like a videotape of one's life. However, brain stimulation very rarely elicited a memory of a specific event, more often evoking vague sights and sounds or repeated experiences such as "seeing a bed" or "hearing a choir sing 'White Christmas.'" Stimulation almost never elicited memories of doing anything—just of seeing and hearing. Also, some patients reported events that they had never actually experienced, such as being chased by a robber or seeing Christ descend from the sky. In short, the stimulation produced something more like a dream than a memory.
2. G. A. Horridge (1962) apparently demonstrated that decapitated cockroaches can learn. First he cut the connections between a cockroach's head and the rest of its body. Then he suspended the cockroach so that its legs dangled just above a surface of water. An electrical circuit was arranged as Figure 13.15 shows so that the roach's leg received a shock whenever it touched the water. Each experimental roach was paired with a control roach that got a leg shock whenever the first roach did; only the experimental roach had any control over the shock, however. (This kind of experiment is known as a "yoked-control" design.)

   Over 5 to 10 minutes, roaches in the experimental group "learned" a response of tucking the leg under the body to avoid shocks. Roaches in the

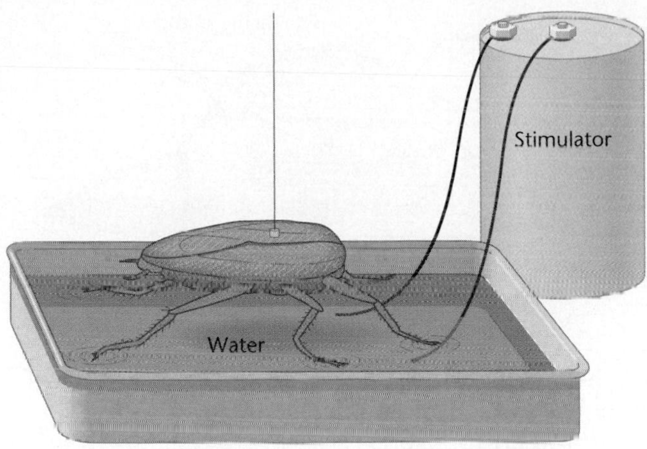

Figure 13.15 Learning in a headless cockroach?
The decapitated cockroach is suspended just above the water; it receives a shock whenever its hind leg touches the water. A cockroach in the control group gets a shock whenever the first roach does regardless of its own behavior. According to some reports, the experimental roach learned to keep its leg out of the water. *(Source: From G. A. Horridge, "Learning of Leg Position by the Ventral Nerve Cord in Headless Insects."* Proceedings of the Royal Society of London, B, 157, *1962, 33–52. Copyright © 1962 The Royal Society of London. Reprinted by permission of the Royal Society of London and G. A. Horridge.)*

control group did not, on the average, change their leg position during the training period. Thus, the changed response apparently qualifies as learning and not as an accidental by-product of the shocks.

These experiments initially seemed a promising way to study learning in a simple nervous system (Eisenstein & Cohen, 1965). Unfortunately, decapitated cockroaches learn slowly and the results vary sharply from one individual to another, limiting the usefulness of the results. After a handful of studies, interest in this line of research faded.

3. In the 1960s and early 1970s, several investigators proposed that each memory is coded as a specific molecule, probably RNA or protein. The boldest test of that hypothesis was an attempt to transfer memories chemically from one individual to another. James McConnell (1962) reported that, when planaria (flatworms) cannibalized other planaria that had been classically conditioned to respond to a light, they apparently "remembered" what the cannibalized planaria had learned. At least they learned the response faster than planaria generally do.

   Inspired by that report, other investigators trained rats to approach a clicking sound for food (Babich, Jacobson, Bubash, & Jacobson, 1965). After the rats were well trained, the experimenters ground up their brains, extracted RNA, and injected it into untrained rats. The recipient rats learned to approach the clicking sound faster than rats in the control group did.

   That report led to a wealth of studies on the transfer of training by brain extracts. In *some* of these experiments, rats that received brain extracts from a trained group showed apparent memory of the task, whereas those that received extracts from an untrained group did not (Dyal, 1971; Fjerdingstad, 1973).

   The results were inconsistent and unreplicable, however, even within a single laboratory (L. T. Smith, 1975). Many laboratories failed to find any hint of a transfer effect. By the mid-1970s, most biological psychologists saw no point in continuing such research.

Learning and the Hebbian Synapse

The research that seems most promising today began with Ivan Pavlov's concept of classical conditioning. Although, as we considered earlier, that theory led Karl Lashley to an unsuccessful search for connections in the cerebral cortex, it also stimulated Donald Hebb to propose a mechanism for change at a synapse.

Hebb suggested that when the axon of neuron A "repeatedly or persistently takes part in firing [cell B], some growth process or metabolic change takes place in one or both cells" that increases the subsequent ability of axon A to excite cell B (Hebb, 1949, p. 62). In other words, an axon that has successfully stimulated cell B in the past becomes even more successful in the future.

Consider how this process relates to classical conditioning. Suppose axon A initially excites cell B slightly, and axon C excites B more strongly. If A and C fire together, their combined effect on B may produce an action potential. You might think of axon A as the CS and axon C as the UCS. Pairing activity in axons A and C increases the future effect of A on B.

A synapse that increases in effectiveness because of simultaneous activity in the presynaptic and postsynaptic neurons is called a **Hebbian synapse.** In Chapter 6, we encountered examples of this type of synapse. In the development of the visual system, if an axon from the left eye consistently fires at the same time as one from the right eye, a neuron in the visual cortex increases its response to both of them. Such synapses may also be critical for many kinds of associative learning. Neuroscientists have discovered much about the mechanisms of Hebbian (or almost Hebbian) synapses.

Single-Cell Mechanisms of Invertebrate Behavior Change

If we are going to look for a needle in a haystack, a good strategy is to look in a small haystack. Therefore, many researchers have turned to studies of invertebrates. Vertebrate and invertebrate nervous systems are organized differently, but the chemistry of the neuron, the principles of the action potential, and even the neurotransmitters are the same. If we identify the physical basis of learning and memory in an invertebrate, we have at least a hypothesis of what *might* work in vertebrates. (Biologists have long used this strategy for studying genetics, embryology, and other biological processes.)

Aplysia as an Experimental Animal

Aplysia, a marine invertebrate related to the common slug, has been a popular animal for studies of the physiology of learning (Figure 13.16). Compared to vertebrates, it has fewer neurons, many of which are large and easy to study. Moreover, unlike vertebrates, *Aplysia* neurons are virtually identical from one individual to another so that different investigators can study the properties of the same neuron.

Figure 13.16 *Aplysia,* a marine mollusk
A full-grown animal is a little larger than the average human hand.

Much of the research on *Aplysia* concerns changes in behavior as a result of experience. Some of those changes may seem simple, and it is a matter of definition whether we call them *learning* or use the broader term *plasticity.* One commonly studied behavior is the withdrawal response: If someone touches the siphon, mantle, or gill of an *Aplysia* (Figure 13.17), the animal vigorously withdraws the irritated structure. Investigators have traced the neural path from the touch receptors through various identifiable interneurons to the motor neurons that direct the withdrawal response. Using this neural pathway, investigators have studied such phenomena as habituation and sensitization.

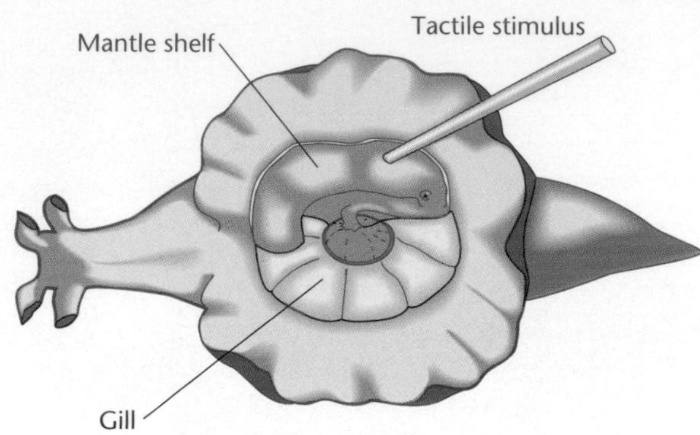

Figure 13.17 Touching an *Aplysia* causes a withdrawal response
The sensory and motor neurons controlling this reaction have been identified and studied.

Habituation in *Aplysia*

Habituation is a decrease in response to a stimulus that is presented repeatedly and accompanied by no change in other stimuli. For example, if your clock chimes every hour, you gradually notice it less and less. Habituation can be demonstrated in an *Aplysia* by repeatedly stimulating its gills with a brief jet of seawater. At first, it withdraws its gills, but after many repetitions, it stops responding. The decline in response is not due to muscle fatigue because, even after habituation has occurred, direct stimulation of the motor neuron produces a full-sized muscle contraction (Kupfermann, Castellucci, Pinsker, & Kandel, 1970). We can also rule out changes in the sensory neuron. The sensory neuron still gives a full, normal response to stimulation; it merely fails to excite the motor neuron as much as before (Kupfermann et al., 1970). We are therefore left with the conclusion that habituation in *Aplysia* depends on a change in the synapse between the sensory neuron and the motor neuron (Figure 13.18).

Sensitization in *Aplysia*

If you experience an unexpected, intense pain, you probably react more strongly than usual to loud sounds, sharp pinches, and other sudden stimuli in the next few days. This phenomenon is **sensitization,** an increase in response to mild stimuli as a result of previous exposure to more intense stimuli. Similarly, a strong stimulus almost anywhere on *Aplysia*'s skin can intensify later withdrawal responses to a touch.

Researchers have traced sensitization to changes at identified synapses (Cleary, Hammer, & Byrne, 1989;

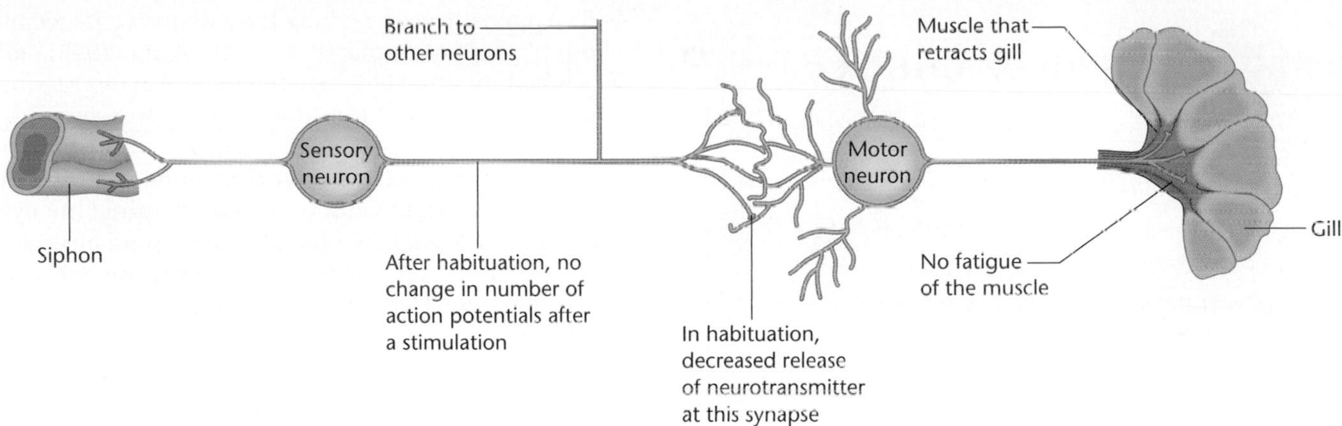

Figure 13.18 Habituation of the gill-withdrawal reflex in *Aplysia*

Touching the siphon causes a withdrawal of the gill. After many repetitions, the response habituates (declines) because of decreased transmission at the synapse between the sensory neuron and the motor neuron. *(Source: Redrawn from "Neuronal Mechanisms of Habituation and Dishabituation of the Gill-Withdrawal Reflex in* Aplysia,*" by V. Castellucci, H. Pinsker, I. Kupfermann, and E. Kandel, Science, 1970, 167, pp. 1745–1748. Copyright © 1970 by AAAS. Used by permission of AAAS and V. Castellucci)*

Dale, Schacher, & Kandel, 1988; Kandel & Schwartz, 1982), as shown in Figure 13.19. Strong stimulation anywhere on the skin excites a particular *facilitating interneuron,* which releases serotonin (5-HT) onto the presynaptic terminals of many sensory neurons. These are called *presynaptic receptors.* When serotonin attaches to these receptors, it closes potassium channels in the membrane. As you will recall from Chapter 2, potassium flows out of the neuron after the peak of the action potential; the exit of potassium restores the neuron to its usual polarization. When serotonin blocks the potassium channels, the effect is a prolonged action potential in the presynaptic cell and therefore more transmitter release. If the sensitizing stimulus occurs repeatedly, the sensory neuron synthesizes new proteins that produce long-term sensitization (C. H. Bailey, Giustetto, Huang, Hawkins, & Kandel, 2000).

The research on *Aplysia* shows us that changes in synaptic activity can produce behavioral plasticity, and in 2000, Eric Kandel won a Nobel Prize for this work. The *Aplysia* research also shows that even sensitization, widely regarded as a fairly simple process, depends on interactions among several neurons and their synapses (Bailey et al., 2000).

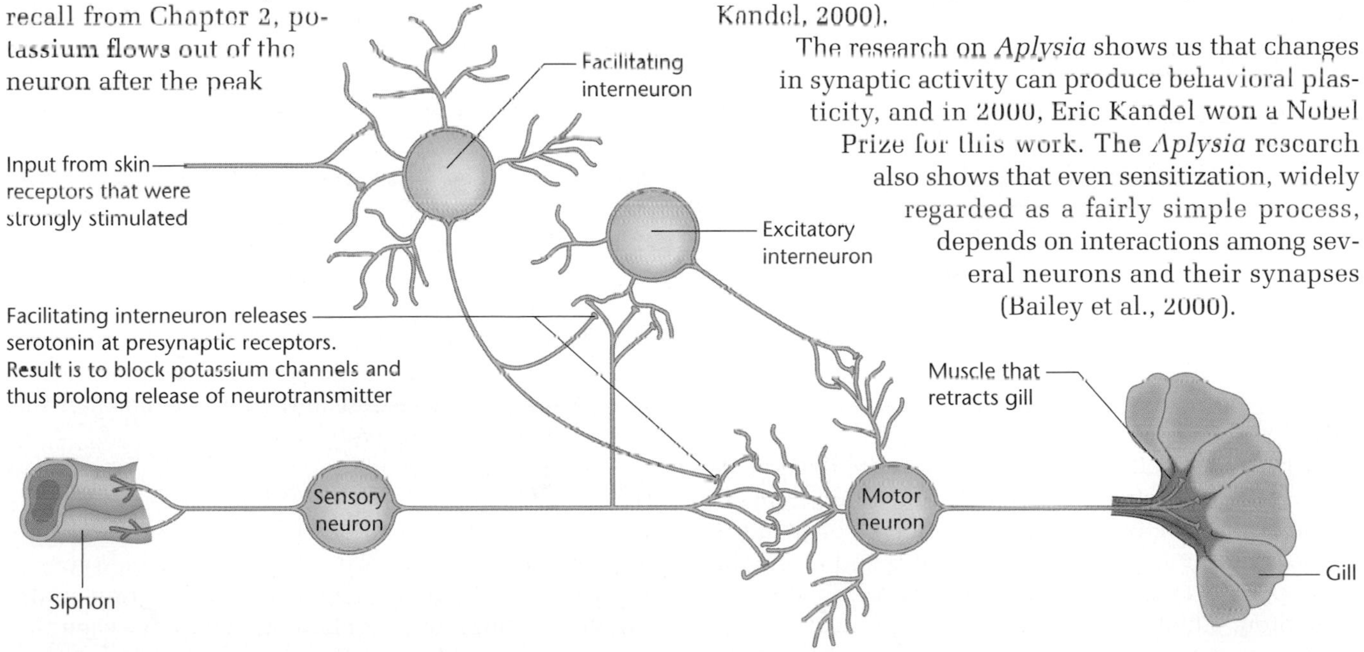

Figure 13.19 Sensitization of the withdrawal response in *Aplysia*

Stimulation of the sensory neuron ordinarily excites the motor neuron, partly by a direct path and partly by stimulation of an excitatory interneuron. Stimulation of a facilitating interneuron releases serotonin to the presynaptic receptors on the sensory neuron, blocking potassium channels and thereby prolonging the release of neurotransmitter. *(Source: After Kandel & Schwartz, 1982)*

1. How can a Hebbian synapse account for the basic phenomena of classical conditioning?
2. What are the advantages of research on *Aplysia* compared with vertebrates?
3. When serotonin blocks potassium channels on the presynaptic terminal, what is the effect on transmission?

Check your answers on page 412.

Long-Term Potentiation in Mammals

Since the work of Sherrington and Cajal, most neuroscientists have assumed that learning depends on some kind of change at the synapses, and the work on *Aplysia* confirms that synaptic changes *can* produce behavioral changes. The first evidence for a similar process among vertebrates came from studies of hippocampal neurons in the 1970s (Bliss & Lømo, 1973). The phenomenon, known as **long-term potentiation (LTP)**, is this: One or more axons connected to a dendrite bombard it with a brief but rapid series of stimuli—such as 100 per second for 1 to 4 seconds. The burst of intense stimulation leaves some of the synapses potentiated (more responsive to new input of the same type) for minutes, days, or weeks.

LTP shows three properties that make it an attractive candidate for a cellular basis of learning and memory:

- **specificity**—If some of the synapses onto a cell have been highly active and others have not, only the active ones become strengthened.
- **cooperativity**—Nearly simultaneous stimulation by two or more axons produces LTP much more strongly than does repeated stimulation by just one axon. As a result of specificity and cooperativity, if axons A and D are repeatedly active together, while axons B and C are usually inactive, the synapses of A and D become strengthened and those of B and C remain the same or become weaker (Sejnowski, Chattarji, & Stanton, 1990).
- **associativity**—Pairing a weak input with a strong input enhances later response to the weak input. In this regard, the synapses subject to LTP are like Hebbian synapses, except that LTP requires only the depolarization of a dendrite, not necessarily an action potential.

The opposite change, long-term depression, occurs in both the hippocampus (Kerr & Abraham, 1995) and the cerebellum (Ito, 1989, 2002). **Long-term depression (LTD)** is a prolonged decrease in response at a synapse. It occurs when axons have been active at a low frequency, such as one to four times per second. For example, recall from Chapter 6 that keeping one eye closed during a sensitive period early in an animal's life causes the visual cortex to decrease its responsiveness to that eye. That phenomenon is an example of LTD (Heynen et al., 2003).

If learning potentiates a synapse, increasing its response rate, what happens as you learn more and more? Does the total amount of activity in the brain keep growing greater and greater? Ordinarily, no, although in a few cases a neuron increases its number of sodium channels to become more active overall (Zhang & Linden, 2003), and in some cases, the hippocampus forms new neurons or expands existing ones (Hall, Thomas, & Everitt, 2000; Shors et al., 2001). However, as a rule, when any synapse undergoes LTP to increase its responsiveness, neighboring synapses decrease their responsiveness, maintaining the total activation at a nearly constant level (Royer & Paré, 2003). We can think of neighboring synapses as competing for a neuron's attention. The synapses with greater than average activity become potentiated, and those with less become depressed.

Biochemical Mechanisms

Determining how LTP or LTD occurs has been a huge research challenge because each neuron has many tiny synapses, sometimes in the tens of thousands. Isolating the chemical changes at any one synapse has taken an enormous amount of creative research. Much of the research has dealt with cells in culture, isolated from the rest of the animal, although a few studies show that the same processes occur in intact animals (Allen, Celikel, & Feldman, 2003; Takahashi, Svoboda, & Malinow, 2003). The mechanisms vary among brain areas (Li, Chen, Xing, Wei, & Rogawski, 2001; Mellor & Nicoll, 2001); we shall discuss LTP in the hippocampus, where it is easiest to demonstrate and where its mechanisms have been most extensively studied.

AMPA and NMDA Synapses

In almost every known case, LTP depends on changes at glutamate synapses. The brain has several types of receptors for glutamate, its most abundant transmitter (Madden, 2002). In past chapters, you have seen that neuroscientists identify different dopamine receptors by number, such as D_1 and D_2, and different GABA receptors by letter, such as $GABA_A$. For glutamate, they named the different receptors after drugs that stimulate them. Here we are interested in two types of glutamate receptors, called AMPA and NMDA. The **AMPA**

receptor is excited by the neurotransmitter glutamate, but it can also respond to a drug called α-amino-3-hydroxy-5-methyl-4-isoxazolepropionic acid (quite a mouthful). The **NMDA receptor** is also ordinarily excited only by glutamate, but it can respond to a drug called N-methyl-D-aspartate.

Both are ionotropic receptors; that is, when they are stimulated, they open a channel to let ions enter the postsynaptic cell. The AMPA receptor opens sodium channels, and it is similar to the other synaptic receptors we have considered. The NMDA receptor, however, is of a type we have not previously discussed: Its response to the transmitter glutamate *depends on the degree of polarization across the membrane.* When glutamate attaches to an NMDA receptor while the membrane is at its resting potential, the ion channel is usually blocked by magnesium ions. (Magnesium ions, positively charged, are attracted to the negative charge inside the cells but do not fit through the NMDA channel.) The NMDA channel opens only if the magnesium leaves, and the surest way to detach the magnesium is to depolarize the membrane, decreasing the negative charge that attracts it (Figure 13.20).

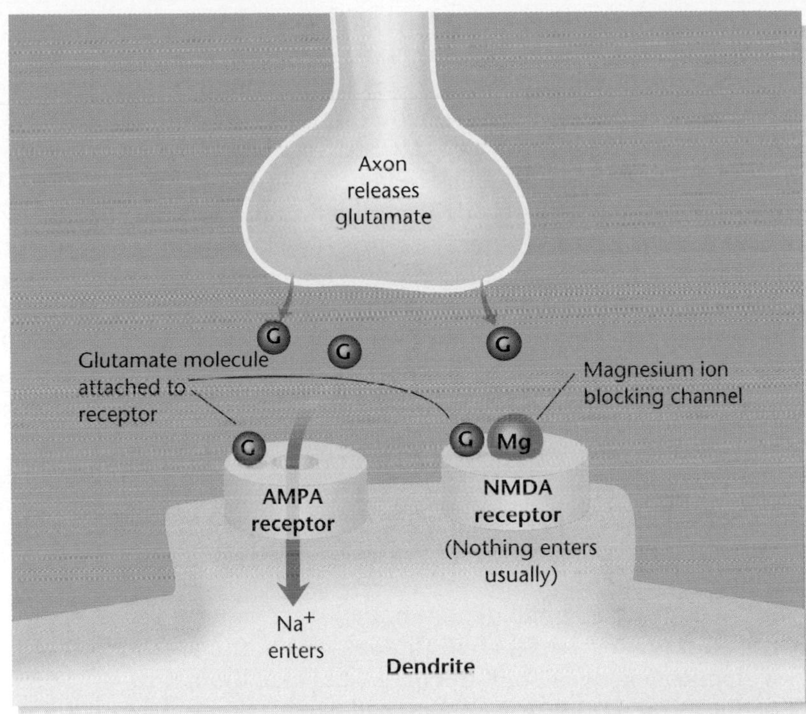

Figure 13.20 The AMPA and NMDA receptors, before LTP
Glutamate attaches to both receptors. At the AMPA receptor, it opens a channel to let sodium ions enter. At the NMDA receptor, it binds but usually fails to open the channel, which is blocked by magnesium ions.

Suppose an axon releases glutamate repeatedly. Better yet, let's activate two axons repeatedly, side by side on the same dendrite. So many sodium ions enter through the AMPA channels that the dendrite becomes significantly depolarized, though it does not produce an action potential. (Remember, dendrites do not produce action potentials.) The depolarization displaces the magnesium molecules, enabling glutamate to open the NMDA channel. At that point, both sodium and calcium enter through the NMDA channel (Figure 13.21).

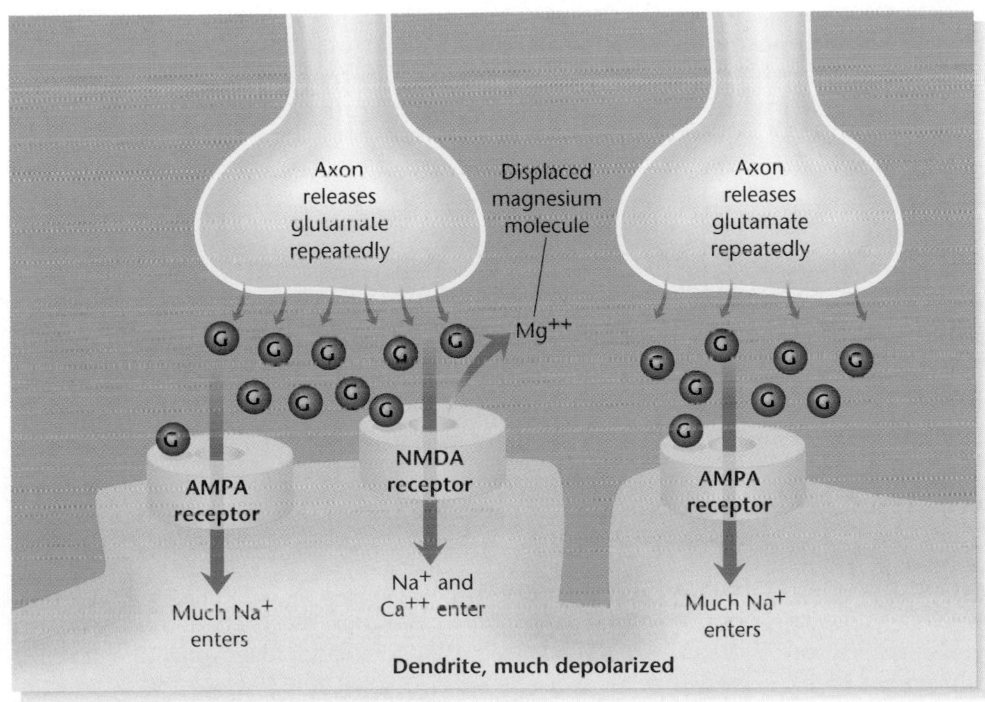

Figure 13.21 The AMPA and NMDA receptors during LTP
If one or more AMPA receptors have been repeatedly stimulated, enough sodium enters to largely depolarize the dendrite's membrane. Doing so displaces the magnesium ions and enables glutamate to open the NMDA receptor, through which sodium and calcium enter.

The entry of calcium is the key to the later changes. When calcium enters through the NMDA channel, it activates a protein called CaMKII (α-calcium-calmodulin-dependent protein kinase II), which migrates to the synapse (Otmakhov et al., 2004). CaMKII is both necessary and sufficient for LTP (Lisman, Schulman, & Cline, 2002). Increasing CaMKII production increases LTP, and mutations that interfere with CaMKII prevent LTP and block learning (Frankland, O'Brien, Ohno, Kirkwood, & Silva, 2001; Irvine, Vernon, & Giese, 2005). The protein CaMKII sets in motion many processes, varying from one neuron to another:

- The dendrite builds more AMPA receptors or moves old ones into better positions (Poncer & Malinow, 2001; Takahashi et al., 2003).
- In some cases, the neuron makes more NMDA receptors (Grosshans, Clayton, Coultrap, & Browning, 2002).
- The dendrite may make more branches, thus forming additional synapses with the same axon (Engert & Bonhoeffer, 1999; Toni, Buchs, Nikonenko, Bron, & Muller, 1999) (Figure 13.22). Recall from Chapter 5 that enriched experience also leads to increased dendritic branching.
- Possibly, some individual AMPA receptors become more responsive than before.

Let's summarize: When glutamate massively stimulates AMPA receptors, the resulting depolarization enables glutamate also to stimulate nearby NMDA receptors. Stimulation of the NMDA receptors lets calcium enter the cell, where it sets into motion a series of changes that potentiate the dendrite's future responsiveness to glutamate, mostly at AMPA receptors. After the NMDA potentiate the AMPA receptors, they revert to their original condition.

The mechanisms of LTD are virtually the opposite of LTP. For example, where LTP leads to expanded dendrites and more synapses, LTD is associated with shrinkage of dendrites and decreased numbers of synaptic receptors (Zhou, Homma, & Poo, 2004).

Once LTP has been established, it no longer depends on NMDA synapses. Drugs that block NMDA synapses prevent the *establishment* of LTP, but they do not interfere with the *maintenance* of LTP that was already established (Gustafsson & Wigström, 1990; Uekita & Okaichi, 2005). In other words, once the NMDA receptors have potentiated the AMPA receptors, the AMPA receptors stay potentiated, regardless of what happens to the NMDAs.

Presynaptic Changes

The changes just described occur in the postsynaptic neuron. In many cases, LTP depends on changes in the presynaptic neuron instead or in addition. Extensive stimulation of a postsynaptic cell causes it to release a **retrograde transmitter** that travels back to the presynaptic cell to modify it. In many cases that retrograde transmitter is nitric oxide (NO). As a result, a presynaptic neuron decreases its threshold for producing action potentials (Ganguly, Kiss, & Poo, 2000), increases its release of neurotransmitter (Zakharenko et al., 2001), expands its axon (Routtenberg, Cantallops, Zaffuto, Serrano, & Namgung, 2000), and releases its transmitter from additional sites along its axon (Reid, Dixon, Takahashi, Bliss, & Fine, 2004). In short, LTP reflects increased activity by the presynaptic neuron as well as increased responsiveness by the postsynaptic neuron.

4. Before LTP: In the normal state, what is the effect of glutamate at the AMPA receptors? At the NMDA receptors?

5. During the formation of LTP: When a burst of intense stimulation releases much more glutamate than usual at two or more incoming axons, what is the effect of the glutamate at the AMPA receptors? At the NMDA receptors? Which ions enter at the NMDA receptors?

6. After LTP has formed: After the neuron has gone through LTP, what is now the effect of glutamate at the AMPA receptors? At the NMDA receptors?

Check your answers on page 412.

LTP and Behavior

LTP occurs at a single synapse. Changing a synapse is a necessary step for learning but hardly sufficient. To explain even a simple learned behavior, we shall need to understand interactions among a huge number of cells in a complex network.

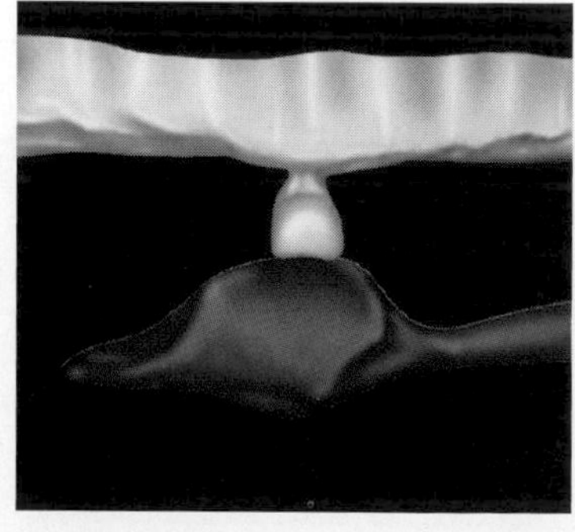

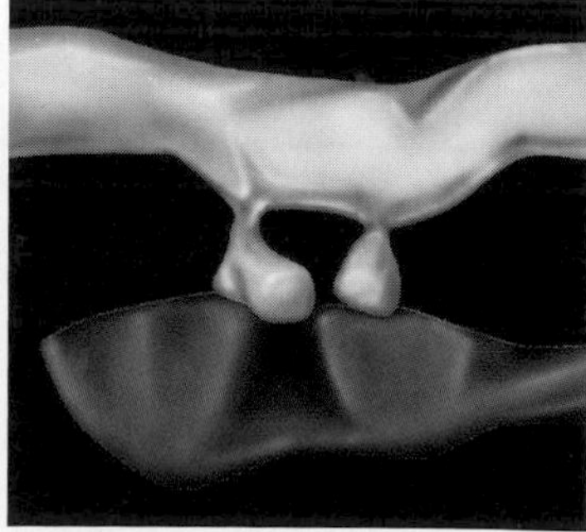

Figure 13.22 One way in which LTP occurs
In some cases, the dendrite makes new branches, which attach to branches of the same axon, thus increasing the overall stimulation.
(Source: Based on Toni, Buchs, Nikonenko, Bron & Muller, 1999)

Still, understanding the mechanisms of LTP may enable researchers to understand what could impair or improve memory. Mice with genes that cause abnormalities of the NMDA receptor learn slowly; those with genes causing extra NMDA receptors have better than normal memory (Tang et al., 1999). LTP increases production of the protein *GAP-43* in the presynaptic neuron, and mice that overproduce this protein show enhanced ability to learn and solve problems (Routtenberg et al., 2000). Drugs that interfere with LTP block learning (Baldwin, Holahan, Sadeghian, & Kelley, 2000), whereas those that facilitate LTP enhance learning (Izquierdo & Medina, 1995). Several pharmaceutical companies are investigating drugs that might improve learning by enhancing LTP (Farah et al., 2004).

Drugs can also enhance memory in other ways. To take the simplest example, caffeine enhances learning and memory by increasing arousal. Many patients with Alzheimer's disease take drugs that facilitate acetylcholine by blocking the enzyme that degrades it (Farah et al., 2004). Other drugs under investigation act on glutamate or dopamine synapses or proteins that alter synaptic receptors.

You may have heard claims that memory can be improved by taking the herb *Ginkgo biloba* or several other chemicals. Drugs must be approved by the Food and Drug Administration, but naturally occurring supplements face almost no regulation at all. Unfortunately, "natural" does not mean "safe" or "effective." Research on ginkgo biloba has not been extensive, but so far, it suggests that the herb offers mild benefits to a limited number of people. Ginkgo biloba dilates blood vessels and therefore increases blood flow to the brain. When given to Alzheimer's patients or other people with memory problems, ginkgo biloba sometimes produces small but measurable benefits (Gold, Cahill, & Wenk, 2002). Similarly, a number of other "memory-boosting" supplements increase blood flow to the brain or increase metabolism. Some studies have shown small memory benefits for these drugs in laboratory animals or aged people (McDaniel, Maier, & Einstein, 2002). At this point, it is best to reserve judgment but encourage more research. It is worth noting, however, that the only demonstrated benefits have been for people with circulatory problems and other disorders, not for young people with normal brains. Little is known about the side effects and risks of these drugs. If you want to improve your grades, the best route is to study harder, not to take pills.

Module 13.2

In Closing: The Physiology of Memory

In this module, we examined mechanisms such as LTP, which seem remote from the complex behaviors we call learning and memory. After we understand the biochemical workings of memory more completely, what can we do with the information? Presumably, we will help people overcome or prevent memory deterioration; we can expect much better therapies for Alzheimer's disease and so forth. Should we also look forward to improving memory for normal people? Would you like to have a supermemory?

Maybe, but let's be cautious. Even though I could add memory chips to my computer to store ever-larger quantities of information, I still don't want to keep everything I write or every e-mail message I receive. Similarly, I'm not sure I would want my brain to retain every experience, even if it had unlimited storage capacity. The ideal supermemory would not just record more information; it would faithfully record the important information and discard the rest. If we can improve memory through drugs, or any other way, we will still want to maintain that selectivity.

Summary

1. A Hebbian synapse is strengthened if it is repeatedly active when the postsynaptic neuron produces action potentials. (p. 405)
2. Habituation of the gill-withdrawal reflex in *Aplysia* depends on a mechanism that decreases the release of transmitter from a particular presynaptic neuron. (p. 406)
3. Sensitization of the gill-withdrawal reflex in *Aplysia* occurs when serotonin blocks potassium channels in a presynaptic neuron and thereby prolongs the release of transmitter from that neuron. (p. 406)
4. Long-term potentiation (LTP) is an enhancement of response at certain synapses because of a brief but intense series of stimuli delivered to a neuron, generally by two or more axons delivering simultaneous inputs. LTP occurs in many brain areas and is particularly prominent in the hippocampus. (p. 408)
5. If axons are active at a very slow rate, their synapses may decrease in responsiveness—a process known as long-term depression (LTD). (p. 408)
6. LTP in hippocampal neurons occurs as follows: Repeated glutamate excitation of AMPA receptors depolarizes the membrane. The depolarization removes magnesium ions that had been blocking NMDA receptors. Glutamate is then able to excite the NMDA receptors, opening a channel for calcium ions to enter the neuron. (p. 408)
7. When calcium enters through the NMDA-controlled channels, it activates a protein that sets in motion a series of events that build more AMPA receptors and increase the growth of dendritic branches. These changes increase the later responsiveness of the dendrite to incoming glutamate. (p. 410)

8. At many synapses, LTP also (or instead) relates to increased release of transmitter from the presynaptic neuron. (p. 410)
9. Procedures that enhance or impair LTP have similar effects on certain kinds of learning. Research on LTP may lead to drugs that help improve memory. (p. 411)

Answers to STOP & CHECK Questions

1. In a Hebbian synapse pairing the activity of a weaker (CS) axon with a stronger (UCS) axon produces an action potential and in the process strengthens the response of the cell to the CS axon. On later trials, it will produce a bigger depolarization of the postsynaptic cell, which we can regard as a conditioned response. (p. 408)
2. *Aplysia* has fewer cells than vertebrates, and the cells and connections are virtually identical from one individual to another. Therefore, researchers can work out the mechanisms of behavior in great detail. (p. 408)
3. Blocking potassium channels prolongs the action potential and therefore prolongs the release of neurotransmitter, producing an increased response. (p. 408)
4. Before LTP, glutamate stimulates AMPA receptors but usually has little effect at the NMDA receptors because magnesium blocks them. (p. 410)
5. During the formation of LTP, the massive glutamate input strongly stimulates the AMPA receptors, thus depolarizing the dendrite. This depolarization enables glutamate to excite the NMDA receptors also. Both calcium and sodium enter there. (p. 410)
6. After LTP has been established, glutamate stimulates the AMPA receptors more than before, mainly because of an increased number of AMPA receptors. At the NMDA receptors, it is again usually ineffective. (p. 410)

Thought Question

If a synapse has already developed LTP once, should it be easier or more difficult to get it to develop LTP again? Why?

Chapter Ending

Key Terms and Activities

Terms

Alzheimer's disease (p. 399)
amnesia (p. 389)
AMPA receptor (p. 408)
amyloid beta protein 42 ($A\beta_{42}$) (p. 400)
anterograde amnesia (p. 390)
associativity (p. 408)
central executive (p. 389)
classical conditioning (p. 384)
conditioned response (CR) (p. 384)
conditioned stimulus (CS) (p. 384)
confabulation (p. 399)
configural learning (p. 397)
consolidation (p. 397)
cooperativity (p. 408)
declarative memory (p. 392)
delayed matching-to-sample task (p. 394)
delayed nonmatching-to-sample task (p. 394)
delayed response task (p. 389)
engram (p. 385)
episodic memory (p. 390)
equipotentiality (p. 386)
explicit memory (p. 392)
habituation (p. 406)
Hebbian synapse (p. 405)
implicit memory (p. 392)
Korsakoff's syndrome (p. 398)
lateral interpositus nucleus (LIP) (p. 386)
long-term depression (LTD) (p. 408)
long-term memory (p. 387)
long-term potentiation (LTP) (p. 408)
mass action (p. 386)
Morris water maze task (p. 395)
NMDA receptor (p. 409)
operant conditioning (p. 384)
phonological loop (p. 389)
plaque (p. 400)

priming (p. 399)
procedural memory (p. 392)
punishment (p. 384)
radial maze (p. 395)
reinforcer (p. 384)
retrograde amnesia (p. 390)
retrograde transmitter (p. 410)
sensitization (p. 406)
short-term memory (p. 387)
specificity (p. 408)
tangle (p. 401)
tau (p. 400)
unconditioned response (UCR) (p. 384)
unconditioned stimulus (UCS) (p. 384)
visuospatial sketchpad (p. 389)
working memory (p. 389)

Suggestion for Further Reading

Eichenbaum, H. (2002). *The cognitive neuroscience of memory.* New York: Oxford University Press. Thoughtful treatment of both the behavioral and physiological aspects of memory.

Websites to Explore

You can go to the Biological Psychology Study Center and click these links. While there, you can also check for suggested articles available on InfoTrac College Edition. The Biological Psychology Internet address is:

http://psychology.wadsworth.com/book/kalatbiopsych9e/

Alzheimer's Research Forum

http://www.alzforum.org/default.asp

BrainInfo: Information about many brain areas, including the hippocampus

http://braininfo.rprc.washington.edu/menumain.html

Exploring Biological Psychology CD

Classical Conditioning (video)
Amnesia and Different Types of Memory (video)
Amnestic Patient (video)
Implicit Memories (Try It Yourself)
Alzheimer's Patient (video)
Long-Term Potentiation (Try It Yourself)
Neural Networks and Me (video)
Chapter Quiz (multiple choice questions)
Critical Thinking (essay questions)

ThomsonNOW™

http://www.thomsonedu.com

Go to this site for the link to ThomsonNOW, your one-stop study shop, Take a Pre-Test for this chapter, and ThomsonNOW will generate a Personalized Study Plan based on your test results. The Study Plan will identify the topics you need to review and direct you to online resources to help you master these topics. You can then take a Post-Test to help you determine the concepts you have mastered and what you still need work on.

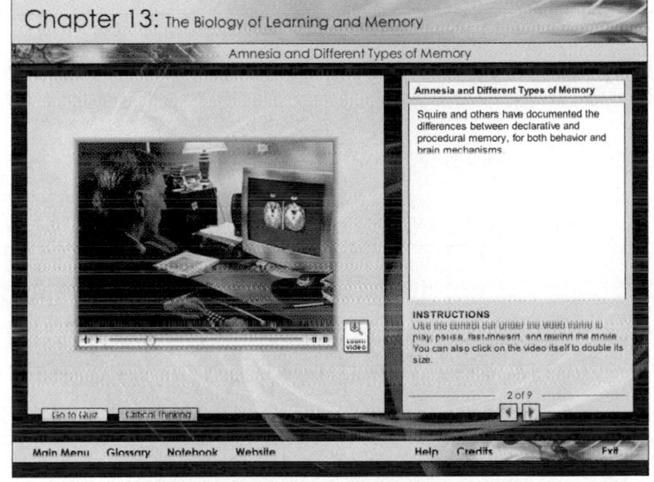

Here is a demonstration of the symptoms of amnesia.

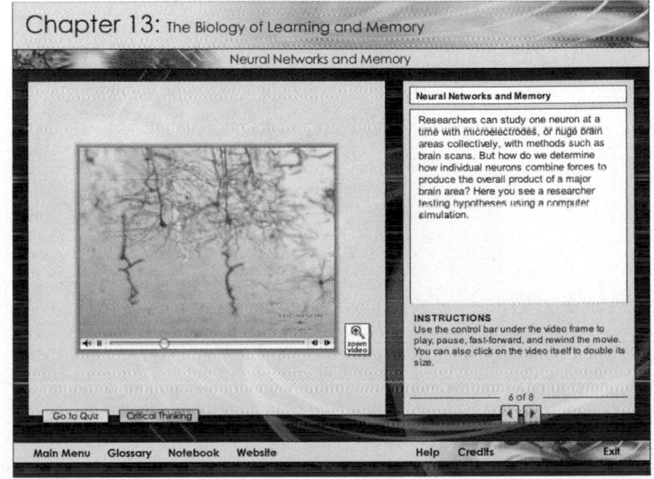

Researchers try to understand memory and amnesia through computer simulations.

Cognitive Functions

14

Chapter Outline

Opposite: Language may have evolved from our tendency to make gestures.
Source: Daly & Newton/Getty Images

Main Ideas

1. The left and right hemispheres of the brain communicate primarily through the corpus callosum, although other smaller commissures also exchange some information between the hemispheres. After damage to the corpus callosum, each hemisphere has access to information only from the opposite half of the body and from the opposite visual field.
2. In most people, the left hemisphere is specialized for language and analytical processing. The right hemisphere is specialized for certain complex visuospatial tasks and synthetic processing.
3. The language specializations of the human brain are enormous elaborations of features that are present in other primates.
4. Abnormalities of the left hemisphere can lead to a great variety of specific language impairments.

Biological explanations of vision, hearing, and movement are fairly detailed. Explanations of motivations, emotions, and memory are less precise, mainly because researchers can less precisely describe or measure the behaviors themselves. Language, thought, and attention are again difficult to measure, much less explain physiologically. Nevertheless, they have been integral topics for neuroscience since its earliest days, beginning with Paul Broca's report in the 1860s that speech depends on part of the left frontal cortex.

Although research on the biology of cognition is difficult, many of the results are fascinating. After damage to the corpus callosum, which connects the two hemispheres, people act as if they have two fields of awareness—separate "minds," you might say. With damage to certain areas of the left hemisphere, people lose their language abilities, while remaining unimpaired in other ways. People with damage to parts of the right hemisphere ignore the left side of their body and the left side of the world. Studies of such people offer clues about how the brain operates and raise stimulating questions.

Module 14.1
Lateralization of Function

Symmetry is common in nature. The sun, stars, and planets are nearly symmetrical, as are most animals and plants. When an atom undergoes radioactive decay, it emits identical rays in exactly opposite directions. However, a few kinds of asymmetry in nature are noteworthy:

- At the "Big Bang," the universe had slightly more matter than antimatter. If matter and antimatter had formed equally, they would have canceled each other out, and no stars or planets could have formed.
- Proteins are made of amino acids, nearly all of which come in mirror-image forms, called D and L. Although both kinds of amino acid form equally easily in a chemistry laboratory, animals and plants use the L forms almost exclusively.
- Most people are right-handed and have somewhat different functions in the two hemispheres of the brain.

This module addresses only the last example. (Sorry, I can't explain the asymmetry of the Big Bang.) Presumably, assigning different functions to the two hemispheres provides some advantage.

Handedness and Its Genetics

Slightly more than 90% of all people—with small differences among ethnic groups—are strongly right-handed. They prefer the right hand for writing, eating, throwing, sewing, sawing, cutting, and so forth. Of the remaining 9%–10%, some are strongly left-handed, but most are somewhat ambidextrous—using the left hand for some activities and the right hand for others. Researchers contrast right-handers to left-handers or to "noncomplete right-handers." In either case, people who are not right-handed form a heterogeneous group.

Chimpanzees and other primates are also mostly right-handed. For most tasks, they show a small preference for the right hand (Hopkins, Dahl, & Pilcher, 2001; Hopkins, Wesley, Izard, Hook, & Schapiro, 2004), but when they make communicative gestures, their preference for the right hand increases (Hopkins et al., 2005).

People become left-handed or non-right-handed for various reasons, including damage or impairment to the left hemisphere of the brain during birth or infancy (Ehrman & Perelle, 2004). The role of genetics has long

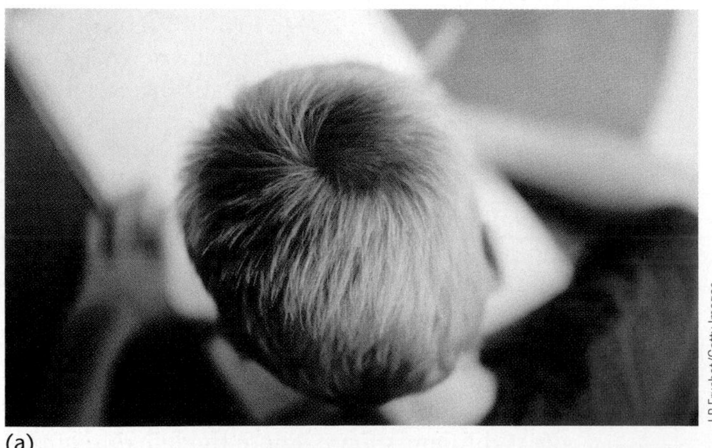

J P Fruchet/Getty Images

(a)

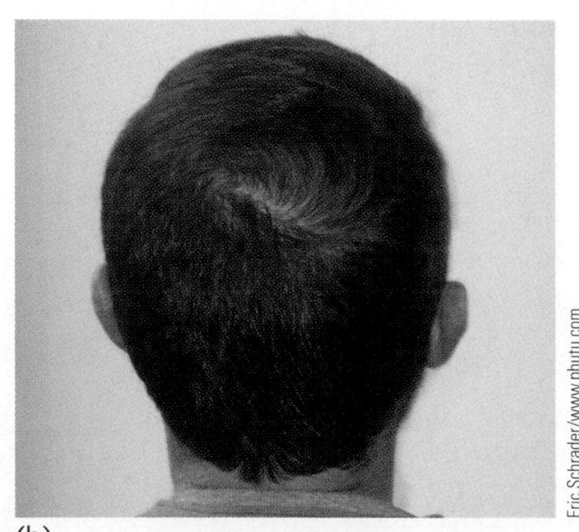

Eric Schrader/www.phutu.com

(b)

Figure 14.1 Hair whorls
Most right-handers have a clockwise hair whorl (a). Left-handers are split about 50–50 between clockwise and counterclockwise hair whorls (b).

been confusing. Left-handed parents often have a right-handed child, and less frequently, two right-handed parents have a left-handed child.

One hypothesis about the genetics of handedness starts with the observation that more than 90% of right-handers have a clockwise hair whorl on their head—that is, a point from which hairs radiate in a clockwise manner. Left-handers and ambidextrous people are split about evenly between clockwise and counterclockwise whorls (Figure 14.1). The direction of the whorl is consistent from infancy through old age and independent of how you wear or brush your hair, so it apparently represents a genetic influence. Amar Klar (2003, 2005) has hypothesized the existence of a dominant gene that produces right-handedness and a clockwise hair whorl. According to this hypothesis, the recessive gene produces random handedness and random hair whorl direction—as likely one way as the other. Suppose that of all human genes for handedness and hair whorl, 58% are of the "right-handed, clockwise" variety, and 42% are of the "random" type. Because the random type is recessive, it shows its effects only in those who have two of this gene. The chance of having two of that gene is 42% x 42%, or almost 18%. If 18% of all people have two of the random gene, about half of those—9%—would be left-handed, and about half would have counterclockwise hair whorls. This hypothesis can make sense of the fact that two left-handed parents can have right-handed children. It also accounts for the fact that monozygotic twins are sometimes discordant—one right-handed and one left-handed.

STOP & CHECK

1. Suppose one monozygotic twin is right-handed and the other is left-handed. According to Klar's hypothesis, when these twins have children of their own, should we expect the left-hander to have a higher percentage of left-handed children, or should the two have equal percentages of left-handed children?
2. How would Klar's hypothesis explain the fact that some right-handed people have counterclockwise hair whorls?

Check your answers on page 428.

The Left and Right Hemispheres

The left hemisphere of the cerebral cortex is connected to skin receptors and muscles mainly on the right side of the body, except for trunk muscles and facial muscles, which are controlled by both hemispheres. The left hemisphere sees only the right half of the world. The right hemisphere is connected to sensory receptors and muscles mainly on the left half of the body. It sees only the left half of the world. Each hemisphere gets auditory information from both ears but slightly stronger information from the contralateral ear. The exceptions to this pattern of crossed input are taste and smell. Each hemisphere gets taste information from its own side of the tongue (Aglioti, Tassinari, Corballis, & Berlucchi, 2000; Pritchard, Macaluso, & Eslinger, 1999) and smell information from the nostril on its own side (Herz, McCall, & Cahill, 1999; Homewood & Stevenson, 2001).

Why all vertebrates evolved so that each hemisphere controls the contralateral (opposite) side of the body, no one knows. Here's a guess: Several kinds of evidence indicate that when the ancestor of vertebrates diverged from the ancestor of insects and other invertebrates, the ancient vertebrate's body "flipped" upside-down relative to the insect's body, along its dorsal–ventral axis. The simplest evidence is that insects have the heart on top, then the digestive system, and a chain of neuron clusters (their counterpart to our spinal cord) on the bottom. Vertebrates have the opposite order. Researchers who have compared the anatomy in finer detail find more precise evidence that our bodies are inverted relative to insects (Arendt & Nübler-Jung, 1994; De Robertis & Sasai, 1996). We don't know why this happened. What it means is that the torso flipped with respect to the legs. Did it also flip with respect to the head? If so, what used to be the left side of the brain was now connected to the muscles and skin on the right side but still connected to taste and smell receptors on the left side (because they are in the head and they flipped sides along with the brain). This hypothesis would explain why each hemisphere is connected to smell and touch receptors on its own side of the head. Admittedly, this idea is speculative, and it raises as many questions as it answers.

At any rate, the left and right hemispheres exchange information through a set of axons called the **corpus callosum** (Figure 14.2; see also Figures 4.10 and 4.13) and through the anterior commissure, the hippocampal commissure, and a couple of other small commissures. Information that initially enters one hemisphere crosses to the opposite hemisphere with only a brief delay.

The two hemispheres are not simply mirror images of each other. In most humans, the left hemisphere is specialized for language; the functions of the right hemisphere are more difficult to summarize, as we shall see later. Such division of labor between the two hemispheres is known as **lateralization.** If you had no corpus callosum, your left hemisphere could react only to information from the right side of your body, and

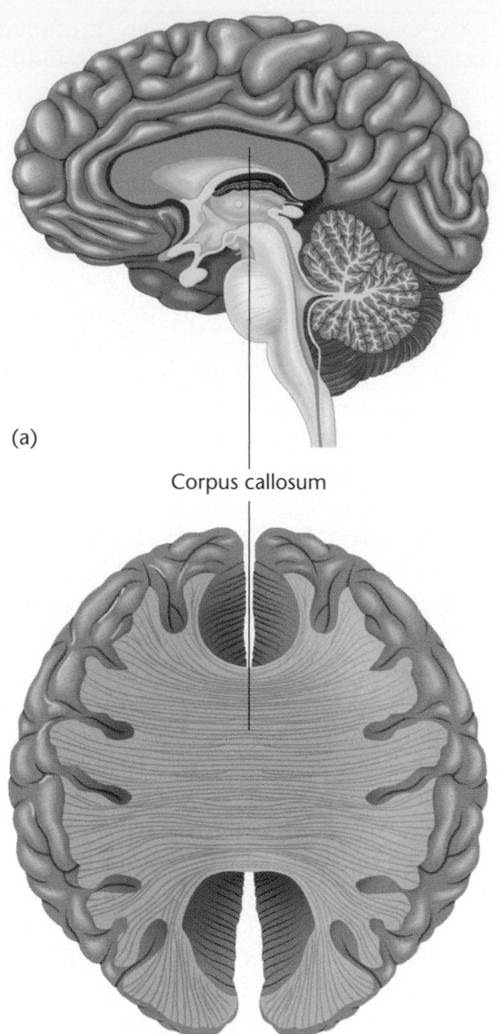

Figure 14.2 Two views of the corpus callosum
The corpus callosum is a large set of axons conveying information between the two hemispheres. **(a)** A sagittal section through the human brain. **(b)** A dissection (viewed from above) in which gray matter has been removed to expose the corpus callosum.

your right hemisphere could react only to information from the left. Because of the corpus callosum, however, each hemisphere receives information from both sides. Only after damage to the corpus callosum (or to one hemisphere) do we see clear evidence of lateralization.

Visual and Auditory Connections to the Hemispheres

Before we can discuss lateralization in any detail, we must consider the way the eyes connect to the brain. The hemispheres are connected to the eyes in such a way that each hemisphere gets input from the opposite half of the visual world; that is, the left hemisphere sees the right side of the world, and the right hemisphere sees the left side. In rabbits and other species with eyes far to the side of the head, the connections from eye to brain are easy to describe: The left eye connects to the right hemisphere, and the right eye connects to the left. *Human eyes are not connected to the brain in this way.* Both of your eyes face forward. You see the left side of the world almost as well with your right eye as with your left eye.

Figure 14.3 illustrates the connections from the eyes to the brain in humans. Light from the right half of the **visual field**—what is visible at any moment—shines onto the left half of *both* retinas, and light from the left visual field shines onto the right half of both retinas. The left half of *each* retina connects to the left hemisphere, which therefore sees the right visual field. Similarly, the right half of each retina connects to the right hemisphere, which sees the left visual field. A small vertical strip down the center of each retina, covering about 5 degrees of visual arc, connects to both hemispheres (Innocenti, 1980; Lavidor & Walsh, 2004). In Figure 14.3, note how half of the axons from each eye cross to the opposite side of the brain at the **optic chiasm** (literally, the optic "cross").

Right visual field ⇒ left half of each retina ⇒ left hemisphere

Left visual field ⇒ right half of each retina ⇒ right hemisphere

The auditory system is organized differently. Each ear sends the information to both sides of the brain because any part of the brain that contributes to localizing sounds must receive input from both ears. However, when the two ears receive different information, each hemisphere does pay more attention to the ear on the opposite side (Hugdahl, 1996).

STOP & CHECK

3. The left hemisphere of the brain is connected to the right eye in rabbits. In humans, the left hemisphere is connected to the left half of each retina. Explain the reason for this species difference.
4. In humans, light from the right visual field shines on the _____ half of each retina, which sends its axons to the _____ hemisphere of the brain.

Check your answers on page 428.

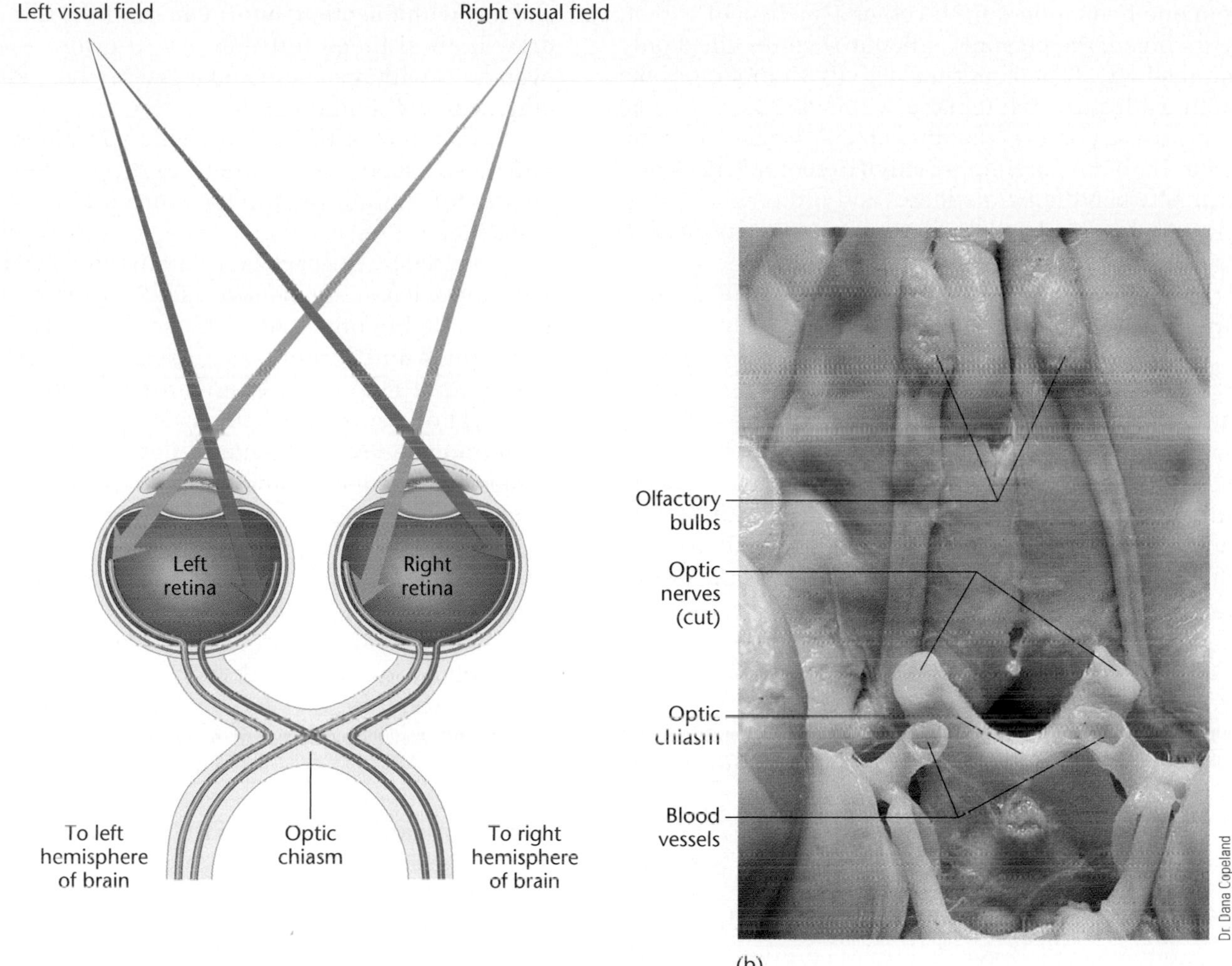

Figure 14.3 Connections from the eyes to the human brain
(a) Route of visual input to the two hemispheres of the brain. Note that the left hemisphere is connected to the left half of each retina and thus gets visual input from the right half of the world; the opposite is true of the right hemisphere. **(b)** Closeup of olfactory bulbs and the optic chiasm. At the optic chiasm, axons from the right half of the left retina cross to the right hemisphere, and axons from the left half of the right retina cross to the left hemisphere.

Cutting the Corpus Callosum

Damage to the corpus callosum prevents the two hemispheres from exchanging information. Occasionally, surgeons sever the corpus callosum as a treatment for severe **epilepsy**, a condition characterized by repeated episodes of excessive synchronized neural activity, mainly because of decreased release of the inhibitory neurotransmitter GABA (During, Ryder, & Spencer, 1995). It can result from a mutation in a gene controlling the GABA receptor (Baulac et al., 2001), from trauma or infection in the brain, brain tumors, or exposure to toxic substances. Often, the cause is not known. About 1%–2% of all people have epilepsy. The symptoms vary depending on the location and type of brain abnormality.

Antiepileptic drugs block sodium flow across the membrane or enhance the effects of GABA. More than 90% of epileptic patients respond well enough to live a normal life. However, if someone continues having frequent seizures despite medication, physicians consider surgically removing the **focus**, or point in the brain where the seizures begin. The location of the focus varies from one person to another.

Removing the focus is not an option if someone has several foci. Therefore, the idea arose to cut the corpus callosum to prevent epileptic seizures from crossing from one hemisphere to the other. One benefit is that, as predicted, the person's epileptic seizures affect only half the body. (The abnormal activity cannot cross the corpus callosum, so it remains within one hemisphere.) A surprising bonus is that the seizures become less frequent. Evidently, epileptic activity rebounds back and forth between the hemispheres and prolongs seizures. If it can't bounce back and forth across the corpus callosum, a seizure may not develop at all.

How does severing the corpus callosum affect other aspects of behavior? People who have undergone surgery to the corpus callosum, referred to as **split-brain people**, maintain their intellect and motivation, and they still walk without difficulty. They also use the two hands together on familiar tasks such as tying shoes. However, if they are asked to pretend they are hitting a golf ball, threading a needle, or attaching a fishhook to a line, they struggle with the less familiar tasks, which have not become automatic for them (Franz, Waldie, & Smith, 2000).

Split-brain patients can use their two hands independently in a way that other people cannot. For example, try drawing ∪ with your left hand while simultaneously drawing ⊃ with your right hand. Most people find this task difficult, but split-brain people do it with ease. Or try drawing circles with both hands simultaneously, but one of them just a little faster than the other (not twice as fast).

try it yourself

Most people find this task difficult; split-brain people spontaneously draw the circles at different speeds (Kennerley, Diedrichsen, Hazeltine, Semjen, & Ivry, 2002).

Incidentally, the difficulty of simultaneously moving your left hand one way and your right hand a different way reflects a cognitive difficulty more than a motor limitation. It is hard to draw a ∪ with one hand and a ⊃ with the other, but if you carefully draw both of them and then try to *trace over* the ∪ with one hand and a ⊃ with the other, you will find it easier.

Evidently, it is difficult to plan two actions at once unless you have clear targets to direct your movements. Split-brain people have no trouble planning two actions at once.

Research by Roger Sperry and his students (Nebes, 1974) revealed subtle behavioral effects when stimuli were limited to one side of the body. In a typical experiment, a split-brain patient stared straight ahead as the experimenter flashed words or pictures on either side of a screen (Figure 14.4). Information that went to one hemisphere could not cross to the other because of the damage to the corpus callosum. The information stayed on the screen long enough to be visible but not long enough for the person to move his or her eyes. The person could then point with the left hand to what the right hemisphere had seen and could point with the right hand to what the left hemisphere had seen. It was as if each side had only half of the answers. The two halves of the brain had different information, and they could not communicate with each other.

The left hemisphere is dominant for speech production in more than 95% of right-handers and nearly 80% of left-handers (McKeever, Seitz, Krutsch, & Van Eys, 1995) (Methods 14.1). It is also better than the right hemisphere at language comprehension for most people, although the right hemisphere does understand speech to some extent (Beeman & Chiarello, 1998). The left and right hemispheres respond about equally to nonlanguage sounds, but parts of the left temporal cortex respond selectively to language (Giraud & Price, 2001). For example, a sentence activates the left hemisphere more than the same words in scrambled order

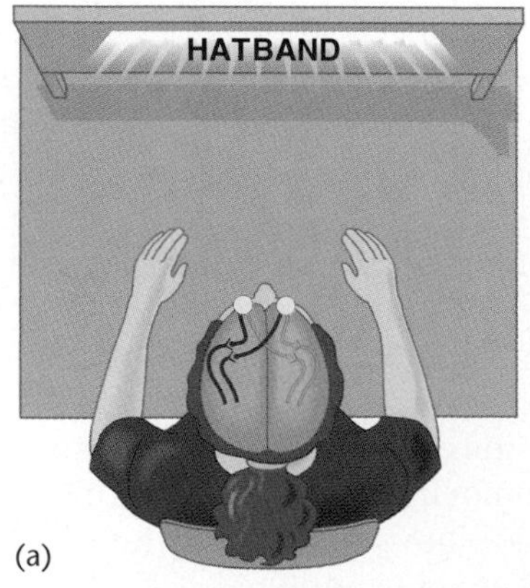

Figure 14.4 Effects of damage to the corpus callosum
(a) When the word *hatband* is flashed on a screen, **(b)** a woman with a split brain can report only what her left hemisphere saw, "band." **(c)** However, with her left hand, she can point to a hat, which is what the right hemisphere saw.

METHODS 14.1
Testing Hemispheric Dominance for Speech

Several methods are available to test which hemisphere is dominant for speech. One is the **Wada Test**, named after its inventor. A physician injects sodium amytal, a barbiturate tranquilizer, into the carotid artery on one side of the head. The drug puts that side of the brain to sleep, enabling researchers to test the capacities of the other hemisphere. For example, a person with left-hemisphere dominance for speech continues speaking after a sodium amytal injection to the right hemisphere, but not after an injection to the left hemisphere. The Wada Test gives highly accurate information about lateralization, but the procedure is risky and sometimes fatal.

A less accurate, but easier and safer, test is the **dichotic listening task**, in which a person wears earphones that present different words to the two ears at the same time. The person tries to say either or both words. People with left-hemisphere dominance for language identify mostly the words heard in the right ear; those with right-hemisphere dominance identify mostly words heard in the left ear.

A third method is the **object naming latency task**, which measures how fast someone can name an object flashed in the left or right visual field (McKeever, Seitz, Krutsch, & Van Eys, 1995). People with left-hemisphere language dominance are faster at naming objects in the right visual field, whereas those with right-hemisphere dominance are faster at naming objects in the left visual field.

A fourth method is to record brain activity while people speak or listen to speech, using PET scans, fMRI scans, or electrical or magnetic evoked responses. This final method is expensive, but it provides the most detailed information about which areas become active during language activities (Vouloumanos, Kiehl, Werker, & Liddle, 2001).

would (Vandenberghe, Nobre, & Price, 2002). Shepherds on one of the Canary Islands have developed a simplified version of Spanish that they whistle, using just four consonants and two vowels, to communicate over long distances. When they listen to these sounds, language areas of their left temporal cortex respond strongly; people who don't understand the language react to it as music, without activating the language areas (Carreiras, Lopez, Rivero, & Corina, 2005).

A split-brain person can name an object after viewing it briefly in the right visual field, seeing it with the left hemisphere. But the same person viewing a display in the left visual field (right hemisphere) usually cannot name or describe it. I say "usually" because a small amount of information travels between the hemispheres through several smaller commissures, as shown in Figure 14.5, and some split-brain patients get enough information to describe some objects in part (Berlucchi, Mangun, & Gazzaniga, 1997; Forster & Corballis, 2000). Nevertheless, a patient who cannot name something points to it correctly with the left hand, even while saying, "I don't know what it was." (Of course, a split-brain person who watches the left hand point out an object can then name it.)

Is there any advantage in having just one hemisphere control speech? Possibly. Many people who have bilateral control of speech stutter (Fox et al., 2000), although not all people who stutter have bilateral control of speech. Perhaps having two speech centers produces competing messages to the speech muscles.

STOP & CHECK

5. Can a split-brain person name an object after feeling it with the left hand? With the right hand? Explain.
6. After a split-brain person sees something in the left visual field, how can he or she describe or identify the object?

Check your answers on page 428.

Split Hemispheres: Competition and Cooperation

Each hemisphere of a split-brain person processes information independently of the other. In the first weeks after surgery, the hemispheres act like separate people sharing one body. One split-brain person repeatedly took items from the grocery shelf with one hand and returned them with the other (Reuter-Lorenz & Miller, 1998).

Another patient—specifically, his left hemisphere—described his experience as follows (Dimond, 1979):

> If I'm reading, I can hold the book in my right hand; it's a lot easier to sit on my left hand, than to hold it with both hands. . . . You tell your hand—I'm going to turn so many pages in a

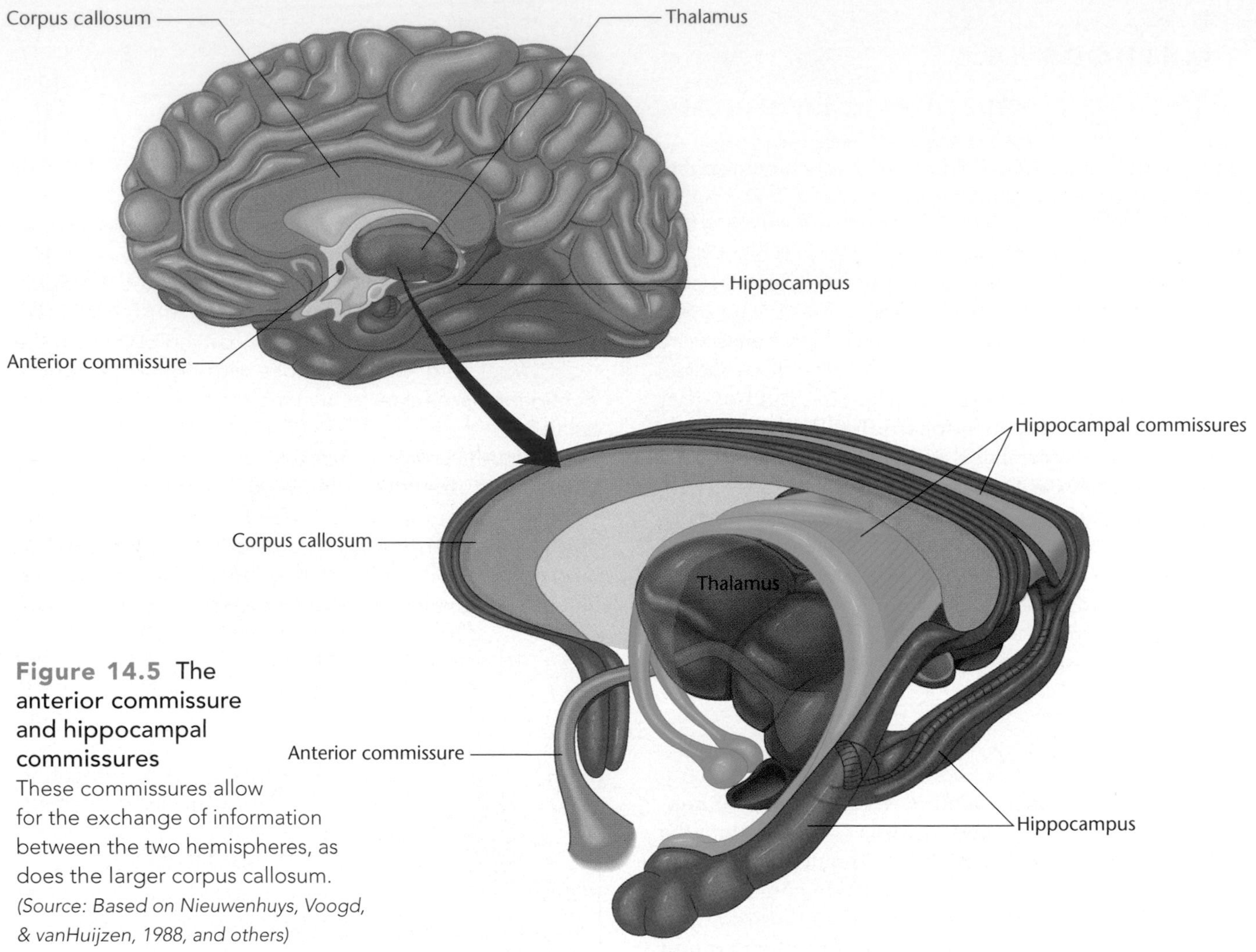

Figure 14.5 The anterior commissure and hippocampal commissures
These commissures allow for the exchange of information between the two hemispheres, as does the larger corpus callosum.
(Source: Based on Nieuwenhuys, Voogd, & vanHuijzen, 1988, and others)

> book—turn three pages—then somehow the left hand will pick up two pages and you're at page 5, or whatever. It's better to let it go, pick it up with the right hand, and then turn to the right page. With your right hand, you correct what the left has done. (p. 211)

Such conflicts are more common soon after surgery than later. The corpus callosum does not heal, but the brain learns to use the smaller connections between the left and right hemispheres (Myers & Sperry, 1985). The left hemisphere somehow suppresses the right hemisphere's interference and takes control in some situations. However, even then, the hemispheres show "differences of opinion" if we test carefully enough. In one study, researchers used computers to "morph" photos to look partly like a split-brain person and partly like another familiar person. Then they asked this split-brain person to identify each photo, after viewing it briefly in one visual field or the other. When he saw it in the right visual field (left hemisphere), he was more likely to say it was himself. When he saw it in the left visual field (right hemisphere), he usually thought it was the other person (Turk et al., 2002).

In other situations, the hemispheres learn to cooperate. A split-brain person who was tested with the apparatus shown in Figure 14.4 used an interesting strategy to answer a yes–no question about what he saw in the left visual field. Suppose an experimenter flashes a picture in the left visual field and asks, "Was it green?" The left (speaking) hemisphere takes a guess: "Yes." That guess might be correct. If not, the right hemisphere, which knows the correct answer, makes the face frown. (Both hemispheres control facial muscles on both sides of the face.) The left hemisphere, feeling the frown, says, "Oh, I'm sorry, I meant 'no.'"

In another experiment, a split-brain patient saw two words flashed at once, one on each side. He was then asked to draw a picture of what he had read. Each hemisphere saw a full word, but the two words could combine to make a different word. For example,

Left Visual Field	Right Visual Field
(Right Hemisphere)	(Left Hemisphere)
hot	dog
honey	moon
sky	scraper
rain	bow

With the right hand, he almost always drew what he had seen in the right visual field (left hemisphere), such as *dog* or *moon*. However, with the left hand, he sometimes drew a literal combination of the two words. For example, after seeing *hot* and *dog*, he drew an overheated dog, not a wiener on a bun, and after seeing *sky* and *scraper*, he drew a sky and a scraper (Figure 14.6). The right hemisphere, which predominantly controls the left hand, drew what it saw in the left visual field (*hot* or *sky*). Ordinarily, the left hemisphere doesn't control the left hand, but through the bilateral mechanisms of the ventromedial spinal pathway (described in Chapter 8), it can move the left hand clumsily, and evidently enough to add what it saw in the right visual field (*dog* or *scraper*). However, neither hemisphere could combine the words into one concept (Kingstone & Gazzaniga, 1995).

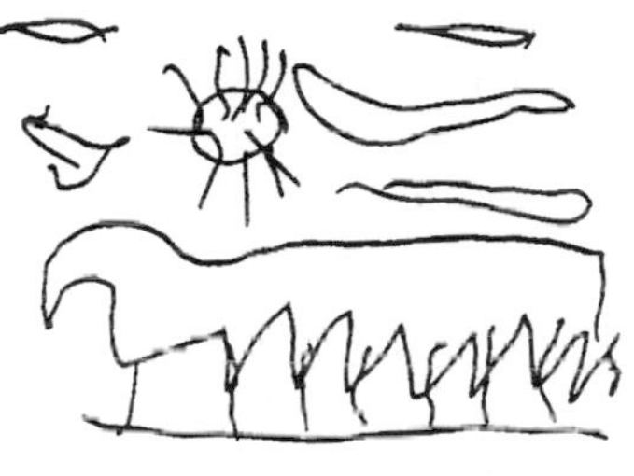

Figure 14.6 Left-hand drawing by a split-brain patient

He saw the word *sky* in the left visual field and *scraper* in the right visual field. His left hemisphere controlled the left hand enough to draw a scraper, and his right hemisphere controlled it enough to draw a sky. Neither hemisphere could combine the two words to make the emergent concept *skyscraper*. *(Source: From "Subcortical Transfer of Higher Order Information: More Illusory Than Real?" by A. Kingstone and M. S. Gazzaniga, 1995. Neuropsychology, 9, pp. 321–328. Copyright © 1995 American Psychological Association. Reprinted with permission)*

The Right Hemisphere

Suppose you watch a series of videotapes of people talking about themselves. Each person speaks twice, once telling the truth and the other time saying nothing but lies. Could you guess which version was the truth? The average score for MIT undergraduates was 47% correct, a bit worse than the 50% they should have had by random guessing. Most other groups did equally badly, except for one group of people who got 60% correct—still not a great score, but at least better than random (Etcoff, Ekman, Magee, & Frank, 2000). Who do you suppose they were? They were people with left-hemisphere brain damage! They could not understand the speech very well, but they were adept at reading gestures and facial expressions. As mentioned in Chapter 12, the right hemisphere is better than the left at perceiving the emotions in people's gestures and tone of voice, such as happiness or sadness (Adolphs, Damasio, & Tranel, 2002). If the left hemisphere is damaged (and therefore prevented from interfering with the right hemisphere), the right hemisphere is free to make reliable judgments (Buck & Duffy, 1980). In contrast, people with damage in parts of the right hemisphere speak in a monotone voice, do not understand other people's emotional expressions, and usually fail to understand humor and sarcasm (Beeman & Chiarello, 1998).

The right hemisphere is dominant for recognizing emotions in others, including both pleasant and unpleasant emotions (Narumoto, Okada, Sadato, Fukui, & Yonekura, 2001). In a split-brain person, the right hemisphere does better than the left at recognizing whether two photographs show the same or different emotions (Stone, Nisenson, Eliassen, & Gazzaniga, 1996). Moreover, according to Jerre Levy and her colleagues' studies of brain-intact people, when the left and right hemispheres perceive different emotions in someone's face, the response of the right hemisphere dominates. For example, examine the faces in Figure 14.7. Each of these combines half of a smiling face with half of a neutral face. Which looks happier to you: face (a) or face (b)? Most people choose face (a), with the smile on the viewer's left (Heller & Levy, 1981; Hoptman & Levy, 1988). Similarly, a frown on the viewer's left looks sadder than a frown on the viewer's right (Sackeim, Putz, Vingiano, Coleman, & McElhiney, 1988). Remember, what you see in your left visual field stimulates your right hemisphere first.

try it yourself

The right hemisphere also appears to be more adept than the left at comprehending spatial relationships. For example, one young woman with damage to her posterior right hemisphere had trouble finding her way around, even in familiar areas. To reach a destination, she needed directions with specific visual details, such as, "Walk to the corner where you see a building with a statue in front of it. Then turn left and go to the corner that has a flagpole and turn right . . . ." Each of these directions had to include an unmistakable feature; if the instruction was "go to the city government building—that's the one with a tower," she might go to a different building that happened to have a tower (Clarke, Assal, & deTribolet, 1993).

How can we best describe the difference in functions between the hemispheres? According to Robert

Figure 14.7 Half of a smiling face combined with half of a neutral face

Which looks happier to you—**(a)** the one with a smile on your left or **(b)** the one with a smile on your right? Your answer may suggest which hemisphere of your brain is dominant for interpreting emotional expressions. *(Source: From "Asymmetry of perception in free viewing of chimeric faces," by J. Levy, W. Heller, M. T. Banich, and L. A. Burton, 1983,* Brain and Cognition, *1983, 2:404–419. Used by permission of Academic Press)*

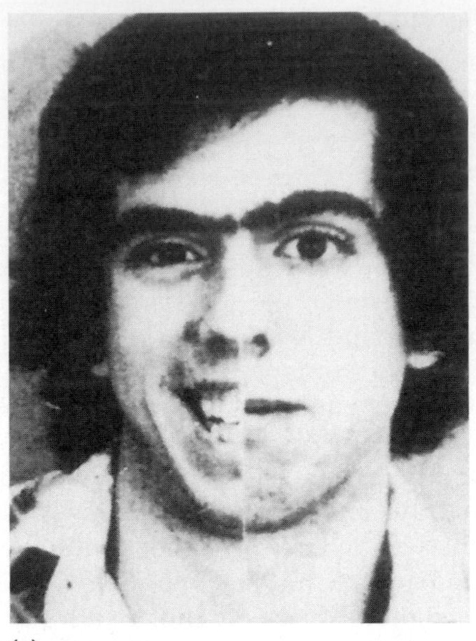
(a)

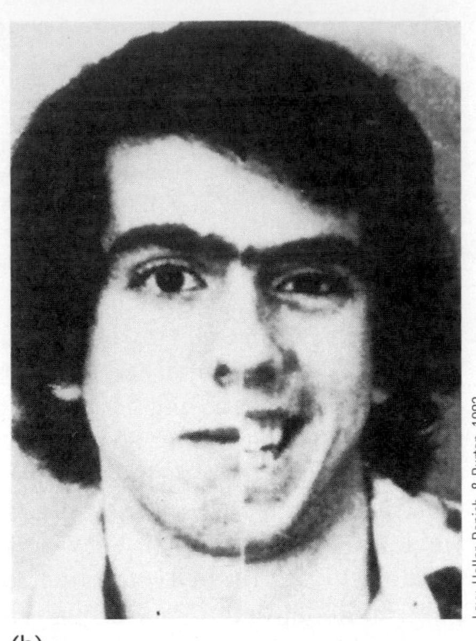
(b)

Levy, Heller, Banich, & Burton, 1983

Ornstein (1997), the left hemisphere focuses more on details and the right hemisphere more on overall patterns. For example, in one study, people with intact brains examined visual stimuli such as the one in Figure 14.8, in which many repetitions of a small letter compose a different large letter. When they were asked to identify the small letters (in this case, B), activity increased in the left hemisphere, but when they were asked to identify the large overall letter (H), activity was greater in the right hemisphere (Fink et al., 1996).

```
B           B
B           B
B           B
B           B
B B B B B B B
B           B
B           B
B           B
B           B
```

Figure 14.8 Stimulus to test analytical and holistic perception

When people were told to name the large composite letter, they had more activity in the right hemisphere. When told to name the small component letters, they had more activity in the left hemisphere. *(Source: Based on Fink, Halligan, et al., 1996)*

Hemispheric Specializations in Intact Brains

The differences between the two hemispheres also can be demonstrated in people without brain damage, although the effects are small. Here is something you can try yourself: Tap with your right hand as many times as you can in a short period of time. Rest and repeat with your left hand. Then repeat with each hand while talking. The Online Try It Yourself activity "Hemisphere Control" will keep track of your totals. For most right-handers and many left-handers, talking decreases the tapping rate with the right hand more than with the left hand (Kinsbourne & McMurray, 1975). Evidently, it is more difficult to do two things at once when both activities depend on the same hemisphere.

ONLINE

STOP & CHECK

7. Which hemisphere is dominant for each of the following in most people: speech, emotional inflection of speech, interpreting other people's emotional expressions, spatial relationships, perceiving overall patterns?

Check your answers on page 428.

Development of Lateralization and Handedness

Because most people's language depends primarily on the left hemisphere, it is natural to ask whether the hemispheres differ anatomically. If so, is the difference present before speech develops or does it develop later? What is the relationship between handedness and hemispheric dominance for speech?

Anatomical Differences Between the Hemispheres

The human brain is specialized to attend to language sounds. If you listen to a repeated syllable ("*pack pack pack pack . . .*") and then suddenly the vowel sound changes ("*. . . pack pack pack peck . . .*"), the change will catch your attention and will evoke larger electrical responses measured on your scalp. Changing from *pack* to *peck* also increases the evoked response from a baby, even a premature infant born only 30 weeks after conception (Cheour-Luhtanen et al., 1996). Evidently, humans attend to language sounds from the start.

Do the hemispheres differ from the start? Norman Geschwind and Walter Levitsky (1968) found that one section of the temporal cortex, called the **planum temporale** (PLAY-num tem-poh-RAH-lee), is larger in the left hemisphere for 65% of people (Figure 14.9). The difference in its size between the left and right hemispheres is slightly greater, on the average, for people who are strongly right-handed (Foundas, Leonard, & Hanna-Pladdy, 2002). Smaller but still significant differences are found between left and right hemispheres of chimpanzees and gorillas, so this difference is apparently part of our ancient genetic heritage (Cantalupo & Hopkins, 2001).

Sandra Witelson and Wazir Pallie (1973) examined the brains of infants who died before age 3 months and found that the left planum temporale was larger in 12 of 14. Later studies using MRI scans found that healthy 5- to 12-year-old children with the biggest ratio of left to right planum temporale performed best on language tests, whereas children with nearly equal hemispheres were better on certain nonverbal tasks (Leonard et al., 1996). People who suffer damage to the left hemisphere in infancy eventually develop less language than those with equal damage to the right hemisphere (Stark & McGregor, 1997). In short, the left hemisphere is specialized for language from the start in most people.

Maturation of the Corpus Callosum

The corpus callosum matures gradually over the first 5 to 10 years of human life (Trevarthen, 1974). The developmental process is not a matter of growing new axons but of selecting certain axons and discarding others. At an early stage, the brain generates far more axons in the corpus callosum than it will have at maturity (Ivy & Killackey, 1981; Killackey & Chalupa, 1986). The reason is that any two neurons connected by the corpus callosum need to have corresponding functions. For example, a neuron in the left hemisphere that responds to light in the center of the fovea should be connected to a right-hemisphere neuron that responds to light in the same location. During early embryonic development, the genes cannot specify exactly where those two neurons will be. Therefore, many connections are made across the corpus callosum, but only those axons that happen to connect very similar cells survive (Innocenti & Caminiti, 1980).

Because the connections take years to develop their mature adult pattern, the behavior of young children in some situations resembles that of split-brain adults. An infant who has one arm restrained will not reach across the midline of the body to pick up a toy on the other side before about age 17 weeks. Evidently, in younger children, each hemisphere has too little access

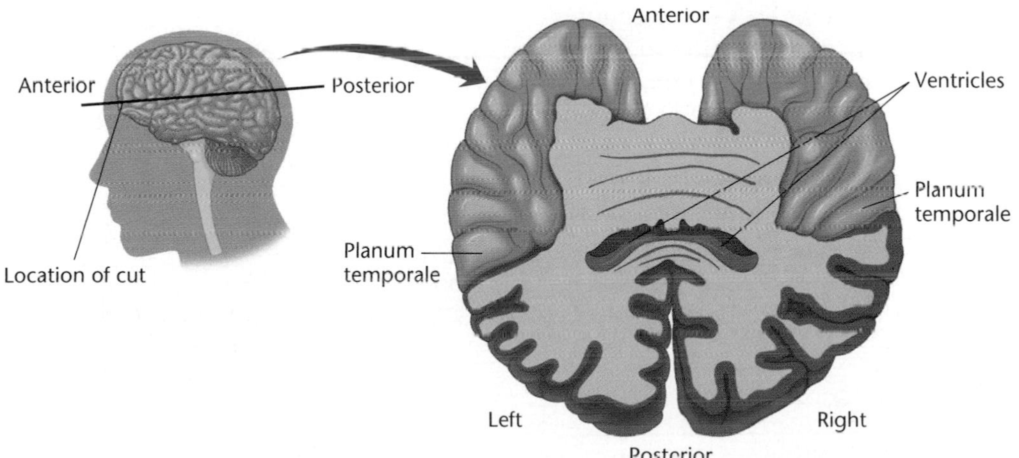

Figure 14.9 Horizontal section through a human brain
This cut, taken just above the surface of the temporal lobe, shows the planum temporale, an area that is critical for speech comprehension. Note that it is substantially larger in the left hemisphere than in the right hemisphere. *(Source: Based on "Human brain: left-right asymmetries in temporal speech region," by N. Geschwind and W. Levitsky, 1968, Science, 161, pp. 186–187. Copyright © 1968 by AAAS and N. Geschwind.)*

to information from the opposite hemisphere (Provine & Westerman, 1979).

In one study, 3- and 5-year-old children were asked to feel two fabrics, either with one hand at two times or with two hands at the same time, and say whether the materials felt the same or different. The 5-year-olds did equally well with one hand or with two. The 3-year-olds made 90% more errors with two hands than with one (Galin, Johnstone, Nakell, & Herron, 1979). The likely interpretation is that the corpus callosum matures sufficiently between ages 3 and 5 to facilitate the comparison of stimuli between the two hands.

Development Without a Corpus Callosum

Rarely, the corpus callosum fails to form or forms incompletely, possibly for genetic reasons. People born without a corpus callosum are unlike people who have it cut later in life. First, whatever prevented formation of the corpus callosum undoubtedly affects brain development in other ways. Second, the absence or near absence of the corpus callosum induces the remaining brain areas to develop abnormally.

People born without a corpus callosum can perform some tasks that split-brain patients fail. They can verbally describe what they feel with either hand and what they see in either visual field; they can also feel one object with the left hand and another with the right hand and say whether they are the same or different (Bruyer, Dupuis, Ophoven, Rectem, & Reynaert, 1985; Sanders, 1989). How do they do so? They do not use their right hemisphere for speech (Lassonde, Bryden, & Demers, 1990). Rather, each hemisphere develops pathways connecting it to both sides of the body, enabling the left (speaking) hemisphere to feel both the left and right hands. Also, the brain's other commissures become larger than usual. In addition to the corpus callosum, people have the **anterior commissure** (see Figures 4.13 and 14.5), which connects the anterior parts of the cerebral cortex, the **hippocampal commissure**, which connects the left and right hippocampi (see Figure 14.5), and the smaller *posterior commissure* (not shown in Figure 14.5). The extra development of these other commissures partly compensates for the lack of a corpus callosum.

STOP & CHECK

8. A child born without a corpus callosum can name something felt with the left hand, but an adult who suffered damage to the corpus callosum cannot. What are two likely explanations?

Check your answer on page 428.

Hemispheres, Handedness, and Language Dominance

For more than 95% of right-handed people, the left hemisphere is strongly dominant for speech (McKeever et al., 1995). Left-handers are more variable. Most left-handers have left-hemisphere dominance for speech, but some have right-hemisphere dominance or a mixture of left and right (Basso & Rusconi, 1998). The same is true for people who were left-handed in early childhood but forced to switch to writing right-handed (Siebner et al., 2002). Many left-handers who have partial right-hemisphere control of speech are also partly reversed for spatial perception, showing more than the usual amount of left-hemisphere contribution. A few left-handers have right-hemisphere dominance for both language and spatial perception (Flöel et al., 2001).

Hand preference relates to some other asymmetries in brain and behavior. Suppose you are hiking through the woods when you come to a fork in the path. Other things being equal, which direction do you choose? You might imagine that you choose randomly, but most people show a tendency to pick one direction more than the other. In one study, people wore a device on their belt that counted the number of times they turned left or right over 3 days. On the average, right-handers turned mostly to the left, and left-handers turned mostly to the right (Mohr, Landis, Bracha, & Brugger, 2003). Animal studies suggest that one turns away from the hemisphere that has more dopamine.

Recovery of Speech After Brain Damage

After brain damage that impairs language, some people recover substantially, but others recover only a little. Why the variation? One factor is age. Other things being equal, the brain is also more plastic early in life than it is later, and young people generally recover better than older people from brain damage. That generalization has exceptions, though. For example, amygdala damage impairs emotional information processing regardless of age, but when it occurs in early childhood, it produces additional deficits not seen in adults, such as impaired understanding of irony and metaphor (Shaw et al., 2004). Evidently, that kind of damage early in life disrupts the organization of other brain areas or impairs learning that usually takes place early in life.

As a rule, children with left-hemisphere damage recover language better than adults with similar damage because the right hemisphere reorganizes to serve some of the left-hemisphere functions to the detriment of its own usual functions. Younger children usually recover language better than older children, although that rule has many exceptions also, depending on the type of medical problem that damaged the left hemisphere (Curtiss, de Bode, & Mathern, 2001).

Language recovery is sometimes surprisingly good for children with **Rasmussen's encephalopathy** (en-seff-ah-LOP-ah-thee), a rare condition in which an autoimmune disorder attacks first the glia and then the neurons of one or the other hemisphere of the brain, usually beginning in childhood or adolescence (Whitney & McNamara, 2000). Symptoms include progressively more frequent epileptic seizures and a gradual loss of brain tissue on one side. Eventually, surgeons remove or disconnect what remains of the damaged hemisphere because it is producing seizures without accomplishing much. After they do so, language sometimes recovers slowly but impressively, even in children over 10 years old at the time of surgery (Boatman et al., 1999; Herz-Pannier et al., 2002). One possible explanation is that Rasmussen's encephalopathy develops so gradually that while the left hemisphere deteriorates over the years, the right hemisphere is already starting to reorganize in a way that enables it to take over language.

Another factor influencing language recovery after brain damage is how speech was lateralized for a given person. For example, someone with partial representation of language in both hemispheres would presumably recover from left-hemisphere damage better than someone who had language representation in the left hemisphere alone. Modern research methods have enabled researchers to support this hypothesis. First they used fMRI to determine how active each hemisphere became while each participant was talking. Then they applied transcranial magnetic stimulation (see Figure 4.37, p. 110) to temporarily suppress activity in one hemisphere or the other. They found that left-hemisphere inactivation blocked speech in those with strong left-hemisphere dominance, right-hemisphere inactivation blocked it in those with right-hemisphere dominance, and neither kind of inactivation eliminated it in people with bilateral control of speech (Knecht et al., 2002).

Avoiding Overstatements

The research on left-brain/right-brain differences sometimes leads to unscientific assertions. Occasionally, you may hear a person say something like, "I don't do well in science because it is a left-brain subject and I am a right-brain person." That kind of statement is based on two reasonable premises and a doubtful one. The scientific ideas are (a) that the hemispheres are specialized for different functions and (b) that certain tasks evoke greater activity in one hemisphere or the other. The doubtful premise is that any individual habitually relies on one hemisphere more than the other.

What evidence do you suppose someone has for believing, "I am a right-brain person"? Did he or she undergo an MRI or PET scan to determine which hemisphere was larger or more active? Not likely. Generally, when people say, "I am right-brained," their only evidence is that they perform well on creative tasks or poorly on logical tasks. (Saying "I am right-brained" sometimes implies that *because* I do poorly on logical tasks, *therefore* I am creative. Unfortunately, illogical is not the same as creative.)

In fact, you use both hemispheres for all but the simplest tasks. Here is the evidence: Suppose you are asked to tap one finger as soon as you see a flash of light. You can tap your right finger a few milliseconds faster than the left if you see a flash in the right visual field, and you can tap your left finger a few milliseconds faster if you see a flash in the left visual field. The reason is that the information doesn't have to cross the corpus callosum. Now suppose we do the same kind of experiment but make the task slightly more complicated. Instead of tapping for any light you see, you tap for just certain kinds of stimuli, so you have to process the information before tapping your finger. The result is that you will tap a bit more slowly, and your reaction time won't depend on which finger is tapping or which visual field sees the stimulus (Forster & Corballis, 2000). Even a slightly difficult task requires you to use both hemispheres anyway, so it doesn't matter where the light started. The same is true in general: Most tasks require cooperation by both hemispheres.

Module 14.1
In Closing: One Brain, Two Hemispheres

Imagine that someone asks you a question to which you honestly reply that you do not know, while your left hand points to the correct answer. It must be an unsettling experience to be in some ways like a single person and in some ways like two.

Often, we try to imagine how some other person feels. We might also wonder what it would feel like to be a dog, a bat, or what it would feel like (if anything) to be an insect. We would like to "get into" someone else's mind, so to speak. For a split-brain person, it would be a matter of getting into another person's *minds* (plural).

Summary

1. Most people are right-handed. According to one hypothesis, a dominant gene produces right-handedness, and a recessive gene leads to random determination of handedness. (p. 416)
2. The corpus callosum is a set of axons connecting the two hemispheres of the brain. (p. 417)
3. The left hemisphere controls speech in most people, and each hemisphere controls mostly the hand on the opposite side, sees the opposite side of the

world, and feels the opposite side of the body. (p. 417)

4. In humans, the left visual field projects onto the right half of each retina, which sends axons to the right hemisphere. The right visual field projects onto the left half of each retina, which sends axons to the left hemisphere. (p. 418)
5. After damage to the corpus callosum, each hemisphere can respond quickly and accurately to questions about the information that reaches it directly and can slowly answer a few questions about information on the other side if it crosses the anterior commissure or one of the other small commissures. (p. 419)
6. Although the two hemispheres of a split-brain person are sometimes in conflict, they find ways to cooperate and cue each other. (p. 421)
7. The right hemisphere is dominant for the emotional inflections of speech and for interpreting other people's emotional expressions in either speech or facial expression. In vision, it attends mostly to overall patterns in contrast to the left hemisphere, which is better for details. (p. 423)
8. The left and right hemispheres differ anatomically even during infancy. Young children have some trouble comparing information from the left and right hands because the corpus callosum is not fully mature. (p. 424)
9. In a child born without a corpus callosum, the rest of the brain develops in unusual ways, and the child does not show the same deficits as an adult who sustains damage to the corpus callosum. (p. 426)
10. The brain of a left-handed person is not simply a mirror image of a right-hander's brain. Most left-handers have left-hemisphere or mixed dominance for speech; few have strong right-hemisphere dominance for speech. (p. 426)
11. Both left and right hemispheres contribute to all but the simplest behaviors. (p. 427)

Answers to STOP & CHECK Questions

1. According to Klar's hypothesis, both twins have two genes for "random" handedness. Although one of them randomly became right-handed and the other left-handed, they will both pass their random handedness genes to their children, and both twins should have an equal percentage of left-handed children. The data confirm that prediction (Klar, 2005). (p. 417)
2. People with the random gene are as likely to be right-handed as left-handed. Of those right-handers with the random gene, about half will have clockwise hair whorls and half will have counterclockwise whorls. (p. 417)
3. In rabbits, the right eye is far to the side of the head and sees only the right visual field. In humans, the eyes point straight ahead and half of each eye sees the right visual field. (p. 418)
4. Left; left (p. 418)
5. A split-brain person cannot describe something after feeling it with the left hand but can with the right. The right hand sends its information to the left hemisphere, which is dominant for language in most people. The left hand sends its information to the right hemisphere, which cannot speak. (p. 421)
6. After seeing something in the left visual field, a split-brain person could point to the correct answer with the left hand. (p. 421)
7. The left hemisphere is dominant for speech; the right hemisphere is dominant for all the other items listed. (p. 424)
8. In children born without a corpus callosum, the left hemisphere develops more than the usual connections with the left hand, and the anterior commissure and other commissures grow larger than usual. (p. 426)

Thought Question

When a person born without a corpus callosum moves the fingers of one hand, he or she also is likely to move the fingers of the other hand involuntarily. What possible explanation can you suggest?

Module 14.2
Evolution and Physiology of Language

Communication is widespread among animals through visual, auditory, tactile, or chemical (pheromonal) displays. Human language stands out from other forms of communication because of its **productivity,** its ability to produce new signals to represent new ideas. That is, certain monkeys have one call to indicate "eagle or hawk in the air—take cover" and another to indicate "beware—snake on the ground." But they have no way to indicate "snake in the tree above you" or "eagle standing on the ground." Humans can discuss all sorts of new events, inventing new expressions when we need them.

Did we evolve this ability out of nothing or from some precursor already present in other species? Why do we have language, whereas other species have at most a rudimentary hint of it? And what brain specializations make language possible? We consider these questions in order.

Nonhuman Precursors of Language

Evolution rarely creates something totally new. Bat wings are modified hands, and porcupine quills are modified hairs. So we would expect human language to be a modification of something we can detect in our closest relatives, chimpanzees.

Common Chimpanzees

After many unsuccessful attempts to teach chimpanzees to speak, researchers achieved better results by teaching them American Sign Language or other visual systems (B. T. Gardner & Gardner, 1975; Premack & Premack, 1972) (Figure 14.10). In one version, chimps learned to press keys bearing symbols to type messages on a computer (Rumbaugh, 1977), such as "Please machine give apple," or (to another chimpanzee), "Please share your chocolate."

Is this use of symbols really language? Not necessarily. For example, when you insert your ATM card into a machine and enter your four-digit PIN, you don't really understand those four digits to mean, "Please machine give money." Similarly, when a chimpanzee presses four symbols on a machine, it may not understand them to mean, "Please machine give apple." The chimps' use of symbols differed from human language in several regards (Rumbaugh, 1990; Terrace, Petitto, Sanders, & Bever, 1979):

- The chimpanzees seldom used the symbols in new, original combinations, as even very young children do. That is, their use of symbols lacked *productivity.*
- The chimpanzees used their symbols almost always to request, only rarely to describe.
- The chimpanzees produced requests far better than they seemed to understand anyone else's requests. In contrast, young children understand far more than they can say.

Bonobos

Such observations made psychologists skeptical about chimpanzee language. Then some surprising results emerged from studies of an endangered species, *Pan paniscus,* known as the bonobo or the pygmy chimpan-

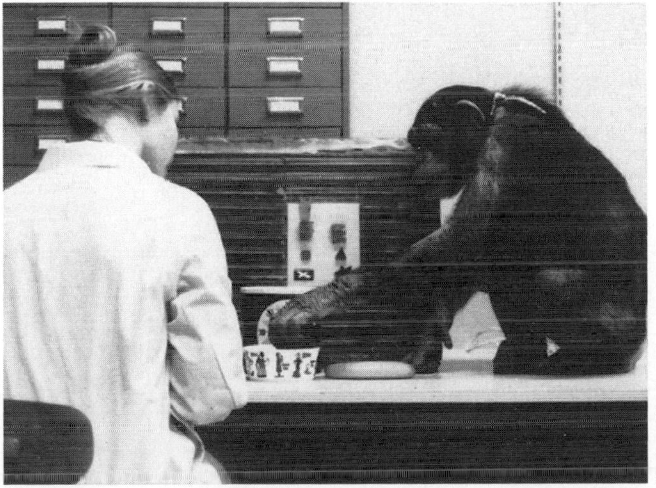

Figure 14.10 One attempt to teach chimpanzees language
One of the Premacks's chimps, Elizabeth, reacts to colored plastic chips that read "Not Elizabeth banana insert—Elizabeth apple wash."

zee (a misleading name because they are practically the same size as common chimpanzees).

Bonobos' social order resembles humans' in several regards. Males and females form strong, sometimes lasting, personal attachments. They often copulate face-to-face. The female is sexually responsive on almost any day and not just during her fertile period. The males contribute significantly to infant care. Adults often share food with one another. They stand comfortably on their hind legs. In short, they resemble humans more than other primates do.

Duane Rumbaugh

Figure 14.11 Language tests for Kanzi, a bonobo *(Pan paniscus)*
He listens to questions through the earphones and points to answers on a board. The experimenter with him does not know what the questions are or what answers are expected. *(Source: From Georgia State University's Language Research Center, operated with the Yerkes Primate Center of Emory.)*

In the mid-1980s, Sue Savage-Rumbaugh, Duane Rumbaugh, and their associates tried to teach a female bonobo named Matata to press symbols that lit when touched; each symbol represents a word (Figure 14.11). Although Matata made little progress, her infant son Kanzi learned just by watching her. When given a chance to use the symbol board, he quickly excelled. Soon researchers noticed that Kanzi understood a fair amount of spoken language. For example, whenever anyone said the word "light," Kanzi would flip the light switch. By age 5½, he understood about 150 English words and could respond to such unfamiliar spoken commands as "Throw your ball in the river" and "Go to the refrigerator and get out a tomato" (Savage-Rumbaugh, 1990; Savage-Rumbaugh, Sevcik, Brakke, & Rumbaugh, 1992). Since then, Kanzi and his younger sister have demonstrated language comprehension comparable to that of a 2- to 2½-year-old child (Savage-Rumbaugh et al., 1993):

- They understand more than they can produce.
- They use symbols to name and describe objects even when they are not requesting them.
- They request items that they do not see, such as "bubbles" (I want to play with the bubble-blower) or "car trailer" (drive me in the car to the trailer).
- They occasionally use the symbols to describe past events. Kanzi once pressed the symbols "Matata bite" to explain the cut that he had received on his hand an hour earlier.
- They frequently make original, creative requests, such as asking one person to chase another while he watches.

Why have Kanzi and Mulika developed such impressive skills where other chimpanzees failed? Perhaps bonobos have more language potential than common chimpanzees. A second explanation is that Kanzi and Mulika began language training when young, unlike the chimpanzees in most other studies. A third reason pertains to the method of training: Perhaps learning by observation and imitation promotes better understanding than the formal training methods of previous studies (Savage-Rumbaugh et al., 1992).

For more information about bonobos, visit this website: **http://www.blockbonobofoundation.org/blinks.htm**

STOP & CHECK

1. How does common chimpanzees' use of symbols differ from language?
2. What are three likely explanations for why the bonobos made more language progress than common chimpanzees?

Check your answers on page 441.

Nonprimates

What about nonprimate species? Elephants learn to imitate the sounds they hear, including the vocalizations of other elephants. Doing so helps them maintain social bonds (Poole, Tyack, Stoeger-Horwath, & Watwood, 2005). Dolphins can learn to respond to gestures and sounds. For example, after the command "Right hoop left Frisbee fetch," a dolphin takes the Frisbee on the left to the hoop on the right (Herman, Pack, & Morrel-Samuels, 1993). However, this system offers the dolphins no opportunity to produce language. They cannot tell humans to take the Frisbee to the hoop (Savage-Rumbaugh, 1993).

Spectacular results have been reported for Alex, an African gray parrot (Figure 14.12). Parrots are, of course, famous for imitating sounds; Irene Pepperberg was the first to argue that parrots can use sounds meaningfully. She kept Alex in a stimulating environment and taught him to say words in conjunction with specific objects. First, she and the other trainers would say a word many times and then offer rewards if Alex approximated the same sound. Here is an excerpt from a conversation with Alex early in training (Pepperberg, 1981, p. 142):

David Carter

Figure 14.12 Language tests for Alex, an African gray parrot
Alex has apparently learned to converse about objects in simple English—for example, giving the correct answer to "What color is the circle?" He receives no food rewards.

Pepperberg: Pasta! (*Takes pasta.*) Pasta! (*Alex stretches from his perch, appears to reach for pasta.*)

Alex: Pa!

Pepperberg: Better . . . what is it?

Alex: Pah-ah.

Pepperberg: Better!

Alex: Pah-ta.

Pepperberg: Okay, here's the pasta. Good try.

Although pasta was used in this example, Pepperberg generally used toys. For example, if Alex said "paper," "wood," or "key," she would give him what he asked for. In no case did she reward him with food for saying "paper" or "wood."

Alex gradually learned to give spoken answers to spoken questions. He was shown a tray of 12 small objects and then asked such questions as "What color is the key?" (answer: "green") and "What object is gray?" (answer: "circle"). In one test, he correctly answered 39 of 48 questions. Even many of his incorrect answers were almost correct. In one case, he was asked the color of the block and he responded with the color of the rock (Pepperberg, 1993). He also can answer questions of the form "How many blue key?" in which he has to examine objects, count the blue keys among objects of two shapes and two colors, and then say the answer, ranging from one to six (Pepperberg, 1994).

Relying on language is not always helpful. Pepperberg put Alex and three other gray parrots on perches; each had a chain of large plastic links from the perch to an almond on the bottom. (Almonds are favorite foods for parrots.) Alex and another language-trained parrot repeatedly told the experimenter, "Want nut." When she declined to bring it to them, they gave up. Two other parrots, untrained in language, used their claws to pull up the chain until they reached the almond (Pepperberg, 2004) (Figure 14.13).

What do we learn from studies of nonhuman language abilities? At a practical level, we gain insights into how best to teach language to those who do not learn it easily, such as people with brain damage or children with autism. At a more theoretical level, these studies point out the ambiguity of our concept of language: We cannot decide whether chimpanzees or parrots have language unless we define language more precisely.

Because bonobos show some potential for language learning, apparently human language evolved from a precursor that was present in the ancient ancestor from which both species derived. What we still don't know is what that precursor ability was doing. Do bonobos, and perhaps other primates, have language-type abilities that they use for communication? Perhaps so; the ability for spoken language probably evolved from early communication by gestures (Corballis, 1999). (Gestures are still important for communication; ask someone what a spiral is and then watch their hands move!)

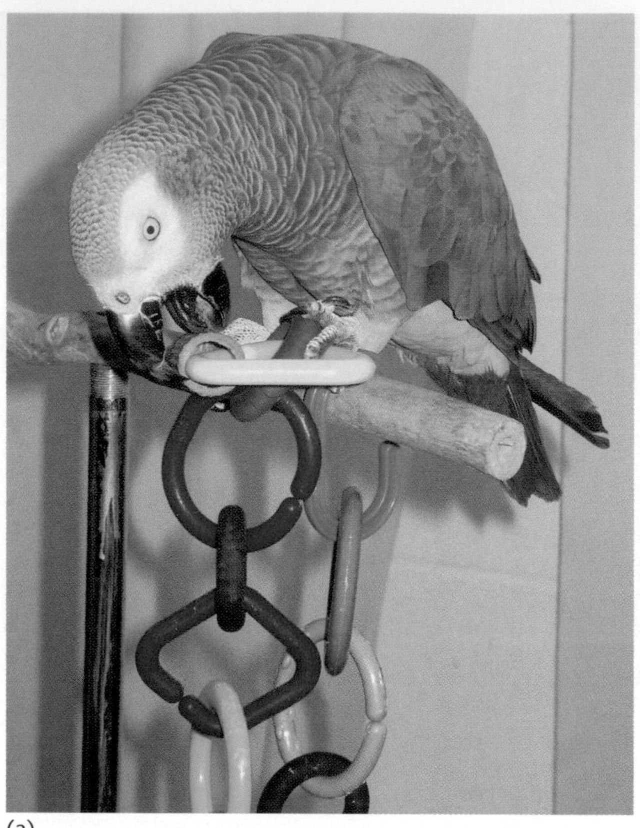

(a)

(b)

Figure 14.13 A gray parrot with a reasoning task
Two parrots not trained in language pulled up chain links to reach the treat. Two with language training persisted in saying, "Want nut," without making any effort on their own.

How Did Humans Evolve Language?

How did we evolve the ability to learn language so much more easily than other species? Most theories fall into two categories: (a) we evolved language as a by-product of overall brain development or (b) we evolved it as an extra part of the brain.

Language as a Product of Overall Intelligence

The simplest view is that humans evolved big brains, and therefore great intelligence, and that language developed as an accidental by-product of increased intelligence. In its simplest form, this hypothesis faces serious problems.

First Problem: People with Full-Sized Brains and Impaired Language

If language is a product of overall brain size, then anyone with a full-sized brain and normal overall intelligence should have normal language. However, not all do. In one family, 16 of 30 people over three generations show severe language deficits despite normal intelligence in other regards. Because of a dominant gene, which has been located, the affected people have serious troubles in pronunciation and virtually all other aspects of language (Fisher, Vargha-Khadem, Watkins, Monaco, & Pembrey, 1998; Gopnik & Crago, 1991; Lai, Fisher, Hurst, Vargha-Khadem, & Monaco, 2001). When they speak, their brains show activity in posterior regions instead of the frontal cortex, as in other people (Vargha-Khadem, Gadian, Copp, & Mishkin, 2005).

They fail to master even simple grammatical rules, as shown in the following dialogue about making plurals:

Experimenter	Respondent
This is a wug; these are . . .	How should I know? *[Later]* These are wug.
This is a zat; these are . . .	These are zacko.
This is a sas; these are . . .	These are sasss. *[Not sasses]*

In another test, experimenters presented sentences and asked whether each sentence was correct and, if not, how to improve it. People in this family accepted many ungrammatical sentences while labeling many correct sentences as incorrect. (Evidently, they were just guessing.) When they tried to correct a sentence, their results were often odd. For example:

Original Item	Attempted Correction
The boy eats three cookie.	The boys eat four cookie.

In short, a genetic condition can seriously impair language without necessarily impairing other aspects of intelligence. Language requires some sort of specialization, not just brain expansion.

Second Problem: Williams Syndrome

What about the reverse? Could someone with mental retardation have good language? Psychologists long assumed that such a pattern was impossible.

Then psychologists discovered a rare condition, affecting about 1 person in 25,000, called **Williams syndrome**, characterized by mental retardation in most regards but, in many cases, skillful use of language. The cause is a deletion of several genes from chromosome 7 (Korenberg et al., 2000), leading to decreased gray matter, especially in brain areas relating to visual processing (Kippenhan et al., 2005; Meyer-Lindenberg et al., 2004; Reiss et al., 2004). Affected people are poor at tasks related to numbers, visuospatial skills (e.g., copying a drawing), and spatial perception (e.g., finding their way home). When asked to estimate the length of a bus, three people with Williams syndrome answered "30 inches," "3 inches or 100 inches maybe," and "2 inches, 10 feet" (Bellugi, Lichtenberger, Jones, Lai, & St George, 2000). Throughout life, they require constant supervision and cannot hold even an unskilled job.

Nevertheless, they are close to normal in several other regards. One is music, such as the ability to clap a complex rhythm and memorize songs (Levitin & Bellugi, 1998). Another is friendliness and the ability to interpret facial expressions, such as relaxed or worried, serious or playful, flirtatious or uninterested (Tager-Flusberg, Boshart, & Baron-Cohen, 1998). Although several brain areas are less well developed than average, they have a larger than average amygdala and several other areas related to emotional processing (Reiss et al., 2004). However, they are not simply overemotional in general; they show low social anxiety but increased anxiety about inanimate objects (Meyer-Lindenberg et al., 2005).

Their most surprising skill is language. Not all people with Williams syndrome have good language abilities (Jarrold, Baddeley, & Hewes, 1998), but some are amazing, considering their impairments in other regards. For example, if asked to "name as many animals as possible in the next minute," most people list familiar animals such as dog, horse, and squirrel. People with Williams syndrome delight in listing odd examples, such as weasel, newt, ibex, unicorn, yak, koala, and triceratops (Bellugi, Wang, & Jernigan, 1994). Figure 14.14 shows the result when a young woman with Williams syndrome and an IQ of 49 was asked to draw an elephant and describe it. Contrast her almost poetic description to the unrecognizable drawing.

Let's not overstate the case. People with Williams syndrome do not handle language perfectly. They develop language slowly at first, and although many of them make spectacular gains in later childhood, their grammar continues to be odd, like that of someone who learned a second language late in life (Clahsen & Almazen, 1998; Karmiloff-Smith et al., 1998). If shown a picture of an unfamiliar object and told its name, they are as likely to think the name refers to some part of the object as to the object itself (Stevens & Karmiloff-Smith, 1997). They use fancy words when a common word would work better, such as "I have to evacuate the glass" instead of "empty" or "pour out" the glass (Bellugi et al., 2000). In any case, observations of Williams syndrome indicate that language is not simply a by-product of overall intelligence.

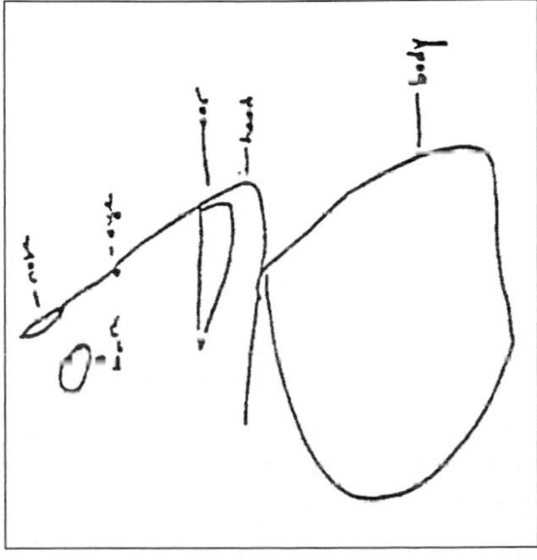

And what an elephant is, it is one of the animals. And what the elephant does, it lives in the jungle. It can also live in the zoo. And what it has, it has long gray ears, fan ears, ears that can blow in the wind. It has a long trunk that can pick up grass, or pick up hay . . . If they're in a bad mood it can be terrible . . . If the elephant gets mad it could stomp; it could charge, like a bull can charge. They have long big tusks. They can damage a car . . . it could be dangerous. When they're in a pinch, when they're in a bad mood it can be terrible. You don't want an elephant as a pet. You want a cat or a dog or a bird . . .

Figure 14.14 A drawing and a description of an elephant by a young woman with Williams syndrome

The labels on the drawing were provided by the investigator based on what the woman said she was drawing. *(Source: From "Williams syndrome: An unusual neuropsychological profile," by U. Bellugi, P. P. Wang, and T. L. Jernigan, In S. H. Broman and J. Grafman, Eds.,* Atypical Cognitive Deficits in Developmental Disorders. *Copyright © 1987 Lawrence Erlbaum. Reprinted by permission.)*

STOP & CHECK

3. What evidence argues against the hypothesis that language evolution depended simply on the overall evolution of brain and intelligence.
4. Describe tasks that people with Williams syndrome do poorly and those that they do well.

Check your answers on page 441.

Language as a Special Module

An alternative view is that language evolved as an extra brain module, a new specialization. This presumed module has been forcefully described by Noam Chomsky (1980) and Steven Pinker (1994) as a **language acquisition device,** a built-in mechanism for acquiring language. The main evidence for this view is the amazing ease with which most children develop language (Trout, 2001). For example, deaf children quickly learn sign language, and if no one teaches them a sign language, they invent one of their own and teach it to one another (Goldin-Meadow, McNeill, & Singleton, 1996; Goldin-Meadow & Mylander, 1998).

Advocates of the language acquisition device concept sometimes go beyond saying that children learn language readily, claiming that they are born with language; all they have to do is to fill in the words and details. Chomsky defends this idea with the **poverty of the stimulus argument:** Children do not hear many examples of some of the grammatical structures they acquire, and therefore, they could not learn them. For example, even young children will phrase the question

> "Is the boy who is unhappy watching Mickey Mouse?"

instead of

> "Is the boy who unhappy is watching Mickey Mouse?"

Chomsky and his followers maintain that children have not had enough opportunity to learn that grammatical rule, so they must be born knowing it. However, it is hard to believe that a child is born knowing the grammars of all the possible human languages (Nowak, Komarova, & Niyogi, 2002). Adherents of the language acquisition device can counter that they just mean that children are born understanding the basic language concepts such as subject, verb, and object. However, if that is all they are born with, we are back to puzzling about how they know how to phrase the question about Mickey Mouse.

Most researchers agree that humans have specially evolved *something* that enables them to learn language easily. The key question is, what? Many researchers doubt even that language is a separate, independent "module," like a speech synthesizer attached to an otherwise unchanged computer. Certain brain areas are, to be sure, necessary for language, but language is not all they do. By analogy, you need your elbow to play tennis, but we wouldn't call your elbow "the tennis joint" (Dick et al., 2001). The parts of your brain important for language are also critical for memory (Ullman, 2001), music perception (Maess, Koelsch, Gunter, & Friederici, 2001), and other tasks.

So back to the original question: How and why did humans evolve language? The honest answer is that we don't know, but language is probably not a by-product of overall intelligence. In fact, the opposite is easier to imagine: Selective pressure for social interactions among people, including those between parents and children, favored the evolution of language, and overall intelligence developed as a by-product of language (Deacon, 1992, 1997). Unfortunately, of course, it is difficult to reconstruct the early evolution of human behavior.

Does Language Learning Have a Critical Period?

If humans are specially adapted to learn language, perhaps we are adapted to learn best during a critical period early in life, just as sparrows learn their song best during an early period. One way to test this hypothesis is to see whether people learn a second language better if they start young. The consistent result is that adults are better than children at memorizing the vocabulary of a second language, but children are much more likely to master the pronunciation and the more unfamiliar aspects of the grammar. For example, the difference between *a* and *the* is difficult for adult Chinese speakers, whose native language doesn't have articles. A child who overhears a language in the neighborhood, without paying much attention, has a better chance of mastering the pronunciation than if he or she tries to learn it as an adult (Au, Knightly, Jun, & Oh, 2002).

However, there is no sharp cutoff for learning a second language; starting at age 2 is better than 4, 4 is better than 6, and 13 is better than 16 (Hakuta, Bialystok, & Wiley, 2003; Harley & Wang, 1997; Weber-Fox & Neville, 1996). Another way to test the critical-period idea is to study people who were not exposed to language at all during infancy. There are a few cases of children who lived in the wild, raised by wolves or whatever, who were later found and returned to human society. Although they were limited in their language learning, the results are difficult to interpret for many reasons.

Clearer data come from studies of deaf children who were unable to learn spoken language and not given an opportunity to learn sign language while they were young. The result is clear: The earlier a child has a chance to learn sign language, the more skilled he or she will become (Harley & Wang, 1997). A child who learns English early can learn sign language later, and a deaf child who learns sign language early can learn English later (except for poor pronunciation), but someone who learns no language while young will never develop much skill at any language, ever (Mayberry, Lock, & Kazmi, 2002). This observation strongly supports the idea of an early critical period for language learning, although it probably does not have a sharp cut-off age.

STOP & CHECK

5. What is the poverty of the stimulus argument, and what is one argument against it?
6. What is the strongest evidence in favor of a critical period for language learning?

Check your answers on page 441.

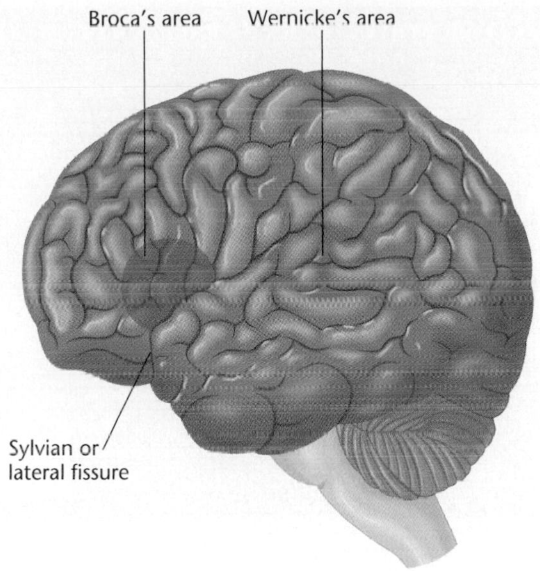

Figure 14.15 Some major language areas of the cerebral cortex
In most people, only the left hemisphere is specialized for language.

Brain Damage and Language

Because almost every healthy child develops language, we infer that the human brain is specialized to facilitate language learning. Most of our knowledge about the brain mechanisms of language has come from studies of people with brain damage.

Broca's Aphasia (Nonfluent Aphasia)

In 1861, the French surgeon Paul Broca treated the gangrene of a patient who had been mute for 30 years. When the man died 5 days later, Broca did an autopsy and found a lesion in the frontal cortex. Over the next few years, Broca examined the brains of additional patients with **aphasia** (severe language impairment); in nearly all cases, he found damage that included this same area, a part of the frontal lobe of the left cerebral cortex near the motor cortex, which is now known as **Broca's area** (Figure 14.15). The usual cause was a stroke (an interruption of blood flow to part of the brain). Broca published his results in 1865, slightly later than papers by other French physicians, Marc and Gustave Dax, who also pointed to the left hemisphere as the seat of language abilities (Finger & Roe, 1996). Broca is given the credit, however, because his description was more detailed and more convincing. This discovery, the first demonstration of a particular function for a particular brain area, paved the way for modern neurology.

We now know that speaking activates a large area of the brain, mostly in the left hemisphere and not just Broca's area (Wallesch, Henriksen, Kornhuber, & Paulson, 1985) (Figure 14.16). Damage limited to Broca's area produces only minor or brief language impairment; serious deficits result from extensive damage that extends into other areas as well. Also the symptoms vary and are not completely predictable from the location of the damage (Dick et al., 2001). For example, some patients have trouble mostly with verbs (Hillis, Wityk, Barker, & Caramazza, 2003).

When people with brain damage suffer serious impairment of language production, we call it **Broca's aphasia**, or **nonfluent aphasia**, regardless of the exact location of the damage. People with Broca's aphasia also have comprehension deficits when the meaning of a sentence depends on prepositions, word endings, or unusual word order—in short, when the sentence structure is complicated.

Difficulty in Language Production

People with Broca's aphasia speak slowly and inarticulately, and they have trouble writing and gesturing (Cicone, Wapner, Foldi, Zurif, & Gardner, 1979). The left frontal cortex is just as important for the sign language of the deaf (Neville et al., 1998; Petitto et al., 2000), and deaf people with Broca's aphasia have trouble producing sign language (Hickok, Bellugi, & Klima, 1996). So the problem relates to language, not just the vocal muscles.

When people with Broca's aphasia speak, they omit most pronouns, prepositions, conjunctions, auxiliary

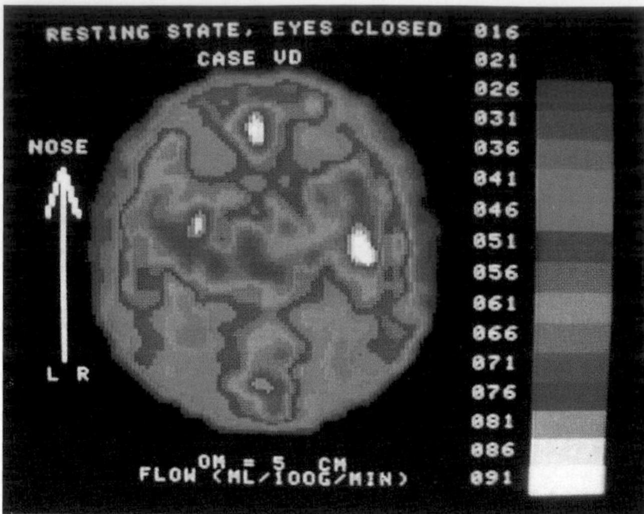

(a)

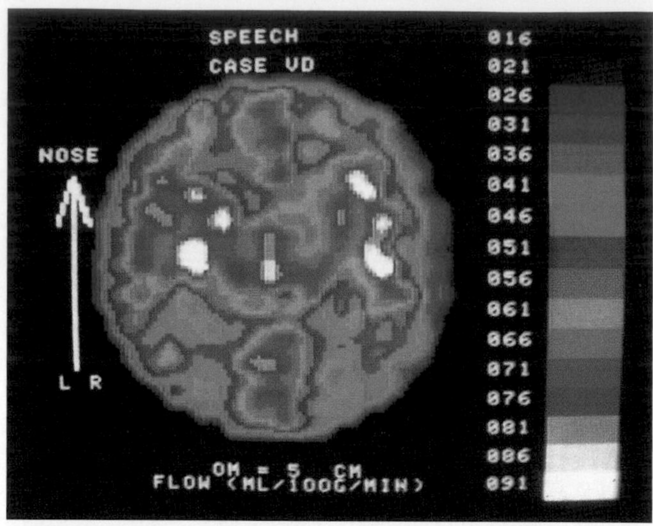

(b)

Figure 14.16 Records showing blood flow for a normal adult

Red indicates the highest level of activity, followed by yellow, green, and blue. **(a)** Blood flow to the brain at rest. **(b)** Blood flow while subject describes a magazine story. **(c)** Difference between **(b)** and **(a).** The results in **(c)** indicate which brain areas increased their activity during language production. Note the increased activity in many areas of the brain, especially on the left side. *(Source: Wallesch, Henriksen, Kornhuber, & Paulson, 1985)*

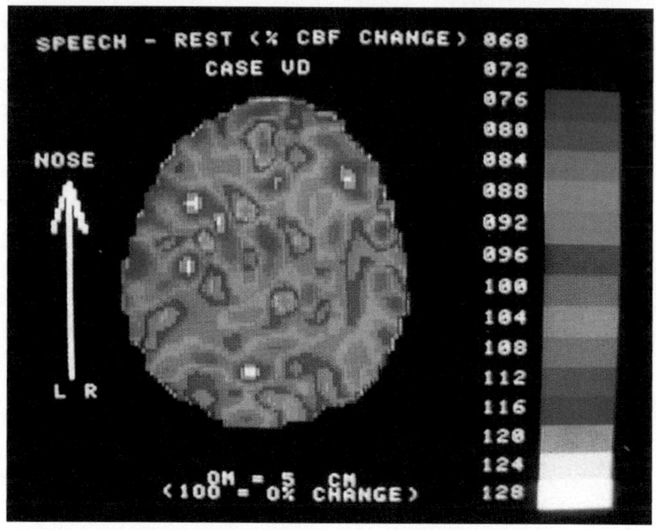

(c)

(helping) verbs, quantifiers, and tense and number endings. At least they do so in English; they use more word endings in languages such as German or Italian, where word endings are more important (Blackwell & Bates, 1995). Prepositions, conjunctions, helping verbs, and so forth are known as the *closed class* of grammatical forms because a language rarely adds new prepositions, conjunctions, and the like. In contrast, new nouns and verbs (the *open class*) enter a language frequently. People with Broca's aphasia seldom use the closed-class words. They find it difficult to repeat a phrase such as "No ifs, ands, or buts," although they can successfully repeat, "The general commands the army." Furthermore, patients who cannot read aloud "To be or not to be" can read "Two bee oar knot two bee" (H. Gardner & Zurif, 1975). Clearly, the trouble is with the word meanings, not just pronunciation.

Why do people with Broca's aphasia omit the grammatical words and endings? Perhaps they have suffered damage to a "grammar area" in the brain, but here is another possibility: When speaking is a struggle, people leave out the weakest elements. Many people who are in great pain speak as if they have Broca's aphasia (Dick et al., 2001).

Problems in Comprehending Grammatical Words and Devices

People with Broca's aphasia have trouble understanding the same kinds of words that they omit when speaking, such as prepositions and conjunctions. They often misunderstand sentences with complex grammar, such as "The girl that the boy is chasing is tall" (Zurif, 1980). However, most English sentences follow the subject-verb-object order, and their meaning is clear even without the prepositions and conjunctions. You can demonstrate this for yourself by taking a paragraph and deleting its prepositions, conjunctions, articles, helping verbs, pronouns, and word endings to see how it might appear to someone with Broca's aphasia. Here is an example, taken from earlier in this chapter:

> What ~~about~~ nonprimate species? Elephant~~s~~ learn ~~to~~ imitate ~~the~~ sound~~s~~ ~~they~~ hear, including ~~the~~ vocalization~~s~~ ~~of~~ other elephant~~s~~. Do~~ing~~ ~~so~~ help~~s~~ ~~them~~ maintain social bond~~s~~. Dolphin~~s~~ ~~can~~ learn

~~to~~ respond ~~to~~ gesture~~s~~ ~~and~~ sound~~s~~. ~~For~~ example, ~~after the~~ command "Right hoop left Frisbee fetch," ~~a~~ dolphin take~~s~~ ~~the~~ Frisbee ~~on the~~ left ~~to the~~ hoop ~~on the~~ right. ~~However, this~~ system offer~~s~~ ~~the~~ dolphin~~s~~ no opportunity ~~to~~ produce language. ~~They can~~not tell human~~s~~ ~~to~~ take ~~the~~ Frisbee ~~to the~~ hoop.

Still, people with Broca's aphasia have not totally lost their knowledge of grammar. For example, they generally recognize that something is wrong with the sentence "He written has songs," even if they cannot say how to improve it (Wulfeck & Bates, 1991). In many ways, their comprehension resembles that of normal people who are distracted. For example, if you listen to someone speaking rapidly with a heavy accent in a noisy room, while trying to do something else at the same time, your comprehension will suffer. You will catch bits and pieces of what the speaker says and fill in the rest by inferences (Blackwell & Bates, 1995; Dick et al., 2001). In fact, even when we hear a sentence clearly, we sometimes ignore the grammar. When people hear "The dog was bitten by the man," many of them assume it was the dog that did the biting (Ferreira, Bailey, & Ferraro, 2002). Patients with Broca's aphasia just rely on inferences instead of grammar more often than the rest of us.

Wernicke's Aphasia (Fluent Aphasia)

In 1874, Carl Wernicke (usually pronounced WER-nih-kee by English speakers, although the German pronunciation is VAYR-nih-keh), a 26-year-old junior assistant in a German hospital, discovered that damage in part of the left temporal cortex produced a different kind of language impairment. Although patients could speak and write, their language comprehension was poor. Damage in and around **Wernicke's area** (see Figure 14.15), located near the auditory part of the cerebral cortex, produces **Wernicke's aphasia**, characterized by impaired ability to remember the names of objects and impaired language comprehension. It is also sometimes known as *fluent aphasia* because the person can still speak smoothly. As with Broca's aphasia, the symptoms and brain damage vary, without a perfect correlation between them. Therefore, we use the term Wernicke's aphasia, or fluent aphasia, to describe a certain pattern of behavior, independent of the location of damage.

The typical characteristics of Wernicke's aphasia are as follows:

1. *Articulate speech.* In contrast to people with Broca's aphasia, those with Wernicke's aphasia speak fluently, except for pauses to try to think of the name of something.
2. *Difficulty finding the right word.* People with Wernicke's aphasia have **anomia** (ay-NOME-ee-uh), difficulty recalling the names of objects. They make up names (e.g., "thingamajig"), substitute one name for another, and use roundabout expressions such as "the thing that we used to do with the thing that was like the other one." When they do manage to find some of the right words, they arrange them improperly, such as, "The Astros listened to the radio tonight" (instead of "I listened to the Astros on the radio tonight") (R. C. Martin & Blossom-Stach, 1986).
3. *Poor language comprehension.* People with Wernicke's aphasia have great trouble understanding spoken and written speech and—in the case of deaf people—sign language (Petitto, 2000). Although many sentences are clear enough without prepositions, word endings, and grammar (which confuse Broca's aphasics), few sentences make sense without nouns and verbs (which trouble Wernicke's patients).

The following conversation is between a woman with Wernicke's aphasia and a speech therapist trying to teach her the names of some objects. (The Duke University Department of Speech Pathology and Audiology provided this dialogue.)

Therapist: *(Holding picture of an apron)* Can you name that one?

Woman: Um . . . you see I can't, I can I can barely do; he would give me sort of umm . . .

T: A clue?

W: That's right . . . just a like, just a . . .

T: You mean, like, "You wear that when you wash dishes or when you cook a meal . . ."?

W: Yeah, something like that.

T: Okay, and what is it? You wear it around your waist, and you cook . . .

W: Cook. Umm, umm, see I can't remember.

T: It's an apron.

W: Apron, apron, that's it, apron.

T: *(Holding another picture)* That you wear when you're getting ready for bed after a shower.

W: Oh, I think that he put under different, something different. We had something, you know, umm, you know.

T: A different way of doing it?

W: No, umm . . . umm . . . *(Pause)*

T: It's actually a bathrobe.

W: Bathrobe. Uh, we didn't call it that, we called it something else.

T: Smoking jacket?

W: No, I think we called it, uh . . .

T: Lounging . . .?

W: No, no, something, in fact, we called it just . . . *(Pause)*

Table 14.1 **Broca's Aphasia and Wernicke's Aphasia**

Type	Pronunciation	Content of Speech	Comprehension
Broca's aphasia	Very poor	Mostly nouns and verbs; omits prepositions and other grammatical connectives	Impaired if the meaning depends on complex grammar
Wernicke's aphasia	Unimpaired	Grammatical but often nonsensical; has trouble finding the right word, especially names of objects	Seriously impaired

T: Robe?

W: Robe. Or something like that.

The patient still knows the names of objects and recognizes them when she hears them; she just has trouble finding them for herself. In some ways, her speech resembles that of a student called upon to speak in a foreign language class after poorly studying the vocabulary list.

Although Wernicke's area and surrounding areas are important, language comprehension also depends on the connections to other brain areas. For example, reading the word *lick* activates not only Wernicke's area but also the part of the motor cortex responsible for tongue movements. Reading *kick* activates the part of the motor cortex controlling foot movements (Hauk, Johnsrude, & Pulvermüller, 2004). It is as if whenever you think about the meaning of an action word, you imagine doing it.

Table 14.1 contrasts Broca's aphasia and Wernicke's aphasia. For more information about aphasia and its many forms, check this website: **http://www.aphasia.org/**

7. Describe the speech production of people with Broca's aphasia and those with Wernicke's aphasia.

8. Is it reasonable to conclude that Broca's patients have lost their grammar?

9. Describe the speech comprehension of people with Broca's aphasia and those with Wernicke's aphasia.

Check your answers on page 441.

Dyslexia

Dyslexia is a specific impairment of reading in a person with adequate vision and adequate skills in other academic areas. It is more common in boys than girls and apparently has genetic influences, although no single gene relates to all cases of dyslexia (Fisher & DeFries, 2002; Kaplan et al., 2002). Dyslexia is more common among English readers than among those who read Italian or other languages with phonetic spelling. However, even among Italians, some people read better than others, and slow-reading Italians have trouble with the same kinds of language tasks as dyslexic English readers (Paulesu et al., 2001). In other words, a certain number of people in any country have trouble reading, but the problems are more severe in a language with as many odd spellings as English has. (For example, consider the words *phlegm, bivouac, khaki, physique,* and *gnat.*)

Many people with dyslexia have mild abnormalities in the structure of many brain areas, including microscopic details (Klingberg et al., 2000). As a rule, a person with dyslexia is more likely to have a bilaterally symmetrical cerebral cortex, whereas in other people, the planum temporale and certain other areas are larger in the left hemisphere (Galaburda, Sherman, Rosen, Aboitiz, & Geschwind, 1985; Hynd & Semrud-Clikeman, 1989; Jenner, Rosen, & Galaburda, 1999). In some people with dyslexia, certain language-related areas are actually larger in the right hemisphere (Duara et al., 1991). They also show signs of weak connections among several brain areas, such that activity in one part of the left cerebral cortex tends to be uncorrelated with activity in other areas of the left cortex, unlike the pattern for normal readers (Horwitz, Rumsey, & Donohue, 1998; Paulesu et al., 1996; Pugh et al., 2000).

Reading is a complicated skill that requires seeing subtle differences as *abode* versus *adobe,* hearing subtle differences as *symphony* versus *sympathy,* and connecting the sound patterns to the visual symbols. In the often confusing literature about dyslexia, the one point that stands out clearly is that different people have different kinds of reading problems, and no one explanation works for all. Some researchers distinguish between *dysphonetic dyslexics* and *dyseidetic dyslexics* (Flynn & Boder, 1991), although many people with dyslexia do not fit neatly into either category (Farmer & Klein, 1995). Dysphonetic dyslexics have trouble sounding out words, so they try to memorize words as wholes, and when they don't recognize a word, they guess based on context. For example, they might read the word *laugh* as "funny." Dyseidetic readers sound out words well enough, but they fail to recognize a word as a whole. They read slowly and have particular trouble with irregularly spelled words.

The most severe cases of dyseidetic dyslexia result from brain damage that restricts the field of vision. People who can see only one letter at a time have many short eye movements, very slow reading, and particular difficulty with long words. In one study, normal people viewed words on a computer screen while a device monitored their eye movements and blurred every letter on the screen except the one the viewer focused on. The result was very slow reading (Rayner & Johnson, 2005).

Various researchers have emphasized different hypotheses to explain dyslexia. The hypothesis of a visual impairment has fallen out of favor, as most people with dyslexia show normal, or close to normal, visual abilities (Cornelissen, Richardson, Mason, Fowler, & Stein, 1995; Skottun, 2000). Another hypothesis suggests a hearing impairment. Brain scans have shown that dyslexics' brains show less than normal responses to speech sounds, especially consonants (Helenius, Salmelin, Richardson, Leinonen, & Lyytinen, 2002; McCrory, Frith, Brunswick, & Price, 2000). Teaching people to pay closer attention to sounds sometimes alleviates dyslexia (Eden et al., 2004; Tallal, 2004). However, it is possible to have dyslexia without hearing problems (Caccappolo-van Vliet, Miozzo, & Stern, 2004).

Many people with dyslexia have particular trouble detecting the temporal order of sounds, such as noticing the difference between beep-click-buzz and beep-buzz-click (Farmer & Klein, 1995; Kujala et al., 2000; Nagarajan et al., 1999). They also have much difficulty making Spoonerisms—that is, trading the first consonants of two words, such as listening to "dear old queen" and saying "queer old dean" or hearing "way of life" and replying "lay of wife" (Paulesu et al., 1996). Doing so, of course, requires close attention to sounds and their order. Many people with dyslexia have trouble with other temporal order tasks as well, such as tapping a regular rhythm with the fingers (Wolff, 1993). In fact, even slow-reading college students, not diagnosed as dyslexic, also have trouble tapping rapid finger rhythms (Carello, LeVasseur, & Schmidt, 2002).

However, granting these temporal order problems, the question remains: How might impaired perception of temporal order lead to dyslexia? Perhaps people with dyslexia have trouble hearing the difference between similar words and therefore confuse them when they try to read them (Carello et al., 2002). However, presumably, someone who could not hear the differences among words would not pronounce them correctly, but most people with dyslexia speak clearly. Therefore, the relation between dyslexia and impaired temporal order processing remains unclear.

Another hypothesis is that the problem in dyslexia is connecting vision to sound. In one study, dyslexics performed normally at watching nonsense words flashed on the screen and saying whether they were the same or different. (For example, *brap-brap* would be the same and *sond-snod* would be different.) They were also equal to normals at listening to two nonsense words and saying whether they were the same. They were impaired only when they had to look at a nonsense word on the screen and then say whether it was the same as a nonsense word they heard (Snowling, 1980). Supporting this hypothesis, brain scans indicate that reading strongly activates areas of the left temporal and parietal cortex for most people, but only weakly activates them in people with dyslexia (Pugh et al., 2001). These areas are believed important for linking visual and auditory information.

A final hypothesis relates dyslexia to a difference in attention. For example, suppose a dot flashes on the left or right part of a screen, and it is your task to identify the location. Sometimes a circle flashes off and on just 100 milliseconds before the dot. If it flashes in the same location as the circle, it improves the performance of most people but not those with dyslexia (Facoetti et al., 2003). Evidently, they do not shift attention in the same way as other people, and reading requires shifting attention from one word to another along the line.

Here is another demonstration of attention and reading. Fixate your eyes on the central dot in each display below and, without moving your eyes left or right, try to read the middle letter of each three-letter display:

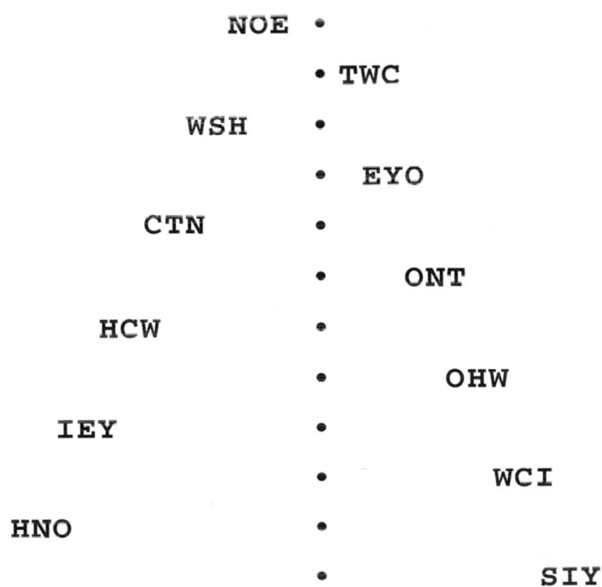

Most people find it easier to read the letters close to the fixation point, but some people with dyslexia are unusually adept at identifying letters well to the right of their fixation point. When they focus on a word, they are worse than average at reading it but better than average at perceiving letters 5 to 10 degrees to the right of it (Geiger, Lettvin, & Zegarra-Moran, 1992; Lorusso et al., 2004). That kind of attentional focus could certainly confuse attempts at reading (De Luca, Di Page, Judica, Spinelli, & Zoccolotti, 1999). Figure 14.17 shows the mean results for normal readers and for people with dyslexia.

For people with this abnormality, an effective treatment might be to teach them to attend to just one word at a time. Some children and adults with dyslexia have been told to place over the page that they are reading a sheet of paper with a window cut out of it that is large enough to expose just one word. In 3 months, 15 dyslexic children improved their reading skills by 1.22 grade levels (Geiger, Lettvin, & Fahle, 1994). Four dyslexic adults also made spectacular progress; one advanced from a third-grade to a tenth-grade reading level in 4 months (Geiger et al., 1992). After about the first 3 weeks of practice, they no longer needed the special cut-out sheet of paper.

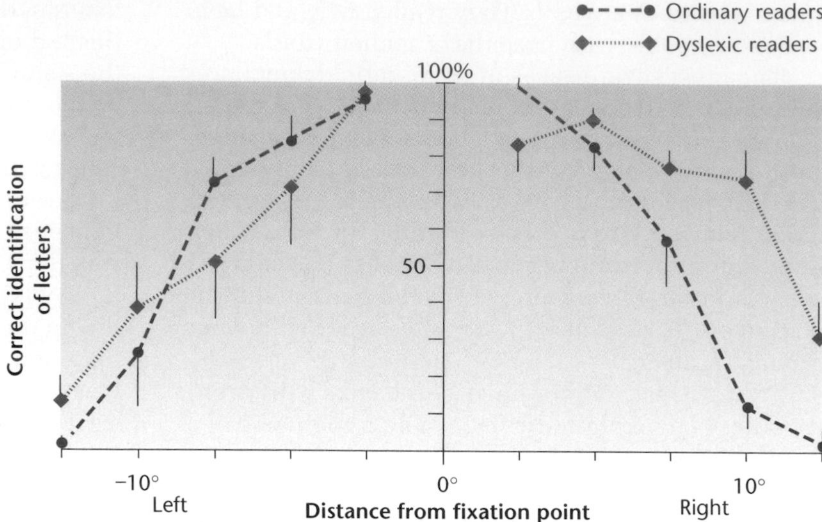

Figure 14.17 Identification of a letter at various distances from the fixation point

Normal readers identify a letter most accurately when it is closest to the fixation point, and their accuracy drops steadily as letters become more remote from that point. Many people with dyslexia show a small impairment for letters just to the right of the fixation point, yet they are substantially more accurate than normal readers are in identifying letters 5 to 10 degrees to the right of fixation. *(Source: Reprinted from "Task-Determined Strategies of Visual Process," by G. Geiger, J. Y. Lettvin, & U. Zegarra-Moran, 1992,* Cognitive Brain Research, *1, pp. 39–52, 1992, with kind permission of Elsevier Science-NL, Sara Burgerhartstraat 25, 1055 KV Amsterdam, The Netherlands.)*

One final twist: Of the four adults with dyslexia who went through this process, three decided that they would rather return to being dyslexic! While dyslexic, they could attend to several tasks at once, such as talking to someone, listening to news on the radio, creating a work of art, and so forth. When they learned to read one word at a time, they found themselves able to perform only one task at a time, and they missed their old way of life. In short, their reading skills were tied to their overall attentional strategies.

For more information about dyslexia, visit this website: **http://www.bda-dyslexia.org.uk**

STOP & CHECK

10. What are four hypotheses about the causes of dyslexia?

Check your answer on page 441.

Module 14.2

In Closing: Language and the Brain

Perhaps the best summary of dyslexia is also the best summary of language impairments in general: Language and reading are sufficiently complicated that people can become impaired in many ways for many reasons. Language is not simply a by-product of overall intelligence, but it is hardly independent of other intellectual functions either.

Summary

1. Chimpanzees can learn to communicate through gestures or nonvocal symbols, although their output does not closely resemble human language. Bonobos have made more language progress than common chimpanzees because of species differences, early onset of training, and different training methods. (p. 429)
2. An African gray parrot has shown surprising language abilities, with a brain organized differently from that of primates. (p. 430)
3. The hypothesis that language emerged as a by-product of overall intelligence or brain size faces major problems: Some people have full-sized brains but impaired language, and people with Williams syndrome have nearly normal language despite mental retardation. (p. 432)
4. People are specialized to learn language easily, but the nature of that specialization is not yet clear. (p. 434)

5. The best evidence for a critical period for language development is the observation that deaf children learn sign language much better if they start early than if their first opportunity comes later in life. However, there does not appear to be a sharp loss of language capacity at any particular age. (p. 434)

6. People with Broca's aphasia (nonfluent aphasia) have difficulty speaking and writing. They find prepositions, conjunctions, and other grammatical connectives especially difficult. They also fail to understand speech when its meaning depends on complex grammar. (p. 435)

7. People with Wernicke's aphasia have trouble understanding speech and recalling the names of objects. (p. 437)

8. Dyslexia (reading impairment) has many forms and no doubt many explanations. The problem may not be purely visual or auditory, but a matter of converting visual signals into auditory information or attending to the right aspects of a visual display. (p. 438)

Answers to STOP & CHECK Questions

1. The chimpanzees seldom arranged the symbols into new combinations, seldom used them to describe anything (only to request), and produced symbols better than they understood anyone else's use of the symbols. (p. 430)

2. Bonobos may be more predisposed to language than common chimpanzees. The bonobos started training at an earlier age. They learned by imitation instead of formal training techniques. (p. 430)

3. Some people have normal brain size but very poor language. Also, some people are mentally retarded but nevertheless develop nearly normal language. (p. 434)

4. Poor: self-care skills, attention, planning, problem solving, numbers, visual-motor skills, and spatial perception. Relatively good: language, interpretation of facial expressions, social behaviors, some aspects of music. (p. 434)

5. The poverty of the stimulus argument is the claim that children say complex sentences without adequate opportunity to learn them, so they must be born with an innate grammar. The argument against this idea is that grammatical rules vary among languages, and children could not be born prepared for all the grammars they might have to learn. (p. 435)

6. Deaf children who are not exposed to sign language until later in life (and who did not learn spoken language either while they were young) never become as proficient at it as those who started younger. (p. 435)

7. People with Broca's aphasia speak slowly and with poor pronunciation, but their speech includes nouns and verbs and is usually meaningful. They omit prepositions, conjunctions, and other grammatical words that have no meaning out of context. People with Wernicke's aphasia speak fluently and grammatically but omit most nouns and verbs and therefore make little sense. (p. 438)

8. No. They can usually recognize incorrect grammar, even if they cannot state how to correct it. Their speech is like that of someone who finds it painful to speak (leaving out words with the least meaning). (p. 438)

9. People with Broca's aphasia understand most speech unless the meaning depends on grammatical devices or complex sentence construction. People with Wernicke's aphasia understand little speech. (p. 438)

10. Four hypotheses are that dyslexia relates to visual problems, hearing problems (especially processing temporal order), connecting vision to hearing, and attention to the proper area of the visual field. (p. 440)

Thought Questions

1. Most people with Broca's aphasia suffer from partial paralysis on the right side of the body. Most people with Wernicke's aphasia do not. Why?

2. In a syndrome called *word blindness,* a person loses the ability to read (even single letters), although the person can still see and speak. What is a possible neurological explanation? That is, can you imagine a pattern of brain damage that might produce this result?

Module 14.3 Attention

Many people today, especially in the United States, are diagnosed with attention-deficit disorder. But what does it mean to have a deficit in attention? Some people with this diagnosis can pay attention to a video game for many hours in a row, even if they don't pay attention to their homework for long. Attention is apparently a multidimensional process.

Alterations in Brain Responses

Attention is closely related to consciousness. As discussed in Chapters 1 and 6, we are conscious of sights and sounds that produce strong responses in the cortex, and we are unconscious of stimuli that produce weaker responses. In many cases, stimuli destined to become conscious or unconscious produce about the same brain activity in the first 200–250 milliseconds (ms); however, in the next few hundred milliseconds, the brain enhances its response for those stimuli that become conscious (Sergent, Baillet, & Dehaene, 2005). How does it select which stimuli to enhance, attend to, and make conscious? Sometimes the answer pertains to the intensity of the stimulus, its similarity to stimuli that have been important in the past, or other features of the stimulus itself. In other cases, people deliberately shift their attention, sometimes in response to instructions. In one study, telling people to pay attention to odors increased the activity of odor-sensitive areas of the cortex even before the odor was presented (Zelano et al., 2005).

One example of attention is binocular rivalry, as discussed in Chapter 1: If you see vertical stripes of one color with one eye and horizontal stripes of a different color with the other eye, you alternate between seeing the horizontal stripes and the vertical stripes. Another example is *change blindness:* If part of a complex scene changes slowly, you probably won't notice it (Rensink, O'Regan, & Clark, 1997). You might also fail to notice a quick change that occurs while you are blinking your eyes or moving them (Henderson & Hollingworth, 2003). The quickest way to get people to notice the change is to instruct them where to direct their attention within the scene. You can experience change blindness with the Online Try It Yourself exercise "Change Blindness."

In these and other tasks, brain activity is greater in the areas responding to the attended stimulus and less in the areas responding to ignored stimuli. Is the brain enhancing responses to the attended stimuli or inhibiting responses to the ignored stimuli? Answering this question might shed light on what it means to have an attention deficit.

In one study, people were told to watch a screen and listen. On each trial, the screen would show either an X or an O while the person also heard "X" or "O." The task was to indicate the letter heard, as quickly as possible, ignoring the visual cue. People did not completely ignore the visual cue, and they responded more quickly when what they saw matched what they heard. The key finding came from brain scans: The auditory cortex responded more strongly to the sound of a letter that was accompanied with an *incompatible* letter, such as hearing "O" while seeing X (Weissman, Warner, & Woldorff, 2004). That is, while attending to a sound in the presence of a distraction, the brain increased its response.

In another study, people looked at faces with names superimposed, as in Figure 14.18. On some trials, they were supposed to attend to the face; on others, they were to attend to the written name. In either case, the instruction was to indicate whether the person was a politician or an actor. The researchers used fMRI to record activity of the fusiform gyrus, which, as you will recall from Chapter 6, responds strongly to faces. On trials when viewers were attending to a face and the name was irrelevant, the fusiform gyrus responded to the face more strongly when the name was incongruent—such as a politician's face and an actor's name. That is, the fusiform gyrus enhanced its response to a relevant, attended face in the presence of distraction. However, when viewers were attending to a printed name, the fusiform gyrus responded to the face equally, regardless of whether it was congruent or incongruent with the name (Egner & Hirsch, 2005). The fusiform gyrus did not inhibit its response to irrelevant, unattended information. This result suggests that attention

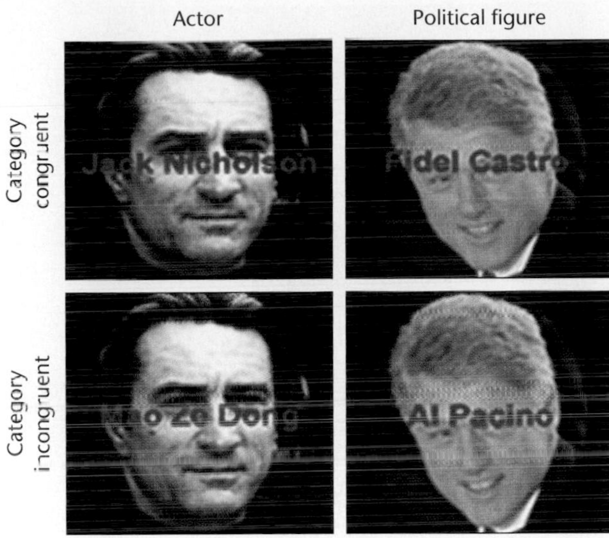

Figure 14.18 Stimuli for study of face-name incongruence

Participants were instructed to attend on some trials to the face and on other trials to the name, identifying it as a politician or actor. Although the name did not match the face, on congruent cases both the person in the picture and the person named had the same profession. On incongruent trials, the name and face had different professions. *(Source: Reprinted with permission from "Cognitive control mechanisms resolve conflict through cortical amplification of task-relevant information." by T. Egner & J. Hirsch,* Nature Neuroscience, 8, *1784–1790. Copyright 2005 Nature Publishing Group.)*

pertains more to enhancing relevant activity than inhibiting irrelevant activity.

STOP & CHECK

1. What is change blindness?
2. What evidence suggests that attention depends on enhancing responses to relevant stimuli as opposed to inhibiting responses to irrelevant stimuli?

Check your answers on page 447.

Neglect

The opposite of attention is inattention, or neglect. Right now, presumably you are attending to what you are reading, ignoring what you see above, below, or to the left or right of this page. People with damage to parts of the right hemisphere show a more widespread **spatial neglect**—a tendency to ignore the left side of the body and its surroundings or the left side of objects. (Damage in the left hemisphere does not produce much neglect of the right side.) They also generally ignore much of what they hear in the left ear and feel in the left hand, especially if they simultaneously feel something in the right hand. They may put clothes on only the right side of the body.

The exact location of the damage within the right hemisphere varies, as do the details of what the person neglects (Hillis et al., 2005; Husain & Rorden, 2003; Karnath, Ferber, & Himmelbach, 2001). People with damage to the inferior part of the right parietal cortex tend to neglect everything to the left of their own body. People with damage to the superior temporal cortex neglect the left side of objects, regardless of their location (Hillis et al., 2005).

If a patient with neglect is shown a long horizontal line and asked to divide it in half, generally the person picks a spot toward the right side of the line, as if part of the left side wasn't there. (With a short line, the person divides it correctly or even to the left of center.) If asked to point "straight ahead," most patients with neglect point to the right of center (Richard, Honoré, Bernati, & Rousseaux, 2004). Some patients with neglect also show deviations in their estimates of the midpoint of a numerical range. For example, what is halfway between 11 and 19? The correct answer is, of course, 15, but people with neglect might say "17." Evidently, they discount the lower numbers as if they were on the left side (Doricchi, Guariglia, Gasparini, & Tomaiuolo, 2005; Zorzi, Priftis, & Umiltà, 2002). At least in Western society, many people visualize the numbers like a line stretching to the right, as in the *x* axis of a graph.

The problem is with attention, not sensation. One patient was shown a letter E, composed of small Hs, as in Figure 14.19(c). She identified it as a big E composed of small Hs, indicating that she saw the whole figure. However, when she was then asked to cross off all the Hs, she crossed off only the ones on the right. When she was shown the figures in Figure 14.19(e), she identified them as an O composed of little Os and an X composed of little Xs. Again, she could see both halves of both figures, but when she was asked to cross off all the elements, she crossed off only the ones on the right. The researchers summarized by saying she saw the forest but only half the trees (Marshall & Halligan, 1995).

Several procedures can increase attention to the neglected side. First, simply telling the person to pay attention to the left side helps temporarily. So does having the person look left while at the same time feeling an object with the left hand (Vaishnavi, Calhoun, & Chatterjee, 2001) or hearing a sound from the left side of the world (Frassinetti, Pavani, & Làdavas, 2002). Something similar is true for unimpaired people also. Suppose you are staring straight ahead and an experimenter is flashing stimuli on the left and right sides. Your task is to identify something about each stimulus,

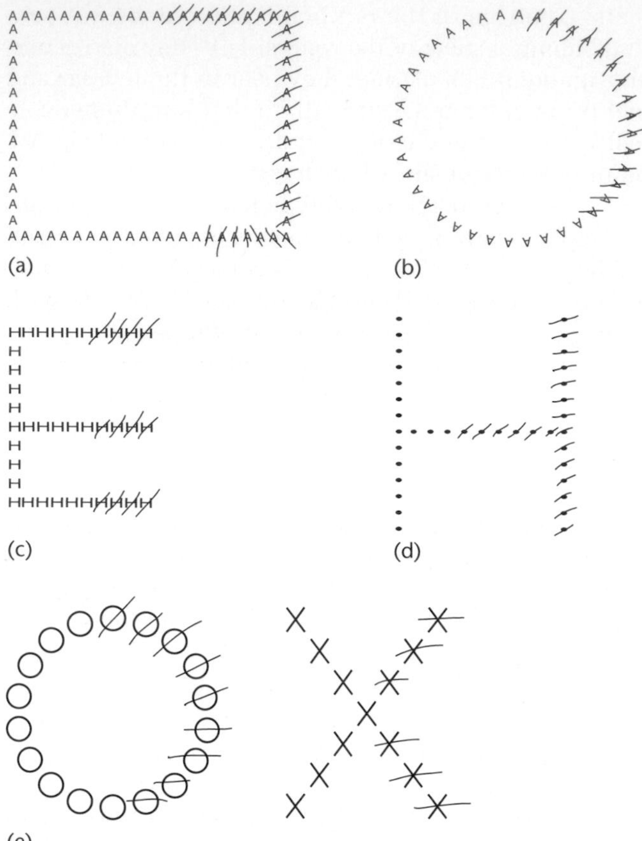

Figure 14.19 Spatial neglect
A patient with neglect of the left side could identify the overall figures indicating that she saw the whole figures. However, when asked to cross off the elements that composed them, she crossed off only the parts on the right. *(Source: Reprinted with permission from "Seeing the forest but only half the trees?" by J. C. Marshall and P. W. Halligan,* Nature, *373, pp. 521–523. Copyright 1995 Nature Publishing Group.)*

such as whether it was on the top or bottom half of the screen. If someone touches you just before a visual stimulus, you will respond slightly faster if the touch was on the same side of the body as the visual stimulus (Kennett, Eimer, Spence, & Driver, 2001). That is, a touch stimulus briefly increases attention to one side of the body or the other.

Other manipulations also shift the attention of patients with neglect to their left side. For example, some patients with neglect report feeling nothing with the left hand, especially if the right hand feels something else at the time. However, if you cross one hand over the other as shown in Figure 14.20, the person is more likely to report feeling the left hand, which is now on the right side of the body (Aglioti, Smania, & Peru, 1999). Also, the person ordinarily has trouble pointing to anything in the left visual field but has somewhat better success if the hand was so far to the left that he or she would have to move it to the right to point to the object (Mattingley, Husain, Rorden, Kennard, & Driver, 1998). Again, the conclusion is that neglect is not due to a loss of sensation but a difficulty in directing attention to the left side.

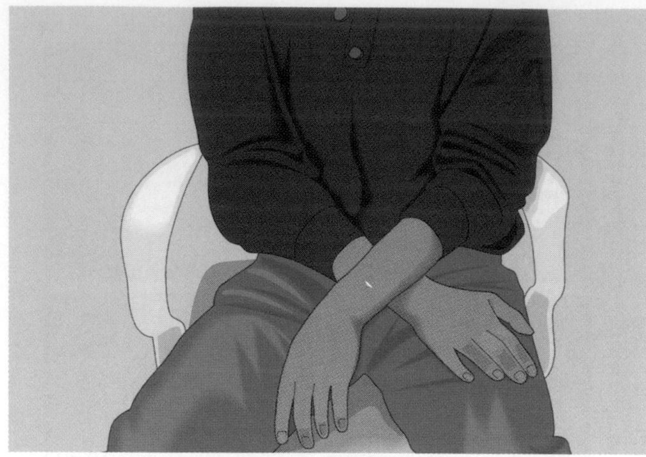

Figure 14.20 A simple way to reduce sensory neglect
Ordinarily, someone with right parietal lobe damage neglects the left arm. However, if the left arm crosses over or under the right, attention to the left arm increases.

Many patients with neglect also have deficits with spatial working memory (Malhotra et al., 2005) and with shifting attention, even when location is irrelevant. For example, one patient could not listen to two sounds and say which one came first, unless the sounds were very prolonged (Cusack, Carlyon, & Robertson, 2000). In short, the problems associated with neglect extend to many kinds of attention, not just the left–right dimension.

STOP & CHECK

3. What is the evidence that spatial neglect is a problem in attention, not sensation?
4. What are several procedures that increase attention to the left side in a person with spatial neglect?

Check your answers on page 447.

Attention-Deficit Hyperactivity Disorder

Attention-deficit hyperactivity disorder (ADHD) is characterized by attention deficits (distractibility), hyperactivity (fidgetiness), impulsiveness, mood swings, short temper, high sensitivity to stress, and impaired ability to make and follow plans (Wender, Wolf, & Wasserstein, 2001). These problems affect social behavior as well as school performance (DuPaul, McGoey, Eckert, & vanBrakle, 2001; Wender et al., 2001). Some people with ADHD have occupational difficulties or antisocial behaviors in adulthood (Mannuzza, Klein, Bessler, Malloy, & LaPadula, 1998).

Psychiatrists and psychologists in the United States apply the ADHD diagnosis to an estimated 3%–10% of children and a smaller number of adults, with males outnumbering females two or three to one. The diagnosis is far less common in many European countries. ADHD is important to study for practical reasons and as a way to understand attention theoretically.

Research is complicated, however, by the difficulty of making a reliable diagnosis. How distractible is too distractible, how fidgety is too fidgety, and how impulsive is too impulsive? We have no medical test to confirm our opinions. Some doctors label only the most extreme cases as ADHD, whereas others apply the label to almost any rambunctious child (Panksepp, 1998). Furthermore, therapists need to distinguish ADHD from other disorders that impair attention, such as lead poisoning, fetal alcohol syndrome, epilepsy, allergies to medicines, sleep deprivation, emotional distress, and damage to the frontal or parietal cortex (Pearl, Weiss, & Stein, 2001).

Measurements of ADHD Behavior

Careful measurements of ADHD people's behavior help clarify our descriptions of the condition. Measurements also enable researchers to quantify improvements that might occur after treatment. Here are three examples of tasks on which people with ADHD differ, on the average, from other people:

- **The choice delay task** Which would you prefer, $5 now or $5.25 tomorrow? Which would you prefer, a cookie now or a slightly larger cookie 15 minutes from now? The details vary, but the choice is between one reward now and a slightly better reward later. Under a variety of circumstances, people with ADHD are more likely than others to choose the smaller but quicker reward (Solanto et al., 2001). This tendency indicates a kind of impulsiveness.
- **The stop signal task** People watch a screen or listen for a sound. When they hear it, they are to press a button as fast as possible. However, sometimes another stimulus occurs a split second after the first one, meaning "disregard the signal; don't press the button." Obviously, anyone would fail to inhibit the response if the signal arrived too late, and most people have no trouble inhibiting it if the "don't press" signal occurs quickly. However, with intermediate delays, most people with ADHD are more likely than others to press the button (Rubia, Oosterlaan, Sergeant, Brandeis, & v. Leeuwen, 1998; Solanto et al., 2001). The interpretation is that people with ADHD have difficulty inhibiting their behaviors. You will understand this test better if you try the Online Try It Yourself exercise "Stop Signal." Be sure to try to respond as quickly as possible on every trial. If you get 100% "correct" even on the longer delays, you have been intentionally slowing your responses to wait for the signal.

ONLINE try it yourself

- **The attentional blink task** People watch a series of black letters flashed on a screen, a new one every 90 ms. In each set, one of the letters is green. Another letter, designated as the "probe" letter, might or might not appear after the green letter. The task is first to name the green letter and then to say whether or not the probe letter appeared after the green letter. For example, in the following examples, suppose the probe letter is "K":

H U R X G V N K B P	**Correct answer: "G, Yes."**
D J C W N E M Q Z U	**Correct answer: "C, No."**

- Most people miss the probe letter (i.e., they say "no" even though K was present) if it appears within 100–700 ms after the green letter. This tendency is called the *attentional blink;* the idea is that you pay attention to the green letter for that period of time after seeing it, so you have trouble paying attention to anything else, as if you had blinked your eyes. The same is even truer for people with ADHD; they usually miss the probe letter even if it arrives almost a second after the green letter (Hollingsworth, McAuliffe, & Knowlton, 2001). The interpretation is that they have trouble controlling their attention; they can't shift it when they need to.

The three tasks measure different kinds of attentional issues. The stop signal and attentional blink tasks measure abilities; the choice delay task measures a preference. (That is, a child who chooses a small cookie now had the ability to choose the larger cookie later but simply preferred the immediate reward.) Furthermore, the choice delay task and stop signal task seem to be measuring impulsiveness, but they measure different kinds of impulsiveness. The stop signal task measures an inability to inhibit an impulse. The choice delay task measures a preference for immediate rewards. A child who acts "impulsive" on both tasks is likely to be diagnosed as ADHD, but many children are impulsive on one task but not the other (Solanto et al., 2001; Sonuga-Barke, 2004).

Possible Causes and Brain Differences

ADHD often runs in families, and twin studies suggest fairly high heritability (Thapar et al., 2003). Several genes have been identified that influence performance on tests of attention (Blasi et al., 2005). ADHD probably depends on multiple genes as well as environmental influences, including prenatal environment. The probability of ADHD is elevated among children of women who smoked cigarettes during pregnancy (Thapar et al., 2003).

On the average, people with ADHD have brain volume about 95% of normal, with a smaller than average right prefrontal cortex (Giedd, Blumenthal, Molloy, & Castellanos, 2001; Stefanatos & Wasserstein, 2001). The cerebellum also tends to be a bit smaller than usual, and cerebellar dysfunction is known to be associated with difficulty switching attention (Ravizza & Ivry, 2001). Still, all these differences are small and inconsistent from one person to another. If someone is uncertain whether a child has ADHD, a brain scan will not provide the answer.

Treatments

Decades ago, physicians discovered that when they gave amphetamine to children with epilepsy to relieve their seizures—at the time, a fairly common treatment—it sometimes reduced hyperactivity as well. Physicians started using amphetamine to reduce hyperactivity, and today, the most common treatment for ADHD is a stimulant drug such as methylphenidate (Ritalin) (Elia, Ambrosini, & Rapoport, 1999) or amphetamine (Adderrall). Stimulant drugs increase attentiveness, improve school performance and social relationships, and decrease impulsiveness. They also improve scores on laboratory tests, including the stop signal task (de Wit, Crean, & Richards, 2000). One study found that stimulant drugs helped adults with ADHD improve their driving, avoid traffic tickets, keep their attention on the road, and decrease their irritability toward other drivers (Jerome & Segal, 2001). Whether these benefits justify giving drugs to so many people is, however, a complex issue.

Amphetamine and methylphenidate increase the availability of dopamine to the postsynaptic receptors. They produce their maximum effects on dopamine about 1 hour after someone takes a pill, and 1 hour is also the time of the maximum behavioral benefit, so researchers are confident that the pills affect behavior through dopamine activity (Volkow et al., 1998). The benefits wear off a few hours later.

Suppose a physician prescribes a stimulant drug, and someone's behavior improves. Many people assume that if the drug helps, the person must have ADHD, but this conclusion does not follow. Several studies have found that stimulant drugs enhance certain aspects of learning and attention even for normal children and adults (R. Elliott et al., 1997; Zahn, Rapoport, & Thompson, 1980).

Many behavioral techniques are available as supplements or substitutes for stimulant drugs. Much of the advice is not surprising (Sohlberg & Mateer, 2001):

- Reduce distractions.
- Use lists, calendars, schedules, and so forth to organize your time.
- Practice strategies to pace yourself.
- Learn to relax. Tension and stress can magnify attention deficits.

For links to many kinds of information about ADHD, check this website: **http://www.add-adhd.org/**

STOP & CHECK

5. Describe the choice delay and stop signal tasks.
6. What is the attentional blink, and how does the attentional blink of a person with ADHD differ from that of most other people?
7. If a doctor is in doubt about whether a child has ADHD, would a brain scan help? Would trying the effects of stimulant drugs help?

Check your answers on page 447.

Module 14.3

In Closing: Attending to Attention

As recently as the 1960s, many psychological researchers, especially those studying learning in rats, were not convinced that the concept of attention was useful at all. They believed that all sensory stimuli influence behavior at all times. New research methods have certainly moved us beyond that point, but a great deal remains to be discovered. As you sit there in an unchanging room, shifting your attention from one item to another, you enhance the brain representation of one stimulus after another, but exactly how do you do that? As researchers attack this question, the answers may have not only practical applications but also deep theoretical implications about the nature of consciousness.

Summary

1. Attention to a stimulus is almost synonymous with being conscious of it. Attention or consciousness relates to increased brain activity in the areas responsive to a stimulus. (p. 442)
2. Damage to parts of the right hemisphere produce spatial neglect for the left side of the body or the left side of objects. (p. 443)
3. Sensory neglect results from a deficit in attention, not sensation. For example, someone with neglect can see an entire letter enough to say what it is, even

though that same person ignores the left half when asked to cross out all the elements that compose it. (p. 443)

4. People with sensory neglect also have difficulties with working memory and with shifting attention from one stimulus to another, even when the stimuli do not vary from left to right. (p. 444)
5. Attention-deficit hyperactivity disorder (ADHD) is a common diagnosis in the United States, although the diagnosis is ambiguous in many cases. The characteristic impulsiveness and impaired attention can be measured by the choice delay task, the stop signal task, and the attentional blink task. (p. 444)
6. The choice delay task measures problems different from those measured by the stop signal and attentional blink tasks. People can be impulsive in different ways or for different reasons. (p. 445)
7. ADHD is probably the result of a number of genes as well as environmental influences. Many people with ADHD have mild brain abnormalities, but the pattern is small and inconsistent. (p. 445)
8. Although stimulant drugs improve cognitive performance of people with ADHD, they also benefit many normal individuals. Therefore, benefits from the drugs should not be used as evidence that someone has ADHD. (p. 446)

Answers to STOP & CHECK Questions

1. Change blindness is the process of failing to notice a change in some scene, usually because the change occurred gradually or while the viewer was moving or blinking his or her eyes. (p. 443)
2. In one experiment, when faces were relevant, the brain's response to a face increased in the presence of an incongruent distracter. However, when faces were irrelevant, the brain did not suppress its response to an incongruent face compared to one congruent with the correct answer. (p. 443)
3. When a patient with neglect sees a large letter composed of small letters, he or she can identify the large letter, even though neglecting part of it when asked to cross off all the small letters. Also, someone who neglects the left hand pays attention to it when it is crossed over the right hand. (p. 444)
4. Simply telling the person to attend to something on the left sometimes helps, temporarily. Having the person look to the left while feeling something on the left side increases attention to the felt object. Crossing the left hand over the right increases attention to the left hand. Moving a hand far to the left makes it easier for the person to point to something in the left visual field because the hand will move toward the right to point at the object. (p. 444)
5. In the choice delay task, someone decides between one reward now and a slightly better one later. In the stop signal task, someone receives a signal to do something, which is sometimes followed by a second signal to disregard the first one and withhold the response. (p. 446)
6. The attentional blink is the period of time after one stimulus has been presented when it is hard to process another stimulus. People with ADHD have a longer than normal attentional blink. (p. 446)
7. In both cases, no. Brain scans differ on the average between people with ADHD and others, but the differences are too inconsistent to be useful in individual cases. Trying the effects of stimulant drugs would not help because the drugs improve attention even for most children who have no attentional problems. (p. 446)

Thought Question

ADHD is diagnosed far more commonly in the United States today than in the past and far more in the United States than in Europe. What possible explanations can you propose? Are any of them testable?

Chapter Ending

Key Terms and Activities

Terms

anomia (p. 437)
anterior commissure (p. 426)
aphasia (p. 435)
attention-deficit hyperactivity disorder (ADHD) (p. 444)
attentional blink task (p. 445)
Broca's aphasia (p. 435)
Broca's area (p. 435)
choice delay task (p. 445)
corpus callosum (p. 417)
dichotic listening task (p. 421)
dyslexia (p. 438)
epilepsy (p. 419)
focus (p. 419)
hippocampal commissure (p. 426)
language acquisition device (p. 434)
lateralization (p. 417)
nonfluent aphasia (p. 435)
object naming latency task (p. 421)
optic chiasm (p. 418)
planum temporale (p. 425)
poverty of the stimulus argument (p. 434)
productivity (p. 429)
Rasmussen's encephalopathy (p. 427)
spatial neglect (p. 443)
split-brain people (p. 420)
stop signal task (p. 445)
visual field (p. 418)
Wada Test (p. 421)
Wernicke's aphasia (p. 437)
Wernicke's area (p. 437)
Williams syndrome (p. 433)

Suggestions for Further Reading

Deacon, T. (1997). *The symbolic species.* New York: Norton. Deep analysis of the evolution of language and intelligence.

Ornstein, R. (1997). *The right mind.* New York: Harcourt Brace. Very readable description of split-brain research and the differences between the left and right hemispheres.

Pinker, S. (1994). *The language instinct.* New York: Morrow. Discussion of both behavioral and biological aspects of language.

Websites to Explore

You can go to the Biological Psychology Study Center and click these links. While there, you can also check for suggested articles available on InfoTrac College Edition. The Biological Psychology Internet address is:

http://psychology.wadsworth.com/book/kalatbiopsych9e/

National Aphasia Association
http://www.aphasia.org/

The Bonobo Foundation
http://www.blockbonobofoundation.org/blinks.htm

The British Dyslexia Association
http://www.bda-dyslexia.org.uk

Exploring Biological Psychology CD

Hemisphere Control (Try It Yourself)
Lateralization and Language (animation)
Split Brain (learning module)
McGurk Effect (Try It Yourself)
Wernicke-Geschwind Model (learning module)
Attention Deficit Disorder (video)
Change Blindness (Try It Yourself)
Stop Signal (Try It Yourself)
Chapter Quiz (multiple-choice questions)
Critical Thinking (essay questions)

ThomsonNOW™

http://www.thomsonedu.com

Go to this site for the link to ThomsonNOW, your one-stop study shop, Take a Pre-Test for this chapter, and ThomsonNOW will generate a Personalized Study Plan based on your test results. The Study Plan will identify the topics you need to review and direct you to online resources to help you master these topics. You can then take a Post-Test to help you determine the concepts you have mastered and what you still need work on.

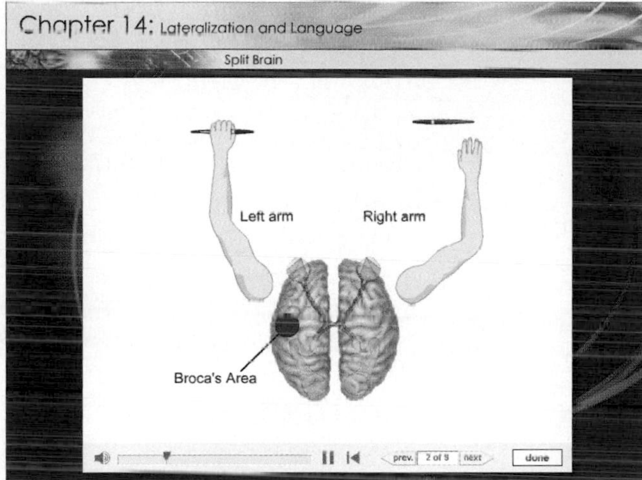

Review the relationship between speech, the two hemispheres, and the two halves of the body.

The McGurk effect shows how we combine visual and auditory cues to understand speech.

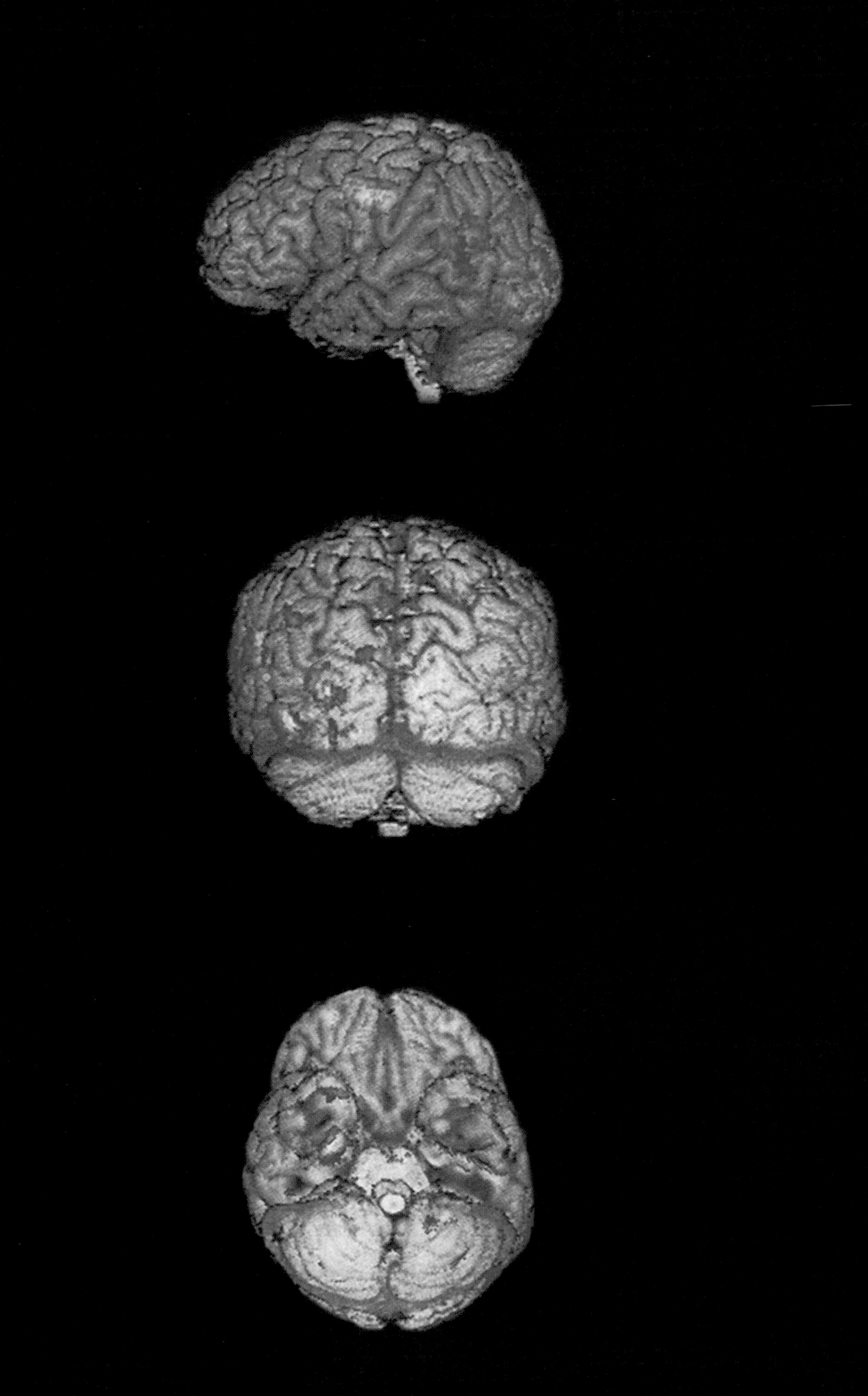

Psychological Disorders

15

Chapter Outline

Opposite: PET scans show the brain areas that increase their activation during visual and auditory hallucinations by a patient with schizophrenia.
Source: Silbersweig et al., 1995

Main Ideas

1. Psychological disorders result from a combination of environmental and biological influences, including genetics.
2. Addiction changes certain brain areas, increasing the tendency to seek the addictive substance and decreasing response to other kinds of reinforcement.
3. The effectiveness of certain drugs implies a relationship between neurotransmitter abnormalities and both depression and schizophrenia. However, serious theoretical issues remain.
4. Schizophrenia may be the result of genetic or other problems that impair early development of the brain.

Are mental illnesses really *illnesses,* analogous to tuberculosis or influenza? Or are they normal reactions to abnormal experiences? They are not exactly either. They are outcomes that combine biological predispositions with experiences, and to control them, we need a good understanding of both aspects.

In this chapter, the emphasis is strongly on the biological components of mental illnesses; *Biological Psychology* is, after all, the title of the book. But this emphasis does not imply that other influences are unimportant.

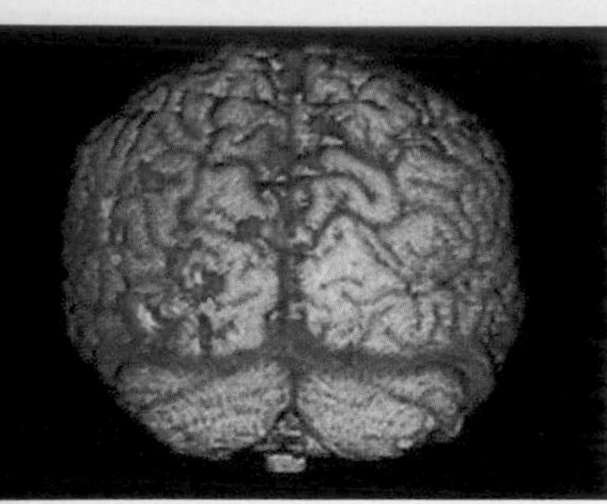

Module 15.1 Substance Abuse and Addictions

The American Psychiatric Association (1994), in its *Diagnostic and Statistical Manual* (4th ed.), defines **substance abuse** as a maladaptive pattern of substance use leading to clinically significant impairment or distress (p. 182). The puzzle of addiction is that people say the addictive behavior is no longer pleasant (or seldom very pleasant), they recognize it as harmful, but nevertheless, they feel a compelling drive to continue the addictive behavior. To understand addiction would be to understand a great deal about motivation in general.

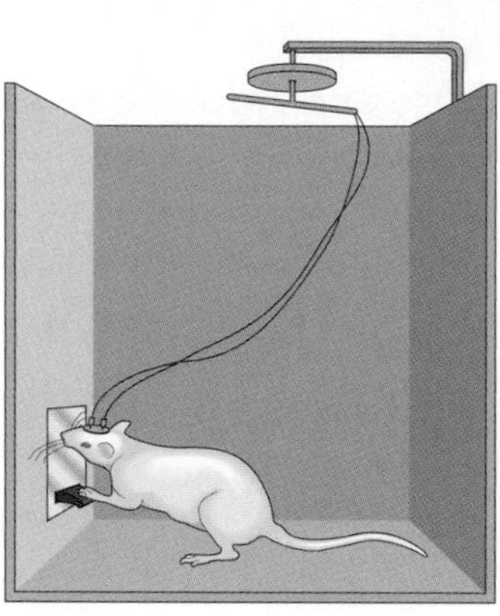

Figure 15.1 A rat pressing a lever for self-stimulation of its brain

Synapses, Reinforcement, and Addiction

Cocaine, heroin, nicotine, and other addictive substances all have one thing in common: They increase activity at dopamine synapses in certain brain areas. The story behind this discovery begins with a pair of young psychologists who were trying to answer a much different question.

Reinforcement and the Nucleus Accumbens

James Olds and Peter Milner (1954) wanted to test whether stimulation of certain brain areas might influence the direction in which a rat turns. However, when they implanted the electrode, they missed their intended target and instead hit an area called the septum. To their surprise, when the rat received the brain stimulation, it sat up, looked around, and sniffed, as if reacting to a favorable stimulus. Olds and Milner later placed rats in Skinner boxes, where they could produce **self-stimulation of the brain** by pressing a lever for electrical brain stimulation (Figure 15.1). With electrodes in the septum and various other places, rats sometimes pressed as often as 2,000 times per hour (Olds, 1958).

Later research found that rats and other species will self-stimulate many brain areas. Virtually all these areas directly or indirectly stimulate axons that release dopamine in the nucleus accumbens (see Figure 3.18) (Wise, 1996). Many other kinds of reinforcing experiences also stimulate dopamine release in that area, including sexual excitement (Damsma, Pfaus, Wenkstern, Philips, & Fibiger, 1992; Lorrain, Riolo, Matuszewich, & Hull, 1999), gambling (Breiter, Aharon, Kahneman, Dale, & Shizgal, 2001), and video games, especially in habitual players (Koepp et al., 1998).

In one fascinating study, young heterosexual men rated the attractiveness of photographed faces, while researchers used fMRI to record activity in their nucleus accumbens. The nucleus accumbens responded when the men looked at female faces that they rated as attractive (Aharon et al., 2001). When they looked a male faces that they rated "attractive," activity in the nucleus accumbens *decreased,* as if viewing them was threatening or unpleasant (Figure 15.2).

Addiction as Increased "Wanting"

It might seem natural to regard the nucleus accumbens as a pleasure area and dopamine as a pleasure chemical. However, not everything that we work for provides joy. For example, you might work hard for a paycheck without feeling much happiness when the paycheck

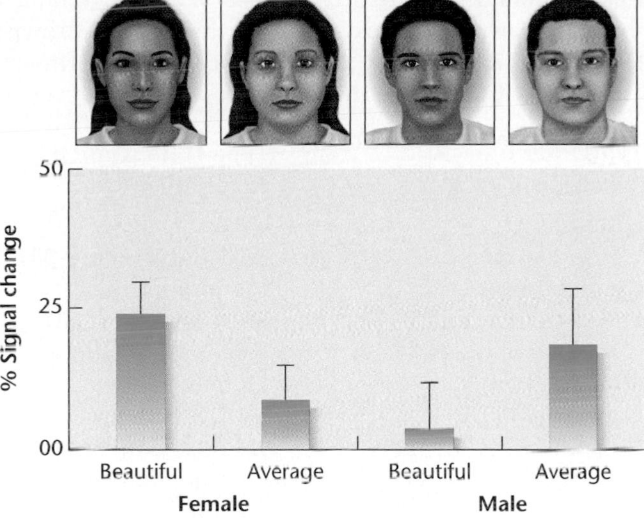

Figure 15.2 Response of nucleus accumbens to photos

Young heterosexual men rated the attractiveness of faces. The nucleus accumbens increased its response when the men saw attractive female faces but decreased at the sight of attractive male faces. *(Source: Reprinted with permission from "Beautiful faces have variable reward value: fMRI and behavioral evidence," by L. Aharon et al., Neuron, 32, pp. 537–551. Copyright 2001 Elsevier Inc.)*

comes. Gambling and video games occupy people's attention by the hour, but the participants usually don't smile. Many drug addicts say that the drug no longer provides much pleasure, even though they continue to be obsessed with obtaining it.

To account for these observations, Kent Berridge and Terry Robinson (1998) distinguished between "liking" and "wanting." According to their view, activity in the nucleus accumbens relates to wanting. To develop an addiction is to increase how much you *want* something, not necessarily how much you like it. Something you want monopolizes your attention. Addictive drugs have a tremendous ability to dominate a user's attention and cravings, even when the drug experience is not pleasant (Berridge & Robinson, 1995).

To evaluate this idea, researchers studied mice with a mutation that increases and prolongs the effects of dopamine. To test how much the mice "like" sweet tastes, researchers watched the facial expressions. Mice make distinctive mouth movements when they eat something tasty—not exactly a smile, but a distinctive expression nevertheless. The mice with increased dopamine showed no more expression of liking than did other mice. However, when they had an opportunity to run down an alley to get a sweet food, they left the start box faster than other mice, paused less in the runway, and ignored distractions better (Peciña, Cagniard, Berridge, Aldridge, & Zhuang, 2003). Other researchers tested mice with deficient production of dopamine. These mice did not approach food. However, if the food was brought to them, they ate as much as normal mice. Evidently, they "liked" the food; they just didn't "want" it enough to walk toward it (Robinson, Sandstrom, Denenberg, & Palmiter, 2005).

Sensitization of the Nucleus Accumbens

As people become addicted to something, it dominates their attention, and the nucleus accumbens responds more strongly to it. That is, the nucleus accumbens becomes *sensitized*. Repeated use of cocaine increases its ability to release dopamine in the nucleus accumbens, also its ability to activate part of the right prefrontal cortex, and the individual's tendency to seek the drug (Robinson & Berridge, 2001; Volkow et al., 2005). Meanwhile, the person responds less than normal to other incentives, including sex. According to one hypothesis, the prefrontal cortex ordinarily sends stimulatory input to the nucleus accumbens to support any potentially reinforcing activity. However, repeated drug use increases the background inhibition in the prefrontal cortex, such that only the strongest stimuli (i.e., the addictive substances) can get through. Everything else is filtered out (Kalivas, Volkow, & Seamans, 2005).

When and how does the brain become sensitized to an addictive substance? Researchers gave rats an opportunity to learn to press a lever to inject themselves with heroin. Then they let some of the rats self-administer heroin during a withdrawal state, while others went through withdrawal without any heroin. At a later time, when rats went through withdrawal a second time, all the rats had an opportunity to press a lever to try to get heroin, although at this time the lever was inoperative. Although both groups of rats pressed the lever, those that had self-administered heroin during the previous withdrawal state pressed far more frequently (Hutcheson, Everitt, Robbins, & Dickinson, 2001). Evidently, receiving an addictive drug during a withdrawal period is a powerful experience that produces sensitization. In effect, the user—rat or human—learns that the drug relieves the distress caused by drug withdrawal and produces heightened effects at that time. Both humans and rats that have abstained from a drug show heightened seeking of the drug—i.e., craving—during periods of stress or after any reminder of the drug (Ciccocioppo, Martin-Fardon, & Weiss, 2004; Ghitza, Fabbricatore, Prokopenko, Pawlak, & West, 2003; Kruzich, Congleton, & See, 2001).

1. What do drug use, sex, gambling, and video-game playing have in common?
2. What evidence suggests that alterations in dopamine influence "wanting" more than "liking"?
3. When addiction develops, how does the nucleus accumbens change its response to the addictive activity and to other reinforcements?
4. Someone who has quit an addictive substance for the first time is strongly counseled not to try it again. Why?

Check your answers on page 458.

Alcohol and Alcoholism

Alcohol has been widely used in most of the world throughout history. In moderate amounts, it helps people relax and may even help prevent heart attacks in older people—although the evidence is hardly conclusive. In greater amounts, it damages the liver and other organs, impairs judgment, and ruins lives. **Alcoholism**, or **alcohol dependence**, is the continued use of alcohol despite medical or social harm, even after people have decided to quit or decrease their drinking. Many people insist "I am not an alcoholic" because they don't drink every day, sometimes drink without getting drunk, and manage to hold a job. However, being an alcoholic does not require severe deterioration. The deciding factor is whether the alcohol interferes with the person's life.

Alcohol inhibits the flow of sodium across the membrane, expands the surface of membranes, decreases serotonin activity (Fils-Aime et al., 1996), facilitates response by the $GABA_A$ receptor (Mihic et al., 1997), blocks glutamate receptors (Tsai et al., 1998), and increases dopamine activity (Phillips et al., 1998). With such diverse effects, no wonder it influences behavior in so many ways.

Genetics

Recall that early-onset Parkinson's disease has a clear genetic basis; late-onset Parkinson's disease does not. The same is true for Alzheimer's disease. With Huntington's disease, people with many C-A-G repeats on the gene for the *huntingtin* protein develop symptoms early in life, whereas those with fewer repeats develop them later or not at all. Similarly, the genetic basis is strong for early-onset alcoholism, especially in men.

Researchers distinguish two types of alcoholism, although not everyone fits one type or the other (J. Brown, Babor, Litt, & Kranzler, 1994; Devor, Abell, Hoffman, Tabakoff, & Cloninger, 1994):

Type I (or Type A) Alcoholism	Type II (or Type B) Alcoholism
Later onset (usually after 25)	Earlier onset (usually before 25)
Gradual onset	More rapid onset
Fewer genetic relatives with alcoholism	More genetic relatives with alcoholism
Men and women about equally	Men far more than women
Generally less severe	Often severe; often associated with criminality

Evidence for a genetic basis of Type II alcoholism includes the findings that (a) monozygotic twins have greater concordance for alcohol abuse than do dizygotic twins (True et al., 1999), and (b) biological children of alcoholics have an increased risk of alcoholism, even if they are adopted by nonalcoholics (Cloninger, Bohman, & Sigvardsson, 1981; Vaillant & Milofsky, 1982). However, many of the biological mothers were drinking during pregnancy; thus, what appears to be a genetic effect could relate partly to prenatal environment. One study found that a person's probability of developing alcoholism correlated strongly with how much alcohol the person's mother drank during pregnancy, regardless of how much she and the father drank after the child was born (Baer, Sampson, Barr, Connor, & Streissguth, 2003).

Genes influence the likelihood of alcoholism in various ways. For example, genes that increase impulsive, risk-taking behavior increase the probability of trying alcohol and other drugs at an early age (Fils-Aime et al., 1996; Virkkunen et al., 1994). Genes that increase the stress response make people more likely to relapse into addiction after an attempt to quit (Kreek, Nielsen, Butelman, & LaForge, 2005). Also, genes that increase adenosine production tend to decrease alcohol intake because adenosine has a calming influence, decreasing stress (Choi et al., 2004).

5. Which type of alcoholism has a stronger genetic basis? Which type has earlier onset?
6. Name three ways a gene could influence alcoholism.

Check your answers on page 458.

Risk Factors

Are some people more likely than others to develop a severe alcohol problem? If so, and if we can identify them, perhaps psychologists could intervene early to prevent alcoholism. We don't know whether early intervention would help, but it is worth a try.

The ideal research requires studying huge numbers of people for years: Measure as many factors as possible for a group of children or adolescents, years later determine which of them developed alcohol problems, and then see which early factors predicted the onset of alcoholism. Such studies find that alcoholism is more likely among those who were described in childhood as impulsive, risk-taking, easily bored, sensation-seeking, and outgoing (Dick, Johnson, Viken, & Rose, 2000; Legrand, Iacono, & McGue, 2005).

Other research follows this design: First identify a group of young men who are not yet problem drinkers. Compare those whose fathers were alcoholics to those who have no close relative with an alcohol problem. Because of the strong familial tendency of alcoholism, researchers expect that many of the sons of alcoholics are future alcoholics themselves. (Researchers focus on men instead of women because almost all Type II alcoholics are men. They study sons of alcoholic fathers instead of mothers to increase the chance of seeing genetic instead of prenatal influences.) The idea is that any behavior more common in the sons of alcoholics is probably a predictor of future alcoholism (Figure 15.3).

Here are the findings:

- Sons of alcoholics show *less* than average intoxication after drinking a moderate amount of alcohol. They report feeling less drunk, show less body sway, and register less change on an EEG (Schuckit & Smith, 1996; Volavka et al., 1996). Presumably, someone who begins to feel tipsy after a drink or two stops at that point; one who "holds his liquor well" continues drinking, perhaps enough to impair his judgment. A follow-up study found that sons of alcoholics who report low intoxication after moderate drinking have a probability greater than 60% of developing alcoholism (Schuckit & Smith, 1997).
- In a difficult situation, alcohol decreases stress for most people, but it decreases it even more for sons of alcoholics (Levenson, Oyama, & Meek, 1987).

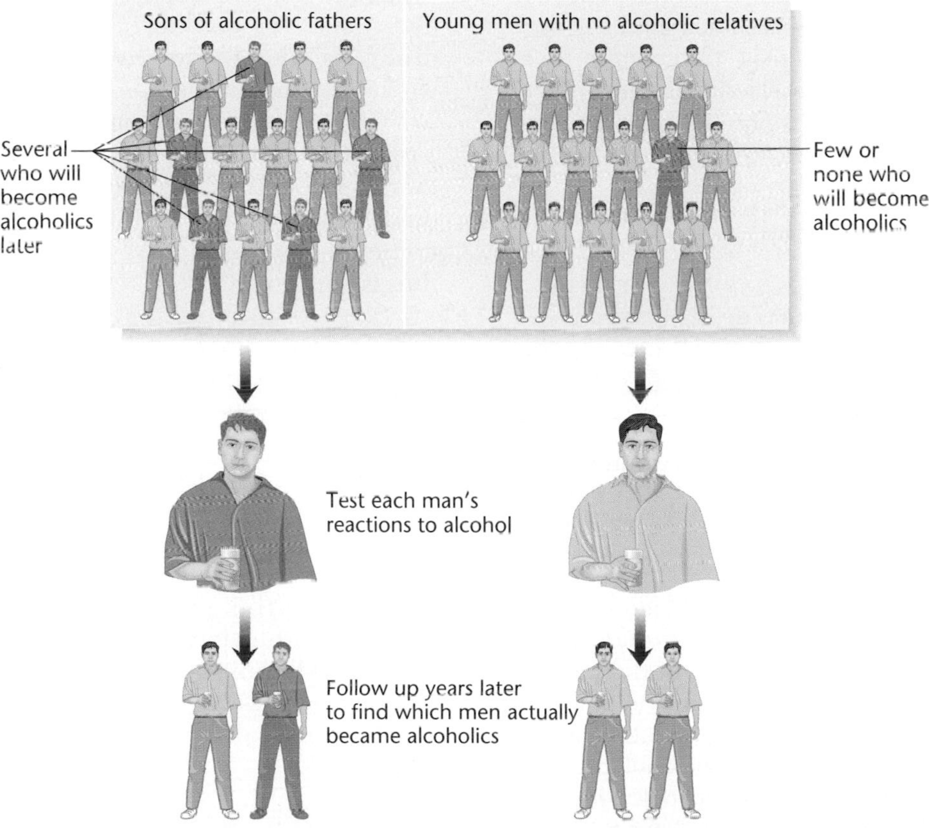

Figure 15.3 Design for studies of predisposition to alcoholism
Sons of alcoholic fathers are compared to other young men of the same age and same current drinking habits. Any behavior that is more common in the first group is presumably a predictor of later alcoholism.

- Sons of alcoholics have some brain peculiarities, including a smaller than normal amygdala in the right hemisphere (Hill et al., 2001). These young men were not yet alcohol abusers, so the brain abnormality represents a predisposition to alcoholism, not a result of it.

STOP & CHECK

7. What are two ways in which sons of alcoholics differ, on average, from sons of nonalcoholics?

Check your answer on page 458.

James W. Kalat

Figure 15.4 Robin Kalat (the author's teenage daughter) finds an alcohol vending machine in Tokyo in 1998

Restrictions against buying alcohol were traditionally weak in a country where most people cannot quickly metabolize acetaldehyde and therefore drink alcohol only in moderation. However, in 2000, Japan banned public alcohol vending machines.

Medications to Combat Substance Abuse

Many people who are trying to overcome substance abuse join Alcoholics Anonymous, Narcotics Anonymous, or similar organizations, and others see psychotherapists. Because many people do not respond well to any of these treatments, researchers have been seeking medications that might decrease the cravings. Many possibilities are still in the experimental phase (Vocci, Acri, & Elkashef, 2005). Here we briefly consider Antabuse and methadone.

Antabuse

After someone drinks ethyl alcohol, enzymes in the liver metabolize it to **acetaldehyde**, a poisonous substance. An enzyme, acetaldehyde dehydrogenase, then converts acetaldehyde to **acetic acid**, a chemical that the body can use as a source of energy:

$$\text{Ethyl alcohol} \dashrightarrow \text{Acetaldehyde} \overset{\text{Acetaldehyde dehydrogenase}}{\dashrightarrow} \text{Acetic acid}$$

People with a weaker gene for acetaldehyde dehydrogenase metabolize acetaldehyde more slowly. If they drink much alcohol, they accumulate acetaldehyde, which can produce flushing of the face, increased heart rate, nausea, headache, abdominal pain, impaired breathing, and damage to internal organs. As you might guess, people who can't metabolize acetaldehyde are unlikely to drink much alcohol. About half of the people in China and Japan have a gene that slows acetaldehyde metabolism; probably for that reason, alcohol abuse has historically been uncommon in those countries (Tu & Israel, 1995) (Figure 15.4). In other words, this gene affects alcohol abuse by altering liver enzymes.

The drug *disulfiram,* which goes by the trade name **Antabuse,** antagonizes the effects of acetaldehyde dehydrogenase by binding to its copper ion. Like many drugs, its effects were discovered by accident. The workers in one rubber-manufacturing plant found that when they got disulfiram on their skin, they developed a rash (Schwartz & Tulipan, 1933). If they inhaled it, they couldn't drink alcohol without getting sick. Soon therapists tried using disulfiram (Antabuse) as a drug, hoping that alcoholics would associate alcohol with illness and stop drinking.

Most studies find that Antabuse is only moderately effective (Hughes & Cook, 1997). When it works, it supplements the alcoholic's own commitment to stop drinking. By taking a daily pill and imagining the illness that could follow a drink of alcohol, the person reaffirms a decision to abstain. In that case, it doesn't matter whether the pill really contains Antabuse or not; someone who never drinks will not experience the threatened illness (Fuller & Roth, 1979). Those who drink in spite of taking the pill become ill, but unfortunately, they are as likely to quit taking the pill as to quit drinking alcohol. Antabuse treatment is more effective if friends make sure the person takes the pill daily (Azrin, Sisson, Meyers, & Godley, 1982).

Methadone

Heroin is an artificial substance invented in the 1800s as a "safer" alternative for people who were trying to quit morphine (an opiate drug). Some physicians even recommended that people using alcohol switch to heroin (Siegel, 1987). They abandoned this idea when they discovered how addictive heroin is.

Still, the idea has persisted that if people can't quit opiates altogether, perhaps they could switch to a less harmful drug. Methadone (METH-uh-don) is similar to heroin and morphine but has the advantage that it can be taken in pill form. (If heroin or morphine is taken as a pill, stomach acids break down most of it.) Methadone in pill form gradually enters the blood and then the brain, so its effects rise slowly, avoiding the "rush" experience. Because it is metabolized slowly, the withdrawal symptoms are also gradual. Furthermore, the user avoids the risk of an injection with an infected needle. Buprenorphine and levomethadyl acetate (LAAM), additional drugs that are similar to methadone, are also used to treat opiate addiction. People using any of these drugs live longer and healthier, on the average, than heroin or morphine users and are far more likely to hold a job (Vocci et al., 2005). However, these drugs do not end the addiction. Anyone who quits methadone or the others is likely to experience cravings.

What is to prevent a drug user from taking the methadone pill, dissolving it in water, and injecting it to get an effect like that of heroin? Physicians found a clever solution: They combine methadone with a small amount of the drug *naloxone,* which blocks the effects of any of these opiate drugs (Vocci et al., 2005). If someone takes a combination of methadone and naloxone as a pill, the stomach acids break down most of the naloxone, leaving methadone, as intended. However, if someone dissolves the pill and injects it, the stomach has no opportunity to break down the naloxone, and the naloxone cancels out the effects of the methadone.

8. Who would be likely to drink more alcohol—someone who metabolizes acetaldehyde to acetic acid rapidly or one who metabolizes it slowly?
9. How does Antabuse work?
10. What is the benefit of adding naloxone to a methadone pill?

Check your answers on page 458.

Module 15.1
In Closing: Addictions

Addictions pose a fascinating paradox: People addicted to alcohol and other drugs insist that they have "lost control" of their behavior. What does that mean? If they don't control their own behavior, who or what does?

In a literal sense, the statement is wrong. All the person's behaviors are a product of his or her own brain. But in another sense, it is right. Someone decides, "I am quitting," and then weeks later or even hours later finds it impossible to resist the urge to return to the addictive activity. Apparently, certain parts of the brain have changed in a way that overwhelms the part that says, "I quit." Addiction blurs our usual distinction between voluntary and involuntary.

Summary

1. Reinforcing brain stimulation, reinforcing experiences, and self-administered drugs increase the activity of axons that release dopamine in the nucleus accumbens. (p. 452)
2. Activity in the nucleus accumbens is not synonymous with pleasure or reward. According to one hypothesis, it relates more to "wanting" than "liking," and addiction represents an increase in wanting. (p. 452)
3. Addiction is associated with sensitization of the nucleus accumbens so that it responds more strongly to the addictive activity and less to other kinds of reinforcement. (p. 453)
4. A key experience in the formation of addictive behavior is trying the substance during withdrawal. The user learns that this is a powerful experience and learns to use the substance as a way of coping with distress. (p. 453)
5. Compared to Type I alcoholism, Type II alcoholism starts faster and sooner, is usually more severe, and affects more men than women. (p. 454)
6. Genes influence alcoholism in several ways, including effects on impulsiveness, responses to stress, and overall calmness. (p. 454)
7. Risk factors for alcoholism, in addition to a family history, include feeling low intoxication after moderate drinking and experiencing much relief from stress after drinking. (p. 455)
8. Ethyl alcohol is metabolized to acetaldehyde, which is then metabolized to acetic acid. People who, for genetic reasons, are deficient in that second reaction tend to become ill after drinking and therefore are unlikely to drink heavily. (p. 456)
9. Antabuse, a drug sometimes used to treat alcohol abuse, blocks the conversion of acetaldehyde to acetic acid. (p. 456)
10. Methadone and similar drugs are sometimes offered as a substitute for opiate drugs. The substitutes have the advantage that if taken as a pill, they satisfy the cravings without severely interrupting the person's ability to carry on with life. (p. 456)

Answers to STOP & CHECK Questions

1. They increase the release of dopamine in the nucleus accumbens. (p. 454)
2. Mice with increased dopamine run faster and more directly to food; mice with decreased dopamine do not approach food. However, both kinds of mice eat the food and show normal facial expressions that presumably indicate liking. (p. 454)
3. The nucleus accumbens becomes selectively sensitized, increasing its response to the addictive activity and decreasing its response to other reinforcing activities. (p. 454)
4. Taking an addictive drug after withdrawing from it is strongly reinforcing and sensitizes drug seeking afterward. (p. 454)
5. For both questions, Type II (p. 454)
6. Genes can influence impulsive, risk-taking personality, the response to stress, and overall calmness. Of course, other possibilities not mentioned in this section also exist. (p. 454)
7. Sons of alcoholics show less intoxication, including less body sway, after drinking a moderate amount of alcohol. They also show greater relief from stress after drinking alcohol. (p. 456)
8. People who metabolize it rapidly would be more likely to drink alcohol because they suffer fewer unpleasant effects. (p. 457)
9. Antabuse blocks the enzyme that converts acetaldehyde to acetic acid and therefore makes people sick if they drink alcohol. Potentially, it could teach people an aversion to alcohol, but more often, it works as a way for the person to make a daily recommitment to abstain from drinking. (p. 457)
10. Naloxone blocks the effects of methadone and other opiates. However, the stomach breaks down naloxone. If someone takes the methadone as a pill, as intended, the naloxone has little effect. However, it has a strong effect if someone dissolves the pill and injects it. Therefore, naloxone prevents people from using the pills for illicit purposes. (p. 457)

Thought Question

The research on sensitization of the nucleus accumbens has dealt with addictive drugs, mainly cocaine. Would you expect a gambling addiction to have similar effects? How could someone test this possibility?

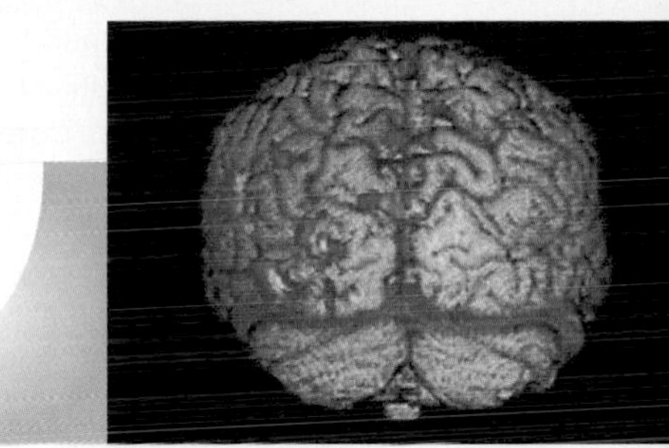

Module 15.2
Mood Disorders

Depression seems easy to diagnose. Depressed people look depressed, act depressed, and say they are depressed (Figure 15.5). The problem is similar symptoms can result from hormonal problems, head injuries (Holsinger et al., 2002), brain tumors, or other illnesses. Many people have depression comorbid with (i.e., combined with) substance abuse, anxiety, schizophrenia, or Parkinson's disease. The consequence for research is inconsistent results because of differences from one patient sample to another. The consequence for an individual patient is the possibility of being treated for one disorder while another one is overlooked.

Bruce Ayers/Getty Images

Figure 15.5 The face of depression
Depression shows in people's face, walk, voice, and mannerisms.

Major Depressive Disorder

At times, almost everyone feels sad, discouraged, lacking in energy. Major depression is a more intense and prolonged experience. According to the *DSM-IV* (American Psychiatric Association, 1994), people with a **major depression** feel sad and helpless every day for weeks at a time. They have little energy, feel worthless, contemplate suicide, have trouble sleeping, cannot concentrate, get little pleasure from sex or food, and in many cases can hardly even imagine being happy again.

Indeed, absence of happiness is a more reliable symptom than increased sadness. In one study, people carried a beeper that sounded at random times to signal them to describe their emotional reactions at the moment. In comparison to other people, depressed people reported the same number of unpleasant experiences but fewer pleasant ones (Peters, Nicolson, Berkhof, Delespaul, & deVries, 2003). In two other studies, people watched films or examined pictures as researchers recorded their reactions. In both cases, depressed people reacted to sad or frightening depictions about the same as anyone else but failed to smile as much at the comedies or pleasant pictures (Rottenberg, Kasch, Gross, & Gotlib, 2002; Sloan, Strauss, & Wisner, 2001).

Major depression is diagnosed about twice as often in women as in men. It can occur at any age, although it is uncommon in children. A survey reported that within any given year about 5% of adults in the United States have "clinically significant" (i.e., fairly severe) depression (Narrow, Rae, Robins, & Regier, 2002). Over the course of a lifetime, more than 10% suffer from major depression.

Genetics and Life Events

Studies of twins and adopted children indicate a moderate degree of heritability for depression (Fu et al., 2002; Wender et al., 1986). However, at least some of the genes are not specific to depression. The close relatives of someone with depression are more likely than other people to suffer not only from depression but also from anxiety disorders, attention-deficit disorder, alcohol or marijuana abuse, obsessive-compulsive disorder, bulimia, migraine headaches, irritable bowel syndrome, and several other conditions (Fu et al., 2002; Hudson et al., 2003).

The risk of depression is particularly elevated among relatives of women with early-onset depression—that is, beginning before age 30 (Bierut et al., 1999; Kendler, Gardner, & Prescott, 1999; Lyons et al., 1998). Compare this pattern to alcoholism, where the risk is highest among relatives of men with early-onset alcoholism.

Although the predisposition to depression undoubtedly depends on many genes, several have been identified. A particular form of one gene leads to an 80% decrease in the brain's ability to produce the neurotransmitter serotonin. A study found that gene in 9 of 87 people with major depression, and only 3 of 219 people in a control group. Furthermore, 2 of those 3 had "mild depression" (X. Zhang et al., 2005). Although it is clear that most people with depression do not have this gene, people who do have it are at high risk for depression.

Another gene of interest is the one controlling the serotonin transporter protein (Pezawas et al., 2005). That protein controls the ability of an axon to reabsorb serotonin after its release—that is, the ability to recycle it for further use. The effect of that gene on depression interacts with people's experiences. Investigators examined the serotonin transporter genes of 847 people, identifying them in terms of two types: the "short" type and the "long" type. They also asked each participant to record certain highly stressful events from age 21 until age 26. Those events included financial setbacks, changes of job or housing, divorce, and so forth. Figure 15.6 shows the results. For people with two short forms of the gene, increasing numbers of stressful experiences led to a big increase in the probability of depression. For those with two long forms, stressful events hardly increased the risk of depression at all. Those with one short and one long gene were intermediate. In other words, the short form of the gene by itself does not lead to depression, nor does a series of stressful events, but a combination of both is hazardous (Caspi et al., 2003). The gene probably alters the way people react to stress.

1. What is the relationship between depression and the short form of the gene controlling the serotonin transporter protein?

Check your answer on page 469.

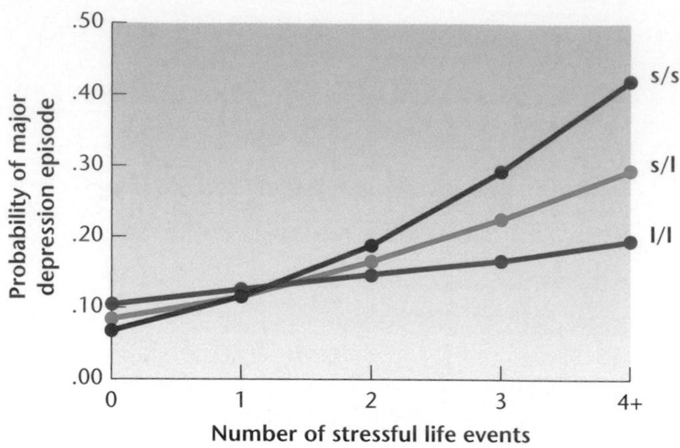

Figure 15.6 Genetics, stress, and depression
The probability of depression increases for people reporting higher numbers of stressful experiences in the previous 5 years; however, the rate of increase depends on their genetics. *(Reprinted with permission from A. Caspi, et al., "Influence of life stress on depression: Moderation by a polymorphism in the 5-HTT gene,"* Science, *301, pp. 386–389 (15). © 2003 AAAS)*

Hormones

Depression occurs in episodes rather than constantly. It lasts months, alleviates for months or years, and then returns. One likely trigger is stress, which releases cortisol, as described in Chapter 12. Cortisol readies the body for action, but prolonged high levels can exhaust the body's energies, impair sleep, impair the immune system, and set the stage for an episode of depression.

The role of sex hormones is less certain. Most women feel some emotional distress for a day or two after giving birth, and about 20% experience **postpartum depression**—that is, depression after giving birth. Most women recover fairly quickly without treatment, but about 0.1% enter a serious, long-lasting depression (Hopkins, Marcus, & Campbell, 1984). Postpartum depression is more common among women who have also suffered major depression at other times and among women who experience severe discomfort around the time of menstruation (Bloch, Rotenberg, Koren, & Klein, 2005).

One study found that after a drug-induced drop in estradiol and progesterone levels, women with a history of postpartum depression suddenly show new symptoms of depression, whereas other women do not (M. Bloch et al., 2000). That is, some women are more vulnerable to depression than others, and hormonal changes can trigger an episode of depression for the vulnerable women. Another study found that estradiol supplements relieved depression in many middle-aged women going through menopause (Soares, Almeida, Joffe, & Cohen, 2001).

Childhood depression is about equally common (actually, equally uncommon) in boys and girls. Beginning at puberty, depression is about twice as common in women as men in all cultures for which we have data (Culbertson, 1997; Cyranowski, Frank, Young, & Shear, 2000; Silberg et al., 1999). The extra vulnerability of women is found even when researchers survey a town for undiagnosed cases, so it is not just a result of women seeking treatment more often than men. Researchers have proposed both biological and social hypotheses to explain the gender difference, but so far, the data do not convincingly support any of the explanations.

Abnormalities of Hemispheric Dominance

Studies of normal people have found a fairly strong relationship between happy mood and increased activity in the left prefrontal cortex (Jacobs & Snyder, 1996). Most depressed people have decreased activity in the left and increased activity in the right prefrontal cortex (Davidson, 1984; Pizzagalli et al., 2002). Here's something you can try: Ask someone to solve a cognitive problem, such as "See how many words you can think of that start with *hu-*" or "Try to remember all the ingredients you've ever seen on a pizza." Then unobtrusively watch the person's eye movements to see whether they gaze right or left. Most people gaze to the right during verbal tasks, but most depressed people gaze to the left, suggesting right-hemisphere dominance (Lenhart & Katkin, 1986).

try it yourself

Many people become seriously depressed after left-hemisphere damage; fewer do after right-hemisphere damage (Vataja et al., 2001). Occasionally, people with right-hemisphere damage become manic, the opposite of depressed (Robinson, Boston, Starkstein, & Price, 1988).

STOP & CHECK

2. Some people offer to train you to use the right hemisphere of your brain more strongly, allegedly to increase creativity. If they were successful, can you see any disadvantage?

Check your answer on page 469.

Viruses

A few cases of depression may be linked to a viral infection. As recently as the 1980s, Borna disease was known only as an infection of European farm animals. Gradually, investigators discovered that a greater variety of species are vulnerable over a wider geographical range. In severe cases, the virus is fatal; in milder cases, **Borna disease** is noted mostly by its behavioral effects, such as periods of frantic activity alternating with periods of inactivity (Figure 15.7).

Many viruses pass between humans and other species, although the effects on humans may be different. In 1985, investigators reported the results of a blood test given to 370 people (Amsterdam et al., 1985). Only 12 people tested positive for Borna disease virus, but all 12 were suffering from major depression or bipolar disorder. These 12 were a small percentage of the 265

(a)

(b)

Bode & Ludwig, 1997

Figure 15.7 Symptoms of Borna disease
Farm animals infected with Borna disease have periods of frantic activity alternating with inactivity, much like a person with bipolar disorder. **(a)** Horse with Borna disease. **(b)** Same horse after recovery. *(Source: Figure 2, p. 174, from Bode L. and Ludwig H. (1997). "Clinical similarities and close genetic relationship of human and animal Borna disease virus."* Archives of Virology (Supplement 13), *167–182, Springer-Verlag. Photo scan by Kevin J. Nolte.)*

depressed people tested; still, *none* of the 105 undepressed people had the virus.

Since then, thousands of people have been tested in Europe, Asia, and North America. The Borna virus was found in about 2% of normal people, 30% of severely depressed patients, and 13% to 14% of people with chronic brain diseases (Bode, Ferszt, & Czech, 1993; Bode, Riegel, Lange, & Ludwig, 1992; Terayama et al., 2003). However, the Borna virus also occurs in people with psychiatric diseases other than depression (Herzog et al., 1997). Evidently, it predisposes people to psychiatric difficulties in general, not specifically depression.

Antidepressant Drugs

It is logical to assume that investigators would first figure out the causes of a psychological disorder and then develop a treatment to address it. But the opposite sequence has been more common: First investigators find a drug or other treatment that seems helpful, and then they try to figure out how it works. Like many other psychiatric drugs, the early antidepressants were discovered by accident.

EXTENSIONS AND APPLICATIONS
Accidental Discoveries of Psychiatric Drugs

Nearly all of the earliest psychiatric drugs were discovered by accident. Disulfiram, for example, was originally used in the manufacture of rubber. Someone noticed that workers in a certain rubber factory avoided alcohol and traced the cause to disulfiram, which had altered the workers' metabolism so they became ill after drinking alcohol. Disulfiram became the drug Antabuse, sometimes prescribed for people who are trying to avoid alcohol.

The use of bromides to control epilepsy was originally based on a theory that was all wrong (Friedlander, 1986; Levitt, 1975). Many people in the 1800s believed that masturbation caused epilepsy and that bromides reduced sexual drive. Therefore, they reasoned, bromides should reduce epilepsy. It turns out that bromides do relieve epilepsy, but for different reasons.

Iproniazid, the first antidepressant drug, was originally marketed to treat tuberculosis, until physicians noticed that it relieved depression. Similarly, chlorpromazine, the first antipsychotic drug, was originally used for other purposes, until physicians noticed its ability to alleviate schizophrenia. For decades, researchers sought new drugs entirely by trial and error. Today, researchers evaluate new potential drugs in test tubes or tissue samples until they find one with a potential for stronger or more specific effects on neurotransmission. The result is the use of fewer laboratory animals.

Types of Antidepressants

Antidepressant drugs fall into four major categories: tricyclics, selective serotonin reuptake inhibitors, MAOIs, and atypical antidepressants (Figure 15.8). The **tricyclics** (e.g., imipramine, trade name Tofranil) operate by preventing the presynaptic neuron from reabsorbing serotonin, dopamine, or norepinephrine after releasing them; thus, the neurotransmitters remain longer in the synaptic cleft and continue stimulating the postsynaptic cell. However, the tricyclics also block histamine receptors, acetylcholine receptors, and certain sodium channels (Horst & Preskorn, 1998). As mentioned in Chapter 9, blocking histamine produces drowsiness. Blocking acetylcholine leads to dry mouth and difficulty urinating. Blocking sodium channels causes heart irregularities, among other problems. People have to limit their use of tricyclic drugs to minimize these side effects. An additional problem is that an overdose of antidepressant drugs can be fatal. Consequently, medications are risky when given to patients with suicidal tendencies.

The **selective serotonin reuptake inhibitors (SSRIs)** are similar to tricyclics but specific to the neurotransmitter serotonin. For example, fluoxetine (trade name Prozac) blocks the reuptake of serotonin. SSRIs produce only mild side effects, mainly mild nausea or headache, but sometimes also nervousness (Feighner et al., 1991). Other common SSRIs include sertraline (Zoloft), fluvoxamine (Luvox), citalopram (Celexa), and paroxetine (Paxil or Seroxat).

The **monoamine oxidase inhibitors (MAOIs)** (e.g., phenelzine, trade name Nardil) block the enzyme monoamine oxidase (MAO), a presynaptic terminal

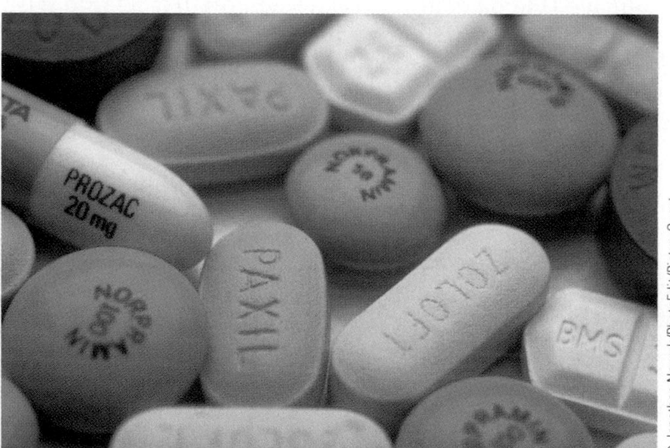

© Jonathan Nourok/PhotoEdit/PictureQuest

Figure 15.8 Antidepressant pills
Tricyclic drugs block the reuptake of catecholamines and serotonin by presynaptic terminals. Selective serotonin reuptake inhibitors, such as Prozac, have similar effects but limited to serotonin. MAOIs block an enzyme that breaks down catecholamines and serotonin.

enzyme that metabolizes catecholamines and serotonin into inactive forms. When MAOIs block this enzyme, the presynaptic terminal has more of its transmitter available for release. Generally, physicians prescribe tricyclics or SSRIs first and then try MAOIs with people who did not respond to the other drugs (Thase, Trivedi, & Rush, 1995). People taking MAOIs must avoid foods containing tyramine—including cheese, raisins, and many others—because a combination of tyramine and MAOIs increases blood pressure. Figure 15.9 summarizes the mechanisms of tricyclics, SSRIs, and MAOIs.

The **atypical antidepressants** are a miscellaneous group of drugs with antidepressant effects and mild side effects (Horst & Preskorn, 1998). One example is bupropion (Wellbutrin), which inhibits reuptake of dopamine and to some extent norepinephrine but not serotonin. Another is venlaxafine, which mostly inhibits the reuptake of serotonin and also somewhat that of norepinephrine and slightly that of dopamine. A third is nefazodone, which specifically blocks serotonin type 2A receptors and also weakly blocks reuptake of serotonin and norepinephrine.

In addition, many people use St. John's wort, an herb. Because it is marketed as a nutritional supplement instead of a drug, the U.S. Food and Drug Administration does not regulate it, and its purity varies from one bottle to another. It has the advantage of being less expensive than antidepressant drugs. An advantage or disadvantage, depending on your point of view, is that it is available without prescription. People can get it easily but often take inappropriate amounts. Apparently, it works the same way as the SSRIs. Depending on which study you believe, it is either a little more effective than SSRIs, about equal to them, or totally ineffective (Barnes, Anderson, & Phillipson, 2001; Hypericum Depression Trial Study Group, 2002). However, it has one little-known and potentially dangerous side effect: All mammals have a liver enzyme that breaks down a variety of plant toxins. St. John's wort increases the effectiveness of that enzyme. Increasing the breakdown of toxins sounds like a good thing, but the enzyme also breaks down most medicines. Therefore, taking St. John's wort decreases the effectiveness of other drugs you might be taking—including other antidepressant drugs, cancer drugs, AIDS drugs, and even birth-control pills (Moore et al., 2000).

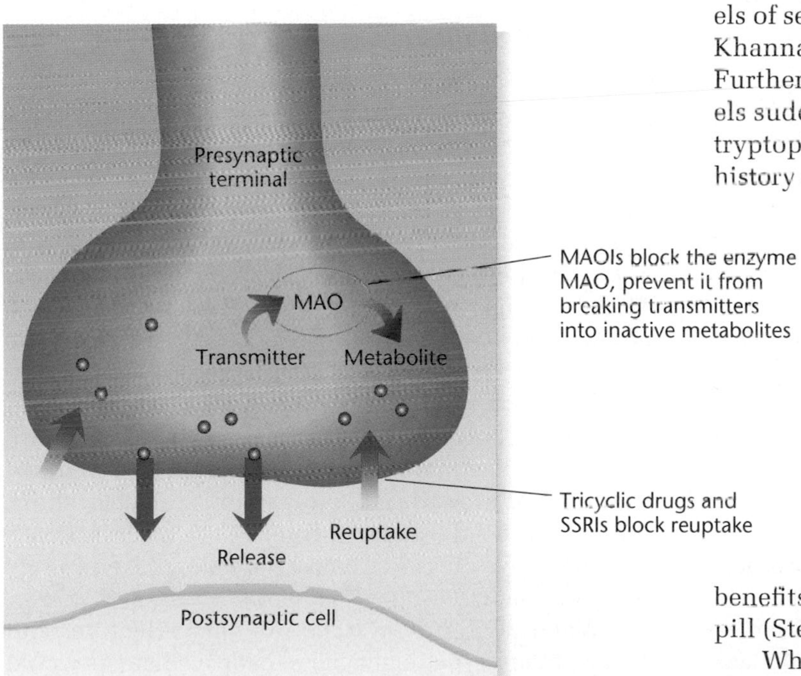

Presynaptic terminal
MAO
Transmitter
Metabolite
Release
Reuptake
Postsynaptic cell
MAOIs block the enzyme MAO, prevent it from breaking transmitters into inactive metabolites
Tricyclic drugs and SSRIs block reuptake

Figure 15.9 Routes of action of antidepressants
Tricyclics block the reuptake of dopamine, norepinephrine, or serotonin. SSRIs specifically block the reuptake of serotonin. MAOIs block the enzyme MAO, which converts dopamine, norepinephrine, or serotonin into inactive chemicals. Atypical antidepressants have varying effects.

Exactly How Do Antidepressants Work?

Given that SSRIs relieve depression by blocking reuptake of serotonin, one might assume that depression results from a lack of serotonin, with deficits in dopamine or other transmitters as well. However, the situation can't be that simple. Blood samples show normal levels of serotonin turnover in depressed patients (Reddy, Khanna, Subhash, Channabasavanna, & Rao, 1992). Furthermore, it is possible to decrease serotonin levels suddenly by consuming all the amino acids except tryptophan, the precursor to serotonin. People with a history of major depression react to that procedure with a temporary bout of depression, but other people tolerate the same decrease in serotonin without feeling depressed (Neumeister et al., 2004).

A further problem is the time course: Antidepressant drugs produce their effects on catecholamine and serotonin synapses within hours, but people need to take the drugs for weeks before they experience any mood elevation. One study found that benefits reported in less than 2 weeks are placebo effects; the patients continue reporting the benefits even if the physician substitutes an inactive pill (Stewart et al., 1998).

What happens over the 2 weeks or more before the drugs produce behavioral effects? One possibility relates to the fact that neurons in parts of the hippocampus and cerebral cortex shrink in some people with depression (Cotter, Mackay, Landau, Kerwin, & Everall, 2001). When drugs increase the release of neurotransmitters, the axons also release a neurotrophin called *brain derived neurotrophic factor* (BDNF) (Guillin et al., 2001). Recall from Chapter 5 that neurotrophins aid in survival, growth, and connections of neurons. The increased release of BDNF promotes the survival and growth of neurons in the hippocampus (Sairanen, Lucas, Ernfors, Castrén, & Castrén, 2005), and these effects may contribute to the benefits of antidepressant drugs. In animal studies, procedures that block the effects of BDNF also block the behavioral effects of the drugs (Santarelli et al., 2003).

Another delayed effect of antidepressant drugs is to desensitize the autoreceptors on the presynaptic neuron. Recall from Chapter 3 that after an axon releases neurotransmitters, some of the molecules flow out of the synapse and attach to autoreceptors on the axon, decreasing further release of the transmitter. In effect, the autoreceptors put on the "brakes." Prolonged use of antidepressant drugs desensitizes the autoreceptors. By removing the brakes, the result is to increase the release of serotonin and other neurotransmitters (Riad et al., 2004).

Still, the honest answer is that we do not know exactly how antidepressant drugs help. The immediate effects on serotonin are clear, but the effects that develop over weeks will need further research.

3. What are the effects of tricyclic drugs?
4. What are the effects of SSRIs?
5. What are the effects of MAOIs?
6. Why do the immediate effects of antidepressants at synapses not explain their effects on behavior?

Check your answers on page 469.

Other Therapies

Antidepressant drugs help many but not all people. About 50% to 60% of all patients with depression who take antidepressants show significant improvement within a few months. Although the various antidepressant drugs differ in their side effects, they differ little in the percentage of people they help. Furthermore, about 30% of patients taking a placebo drug also improve within the same time (Hollon, Thase, & Markowitz, 2002), so many of those who improve while taking drugs would have improved without them. For children and adolescents, antidepressants produce even weaker benefits and sometimes serious side effects (Jureidini et al., 2004).

An alternative to antidepressant drugs is cognitive therapy or other psychotherapy. Brain scans show that both antidepressant drugs and psychotherapy increase metabolism in the same brain areas (Brody et al., 2001; S. D. Martin et al., 2001). That similarity should not be terribly surprising if we accept the mind-body monism position. If mental activity is the same thing as brain activity, then changing someone's thoughts should indeed change brain chemistry.

Like antidepressant drugs, psychotherapy benefits 50% to 60% of all patients within a few months (Hollon et al., 2002). Of patients who receive both drugs and psychotherapy, about the same percentage improve (Thase et al., 1997). Even a program of regular, nonstrenuous exercise relieves many cases of mild depression (Leppämäki, Partonen, & Lönnqvist, 2002). Evidently, about 30% of people with depression improve without any treatment, another 20% to 30% respond well to treatment, and the rest are more challenging. The drugs have the advantages of being inexpensive and convenient; they also show benefits within 2 or 3 weeks, whereas the benefits of psychotherapy generally develop over months. However, psychotherapy has more enduring benefits. According to one report, 76% of patients who recover by taking drugs will relapse into depression within the next year, as opposed to 31% of those who recover through psychotherapy (Hollon et al., 2005).

What can anyone offer to those who respond to neither drugs nor psychotherapy? Let us consider two possibilities: electroconvulsive therapy and sleep alterations.

Electroconvulsive Therapy (ECT)

Treatment through an electrically induced seizure, known as **electroconvulsive therapy (ECT)**, has had a stormy history (Fink, 1985). It originated with the observation that for people with both epilepsy and schizophrenia, as symptoms of one disorder increase, symptoms of the other often decrease (Trimble & Thompson, 1986). In the 1930s, a Hungarian physician, Ladislas Meduna, tried to relieve schizophrenia by inducing convulsions. Soon, other physicians were doing the same, inducing seizures with a large dose of insulin. Insulin shock is a dreadful experience, however, and difficult to control. An Italian physician, Ugo Cerletti, after years of experimentation with animals, developed a method of inducing seizures with an electric shock through the head (Cerletti & Bini, 1938). Electroconvulsive therapy is quick, and most patients awaken calmly without remembering it.

When ECT proved to be not very effective with schizophrenia, you might guess that psychiatrists would abandon it. Instead, they tried it for other mental hospital patients, despite having no theoretical basis. ECT did indeed relieve depression in many cases. However, its misuse during the 1950s earned it a bad reputation, as some patients were given ECT hundreds of times without their consent.

When antidepressant drugs became available in the late 1950s, the use of ECT declined abruptly. However, it made a partial comeback in the 1970s. ECT to-

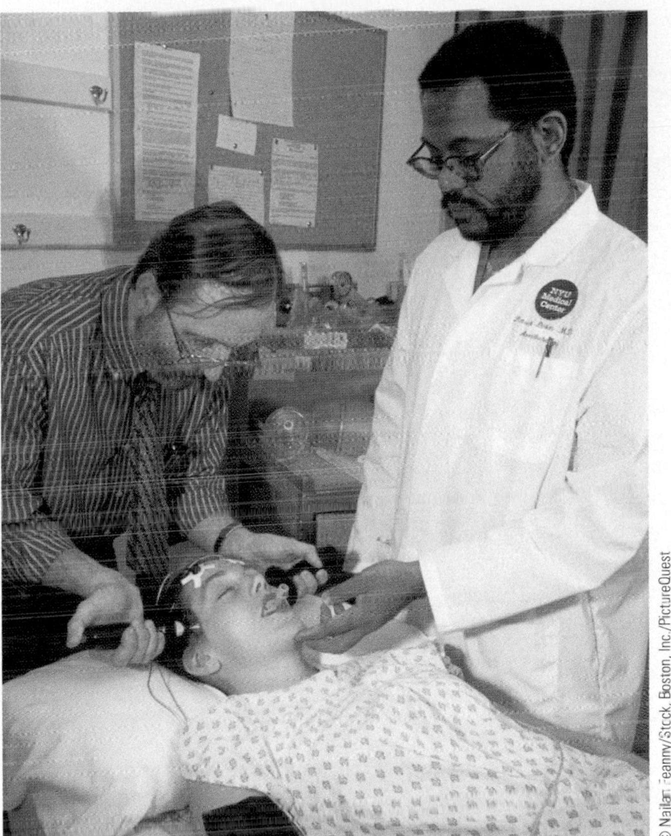

© Najlah Feanny/Stock, Boston, Inc./PictureQuest

Figure 15.10 Electroconvulsive therapy (ECT)
In contrast to an earlier era, ECT today is administered with muscle relaxants or anesthetics to minimize discomfort and only if the patient gives informed consent.

day is used only with informed consent, usually for patients who have not responded to antidepressant drugs (Scovern & Kilmann, 1980; Weiner, 1979). It is also sometimes recommended for patients with strong suicidal tendencies because it works faster than antidepressant drugs: Feeling better in 1 week instead of 2 could make the difference between life and death.

ECT is usually applied every other day for about 2 weeks, sometimes longer. Patients are given muscle relaxants or anesthetics to minimize discomfort and the possibility of injury (Figure 15.10). Because the shock is less intense than in earlier years, the risk of provoking a heart attack is low except in elderly patients.

The most common side effect of ECT is memory loss, but if physicians limit the shock to the right hemisphere, the antidepressant effects occur without memory impairment (McElhiney et al., 1995). (Recall that right-hemisphere activity is more associated with unpleasant mood.)

Besides the threat of memory loss, the other serious drawback to ECT is the high risk of relapsing into another episode of depression within a few months (Riddle & Scott, 1995). After ECT has relieved depression, the usual strategy is to try to prevent a relapse by means of drugs, psychotherapy, or periodic ECT treatments (Swoboda, Conca, König, Waanders, & Hansen, 2001).

More than half a century after the introduction of ECT, no one is yet sure how it relieves depression. A study in rats showed that it alters the expression of at least 120 genes in the hippocampus and frontal cortex alone. Some of the biggest effects pertained to genes related to neurotrophins, arachidonic acid, generation of new neurons, and responsiveness to exercise (Altar et al., 2004). Each of those pathways is known to have strong links to depression.

A similar treatment is repetitive transcranial magnetic stimulation. An intense magnetic field is applied to the scalp, stimulating the neurons just below the magnet. This procedure resembles ECT both in its level of effectiveness and in the fact that no one knows why it is effective (George et al., 1997).

Altered Sleep Patterns

Most people who are depressed report sleep problems, and people with sleep problems are more likely than others to become depressed (Ford & Cooper-Patrick, 2001). Most people with depression have sleep patterns resembling those of healthy people who have gone to bed later than usual: They fall asleep but awaken early, unable to get back to sleep. They also enter REM sleep within 45 minutes after going to sleep, as Figure 15.11 illustrates. Healthy people do so also if they go to bed later than usual. In addition, people who are depressed have more than the average number of eye movements per minute during REM sleep. Many of their relatives show these same sleep patterns, and the relatives who show these patterns are more likely to become depressed themselves than are relatives who sleep normally (Modell, Ising, Holsboer, & Lauer, 2005). In short, altered sleep is a lifelong trait of people who are predisposed to depression.

Surprisingly, although a sleepless night annoys most people, a night of total sleep deprivation is the quickest known method of relieving depression (Ringel & Szuba, 2001). Unfortunately, about half of the people who experience this relief become depressed again after the next night's sleep. It is possible to extend the benefits by altering the sleep schedule on subsequent days. For example, go without sleep altogether for one day and then start a schedule of sleeping from 5 P.M. until midnight instead of the usual time. This schedule relieves depression for at least a week in most patients and often longer (Riemann et al., 1999). Combining sleep alteration with drug therapies can provide long-lasting benefits (Wirz-Justice & Van den Hoofdakker, 1999).

Researchers cannot yet explain how sleep deprivation or rescheduling produces mood benefits. A better understanding might lead to other treatments for depression.

Figure 15.11 Circadian rhythms and depression
If people who are not depressed go to bed at their normal time, they get much stage 4 sleep for the first few hours and increasing amounts of REM sleep later in the night. Most people with depression have their circadian rhythms advanced by several hours; they sleep as someone else would at a later time. *(Source: Illustration of sleep patterns of normal and depressed people from Sleep by J. Allan Hobson, © 1989, 1995 by J. Allan Hobson. Reprinted by permission of Henry Holt and Company, LLC.)*

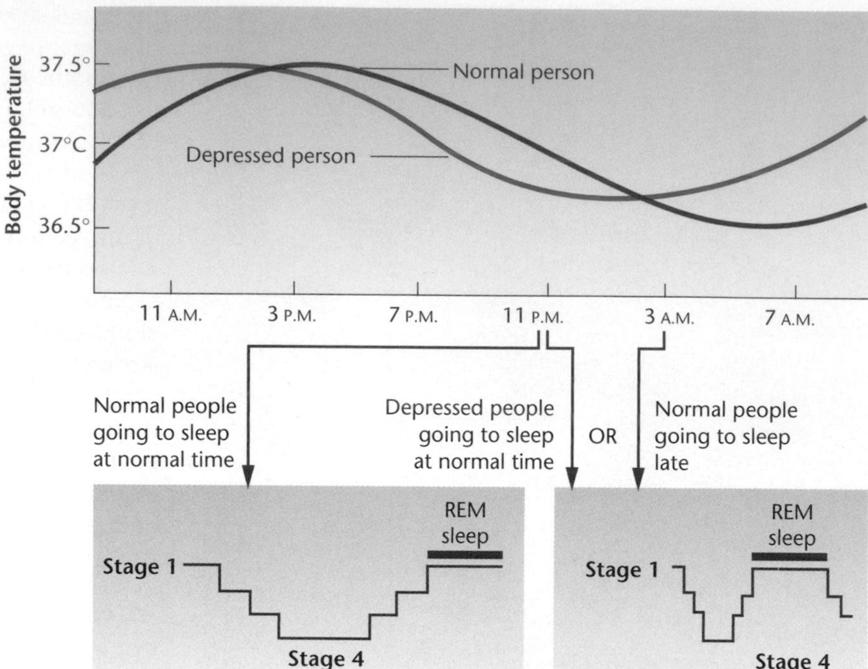

STOP & CHECK

7. For what kinds of patients is ECT recommended?
8. What change in sleep habits sometimes relieves depression?

Check your answers on page 469.

Bipolar Disorder

Depression can be either unipolar or bipolar. People with **unipolar disorder** vary between normality and one pole—depression. People with **bipolar disorder**—formerly known as **manic-depressive disorder**—alternate between two poles—depression and its opposite, mania. **Mania** is characterized by restless activity, excitement, laughter, self-confidence, rambling speech, and loss of inhibitions. Some manic people are dangerous to themselves and others. Figure 15.12 shows the brain's increase in glucose use during mania and its decrease during depression (Baxter et al., 1985).

People who have full-blown episodes of mania are said to have **bipolar I disorder.** People with **bipolar II disorder** have much milder manic phases, called hypomania, which are characterized mostly by agitation or anxiety. About 1% of people have at least a mild case of bipolar disorder at some time in life, with an average age of onset in the early 20s (Craddock & Jones, 1999). In addition to the mood swings, most people with bipolar disorder have attention deficits, poor impulse control, and impairments of verbal memory (Quraishi & Frangou, 2002).

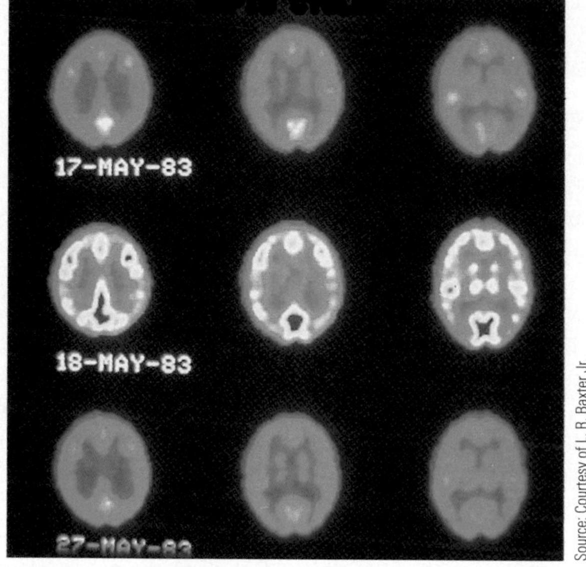

Figure 15.12 PET scans for a patient with bipolar disorder
Horizontal planes through three levels of the brain are shown for each day. On May 17 and May 27, when the patient was depressed, brain metabolic rates were low. On May 18, when the patient was in a cheerful, hypomanic mood, the brain metabolic rate was high. Red indicates the highest metabolic rate, followed by yellow, green, and blue. *(Source: Reprinted with permission from "A functional neuroanatomy of hallucinations in schizophrenia," by L. R. Baxter, Nature 378, 176–179. Copyright 1995 Nature Publishing Group.)*

Genetics

Several lines of evidence suggest a hereditary basis for bipolar disorder (Craddock & Jones, 1999). If one monozygotic twin has bipolar disorder, the other has at least a 50% chance of getting it also, whereas dizygotic twins, brothers, sisters, or children have about a 5% to 10% probability. Adopted children who develop bipolar disorder are likely to have biological relatives with mood disorders. Comparisons of chromosomes have identified several genes that are somewhat more common than average among people with bipolar disorder (e.g., Neves-Pereira et al., 2002). However, each of these genes merely increases the risk; no gene is strongly linked to bipolar disorder.

Treatments

The first successful treatment for bipolar disorder, and still a common one, is **lithium** salts. Lithium's benefits were discovered accidentally by an Australian investigator, J. F. Cade, who believed uric acid might relieve mania and depression. Cade mixed uric acid (a component of urine) with a lithium salt to help it dissolve and then gave the solution to patients. It was indeed helpful, although investigators eventually realized that lithium was the effective agent, not uric acid.

Lithium stabilizes mood, preventing a relapse into either mania or depression. The dose must be regulated carefully, as a low dose is ineffective and a high dose is toxic (Schou, 1997). Two other effective drugs are valproate (trade names Depakene, Depakote, and others) and carbamazepine. Valproate and carbamazepine, originally marketed for the treatment of epilepsy, are often recommended for patients with bipolar II disorder, characterized by mild manic phases. Lithium appears to be more effective for people with bipolar I disorder (Kleindienst & Greil, 2000).

Lithium, valproate, and carbamazepine have many effects on the brain. A good research strategy is to assume that they relieve bipolar disorder because of some effect they have in common. For example, valproate and carbamazepine increase activity at GABA synapses but lithium does not, so that effect is presumably not critical. Valproate promotes the growth of axons and dendrites; the other drugs have not been tested in this regard (Hao et al., 2004). In contrast, all three drugs block the synthesis of a brain chemical called *arachidonic acid,* which is produced during brain inflammation (Rapoport & Bosetti, 2002). The effects of arachidonic acid are also counteracted by polyunsaturated fatty acids, such as those in seafood, and epidemiological studies suggest that people who eat at least a pound (0.45 kg) of seafood per week have a decreased risk of bipolar disorder (Noaghiul & Hibbeln, 2003).

Another treatment is still in the experimental stage: In one research study, patients with bipolar disorder were tested with a kind of MRI, called echo-planar magnetic resonance spectroscopic imaging, that generates weak electromagnetic fields throughout the head. Several patients spontaneously reported feeling better after the research, and later studies found that most patients with bipolar disorder experience mood benefits at least temporarily and sometimes for days (Rohan et al., 2004).

A further treatment deserves more attention: Patients with bipolar disorder during the depressed phase tend to go to bed late and stay in bed for many hours. During the manic phase, they go to bed early but awaken quickly, sleeping perhaps only 3 or 4 hours. Researchers had one patient with bipolar disorder keep a consistent sleeping schedule in a dark, quiet room. That procedure greatly reduced the intensity of his mood swings (Wehr et al., 1998). The researchers speculate that the artificial lights, television, and other technology of our society tempt us to stay up late at night and thereby increase the prevalence of bipolar disorder.

9. What are two common treatments for bipolar disorder?

10. What food should be recommended for patients with bipolar disorder and why?

Check your answers on page 469.

Seasonal Affective Disorder

Another form of depression is **seasonal affective disorder (SAD),** which is depression that regularly recurs during a particular season, such as winter. SAD is most prevalent near the poles, where the winter nights are long (Haggarty et al., 2002), less common in moderate climates, and unheard of in the tropics. Most people feel happier and more active during the summer, when there are many hours of sunlight, than during winter (Madden, Heath, Rosenthal, & Martin, 1996). SAD exaggerates this common tendency.

SAD differs from other types of depression in many ways; for example, patients with SAD have phase-delayed sleep and temperature rhythms—becoming sleepy and wakeful a bit later than normal—unlike most other patients with depression, whose rhythms are phase-advanced (Teicher et al., 1997) (Figure 15.13). Also SAD is seldom as severe as major depression.

It is possible to treat SAD with very bright lights (e.g., 2,500 lux) for an hour or more each day. The bright light treatment is effective in morning, afternoon, or

Figure 15.13 Circadian rhythms for normal, depressed, and SAD people
Patients with SAD are phase-delayed while most other patients with depression are phase-advanced.

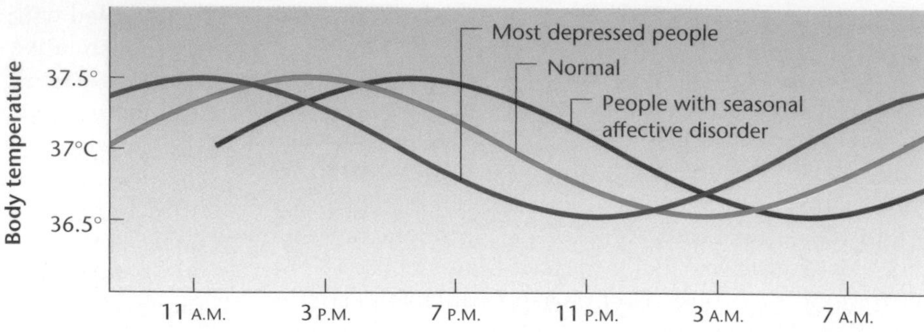

evening (Eastman, Young, Fogg, Liu, & Meaden, 1998; Lewy et al., 1998; Terman, Terman, & Ross, 1998). The most likely explanations are that bright light affects serotonin synapses and alters circadian rhythms. Regardless of how it works, it produces substantial benefits. Many therapists recommend bright light therapy for nonseasonal depression as well. Research on that possibility has been sparse—possibly because drug companies are not interested in sponsoring it—but so far, the results indicate that bright light relieves depression at least as well as drugs or psychotherapy and possibly better. Bright light is less expensive than the other therapies and produces its benefits more rapidly, often within 1 week (Kripke, 1998). Combining bright light with another form of therapy magnifies the benefits (Kripke, 1998; Loving, Kripke, & Shuchter, 2002).

The following website provides much information about light therapy and biological rhythms: **http://www.sltbr.org/**

STOP & CHECK

11. What are the advantages of light treatment compared to antidepressant drugs?

Check your answer on page 469.

Module 15.2

In Closing: The Biology of Mood Swings

Do you feel sad because of events that have happened to you or because of your brain chemistry? According to biological psychologists, that is a meaningless question. Your experiences *are* changes in your brain state; you cannot have one without the other. The better question is: Are some people more likely than others to become depressed because of a preexisting condition in their brain structure or chemistry? The answer to that one is "probably." It is difficult to get from "probably" to "definitely" because it is difficult to do research on human moods. At each stage in life, brain structure and chemistry alter one's reactions to events, and events in turn alter the brain, affecting the reaction to the next event. Studying an adult brain has the same challenge as watching only a few minutes in the middle of a complex movie and trying to guess how events led up to that point.

Summary

1. People with major depression find that almost nothing makes them happy. Depression occurs as a series of episodes. (p. 459)
2. Depression shows a strong family tendency, especially for relatives of women with early-onset depression. (p. 460)
3. One gene has been shown to increase the probability of depression only among people who have had stressful experiences. (p. 460)
4. Depression is associated with decreased activity in the left hemisphere of the cortex. (p. 461)
5. Four kinds of antidepressant drugs are in wide use. Tricyclics block reuptake of serotonin and catecholamines but produce strong side effects. SSRIs block reuptake of serotonin. MAOIs block an enzyme that breaks down catecholamines and serotonin. Atypical antidepressants are a miscellaneous group with diverse effects. (p. 462)
6. The antidepressants alter synaptic activity quickly, but their effects on behavior build up over weeks. (p. 463)
7. The behavioral effects of antidepressant drugs probably depend on two slow changes in the brain. The drugs increase the release of BDNF, which promotes neuron growth and survival. They also desensitize autoreceptors and thereby increase release of neurotransmitters. (p. 463)
8. Other therapies for depression include psychotherapy, electroconvulsive therapy, and altered sleep patterns. (p. 464)

9. People with bipolar disorder alternate between depression and mania. Bipolar disorder has a probable genetic basis. Effective therapies include lithium salts and certain anticonvulsant drugs. (p. 466)
10. Seasonal affective disorder is marked by recurrent depression during one season of the year. Exposure to bright lights is usually effective in treating it and can help people with other kinds of depression also. (p. 467)

Answers to STOP & CHECK Questions

1. People with the short form of the gene are more likely than other people to react to stressful experiences by becoming depressed. However, in the absence of stressful experiences, their probability is not increased. (p. 460)
2. People with predominant right-hemisphere activity and decreased left-hemisphere activity tend to become depressed. (p. 461)
3. Tricyclic drugs block reuptake of serotonin and catecholamines. They also block histamine receptors, acetylcholine receptors, and certain sodium channels, thereby producing unpleasant side effects. (p. 464)
4. SSRIs selectively inhibit the reuptake of serotonin. (p. 464)
5. MAOIs block the enzyme MAO, which breaks down catecholamines and serotonin. The result is increased availability of these transmitters. (p. 464)
6. The antidepressants produce their known effects on the synapses quickly, but their behavioral benefits develop gradually over 2 to 3 weeks. (p. 464)
7. ECT is recommended for depressed people who did not respond to other therapies and for those who are an immediate suicide risk (because ECT acts faster than other therapies). (p. 466)
8. Getting people with depression to go to bed earlier sometimes relieves depression. (p. 466)
9. The common treatments for bipolar disorder are lithium salts and certain anticonvulsant drugs. (p. 467)
10. Patients with bipolar disorder probably should eat at least a pound of seafood per week to get the polyunsaturated fatty acids that combat arachidonic acid. (p. 467)
11. Light therapy is cheaper, has no side effects, and produces its benefits more quickly. (p. 468)

Thought Question

Some people have suggested that ECT relieves depression by causing people to forget the events that caused it. What evidence opposes this hypothesis?

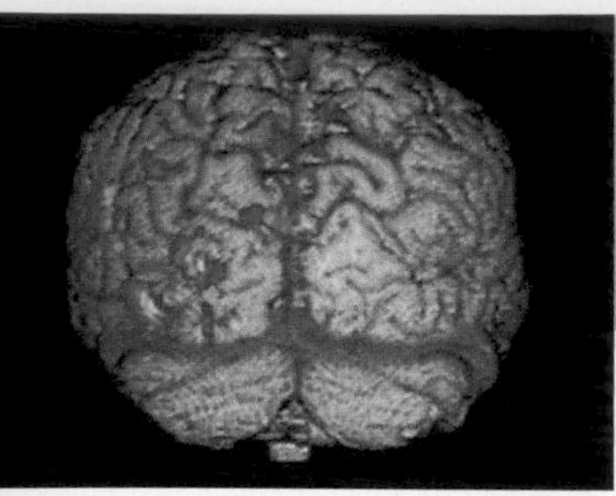

Module 15.3
Schizophrenia

Here is a conversation between two people diagnosed with schizophrenia (Haley, 1959, p. 321):

A: Do you work at the air base?

B: You know what I think of work. I'm 33 in June, do you mind?

A: June?

B: 33 years old in June. This stuff goes out the window after I live this, uh—leave this hospital. So I can't get my vocal cords back. So I lay off cigarettes. I'm in a spatial condition, from outer space myself . . . .

A: I'm a real spaceship from across.

B: A lot of people talk that way, like crazy, but "Believe It or Not," by Ripley, take it or leave it—alone—it's in the *Examiner,* it's in the comic section, "Believe It or Not," by Ripley, Robert E. Ripley, Believe it or not, but we don't have to believe anything, unless I feel like it. Every little rosette—too much alone.

A: Yeah, it could be possible.

B: I'm a civilian seaman.

A: Could be possible. I takę my bath in the ocean.

B: Bathing stinks. You know why? 'Cause you can't quit when you feel like it. You're in the service.

People with schizophrenia say and do things that other people (including other people with schizophrenia) find difficult to understand. The causes of the disorder are not well understood, but they apparently include a large biological component.

Characteristics

According to the *DSM-IV,* **schizophrenia** is a disorder characterized by deteriorating ability to function in everyday life and by some combination of hallucinations, delusions, thought disorder, movement disorder, and inappropriate emotional expressions (American Psychiatric Association, 1994). The symptoms vary greatly. Hallucinations and delusions are prominent for some; thought disorders are dominant for others; some have clear signs of brain damage, but others do not. In short, you could easily find several people diagnosed with schizophrenia who have almost nothing in common (Andreasen, 1999). Schizophrenia can be either acute or chronic. An **acute** condition has a sudden onset and good prospects for recovery. A **chronic** condition has a gradual onset and a long-term course.

Schizophrenia was originally called *dementia praecox,* which is Latin for "premature mental deterioration." In 1911, Eugen Bleuler introduced the term *schizophrenia.* Although the term is Greek for "split mind," it is *not* related to *dissociative identity disorder* (previously known as *multiple personality),* in which someone alternates among different personalities. What Bleuler meant by *schizophrenia* was a split between the emotional and intellectual aspects of experience: The person's emotional expression or lack of it seems unconnected with current experiences. For example, someone might giggle or cry for no apparent reason or show no reaction to bad news. Not all patients show this detachment of emotion from intellect, but the term lives on.

This website provides a good source of information on many aspects of schizophrenia: **http://www.schizophrenia.com/**

Behavioral Symptoms

Schizophrenia is characterized by **positive symptoms** (behaviors that are present that should be absent) and **negative symptoms** (behaviors that are absent that should be present). Negative symptoms include weak social interactions, emotional expression, speech, and working memory. Negative symptoms are usually stable over time and difficult to treat. Positive symptoms fall into two clusters: psychotic and disorganized (Andreasen, Arndt, Alliger, Miller, & Flaum, 1995). The *psychotic* cluster consists of **delusions** (unfounded beliefs, such as the conviction that one is being persecuted or that outer space aliens are trying to control one's behavior) and **hallucinations** (abnormal sensory experiences, such as hearing voices when one is alone). PET scans have determined that hallucinations occur during periods of increased activity in the thalamus, hippocampus, and parts of the cortex, including many of the areas activated by actual hearing (Shergill, Brammer, Williams, Murray, & McGuire, 2000; Silbersweig et al., 1995).

The *disorganized* cluster of positive symptoms consists of inappropriate emotional displays, bizarre behaviors, and thought disorder. The most typical **thought disorder** of schizophrenia is a difficulty understanding and using abstract concepts. Related symptoms include deficits in attention and working memory. Most people with schizophrenia show serious impairments on a task where they have to remember to choose, say, ♣ over ■, ■ over ⌘, but ⌘ over ♣ (Hanlon et al., 2005). (It is analogous to the children's game "Rock-Paper-Scissors," where scissors cut paper, paper covers rock, but rock breaks scissors.) The fact that this task is known to depend on the hippocampus suggests a link between schizophrenia and dysfunction of the hippocampus.

Which of the various symptoms, if any, is the primary problem? According to Nancy Andreasen (1999), a leading investigator of schizophrenia (see photo and quote on pages inside the back cover), the main problem is disordered thoughts, which result from abnormal interactions between the cortex and the thalamus and cerebellum. The disordered thinking may lead to the hallucinations, delusions, and other symptoms.

EXTENSIONS AND APPLICATIONS

Differential Diagnosis of Schizophrenia

Suppose you're a psychiatrist and you meet a patient who has recently deteriorated in everyday functioning and has hallucinations, delusions, thought disorder, and disorganized speech. You are ready to enter a diagnosis of schizophrenia and begin treatment, right?

Not so fast. First you should make a **differential diagnosis,** ruling out other conditions that might produce similar symptoms. Here are a few conditions that sometimes resemble schizophrenia:

- *Mood disorder with psychotic features:* People with depression frequently have delusions, especially delusions of guilt or failure. Some report hallucinations also.
- *Substance abuse:* Many of the positive symptoms of schizophrenia can develop from prolonged use of amphetamine, methamphetamine, cocaine, LSD, or phencyclidine ("angel dust"). Someone who stops taking the drugs is likely, though not certain, to recover from these symptoms. Substance abuse is more likely than schizophrenia to produce visual hallucinations.
- *Brain damage:* Lesions to the temporal or prefrontal cortex, or tumors there, can produce symptoms resembling schizophrenia.
- *Undetected hearing deficits:* Sometimes someone who is starting to have trouble hearing thinks that everyone else is whispering and starts to worry, "They're whispering about me!" Delusions of persecution can develop.
- *Huntington's disease:* The symptoms of Huntington's disease include hallucinations, delusions, and disordered thinking, as well as motor symptoms. A rare type of schizophrenia, *catatonic schizophrenia,* includes motor abnormalities, so a mixture of psychological and motor symptoms could represent either schizophrenia or Huntington's disease.
- *Nutritional abnormalities:* Niacin deficiency can produce hallucinations and delusions (Hoffer, 1973); so can deficiency of vitamin C or an allergy to milk proteins (not the same as lactose intolerance). Some people who cannot tolerate wheat gluten or other proteins react with hallucinations and delusions (Reichelt, Seim, & Reichelt, 1996).

Demographic Data

About 1% of people suffer from schizophrenia at any given time (Narrow et al., 2002). The estimate rises or falls depending on whether we include mild or only severe cases. Since the mid-1900s, the reported prevalence of schizophrenia has been declining in many countries (Suvisaari, Haukka, Tanskanen, & Lönnqvist, 1999; Torrey & Miller, 2001). Has schizophrenia actually become less common, or are psychiatrists just diagnosing it differently? No one knows, and this is not an easy question to answer. However, even when it is diagnosed today, it appears to be less severe than it often used to be. Perhaps our society is doing something to prevent schizophrenia, even though we don't know what it is.

Schizophrenia occurs in all ethnic groups and all parts of the world, although it is 10 to 100 times more common in the United States and Europe than in most Third World countries (Torrey, 1986). Part of that discrepancy could be due to differences in recordkeeping, but other possibilities exist. Lifetime prevalence of schizophrenia is more common for men than women by a ratio of about 7 to 5. On the average, it is also more severe in men and has an earlier onset—usually in the early 20s for men and the late 20s for women (Aleman, Kahn, & Selten, 2003).

One more little unexplained oddity: The older a father is at the time of a baby's birth, the greater the risk of schizophrenia in that baby (Byrne, Agerbo, Ewald, Eaton, & Mortensen, 2003; Malaspina et al., 2001). The age of the mother is apparently unimportant. One hypothesis is that older fathers have more mutations in their genes, but the evidence for this explanation is not strong.

1. Why are hallucinations considered a "positive symptom"?
2. Has the reported prevalence of schizophrenia been increasing, decreasing, or staying the same?

Check your answers on page 481.

Genetics

Huntington's disease (Chapter 8) can be called a genetic disease: Almost everyone with Huntington's disease has an abnormality in the same gene, and anyone with that abnormal gene will get Huntington's disease. At one time, many researchers believed that schizophrenia might be a genetic disease in the same sense. However, accumulating evidence indicates that schizophrenia is not a one-gene disorder.

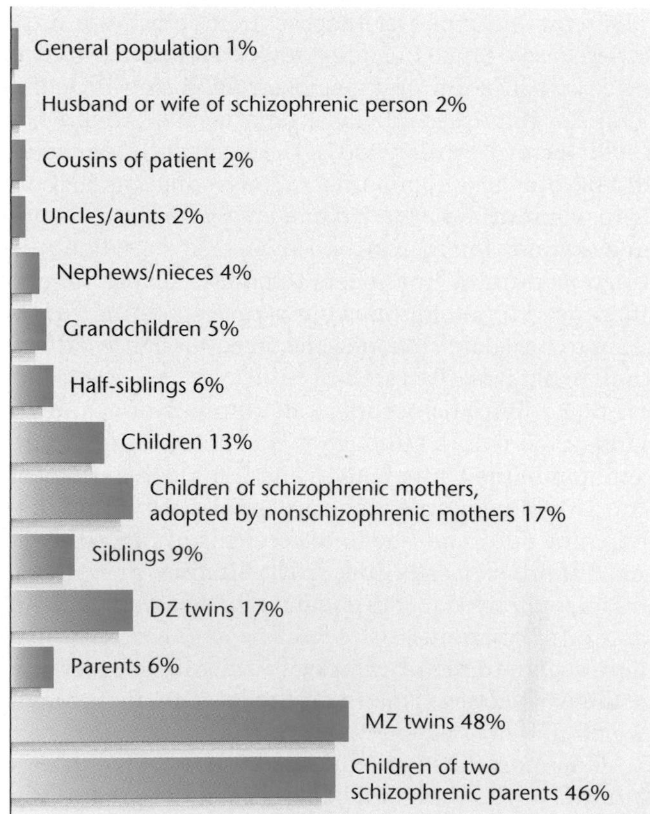

Figure 15.14 Probabilities of developing schizophrenia
People with a closer genetic relationship to someone with schizophrenia have a higher probability of developing it themselves. *(Source: Based on data from Gottesman, 1991)*

Twin Studies

The more closely you are biologically related to someone with schizophrenia, the greater your own probability of schizophrenia, as shown in Figure 15.14 (Gottesman, 1991). One of the most important points in Figure 15.14, confirmed by other studies (Cardno et al., 1999), is that monozygotic twins have a much higher **concordance** (agreement) for schizophrenia than do dizygotic twins. Furthermore, twin pairs who are really monozygotic, but thought they weren't, are more concordant than twin pairs who thought they were, but really aren't (Kendler, 1983). That is, *being* monozygotic is more critical than *being treated as* monozygotic.

The high concordance for monozygotic twins has long been taken as strong evidence for a genetic influence. However, note two limitations:

- Monozygotic twins have only about 50% concordance, not 100%. Monozygotic twins could differ because a gene is activated in one individual and suppressed in another (Tsujita et al., 1998), or they could differ because of some environmental influence.
- In Figure 15.14, note the greater similarity between dizygotic twins than between siblings. Dizygotic twins have the same genetic resemblance as siblings but greater environmental similarity, including that of prenatal and early postnatal life.

Adopted Children Who Develop Schizophrenia

When an adopted child develops schizophrenia, it is more common among his or her biological relatives than adopting relatives. One Danish study found schizophrenia in 12.5% of the immediate biological relatives and none of the adopting relatives (Kety et al., 1994). Note in Figure 15.14 that children of a schizophrenic mother have a moderately high probability of schizophrenia, even if adopted by nonschizophrenic parents.

These results suggest a genetic basis, but they are also consistent with a prenatal influence. Consider a pregnant woman with schizophrenia. True, she passes her genes to her child, but she also provides the prenatal environment, which may be less than healthy. Many women with schizophrenia have poor nutrition, smoke and drink heavily, and fail to get medical care during pregnancy. If their children develop schizophrenia, we cannot be sure that the influence is genetic.

Efforts to Locate a Gene

There are reasons for skepticism about a strong role for genetics. One of the biggest is that people with schizophrenia tend to die younger than other people and tend to have fewer children than average. Furthermore, their brothers and sisters have no more children than average, so natural selection should be decreasing the prevalence of the responsible genes (Haukka, Suvisaari, & Lönnqvist, 2003).

The strongest evidence for a genetic influence would be to locate a gene that is consistently linked with schizophrenia. Recall from earlier chapters that researchers have located a gene that is strongly linked with Huntington's disease and genes linked with the early-onset forms of Parkinson's and Alzheimer's diseases. Researchers have also identified a genetic basis for childhood-onset schizophrenia (Burgess et al., 1998). However, childhood-onset schizophrenia is uncommon and differs in several regards from the more common, adult-onset variety (Nopoulos, Giedd, Andreasen, & Rapoport, 1998; Rapoport et al., 1999; P. M. Thompson et al., 2001).

Attempts to link adult-onset schizophrenia to an identified gene have produced many hard-to-replicate or unimpressive results. For example, one study found a gene that was present in 70% of schizophrenic patients and 60% of other people (Saleem et al., 2001). If we assume that 1% of the population has schizophrenia, the math works out that someone without this gene has a 0.7% risk of schizophrenia and someone with the gene has a 1.2% risk.

If schizophrenia has a strong genetic influence, but we cannot locate a gene responsible for it, one possibility is that it depends on different genes in different families. Another possibility is that it depends on a combination of genes, such that no one gene by itself has a big effect. For example, one gene of interest is *DISC1* (for "disrupted in schizophrenia 1"). One form of this gene alters the structure and decreases the gray matter of the hippocampus (Calicott et al., 2005). However, not everyone with the disrupted form of that gene develops schizophrenia. Researchers have found that it interacts with another gene (*PDE4B*), and they surmise that people with disrupted forms of both genes would be at the highest risk of schizophrenia (Millar et al., 2005).

Another promising study identified a gene linked to high levels of negative symptoms of schizophrenia (Fanous et al., 2005). Perhaps in the past, researchers have made a mistake by seeking a gene responsible for schizophrenia in general. The search might be more fruitful if we concentrate on particular symptoms or types of schizophrenia.

Another possibility is that some cases of schizophrenia result from environmental influences instead of, or in addition to, genetics. The greater the influence of environmental factors, the harder it will be to locate specific genes responsible for schizophrenia.

3. The concordance for schizophrenia is greater for dizygotic twins than for siblings. What is a likely explanation?
4. The fact that adopted children who develop schizophrenia usually have biological relatives with schizophrenia implies a probable genetic basis. What other interpretation is possible?

Check your answers on page 481.

The Neurodevelopmental Hypothesis

According to the **neurodevelopmental hypothesis** now popular among researchers, schizophrenia is based on abnormalities in the prenatal (before birth) or neonatal (newborn) development of the nervous system, which lead to subtle abnormalities of brain anatomy and major abnormalities in behavior (Weinberger, 1996). The abnormalities could result from genetics, difficulties during pregnancy or birth, or a combination of both kinds of influences. The hypothesis holds that stressful experiences later in life aggravate the symptoms but do not cause schizophrenia.

The supporting evidence is that (a) several kinds of prenatal or neonatal difficulties are linked to later schizophrenia; (b) people with schizophrenia have minor brain abnormalities that apparently originate early in life; and (c) it is plausible that abnormalities of early development could impair behavior in adulthood.

Prenatal and Neonatal Environment

The risk of schizophrenia is elevated among people who had problems that could have affected their brain development, including poor nutrition of the mother during pregnancy, premature birth, low birth weight, and complications during delivery, such as excessive bleeding. However, each of these influences has only a small effect on schizophrenia (Cannon, Jones, & Murray, 2002). Schizophrenia has also been linked to head injuries in early childhood (AbdelMalik, Husted, Chow, & Bassett, 2003), although we do not know whether the head injuries led to schizophrenia or early symptoms of schizophrenia increased the risk of head injuries.

If a mother is Rh-negative and her baby is Rh-positive, a small amount of the baby's Rh-positive blood factor may leak into the mother's blood supply, triggering immunological rejection. The response is weak with the woman's first Rh-positive baby but stronger in later pregnancies, and it is more intense with boy than girl babies. Second- and later-born boy babies with Rh incompatibility have an increased risk of hearing deficits, mental retardation, and several other problems, and about twice the usual probability of schizophrenia (Hollister, Laing, & Mednick, 1996).

An implication of prenatal difficulties also stems from the **season-of-birth effect:** the tendency for people born in winter to have a slightly (5% to 8%) greater probability of developing schizophrenia than people born at other times of the year. This tendency is particularly pronounced in latitudes far from the equator (Davies, Welham, Chant, Torrey, & McGrath, 2003; Torrey, Miller, et al., 1997).

What might account for the season-of-birth effect? One possibility is complications of delivery or early nutrition. Another is viral infection. Influenza and other viral epidemics are most common in the fall. Therefore, the reasoning goes, many pregnant women become infected in the fall with a virus that impairs a crucial stage of brain development in a baby who will be born in the winter. A virus that affects the mother does not cross the placenta into the fetus's brain, but the mother's cytokines do cross, and excessive cytokines can impair brain development (Zuckerman, Rehavi, Nachman, & Weiner, 2003). The mother's infection also causes a fever, which can damage the fetal brain. A fever of just 38.5°C (101°F) slows the division of fetal neurons (Laburn, 1996). (Exercise during pregnancy does *not* overheat the abdomen and is not dangerous to the fetus. Hot baths and saunas are risky, however.) When mice are infected with influenza during pregnancy, their offspring develop a number of behavioral abnormalities, including deficient exploration and deficient social reactions to other mice (Shi, Fatemi, Sidwell, & Patterson, 2003).

To test the role of prenatal infection, it would be best to examine which mothers had infections and at which stage of pregnancy and then relate those data to the eventual psychiatric outcome of their children. No one keeps good records of individual cases of influenza. However, researchers examined the records of tens of thousands of people in Scotland, England, and Denmark over several decades. They found increased schizophrenia rates among people born 2 to 3 months after major influenza epidemics, such as the one in the autumn of 1957 (Adams, Kendell, Hare, & Munk-Jørgensen, 1993). Other studies retrieved blood samples that hospitals had taken from pregnant women and stored for decades. The researchers found increased probability of influenza virus, and increased levels of immune system proteins, among the mothers whose children eventually developed schizophrenia (A. S. Brown et al., 2004; Buka et al., 2001). Another study examined mothers who had rubella (German measles) during pregnancy and found that 11 of 53 of their children developed schizophrenia or related disorders (A. S. Brown et al., 2001).

Another kind of infection is a parasite, *Toxoplasma gondii.* This parasite reproduces only in cats, but other animals including humans can be infected. If it infects the brain of an infant or child, it can impair brain development and lead to memory disorder, hallucinations, and delusions (Torrey & Yolken, 2005). According to a survey of mothers, people who developed schizophrenia in adulthood were more likely than other people to have had a pet cat in childhood (Torrey, Rawlings, & Yolken, 2000). Also, blood tests found antibodies to the Toxoplasma parasite in a much higher percentage of people with schizophrenia than in the general population (Leweke et al., 2004; Yolken et al., 2001).

In short, some cases of schizophrenia may develop as a result of infections with viruses or parasites. This mechanism is an alternative or supplement to genetics and other influences.

Mild Brain Abnormalities

In accord with the neurodevelopmental hypothesis, some (though not all) people with schizophrenia show mild abnormalities of brain anatomy. The abnormalities are small; they vary from person to person; and the results depend on age, symptoms, and so forth. Consequently, although many studies report brain abnormalities in schizophrenia, they disagree about the location of those abnormalities. Figure 15.15 summarizes 15 studies, including a total of 390 people with schizophrenia. Brain areas marked in yellow showed decreased volume in the most studies; those in various shades of red showed decreases in fewer studies;

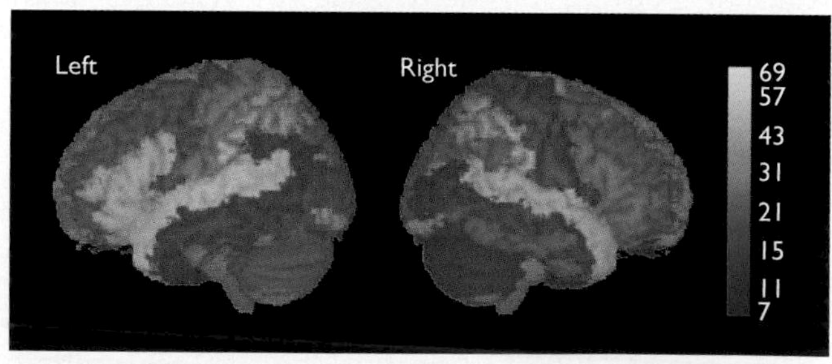

Figure 15.15 Cortical areas showing decreased volume in patients with schizophrenia
Areas marked in yellow showed decreased volume in the largest percentage of studies; those in various shades of red showed decreases in fewer studies. *(Source: From "Regional deficits in brain volume in schizophrenia: A meta-analysis of voxel-based morphometry studies," by R. Honea, T. J. Crow, D. Passingham, and C. E. Mackay,* American Journal of Psychiatry, 162, 2005. *Reprinted with permission from the American Journal of Psychiatry, Copyright (2005). American Psychiatric Association)*

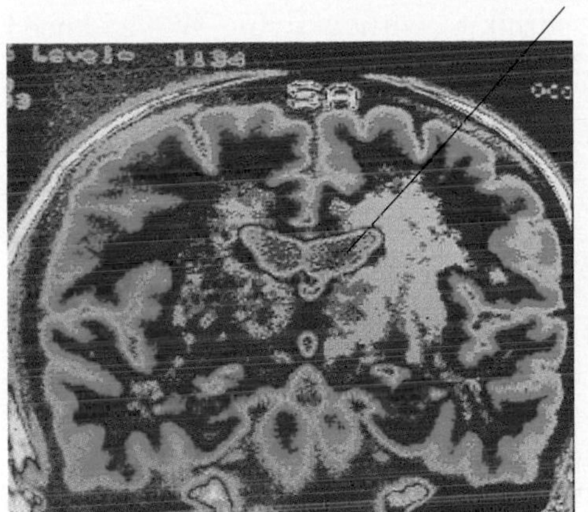

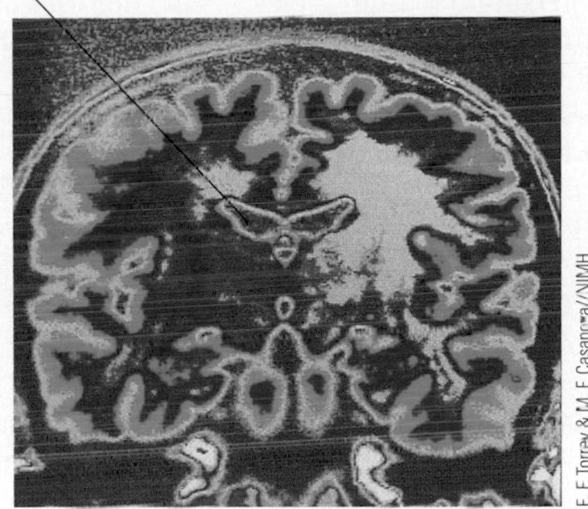

Figure 15.16 Coronal sections for identical twins The twin on the left has schizophrenia; the twin on the right does not. The ventricles (near the center of each brain) are larger in the twin with schizophrenia

and those in gray appeared normal in all studies (Honea, Crow, Passingham, & Mackay, 2005). Note that the strongest deficits were in the left temporal and frontal areas of the cortex. Note also that most cortical areas showed mild abnormalities in at least one or two studies.

Furthermore, the ventricles (fluid-filled spaces within the brain) are larger than normal in people with schizophrenia (Wolkin et al., 1998; Wright et al., 2000) (Figure 15.16). The increased size of the ventricles implies less space taken by brain cells. Signs of brain damage are especially common in people who had a history of complications during pregnancy or at birth (Stefanis et al., 1999).

The areas with consistent signs of abnormality include some that mature slowly, such as the dorsolateral prefrontal cortex (Berman, Torrey, Daniel, & Weinberger, 1992; Fletcher et al., 1998; Gur, Cowell, et al., 2000). As you might predict, people with schizophrenia perform poorly at working memory tasks, which depend on the prefrontal cortex (Goldberg, Weinberger, Berman, Pliskin, & Podd, 1987; Spindler, Sullivan, Menon, Lim, & Pfefferbaum, 1997). Most patients with schizophrenia show deficits of memory and attention similar to those of people with damage to the temporal or prefrontal cortex (Park, Holzman, & Goldman-Rakic, 1995) (Methods 15.1).

At a microscopic level, the most reliable finding is that cell bodies are smaller than normal, especially in the hippocampus and prefrontal cortex (Pierri, Volk, Auh, Sampson, & Lewis, 2001; Rajkowska, Selemon, & Goldman-Rakic, 1998; Selemon, Rajkowska, & Goldman-Rakic, 1995; Weinberger, 1999).

Lateralization also differs from the normal pattern. In most people, the left hemisphere is slightly larger than the right, especially in the planum temporale of the temporal lobe, but in people with schizophrenia, the right planum temporale is equal or larger (Kasai et al., 2003; Kwon et al., 1999). People with schizophrenia have lower than normal overall activity in the left hemisphere (Gur & Chin, 1999) and are more likely than other people to be left-handed (Satz & Green, 1999). All these results suggest a subtle change in early brain development.

METHODS 15.1
The Wisconsin Card Sorting Task

Neuropsychologists use many behavioral tests to measure the functioning of the prefrontal cortex. One is the Wisconsin Card Sorting Task. A person is handed a shuffled deck of cards that differ in number, color, and shape of objects—for example, three red circles, five blue triangles, four green squares. First the person is asked to sort them by one rule, such as separate them by color. Then the rule changes, and the person is supposed to sort them by a different rule, such as number. Shifting to a new rule requires suppressing the old one and evokes activity in the prefrontal cortex (Konishi et al., 1998). People with damage to the prefrontal cortex can sort by whichever rule is first, but then they have trouble shifting to a new rule. People with schizophrenia have the same difficulty.

The reasons behind the brain abnormalities are not certain. Most researchers have been careful to limit their studies to patients with schizophrenia who have never taken, or who have not recently taken, antipsychotic drugs, so the deficits are not a result of treatments for schizophrenia. However, one study found volume deficits only in patients who were also alcohol abusers (Sullivan et al., 2000). Another study found equal deficits in patients who did and those who did not abuse alcohol (Mathalon, Pfefferbaum, Lim, Rosenbloom, & Sullivan, 2003). Unfortunately, most studies have not examined the possible role of alcohol and other drugs, so we do not know how much of the brain deficit may be due to substance abuse.

The results are inconclusive as to whether the brain damage associated with schizophrenia is *progressive*—that is, whether it increases over time. The brain damage associated with Parkinson's disease, Huntington's disease, and Alzheimer's disease gets worse as the person ages. Brain abnormalities are found in young people shortly after a diagnosis of schizophrenia (Lieberman et al., 2001), and most studies find that the brain abnormalities are no greater in older patients (Andreasen et al., 1990; Censits, Ragland, Gur, & Gur, 1997; Russell, Munro, Jones, Hemsley, & Murray, 1997; Selemon et al., 1995). One study reported some shrinkage of the cerebral cortex and expansion of the ventricles during the first year after patients were first diagnosed (Cahn et al., 2002), and a few studies have reported slightly increased damage as patients age (Hulshoff et al., 2001; Mathalon, Sullivan, Lim, & Pfefferbaum, 2001). Nevertheless, other researchers doubt these results (Weinberger & McClure, 2002) because brains of people with schizophrenia do not show the signs that accompany neuron death—proliferation of glia cells and activation of the genes responsible for repair after injury (Arnold, 2000; Benes, 1995; Lim et al., 1998). Possibly, the neurons are shrinking without dying. We shall need more research.

Early Development and Later Psychopathology

One question may have struck you. How can we reconcile the idea of abnormalities in early development with the fact that the disorder is usually diagnosed after age 20? The time course may not be so puzzling as it seems at first (Weinberger, 1996). Most of the people who develop schizophrenia in their 20s or later had shown other problems since childhood, including deficits in attention, memory, and impulse control (Keshavan, Diwadkar, Montrose, Rajarethinam, & Sweeney, 2005). Furthermore, the prefrontal cortex, an area that shows consistent signs of deficit in schizophrenia, matures slowly, not reaching full competence until the late teens (D. A. Lewis, 1997; Sowell, Thompson, Holmes, Jernigan, & Toga, 1999). In one study, researchers damaged this area in infant monkeys and tested the monkeys later. At age 1 year, the monkeys' behavior was nearly normal, but by age 2 years, it had deteriorated markedly (P. S. Goldman, 1971, 1976). That is, the effects of the brain damage actually grew worse. Presumably, the effects of brain damage were minimal at age 1 year because the dorsolateral prefrontal cortex doesn't do much at that age anyway. Later, when it should begin assuming important functions, the damage begins to make a difference (Figure 15.17).

The current status of the neurodevelopmental hypothesis is best described as plausible but not firmly established. Additional research will be necessary to test the hypothesis more thoroughly.

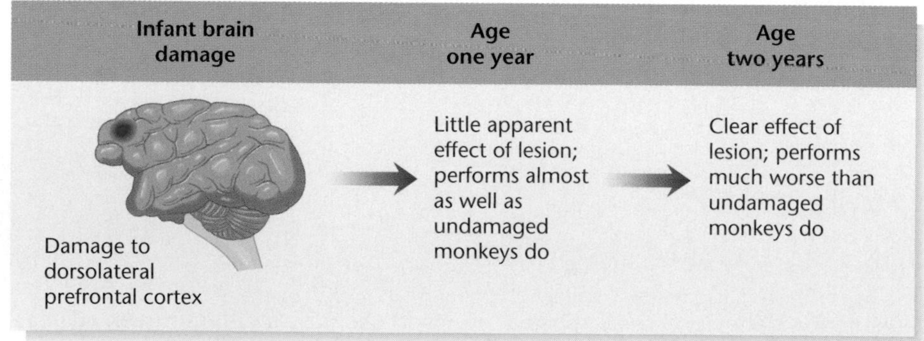

Figure 15.17 Delayed effects of brain damage in infant monkeys
After damage to the dorsolateral prefrontal cortex, monkeys are unimpaired at age 1 year but impaired later, when this area ordinarily matures. Researchers speculate that similar damage in humans might produce behavioral deficits not apparent until adulthood; thus, an abnormality of early brain development might produce schizophrenia in adults. *(Source: Based on P. S. Goldman, 1976)*

STOP & CHECK

5. What is the season-of-birth effect?
6. If schizophrenia is due to abnormal brain development, why do behavioral symptoms not become apparent until later in life?

Check your answers on page 481.

Neurotransmitters and Drugs

Before antipsychotic drugs became available in the mid-1950s, most people with schizophrenia were confined to mental hospitals, where most deteriorated for the rest of their lives. Today, the mental hospitals are far less crowded because of drugs and outpatient treatment. The nature of those drugs presumably tells us something about the nature of schizophrenia, although exactly what it tells us remains unclear.

Antipsychotic Drugs and Dopamine

In the 1950s, psychiatrists discovered that **chlorpromazine** (trade name Thorazine) relieves the positive symptoms of schizophrenia for most, though not all, patients. The typical course is that someone begins to experience relief after 2 or 3 weeks on the drug and must continue taking it indefinitely lest the symptoms return. Researchers later discovered other **antipsychotic**, or **neuroleptic, drugs** (drugs that tend to relieve schizophrenia and similar conditions) in two chemical families: the **phenothiazines** (FEE-no-THI-uh-zeens), which include chlorpromazine, and the **butyrophenones** (BYOO-tir-oh-FEE-noans), which include haloperidol (trade name Haldol). As Figure 15.18 illustrates, each of these drugs blocks dopamine synapses.

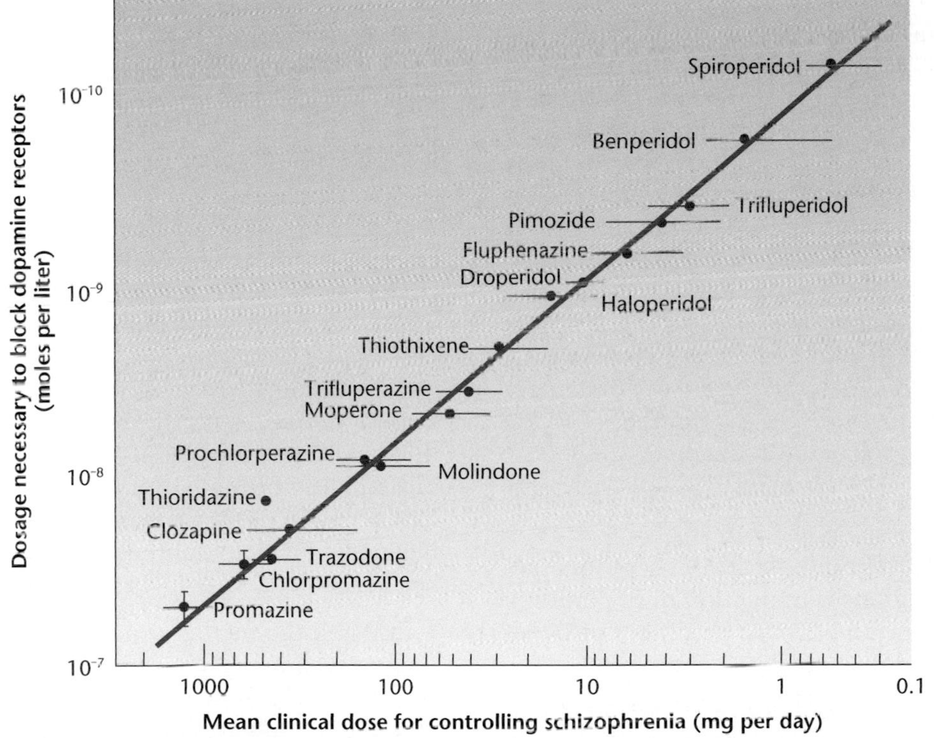

Figure 15.18 Dopamine-blocking effects of antipsychotic drugs
Drugs are arranged along the horizontal axis in terms of the average daily dose prescribed for patients with schizophrenia. (Horizontal lines indicate common ranges.) *Larger* doses are to the left and *smaller* doses are to the right so that *more effective* drugs are to the right. Along the vertical axis is a measurement of the amount of each drug required to achieve a certain degree of blockage of postsynaptic dopamine receptors. Again, *larger* doses are toward the bottom and *smaller* doses are toward the top so that the drugs on top are *more effective*. *(Source: From "Antipsychotic Drug Doses and Neuroleptic/Dopamine Receptors," by P. Seeman, T. Lee, M. Chau Wong, and K. Wong,* Nature, *261, 1976, pp. 717–719. Copyright © 1976 Macmillan Magazines Limited. Reprinted by permission of Nature and Phillip Seeman)*

For each drug, researchers determined the mean dose prescribed for patients with schizophrenia (displayed along the horizontal axis) and the amount needed to block dopamine receptors (displayed along the vertical axis). As the figure shows, the drugs that are most effective against schizophrenia (and therefore used in the smallest doses) are the most effective at blocking dopamine receptors (Seeman, Lee, Chau-Wong, & Wong, 1976).

That finding inspired the **dopamine hypothesis of schizophrenia,** which holds that schizophrenia results from excess activity at dopamine synapses in certain brain areas. Further support for this hypothesis comes from the fact that large, repeated doses of amphetamine, methamphetamine, and cocaine can induce **substance-induced psychotic disorder,** characterized by hallucinations and delusions (positive symptoms of schizophrenia). Each of these drugs increases or prolongs the activity at dopamine synapses. LSD also produces psychotic symptoms; LSD is best known for its effects on serotonin synapses, but it also increases activity at dopamine synapses.

One group of researchers set out to measure the number of dopamine receptors occupied at a given moment. They used a radioactively labeled drug, IBZM, that binds to dopamine type D_2 receptors. Because IBZM binds only to receptors that dopamine did not already bind, measuring the radioactivity counts the number of vacant dopamine receptors. Then the researchers used a second drug, AMPT, that blocks all synthesis of dopamine and again used IBZM to count the number of vacant D_2 receptors. Because AMPT had prevented production of dopamine, *all* D_2 receptors should be vacant at this time, so the researchers got a count of the total. Then they subtracted the first count from the second count, yielding the number of D_2 receptors occupied by dopamine at the first count:

- First count: IBZM binds to all D_2 receptors not already attached to dopamine.
- Second count: IBZM binds to all D_2 receptors (because AMPT eliminated production of dopamine).
- Second count minus first count = number of D_2 receptors bound to dopamine at the first count.

The researchers found that people with schizophrenia had about twice as many D_2 receptors occupied as normal (Abi-Dargham et al., 2000). Another study found that among patients with schizophrenia, the greater the amount of D_2 receptor activation in the prefrontal cortex, the greater the cognitive impairment (Meyer-Lindenberg et al., 2002).

However, the dopamine hypothesis has some limitations and problems. Direct measurements of dopamine and its metabolites generally find approximately normal levels in people with schizophrenia (Jaskiw & Weinberger, 1992). Also, recall from the depression module that antidepressant drugs alter the activity at dopamine and serotonin synapses quickly but improve mood only after 2 or 3 weeks of treatment. The same is true for schizophrenia: Antipsychotic drugs block dopamine synapses within minutes, but their effects on behavior build up gradually over 2 or 3 weeks. So blocking dopamine synapses may be an important first step for an antipsychotic drug, but clearly, something else must develop later.

Role of Glutamate

According to the **glutamate hypothesis of schizophrenia,** the problem relates in part to deficient activity at glutamate synapses, especially in the prefrontal cortex. In many brain areas, dopamine inhibits glutamate release, or glutamate stimulates neurons that inhibit dopamine release. Therefore, increased dopamine would produce the same effects as decreased glutamate. So the antipsychotic effects of drugs that block dopamine are compatible with either the excess-dopamine hypothesis or the deficient-glutamate hypothesis. One experiment examined mice that had a severe deficit of NMDA-type glutamate receptors but normal amounts of dopamine. Dopamine-blocking drugs such as haloperidol decreased the behavioral abnormalities of these mice (Mohn, Gainetdinov, Caron, & Koller, 1999).

Schizophrenia is associated with lower than normal release of glutamate and fewer than normal receptors in the prefrontal cortex and hippocampus (Akbarian et al., 1995; Ibrahim et al., 2000; Tsai et al., 1995). Further support comes from the effects of **phencyclidine (PCP)** ("angel dust"), a drug that inhibits the NMDA glutamate receptors. At low doses, it produces intoxication and slurred speech. At larger doses, it produces both positive and negative symptoms of schizophrenia, including hallucinations, thought disorder, loss of emotions, and memory loss. PCP is an interesting model for schizophrenia in other regards also (Farber, Newcomer, & Olney, 1999; Olney & Farber, 1995):

- PCP and the related drug *ketamine* produce little if any psychotic response in preadolescents. Just as the symptoms of schizophrenia usually begin to emerge well after puberty, so do the psychotic effects of PCP and ketamine.
- LSD, amphetamine, and cocaine produce temporary schizophrenic symptoms in almost anyone, and not much worse in people with a history of schizophrenia than in anyone else. However, for someone who has recovered from schizophrenia, PCP induces a long-lasting relapse.

It might seem that the best test of the glutamate hypothesis would be to administer glutamate itself. However, recall from Chapter 5 that strokes kill neurons by overstimulating glutamate synapses. Increasing overall brain glutamate would be risky.

However, the NMDA glutamate receptor has a primary site that is activated by glutamate and a secondary site that is activated by glycine (Figure 15.19). Glycine by itself does not activate the receptor, but it increases the effectiveness of glutamate. Thus, an increase in glycine can increase the activity at NMDA synapses without overstimulating glutamate throughout the brain. Although glycine is not an effective antipsychotic drug by itself, it increases the effects of other antipsychotic drugs, especially with regard to negative symptoms (Heresco-Levy et al., 1999; Heresco-Levy & Javitt, 2004). Schizophrenia is a sufficiently complex disorder that both dopamine and glutamate may play important roles, perhaps to different degrees in different individuals.

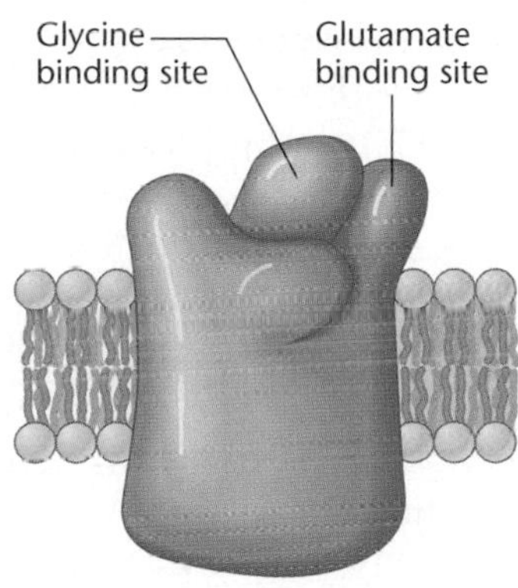

Figure 15.19 An NMDA glutamate receptor
NMDA glutamate receptors have a primary binding site for glutamate and a secondary binding site for glycine. Glycine increases the effect of glutamate.

New Drugs

The drugs that block dopamine synapses produce their benefits by acting on neurons in the **mesolimbocortical system,** a set of neurons that project from the midbrain tegmentum to the limbic system. However, the drugs also block dopamine neurons in the *mesostriatal system,* which projects to the basal ganglia (Figure 15.20). The result is **tardive dyskinesia** (TARD-eev dis-kih-NEE-zhee-uh), characterized by tremors and other involuntary movements that develop gradually and to varying degrees among different patients (Kiriakakis, Bhatia, Quinn, & Marsden, 1998).

Once tardive dyskinesia emerges, it can last long after the person quits the drug (Kiriakakis et al., 1998). Consequently, the best strategy is to prevent it from starting. Certain new drugs called **second-generation antipsychotics,** or atypical antipsychotics, alleviate schizophrenia but seldom if ever produce movement problems (Figure 15.21). The most common of these drugs are clozapine, amisulpride, risperidone, olanzapine, and aripiprazole. They are more effective than the older drugs at treating the negative symptoms of schizophrenia, and they are now used more widely (J. M. Davis, Chen, & Glick, 2003; Edlinger et al., 2005). Unfortunately, they produce their own side effects, including weight gain, increased risk of diabetes (Newcomet et al., 2002) and an impairment of the immune system.

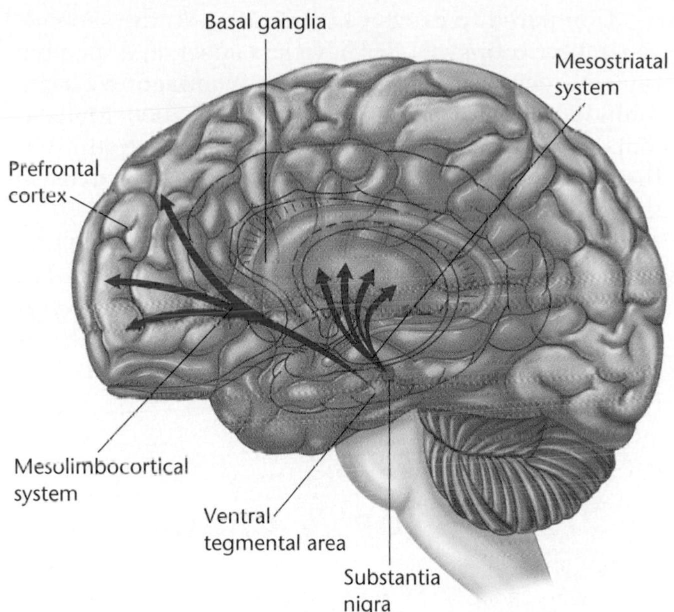

Figure 15.20 Two major dopamine pathways
Overactivity of the mesolimbocortical system is linked to the symptoms of schizophrenia; the path to the basal ganglia is associated with tardive dyskinesia, a movement disorder. *(Source: Adapted from Valzelli, 1980)*

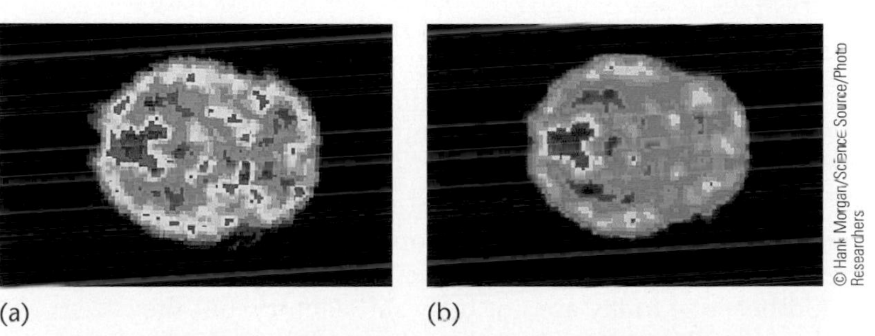

Figure 15.21 PET scans of a patient with schizophrenia
These PET scans of a patient with schizophrenia **(a)** taking clozapine and **(b)** during a period off the drug demonstrate that clozapine increases brain activity in many brain areas. (Red indicates the highest activity, followed by yellow, green, and blue.)

Compared to drugs like haloperidol, the second-generation antipsychotics have less effect on dopamine type D_2 receptors but more strongly antagonize serotonin type 5-HT_2 receptors (Kapur et al., 2000; Meltzer, Matsubara, & Lee, 1989; Mrzljak et al., 1996; Roth, Willins, Kristiansen, & Kroeze, 1999). They also increase the release of glutamate (Melone et al., 2001).

In short, schizophrenia is neither a one-gene disorder nor a one-neurotransmitter disorder. In addition to abnormalities in dopamine, glutamate, and serotonin, people with schizophrenia also show deficits in GABA activity (Hashimoto et al., 2003; D. A. Lewis, Hashimoto, & Volk, 2005).

STOP & CHECK

7. How fast do antipsychotic drugs affect dopamine synapses? How fast do they alter behavior?
8. What drugs induce mainly the positive symptoms of schizophrenia? What drug can induce both positive and negative symptoms?
9. Why are so many drug results equally compatible with the dopamine hypothesis and the glutamate hypothesis?

Check your answers on page 481.

Module 15.3

In Closing: The Fascination of Schizophrenia

A good mystery novel presents an array of clues, mixing important clues with irrelevant information, and the reader's challenge is to figure out who committed the crime. Schizophrenia research is similar, except that we want to know *what* is to blame, not *who.* As with a mystery novel, we have to sort through an enormous number of clues and false leads, looking for a pattern. One difference is that, unlike the reader of a mystery novel, we have the option of collecting new evidence of our own.

I trust it is clear to you that researchers have not yet solved the mystery of schizophrenia. But it should also be clear that they have made progress. The hypotheses of today are not fully satisfactory, but they have much more support than the hypotheses of decades past. Our research also provides a few guidelines on how to prevent schizophrenia. For example, pregnant women should get good nutrition and receive immunization against influenza. The future looks exciting for this area of research.

Summary

1. Positive symptoms of schizophrenia (behaviors that are not present in most other people) include hallucinations, delusions, inappropriate emotions, bizarre behaviors, and thought disorder. (p. 470)
2. Negative symptoms (normal behaviors absent that should be present) include deficits of social interaction, emotional expression, and speech. (p. 470)
3. Studies of twins and adopted children imply a genetic predisposition to schizophrenia. However, the adoption studies do not distinguish between the roles of genetics and prenatal environment. (p. 472)
4. So far, researchers have not located any gene that is strongly linked with schizophrenia in general, perhaps because it depends on a combination of genes. One gene has been linked to the negative symptoms. (p. 473)
5. According to the neurodevelopmental hypothesis, either genes or difficulties early in life impair brain development in ways that lead to behavioral abnormalities beginning in early adulthood. (p. 473)
6. The probability of schizophrenia is slightly higher than average for those who were subjected to difficulties before or at the time of birth or during early infancy. Childhood infection with a parasite that invades the brain is another possibility. (p. 473)
7. Some people with schizophrenia show mild abnormalities of early brain development, especially in the temporal and frontal lobes. Most (but not all) studies conclude that the brain damage is nonprogressive; that is, it does not increase over time, as brain damage does with Alzheimer's disease and Huntington's disease. (p. 474)
8. Parts of the prefrontal cortex are very slow to mature. It is plausible that early disruption of those areas might produce behavioral symptoms that become manifest as schizophrenia in young adults. (p. 476)
9. According to the dopamine hypothesis, schizophrenia is due to excess dopamine activity. The main support for this hypothesis is that drugs that block dopamine synapses reduce the positive symptoms of schizophrenia and drugs that increase dopamine activity can induce the positive symptoms. However, direct measurements of dopamine and its receptors have not strongly supported this theory. (p. 477)
10. According to the glutamate hypothesis, the problem is deficient glutamate activity. Evidence supporting this view is that phencyclidine, which blocks NMDA glutamate synapses, produces both

positive and negative symptoms of schizophrenia, especially in people predisposed to schizophrenia. (p. 478)

11. Prolonged use of antipsychotic drugs may produce tardive dyskinesia, a movement disorder. Second-generation antipsychotic drugs relieve both positive and negative symptoms without producing tardive dyskinesia. Most psychiatrists now prescribe second-generation drugs. (p. 479)

Answers to STOP & CHECK Questions

1. Hallucinations are considered a positive symptom because they are present when they should be absent. A "positive" symptom is not a "good" symptom. (p. 472)
2. Schizophrenia has been decreasing in reported prevalence. (p. 472)
3. Dizygotic twins shared more of their environment, including prenatal environment. (p. 473)
4. A biological mother can influence her child's development through prenatal environment as well as genetics, even if the child is adopted early. (p. 473)
5. The season-of-birth effect is the observation that schizophrenia is slightly more common among people who were born in the winter. (p. 477)
6. Parts of the prefrontal cortex are very slow to reach maturity; therefore, early disruption of this area's development might not produce any symptoms early in life, when the prefrontal cortex is contributing little anyway. (p. 477)
7. They alter dopamine synaptic activity within minutes. They take 2 or more weeks to alter behavior. (p. 480)
8. Amphetamine, cocaine, and LSD in large doses induce positive symptoms, such as hallucinations and delusions. Phencyclidine induces both positive and negative symptoms. (p. 480)
9. Dopamine inhibits glutamate cells in many areas, and glutamate stimulates neurons that inhibit dopamine. Therefore, the effects of increasing dopamine are similar to those of decreasing glutamate. (p. 480)

Thought Questions

1. How might denervation supersensitivity (discussed in Chapter 5) help explain tardive dyskinesia?
2. Why might it be difficult to find effective drugs for someone who suffers from both depression and schizophrenia?

Chapter Ending

Key Terms and Activities

Terms

acetaldehyde (p. 456)
acetic acid (p. 456)
acute (p. 470)
alcoholism (or alcohol dependence) (p. 454)
Antabuse (p. 456)
antipsychotic (or neuroleptic) drug (p. 477)
atypical antidepressants (p. 463)
bipolar disorder (or manic-depressive disorder) (p. 466)
bipolar I disorder (p. 466)
bipolar II disorder (p. 466)
Borna disease (p. 461)
butyrophenone (p. 477)
chlorpromazine (p. 477)
chronic (p. 470)
concordance (p. 472)
delusion (p. 470)
differential diagnosis (p. 471)
dopamine hypothesis of schizophrenia (p. 478)
electroconvulsive therapy (ECT) (p. 464)
glutamate hypothesis of schizophrenia (p. 478)
hallucination (p. 470)
lithium (p. 467)
major depression (p. 459)
mania (p. 466)
mesolimbocortical system (p. 479)
monoamine oxidase inhibitors (MAOIs) (p. 462)
negative symptom (p. 470)
neurodevelopmental hypothesis (p. 473)
phencyclidine (PCP) (p. 478)
phenothiazine (p. 477)
positive symptom (p. 470)
postpartum depression (p. 460)
schizophrenia (p. 470)
seasonal affective disorder (SAD) (p. 467)
season-of-birth effect (p. 474)
second-generation antipsychotics (p. 479)
selective serotonin reuptake inhibitors (SSRIs) (p. 462)
self-stimulation of the brain (p. 452)
substance abuse (p. 452)
substance-induced psychotic disorder (p. 478)
tardive dyskinesia (p. 479)
thought disorder (p. 471)
tricyclic (p. 462)
Type I alcoholism (p. 454)
Type II alcoholism (p. 454)
unipolar disorder (p. 466)

Suggestions for Further Reading

Andreasen, N. C. (2001). *Brave new brain.* New York: Oxford University Press. Excellent discussion of biological research on psychiatric disorders by one of the leading researchers dealing with schizophrenia.

Charney, D. S., & Nestler, E. J. (Eds.). (2004). *Neurobiology of mental illness* (2nd ed.). New York: Oxford University Press. An extensive reference work on all types of psychiatric disorders.

McKim, W. A. (2003). *Drugs and behavior* (5th ed.). Upper Saddle River, NJ: Prentice Hall. Concise, highly informative text on drugs and drug abuse.

Websites to Explore

You can go to the Biological Psychology Study Center and click these links. While there, you can also check for suggested articles available on InfoTrac College Edition. The Biological Psychology Internet address is:

http://psychology.wadsworth.com/book/kalatbiopsych9e/

Society for Light Treatment and Biological Rhythms

http://www.sltbr.org/

Schizophrenia Information and Support

http://www.schizophrenia.com/

Exploring Biological Psychology CD

Understanding Addiction (video)
CNS Stimulants (animation)
Major Depressive Disorder: Barbara (two videos)
Antidepressant Drugs (animation)
Bipolar Disorder: Mary (three videos)
Bipolar Disorder: Etta (two videos)
Chapter Quiz (multiple-choice questions)
Critical Thinking (essay questions)

ThomsonNOW

http://www.thomsonedu.com

Go to this site for the link to ThomsonNOW, your one-stop study shop. Take a Pre-Test for this chapter, and ThomsonNOW will generate a Personalized Study Plan based on your test results. The Study Plan will identify the topics you need to review and direct you to online resources to help you master these topics. You can then take a Post-Test to help you determine the concepts you have mastered and what you still need work on.

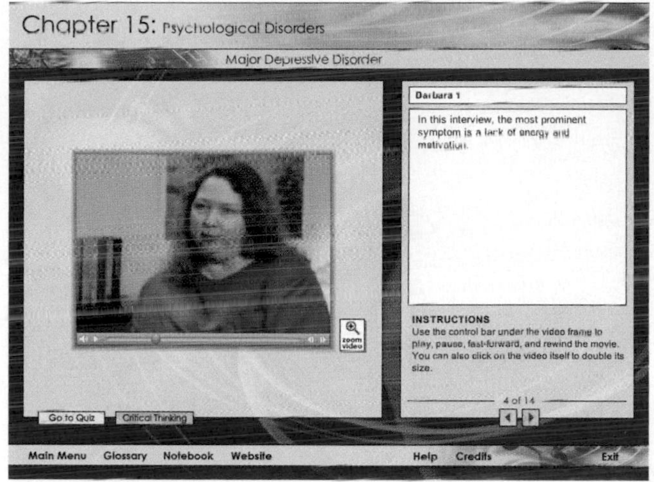

An interview shows how depression robs someone of the joy of living.

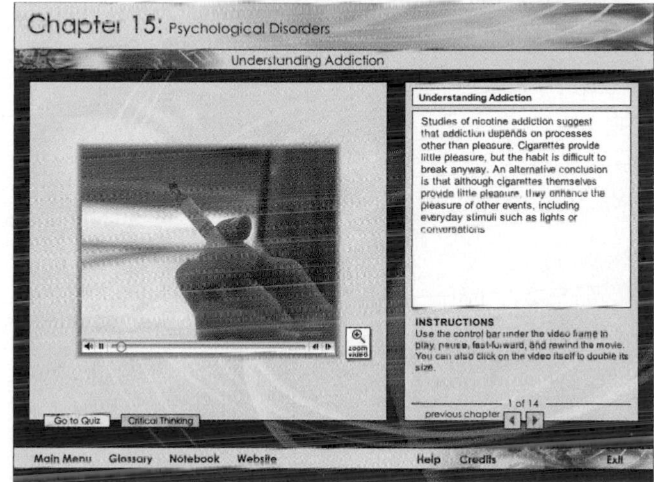

This video highlights research on nicotine addiction.

Brief, Basic Chemistry

Main Ideas

1. All matter is composed of a limited number of elements that combine in endless ways.
2. Atoms, the component parts of an element, consist of protons, neutrons, and electrons. Most atoms can gain or lose electrons, or share them with other atoms.
3. The chemistry of life is predominantly the chemistry of carbon compounds.

Introduction

To understand certain aspects of biological psychology, particularly the action potential and the molecular mechanisms of synaptic transmission, you need to know a little about chemistry. If you have taken a high school or college course and remember the material reasonably well, you should have no trouble with the chemistry in this text. If your knowledge of chemistry is pretty hazy, this appendix will help. (If you plan to take other courses in biological psychology, you should study as much biology and chemistry as possible.)

Elements and Compounds

If you look around, you will see an enormous variety of materials—dirt, water, wood, plastic, metal, cloth, glass, your own body. Every object is composed of a small number of basic building blocks. If a piece of wood catches fire, it breaks down into ashes, gases, and water vapor. The same is true of your body. An investigator could take those ashes, gases, and water and break them down by chemical and electrical means into carbon, oxygen, hydrogen, nitrogen, and a few other materials. Eventually, however, the investigator arrives at a set of materials that cannot be broken down further: Pure carbon or pure oxygen, for example, cannot be converted into anything simpler, at least not by ordinary chemical means. (High-power bombardment with subatomic particles is another story.) The matter we see is composed of **elements** (materials that cannot be broken down into other materials) and **compounds** (materials made up by combining elements).

Chemists have found 92 elements in nature, and they have constructed more in the laboratory. (Actually, one of the 92—technetium—is so rare as to be virtually unknown in nature.) Figure A.1, the periodic table, lists each of these elements. Of these, only a few are important for life on Earth. Table A.1 shows the elements commonly found in the human body.

Note that each element has a one- or two-letter abbreviation, such as O for oxygen, H for hydrogen, and Ca for calcium. These are internationally accepted symbols that facilitate communication among chemists who speak different languages. For example, element number 19 is called potassium in English, potassio in Italian, kālijs in Latvian, and draslík in Czech. But chemists in all countries use the symbol K (from *kalium,* the Latin word for "potassium"). Similarly,

Table A.1 The Elements That Compose Almost All of the Human Body

Element	Symbol	Percentage by Weight in Human Body
Oxygen	O	65
Carbon	C	18
Hydrogen	H	10
Nitrogen	N	3
Calcium	Ca	2
Phosphorus	P	1.1
Potassium	K	0.35
Sulfur	S	0.25
Sodium	Na	0.15
Chlorine	Cl	0.15
Magnesium	Mg	0.05
Iron	Fe	Trace
Copper	Cu	Trace
Iodine	I	Trace
Fluorine	F	Trace
Manganese	Mn	Trace
Zinc	Zn	Trace
Selenium	Se	Trace
Molybdenum	Mo	Trace

Periodic Table of the Elements

Period	Alkali Metals 1 IA	Alkaline Earth Metals 2 IIA	Transition Elements 3 IIIB	4 IVB	5 VB	6 VIB	7 VIIB	8 VIIIB	9 VIIIB	10 VIIIB	11 IB	12 IIB	13 IIIA	14 IVA	15 VA	16 VIA	Halogens 17 VIIA	Noble Gases 18 VIIA
1	1 **H** hydrogen 1.008																	2 **He** helium 4.003
2	3 **Li** lithium 6.941	4 **Be** beryllium 9.012											5 **B** boron 10.81	6 **C** carbon 12.011	7 **N** nitrogen 14.007	8 **O** oxygen 16.0	9 **F** fluorine 18.999	10 **Ne** neon 20.179
3	11 **Na** sodium 22.99	12 **Mg** magnesium 24.305											13 **Al** aluminum 26.982	14 **Si** silicon 28.085	15 **P** phosphorous 30.974	16 **S** sulfur 32.060	17 **Cl** chlorine 35.453	18 **Ar** argon 39.948
4	19 **K** potassium 39.098	20 **Ca** calcium 40.08	21 **Sc** scandium 44.955	22 **Ti** titanium 47.90	23 **V** vanadium 50.941	24 **Cr** chromium 51.996	25 **Mn** manganese 54.938	26 **Fe** iron 55.847	27 **Co** cobalt 58.933	28 **Ni** nickel 58.70	29 **Cu** copper 63.546	30 **Zn** zinc 65.38	31 **Ga** gallium 69.72	32 **Ge** germanium 72.59	33 **As** arsenic 74.922	34 **Se** selenium 78.96	35 **Br** bromine 79.904	36 **Kr** krypton 83.80
5	37 **Rb** rubidium 85.468	38 **Sr** strontium 87.62	39 **Y** yttrium 88.906	40 **Zr** zirconium 91.22	41 **Nb** niobium 92.906	42 **Mo** molybdenum 95.940	43 **Tc** technetium (97)	44 **Ru** ruthenium 101.07	45 **Rh** rhodium 102.905	46 **Pd** palladium 106.40	47 **Ag** silver 107.868	48 **Cd** cadmium 112.41	49 **In** indium 114.82	50 **Sn** tin 118.69	51 **Sb** antimony 121.75	52 **Te** tellurium 127.60	53 **I** iodine 126.904	54 **Xe** xenon 131.30
6	55 **Cs** cesium 132.905	56 **Ba** barium 137.33	57 **La** lanthanum 138.906 †	72 **Hf** hafnium 178.49	73 **Ta** tantalum 180.948	74 **W** tungsten 183.85	75 **Re** rhenium 186.207	76 **Os** osmium 190.20	77 **Ir** iridium 192.22	78 **Pt** platinum 195.09	79 **Au** gold 196.967	80 **Hg** mercury 200.59	81 **Tl** thallium 204.37	82 **Pb** lead 207.20	83 **Bi** bismuth 208.980	84 **Po** polonium (209)	85 **At** astatine (210)	86 **Rn** radon (222)
7	87 **Fr** francium (223)	88 **Ra** radium 226.025	89 **Ac** actinium (227) ‡	104 **Rf** rutherfordium (261)	105 **Db** dubnium (262)	106 **Sg** seaborgium (266)	107 **Bh** bohrium (264)	108 **Hs** hassium (269)	109 **Mt** meitnerium (268)	110 **Ds** darmstadtium (271)	111 **Rg** roentgenium (272)	112 **Uub** ununbium (285)	113 **Uut** ununtrium (284)	114 **Uuq** ununquadium (289)	115 **Uup** ununpentium (288)	116 **Uuh** ununhexium (292)	117 **Uus** ununseptium (?)	118 **Uuo** ununoctium (?)

Inner Transition Elements

† Lanthanides 6	58 **Ce** cerium 140.12	59 **Pr** praseodymium 140.908	60 **Nd** neodymium 144.24	61 **Pm** prometheum (145)	62 **Sm** samarium 150.40	63 **Eu** europium 151.96	64 **Gd** gadolinium 157.25	65 **Tb** terbium 158.925	66 **Dy** dysprosium 162.50	67 **Ho** holmium 164.93	68 **Er** erbium 167.26	69 **Tm** thulium 168.934	70 **Yb** ytterbium 173.04	71 **Lu** lutetium 174.97
‡ Actinides 7	90 **Th** thorium 232.038	91 **Pa** protactinium 231.036	92 **U** uranium 238.029	93 **Np** neptunium (237)	94 **Pu** plutonium (244)	95 **Am** americium (243)	96 **Cm** curium (247)	97 **Bk** berkelium (247)	98 **Cf** californium (251)	99 **Es** einsteinium (254)	100 **Fm** fermium (257)	101 **Md** mendelevium (258)	102 **No** nobelium (255)	103 **Lr** lawrencium (260)

Key

atomic number	1	
	H	symbol of element
element name	hydrogen	
	1.008	atomic weight

Figure A.1 The periodic table of chemistry

It is called "periodic" because certain properties show up at periodic intervals. For example, the column from lithium down consists of metals that readily form salts. The column at the far right consists of gases that do not readily form compounds. Elements 112–118 have only tentative names and symbols.

the symbol for sodium is Na (from *natrium,* the Latin word for "sodium"), and the symbol for iron is Fe (from the Latin word *ferrum*).

A compound is represented by the symbols for the elements that compose it. For example, NaCl stands for sodium chloride (common table salt). H_2O, the symbol for water, indicates that water consists of two parts of hydrogen and one part of oxygen.

Atoms and Molecules

A block of iron can be chopped finer and finer until it is divided into tiny pieces that cannot be broken down any further. These pieces are called **atoms.** Every element is composed of atoms. A compound, such as water, can also be divided into tinier and tinier pieces. The smallest possible piece of a compound is called a **molecule.** A molecule of water can be further decomposed into two atoms of hydrogen and one atom of oxygen, but when that happens the compound is broken and is no longer water. A molecule is the smallest piece of a compound that retains the properties of the compound.

An atom is composed of subatomic particles, including protons, neutrons, and electrons. A proton has a positive electrical charge, a neutron has a neutral charge, and an electron has a negative charge. The nucleus of an atom—its center—contains one or more protons plus a number of neutrons. Electrons are found in the space around the nucleus. Because an atom has the same number of protons as electrons, the electrical charges balance out. (Ions, which we will soon consider, have an imbalance of positive and negative charges.)

The difference between one element and another is in the number of protons in the nucleus of the atom. Hydrogen has just one proton, for example, and oxygen has eight. The number of protons is the **atomic number** of the element; in the periodic table it is recorded at the top of the square for each element. The number at the bottom is the element's **atomic weight,** which indicates the weight of an atom relative to the weight of one proton. A proton has a weight of one unit, a neutron has a weight just trivially greater than one, and an electron has a weight just trivially greater than zero. The atomic weight of the element is the number of protons in the atom plus the average number of neutrons. For example, most hydrogen atoms have one proton and no neutrons; a few atoms per thousand have one or two neutrons, giving an average atomic weight of 1.008. Sodium ions have 11 protons; most also have 12 neutrons, and the atomic weight is slightly less than 23. (Can you figure out the number of neutrons in the average potassium atom? Refer to Figure A.1.)

Ions and Chemical Bonds

An atom that has gained or lost one or more electrons is called an **ion.** For example, if sodium and chloride come together, the sodium atoms readily lose one electron each and the chloride atoms gain one each. The result is a set of positively charged sodium ions (indicated Na^+) and negatively charged chloride ions (Cl^-). Potassium atoms, like sodium atoms, tend to lose an electron and to become positively charged ions (K^+); calcium ions tend to lose two electrons and gain a double positive charge (Ca^{++}).

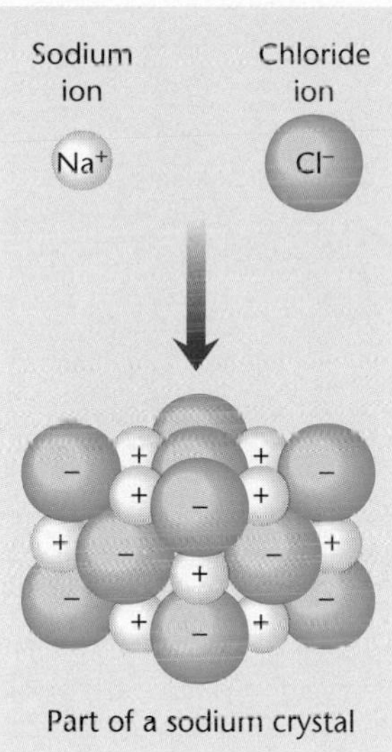

Figure A.2 The crystal structure of sodium chloride
Each sodium ion is surrounded by chloride ions, and each chloride ion is surrounded by sodium ions; no ion is bound to any other single ion in particular.

Because positive charges attract negative charges, sodium ions attract chloride ions. When dry, sodium and chloride form a crystal structure, as Figure A.2 shows. (In water solution, the two kinds of ions move about haphazardly, occasionally attracting one another but then pulling apart.) The attraction of positive ions for negative ions forms an **ionic bond.** In other cases, instead of transferring an electron from one atom to another, some pairs of atoms share electrons with each other, forming a **covalent bond.** For example, two hydrogen atoms bind, as shown in Figure A.3, and two hydrogen atoms bind with an oxygen atom, as shown in Figure A.4. Atoms that are attached by a covalent bond cannot move independently of one another.

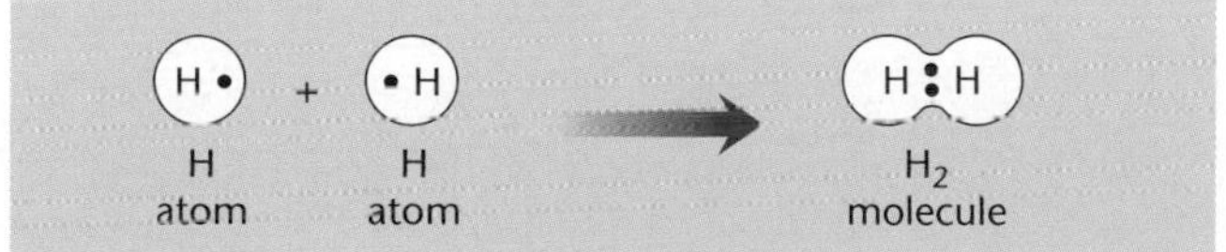

Figure A.3 Structure of a hydrogen molecule
A hydrogen atom has one electron; in the compound the two atoms share the two electrons equally.

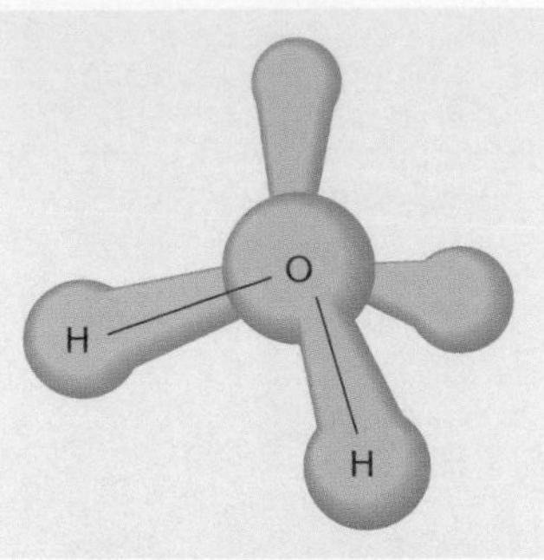

Figure A.4 Structure of a water molecule
The oxygen atom shares a pair of electrons with each hydrogen atom. Oxygen holds the electrons more tightly, making the oxygen part of the molecule more negatively charged than the hydrogen part of the molecule.

Reactions of Carbon Atoms

Living organisms depend on the enormously versatile compounds of carbon. Because of the importance of these compounds for life, the chemistry of carbon is known as organic chemistry.

Carbon atoms form covalent bonds with hydrogen, oxygen, and a number of other elements. They also form covalent bonds with other carbon atoms. Two carbon atoms may share from one to three pairs of electrons. Such bonds can be indicated as follows:

C–C Two atoms share one pair of electrons.
C=C Two atoms share two pairs of electrons.
C≡C Two atoms share three pairs of electrons.

Each carbon atom ordinarily forms four covalent bonds, either with other carbon atoms, with hydrogen atoms, or with other atoms. Many biologically important compounds include long chains of carbon compounds linked to one another, such as:

```
   H  H  H               H  H  H  H  H  H
   |  |  |               |  |  |  |  |  |
H—C—C—C—OH           H—C=C—C=C—C=C—H
   |  |  |
   H  H  H
```

Note that each carbon atom has a total of four bonds, counting each double bond as two. In some molecules, the carbon chain loops around to form a ring:

```
   H       H            H       H
    \     /              \     /
     C———C                C———C
    /  H H \             //     \\
H—C—H     H—C—H      H—C         C—H
    \  H H  /             \     /
     C———C                C===C
    /     \              /     \
   H       H            H       H
```

Ringed structures are common in organic chemistry. To simplify the diagrams chemists often omit the hydrogen atoms. You can simply assume that each carbon atom in the diagram has four covalent bonds and that all the bonds not shown are with hydrogen atoms. To further simplify the diagrams, chemists often omit the carbon atoms themselves, showing only the carbon-to-carbon bonds. For example, the two molecules shown in the previous diagram might be rendered as follows:

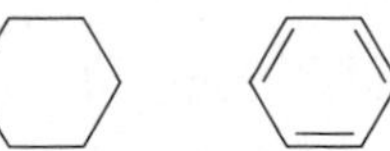

If a particular carbon atom has a bond with some atom other than hydrogen, the diagram shows the exception. For example, in each of the two molecules diagrammed below, one carbon has a bond with an oxygen atom, which in turn has a bond with a hydrogen atom. All the bonds that are not shown are carbon–hydrogen bonds.

```
O—H        O—H
```

Figure A.5 illustrates some carbon compounds that are critical for animal life. Purines and pyrimidines form the central structure of DNA and RNA, the chemicals responsible for heredity. Proteins, fats, and carbohydrates are the primary types of fuel that the body uses. Figure A.6 displays the chemical structures of seven neurotransmitters that are extensively discussed in this text.

Chemical Reactions in the Body

A living organism is an immensely complicated, coordinated set of chemical reactions. Life requires that the rate of each reaction be carefully regulated. In many cases one reaction produces a chemical that enters into another reaction, which produces another chemical that enters into another reaction, and so forth. If any one of those reactions is too rapid compared to the others, the chemical it produces will accumulate to possibly harmful levels. If a reaction is too slow, it will not produce enough product and the next reaction will be stalled.

Enzymes are proteins that control the rate of chemical reactions. Each reaction is controlled by a particular enzyme. Enzymes are a type of catalyst. A catalyst is any chemical that facilitates a reaction among other chemicals, without being altered itself in the process.

The Role of ATP

The body relies on **ATP (adenosine triphosphate)** as its main way of sending energy where it is needed

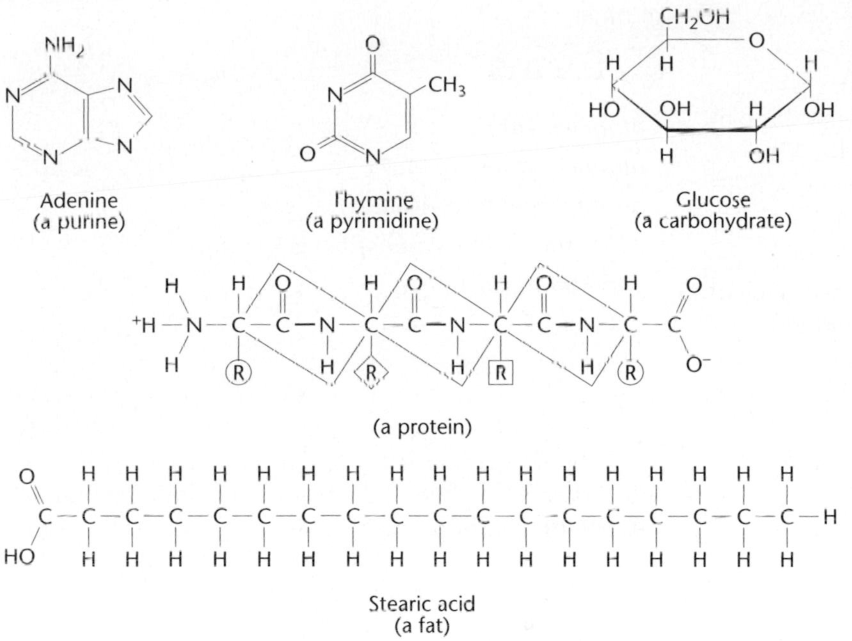

Adenine
(a purine)

Thymine
(a pyrimidine)

Glucose
(a carbohydrate)

(a protein)

Stearic acid
(a fat)

Figure A.5 Structures of some important biological molecules
The R in the protein represents a point of attachment for various chains that differ from one amino acid to another. Actual proteins are much longer than the chemical shown here.

$CH_3C(=O)—O—CH_2CH_2N(CH_3)_3$ Acetylcholine

$CH_2CH_2NH_2$ Dopamine

$CHCH_2NH_2$ Norepinephrine

$CHCH_2NH—CH_3$ Epinephrine

$CH_2CH_2NH_2$ Serotonin (5-hydroxytryptamine)

Glutamate

$NH_2—CH_2—CH_2—CH_2—C$ GABA (γ-amino-butyric acid)

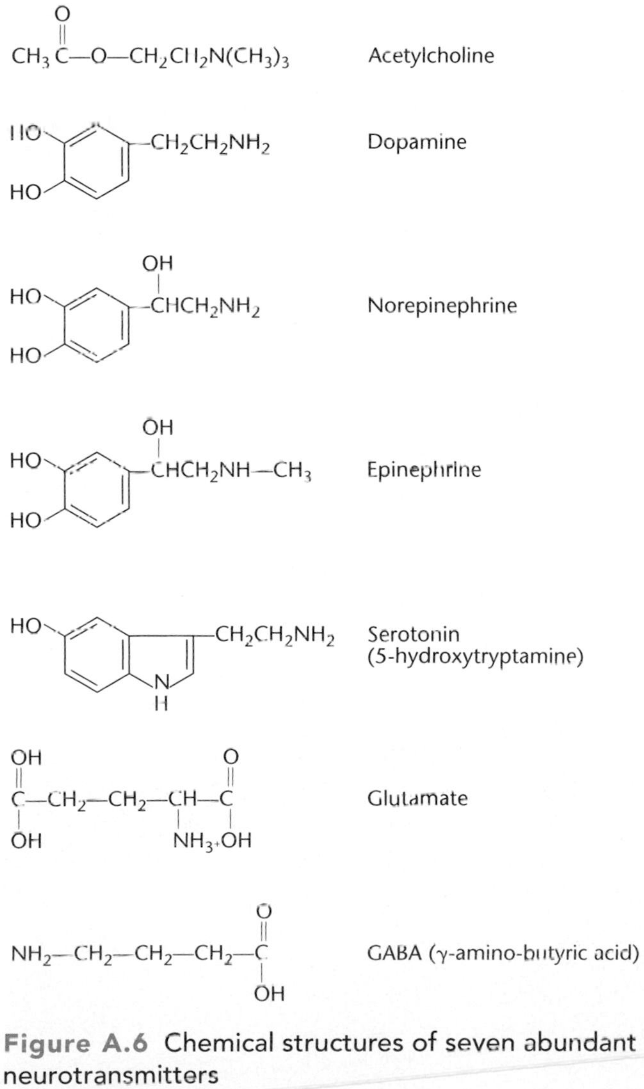

Figure A.6 Chemical structures of seven abundant neurotransmitters

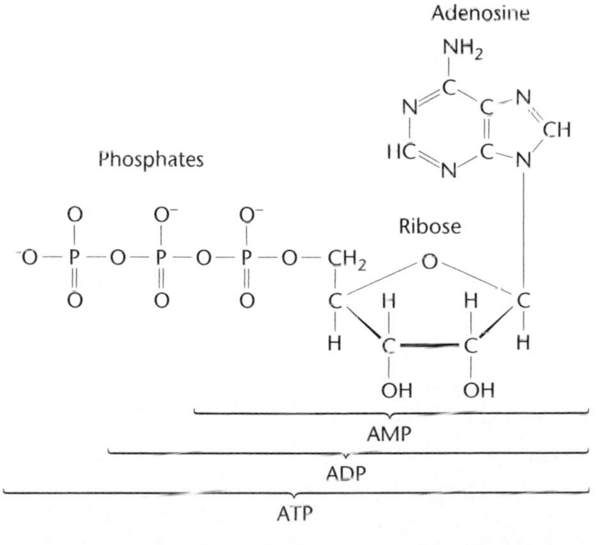

(Figure A.7). Much of the energy derived from food goes into forming ATP molecules that eventually provide energy for the muscles and other body parts.

ATP consists of adenosine bound to ribose and three phosphate groups (PO_3). Phosphates form high-energy covalent bonds. That is, a large amount of energy is required to form the bonds and a large amount of energy is released when they break. ATP can break off one or two of its three phosphates to provide energy.

Adenosine

Phosphates

Ribose

AMP

ADP

ATP

Figure A.7 ATP, composed of adenosine, ribose, and three phosphates
ATP can lose one phosphate group to form ADP (adenosine diphosphate) and then lose another one to form AMP (adenosine monophosphate). Each time it breaks off a phosphate group, it releases energy.

Summary

1. Matter is composed of 92 elements that combine to form an endless variety of compounds. (p. 485)
2. An atom is the smallest piece of an element. A molecule is the smallest piece of a compound that maintains the properties of the compound. (p. 487)
3. The atoms of some elements can gain or lose an electron, thus becoming ions. Positively charged ions attract negatively charged ions, forming an ionic bond. In some cases two or more atoms may share electrons, thus forming a covalent bond. (p. 487)
4. The principal carrier of energy in the body is a chemical called ATP. (p. 488)

Terms

atom (p. 487)
atomic number (p. 487)
atomic weight (p. 487)
ATP (adenosine triphosphate) (p. 488)
compound (p. 485)
covalent bond (p. 487)
element (p. 485)
enzyme (p. 488)
ion (p. 487)
ionic bond (p. 487)
molecule (p. 487)

Society for Neuroscience Policies on the Use of Animals and Human Subjects in Neuroscience Research

B

Policy on the Use of Animals in Neuroscience Research

The Policy on the Use of Animals in Neuroscience Research affects a number of the Society's functions that involve making decisions about animal research conducted by individual members. These include the scheduling of scientific presentations at the Annual Meeting, the review and publication of original research papers in *The Journal of Neuroscience,* and the defense of members whose ethical use of animals in research is questioned by antivivisectionists. The responsibility for implementing the policy in each of these areas will rest with the relevant administrative body (Program Committee, Publications Committee, Editorial Board, and Committee on Animals in Research, respectively), in consultation with Council.

Introduction

The Society for Neuroscience, as a professional society for basic and clinical researchers in neuroscience, endorses and supports the appropriate and responsible use of animals as experimental subjects. Knowledge generated by neuroscience research on animals has led to important advances in the understanding of diseases and disorders that affect the nervous system and in the development of better treatments that reduce suffering in humans and animals. This knowledge also makes a critical contribution to our understanding of ourselves, the complexities of our brains, and what makes us human. Continued progress in understanding how the brain works and further advances in treating and curing disorders of the nervous system require investigation of complex functions at all levels in the living nervous system. Because no adequate alternatives exist, much of this research must be done on animal subjects. The Society takes the position that neuroscientists have an obligation to contribute to this progress through responsible and humane research on animals.

Several functions of the Society are related to the use of animals in research. A number of these involve decisions about research conducted by individual members of the Society, including the scheduling of scientific presentations at the Annual Meeting, the review and publication of original research papers in *The Journal of Neuroscience,* and the defense of members whose ethical use of animals in research is questioned by antivivisectionists. Each of these functions, by establishing explicit support of the Society for the research of individual members, defines a relationship between the Society and its members. The purpose of this document is to outline the policy that guides that relationship. Compliance with the following policy will be an important factor in determining the suitability of research for presentation at the Annual Meeting or for publication in *The Journal of Neuroscience,* and in situations where the Society is asked to provide public and active support for a member whose use of animals in research has been questioned.

General Policy

Neuroscience research uses complicated, often invasive methods, each of which is associated with different problems, risks, and specific technical considerations. An experimental method that would be deemed inappropriate for one kind of research may be the method of choice for another kind of research. It is therefore impossible for the Society to define specific policies and procedures for the care and use of all research animals and for the design and conduct of every neuroscience experiment.

The U.S. *Public Health Service Policy on Humane Care and Use of Laboratory Animals* (PHS Policy) and the *Guide for the Care and Use of Laboratory Animals* (the Guide) describe a set of general policies and procedures designed to ensure the humane and appropriate use of live vertebrate animals in all forms of biomedical research. The Society finds the policies and procedures set forth in the PHS Policy and the Guide to be both necessary and sufficient to ensure a high standard of animal care and use and adopts them as its official "Policy on the Use of Animals in Neuroscience Research" (Society Policy). All Society members are expected to conduct their animal research in compliance with the Society Policy and are required to verify that they have done so when submitting abstracts for presentation at the Annual Meeting or manuscripts for publication in *The Journal of Neuroscience.* Adherence to the Society Policy is also an important step toward receiving help from the Society in responding to questions about a member's use of animals in research. A complete description of the Society's policy and procedures for defending members whose research comes under attack is given in the Society's *Handbook for the Use of Animals in Neuroscience Research.*

Local Committee Review

An important element of the Society Policy is the establishment of a local committee that is charged with reviewing and approving all proposed animal care and use procedures. In addition to scientists experienced in research involving animals and a veterinarian, the membership of this local committee should include an individual who is not affiliated with the member's institution in any other way. In reviewing a proposed use of animals, the committee should evaluate the adequacy of institutional policies, animal husbandry, veterinary care, and the physical plant. Specific attention should be paid to proposed procedures for animal procurement, quarantine and stabilization, separation by species, disease diagnosis and treatment, anesthesia and analgesia, surgery and postsurgical care, and euthanasia. The review committee also should ensure that procedures involving live vertebrate animals are designed and performed with due consideration of their relevance to human or animal health, the advancement of knowledge, or the good of society. This review and approval of a member's use of live vertebrate animals in research by a local committee is an essential component of the Society Policy. Assistance in developing appropriate animal care and use procedures and establishing a local review committee can be obtained from the documents listed here and from the Society.

Other Laws, Regulations, and Policies

In addition to complying with the policy described above, Regular Members (i.e., North American residents) of the Society must also adhere to all relevant national, state, or local laws and/or regulations that govern their use of animals in neuroscience research. Thus, U.S. members must observe the U.S. Animal Welfare Act (as amended in 1985) and its implementing regulations from the U.S. Department of Agriculture. Canadian members must abide by the *Guide to the Care and Use of Experimental Animals,* and members in Mexico must comply with the *Reglamento de la Ley General de Salud en Materia de Investigacion para la Salud* of the Secretaria de Salud (published on Jan. 6, 1987). Similarly, in addition to complying with the laws and regulations of their home countries, Foreign Members of the Society should adhere to the official Society Policy outlined here.

Recommended References

"Anesthesia and paralysis in experimental animals." *Visual Neuroscience,* 1:421–426. 1984.

The Biomedical Investigator's Handbook for Researchers Using Animal Models. 1987. Foundation for Biomedical Research, 818 Connecticut Ave., N.W., Suite 303, Washington, D.C. 20006.

Guide for the Care and Use of Laboratory Animals, 7th edition. 1996. NRC (National Research Council), Institute of Laboratory Animal Resources, National Academy of Sciences, 2101 Constitution Ave., N.W., Washington, D.C. 20418.

Guide to the Care and Use of Experimental Animals, 2nd edition, vol. 1. 1993. Canadian Council on Animal Care, 350 Albert St., Suite 315, Ottawa, Ontario, Canada K1R 1B1.

Handbook for the Use of Animals in Neuroscience Research. 1991. Society for Neuroscience, 11 Dupont Circle, N.W., Suite 500, Washington, D.C. 20036.

OPRR Public Health Service Policy on Humane Care and Use of Laboratory Animals (revised Sept. 1986). Office for Protection from Research Risks, NIH, 6100 Executive Blvd., Suite 3B01-MSC 7507, Rockville, MD 20892-7507.

Preparation and Maintenance of Higher Mammals During Neuroscience Experiments. Report of a National Institutes of Health Workshop. NIH Publication No. 91-3207, March 1991. National Eye Institute, Bldg. 31, Rm. 6A47, Bethesda, MD 20892.

Seventh Title of the Regulations of the General Law of Health, Regarding Health Research. In: *Laws and Codes of Mexico.* Published in the Porrua Collection, 12th updated edition, pp. 430–431. Porrua Publishers, Mexico, 1995.

The following principles, based largely on the PHS *Policy on Humane Care and Use of Laboratory Animals,* can be a useful guide in the design and implementation of experimental procedures involving laboratory animals.

Animals selected for a procedure should be of an appropriate species and quality and the minimum number required to obtain valid results.

Proper use of animals, including the avoidance or minimization of discomfort, distress, and pain, when consistent with sound scientific practices, is imperative.

Procedures with animals that may cause more than momentary or slight pain or distress should be performed with appropriate sedation, analgesia, or anesthesia. Surgical or other painful procedures should not be performed on unanesthetized animals paralyzed by chemical agents.

Postoperative care of animals shall be such as to minimize discomfort and pain and, in any case, shall be equivalent to accepted practices in schools of veterinary medicine.

Animals that would otherwise suffer severe or chronic pain or distress that cannot be relieved should be painlessly killed at the end of the procedure or, if appropriate, during the procedure. If the study requires the death of the animal, the animal must be killed in a humane manner.

Living conditions should be appropriate for the species and contribute to the animals' health and comfort. Normally, the housing, feeding, and care of all animals used for biomedical purposes must be directed by a veterinarian or other scientist trained and experienced in the proper care, handling, and use of the species being maintained or studied. In any case, appropriate veterinary care shall be provided.

Exceptions to these principles require careful consideration and should only be made by an appropriate review group such as an institutional animal care and use committee.

Policy on the Use of Human Subjects in Neuroscience Research

Experimental procedures involving human subjects must have been conducted in conformance with the policies and principles contained in the Federal Policy for the Protection of Human Subjects (United States Office of Science and Technology Policy) and in the Declaration of Helsinki. When publishing a paper in *The Journal of Neuroscience* or submitting an abstract for presentation at the Annual Meeting, authors must sign a statement of compliance with this policy.

Recommended References

Declaration of Helsinki. (Adopted in 1964 by the 18th World Medical Assembly in Helsinki, Finland, and revised by the 29th World Medical Assembly in Tokyo in 1975.) In: *The Main Issue in Bioethics Revised Edition.* Andrew C. Varga, Ed. New York: Paulist Press, 1984.

Federal Policy for the Protection of Human Subjects; Notices and Rules. *Federal Register.* Vol. 56, No. 117 (June 18, 1991), pp. 28002–28007.

http://www.apa.org/science/anguide.html
This Web site presents the ethical guidelines adopted by the American Psychological Association. They are largely similar to those of the Neuroscience Society.

References

Numbers in parentheses following entries indicate the chapter in which a reference is cited.

Abbar, M., Couret, P., Bellivier, F., Leboyer, M., Boulenger, J. P., Castelhau, D., et al. (2001). Suicide attempts and the tryptophan hydroxylase gene. *Molecular Psychiatry, 6,* 268–273. (12)

AbdelMalik, P., Husted, J, Chow, E. W. C., & Bassett, A. S. (2003). Childhood head injury and expression of schizophrenia in multiply affected families. *Archives of General Psychiatry, 60,* 231–236. (15)

Abercrombie, H. C., Kalin, N. H., Thurow, M. E., Rosenkranz, M. A., & Davidson, R. J. (2003). Cortisol variation in humans affects memory for emotionally laden and neutral information. *Behavioral Neuroscience, 117,* 505–516. (12)

Abi-Dargham, A., Rodenhiser, J., Printz, D., Zea-Ponce, Y., Gil, R., Kegeles, L. S., et al. (2000). Increased baseline occupancy of D_2 receptors by dopamine in schizophrenia. *Proceedings of the National Academy of Sciences, USA, 97,* 8104–8109. (15)

Abraham, N. M., Spors, H., Carleton, A., Margrie, T. W., Kuner, T., & Schaefer, A. T. (2004). Maintaining accuracy at the expense of speed: Stimulus similarity defines odor discrimination time in mice. *Neuron, 44,* 865–876. (7)

Adamec, R. E., Stark-Adamec, C., & Livingston, K. E. (1980). The development of predatory aggression and defense in the domestic cat (*Felis catus*): 3. Effects on development of hunger between 180 and 365 days of age. *Behavioral and Neural Biology, 30,* 435–447. (12)

Adams, D. B., Gold, A. R., & Burt, A. D. (1978). Rise in female-initiated sexual activity at ovulation and its suppression by oral contraceptives. *New England Journal of Medicine, 299,* 1145–1150. (11)

Adams, R. B., Jr., Gordon, H. L., Baird, A. A., Ambady, N., & Kleck, R. E. (2003). Effects of gaze on amygdala sensitivity to anger and fear faces. *Science, 300,* 1536. (12)

Adams, R. B., Jr., & Kleck, R. E. (2005). Effects of direct and averted gaze on the perception of facially communicated emotion. *Emotion, 5,* 3–11. (12)

Adams, W., Kendell, R. E., Hare, E. H., & Munk-Jørgensen, P. (1993). Epidemiological evidence that maternal influenza contributes to the aetiology of schizophrenia. *British Journal of Psychiatry, 163,* 522–534. (15)

Ader, R. (2001). Psychoneuroimmunology. *Current Directions in Psychological Science, 10,* 94–98. (12)

Adkins, E. K., & Adler, N. T. (1972). Hormonal control of behavior in the Japanese quail. *Journal of Comparative and Physiological Psychology, 81,* 27–36. (11)

Adkins-Regan, E. (1988). Sex hormones and sexual orientation in animals. *Psychobiology, 16,* 335–347. (11)

Adler, E., Hoon, M. A., Mueller, K. L., Chandrashekar, J., Ryba, N. J. P., & Zuker, C. S. (2000). A novel family of mammalian taste receptors. *Cell, 100,* 693–702. (7)

Adolphs, R., Baron-Cohen, S., & Tranel, D. (2002). Impaired recognition of social emotions following amygdala damage. *Journal of Cognitive Neuroscience, 14,* 1264–1274. (12)

Adolphs, R., Damasio, H., & Tranel, D. (2002). Neural systems for recognition of emotional prosody: A 3-D lesion study. *Emotion, 2,* 23–51. (14)

Adolphs, R., Denburg, N. L., & Tranel, D. (2001). The amygdala's role in long-term declarative memory for gist and detail. *Behavioral Neuroscience,115,* 983–992. (12)

Adolphs, R., Gosselin, F., Buchanan, T. W., Tranel, D., Schyns, P., & Damasio, A. R. (2005). A mechanism for impaired fear recognition after amygdala damage. *Nature, 433,* 68–72. (12)

Adolphs, R., Tranel, D., & Buchanan, T. W. (2005). Amygdala damage impairs emotional memory for gist but not details of complex stimuli. *Nature Neuroscience, 8,* 512–518. (12)

Adolphs, R., Tranel, D., & Damasio, A. R. (1998). The human amygdala in social judgment. *Nature, 393,* 470–474. (12)

Adolphs, R., Tranel, D., & Damasio, A. R. (2003). Dissociable neural systems for recognizing emotions. *Brain and Cognition, 52,* 61–69. (12)

Adolphs, R., Tranel, D., Damasio, H., & Damasio, A. (1994). Impaired recognition of emotion in facial expressions following bilateral damage to the human amygdala. *Nature, 372,* 669–672. (12)

Adolphs, R., Tranel, D., Damasio, H., & Damasio, A. (1995). Fear and the human amygdala. *Journal of Neuroscience, 15,* 5879–5891. (12)

Aggleton, J. P., Blindt, H. S., & Rawlins, J. N. P. (1989). Effects of amygdaloid and amygdaloid-hippocampal lesions on object recognition and spatial working memory in rats. *Behavioral Neuroscience, 103,* 962–974. (13)

Aglioti, S., Smania, N., Atzei, A., & Berlucchi, G. (1997). Spatio-temporal properties of the pattern of evoked phantom sensations in a left index amputee patient. *Behavioral Neuroscience, 111,* 867–872. (5)

Aglioti, S., Smania, N., & Peru, A. (1999). Frames of reference for mapping tactile stimuli in brain-damaged patients. *Journal of Cognitive Neuroscience, 11,* 67–79. (14)

Aglioti, S., Tassinari, G., Corballis, M. C., & Berlucchi, G. (2000). Incomplete gustatory localization as shown by analysis of taste discrimination after callosotomy. *Journal of Cognitive Neuroscience, 12,* 238–245. (7, 14)

Aharon, I., Etcoff, N., Ariely, D., Chabris, C. F., O'Connor, E., & Breiter, H. C. (2001). Beautiful faces have variable reward value: fMRI and behavioral evidence. *Neuron, 32,* 537–551. (15)

Ahlskog, J. E., & Hoebel, B. G. (1973). Overeating and obesity from damage to a noradrenergic system in the brain. *Science, 182,* 166–169. (10)

Ahlskog, J. E., Randall, P. K., & Hoebel, B. G. (1975). Hypothalamic hyperphagia: Dissociation from hyperphagia following destruction of noradrenergic neurons. *Science, 190,* 399–401. (10)

Ahmed, I. I., Shryne, J. E., Gorski, R. A., Branch, B. J., & Taylor, A. N. (1991). Prenatal ethanol and the prepubertal sexually dimorphic nucleus of the preoptic area. *Physiology & Behavior, 49,* 427–432. (11)

Airaksinen, M. S., & Saarma, M. (2002). The GDNF family: Signalling, biological functions and therapeutic value. *Nature Reviews Neuroscience, 3,* 383–394. (5)

Akbarian, S., Kim, J. J., Potkin, S. G., Hagman, J. O., Tafazzoli, A., Bunney, W. E., Jr., et al. (1995). Gene expression for glutamic acid decarboxylase is reduced without loss of neurons in prefrontal cortex of schizophrenics. *Archives of General Psychiatry, 52,* 258–266. (15)

Albright, T. D., Jessell, T. M., Kandel, E. R., & Posner, M. I. (2001). Progress in the neural sciences in the century after Cajal (and the mysteries that remain). *Annals of the New York Academy of Sciences, 929,* 11–40. (2)

Aldrich, M. S. (1998). Diagnostic aspects of narcolepsy. *Neurology, 50*(Suppl. 1), S2–S7. (9)

Aleman, A., Kahn, R. S., & Selten, J. P. (2003). Sex differences in the risk of schizophrenia. *Archives of General Psychiatry, 60,* 565–571. (15)

Allen, C. B., Celikel, T., & Feldman, D. E. (2003). Long-term depression induced by sensory deprivation during cortical map plasticity *in vivo*. *Nature Neuroscience, 6,* 291–299. (13)

Allen, J. S., Damasio, H., Grabowski, T. J., Bruss, J., & Zhang, W. (2003). Sexual dimorphism and asymmetries in the gray-white composition of the human cerebrum. *NeuroImage, 18,* 880–894. (4, 11)

Allison, T., & Cicchetti, D. V. (1976). Sleep in mammals: Ecological and constitutional correlates. *Science, 194,* 732–734. (9)

Almli, C. R., Fisher, R. S., & Hill, D. L. (1979). Lateral hypothalamus destruction in infant rats produces consummatory deficits without sensory neglect or attenuated arousal. *Experimental Neurology, 66,* 146–157. (10)

Al-Rashid, R. A. (1971). Hypothalamic syndrome in acute childhood leukemia. *Clinical Pediatrics, 10,* 53–54. (10)

Altar, C. A., Laeng, P., Jurata, L. W., Brockman, J. A., Lemire, A., Bullard, J., et al. (2004). Electroconvulsive seizures regulate gene expression of distinct neurotrophic signaling pathways. *Journal of Neuroscience, 24,* 2667–2677. (15)

Amateau, S. K., & McCarthy, M. M. (2004). Inductiion of PGE_2 by estradiol mediates developmental masculinization of sex behavior. *Nature Neuroscience, 7,* 643–650. (11)

Amedi, A., Floel, A., Knecht, S., Zohary, E., & Cohen, L. G. (2004). Transcranial magnetic stimulation of the occipital pole interferes with verbal processing in blind subjects. *Nature Neuroscience, 7,* 1266–1270. (5)

Amedi, A., Raz, N., Pianka, P., Malach, R., & Zohary, E. (2003). Early "visual" cortex activation correlates with superior verbal memory performance in the blind. *Nature Neuroscience, 6,* 758–766. (5)

American Psychiatric Association. (1994). *Diagnostic and statistical manual of mental disorders* (4th ed.). Washington, DC: Author. (12, 15)

Amidzic, O., Riehle, H. J., Fehr, T., Wienbruch, C., & Elbert, T. (2001). Pattern of focal γ-bursts in chess players. *Nature, 412,* 603. (4)

Amiry-Moghaddam, M., & Ottersen, O. P. (2003). The molecular basis of water transport in the brain. *Nature Reviews Neuroscience, 4,* 991–1001. (2)

Amoore, J. E. (1977). Specific anosmia and the concept of primary odors. *Chemical Senses and Flavor, 2,* 267–281. (7)

Amsterdam, J. D., Winokur, A., Dyson, W., Herzog, S., Gonzalez, F., Rott, R., et al. (1985). Borna disease virus. *Archives of General Psychiatry, 42,* 1093–1096. (15)

Andersen, J. L., Klitgaard, H., & Saltin, B. (1994). Myosin heavy chain isoforms in single fibres from m. vastus lateralis of sprinters: Influence of training. *Acta Physiologica Scandinavica, 151,* 135–142. (8)

Andersen, S. L., Arvanitogiannis, A., Pliakas, A. M., LeBlanc, C., & Carlezon, W. A., Jr. (2002). Altered responsiveness to cocaine in rats exposed to methylphenidate during development. *Nature Neuroscience, 5,* 13–14. (3)

Andersen, T. S., Tiippana, K., & Sams, M. (2004). Factors influencing audiovisual fission and fusion illusions. *Cognitive Brain Research, 21,* 301–308. (4)

Anderson, A. K., & Phelps, E. A. (2001). Lesions of the human amygdala impair enhanced perception of emotionally salient events. *Nature, 411,* 305–309. (12)

Anderson, A. K., & Phelps, E. A. (2002). Is the human amygdala critical for the subjective experience of emotion? Evidence of intact dispositional affect in patients with amygdala lesions. *Journal of Cognitive Neuroscience, 14,* 709–720. (12)

Anderson, S. W., Bechara, A., Damasio, H., Tranel, D., & Damasio, A. R. (1999). Impairment of social and moral behavior related to early damage in human prefrontal cortex. *Nature Neuroscience, 2,* 1032–1037. (12)

Andersson, K.-E. (2001). Pharmacology of penile erection. *Pharmacological Reviews, 53,* 417–450. (11)

Andreasen, N. C. (1988). Brain imaging: Applications in psychiatry. *Science, 239,* 1381–1388. (4)

Andreasen, N. C. (1999). A unitary model of schizophrenia. *Archives of General Psychiatry, 56,* 781–787. (15)

Andreasen, N. C., Arndt, S., Alliger, R., Miller, D., & Flaum, M. (1995). Symptoms of schizophrenia: Methods, meanings, and mechanisms. *Archives of General Psychiatry, 52,* 341–351. (15)

Andreasen, N. C., Swayze, V. W., II, Flaum, M., Yates, W. R., Arndt, S., & McChesney, C. (1990). Ventricular enlargement in schizophrenia evaluated with computed tomographic scanning. *Archives of General Psychiatry, 47,* 1008–1015. (15)

Andrew, D., & Craig, A. D. (2001). Spinothalamic lamina I neurons selectively sensitive to histamine: A central neural pathway for itch. *Nature Neuroscience, 4,* 72–77. (7)

Andrews, T. J., Halpern, S. D., & Purves, D. (1997). Correlated size variations in human visual cortex, lateral geniculate nucleus, and optic tract. *Journal of Neuroscience, 17,* 2859–2868. (6)

Angulo, M. C., Kozlov, A. S., Charpak, S., & Audinat, E. (2004). Glutamate released from glial cells synchronizes neuronal activity in the hippocampus. *Journal of Neuroscience, 24,* 6920–6927. (2)

Antanitus, D. S. (1998). A theory of cortical neuron-astrocyte interaction. *The Neuroscientist, 4,* 154–159. (2)

Antle, M. C., & Mistlberger, R. E. (2000). Circadian clock resetting by sleep deprivation without exercise in the Syrian hamster. *Journal of Neuroscience, 20,* 9326–9332. (9)

Apostolakis, E. M., Garai, J., Fox, C., Smith, C. L., Watson, S. J., Clark, J. H., & O'Malley, B. W. (1996). Dopaminergic regulation of progesterone receptors: Brain D_5 dopamine receptors mediate induction of lordosis by D_1-like agonists in rats. *Journal of Neuroscience, 16,* 4823–4834. (11)

Appolinario, J. C., Bacaltchuk, J., Sichieri, R., Claudino, A. M., Godoy-Matos, A., Morgan, C., et al. (2003). A randomized, double-blind, placebo-controlled study of sibutramine in the treatment of binge-eating disorder. *Archives of General Psychiatry, 60,* 1109–1116. (10)

Araneda, R. C., Kini, A. D., & Firestein, S. (2000). The molecular receptive range of an odorant receptor. *Nature Neuroscience, 3,* 1248–1255. (7)

Archer, J. (2000). Sex differences in aggression between heterosexual partners: A meta-analytic review. *Psychological Bulletin, 126,* 651–680. (12)

Arendt, D., & Nübler-Jung, K. (1994). Inversion of dorsoventral axis? *Nature, 371,* 26. (14)

Arendt, D., Tessmar-Raible, K., Snyman, H., Dorresteijn, A. W., & Wittbrodt, J. (2004). Ciliary photoreceptors with a vertebrate-type opsin in an invertebrate brain. *Science, 306,* 869–871. (6)

Arendt, J. (1997). Safety of melatonin in long-term use(?). *Journal of Biological Rhythms, 12,* 673–681. (9)

Arkin, A. M., Toth, M. F., Baker, J., & Hastey, J. M. (1970). The frequency of sleep talking in the laboratory among chronic sleep talkers and good dream recallers. *Journal of Nervous and Mental Disease, 151,* 369–374. (9)

Arnold, A. P. (2004). Sex chromosomes and brain gender. *Nature Reviews Neuroscience, 5,* 701–708. (1, 6, 11)

Arnold, A. P., & Breedlove, S. M. (1985). Organizational and activational effects of sex steroids on brain and behavior: A reanalysis. *Hormones and Behavior, 19,* 469–498. (11)

Arnold, S. E. (2000). Cellular and molecular neuropathology of the parahippocampal region in schizophrenics. *Annals of the New York Academy of Sciences, 911,* 275–292. (15)

Aron, A., Fisher, H., Mashek, D. J., Strong, G., Li, H., & Brown, L. L. (2005). Reward, motivation, and emotion systems associated with early-stage intense romantic love. *Journal of Neurophysiology, 94,* 327–337. (12)

Arvidson, K., & Friberg, U. (1980). Human taste: Response and taste bud number in fungiform papillae. *Science, 209,* 807–808. (7)

Ascherio, A., Weisskopf, M. G., O'Reilly, E. J., McCullough, M., Calle, E. E., Rodriguez, C., et al. (2004). Coffee consumption, gender, and Parkinson's disease mortality in the cancer prevention study II cohort: The modifying effects of estrogen. *American Journal of Epidemiology, 160,* 977–984. (8)

Aserinsky, E., & Kleitman, N. (1955). Two types of ocular motility occurring in sleep. *Journal of Applied Physiology, 8,* 1–10. (7, 9)

Aston-Jones, G., Chen, S., Zhu, Y., & Oshinsky, M. L. (2001). A neural circuit for circadian regulation of arousal. *Nature Neuroscience, 4,* 732–738. (9)

Au, T. K., Knightly, L. M., Jun, S.-A., & Oh, J. S. (2002). Overhearing a language during childhood. *Psychological Science, 13,* 238–243. (14)

Azrin, N. H., Sisson, R. W., Meyers, R., & Godley, M. (1982). Alcoholism treatment by disulfiram and community reinforcement therapy. *Journal of Behavior Therapy and Experimental Psychiatry, 13,* 105–112. (15)

Babich, F. R., Jacobson, A. L., Bubash, S., & Jacobson, A. (1965). Transfer of a response to naive rats by injection of ribonucleic acid extracted from trained rats. *Science, 149,* 656–657. (13)

Babiloni, C., Brancucci, A., Pizzella, V., Romani, G. L., Tecchio, F., Torquati, K., et al. (2005). Contingent negative variation in the parasylvian cortex increases during expectancy of painful sensorimotor events: A magnetoencephalographic study. *Behavioral Neuroscience, 119,* 49–502. (7)

Babkoff, H., Caspy, T., Mikulincer, M., & Sing, H. C. (1991). Monotonic and rhythmic influences: A challenge for sleep deprivation research. *Psychological Bulletin, 109,* 411–428. (9)

Backlund, E.-O., Granberg, P.-O., Hamberger, B., Sedvall, G., Seiger, A., & Olson, L. (1985). Transplantation of adrenal medullary tissue to striatum in Parkinsonism. In A. Björklund & U. Stenevi (Eds.), *Neural grafting in the mammalian CNS* (pp. 551–556). Amsterdam: Elsevier. (8)

Bäckman, J., & Alerstam, T. (2001). Confronting the winds: Orientation and flight behavior of roosting swifts, *Apus apus. Proceedings of the Royal Society of London. Series B—Biological Sciences, 268,* 1081–1087. (9)

Baddeley, A. D., & Hitch, G. (1974). Working memory. In G. H. Bower (Ed.), *Psychology of learning and motivation* (Vol. 8, pp. 47–89). New York: Academic Press. (13)

Baddeley, A. D., & Hitch, G. J. (1994). Developments in the concept of working memory. *Neuropsychology, 8,* 485–493. (13)

Baer, J. S., Sampson, P. D., Barr, H. M., Connor, P. D., & Streissguth, A. P. (2003). A 21-year longitudinal analysis of the effects of prenatal alcohol exposure on young adult drinking. *Archives of General Psychiatry, 60,* 377–385. (15)

Baghdoyan, H. A., Spotts, J. L., & Snyder, S. G. (1993). Simultaneous pontine and basal forebrain microinjections of carbachol suppress REM sleep. *Journal of Neuroscience, 13,* 229–242. (9)

Bailey, C. H., Giustetto, M., Huang, Y.-Y., Hawkins, R. D., & Kandel, E. R. (2000). Is heterosynaptic modulation essential for stabilizing Hebbian plasticity and memory? *Nature Reviews Neuroscience, 1,* 11–20. (13)

Bailey, J. M., & Pillard, R. C. (1991). A genetic study of male sexual orientation. *Archives of General Psychiatry, 48,* 1089–1096. (11)

Bailey, J. M., Pillard, R. C., Dawood, K., Miller, M. B., Farrer, L. A., Trivedi, S., et al. (1999). A family history study of male sexual orientation using three independent samples. *Behavior Genetics, 29,* 79–86. (11)

Bailey, J. M., Pillard, R. C., Neale, M. C., & Agyei, Y. (1993). Heritable factors influence sexual orientation in women. *Archives of General Psychiatry, 50,* 217–223. (11)

Bailey, J. M., Willerman, L., & Parks, C. (1991). A test of the maternal stress theory of human male homosexuality. *Archives of Sexual Behavior, 20,* 277–293. (11)

Bakker, J., Honda, S.-I., Harada, N., & Balthazart, J. (2002). The aromatase knockout mouse provides new evidence that estradiol is required during development in the female for the expression of sociosexual behaviors in adulthood. *Journal of Neuroscience, 22,* 9104–9112. (11)

Baldwin, A. E., Holahan, M. R., Sadeghian, K., & Kelley, A. E. (2000). *N*-methyl-D-aspartate receptor-dependent plasticity within a distributed corticostriatal network mediates appetitive instrumental learning. *Behavioral Neuroscience, 114,* 84–98. (13)

Ballard, P. A., Tetrud, J. W., & Langston, J. W. (1985). Permanent human Parkinsonism due to 1-methyl-4-phenyl-1,2,3,6-tetrahydropyridine (MPTP). *Neurology, 35,* 949–956. (8)

Bao, S., Chan, V. T., & Merzenich, M. M. (2001). Cortical remodeling induced by activity of ventral tegmental dopamine neurons. *Nature, 412,* 79–83. (5)

Baquet, Z. C., Gorski, J. A., & Jones, K. R. (2004). Early striatal dendrite deficits followed by neuron loss with advanced age in the absence of anterograde cortical brain-derived neurotrophic factor. *Journal of Neuroscience, 24,* 4250–4258. (5)

Barbour, D. L., & Wang, X. (2003). Contrast tuning in auditory cortex. *Science, 299,* 1073–1075. (7)

Barinaga, M. (1996). Finding new drugs to treat stroke. *Science, 272,* 664–666. (5)

Barnea, G., O'Donnell, S., Mancia, F., Sun, X., Nemes, A., Mendelsohn, M., et al. (2004). Odorant receptors on axon termini in the brain. *Science, 304,* 1468. (7)

Barnes, B. M. (1996, September/October). Sang froid. *The Sciences, 36*(5), 13–14. (9)

Barnes, J., Anderson, L. A., & Phillipson, J. D. (2001). St John's wort (*Hypericum perforatum L.*): A review of its chemistry, pharmacology and clinical properties. *Journal of Pharmacy and Pharmacology, 53,* 583–600. (15)

Barone, F. C., Feuerstein, G. Z., & White, R. F. (1997). Brain cooling during transient focal ischemia provides complete neuroprotection. *Neuroscience and Biobehavioral Reviews, 21,* 31–44. (5)

Barton, R. A., & Harvey, P. H. (2000). Mosaic evolution of brain structure in mammals. *Nature, 405,* 1055–1058. (4)

Bartoshuk, L. M. (1991). Taste, smell, and pleasure. In R. C. Bolles (Ed.), *The hedonics of taste* (pp. 15–28). Hillsdale, NJ: Erlbaum. (7)

Bartoshuk, L. M., Gentile, R. L., Moskowitz, H. R., & Meiselman, H. L. (1974). Sweet taste induced by miracle fruit (*Synsephalum dulcificum*). *Physiology & Behavior, 12,* 449–456. (7)

Basheer, R., Rainnie, D. G., Porkka-Heiskanen, T., Ramesh, V., & McCarley, R. W. (2001). Adenosine, prolonged wakefulness, and A1-activated NF-kB DNA binding in the basal forebrain of the rat. *Neuroscience, 104,* 731–739. (9)

Basil, J. A., Kamil, A. C., Balda, R. P., & Fite, K. V. (1996). Differences in hippocampal volume among food storing corvids. *Brain, Behavior and Evolution, 47,* 156–164. (13)

Basso, A., & Rusconi, M. L. (1998). Aphasia in left-handers. In P. Coppens, Y. Lebrun, & A. Basso (Eds.), *Aphasia in atypical populations* (pp. 1–34). Mahwah, NJ: Erlbaum. (14)

Bastien, C., & Campbell, K. (1992). The evoked K-complex: All-or-none phenomenon? *Sleep, 15,* 236–245. (9)

Battersby, S. (1997). Plus c'est le même chews. *Nature, 385,* 679. (10)

Baulac, S., Huberfeld, G., Gourfinkel-An, I., Mitropoulou, G., Beranger, A., Prud' homme, J.-F., et al. (2001). First genetic evidence of GABAA receptor dysfunction in epilepsy: A mutation in the γ2-

subunit gene. *Nature Genetics, 28,* 46–48. (14)

Baum, A., Gatchel, R. J., & Schaeffer, M. A. (1983). Emotional, behavioral, and physiological effects of chronic stresss at Three Mile Island. *Journal of Consulting and Clinical Psychology, 51,* 565–582. (12)

Baum, M. J., & Vreeburg, J. T. M. (1973). Copulation in castrated male rats following combined treatment with estradiol and dihydrotestosterone. *Science, 182,* 283–285. (11)

Baxter, L. R., Phelps, M. E., Mazziotta, J. C., Schwartz, J. M., Gerner, R. H., Selin, C. E., et al. (1985). Cerebral metabolic rates for glucose in mood disorders. *Archives of General Psychiatry, 42,* 441–447. (15)

Baxter, M. G., & Murray, E. A. (2002). The amygdala and reward. *Nature Reviews Neuroscience, 3,* 563–573. (12)

Bayley, P. J., Frascino, J. C., & Squire, L. R. (2005). Robust habit learning in the absence of awareness and independent of the medial temporal lobe. *Nature, 436,* 550–553. (13)

Baylis, G. C., & Driver, J. (2001). Shape-coding in IT cells generalizes over contrast and mirror reversal but not figure-ground reversal. *Nature Neuroscience, 4,* 937–942. (6)

Beal, M. F., & Ferrante, R. J. (2004). Experimental therapeutics in transgenic mouse models of Huntington's disease. *Nature Reviews Neuroscience, 5,* 373–384. (8)

Bechara, A., Damasio, H., Damasio, A. R., & Lee, G. P. (1999). Different contributions of the human amygdala and ventromedial prefrontal cortex to decision-making. *Journal of Neuroscience, 19,* 5473–5481. (12)

Becker, C., Thiébot, M.-H., Touitou, Y., Hamon, M., Cesselin, F., & Benoliel, J.-J. (2001). Enhanced cortical extracellular levels of cholecystokinin-like material in a model of anticipation of social defeat in the rat. *Journal of Neuroscience, 21,* 262–269. (12)

Becker, H. C. (1988). Effects of the imidazobenzodiazepine Ro15-4513 on the stimulant and depressant actions of ethanol on spontaneous locomotor activity. *Life Sciences, 43,* 643–650. (12)

Beebe, D. W., & Gozal, D. (2002). Obstructive sleep apnea and the prefrontal cortex: Towards a comprehensive model linking nocturnal upper airway obstruction to daytime cognitive and behavioral deficits. *Journal of Sleep Research, 11,* 1–16. (9)

Beeman, M. J., & Chiarello, C. (1998). Complementary right- and left-hemisphere language comprehension. *Current Directions in Psychological Science, 7,* 2–8. (14)

Behl, C. (2002). Oestrogen as a neuroprotective hormone. *Nature Reviews Neuroscience, 3,* 433–442. (11)

Békésy, G.—*See* von Békésy, G.

Bellugi, U., Lichtenberger, L., Jones, W., Lai, Z., & St George, M. (2000). I. The neurocognitive profile of Williams syndrome: A complex pattern of strengths and weaknesses. *Journal of Cognitive Neuroscience, 12*(Suppl.), 7–29. (14)

Bellugi, U., Wang, P. P., & Jernigan, T. L. (1994). Williams syndrome: An unusual neuropsychological profile. In S. H. Broman & J. Grafman (Eds.), *Atypical cognitive deficits in developmental disorders* (pp. 23–56). Hillsdale, NJ: Erlbaum. (14)

Benedetti, F., Arduino, C., & Amanzio, M. (1999). Somatotopic activation of opioid systems by target-directed expectations of analgesia. *Journal of Neuroscience, 19,* 3639–3648. (7)

Benes, F. M. (1995). Is there a neuroanatomic basis for schizophrenia? An old question revisited. *The Neuroscientist, 1,* 104–115. (15)

Benes, F. M., Turtle, M., Khan, Y., & Farol, P. (1994). Myelination of a key relay zone in the hippocampal formation occurs in the human brain during childhood, adolescence, and adulthood. *Archives of General Psychiatry, 51,* 477–484. (5)

Benjamin, J., Li, L., Patterson, C., Greenberg, B. D., Murphy, D. L., & Hamer, D. H. (1996). Population and familial association between the D4 dopamine receptor gene and measures of novelty seeking. *Nature Genetics, 12,* 81–84. (3)

Benn, S. C., & Woolf, C. J. (2004). Adult neuron survival strategies—Slamming on the brakes. *Nature Reviews Neuroscience, 5,* 686–700. (5)

Benoit, S. C., Air, E. L., Coolen, L. M., Strauss, R., Jackman, A., Clegg, D. J., et al. (2002). The catabolic action of insulin in the brain is mediated by melanocortins. *Journal of Neuroscience, 22,* 9048–9052. (10)

Benschop, R. J., Godaert, G. L. R., Geenen, R., Brosschot, J. F., DeSmet, M. B. M., Olff, M., et al. (1995). Relationships between cardiovascular and immunologic changes in an experimental stress model. *Psychological Medicine, 25,* 323–327. (12)

Berdoy, M., Webster, J. P., & Macdonald, D. W. (2000). Fatal attraction in rats infected with *Toxoplasma gondii. Proceedings of the Royal Society of London, B, 267,* 1591–1594. (12)

Berenbaum, S. A. (1999). Effects of early androgens on sex-typed activities and interests in adolescents with congenital adrenal hyperplasia. *Hormones and Behavior, 35,* 102–110. (11)

Berenbaum, S. A., Duck, S. C., & Bryk, K. (2002). Behavioral effects of prenatal *versus* postnatal androgen excess in children with 21 hydroxylase-deficient congenital adrenal hyperplasia. *Journal of Clinical Endocrinology & Metabolism, 85,* 727–733. (11)

Berger, R. J., & Phillips, N. H. (1995). Energy conservation and sleep. *Behavioural Brain Research, 69,* 65–73. (9)

Berger-Sweeney, J., & Hohmann, C. F. (1997). Behavioral consequences of abnormal cortical development: Insights into developmental disabilities. *Behavioural Brain Research, 86,* 121–142. (5)

Berlucchi, G., Mangun, G. R., & Gazzaniga, M. S. (1997). Visuospatial attention and the split brain. *News in Physiological Sciences, 12,* 226–231. (14)

Berman, K. F., Torrey, E. F., Daniel, D. G., & Weinberger, D. R. (1992). Regional cerebral blood flow in monozygotic twins discordant and concordant for schizophrenia. *Archives of General Psychiatry, 49,* 927–934. (15)

Bernhardt, P. C. (1997). Influences of serotonin and testosterone in aggression and dominance: Convergence with social psychology. *Current Directions in Psychological Science, 6,* 44–48. (12)

Bernstein, J. J., & Gelderd, J. B. (1970). Regeneration of the long spinal tracts in the goldfish. *Brain Research, 20,* 33–38. (5)

Berntsen, D., & Rubin, D. C. (2002). Emotionally charged autobiographical memories across the life span: The recall of happy, sad, traumatic and involuntary memories. *Psychology and Aging, 17,* 636–652. (13)

Berntson, G. G., Shafi, R., & Sarter, M. (2002). Specific contributions of the basal forebrain corticopetal cholinergic system to electroencephalographic activity and sleep/waking behaviour. *European Journal of Neuroscience, 16,* 2453–2461. (9)

Berridge, C. W., Stellick, R. L., & Schmeichel, B. E. (2005). Wake-promoting actions of medial basal forebrain β_2 receptor stimulation. *Behavioral Neuroscience, 119,* 743–751. (9)

Berridge, K. C., & Robinson, T. E. (1995). The mind of an addicted brain: Neural sensitization of wanting versus liking. *Current Directions in Psychological Science, 4,* 71–76. (15)

Berridge, K. C., & Robinson, T. E. (1998). What is the role of dopamine in reward: Hedonic impact, reward learning, or incentive salience? *Brain Research Reviews, 28,* 309–369. (15)

Berson, D. M., Dunn, F. A., & Takao, M. (2002). Phototransduction by retinal ganglion cells that set the circadian clock. *Science, 295,* 1070–1073. (9)

Bertram, L., Blacker, D., Mullin, K., Keeney, D., Jones, J., Basu, S., et al. (2000). Evidence for genetic linkage of Alzheimer's disease to chromosome 10q. *Science, 290,* 2302–2303. (13)

Betarbet, R., Sherer, T. B., MacKenzie, G., Garcia-Osuna, M., Panov, A. V., & Greenamyre, J. T. (2000). Chronic systemic pesticide exposure reproduces features of Parkinson's disease. *Nature Neuroscience, 3,* 1301–1306. (8)

Berti, A., Bottini, G., Gandola, M., Pia, L., Smassia, N., Stracciari, A, et al. (2005). Shared cortical anatomy for motor awareness and motor control. *Science, 309,* 488–491. (8)

Biben, M. (1979). Predation and predatory play behaviour of domestic cats. *Animal Behaviour, 27,* 81–94. (12)

Biernaskie, J., Chernenko, G., & Corbett, D. (2004). Efficacy of rehabilitative experience declines with time after focal ischemic brain injury. *Journal of Neuroscience, 24,* 1245–1254. (5)

Bierut, L. J., Heath, A. C., Bucholz, K. K., Dinwiddie, S. H., Madden, P. A. F., Statham, D. J., et al. (1999). Major depressive disorder in a community-based twin sample. *Archives of General Psychiatry, 56,* 557–563. (15)

Billington, C. J., & Levine, A. S. (1992). Hypothalamic neuropeptide Y regulation of feeding and energy metabolism. *Current Opinion in Neurobiology, 2,* 847–851. (10)

Binder, G. K., & Griffin, D. E. (2001). Interferon-γ-mediated site-specific clearance of alphavirus from CNS neurons. *Science, 293,* 303–306. (2)

Bischof, M., & Bassetti, C. L. (2004). Total dream loss: A distinct neuropsychological dysfunction after bilateral PCA stroke. *Annals of Neurology, 56,* 583–586. (9)

Blackless, M., Charuvastra, A., Derryck, A., Fausto-Sterling, A., Lauzanne, K., & Lee, E. (2000). How sexually dimorphic are we? Review and synthesis. *American Journal of Human Biology, 12,* 151–166. (11)

Blackwell, A., & Bates, E. (1995). Inducing agrammatic profiles in normals: Evidence for the selective vulnerability of morphology under cognitive resource limitation. *Journal of Cognitive Neuroscience, 7,* 228–257. (14)

Blagrove, M., Thayer, B., & Blakemore, S. (2004). The perception of self- versus experimenter-produced tactile stimuli when waking from REM and NREM sleep: Implications for the psychophysiology of dream formation. *Sleep, 27* (Suppl.), A60–A61. (9)

Blair, H. T., Huynh, V. K., Vaz, V. T., Van, J., Patel, R. R., Hiteshi, A. K., et al. (2005). Unilateral storage of fear memories by the amygdala. *Journal of Neuroscience, 25,* 4198–4205. (12)

Blake, R., & Hirsch, H. V. B. (1975). Deficits in binocular depth perception in cats after alternating monocular deprivation. *Science, 190,* 1114–1116. (6)

Blake, R., Palmeri, T. J., Marois, R., & Kim, C.-Y. (2005). On the perceptual reality of synesthetic color. In L. C. Robertson & N. Sagiv (Eds.), *Synesthesia* (pp. 47–73). Oxford, England: Oxford University Press. (7)

Blakemore, S.-J., Wolpert, D. M., & Frith, C. D. (1998). Central cancellation of self-produced tickle sensation. *Nature Neuroscience, 1,* 635–640. (7)

Blanke, O., Ortigue, S., Landis, T., & Seeck, M. (2002). Stimulating illusory own-body perceptions. *Nature, 419,* 269–270. (7)

Blasi, G., Mattay, V. S., Bertolino, A., Elvevåg, B., Callicott, J. H., Das, S., et al. (2005). Effect of catechol-O-methyltransferase *val*[158]*met* genotype on attentional control. *Journal of Neuroscience, 25,* 5038–5045. (14)

Bliss, T. V. P., & Lømo, T. (1973). Long-lasting potentiation of synaptic transmission in the dentate area of the anaesthetized rabbit following stimulation of the perforant path. *Journal of Physiology (London), 232,* 331–356. (13)

Bloch, G. J., Butler, P. C., & Kohlert, J. G. (1996). Galanin microinjected into the medial preoptic nucleus facilitates female- and male-typical sexual behaviors in the female rat. *Physiology & Behavior, 59,* 1147–1154. (11)

Bloch, G. J., & Mills, R. (1995). Prepubertal testosterone treatment of neonatally gonadectomized male rats: Defeminization and masculinization of behavioral and endocrine function in adulthood. *Neuroscience and Biobehavioral Reviews, 19,* 187–200. (11)

Bloch, G. J., Mills, R., & Gale, S. (1995). Prepubertal testosterone treatment of female rats: Defeminization of behavioral and endocrine function in adulthood. *Neuroscience and Biobehavioral Reviews, 19,* 177–186. (11)

Bloch, M., Rotenberg, N., Koren, D., & Klein, E. (2005). Risk factors associated with the development of postpartum mood disorders. *Journal of Affective Disorders, 88,* 9–18. (15)

Bloch, M., Schmidt, P. J., Danaceau, M., Murphy, J., Nieman, L., & Rubinow, D. R. (2000). Effects of gonadal steroids in women with a history of postpartum depression. *American Journal of Psychiatry, 157,* 924–930. (15)

Blonder, L. X., Smith, C. D., Davis, C. E., Kesler/West, M. L., Garrity, T. F., Avison, M. J., et al. (2004). Regional brain response to faces of humans and dogs. *Cognitive Brain Research, 20,* 384–394. (6)

Blum, D. (1994). *The monkey wars.* New York: Oxford University Press. (1)

Blum, I., Lerman, M., Misrachi, I., Nordenberg, Y., Grosskopf, I., Weizman, A., et al. (2004). Lack of plasma norepinephrine cyclicity, increased estradiol during the follicular phase, and of progesterone and gonadotrophins at ovulation in women with prementrual syndrome. *Neuropsychobiology, 50,* 10–15. (11)

Blum, K., Cull, J. G., Braverman, E. R., & Comings, D. E. (1996). Reward deficiency syndrome. *American Scientist, 84,* 132–145. (3)

Boatman, D., Freeman, J., Vining, E., Pulsifer, M., Miglioretti, D., Minahan, R., et al. (1999). Language recovery after left hemispherectomy in children with late-onset seizures. *Annals of Neurology, 46,* 579–586. (14)

Bobrow, D., & Bailey, J. M. (2000). Is male homosexuality maintained via kin selection? *Evolution and Human Behavior, 22,* 361–368. (11)

Bode, L., Ferszt, R., & Czech, G. (1993). Borna disease virus infection and affective disorders in man. *Archives of Virology* (Suppl. 7), 159–167. (15)

Bode, L., & Ludwig, H. (1997). Clinical similarities and close genetic relationship of human and animal Borna disease virus. *Archives of Virology* (Suppl. 13), 167–182. (15)

Bode, L., Riegel, S., Lange, W., & Ludwig, H. (1992). Human infections with Borna disease virus: Seroprevalence in patients with chronic diseases and healthy individuals. *Journal of Medical Virology, 36,* 309–315. (15)

Bogaert, A. F. (2003a). The interaction of fraternal birth order and body size in male sexual orientation. *Behavioral Neuroscience, 117,* 381–384. (11)

Bogaert, A. F. (2003b). Number of older brothers and sexual orientation: New tests and the attraction/behavior distinction in two national probability samples. *Journal of Personality and Social Psychology, 84,* 644–652. (11)

Bohbot, V. D., Allen, J. J. B., & Nadel, L. (2000). Memory deficits characterized by patterns of lesions to the hippocampus and parahippocampal cortex. *Annals of the New York Academy of Sciences, 911,* 355–368. (13)

Bohn, M. C., Cupit, L., Marciano, F., & Gash, D. M. (1987). Adrenal medulla grafts enhance recovery of striatal dopaminergic fibers. *Science, 237,* 913–916. (8)

Boivin, D. B., Duffy, J. F., Kronauer, R. E., & Czeisler, C. A. (1996). Dose-response relationships for resetting of human circadian clock by light. *Nature, 379,* 540–542. (9)

Bolaños, C. A., Barrot, M., Berton, O., Wallace-Black, D., & Nestler, E. J. (2003). Methylphenidate treatment during pre- and periadolescence alters behavioral responses to emotional stimuli at adulthood. *Biological Psychiatry, 54,* 1317–1329. (3)

Bonifati, V., Rizzu, P., van Baren, M. J., Schaap, O., Breedlove, G. J., Krieger, E., et al. (2003). Mutations in the *DJ-1* gene associated with autosomal recessive early-onset Parkinsonism. *Science, 299,* 256–259. (8)

Booth, F. W., & Neufer, P. D. (2005, January/February). Exercise controls gene expression. *American Scientist, 93,* 28–35. (8)

Borodinsky, L. N., Root, C. M., Cronin, J. A., Sann, S. B., Gu, X., & Spitzer, N. C. (2004). Activity-dependent homeostatic specification of transmitter expression in embryonic neurons. *Nature, 429,* 523–530. (3)

Bouchard, T. J., Jr., & McGue, M. (2003). Genetic and environmental influences on human psychological differences. *Journal of Neurobiology, 54,* 4–45. (1)

Boucher, T. J., Okuse, K., Bennett, D. L. H., Munson, J. B., Wood, J. N., & McMahon, S. B. (2000). Potent analgesic effects of GDNF in neuropathic pain states. *Science, 290,* 124–127. (7)

Boucsein, K., Weniger, G., Mursch, K., Steinhoff, B. J., & Irle, E. (2001). Amygdala lesion in temporal lobe epilepsy subjects impairs associative learning of emotional facial expressions. *Neuropsychologia, 39,* 231–236. (12)

Boutrel, B., Franc, B., Hen, R., Hamon, M., & Adrien, J. (1999). Key role of 5-HT1B receptors in the regulation of paradoxical sleep as evidenced in 5-HT1B knockout mice. *Journal of Neuroscience, 19,* 3204–3212. (9)

Bowles, S., & Posel, B. (2005). Genetic relatedness predicts South African migrant workers' remittances to their families. *Nature, 434,* 380–383. (1)

Bowmaker, J. K. (1998). Visual pigments and molecular genetics of color blindness. *News in Physiological Sciences, 13,* 63–69. (6)

Bowmaker, J. K., & Dartnall, H. J. A. (1980). Visual pigments of rods and cones in a human retina. *Journal of Physiology (London), 298,* 501–511. (6)

Brandt, T. (1991). Man in motion: Historical and clinical aspects of vestibular function. *Brain, 114,* 2159–2174. (7)

Brasted, P. J., Watts, C., Robbins, T. W., & Dunnett, S. B. (1999). Associative plasticity in striatal transplants. *Proceedings of the National Academy of Sciences, USA, 96,* 10524–10529. (8)

Braun, A. R., Balkin, T. J., Wesensten, N. J., Gwadry, F., Carson, R. E., Varga, M., et al. (1998). Dissociated pattern of activity in visual cortices and their projections during human rapid eye movement sleep. *Science, 279,* 91–95. (8, 9)

Braus, H. (1960). Anatomie des Menschen, 3. Band: Periphere Leistungsbahnen II. Centrales Nervensystem, Sinnesorgane. 2. Auflage [Human anatomy: Vol. 3. Peripheral pathways II. Central nervous system, sensory organs (2nd ed.)]. Berlin: Springer-Verlag. (4)

Bray, G. A., Nielsen, S. J., & Popkin, B. M. (2004). Consumption of high-fructose corn syrup in beverages may play a role in the epidemic of obesity. *American Journal of Clinical Nutrition, 79,* 537–543. (10)

Breiter, H. C., Aharon, I., Kahneman, D., Dale, A., & Shizgal, P. (2001). Functional imaging of neural responses to expectancy and experience of monetary gains and losses. *Neuron, 30,* 619–639. (15)

Bremner, J. D., Vythilingam, M., Anderson, G., Vermetten, E., McGlashan, T., Heninger, G., et al. (2003). Assessment of the hypothalamic-pituitary-adrenal axis over a 24-hour diurnal period and in response to neuroendocrine challenges in women with and without childhood sexual abuse and posttraumatic stress disorder. *Biological Psychiatry, 54,* 710–718. (12)

Brennan, P. A., Grekin, E. R., & Mednick, S. A. (1999). Maternal smoking during pregnancy and adult male criminal outcomes. *Archives of General Psychiatry, 56,* 215–219. (5, 12)

Bridgeman, B., & Staggs, D. (1982). Plasticity in human blindsight. *Vision Research, 22,* 1199–1203. (6)

Brightman, M. W. (1997). Blood-brain barrier: Penetration by solutes and cells. In G. Adelman & B. H. Smith (Eds.), *Elsevier encyclopedia of neuroscience.* New York: Elsevier. (2)

Brinkmann, R. R., Mezei, M. M., Theilmann, J., Almqvist, E., & Hayden, M. R. (1997). The likelihood of being affected with Huntington disease by a particular age, for a specific CAG size. *American Journal of Human Genetics, 60,* 1202–1210. (8)

Brody, A. L., Saxena, S., Stoesssel, P., Gillies, L. A., Fairbanks, L. A., Alborzian, S., et al. (2001). Regional brain metabolic changes in patients with major depression treated with either paroxetine or interpersonal therapy. *Archives of General Psychiatry, 58,* 631–640. (15)

Brooks, D. C., & Bizzi, E. (1963). Brain stem electrical activity during deep sleep. *Archives Italiennes de Biologie, 101,* 648–665. (9)

Brooks, J. H., & Reddon, J. R. (1996). Serum testosterone in violent and nonviolent young offenders. *Journal of Clinical Psychology, 52,* 475–483. (12)

Broughton, R., Billlings, R., Cartwright, R., Doucette, D., Edmeads, J., Edwardh, M., et al. (1994). Homicidal somnambulism: A case report. *Sleep, 17,* 253–264. (9)

Brown, A. S., Begg, M. D., Gravenstein, S., Schaefer, C. A., Wyatt, R. J., Bresnahan, M., et al. (2004). Serologic evidence of prenatal influenza in the etiology of schizophrenia. *Archives of General Psychiatry, 61,* 774–780. (15)

Brown, A. S., Cohen, P., Harkavy-Friedman, J., Babulas, V., Malaspina, D., Gorman, J. M., et al. (2001). Prenatal rubella, premorbid abnormalities, and adult schizophrenia. *Biological Psychiatry, 49,* 473–486. (15)

Brown, G. L., Ebert, M. H., Goyer, P. F., Jimerson, D. C., Klein, W. J., Bunney, W. E., et al. (1982). Aggression, suicide, and serotonin: Relationships of CSF amine metabolites. *American Journal of Psychiatry, 139,* 741–746. (12)

Brown, J., Babor, T. F., Litt, M. D., & Kranzler, H. R. (1994). The type A/type B distinction. *Annals of the New York Academy of Sciences, 708,* 23–33. (15)

Brown, J. R., Ye, H., Bronson, R. T., Dikkes, P., & Greenberg, M. E. (1996). A defect in nurturing in mice lacking the immediate early gene *fos B. Cell, 86,* 297–309. (11)

Bruesch, S. R., & Arey, L. B. (1942). The number of myelinated and unmyelinated fibers in the optic nerve of vertebrates. *Journal of Comparative Neurology, 77,* 631–665. (6)

Brüning, J. C., Gautham, D., Burks, D. J., Gillette, J., Schubert, M., Orban, P. C., et al. (2000). Role of brain insulin receptor in control of body weight and reproduction. *Science, 289,* 2122–2125. (10)

Bruyer, R., Dupuis, M., Ophoven, E., Rectem, D., & Reynaert, C. (1985). Anatomical and behavioral study of a case of asymptomatic callosal agenesis. *Cortex, 21,* 417–430. (14)

Buck, L., & Axel, R. (1991). A novel multigene family may encode odorant receptors: A molecular basis for odor recognition. *Cell, 65,* 175–187. (7)

Buck, R., & Duffy, R. J. (1980). Nonverbal communication of affect in brain-damaged patients. *Cortex, 16,* 351–362. (14)

Budney, A. J., Hughes, J. R., Moore, B. A., & Novy, P. L. (2001). Marijuana abstinence effects in marijuana smokers maintained in their home environment. *Archives of General Psychiatry, 58,* 917–924. (3)

Buell, S. J., & Coleman, P. D. (1981). Quantitative evidence for selective dendritic growth in normal human aging but not in senile dementia. *Brain Research, 214,* 23–41. (5)

Buka, S. L., Tsuang, M. T., Torrey, E. F., Klebanoff, M. A., Bernstein, D., & Yolken, R. H. (2001). Maternal infections and subsequent psychosis among offspring. *Archives of General Psychiatry, 58,* 1032–1037. (15)

Bundgaard, M. (1986). Pathways across the vertebrate blood-brain barrier: Morphological viewpoints. *Annals of the New York Academy of Sciences, 481,* 7–19. (2)

Burgess, C. E., Lindblad, K., Sigransky, E., Yuan, Q.-P., Long, R. T., Breschel, T., et al. (1998). Large CAG/CTG repeats are associated with childhood-onset schizophrenia. *Molecular Psychiatry, 3,* 321–327. (15)

Burgess, P. W., & McNeil, J. E. (1999). Content-specific confabulation. *Cortex, 35,* 163–182. (13)

Burr, D. C., Morrone, M. C., & Ross, J. (1994). Selective suppression of the magnocellular visual pathway during saccadic eye movements. *Nature, 371,* 511–513. (6)

Burrell, B. (2004). *Postcards from the brain museum.* New York: Broadway Books. (4)

Burton, H., Snyder, A. Z., Conturo, T. E., Akbudak, E., Ollinger, J. M., & Raichle, M. E. (2002). Adaptive changes in early and late blind: A fMRI study of Braille reading. *Journal of Neurophysiology, 87,* 589–607. (5)

Burton, R. F. (1994). *Physiology by numbers.* Cambridge, England: Cambridge University Press. (10)

Buss, D. M. (1994). The strategies of human mating. *American Scientist, 82,* 238–249. (11)

Buss, D. M. (2000). Desires in human mating. *Annals of the New York Academy of Sciences, 907,* 39–49. (11)

Buss, D. M. (2001). Cognitive biases and emotional wisdom in the evolution of conflict between the sexes. *Current Directions in Psychological Science, 10,* 219–223. (11)

Byl, N. N., McKenzie, A., & Nagarajan, S. S. (2000). Differences in somatosensory hand organization in a healthy flutist and a flutist with focal hand dystonia: A case report. *Journal of Hand Therapy, 13,* 302–309. (5)

Byne, W., Tobet, S., Mattiace, L. A., Lasco, M. S., Kemether, E., Edgar, M. A., et al. (2001). The interstitial nuclei of the human anterior hypothalamus: An investigation of variation with sex, sexual orientation, and HIV status. *Hormones and Behavior, 40,* 86–92. (11)

Byrne, M., Agerbo, E., Ewald, H., Eaton, W. W., & Mortensen, P. B. (2003). Parental age and risk of schizophrenia. *Archives of General Psychiatry, 60,* 673–678. (15)

Caccappolo-van Vliet, E., Miozzo, M., & Stern, Y. (2004). Phonological dyslexia: A test case for reading models. *Psychological Science, 15,* 583–590. (14)

Cadoret, R. J., Yates, W. R., Troughton, E., Woodworth, G., & Stewart, M. A. (1995). Genetic-environmental interaction in the genesis of aggressivity and conduct disorders. *Archives of General Psychiatry, 52,* 916–924. (12)

Cahill, L., & McGaugh, J. L. (1998). Mechanisms of emotional arousal and lasting declarative memory. *Trends in Neurosciences, 21,* 294–299. (13)

Cahn, R., Borziex, M.-G., Aldinio, C., Toffano, G., & Cahn, J. (1989). Influence of monosialoganglioside inner ester on neurologic recovery after global cerebral ischemia in monkeys. *Stroke, 20,* 652–656. (5)

Cahn, W., Hulshoff, H. E., Lems, E. B. T. E., van Haren, N. E. M., Schnack, H. G., van der Linden, J. A., et al. (2002). Brain volume changes in first-episode schizophrenia. *Archives of General Psychiatry, 59,* 1002–1010. (15)

Caicedo, A., & Roper, S. D. (2001). Taste receptor cells that discriminate between bitter stimuli. *Science, 291,* 1557–1560. (7)

Cajal, S. R. (1937). Recollections of my life. *Memoirs of the American Philosophical Society, 8.* (Original work published 1901–1917) (2)

Calder, A. J., Keane, J., Manes, F., Antoun, N., & Young, A. W. (2000). Impaired recognition and experience of disgust following brain injury. *Nature Neuroscience, 3,* 1077–1078. (12)

Caldwell, J. A., Mu, Q., Smith, J. K., Mishory, A., Caldwell, J. L., Peters, G., et al. (2005). Are individual differences in fatigue vulnerability related to baseline differences in cortical activation? *Behavioral Neuroscience, 119,* 694–707. (9)

Calignano, A., LaRana, G., Giuffrida, A., & Piomelli, D. (1998). Control of pain initiation by endogenous cannabinoids. *Nature, 394,* 277–281. (3)

Callicott, J. H., Straub, R. E., Pezawas, L., Egan, M. F., Mattay, V. S., Hariri, A. R., et al. (2005). Variation in *DISC1* affects hippocampal structure and function and increases risk for schizophrenia. *Proceedings of the National Academy of Sciences, USA, 102,* 8627–8632. (15)

Cameron, H. A., & McKay, R. D. G. (1999). Restoring production of hippocampal neurons in old age. *Nature Neuroscience, 2,* 894–897. (12)

Cameron, N. M., Champagne, F. A., Parent, C., Fish, E. W., Ozaki-Kuroda, K., & Meaney, M. J. (2005). The programming of individual differences in defensive responses and reproductive strategies in the rat through variations in maternal care. *Neuroscience and Biobehavioral Reviews, 29,* 843–865. (5)

Campbell, S. (2000). Is there an intrinsic period of the circadian clock? *Science, 288,* 1174. (9)

Campbell, S. S., & Tobler, I. (1984). Animal sleep: A review of sleep duration across phylogeny. *Neuroscience and Biobehavioral Reviews, 8,* 269–300. (9)

Camperio-Ciani, A., Corna, F., & Capiluppi, C. (2004). Evidence for maternally inherited factors favouring male homosexuality and promoting female fecundity. *Proceedings of the Royal Society of London, B, 271,* 2217–2221. (11)

Campfield, L. A., Smith, F. J., & Burn, P. (1998). Strategies and potential molecular targets for obesity treatment. *Science, 280,* 1383–1387. (10)

Campfield, L. A., Smith, F. J., Guisez, Y., Devos, R., & Burn, P. (1995). Recombinant mouse OB protein: Evidence for a peripheral signal linking adiposity and central neural networks. *Science, 269,* 546–552. (10)

Canepari, M., Rossi, R., Pellegrino, M. A., Orell, R. W., Cobbold, M., Harridge, S., et al. (2005). Effects of resistance training on myosin function studies by the in vitro motility assay in young and older men. *Journal of Applied Physiology, 98,* 2390–2395. (8)

Canli, T., Sivers, H., Whitfield, S. L., Gotlib, I. H., & Gabrieli, J. d. E. (2002). Amygdala response to happy faces as a function of extraversion. *Science, 296,* 2191. (12)

Cannon, M., Jones, P. B., & Murray, R. M. (2002). Obstetric complications and schizophrenia: Historical and meta-analytic review. *American Journal of Psychiatry, 159,* 1080–1092. (15)

Cannon, W. B. (1929). Organization for physiological homeostasis. *Physiological Reviews, 9,* 399–431. (10)

Cannon, W. B. (1945). *The way of an investigator.* New York: Norton. (inside cover)

Cantalupo, C., & Hopkins, W. D. (2001). Asymmetric Broca's area in great apes. *Nature, 414,* 505. (14)

Cao, Y. Q., Mantyh, P. W., Carlson, E. J., Gillespie, A.-M., Epstein, C. J., & Basbaum, A. I. (1998). Primary afferent tachykinins are required to experience moderate to intense pain. *Nature, 392,* 390–394. (7)

Cardno, A. G., Marshall, E. J., Coid, B., Macdonald, A. M., Ribchester, T. R., Davies, N. J., et al. (1999). Heritability estimates for psychotic disorders. *Archives of General Psychiatry, 56,* 162–168. (15)

Carello, C., LeVasseur, V. M., & Schmidt, R. C. (2002). Movement sequencing and phonological fluency in (putatively) nonimpaired readers. *Psychological Science, 13,* 375–379. (14)

Carlezon, W. A., Jr., Mague, S. D., & Andersen, S. L. (2003). Enduring behavioral effects of early exposure to methylphenidate in rats. *Biological Psychiatry, 54,* 1330–1337. (3)

Carlezon, W. A., Jr., Thome, J., Olson, V. G., Lane-Ladd, S. B., Brodkin, E. S., Hiroi, N., et al. (1998). Regulation of cocaine reward by CREB. *Science, 282,* 2272–2275. (3)

Carlsson, A. (2001). A paradigm shift in brain research. *Science, 294,* 1021–1024. (3)

Carpenter, G. A., & Grossberg, S. (1984). A neural theory of circadian rhythms: Aschoff's rule in diurnal and nocturnal mammals. *American Journal of Physiology, 247,* R1067–R1082. (9)

Carreiras, M., Lopez, J., Rivero, F., & Corina, D. (2005). Neural processing of a whistled language. *Nature, 433,* 31–32. (14)

Carruth, L. L., Reisert, I., & Arnold, A. P. (2002). Sex chromosome genes directly affect brain sexual differentiation. *Nature Neuroscience, 5,* 933–934. (11)

Carter, C. S. (1992). Hormonal influences on human sexual behavior. In J. B. Becker, S. M. Breedlove, & D. Crews (Eds.), *Behavioral endocrinology* (pp. 131–142). Cambridge, MA: MIT Press. (11)

Caspi, A., McClay, J., Moffitt, T. E., Mill, J., Martin, J., Craig, I. W., et al. (2002). Role of genotype in the cycle of violence in maltreated children. *Science, 297,* 851–854. (12)

Caspi, A., Sugden, K., Moffitt, T. E., Taylor, A., Craig, I. W., Harrington, H., et al. (2003). Influence of life stress on depression: Moderation by a polymorphism in the 5-HTT gene. *Science, 301,* 386–389. (15)

Cassia, V. M., Turati, C., & Simion, F. (2004). Can a nonspecific bias toward top-heavy patterns explain newborns' face preference? *Psychological Science, 15,* 379–383. (6)

Castellucci, V. F., Pinsker, H., Kupfermann, I., & Kandel, E. (1970). Neuronal mechanisms of habituation and dishabituation of the gill-withdrawal reflex in *Aplysia. Science, 167,* 1745–1748. (13)

Castner, S. A., & Goldman-Rakic, P. S. (2004). Enhancement of working memory in aged monkeys by a sensitizing regimen of dopamine D_1 receptor stimulation. *Journal of Neuroscience, 24,* 1446–1450. (13)

Catalano, S. M., & Shatz, C. J. (1998). Activity-dependent cortical target selection by thalamic axons. *Science, 281,* 559–562. (5)

Catchpole, C. K., & Slater, P. J. B. (1995). *Bird song: Biological themes and variations.* Cambridge, England: Cambridge University Press. (1)

Caterina, M. J., Leffler, A., Malmberg, A. B., Martin, W. J., Trafton, J., Petersen-Zeitz, et al. (2000). Impaired nociception and pain sensation in mice lacking the capsaicin receptor. *Science, 288,* 306–313. (7)

Catterall, W. A. (1984). The molecular basis of neuronal excitability. *Science, 223,* 653–661. (2)

Cavigelli, S. A., & McClintock, M. K. (2003). Fear of novelty in infant rats predicts adult corticosterone dynamics and an early death. *Proceedings of the National Academy of Sciences, USA, 100,* 16131–16136. (12)

Censits, D. M., Ragland, J. D., Gur, R. C., & Gur, R. E. (1997). Neuropsychological evidence supporting a neurodevelopmental model of schizophrenia: A longitudinal study. *Schizophrenia Research, 24,* 289–298. (15)

Cerlotti, U., & Bini, L. (1938). L'Elettroshock [Electroshock]. *Archivio Generale di Neurologia e Psichiatria e Psicoanalisi, 19,* 266–268. (15)

Chalmers, D. J. (1995). Facing up to the problem of consciousness. *Journal of Consciousness Studies, 2,* 200–219. (1)

Chalmers, D. L. (2004). How can we construct a science of consciousness? In M. S. Gazzaniga (Ed.), *The cognitive neurosciences* (3rd ed., pp. 1111–1119). Cambridge, MA: MIT Press. (1)

Chang, E. F., & Merzenich, M. M. (2003). Environmental noise retards auditory cortical development. *Science, 300,* 498–502. (7)

Chapin, J. K., Moxon, K. A., Markowitz, R. S., & Nicolelis, M. A. L. (1999). Real-time control of a robot arm using simultaneously recorded neurons in the motor cortex. *Nature Neuroscience, 2,* 664–670. (8)

Chaudhari, N., Landin, A. M., & Roper, S. D. (2000). A metabotropic glutamate receptor variant functions as a taste receptor. *Nature Neuroscience, 3,* 113–119. (7)

Chawla, D., Rees, G., & Friston, K. J. (1999). The physiological basis of attentional modulation in extrastriate visual areas. *Nature Neuroscience, 2,* 671–676. (6)

Cheer, J. F., Wassum, K. M., Heien, M. L. A. V., Phillips, P. E. M., & Wightman, R. M. (2004). Cannabinoids enhance subsecond dopamine release in the nucleus accumbens of awake rats. *Journal of Neuroscience, 24,* 4393–4400. (3)

Chen, L. M., Friedman, R. M., & Roe, A. W. (2003). Optical imaging of a tactile illusion in area 3b of the primary somatosensory cortex. *Science, 302,* 881–885. (7)

Cheour-Luhtanen, M., Alho, K., Sainio, K., Rinne, T., Reinikainen, K., Pohjavuoir, M., et al. (1996). The ontogenetically earliest discriminative response of the human brain. *Psychophysiology, 33,* 478–481. (14)

Chevaleyre, V., & Castillo, P. E. (2004). Endocannabinoid-mediated metaplasiticity in the hippocampus. *Neuron, 43,* 871–881. (3)

Chiueh, C. C. (1988). Dopamine in the extrapyramidal motor function: A study based upon the MPTP-induced primate model of Parkinsonism. *Annals of the New York Academy of Sciences, 515,* 226–248. (8)

Cho, K. (2001). Chronic "jet lag" produces temporal lobe atrophy and spatial cognitive deficits. *Nature Neuroscience, 4,* 567–568. (9)

Choi, D.-S., Cascini, M.-G., Mailliard, W., Young, H., Paredes, P., McMahon, T., et al. (2004). The type I equilibrative nucleoside transporter regulates ethanol intoxication and preference. *Nature Neuroscience, 7,* 855–861. (15)

Choi-Lundberg, D. L., Lin, Q., Chang, Y.-N., Chiang, Y. L., Hay, C. M., Mohajeri, H., et al. (1997). Dopaminergic neurons protected from degeneration by GDNF gene therapy. *Science, 275,* 838–841. (5)

Chollet, F., & Weiller, C. (1994). Imaging recovery of function following brain injury. *Current Opinion in Neurobiology, 4,* 226–230. (5)

Chomsky, N. (1980). *Rules and representations.* New York: Columbia University Press. (14)

Christian, K. M., & Thompson, R. F. (2005). Long-term storage of an associative memory trace in the cerebellum. *Behavioral Neuroscience, 119,* 526–537. (13)

Chuang, H., Prescott, E. D., Kong, H., Shields, S., Jordt, S.-E., Basbaum, A. I., et al. (2001). Bradykinin and nerve growth factor release the capsaicin receptor from PtdIns(4,5)P2-mediated inhibition. *Nature, 411,* 957–962. (7)

Ciccocioppo, R., Martin-Fardon, R., & Weiss, F. (2004). Stimuli associated with a single cocaine experience elicit long-lasting cocaine-seeking. *Nature Neuroscience, 7,* 495–498. (15)

Cicone, N., Wapner, W., Foldi, N. S., Zurif, E., & Gardner, H. (1979). The relation between gesture and language in aphasic communication. *Brain and Language, 8,* 324–349. (14)

Cisek, P., & Kalaska, J. F. (2004). Neural correlates of mental rehearsal in dorsal premotor cortex. *Nature, 431,* 993–996. (8)

Clahsen, H., & Almazen, M. (1998). Syntax and morphology in Williams syndrome. *Cognition, 68,* 167–198. (14)

Clark, B. A., Monsivais, P., Branco, T., London, M., & Häuser, M. (2005). The site of action potential initiation in cerebellar Purkinje neurons. *Nature Neuroscience, 8,* 137–139. (2)

Clark, D. A., Mitra, P. P., & Wang, S. S.-H. (2001). Scalable architecture in mammalian brains. *Nature, 411,* 189–193. (5)

Clark, R. E., & Lavond, D. G. (1993). Reversible lesions of the red nucleus during acquisition and retention of a classically conditioned behavior in rabbits. *Behavioral Neuroscience, 107,* 264–270. (13)

Clark, W. S. (2004). Is the zone-tailed hawk a mimic? *Birding, 36,* 494–498. (1)

Clarke, S., Assal, G., & deTribolet, N. (1993). Left hemisphere strategies in visual recognition, topographical orientation and time planning. *Neuropsychologia, 31,* 99–113. (14)

Clayton, E. C., & Williams, C. L. (2000). Glutamatergic influences on the nucleus paragigantocellularis: Contribution to performance in avoidance and spatial memory tasks. *Behavioral Neuroscience, 114,* 707–712. (9)

Cleary, J. P., Walsh, D. M., Hofmeister, J. J., Shankar, G. M., Kuskowski, M. A., Selkoe, D. J., et al. (2005). Natural oligomers of the amyloid-β protein specifically disrupt cognitive function. *Nature Neuroscience, 8,* 79–84. (13)

Cleary, L. J., Hammer, M., & Byrne, J. H. (1989). Insights into the cellular mechanisms of short-term sensitization in *Aplysia.* In T. J. Carew & D. B. Kelley (Eds.), *Perspectives in neural systems and behavior* (pp. 105–119). New York: Liss. (13)

Clohessy, A. B., Posner, M. I., Rothbart, M. K., & Veccra, S. P. (1991). The development of inhibition of return in early infancy. *Journal of Cognitive Neuroscience, 3,* 345–350. (6)

Cloninger, C. R., Bohman, M., & Sigvardsson, S. (1981). Inheritance of alcohol abuse: Cross-fostering of adopted men. *Archives of General Psychiatry, 38,* 861–868. (15)

Clutton-Brock, T. H., O'Riain, M. J., Brotherton, P. N. M., Gaynor, D., Kansky, R., Griffin, A. S., et al. (1999). Selfish sentinels in cooperative mammals. *Science, 284,* 1640–1644. (1)

Cobos, P., Sánchez, M., Pérez, N., & Vila, J. (2004). Effects of spinal cord injuries on the subjective component of emotions. *Cognition and Emotion, 18,* 281–287. (12)

Cohen, B., Novick, D., & Rubinstein, M. (1996). Modulation of insulin activities by leptin. *Science, 274,* 1185–1188. (10)

Cohen, D., & Nicolelis, M. A. L. (2004). Reduction of single-neuron firing uncertainty by cortical ensembles during motor skill learning. *Journal of Neuroscience, 24,* 3574–3582. (8)

Cohen, L. G., Celnik, P., Pascual-Leone, A., Corwell, B., Faiz, L., Dambrosia, J., et al. (1997). Functional relevance of cross-modal plasticity in blind humans. *Nature, 389,* 180–183. (5)

Cohen, S., Frank, E., Doyle, W. J., Skoner, D. P., Rabin, B. S., & Swaltney, J. M., Jr. (1998). Types of stressors that increase susceptibility to the common cold in healthy adults. *Health Psychology, 17,* 214–223. (12)

Cohen-Kettenis, P. T. (2005). Gender change in 46,XY persons with 5α-reductase-2 deficiency and 17β-hydroxysteroid dehydrogenase-3 deficiency. *Archives of Sexual Behavior, 34,* 399–410. (11)

Cohen-Tannoudji, M., Babinet, C., & Wassef, M. (1994). Early determination of a mouse somatosensory cortex marker. *Nature, 368,* 460–463. (5)

Colantuoni, C., Rada, P., McCarthy, J., Patten, C., Avena, N. M., Chadeayne, A., et al. (2002). Evidence that intermittent, excessive sugar intake causes endogenous opioid dependence. *Obesity Research, 10,* 478–488. (10)

Colantuoni, C., Schwenker, J., McCarthy, J., Rada, P., Ladenheim, B., Cadet, J.-L., et al. (2001). Excessive sugar intake alters binding to dopamine and mu-opioid receptors in the brain. *NeuroReport, 12,* 3549–3552. (10)

Colapinto, J. (1997, December 11). The true story of John/Joan. *Rolling Stone,* pp. 54–97. (11)

Colbourne, F., & Corbett, D. (1995). Delayed postischemic hypothermia: A six-month survival study using behavioral and histological assessments of neuroprotection. *Journal of Neuroscience, 15,* 7250–7260. (5)

Colbourne, F., Sutherland, G. R., & Auer, R. N. (1999). Electron microscopic evidence against apoptosis as the mechanism of neuronal death in global ischemia. *Journal of Neuroscience, 19,* 4200–4210. (5)

Colcombe, S. J., Erickson, K. I., Raz, N., Webb, A. G., Cohen, N. J., McAuley, E., et al. (2003). Aerobic fitness reduces brain tissue loss in aging humans. *Journal of Gerontology: Medical Sciences, 58A,* 176–180. (5)

Colgreave, N. (2002). Sex releases the speed limit on evolution. *Nature, 420,* 664–666. (11)

Collier, T. J., Sortwell, C. E., & Daley, B. F. (1999). Diminished viability, growth, and behavioral efficacy of fetal dopamine neuron grafts in aging rats with long-term dopamine depletion: An argument for neurotrophic supplementation. *Journal of Neuroscience, 19,* 5563–5573. (8)

Considine, R. V., Sinha, M. K., Heiman, M. L., Kriauciunas, A., Stephens, T. W., Nyce, M. R., et al. (1996). Serum immunoreactive-leptin concentrations in normal-weight and obese humans. *New England Journal of Medicine, 334,* 292–295. (10)

Conti, A. C., Raghupathi, R., Trojanowski, J. Q., & McIntosh, T. K. (1998). Experimental brain injury induces regionally distinct apoptosis during the acute and delayed post-traumatic period. *Journal of Neuroscience, 18,* 5663–5672. (5)

Cooke, B. M., Tabibnia, G., & Breedlove, S. M. (1999). A brain sexual dimorphism controlled by adult circulating androgens. *Proceedings of the National Academy of Sciences, USA, 96,* 7538–7540. (11)

Coppola, D. M., Purves, H. R., McCoy, A. N., & Purves, D. (1998). The distribution of oriented contours in the real world. *Proceedings of the National Academy of Sciences, USA, 95,* 4002–4006. (6)

Corballis, M. C. (1999). The gestural origins of language. *American Scientist, 87,* 138–145. (14)

Corder, E. H., Saunders, A. M., Strittmatter, W. J., Schmechel, D. E., Gaskell, P. C., Small, G. W., et al. (1993). Gene dose of apolipoprotein E type 4 allele and the risk of Alzheimer's disease in late onset families. *Science, 261,* 921–923. (13)

Corkin, S. (1984). Lasting consequences of bilateral medial temporal lobectomy: Clinical course and experimental findings in H. M. *Seminars in Neurology, 4,* 249–259. (13)

Corkin, S. (2002). What's new with the amnesic patient H. M.? *Nature Reviews Neuroscience, 3,* 153–159. (13)

Corkin, S., Rosen, T. J., Sullivan, E. V., & Clegg, R. A. (1989). Penetrating head injury in young adulthood exacerbates cognitive decline in later years. *Journal of Neuroscience, 9,* 3876–3883. (5)

Cornelissen, P., Richardson, A., Mason, A., Fowler, S., & Stein, J. (1995). Contrast sensitivity and coherent motion detection measured at photopic luminance levels in dyslexics and controls. *Vision Research, 35,* 1483–1494. (14)

Cornette, L., Dupont, P., Rosier, A., Sunaert, S., Van Hecke, P., Michiels, J., et al. (1998). Human brain regions involved in direction discrimination. *Journal of Neurophysiology, 79,* 2749–2765. (6)

Cosmelli, D., David, O., Lachaux, J.-P., Martinerie, J., Garnero, L., Renault, B., et al. (2004). Waves of consciousness: Ongoing cortical patterns during binocular rivalry. *NeuroImage, 23,* 128–140. (1)

Coss, R. G., Brandon, J. G., & Globus, A. (1980). Changes in morphology of dendritic spines on honeybee calycal interneurons associated with cumulative nursing and foraging experiences. *Brain Research, 192,* 49–59. (5)

Costa, M., Braun, C., & Birbaumer, N. (2003). Gender differences in response to pictures of nudes: A magnetoencephalography study. *Biological Psychology, 63,* 129–147. (4)

Cotman, C. W., & Nieto-Sampedro, M. (1982). Brain function, synapse renewal, and plasticity. *Annual Review of Psychology, 33,* 371–401. (5)

Cotter, D., Mackay, D., Landau, S., Kerwin, R., & Everall, I. (2001). Reduced glial cell density and neuronal size in the anterior cingulate cortex in major depressive disorder. *Archives of General Psychiatry, 58,* 545–553. (15)

Courchesne, E., Townsend, J., Akshoomoff, N. A., Saitoh, O., Yeung-Courchesne, R., Lincoln, A. J., et al. (1994). Impairment in shifting attention in autistic and cerebellar patients. *Behavioral Neuroscience, 108,* 848–865. (4)

Cowart, B. J. (2005, Spring). Taste, our body's gustatory gatekeeper. *Cerebrum, 7*(2), 7–22. (7)

Cowey, A., & Stoerig, P. (1995). Blindsight in monkeys. *Nature, 373,* 247–249. (6)

Cowley, M. A., Smith, R. G., Diano, S., Tschöp, M., Pronchuk, N., Grove, K. L., et al. (2003). The distribution and mechanism of action of ghrelin in the CNS demonstrates a novel hypothalamic circuit regulating energy homeostasis. *Neuron, 37,* 649–661. (10)

Cox, D., Meyers, E., & Sinha, P. (2004). Contextually evoked object-specific responses in human visual cortex. *Science, 304,* 115–117. (6)

Crabbe, J. C., Wahlsten, D., & Dudek, B. C. (1999). Genetics of mouse behavior: Interactions with laboratory environment. *Science, 284,* 1670–1672. (1)

Craddock, N., & Jones, I. (1999). Genetics of bipolar disorder. *Journal of Medical Genetics, 36,* 585–594. (15)

Craig, A. D., Krout, K., & Andrew, D. (2001). Quantitative response characteristics of thermoreceptive and nociceptive lamina I spinothalamic neurons in the cat. *Journal of Neurophysiology, 86,* 1459–1480. (7)

Craig, A. M., & Boudin, H. (2001). Molecular heterogeneity of central synapses: Afferent and target regulation. *Nature Neuroscience, 4,* 569–578. (3)

Crair, M. C., Gillespie, D. C., & Stryker, M. P. (1998). The role of visual experience in the development of columns in cat visual cortex. *Science, 279,* 566–570. (6)

Crair, M. C., & Malenka, R. C. (1995). A critical period for long-term potentiation at thalamocortical synapses. *Nature, 375,* 325–328. (6)

Cravchik, A., & Goldman, D. (2000). Neurochemical individuality. *Archives of General Psychiatry, 57,* 1105–1114. (3)

Cremers, C. W. R. J., & van Rijn, P. M. (1991). Acquired causes of deafness in childhood. *Annals of the New York Academy of Sciences, 630,* 197–202. (7)

Crick, F. C., & Koch, C. (2004). A framework for consciousness. In M. S. Gazzaniga (Ed.), *The cognitive neurosciences* (3rd ed., pp. 1133–1143). Cambridge, MA: MIT Press. (1)

Crick, F., & Mitchison, G. (1983). The function of dream sleep. *Nature, 304,* 111–114. (9)

Critchley, H. D., Mathias, C. J., & Dolan, R. J. (2001). Neuroanatomical basis for first- and second-order representations of bodily states. *Nature Neuroscience, 4,* 207–212. (12)

Critchley, H. D., & Rolls, E. T. (1996). Hunger and satiety modify the responses of olfactory and visual neurons in the primate orbito-frontal cortex. *Journal of Neurophysiology, 75,* 1673–1686. (10)

Crosio, C., Cermakian, N., Allis, C. D., & Sassone-Corsi, P. (2000). Light induces chromatin modification in cells of the mammalian circadian clock. *Nature Neuroscience, 3,* 1241–1247. (9)

Crossin, K. L., & Krushel, L. A. (2000). Cellular signaling by neural cell adhesion molecules of the immunoglobulin family. *Developmental Dynamics, 218,* 260–279. (5)

Culbertson, F. M. (1997). Depression and gender. *American Psychologist, 52,* 25–31. (15)

Culebras, A. (1996). *Clinical handbook of sleep disorders.* Boston: Butterworth-Heinemann. (9)

Cummings, D. E., Clement, K., Purnell, J. Q., Vaisse, C., Foster, K. E., Frayo, R. S., et al. (2002). Elevated plasma ghrelin levels in Prader-Willi syndrome. *Nature Medicine, 8,* 643–644. (10)

Curtis, A. L., Bello, N. T., & Valentine, R. J. (2001). Evidence for functional release of endogenous opioids in the locus ceruleus during stress termination. *Journal of Neuroscience, 21,* RC 152: 1–5. (3)

Curtiss, S., de Bode, S., & Mathern, G. W. (2001). Spoken language outcomes after hemispherectomy: Factoring in etiology. *Brain and Language, 79,* 379–396. (14)

Cusack, R., Carlyon, R. P., & Robertson, I. H. (2000). Neglect between but not within auditory objects. *Journal of Cognitive Neuroscience, 12,* 1056–1065. (14)

Cutler, W. B., Preti, G., Krieger, A., Huggins, G. R., Garcia, C. R., & Lawley, H. J. (1986). Human axillary secretions influence women's menstrual cycles: The role of donor extract from men. *Hormones and Behavior, 20,* 463–473. (7)

Cynader, M., & Chernenko, G. (1976). Abolition of direction selectivity in the visual cortex of the cat. *Science, 193,* 504–505. (6)

Cyranowski, J. M., Frank, E., Young, E., & Shear, K. (2000). Adolescent onset of the gender difference in lifetime rates of major depression. *Archives of General Psychiatry, 57,* 21–27. (15)

Czeisler, C. A., Duffy, J. F., Shanahan, T. L., Brown, E. N., Mitchell, J. F., Rimmer, D. W., et al. (1999). Stability, precision, and near-24-hour period of the human circadian pacemaker. *Science, 284,* 2177–2181. (9)

Czeisler, C. A., Johnson, M. P., Duffy, J. F., Brown, E. N., Ronda, J. M., & Kronauer, R. E. (1990). Exposure to bright light and darkness to treat physiologic maladaptation to night work. *New England Journal of Medicine, 322,* 1253–1259. (9)

Czeisler, C. A., Weitzman, E. D., Moore-Ede, M. C., Zimmerman, J. C., & Knauer, R. S. (1980). Human sleep: Its duration and organization depend on its circadian phase. *Science, 210,* 1264–1267. (9)

Dabbs, J. M., Jr., Carr, T. S., Frady, R. L., & Riad, J. K. (1995). Testosterone, crime, and misbehavior among 692 male prison inmates. *Personality and Individual Differences, 18,* 627–633. (12)

Dale, N., Schacher, S., & Kandel, E. R. (1988). Long-term facilitation in *Aplysia* involves increase in transmitter release. *Science, 239,* 282–285. (13)

Dalterio, S., & Bartke, A. (1979). Perinatal exposure to cannabinoids alters male reproductive function in mice. *Science, 205,* 1420–1422. (11)

Dalton, K. (1968). Ante-natal progesterone and intelligence. *British Journal of Psychiatry, 114,* 1377–1382. (11)

Dalton, P., Doolittle, N., & Breslin, P. A. (2002). Gender-specific induction of enhanced sensitivity to odors. *Nature Neuroscience, 5,* 199–200. (7)

Damasio, A. R. (1994). *Descartes' error.* New York: Putnam's Sons. (12)

Damasio, A. (1999). *The feeling of what happens.* New York: Harcourt Brace. (12)

Damsma, G., Pfaus, J. G., Wenkstern, D., Phillips, A. G., & Fibiger, H. C. (1992). Sexual behavior increases dopamine transmission in the nucleus accumbens and striatum of male rats: A comparison with novelty and locomotion. *Behavioral Neuroscience, 106,* 181–191. (15)

Darwin, C. (1859). *The origin of species.* New York: D. Appleton. (1)

Davalos, D., Grutzendler, J., Yang, G., Kim, J. V., Zuo, Y., Jung, S., et al. (2005). ATP mediates rapid microglial response to local brain injury *in vivo*. *Nature Neuroscience, 8,* 752–758. (2)

Davidson, R. J. (1984). Affect, cognition, and hemispheric specialization. In C. E. Izard, J. Kagan, & R. B. Zajonc (Eds.), *Emotions, cognition, & behavior* (pp. 320–365). Cambridge, England: Cambridge University Press. (15)

Davidson, R. J., & Fox, N. A. (1982). Asymmetrical brain activity discriminates between positive and negative affective stimuli in human infants. *Science, 218,* 1235–1237. (12)

Davidson, R. J., & Henriques, J. (2000). Regional brain function in sadness and depression. In J. C. Borod (Ed.), *The neuropsychology of emotion* (pp. 269–297). London: Oxford University Press. (12)

Davies, G., Welham, J., Chant, D., Torrey, E. F., & McGrath, J. (2003). A systematic review and meta-analysis of Northern hemisphere season of birth effects in schizophrenia. *Schizophrenia Bulletin, 29,* 587–593. (15)

Davies, P. (2000). A very incomplete comprehensive theory of Alzheimer's disease. *Annals of the New York Academy of Sciences, 924,* 8–16. (13)

Davis, E. C., Shryne, J. E., & Gorski, R. A. (1995). A revised critical period for the sexual differentiation of the sexually dimorphic nucleus of the preoptic area in the rat. *Neuroendocrinology, 62,* 579–585. (11)

Davis, J. M., Chen, N., & Glick, I. D. (2003). A meta-analysis of the efficacy of second-generation antipsychotics. *Archives of General Psychiatry, 60,* 553–564. (15)

Davis, K. D., Kiss, Z. H. T., Luo, L., Tasker, R. R., Lozano, A. M., & Dostrovsky, J. O. (1998). Phantom sensations generated by thalamic microstimulation. *Nature, 391,* 385–387. (5)

Dawkins, R. (1989). *The selfish gene* (new ed.). Oxford, England: Oxford University Press. (1)

Dawson, T. M., & Dawson, V. L. (2003). Molecular pathways of neurodegeneration in Parkinson's disease. *Science, 302,* 819–822. (8)

Dawson, T. M., Gonzalez-Zulueta, M., Kusel, J., & Dawson, V. L. (1998). Nitric oxide: Diverse actions in the central and peripheral nervous system. *The Neuroscientist, 4,* 96–112. (3)

Day, S. (2005). Some demographic and socio-cultural aspects of synesthesia. In L. C. Robertson & N. Sagiv (Eds.), *Synesthesis* (pp. 11–33). Oxford, England: Oxford University Press. (7)

de Castro, J. M. (2000). Eating behavior: Lessons from the real world of humans. *Nutrition, 16,* 800–813. (10)

de Castro, J. M. (2002). Independence of heritable influences on the food intake of free-living humans. *Nutrition, 18,* 11–16. (10)

de Castro, J. M., & Plunkett, S. (2002). A general model of intake regulation. *Neuroscience and Biobehavioral Reviews, 26,* 581–595. (10)

de Jong, W. W., Hendriks, W., Sanyal, S., & Nevo, E. (1990). The eye of the blind mole rat (*Spalax ehrenbergi*): Regressive evolution at the molecular level. In E. Nevo & O. A. Reig (Eds.), *Evolution of subterranean mammals at the organismal and molecular levels* (pp. 383–395). New York: Liss. (9)

de Jonge, F. H., Louwerse, A. L., Ooms, M. P., Evers, P., Endert, E., & Van De Poll, N. E. (1989). Lesions of the SDN-POA inhibit sexual behavior of male Wistar rats. *Brain Research Bulletin, 23,* 483–492. (11)

de la Iglesia, H. O., Meyer, J., Carpino, A., Jr., & Schwartz, W. J. (2000). Antiphase oscillation of the left and right suprachiasmatic nuclei. *Science, 290,* 799–801. (9)

De Luca, M., Di Page, E., Judica, A., Spinelli, D., & Zoccolotti, P. (1999). Eye movement patterns in linguistic and non-linguistic tasks in developmental surface dyslexia. *Neuropsychologia, 37,* 1407–1420. (14)

De Robertis, E. M., & Sasai, Y. (1996). A common plan for dorsoventral patterning in *Bilaeria*. *Nature, 380,* 37–40. (14)

de Wit, H., Crean, J., & Richards, J. B. (2000). Effects of d-amphetamine and ethanol on a measure of behavioral inhibition in humans. *Behavioral Neuroscience, 114,* 830–837. (14)

Deacon, T. W. (1990). Problems of ontogeny and phylogeny in brain-size evolution. *International Journal of Primatology, 11,* 237–282. (4)

Deacon, T. W. (1992). Brain-language coevolution. In J. A. Hawkins & M. Gell-Mann (Eds.), *The evolution of human languages* (pp. 49–83). Reading, MA: Addison-Wesley. (14)

Deacon, T. W. (1997). *The symbolic species.* New York: Norton. (4, 14)

DeArmond, S. J., Fusco, M. M., & Dewey, M. M. (1974). *Structure of the human brain.* New York: Oxford University Press. (10)

DeCoursey, P. (1960). Phase control of activity in a rodent. *Cold Spring Harbor symposia on quantitative biology, 25,* 49–55. (9)

DeFelipe, C., Herrero, J. F., O'Brien, J. A., Palmer, J. A., Doyle, C. A., Smith, A. J. H., et al. (1998). Altered nociception, analgesia and aggression in mice lacking the receptor for substance P. *Nature, 392,* 394–397. (7)

Dehaene, S., & Changeux, J.-P. (2004). Neural mechanisms for access to consciousness. In M. S. Gazzaniga (Ed.), *The cognitive neurosciences* (3rd ed., pp. 1145–1157). Cambridge, MA: MIT Press. (1)

Dehaene, S., Naccache, L., Cohen, L., LeBihan, D., Mangin, J.-F., Poline, J.-B., et al. (2001). Cerebral mechanisms of word masking and unconscious repetition priming. *Nature Neuroscience, 4,* 752–758. (1)

Del Cerro, M. C. R., Perez Izquierdo, M. A., Rosenblatt, J. S., Johnson, B. M., Pacheco, P., & Komisaruk, B. R. (1995). Brain 2-deoxyglucose levels related to maternal behavior-inducing stimuli in the rat. *Brain Research, 696,* 213–220. (11)

Del Punta, K., Leinders-Zufall, T., Rodriguez, I., Jukam, D., Wysocki, C. J., Ogawa, S., et al. (2002). Deficient pheromone responses in mice lacking a cluster of vomeronasal receptor genes. *Nature, 419,* 70–74. (7)

Delahanty, D. L., Raimonde, A. J., & Spoonster, E. (2000). Initial posttraumatic urinary cortisol levels predict subsequent PTSD symptoms in motor vehicle accident victims. *Biological Psychiatry, 48,* 940–947. (12)

Delgado, J. M. R. (1981). Neuronal constellations in aggressive behavior. In L. Valzelli & L. Morgese (Eds.), *Aggression and violence: A psycho/biological and clinical approach* (pp. 82–98). Milan, Italy: Edizioni Saint Vincent. (12)

Deliagina, T. G., Orlovsky, G. N., & Pavlova, G. A. (1983). The capacity for generation of rhythmic oscillations is distributed in the lumbosacral spinal cord of the cat. *Experimental Brain Research, 53,* 81–90. (8)

Dement, W. (1960). The effect of dream deprivation. *Science, 131,* 1705–1707. (9)

Dement, W. (1972). *Some must watch while some must sleep.* San Francisco: Freeman. (9; inside cover)

Dement, W. C. (1990). A personal history of sleep disorders medicine. *Journal of Clinical Neurophysiology, 7,* 17–47. (9)

Dement, W., Ferguson, J., Cohen, H., & Barchas, J. (1969). Non-chemical methods and data using a biochemical model: The REM quanta. In A. J. Mandell & M. P. Mandell (Eds.), *Psychochemical research in man* (pp. 275–325). New York: Academic Press. (9)

Dement, W., & Kleitman, N. (1957a). Cyclic variations in EEG during sleep and their relation to eye movements, body motility, and dreaming. *Electroencephalography and Clinical Neurophysiology, 9,* 673–690. (9)

Dement, W., & Kleitman, N. (1957b). The relation of eye movements during sleep to dream activity: An objective method for the study of dreaming. *Journal of Experimental Psychology, 53,* 339–346. (9)

Dennett, D. C. (1991). *Consciousness explained.* Boston: Little, Brown. (1)

Denys, K., Vanduffel, W., Fize, D., Nelissen, K., Peuskens, H., Van Essen, D., et al. (2004). The processing of visual shape in the cerebral cortex of human and nonhuman primates: A functional magnetic resonance imaging study. *Journal of Neuroscience, 24,* 2551–2565. (6)

deQuervain, D. J.-F., Roozendaal, B., & McGaugh, J. L. (1998). Stress and glucocorticoids impair retrieval of long-term spatial memory. *Nature, 394,* 787–790. (13)

Derégnaucourt, S., Mitra, P. P., Fehér, O., Pytte, C., & Tchernichovski, O. (2005). How sleep affects the developmental learning of bird song. *Nature, 433,* 710–716. (9)

DeSimone, J. A., Heck, G. L., & Bartoshuk, L. M. (1980). Surface active taste modifiers: A comparison of the physical and psycho-physical properties of gymnemic acid and sodium lauryl sulfate. *Chemical Senses, 5,* 317–330. (7)

DeSimone, J. A., Heck, G. L., Mierson, S., & DeSimone, S. K. (1984). The active ion transport properties of canine lingual epithelia in vitro. *Journal of General Physiology, 83,* 633–656. (7)

Detre, J. A., & Floyd, T. F. (2001). Functional MRI and its applications to the clinical neurosciences. *The Neuroscientist, 7,* 64–79. (4)

Deutsch, J. A., & Ahn, S. J. (1986). The splanchnic nerve and food intake regulation. *Behavioral and Neural Biology, 45,* 43–47. (10)

Deutsch, J. A., Young, W. G., & Kalogeris, T. J. (1978). The stomach signals satiety. *Science, 201,* 165–167. (10)

DeValois, R. L., Albrecht, D. G., & Thorell, L. G. (1982). Spatial frequency selectivity of cells in macaque visual cortex. *Vision Research, 22,* 545–559. (6)

DeValois, R. L., & Jacobs, G. H. (1968). Primate color vision. *Science, 162,* 533–540. (6)

Devane, W. A., Dysarz, F. A., III, Johnson, M. R., Melvin, L. S., & Howlett, A. C. (1988). Determination and characterization of a cannabinoid receptor in rat brain. *Molecular Pharmacology, 34,* 605–613. (3)

Devor, E. J., Abell, C. W., Hoffman, P. L., Tabakoff, B., & Cloninger, C. R. (1994). Platelet MAO activity in Type I and Type II alcoholism. *Annals of the New York Academy of Sciences, 708,* 119–128. (15)

Devor, M. (1996). Pain mechanisms. *The Neuroscientist, 2,* 233–244. (7)

DeYoe, E. A., Felleman, D. J., Van Essen, D. C., & McClendon, E. (1994). Multiple processing streams in occipitotemporal visual cortex. *Nature, 371,* 151–154. (6)

Di Lorenzo, P. M., Hallock, R. M., & Kennedy, D. P. (2003). Temporal coding of sensation: Mimicking taste quality with electrical stimulation of the brain. *Behavioral Neuroscience, 117,* 1423–1433. (2, 7)

Diamond, M., & Sigmundson, H. K. (1997). Management of intersexuality: Guidelines for dealing with persons with ambiguous genitalia. *Archives of Pediatrics and Adolescent Medicine, 151,* 1046–1050. (11)

Diamond, M. C., Scheibel, A. B., Murphy, G. M., & Harvey, T. (1985). On the brain of a scientist: Albert Einstein. *Experimental Neurology, 88,* 198–204. (4)

Dichgans, J. (1984). Clinical symptoms of cerebellar dysfunction and their topodiagnostic significance. *Human Neurobiology, 2,* 269–279. (8)

Dick, D. M., Johnson, J. K., Viken, R. J., & Rose, R. J. (2000). Testing between-family associations in within-family comparisons. *Psychological Science, 11,* 409–413. (15)

Dick, F., Bates, E., Wulfeck, B., Utman, J. A., Dronkers, N., & Gernsbacher, M. A. (2001). Language deficits, localization, and grammar: Evidence for a distributive model of language breakdown in aphasic patients and neurologically intact individuals. *Psychological Review, 108,* 759–788. (14)

Dickens, W. T., & Flynn, J. R. (2001). Heritability estimates versus large environmental effects: The IQ paradox resolved. *Psychological Review, 108,* 346–369. (1)

Dierks, T., Linden, D. E. J., Jandl, M., Formisano, E., Goebel, R., Lanfermann, H., et al. (1999). Activation of Heschl's gyrus during auditory hallucinations. *Neuron, 22,* 615–621. (4)

Dijk, D.-J., & Cajochen, C. (1997). Melatonin and the circadian regulation of sleep initiation, consolidation, structure, and the sleep EEG. *Journal of Biological Rhythms, 12,* 627–635. (9)

Diller, L., Packer, O. S., Verweij, J., McMahon, M. J., Williams, D. R., & Dacey, D. M. (2004). L and M cone contributions to the midget and parasol ganglion cell receptive fields of macaque monkey retina. *Journal of Neuroscience, 24,* 1079–1088. (6)

DiMarzo, V., Fontana, A., Cadas, H., Schinelli, S., Cimino, G., Schwartz, J.-C., et al. (1994). Formation and inactivation of endogenous cannabinoid anandamide in central neurons. *Nature, 372,* 686–691. (3)

DiMarzo, V., Goparaju, S. K., Wang, L., Liu, J., Bátkai, S., Járai, Z., et al. (2001). Leptin-regulated endocannabinoids are involved in maintaining food intake. *Nature, 410,* 822–825. (3)

Dimond, S. J. (1979). Symmetry and asymmetry in the vertebrate brain. In D. A. Oakley & H. C. Plotkin (Eds.), *Brain, behaviour, and evolution* (pp. 189–218). London: Methuen. (14)

Dong, E., Maatsumoto, K., Tohda, M., Kaneko, Y., & Watanabe, H. (1999). Diazepam binding inhibitor (DBI) gene expression in the brains of socially isolated and group-housed mice. *Neuroscience Research, 33,* 171–177. (12)

Doricchi, F., Guariglia, P., Gasparini, M., & Tomaiuolo, F. (2005). Dissociation between physical and mental number line bisection in right hemisphere brain damage. *Nature Neuroscience, 8,* 1663–1665. (14)

Dörner, G. (1974). Sex-hormone-dependent brain differentiation and sexual functions. In G. Dörner (Ed.), *Endocrinology of sex* (pp. 30–37). Leipzig: Barth. (11)

Doty, R. L., Applebaum, S., Zusho, H., & Settle, R. G. (1985). Sex differences in odor identification ability: A cross-cultural analysis. *Neuropsychologia, 23,* 667–672. (7)

Dowling, J. E. (1987). *The retina.* Cambridge, MA: Harvard University Press. (6)

Dowling, J. E., & Boycott, B. B. (1966). Organization of the primate retina. *Proceedings of the Royal Society of London, B, 166,* 80–111. (6)

Downar, J., Mikulis, D. J., & Davis, K. D. (2003). Neural correlates of the prolonged salience of painful stimulation. *NeuroImage, 20,* 1540–1551. (7)

Drachman, D. B. (1978). Myasthenia gravis. *New England Journal of Medicine, 298,* 136–142, 186–193. (8)

Draganski, B., Gaser, C., Busch, V., Schuierer, G., Bogdahn, U., & May, A. (2004). Changes in grey matter induced by training. *Nature, 427,* 311–312. (5)

Dragoi, V., Rivadulla, C., & Sur, M. (2001). Foci of orientation plasticity in visual cortex. *Nature, 411,* 80–86. (6)

Dreger, A. D. (1998). *Hermaphrodites and the medical invention of sex.* Cambridge, MA: Harvard University Press. (11)

Drewnowski, A., Henderson, S. A., Shore, A. B., & Barratt-Fornell, A. (1998). Sensory responses to 6-*n*-propylthiouracil (PROP) or sucrose solutions and food preferences in young women. *Annals of the New York Academy of Sciences, 855,* 797–801. (7)

Driver, J., & Frith, C. (2000). Shifting baselines in attention research. *Nature Reviews Neuroscience, 1,* 147–148. (6)

Duara, R., Kushch, A., Gross-Glenn, K., Barker, W. W., Jallad, B., Pascal, S., et al. (1991). Neuroanatomic differences between dyslexic and normal readers on magnetic resonance imaging scans. *Archives of Neurology, 48,* 410–416. (14)

Ducommun, C. Y., Michel, C. M., Clarke, S., Adriani, M., Seeck, M., Landis, T., et al. (2004). Cortical motion deafness. *Neuron, 43,* 765–777. (7)

Dudchenko, P. A., & Taube, J. S. (1997). Correlation between head direction cell activity and spatial behavior on a radial arm maze. *Behavioral Neuroscience, 111,* 3–19. (13)

Duelli, R., & Kuschinsky, W. (2001). Brain glucose transporters: Relationship to local energy demand. *News in Physiological Sciences, 16,* 71–76. (2)

Dunnett, S. B., & Björklund, A. (1999). Prospects for new restorative and neuroprotective treatments in Parkinson's disease. *Nature, 399*(Suppl.), A32–A39. (8)

Dunnett, S. B., Ryan, C. N., Levin, P. D., Reynolds, M., & Bunch, S. T. (1987). Functional consequences of embryonic neocortex transplanted to rats with prefrontal cortex lesions. *Behavioral Neuroscience, 101,* 489–503. (8)

DuPaul, G. J., McGoey, K. E., Eckert, T. L., & vanBrakle, J. (2001). Preschool children with attention-deficit/hyperactivity disorder: Impairments in behavioral, social, and school functioning. *Journal of the American Academy of Child & Adolescent Psychiatry, 40,* 508–515. (14)

During, M. J., Ryder, K. M., & Spencer, D. D. (1995). Hippocampal GABA transporter function in temporal-lobe epilepsy. *Nature, 376,* 174–177. (14)

Dyal, J. A. (1971). Transfer of behavioral bias: Reality and specificity. In E. J. Fjerdingstad (Ed.), *Chemical transfer of learned information* (pp. 219–263). New York: American Elsevier. (13)

Earnest, D. J., Liang, F.-Q., Ratcliff, M., & Cassone, V. M. (1999). Immortal time: Circadian clock properties of rat suprachiasmatic cell lines. *Science, 283,* 693–695. (9)

Eastman, C. I., Hoese, E. K., Youngstedt, S. D., & Liu, L. (1995). Phase-shifting human circadian rhythms with exercise during the night shift. *Physiology & Behavior, 58,* 1287–1291. (9)

Eastman, C. I., Young, M. A., Fogg, L. F., Liu, L., & Meaden, P. M. (1998). Bright light treatment of winter depression. *Archives of General Psychiatry, 55,* 883–889. (15)

Eaves, L. J., Martin, N. G., & Heath, A. C. (1990). Religious affiliation in twins and their parents: Testing a model of cultural inheritance. *Behavior Genetics, 20,* 1–22. (1)

Ebstein, R. P., Novick, O., Umansky, R., Priel, B., Osher, Y., Blaine, D., et al. (1996). Dopamine D4 receptor (D4DR) exon III polymorphism associated with the personality trait of Novelty Seeking. *Nature Genetics, 12,* 78–80. (3)

Eccles, J. C. (1964). *The physiology of synapses.* Berlin: Springer-Verlag. (3)

Eccles, J. C. (1986). Chemical transmission and Dale's principle. In T. Hökfelt, K.

Fuxe, & B. Pernow (Eds.), *Progress in brain research* (Vol. 68, pp. 3–13). Amsterdam: Elsevier. (3)

Eckhorn, R., Bauer, R., Jordan, W., Brosch, M., Kruse, W., Munk, M., et al. (1988). Coherent oscillations: A mechanism of feature linking in the visual cortex? *Biological Cybernetics, 60,* 121–130. (4)

Edelman, G. M. (1987). *Neural Darwinism.* New York: Basic Books. (5)

Edelman, G. (2001). Consciousness: The remembered present. *Annals of the New York Academy of Sciences, 929,* 111–122. (1)

Eden, G. F., Jones, K. M., Cappell, K., Gareau, L., Wood, F. B., Zeffiro, T. A., et al. (2004). Neural changes following remediation in adult developmental dyslexia. *Neuron, 44,* 411–422. (14)

Edgley, S. A., Jankowska, E., & Hammar, I. (2004). Ipsilateral actions of feline corticospinal tract neurons on limb motoneurons. *Journal of Neuroscience, 24,* 7804–7813. (8)

Edinger, J. D., McCall, W. V., Marsh, G. R., Radtke, R. A., Erwin, C. W., & Lininger, A. (1992). Periodic limb movement variability in older DIMS patients across consecutive nights of home monitoring. *Sleep, 15,* 156–161. (9)

Edinger, K. L., & Frye, C. A. (2004). Testosterone's analgesic, anxiolytic, and cognitive-enhancing effects may be due in part to actions of its 5α-reduced metabolites in the hippocampus. *Behavioral Neuroscience, 118,* 1352–1364. (11)

Edlinger, M., Hausmann, A., Kemmler, G., Kurz, M., Kurzhaler, I., Walch, T., et al. (2005). Trends in the pharmacological treatment of patients with schizophrenia over a 12 year observation period. *Schizophrenia Research, 77,* 25–34. (15)

Edman, G., Åsberg, M., Levander, S., & Schalling, D. (1986). Skin conductance habituation and cerebrospinal fluid 5-hydroxy-indoleacetic acid in suicidal patients. *Archives of General Psychiatry, 43,* 586–592. (12)

Egner, T., & Hirsch, J. (2005). Cognitive control mechanisms resolve conflict through cortical amplification of task-relevant information. *Nature Neuroscience, 8,* 1784–1790. (14)

Ehrhardt, A. A., & Money, J. (1967). Progestin-induced hermaphroditism: IQ and psychosexual identity in a study of ten girls. *Journal of Sex Research, 3,* 83–100. (11)

Ehrlich, P. R., Dobkin, D. S., & Wheye, D. (1988). *The birder's handbook.* New York: Simon & Schuster. (10)

Ehrman, L., & Perelle, I. B. (2004). Commentary on Klar. *Genetics, 167,* 2139. (14)

Eichenbaum, H. (2000). A cortical-hippocampal system for declarative memory. *Nature Reviews Neuroscience, 1,* 41–50. (13)

Eichenbaum, H. (2002). *The cognitive neuroscience of memory.* New York: Oxford University Press. (13)

Eidelberg, E., & Stein, D. G. (1974). Functional recovery after lesions of the nervous system. *Neurosciences Research Program Bulletin, 12,* 191–303. (5)

Eisenstein, E. M., & Cohen, M. J. (1965). Learning in an isolated prothoracic insect ganglion. *Animal Behaviour, 13,* 104–108. (13)

Ek, M., Engblom, D., Saha, S., Blomqvist, A., Jakobsson, P.-J., & Ericsson-Dahlstrand, A. (2001). Pathway across the blood-brain barrier. *Nature, 410,* 430–431. (10)

Elbert, T., Candia, V., Altenmüller, E., Rau, H., Sterr, A., Rockstroh, B., et al. (1998). Alteration of digital representations in somatosensory cortex in focal hand dystonia. *Neuroreport, 9,* 3571–3575. (5)

Elbert, T., Pantev, C., Wienbruch, C., Rockstroh, B., & Taub, E. (1995). Increased cortical representation of the fingers of the left hand in string players. *Science, 270,* 305–307. (5)

Eldridge, L. L., Engel, S. A., Zeineh, M. M., Bookheimer, S. Y., & Knowlton, B. J. (2005). A dissociation of encoding and retrieval processes in the human hippocampus. *Journal of Neuroscience, 25,* 3280–3286. (13)

Elia, J., Ambrosini, P. J., & Rapoport, J. L. (1999). Treatment of attention-deficit hyperactivity disorder. *New England Journal of Medicine, 340,* 780–788. (14)

Elias, C. F., Lee, C., Kelly, J., Aschkenazi, C., Ahima, R. S., Couceyro, P. R., et al. (1998). Leptin activates hypothalamic CART neurons projecting to the spinal cord. *Neuron, 21,* 1375–1385. (10)

Ellacott, K. L. J., & Cone, R. D. (2004). The central melanocortin system and the integration of short- and long-term regulators of energy homeostasis. *Recent Progress in Hormone Research, 59,* 395–408. (10)

Elliott, R., Sahakian, B. J., Matthews, K., Bannerjea, A., Rimmer, J., & Robbins, T. W. (1997). Effects of methylphenidate on spatial working memory and planning in healthy young adults. *Psychopharmacology, 131,* 196–206. (14)

Elliott, T. R. (1905). The action of adrenalin. *Journal of Physiology (London), 32,* 401–467. (3)

Ellis, L., & Ames, M. A. (1987). Neurohormonal functioning and sexual orientation: A theory of homosexuality–heterosexuality. *Psychological Bulletin, 101,* 233–258. (11)

Ellis, L., Ames, M. A., Peckham, W., & Burke, D. (1988). Sexual orientation of human offspring may be altered by severe maternal stress during pregnancy. *Journal of Sex Research, 25,* 152–157. (11)

Ellis, L., & Cole-Harding, S. (2001). The effects of prenatal stress, and of prenatal alcohol and nicotine exposure, on human sexual orientation. *Physiology & Behavior, 74,* 213–226. (11)

Elovainio, M., Kivimäki, M., Viikari, J., Ekelund, J., & Keltikangas-Järvinen, L. (2005). The mediating role of novelty seeking in the association between the type 4 dopamine receptor gene polymorphism and cigarette-smoking behavior. *Personality and Individual Differences, 38,* 639–645. (3)

Elston, G. N. (2000). Pyramidal cells of the frontal lobe: All the more spinous to think with. *Journal of Neuroscience, 20,* RC95: 1–4. (4)

Emery, N. J., Capitanio, J. P., Mason, W. A., Machado, C. J., Mendoza, S. P., & Amaral, D. G. (2001). The effects of bilateral lesions of the amygdala on dyadic social interactions in rhesus monkeys (*Macaca mulatta*). *Behavioral Neuroscience, 115,* 515–544. (12)

Emmorey, K., Allen, J. S., Bruss, J., Schenker, N., & Damasio, H. (2003). A morphometric analysis of auditory brain regions in congenitally deaf adults. *Proceedings of the National Academy of Sciences, USA, 100,* 10049–10054. (7)

Endo, T., Schwierin, B., Borbély, A. A., & Tobler, I. (1997). Selective and total sleep deprivation: Effect on the sleep EEG in the rat. *Psychiatry Research, 66,* 97–110. (9)

Engel, S. A. (1999). Using neuroimaging to measure mental representations: Finding color-opponent neurons in visual cortex. *Current Directions in Psychological Science, 8,* 23–27. (6)

Engert, F., & Bonhoeffer, T. (1999). Dendritic spine changes associated with hippocampal long-term synaptic plasticity. *Nature, 399,* 66–70. (13)

Ensor, D. M., Morley, J. S., Redfern, R. M., & Miles, J. B. (1993). The activity of an analogue of MPF (β-endorphin 28-31) in a rat model of Parkinson's disease. *Brain Research, 610,* 166–168. (8)

Epping-Jordan, M. P., Watkins, S. S., Koob, G. F., & Markou, A. (1998). Dramatic decreases in brain reward function during nicotine withdrawal. *Nature, 393,* 76–79. (3)

Erickson, C., & Lehrman, D. (1964). Effect of castration of male ring doves upon ovarian activity of females. *Journal of Comparative and Physiological Psychology, 58,* 164–166. (11)

Erickson, R. P. (1982). The across-fiber pattern theory: An organizing principle for molar neural function. *Contributions to Sensory Physiology, 6,* 79–110. (7)

Erickson, R. P., DiLorenzo, P. M., & Woodbury, M. A. (1994). Classification of taste responses in brain stem: Membership in fuzzy sets. *Journal of Neurophysiology, 71,* 2139–2150. (7)

Ericsson, K. A., & Charness, N. (1994). Expert performance: Its structure and acquisition. *American Psychologist, 49,* 725–747. (5)

Eriksson, P. S., Perfilieva, E., Björk-Eriksson, T., Alborn, A.-M., Nordborg, C., Peterson, D. A., et al. (1998). Neurogenesis in the adult human hippocampus. *Nature Medicine, 4,* 1313–1317. (5)

Ertekin-Taner, N., Graff-Radford, N., Younkin, L. H., Eckman, C., Baker, M., Adamson, J., et al. (2000). Linkage of plasma Aß42 to a quantitative locus on chromosome 10 in late-onset Alzheimer's disease pedigrees. *Science, 290,* 2303–2304. (13)

Eslamboli, A., Georgievska, B., Ridley, R. M., Baker, H. F., Muzyczka, N., Burger, C., et al. (2005). Continuous low-level glial cell line-derived neurotrophic factor delivery using recombinant adeno-associated viral vectors provides neuroprotection and induces behavioral recovery in a primate model of Parkinson's disease. *Journal of Neuroscience, 25,* 769–777. (8)

Esslen, M., Pascual-Marqui, R. D., Hell, D., Kochi, K., & Lehmann, D. (2004). Brain areas and time course of emotional processing. *NeuroImage, 21,* 1189–1203. (12)

Etcoff, N. L., Ekman, P., Magee, J. J., & Frank, M. G. (2000). Lie detection and language comprehension. *Nature, 405,* 139. (12, 14)

Etgen, A. M., Chu, H.-P., Fiber, J. M., Karkanias, G. B., & Morales, J. M. (1999). Hormonal integration of neurochemical and sensory signals governing female reproductive behavior. *Behavioural Brain Research, 105,* 93–103. (11)

Evans, D. A., Funkenstein, H. H., Albert, M. S., Scherr, P. A., Cook, N. R., Chown, M. J., et al. (1989). Prevalence of Alzheimer's disease in a community population of older persons. *Journal of the American Medical Association, 262,* 2551–2556. (13)

Evarts, E. V. (1979). Brain mechanisms of movement. *Scientific American, 241*(3), 164–179. (8)

Everson, C. A. (1995). Functional consequences of sustained sleep deprivation in the rat. *Behavioural Brain Research, 69,* 43–54. (9)

Eyre, J. A., Taylor, J. P., Villagra, F., Smith, M., & Miller, S. (2001). Evidence of activity dependent withdrawal of corticospinal projections during human development. *Neurology, 57,* 1543–1554. (8)

Facoetti, A., Lorusso, M. L., Paganoni, P., Cattaneo, C., Galli, R., Umiltà, C., et al. (2003). Auditory and visual automatic attention deficits in developmental dyslexia. *Cognitive Brain Research, 16,* 185–191. (14)

Fadda, F. (2000). Tryptophan-free diets: A physiological tool to study brain serotonin function. *News in Physiological Sciences, 15,* 260–264. (3)

Fadool, D. A., Tucker, K., Perkins, R., Fasciani, G., Thompson, R. N., Parsons, A. D., et al. (2004). Kv1.3 channel gene-targeted deletion produces "super-smeller mice" with altered glomeruli, interacting scaffolding proteins, and biophysics. *Neuron, 41,* 389–404. (7)

Fagiolini, M., & Hensch, T. K. (2000). Inhibitory threshold for critical-period activation in primary visual cortex. *Nature, 404,* 183–186. (6)

Fairbanks, L. A., Jorgensen, M. J., Huff, A., Blau, K., Hung, Y.-Y., & Mann, J. J. (2004). Adolescent impulsivity predicts adult dominance attainment in male vervet monkeys. *American Journal of Primatology, 64,* 1–17. (12)

Falleti, M. G., Maruff, P., Collie, A., Darby, D. G., & McStephen, M. (2003). Qualitative similarities in cognitive impairment associated with 24 h of sustained wakefulness and a blood alcohol concentration of 0.05%. *Journal of Sleep Research, 12,* 265–274. (9)

Famy, C., Streissguth, A. P., & Unis, A. S. (1998). Mental illness in adults with fetal alcohol syndrome or fetal alcohol effects. *American Journal of Psychiatry, 155,* 552–554. (5)

Fan, P. (1995). Cannabinoid agonists inhibit the activation of 5-HT3 receptors in rat nodose ganglion neurons. *Journal of Neurophysiology, 73,* 907–910. (3)

Fan, W., Ellacott, K. L. J., Halatchev, I. G., Takahashi, K., Yu, P., & Cone, R. D. (2004). Cholecystokinin-mediated suppression of feeding involves the brainstem melanocortin system. *Nature Neuroscience, 7,* 335–336. (10)

Fang, F., & He, S. (2005). Cortical responses to invisible objects in the human dorsal and ventral pathways. *Nature Neuroscience, 8,* 1380–1385. (6)

Fanous, A. H., van den Oord, E. J., Riley, B. P., Aggen, S. H., Neale, M. C., O'Neill, F. A., et al. (2005). Relationship between a high-risk haplotype in the *DTNBP1* (dysbindin) gene and clinical features of schizophrenia. *American Journal of Psychiatry, 162,* 1824–1832. (15)

Fantz, R. L. (1963). Pattern vision in newborn infants. *Science, 140,* 296–297. (6)

Farah, M. J. (1990). *Visual agnosia.* Cambridge, MA: MIT Press. (6)

Farah, M. J., Illes, J., Cook-Deegan, R., Gardner, H., Kandel, E., King, P., et al. (2004). Neurocognitive enhancement: What can we do and what should we do? *Nature Reviews Neuroscience, 5,* 421–425. (9)

Farah, M. J., Wilson, K. D., Drain, M., & Tanaka, J. N. (1998). What is "special" about face perception? *Psychological Review, 105,* 482–498. (6)

Farber, N. B., Newcomer, J. W., & Olney, J. W. (1999). Glycine agonists: What can they teach us about schizophrenia? *Archives of General Psychiatry, 56,* 13–17. (15)

Farmer, M. E., & Klein, R. M. (1995). The evidence for a temporal processing deficit linked to dyslexia: A review. *Psychonomic Bulletin & Review, 2,* 460–493. (14)

Farooqi, I. S., Keogh, J. M., Kamath, S., Jones, S., Gibson, W. T., Trussell, R., et al. (2001). Partial leptin deficiency and human adiposity. *Nature, 414,* 34–35. (10)

Farooqi, I. S., & O'Rahilly, S. (2004). Monogenic human obesity syndromes. *Recent Progress in Hormone Research, 59,* 409–424. (10)

Featherstone, R. E., Fleming, A. S., & Ivy, G. O. (2000). Plasticity in the maternal circuit: Effects of experience and partum condition on brain astrocyte number in female rats. *Behavioral Neuroscience, 114,* 158–172. (11)

Federman, D. D. (1967). *Abnormal sexual development.* Philadelphia: Saunders. (11)

Feeney, D. M. (1987). Human rights and animal welfare. *American Psychologist, 42,* 593–599. (1)

Feeney, D. M., & Sutton, R. L. (1988). Catecholamines and recovery of function after brain damage. In D. G. Stein & B. A. Sabel (Eds.), *Pharmacological approaches to the treatment of brain and spinal cord injury* (pp. 121–142). New York: Plenum Press. (5)

Feeney, D. M., Sutton, R. L., Boyeson, M. G., Hovda, D. A., & Dail, W. G. (1985). The locus coeruleus and cerebral metabolism: Recovery of function after cerebral injury. *Physiological Psychology, 13,* 197–203. (5)

Feighner, J. P., Gardner, E. A., Johnston, J. A., Batey, S. R., Khayrallah, M. A., Ascher, J. A., et al. (1991). Double-blind comparison of bupropion and fluoxetine in depressed out-patients. *Journal of Clinical Psychiatry, 52,* 329–335. (15)

Fendrich, R., Wessinger, C. M., & Gazzaniga, M. S. (1992). Residual vision in a scotoma: Implications for blindsight. *Science, 258,* 1489–1491. (6)

Fentress, J. C. (1973). Development of grooming in mice with amputated forelimbs. *Science, 179,* 704–705. (8)

Ferguson, C. P., & Pigott, T. A. (2000). Anorexia and bulimia nervosa: Neurobiology and pharmacotherapy. *Behavior Therapy, 31,* 237–263. (10)

Ferguson, N. B. L., & Keesey, R. E. (1975). Effect of a quinine-adulterated diet upon body weight maintenance in male rats with ventromedial hypothalamic lesions. *Journal of Comparative and Physiological Psychology, 89,* 478–488. (10)

Fergusson, D. M., Woodward, L. J., & Horwood, J. (1998). Maternal smoking during pregnancy and psychiatric adjustment in late adolescence. *Archives of General Psychiatry, 55,* 721–727. (5, 12)

Ferreira, F., Bailey, K. G. D., & Ferraro, V. (2002). Good-enough representations in language comprehension. *Current Directions in Psychological Science, 11,* 11–15. (14)

Fettiplace, R. (1990). Transduction and tuning in auditory hair cells. *Seminars in the Neurosciences, 2,* 33–40. (7)

Field, E. F., Whishaw, I. Q., Forgie, M. L., & Pellis, S. M. (2004). Neonatal and pubertal, but not adult, ovarian steroids are necessary for the development of female-typical patterns of dodging to protect a food item. *Behavioral Neuroscience, 118,* 1293–1304. (11)

Fields, R. D., Schwab, M. E., & Silver, J. (1999). Does CNS myelin inhibit axon regeneration? *The Neuroscientist, 5,* 12–18. (5)

Filbin, M. T. (2003). Myelin-associated inhibitors of axonal regeneration in the adult mammalian CNS. *Nature Reviews Neuroscience, 4,* 703–713. (5)

Fils-Aime, M.-L., Eckardt, M. J., George, D. T., Brown, G. L., Mefford, I., & Linnoila, M. (1996). Early-onset alcoholics have lower cerebrospinal fluid 5-hydroxyindoleacetic acid levels than late-onset alcoholics. *Archives of General Psychiatry, 53,* 211–216. (15)

Fine, I., Smallman, H. S., Doyle, P., & MacLeod, D. I. A. (2002). Visual function before and after the removal of bilateral congenital cataracts in adulthood. *Vision Research, 42,* 191–210. (6)

Fine, I. Wade, A. R., Brewer, A. A., May, M. G., Goodman, D. F., Boynton, G. M., et al. (2003). Long-term deprivation affects visual perception and cortex. *Nature Neuroscience, 6,* 915–916. (6)

Finette, B. A., O'Neill, J. P., Vacek, P. M., & Albertini, R. J. (1998). Gene mutations with characteristic deletions in cord blood T lymphocytes associated with passive maternal exposure to tobacco smoke. *Nature Medicine, 4,* 1144–1151. (5)

Finger, S., & Roe, D. (1996). Gustave Dax and the early history of cerebral dominance. *Archives of Neurology, 53,* 806–813. (14)

Fink, G., Sumner, B. E. H., Rosie, R., Grace, O., & Quinn, J. P. (1996). Estrogen control of central neurotransmission: Effect on mood, mental state, and memory. *Cellular and Molecular Neurobiology, 16,* 325–344. (11)

Fink, G. R., Halligan, P. W., Marshall, J. C., Frith, C. D., Frackowiak, R. S. J., & Dolan, R. J. (1996). Where in the brain does visual attention select the forest and the trees? *Nature, 382,* 626–628. (14)

Fink, M. (1985). Convulsive therapy: Fifty years of progress. *Convulsive Therapy, 1,* 204–216. (15)

Finlay, B. L., & Darlington, R. B. (1995). Linked regularities in the development and evolution of mammalian brains. *Science, 268,* 1578–1584. (4)

Finlay, B. L., & Pallas, S. L. (1989). Control of cell number in the developing mammalian visual system. *Progress in Neurobiology, 32,* 207–234. (5)

Fisher, S. E., & DeFries, J. C. (2002). Developmental dyslexia: Genetic dissection of a complex cognitive trait. *Nature Reviews Neuroscience, 3,* 767–780. (14)

Fisher, S. E., Vargha-Khadem, F., Watkins, K. E., Monaco, A. P., & Pembrey, M. E. (1998). Localisation of a gene implicated in a severe speech and language disorder. *Nature Genetics, 18,* 168–170. (14)

Fitts, D. A., Starbuck, E. M., & Ruhf, A. (2000). Circumventricular organs and ANGII-induced salt appetite: Blood pressure and connectivity. *American Journal of Physiology, 279,* R2277–R2286. (10)

Fitzgerald, P. B., Brown, T. L., & Daskalakis, Z. J. (2002). The application of transcranial magnetic stimulation in psychiatry and neurosciences research. *Acta Psychiatrica Scandinavica, 105,* 324–340. (4)

Fjerdingstad, E. J. (1973). Transfer of learning in rodents and fish. In W. B. Essman & S. Nakajima (Eds.), *Current biochemical approaches to learning and memory* (pp. 73–98). Flushing, NY: Spectrum. (13)

Flack, W. F., Jr., Laird, J. D., & Cavallaro, L. A. (1999). Separate and combined effects of facial expressions and bodily postures on emotional feelings. *European Journal of Social Psychology, 29,* 203–217. (12)

Flatz, G. (1987). Genetics of lactose digestion in humans. *Advances in Human Genetics, 16,* 1–77. (10)

Fleet, W. S., & Heilman, K. M. (1986). The fatigue effect in hemispatial neglect. *Neurology, 36*(Suppl. 1), 258. (5)

Fletcher, P. C., McKenna, P. J., Frith, C. D., Grasby, P. M., Friston, K. J., & Dolan, R. J. (1998). Brain activations in schizophrenia during a graded memory task studied with functional neuroimaging. *Archives of General Psychiatry, 55,* 1001–1008. (15)

Fletcher, R., & Voke, J. (1985). *Defective colour vision.* Bristol, England: Hilger. (6)

Flint, J. (2004). The genetic basis of neuroticism. *Neuroscience and Biobehavioral Reviews, 28,* 307–316. (12)

Flöel, A., Knecht, S., Lohmann, H., Deppe, M., Sommer, J., Dräger, B., et al. (2001). Language and spatial attention can lateralize to the same hemisphere in healthy humans. *Neurology, 57,* 1018–1024. (14)

Flor, H., Elbert, T., Knecht, S., Wienbruch, C., Pantev, C., Birbaumer, N., et al. (1995). Phantom-limb pain as a perceptual correlate of cortical reorganization following arm amputation. *Nature, 375,* 482–484. (5)

Florence, S. L., & Kaas, J. H. (1995). Large-scale reorganization at multiple levels of the somatosensory pathway follows therapeutic amputation of the hand in monkeys. *Journal of Neuroscience, 15,* 8083–8095. (5)

Florence, S. L., Taub, H. B., & Kaas, J. H. (1998). Large-scale sprouting of cortical connections after peripheral injury in adult macaque monkeys. *Science, 282,* 1117–1121. (5)

Flynn, J. M., & Boder, E. (1991). Clinical and electrophysiological correlates of dysphonetic and dyseidetic dyslexia. In J. F. Stein (Ed.), *Vision and visual dyslexia* (pp. 121–131). Vol. 13 of J. R. Cronly-Dillon (Ed.), *Vision and visual dysfunction.* Boca Raton, FL: CRC Press. (14)

Fogassi, L., Ferrari, P. F., Gesierich, B., Rozzi, S., Chersi, F., & Rizzolatti, G. (2005). Parietal lobe: From action understanding to intention understanding. *Science, 308,* 662–667. (8)

Folkard, S., Hume, K. I., Minors, D. S., Waterhouse, J. M., & Watson, F. L. (1985). Independence of the circadian rhythm in alertness from the sleep/wake cycle. *Nature, 313,* 678–679. (9)

Follesa, P., Serra, M., Cagetti, E., Pisu, M. G., Porta, S., Floris, S., et al. (2000). Allopregnanolone synthesis in cerebellar granule cells: Roles in regulation of GABAA receptor expression and function during progesterone treatment and withdrawal. *Molecular Pharmacology, 57,* 1262–1270. (11)

Ford, D. E., & Cooper-Patrick, L. (2001). Sleep disturbances and mood disorders: An epidemiological perspective. *Depression and Anxiety, 14,* 3–6. (15)

Forger, N. G., & Breedlove, S. M. (1987). Motoneuronal death during human fetal development. *Journal of Comparative Neurology, 264,* 118–122. (5)

Forger, N. G., Rosen, G. J., Waters, E. M., Jacob, D., Simerly, R. B., & de Vries, G. J. (2004). Deletion of *Bax* eliminates sex differences in the mouse forebrain. *Proceedings of the National Academy of Sciences, USA, 101,* 13666–13671. (11)

Forster, B., & Corballis, M. C. (2000). Interhemispheric transfer of colour and shape information in the presence and absence of the corpus callosum. *Neuropsychologia, 38,* 32–45. (14)

Fortin, N. J., Agster, K. L., & Eichenbaum, H. B. (2002). Critical role of the hippocampus in memory for sequences of events. *Nature Neuroscience, 5,* 458–462. (13)

Fosse, R., Stickgold, R., & Hobson, J. A. (2001). The mind in REM sleep: Reports of emotional experience. *Sleep, 24,* 947–955. (15)

Fotopoulou, A., Solms, M., & Turnbull, O. (2004). Wishful reality distortions in confabulation: A case report. *Neuropsychologia, 47*, 727–744. (13)

Foundas, A. L., Leonard, C. M., & Hanna-Pladdy, B. (2002). Variability in the anatomy of the planum temporale and posterior ascending ramus: Do right- and left-handers differ? *Brain and Language, 83*, 403–424. (14)

Fox, P. T., Ingham, R. J., Ingham, J. C., Zamarripa, F., Xiong, J.-H., & Lancaster, J. L. (2000). Brain correlates of stuttering and syllable production: A PET performance-correlation analysis. *Brain, 123*, 1985–2004. (14)

Frangou, S., Chitins, X., & Williams, S. C. R. (2004). Mapping IQ and gray matter density in healthy young people. *NeuroImage, 23*, 800–805. (4)

Frank, R. A., Mize, S. J. S., Kennedy, L. M., de los Santos, H. C., & Green, S. J. (1992). The effect of *Gymnema sylvestre* extracts on the sweetness of eight sweeteners. *Chemical Senses, 17*, 461–479. (7)

Frankland, P. W., & Bontempi, B. (2005). The organization of recent and remote memories. *Nature Reviews Neuroscience, 6*, 119–130. (13)

Frankland, P. W., Josselyn, S. A., Bradwejn, J., Vaccarino, F. J., & Yeomans, J. S. (1997). Activation of amygdala cholecystokinin B receptors potentiates the acoustic startle response in the rat. *Journal of Neuroscience, 17*, 1838–1847. (12)

Frankland, P. W., O'Brien, C., Ohno, M., Kirkwood, A., & Silva, A. J. (2000). α-CaMKII-dependent plasticity in the cortex is required for permanent memory. *Nature, 411*, 309–313. (13)

Franz, E. A., Waldie, K. E., & Smith, M. J. (2000). The effect of callosotomy on novel versus familiar bimanual actions: A neural dissociation between controlled and automatic processes? *Psychological Science, 11*, 82–85. (14)

Frassinetti, F., Pavani, F., & Làdavas, E. (2002). Acoustical vision of neglected stimuli: Interaction among spatially converging audiovisual inputs in neglect patients. *Journal of Cognitive Neuroscience, 14*, 62–69. (14)

Freed, C. R., Greene, P. E., Breeze, R. E., Tsai, W.-Y., DuMouchel, W., Kao, R., et al. (2001). Transplantation of embryonic dopamine neurons for severe Parkinson's disease. *New England Journal of Medicine, 344*, 710–719. (8)

Freedman, M. S., Lucas, R. J., Soni, B., von Schantz, M., Muñoz, M., David-Gray, Z., et al. (1999). Regulation of mammalian circadian behavior by non-rod, non-cone, ocular photoreceptors. *Science, 284*, 502–504. (9)

Freedman, R. D., & Thibos, L. N. (1975). Contrast sensitivity in humans with abnormal visual experience. *Journal of Physiology, 247*, 687–710. (6)

Frese, M., & Harwich, C. (1984). Shiftwork and the length and quality of sleep. *Journal of Occupational Medicine, 26*, 561–566. (9)

Fridberger, A., Boutet de Monvel, J., Zheng, J., Hu, N., Zou, Y., Ren, T., et al. (2004). Organ of Corti potentials and the motion of the basilar membrane. *Journal of Neuroscience, 24*, 10057–10063. (7)

Fried, I., Katz, A., McCarthy, G., Sass, K. J., Williamson, P., Spencer, S. S., et al. (1991). Functional organization of human supplementary motor cortex studied by electrical stimulation. *Journal of Neuroscience, 11*, 3656–3666. (8)

Fried, I., Wilson, C. L., Morrow, J. W., Cameron, K. A., Behnke, E. D., Ackerson, L. C., et al. (2001). Increased dopamine release in the human amygdala during performance of cognitive tasks. *Nature Neuroscience, 4*, 201–206. (13)

Fried, P. A., Watkinson, B., & Gray, R. (2003). Differential effects on cognitive functioning in 13- to 16-year-olds prenatally exposed to cigarettes and marihuana. *Neurotoxicology and Teratology, 25*, 427–436. (5)

Fried, S., Münch, T. A., & Werblin, F. S. (2002). Mechanisms and circuitry underlying directional selectivity in the retina. *Nature, 420*, 411–414. (6)

Friedburg, D., & Klöppel, K. P. (1996). Frühzeitige Korrektion von Hyperopie und Astigmatismus bic Kindern führt zu besserer Entwicklung des Sehschärfe [Early correction of hyperopia and astigmatism in children improves development of visual acuity]. *Klinische Monatsblatt der Augenheilkunde, 209*, 21–24. (6)

Friedlander, W. J. (1986). Who was "the father of bromide treatment of epilepsy"? *Archives of Neurology, 43*, 505–507. (15)

Friedman, M. I., & Stricker, E. M. (1976). The physiological psychology of hunger: A physiological perspective. *Psychological Review, 83*, 409–431. (10)

Fritsch, G., & Hitzig, E. (1870). Über die elektrische Erregbarkeit des Grosshirns [Concerning the electrical stimulability of the cerebrum]. *Archiv für Anatomie Physiologie und Wissenschaftliche Medicin*, 300–332. (8)

Fritz, J., Shamma, S., Elhilali, M., & Klein, D. (2003). Rapid task-related plasticity of spectrotemporal receptive fields in primary auditory cortex. *Nature Neuroscience, 6*, 1216–1223. (5)

Fu, L.-Y., Acuna-Goycolea, C., & van den Pol, A. N. (2004). Neuropeptide Y inhibits hypocretin/orexin neurons by multiple presynaptic and postsynaptic mechanisms: Tonic depression of the hypothalamic arousal system. *Journal of Neuroscience, 24*, 8741–8751. (10)

Fu, Q., Heath, A. C., Bucholz, K. K., Nelson, E., Goldberg, J., Lyons, M. J., et al. (2002). Shared genetic risk of major depression, alcohol dependence, and marijuana dependence. *Archives of General Psychiatry, 59*, 1125–1132. (15)

Fu, W., Sugai, T., Yoshimura, H., & Onoda, N. (2004). Convergence of olfactory and gustatory connections onto the endopiriform nucleus in the rat. *Neuroscience, 126*, 1033–1041. (7)

Fuller, R. K., & Roth, H. P. (1979). Disulfiram for the treatment of alcoholism: An evaluation in 128 men. *Annals of Internal Medicine, 90*, 901–904. (15)

Furey, M. L., Pietrini, P., & Haxby, J. V. (2000). Cholinergic enhancement and increased selectivity of perceptual processing during working memory. *Science, 290*, 2315–2319. (13)

Fuster, J. M. (1989). *The prefrontal cortex* (2nd ed.). New York: Raven Press. (4)

Gabrieli, J. D. E., Corkin, S., Mickel, S. F., & Growdon, J. H. (1993). Intact acquisition of mirror-tracing skill in Alzheimer's disease and in global amnesia. *Behavioral Neuroscience, 107*, 899–910. (13)

Gage, F. H. (2000). Mammalian neural stem cells. *Science, 287*, 1433–1438. (5)

Gais, S., Plihal, W., Wagner, U., & Born, J. (2000). Early sleep triggers memory for early visual discrimination skills. *Nature Neuroscience, 3*, 1335–1339. (9)

Galaburda, A. M., Sherman, G. F., Rosen, G. D., Aboitiz, F., & Geschwind, N. (1985). Developmental dyslexia: Four consecutive patients with cortical anomalies. *Annals of Neurology, 18*, 222–233. (14)

Galante, M., & Diana, M. A. (2004). Group I metabotropic glutamate receptors inhibit GABA release at interneuron Purkinje synapses through endocannabinoid production. *Journal of Neuroscience, 24*, 4865–4874. (3)

Gale, G. D., Anagnostaras, S. G., Godsil, B. P., Mitchell, S., Nozawa, T., Sage, J. R., et al. (2004). Role of the basolateral amygdala in the storage of fear memories across the adult lifetime of rats. *Journal of Neuroscience, 24*, 3810–3815. (12)

Galef, B. G., Jr. (1992). Weaning from mother's milk to solid foods: The developmental psychobiology of self-selection of foods by rats. *Annals of the New York Academy of Sciences, 662*, 37–52. (10)

Galin, D., Johnstone, J., Nakell, L., & Herron, J. (1979). Development of the capacity for tactile information transfer between hemispheres in normal children. *Science, 204*, 1330–1332. (14)

Gan, W.-B., Kwon, E., Feng, G., Sanes, J. R., & Lichtman, J. W. (2003). Synaptic dynamism measured over minutes to months: Age-dependent decline in an autonomic ganglion. *Nature Neuroscience, 6*, 956–960. (5)

Gangestad, S. W., & Simpson, J. A. (2000). The evolution of human mating: Trade-offs and strategic pluralism. *Behavioral and Brain Sciences, 23*, 573–644. (11)

Gangestad, S. W., Simpson, J. A., Cousins, A. J., Garver-Apgar, C. E., & Christensen,

P. N. (2004). Women's preferences for male behavioral displays change across the menstrual cycle. *Psychological Science, 15,* 203–207. (11)

Ganguly, K., Kiss, L., & Poo, M. (2000). Enhancement of presynaptic neuronal excitability by correlated presynaptic and postsynaptic spiking. *Nature Neuroscience, 3,* 1018–1026. (13)

Gao, J.-H., Parsons, L. M., Bower, J. M., Xiong, J., Li, J., & Fox, P. T. (1996). Cerebellum implicated in sensory acquisition and discrimination rather than motor control. *Science, 272,* 545–547. (8)

Garcia, R., Vouimba, R.-M., Baudry, M., & Thompson, R. F. (1999). The amygdala modulates prefrontal cortex activity relative to conditioned fear. *Nature, 402,* 294–296. (12)

García-Pérez, M. A., & Peli, E. (2001). Intrasaccadic perception. *Journal of Neuroscience, 21,* 7313–7322. (6)

Gardner, E. P., Ro, J. Y., Debowy, D., & Ghosh, S. (1999). Facilitation of neuronal activity in somatosensory and posterior parietal cortex during prehension. *Experimental Brain Research, 127,* 329–354. (8)

Gardner, B. T., & Gardner, R. A. (1975). Evidence for sentence constituents in the early utterances of child and chimpanzee. *Journal of Experimental Psychology: General, 104,* 244–267. (14)

Gardner, H., & Zurif, E. B. (1975). Bee but not be: Oral reading of single words in aphasia and alexia. *Neuropsychologia, 13,* 181–190. (14)

Garpenstrand, H., Annas, P., Ekblom, J., Oreland, L., & Fredrikson, M. (2001). Human fear conditioning is related to dopaminergic and serotonergic biological markers. *Behavioral Neuroscience, 115,* 358–364. (12)

Gaser, C., & Schlaug, G. (2003). Brain structures differ between musicians and non-musicians. *Journal of Neuroscience, 23,* 9240–9245. (5)

Gash, D. M., Zhang, Z., Ovadia, A., Cass, W. A., Yi, A., Simmerman, L., et al. (1996). Functional recovery in Parkinsonian monkeys treated with GDNF. *Nature, 380,* 252–255. (8)

Gauthier, I., Tarr, M. J., Anderson, A. W., Skudlarski, P., & Gore, J. C. (1999). Activation of the middle fusiform "face area" increases with experience in recognizing novel objects. *Nature Neuroscience, 2,* 568–573. (6)

Geiger, G., Lettvin, J. Y., & Fahle, M. (1994). Dyslexic children learn a new visual strategy for reading: A controlled experiment. *Vision Research, 34,* 1223–1233. (14)

Geiger, G., Lettvin, J. Y., & Zegarra-Moran, O. (1992). Task-determined strategies of visual process. *Cognitive Brain Research, 1,* 39–52. (14)

Geisler, F. H., Coleman, W. P., Grieco, G., Poonian, D., & the Sygen Study Group (2001). The Sygen® multicenter acute spinal cord injury study. *Spine, 26* (Suppl.), S87–S98. (5)

George, M. S., Wasserman, E. M., Kimbrell, T. A., Little, J. T., Williams, W. E., Danielson, A. L., et al. (1997). Mood improvement following daily left prefrontal repetitive transcranial magnetic stimulation in patients with depression: A placebo-controlled crossover trial. *American Journal of Psychiatry, 154,* 1752–1756. (15)

Gerald, M. S., Higley, S., Westergaard, G. C., Suomi, S. J., & Higley, J. D. (2002). Variation in reproductive outcomes for captive male rhesus macaques (*Macaca mulatta*) differing in CSF 5-hydroxyindoleacetic acid concentrations. *Brain Behavior and Evolution, 60,* 117–124. (12)

Gerardin, D. C. C., & Pereira, O. C. M. (2002). Reproductive changes in male rats treated perinatally with an aromatase inhibitor. *Pharmacology Biochemistry and Behavior, 71,* 309–313. (11)

Gerdeman, G. L., Ronesi, J., & Lovinger, D. M. (2002). Post-synaptic endocannabinoid release is critical to long-term depression in the striatum. *Nature Neuroscience, 5,* 446–451. (3)

Gerwig, M., Hajjar, K., Dimitrova, A., Maschke, M., Kolb, F. P., Frings, M., et al. (2005). Timing of conditioned eyeblink responses is impaired in cerebellar patients. *Journal of Neuroscience, 25,* 3919–3931. (13)

Geschwind, N., & Levitsky, W. (1968). Human brain: Left-right asymmetries in temporal speech region. *Science, 161,* 186–187. (14)

Ghitza, U. E., Fabbricatore, A. T., Prokopenko, V., Pawlak, A. P., & West, M. O. (2003). Persistent cue-evoked activity of accumbens neurons after prolonged abstinence from self-administered cocaine. *Journal of Neuroscience, 23,* 7239–7245. (15)

Gibbs, F. P. (1983). Temperature dependence of the hamster circadian pacemaker. *American Journal of Physiology, 244,* R607–R610. (9)

Gibbs, J., Young, R. C., & Smith, G. P. (1973). Cholecystokinin decreases food intake in rats. *Journal of Comparative and Physiological Psychology, 84,* 488–495. (10)

Giedd, J. N., Blumenthal, J., Molloy, E., & Castellanos, F. X. (2001). Brain imaging of attention deficit/hyperactivity disorder. *Annals of the New York Academy of Sciences, 931,* 33–49. (7)

Gifkins, A., Greba, Q., & Kokkinidis, L. (2002). Ventral tegmental area dopamine neurons mediate the shock sensitization of acoustic startle: A potential site of action for benzodiazepine anxiolytics. *Behavioral Neuroscience, 116,* 785–794. (12)

Gilbertson, M. W., Shenton, M. E., Ciszewski, A., Kasai, K., Lasko, N. B., Orr, S. P., et al. (2002). Smaller hippocampal volume predicts pathological vulnerability to psychological trauma. *Nature Neuroscience, 5,* 1242–1247. (12)

Gilmour, D., Knaut, H., Maischein, H.-M., & Nüsslein-Volhard, C. (2004). Towing of sensory axons by their migrating target cells *in vivo*. *Nature Neuroscience, 7,* 491–492. (5)

Gillette, M. U., & McArthur, A. J. (1996). Circadian actions of melatonin at the suprachiasmatic nucleus. *Behavioural Brain Research, 73,* 135–139. (9)

Giraud, A. L., & Price, C. J. (2001). The constraints functional neuroimaging places on classical models of auditory word processing. *Journal of Cognitive Neuroscience, 13,* 754–765. (14)

Giraux, P., Sirigu, A., Schneider, F., & Dubernard, J.-M. (2001). Cortical reorganization in motor cocrtex after graft of both hands. *Nature Neuroscience, 4,* 691–692. (5)

Giros, B., Jaber, M., Jones, S. R., Wightman, R. M., & Caron, M. G. (1996). Hyperlocomotion and indifference to cocaine and amphetamine in mice lacking the dopamine transporter. *Nature, 379,* 606–612. (3)

Giuliani, D., & Ferrari, F. (1996). Differential behavioral response to dopamine D2 agonists by sexually naive, sexually active, and sexually inactive male rats. *Behavioral Neuroscience, 110,* 802–808. (11)

Gläscher, J., & Adolphs, R. (2003). Processing of the arousal of subliminal and supraliminal emotional stimuli by the human amygdala. *Journal of Neuroscience, 23,* 10274–10282. (12)

Glass, M. (2001). The role of cannabinoids in neurodegenerative diseases. *Progress in Neuro-Psychopharmacology & Biological Psychiatry, 25,* 743–765. (8)

Glendenning, K. K., Baker, B. N., Hutson, K. A., & Masterton, R. B. (1992). Acoustic chiasm V: Inhibition and excitation in the ipsilateral and contralateral projections of LSO. *Journal of Comparative Neurology, 319,* 100–122. (7)

Glick, S. D. (1974). Changes in drug sensitivity and mechanisms of functional recovery following brain damage. In D. G. Stein, J. J. Rosen, & N. Butters (Eds.), *Plasticity and recovery of function in the central nervous system* (pp. 339–372). New York: Academic Press. (5)

Goate, A., Chartier-Harlin, M. C., Mullan, M., Brown, J., Crawford, F., Fidani, L., et al. (1991). Segregation of a missense mutation in the amyloid precursor protein gene with familial Alzheimer's disease. *Nature, 349,* 704–706. (13)

Goddard, M. R., Godfray, H. C. J., & Burt, A. (2005). Sex increases the efficacy of natural selection in experimental yeast populations. *Nature, 434,* 636–640. (11)

Gödecke, I., & Bonhoeffer, T. (1996). Development of identical orientation maps for two eyes without common visual experience. *Nature, 379,* 251–254. (6)

Gogos, J. A., Osborne, J., Nemes, A., Mendelsohn, M., & Axel, R. (2000). Genetic ablation and restoration of the olfactory topographic map. *Cell, 103,* 609–620. (5)

Gold, P. E., Cahill, L., & Wenk, G. L. (2002). Gingko biloba: A cognitive enhancer? *Psychological Science in the Public Interest, 3,* 2–11. (13)

Gold, R. M. (1973). Hypothalamic obesity: The myth of the ventromedial hypothalamus. *Science, 182,* 488–490. (10)

Goldberg, T. E., Weinberger, D. R., Berman, K. F., Pliskin, N. H., & Podd, M. H. (1987). Further evidence for dementia of the prefrontal type in schizophrenia? *Archives of General Psychiatry, 44,* 1008–1014. (15)

Goldin-Meadow, S., McNeill, D., & Singleton, J. (1996). Silence is liberating: Removing the handcuffs on grammatical expression in the manual modality. *Psychological Review, 103,* 34–55. (14)

Goldin-Meadow, S., & Mylander, C. (1998). Spontaneous sign systems created by deaf children in two cultures. *Nature, 391,* 279–281. (14)

Goldman, P. S. (1971). Functional development of the prefrontal cortex in early life and the problem of neuronal plasticity. *Experimental Neurology, 32,* 366–387. (15)

Goldman, P. S. (1976). The role of experience in recovery of function following orbital prefrontal lesions in infant monkeys. *Neuropsychologia, 14,* 401–412. (15)

Goldman-Rakic, P. S. (1987). Development of cortical circuitry and cognitive function. *Child Development, 58,* 601–622. (5)

Goldman-Rakic, P. S. (1988). Topography of cognition: Parallel distributed networks in primate association cortex. *Annual Review of Neuroscience, 11,* 137–156. (4; inside cover)

Goldstein, A. (1980). Thrills in response to music and other stimuli. *Physiological Psychology, 8,* 126–129. (7)

Goldstein, J. M., Seidman, L. J., Horton, N. J., Makris, N., Kennedy, D. N., Caviness, V. S., Jr., et al. (2001). Normal sexual dimorphism of the adult human brain assessed by in vivo magnetic resonance imaging. *Cerebral Cortex, 11,* 490–497. (11)

Goldstein, L. B. (1993). Basic and clinical studies of pharmacologic effects on recovery from brain injury. *Journal of Neural Transplantation & Plasticity, 4,* 175–192. (5)

Gollin, E. S. (1960). Developmental studies of visual recognition of incomplete objects. *Perceptual and Motor Skills, 11,* 289–298. (13)

González, B., Rodríguez, M., Ramirez, C., & Sabate, M. (2005). Disturbance of motor imagery after cerebellar stroke. *Behavioral Neuroscience, 199,* 622–626. (8)

Gonzalez, S. L., Labombarda, F., Deniselle, M. C. G., Guennoun, R., Schumacher, M., & De Nicola, A. F. (2004). Progesterone up-regulates neuronal brain-derived neurotrophic factor expression in the injured spinal cord. *Neuroscience, 125,* 605–614. (5)

Good, C. D., Johnsrude, I., Ashburner, J., Henson, R. N. A., Friston, K. J., & Frackowiak, R. S. J. (2001). Cerebral asymmetry and the effects of sex and handedness on brain structure: A voxel-based morphometric analysis of 465 normal adult human brains. *NeuroImage, 14,* 685–700. (11)

Goodale, M. A. (1996). Visuomotor modules in the vertebrate brain. *Canadian Journal of Physiology and Pharmacology, 74,* 390–400. (6, 8)

Goodale, M. A., Milner, A. D., Jakobson, L. S., & Carey, D. P. (1991). A neurological dissociation between perceiving objects and grasping them. *Nature, 349,* 154–156. (6, 8)

Gopnik, M., & Crago, M. B. (1991). Familial aggregation of a developmental language disorder. *Cognition, 39,* 1–50. (14)

Gorski, J. A., Zeiler, S. R., Tamowski, S., & Jones, K. R. (2003). Brain-derived neurotrophic factor is required for the maintenance of cortical dendrites. *Journal of Neuroscience, 23,* 6856–6865. (5)

Gorski, R. A. (1980). Sexual differentiation of the brain. In D. T. Krieger & J. C. Hughes (Eds.), *Neuroendocrinology* (pp. 215–222). Sunderland, MA: Sinauer. (11)

Gorski, R. A. (1985). The 13th J. A. F. Stevenson memorial lecture. Sexual differentiation of the brain: Possible mechanisms and implications. *Canadian Journal of Physiology and Pharmacology, 63,* 577–594. (11)

Gorski, R. A., & Allen, L. S. (1992). Sexual orientation and the size of the anterior commissure in the human brain. *Proceedings of the National Academy of Sciences, USA, 89,* 7199–7202. (11)

Gosler, A. G., Greenwood, J. J. D., & Perrins, C. (1995). Predation risk and the cost of being fat. *Nature, 377,* 621–623. (10)

Gothe, J., Brandt, S. A., Irlbacher, K., Röricht, S., Sabel, B. A., & Meyer, B.-U. (2002). Changes in visual cortex excitability in blind subjects as demonstrated by transcranial magnetic stimulation. *Brain, 125,* 479–490. (5)

Gottesmann, C. (2004). Brain inhibitory mechanisms involved in basic and higher integrated sleep processes. *Brain Research Reviews, 45,* 230–249. (9)

Gottesman, I. I. (1991). *Schizophrenia genesis.* New York: Freeman. (15)

Gould, E., Reeves, A. J., Graziano, M. S. A., & Gross, C. G. (1999). Neurogenesis in the neocortex of adult primates. *Science, 286,* 548–552. (5)

Gozal, D., Daniel, J. M., & Dohanich, G. P. (2001). Behavioral and anatomical correlates of chronic episodic hypoxia during sleep in the rat. *Journal of Neuroscience, 21,* 2442–2450. (15)

Grant, A. J., & Kline, D. L. (2003). Electrophysiological responses from Culicoides (Diptera: Ceratopogonidae) to stimulation with carbon dioxide. *Journal of Medical Entomology, 40,* 284–292. (7)

Gratacòs, M., Nadal, M., Martin-Santos, R., Pujana, M. A., Gago, J., Peral, B., et al. (2001). A polymorphic genomic duplication on human chromosome 15 is a susceptibility factor for panic and phobic disorders. *Cell, 106,* 367–379. (12)

Graves, J. A. M. (1994). Mammalian sex-determining genes. In R. V. Short & E. Balaban (Eds.), *The differences between the sexes* (pp. 397–418). Cambridge, England: Cambridge University Press. (11)

Gray, C. M., König, P., Engel, A. K., & Singer, W. (1989). Oscillatory responses in cat visual cortex exhibit inter-columnar synchronization which reflects global stimulus properties. *Nature, 338,* 334–337. (4)

Gray, J. A. (1970). The psychophysiological basis of introversion–extraversion. *Behavioural Research Therapy, 8,* 249–266. (12)

Graybiel, A. M. (1998). The basal ganglia and chunking of action repertoires. *Neurobiology of Learning and Memory, 70,* 119–136. (8)

Graybiel, A. M., Aosaki, T., Flaherty, A. W., & Kimura, M. (1994). The basal ganglia and adaptive motor control. *Science, 265,* 1826–1831. (4)

Graziadei, P. P. C., & deHan, R. S. (1973). Neuronal regeneration in frog olfactory system. *Journal of Cell Biology, 59,* 525–530. (5)

Graziano, M. S. A., Taylor, C. S. R., & Moore, T. (2002). Complex movements evoked by microstimulation of precentral cortex. *Neuron, 34,* 841–851. (4, 8)

Greene, J. D., Nystrom, L. E., Engell, A. D., Darley, J. M., & Cohen, J. D. (2004). The neural bases of cognitive conflict and control in moral judgment. *Neuron, 44,* 389–400. (13)

Greengard, P. (2001). The neurobiology of slow synaptic transmission. *Science, 294,* 1024–1030. (3)

Greenlee, M. W., Lang, H.-J., Mergner, T., & Seeger, W. (1995). Visual short-term memory of stimulus velocity in patients with unilateral posterior brain damage. *Journal of Neuroscience, 15,* 2287–2300. (6)

Greenough, W. T. (1975). Experiential modification of the developing brain. *American Scientist, 63,* 37–46. (5)

Gribkoff, V. K., Starrett, J. E., Jr., Dworetzky, S. I., Hewawasam, P., Boissard, C. G., Cook, D. A., et al. (2001). Targeting acute ischemic stroke with a calcium-sensitive opener of maxi-K potassium channels. *Nature Medicine, 7,* 471–477. (5)

Grice, D. E., Halmi, K. A., Fichter, M. M., Strober, M., Woodside, D. B., Treasure, J. T., et al. (2002). Evidence for a susceptibility gene for anorexia nervosa on chromosome 1. *American Journal of Human Genetics, 70,* 787–792. (10)

Griffin, D. R. (2001). *Animal minds: Beyond cognition to consciousness.* Chicago: University of Chicago Press. (1)

Griffin, D. R., Webster, F. A., & Michael, C. R. (1960). The echolocation of flying insects by bats. *Animal Behaviour, 8,* 141–154. (7)

Griffiths, T. D., Uppenkamp, S., Johnsrude, I., Josephs, O., & Patterson, R. D. (2001). Encoding of the temporal regularity of sound in the human brainstem. *Nature Neuroscience, 4,* 633–637. (7)

Grillon, C., Morgan, C. A., III, Davis, M., & Southwick, S. M. (1998). Effect of darkness on acoustic startle in Vietnam veterans with PTSD. *American Journal of Psychiatry, 155,* 812–817. (12)

Grill-Spector, K., Knouf, N., & Kanwisher, N. (2004). The fusiform face area subserves face perception, not generic within category identification. *Nature Neuroscience, 7,* 555–562. (6)

Grinvald, E., & Hildesheim, R. (2004). VSDI: A new era in functional imaging of cortical dynamics. *Nature Reviews Neuroscience, 5,* 874–885. (4)

Gross, C. G. (1999). The fire that comes from the eye. *The Neuroscientist, 5,* 58–64. (6)

Gross, C. G., & Graziano, M. S. A. (1995). Multiple representations of space in the brain. *The Neuroscientist, 1,* 43–50. (4)

Gross, C., & Hen, R. (2004). The developmental origins of anxiety. *Nature Reviews Neuroscience, 5,* 545–552. (12)

Grosshans, D. R., Clayton, D. A., Coultrap, S. J., & Browning, M. D. (2002). LTP leads to rapid surface expression of NMDA but not AMPA receptors in adult rat CA1. *Nature Neuroscience, 5,* 27–33. (13)

Grossman, E. D., & Blake, R. (2001). Brain activity evoked by inverted and imagined biological motion. *Vision Research, 41,* 1475–1482. (6)

Grossman, E., Donnelly, M., Price, R., Pickens, D., Morgan, V., Neighbor, G., et al. (2000). Brain areas involved in perception of biological motion. *Journal of Cognitive Neuroscience, 12,* 711–720. (6)

Grossman, S. P., Dacey, D., Halaris, A. E., Collier, T., & Routtenberg, A. (1978). Aphagia and adipsia after preferential destruction of nerve cell bodies in hypothalamus. *Science, 202,* 537–539. (10)

Grutzendler, J., Kasthuri, N., & Gan, W.-B. (2002). Long-term dendritic spine stability in the adult cortex. *Nature, 420,* 812–816. (5)

Gubernick, D. J., & Alberts, J. R. (1983). Maternal licking of young: Resource exchange and proximate controls. *Physiology & Behavior, 31,* 593–601. (11)

Guidotti, A., Ferrero, P., Fujimoto, M., Santi, R. M., & Costa, E. (1986). Studies on endogenous ligands (endocoids) for the benzodiazepine/beta carboline binding sites. *Advances in Biochemical Pharmacology, 41,* 137–148. (12)

Guidotti, A., Forchetti, C. M., Corda, M. G., Konkel, D., Bennett, C. D., & Costa, E. (1983). Isolation, characterization, and purification to homogeneity of an endogenous polypeptide with agonistic action on benzodiazepine receptors. *Proceedings of the National Academy of Sciences, USA, 80,* 3531–3535. (12)

Guillery, R. W., Feig, S. L., & Lozsádi, D. A. (1998). Paying attention to the thalamic reticular nucleus. *Trends in Neurosciences, 21,* 28–32. (4, 9)

Guillery, R. W., Feig, S. L., & van Lieshout, D. P. (2001). Connections of higher order visual relays in the thalamus: A study of corticothalamic pathways in cats. *Journal of Comparative Neurology, 438,* 66–85. (6)

Guillin, O., Diaz, J., Carroll, P., Griffon, N., Schwartz, J-C., & Sokoloff P. (2001). BDNF controls dopamine D_3 receptor expression and triggers behavioural sensitization. *Nature, 412,* 86–89. (15)

Guisinger, S. (2003). Adapted to flee famine: Adding an evolutionary perspective to anorexia nervosa. *Psychological Review, 110,* 745–761. (10)

Guo, S.-W., & Reed, D. R. (2001). The genetics of phenylthiocarbamide perception. *Annals of Human Biology, 28,* 111–142. (7)

Gur, R. E., & Chin, S. (1999). Laterality in functional brain imaging studies of schizophrenia. *Schizophrenia Bulletin, 25,* 141–156. (15)

Gur, R. E., Cowell, P. E., Latshaw, A., Turetsky, B. I., Grossman, R. I., Arnold, S. E., et al. (2000). Reduced dorsal and orbital prefrontal gray matter volumes in schizophrenia. *Archives of General Psychiatry, 57,* 761–768. (15)

Gur, R. E., Turetsky, B. I., Cowell, P. E., Finkelman, C., Maany, V., Grossman, R. I., et al. (2000). Temporolimbic volume reductions in schizophrenia. *Archives of General Psychiatry, 57,* 769–775. (15)

Gusella, J. F., & MacDonald, M. E. (2000). Molecular genetics: Unmasking polyglutamine triggers in neurodegenerative disease. *Nature Reviews Neuroscience, 1,* 109–115. (8)

Gustafsson, B., & Wigström, H. (1990). Basic features of long-term potentiation in the hippocampus. *Seminars in the Neurosciences, 2,* 321–333. (13)

Gutschalk, A., Patterson, R. D., Scherg, M., Uppenkamp, S., & Rupp, A. (2004). Temporal dynamics of pitch in human auditory cortex. *NeuroImage, 22,* 755–766. (7)

Gwinner, E. (1986). Circannual rhythms in the control of avian rhythms. *Advances in the Study of Behavior, 16,* 191–228. (9)

Haas, H., & Panula, P. (2003). The role of histamine and the tuberomamillary nucleus in the nervous system. *Nature Reviews Neuroscience, 4,* 121–130. (9)

Hadjikhani, N., Liu, A. K., Dale, A. M., Cavanagh, P., & Tootell, R. B. H. (1998). Retinotopy and color sensitivity in human visual cortical area V8. *Nature Neuroscience, 1,* 235–241. (6)

Hafting, T., Fyhn, M., Molden, S., Moser, M.-B., & Moser, E. I. (2005). Microstructure of a spatial map in the entorhinal cortex. *Nature, 436,* 801–806. (13)

Hagenbuch, B., Gao, B., & Meier, P. J. (2002). Transport of xenobiotics across the blood-brain barrier. *News in Physiological Sciences, 17,* 231–234. (2)

Haggarty, J. M., Cernovsky, Z., Husni, M., Minor, K., Kermean, P., & Merskey, H. (2002). Seasonal affective disorder in an arctic community. *Acta Psychiatrica Scandinavica, 105,* 378–384. (15)

Haier, R. J., Jung, R. E., Yeo, R. A., Head, K., & Alkire, M. T. (2004). Structural brain variation and general intelligence. *NeuroImage, 23,* 425–433. (4)

Haimov, I., & Arendt, J. (1999). The prevention and treatment of jet lag. *Sleep Medicine Reviews, 3,* 229–240. (9)

Haimov, I., & Lavie, P. (1996). Melatonin—A soporific hormone. *Current Directions in Psychological Science, 5,* 106–111. (9)

Hains, B. C., Everhart, A. W., Fullwood, S. D., & Hulsebosch, C. E. (2002). Changes in serotonin, serotonin transporter expression and serotonin denervation supersensitivity: Involvement in chronic central pain after spinal hemisection in the rat. *Experimental Neurology, 175,* 347–362. (5)

Haist, F., Gore, J. B., & Mao, H. (2001). Consolidation of human memory over decades revealed by functional magnetic resonance imaging. *Nature Neuroscience, 4,* 1139–1145. (13)

Hakuta, K., Bialystok, E., & Wiley, E. (2003). Critical evidence: A test of the critical-period hypothesis for second-language acquisition. *Psychological Science, 14,* 31–38. (14)

Halaas, J. L, Gajiwala, K. S., Maffei, M., Cohen, S. L., Chait, B. T., Rabinowitz, D., et al. (1995). Weight-reducing effects of the plasma protein encoded by the obese gene. *Science, 269,* 543–546. (10)

Halari, R., Hines, M., Kumari, V., Mehrotra, R., Wheeler, M., Ng, V., et al. (2005). Sex differences and individual differences in cognitive performance and their relationship to endogenous gonadal hormones and gonadotropins. *Behavioral Neuroscience, 119,* 104–117. (11)

Hale, S., Myerson, J., Rhee, S. H., Weiss, C. S., & Abrams, R. A. (1996). Selective interference with the maintenance of location information in working memory. *Neuropsychology, 10,* 228–240. (13)

Haley, J. (1959). An interactional description of schizophrenia. *Psychiatry, 22,* 321–332. (15)

Hall, J., Thomas, K. L., & Everitt, B. J. (2000). Rapid and selective induction of BDNF expression in the hippocampus during contextual learning. *Nature Neuroscience, 3,* 533–535. (13)

Hallem, E. A., Fox, A. N., Zwiebel, L. J., & Carlson, J. R. (2004). Mosquito receptor for human-sweat odorant. *Nature, 427,* 212–213. (7)

Haller, J., Tóth, M., & Halász, J. (2005). The activation of raphe serotonergic neurons in normal and hypoarousal-driven aggression: A double labeling study in rats. *Behavioural Brain Research, 161,* 88–94. (12)

Halpern, D. F. (2004). A cognitive-process taxonomy for sex differences in cognitive abilities. *Current Directions in Psychological Science, 13,* 135–139. (11)

Halpern, S. D., Andrews, T. J., & Purves, D. (1999). Interindividual variation in human visual performance. *Journal of Cognitive Neuroscience, 11,* 521–534. (6)

Hamann, S. B., & Squire, L. R. (1995). On the acquisition of new declarative knowledge in amnesia. *Behavioral Neuroscience, 109,* 1027–1044. (13)

Hamer, D. H., Hu, S., Magnuson, V. L., Hu, N., & Pattatucci, A. M. L. (1993). A linkage between DNA markers on the X chromosome and male sexual orientation. *Science, 261,* 321–327. (11)

Hamilton, W. D. (1964). The genetical evolution of social behavior (I and II). *Journal of Theoretical Biology, 7,* 1–16; 17–52. (1)

Hampson, R. E., Simeral, J. D., & Deadwyler, S. A. (1999). Distribution of spatial and nonspatial information in dorsal hippocampus. *Nature, 402,* 610–614. (13)

Han, C. J., & Robinson, J. K. (2001). Cannabinoid modulation of time estimation in the rat. *Behavioral Neuroscience, 115,* 243–246. (3)

Hanaway, J., Woolsey, T. A., Gado, M. H., & Roberts, M. P., Jr. (1998). *The brain atlas.* Bethesda, MD: Fitzgerald Science Press. (12)

Hanlon, F. M., Weisend, M. P., Yeo, R. A., Huang, M., Lee, R. R., Thoma, R. J., et al. (2005). A specific test of hippocampal deficit in schizophrenia. *Behavioral Neuroscience, 119,* 863–875. (15)

Hannibal, J., Hindersson, P., Knudsen, S. M., Georg, B., & Fahrenkrug, J. (2001). The photopigment melanopsin is exclusively present in pituitary adenylate cyclase-activating polypeptide-containing retinal ganglion cells of the retinohypothalamic tract. *Journal of Neuroscience, 21,* RC191: 1–7. (9)

Hao, Y., Creson, T., Zhang, L., Li, P., Du, F., Yuan, P., et al. (2004). Mood stabilizer valproate promotes ERK pathway-dependent cortical neuroal growth and neurogenesis. *Journal of Neuroscience, 24,* 6590–6599. (15)

Haqq, C. M., & Donahoe, P. K. (1998). Regulation of sexual dimorphism in mammals. *Physiological Reviews, 78,* 1–33. (11)

Hara, J., Beuckmann, C. T., Nambu, T., Willie, J. T., Chemelli, R. M., Sinton, C. M., et al. (2001). Genetic ablation of orexin neurons in mice results in narcolepsy, hypophagia, and obesity. *Neuron, 30,* 345–354. (9)

Hardy, J., & Selkoe, D. J. (2002). The amyloid hypothesis of Alzheimer's disease: Progress and problems on the way to therapeutics. *Science, 297,* 353–356. (13)

Hari, R. (1994). Human cortical functions revealed by magnetoencephalography. *Progress in Brain Research, 100,* 163–168. (4)

Harley, B., & Wang, W. (1997). The critical period hypothesis: Where are we now? In A. M. B. deGroot & J. F. Knoll (Eds.), *Tutorials in bilingualism* (pp. 19–51). Mahwah, NJ: Erlbaum. (14)

Hariri, A. R., Mattay, V. S., Tessitore, A., Fera, F., & Weinberger, D. R. (2003). Neocortical modulation of the amygdala response to fearful stimuli. *Biological Psychology, 53,* 494–501. (12, 13)

Hariri, A. R., Mattay, V. S., Tessitore, A., Kolachana, B., Fera, F., Goldman, D., et al. (2002). Serotonin transporter genetic variation and the response of the human amygdala. *Science, 297,* 400–403. (12)

Harmer, C. J., Thilo, K. V., Rothwell, J. C., & Goodwin, G. M. (2001). Transcranial magnetic stimulation of medial-frontal cortex impairs the processing of angry facial expressions. *Nature Neuroscience, 4,* 17–18. (12)

Harper, L. V. (2005). Epigenetic inheritance and the intergenerational transfer of experience. *Psychological Bulletin, 131,* 340–360. (1)

Harper, S. Q., Staber, P. D., He, X., Eliason, S. L., Martino, I. H., Mao, Q., et al. (2005). RNA interference improves motor and neuropathological abnormalities in a Huntington's disease mouse model. *Proceedings of the National Academy of Sciences, USA, 102,* 5820–5825. (8)

Harris, C. H. (2002). Sexual and romantic jealousy in heterosexual and homosexual adults. *Psychological Science, 13,* 7–12. (11)

Harris, C. R. (1999, July/August). The mystery of ticklish laughter. *American Scientist, 87*(4), 344–351. (7)

Harris, K. M., & Stevens, J. K. (1989). Dendritic spines of CA1 pyramidal cells in the rat hippocampus: Serial electron microscopy with reference to their biophysical characteristics. *Journal of Neuroscience, 9,* 2982–2997. (2)

Harris, R. A., Brodie, M. S., & Dunwiddie, T. V. (1992). Possible substrates of ethanol reinforcement: GABA and dopamine. *Annals of the New York Academy of Sciences, 654,* 61–69. (3)

Hart, B. L. (Ed.). (1976). *Experimental psychobiology.* San Francisco: Freeman. (10)

Hartline, H. K. (1949). Inhibition of activity of visual receptors by illuminating nearby retinal areas in the limulus eye. *Federation Proceedings, 8,* 69. (6)

Harvey, A. G., & Bryant, R. A. (2002). Acute stress disorder: A synthesis and critique. *Psychological Bulletin, 128,* 886–902. (12)

Hashimoto, T., Volk, D. W., Eggan, S. M., Mirnics, K., Pierri, J. N., Sun, Z., et al. (2003). Gene expression deficits in a subclass of GABA neurons in the prefrontal cortex of subjects with schizophrenia. *Journal of Neuroscience, 23,* 6315–6326. (15)

Håstad, O., Victorsson, J., & Ödeen, A. (2005). Differences in color vision make passerines less conspicuous in the eyes of their predators. *Proceedings of the National Academy of Sciences, USA, 102,* 6391–6394. (6)

Haueisen, J., & Knösche, T. R. (2001). Involuntary motor activity in pianists evoked by music perception. *Journal of Cognitive Neuroscience, 13,* 786–792. (8)

Hauk, O., Johnsrude, I., & Pulvermüller, F. (2004). Somatatopic representation of action words in human motor and premotor cortex. *Neuron, 41,* 301–307. (14)

Haukka, J., Suvisaara, J., & Lönnqvist, J. (2003). Fertility of patients with schizophrenia, their siblings, and the general population: A cohort study from 1950 to 1959 in Finland. *American Journal of Psychiatry, 160,* 460–463. (15)

Hausknecht, K. A., Acheson, A., Farrar, A. M., Kieres, A. K., Shen, R.-Y., Richards, J. B., et al. (2005). Prenatal alcohol exposure causes attention deficits in male rats. *Behavioral Neuroscience, 119,* 302–310. (5)

Häusser, M., Spruston, N., & Stuart, G. J. (2000). Diversity and dynamics of dendritic signaling. *Science, 290,* 739–744. (2)

Haydon, P. G. (2001). Glia: Listening and talking to the synapse. *Nature Reviews Neuroscience, 2,* 185–193. (2)

He, W., Yasumatsu, K., Varadarajan, V., Yamada, A., Lem, J., Ninomiya, Y., et al. (2004). Umami taste receptors are mediated by α-transducin and α-gustducin. *Journal of Neuroscience, 24,* 7674–7680. (7)

Hebb, D. O. (1949). *Organization of behavior.* New York: Wiley. (13; inside cover)

Heffner, H. E., & Koay, G. (2005). Tinnitus and hearing loss in hamsters (*Mesocricetus auratus*) exposed to loud sound. *Behavioral Neuroscience, 119,* 734–742. (7)

Hegdé, J., & Van Essen, D. C. (2000). Selectivity for complex shapes in primate visual area V2. *Journal of Neuroscience, 20,* RC61: 1–6. (6)

Heims, H. C., Critchley, H. D., Dolan, R., Mathias, C. J., & Cipolotti, L. (2004). Social and motivational functioning is not critically dependent on feedback of autonomic responses: Neuropsychological evidence from patients with pure autonomic failure. *Neuropsychologia, 42,* 1979–1988. (12)

Heisler, L. K., Cowley, M. A., Tecott, L. H., Fan, W., Low, M. J., Smart, J. L., et al. (2002). Activation of central melanocortin pathways by fenfluramine. *Science, 297,* 609–611. (10)

Helenius, P., Salmelin, R., Richardson, U., Leinonen, S., & Lyytinen, H. (2002). Abnormal auditory cortical activation in dyslexia 100 msec after speech onset. *Journal of Cognitive Neuroscience, 14,* 603–617. (14)

Heller, W., & Levy, J. (1981). Perception and expression of emotion in right-handers and left-handers. *Neuropsychologia, 19,* 263–272. (14)

Henderson, J. M., & Hollingworth, A. (2003). Global transsaccadic change blindness during scene perception. *Psychological Science, 14,* 493–497. (14)

Hendrie, H. C. (2001). Exploration of environmental and genetic risk factors for Alzheimer's disease: The value of cross-cultural studies. *Current Directions in Psychological Science, 10,* 98–101. (13)

Hendry, S. H. C., & Reid, R. C. (2000). The koniocellular pathway in primate vision. *Annual Review of Neuroscience, 23,* 127–153. (6)

Hennig, J., Reuter, M., Netter, P., Burk, C., & Landt, O. (2005). Two types of aggression are differentially related to serotonergic activity and the A779C *TPH* polymorphism. *Behavioral Neuroscience, 119,* 16–25. (12)

Hennig, R., & Lømo, T. (1985). Firing patterns of motor units in normal rats. *Nature, 314,* 164–166. (8)

Heresco-Levy, U., Javitt, D. C., Ermilov, M., Mordel, C., Silipo, G., & Lichtenstein, M. (1999). Efficacy of high-dose glycine in the treatment of enduring negative symptoms of schizophrenia. *Archives of General Psychiatry, 56,* 29–36. (15)

Heresco-Levy, U., & Javitt, D. C. (2004). Comparative effects of glycine and D-cycloserine on persistent negative symptoms in schizophrenia: A retrospective analysis. *Schizophrenia Research, 66,* 89–96. (15)

Herkenham, M. (1992). Cannabinoid receptor localization in brain: Relationship to motor and reward systems. *Annals of the New York Academy of Sciences, 654,* 19–32. (3)

Herkenham, M., Lynn, A. B., de Costa, B. R., & Richfield, E. K. (1991). Neuronal localization of cannabinoid receptors in the basal ganglia of the rat. *Brain Research, 547,* 267–274. (3)

Herman, L. M., Pack, A. A., & Morrel-Samuels, P. (1993). Representational and conceptual skills of dolphins. In H. L. Roitblat, L. M. Herman, & P. E. Nachtigall (Eds.), *Language and communication: Comparative perspectives* (pp. 403–442). Hillsdale, NJ: Erlbaum. (14)

Hernán, M. A., Takkouche, B., Caamaño-Isorna, F., & Gestal-Otero, J. J. (2002). A meta-analysis of coffee drinking, cigarette smoking, and the risk of Parkinson's disease. *Annals of Neurology, 52,* 276–284. (8)

Herrero, S. (1985). *Bear attacks: Their causes and avoidance.* Piscataway, NJ: Winchester. (7)

Hertz-Pannier, L., Chiron, C., Jampaqué, I., Renaux-Kieffer, V., Van de Moortele, P.-F., Delalande, O., et al. (2002). Late plasticity for language in a child's non-dominant hemisphere. A pre- and post-surgery fMRI study. *Brain, 125,* 361–372. (14)

Herz, R. S. (2004). A naturalistic analysis of autobiographical memories triggered by olfactory, visual, and auditory stimuli. *Chemical Senses, 29,* 217–224. (7)

Herz, R. S., & Inzlicht, M. (2002). Sex differences in response to physical and social factors involved in human mate selection: The importance of smell for women. *Evolution and Human Behavior, 23,* 359–364. (7)

Herz, R. S., McCall, C., & Cahill, L. (1999). Hemispheric lateralization in the processing of odor pleasantness versus odor names. *Chemical Senses, 24,* 691–695. (14)

Herzog, S., Pfeuffer, I., Haberzettl, K., Feldmann, H., Frese, K., Bechter, K., et al. (1997). Molecular characterization of Borna disease virus from naturally infected animals and possible links to human disorders. *Archives of Virology* (Suppl. 13), 183–190. (15)

Hess, B. J. M. (2001). Vestibular signals in self-orientation and eye movement control. *News in Physiological Sciences, 16,* 234–238. (7)

Hettinger, T. P., & Frank, M. E. (1992). Information processing in mammalian gustatory systems. *Current Opinion in Neurobiology, 2,* 469–478. (7)

Heynen, A. J., Yoon, B.-J., Liu, C.-H., Chung, H. J., Huganir, R. I., & Bear, M. F. (2003). Molecular mechanism for loss of visual cortical responsiveness following brief monocular deprivation. *Nature Neuroscience, 6,* 854–862. (13)

Hickok, G., Bellugi, U., & Klima, E. S. (1996). The neurobiology of sign language and its implications for the neural basis of language. *Nature, 381,* 699–702. (14)

Higley, J. D., Mehlman, P. T., Higley, S. B., Fernald, B., Vickers, J., Lindell, S. G., et al. (1996). Excessive mortality in young free-ranging male nonhuman primates with low cerebrospinal fluid 5-hydroxyindoleacetic acid concentrations. *Archives of General Psychiatry, 53,* 537–543. (12)

Hill, S. Y., De Bellis, M. D., Keshavan, M. S., Lowers, L., Shen, S., Hall, J., et al. (2001). Right amygdala volume in adolescents and young adult offspring from families at high risk for developing alcoholism. *Biological Psychiatry, 49,* 894–905. (15)

Hillis, A. E., Newhart, M., Heidler, J., Barker, P. B., Herskovits, E. H., & Degaonkar, M. (2005). Anatomy of spatial attention: Insights from perfusion imaging and hemispatial neglect in acute stroke. *Journal of Neuroscience, 25,* 3161–3167. (14)

Hillis, A. E., Wityk, R. J., Barker, P. B., & Caramazza, A. (2003). Neural regions essential for writing verbs. *Nature Neuroscience, 6,* 19–20. (14)

Hines, M., Golombok, S., Rust, J., Johnston, K. J., Golding, J., & the Avon Longitudinal Study of Parents and Children Study Team. (2002). Testosterone during pregnancy and gender role behavior of preschool children: A longitudinal, population study. *Child Development, 73,* 1678–1687. (11)

Hinkle, D. A., & Connor, C. E. (2002). Three-dimensional orientation tuning in macaque area V4. *Nature Neuroscience, 5,* 665–670. (6)

Hitchcock, J. M., & Davis, M. (1991). Efferent pathway of the amygdala involved in conditioned fear as measured with the fear-potentiated startle paradigm. *Behavioral Neuroscience, 105,* 826–842. (12)

Hiyama, T. Y., Watanabe, E., Okado, H., & Noda, M. (2004). The subfornical organ is the primary locus of sodium-level sensing by Na_x sodium channels for the control of salt-intake behavior. *Journal of Neuroscience, 24,* 9276–9281. (10)

Hjelmstad, G. O. (2004). Dopamine excites nucleus accumbens neurons through the differential modulation of glutamate and GABA release. *Journal of Neuroscience, 24,* 8621–8628. (3)

Hobson, J. A. (1989). *Sleep.* New York: Scientific American Library. (15)

Hobson, J. A., & McCarley, R. W. (1977). The brain as a dream state generator: An activation-synthesis hypothesis of the dream process. *American Journal of Psychiatry, 134,* 1335–1348. (9)

Hobson, J. A., Pace-Schott, E. F., & Stickgold, R. (2000). Dreaming and the brain: Toward a cognitive neuroscience of conscious states. *Behavioral and Brain Sciences, 23,* 793–1121. (9)

Hock, C., Konietzko, U., Streffer, J. R., Tracy, J., Signorell, A., Müller-Tillmanns, B., et al.

(2003). Antibodies against β-amyloid slow cognitive decline in Alzheimer's disease. *Neuron, 38,* 547–554. (13)

Hoebel, B. G. (1988). Neuroscience and motivation: Pathways and peptides that define motivational systems. In R. C. Atkinson, R. J. Herrnstein, G. Lindzey, & R. D. Luce (Eds.), *Stevens' handbook of experimental psychology* (2nd ed., pp. 547–625). New York: Wiley. (10)

Hoebel, B. G., & Hernandez, L. (1993). Basic neural mechanisms of feeding and weight regulation. In A. J. Stunkard & T. A. Wadden (Eds.), *Obesity: Theory and therapy* (2nd ed., pp. 43–62). New York: Raven Press. (10)

Hoebel, B. G., Rada, P. V., Mark, G. P., & Pothos, E. (1999). Neural systems for reinforcement and inhibition of behavior: Relevance to eating, addiction, and depression. In D. Kahneman, E. Diener, & N. Schwartz (Eds.), *Well-being: Foundations of hedonic psychology* (pp. 560–574). New York: Russell Sage Foundation. (10)

Hoek, H. W., & van Hoeken, D. (2003). Review of the prevalence and incidence of eating disorders. *International Journal of Eating Disorders, 34,* 383–396. (10)

Hoffer, A. (1973). Mechanism of action of nicotinic acid and nicotinamide in the treatment of schizophrenia. In D. Hawkins & L. Pauling (Eds.), *Orthomolecular psychiatry* (pp. 202–262). San Francisco: Freeman. (15)

Hoffman, P. L., Tabakoff, B., Szabó, G., Suzdak, P. D., & Paul, S. M. (1987). Effect of an imidazobenzodiazepine, Ro15-4513, on the incoordination and hypothermia produced by ethanol and pento-barbital. *Life Sciences, 41,* 611–619. (12)

Hoffman, R. (2001). Thermophiles in Kamchatka. *American Scientist, 89,* 20–23. (10)

Hoffmann, F., & Curio, G. (2003). REM-Schlaf und rezidivierende Erosio corneae—eine Hypothese [REM sleep and recurrent corneal erosion—A hypothesis]. *Klinische Monatsblatter fur Augenheilkunde, 220,* 51–53. (9)

Hohmann, A. G., Suplita, R. L., Bolton, N. M., Neely, M. H., Fegley, D., Mangieri, R., et al. (2005). An endocannabinoid mechanism for stress-induced analgesia. *Nature, 435,* 1108–1112. (7)

Hokfelt, T., Johansson, O., & Goldstein, M. (1984). Chemical anatomy of the brain. *Science, 225,* 1326–1334. (3)

Holcombe, A. O., & Cavanagh, P. (2001). Early binding of feature pairs for visual perception. *Nature Neuroscience, 4,* 127–128. (4)

Hollingsworth, D. E., McAuliffe, S. P., & Knowlton, B. J. (2001). Temporal allocation of visual attention in adult attention deficit hyperactivity disorder. *Journal of Cognitive Neuroscience, 13,* 298–305. (14)

Hollister, J. M., Laing, P., & Mednick, S. A. (1996). Rhesus incompatibility as a risk factor for schizophrenia in male adults. *Archives of General Psychiatry, 53,* 19–24. (15)

Hollon, S. D., De Rubeis, R. J., Shelton, R. C., Amsterdam, J. D., Salomon, R. M., O'Reardon, J. P., et al. (2005). Prevention of relapse following cognitive therapy vs. medications in moderate to severe depression. *Archives of General Psychiatry, 62,* 417–422. (15)

Hollon, S. D., Thase, M. E., & Markowitz, J. C. (2002). Treatment and prevention of depression. *Psychological Science in the Public Interest, 3,* 39–77. (15)

Holsinger, T., Steffens, D. C., Phillips, C., Helms, M. J., Havlik, R. J., Breitner, J. et al. (2002). Head injury in early adulthood and the lifetime risk of depression. *Archives of General Psychiatry, 59,* 17–22. (15)

Holstege, G., Georgiadis, J. R., Paans, A. M. J., Meiners, L. C., van der Graaf, F. H. C. E., & Reinders, A. A. T. S. (2003). Brain activation during human male ejaculation. *Journal of Neuroscience, 23,* 9185–9193. (11)

Holy, T. E., Dulac, C., & Meister, M. (2000). Responses of vomeronasal neurons to natural stimuli. *Science, 289,* 1569–1572. (7)

Homewood, J., & Stevenson, R. J. (2001). Differences in naming accuracy of odors presented to the left and right nostrils. *Biological Psychology, 58,* 65–73. (14)

Honea, R., Crow, T. J., Passingham, D., & Mackay, C. E. (2005). Regional deficits in brain volume in schizophrenia: A meta-analysis of voxel-based morphometry studies. *American Journal of Psychiatry, 162,* 2233–2245. (15)

Hoover, J. E., & Strick, P. L. (1993). Multiple output channels in the basal ganglia. *Science, 259,* 819–821. (8)

Hopkins, J., Marcus, M., & Campbell, S. B. (1984). Postpartum depression: A critical review. *Psychological Bulletin, 95,* 498–515. (15)

Hopkins, W. D., Dahl, J. F., & Pilcher, D. (2001). Genetic influence on the expression of hand preferences in chimpanzees (*Pan troglodytes*): Evidence in support of the right-shift theory and developmental instability. *Psychological Science, 12,* 299–303. (14)

Hopkins, W. D., Russell, J., Freeman, H., Buehler, N., Reynolds, E., & Schapiro, S. J. (2005). The distribution and development of handedness for manual gestures in captive chimpanzees (*Pan troglodytes*). *Psychological Science, 16,* 487–493. (14)

Hopkins, W. D., Wesley, M. J., Izard, M. K., Hook, M., & Schapiro, S. J. (2004). Chimpanzees (*Pan troglodytes*) are predominantly right-handed: Replication in three populations of apes. *Behavioral Neuroscience, 118,* 659–663. (14)

Hoptman, M. J., & Levy, J. (1988). Perceptual asymmetries in left- and right-handers for cartoon and real faces. *Brain and Cognition, 8,* 178–188. (14)

Horne, J. A. (1992). Sleep and its disorders in children. *Journal of Child Psychology & Psychiatry & Allied Disciplines, 33,* 473–487. (9)

Horne, J. A., & Minard, A. (1985). Sleep and sleepiness following a behaviourally "active" day. *Ergonomics, 28,* 567–575. (9)

Horner, P. J., & Gage, F. H. (2000). Regenerating the damaged central nervous system. *Nature, 407,* 963–970. (5)

Horridge, G. A. (1962). Learning of leg position by the ventral nerve cord in headless insects. *Proceedings of the Royal Society of London, B, 157,* 33–52. (13)

Horst, W. D., & Preskorn, S. H. (1998). Mechanisms of action and clinical characteristics of three atypical antidepressants: Venlafaxine, nefazodone, bupropion. *Journal of Affective Disorders, 51,* 237–254. (15)

Horton, J. C., & Hocking, D. R. (1996). An adult-like pattern of ocular dominance columns in striate cortex of newborn monkeys prior to visual experience. *Journal of Neuroscience, 16,* 1791–1807. (6)

Horvath, T. L. (2005). The hardship of obesity: A soft-wired hypothalamus. *Nature Neuroscience, 8,* 561–565. (10)

Horvitz, J. C., & Eyny, Y. S. (2000). Dopamine D2 receptor blockade reduces response likelihood but does not affect latency to emit a learned sensory-motor response: Implications for Parkinson's disease. *Behavioral Neuroscience, 114,* 934–939. (8)

Horwitz, B., Rumsey, J. M., & Donohue, B. C. (1998). Functional connectivity of the angular gyrus in normal reading and dyslexia. *Proceedings of the National Academy of Sciences, USA, 95,* 8939–8944. (14)

Hoshi, E., & Tanji, J. (2000). Integration of target and body-part information in the premotor cortex when planning action. *Nature, 408,* 466–470. (8)

Hovda, D. A., & Feeney, D. M. (1989). Amphetamine-induced recovery of visual cliff performance after bilateral visual cortex ablation in cats: Measurements of depth perception thresholds. *Behavioral Neuroscience, 103,* 574–584. (5)

Howland, H. C., & Sayles, N. (1984). Photorefractive measurements of astigmatism in infants and young children. *Investigative Ophthalmology and Visual Science, 25,* 93–102. (6)

Howlett, A. C., Breivogel, C. S., Childers, S. R., Deadwyler, S. A., Hampson, R. E., & Porrino, L. J. (2004). Cannabinoid physiology and pharmacology: 30 years of progress. *Neuropharmacology, 47,* 345–358. (3)

Hrdy, S. B. (2000). The optimal number of fathers. *Annals of the New York Academy of Sciences, 907,* 75–96. (11)

Hróbjartsson, A., & Gøtzsche, P. C. (2001). Is the placebo powerless? *New England Journal of Medicine, 344,* 1594–1602. (7)

Hsu, M., Sik, A., Gallyas, F., Horváth, Z., & Buzsáki, G. (1994). Short-term and long-term changes in the postischemic hippocampus. *Annals of the New York Academy of Sciences, 743,* 121–140. (5)

Hua, J. Y., & Smith, S. J. (2004). Neural activity and the dynamics of central nervous system development. *Nature Neuroscience, 7,* 327–332. (5)

Huang, W., Sved, A. F., & Stricker, E. M. (2000). Water ingestion provides an early signal inhibiting osmotically stimulated vasopressin secretion in rats. *American Journal of Physiology, 279,* R756–R760. (10)

Huang, Y.-J., Maruyama, Y., Lu, K.-S., Pereira, E., Plonsky, I., Baur, J. E., et al. (2005). Mouse taste buds use serotonin as a neurotransmitter. *Journal of Neuroscience, 25,* 843–847. (3)

Hubbard, E. M., Arman, A. C., Ramachandran, V. S., & Boynton, G. M. (2005). Individual differences among grapheme-color synesthetes: Brain-behavior correlations. *Neuron, 45,* 975–985. (7)

Hubbard, E. M., Piazza, M., Pinel, P., & Dehaene, S. (2005). Interactions between number and space in parietal cortex. *Nature Reviews Neuroscience, 6,* 435–448. (4)

Hubel, D. H. (1963, November). The visual cortex of the brain. *Scientific American, 209*(5), 54–62. (6)

Hubel, D. H., & Wiesel, T. N. (1959). Receptive fields of single neurons in the cat's striate cortex. *Journal of Physiology, 148,* 574–591. (6)

Hubel, D. H., & Wiesel, T. N. (1965). Binocular interaction in striate cortex of kittens reared with artificial squint. *Journal of Neurophysiology, 28,* 1041–1059. (6)

Hubel, D. H., & Wiesel, T. N. (1977). Functional architecture of macaque monkey visual cortex. *Proceedings of the Royal Society of London, B, 198,* 1–59. (6)

Hubel, D. H., & Wiesel, T. N. (1998). Early exploration of the visual cortex. *Neuron, 20,* 401–412. (6)

Huber, R., Ghilardi, M. F., Massimini, M., & Tononi, G. (2004). Local sleep and learning. *Nature, 430,* 78–81. (9)

Hudson, J. I., Mangweth, B., Pope, H. G., Jr., De Col, C., Hausmann, A., Gutweniger, S., et al. (2003). Family study of affective spectrum disorder. *Archives of General Psychiatry, 60,* 170–177. (15)

Hudspeth, A. J. (1985). The cellular basis of hearing: The biophysics of hair cells. *Science, 230,* 745–752. (7)

Hugdahl, K. (1996). Brain laterality—beyond the basics. *European Psychologist, 1,* 206–220. (14)

Hughes, H. C., Nozawa, G., & Kitterle, F. (1996). Global precedence, spatial frequency channels, and the statistics of natural images. *Journal of Cognitive Neuroscience, 8,* 197–230. (6)

Hughes, J. C., & Cook, C. C. H. (1997). The efficacy of disulfiram: A review of outcome studies. *Addiction, 92,* 381–395. (15)

Hull, E. M., Du, J., Lorrain, D. S., & Matuszewich, L. (1997). Testosterone, preoptic dopamine, and copulation in male rats. *Brain Research Bulletin, 44,* 327–333. (11)

Hull, E. M., Eaton, R. C., Markowski, V. P., Moses, J., Lumley, L. A., & Loucks, J. A. (1992). Opposite influence of medial preoptic D_1 and D_2 receptors on genital reflexes: Implications for copulation. *Life Sciences, 51,* 1705–1713. (11)

Hull, E. M., Lorrain, D. S., Du, J., Matuszewich, L., Lumley, L. A., Putnam, S. K., et al. (1999). Hormone-neurotransmitter interactions in the control of sexual behavior. *Behavioural Brain Research, 105,* 105–116. (11)

Hull, E. M., Nishita, J. K., Bitran, D., & Dalterio, S. (1984). Perinatal dopamine-related drugs demasculinize rats. *Science, 224,* 1011–1013. (11)

Hulshoff, H. E., Schnack, H. G., Mandl, R. C. W., van Haren, N. E. M., Koning, H., Collins, L., et al. (2001). Focal gray matter density changes in schizophrenia. *Archives of General Psychiatry, 58,* 1118–1125. (15)

Hunt, E., Streissguth, A. P., Kerr, B., & Carmichael-Olson, H. (1995). Mothers' alcohol consumption during pregnancy: Effects on spatial-visual reasoning in 14-year-old children. *Psychological Science, 6,* 339–342. (5)

Hunt, S. P., & Mantyh, P. W. (2001). The molecular dynamics of pain control. *Nature Reviews Neuroscience, 2,* 83–91. (7)

Hunter, W. S. (1923). *General psychology* (Rev. ed.). Chicago: University of Chicago Press. (4)

Huntington's Disease Collaborative Research Group. (1993). A novel gene containing a trinucleotide repeat that is expanded and unstable on Huntington's disease chromosomes. *Cell, 72,* 971–983. (8)

Hurovitz, C. S., Dunn, S., Domhoff, G. W., & Fiss, H. (1999). The dreams of blind men and women: A replication and extension of previous findings. *Dreaming, 9,* 183–193. (6)

Hurvich, L. M., & Jameson, D. (1957). An opponent-process theory of color vision. *Psychological Review, 64,* 384–404. (6)

Husain, M., & Rorden, C. (2003). Non-spatially lateralized mechanisms in hemispatial neglect. *Nature Reviews Neuroscience, 4,* 26–36. (14)

Hutcheson, D. M., Everitt, B. J., Robbins, T. W., & Dickinson, A. (2001). The role of withdrawal in heroin addiction: Enhances reward or promotes avoidance? *Nature Neuroscience, 4,* 943–947. (15)

Hyde, K. L., & Peretz, I. (2004). Brains that are out of tune but in time. *Psychological Science, 15,* 356–360. (7)

Hynd, G. W., & Semrud-Clikeman, M. (1989). Dyslexia and brain morphology. *Psychological Bulletin, 106,* 447–482. (14)

Hypericum Depression Trial Study Group. (2002). Effect of *Hypericum perforatum* (St. John's wort) in major depressive disorder. *Journal of the American Medical Association, 287,* 1807–1814. (15)

Ibrahim, H. M., Hogg, A. J., Jr., Healy, D. J., Haroutunian, V., Davis, K. L., & Meador-Woodruff, J. H. (2000). Ionotropic glutamate receptor binding and subunit mRNA expression in thalamic nuclei in schizophrenia. *American Journal of Psychiatry, 157,* 1811–1823. (15)

Iggo, A., & Andres, K. H. (1982). Morphology of cutaneous receptors. *Annual Review of Neuroscience, 5,* 1–31. (7)

Ikeda, H., Heinke, B., Ruscheweyh, R., & Sandkühler, J. (2003). Synaptic plasticity in spinal lamina I projection neurons that mediate hyperalgesia. *Science, 299,* 1237–1240. (7)

Ikegaya, Y., Aaron, G., Cossart, R., Aronov, D., Lampl, I., Ferster, D., et al. (2004). Synfire chains and cortical songs: Temporal modules of cortical activity. *Science, 304,* 559–564. (2)

Ikonomidou, C., Bittigau, P. Ishimaru, M. J., Wozniak, D. F., Koch, C., Genz, K., et al. (2000). Ethanol-induced apoptotic neurodegeneration and fetal alcohol syndrome. *Science, 287,* 1056–1060. (5)

Imamura, K., Mataga, N., & Mori, K. (1992). Coding of odor molecules by mitral/tufted cells in rabbit olfactory bulb: I. Aliphatic compounds. *Journal of Neurophysiology, 68,* 1986–2002. (7)

Imperato-McGinley, J., Guerrero, L., Gautier, T., & Peterson, R. E. (1974). Steroid 5 alpha-reductase deficiency in man: An inherited form of male pseudohermaphroditism. *Science, 186,* 1213–1215. (11)

Innocenti, G. M. (1980). The primary visual pathway through the corpus callosum: Morphological and functional aspects in the cat. *Archives Italiennes de Biologie, 118,* 124–188. (14)

Innocenti, G. M., & Caminiti, R. (1980). Postnatal shaping of callosal connections from sensory areas. *Experimental Brain Research, 38,* 381–394. (14)

Inouye, S. T., & Kawamura, H. (1979). Persistence of circadian rhythmicity in a mammalian hypothalamic "island" containing the suprachiasmatic nucleus. *Proceedings of the National Academy of Sciences, USA, 76,* 5962–5966. (9)

Irvine, E. E., Vernon, J., & Giese, K. P. (2005). αCaMKII autophosphorylation contributes to rapid learning but is not necessary for memory. *Nature Neuroscience, 8,* 411–412. (13)

Irwin, D. E., & Brockmole, J. R. (2004). Suppressing *where* but not *what*: The effect of saccades on dorsal- and ventral-stream visual processing. *Psychological Science, 15,* 467–473. (6)

Ito, M. (1984). *The cerebellum and neural control.* New York: Raven Press. (8)

Ito, M. (1989). Long-term depression. *Annual Review of Neuroscience, 12,* 85–102. (13)

Ito, M. (2002). The molecular organization of cerebellar long-term depression. *Nature Reviews Neuroscience, 3,* 896–902. (13)

Ivry, R. B., & Diener, H. C. (1991). Impaired velocity perception in patients with lesions of the cerebellum. *Journal of Cognitive Neuroscience, 3,* 355–366. (8)

Ivy, G. O., & Killackey, H. P. (1981). The ontogeny of the distribution of callosal projection neurons in the rat parietal cortex. *Journal of Comparative Neurology, 195,* 367–389. (14)

Iwema, C. L., Fang, H., Kurtz, D. B., Youngentob, S. L., & Schwob, J. E. (2004). Odorant receptor expression patterns are restored in lesion-recovered rat olfactory epithelium. *Journal of Neuroscience, 24,* 356–369. (7)

Izquierdo, I., & Medina, J. H. (1995). Correlation between the pharmacology of long-term potentiation and the pharmacology of memory. *Neurobiology of Learning and Memory, 63,* 19–32. (13)

Jacobs, B., Schall, M., & Scheibel, A. B. (1993). A quantitative dendritic analysis of Wernicke's area in humans: II. Gender, hemispheric, and environmental factors. *Journal of Comparataive Neurology, 327,* 97–111. (5)

Jacobs, B., & Scheibel, A. B. (1993). A quantitative dendritic analysis of Wernicke's area in humans: I. Lifespan changes. *Journal of Comparative Neurology, 327,* 83–96. (5)

Jacobs, G. D., & Snyder, D. (1996). Frontal brain asymmetry predicts affective style in men. *Behavioral Neuroscience, 110,* 3–6. (15)

James, W. (1884). What is an emotion? *Mind, 9,* 188–205. (12)

James, W. (1894). The physical basis of emotion. *Psychological Review, 1,* 516–529. (12)

James, W. (1961). *Psychology: The briefer course.* New York: Harper. (Original work published 1892) (12)

Jameson, K. A., Highnote, S. M., & Wasserman, L. M. (2001). Richer color experience in observers with multiple photopigment opsin genes. *Psychonomic Bulletin & Review, 8,* 244–261. (6)

Jandacek, R. J., & Woods, S. C. (2004). Pharmaceutical approaches to the treatment of obesity. *Drug Discovery Today, 9,* 874–880. (10)

Janus, C., Pearson, J., McLaurin, J., Mathews, P. M., Jiang, Y., Schmidt, S. D., et al. (2000). Aβ peptide immunization reduces behavioural impairment and plaques in a model of Alzheimer's disease. *Nature, 408,* 979–982. (13)

Jarrard, L. E., Okaichi, H., Steward, O., & Goldschmidt, R. B. (1984). On the role of hippocampal connections in the performance of place and cue tasks: Comparisons with damage to hippocampus. *Behavioral Neuroscience, 98,* 946–954. (13)

Jarrold, C., Baddeley, A. D., & Hewes, A. K. (1998). Verbal and nonverbal abilities in the Williams syndrome phenotype: Evidence for diverging developmental trajectories. *Journal of Child Psychology and Psychiatry and Allied Disciplines, 39,* 511–523. (14)

Jaskiw, G. E., & Weinberger, D. R. (1992). Dopamine and schizophrenia—a cortically corrective perspective. *Seminars in the Neurosciences, 4,* 179–188. (15)

Jenner, A. R., Rosen, G. D., & Galaburda, A. M. (1999). Neuronal asymmetries in primary visual cortex of dyslexic and nondyslexic brains. *Annals of Neurology, 46,* 189–196. (14)

Jerison, H. J. (1985). Animal intelligence as encephalization. *Philosophical Transactions of the Royal Society of London, B, 308,* 21–35. (4)

Jerome, L., & Segal, A. (2001). Benefit of long-term stimulants on driving in adults with ADHD. *Journal of Nervous and Mental Disease, 189,* 63–64. (14)

Jimerson, D. C., & Wolfe, B. E. (2004). Neuropeptides in eating disorders. *CNS Spectrums, 9,* 516–522. (10)

Johns, T. R., & Thesleff, S. (1961). Effects of motor inactivation on the chemical sensitivity of skeletal muscle. *Acta Physiologica Scandinavica, 51,* 136–141. (5)

Johnson, E. N., Hawken, M. J., & Shapley, R. (2001). The spatial transformation of color in the primary visual cortex of the macaque monkey. *Nature Neuroscience, 4,* 409–416. (6)

Johnson, L. C. (1969). Physiological and psychological changes following total sleep deprivation. In A. Kales (Ed.), *Sleep: Physiology & pathology* (pp. 206–220). Philadelphia: Lippincott. (9)

Johnson, M. H., Posner, M. I., & Rothbart, M. K. (1991). Components of visual orienting in early infancy: Contingency learning, anticipatory looking, and disengaging. *Journal of Cognitive Neuroscience, 3,* 335–344. (6)

Johnson, M. T. V., Kipnis, A. N., Coltz, J. D., Gupta, A., Silverstein, P., Zwiebel, F., et al. (1996). Effects of levodopa and viscosity on the velocity and accuracy of visually guided tracking in Parkinson's disease. *Brain, 119,* 801–813. (8)

Jonas, P., Bischofberger, J., & Sandkühler, J. (1998). Corelease of two fast neurotransmitters at a central synapse. *Science, 281,* 419–424. (3)

Jonas, S. (1995). Prophylactic pharmacologic neuroprotection against focal cerebral ischemia. *Annals of the New York Academy of Sciences, 765,* 21–25. (5)

Jones, C. M., Braithwaite, V. A., & Healy, S. D. (2003). The evolution of sex differences in spatial ability. *Behavioral Neuroscience, 117,* 403–411. (11)

Jones, C. R., Campbell, S. S., Zone, S. E., Cooper, F., DeSano, A., Murphy, P. J., et al. (1999). Familial advanced sleep-phase syndrome: A short-period circadian rhythm variant in humans. *Nature Medicine, 5,* 1062–1065. (9)

Jones, E. G., & Pons, T. P. (1998). Thalamic and brainstem contributions to large-scale plasticity of primate somatosensory cortex. *Science, 282,* 1121–1125. (5)

Jones, H. S., & Oswald, I. (1968). Two cases of healthy insomnia. *Electroencephalography and Clinical Neurophysiology, 24,* 378–380. (9)

Jordan, H. A. (1969). Voluntary intragastric feeding. *Journal of Comparative and Physiological Psychology, 68,* 498–506. (10)

Joseph, J. A., Shukitt-Hale, B., Denisova, N. A., Prior, R. L., Cao, G., Martin, A., et al. (1998). Long-term dietary strawberry, spinach, or vitamin E supplementation retards the onset of age-related neuronal signal-transduction and cognitive behavioral deficits. *Journal of Neuroscience, 18,* 8047–8055. (13)

Jouvet, M. (1960). Telencephalic and rhombencephalic sleep in the cat. In G. E. W. Wolstenholme & M. O'Connor (Eds.), *CIBA Foundation symposium on the nature of sleep* (pp. 188–208). Boston: Little, Brown. (9)

Joyner, A. L., & Guillemot, F. (1994). Gene targeting and development of the nervous system. *Current Opinion in Neurobiology, 4,* 37–42. (4)

Jueptner, M., & Weiller, C. (1998). A review of differences between basal ganglia and cerebellar control of movements as revealed by functional imaging studies. *Brain, 121,* 1437–1449. (8)

Jureidini, J. N., Doecke, C. J., Mansfield, P. R., Haby, M. M., Menkes, D. B., & Tonkin, A. L. (2004). Efficacy and safety of antidepressants for children and adolescents. *British Medical Journal, 328,* 879–883. (15)

Kaas, J. H. (1983). What, if anything, is SI? Organization of first somatosensory area of cortex. *Physiological Reviews, 63,* 206–231. (7)

Kaas, J. H., Merzenich, M. M., & Killackey, H. P. (1983). The reorganization of somatosensory cortex following peripheral nerve damage in adult and developing mammals. *Annual Review of Neuroscience, 6,* 325–356. (5)

Kaas, J. H., Nelson, R. J., Sur, M., Lin, C.-S., & Merzenich, M. M. (1979). Multiple representations of the body within the primary somatosensory cortex of primates. *Science, 204,* 521–523. (4)

Kakei, S., Hoffman, D. S., & Strick, P. L. (2001). Direction of action is represented in the ventral premotor cortex. *Nature Neuroscience, 4,* 1020–1025. (8)

Kales, A., Scharf, M. B., & Kales, J. D. (1978). Rebound insomnia: A new clinical syndrome. *Science, 201,* 1039–1041. (9)

Kalin, N. H., Shelton, S. E., & Davidson, R. J. (2004). The role of the central nucleus of the amygdala in mediating fear and anxiety in the primate. *Journal of Neuroscience, 24,* 5506–5515. (12)

Kalin, N.H., Shelton, S. E., Davidson, R. J., & Kelley, A. E. (2001). The primate amygdala mediates acute fear but not the behavioral and physiological components of anxious temperament. *Journal of Neuroscience, 21,* 2067–2074. (12)

Kalivas, P. W., Volkow, N., & Seamans, J. (2005). Unmanageable motivation in addiction: A pathology in prefrontal-accumbens glutamate transmission. *Neuron, 45,* 647–650. (15)

Kalsner, S. (2001). Autoreceptors do not regulate routinely neurotransmitter release: Focus on adrenergic systems. *Journal of Neurochemistry, 78,* 676–684. (3)

Kamitani, Y., & Tong, F. (2005). Decoding the visual and subjective contents of the human brain. *Nature Neuroscience, 8,* 679–685. (6)

Kandel, E. R., & Schwartz, J. H. (1982). Molecular biology of learning: Modulation of transmitter release. *Science, 218,* 433–443. (13)

Kanwisher, N. (2000). Domain specificity in face perception. *Nature Neuroscience, 3,* 759–763. (6)

Kanwisher, N., & Wojciulik, E. (2000). Visual attention: Insights from brain imaging. *Nature Reviews Neuroscience, 1,* 91–100. (6)

Kaplan, D. E., Gayán, J., Ahn, J., Won, T.-W., Pauls, D., Olson, R. K., et al. (2002). Evidence for linkage and association with reading disability, on 6p21.3-22. *American Journal of Human Genetics, 70,* 1287–1298. (14)

Kaplan, J. R., Muldoon, M. F., Manuck, S. B., & Mann, J. J. (1997). Assessing the observed relationship between low cholesterol and violence-related mortality. *Annals of the New York Academy of Sciences, 836,* 57–80. (12)

Kapur, S., Zipusky, R., Jones, C., Shammi, C. S., Remington, G., & Seeman, P. (2000). A positron emission tomography study of quetiapine in schizophrenia. *Archives of General Psychiatry, 57,* 553–559. (15)

Kargo, W. J., & Nitz, D. A. (2004). Improvements in the signal-to-noise ratio of motor cortex cells distinguish early versus late phases of motor skill learning. *Journal of Neuroscience, 24,* 5560–5569. (8)

Karmiloff-Smith, A., Tyler, L. K., Voice, K., Sims, K., Udwin, O., Howlin, P., et al. (1998). Linguistic dissociations in Williams syndrome: Evaluating receptive syntax in on-line and off-line tasks. *Neuropsychologia, 36,* 343–351. (14)

Karnath, H.-O., Ferber, S., & Himmelbach, M. (2001). Spatial awareness is a function of the temporal not the posterior parietal lobe. *Nature, 411,* 950–953. (14)

Karrer, T., & Bartoshuk, L. (1991). Capsaicin desensitization and recovery on the human tongue. *Physiology & Behavior, 49,* 757–764. (7)

Kas, M. J. H., Tiesjema, B., van Dijk, G., Garner, K. M., Barsh, G. S., Ter Brake, O., et al. (2004). Induction of brain region-specific forms of obesity by agouti. *Journal of Neuroscience, 24,* 10176–10181. (10)

Kasai, K., Shenton, M. E., Salisbury, D. F., Hirayasu, Y., Onitsuka, T., Spencer, M. H., et al. (2003). Progressive decrease of left Heschl gyrus and planum temporale gray matter volume in first-episode schizophrenia. *Archives of General Psychiatry, 60,* 766–775. (15)

Kasai, T., & Morotomi, T. (2001). Event-related brain potentials during selective attention to depth and form in global stereopsis. *Vision Research, 41,* 1379–1388. (6)

Katkin, E. S., Wiens, S., & Öhman, A. (2001). Nonconscious fear conditioning, visceral perception, and the development of gut feelings. *Psychological Science, 12,* 366–370. (12)

Kawasaki, H., Adolphs, R., Kaufman, O., Damasio, H., Damasio, A. R., Granner, M., et al. (2001). Single-neuron responses to emotional visual stimuli recorded in human ventral prefrontal cortex. *Nature Neuroscience, 4,* 15–16. (12)

Keefe, F. J., & France, C. R. (1999). Pain: Biopsychosocial mechanisms and management. *Current Directions in Psychological Science, 8,* 137–141. (7)

Keele, S. W., & Ivry, R. (1990). Does the cerebellum provide a common computation for diverse tasks? *Annals of the New York Academy of Sciences, 608,* 179–207. (8)

Keirstead, H. S., Nistor, G., Bernal, G., Totoiu, M., Cloutier, F., Sharp, K., et al. (2005). Human embryonic stem cell-derived oligodendrocyte progenitor cell transplants remyelinate and restore locomotion after spinal cord injury. *Journal of Neuroscience, 25,* 4694–4705. (5)

Kelly, T. L., Neri, D. F., Grill, J. T., Ryman, D., Hunt, P. D., Dijk, D.-J., et al. (1999). Nonentrained circadian rhythms of melatonin in submariners scheduled to an 18-hour day. *Journal of Biological Rhythms, 14,* 190–196. (9)

Kendler, K. S. (1983). Overview: A current perspective on twin studies of schizophrenia. *American Journal of Psychiatry, 140,* 1413–1425. (15)

Kendler, K. S. (2001). Twin studies of psychiatric illness. *Archives of General Psychiatry, 58,* 1005–1014. (1)

Kendler, K. S., Gardner, C. O., & Prescott, C. A. (1999). Clinical characteristics of major depression that predict risk of depression in relatives. *Archives of General Psychiatry, 56,* 322–327. (15)

Kendler, K. S., Myers, J., Prescott, C. A., & Neale, M. C. (2001). The genetic epidemiology of irrational fears and phobias in men. *Archives of General Psychiatry, 58,* 257–265. (12)

Kendler, K. S., Thornton, L. M., Gilman, S. E., & Kessler, R. C. (2000). Sexual orientation in a U.S. national sample of twin and nontwin sibling pairs. *American Journal of Psychiatry, 157,* 1843–1846. (11)

Kennard, C., Lawden, M., Morland, A. B., & Ruddock, K. H. (1995). Colour identification and colour constancy are impaired in a patient with incomplete achromatopsia associated with prestriate cortical lesions. *Proceedings of the Royal Society of London, B, 260,* 169–175. (6)

Kennaway, D. J., & Van Dorp, C. F. (1991). Free-running rhythms of melatonin, cortisol, electrolytes, and sleep in humans in Antarctica. *American Journal of Physiology, 260,* R1137–R1144. (9)

Kennerley, S. W., Diedrichsen, J., Hazeltine, E., Semjen, A., & Ivry, R. B. (2002). Callosotomy patients exhibit temporal uncoupling during continuous bimanual movements. *Nature Neuroscience, 5,* 376–381. (14)

Kennett, S., Eimer, M., Spence, C., & Driver, J. (2001). Tactile-visual links in exogenous spatial attention under different postures: Convergent evidence from psychophysics and ERPs. *Journal of Cognitive Neuroscience, 13,* 462–478. (14)

Kerr, D. S., & Abraham, W. C. (1995). Cooperative interactions among afferents govern the induction of homosynaptic long-term depression in the hippocampus. *Proceedings of the National Academy of Sciences, USA, 92,* 11637–11641. (13)

Keshavan, M. S., Diwadkar, V. A., Montrose, D. M., Rajarethinam, R., & Sweeney, J. A. (2005). Premorbid indicators and risk for schizophrenia: A selective review and update. *Schizophrenia Research, 79,* 45–57. (15)

Kesner, R. P., Gilbert, P. E., & Barua, L. A. (2002). The role of the hippocampus in meaning for the temporal order of a sequence of odors. *Behavioral Neuroscience, 116,* 286–290. (13)

Kesslak, J. P., So, V., Choi, J., Cotman, C. W., & Gomez-Pinilla, F. (1998). Learning up-regulates brain-derived neurotrophic factor messenger ribonucleic acid: A mechanism to facilitate encoding and circuit maintenance? *Behavioral Neuroscience, 112,* 1012–1019. (5)

Kety, S. S., Wender, P. H., Jacobson, B., Ingraham, L. J., Jansson, L., Faber, B., et al. (1994). Mental illness in the biological and adoptive relatives of schizophrenic adoptees. *Archives of General Psychiatry, 51,* 442–455. (15)

Keverne, E. B. (1999). The vomeronasal organ. *Science, 286,* 716–720. (7)

Kiecolt-Glaser, J. K., & Glaser, R. (1993). Mind and immunity. In D. Goleman & J. Gurin (Eds.), *Mind/body medicine* (pp. 39–61). Yonkers, NY: Consumer Reports Books. (12)

Kikuchi-Yorioka, Y., & Sawaguchi, T. (2000). Parallel visuospatial and audiospatial working memory processes in the monkey dorsolateral prefrontal cortex. *Nature Neuroscience, 3,* 1075–1076. (13)

Kilgour, A. R., de Gelder, B., & Lederman, S. J. (2004). Haptic face recognition and prosopagnosia. *Neuropsychologia, 42,* 707–712. (6)

Killackey, H. P., & Chalupa, L. M. (1986). Ontogenetic change in the distribution of callosal projection neurons in the postcentral gyrus of the fetal rhesus monkey. *Journal of Comparative Neurology, 244,* 331–348. (14)

Killeffer, F. A., & Stern, W. E. (1970). Chronic effects of hypothalamic injury. *Archives of Neurology, 22,* 419–429. (10)

Kim, J.-H., Auerbach, J. M., Rodriguez-Gómez, J. A., Velasco, I., Gavin, D., Lumelsky, N., et al. (2002). Dopamine neurons derived from embryonic stem cells function in an animal model of Parkinson's disease. *Nature, 418,* 50–56. (8)

Kim, U., Jorgenson, E., Coon, H., Leppert, M., Risch, N., & Drayna, D. (2003). Positional cloning of the human quantitative trait locus underlying taste sensitivity to phenylthiocarbamide. *Science, 299,* 1221–1225. (7)

Kim, Y.-H., Park, J.-H., Hong, S. H., & Koh, J.-Y. (1999). Nonproteolytic neuroprotection by human recombinant tissue plasminogen activator. *Science, 284,* 647–650. (5)

Kimble, G. A. (1967). Attitudinal factors in classical conditioning. In G. A. Kimble (Ed.), *Foundations of conditioning and learning* (pp. 642–659). New York: Appleton-Century-Crofts. (4)

King, B. M., Smith, R. L., & Frohman, L. A. (1984). Hyperinsulinemia in rats with ventromedial hypothalamic lesions: Role of hyperphagia. *Behavioral Neuroscience, 98,* 152–155. (10)

King, M., Su, W., Chang, A., Zuckerman, A., & Pasternak, G. W. (2001). Transport of opioids from the brain to the periphery by P-glycoprotein: Peripheral actions of central drugs. *Nature Neuroscience, 4,* 268–274. (2)

Kingstone, A., & Gazzaniga, M. S. (1995). Subcortical transfer of higher order information: More illusory than real? *Neuropsychology, 9,* 321–328. (14)

Kinnamon, J. C. (1987). Organization and innervation of taste buds. In T. E. Finger & W. L. Silver (Eds.), *Neurobiology of taste and smell* (pp. 277–297). New York: Wiley. (7)

Kinomura, S., Larsson, J., Gulyás, B., & Roland, P. E. (1996). Activation by attention of the human reticular formation and thalamic intralaminar nuclei. *Science, 271,* 512–515. (9)

Kinsbourne, M., & McMurray, J. (1975). The effect of cerebral dominance on time sharing between speaking and tapping by preschool children. *Child Development, 46,* 240–242. (14)

Kinsey, A. C., Pomeroy, W. B., & Martin, C. E. (1948). *Sexual behavior in the human male.* Philadelphia: Saunders. (11)

Kinsey, A. C., Pomeroy, W. B., Martin, C. E., & Gebhard, P. H. (1953). *Sexual behavior in the human female.* Philadelphia: Saunders. (11)

Kippenhan, J. S., Olsen, R. K., Mervis, C. B., Morris, C. A., Kohn, P., Meyer-Lindenberg, A., et al. (2005). Genetic contributions to human gyrification: Sulcal morphometry in Williams syndrome. *Journal of Neuroscience, 25,* 7840–7846. (14)

Kiriakakis, V., Bhatia, K. P., Quinn, N. P., & Marsden, C. D. (1998). The natural history of tardive dyskinesia: A long-term follow-up study of 107 cases. *Brain, 121,* 2053–2066. (15)

Kirkpatrick, P. J., Smielewski, P., Czosnyka, M., Menon, D. K., & Pickard, J. D. (1995). Near-infrared spectroscopy in patients with head injury. *Journal of Neurosurgery, 83,* 963–970. (5)

Kirkwood, A., Lee, H.-K., & Bear, M. F. (1995). Co-regulation of long-term potentiation and experience-dependent synaptic plasticity in visual cortex by age and experience. *Nature, 375,* 328–331. (6)

Kiyashchenko, L. I., Mileykovskiy, B. Y., Maidment, N., Lam, H. A., Wu, M.-F., John, J., et al. (2002). Release of hypocretin (orexin) during waking and sleeping states. *Journal of Neuroscience, 22,* 5282–5286. (9)

Klar, A. J. S. (2003). Human handedness and scalp hair-whorl direction develop from a common genetic mechanism. *Genetics, 165,* 269–276. (14)

Klar, A. J. S. (2005). A 1927 study supports a current genetic model for inheritance of human scalp hair-whorl orientation and hand-use preference traits. *Genetics, 170,* 2027–2030. (14)

Klein, D. F. (1993). False suffocation alarms, spontaneous panics, and related conditions. *Archives of General Psychiatry, 50,* 306–317. (12)

Kleindienst, N., & Greil, W. (2000). Differential efficacy of lithium and carbamazepine in the prophylaxis of bipolar disorder: Results of the MAP study. *Neuropsychobiology, 42*(Suppl. 1), 2–10. (15)

Kleitman, N. (1963). *Sleep and wakefulness* (Rev. ed.). Chicago: University of Chicago Press. (9)

Klingberg, T., Forssberg, H., & Westerberg, H. (2002). Increased brain activity in frontal and parietal cortex underlies the development of visuospatial working memory capacity during childhood. *Journal of Cognitive Neuroscience, 14,* 1–10. (13)

Klingberg, T., Hedehus, M., Temple, E., Salz, T., Gabrielli, J. D. E., Moseley, M. E., et al. (2000). Microstructure of temporoparietal white matter as a basis for reading ability: Evidence from diffusion tensor magnetic resonance imaging. *Neuron, 25,* 493–500. (14)

Kluger, M. J. (1991). Fever: Role of pyrogens and cryogens. *Physiological Reviews, 71,* 93–127. (10)

Klüver, H., & Bucy, P. C. (1939). Preliminary analysis of functions of the temporal lobes in monkeys. *Archives of Neurology and Psychiatry, 42,* 979–1000. (4)

Knecht, S., Flöel, A., Dräger, B., Breitenstein, C., Sommer, J., Henningsen, H., et al. (2002). Degree of language lateralization determines susceptibility to unilateral brain lesions. *Nature Neuroscience, 5,* 695–699. (14)

Knoll, J. (1993). The pharmacological basis of the beneficial effects of (2) deprenyl (selegiline) in Parkinson's and Alzheimer's diseases. *Journal of Neural Transmission* (Suppl. 40), 69–91. (8)

Knyazev, G. G., Slobodskaya, H. R., & Wilson, G. D. (2002). Psychophysiological correlates of behavioural inhibition and activation. *Personality and Individual Differences, 33,* 647–660. (12)

Koepp, M. J., Gunn, R. N., Lawrence, A. D., Cunningham, V. J., Dagher, A., Jones, T., et al. (1998). Evidence for striatal dopamine release during a video game. *Nature, 393,* 266–268. (15)

Kolb, B., Côté, S., Ribeiro-da-Silva, A., & Cuello, A. C. (1997). Nerve growth factor treatment prevents dendritic atrophy and promotes recovery of function after cortical injury. *Neuroscience, 76,* 1139–1151. (8)

Kolb, B., Gorny, G., Côté, S., Ribeiro-da-Silva, A., & Cuello, A. C. (1997). Nerve growth factor stimulates growth of cortical pyramidal neurons in young adult rats. *Brain Research, 751,* 289–294. (5)

Kolb, B., Gorny, G., Li, Y., Samaha, A.-N., & Robinson, T. E. (2003). Amphetamine or cocaine limits the ability of later experience to promote structural plasticity in the neocortex and nucleus accumbens. *Proceedings of the National*

Academy of Sciences, USA, 100, 10523–10528. (5)

Komisaruk, B. R., Adler, N. T., & Hutchison, J. (1972). Genital sensory field: Enlargement by estrogen treatment in female rats. *Science, 178,* 1295–1298. (11)

Komura, Y., Tamura, R., Uwano, T., Nishijo, H., Kaga, K., & Ono, T. (2001). Retrospective and prospective coding for predicted reward in the sensory thalamus. *Nature, 412,* 546–549. (4)

Kondo, I., Marvizon, J. C. G., Song, B., Salgado, F., Codeluppi, S., Hua, X.-Y., et al. (2005). Inhibition by spinal μ- and δ-opioid agonists of afferent-evoked substance P release. *Journal of Neuroscience, 25,* 3651–3660. (7)

Kong, J., Shepel, P. N., Holden, C. P., Mackiewicz, M., Pack, A. I., & Geiger, J. D. (2002). Brain glycogen decreases with increased periods of wakefulness: Implications for homeostatic drive to sleep. *Journal of Neuroscience, 22,* 5581–5587. (9)

Konishi, M. (1995). Neural mechanisms of auditory image formation. In M. S. Gazzaniga (Ed.), *The cognitive neurosciences* (pp. 269–277). Cambridge, MA: MIT Press. (7)

Konishi, S., Nakajima, K., Uchida, I., Kameyama, M., Nakahara, K., Sekihara, K., et al. (1998). Transient activation of inferior prefrontal cortex during cognitive set shifting. *Nature Neuroscience, 1,* 80–84. (15)

Kordower, J. H., Emborg, M. E., Bloch, J., Ma, S.Y., Chu, Y., Leventhal, L., et al. (2000). Neurodegeneration prevented by lentiviral vector delivery of GDNF in primate models of Parkinson's disease. *Science, 290,* 767–773. (8)

Korenberg, J. R., Chen, X.-N., Hirota, H., Lai, Z., Bellugi, U., Burian, D., et al. (2000). VI. Genome structure and cognitive map of Williams syndrome. *Journal of Cognitive Neuroscience, 12*(Suppl.), 89–107. (14)

Kornhuber, H. H. (1974). Cerebral cortex, cerebellum, and basal ganglia: An introduction to their motor functions. In F. O. Schmitt & F. G. Worden (Eds.), *The neurosciences: Third study program* (pp. 267–280). Cambridge, MA: MIT Press. (8)

Korpi, E. R., & Sinkkonen, S. T. (2006). $GABA_A$ receptor subtypes as targets for neuropsychiatric drug development. *Pharmacology & Therapeutics, 109,* 12–32. (12)

Kosfeld, M., Heinrichs, M., Zak, P. J., Fischbacher, U., & Fehr, E. (2005). Oxytocin increases trust in humans. *Nature, 435,* 673–676. (11)

Kosslyn, S. M., Ganis, G., & Thompson, W. L. (2001). Neural foundations of imagery. *Nature Reviews Neuroscience, 2,* 635–642. (6)

Kosslyn, S. M., & Thompson, W. L. (2003). When is early visual cortex activated during visual mental imagery? *Psychological Bulletin, 129,* 723–746. (6)

Kostrzewa, R. M. (1995). Dopamine receptor supersensitivity. *Neuroscience and Biobehavioral Reviews, 19,* 1–17. (5)

Kourtzi, Z., & Kanwisher, N. (2000). Activation in human MT/MST by static images with implied motion. *Journal of Cognitive Neuroscience, 12,* 48–55. (6)

Kozloski, J., Hamzei-Sichani, F., & Yuste, R. (2001). Stereotyped position of local synaptic targets in neocortex. *Science, 293,* 868–872. (5)

Kraemer, D. J. M., Macrae, C. N., Green, A. E., & Kelley, W. M. (2005). Sound of silence activates auditory cortex. *Nature, 434,* 158. (7)

Krakauer, A. H. (2005). Kin selection and cooperative courtship in wild turkeys. *Nature, 434,* 69–72. (1)

Kraly, F. S., Kim, Y.-M., Dunham, L. M., & Tribuzio, R. A. (1995). Drinking after intragastric NaCl without increase in systemic plasma osmolality in rats. *American Journal of Physiology, 269,* R1085–R1092. (10)

Kreek, M. J., Nielsen, D. A., Butelman, H. R., & LaForge, K. S. (2005). Genetic influences on impulsivity, risk taking, stress responsivity and vulnerability to drug abuse and addiction. *Nature Neuroscience, 8,* 1450–1457. (15)

Kreitzer, A. C., Carter, A. G., & Regehr, W. G. (2002). Inhibition of interneuron firing extends the spread of endocannabinoid signaling in the cerebellum. *Neuron, 34,* 787–796. (3)

Kreitzer, A. C., & Regehr, W. G. (2001). Retrograde inhibition of presynaptic calcium influx by endogenous cannabinoids at excitatory synapses onto Purkinje cells. *Neuron, 29,* 717–727. (3)

Kringelbach, M. L. (2005). The human orbitofrontal cortex: Linking reward to hedonic experience. *Nature Reviews Neuroscience, 6,* 691–702. (12)

Kripke, D. F. (1998). Light treatment for nonseasonal depression: Speed, efficacy, and combined treatment. *Journal of Affective Disorders, 49,* 109–117. (15)

Kruesi, M. J. P., Hibbs, E. D., Zahn, T. P., Keysor, C. S., Hamburger, S. D., Bartko, J. J., et al. (1992). A 2-year prospective follow-up of children and adolescents with disruptive behavior disorders. *Archives of General Psychiatry, 49,* 429–435. (12)

Krupa, D. J., Thompson, J. K., & Thompson, R. F. (1993). Localization of a memory trace in the mammalian brain. *Science, 260,* 989–991. (13)

Krupa, D. J., Wiest, M. C., Shuler, M. G., Laubach, M., & Nicolelis, M. A. L. (2004). Layer-specific somatosensory cortical activation during active tactile discrimination. *Science, 304,* 1989–1992. (7)

Kruzich, P. J., Congleton, K. M., & See, R. E. (2001). Conditioned reinstatement of drug-seeking behavior with a discrete compound stimulus classically conditioned with intravenous cocaine. *Behavioral Neuroscience, 115,* 1086–1092. (15)

Kubota, Y., Sato, W., Murai, T., Toichi, M., Ikeda, A., & Sengoku, A. (2000). Emotional cognition without awareness after unilateral temporal lobectomy in humans. *Journal of Neuroscience, 20,* RC97, 1–5. (12)

Kuhlmann, S., Piel, M., & Wolf, O. T. (2005). Impaired memory retrieval after psychosocial stress in healthy young men. *Journal of Neuroscience, 25,* 2977–2982. (12)

Kuhlman, S. J., Silver, R., LeSauter, J., Bult-Ito, A., & McMahon, D. G. (2003). Phase resetting light pulses induce *Per1* and persistent spike activity in a subpopulation of biological clock neurons. *Journal of Neuroscience, 23,* 1441–1450. (9)

Kujala, T., Myllyviita, K., Tervaniemi, M., Alho, K., Kallio, J., & Näätänen, R. (2000). Basic auditory dysfunction in dyslexia as demonstrated by brain activity measurements. *Psychophysiology, 37,* 262–266. (14)

Kumaran, D., & Maguire, E. A. (2005). The human hippocampus: Cognitive maps or relational memory? *Journal of Neuroscience, 25,* 7254–7259. (13)

Kupfermann, I., Castellucci, V., Pinsker, H., & Kandel, E. (1970). Neuronal correlates of habituation and dishabituation of the gill withdrawal reflex in *Aplysia. Science, 167,* 1743–1745. (13)

Kurahashi, T., Lowe, G., & Gold, G. H. (1994). Suppression of odorant responses by odorants in olfactory receptor cells. *Science, 265,* 118–120. (7)

Kuypers, H. G. J. M. (1989). Motor system organization. In G. Adelman (Ed.), *Neuroscience year* (pp. 107–110). Boston: Birkhäuser. (8)

Kwon, J. S., McCarley, R. W., Hirayasu, Y., Anderson, J. E., Fischer, I. A., Kikinis, R., et al. (1999). Left planum temporale volume reduction in schizophrenia. *Archives of General Psychiatry, 56,* 142–148. (15)

LaBar, K. S., & Phelps, E. A. (1998). Arousal-mediated memory consolidation: Role of the medial temporal lobe in humans. *Psychological Science, 9,* 490–493. (13)

Laburn, H. P. (1996). How does the fetus cope with thermal challenges? *News in Physiological Sciences, 11,* 96–100. (5, 15)

Lacroix, L., Spinelli, S., Heidbreder, C. A., & Feldon, J. (2000). Differential role of the medial and lateral prefrontal cortices in fear and anxiety. *Behavioral Neuroscience, 114,* 1119–1130. (12)

Laeng, B., & Caviness, V. S. (2001). Prosopagnosia as a deficit in encoding curved surfaces. *Journal of Cognitive Neuroscience, 13,* 556–576. (6)

Laeng, B., Svartdal, F., & Oelmann, H. (2004). Does color synesthesia pose a paradox for early-selection theories of attention? *Psychological Science, 15,* 277–281. (7)

Lagoda, G., Muschamp, J. W., Vigdorchik, A., & Hull, E. (2004). A nitric oxide synthesis inhibitor in the medial preoptic area inhibits copulation and stimulus sensitization in male rats. *Behavioral Neuroscience, 118,* 1317–1323. (11)

Lai, C. S. L., Fisher, S. E., Hurst, J. A., Vargha-Khadem, F., & Monaco, A. P. (2001). A forkhead-domain gene is mutated in a severe speech and language disorder. *Nature, 413,* 519–523. (14)

Lake, R. I. E., Eaves, L. J., Maes, H. H. M., Heath, A. C., & Martin, N. G. (2000). Further evidence against the environmental transmission of individual differences in neuroticism from a collaborative study of 45,850 twins and relatives on two continents. *Behavior Genetics, 30,* 223–233. (1)

LaLumiere, R. T., Buen, T.-V., & McGaugh, J. L. (2003). Post training intra-basolateral amygdala infusions of norepinephrine enhance consolidation of memory for contextual fear conditioning. *Journal of Neuroscience, 23,* 6754–6758. (13)

Lam, H.-M., Chiu, J., Hsieh, M.-H., Meisel, L., Oliveira, I. C., Shin, M., & Coruzzi, G. (1998). Glutamate-receptor genes in plants. *Nature, 396,* 125–126. (3)

Lambie, J. A., & Marcel, A. J. (2002). Consciousness and the varieties of emotion experience: A theoretical framework. *Psychological Review, 109,* 219–259. (1)

Land, E. H., Hubel, D. H., Livingstone, M. S., Perry, S. H., & Burns, M. M. (1983). Colour-generating interactions across the corpus callosum. *Nature, 303,* 616–618. (6)

Landis, D. M. D. (1987). Initial junctions between developing parallel fibers and Purkinje cells are different from mature synaptic junctions. *Journal of Comparative Neurology, 260,* 513–525. (3)

Lang, P. J. (1994). The varieties of emotional experience: A meditation on James-Lange theory. *Psychological Review, 101,* 211–221. (12)

Lang, R. A., Flor-Henry, P., & Frenzel, R. R. (1990). Sex hormone profiles in pedophilic and incestuous men. *Annals of Sex Research, 3,* 59–74. (11)

Larsen, R. J., Kasimatis, M., & Frey, K. (1992). Facilitating the furrowed brow—An unobtrusive test of the facial feedback hypothesis applied to unpleasant affect. *Cognition & Emotion, 6,* 321–338. (12)

Lashley, K. S. (1929). *Brain mechanisms and intelligence.* Chicago: University of Chicago Press. (13)

Lashley, K. S. (1930). Basic neural mechanisms in behavior. *Psychological Review, 37,* 1–24. (inside cover)

Lashley, K. S. (1950). In search of the engram. *Symposia of the Society for Experimental Biology, 4,* 454–482. (13)

Lassonde, M., Bryden, M. P., & Demers, P. (1990). The corpus callosum and cerebral speech lateralization. *Brain and Language, 38,* 195–206. (14)

Lau, H. C., Rogers, R. D., Haggard, P., & Passingham, R. E. (2004). Attention to intention. *Science, 303,* 1208–1210. (8)

Laugerette, F., Passilly-Degrace, P., Patris, B., Niot, I., Febbraio, M., Montmayeur, J.-P., et al. (2005). CD36 involvement in orosensory detection of dietary lipids, spontaneous fat preference, and digestive secretions. *Journal of Clinical Investigation, 115,* 3177–3184. (7)

Laurent, J.-P., Cespuglio, R., & Jouvet, M. (1974). Dèlimitation des voies ascendantes de l'activité ponto-géniculo-occipitale chez le chat [Demarcation of the ascending paths of ponto-geniculo-occipital activity in the cat]. *Brain Research, 65,* 29–52. (9)

Lavidor, M., & Walsh, V. (2004). The nature of foveal representation. *Nature Reviews Neuroscience, 5,* 729–735. (14)

Le Grand, R., Mondloch, C. J., Maurer, D., & Brent, H. P. (2001). Early visual experience and face processing. *Nature, 410,* 890. (6)

Le Grand, R., Mondloch, C. J., Maurer, D., & Brent, H. P. (2003). Expert face processing requires visual input to the right hemisphere during infancy. *Nature Neuroscience, 6,* 1108–1112. (6)

Lebedev, M. A., Carmena, J. M., O'Doherty, J. E., Zacksenhouse, M., Henriquez, C. S., Principe, J. C., et al. (2005). Cortical ensemble adaptation to represent velocity of an artificial actuator controlled by a brain-machine interface. *Journal of Neuroscience, 25,* 4681–4693. (8)

LeDoux, J. (1996). *The emotional brain.* New York: Simon & Schuster. (12)

LeDoux, J. E., Iwata, J., Cicchetti, P., & Reis, D. J. (1988). Different projections of the central amygdaloid nucleus mediate autonomic and behavioral correlates of conditioned fear. *Journal of Neuroscience, 8,* 2517–2529. (12)

Lee, J.-M., Zipfel, G. J., & Choi, D. W. (1999). The changing landscape of ischaemic brain injury mechanisms. *Nature, 399*(Suppl.), A7–A14. (5)

Lee, M. G., Hassani, O. K., & Jones, B. E. (2005). Discharge of identified orexin/hypocretin neurons across the sleep-waking cycle. *Journal of Neuroscience, 25,* 6716–6720. (9)

Lee, S.-H., Blake, R., & Heeger, D. J. (2005). Traveling waves of activity in primary visual cortex during binocular rivalry. *Nature Neuroscience, 8,* 22–23. (1)

Legrand, L. N., Iacono, W. G., & McGue, M. (2005, March/April). Predicting addiction. *American Scientist, 93,* 140–147. (15)

Lehky, S. R. (2000). Deficits in visual feature binding under isoluminant conditions. *Journal of Cognitive Neuroscience, 12,* 383–392. (4)

Lehrman, D. S. (1964). The reproductive behavior of ring doves. *Scientific American, 211*(5), 48–54. (11)

Leibowitz, S. F., & Alexander, J. T. (1991). Analysis of neuropeptide Y-induced feeding: Dissociation of Y_1 and Y_2 receptor effects on natural meal patterns. *Peptides, 12,* 1251–1260. (10)

Leibowitz, S. F., Hammer, N. J., & Chang, K. (1981). Hypothalamic paraventricular nucleus lesions produce overeating and obesity in the rat. *Physiology & Behavior, 27,* 1031–1040. (10)

Leibowitz, S. F., & Hoebel, B. G. (1998). Behavioral neuroscience of obesity. In G. A. Bray, C. Bouchard, & P. T. James (Eds.), *Handbook of obesity* (pp. 313–358). New York: Dekker. (10)

Lein, E. S., & Shatz, C. J. (2001). Neurotrophins and refinement of visual circuitry. In W. M. Cowan, T. C. Südhof, & C. F. Stevens (Eds.), *Synapses* (pp. 613–649). Baltimore, MD: Johns Hopkins University Press. (6)

Leinders-Zufall, T., Lane, A. P., Puche, A. C., Ma, W., Novotny, M. V., Shipley, M. T., et al. (2000). Ultrasensitive pheromone detection by mammalian vomeronasal neurons. *Nature, 405,* 792–796. (7)

Lenhart, R. E., & Katkin, E. S. (1986). Psychophysiological evidence for cerebral laterality effects in a high-risk sample of students with subsyndromal bipolar depressive disorder. *American Journal of Psychiatry, 143,* 602–607. (15)

Lennie, P. (1998). Single units and visual cortical organization. *Perception, 27,* 889–935. (6)

Lenz, F. A., & Byl, N. N. (1999). Reorganization in the cutaneous core of the human thalamic principal somatic sensory nucleus (ventral caudal) in patients with dystonia. *Journal of Neurophysiology, 82,* 3204–3212. (5)

Leon, L. R. (2002). Invited review: Cytokine regulation of fever: Studies using gene knockout mice. *Journal of Applied Physiology, 92,* 2648–2655. (10)

Leonard, C. M., Lombardino, L. J., Mercado, L. R., Browd, S. R., Breier, J. I., & Agee, O. F. (1996). Cerebral asymmetry and cognitive development in children: A magnetic resonance imaging study. *Psychological Science, 7,* 89–95. (14)

Leopold, D. A., & Logothetis, N. K. (1996). Activity changes in early visual cortex reflect monkeys' percepts during binocular rivalry. *Nature, 379,* 549–553. (6)

Leppämäki, S., Partonen, T., & Lönnqvist, J. (2002). Bright-light exposure combined with physical exercise elevates mood. *Journal of Affective Disorders, 72,* 139–144. (15)

Leshem, M. (1999). The ontogeny of salt hunger in the rat. *Neuroscience and Biobehaioral Reviews, 23,* 649–659. (10)

Lesse, S. (1984). Psychosurgery. *American Journal of Psychotherapy, 38,* 224–228. (4)

Lester, B. M., LaGasse, L. L., & Seifer, R. (1998). Cocaine exposure and children: The meaning of subtle effects. *Science, 282,* 633–634. (5)

Lettvin, J. Y., Maturana, H. R., McCulloch, W. S., & Pitts, W. H. (1959). What the frog's eye tells the frog's brain. *Proceedings of the Institute of Radio Engineers, 47,* 1940–1951. (7)

Leung, H.-C., Gore, J. C., & Goldman-Rakic, P. S. (2002). Sustained mnemonic response in the human middle frontal gyrus during on-line storage of spatial memoranda. *Journal of Cognitive Neuroscience, 14,* 659–671. (13)

Leutgeb, S., Leutgeb, J. K., Barnes, C. A., Moser, E. I., McNaughton, B. L., & Moser, M.-B. (2005). Independent codes for spatial and episodic memory in hippocampal neuronal ensembles. *Science, 309,* 619–623. (13)

LeVay, S. (1991). A difference in hypothalamic structure between heterosexual and homosexual men. *Science, 253,* 1034–1037. (11)

LeVay, S. (1993). *The sexual brain.* Cambridge, MA: MIT Press. (11)

Levenson, R. W., Oyama, O. N., & Meek, P. S. (1987). Greater reinforcement from alcohol for those at risk: Parental risk, personality risk, and sex. *Journal of Abnormal Psychology, 96,* 242–253. (15)

LeVere, T. E. (1975). Neural stability, sparing and behavioral recovery following brain damage. *Psychological Review, 82,* 344–358. (5)

LeVere, T. E., & Morlock, G. W. (1973). Nature of visual recovery following posterior neodecortication in the hooded rat. *Journal of Comparative and Physiological Psychology, 83,* 62–67. (5)

Levi-Montalcini, R. (1987). The nerve growth factor 35 years later. *Science, 237,* 1154–1162. (5)

Levi-Montalcini, R. (1988). *In praise of imperfection.* New York: Basic Books. (5; inside cover)

Levin, E. D., & Rose, J. E. (1995). Acute and chronic nicotine interactions with dopamine systems and working memory performance. *Annals of the New York Academy of Sciences, 757,* 245–252. (3)

Levine, J. A., Lannngham-Foster, L. M., McCrady, S. K., Krizan, A. C., Olson, L. R., Kane, P. H., et al. (2005). Interindividual variation in posture allocation: Possible role in human obesity. *Science, 307,* 584–586. (10)

Levine, J. D., Fields, H. L., & Basbaum, A. I. (1993). Peptides and the primary afferent nociceptor. *Journal of Neuroscience, 13,* 2273–2286. (3)

Levitin, D. J., & Bellugi, U. (1998). Musical abilities in individuals with Williams syndrome. *Music Perception, 15,* 357–389. (14)

Levitt, R. A. (1975). *Psychopharmacology.* Washington, DC: Hemisphere. (15)

Levitt-Gilmour, T. A., & Salpeter, M. M. (1986). Gradient of extrajunctional acetylcholine receptors early after denervation of mammalian muscle. *Journal of Neuroscience, 6,* 1606–1612. (5)

Levitzki, A. (1988). From epinephrine to cyclic AMP. *Science, 241,* 800–806. (3)

Levivier, M., Przedborski, S., Bencsics, C., & Kang, U. J. (1995). Intrastriatal implantation of fibroblasts genetically engineered to produce brain-derived neurotrophic factor prevents degeneration of dopaminergic neurons in a rat model of Parkinson's disease. *Journal of Neuroscience, 15,* 7810–7820. (5)

Levy, J., Heller, W., Banich, M. T., & Burton, L. A. (1983). Asymmetry of perception in free viewing of chimeric faces. *Brain and Cognition, 2,* 404–419. (14)

Levy, L. J., Astur, R. S., & Frick, K. M. (2005). Men and women differ in object memory but not performance of a virtual radial maze. *Behavioral Neuroscience, 119,* 853–862. (11)

Levy-Lahad, E., Wijsman, E. M., Nemens, E., Anderson, L., Goddard, K. A. B., Weber, J. L., et al. (1995). A familial Alzheimer's disease locus on chromosome 1. *Science, 269,* 970–973. (13)

Leweke, F. M., Gerth, C. W., Koethe, D., Klosterkötter, J., Ruslanova, I., Krivogorsky, B., et al. (2004). Antibodies to infectious agents in individuals with recent onset schizophrenia. *European Archives of Psychiatry and Clinical Neuroscience, 254,* 4–8. (15)

Lewis, D. A. (1997). Development of the prefrontal cortex during adolescence: Insights into vulnerable neural circuits in schizophrenia. *Neuropsychopharmacology, 16,* 385–398. (5, 15)

Lewis, D. A., Hashimoto, T., & Volk, D. W. (2005). Cortical inhibitory neurons and schizophrenia. *Nature Reviews Neuroscience, 6,* 312–324. (15)

Lewis, E. R., Everhart, T. E., & Zeevi, Y. Y. (1969). Studying neural organization in *Aplysia* with the scanning electron microscope. *Science, 165,* 1140–1143. (3)

Lewis, T. L., & Maurer, D. (2005). Multiple sensitive periods in human visual development: Evidence from visually deprived children. *Developmental Psychobiology, 46,* 163–183. (6)

Lewis, V. G., Money, J., & Epstein, R. (1968). Concordance of verbal and nonverbal ability in the adrenogenital syndrome. *Johns Hopkins Medical Journal, 122,* 192–195. (11)

Lewy, A. J., Bauer, V. K., Cutler, N. L., Sack, R. L., Ahmed, S., Thomas, K. H., et al. (1998). Morning vs. evening light treatment of patients with winter depression. *Archives of General Psychiatry, 55,* 890–896. (15)

Li, H., Chen, A., Xing, G., Wei, M.-L., & Rogawski, M. A. (2001). Kainate receptor-mediated heterosynaptic facilitation in the amygdala. *Nature Neuroscience, 4,* 612–620. (13)

Libet, B., Gleason, C. A., Wright, E. W., & Pearl, D. K. (1983). Time of conscious intention to act in relation to onset of cerebral activities (readiness potential): The unconscious initiation of a freely voluntary act. *Brain, 106,* 623–642. (8)

Lieberman, J., Chakos, M., Wu, H., Alvir, J., Hoffman, E., Robinson, D., et al. (2001). Longitudinal study of brain morphology in first episode schizophrenia. *Biological Psychiatry, 49,* 487–499. (15)

Lim, K. O., Adalsteinsson, E., Spielman, D., Sullivan, E. V., Rosenbloom, M. J., & Pfefferbaum, A. (1998). Proton magnetic resonance spectroscopic imaging of cortical gray and white matter in schizophrenia. *Archives of General Psychiatry, 55,* 346–352. (15)

Lim, M. M., Wang, Z., Olazábal, D. E., Ren, X., Terwilliger, E. F., & Young, L. J. (2004). Enhanced partner preference in a promiscuous species by manipulating the expression of a single gene. *Nature, 429,* 754–757. (11)

Lin, J.-S., Hou, Y., Sakai, K., & Jouvet, M. (1996). Histaminergic descending inputs to the mesopontine tegmentum and their role in the control of cortical activation and wakefulness in the cat. *Journal of Neuroscience, 16,* 1523–1537. (9)

Lin, L., Faraco, J., Li, R., Kadotani, H., Rogers, W., Lin, X., et al. (1999). The sleep disorder canine narcolepsy is caused by a mutation in the hypocretin (orexin) receptor 2 gene. *Cell, 98,* 365–376. (9)

Lindberg, N. O., Coburn, C., & Stricker, E. M. (1984). Increased feeding by rats after subdiabetogenic streptozotocin treatment: A role for insulin in satiety. *Behavioral Neuroscience, 98,* 138–145. (10)

Lindemann, B. (1996). Taste reception. *Physiological Reviews, 76,* 719–766. (7)

Lindsay, P. H., & Norman, D. A. (1972). *Human information processing.* New York: Academic Press. (7)

Lindvall, O., Kokaia, Z., & Martinez-Serrano, A. (2004). Stem cell therapy for human neurodegenerative disorders—How to make it work. *Nature Medicine, 10,* S42–S50. (8)

Liou, Y.-C., Tocilj, A., Davies, P. L., & Jia, Z. (2000). Mimicry of ice structure by surface hydroxyls and water of a β-helix antifreeze protein. *Nature, 406,* 322–324. (10)

Lisman, J., Schulman, H., & Cline, H. (2002). The molecular basis of CaMKII function in synaptic and behavioural memory. *Nature Reviews Neuroscience, 3,* 175–190. (13)

Liu, G., & Tsien, R. W. (1995). Properties of synaptic transmission at single hippocampal synaptic boutons. *Nature, 375,* 404–408. (3)

Liu, L. Y., Coe, C. L., Swenson, C. A., Kelly, E. A., Kita, H., & Busse, W. W. (2002). School examinations enhance airway inflammation to antigen challenge. *American Journal of Respiratory and Critical Care Medicine, 165,* 1062–1067. (12)

Liu, P., & Bilkey, D. K. (2001). The effect of excitotoxic lesions centered on the hippocampus or perirhinal cortex in object recognition and spatial memory tasks. *Behavioral Neuroscience, 115,* 94–111. (13)

Liu, X., Zwiebel, L. J., Hinton, D., Benzer, S., Hall, J. C., & Rosbash, M. (1992). The period gene encodes a predominantly nuclear protein in adult Drosophila. *Journal of Neuroscience, 12,* 2735–2744. (9)

Livingstone, M. S. (1988, January). Art, illusion and the visual system. *Scientific American, 258*(1), 78–85. (6)

Livingstone, M. S., & Hubel, D. (1988). Segregation of form, color, movement, and depth: Anatomy, physiology, and perception. *Science, 240,* 740–749. (6)

Ljungberg, M. C., Stern, C., & Wilkin, C. P. (1999). Survival of genetically engineered, adult-derived rat astrocytes grafted into the 6-hydroxydopamine lesioned adult rat striatum. *Brain Research, 816,* 29–37. (8)

Lockwood, A. H., Salvi, R. J., Coad, M. L., Towsley, M. L., Wack, D. S., & Murphy, B. W. (1998). The functional neuroanatomy of tinnitus: Evidence for limbic system links and neural plasticity. *Neurology, 50,* 114–120. (7)

Loewenstein, W. R. (1960, August). Biological transducers. *Scientific American, 203*(2), 98–108. (7)

Loewi, O. (1960). An autobiographic sketch. *Perspectives in Biology, 4,* 3–25. (3)

Logan, C. G., & Grafton, S. T. (1995). Functional anatomy of human eyeblink conditioning determined with regional cerebral glucose metabolism and positron-emission tomography. *Proceedings of the National Academy of Sciences, USA, 92,* 7500–7504. (13)

Logothetis, N. K., Pauls, J., Augath, M., Trinath, T., & Oeltermann, A. (2001). Neurophysiological investigtion of the basis of the fMRI signal. *Nature, 412,* 150–157. (4)

London, E. D., Cascella, N. G., Wong, D. F., Phillips, R. L., Dannals, R. F., Links, J. M., et al. (1990). Cocaine-induced reduction of glucose utilization in human brain. *Archives of General Psychiatry, 47,* 567–574. (3)

Long, M. A., Jutras, M. J., Connors, B. W., & Burwell, R. D. (2005). Electrical synapses coordinate activity in the suprachiasmatic nucleus. *Nature Neuroscience, 8,* 61–66. (9)

Lord, G. M., Matarese, G., Howard, J. K., Baker, R. J., Bloom, S. R., & Lechler, R. I. (1998). Leptin modulates the T-cell immune response and reverses starvation-induced immunosuppression. *Nature, 394,* 897–901. (10)

Lorenzo, A., Yuan, M., Zhang, Z., Paganetti, P. A., Sturchler-Pierrat, C., Staufenbiel, M., et al. (2000). Amyloid ß interacts with the amyloid precursor protein: A potential toxic mechanism in Alzheimer's disease. *Nature Neuroscience, 3,* 460–464. (13)

Lorrain, D. S., Riolo, J. V., Matuszewich, L., & Hull, E. M. (1999). Lateral hypothalamic serotonin inhibits nucleus accumbens dopamine: Implications for sexual refractoriness. *Journal of Neuroscience, 19,* 7648–7652. (15)

Lorusso, M. L., Facoetti, A., Pesenti, S., Cattaneo, C., Molteni, M., & Geiger, G. (2004). Wider recognition in peripheral vision common to different subtypes of dyslexia. *Vision Research, 44,* 2413–2424. (14)

Lott, I. T. (1982). Down's syndrome, aging, and Alzheimer's disease: A clinical review. *Annals of the New York Academy of Sciences, 396,* 15–27. (13)

Lotto, R. B., & Purves, D. (1999). The effects of color on brightness. *Nature Neuroscience, 2,* 1010–1014. (6)

Lotto, R. B., & Purves, D. (2002). The empirical basis of color perception. *Consciousness and Cognition, 11,* 609–629. (6)

Lotze, M., Grodd, W., Birbaumer, N., Erb, M., Huse, E., & Flor, H. (1999). Does use of a myoelectric prosthesis prevent cortical reorganization and phantom limb pain? *Nature Neuroscience, 2,* 501–502. (5)

Loving, R. T., Kripke, D. F., & Shuchter, S. R. (2002). Bright light augments antidepressant effects of medication and wake therapy. *Depression and Anxiety, 16,* 1–3. (15)

Lucas, B. K., Ormandy, C. J., Binart, N., Bridges, R. S., & Kelly, P. A. (1998). Null mutation of the prolactin receptor gene produces a defect in maternal behavior. *Endocrinology, 139,* 4202–4107. (11)

Lucas, R. J., Douglas, R. H., & Foster, R. G. (2001). Characterization of an ocular photopigment capable of driving pupillary constriction in mice. *Nature Neuroscience, 4,* 621–626. (9)

Lucas, R. J., Freedman, M. S., Muñoz, M., Garcia-Fernández, J.-M., & Foster, R. G. (1999). Regulation of the mammalian pineal by non-rod, non-cone ocular photoreceptors. *Science, 284,* 505–507. (9)

Luders, E., Narr, K. L., Thompson, P. M., Rex, D. E., Jancke, L., Steinmetz, H., et al. (2004). Gender differences in cortical complexity. *Nature Neuroscience, 7,* 799–800. (4)

Lund, R. D., Lund, J. S., & Wise, R. P. (1974). The organization of the retinal projection to the dorsal lateral geniculate nucleus in pigmented and albino rats. *Journal of Comparative Neurology, 158,* 383–404. (6)

Lupien, S. J., de Leon, M., de Santi, S., Convit, A., Tarshish, C., Nair, N. P. V., et al. (1998). Cortisol levels during human aging predict hippocampal atrophy and memory deficits. *Nature Neuroscience, 1,* 69–73. (12)

Lyman, C. P., O'Brien, R. C., Greene, G. C., & Papafrangos, E. D. (1981). Hibernation and longevity in the Turkish hamster *Mesocricetus brandti. Science, 212,* 668–670. (9)

Lyons, M. J., Eisen, S. A., Goldberg, J., True, W., Lin, N., Meyer, J. M., et al. (1998). A registry-based twin study of depression in men. *Archives of General Psychiatry, 55,* 468–472. (15)

Lyons, M. J., True, W. R., Eisen, S. A., Goldberg, J., Meyer, J. M., Faraone, S. V., et al. (1995). Differential heritability of adult and juvenile antisocial traits. *Archives of General Psychiatry, 52,* 906–915. (12)

Lytle, L. D., Messing, R. B., Fisher, L., & Phebus, L. (1975). Effects of long-term corn consumption on brain serotonin and the response to electric shock. *Science, 190,* 692–694. (12)

MacAndrew, D. K., Klatzky, R. L., Fiez, J. A., McClelland, J. L., & Becker, J. T. (2002). The phonological-similarity effect differentiates between two working memory tasks. *Psychological Science, 13,* 465–468. (4)

Macdonald, R. L., Weddle, M. G., & Gross, R. A. (1986). Benzodiazepine, ß-carboline, and barbiturate actions on GABA responses. *Advances in Biochemical Psychopharmacology, 41,* 67–78. (12)

Macey, P. M., Henderson, L. A., Macey, K. E., Alger, J. R., Frysinger, R. C., Woo, M. A., et al. (2002). Brain morphology associated with obstructive sleep apnea. *American Journal of Respiratory & Critical Care Medicine, 166,* 1382–1387. (9)

MacFarlane, J. G., Cleghorn, J. M., & Brown, G. M. (1985a, September). *Circadian rhythms in chronic insomnia.* Paper presented at the World Congress of Biological Psychiatry, Philadelphia. (9)

MacFarlane, J. G., Cleghorn, J. M., & Brown, G. M. (1985b). Melatonin and core temperature rhythms in chronic insomnia. In G. M. Brown & S. D. Wainwright (Eds.), *The pineal gland: Endocrine aspects* (pp. 301–306). New York: Pergamon Press. (9)

MacLean, P. D. (1949). Psychosomatic disease and the "visceral brain": Recent developments bearing on the Papez theory of emotion. *Psychosomatic Medicine, 11,* 338–353. (12)

MacLusky, N. J., & Naftolin, F. (1981). Sexual differentiation of the central nervous system. *Science, 211,* 1294–1303. (11)

Macphail, E. M. (1985). Vertebrate intelligence: The null hypothesis. *Philosophical Transactions of the Royal Society of London, B, 308,* 37–51. (4)

Macrae, C. N., Alnwick, K. A., Milne, A. B., & Schloerscheidt, A. M. (2002). Person perception across the menstrual cycle. *Psychological Science, 13,* 532–536. (11)

Madden, D. R. (2002). The structure and function of glutamate receptor ion channels. *Nature Reviews Neuroscience, 3,* 91–101. (13)

Madden, P. A. F., Heath, A. C., Rosenthal, N. E., & Martin, N. G. (1996). Seasonal changes in mood and behavior. *Archives of General Psychiatry, 53,* 47–55. (15)

Maes, M., Scharpé, S., Verkerk, R., D'Hondt, P., Peeters, D., Cosyns, P., et al. (1995). Seasonal availability in plasma L-tryptophan availability in healthy volunteers. *Archives of General Psychiatry, 52,* 937–946. (12)

Maess, B., Koelsch, S., Gunter, T. C., & Friederici, A. D. (2001). Musical syntax is processed in Broca's area: An MEG study. *Nature Neuroscience, 4,* 540–545. (14)

Magee, J. C., & Cook, E. P. (2000). Somatic EPSP amplitude is independent of synapse location in hippocampal pyramidal neurons. *Nature Neuroscience, 3,* 895–903. (3)

Mague, S. D., Andersen, S. L., & Carlezon, W. A., Jr. (2005). Early developmental exposure to methylphenidate reduces cocaine-induced potentiation of brain stimulation rewards in rats. *Biological Psychiatry, 57,* 120–125. (3)

Maguire, E. A., & Frith, C. D. (2003). Lateral asymmetry in the hippocampal response to the remoteness of autobiographical memories. *Journal of Neuroscience, 23,* 5302–5307. (13)

Maguire, E. A., Gadian, D. G., Johnsrude, I. S., Good, C. D., Ashburner, J., Frackowiak, R. S. J., et al. (2000). Navigation-related structural change in the hippocampi of taxi drivers. *Proceedings of the National Academy of Sciences, USA, 97,* 4398–4403. (13)

Mahowald, M. W., & Schenck, C. H. (1992). Dissociated states of wakefulness and sleep. *Neurology, 42*(Suppl. 6), 44–52. (9)

Maier, S. F., & Watkins, L. R. (1998). Cytokines for psychologists: Implications of bidirectional immune-to-brain communication for understanding behavior, mood, and cognition. *Psychological Review, 105,* 83–107. (12)

Mair, R. G., Burk, J. A., & Porter, M. C. (2003). Impairment of radial maze delayed nonmatching after lesions of anterior thalamus and parahippocampal cortex. *Behavioral Neuroscience, 117,* 596–605. (13)

Malaspina, D., Harlap, S., Fennig, S., Heiman, D., Nahon, D., Feldman, D., et al. (2001). Advancing paternal age and the risk of schizophrenia. *Archives of General Psychiatry, 58,* 361–367. (15)

Malhotra, P., Jäger, H. R., Parton, A., Greenwood, R., Playford, E. D., Brown, M. M., et al. (2005). Spatial working memory capacity in unilateral neglect. *Brain, 128,* 424–435. (14)

Mallis, M. M., & DeRoshia, C. W. (2005). Circadian rhythms, sleep, and performance in space. *Aviation, Space, and Environmental Medicine, 76*(Suppl. 6), B94–B107. (9)

Malmberg, A. B., Chen, C., Tonegawa, S., & Basbaum, A. I. (1997). Preserved acute pain and reduced neuropathic pain in mice lacking PKCγ. *Science, 278,* 179–283. (7)

Manfredi, M., Stocchi, F., & Vacca, L. (1995). Differential diagnosis of Parkinsonism. *Journal of Neural Transmission*(Suppl. 45), 1–9. (8)

Mangiapane, M. L., & Simpson, J. B. (1980). Subfornical organ: Forebrain site of pressor and dipsogenic action of angiotensin II. *American Journal of Physiology, 239,* R382–R389. (10)

Mann, J. J., Arango, V., & Underwood, M. D. (1990). Serotonin and suicidal behavior. *Annals of the New York Academy of Sciences, 600,* 476–485. (12)

Mannuzza, S., Klein, R. G., Bessler, A., Malloy, P., & LaPadula, M. (1998). Adult psychiatric status of hyperactive boys grown up. *American Journal of Psychiatry, 155,* 493–498. (5)

Maquet, P., Laureys, S., Peigneux, P., Fuchs, S., Petiau, C., Phillips, C., et al. (2000). Experience-dependent changes in cerebral activation during human REM sleep. *Nature Neuroscience, 3,* 831–836. (9)

Maquet, P., Peters, J.-M., Aerts, J., Delfiore, G., Degueldre, C., Luxen, A., et al. (1996). Functional neuroanatomy of human rapid-eye-movement sleep and dreaming. *Nature, 383,* 163–166. (8, 9)

Marcar, V. L., Zihl, J., & Cowey, A. (1997). Comparing the visual deficits of a motion blind patient with the visual deficits of monkeys with area MT removed. *Neuropsychologia, 35,* 1459–1465. (6)

Marín, O., & Rubenstein, J. L. R. (2001). A long, remarkable journey: Tangential migration in the telencephalon. *Nature Reviews Neuroscience, 2,* 780–790. (5)

Marin, O., Smeets, W. J. A. J., & González, A. (1998). Evolution of the basal ganglia in tetrapods: A new perspective based on recent studies in amphibians. *Trends in Neurosciences, 21,* 487–494. (4)

Mark, V. H., & Ervin, F. R. (1970). *Violence and the brain.* New York: Harper & Row. (12)

Marshall, J. C., & Halligan, P. W. (1995). Seeing the forest but only half the trees? *Nature, 373,* 521–523. (14)

Marshall, J. F. (1985). Neural plasticity and recovery of function after brain injury. *International Review of Neurobiology, 26,* 201–247. (5)

Marsicano, G., Goodenough, S., Monory, K., Hermann, H., Eder, M., Cannich, A., et al. (2003). CB1 cannabinoid receptors and on-demand defense against excitotoxicity. *Science, 302,* 84–88. (3)

Martin, A. R. (1977). Junctional transmission: II. Presynaptic mechanisms. In E. R. Kandel (Ed.), *Handbook of physiology* (Sect. 1, Vol. 1, Pt. 1, pp. 329–355). Bethesda, MD: American Physiological Society. (3)

Martin, E. R., Scott, W. K., Nance, M. A., Watts, R. L., Hubble, J. P., Koller, W. C., et al. (2001). Association of single-nucleotide polymorphisms of the tau gene with late-onset Parkinson disease. *Journal of the American Medical Association, 286,* 2245–2250. (8)

Martin, G., Rojas, L. M., Ramírez, Y., & McNeil, R. (2004). The eyes of oilbirds (*Steatornis caripensis*): Pushing at the limits of sensitivity. *Naturwissenschaften, 91,* 26–29. (6)

Martin, J. T., & Nguyen, D. H. (2004). Anthropometric analysis of homosexuals and heterosexuals: Implications for early hormone exposure. *Hormones and Behavior, 45,* 31–39. (11)

Martin, P. R., Lee, B. B., White, A. J. R., Solomon, S. G., & Rütiger, L. (2001). Chromatic sensitivity of ganglion cells in the peripheral primate retina. *Nature, 410,* 933–936. (6)

Martin, R. C., & Blossom-Stach, C. (1986). Evidence of syntactic deficits in a fluent aphasic. *Brain and Language, 28,* 196–234. (14)

Martin, S. D., Martin, E., Rai, S. S., Richardson, M. A., Royall, R., & Eng, C. (2001). Brain blood flow changes in depressed patients treated with interpersonal psychotherapy or venlafaxine hydrochloride. *Archives of General Psychiatry, 58,* 641–648. (15)

Martindale, C. (2001). Oscillations and analogies: Thomas Young, MD, FRS, genius. *American Psychologist, 56,* 342–345. (6)

Martinez, L. M., & Alonso, J.-M. (2001). Construction of complex receptive fields in cat primary visual cortex. *Neuron, 32,* 515–525. (6)

Martinez-Vargas, M. C., & Erickson, C. J. (1973). Some social and hormonal determinants of nest-building behaviour in the ring dove (*Streptopelia risoria*). *Behaviour, 45,* 12–37. (11)

Masland, R. H. (2001). The fundamental plan of the retina. *Nature Neuroscience, 4,* 877–886. (6)

Mason, D. A., & Frick, P. J. (1994). The heritability of antisocial behavior: A meta-analysis of twin and adoption studies. *Journal of Psychopathology and Behavioral Assessment, 16,* 301–323. (12)

Massimini, M., Ferrarelli, F., Huber, R., Esser, S. K., Singh, H., & Tononi, G. (2005). Breakdown of cortical effective connectivity during sleep. *Science, 309,* 2228–2232. (9)

Mathalon, D. H., Pfefferbaum, A., Lim, K. O., Rosenbloom, M. J., & Sullivan, E. V. (2003). Compounded brain volume deficits in schizophrenia-alcoholism comorbidity. *Archives of General Psychiatry, 60,* 245–252. (15)

Mathalon, D. H., Sullivan, E. V., Lim, K. O., & Pfefferbaum, A. (2001). Progressive brain volume changes and the clinical course of schizophrenia in men. *Archives of General Psychiatry, 58,* 148–157. (15)

Matsumoto, Y., Mishima, K., Satoh, K., Tozawa, T., Mishima, Y., Shimizu, T., et al. (2001). Total sleep deprivation induces an acute and transient increase in NK cell activity in healthy young volunteers. *Sleep, 24,* 804–809. (9)

Matsunami, H., Montmayeur, J.-P., & Buck, L. B. (2000). A family of candidate taste receptors in human and mouse. *Nature, 404,* 601–604. (7)

Mattay, V. S., Berman, K. F., Ostrem, J. L., Esposito, G., Van Horn, J. D., Bigelow, L. B., et al. (1996). Dextroamphetamine enhances "neural network-specific" physiological signals: A positron-emission tomography rCBF study. *Journal of Neuroscience, 15,* 4816–4822. (3)

Mattingley, J. B., Husain, M., Rorden, C., Kennard, C., & Driver, J. (1998). Motor role of human inferior parietal lobe revealed in unilateral neglect patients. *Nature, 392,* 179–182. (14)

Matuszewich, L., Lorrain, D. S., & Hull, E. M. (2000). Dopamine release in the medial preoptic area of female rats in response to hormonal manipulation and sexual activity. *Behavioral Neuroscience, 114,* 772–782. (11)

Maurice, D. M. (1998). The Von Sallmann lecture of 1996: An ophthalmological explanation of REM sleep. *Experimental Eye Research, 66,* 139–145. (9)

May, P. R. A., Fuster, J. M., Haber, J., & Hirschman, A. (1979). Woodpecker drilling behavior: An endorsement of the rotational theory of impact brain injury. *Archives of Neurology, 36,* 370–373. (5)

Mayberry, R. I., Lock, E., & Kazmi, H. (2002). Linguistic ability and early language exposure. *Nature, 417,* 38. (14)

Mayer, A. D., & Rosenblatt, J. S. (1979). Hormonal influences during the ontogeny of maternal behavior in female rats. *Journal of Comparative and Physiological Psychology, 93,* 879–898. (11)

Mayne, T. J. (1999). Negative affect and health: The importance of being earnest. *Cognition and Emotion, 13,* 601–635. (12)

McBurney, D. H., & Bartoshuk, L. M. (1973). Interactions between stimuli with different taste qualities. *Physiology & Behavior,* 10, 1101–1106. (7)

McCann, U. D., Lowe, K. A., & Ricaurte, G. A. (1997). Long-lasting effects of recreational drugs of abuse on the central nervous system. *The Neuroscientist, 3,* 399–411. (3)

McCarley, R. W., & Hobson, J. A. (1977). The neurobiological origins of psychoanalytic dream theory. *American Journal of Psychiatry, 134,* 1211–1221. (9)

McCarley, R. W., & Hoffman, E. (1981). REM sleep, dreams, and the activation synthesis hypothesis. *American Journal of Psychiatry, 138,* 904–912. (9)

McCarthy, G., Puce, A., Gore, J. C., & Allison, T. (1997). Face-specific processing in the human fusiform gyrus. *Journal of Cognitive Neuroscience, 9,* 605–610. (6)

McCaughey, S. A., & Scott, T. R. (2000). Rapid induction of sodium appetite modifies taste-evoked activity in the rat nucleus of the solitary tract. *American Journal of Physiology, 279,* R1121–1131. (10)

McClellan, A. D. (1998). Spinal cord injury: Lessons from locomotor recovery and axonal regeneration in lower vertebrates. *The Neuroscientist, 4,* 250–263. (5)

McClintock, M. K. (1971). Menstrual synchrony and suppression. *Nature, 229,* 244–245. (7)

McConnell, J. V. (1962). Memory transfer through cannibalism in planarians. *Journal of Neuropsychiatry, 3*(Suppl. 1), 42–48. (13)

McConnell, S. K. (1992). The genesis of neuronal diversity during development of cerebral cortex. *Seminars in the Neurosciences, 4,* 347–356. (5)

McCrory, E., Frith, U., Brunswick, N., & Price, C. (2000). Abnormal functional activation during a simple word repetition task: A PET study of adult dyslexics. *Journal of Cognitive Neuroscience, 12,* 753–762. (14)

McDaniel, M. A., Maier, S. F., & Einstein, G. O. (2002). "Brain-specific" nutrients: A memory cure? *Psychological Science in the Public Interest, 3,* 12–38. (13)

McDonald, M. P., Willard, L. B., Wenk, G. L., & Crawley, J. N. (1998). Coadministration of galanin antagonist M40 with a muscarinic M_1 agonist improves delayed nonmatching to position choice accuracy in rats with cholinergic lesions. *Journal of Neuroscience, 18,* 5078–5085. (13)

McElhiney, M. C., Moody, B. J., Steif, B. L., Prudic, J., Devanand, D. P., Nobler, M. S., et al. (1995). Autobiographical memory and mood: Effects of electroconvulsive therapy. *Neuropsychology, 9,* 501–517. (15)

McEwen, B. S. (2000). The neurobiology of stress: From serendipity to clinical relevance. *Brain Research, 886,* 172–189. (10, 12)

McEwen, B. S. (2001). Invited review: Estrogen effects on the brain: Multiple sites and molecular mechanisms. *Journal of Applied Physiology, 91,* 2785–2801. (11)

McGaughy, J., Koene, R. A., Eichenbaum, H., & Hasselmo, M. E. (2005). Cholinergic deafferentation of the entorhinal cortex in rats impairs encoding of novel but not familiar stimuli in a delayed non-match-to-sample task. *Journal of Neuroscience, 25,* 10273–10281. (13)

McGregor, I. S., Hargreaves, G. A., Apfelbach, R., & Hunt, G. E. (2004). Neural correlates of cat odor-induced anxiety in rats: Region-specific effects of the benzodiazepine midazolam. *Journal of Neuroscience, 24,* 4134–4144. (12)

McGuire, S., & Clifford, J. (2000). Genetic and environmental contributions to loneliness in children. *Psychological Science, 11,* 487–491. (1)

McHugh, P. R., & Moran, T. H. (1985). The stomach: A conception of its dynamic role in satiety. *Progress in Psychobiology and Physiological Psychology, 11,* 197–232. (10)

McKeever, W. F., Seitz, K. S., Krutsch, A. J., & Van Eys, P. L. (1995). On language laterality in normal dextrals and sinistrals: Results from the bilateral object naming latency task. *Neuropsychologia, 33,* 1627–1635. (14)

McKemy, D. D., Neuhausser, W. M., & Julius, D. (2002). Identification of a cold receptor reveals a general role for TRP channels in thermosensation. *Nature, 416,* 52–58. (7)

McKinnon, W., Weisse, C. S., Reynolds, C. P., Bowles, C. A., & Baum, A. (1989). Chronic stress, leukocyte-subpopulations, and humoral response to latent viruses. *Health Psychology, 8,* 389–402. (12)

McNaughton, N., & Corr, P. J. (2004). A two-dimensional neuropsychology of defense: Fear/anxiety and defensive distance. *Neuroscience and Biobehavioral Reviews, 28,* 285–305. (12)

McPartland, J., DiMarzo, V., de Petrocellis, L., Mercer, A., & Glass, M. (2001). Cannabinoid receptors are absent in insects. *Journal of Comparative Neurology, 436,* 423–429. (3)

Meddis, R., Pearson, A. J. D., & Langford, G. (1973). An extreme case of healthy insomnia. *EEG and Clinical Neurophysiology, 35,* 213–214. (9)

Mednick, S. C., Nakayama, K., Cantero, J. L., Atienza, M., Levin, A. A., Pathak, N., et al. (2002). The restorative effect of naps on perceptual deterioration. *Nature Neuroscience, 5,* 677–681. (9)

Meister, M., Wong, R. O. L., Baylor, D. A., & Shatz, C. J. (1991). Synchronous bursts of action potentials in ganglion cells of the developing mammalian retina. *Science, 252,* 939–943. (5)

Mellor, J., & Nicoll, R. A. (2001). Hippocampal mossy fiber LTP is independent of postsynaptic calcium. *Nature Neuroscience, 4,* 125–126. (13)

Melone, M., Vitellaro-Zuccarello, L., Vallejo-Illarramendi, A., Pérez-Samartin, A., Matute, C., Cozzi, A., et al. (2001). The expression of glutamate transporter

GLT-1 in the rat cerebral cortex is downregulated by the antipsychotic drug clozapine. *Molecular Psychiatry, 6,* 380–386. (15)

Meltzer, H. Y., Matsubara, S., & Lee, J.-C. (1989). Classification of typical and atypical antipsychotic drugs on the basis of dopamine D-1, D-2 and serotonin$_2$ pKi values. *Journal of Pharmacology and Experimental Therapeutics, 251,* 238–246. (15)

Melzack, R., & Wall, P. D. (1965). Pain mechanisms: A new theory. *Science, 150,* 971–979. (7)

Mergen, M., Mergen, H., Ozata, M., Oner, R., & Oner, C. (2001). A novel melanocortin 4 receptor (MC4R) gene mutation associated with morbid obesity. *Journal of Clinical Endocrinology & Metabolism, 86,* 3448–3451. (10)

Merton, P. A. (1972). How we control the contraction of our muscles. *Scientific American, 226*(5), 30–37. (8)

Merzenich, M. M., Nelson, R. J., Stryker, M. P., Cynader, M. S., Schoppman, A., & Zook, J. M. (1984). Somatosensory cortical map changes following digit amputation in adult monkeys. *Journal of Comparative Neurology, 224,* 591–605. (5)

Mesulam, M.-M. (1995). Cholinergic pathways and the ascending reticular activating system of the human brain. *Annals of the New York Academy of Sciences, 757,* 169–179. (4, 9)

Meyer-Bahlburg, H. F. L. (2005). Gender identity outcome in female-raised 46,XY persons with penile agenesis, cloacal exstrophy of the bladder, or penile ablation. *Archives of Sexual Behavior, 34,* 423–438. (11)

Meyer-Lindenberg, A., Hariri, A. R., Munoz, K. E., Mervis, C. B., Mattay, V. S., Morris, C. A., et al. (2005). Neural correlates of genetically abnormal social cognition in Williams syndrome. *Nature Neuroscience, 8,* 991–993. (14)

Meyer-Lindenberg, A., Kohn, P., Mervis, C. B., Kippenhan, J. S., Olsen, R. K., Morris, C. A., et al. (2004). Neural basis of genetically determined visuospatial construction deficit in Williams syndrome. *Neuron, 43,* 623–631. (14)

Meyer-Lindenberg, A., Miletich, R. S., Kohn, P. D., Esposito, G., Carson, R. E., Quarantelli, M., et al. (2002). Reduced prefrontal activity predicts exaggerated striatal dopaminergic function in schizophrenia. *Nature Neuroscience, 5,* 267–271. (15)

Mezzanotte, W. S., Tangel, D. J., & White, D. P. (1992). Waking genioglossal electromyogram in sleep apnea patients versus normal controls (a neuromuscular compensatory mechanism). *Journal of Clinical Investigation, 89,* 1571–1579. (9)

Mihalcescu, I., Hsing, W., & Leibler, S. (2004). Resilient circadian oscillator revealed in individual cyanobacteria. *Nature, 430,* 81–85. (9)

Mihic, S. J., Ye, Q., Wick, M. J., Koltchine, V. V., Krasowski, M. D., Finn, S. E., et al. (1997). Sites of alcohol and volatile anaesthetic action on GABA$_A$ and glycine receptors. *Nature, 389,* 385–389. (15)

Milberger, S., Biederman, J., Faraone, S. V., Chen, L., & Jones, J. (1996). Is maternal smoking during pregnancy a risk factor for attention deficit hyperactivity disorder in children? *American Journal of Psychiatry, 153,* 1138–1142. (5)

Miles, F. A., & Evarts, E. V. (1979). Concepts of motor organization. *Annual Review of Psychology, 30,* 327–362. (8)

Millán, J. del R., Renkens, F., Mouriño, J., & Gerstner, W. (2004). Brain-actuated interaction. *Artificial Intelligence, 159,* 241–259. (8)

Millar, J. K., Pickard, B. S., Mackie, S., James, R., Christie, S., Buchanan, S. R., et al. (2005). DISC1 and PDE4B are interacting genetic factors in schizophrenia that regulate cAMP signaling. *Science, 310,* 1187–1191. (15)

Miller, E. (2000). The prefrontal cortex and cognitive control. *Nature Reviews Neuroscience, 1,* 59–65. (4)

Miller, W. C., & DeLong, M. R. (1988). Parkinsonian symptomatology: An anatomical and physiological analysis. *Annals of the New York Academy of Sciences, 515,* 287–302. (8)

Milner, B. (1959). The memory defect in bilateral hippocampal lesions. *Psychiatric Research Reports, 11,* 43–58. (13)

Minokoshi, Y., Alquier, T., Furukawa, N., Kim, Y.-B., Lee, A., Xue, B., et al. (2004). AMP-kinase regulates food intake by responding to hormonal and nutrient signals in the hypothalamus. *Nature, 428,* 569–574. (10)

Mirescu, C., Peters, J. D., & Gould, E. (2004). Early life experience alters response of adult neurogenesis to stress. *Nature Neuroscience, 7,* 841–846. (12)

Misrahi, M., Meduri, G., Pissard, S., Bouvattier, C., Beau, I., Loosfelt, H., et al. (1997). Comparison of immunocytochemical and molecular features with the phenotype in a case of incomplete male pseudohermaphroditism associated with a mutation of the luteinizing hormone receptor. *Journal of Clinical Endocrinology & Metabolism, 82,* 2159–2165. (11)

Mitchell, D. E. (1980). The influence of early visual experience on visual perception. In C. S. Harris (Ed.), *Visual coding and adaptability* (pp. 1–50). Hillsdale, NJ: Erlbaum. (6)

Mitchell, D. E., Gingras, G., & Kind, P. C. (2001). Initial recovery of vision after early monocular deprivation in kittens is faster when both eyes are open. *Proceedings of the National Academy of Sciences, USA, 98,* 11662–11667. (6)

Miyahara, E., Pokorny, J., Smith, V. C., Baron, R., & Baron, E. (1998). Color vision in two observers with highly biased LWS/MWS cone ratios. *Vision Research, 38,* 601–612. (6)

Miyazawa, A., Fujiyoshi, Y., & Unwin, N. (2003). Structure and gating mechanism of the acetylcholine receptor pore. *Nature, 423,* 949–955. (3)

Mizoguchi, K., Ishige, A., Takeda, S., Aburada, M., & Tabira, T. (2004). Endogenous glucocorticoids are essential for maintaining prefrontal cortical cognitive function. *Journal of Neuroscience, 24,* 5492–5499. (12)

Mochizuki, T., Crocker, A., McCormack, S., Yanagisawa, M., Sakurai, T., & Scammell, T. E. (2004). Behavioral state instability in orexin knock-out mice. *Journal of Neuroscience, 24,* 6291–6300. (9)

Modell, S., Ising, M., Holsboer, F., & Lauer, C. J. (2005). The Munich vulnerability study on affective disorders: Premorbid polysomnographic profile of affected high-risk probands. *Biological Psychiatry, 58,* 694–699. (15)

Moeller, F. G., Dougherty, D. M., Swann, A. C., Collins, D., Davis, C. M., & Cherek, D. R. (1996). Tryptophan depletion and aggressive responding in healthy males. *Psychopharmacology, 126,* 97–103. (12)

Mohn, A., Gainetdinov, R. R., Caron, M. G., & Koller, B. H. (1999). Mice with reduced NMDA receptor expression display behaviors related to schizophrenia. *Cell, 98,* 427–436. (15)

Mohr, C., Landis, T., Bracha, H. S., & Brugger, P. (2003). Opposite turning behavior in right-handers and non-right-handers suggests a link between handedness and cerebral dopamine asymmetries. *Behavioral Neuroscience, 117,* 1448–1452. (14)

Moita, M. A. P., Rosis, S., Zhou, Y., LeDoux, J. E., & Blair, H. T. (2004). Putting fear in its place: Remapping of hippocampus place cells during fear conditioning. *Journal of Neuroscience, 24,* 7015–7023. (13)

Money, J. (1967). Sexual problems of the chronically ill. In C. W. Wahl (Ed.), *Sexual problems: Diagnosis and treatment in medical practice* (pp. 266–287). New York: Free Press. (8)

Money, J., & Ehrhardt, A. A. (1972). *Man & woman, boy & girl.* Baltimore, MD: Johns Hopkins University Press. (11)

Money, J., & Lewis, V. (1966). IQ, genetics and accelerated growth: Adrenogenital syndrome. *Bulletin of the Johns Hopkins Hospital, 118,* 365–373. (11)

Money, J., & Schwartz, M. (1978). Biosocial determinants of gender identity differentiation and development. In J. B. Hutchison (Ed.), *Biological determinants of sexual behaviour* (pp. 765–784). Chichester, England: Wiley. (11)

Monteleone, P., Luisi, S., Tonetti, A., Bernardi, F., Genazzani, A. D., Luisi, M., et al. (2000). Allopregnanolone concentrations and premenstrual syndrome. *European Journal of Endocrinology, 142,* 269–273. (11)

Monti-Bloch, L., Jennings-White, C., & Berliner, D. L. (1998). The human vomeronasal system: A review. *Annals of the New York Academy of Sciences, 855,* 373–389. (7)

Monti-Bloch, L., Jennings-White, C., Dolberg, D. S., & Berliner, D. L. (1994). The human vomeronasal system. *Psychoneuroendocrinology, 19,* 673–686. (7)

Montoya, A. G., Sorrentino, R., Lucas, S. E., & Price, B. H. (2002). Long-term neuropsychiatric consequences of "Ecstasy" (MDMA): A review. *Harvard Review of Psychiatry, 10,* 212–220. (3)

Moorcroft, W. H. (1993). *Sleep, dreaming, & sleep disorders* (2nd ed.). Lanham, MD: University Press of America. (9)

Moore, L. B., Goodwin, B., Jones, S. A., Wisely, G. B., Serabjit-Singh, C. J., Willson, T. M., et al. (2000). St. John's wort induces hepatic drug metabolism through activation of the pregnane X receptor. *Proceedings of the National Academy of Sciences, USA, 97,* 7500–7502. (15)

Moore, T., Rodman, H. R., Repp, A. B., & Gross, C. G. (1995). Localization of visual stimuli after striate cortex damage in monkeys: Parallels with human blindsight. *Proceedings of the National Academy of Sciences, USA, 92,* 8215–8218. (6)

Moore-Ede, M. C., Czeisler, C. A., & Richardson, G. S. (1983). Circadian timekeeping in health and disease. *New England Journal of Medicine, 309,* 469–476. (9)

Morgan, D., Diamond, D. M., Gottschall, P. E., Ugen, K. E., Dickey, C., Hardy, J., et al. (2000). Aß peptide vaccination prevents memory loss in an animal model of Alzheimer's disease. *Nature, 408,* 982–985. (13)

Mori, K., Mataga, N., & Imamura, K. (1992). Differential specificities of single mitral cells in rabbit olfactory bulb for a homologous series of fatty acid odor molecules. *Journal of Neurophysiology, 67,* 786–789. (7)

Morland, A. B., Lê, S., Carroll, E., Hoffmann, M. B., & Pambakian, A. (2004). The role of spared calcarine cortex and lateral occipital cortex in the responses of human hemianopes to visual motion. *Journal of Cognitive Neuroscience, 16,* 204–218. (6)

Morley, J. E., Levine, A. S., Grace, M., & Kneip, J. (1985). Peptide YY (PYY), a potent orexigenic agent. *Brain Research, 341,* 200–203. (10)

Morris, J. A., Jordan, C. L., & Breedlove, S. M. (2004). Sexual differentiation of the vertebrate nervous system. *Nature Neuroscience, 7,* 1034–1039. (11)

Morris, J. S., deBonis, M., & Dolan, R. J. (2002). Human amygdala responses to fearful eyes. *NeuroImage, 17,* 214–222. (12)

Morris, M., Lack, L., & Dawson, D. (1990). Sleep-onset insomniacs have delayed temperature rhythms. *Sleep, 13,* 1–14. (9)

Morrison, A. R., Sanford, L. D., Ball, W. A., Mann, G. L., & Ross, R. J. (1995). Stimulus-elicited behavior in rapid eye movement sleep without atonia. *Behavioral Neuroscience, 109,* 972–979. (9)

Morrone, M. C., Ross, J., & Burr, D. (2005). Saccadic eye movements cause compression of time as well as space. *Nature Neuroscience, 8,* 950–954. (6)

Morton, A. J., Wood, N. I., Hastings, M. H., Hurelbink, C., Barker, R. A., & Maywood, E. S. (2005). Disintegration of the sleep–wake cycle and circadian timing in Huntington's disease. *Journal of Neuroscience, 25,* 157–163. (9)

Moruzzi, G., & Magoun, H. W. (1949). Brain stem reticular formation and activation of the EEG. *Electroencephalography and Clinical Neurophysiology, 1,* 455–473. (9)

Moscovitch, M. (1992). Memory and working-with-memory: A component process model based on modules and central systems. *Journal of Cognitive Neuroscience, 4,* 257–267. (13)

Moscovitch, M., Winocur, G., & Behrmann, M. (1997). What is special about face recognition? Nineteen experiments on a person with visual object agnosia and dyslexia but normal face recognition. *Journal of Cognitive Neuroscience, 9,* 555–604. (6)

Moss, C. F., & Simmons, A. M. (1986). Frequency selectivity of hearing in the green treefrog, *Hyla cinerea*. *Journal of Comparative Physiology, A, 159,* 257–266. (7)

Moss, S. J., & Smart, T. G. (2001). Constructing inhibitory synapses. *Nature Reviews Neuroscience, 2,* 240–250. (3)

Mrosovsky, N. (1990). *Rheostasis: The physiology of change.* New York: Oxford University Press. (10)

Mrzljak, L., Bergson, C., Pappy, M., Huff, R., Levenson, R., & Goldman-Rakic, P. S. (1996). Localization of dopamine D4 receptors in GABAergic neurons of the primate brain. *Nature, 381,* 245–248. (15)

Mueller, K. L., Hoon, M. A., Erlenbach, I., Chandrashekar, J., Zuker, C. S., & Ryba, N. J. P. (2005). The receptors and coding logic for bitter taste. *Nature, 434,* 225–229. (7)

Mukamel, R., Gelbard, H., Arieli, A., Hasson, U., Fried, I., & Malach, R. (2005). Coupling between neuronal firing, field potentials, and fMRI in human auditory cortex. *Science, 309,* 951–954. (4)

Mulligan, S. J., & MacVicar, B. A. (2004). Calcium transients in astrocyte end feet cause cerebrovascular constrictions. *Nature, 431,* 195–199. (2)

Munk, M. H. J., Roelfsema, P. R., König, P., Engel, A. K., & Singer, W. (1996). Role of reticular activation in the modulation of intracortical synchronization. *Science, 272,* 271–274. (9)

Munoz, D. P., & Everling, S. (2004). Look away: The anti-saccade task and the voluntary control of eye movement. *Nature Reviews Neuroscience, 5,* 218–228. (6)

Münzberg, H., & Myers, M. G., Jr. (2005). Molecular and anatomical determinants of central leptin resistance. *Nature Neuroscience, 8,* 566–570. (10)

Murphy, F. C., Nimmo-Smith, I., & Lawrence, A. D. (2003). Functional neuroanatomy of emotions: A meta-analysis. *Cognitive, Affective, & Behavioral Neuroscience, 3,* 207–233. (12)

Murphy, M. R., Checkley, S. A., Seckl, J. R., & Lightman, S. L. (1990). Naloxone inhibits oxytocin release at orgasm in man. *Journal of Clinical Endocrinology & Metabolism, 71,* 1056–1058. (11)

Murrell, J., Farlow, M., Ghetti, B., & Benson, M. D. (1991). A mutation in the amyloid precursor protein associated with hereditary Alzheimer's disease. *Science, 254,* 97–99. (13)

Myers, A., Holmans, P., Marshall, H., Kwon, J., Meyer, D., Ramic, D., et al. (2000). Susceptibility locus for Alzheimer's disease on chromosome 10. *Science, 290,* 2304–2305. (13)

Myers, J. J., & Sperry, R. W. (1985). Interhemispheric communication after section of the forebrain commissures. *Cortex, 21,* 249–260. (14)

Nadal, A., Díaz, M., & Valverde, M. A. (2001). The estrogen trinity: Membrane, cytosolic, and nuclear effects. *News in Physiological Sciences, 16,* 251–255. (11)

Nadarajah, B., & Parnavelas, J. G. (2002). Modes of neuronal migration in the developing cerebral cortex. *Nature Reviews Neuroscience, 3,* 423–432. (5)

Nader, K., Bechara, A., Roberts, D. C.. S., & van der Kooy, D. (1994). Neuroleptics block high- but not low-dose heroin place preferences: Further evidence for a two-system model of motivation. *Behavioral Neuroscience, 108,* 1128–1138. (3)

Nadkarni, S., & Jung, P. (2003). Spontaneous oscillations of dressed neurons: A new mechanism for epilepsy? *Physical Review Letters, 91,* 268101. (2)

Nagarajan, S., Mahncke, H., Salz, T., Tallal, P., Roberts, T., & Merzenich, M. M. (1999). Cortical auditory signal processing in poor readers. *Proceedings of the National Academy of Sciences, USA, 96,* 6483–6488. (14)

Nagayama, T., Sinor, A. D., Simon, R. P., Chen, J., Graham, S. H., Jin, K., et al. (1999). Cannabinoids and neuroprotection in global and focal cerebral ischemia and in neuronal cultures. *Journal of Neuroscience, 19,* 2987–2995. (5)

Naggert, J. K., Fricker, L. D., Varlamov, O., Nishina, P. M., Rouille, Y., Steiner, D. F., et al. (1995). Hyperproinsulinaemia in obese fat/fat mice associated with a carboxypeptidase E mutation which reduces enzyme activity. *Nature Genetics, 10,* 135–142. (10)

Nakashima, Y., Kuwamura, T., & Yogo, Y. (1995). Why be a both-ways sex changer? *Ethology, 101,* 301–307. (11)

Narrow, W. E., Rae, D. S., Robins, L. N., & Regier, D. A. (2002). Revised prevalence estimates of mental disorders in the United States. *Archives of General Psychiatry, 59,* 115–123. (15)

Narumoto, J., Okada, T., Sadato, N., Fukui, K., & Yonekura, Y. (2001). Attention to emotion modulates fMRI activity in human right superior temporal sulcus. *Cognitive Brain Research, 12,* 225–231. (12, 14)

Nathans, J., Davenport, C. M., Maumenee, I. H., Lewis, R. A., Hejtmancik, J. F., Litt, M., et al. (1989). Molecular genetics of human blue cone monochromacy. *Science, 245,* 831–838. (6)

Naylor, E., Bergmann, B. M., Krauski, K., Zee, P. C., Takahashi, J. S., Vitaterna, M. H., et al. (2000). The circadian clock mutation alters sleep homeostasis in the mouse. *Journal of Neuroscience, 20,* 8138–8143. (9)

Nebes, R. D. (1974). Hemispheric specialization in commissurotomized man. *Psychological Bulletin, 81,* 1–14. (14)

Nef, P. (1998). How we smell: The molecular and cellular bases of olfaction. *News in Physiological Sciences, 13,* 1–5. (7)

Neitz, M., Kraft, T. W., & Neitz, J. (1998). Expression of L cone pigment gene subtypes in females. *Vision Research, 38,* 3221–3225. (6)

Nelson, C. A., Wewerka, S., Thomas, K. M., Tribby-Walbridge, S., deRegnier, R., & Georgieff, M. (2000). Neurocognitive sequelae of infants of diabetic mothers. *Behavioral Neuroscience, 114,* 950–956. (5)

Nelson, D. O., & Prosser, C. L. (1981). Intracellular recordings from thermosensitive preoptic neurons. *Science, 213,* 787–789. (10)

Netter, F. H. (1983). *CIBA collection of medical illustrations: Vol. 1. Nervous system.* New York: CIBA. (11)

Neumeister, A., Nugent, A. C., Waldeck, T., Geraci, M., Schwarz, M., Bonne, O., et al. (2004). Neural and behavioral responses to tryptophan depletion in unmedicated patients with remitted major depressive disorder and controls. *Archives of General Psychiatry, 61,* 765–773. (15)

Neves-Pereira, M., Mundo, E., Muglia, P., King, N., Macciardi, F., & Kennedy, J. L. (2002). The brain-derived neurotrophic factor gene confers susceptibility to bipolar disorder: Evidence from a family-based association study. *American Journal of Human Genetics, 71,* 651–655. (15)

Neville, H. J., Bavelier, D., Corina, D., Rauschecker, J., Karni, A., Lalwani, A., et al. (1998). Cerebral organization for language in deaf and hearing subjects: Biological constraints and effects of experience. *Proceedings of the National Academy of Sciences, USA,* 95, 922–929. (14)

Newcomer, J. W., Haupt, D. W., Fucetola, R., Melson, A. K., Schweiger, J. A., Cooper, B. P., et al. (2002). Abnormalities in glucose regulation during antipsychotic treatment of schizophrenia. *Archives of General Psychiatry, 59,* 337–345. (15)

Newcomer, J. W., Selke, G., Melson, A. K., Hershey, T., Craft, S., Richards, K., et al. (1999). Decreased memory performance in healthy humans induced by stress-level cortisol treatment. *Archives of General Psychiatry, 56,* 527–533. (13)

Nicholas, M. K., & Arnason, B. G. W. (1992). Immunologic responses in central nervous system transplantation. *Seminars in the Neurosciences, 4,* 273–283. (8)

Nicklas, W. J., Saporito, M., Basma, A., Geller, H. M., & Heikkila, R. E. (1992). Mitochondrial mechanisms of neurotoxicity. *Annals of the New York Academy of Sciences, 648,* 28–36. (8)

Nicolelis, M. A. L. (2001). Actions from thoughts. *Nature, 409,* 403–407. (8)

Nicolelis, M. A. L., Ghazanfar, A. A., Stambaugh, C. R., Oliveira, L. M. O., Laubach, M., Chapin, J. K., et al. (1998). Simultaneous encoding of tactile information by three primate cortical areas. *Nature Neuroscience, 1,* 621–630. (4)

Nie, Z., Schweitzer, P., Roberts, A. J., Madamba, S. G., Moore, S. D., & Siggins, G. R. (2004). Ethanol augments GABAergic transmission in the central amygdala via CRF1 receptors. *Science, 303,* 1512–1514. (12)

Nieuwenhuys, R., Voogd, J., & vanHuijzen, C. (1988). *The human central nervous system* (3rd Rev. ed.). Berlin: Springer-Verlag. (4, 10, 12, 14)

Niki, K., & Luo, J. (2002). An fMRI study on the time-limited role of the medial temporal lobe in long-term topographical autobiographic memory. *Journal of Cognitive Neuroscience, 14,* 500–507. (13)

Nilsson, G. E. (1999, December). The cost of a brain. *Natural History, 108,* 66–73. (4)

Nishimaru, H., Restrepo, C. E., Ryge, J., Yanagawa, Y., & Kiehn, O. (2005). Mammalian motor neurons corelease glutamate and acetylcholine at central synapses. *Proceedings of the National Academy of Sciences, USA, 102,* 5245–5249. (3)

Noaghiul, S., & Hibbeln, J. R. (2003). Cross-national comparisons of seafood consumption and rates of bipolar disorders. *American Journal of Psychiatry, 160,* 2222–2227. (15)

Noble, E. P., Ozkaragoz, T. Z., Ritchie, T. L., Zhang, X., Belin, T. R., & Sparkes, R. S. (1998). D_2 and D_4 dopamine receptor polymorphisms and personality. *American Journal of Medical Genetics, 81,* 257–267. (3)

Nopoulos, P., Flaum, M., O'Leary, D., & Andreasen, N. C. (2000). Sexual dimorphism in the human brain: Evaluation of tissue volume, tissue composition and surface anatomy using magnetic resonance imaging. *Psychiatry Research: Neuroimaging Section, 98,* 1–13. (11)

Nopoulos, P. C., Giedd, J. N., Andreasen, N. C., & Rapoport, J. L. (1998). Frequency and severity of enlarged cavum septi pellucidi in childhood-onset schizophrenia. *American Journal of Psychiatry, 155,* 1074–1079. (15)

Nordenström, A., Servin, A., Bohlin, G., Laarsson, A., & Wedell, A. (2002). Sex-typed toy play behavior correlates with the degree of prenatal androgen exposure assessed by *CYP21* genotype in girls with congenital adrenal hyperplasia. *Journal of Clinical Endocrinology & Metabolism, 87,* 5119–5124. (11)

Norman, R. A., Tataranni, P. A., Pratley, R., Thompson, D. B., Hanson, R. L., Prochazka, M., et al. (1998). Autosomal genomic scan for loci linked to obesity and energy metabolism in Pima Indians. *American Journal of Human Genetics, 62,* 659–668. (10)

North, R. A. (1989). Neurotransmitters and their receptors: From the clone to the clinic. *Seminars in the Neurosciences, 1,* 81–90. (2)

North, R. A. (1992). Cellular actions of opiates and cocaine. *Annals of the New York Academy of Sciences, 654,* 1–6. (3)

Nosenko, N. D., & Reznikov, A. G. (2001). Prenatal stress and sexual differentiation of monoaminergic brain systems. *Neurophysiology, 33,* 197–206. (11)

Nottebohm, F. (2002). Why are some neurons replaced in adult brain? *Journal of Neuroscience, 22,* 624–628. (5)

Nowak, M. A., Komarova, N. L., & Niyogi, P. (2002). Computational and evolutionary aspects of language. *Nature, 417,* 611–617. (14)

Nunn, J. A., Gregory, L. J., Brammer, M., Williams, S. C. R., Parslow, D. M., Morgan, M. J., et al. (2002). Functional magnetic resonance imaging of synesthesia: Activation of V4/V8 by spoken words. *Nature Neuroscience, 5,* 371–375. (7)

Ó Scalaidhe, S. P., Wilson, F. A. W., & Goldman-Rakic, P. S. (1997). Areal segregation of face-processing neurons in prefrontal cortex. *Science, 278,* 1135–1138. (6)

O'Connor, D. H., Fukui, M. M., Pinsk, M. A., & Kastner, S. (2002). Attention modulates responses in the human lateral geniculate nucleus. *Nature Neuroscience, 5,* 1203–1209. (6)

O'Dowd, B. F., Lefkowitz, R. J., & Caron, M. G. (1989). Structure of the adrenergic and related receptors. *Annual Review of Neuroscience, 12,* 67–83. (3)

Ohayon, M. M., & Partinen, M. (2002). Insomnia and global sleep dissatisfaction in Finland. *Journal of Sleep Research, 11,* 339–346. (9)

Ohno-Shosaku, T., Maejima, T., & Kano, M. (2001). Endogenous cannabinoids mediate retrograde signals from depolarized postsynaptic neurons to presynaptic terminals. *Neuron, 29,* 729–738. (3)

Oka, Y., Omura, M., Kataoka, H., & Touhara, K. (2004). Olfactory receptor antagonism between odorants. *The EMBO Journal, 23,* 120–126. (7)

O'Kane, G., Kensinger, E. A., & Corkin, S. (2004). Evidence for semantic learning in profound amnesia: An investigation with patient H. M. *Hippocampus, 14,* 417–425. (13)

O'Keefe, J., & Burgess, N. (1996). Geometric determinants of the place fields of hippocampal neurons. *Nature, 381,* 425–434. (13)

Olanow, C. W., Goetz, C. G., Kordower, J. H., Stoessl, A. J., Sossi, V., Brin, M. F., et al. (2003). A double-blind controlled trial of bilateral fetal nigral transplantation in Parkinson's disease. *Annals of Neurology, 54,* 403–414. (8)

Olausson, H., Lamarre, Y., Backlund, H., Morin, C., Wallin, B. G., Starck, G., et al. (2002). Unmyelinated tactile afferents signal touch and project to insular cortex. *Nature Neuroscience, 5,* 900–904. (7)

Olds, J. (1958). Satiation effects in self-stimulation of the brain. *Journal of Comparative and Physiological Psychology, 51,* 675–678. (15)

Olds, J., & Milner, P. (1954). Positive reinforcement produced by electrical stimulation of the septal area and other regions of the rat brain. *Journal of Comparative and Physiological Psychology, 47,* 419–428. (15)

O'Leary, A. (1990). Stress, emotion, and human immune function. *Psychological Bulletin, 108,* 363–382. (12)

Olney, J. W., & Farber, N. B. (1995). Glutamate receptor dysfunction and schizophrenia. *Archives of General Psychiatry, 52,* 998–1007. (15)

Olson, D. J., Kamil, A. C., Balda, R. P., & Nims, P. J. (1995). Performance of four seed-caching corvid species in operant tests of nonspatial and spatial memory. *Journal of Comparative Psychology, 109,* 173–181. (13)

Olson, E. J., Boeve, B. F., & Silber, M. H. (2000). Rapid eye movement sleep behaviour disorder: Demographic, clinical and laboratory findings in 93 cases. *Brain, 123,* 331–339. (9)

Olton, D. S., & Papas, B. C. (1979). Spatial memory and hippocampal function. *Neuropsychologia, 17,* 669–682. (13)

Olton, D. S., Walker, J. A., & Gage, F. H. (1978). Hippocampal connections and spatial discrimination. *Brain Research, 139,* 295–308. (13)

O'Reilly, R. C., & Rudy, J. W. (2001). Conjunctive representations in learning and memory: Principles of cortical and hippocampal function. *Psychological Review, 108,* 311–345. (13)

Ornstein, R. (1997). *The right mind.* New York: Harcourt Brace. (14)

Osborne, L. C., Bialek, W., & Lisberger, S. G. (2004). Time course of information about motion direction in visual area MT of macaque monkeys. *Journal of Neuroscience, 24,* 3210–3222. (6)

Oswald, A.-M., Chacron, M. J., Doiron, B., Bastian, J., & Maler, L. (2004). Parallel processing of sensory input by bursts and isolated spikes. *Journal of Neuroscience, 24,* 4351–4362. (2)

Otmakhov, N., Tao-Cheng, J.-H., Carpenter, S., Asrican, B., Dosemici, A., & Reese, T. S. (2004). Persistent accumulation of calcium/calmodulin-dependent protein kinase II in dendritic spines after induction of NMDA receptor-dependent chemical long-term potentiation. *Journal of Neuroscience, 25,* 9324–9331. (13)

Ouchi, Y., Yoshikawa, E., Okada, H., Futatsubashi, M., Sekine, Y., Iyo, M., et al. (1999). Alterations in binding site density of dopamine transporter in the striatum, orbitofrontal cortex, and amygdala in early Parkinson's disease: Compartment analysis for ß-CFT binding with positron emission tomography. *Annals of Neurology, 45,* 601–610. (8)

Paladini, C. A., Fiorillo, C. D., Morikawa, H., & Williams, J. T. (2001). Amphetamine selectively blocks inhibitory glutamate transmission in dopamine neurons. *Nature Neuroscience, 4,* 275–281. (3)

Palinkas, L. A. (2003). The psychology of isolated and confined environments. *American Psychologist, 58,* 353–363. (9)

Palva, S., Linkenkaer-Hansen, K., Näätänen, R., & Palva, J. M. (2005). Early neural correlates of conscious somatosensory perception. *Journal of Neuroscience, 25,* 5248–5258. (7)

Panda, S., Sato, T. K., Castrucci, A. M., Rollag, M. D., DeGrip, W. J., Hogenesch, J. B., et al. (2002). Melanopsin (*Opn4*) requirement for normal light-induced circadian phase shifting. *Science, 298,* 2213–2216. (9)

Pandey, G. N., Pandey, S. C., Dwivedi, Y., Sharma, R. P., Janicak, P. G., & Davis, J. M. (1995). Platelet serotonin-2A receptors: A potential biological marker for suicidal behavior. *American Journal of Psychiatry, 152,* 850–855. (12)

Pankevich, D. E., Baum, M. J., & Cherry, J. A. (2004). Olfactory sex discrimination persists, whereas the preference for urinary odorants from estrous females disappears in male mice after vomeronasal organ removal. *Journal of Neuroscience, 24,* 9451–9457. (7)

Panksepp, J. (1998). Attention deficit hyperactivity disorders, psychostimulants, and intolerance of childhood playfulness: A tragedy in the making? *Current Directions in Psychological Science, 7,* 91–98. (14)

Panov, A. V., Gutekunst, C.-A., Leavitt, B. R., Hayden, M. R, Burke, J. R., Strittmatter, W. J., et al. (2002). Early mitochondrial calcium defects in Huntington's disease are a direct effect of polyglutamines. *Nature Neuroscience, 5,* 731–736. (8)

Pappone, P. A., & Cahalan, M. D. (1987). Pandinus imperator scorpion venom blocks voltage-gated potassium channels in nerve fibers. *Journal of Neuroscience, 7,* 3300–3305. (2)

Pardal, R., & López-Barneo, J. (2002). Low glucose-sensing cells in the carotid body. *Nature Neuroscience, 5,* 197–198. (10)

Paré, M., Smith, A. M., & Rice, F. L. (2002). Distribution and terminal arborizations of cutaneous mechanoreceptors in the glabrous finger pads of the monkey. *Journal of Comparative Neurology, 445,* 347–359. (7)

Paredes, R. G., & Vazquez, B. (1999). What do female rats like about sex? Paced mating. *Behavioural Brain Research, 105,* 117–127. (11)

Parent, M. B., Habib, M. K., & Baker, G. B. (1999). Task-dependent effects of the antidepressant/antipanic drug phenelzine on memory. *Psychopharmacology, 142,* 280–288. (9)

Park, S., Holzman, P. S., & Goldman-Rakic, P. S. (1995). Spatial working memory deficits in the relatives of schizophrenic patients. *Archives of General Psychiatry, 52,* 821–828. (15)

Park, T. J., Comer, C., Carol, A., Lu, Y., Hong, H.-S., & Rice, F. L. (2003). Somatosensory organization and behavior in naked mole-rats: II. Peripheral structures, innervation, and selective lack of neuropeptides associated with thermoregulation and pain. *Journal of Comparative Neurology, 465,* 104–120. (10)

Parker, G. H. (1922). *Smell, taste, and allied senses in the vertebrates.* Philadelphia: Lippincott. (7)

Parkes, L., Lund, J., Angelucci, A., Solomon, J. A., & Morgan, M. (2001). Compulsory averaging of crowded orientation signals in human vision. *Nature Neuroscience, 4,* 739–744. (6)

Parr-Brownlie, L. C., & Hyland, B. I. (2005). Bradykinesia induced by dopamine D_2 receptor blockade is associated with reduced motor cortex activity in the rat. *Journal of Neuroscience, 25,* 5700–5709. (8)

Parrott, A. C. (2001). Human psychopharmacology of Ecstasy (MDMA): A review of 15 years of empirical research. *Human Psychopharmacology: Clinical and Experimental, 16,* 557–577. (3)

Pascalis, O., Scott, L. S., Kelly, D. J., Shannon, R. W., Nicholson, E., Coleman, M., et al. (2005). Plasticity of face processing in infancy. *Proceedings of the National Academy of Sciences, USA, 102,* 5297–5300. (6)

Pascual-Leone, A., & Walsh, V. (2001). Fast backprojections from the motion to the primary visual area necessary for visual awareness. *Science, 292,* 510–512. (6)

Pasterski, V. L., Geffner, M. E., Brain, C., Hindmarsh, P., Brook, C., & Hines, M. (2005). Prenatal hormones and postnatal socialization by parents as determinants of male-typical toy play in girls with congenital adrenal hyperplasia. *Child Development, 76,* 264–278. (11)

Patte, C., Gandolfo, P., Leprince, J., Thoumas, J. L., Fontaine, M., Vaudry, H., et al. (1999). GABA inhibits endozepine release from cultured rat astrocytes. *Glia, 25,* 404–411. (12)

Paulesu, E., Démonet, J.-F., Fazio, F., McCrory, E., Chanoine, V., Brunswick, N., et al. (2001). Dyslexia: Cultural diversity and biological unity. *Science, 291,* 2165–2167. (14)

Paulesu, E., Frith, U., Snowling, M., Gallagher, A., Morton, J., Frackowiak, R. S. J., et al. (1996). Is developmental dyslexia a disconnection syndrome? *Brain, 119,* 143–157. (14)

Paus, T., Marrett, S., Worsley, K. J., & Evans, A. C. (1995). Extraretinal modulation of cerebral blood flow in the human visual cortex: Implications for saccadic suppression. *Journal of Neurophysiology, 74,* 2179–2183. (6)

Pavlov, I. P. (1927). *Conditioned reflexes.* Oxford, England: Oxford University Press. (13)

Pearl, P. L., Weiss, R. E., & Stein, M. A. (2001). Medical mimics. *Annals of the New York Academy of Sciences, 931,* 97–112. (14)

Peciña, S., Cagniard, B., Berridge, K. C., Aldridge, J. W., & Zhuang, X. (2003). Hyperdopaminergic mutant mice have higher "wanting" but not "liking" for sweet rewards. *Journal of Neuroscience, 23,* 9395–9402. (15)

Pedersen, C. A., Caldwell, J. D., Walker, C., Ayers, G., & Mason, G. A. (1994). Oxytocin activates the postpartum onset of rat maternal behavior in the ventral tegmentum and medial preoptic areas. *Behavioral Neuroscience, 108,* 1163–1171. (11)

Pegna, A. J., Khateb, A., Lazeyrus, F., & Seghier, M. L. (2004). Discriminating emotional faces without primary visual cortices involves the right amygdala. *Nature Neuroscience, 8,* 24–25. (12)

Peigneux, P., Laureys, S., Fuchs, S., Collette, F., Perrin, F., Reggers, J., et al. (2004). Are spatial memories strengthened in the human hippocampus during slow wave sleep? *Neuron, 44,* 535–545. (9)

Pellis, S. M., O'Brien, D. P., Pellis, V. C., Teitelbaum, P., Wolgin, D. L., & Kennedy, S. (1988). Escalation of feline predation along a gradient from avoidance through "play" to killing. *Behavioral Neuroscience, 102,* 760–777. (12)

Pellymounter, M. A., Cullen, M. J., Baker, M. B., Hecht, R., Winters, D., Boone, T., et al. (1995). Effects of the obese gene product on body weight regulation in *ob/ob* mice. *Science, 269,* 540–543. (10)

Penagos, H., Melcher, J. R., & Oxenham, A. J. (2004). A neural representation of pitch salience in nonprimary human auditory cortex revealed with functional magnetic resonance imaging. *Journal of Neuroscience, 24,* 6810–6815. (7)

Penfield, W. (1955). The permanent record of the stream of consciousness. *Acta Psychologica, 11,* 47–69. (13)

Penfield, W., & Milner, B. (1958). Memory deficit produced by bilateral lesions in the hippocampal zone. *Archives of Neurology and Psychiatry, 79,* 475–497. (13)

Penfield, W., & Perot, P. (1963). The brain's record of auditory and visual experience. *Brain, 86,* 595–696. (13)

Penfield, W., & Rasmussen, T. (1950). *The cerebral cortex of man.* New York: Macmillan. (4, 8)

Pennington, B. F., Filipek, P. A., Lefly, D., Chhabildas, N., Kennedy, D. N., Simon, J. H., et al. (2000). A twin MRI study of size variations in the human brain. *Journal of Cognitive Neuroscience, 12,* 223–232. (4)

Penton-Voak, I. S., Perrett, D. I., Castles, D. L., Kobayashi, T., Burt, D. M., Murray, L. K., et al. (1999). Menstrual cycle alters face preference. *Nature, 399,* 741–742. (11)

Pepperberg, I. M. (1981). Functional vocalizations by an African grey parrot. *Zeitschrift für Tierpsychologie, 55,* 139–160. (14)

Pepperberg, I. M. (1993). Cognition and communication in an African Grey parrot (*Psittacus erithacus*): Studies on a nonhuman, nonprimate, nonmammalian subject. In H. L. Roitblat, L. M. Herman, & P. E. Nachtigall (Eds.), *Language and communication: Comparative perspectives* (pp. 221–248). Hillsdale, NJ: Erlbaum. (14)

Pepperberg, I. M. (1994). Numerical competence in an African gray parrot (*Psittacus erithacus*). *Journal of Comparative Psychology, 108,* 36–44. (14)

Pepperberg, I. M. (2004). "Insightful" string-pulling in Grey parrots (*Psittacus erithacus*) is affected by vocal competence. *Animal Cognition, 7,* 263–266. (14)

Pericak-Vance, M. A., Bebout, J. L., Gaskell, P. C., Jr., Yamaoka, L. H., Hung, W.-Y., Alberts, M. J., et al. (1991). Linkage studies in familial Alzheimer disease: Evidence for chromosome 19 linkage. *American Journal of Human Genetics, 48,* 1034–1050. (13)

Perlow, M. J., Freed, W. J., Hoffer, B. J., Seiger, A., Olson, L., & Wyatt, R. J. (1979). Brain grafts reduce motor abnormalities produced by destruction of nigrostriatal dopamine system. *Science, 204,* 643–647. (8)

Perrone, J. A., & Thiele, A. (2001). Speed skills: Measuring the visual speed analyzing properties of primate MT neurons. *Nature Neuroscience, 4,* 526–532. (6)

Pert, C. B. (1997). *Molecules of emotion.* New York: Touchstone. (2)

Pert, C. B., & Snyder, S. H. (1973). The opiate receptor: Demonstration in nervous tissue. *Science, 179,* 1011–1014. (3, 7)

Pesenti, M., Zago, L., Crivello, F., Mellet, E., Samson, D., Duroux, B., et al. (2001). Mental calculation in a prodigy is sustained by right prefrontal and medial temporal areas. *Nature Neuroscience, 4,* 103–107. (4)

Pesold, C., & Treit, D. (1995). The central and basolateral amygdala differentially mediate the anxiolytic effect of benzodiazepines. *Brain Research, 671,* 213–221. (12)

Peters, F., Nicolson, N. A., Berkhof, J., Delespaul, P., & deVries, M. (2003). Effects of daily events on mood states in major depressive disorder. *Journal of Abnormal Psychology, 112,* 203–211. (15)

Peters, R. H., Sensenig, L. D., & Reich, M. J. (1973). Fixed-ratio performance following ventromedial hypothalamic lesions in rats. *Physiological Psychology, 1,* 136–138. (10)

Peterson, L. R., & Peterson, M. J. (1959). Short-term retention of individual verbal items. *Journal of Experimental Psychology, 58,* 193–198. (13)

Petitto, L. A., Zatorre, R. J., Gauna, K., Nikelski, E. J., Dostie, D., & Evans, A. C. (2000). Speech-like cerebral activity in profoundly deaf people processing signed languages: Implications for the neural basis of human language. *Proceedings of the National Academy of Sciences, USA, 97,* 13961–13966. (14)

Petrovic, P., Kalso, E., Petersson, K. M., & Ingvar, M. (2002). Placebo and opioid analgesia—Imaging a shared neuronal network. *Science, 295,* 1737–1740. (7)

Pezawas, L., Meyer-Lindenberg, A., Drabant, E. M., Verchinski, B. A., Munoz, K. E., Kolachana, B. S., et al. (2005). 5-HTTLPR polymorphism impacts human cingulate-amygdala interactions: A genetic susceptibility mechanism for depression. *Nature Neuroscience, 8,* 828–834. (15)

Pezawas, L., Verchinski, B. A., Mattay, V. S., Callicott, J. H., Kolachana, B. S., Straub, R. E., et al. (2004). The brain-derived neurotrophic factor val66met polymorphism and variation in human cortical morphology. *Journal of Neuroscience, 24,* 10099–10102. (4)

Pfaus, J. G., Shadiack, A., Van Soest, T., Tse, M., & Molinoff, P. (2004). Selective facilitation of sexual solicitation in the female rat by a melanocortin receptor agonist. *Proceedings of the National Academy of Sciences, USA, 101,* 10201–10204. (11)

Pham, K., McEwen, B. S., LeDoux, J. E., & Nader, K. (2005). Fear learning transiently impairs hippocampal cell proliferation. *Neuroscience, 130,* 17–24. (12)

Phan, K. L., Wager, T., Taylor, S. F., & Liberzon, I. (2002). Functional neuroanatomy of emotion: A meta-analysis of emotion activation studies in PET and fMRI. *NeuroImage, 16,* 331–348. (12)

Phelps, M. E., & Mazziotta, J. C. (1985). Positron emission tomography: Human brain function and biochemistry. *Science, 228,* 799–809. (4)

Philippot, P., Chapelle, G., & Blairy, S. (2002). Respiratory feedback in the generation of emotions. *Cognition and Emotion, 16,* 605–627. (12)

Phillips, M. L., Young, A. W., Senior, C., Brammer, M., Andrew, C., Calder, A. J., et al. (1997). A specific neural substrate for perceiving facial expressions of disgust. *Nature, 389,* 495–498. (12)

Phillips, T. J., Brown, K. J., Burkhart-Kasch, S., Wenger, C. D., Kelly, M. A., Rubinstein, M., et al. (1998). Alcohol preference and sensitivity are markedly reduced in mice lacking dopamine D_2 receptors. *Nature Neuroscience, 1,* 610–615. (15)

Piazza, M., Izard, V., Pinel, P., Le Bihan, D., & Dehaene, S. (2004). Tuning curves for approximate numerosity in the human intraparietal sulcus. *Neuron, 44,* 547–555. (4)

Piccini, P., Burn, D. J., Ceravolo, R., Maraganore, D., & Brooks, D. J. (1999). The role of inheritance in sporadic Parkinson's disease: Evidence from a longitudinal study of dopaminergic function in twins. *Annals of Neurology, 45,* 577–582. (8)

Pich, E. M., Pagliusi, S. R., Tessari, M., Talabot-Ayer, D., van Huijsduijnen, R. H., & Chiamulera, C. (1997). Common neural substrates for the addictive properties of nicotine and cocaine. *Science, 275,* 83–86. (3)

Pierri, J. N., Volk, C. L. E., Auh, S., Sampson, A., & Lewis, D. A. (2001). Decreased somal size of deep layer 3 pyramidal neurons in the prefrontal cortex of subjects with schizophrenia. *Archives of General Psychiatry, 58,* 466–473. (15)

Pillon, B., Ertle, S., Deweer, B., Sarazin, M., Agid, Y., & Dubois, B. (1996). Memory for spatial location is affected in Parkinson's disease. *Neuropsychologia, 34,* 77–85. (8)

Pinckard, K. L., Stellflug, J., Resko, J. A., Roselli, C. E., & Stormshak, F. (2000). Review: Brain aromatization and other factors affecting male reproductive behavior with emphasis on the sexual orientation of rams. *Domestic Animal Endocrinology, 18,* 83–96. (11)

Pinker, S. (1994). *The language instinct.* New York: HarperCollins. (14)

Pizzagalli, D. A., Nitschke, J. B., Oakes, T. R., Hendrick, A. M., Horras, K. A., Larson, C. L., et al. (2002). Brain electrical tomography in depression: The importance of symptom severity, anxiety, and melancholic features. *Biological Psychiatry, 52,* 73–85. (15)

Pizzorusso, T., Medini, P., Berardi, N., Chierzi, S., Fawcett, J. W., & Maffei, L. (2002). Reactivation of ocular dominance plasticity in the adult visual cortex. *Science, 298,* 1248–1251. (6)

Plihal, W., & Born, J. (1997). Effects of early and late nocturnal sleep on declarative and procedural memory. *Journal of Cognitive Neuroscience, 9,* 534–547. (9)

Plomin, R., Corley, R., DeFries, J. C., & Fulker, D. (1990). Individual differences in television viewing in early childhood: Nature as well as nurture. *Psychological Science, 1,* 371–377. (1)

Poldrack, R. A., Sabb, F. W., Foerde, K., Tom, S. M., Asarnow, R. F., Bookheimer, S. Y., et al. (2005). The neural correlates of motor skill automaticity. *Journal of Neuroscience, 25,* 5356–5364. (8)

Poling, A., Schlinger, H., & Blakely, E. (1988). Failure of the partial inverse benzodiazepine agonist Ro15-4513 to block the lethal effects of ethanol in rats. *Pharmacology, 31,* 945–947. (12)

Polley, D. B., Kvašňák, E., & Frostig, R. D. (2004). Naturalistic experience transforms sensory maps in the adult cortex of caged animals. *Nature, 429,* 67–71. (5)

Poltorak, M., Wright, R., Hemperly, J. J., Torrey, E. F., Issa, F., Wyatt, R. J., et al. (1997). Monozygotic twins discordant for schizophrenia are discordant for N-CAM and L1 in CSF. *Brain Research, 751,* 152–154. (5)

Poncer, J. C., & Malinow, R. (2001). Postsynaptic conversion of silent synapses during LTP affects synaptic gain and transmission dynamics. *Nature Neuroscience, 4,* 989–996. (13)

Pons, T. P., Garraghty, P. E., Ommaya, A. K., Kaas, J. H., Taub, E., & Mishkin, M. (1991). Massive cortical reorganization after sensory deafferentation in adult macaques. *Science, 252,* 1857–1860. (5)

Pontieri, F. E., Tanda, G., Orzi, F., & DiChiara, G. (1996). Effects of nicotine on the nucleus accumbens and similarity to those of addictive drugs. *Nature, 382,* 255–257. (3)

Poo, M.-m. (2001). Neurotrophins as synaptic modulators. *Nature Reviews Neuroscience, 2,* 24–32. (5)

Poole, J. H., Tyack, P. L., Stoeger-Horwath, A. S., & Watwood, S. (2005). Elephants are capable of vocal learning. *Nature, 434,* 455–456. (14)

Pope, H. G., Jr., Gruber, A. J., Hudson, J. I., Huestis, M. A., & Yurgelun-Todd, D. (2001). Neuropsychological performance in long-term cannabis users. *Archives of General Psychiatry, 58,* 909–915. (3)

Poremba, A., Saunders, R. C., Crane, A. M., Cook, M., Sokoloff, L., & Mishkin, M. (2003). Functional mapping of the primate auditory system. *Science, 299,* 568–572. (7)

Porrino, L. J., Daunais, J. B., Rogers, G. A., Hampson, R. E., & Deadwyler, S. A. (2005). Facilitation of task performance and removal of the effects of sleep deprivation by an ampakine (CX717) in nonhuman primates. *PLOS Biology, 3,* e299. (9)

Posner, S. F., Baker, L., Heath, A., & Martin, N. G. (1996). Social contact, social attitudes, and twin similarity. *Behavior Genetics, 26,* 123–133. (1)

Posthuma, D., De Geus, E. J. C., Baaré, W. F. C., Pol, H. E. H., Kahn, R. S., & Boomsma, D. I. (2002). The association between brain volume and intelligence is of genetic origin. *Nature Neuroscience, 5,* 83–84. (4)

Potegal, M. (1994). Aggressive arousal: The amygdala connection. In M. Potegal & J. F. Knutson (Eds.), *The dynamics of aggression* (pp. 73–111). Hillsdale, NJ: Erlbaum. (12)

Potegal, M., Ferris, C., Hebert, M., Meyerhoff, J. M., & Skaredoff, L. (1996). Attack priming in female Syrian golden hamsters is associated with a *c-fos* coupled process within the corticomedial amygdala. *Neuroscience, 75,* 869–880. (12)

Potegal, M., Hebert, M., DeCoster, M., & Meyerhoff, J. L. (1996). Brief, high-frequency stimulation of the corticomedial amygdala induces a delayed and prolonged increase of aggressiveness in male Syrian golden hamsters. *Behavioral Neuroscience, 110,* 401–412. (12)

Pouget, A., Dayan, P., & Zemel, R. (2000). Information processing with population codes. *Nature Reviews Neuroscience, 1,* 125–132. (7)

Premack, A. J., & Premack, D. (1972). Teaching language to an ape. *Scientific American, 227*(4), 92–99. (14)

Preti, G., Cutler, W. B., Garcia, C. R., Huggins, G. R., & Lawley, H. J. (1986). Human axillary secretions influence women's menstrual cycles: The role of donor extract of females. *Hormones and Behavior, 20,* 474–482. (7)

Price, C. J., Warburton, E. A., Moore, C. J., Frackowiak, R. S. J., & Friston, K. J. (2001). Dynamic diaschisis: Anatomically remote and context-sensitive human brain lesions. *Journal of Cognitive Neuroscience, 13,* 419–429. (5)

Price, M. P., Lewin, G. R., McIlwrath, S. L., Cheng, C., Xie, J., Heppenstall, P. A., et al. (2000). The mammalian sodium channel BNC1 is required for normal touch sensation. *Nature, 407,* 1007–1011. (7)

Pritchard, T. C., Hamilton, R. B., Morse, J. R., & Norgren, R. (1986). Projections of thalamic gustatory and lingual areas in the monkey, *Macaca fascicularis. Journal of Comparative Neurology, 244,* 213–228. (7)

Pritchard, T. C., Macaluso, D. A., & Eslinger, P. J. (1999). Taste perception in patients with insular cortex lesions. *Behavioral Neuroscience, 113,* 663–671. (7, 14)

Provine, R. R. (1979). "Wing-flapping" develops in wingless chicks. *Behavioral and Neural Biology, 27,* 233–237. (8)

Provine, R. R. (1981). Wing-flapping develops in chickens made flightless by feather mutations. *Developmental Psychobiology, 14,* 48 B 1–486. (8)

Provine, R. R. (1984). Wing-flapping during development and evolution. *American Scientist, 72,* 448–455. (8)

Provine, R. R. (1986). Yawning as a stereotyped action pattern and releasing stimulus. *Ethology, 72,* 109–122. (8)

Provine, R. R., & Westerman, J. A. (1979). Crossing the midline: Limits of early eye-hand behavior. *Child Development, 50,* 437–441. (14)

Prutkin, J., Duffy, V. B., Etter, L., Fast, K., Gardner, E., Lucchina, L. A., et al. (2000). Genetic variation and inferences about perceived taste intensity in mice and men. *Physiology & Behavior, 69,* 161–173. (7)

Ptak, R., Gutbrod, K., Perrig, W., & Schnider, A. (2001). Probabilistic contingency learning with limbic or prefrontal damage. *Behavioral Neuroscience, 115,* 993–1001. (13)

Puca, A. A., Daly, M. J., Brewster, S. J., Matise, T. C., Barrett, J., Shea-Drinkwater, M., et al. (2001). A genome-wide scan for linkage to human exceptional longevity identifies a locus on chromosome 4. *Proceedings of the National Academy of Sciences, USA, 98,* 10505–10508. (1)

Puchalla, J. L., Schneidman, E., Harris, R. A., & Berry, M. J. (2005). Redundancy in the population code of the retina. *Neuron, 46,* 493–504. (6)

Pugh, K. R., Mencl. W. E., Jenner, A. R., Lee, J. R., Katz, L., Frost, S. J., et al. (2001). Neuroimaging studies of reading development and reading disability. *Learning Disabilities Research & Practice, 16,* 240–249. (14)

Pugh, K. R., Mencl, W. E., Shaywitz, B. A., Shaywitz, S. E., Fulbright, R. K., Constable, R. T., et al. (2000). The angular gyrus in developmental dyslexia: Task-specific differences in functional connectivity within parietal cortex. *Psychological Science, 11,* 51–56. (14)

Purcell, D. W., Blanchard, R., & Zucker, K. J. (2000). Birth order in a contemporary sample of gay men. *Archives of Sexual Behavior, 29,* 349–356. (11)

Purves, D., & Hadley, R. D. (1985). Changes in the dendritic branching of adult mammalian neurones revealed by repeated imaging *in situ. Nature, 315,* 404–406. (5)

Purves, D., & Lotto, R. B. (2003). *Why we see what we do: An empirical theory of vision.* Sunderland, MA: Sinauer Associates. (6)

Purves, D., Shimpi, A., & Lotto, R. B. (1999). An empirical explanation of the Cornsweet effect. *Journal of Neuroscience, 19,* 8542–8551. (6)

Putnam, S. K., Du, J., Sato, S., & Hull, E. M. (2001). Testosterone restoration of copulatory behavior correlates with medial preoptic dopamine release in castrated male rats. *Hormones and Behavior, 39,* 216–224. (11)

Quraishi, S., & Frangou, S. (2002). Neuropsychology of bipolar disorder: A review. *Journal of Affective Disorders, 72,* 209–226. (15)

Rada, P. V., & Hoebel, B. G. (2000). Supraadditive effect of δ-fenfluramine plus phentermine on extracellular acetylcholine in the nucleus accumbens: Possible mechanism for inhibition of excessive feeding and drug abuse. *Pharmacology Biochemistry and Behavior, 65,* 369–373. (10)

Ragsdale, D. S., McPhee, J. C., Scheuer, T., & Catterall, W. A. (1994). Molecular determinants of state-dependent block of Na^+ channels by local anesthetics. *Science, 265,* 1724–1728. (2)

Rahman, Q., Andersson, D., & Govier, E. (2005). A specific sexual orientation-related difference in navigation strategy. *Behavioral Neuroscience, 119,* 311–316. (11)

Rahman, Q., Kumari, V., & Wilson, G. D. (2003). Sexual orientation-related differences in prepulse inhibition of the human startle response. *Behavioral Neuroscience, 117,* 1096–1102. (11)

Rahman, Q., & Wilson, G. D. (2003). Born gay? The psychobiology of human sexual orientation. *Personality and Individual Differences, 34,* 1337–1382. (11)

Raine, A., Reynolds, C., Venables, P. H., Mednick, S. A., & Farrington, D. P. (1998). Fearlessness, stimulation-seeking, and large body size at age 3 as early predispositions to childhood aggression at age 11 years. *Archives of General Psychiatry, 55,* 745–751. (12)

Rainnie, D. G., Grunze, H. C. R., McCarley, R. W., & Greene, R. W. (1994). Adenosine inhibition of mesopontine cholinergic neurons: Implications for EEG arousal. *Science, 263,* 689–692. (9)

Rainville, P., Duncan, G. H., Price, D. D., Carrier, B., & Bushnell, M. C. (1997). Pain affect encoded in human anterior cingulate but not somatosensory cortex. *Science, 277,* 968–971. (7)

Raisman, G. (2004). Myelin inhibitors: Does NO mean GO? *Nature Reviews Neuroscience, 5,* 157–161. (5)

Rajkowska, G., Selemon, L. D., & Goldman-Rakic, P. S. (1998). Neuronal and glial somal size in the prefrontal cortex. *Archives of General Psychiatry, 55,* 215–224. (15)

Rakic, P. (1998). Cortical development and evolution. In M. S. Gazzaniga & J. S. Altman (Eds.), *Brain and mind: Evolutionary perspectives* (pp. 34–40). Strasbourg, France: Human Frontier Science Program. (5)

Rakic, P. (2002). Neurogenesis in adult primate neocortex: An evaluation of the evidence. *Nature Reviews Neuroscience, 3,* 65–71. (5)

Rakic, P. (2004). Immigration denied. *Nature, 427,* 685–686. (5)

Rakic, P., & Lidow, M. S. (1995). Distribution and density of monoamine receptors in the primate visual cortex devoid of retinal input from early embryonic stages. *Journal of Neuroscience, 15,* 2561–2574. (6)

Ralph, M. R., Foster, R. G., Davis, F. C., & Menaker, M. (1990). Transplanted suprachiasmatic nucleus determines circadian period. *Science, 247,* 975–978. (9)

Ralph, M. R., & Menaker, M. (1988). A mutation of the circadian system in golden hamsters. *Science, 241,* 1225–1227. (9)

Ram, A., Pandey, H. P., Matsumura, H., Kasahara-Orita, K., Nakajima, T., Takahata, R., et al. (1997). CSF levels of prostaglandins, especially the level of prostaglandin D_2, are correlated with increasing propensity towards sleep in rats. *Brain Research, 751,* 81–89. (9)

Ramachandran, V. S., & Blakeslee, S. (1998). *Phantoms in the brain.* New York: Morrow. (5)

Ramachandran, V. S., & Hirstein, W. (1998). The perception of phantom limbs: The D. O. Hebb lecture. *Brain, 121,* 1603–1630. (5)

Ramírez, B. G., Blázquez, C., Gómez del Pulgar, T., Guzmán, M., & de Ceballos, M. L. (2005). Prevention of Alzheimer's disease pathology by cannabinoids: Neuroprotection mediated by blockade of microglial activation. *Journal of Neuroscience, 25,* 1904–1913. (13)

Ramirez, J. J. (2001). The role of axonal sprouting in functional reorganization after CNS injury: Lessons from the hippocampal formation. *Restorative Neurology and Neuroscience, 19,* 237–262. (5)

Ramirez, J. J., Bulsara, K. R., Moore, S. C., Ruch, K., & Abrams, W. (1999). Progressive unilateral damage of the entorhinal cortex enhances synaptic efficacy of the crossed entorhinal afferent to dentate granule cells. *Journal of Neuroscience, 19*: RC42, 1–6. (5)

Ramirez, J. J., Fass, B., Karpiak, S. E., & Steward, O. (1987a). Ganglioside treatments reduce locomotor hyperactivity after bilateral lesions of the entorhinal cortex. *Neuroscience Letters, 75,* 283–287. (5)

Ramirez, J. J., Fass, B., Kilfoil, T., Henschel, B., Grones, W., & Karpiak, S. E. (1987b). Ganglioside-induced enhancement of behavioral recovery after bilateral lesions of the entorhinal cortex. *Brain Research, 414,* 85–90. (5)

Ramirez, J. J., McQuilkin, M., Carrigan, T., MacDonald, K., & Kelley, M. S. (1996). Progressive entorhinal cortex lesions accelerate hippocampal sprouting and spare spatial memory in rats. *Proceedings of the National Academy of Sciences, USA, 93,* 15512–15517. (5)

Ramnani, N., & Owen, A. M. (2004). Anterior prefrontal cortex: Insights into function from anatomy and neuroimaging. *Nature Reviews Neuroscience, 5,* 184–194. (4)

Ramón y Cajal, S. (1937). *Recollections of my life. Memoirs of the American Philosophical Society, 8,* parts 1 and 2. (inside cover)

Randolph, C., Tierney, M. C., & Chase, T. N. (1995). Implicit memory in Alzheimer's disease. *Journal of Clinical and Experimental Neuropsychology, 17,* 343–351. (13)

Ranson, S. W., & Clark, S. L. (1959). *The anatomy of the nervous system: Its development and function* (10th ed.). Philadelphia: Saunders. (4)

Rapkin, A. J., Morgan, M., Goldman, L., Brann, D. W., Simone, D., & Mahesh, V. B. (1997). Progesterone metabolite allopregnanolone in women with premenstrual syndrome. *Obstetrics & Gynecology, 90,* 709–714. (11)

Rapoport, J. L., Giedd, J. N., Blumenthal, J., Hamburger, S., Jeffries, N., Fernandez, T., et al. (1999). Progressive cortical change during adolescence in childhood-onset schizophrenia. *Archives of General Psychiatry, 56,* 649–654. (15)

Rapoport, S. I., & Bosetti, F. (2002). Do lithium and anticonvulsants target the brain arachidonic acid cascade in bipolar patients? *Archives of General Psychiatry, 59,* 592–596. (15)

Rapoport, S. I., & Robinson, P. J. (1986). Tight-junctional modification as the basis of osmotic opening of the blood-brain barrier. *Annals of the New York Academy of Sciences, 481,* 250–267. (2)

Rattenborg, N. C., Amlaner, C. J., & Lima, S. L. (2000). Behavioral, neurophysiological and evolutionary perspectives on unihemispheric sleep. *Neuroscience and Biobehavioral Reviews, 24,* 817–842. (9)

Rattenborg, N. C., Mandt, B. H., Obermeyer, W. H., Winsauer, P. J., Huber, R., Wikelski, M., et al. (2004). Migratory sleeplessness in the white-crowned sparrow (*Zonotrichia leucophrys gambelii*). *PLOS Biology, 2,* 924–936. (9)

Raum, W. J., McGivern, R. F., Peterson, M. A., Shryne, J. H., & Gorski, R. A. (1990). Prenatal inhibition of hypothalamic sex steroid uptake by cocaine: Effects on neurobehavioral sexual differentiation in male rats. *Developmental Brain Research, 53,* 230–236. (11)

Ravizza, S. M., & Ivry, R. B. (2001). Comparison of the basal ganglia and cerebellum in shifting attention. *Journal of Cognitive Neuroscience, 13,* 285–297. (14)

Rayner, K., & Johnson, R. L. (2005). Letter-by-letter acquired dyslexia is due to the serial encoding of letters. *Psychological Science, 16,* 530–534. (14)

Rechtschaffen, A., & Bergmann, B. M. (1995). Sleep deprivation in the rat by the disk-over-water method. *Behavioural Brain Research, 69,* 55–63. (9)

Reddy, P. L., Khanna, S., Subhash, M. N., Channabasavanna, S. M., & Rao, B. S. S. R. (1992). CSF amine metabolites in depression. *Biological Psychiatry, 31,* 112–118. (15)

Reed, J. M., & Squire, L. R. (1999). Impaired transverse patterning in human amnesia is a special case of impaired memory for two-choice discrimination tasks. *Behavioral Neuroscience, 113,* 3–9. (13)

Rees, G., Kreiman, G., & Koch, C. (2002). Neural correlates of consciousness in humans. *Nature Reviews Neuroscience, 3,* 261–270. (9)

Reeves, A. G., & Plum, F. (1969). Hyperphagia, rage, and dementia accompanying a ventromedial hypothalamic neoplasm. *Archives of Neurology, 20,* 616–624. (10)

Refinetti, R. (2000). *Circadian physiology.* Boca Raton, FL: CRC Press. (9)

Refinetti, R., & Carlisle, H. J. (1986). Complementary nature of heat production and heat intake during behavioral thermoregulation in the rat. *Behavioral and Neural Biology, 46,* 64–70. (10)

Refinetti, R., & Menaker, M. (1992). The circadian rhythm of body temperature. *Physiology & Behavior, 51,* 613–637. (9)

Regan, T. (1986). The rights of humans and other animals. *Acta Physiologica Scandinavica, 128*(Suppl. 554), 33–40. (1)

Reichelt, K. L., Seim, A. R., & Reichelt, W. H. (1996). Could schizophrenia be reasonably explained by Dohan's hypothesis on genetic interaction with a dietary peptide overload? *Progress in Neuro-Psychopharmacology & Biological Psychiatry, 20,* 1083–1114. (15)

Reichling, D. B., Kwiat, G. C., & Basbaum, A. I. (1988). Anatomy, physiology, and pharmacology of the periaqueductal gray contribution to antinociceptive controls. In H. L. Fields & J.-M. Besson (Eds.), *Progress in brain research* (Vol. 77, pp. 31–46). Amsterdam: Elsevier. (7)

Reick, M., Garcia, J. A., Dudley, C., & McKnight, S. L. (2001). NPAS2: An analog of clock operative in the mammalian forebrain. *Science, 293,* 506–509. (9)

Reid, C. A., Dixon, D. B., Takahashi, M., Bliss, T. V. P., & Fine, A. (2004). Optical quantal analysis indicates that long-term potentiation at single hippocampal mossy fiber synapses is expressed through increased release probability, recruitment of new release sites, and activation of silent synapses. *Journal of Neuroscience, 24,* 3618–3626. (13)

Reiss, A. L., Eckert, M. A., Rose, F. E., Karchemskiy, A., Kesler, S., Chang, M., et al. (2004). An experiment of nature: Brain anatomy parallels cognition and behavior in Williams syndrome. *Journal of Neuroscience, 24,* 5009–5015. (14)

Reiter, R. J. (2000). Melatonin: Lowering the high price of free radicals. *News in Physiological Sciences, 15,* 246–250. (9)

Rema, V., Armstrong-Jones, M., & Ebner, F. F. (2003). Experience-dependent plasticity is impaired in adult rat barrel cortex after whiskers are unused in early postnatal life. *Journal of Neuroscience, 23,* 358–366. (5)

Rensink, R. A., O'Regan, J. K., & Clark, J. J. (1997). To see or not to see: The need for attention to perceive changes in scenes. *Psychological Science, 8,* 368–373. (14)

Reuter-Lorenz, P., & Davidson, R. J. (1981). Differential contributions of the two cerebral hemispheres to the perception of happy and sad faces. *Neuropsychologia, 19,* 609–613. (12)

Reuter-Lorenz, P. A., & Miller, A. C. (1998). The cognitive neuroscience of human laterality: Lessons from the bisected brain. *Current Directions in Psychological Science, 7,* 15–20. (14)

Rhees, R. W., Shryne, J. E., & Gorski, R. A. (1990). Onset of the hormone-sensitive perinatal period for sexual differentiation of the sexually dimorphic nucleus of the preoptic area in female rats. *Journal of Neurobiology, 21,* 781–786. (11)

Rhodes, J. S., van Praag, H., Jeffrey, S., Girard, I., Mitchell, G. S., Garland, T., Jr., et al. (2003). Exercise increases hippocampal neurogenesis to high levels but does not improve spatial learning in mice bred for increased voluntary wheel running. *Behavioral Neuroscience, 117,* 1006–1016. (5)

Riad, M., Zimmer, L., Rbah, L., Watkins, K. C., Hamon, M., & Descarries, L. (2004). Acute treatment with the antidepressant fluoxetine internalizes 5-HT_{1A} autoreceptors and reduces the *in vivo* binding of the PET radioligand [^{18}F] MPPF in the nucleus raphe dorsalis of the rat. *Journal of Neuroscience, 24,* 5420–5426. (15)

Riccio, D. C., Millin, P. M., & Gisquet-Verrier, P. (2003). Retrograde amnesia: Forgetting back. *Current Directions in Psychological Science, 12,* 41–44. (13)

Rice, G., Anderson, C., Risch, N., & Ebers, G. (1999). Male homosexuality: Absence of linkage to microsatellite markers at Xq28. *Science, 284,* 665–667. (11)

Richard, C., Honoré, J., Bernati, T., & Rousseaux, M. (2004). Straight-ahead pointing correlates with long-line bisection in neglect patients. *Cortex, 40,* 75–83. (14)

Richter, C. P. (1922). A behavioristic study of the activity of the rat. *Comparative Psychology Monographs, 1,* 1–55. (9)

Richter, C. P. (1936). Increased salt appetite in adrenalectomized rats. *American Journal of Physiology, 115,* 155–161. (10)

Richter, C. P. (1950). Taste and solubility of toxic compounds in poisoning of rats and humans. *Journal of Comparative and Physiological Psychology, 43,* 358–374. (7)

Richter, C. P. (1967). Psychopathology of periodic behavior in animals and man. In J. Zubin & H. F. Hunt (Eds.), *Comparative psychopathology* (pp. 205–227). New York: Grune & Stratton. (9)

Richter, C. P. (1975). Deep hypothermia and its effect on the 24-hour clock of rats and hamsters. *Johns Hopkins Medical Journal, 136,* 1–10. (9)

Richter, C. P., & Langworthy, O. R. (1933). The quill mechanism of the porcupine. *Journal für Psychologie und Neurologie, 45,* 143–153. (4)

Rickard, T. C., & Grafman, J. (1998). Losing their configural mind: Amnesic patients fail on transverse patterning. *Journal of Cognitive Neuroscience, 10,* 509–524. (13)

Riddle, W. J. R., & Scott, A. I. F. (1995). Relapse after successful electroconvulsive therapy: The use and impact of continuation antidepressant drug treatment. *Human Psychopharmacology, 10,* 201–205. (15)

Riemann, D., König, A., Hohagen, F., Kiemen, A., Voderholzer, U., Backhaus, J., et al. (1999). How to preserve the antidepressive effect of sleep deprivation: A comparison of sleep phase advance and sleep phase delay. *European Archives of Psychiatry and Clinical Neuroscience, 249,* 231–237. (15)

Ringel, B. L., & Szuba, M. P. (2001). Potential mechanisms of the sleep therapies for depression. *Depression and Anxiety, 14,* 29–36. (15)

Rinn, W. E. (1984). The neuropsychology of facial expression: A review of the neurological and psychological mechanisms for producing facial expressions. *Psychological Bulletin, 95,* 52–77. (8)

Rittenhouse, C. D., Shouval, H. Z., Paradiso, M. A., & Bear, M. F. (1999). Monocular deprivation induces homosynaptic long-term depression in visual cortex. *Nature, 397,* 347–350. (6)

Ro, T., Shelton, D., Lee, O.L., & Chang, E. (2004). Extrageniculate mediation of unconscious vision in transcranial magnetic stimulation-induced blindsight. *Proceedings of the National Academy of Sciences, USA, 101,* 9933–9935. (6)

Robbins, T. W., & Everitt, B. J. (1995). Arousal systems and attention. In M. S. Gazzaniga (Ed.), *The cognitive neurosciences* (pp. 703–720). Cambridge, MA: MIT Press. (9)

Robertson, I. H. (2005, Winter). The deceptive world of subjective awareness. *Cerebrum, 7*(1), 74–83. (4)

Robertson, L. C. (2003). Binding, spatial attention and perceptual awareness. *Nature Reviews Neuroscience, 4,* 93–102. (4)

Robertson, L., Treisman, A., Friedman-Hill, S., & Grabowecky, M. (1997). The interaction of spatial and object pathways: Evidence from Balint's syndrome. *Journal of Cognitive Neuropsychology, 9,* 295–317. (4)

Robillard, T. A. J., & Gersdorff, M. C. H. (1986). Prevention of pre- and perinatal acquired hearing defects: Part I. Study of causes. *Journal of Auditory Research, 26,* 207–237. (7)

Robinson, R., Sandstrom, S. M., Denenberg, V. H., & Palmiter, R. D. (2005). Distinguishing whether dopamine regulates liking, wanting, and/or learning about rewards. *Behavioral Neuroscience, 119,* 5–15. (15)

Robinson, R. G., Boston, J. D., Starkstein, S. E., & Price, T. R. (1988). Comparison of mania and depression after brain injury: Causal factors. *American Journal of Psychiatry, 145,* 172–178. (15)

Robinson, T. E., & Berridge, K. C. (2001). Incentive-sensitization and addiction. *Addiction, 96,* 103–114. (15)

Rocha, B. A., Fumagalli, F., Gainetdinov, R. R., Jones, S. R., Ator, R., Giros, B., et al. (1998). Cocaine self-administration in dopamine-transporter knockout mice. *Nature Neuroscience, 1,* 132–137. (3)

Rochira, V., Balestrieri, A., Madeo, B., Baraldi, E., Faustini-Fustini, M., Granata, A. R. M., et al. (2001). Congenital estrogen deficiency: In search of the estrogen role in human male reproduction. *Molecular and Cellular Endocrinology, 178,* 107–115. (11)

Rodrigue, K. M., & Raz, N. (2004). Shrinkage of the entorhinal cortex over five years predicts memory performance in healthy adults. *Journal of Neuroscience, 24,* 956–963. (13)

Rodriguez, E., George, N., Lachaux, J.-P., Martinerie, J., Renault, B., & Varela, F. J. (1999). Perception's shadow: Long-distance synchronization of human brain activity. *Nature, 397,* 430–433. (4)

Rodriguez, I., Del Punta, K., Rothman, A., Ishii, T., & Mombaerts, P. (2002). Multiple new and isolated families within the mouse superfamily of Vlr vomeronasal receptors. *Nature Neuroscience, 5,* 134–140. (7)

Rodriguez, I., Greer, C. A., Mok, M. Y., & Mombaerts, P. A. (2000). A putative pheromone receptor gene expressed in human olfactory mucosa. *Nature Genetics, 26,* 18–19. (7)

Roelfsema, P. R., Engel, A. K., König, P., & Singer, W. (1997). Visuomotor integration is associated with zero time-lag synchronization among cortical areas. *Nature, 385,* 157–161. (4)

Roelfsema, P. R., Lamme, V. A. F., & Spekreijse, H. (2004). Synchrony and variation of firing rates in the primary visual cortex during contour grouping. *Nature Neuroscience, 7,* 982–991. (4)

Roenneberg, T., Kuehnle, T., Pramstaller, P. P., Ricken, J., Havel, M., Ricken, J., et al. (2004). A marker for the end of adolescence. *Current Biology, 14,* R1038–R1039. (9)

Roffwarg, H. P., Muzio, J. N., & Dement, W. C. (1966). Ontogenetic development of human sleep-dream cycle. *Science, 152,* 604–609. (9)

Rohan, M., Parow, A., Stoll, A. L., Demopulos, C., Friedman, S., Dager, S., et al. (2004). Low-field magnetic stimulation in bipolar depression using an MRI-based stimulator. *American Journal of Psychiatry, 161,* 93–98. (15)

Rollenhagen, J. E., & Olson, C. R. (2000). Mirror-image confusion in single neurons of the macaque inferotemporal cortex. *Science, 287,* 1506–1508. (6)

Rolls, E. T. (1995). Central taste anatomy and neurophysiology. In R. L. Doty (Ed.), *Handbook of olfaction and gustation* (pp. 549–573). New York: Dekker. (7)

Rolls, E. T. (1996a) The representation of space in the primate hippocampus, and its relation to memory. In K. Ishikawa, J. L. McGaugh, and H. Sakata (Eds.), *Brain processes and memory* (pp. 203–227). Amsterdam: Elsevier. (13)

Rolls, E. T. (1996b). A theory of hippocampal function in memory. *Hippocampus, 6,* 601–620. (13)

Rome, L. C., Loughna, P. T., & Goldspink, G. (1984). Muscle fiber activity in carp as a function of swimming speed and muscle temperature. *American Journal of Psychiatry, 247,* R272–R279. (8)

Romer, A. S. (1962). *The vertebrate body.* Philadelphia: Saunders. (5)

Rommel, S. A., Pabst, D. A., & McLellan, W. A. (1998). Reproductive thermoregulation in marine mammals. *American Scientist, 86,* 440–448. (10)

Roorda, A., Metha, A. B., Lennie, P., & Williams, D. R. (2001). Packing arrangement of the three cone classes in primate retina. *Vision Research, 41,* 1291–1306. (6)

Roorda, A., & Williams, D. R. (1999). The arrangement of the three cone classes in the living human eye. *Nature, 397,* 520–522. (6)

Rose, J. E., Brugge, J. F., Anderson, D. J., & Hind, J. E. (1967). Phase-locked response to low-frequency tones in single auditory nerve fibers of the squirrel monkey. *Journal of Neurophysiology, 30,* 769–793. (7)

Rosen, A. C., Prull, M. W., Gabrieli, J. D. E., Stoub, T., O'Hara, R., Friedman, L., et al. (2003). Differential associations between entorhinal and hippocampal volume and memory performance in older adults. *Behavioral Neuroscience, 117,* 1150–1160. (13)

Rosen, A. C., Prull, M. W., O-Hara, R., Race, E. A., Desmond, J. E., Glover, G. H., et al. (2002). Variable effects of aging on frontal lobe contributions to memory. *NeuroReport, 13,* 2425–2428. (13)

Rosen, H. J., Perry, R. J., Murphy, J., Kramer, J. H., Mychack, P., Schuff, N., et al. (2002). Emotion comprehension in the temporal variant of frontotemporal dementia. *Brain, 125,* 2286–2295. (12)

Rosenbaum, D. A. (2005). The Cinderella of psychology. *American Psychologist, 60,* 308–317. (8)

Rosenblatt, J. S. (1967). Nonhormonal basis of maternal behavior in the rat. *Science, 156,* 1512–1514. (11)

Rosenblatt, J. S. (1970). Views on the onset and maintenance of maternal behavior in the rat. In L. R. Aronson, E. Tobach, D. S. Lehrman, & J. S. Rosenblatt (Eds.), *Development and evolution of behavior* (pp. 489–515). San Francisco: Freeman. (11)

Rosenblatt, J. S., Olufowobi, A., & Siegel, H. I. (1998). Effects of pregnancy hormones on maternal responsiveness, responsiveness to estrogen stimulation of maternal behavior, and the lordosis response to estrogen stimulation. *Hormones and Behavior, 33,* 104–114. (11)

Rosenzweig, E. S., Redish, A. D., McNaughton, B. L., & Barnes, C. A. (2003). Hippocampal map realignment and spatial learning. *Nature Neuroscience, 6,* 609–615. (13)

Rosenzweig, M. R., & Bennett, E. L. (1996). Psychobiology of plasticity: Effects of training and experience on brain and behavior. *Behavioural Brain Research, 78,* 57–65. (5)

Rösler, A., & Witztum, E. (1998). Treatment of men with paraphilia with a long-acting analogue of gonadotropin-releasing hormone. *New England Journal of Medicine, 338,* 416–422. (11)

Ross, E. D., Homan, R. W., & Buck, R. (1994). Differential hemispheric lateralization of primary and social emotions. *Neuropsychiatry, Neuropsychology, and Behavioral Neurology, 7,* 1–19. (12)

Rossi, D. J., Oshima, T., & Attwell, D. (2000). Glutamate release in severe brain ischaemia is mainly by reversed uptake. *Nature, 403,* 316–321. (5)

Rossi, S., Miniussi, C., Pasqualetti, P., Babiloni, C., Rossini, P. M., & Cappa, S. F. (2004). Age-related functioinal changes of prefrontal cortex in long-term memory: A repetitive transcranial magnetic stimulation study. *Journal of Neuroscience, 24,* 7939–7944. (13)

Rossion, B., Gauthier, I., Goffaux, V., Tarr, M. J., & Crommelinck, M. (2002). Expertise training with novel objects leads to left-lateralized facelike electrophysiological responses. *Psychological Science, 13,* 250–257. (6)

Rosvold, H. E., Mirsky, A. F., & Pribram, K. H. (1954). Influence of amygdalectomy on social behavior in monkeys. *Journal of Comparative and Physiological Psychology, 47,* 173–178. (12)

Roth, B. L., Willins, D. L., Kristiansen, K., & Kroeze, W. K. (1999). Activation is hallucinogenic and antagonism is therapeutic: Role of 5-HT_{2A} receptors in atypical antipsychotic drug actions. *The Neuroscientist, 5,* 254–262. (15)

Rottenberg, J., Kasch, K. L., Gross, J. J., & Gotlib, I. H. (2002). Sadness and amusement reactivity differentially predict concurrent and prospective functioning in major depressive disorder. *Emotion, 2,* 135–146. (15)

Routtenberg, A., Cantallops, I., Zaffuto, S., Serrano, P., & Namgung, U. (2000). Enhanced learning after genetic overexpression of a brain growth protein. *Proceedings of the National Academy of Sciences, USA, 97,* 7657–7662. (13)

Rovainen, C. M. (1976). Regeneration of Müller and Mauthner axons after spinal transection in larval lampreys. *Journal of Comparative Neurology, 168,* 545–554. (5)

Rowland, D. L., & Burnett, A. L. (2000). Pharmacotherapy in the treatment of male sexual dysfunction. *Journal of Sex Research, 37,* 226–243. (11)

Roy, A., DeJong, J., & Linnoila, M. (1989). Cerebrospinal fluid monoamine metabolites and suicidal behavior in depressed patients. *Archives of General Psychiatry, 46,* 609–612. (12)

Royer, S., & Paré, D. (2003). Conservation of total synaptic weight through balanced synaptic depression and potentiation. *Nature, 422,* 518–522. (13)

Rozin, P. (1990). Getting to like the burn of chili pepper. In B. G. Green, J. R. Mason, & M. R. Kare (Eds.), *Chemical senses* (Vol. 2, pp. 231–269). New York: Dekker. (10)

Rozin, P., Dow, S., Moscovitch, M., & Rajaram, S. (1998). What causes humans to begin and end a meal? A role for memory for what has been eaten, as evidenced by a study of multiple meal eating in amnesic patients. *Psychological Science, 9,* 392–396. (13)

Rozin, P., & Kalat, J. W. (1971). Specific hungers and poison avoidance as adaptive specializations of learning. *Psychological Review, 78,* 459–486. (10, 13)

Rozin, P., & Pelchat, M. L. (1988). Memories of mammaries: Adaptations to weaning from milk. *Progress in Psychobiology and Physiological Psychology, 13,* 1–29. (10)

Rozin, P., & Schull, J. (1988). The adaptive-evolutionary point of view in experimental psychology. In R. C. Atkinson, R. J. Herrnstein, G. Lindzey, & R. D. Luce (Eds.), *Stevens' handbook of experimental psychology* (2nd ed.): Vol. 1. *Perception and motivation* (pp. 503–546). New York: Wiley. (13)

Rozin, P., & Vollmecke, T. A. (1986). Food likes and dislikes. *Annual Review of Nutrition, 6,* 433–456. (10)

Rozin, P., & Zellner, D. (1985). The role of Pavlovian conditioning in the acquisition of food likes and dislikes. *Annals of the New York Academy of Sciences, 443,* 189–202. (10)

Rubens, A. B., & Benson, D. F. (1971). Associative visual agnosia. *Archives of Neurology, 24,* 305–316. (6)

Rubia, K., Oosterlaan, J., Sergeant, J. A., Brandeis, D., & v. Leeuwen, T. (1998). Inhibitory dysfunction in hyperactive boys. *Behavioural Brain Research, 94,* 25–32. (14)

Rubin, B. D., & Katz, L. C. (2001). Spatial coding of enantiomers in the rat olfactory bulb. *Nature Neuroscience, 4,* 355–356. (7)

Rubinow, M. J., Arseneau, L. M., Beverly, J. L., & Juraska, J. M. (2004). Effect of the estrous cycle on water maze acquisition depends on the temperature of the water. *Behavioral Neuroscience, 118,* 863–868. (10)

Ruby, N. F., Brennan, T. J., Xie, X., Cao, V., Franken, P., Heller, H. C., et al. (2002). Role of melanopsin in circadian responses to light. *Science, 298,* 2211–2213. (9)

Rudolph, U., Crestani, F., Benke, D., Brünig, I., Benson, J. A., Fritschy, J.-M., et al. (1999). Benzodiazepine actions mediated by specific γ-aminobutyric acidA receptor subtypes. *Nature, 401,* 796–800. (12)

Rujescu, D., Giegling, I., Bondy, B., Gietl, A., Zill, P., & Möller, H.-J. (2002). Association of anger-related traits with SNPs in the TPH gene. *Molecular Psychiatry, 7,* 1023–1029. (12)

Rumbaugh, D. M. (Ed.). (1977). *Language learning by a chimpanzee: The Lana Project.* New York: Academic Press. (14)

Rumbaugh, D. M. (1990). Comparative psychology and the great apes: Their competency in learning, language, and numbers. *Psychological Record, 40,* 15–39. (14)

Rupprecht, R., di Michele, F., Hermann, B., Ströhle, A., Lancel, M., Romeo, E., et al. (2001). Neuroactive steroids: Molecular mechanisms of action and implications for neuropsychopharmacology. *Brain Research Reviews, 37,* 59–67. (11)

Rusak, B., & Zucker, I. (1979). Neural regulation of circadian rhythms. *Physiological Reviews, 59,* 449–526. (9)

Russell, A. J., Munro, J. C., Jones, P. B., Hemsley, D. R., & Murray, R. M. (1997). Schizophrenia and the myth of intellectual decline. *American Journal of Psychiatry, 154,* 635–639. (15)

Russell, M. J., Switz, G. M., & Thompson, K. (1980). Olfactory influences on the human menstrual cycle. *Pharmacology, Biochemistry, and Behavior, 13,* 737–738. (7)

Rutter, M., Pickles, A., Murray, R., & Eaves, L. (2001). Testing hypotheses on specific environmental causal effects on behavior. *Psychological Bulletin, 127,* 291–324. (1)

Rüttiger, L., Braun, D. I., Gegenfurtner, K. R., Petersen, D., Schönle, P., & Sharpe, L. T. (1999). Selective color constancy deficits after circumscribed unilateral brain lesions. *Journal of Neuroscience, 19,* 3094–3106. (6)

Saad, W. A., Luiz, A. C., Camargo, L. A. A., Renzi, A., & Manani, J. V. (1996). The lateral preoptic area plays a dual role in the regulation of thirst in the rat. *Brain Research Bulletin, 39,* 171–176. (10)

Sabel, B. A. (1997). Unrecognized potential of surviving neurons: Within-systems plasticity, recovery of function, and the hypothesis of minimal residual structure. *The Neuroscientist, 3,* 366–370. (5)

Sabel, B. A., Slavin, M. D., & Stein, D. G. (1984). GM_1 ganglioside treatment facilitates behavioral recovery from bilateral brain damage. *Science, 225,* 340–342. (5)

Sabo, K. T., & Kirtley, D. D. (1982). Objects and activities in the dreams of the blind. *International Journal of Rehabilitation Research, 5,* 241–242. (4)

Sack, R. L., & Lewy, A. J. (2001). Circadian rhythm sleep disorders: Lessons from the blind. *Sleep Medicine Reviews, 5,* 189–206. (9)

Sackeim, H. A., Putz, E., Vingiano, W., Coleman, E., & McElhiney, M. (1988). Lateralization in the processing of emotionally laden information: I. Normal functioning. *Neuropsychiatry, Neuropsychology, and Behavioral Neurology, 1,* 97–110. (14)

Sadato, N., Pascual-Leone, A., Grafman, J., Deiber, M.-P., Ibañez, V., & Hallett, M. (1998). Neural networks for Braille reading by the blind. *Brain, 121,* 1213–1229. (5)

Sadato, N., Pascual-Leone, A., Grafman, J., Ibañez, V., Deiber, M.-P., Dold, G., et al. (1996). Activation of the primary visual cortex by Braille reading in blind subjects. *Nature, 380,* 526–528. (5)

Sairanen, M., Lucas, G., Ernfors, P., Castrén, M., & Castrén, E. (2005). Brain-derived neurotrophic factor and antidepressant drugs have different but coordinated effects on neuronal turnover, proliferation, and survival in the adult dentate gyrus. *Journal of Neuroscience, 25,* 1089–1094. (15)

Sakai, K., Rowe, J. B., & Passingham, R. E. (2002). Active maintenance in prefrontal area 46 creates distractor-resistant memory. *Nature Neuroscience, 5,* 479–484. (13)

Saleem, Q., Dash, D., Gandhi, C., Kishore, A., Benegal, V., Sherrin, T., et al. (2001). Association of CAG repeat loci on chromosome 22 with schizophrenia and bipolar disorder. *Molecular Psychiatry, 6,* 694–700. (15)

Salmelin, R., Hari, R., Lounasmaa, O. V., & Sams, M. (1994). Dynamics of brain activation during picture naming. *Nature, 368,* 463–465. (4)

Sánchez, I., Mahlke, C., & Yuan, J. (2003). Pivotal role of oligomerization in expanded polyglutamine neurodegenerative disorders. *Nature, 421,* 373–379. (8)

Sander, K., & Scheich, H. (2001). Auditory perception of laughing and crying activates human amygdala regardless of attentional state. *Cognitive Brain Research, 12,* 181–198. (12)

Sanders, R. J. (1989). Sentence comprehension following agenesis of the corpus callosum. *Brain and Language, 37,* 59–72. (14)

Sanders, S. K., & Shekhar, A. (1995). Anxiolytic effects of chlordiazepoxide blocked by injection of $GABA_A$ and benzodiazepine receptor antagonists in the region of the anterior basolateral amygdala of rats. *Biological Psychiatry, 37,* 473–476. (12)

Sandstrom, N. J., Kaufman, J., & Huettel, S. A. (1998). Males and females use different distal cues in a virtual environment navigation task. *Cognitive Brain Research, 6,* 351–360. (11)

Sanes, J. N., Donoghue, J. P., Thangaraj, V., Edelman, R. R., & Warach, S. (1995). Shared neural substrates controlling hand movements in human motor cortex. *Science, 268,* 1775–1777. (8)

Sanes, J. R. (1993). Topographic maps and molecular gradients. *Current Opinion in Neurobiology, 3,* 67–74. (5)

Sanger, T. D., Pascual-Leone, A., Tarsy, D., & Schlaug, G. (2001). Nonlinear sensory cortex response to simultaneous tactile stimuli in writer's cramp. *Movement Disorders, 17,* 105–111. (5)

Sanger, T. D., Tarsy, D., & Pascual-Leone, A. (2001). Abnormalities of spatial and temporal sensory discrimination in writer's cramp. *Movement Disorders, 16,* 94–99. (5)

SantaCruz, K., Lewis, J., Spires, T., Paulson, J., Kotilinek, L., Ingelsson, M., et al. (2005). Tau suppression in a neurodegenerative mouse model improves memory function. *Science, 309,* 476–481. (13)

Santarelli, L., Saxe, M., Gross, C., Surget, A., Battaglia, F., Sulawa, S., et al. (2003). Requirement of hippocampal neurogenesis for the behavioral effects of antidepressants. *Science, 301,* 805–809. (15)

Santini, E., Ge, H., Ren, K., Pena de Ortiz, S., & Quirk, G. J. (2004). Consolidation of fear extinction requires protein synthesis in the medial prefrontal cortex. *Journal of Neuroscience, 24,* 5704–5710. (13)

Sapolsky, R. M. (1992). *Stress, the aging brain, and the mechanisms of neuron death.* Cambridge, MA: MIT Press. (12)

Sapolsky, R. M. (1998). *Why zebras don't get ulcers.* New York: Freeman. (12)

Sáry, G., Vogels, R., & Orban, G. A. (1993). Cue-invariant shape selectivity of macaque inferior temporal neurons. *Science, 260,* 995–997. (6)

Satinoff, E. (1964). Behavioral thermoregulation in response to local cooling of the rat brain. *American Journal of Physiology, 206,* 1389–1394. (10)

Satinoff, E. (1991). Developmental aspects of behavioral and reflexive thermoregulation. In H. N. Shanir, G. A. Barr, & M. A. Hofer (Eds.), *Developmental psychobiology: New methods and changing concepts* (pp. 169–188). New York: Oxford University Press. (10)

Satinoff, E., McEwen, G. N., Jr., & Williams, B. A. (1976). Behavioral fever in newborn rabbits. *Science, 193,* 1139–1140. (10)

Satinoff, E., & Rutstein, J. (1970). Behavioral thermoregulation in rats with anterior hypothalamic lesions. *Journal of Comparative and Physiological Psychology, 71,* 77–82. (10)

Satinoff, E., Valentino, D., & Teitelbaum, P. (1976). Thermoregulatory cold-defense deficits in rats with preoptic/anterior hypothalamic lesions. *Brain Research Bulletin, 1,* 553–565. (10)

Sato, W., Yoshikawa, S., Kochiyama, T., & Matsumura, M. (2004). The amygdala processes the emotional significance of facial expressions: An fMRI investigation using the interaction between expression and face direction. *NeuroImage, 22,* 1006–1013. (12)

Satz, P., & Green, M. F. (1999). Atypical handedness in schizophrenia: Some methodological and theoretical issues. *Schizophrenia Bulletin, 25,* 63–78. (15)

Saucier, D. M., Green, S. M., Leason, J., MacFadden, A., Bell, S., & Elias, L. J. (2002). Are sex differences in navigation caused by sexually dimorphic strategies or by differences in the ability to use the strategies? *Behavioral Neuroscience, 116,* 403–410. (11)

Savage-Rumbaugh, E. S. (1990). Language acquisition in a nonhuman species: Implications for the innateness debate. *Developmental Psychobiology, 23,* 599–620. (14)

Savage-Rumbaugh, E. S. (1991). Language learning in the bonobo: How and why they learn. In N. A. Kresnegor, D. M. Rumbaugh, R. L. Schiefelbusch, & M. Studdert-Kennedy (Eds.), *Biological and behavioral determinants of language development* (pp. 209–233). Hillsdale, NJ: Erlbaum. (14)

Savage-Rumbaugh, E. S. (1993). Language learnability in man, ape, and dolphin. In H. L. Roitblat, L. M. Herman, & P. E. Nachtigall (Eds.), *Language and com-*

munication: Comparative perspectives (pp. 457–473). Hillsdale, NJ: Erlbaum. (14)

Savage-Rumbaugh, E. S., Murphy, J., Sevcik, R. A., Brakke, K. E., Williams, S. L., & Rumbaugh, D. M. (1993). Language comprehension in ape and child. *Monographs of the Society for Research in Child Development, 58*(Serial no. 233). (14)

Savage-Rumbaugh, E. S., Sevcik, R. A., Brakke, K. E., & Rumbaugh, D. M. (1992). Symbols: Their communicative use, communication, and combination by bonobos (*Pan paniscus*). In L. P. Lipsitt & C. Rovee-Collier (Eds.), *Advances in infancy research* (Vol. 7, pp. 221–278). Norwood, NJ: Ablex. (14)

Savic, I., Berglund, H., Gulyas, B., & Roland, P. (2001). Smelling of odorous sex hormone-like compounds causes sex-differentiated hypothalamic activations in humans. *Neuron, 31,* 661–668. (7)

Savitz, J. B., & Ramesar, R. S. (2004). Genetic variants implicated in personality: A review of the more promising candidates. *American Journal of Medical Genetics Part B, 131B,* 20–32. (3)

Sawamoto, N., Honda, M., Hanakawa, T., Fukuyama, H., & Shibasaki, H. (2002). Cognitive slowing in Parkinson's disease: A behavioral evaluation independent of motor slowing. *Journal of Neuroscience, 22,* 5198–5203. (8)

Scamell, T., Gerashchenko, D., Urade, Y., Onoe, H., Saper, C., & Hayaishi, O. (1998). Activation of ventrolateral preoptic neurons by the somnogen prostaglandin D_2. *Proceedings of the National Academy of Sciences, USA, 95,* 7754–7759. (9)

Scannevin, R. H., & Huganir, R. L. (2000). Postsynaptic organization and regulation of excitatory synapses. *Nature Reviews Neuroscience, 1,* 133–141. (3)

Schacter, D. L. (1983). Amnesia observed: Remembering and forgetting in a natural environment. *Journal of Abnormal Psychology, 92,* 236–242. (13)

Schacter, D. L. (1985). Priming of old and new knowledge in amnesic patients and normal subjects. *Annals of the New York Academy of Sciences, 444,* 41–53. (13)

Schärli, H., Harman, A. M., & Hogben, J. H. (1999). Blindsight in subjects with homonymous visual field defects. *Journal of Cognitive Neuroscience, 11,* 52–66. (6)

Scheibel, A. B. (1983). Dendritic changes. In B. Reisberg (Ed.), *Alzheimer's disease* (pp. 69–73). New York: Free Press. (13)

Schellenberg, G. D., Bird, T. D., Wijsman, E. M., Orr, H. T., Anderson, L., Nemens, E., et al. (1992). Genetic linkage evidence for a familial Alzheimer's disease locus on chromosome 14. *Science, 258,* 668–671. (13)

Schenck, C. H., & Mahowald, M. W. (1996). Long-term, nightly benzodiazepine treatment of injurious parasomnias and other disorders of disrupted nocturnal sleep in 170 adults. *American Journal of Medicine, 100,* 333–337. (9)

Schenk, D., Barbour, R., Dunn, W., Gordon, G., Grajeda, H., Guido, T., et al. (1999). Immunization with amyloid-β attenuates Alzheimer-disease-like pathology in the PDAPP mouse. *Nature, 400,* 173–177. (13)

Scherer, S. S. (1986). Reinnervation of the extraocular muscles in goldfish is nonselective. *Journal of Neuroscience, 6,* 764–773. (5)

Schienle, A., Stark, R., Walter, B., Blecker, C., Ott, U., Kirsch, P., et al. (2002). The insula is not specifically involved in disgust processing: An fMRI study. *NeuroReport, 13,* 2023–2026. (12)

Schiermeier, Q. (1998). Animal rights activists turn the screw. *Nature, 396,* 505. (1)

Schiffman, S. S. (1983). Taste and smell in disease. *New England Journal of Medicine, 308,* 1275–1279, 1337–1343. (7)

Schiffman, S. S., & Erickson, R. P. (1971). A psychophysical model for gustatory quality. *Physiology & Behavior, 7,* 617–633. (7)

Schiffman, S. S., & Erickson, R. P. (1980). The issue of primary tastes versus a taste continuum. *Neuroscience and Biobehavioral Reviews, 4,* 109–117. (7)

Schiffman, S. S., Lockhead, E., & Maes, F. W. (1983). Amiloride reduces the taste intensity of Na^+ and Li^+ salts and sweeteners. *Proceedings of the National Academy of Sciences, USA, 80,* 6136–6140. (7)

Schiffman, S. S., McElroy, A. E., & Erickson, R. P. (1980). The range of taste quality of sodium salts. *Physiology & Behavior, 24,* 217–224. (7)

Schlinger, H. D., Jr. (1996). How the human got its spots. *Skeptic, 4,* 68–76. (1)

Schmid, A., Koch, M., & Schnitzler, H.-U. (1995). Conditioned pleasure attenuates the startle response in rats. *Neurobiology of Learning and Memory, 64,* 1–3. (12)

Schmidt, L. A.(1999). Frontal brain electrical activity in shyness and sociability. *Psychological Science, 10,* 316–320. (12)

Schmidt, P. J., Nieman, L. K., Danaceau, M. A., Adams, L. F., & Rubinow, D. R. (1998). Differential behavioral effects of gonadal steroids in women with and in those without premenstrual syndrome. *New England Journal of Medicine, 338,* 209–216. (11)

Schmidt-Hieber, C, Jonas, P., & Bischofberger, J. (2004). Enhanced synaptic plasticity in newly generated granule cells of the adult hippocampus. *Nature, 429,* 184–187. (5)

Schneider, B. A., Trehub, S. E., Morrongiello, B. A., & Thorpe, L. A. (1986). Auditory sensitivity in preschool children. *Journal of the Acoustical Society of America, 79,* 447–452. (7)

Schneider, P., Scherg, M., Dosch, G., Specht, H. J., Gutschalk, A., & Rupp, A. (2002). Morphology of Heschl's gyrus reflects enhanced activation in the auditory cortex of musicians. *Nature Neuroscience, 5,* 688–694. (5)

Schnider, A. (2003). Spontaneous confabulation and the adaptation of thought to ongoing reality. *Nature Reviews Neuroscience, 4,* 662–671. (13)

Schnider, A., & Ptak, R. (1999). Spontaneous confabulators fail to suppress currently irrelevant memory traces. *Nature Neuroscience, 2,* 677–681. (13)

Schoenemann, P. T., Budinger, T. F., Sarich, V. M., & Wang, W. S.-Y. (2000). Brain size does not predict general cognitive ability within families. *Proceedings of the National Academy of Sciences, USA, 97,* 4932–4937. (4)

Schoenemann, P. T., Sheehan, M. J., & Glotzer, L. D. (2005). Prefrontal white matter volume is disproportionately larger in humans than in other primates. *Nature Neuroscience, 8,* 242–252. (4)

Schou, M. (1997). Forty years of lithium treatment. *Archives of General Psychiatry, 54,* 9–13. (15)

Schoups, A., Vogels, R., Qian, N., & Orban, G. (2001). Practising orientation identification improves orientation coding in V1 neurons. *Nature, 412,* 549–553. (6)

Schradin, C., & Anzenberger, G. (1999). Prolactin, the hormone of paternity. *News in Physiological Sciences, 14,* 223–231. (11)

Schroeder, J. A., & Flannery-Schroeder, E. (2005). Use of herb *Gymnema sylvestre* to illustrate the principles of gustatory sensation: An undergraduate neuroscience laboratory exercise. *Journal of Undergraduate Neuroscience Education, 3,* A59–A62. (7)

Schuckit, M. A., & Smith, T. L. (1996). An 8-year follow-up of 450 sons of alcoholic and control subjects. *Archives of General Psychiatry, 53,* 202–210. (15)

Schuckit, M. C., & Smith, T. L. (1997). Assessing the risk for alcoholism among sons of alcoholics. *Journal of Studies on Alcohol, 58,* 141–145. (15)

Schulkin, J. (1991). *Sodium hunger: The search for a salty taste.* Cambridge, England: Cambridge University Press. (10)

Schulz, J. B., Weller, M., & Moskowitz, M. A. (1999). Caspases as treatment targets in stroke and neurodegenerative diseases. *Annals of Neurology, 45,* 421–429. (5)

Schwab, M. E. (1998). Regenerative nerve fiber growth in the adult central nervous system. *News in Physiological Sciences, 13,* 294–298. (5)

Schwartz, C. E., Wright, C. I., Shin, L. M., Kagan, J., & Rauch, S. L. (2003). Inhibited and uninhibited infants "grown up": Adult amygdalar response to novelty. *Science, 300,* 1952–1953. (12)

Schwartz, G. J. (2000). The role of gastrointestinal vagal afferents in the control of food intake: Current prospects. *Nutrition, 16,* 866–873. (10)

Schwartz, L., & Tulipan, L. (1933). An outbreak of dermatitis among workers in a rubber manufacturing plant. *Public Health Reports, 48,* 809–814. (15)

Schwartz, M. B., & Brownell, K. D. (1995). Matching individuals to weight loss treatments: A survey of obesity experts. *Journal of Consulting and Clinical Psychology, 63,* 149–153. (10)

Schwartz, M. F. (1995). Re-examining the role of executive functions in routine action production. *Annals of the New York Academy of Sciences, 769,* 321–335. (8)

Schwartz, W. J., & Gainer, H. (1977). Suprachiasmatic nucleus: Use of 14C-labeled deoxyglucose uptake as a functional marker. *Science, 197,* 1089–1091. (9)

Scott, S. H. (2004). Optimal feedback control and the neural basis of volitional motor control. *Nature Reviews Neuroscience, 5,* 532–544. (8)

Scott, T. R., & Verhagen, J. V. (2000). Taste as a factor in the management of nutrition. *Nutrition, 16,* 874–885. (10)

Scott, W. K., Nance, M. A., Watts, R. L., Hubble, J. P., Koller, W. C., Lyons, K., et al. (2001). Complete genomic screen in Parkinson disease. *Journal of the American Medical Association, 286,* 2239–2244. (8)

Scovern, A. W., & Kilmann, P. R. (1980). Status of electroconvulsive therapy: Review of the outcome literature. *Psychological Bulletin, 87,* 260–303. (15)

Scoville, W. B., & Milner, B. (1957). Loss of recent memory after bilateral hippocampal lesions. *Journal of Neurology, Neurosurgery, and Psychiatry, 20,* 11–21. (13)

Searle, J. R. (1992). *The rediscovery of the mind.* Cambridge, MA: MIT Press. (1)

Seeley, R. J., Kaplan, J. M., & Grill, H. J. (1995). Effect of occluding the pylorus on intraoral intake: A test of the gastric hypothesis of meal termination. *Physiology & Behavior, 58,* 245–249. (10)

Seeman, P., Lee, T., Chau-Wong, M., & Wong, K. (1976). Antipsychotic drug doses and neuroleptic/dopamine receptors. *Nature, 261,* 717–719. (15)

Seger, C. A., & Cincotta, C. M. (2005). The roles of the caudate nucleus in human classification learning. *Journal of Neuroscience, 25,* 2941–2951. (8)

Segerstrom, S. C., & Miller, G. E. (2004). Psychological stress and the human immune system: A meta-analytic study of 30 years of inquiry. *Psychological Bulletin, 130,* 601–630. (12)

Segu, L., Buhot, M.-C., & Hen, R. (1994). Enhanced aggressive behavior in mice lacking 5-HT1B receptor. *Science, 265,* 1875–1878. (12)

Sehgal, A., Ousley, A., Yang, Z., Chen, Y., & Schotland, P. (1999). What makes the circadian clock tick: Genes that keep time? *Recent Progress in Hormone Research, 54,* 61–85. (9)

Seifritz, E., Esposito, F., Hennel, F., Mustovic, H., Neuhoff, J. G., Bilecen, D., et al. (2002). Spatiotemporal pattern of neural processing in the human auditory cortex. *Science, 297,* 1706–1708. (7)

Sejnowski, T. J., Chattarji, S., & Stanton, P. K. (1990). Homosynaptic long-term depression in hippocampus and neocortex. *Seminars in the Neurosciences, 2,* 355–363. (13)

Sejnowski, T. J., & Destexhe, A. (2000). Why do we sleep? *Brain Research, 886,* 208–223. (9)

Selemon, L. D., Rajkowska, G., & Goldman-Rakic, P. S. (1995). Abnormally high neuronal density in the schizophrenic cortex. *Archives of General Psychiatry, 52,* 805–818. (15)

Selkoe, D. J. (1999). Translating cell biology into therapeutic advances in Alzheimer's disease. *Nature, 399*(Suppl.), A23–A31. (13)

Selkoe, D. J. (2000). Toward a comprehensive theory for Alzheimer's disease. *Annals of the New York Academy of Sciences, 924,* 17–25. (13)

Selye, H. (1979). Stress, cancer, and the mind. In J. Taché, H. Selye, & S. B. Day (Eds.), *Cancer, stress, and death* (pp. 11–27). New York: Plenum Press. (12)

Selzer, M. E. (1978). Mechanisms of functional recovery and regeneration after spinal cord transection in larval sea lamprey. *Journal of Physiology, 277,* 395–408. (5)

Semendeferi, K., Lu, A., Schenker, N., & Damasio, H. (2002). Humans and great apes share a large frontal cortex. *Nature Neuroscience, 5,* 272–276. (4)

Sergent, C., Baillet, S., & Dehaene, S. (2005). Timing of the brain events underlying access to consciousness during the attentional blink. *Nature Neuroscience, 8,* 1391–1400. (14)

Serizawa, S., Ishii, T., Nakatani, H., Tsuboi, A., Nagawa, F., Asano, M., et al. (2000). Mutually exclusive expression of ododrant receptor transgenes. *Nature Neuroscience, 3,* 687–693. (7)

Serizawa, S., Miyamichi, K., Nakatani, H., Suzuki, M., Saito, M., Yoshihara, Y., et al. (2003). Negative feedback regulation ensures the one receptor-one olfactory neuron rule in mouse. *Science, 302,* 2088–2094. (7)

Serruya, M. D., Hatsopoulos, N. G., Paninski, L., Fellows, M. R., & Donoghue, J. P. (2002). Instant neural control of a movement signal. *Nature, 416,* 141–142. (8)

Shadlen, M. N., & Newsome, W. T. (1996). Motion perception: Seeing and deciding. *Proceedings of the National Academy of Sciences, USA, 93,* 628–633. (8)

Shah, A., & Lisak, R. P. (1993). Immunopharmacologic therapy in myasthenia gravis. *Clinical Neuropharmacology, 16,* 97–103. (8)

Shah, N. M., Pisapia, D. J., Maniatis, S., Mendelsohn, M. M., Nemes, A., & Axel, R. (2004). Visualizing sexual dimorphism in the brain. *Neuron, 43,* 313–319. (11)

Shakelford, T. K., Buss, D. M., & Bennett, K. (2002). Forgiveness or breakup: Sex differences in responses to a partner's infidelity. *Cognition and Emotion, 16,* 299–307. (11)

Shalev, A. Y., Peri, T., Brandes, D., Freedman, S., Orr, S. P., & Pitman, R. K. (2000). Auditory startle response in trauma survivors with posttraumatic stress disorder: A prospective study. *American Journal of Psychiatry, 157,* 255–261. (12)

Shapiro, C. M., Bortz, R., Mitchell, D., Bartel, P., & Jooste, P. (1981). Slow-wave sleep: A recovery period after exercise. *Science, 214,* 1253–1254. (9)

Shapley, R. (1995). Parallel neural pathways and visual function. In M. S. Gazzaniga (Ed.), *The cognitive neurosciences* (pp. 315–324). Cambridge, MA: MIT Press. (6)

Sharma, J., Angelucci, A., & Sur, M. (2000). Induction of visual orientation modules in auditory cortex. *Nature, 404,* 841–847. (5)

Shatz, C. J. (1992, September). The developing brain. *Scientific American, 267*(9), 60–67. (5)

Shatz, C. J. (1996). Emergence of order in visual-system development. *Proceedings of the National Academy of Sciences, USA, 93,* 602–608. (6)

Shaw, P., Lawrence, E. J., Radbourne, C., Bramham, J., Polkey, C. E., & David, A. S. (2004). The impact of early and late damage to the human amygdala on "theory of mind" reasoning. *Brain, 127,* 1535–1548. (14)

Shearman, L. P., Sriram, S., Weaver, D. R., Maywood, E. S., Chaves, I., Zheng, B., et al. (2000). Interacting molecular loops in the mammalian circadian clock. *Science, 288,* 1013–1019. (9)

Sheehan, T. P., Cirrito, J., Numan, M. J., & Numan, M. (2000). Using *c-Fos* immunocytochemistry to identify forebrain regions that may inhibit maternal behavior in rats. *Behavioral Neuroscience, 114,* 337–352. (11)

Shergill, S. S., Brammer, M. J., Williams, S. C. R., Murray, R. M., & McGuire, P. K. (2000). Mapping auditory hallucinations in schizophrenia using functional magnetic resonance imaging. *Archives of General Psychiatry, 57,* 1033–1038. (15)

Sherrington, C. S. (1906). *The integrative action of the nervous system.* New York: Scribner's. (2nd ed.). New Haven, CT: Yale University Press, 1947. (3)

Sherrington, C. S. (1941). *Man on his nature.* New York: Macmillan. (inside cover)

Sherrington, R., Rogaev, E. I., Liang, Y., Rogaeva, E. A., Levesque, G., Ikeda, M., et al. (1995). Cloning of a gene bearing missense mutations in early-onset familial Alzheimer's disease. *Nature, 375,* 754–760. (13)

Shi, L., Fatemi, S. H., Sidwell, R. W., & Patterson, P. H. (2003). Maternal influenza infection causes marked behavioral and pharmacological changes in the offspring. *Journal of Neuroscience, 23,* 297–302. (15)

Shik, M. L., & Orlovsky, G. N. (1976). Neurophysiology of locomotor automatism. *Physiological Reviews, 56,* 465–501. (8)

Shimojo, S., Kamitani, Y., & Nishida, S. (2001). Afterimage of perceptually filled-in surface. *Science, 293,* 1677–1680. (6)

Shimura, H., Schlossmacher, M. G., Hattori, N., Frosch, M. P., Trockenbacher, A., Schneider, R., et al. (2001). Ubiquitination of a new form of α-synuclein by parkin from human brain: Implications for Parkinson's disease. *Science, 293,* 263–269. (8)

Shine, R., Phillips, B., Waye, H., LeMaster, M., & Mason, R. T. (2001). Benefits of female mimicry in snakes. *Nature, 414,* 267. (10)

Shirasaki, R., Katsumata, R., & Murakami, F. (1998). Change in chemoattractant responsiveness of developing axons at an intermediate target. *Science, 279,* 105–107. (5)

Shirley, S. G., & Persaud, K. C. (1990). The biochemistry of vertebrate olfaction and taste. *Seminars in the Neurosciences, 2,* 59–68. (7)

Shiv, B., Loewenstein, G., Bechara, A., Damasio, H., & Damasio, A. R. (2005). Investment behavior and the negative side of emotion. *Psychological Science, 16,* 435–439. (12)

Shoham, S., Halgren, E., Maynard, E. M., & Normann, R. A. (2001). Motor-cortical activity in tetraplegics. *Nature, 413,* 793. (8)

Shors, T. J., Miesegaes, G., Beylin, A., Zhao, M., Rydel, T., & Gould, E. (2001). Neurogenesis in the adult is involved in the formation of trace memories. *Nature, 410,* 372–376. (13)

Shoulson, I. (1990). Huntington's disease: Cognitive and psychiatric features. *Neuropsychiatry, Neuropsychology, and Behavioral Neurology, 3,* 15–22. (8)

Shuman, M., & Kanwisher, N. (2004). Numerical magnitude in the human parietal lobe: Tests of representation generality and domain specificity. *Neuron, 44,* 557–569. (4)

Shutts, D. (1982). *Lobotomy: Resort to the knife.* New York: Van Nostrand Reinhold. (4)

Siderowf, A., & Stern, M. (2003). Update on Parkinson disease. *Annals of Internal Medicine, 138,* 651–658. (8)

Siebner, H. R., Limmer, C., Peinemann, A., Drzezga, A., Bloom, B. R., Schwaiger, M., et al. (2002). Long-term consequences of switching handedness: A positron emission tomography study on handwriting in "converted" left handers. *Journal of Neuroscience, 22,* 2816–2825. (14)

Siegel, A., & Pott, C. B. (1988). Neural substrates of aggression and flight in the cat. *Progress in Neurobiology, 31,* 261–283. (12)

Siegel, J. M. (1995). Phylogeny and the function of REM sleep. *Behavioural Brain Research, 69,* 29–34. (9)

Siegel, J. M. (2001). The REM sleep-memory consolidation hypothesis. *Science, 294,* 1058–1063. (9)

Siegel, S. (1987). Alcohol and opiate dependence: Reevaluation of the Victorian perspective. *Research Advances in Alcohol and Drug Problems, 9,* 279–314. (15)

Silberg, J., Pickles, A., Rutter, M., Hewitt, J., Simonoff, E., Maes, H., et al. (1999). The influence of genetic factors and life stress on depression among adolescent girls. *Archives of General Psychiatry, 56,* 225–232. (15)

Silbersweig, D. A., Stern, E., Frith, C., Cahill, C., Holmes, A., Grootoonk, S., et al. (1995). A functional neuroanatomy of hallucinations in schizophrenia. *Nature, 378,* 176–179. (15)

Simon, E. (2000). Interface properties of circumventricular organs in salt and fluid balance. *News in Physiological Sciences, 15,* 61–67. (10)

Sincich, L. C., Park, K. F., Wohlgemuth, M. J., & Horton, J. C. (2004). Bypassing V1: A direct geniculate input to area MT. *Nature Neuroscience, 7,* 1123–1128. (6)

Sinclair, J. R., Jacobs, A. L., & Nirenberg, S. (2004). Selective ablation of a class of amacrine cells alers spatial processing in the retina. *Journal of Neuroscience, 24,* 1459–1467. (6)

Singer, T., Seymour, B., O'Doherty, J., Kaube, H., Dolan, R. J., & Frith, C. D. (2004). Empathy for pain involves the affective but not sensory components of pain. *Science, 303,* 1157–1162. (7)

Singer, W. (1986). Neuronal activity as a shaping factor in postnatal development of visual cortex. In W. T. Greenough & J. M. Jusaska (Eds.), *Developmental neuropsychobiology* (pp. 271–293). Orlando, FL: Academic Press. (6)

Singh, S., & Mallic, B. N. (1996). Mild electrical stimulation of pontine tegmentum around locus coeruleus reduces rapid eye movement sleep in rats. *Neuroscience Research, 24,* 227–235. (9)

Singleton, A. B., Farrer, M., Johnson, J., Singleton, A., Hague, S., Kachergus, J., et al. (2003). α-synuclein locus triplication causes Parkinson's disease. *Science, 302,* 841. (8)

Sirigu, A., Daprati, E., Ciancia, S., Giraux, P., Nighoghossian, N., Posda, A., et al. (2004). Altered awareness of voluntary action after damage to the parietal cortex. *Nature Neuroscience, 7,* 80–84. (8)

Sirigu, A., Grafman, J., Bressler, K., & Sunderland, T. (1991). Multiple representations contribute to body knowledge processing. Evidence from a case of autopagnosia. *Brain, 114,* 629–642. (7)

Sjöström, M., Friden, J., & Ekblom, B. (1987). Endurance, what is it? Muscle morphology after an extremely long distance run. *Acta Physiologica Scandinavica, 130,* 513–520. (8)

Skotko, B. G., Kensinger, E. A., Locascio, J. J., Einstein, G., Rubin, D. C., Tupler, L. A., et al. (2004). Puzzling thoughts for H. M.: Can new semantic information be anchored to old semantic memories? *Neuropsychology, 18,* 756–769. (13)

Skottun, B. C. (2000). The magnocellular deficit theory of dyslexia: The evidence from contrast sensitivity. *Vision Research, 40,* 111–127. (14)

Sloan, D. M., Strauss, M. E., & Wisner, K. L. (2001). Diminished response to pleasant stimuli by depressed women. *Journal of Abnormal Psychology, 110,* 488–493. (15)

Slob, A. K., Bax, C. M., Hop, W. C. J., Rowland, D. L., & van der Werff ten Bosch, J. J. (1996). Sexual arousability and the menstrual cycle. *Psychoneuroendocrinology, 21,* 545–558. (11)

Slotkin, T. A. (1998). Fetal nicotine or cocaine exposure: Which is worse? *Journal of Pharmacology and Experimental Therapeutics, 285,* 931–945. (5)

Smith, C. A. D., Gough, A. C., Leigh, P. N., Summers, B. A., Harding, A. E., Maranganore, D. M., et al. (1992). Debrisoquine hydroxylase gene polymorphism and susceptibility to Parkinson's disease. *Lancet, 339,* 1375–1377. (8)

Smith, D. E., Rapp, P. R., McKay, H. M., Roberts, J. A., & Tuszynski, M. H. (2004). Memory impairment in aged primates is associated with focal death of cortical neurons and atrophy of subcortical neurons. *Journal of Neuroscience, 24,* 4373–4381. (13)

Smith, G. P. (1998). Pregastric and gastric satiety. In G. P. Smith (Ed.), *Satiation: From gut to brain* (pp. 10–39). New York: Oxford University Press. (10)

Smith, G. P., & Gibbs, J. (1998). The satiating effects of cholecystokinin and bombesin-like peptides. In G. P. Smith (Ed.), *Satiation: From gut to brain* (pp. 97–125). New York: Oxford University Press. (10)

Smith, L. T. (1975). The interanimal transfer phenomenon: A review. *Psychological Bulletin, 81,* 1078–1095. (13)

Smith, M. A., Brandt, J., & Shadmehr, R. (2000). Motor disorder in Huntington's disease begins as a dysfunction in error feedback control. *Nature, 403,* 544–549. (8)

Smulders, T. V., Shiflett, M. W., Sperling, A. J., & DeVoogd, T. J. (2000). Seasonal changes in neuron numbers in the hippocampal formation of a food-hoarding bird: The black capped chickadee. *Journal of Neurobiology, 44,* 414–422. (5)

Snowling, M. J. (1980). The development of grapheme-phoneme correspondence in normal and dyslexic readers. *Journal of Experimental Child Psychology, 29,* 294–305. (14)

Snyder, E. M., Nong, Y., Almeida, C. G., Paul, S., Moran, T., Choi, E. Y., et al. (2005). Regulation of NMDA receptor trafficking by amyloid-β. *Nature Neuroscience, 8,* 1051–1058. (13)

Snyder, L. H., Grieve, K. L., Brotchie, P., & Andersen, R. A. (1998). Separate body- and world-referenced representations of visual space in parietal cortex. *Nature, 394,* 887–891. (8)

Soares, C. deN., Almeida, O. P., Joffe, H., & Cohen, L. S. (2001). Efficacy of estradiol for the treatment of depressive disorders in perimenopausal women. *Archives of General Psychiatry, 58,* 529–534. (15)

Sohlberg, M. M., & Mateer, C. A. (2001). Improving attention and managing attentional problems. *Annals of the New York Academy of Sciences, 931,* 359–375. (14)

Solanto, M. V., Abikoff, H., Sonuga-Barke, E., Schachar, R., Logan, G. D., Wigal, T., et al. (2001). The ecological validity of delay aversion and response inhibition as measures of impulsivity in AD/HD: A supplement to the NIMH multimodal treatment study of AD/HD. *Journal of Abnormal Child Psychology, 29,* 215–228. (14)

Solms, M. (1997). *The neuropsychology of dreams.* Mahwah, NJ: Erlbaum. (9)

Solms, M. (2000). Dreaming and REM sleep are controlled by different brain mechanisms. *Behavioral and Brain Sciences, 23,* 843–850. (9)

Somero, G. N. (1996). Temperature and proteins: Little things can mean a lot. *News in Physiological Sciences, 11,* 72–77. (10)

Somerville, L. H., Kim, H., Johnstone, T., Alexander, A. L., & Whalen, P. J. (2004). Human amygdala responses during presentation of happy and neutral faces: Correlations with state anxiety. *Biological Psychology, 55,* 897–903. (12)

Somjen, G. G. (1988). Nervenkitt: Notes on the history of the concept of neuroglia. *Glia, 1,* 2–9. (2)

Song, H., Stevens, C. F., & Gage, F. H. (2002). Neural stem cells from adult hippocampus develop essential properties of functional CNS neurons. *Nature Neuroscience, 5,* 438–445. (5)

Sonuga-Barke, E. J. S. (2004). Causal models of attention-deficit/hyperactivity disorder: From common simple deficits to multiple developmental pathways. *Biological Psychology, 57,* 1231–1238. (14)

Sowell, E. R., Thompson, P. M., Holmes, C. J., Jernigan, T. L., & Toga, A. W. (1999). In vivo evidence for post-adolescent brain maturation in frontal and striatal regions. *Nature Neuroscience, 2,* 859–861. (5)

Sowell, E. R., Thompson, P. M., Tessner, K. D., & Toga, A. W. (2001). Mapping continued brain growth and gray matter density reduction in dorsal frontal cortex: Inverse relationships during postadolescent brain maturation. *Journal of Neuroscience, 21,* 8819–8829. (15)

Spangler, R., Wittkowski, K. M., Goddard, N. L., Avena, N. M., Hoebel, B. G., & Leibowitz, S. F. (2004). Opiate-like effects of sugar on gene expression in reward areas of the rat brain. *Molecular Brain Research, 124,* 134–142. (10)

Spencer, R. M. C., Zelaznik, H. N., Diedrichsen, J., & Ivry, R. B. (2003). Disrupted timing of discontinuous but not continuous movements by cerebellar lesions. *Science, 300,* 1437–1439. (8)

Sperry, R. W. (1943). Visuomotor coordination in the newt (*Triturus viridescens*) after regeneration of the optic nerve. *Journal of Comparative Neurology, 79,* 33–55. (5)

Sperry, R. W. (1975). In search of psyche. In F. G. Worden, J. P. Swazey, & G. Adelman (Eds.), *The neurosciences: Paths of discovery* (pp. 425–434). Cambridge, MA: MIT Press. (inside cover)

Spiegel, T. A. (1973). Caloric regulation of food intake in man. *Journal of Comparative and Physiological Psychology, 84,* 24–37. (10)

Spindler, K. A., Sullivan, E. V., Menon, V., Lim, K. O., & Pfefferbaum, A. (1997). Deficits in multiple systems of working memory in schizophrenia. *Schizophrenia Research, 27,* 1–10. (15)

Spreux-Varoquaux, O., Alvarez, J.-C., Berlin, I., Batista, G., Despierre, P.-G., Gilton, A., et al. (2001). Differential abnormalities in plasma 5-HIAA and platelet serotonin concentrations in violent suicide attempters. *Life Sciences, 69,* 647–657. (12)

Spurzheim, J. G. (1908). *Phrenology* (Rev. ed.). Philadelphia: Lippincott. (4)

Squire, L. R. (1992). Memory and the hippocampus: A synthesis from findings with rats, monkeys, and humans. *Psychological Review, 99,* 195–231. (13)

Squire, L. R., Amaral, D. G., & Press, G. A. (1990). Magnetic resonance imaging of the hippocampal formation and mammillary nuclei distinguish medial temporal lobe and diencephalic amnesia. *Journal of Neuroscience, 10,* 3106–3117. (13)

Squires, T. M. (2004). Optimizing the vertebrate vestibular semicircular canal: Could we balance any better? *Physical Review Letters, 93,* 198106. (7)

St George-Hyslop, P. H. (2000). Genetic factors in the genesis of Alzheimer's disease. *Annals of the New York Academy of Sciences, 924,* 1–7. (13)

Stahl, J. E., Furie, K. L., Gleason, S., & Gazelle, G. S. (2003). Stroke: Effect of implementing an evaluation and treatment protocol compliant with NINDS recommendations. *Radiology, 228,* 659–668. (5)

Stanford, L. R. (1987). Conduction velocity variations minimize conduction time differences among retinal ganglion cell axons. *Science, 238,* 358–360. (2)

Stanley, B. G., Schwartz, D. H., Hernandez, L., Leibowitz, S. F., & Hoebel, B. G. (1989). Patterns of extracellular 5-hydroxyindoleacetic acid (5-HIAA) in the paraventricular hypothalamus (PVN): Relation to circadian rhythm and deprivation-induced eating behavior. *Pharmacology, Biochemistry, & Behavior, 33,* 257–260. (12)

Stark, R. E., & McGregor, K. K. (1997). Follow-up study of a right- and a left-hemispherectomized child: Implications for localization and impairment of language in children. *Brain and Language, 60,* 222–242. (14)

Starke, K. (2001). Presynaptic autoreceptors in the third decade: Focus on α_2-adrenoceptors. *Journal of Neurochemistry, 78,* 685–693. (3)

Starr, C., & Taggart, R. (1989). *Biology: The unity and diversity of life.* Pacific Grove, CA: Brooks/Cole. (3, 4, 7, 8, 11)

Stefanatos, G. A., & Wasserstein, J. (2001). Attention deficit/hyperactivity disorder as a right hemisphere syndrome. *Annals of the New York Academy of Sciences, 931,* 172–195. (14)

Stefanis, N., Frangou, S., Yakeley, J., Sharma, T., O'Connell, P., Morgan, K., et al. (1999). Hippocampal volume reduction in schizophrenia: Effects of genetic risk and pregnancy and birth complications. *Biological Psychiatry, 46,* 689–696. (15)

Stein, D. G., & Fulop, Z. L. (1998). Progesterone and recovery after traumatic brain injury: An overview. *The Neuroscientist, 4,* 435–442. (5)

Stein, M. B., Hanna, C., Koverola, C., Torchia, M., & McClarty, B. (1997). Structural brain changes in PTSD. *Annals of the New York Academy of Sciences, 821,* 76–82. (12)

Steiner, T., Ringleb, P., & Hacke, W. (2001). Treatment options for large hemispheric stroke. *Neurology, 57*(Suppl. 2), S61–S68. (5)

Stella, N., Schweitzer, P., & Piomelli, D. (1997). A second endogenous cannabinoid that modulates long-term potentiation. *Nature, 382,* 677–678. (3)

Stephens, T. W., Basinski, M., Bristow, P. K., Bue-Valleskey, J. M., Burgett, S. G., Craft, L., et al. (1995). The role of neuropeptide Y in the antiobesity action of the obese gene product. *Nature, 377,* 530–532. (10)

Stevens, C. F. (2001). An evolutionary scaling law for the primate visual system and its basis in cortical function. *Nature, 411,* 193–195. (6)

Stevens, T., & Karmiloff-Smith, A. (1997). Word learning in a special population: Do individuals with Williams syndrome obey lexical constraints? *Journal of Child Language, 24,* 737–765. (14)

Stewart, J. W., Quitkin, F. M., McGrath, P. J., Amsterdam, J., Fava, M., Fawcett, J., et al. (1998). Use of pattern analysis to predict differential relapse of remitted patients with major depression during 1 year of treatment with fluoxetine or placebo. *Archives of General Psychiatry, 55,* 334–343. (15)

Stickgold, R., James, L., & Hobson, J. A. (2000). Visual discrimination learning requires sleep after training. *Nature Neuroscience, 3,* 1237–1238. (9)

Stickgold, R., Malia, A., Maguire, D., Roddenberry, D., & O'Connor, M. (2000). Replaying the game: Hypnagogic images in normals and amnesics. *Science, 290,* 350–353. (13)

Stickgold, R., Whidbee, D., Schirmer, B., Patel, V., & Hobson, J. (2000). Visual discrimination task improvement: A multistep process occurring during sleep. *Journal of Cognitive Neuroscience, 12,* 246–254. (9)

Stockman, A., & Sharpe, L. T. (1998). Human cone spectral sensitivities: A progress report. *Vision Research, 38,* 3193–3206. (6)

Stone, V. E., Nisenson, L., Eliassen, J. C., & Gazzaniga, M. S. (1996). Left hemisphere representations of emotional facial expressions. *Neuropsychologia, 34,* 23–29. (14)

Storey, K. B., & Storey, J. M. (1999, May/June). Lifestyles of the cold and frozen. *The Sciences, 39*(3), 33–37. (10)

Stout, A. K., Raphael, H. M., Kanterewicz, B. I., Klann, E., & Reynolds, I. J. (1998). Glutamate-induced neuron death requires mitochondrial calcium uptake. *Nature Neuroscience, 1,* 366–373. (5)

Stowers, L., Holy, T. E., Meister, M., Dulac, C., & Koentges, G. (2002). Loss of sex discrimination and male-male aggression in mice deficient for TRP2. *Science, 295,* 1493–1500. (7)

Strack, F., Martin, L. L., & Stepper, S. (1988). Inhibiting and facilitating conditions of the human smile: A nonobtrusive test of the facial feedback hypothesis. *Journal of Personality and Social Psychology, 54,* 768–777. (12)

Strichartz, G., Rando, T., & Wang, G. K. (1987). An integrated view of the molecular toxinology of sodium channel gating in excitable cells. *Annual Review of Neuroscience, 10,* 237–267. (2)

Stricker, E. M. (1969). Osmoregulation and volume regulation in rats: Inhibition of hypovolemic thirst by water. *American Journal of Physiology, 217,* 98–105. (10)

Stricker, E. M., Swerdloff, A. F., & Zigmond, M. J. (1978). Intrahypothalamic injections of kainic acid produce feeding and drinking deficits in rats. *Brain Research, 158,* 470–473. (10)

Strickland, T. L., Miller, B. L., Kowell, A., & Stein, R. (1998). Neurobiology of cocaine induced organic brain impairment: Contributions from functional neuroimaging. *Neuropsychology Review, 8,* 1–9. (3)

Strittmatter, W. J., & Roses, A. D. (1995). Apolipoprotein E: Emerging story in the pathogenesis of Alzheimer's disease. *The Neuroscientist, 1,* 298–306. (13)

Strotmann, J., Levai, O., Fleischer, J., Schwarzenbacher, K., & Breer, H. (2004). Olfactory receptor proteins in axonal processes of chemosensory neurons. *Journal of Neuroscience, 224,* 7754–7761. (7)

Stryker, M. P., & Sherk, H. (1975). Modification of cortical orientation selectivity in the cat by restricted visual experience: A reexamination. *Science, 190,* 904–906. (6)

Stryker, M. P., Sherk, H., Leventhal, A. G., & Hirsch, H. V. B. (1978). Physiological consequences for the cat's visual cortex of effectively restricting early visual experience with oriented contours. *Journal of Neurophysiology, 41,* 896–909. (6)

Strzelczuk, M., & Romaniuk, A. (1996). Fear induced by the blockade of $GABA_A$-ergic transmission in the hypothalamus of the cat: Behavioral and neurochemical study. *Behavioural Brain Research, 72,* 63–71. (12)

Studer, L., Tabar, V., & McKay, R. D. G. (1998). Transplantation of expanded mesencephalic precursors leads to recovery in Parkinsonian rats. *Nature Neuroscience, 1,* 290–295. (8)

Stunkard, A. J., Sorensen, T. I. A., Hanis, C., Teasdale, T. W., Chakraborty, R., Schull, W. J., et al. (1986). An adoption study of human obesity. *New England Journal of Medicine, 314,* 193–198. (10)

Stuss, D. T., & Benson, D. F. (1984). Neuropsychological studies of the frontal lobes. *Psychological Bulletin, 95,* 3–28. (4)

Sullivan, E. V., Deshmukh, A., Desmond, J. E., Mathalon, D. H., Rosenbloom, M. J., Lim, K. O., et al. (2000). Contribution of alcohol abuse to cerebellar volume deficits in men with schizophrenia. *Archives of General Psychiatry, 57,* 894–902. (15)

Sunaert, S., Van Hecke, P., Marchal, G., & Orban, G. A. (1999). Motion-responsive regions of the human brain. *Experimental Brain Research, 127,* 355–370. (6)

Sunaert, S., Van Hecke, P., Marchal, G., & Orban, G. A. (2000). Attention to speed of motion, speed discrimination, and task difficulty: An fMRI study. *NeuroImage, 11,* 612–623. (6)

Supèr, H., Spekreijse, H., & Lamme, V. A. F. (2001). Two distinct modes of sensory processing observed in monkey primary visual cortex (V1). *Nature Neuroscience, 4,* 304–310. (6)

Sur, M., & Leamey, C. A. (2001). Development and plasticity of cortical areas and networks. *Nature Reviews Neuroscience, 2,* 251–262. (6)

Sutton, L. C., Lea, E., Will, M. J., Schwartz, B. A., Hartley, C. E., Poole, J. C., et al. (1997). Inescapable shock-induced potentiation of morphine analgesia. *Behavioral Neuroscience, 111,* 1105–1113. (7)

Sutton, R. L., Hovda, D. A., & Feeney, D. M. (1989). Amphetamine accelerates recovery of locomotor function following bilateral frontal cortex ablation in rats. *Behavioral Neuroscience, 103,* 837–841. (5)

Suvisaari, J. M., Haukka, J. K., Tanskanen, A. J., & Lönnqvist, J. K. (1999). Decline in the incidence of schizophrenia in Finnish cohorts born from 1954 to 1965. *Archives of General Psychiatry, 56,* 733–740. (15)

Suzdak, P. D., Glowa, J. R., Crawley, J. N., Schwartz, R. D., Skolnick, P., & Paul, S. M. (1986). A selective imidazobenzodiazepine antagonist of ethanol in the rat. *Science, 234,* 1243–1247. (12)

Swaab, D. F., Chung, W. C. J., Kruijver, F. P. M., Hofman, M. A., & Ishunina, T. A. (2001). Structural and functional sex differences in the human hypothalamus. *Hormones and Behavior, 40,* 93–98. (11)

Swaab, D. F., & Hofman, M. A. (1990). An enlarged suprachiasmatic nucleus in homosexual men. *Brain Research, 537,* 141–148. (11)

Swaab, D. F., Slob, A. K., Houtsmuller, E. J., Brand, T., & Zhou, J. N. (1995). Increased number of vasopressin neurons in the suprachiasmatic nucleus (SCN) of "bisexual" adult male rats following perinatal treatment with the aromatase blocker ATD. *Developmental Brain Research, 85,* 273–279. (11)

Swoboda, E., Conca, A., König, P., Waanders, R., & Hansen, M. (2001). Maintenance electroconvulsive therapy in affective and schizoaffective disorders. *Neuropsychobiology, 43,* 23–28. (15)

Szymusiak, R. (1995). Magnocellular nuclei of the basal forebrain: Substrates of sleep and arousal regulation. *Sleep, 18,* 478–500. (9)

Tabrizi, S. J., Cleeter, M. W. J., Xuereb, J., Taanman, J.-W., Cooper, J. M., & Schapira, A. H. V. (1999). Biochemical abnormalities and excitotoxicity in Huntington's disease brain. *Annals of Neurology, 45,* 25–32. (8)

Taddese, A., Nah, S. Y., & McCleskey, E. W. (1995). Selective opioid inhibition of small nociceptive neurons. *Science, 270,* 1366–1369. (7)

Tagawa, Y., Kanold, P. O., Majdan, M., & Shatz, C. J. (2005). Multiple periods of functional ocular dominance plasticity in mouse visual cortex. *Nature Neuroscience, 8,* 380–388. (6)

Tager-Flusberg, H., Boshart, J., & Baron-Cohen, S. (1998). Reading the windows to the soul: Evidence of domain-specific sparing in Williams syndrome. *Journal of Cognitive Neuroscience, 10,* 631–639. (14)

Tai, Y. F., Scherfler, C., Brooks, D. J., Sawamoto, N., & Castiello, U. (2004). The human premotor cortex is "mirror" only for biological actions. *Current Biology, 14,* 117–120. (8)

Taillard, J., Philip, P., Coste, O., Sagaspe, P., & Bioulac, B. (2003). The circadian and homeostatic modulation of sleep pressure during wakefulness differs between morning and evening chronotypes. *Journal of Sleep Research, 12,* 275–282. (9)

Takahashi, H., Yahata, N., Koeda, M., Matsuda, T., Asai, K., & Okubo, Y. (2004). Brain activation associated with evaluative processes of guilt and embarrassment: An fMRI study. *NeuroImage, 23,* 967–974. (12)

Takahashi, T., Svoboda, K., & Malinow, R. (2003). Experience strengthening transmission by driving AMPA receptors into synapses. *Science, 299,* 1585–1588. (13)

Takeuchi, A. (1977). Junctional transmission: I. Postsynaptic mechanisms. In E. R. Kandel (Ed.), *Handbook of physiology Section 1: Neurophysiology, Vol. 1. Cellular biology of neurons* (Pt. 1, pp. 295–327). Bethesda, MD: American Physiological Society. (3)

Tallal, P. (2004). Improving language and literacy is a matter of time. *Nature Reviews Neuroscience, 5,* 721–728. (14)

Tanaka, J., Hayashi, Y., Nomura, S., Miyakubo, H., Okumura, T., & Sakamaki, K. (2001). Angiotensinergic and noradrenergic mechanisms in the hypothalamic paraventricular nucleus participate in the drinking response induced by activation of the subfornical organ in rats. *Behavioural Brain Research, 118,* 117–122. (10)

Tanaka, J., Hori, K., & Nomura, M. (2001). Dipsogenic response induced by angiotensinergic pathways from the lateral hypothalamic area to the subfornical organ in rats. *Behavioural Brain Research, 118,* 111–116. (10)

Tanaka, K., Sugita, Y., Moriya, M., & Saito, H.-A. (1993). Analysis of object motion in the ventral part of the medial superior temporal area of the macaque visual cortex. *Journal of Neurophysiology, 69,* 128–142. (6)

Tanaka, Y., Kamo, T., Yoshida, M., & Yamadori, A. (1991). "So-called" cortical deafness. *Brain, 114,* 2385–2401. (7)

Tang, Y.-P., Shimizu, E., Dube, G. R., Rampon, C., Kerchner, G. A., Zhuo, M., et al. (1999). Genetic enhancement of learning and memory in mice. *Nature, 401,* 63–69. (13)

Tanji, J., & Shima, K. (1994). Role for supplementary motor area cells in planning several movements ahead. *Nature, 371,* 413–416. (8)

Tanner, C. M., Ottman, R., Goldman, S. M., Ellenberg, J., Chan, P., Mayeux, R., et al. (1999). Parkinson disease in twins: An etiologic study. *Journal of the American Medical Association, 281,* 341–346. (8)

Tarr, M. J., & Gauthier, I. (2000). FFA: A flexible fusiform area for subordinate-level visual processing automatized by experience. *Nature Neuroscience, 3,* 764–769. (6)

Taub, E., & Berman, A. J. (1968). Movement and learning in the absence of sensory feedback. In S. J. Freedman (Ed.), *The neuropsychology of spatially oriented behavior* (pp. 173–192). Homewood, IL: Dorsey. (5)

Taylor, J. P., Hardy, J., & Fischbeck, K H. (2002). Toxic proteins in neurodegenerative disease. *Science, 296,* 1991–1995. (13)

Teff, K. L., Elliott, S. S., Tschöp, M., Kieffer, T. J., Rader, D., Heiman, M., et al. (2004). Dietary fructose reduces circulating insulin and leptin, attenuates postprandial suppression of ghrelin, and increases triglycerides in women. *Journal of Clinical Endocrinology & Metabolism, 89,* 2963–2972. (10)

Teicher, M. H., Glod, C. A., Magnus, E., Harper, D., Benson, G., Krueger, K., et al. (1997). Circadian rest–activity disturbances in seasonal affective disorder. *Archives of General Psychiatry, 54,* 124–130. (15)

Teitelbaum, P. (1955). Sensory control of hypothalamic hyperphagia. *Journal of Comparative and Physiological Psychology, 48,* 156–163. (10)

Teitelbaum, P. (1961). Disturbances in feeding and drinking behavior after hypothalamic lesions. In M. R. Jones (Ed.), *Nebraska Symposia on Motivation 1961* (pp. 39–69). Lincoln: University of Nebraska Press. (10)

Teitelbaum, P., & Epstein, A. N. (1962). The lateral hypothalamic syndrome. *Psychological Review, 69,* 74–90. (10)

Teitelbaum, P., Pellis, V. C., & Pellis, S. M. (1991). Can allied reflexes promote the integration of a robot's behavior? In J. A. Meyer & S. W. Wilson (Eds.), *From animals to animats: Simulation of animal behavior* (pp. 97–104). Cambridge, MA: MIT Press/Bradford Books. (8)

Terayama, H., Nishino, Y., Kishi, M., Ikuta, K., Itoh, M., & Iwahashi, K. (2003). Detection of anti-Borna virus (BDV) antibodies from patients with schizophrenia and mood disorders in Japan. *Psychiatry Research, 120,* 201–206. (15)

Terman, M., Terman, J. S., & Ross, D. C. (1998). A controlled trial of timed bright light and negative air ionization for treatment of winter depression. *Archives of General Psychiatry, 55,* 875–882. (15)

Terrace, H. S., Petitto, L. A., Sanders, R. J., & Bever, T. G. (1979). Can an ape create a sentence? *Science, 206,* 891–902. (14)

Tetrud, J. W., Langston, J. W., Garbe, P. L., & Ruttenber, A. J. (1989). Mild Parkinsonism in persons exposed to 1-methyl-4-phenyl-1,2,3,6-tetrahydropyridine (MPTP). *Neurology, 39,* 1483–1487. (8)

Thanickal, T. C., Moore, R. Y., Nienhuis, R., Ramanathan, L., Gulyani, S., Aldrich, M., et al. (2000). Reduced number of hypocretin neurons in human narcolepsy. *Neuron, 27,* 469–474. (9)

Thapar, A., Fowler, T., Rice, F., Scourfield, J., van den Bree, M., Thomas, H., et al. (2003). Maternal smoking during pregnancy and attention deficit hyperactivity disorder symptoms in offspring. *American Journal of Psychiatry, 160,* 1985–1989. (14)

Thase, M. E., Greenhouse, J. B., Frank, E., Reynolds, C. F., III, Pilkonis, P. A., Hurley, K., et al. (1997). Treatment of major depression with psychotherapy or psychotherapy - psychopharmacology combinations. *Archives of General Psychiatry, 54,* 1009–1015. (15)

Thase, M. E., Trivedi, M. H., & Rush, A. J. (1995). MAOIs in the contemporary treatment of depression. *Neuropsychopharmacology, 12,* 185–219. (15)

Thiele, A., Henning, P., Kubischik, K.-P., & Hoffman, K.-P. (2002). Neural mechanisms of saccadic suppression. *Science, 295,* 2460–2462. (6)

Thier, P., Dicke, P. W., Haas, R., & Barash, S. (2000). Encoding of movement time by populations of cerebellar Purkinje cells. *Nature, 405,* 72–76. (8)

Thilo, K. V., Santoro, L., Walsh, V., & Blakemore, C. (2004). The site of saccadic suppression. *Nature Neuroscience, 7,* 13–14. (6)

Thomas, K. M., Drevets, W. C., Dahl, R. E., Ryan, N. D., Birmaher, B., Eccard, C. H., et al. (2001). Amygdala response to fearful faces in anxious and depressed children. *Archives of General Psychiatry, 58,* 1057–1063. (12)

Thomas, P. K. (1988). Clinical aspects of PNS regeneration. In S. G. Waxman (Ed.), *Advances in neurology* (Vol. 47, pp. 9–29). New York: Raven Press. (5)

Thompson, P. M., Hayashi, K. M., Simon, S. L., Geaga, J. A., Hong, M. S., Sui, Y., et al. (2004). Structural abnormalities in the brains of human subjects who use methamphetamine. *Journal of Neuroscience, 24,* 6028–6036. (3)

Thompson, P. M., Vidal, C., Giedd, J. N., Gochman, P., Blumenthal, J., Nicolson, R., et al. (2001). Mapping adolescent brain change reveals dynamic wave of accelerated gray matter loss in very early-onset schizophrenia. *Proceedings of the National Academy of Sciences, USA, 98,* 11650–11655. (15)

Thompson, R. F. (1986). The neurobiology of learning and memory. *Science, 233,* 941–947. (13)

Ticku, M. K., & Kulkarni, S. K. (1988). Molecular interactions of ethanol with GABAergic system and potential of Ro15-4513 as an ethanol antagonist. *Pharmacology Biochemistry and Behavior, 30,* 501–510. (12)

Timms, B. G., Howdeshell, K. L., Barton, L., Richter, C. A., & vom Saal, F. S. (2005). Estrogenic chemicals in plastic and oral contraceptives disrupt development of the fetal mouse prostate and urethra. *Pro-*

ceedings of the National Academy of Sciences, USA, 102, 7014–7019. (11)

Tinbergen, N. (1951). *The study of instinct.* Oxford, England: Oxford University Press. (1)

Tinbergen, N. (1973). The search for animal roots of human behavior. In N. Tinbergen (Ed.), *The animal in its world* (Vol. 2, pp. 161–174). Cambridge, MA: Harvard University Press. (1)

Tingate, T. R., Lugg, D. J., Muller, H. K., Stowe, R. P., & Pierson, D. L. (1997). Antarctic isolation: Immune and viral studies. *Immunology and Cell Biology, 75,* 275–283. (12)

Tippin, J., & Henn, F. A. (1982). Modified leukotomy in the treatment of intractable obsessional neurosis. *American Journal of Psychiatry, 139,* 1601–1603. (4)

Toh, K. L., Jones, C. R., He, Y., Eide, E. J., Hinz, W. A., Virshup, D. M., et al. (2001). An h*Per2* phosphorylation site mutation in familial advanced sleep phase syndrome. *Science, 291,* 1040–1043. (9)

Tominaga, M., Caterina, M. J., Malmberg, A. B., Rosen, T. A., Gilbert, H., Skinner, K., et al. (1998). The cloned capsaicin receptor integrates multiple pain-producing stimuli. *Neuron, 21,* 531–543. (7)

Tomizawa, K., Iga, N., Lu, Y.-F., Morikawa, A., Matsushita, M., Li, S.-T., et al. (2003). Oxytocin improves long-lasting spatial memory during motherhood through MAP kinase cascade. *Nature Neuroscience, 6,* 384–390. (11)

Toni, N., Buchs, P.-A., Nikonenko, I., Bron, C. R., & Muller, D. (1999). LTP promotes formation of multiple spine synapses between a single axon terminal and a dendrite. *Nature, 402,* 421–425. (13)

Torrey, E. F. (1986). Geographic variations in schizophrenia. In C. Shagass, R. C. Josiassen, W. H. Bridger, K. J. Weiss, D. Stoff, & G. M. Simpson (Eds.), *Biological psychiatry 1985* (pp. 1080–1082). New York: Elsevier. (15)

Torrey, E. F., & Miller, J. (2001). *The invisible plague: The rise of mental illness from 1750 to the present.* New Brunswick, NJ: Rutgers University Press. (15)

Torrey, E. F., Miller, J., Rawlings, R., & Yolken, R. H. (1997). Seasonality of births in schizophrenia and bipolar disorder: A review of the literature. *Schizophrenia Research, 28,* 1–38. (15)

Torrey, E. F., Rawlings, R., & Yolken, R. H. (2000). The antecedents of psychosis: A case-control study of selected risk factors. *Schizophrenia Research, 46,* 17–23. (15)

Torrey, E. F., & Yolken, R. H. (2005). *Toxoplasma gondii* as a possible cause of schizophrenia. *Biological Psychiatry, 57,* 128S. (15)

Townsend, J., Courchesne, E., Covington, J., Westerfield, M., Harris, N. S., Lyden, P., et al. (1999). Spatial attention deficits in patients with acquired or developmental cerebellar abnormality. *Journal of Neuroscience, 19,* 5632–5643. (8)

Trachtenberg, J. T., Chen, B. E., Knott, G. W., Feng, G., Sanes, J. R., Welker, E., et al. (2002). Long-term *in vivo* imaging of experience-dependent synaptic plasticity in adult cortex. *Nature, 420,* 788–794. (5)

Tran, P. B., & Miller, R. J. (2003). Chemokine receptors: Signposts to brain development and disease. *Nature Reviews Neuroscience, 4,* 444–455. (5)

Tranel, D., & Damasio, A. (1993). The covert learning of affective valence does not require structures in hippocampal system or amygdala. *Journal of Cognitive Neuroscience, 5,* 79–88. (13)

Travers, S. P., Pfaffmann, C., & Norgren, R. (1986). Convergence of lingual and palatal gustatory neural activity in the nucleus of the solitary tract. *Brain Research, 365,* 305–320. (7)

Trefilov, A., Berard, J., Krawczak, M., & Schmidtke, J. (2000). Natal dispersal in rhesus macaques is related to serotonin transporter gene promoter variation. *Behavior Genetics, 30,* 295–301. (12)

Treig, T., Werner, C., Sachse, M., & Hesse, S. (2003). No benefit from D-amphetamine when added to physiotherapy after stroke: A randomized, placebo-controlled study. *Clinical Rehabilitation, 17,* 590–599. (5)

Treisman, A. (1999). Feature binding, attention and object perception. In G. W. Humphreys, J. Duncan, & A. Treisman (Eds.), *Attention, space, and action* (pp. 91–111). Oxford, England: Oxford University Press. (4)

Trejo, J. L., Carro, E., & Torres-Alemán, I. (2001). Circulating insulin-like growth factor I mediates exercise-induced increases in the number of new neurons in the adult hippocampus. *Journal of Neuroscience, 21,* 1628–1634. (5)

Trevena, J. A., & Miller, J. (2002). Cortical movement preparation before and after a conscious decision to move. *Consciousness and Cognition, 11,* 162–190. (8)

Trevarthen, C. (1974). Cerebral embryology and the split brain. In M. Kinsbourne & W. L. Smith (Eds.), *Hemispheric disconnection and cerebral function* (pp. 208–236). Springfield, IL: Thomas. (14)

Trimble, M. R., & Thompson, P. J. (1986). Neuropsychological and behavioral sequelae of spontaneous seizures. *Annals of the New York Academy of Sciences, 462,* 284–292. (15)

Trivers, R. L. (1985). *Social evolution.* Menlo Park, CA: Benjamin/Cummings. (1)

Trout, J. D. (2001). The biological basis of speech: What to infer from talking to the animals. *Psychological Review, 108,* 523–549. (14)

True, W. R., Xian, H., Scherer, J. F., Madden, P. A. F., Bucholz, K. K., Heath, A. C., et al. (1999). Common genetic vulnerability for nicotine and alcohol dependence in men. *Archives of General Psychiatry, 56,* 655–661. (15)

Tsai, G., Passani, L. A., Slusher, B. S., Carter, R., Baer, L., Kleinman, J. E., et al. (1995). Abnormal excitatory neurotransmitter metabolism in schizophrenic brains. *Archives of General Psychiatry, 52,* 829–836. (15)

Tsai, G. E., Ragan, P., Chang, R., Chen, S., Linnoila, M. I., & Coyle, J. T. (1998). Increased glutamatergic neurotransmission and oxidative stress after alcohol withdrawal. *American Journal of Psychiatry, 155,* 726–732. (15)

Ts'o, D. Y., & Roe, A. W. (1995). Functional compartments in visual cortex: Segregation and interaction. In M. S. Gazzaniga (Ed.), *The cognitive neurosciences* (pp. 325–337). Cambridge, MA: MIT Press. (6)

Tsujita, T., Niikawa, N., Yamashita, H., Imamura, A., Hamada, A., Nakane, Y., et al. (1998). Genomic discordance between monozygotic twins discordant for schizophrenia. *American Journal of Psychiatry, 155,* 422–424. (15)

Tsunoda, K., Yamane, Y., Nishizaki, M., & Tanifuji, M. (2001). Complex objects are represented in macaque inferotemporal cortex by the combination of feature columns. *Nature Neuroscience, 4,* 832–838. (6)

Tu, G. C., & Israel, Y. (1995). Alcohol consumption by Orientals in North America is predicted largely by a single gene. *Behavior Genetics, 25,* 59–65. (15)

Tucker, D. M., Luu, P., & Pribram, K. H. (1995). Social and emotional self-regulation. *Annals of the New York Academy of Sciences, 769,* 213–239. (8)

Turk, D. J., Heatherton, T. F., Kelley, W. M., Funnell, M. G., Gazzaniga, M. S., & Macrae, C. N. (2002). Mike or me? Self-recognition in a split-brain patient. *Nature Neuroscience, 5,* 841–842. (14)

Turner, R. S., & Anderson, M. E. (2005). Context-dependent modulation of movement-related discharge in the primate globus pallidus. *Journal of Neuroscience, 25,* 2965–2976. (8)

Uchida, N., Takahashi, Y. K., Tanifuji, M., & Mori, K., (2000). Odor maps in the mammalian olfactory bulb: Domain organization and odorant structural features. *Nature Neuroscience, 3,* 1035–1043. (7)

Udry, J. R., & Morris, N. M. (1968). Distribution of coitus in the menstrual cycle. *Nature, 220,* 593–596. (11)

Uekita, T., & Okaichi, H. (2005). NMDA antagonist MK-801 does not interfere with the use of spatial representation in a familiar environment. *Behavioral Neuroscience, 119,* 548–556. (13)

Ulanovsky, N., Las, L., & Nelken, I. (2003). Processing of low-probability sounds by cortical neurons. *Nature Neurosciences, 6,* 391–398. (7)

Ullman, M. T. (2001). A neurocognitive perspective on language: The declarative/

procedural model. *Nature Reviews Neuroscience, 2,* 717–726. (14)

Unterberg, A. W., Stover, J., Kress, B., & Kiening, K. L. (2004). Edema and brain trauma. *Neuroscience, 129,* 1021–1029. (5)

Urry, H. L., Nitschke, J. B., Dolski, I., Jackson, D. C., Dalton, K. M., Mueller, C. J., et al. (2004). Making a life worth living: Neural correlates of well-being. *Psychological Science, 15,* 367–372. (12)

U.S.-Venezuela Collaborative Research Project. (2004). Venezuelan kindreds reveal that genetic and environmental factors modulate Huntington's disease age of onset. *Proceedings of the National Academy of Sciences, USA, 101,* 3498–3503. (8)

Uwano, T., Nishijo, H., Ono, T., & Tamura, R. (1995). Neuronal responsiveness to various sensory stimuli, and associative learning in the rat amygdala. *Neuroscience, 68,* 339–361. (12)

Vaillant, G. E., & Milofsky, E. S. (1982). The etiology of alcoholism: A prospective viewpoint. *American Psychologist, 37,* 494–503. (15)

Vaishnavi, S., Calhoun, J., & Chatterjee, A. (2001). Binding personal and peripersonal space: Evidence from tactile extinction. *Journal of Cognitive Neuroscience, 13,* 181–189. (14)

Valente, E. M., Abou-Sleiman, P. M., Caputo, V., Muquit, M. M. K., Harvey, K., Gispert, S., et al. (2004). Hereditary early-onset Parkinson's disease caused by mutations in *PINK1. Science, 304,* 1158–1160. (8)

Valzelli, L. (1973). The "isolation syndrome" in mice. *Psychopharmacologia, 31,* 305–320. (12)

Valzelli, L. (1980). *An approach to neuroanatomical and neurochemical psychophysiology.* Torino, Italy: C. G. Edizioni Medico Scientifiche. (10, 15)

Valzelli, L., & Bernasconi, S. (1979). Aggressiveness by isolation and brain serotonin turnover changes in different strains of mice. *Neuropsychobiology, 5, 129–135.* (12)

van den Pol, A. N. (1999). Hypothalamic hypocretin (orexin): Robust innervation of the spinal cord. *Journal of Neuroscience, 19,* 3171–3182. (10)

van Dellen, A., Blakemore, C., Deacon, R., York, D., & Hannan, A. J. (2000). Delaying the onset of Huntington's in mice. *Nature, 404,* 721–722. (8)

Van der Does, A. J. W. (2001). The effects of tryptophan depletion on mood and psychiatric symptoms. *Journal of Affective Disorders, 64,* 107–119. (12)

van der Stelt, M., Veldhuis, W. B., Maccarrone, M., Bär, P., Nicolay, K., Veldink, G. A., et al. (2002). Acute neuronal injury, excitotoxicity, and the endocannabinoid system. *Molecular Neurobiology, 26,* 317–346. (5)

van der Vegt, B. J., Lieuwes, N., van de Wall, E. H. E. M., Kato, K., Moya-Albiol, L., Martínez-Sanchis, W., et al. (2003). Activation of serotonergic neurotransmission during the performance of aggressive behavior in rats. *Behavioral Neuroscience, 117,* 667–674. (12)

Van Essen, D. C., & DeYoe, E. A. (1995). Concurrent processing in the primate visual cortex. In M. S. Gazzaniga (Ed.), *The cognitive neurosciences* (pp. 383–400). Cambridge, MA: MIT Press. (6)

Van Horn, J. D., Grafton, S. T., Rockmore, D., & Gazzaniga, M. S. (2004). Sharing neuroimaging studies of human cognition. *Nature Neuroscience, 7,* 473–481. (4)

van Honk, J., Tuiten, A., Hermans, E., Putman, P., Koppenschaar, H., Thijssen, J., et al. (2001). A single administration of testosterone induces cardiac accelerative responses to angry faces in healthy young women. *Behavioral Neuroscience, 115,* 238–242. (12)

Van Petta, C. (2004). Relationship between hippocampal volume and memory ability in healthy individuals across the lifespan: Review and meta-analysis. *Neuropsychologia, 42,* 1394–1413. (13)

van Praag, H., Kempermann, G., & Gage, F. H. (1999). Running increases cell proliferation and neurogenesis in the adult mouse dentate gyrus. *Nature Neuroscience, 2,* 266–270. (5)

van Praag, H., Kempermann, G., & Gage, F. H. (2000). Neural consequences of environmental enrichment. *Nature Reviews Neuroscience, 1,* 191–198. (5)

van Praag, H., Schinder, A. F., Christie, B. R., Toni, N., Palmer, T. D., & Gage, F. H. (2002). Functional neurogenesis in the adult hippocampus. *Nature, 415,* 1030–1034. (5)

Van Wanrooij, M. M., & Van Opstal, A. J. (2004). Contribution of head shadow and pinna cues to chronic monaural sound localization. *Journal of Neuroscience, 24,* 4163–4171. (7)

Van Wanrooij, M. M., & Van Opstal, A. J. (2005). Relearning sound localization with a new ear. *Journal of Neuroscience, 25,* 5413–5424. (7)

Van Zoeren, J. G., & Stricker, E. M. (1977). Effects of preoptic, lateral hypothalamic, or dopamine-depleting lesions on behavioral thermoregulation in rats exposed to the cold. *Journal of Comparative and Physiological Psychology, 91,* 989–999. (10)

van Zutphen, B. (2001). European researchers encourage improvement in lab animal welfare. *Nature, 409,* 452. (1)

Vandenberghe, R., Nobre, A. C., & Price, C. J. (2002). The response of left temporal cortex to sentences. *Journal of Cognitive Neuroscience, 14,* 550–560. (14)

Vanduffel, W., Fize, D., Mandeville, J. B., Nelissen, K., Van Hecke, P., Rosen, B. R., et al. (2001). Visual motion processing investigated using contrast agent-enhanced fMRI in awake behaving monkeys. *Neuron, 32,* 565–577. (6)

Varela, F., Lachaux, J.-P., Rodriguez, E., & Martinerie, J. (2001). The brainweb: Phase synchronization and large-scale integration. *Nature Reviews Neuroscience, 2,* 229–239. (4)

Vargha-Khadem, F., Gadian, D. G., Copp, A., & Mishkin, M. (2005). *FOXP2* and the neuroanatomy of speech and language. *Nature Reviews Neuroscience, 6,* 131–138. (14)

Vataja, R., Pohjasvaara, T., Leppävuori, A., Mäantylä, R., Aronen, H. J., Salonen, O., et al. (2001). Magnetic resonance imaging correlates of depression after ischemic stroke. *Archives of General Psychiatry, 58,* 925–931. (15)

Vawter, M. P., Evans, S., Choudary, P., Tomita, H., Meador-Woodruff, J., Molnar, M., et al. (2004). Gender-specific gene expression in post-mortem human brain. Localization to sex chromosomes. *Neuropsychopharmacology, 29,* 373–384. (11)

Verhage, M., Maia, A. S., Plomp, J. J., Brussard, A. B., Heeroma, J. H., Vermeer, H., et al. (2000). Synaptic assembly of the brain in the absence of neurotransmitter secretion. *Science, 287,* 864–869. (5)

Verrey, F., & Beron, J. (1996). Activation and supply of channels and pumps by aldosterone. *News in Physiological Sciences, 11,* 126–133. (10)

Victor, M., Adams, R. D., & Collins, G. H. (1971). *The Wernicke-Korsakoff syndrome.* Philadelphia: Davis. (13)

Virkkunen, M., DeJong, J., Bartko, J., Goodwin, F. K., & Linnoila, M. (1989). Relationship of psychobiological variables to recidivism in violent offenders and impulsive fire setters. *Archives of General Psychiatry, 46,* 600–603. (12)

Virkkunen, M., Eggert, M., Rawlings, R., & Linnoila, M. (1996). A prospective follow-up study of alcoholic violent offenders and fire setters. *Archives of General Psychiatry, 53,* 523–529. (12)

Virkkunen, M., Nuutila, A., Goodwin, F. K., & Linnoila, M. (1987). Cerebrospinal fluid monoamine metabolite levels in male arsonists. *Archives of General Psychiatry, 44,* 241–247. (12)

Virkkunen, M., Rawlings, R., Tokola, R., Poland, R. E., Guidotti, A., Nemeroff, C., et al. (1994). CSF biochemistries, glucose metabolism, and diurnal activity rhythms in alcoholic, violent offenders, fire setters, and healthy volunteers. *Archives of General Psychiatry, 51,* 20–27. (15)

Visser, E. K., Beersma, G. M., & Daan, S. (1999). Melatonin suppression by light in humans is maximal when the nasal part of the retina is illuminated. *Journal of Biological Rhythms, 14,* 116–121. (9)

Vliegen, J., Van Grootel, T. J., & Van Opstal, A. J. (2004). Dynamic sound localization during rapid eye–head gaze shifts. *Journal of Neuroscience, 24,* 9291–9302. (7)

Vocci, F. J., Acri, J., & Elkashef, A. (2005). Medication development for addictive disorders: The state of the science. *American Journal of Psychiatry, 162,* 1432–1440. (15)

Vogels, R., Biederman, I., Bar, M., & Lorincz, A. (2001). Inferior temporal neurons show greater sensitivity to nonaccidental than to metric shape differences. *Journal of Cognitive Neuroscience, 13,* 444–453. (6)

Volavka, J., Czobor, P., Goodwin, D. W., Gabrielli, W. F., Penick, E. C., Mednick, S. A., et al. (1996). The electroencephalogram after alcohol administration in high-risk men and the development of alcohol use disorders 10 years later. *Archives of General Psychiatry, 53,* 258–263. (15)

Volkow, N. D., Wang, G.-J., Fischman, M. W., Foltin, R. W., Fowler, J. S., Abumrad, N. N., Vitkum, S., Logan, J., Gatley, S. J., Pappas, N., Hitzemann, R., & Shea, C. E. (1997). Relationship between subjective effects of cocaine and dopamine transporter occupancy. *Nature, 386,* 827–830. (3)

Volkow, N. D., Wang, G.-J., & Fowler, J. S. (1997). Imaging studies of cocaine in the human brain and studies of the cocaine addict. *Annals of the New York Academy of Sciences, 820,* 41–55. (3)

Volkow, N. D., Wang, G.-J., Fowler, J. S., Gatley, S. J., Logan, J., Ding, Y.-S., et al. (1998). Dopamine transporter occupancies in the human brain induced by therapeutic doses of oral methylphenidate. *American Journal of Psychiatry, 155,* 1325–1331. (3, 14)

Volkow, N. D., Wang, G.-J., Fowler, J. S., Logan, J., Gatley, S. J., Hitzemann, R., et al. (1997). Decreased striatal dopaminergic responsiveness in detoxified cocaine-dependent subjects. *Nature, 386,* 830–833. (3)

Volkow, N. D., Wang, G.-J., Ma, Y., Fowler, J. S., Wong, C., Ding, Y.-S., et al. (2005). Activation of orbital and medial prefrontal cortex by methylphenidate in cocaine-addicted subjects but not in controls: Relevance to addiction. *Journal of Neuroscience, 25,* 3932–3939. (15)

Volkow, N. D., & Wise, R. A. (2005). How can drug addiction help us understand obesity? *Nature Neuroscience, 8,* 555–560. (10)

Volterra, A., & Meldolesi, J. (2005). Astrocytes, from brain glue to communication elements: The revolution continues. *Nature Reviews Neuroscience, 6,* 626–640. (2)

von Békésy, G. (1956). Current status of theories of hearing. *Science, 123,* 779–783. (7)

von Gall, C., Garabette, M. L., Kell, C. A., Frenzel, S., Dehghani, F., Schumm-Draeger, P. M., et al. (2002). Rhythmic gene expression in pituitary depends on heterologous sensitization by the neurohormone melatonin. *Nature Neuroscience, 5,* 234–238. (9)

von Melchner, L., Pallas, S. L., & Sur, M. (2000). Visual behaviour mediated by retinal projections directed to the visual pathway. *Nature, 404,* 871–876. (5)

Vouloumanos, A., Kiehl, K. A., Werker, J. F., & Liddle, P. F. (2001). Detection of sounds in the auditory stream: Event-related fMRI evidence for differential activation to speech and nonspeech. *Journal of Cognitive Neuroscience, 13,* 994–1005. (14)

Vrba, E. S. (1998). Multiphasic growth models and the evolution of prolonged growth exemplified by human brain evolution. *Journal of Theoretical Biology, 190,* 227–239. (5)

Vuilleumier, P. (2005). Cognitive science: Staring fear in the face. *Nature, 433,* 22–23. (12)

Vuilleumier, P., Armony, J. L., Driver, J., & Dolan, R. J. (2001). Effects of attention and emotion on face processing in the human brain: An event-related fMRI study. *Neuron, 30,* 829–841. (12)

Wager, T. D., Rilling, J. K., Smith, E. E., Sokolik, A., Casey, K. L., Davidson, R. J., et al. (2004). Placebo-induced changes in fMRI in the anticipation and experience of pain. *Science, 303,* 1162–1167. (7)

Wagner, A. D., Schacter, D. L., Rotte, M., Koutstaal, W., Maril, A., Dale, A. M., et al. (1998). Building memories: Remembering and forgetting of verbal experiences as predicted by brain activity. *Science, 281,* 1188–1191. (4)

Wagner, U., Gais, S., Halder, H., Verleger, R., & Born, J. (2004). Sleep inspires insight. *Nature, 427,* 352–355. (9)

Waisbren, S. R., Brown, M. J., de Sonneville, L. M. J., & Levy, H. L. (1994). Review of neuropsychological functioning in treated phenylketonuria: An information-processing approach. *Acta Paediatrica, 83*(Suppl. 407), 98–103. (1)

Waldvogel, J. A. (1990). The bird's eye view. *American Scientist, 78,* 342–353. (6)

Wallesch, C.-W., Henriksen, L., Kornhuber, H.-H., & Paulson, O. B. (1985). Observations on regional cerebral blood flow in cortical and subcortical structures during language production in normal man. *Brain and Language, 25,* 224–233. (14)

Wallman, J., & Pettigrew, J. D. (1985). Conjugate and disjunctive saccades in two avian species with contrasting oculomotor strategies. *Journal of Neuroscience, 5,* 1418–1428. (6)

Walsh, G. S., Orike, N., Kaplan, D. R., & Miller, F. D. (2004). The invulnerability of adult neurons: A critical role of p73. *Journal of Neuroscience, 24,* 9638–9647. (5)

Walsh, V., & Cowey, A. (2000). Transcranial magnetic stimulation and cognitive neuroscience. *Nature Reviews Neuroscience, 1,* 73–79. (4)

Wang, A., Liang, Y., Fridell, R. A., Probst, F. J., Wilcox, E. R., Touchman, J. W., et al. (1998). Associations of unconventional myosin *MYO15* mutations with human nonsyndromic deafness *DFNB3*. *Science, 280,* 1447–1451. (7)

Wang, H., & Tessier-Lavigne, M. (1999). En passant neurotrophic action of an intermediate axonal target in the developing mammalian CNS. *Nature, 401,* 765–769. (5)

Wang, Q., Schoenlein, R. W., Peteanu, L. A., Mathies, R. A., & Shank, C. V. (1994). Vibrationally coherent photochemistry in the femtosecond primary event of vision. *Science, 266,* 422–424. (6)

Wang, T., Okano, Y., Eisensmith, R., Huang, S. Z., Zeng, Y. T., Wilson, H. Y. L., et al. (1989). Molecular genetics of phenylketonuria in Orientals: Linkage disequilibrium between a termination mutation and haplotype 4 of the phenylalanine hydroxylase gene. *American Journal of Human Genetics, 45,* 675–680. (1)

Wang, X., Lu, T., Snider, R. K., & Liang, L. (2005). Sustained firing in auditory cortex evoked by preferred stimuli. *Nature, 435,* 341–346. (7)

Warach, S. (1995). Mapping brain pathophysiology and higher cortical function with magnetic resonance imaging. *The Neuroscientist, 1,* 221–235. (4)

Ward, I. L., Bennett, A. L., Ward, O. B., Hendricks, S. E., & French, J. A. (1999). Androgen threshold to activate copulation differs in male rats prenatally exposed to alcohol, stress, or both factors. *Hormones and Behavior, 36,* 129–140. (11)

Ward, I. L., Romeo, R. D., Denning, J. H., & Ward, O. B. (1999). Fetal alcohol exposure blocks full masculinization of the dorsolateral nucleus in rat spinal cord. *Physiology & Behavior, 66,* 571–575. (11)

Ward, I. L., Ward, B., Winn, R. J., & Bielawski, D. (1994). Male and female sexual behavior potential of male rats prenatally exposed to the influence of alcohol, stress, or both factors. *Behavioral Neuroscience, 108,* 1188–1195. (11)

Ward, I. L., & Ward, O. B. (1985). Sexual behavior differentiation: Effects of prenatal manipulations in rats. In N. Adler, D. Pfaff, & R. W. Goy (Eds.), *Handbook of behavioral neurobiology, Vol. 7* (pp. 77–98). New York: Plenum Press. (11)

Ward, O. B., Monaghan, E. P., & Ward, I. L. (1986). Naltrexone blocks the effects of prenatal stress on sexual behavior differentiation in male rats. *Pharmacology Biochemistry and Behavior, 25,* 573–576. (11)

Ward, O. B., Ward, I. L., Denning, J. H., French, J. A., & Hendricks, S. E. (2002). Postparturitional testosterone surge in male offspring of rats stressed and/or fed ethanol during late pregnancy. *Hormones and Behavior, 41,* 229–235. (11)

Ward, R., Danziger, S., Owen, V., & Rafal, R. (2002). Deficits in spatial coding and feature binding following damage to spatiotopic maps in the human pulvinar. *Nature Neuroscience, 5,* 99–100. (4)

Warren, R. M. (1999). *Auditory perception.* Cambridge, England: Cambridge University Press. (7)

Warrington, E. K., & Weiskrantz, L. (1968). New method for testing long-term retention with special reference to amnesic patients. *Nature, 217,* 972–974. (13)

Wässle, H. (2004). Parallel processing in the mammalian retina. *Nature Neuroscience, 5,* 747–757. (6)

Waxman, S. G., & Ritchie, J. M. (1985). Organization of ion channels in the myelinated nerve fiber. *Science, 228,* 1502–1507. (2)

Weaver, D. R. (1997). Reproductive safety of melatonin: A "wonder drug" to wonder about. *Journal of Biological Rhythms, 12,* 682–689. (9)

Webb, W. B. (1974). Sleep as an adaptive response. *Perceptual and Motor Skills, 38,* 1023–1027. (9)

Weber-Fox, C. M., & Neville, H. J. (1996). Maturational constraints on functional specializations for language processing: ERP and behavioral evidence in bilingual speakers. *Journal of Cognitive Neuroscience, 8,* 231–256. (14)

Wegener, D., Freiwald, W. A., & Kreiter, A. K. (2004). The influence of sustained selective attention on stimulus selectivity in macaque visual area MT. *Journal of Neuroscience, 24,* 6106–6114. (6)

Wehr, T. A., Turner, E. H., Shimada, J. M., Lowe, C. H., Barker, C., & Leinbenluft, E. (1998). Treatment of a rapidly cycling bipolar patient by using extended bed rest and darkness to stabilize the timing and duration of sleep. *Biological Psychiatry, 43,* 822–828. (15)

Wei, F., Wang, G.-D., Kerchner, G. A., Kim, S. J., Xu, H.-M., Chen, Z.-F., et al. (2001). Genetic enhancement of inflammatory pain by forebrain NR2B overexpression. *Nature Neuroscience, 4,* 164–169. (7)

Weidensaul, S. (1999). *Living on the wind.* New York: North Point Press. (10)

Weinberger, D. R. (1996). On the plausibility of "the neurodevelopmental hypothesis" of schizophrenia. *Neuropsychopharmacology, 14,* 1S–11S. (15)

Weinberger, D. R. (1999). Cell biology of the hippocampal formation in schizophrenia. *Biological Psychiatry, 45,* 395–402. (15)

Weinberger, D. R., & McClure, R. K. (2002). Neurotoxicity, neuroplasticity, and magnetic resonance imaging morphometry: What is happening in the schizophrenic brain? *Archives of General Psychiatry, 59,* 553–558. (15)

Weindl, A. (1973). Neuroendocrine aspects of circumventricular organs. In W. F. Ganong & L. Martini (Eds.), *Frontiers in neuroendocrinology 1973* (pp. 3–32). New York: Oxford University Press. (10)

Weiner, R. D. (1979). The psychiatric use of electrically induced seizures. *American Journal of Psychiatry, 136,* 1507–1517. (15)

Weingarten, P., & Zhou, Q.-Y. (2001). Protection of intracellular dopamine cytotoxicity by dopamine disposition and metabolism factors. *Journal of Neurochemistry, 77,* 776–785. (8)

Weiskrantz, L., Warrington, E. K., Sanders, M. D., & Marshall, J. (1974). Visual capacity in the hemianopic field following a restricted occipital ablation. *Brain, 97,* 709–728. (6)

Weiss, P. (1924). Die funktion transplantierter amphibienextremitäten. Aufstellung einer resonanztheorie der motorischen nerventätigkeit auf grund abstimmter endorgane [The function of transplanted amphibian limbs. Presentation of a resonance theory of motor nerve action upon tuned end organs]. *Archiv für Mikroskopische Anatomie und Entwicklungsmechanik, 102,* 635–672. (5)

Weissman, D. H., Warner, L. M., & Woldorff, M. G. (2004). The neural mechanisms for minimizing cross-modal distraction. *Journal of Neuroscience, 24,* 10941–10949. (14)

Weller, L., Weller, A., Koresh-Kamin, H., & Ben-Shoshan, R. (1999). Menstrual synchrony in a sample of working women. *Psychoneuroendocrinology, 24,* 449–459. (7)

Weller, L., Weller, A., & Roizman, S. (1999). Human menstrual synchrony in families and among close friends: Examining the importance of mutual exposure. *Journal of Comparative Psychology, 113,* 261–268. (7)

Wender, P. H., Kety, S. S., Rosenthal, D., Schulsinger, F., Ortmann, J., & Lunde, I. (1986). Psychiatric disorders in the biological and adoptive families of adopted individuals with affective disorders. *Archives of General Psychiatry, 43,* 923–929. (15)

Wender, P. H., Wolf, L. E., & Wasserstein, J. (2001). Adults with ADHD. *Annals of the New York Academy of Sciences, 931,* 1–16. (14)

Wessinger, C. M., Fendrich, R., & Gazzaniga, M. S. (1997). Islands of residual vision in hemianopic patients. *Journal of Cognitive Neuropsychology, 9,* 203–221. (6)

Wessinger, C. M., VanMeter, J., Tian, B., Van Lare, J., Pekar, J., & Rauschecker, J. P. (2001). Hierarchical organization of the human auditory cortex revealed by functional magnetic resonance imaging. *Journal of Cognitive Neuroscience, 13,* 1–7. (7)

Westbrook, G. L., & Jahr, C. E. (1989). Glutamate receptors in excitatory neurotransmission. *Seminars in the Neurosciences, 1,* 103–114. (3)

Westergaard, G. C., Cleveland, A., Trenkle, M. K., Lussier, I. D., & Higley, J. D. (2003). CSF 5-HIAA concentration as an early screening tool for predicting significant life history outcomes in female specific-pathogen-free (SPF) rhesus macaques (*Macaca mulatta*) maintained in captive breeding groups. *Journal of Medical Primatology, 32,* 95–104. (12)

Whalen, P. J. (1998). Fear, vigilance, and ambiguity: Initial neuroimaging studies of the human amygdala. *Current Directions in Psychological Science, 7,* 177–188. (12)

Whalen, P. J., Kagan, J., Cook, R. G., Davis, F. C., Kim, H., Polis, S., et al. (2004). Human amygdala responsivity to masked fearful eye whites. *Science, 306,* 2061. (12)

Wheeler, M. E., & Treisman, A. (2002). Binding in short-term visual memory. *Journal of Experimental Psychology: General, 131,* 48–64. (4)

White, L. E., Coppola, D. M., & Fitzpatrick, D. (2001). The contribution of sensory experience to the maturation of orientation selectivity in ferret visual cortex. *Nature, 411,* 1049–1052. (6)

Whitman, B. W., & Packer, R. J. (1993). The photic sneeze reflex: Literature review and discussion. *Neurology, 43,* 868–871. (8)

Whitney, K. D., & McNamara, J. O. (2000). GluR3 autoantibodies destroy neural cells in a complement-dependent manner modulated by complement regulatory proteins. *Journal of Neuroscience, 20,* 7307–7316. (14)

Whyte, J., Katz, D., Long, D., DiPasquale, M. C., Polansky, M., Kalmar, K., et al. (2005). Predictors of outcome in prolonged posttraumatic disorders of consciousness and assessment of medication effects: A multicenter study. *Archives of Physical Medicine and Rehabilitation, 86,* 453–462. (5)

Wichmann, T., Vitek, J. L., & DeLong, M. R. (1995). Parkinson's disease and the basal ganglia: Lessons from the laboratory and from neurosurgery. *The Neuroscientist, 1,* 236–244. (8)

Wicker, B., Keysers, C., Plailly, J., Royet, J.-P., Gallese, V., & Rizzolatti, G. (2003). Both of us disgusted in *my* insula: The common neural basis of seeing and feeling disgust. *Neuron, 40,* 655–664. (12)

Wiedemann, K., Jahn, H., Yassouridis, A., & Kellner, M. (2001). Anxiolyticlike effects of atrial natriuretic peptide on cholecystokinin tetrapeptide-induced panic attacks. *Archives of General Psychiatry, 58,* 371–377. (12)

Wiesel, T. N. (1982). Postnatal development of the visual cortex and the influence of environment. *Nature, 299,* 583–591. (6; inside cover)

Wiesel, T. N., & Hubel, D. H. (1963). Single-cell responses in striate cortex of kittens deprived of vision in one eye. *Journal of Neurophysiology, 26,* 1003–1017. (6)

Wild, H. M., Butler, S. R., Carden, D., & Kulikowski, J. J. (1985). Primate cortical area V4 important for colour constancy but not wavelength discrimination. *Nature, 313,* 133–135. (6)

Wilens, T. E., Faraone, S. V., Biederman, J., & Gunawardene, S. (2003). Does stimulant therapy of attention-deficit/hyperactivity disorder beget later substance abuse? A meta-analytic review of the literature. *Pediatrics, 111,* 179–185. (3)

Willerman, L., Schultz, R., Rutledge, J. N., & Bigler, E. D. (1991). In vivo brain size and intelligence. *Intelligence, 15,* 223–228. (5)

Williams, C. L. (1986). A reevaluation of the concept of separable periods of organizational and activational actions of estrogens in development of brain and behavior. *Annals of the New York Academy of Sciences, 474,* 282–292. (11)

Williams, G., Cai, X. J., Elliott, J. C., & Harrold, J. A. (2004). Anabolic neuropeptides. *Physiology & Behavior, 81,* 211–222. (10)

Williams, M. A., Morris, A. P., McGlone, F., Abbott, D. F., & Mattingley, J. B. (2004). Amygdala responses to fearful and happy facial expressions under conditions of binocular suppression. *Journal of Neuroscience, 24,* 2898–2904. (12)

Williams, M. T., Davis, H. N., McCrea, A. E., Long, S. J., & Hennessy, M. B. (1999). Changes in the hormonal concentrations of pregnant rats and their fetuses following multiple exposures to a stressor during the third trimester. *Neurotoxicology and Teratology, 21,* 403–414. (11)

Williams, R. W., & Herrup, K. (1988). The control of neuron number. *Annual Review of Neuroscience, 11,* 423–453. (2, 8)

Williams, T. (1999, May/June). Management by majority. *Audubon, 101*(3), 40–49. (1)

Williams, Z. M., Bush, G., Rauch, S. L., Cosgrove, G. R., & Eskandar, E. N. (2004). Human anterior cingulate neurons and the integration of monetary reward with motor responses. *Nature Neuroscience, 7,* 1370–1375. (12)

Williamson, D. A., Ravussin, E., Wong, M.-L., Wagner, A., DiPaoli, A., Caglayan, S., et al. (2005). Microanalysis of eating behavior of three leptin deficient adults treated with leptin therapy. *Appetite, 45,* 75–80. (10)

Willingham, D. B., Koroshetz, W. J., & Peterson, E. W. (1996). Motor skills have diverse neural bases: Spared and impaired skill acquisition in Huntington's disease. *Neuropsychology, 10,* 315–321. (8)

Willis, G. L., & Armstrong, S. M. (1999). A therapeutic role for melatonin antagonism in experimental models of Parkinson's disease. *Physiology & Behavior, 66,* 785–795. (9)

Willson, M. C., Wilman, A. H., Bell, E. C., Asghar, S. J., & Silverstone, P. H. (2004). Dextroamphetamine causes a change in regional brain activity in vivo during cognitive tasks: A functional magnetic resonance imaging study of blood oxygen level-dependent response. *Biological Psychiatry, 56,* 284–291. (3)

Wilson, B. A., Baddeley, A. D., & Kapur, N. (1995). Dense amnesia in a professional musician following herpes simplex virus encephalitis. *Journal of Clinical and Experimental Neuropsychology, 17,* 668–681. (13)

Wilson, D. S., & Sober, E. (1994). Reintroducing group selection to the human behavioral sciences. *Behavioral and Brain Sciences, 17,* 585–654. (1)

Wilson, J. D., George, F. W., & Griffin, J. E. (1981). The hormonal control of sexual development. *Science, 211,* 1278–1284. (11)

Wilson, R. I., & Nicoll, R. A. (2001). Endogenous cannabinoids mediate retrograde signalling at hippocampal synapses. *Nature, 410,* 588–592. (3)

Wilson, R. I., & Nicoll, R. A. (2002). Endocannabinoid signaling in the brain. *Science, 296,* 678–682. (3)

Winer, G. A., Cottrell, J. F., Gregg, V., Fournier, J. S., & Bica. L. A. (2002). Fundamentally misunderstanding visual perception: Adults' belief in visual emissions. *American Psychologist, 57,* 417–424. (6)

Winfree, A. T. (1983). Impact of a circadian clock on the timing of human sleep. *American Journal of Physiology, 245,* R497–R504. (9)

Winocur, G., & Hasher, L. (1999). Aging and time-of-day effects on cognition in rats. *Behavioral Neuroscience, 113,* 991–997. (9)

Winocur, G., & Hasher, L. (2004). Age and time-of-day effects on learning and memory in a non-matching-to-sample test. *Neurobiology of Aging, 25,* 1107–1115. (9)

Winston, J. S., Strange, B. A., O'Doherty, J., & Dolan, R. J. (2002). Automatic and intentional brain responses during evaluation of trustworthiness of faces. *Nature Neuroscience, 5,* 277–283. (12)

Wirdefeldt, K., Gatz, M., Pawitan, Y., & Pedersen, N. L. (2004). Risk and protective factors for Parkinson's disease: A study in Swedish twins. *Annals of Neurology, 57,* 27–33. (8)

Wirz-Justice, A., & Van den Hoofdakker, R. H. (1999). Sleep deprivation in depression: What do we know, where do we go? *Biological Psychiatry, 46,* 445–453. (15)

Wirz-Justice, A., Werth, E., Renz, C., Müller, S., & Kräuchi, K. (2002). No evidence for a phase delay in human circadian rhythms after a single morning melatonin administration. *Journal of Pineal Research, 32,* 1–5. (9)

Wise, R. A. (1996). Addictive drugs and brain stimulation reward. *Annual Review of Neuroscience, 19,* 319–340. (15)

Wise, R. A., & Bozarth, M. A. (1987). A psychomotor stimulant theory of addiction. *Psychological Review, 94,* 469–492. (3)

Witelson, S. F., Glezer, I. I., & Kigar, D. L. (1995). Women have greater density of neurons in posterior temporal cortex. *Journal of Neuroscience, 15,* 3418–3428. (11)

Witelson, S. F., Kigar, D. L., & Harvey, T. (1999). The exceptional brain of Albert Einstein. *Lancet, 353,* 2149–2153. (4)

Witelson, S. F., & Pallie, W. (1973). Left hemisphere specialization for language in the newborn: Neuroanatomical evidence of asymmetry. *Brain, 96,* 641–646. (14)

Wolf, S. (1995). Dogmas that have hindered understanding. *Integrative Physiological and Behavioral Science, 30,* 3–4. (12)

Wolff, P. H. (1993). Impaired temporal resolution in developmental dyslexia. *Annals of the New York Academy of Sciences, 682,* 87–103. (14)

Wolkin, A., Rusinek, H., Vaid, G., Arena, L., Lafargue, T., Sanfilipo, M., et al. (1998). Structural magnetic resonance image averaging in schizophrenia. *American Journal of Psychiatry, 155,* 1064–1073. (15)

Wolpaw, J. R., & McFarland, D. J. (2004). Control of a two-dimensional movement signal by a noninvasive brain-computer interface in humans. *Proceedings of the National Academy of Sciences, USA, 101,* 17849–17861. (8)

Wolpert, L. (1991). *The triumph of the embryo.* Oxford, England: Oxford University Press. (5)

Wong-Riley, M. T. T. (1989). Cytochrome oxidase: An endogenous metabolic marker for neuronal activity. *Trends in Neurosciences, 12,* 94–101. (2)

Wooding, S., Kim, U., Bamshad, M J., Larsen, J., Jorde, L. B., & Drayna, D. (2004). Natural selection and molecular evolution in *PTC*, a bitter-taste receptor gene. *American Journal of Human Genetics, 74,* 637–646. (1)

Woods, S. C., & Seeley, R. J. (2000). Adiposity signals and the control of energy homeostasis. *Nutrition, 16,* 894–902. (10)

Woodson, J. C., & Balleine, B. W. (2002). An assessment of factors contributing to instrumental performance for sexual reward in the rat. *Quarterly Journal of Experimental Psychology, 55B,* 75–88. (11)

Woodson, J. C., & Gorski, R. A. (2000). Structural sex differences in the mammalian brain: Reconsidering the male/female dichotomy. In A. Matsumoto (Ed.), *Sexual differentiation of the brain* (pp. 229–255). Boca Raton, FL: CRC Press. (11)

Woodworth, R. S. (1934). *Psychology* (3rd ed.). New York: Holt. (2)

Woolf, N. J. (1991). Cholinergic systems in mammalian brain and spinal cord. *Progress in Neurobiology, 37,* 475–524. (4)

Woolf, N. J. (1996). Global and serial neurons form a hierarchically arranged interface proposed to underlie memory and cognition. *Neuroscience, 74,* 625–651. (9)

Wright, I. C., Rabe-Hesketh, S., Woodruff, P. W. R., David, A. S., Murray, R. M., & Bullmore, E. T. (2000). Meta-analysis of regional brain volumes in schizophrenia. *American Journal of Psychiatry, 157,* 16–25. (15)

Wulfeck, B., & Bates, E. (1991). Differential sensitivity to errors of agreement and word order in Broca's aphasia. *Journal of Cognitive Neuroscience, 3,* 258–272. (14)

Wurtman, J. J. (1985). Neurotransmitter control of carbohydrate consumption. *Annals of the New York Academy of Sciences, 443,* 145–151. (3)

Wüst, S., Kasten, E., & Sabel, B. A. (2002). Blindsight after optic nerve injury indicates functionality of spared fibers. *Journal of Cognitive Neuroscience, 14,* 243–253. (6)

Wynne, C. D. L. (2004). The perils of anthropomorphism. *Nature, 428,* 606. (1)

Xiao, Y., Wang, Y., & Felleman, D. J. (2003). A spatially organized representation of colour in macaque cortical area V2. *Nature, 421,* 535–539. (6)

Xu, Y., Padiath, Q. S., Shapiro, R. E., Jones, C. R., Wu, S. C., Saigoh, N., et al. (2005). Functional consequences of a *CK1δ* mutation causing familial advanced sleep phase syndrome. *Nature, 434,* 640–644. (9)

Yabuta, N. H., Sawatari, A., & Callaway, E. M. (2001). Two functional channels from primary visual cortex to dorsal visual cortical areas. *Science, 292,* 297–300. (6)

Yamaguchi, S., Isejima, H., Matsuo, T., Okura, R., Yagita, K., Kobayashi, M., et al. (2003). Synchronization of cellular clocks in the suprachiasmatic nucleus. *Science, 302,* 1408–1412. (9)

Yamamoto, S., & Kitazawa, S. (2001). Reversal of subjective temporal order due to arm crossing. *Nature Neuroscience, 4,* 759–765. (2)

Yamamoto, T. (1984). Taste responses of cortical neurons. *Progress in Neurobiology, 23,* 273–315. (7)

Yamamoto, Y., Akiyoshi, J., Kiyota, A., Katsuragi, S., Tsutsumi, T., Isogawa, K., et al. (2000). Increased anxiety behavior in OLETF rats without cholecystokinin-A receptor. *Brain Research Bulletin, 53,* 789–792. (12)

Yanagisawa, K., Bartoshuk, L. M., Catalanotto, F. A., Karrer, T. A., & Kveton, J. F. (1998). Anesthesia of the chorda tympani nerve and taste phantoms. *Physiology & Behavior, 63,* 329–335. (7)

Yang, F., Lim, G. P., Begum, A. N., Ubeda, O. J., Simmons, M. R., Ambegaokar, S. S., et al. (2005). Curcumin inhibits formation of amyloid β oligomers and fibrils, binds plaques, and reduces amyloid *in vivo. Journal of Biological Chemistry, 280,* 5892–5901. (13)

Yehuda, R. (1997). Sensitization of the hypothalamic-pituitary-adrenal axis in posttraumatic stress disorder. *Annals of the New York Academy of Sciences, 821,* 57–75. (12)

Yehuda, R. (2002). Post-traumatic stress disorder. *New England Journal of Medicine, 346,* 108–114. (12)

Yeomans, J. S., & Frankland, P. W. (1996). The acoustic startle reflex: Neurons and connections. *Brain Research Reviews,* 21, 301–314. (12)

Yolken, R. H., Bachmann, S., Rouslanova, I., Lillehoj, E., Ford, G., Torrey, E. F., et al. (2001). Antibodies to *Toxoplasma gondii* in individuals with first-episode schizophrenia. *Clinical Infectious Diseases, 32,* 842–844. (15)

Yost, W. A., & Nielsen, D. W. (1977). *Fundamentals of hearing.* New York: Holt, Rinehart & Winston. (7)

Young, A. B. (1995). Huntington's disease: Lessons from and for molecular neuroscience. *The Neuroscientist, 1,* 51–58. (8)

Young, J. P., Herath, P., Eickhoff, S., Choi, J., Grefkes, C., Zilles, K., et al. (2004). Somatotopy and attentional modulation of the human parietal and opercular regions. *Journal of Neuroscience, 24,* 5391–5399. (7)

Young, S. N., & Leyton, M. (2002). The role of serotonin in human mood and social interaction: Insight from altered tryptophan levels. *Pharmacology, Biochemistry and Behavior, 71,* 857–865. (12)

Yousem, D. M., Maldjian, J. A., Siddiqi, F., Hummel, T., Alsop, D. C., Geckle, R. J., et al. (1999). Gender effects on odor-stimulated functional magnetic resonance imaging. *Brain Research, 818,* 480–487. (7)

Yovel, G., & Kanwisher, N. (2004). Face perception: Domain specific, not process specific. *Neuron, 44,* 889–898. (6)

Yu, T. W., & Bargmann, C. I. (2001). Dynamic regulation of axon guidance. *Nature Neuroscience Supplement, 4,* 1169–1176. (5)

Zahn, T. P., Rapoport, J. L., & Thompson, C. L. (1980). Autonomic and behavioral effects of dextroamphetamine and placebo in normal and hyperactive prepubertal boys. *Journal of Abnormal Child Psychology, 8,* 145–160. (14)

Zakharenko, S. S., Zablow, L., & Siegelbaum, S. A. (2001). Visualization of changes in presynaptic function during long-term synaptic plasticity. *Nature Neuroscience, 4,* 711–717. (13)

Zatorre, R. J., Bouffard, M., & Belin, P. (2004). Sensitivity to auditory object features in human temporal neocortex. *Journal of Neuroscience, 24,* 3637–3642. (7)

Zeevalk, G. D., Manzino, L., Hoppe, J., & Sonsalla, P. (1997). In vivo vulnerability of dopamine neurons to inhibition of energy metabolism. *European Journal of Pharmacology, 320,* 111–119. (8)

Zeitzer, J. M., Buckmaster, C. L., Parker, K. J., Hauck, C. M., Lyons, D. M., & Mignot, E. (2003). Circadian and homeostatic regulation of hypocretin in a primate model: Implications for the consolidation of wakefulness. *Journal of Neuroscience, 23,* 3555–3560. (9)

Zeki, S. (1980). The representation of colours in the cerebral cortex. *Nature, 284,* 412–418. (6)

Zeki, S. (1983). Colour coding in the cerebral cortex: The responses of wavelength-selective and colour-coded cells in monkey visual cortex to changes in wavelength composition. *Neuroscience, 9,* 767–781. (6)

Zeki, S., McKeefry, D. J., Bartels, A., & Frackowiak, R. S. J. (1998). Has a new color area been discovered? *Nature Neuroscience, 1,* 335. (6)

Zeki, S., & Shipp, S. (1988). The functional logic of cortical connections. *Nature, 335,* 311–317. (6)

Zelano, C., Bensafi, M., Porter, J., Mainland, J., Johnson, B., Bremner, E., et al. (2005). Attentional modulation in human primary olfactory cortex. *Nature Neuroscience, 8,* 114–120. (14)

Zhang, J. (2003). Evolution of the human *ASPM* gene, a major determinant of brain size. *Genetics, 165,* 2063–2070. (4)

Zhang, L. I., Bao, S., & Merzenich, M. M. (2001). Persistent and specific influences of early acoustic environments on primary auditory cortex. *Nature Neuroscience, 4,* 1123–1130. (5)

Zhang, W., & Linden, D. J. (2003). The other side of the engram: Experience-driven changes in neuronal intrinsic excitability. *Nature Reviews Neuroscience, 4,* 885–900. (13)

Zhang, X., & Firestein, S. (2002). The olfactory receptor gene superfamily of the mouse. *Nature Neuroscience, 5,* 124–133. (7)

Zhang, X., Gainetdinov, R. R., Beaulieu, J.-M., Sotnikova, T. D., Burch, L. H., Williams, R. B., et al. (2005). Loss-of-function mutation in tryptophan hydroxylase-2 identified in unipolar major depression. *Neuron, 45,* 11–16. (15)

Zhang, X., Smith, D. L., Meriin, A. B., Engemann, S., Russel, D. E., Roark, M., et al. (2005). A potent small molecule inhibits polyglutamine aggregation in Huntington's disease neurons and suppresses neurodegeneration *in vivo. Proceedings of the National Academy of Sciences, USA, 102,* 892–897. (8)

Zhang, Y., Proenca, R., Maffei, M., Barone, M., Leopold, L., & Friedman, J. M. (1994).

Positional cloning of the mouse obese gene and its human homologue. *Nature, 372,* 425–432. (10)

Zhao, Z., & Davis, M. (2004). Fear-potentiated startle in rats is mediated by neurons in the deep layers of the superior colliculus/deep mesencephalic nucleus of the rostral midbrain through the glutamate non-NMDA receptors. *Journal of Neuroscience, 24,* 10326–10334. (12)

Zheng, B., Larkin, D. W., Albrecht, U., Sun, Z. S., Sage, M., Eichele, G., et al. (1999). The *mPer2* gene encodes a functional component of the mammalian circadian clock. *Nature, 400,* 169–173. (9)

Zhou, F., Zhu, X., Castellani, R. J., Stimmelmayr, R., Perry, G., Smith, M. A., et al. (2001). Hibernation, a model of neuroprotection. *American Journal of Pathology, 158,* 2145–2151. (9)

Zhou, Q., Homma, K. J., & Poo, M. (2004). Shrinkage of dendritic spines associated with long-term depression of hippocampal synapses. *Neuron, 44,* 749–757. (13)

Zhu, L. X., Sharma, S., Stolina, M., Gardner, B., Roth, M. D., Tashkin, D. P., et al. (2000). δ9-Tetrahydrocannabinol inhibits antitumor immunity by a CB2 receptor-mediated, cytokine-dependent pathway. *Journal of Immunology, 165,* 373–380. (3)

Zihl, J., von Cramon, D., & Mai, N. (1983). Selective disturbance of movement vision after bilateral brain damage. *Brain, 106,* 313–340. (6)

Zola, S. M., Squire, L. R., Teng, E., Stefanacci, L., Buffalo, E. A., & Clark, R. E. (2000). Impaired recognition memory in monkeys after damage limited to the hippocampal region. *Journal of Neuroscience, 20,* 451–463. (13)

Zorrilla, E. P., Luborsky, L., McKay, J. R., Rosenthal, R., Houldin, A., Tax, A., et al. (2001). The relationship of depression and stressors to immunological assays: A meta-analytic review. *Brain, Behavior, and Immunity, 15,* 199–226. (12)

Zorzi, M., Priftis, K., & Umiltà, C. (2002). Neglect disrupts the mental number line. *Nature, 417,* 138. (14)

Zou, Z., Horowitz, L. F., Montmayeur, J.-P., Snapper, S., & Buck, L. B. (2001). Genetic tracing reveals a stereotyped sensory map in the olfactory cortex. *Nature, 414,* 173–179. (7)

Zubieta, J.-K., Ketter, T. A., Bueller, J. A., Xu, Y., Kilbourn, M. R., Young, E. A., et al. (2003). Regulation of human affective responses by anterior cingulate and limbic υ-opioid neurotransmission. *Archives of General Psychiatry, 60,* 1145–1153. (7)

Zuccato, C., Ciammola, A., Rigamonti, D., Leavitt, B. R., Goffredo, D., Conti, L., et al. (2001). Loss of huntingtin-mediated BDNF gene transcription in Huntington's disease. *Science, 293,* 493–498. (8)

Zucker, K. J., Bradley, S. J., Oliver, G., Blake, J., Fleming, S., & Hood, J. (1996). Psychosexual development of women with congenital adrenal hyperplasia. *Hormones and Behavior, 30,* 300–318. (11)

Zuckerman, L., Rehavi, M., Nachman, R., & Weiner, I. (2003). Immune activation during pregnancy in rats leads to a postpubertal emergence of disrupted latent inhibition, dopaminergic hyperfunction, and altered limbic morphology in the offspring: A novel neurodevelopmental model of schizophrenia. *Neuropsychopharmacology, 28,* 1778–1789. (15)

Zurif, E. B. (1980). Language mechanisms: A neuropsychological perspective. *American Scientist, 68,* 305–311. (1)

Name Index

Subject Index/Glossary

Note: Italicized page numbers refer to figures, illustrations, and tables.